AUDITING
An Integrated Approach

Eighth Edition

AUDITING
An Integrated Approach

ALVIN A. ARENS
Price Waterhouse
Auditing Professor
Michigan State University

JAMES K. LOEBBECKE
Kenneth A. Sorensen
Peat Marwick Professor of Accounting
University of Utah

With Contributing Authors
RANDAL J. ELDER
Syracuse University

MARK S. BEASLEY
North Carolina State University

Prentice Hall, Upper Saddle River, New Jersey 07458

Library of Congress Cataloging-in-Publication Data

Arens, Alvin A.
    Auditing, an integrated approach / Alvin A. Arens, James K. Loebbecke—8th ed.
        p.   cm.
    Includes index.
    ISBN 0-13-082735-5
    1. Auditing. I. Loebbecke, James K. II. Title.

    HF5667 A69 1999
    657'45—dc21

                                                    99-046401

Executive Editor: Annie Todd
Assistant Editor: Kathryn Sheehan
Editorial Assistant: Fran Toepfer
Editor-In-Chief: PJ Boardman
Executive Marketing Manager: Beth Toland
Associate Managing Editor: Sondra Greenfield
Senior Manufacturing Supervisor: Paul Smolenski
Manufacturing Manager: Vincent Scelta
Design Director: Pat Smythe
Interior Design: Michael Jung
Cover Design: Michael J. Fruhbeis
Cover Illustration: Digital Productions, Inc.
Composition: Graphic World, Inc.

This book contains quotations and adaptations from publications copyrighted by the American
Institute of Certified Public Accountants, Inc. Such passages have been reprinted or adapted
with permission of the American Institute of Certified Public Accountants.

ISBN: 0-13-082735-5

Prentice-Hall International (UK) Limited, *London*
Prentice-Hall of Australia Pty. Limited, *Sydney*
Prentice-Hall Canada, Inc., *Toronto*
Prentice-Hall Hispanoamericana, S.A., *Mexico*
Prentice-Hall of India Private Limited, *New Delhi*
Prentice-Hall of Japan, Inc., *Tokyo*
Prentice-Hall (*Singapore*) Pte., Ltd
Editora Prentice-Hall do Brasil, Ltda., *Rio de Janeiro*

Printed in the United States of America

10 9 8 7 6 5 4 3 2

CONTENTS

Preface xv

PART I   The Auditing Profession

1   THE DEMAND FOR AUDIT AND ASSURANCE SERVICES   1
Learning Objectives   1
Assurance Services   2
Economic Demand for Auditing   7
Nature of Auditing   9
Distinction between Auditing and Accounting   11
Types of Audits   11
Types of Auditors   13
Certified Public Accountant   14
Summary   15
Essential Terms   16
Review Questions   16
Multiple Choice Questions from CPA Examinations   17
Discussion Questions and Problems   18
Internet Problem 1-1: Assurance Services   21

2   THE CPA PROFESSION   23
Learning Objectives   23
Certified Public Accounting Firms   24
Activities of CPA Firms   25
Structure of CPA Firms   26
AICPA   28
Generally Accepted Auditing Standards   29
Statements on Auditing Standards   31
Quality Control   33

Securities and Exchange Commission   36
Summary   37
Essential Terms   37
Review Questions   38
Multiple Choice Questions from CPA Examinations   38
Discussion Questions and Problems   39
Internet Problem 2-1: CPA Vision Project   41

3   AUDIT REPORTS   43
Learning Objectives   43
Standard Unqualified Audit Report   44
Unqualified Audit Report with Explanatory Paragraph or Modified
    Wording   47
Departures from an Unqualified Audit Report   50
Materiality   52
Discussion of Conditions Requiring a Departure   55
Auditor's Decision Process for Audit Reports   59
Summary   62
Essential Terms   62
Review Questions   62
Multiple Choice Questions from CPA Examinations   63
Discussion Questions and Problems   65
Case   71
Internet Problem 3-1: Research Annual Reports   73

4   PROFESSIONAL ETHICS   75
Learning Objectives   75
What are Ethics?   76
Ethical Dilemmas   77
Special Need for Ethical Conduct in Professions   80
Code of Professional Conduct   82
Independence   86
Other Rules of Conduct   92
Enforcement   99
Summary   100
Essential Terms   101
Review Questions   101
Multiple Choice Questions from CPA Examinations   102
Discussion Questions and Problems   103
Cases   106
Internet Problem 4-1: AICPA *Code of Professional Conduct*—**Ethics Rulings
    and Case   109**

5   LEGAL LIABILITY   111
Learning Objectives   111
Changed Legal Environment   112

Distinction among Business Failure, Audit Failure, and Audit Risk   113

Legal Concepts Affecting Liability   114

Liability to Clients   115

Liability to Third Parties under Common Law   119

Civil Liability under the Federal Securities Laws   121

Criminal Liability   125

The Profession's Response to Legal Liability   127

Protecting Individual CPAs from Legal Liability   128

Summary   130

Essential Terms   130

Review Questions   131

Multiple Choice Questions from CPA Examinations   132

Discussion Questions and Problems   133

Cases   137

Internet Problem 5-1: SEC Enforcement   139

PART II   The Audit Process

6   AUDIT RESPONSIBILITIES AND OBJECTIVES   141

Learning Objectives   141

Objective of Conducting an Audit of Financial Statements   142

Management's Responsibilities   143

Auditor's Responsibilities   143

Financial Statement Cycles   149

Setting Audit Objectives   154

Transaction-Related Audit Objectives   156

Balance-Related Audit Objectives   158

How Audit Objectives Are Met   160

Summary   163

Essential Terms   164

Review Questions   164

Multiple Choice Questions from CPA Examinations   165

Discussion Questions and Problems   167

Case   172

Internet Problem 6-1: Assertions and Evidence Associated with New Assurance Services   173

7   AUDIT EVIDENCE   175

Learning Objectives   175

Nature of Evidence   176

Audit Evidence Decisions   176

Persuasiveness of Evidence   178

Types of Audit Evidence   181

Analytical Procedures   188

Five Types of Analytical Procedures   190

Using Statistical Techniques and Computer Software   194

Appendix A: Common Financial Ratios   196
Short-Term Debt-Paying Ability   196
Short-Term Liquidity   197
Ability to Meet Long-Term Debt Obligations and Preferred Dividends   198
Operating and Performance Ratios   198
Illustration   200
Essential Terms   203
Review Questions   204
Multiple Choice Questions from CPA Examinations   205
Discussion Questions and Problems   206
Case   214
Internet Problem 7-1: Analytical Procedures—Industry Comparisons   215

8   AUDIT PLANNING AND DOCUMENTATION   217
Learning Objectives   217
Planning   218
Preplan the Audit   219
Obtain Background Information   224
Obtain Information about Client's Legal Obligations   226
Perform Preliminary Analytical Procedures   227
Summary of the Purposes of Audit Planning   228
Working Papers   230
Summary of Working Papers   237
Essential Terms   238
Review Questions   238
Multiple Choice Questions from CPA Examinations   240
Discussion Questions and Problems   241
Case   246
Internet Problem 8-1: Industry Research and Client Acceptance   247

9   MATERIALITY AND RISK   249
Learning Objectives   249
Materiality   250
Set Preliminary Judgment about Materiality   251
Allocate Preliminary Judgment about Materiality to Segments (Tolerable Misstatement)   254
Estimate Misstatement and Compare with Preliminary Judgment   256
Risk   257
Types of Risks   259
Factors Affecting Acceptable Audit Risk   261
Factors Affecting Inherent Risk   264
Other Materiality and Risk Considerations   267
Evaluating Results   271
Essential Terms   273
Review Questions   274
Multiple Choice Questions from CPA Examinations   275

Discussion Questions and Problems   276
Cases   283
Internet Problem 9-1: Materiality and Tolerable Misstatement   286

10   INTERNAL CONTROL AND CONTROL RISK   287

Learning Objectives   287
Client and Auditor Concerns   288
Components of Internal Control   292
Procedures to Obtain an Understanding of Internal Control   301
Assess Control Risk   305
Tests of Controls   311
Decide Planned Detection Risk and Design Substantive Tests   313
Summary   313
Essential Terms   315
Review Questions   316
Multiple Choice Questions from CPA Examinations   317
Discussion Questions and Problems   319
Case   324
Integrated Case Application—Pinnacle Manufacturing: Part I   325
Internet Problem 10-1: Corporate Governance   328

11   THE IMPACT OF INFORMATION TECHNOLOGY ON THE AUDIT PROCESS   329

Learning Objectives   329
How Information Technologies Enhance Internal Control   330
Assessing Risks of Information Technology   331
Internal Controls Specific to Information Technology   332
Impact of Information Technology on the Audit Process   338
Issues for Different IT Environments   343
Summary   346
Essential Terms   346
Review Questions   347
Multiple Choice Questions from CPA Examinations   348
Discussion Questions and Problems   349
Case   355
Internet Problem 11-1: COBIT   357

12   OVERALL AUDIT PLAN AND AUDIT PROGRAM   359

Learning Objectives   359
Types of Tests   360
Selecting Which Types of Tests to Perform   366
Evidence Mix   370
Design of the Audit Program   371
Summary of the Audit Process   379
Essential Terms   383
Review Questions   383

Multiple Choice Questions from CPA Examinations   385
Discussion Questions and Problems   386
Cases   391

PART III Application of the Audit Process to the Sales and Collection Cycle

13 **AUDIT OF THE SALES AND COLLECTION CYCLE: TESTS OF CONTROLS AND SUBSTANTIVE TESTS OF TRANSACTIONS   397**
Learning Objectives   397
Accounts and Classes of Transactions in the Sales and Collection Cycle   398
Business Functions in the Cycle and Related Documents and Records   399
Methodology for Designing Tests of Controls and Substantive Tests of Transactions for Sales   403
Sales Returns and Allowances   411
Methodology for Designing Tests of Controls and Substantive Tests of Transactions for Cash Receipts   412
Audit Tests for Uncollectible Accounts   414
Additional Internal Controls over Account Balances   415
Effect of Results of Tests of Controls and Substantive Tests of Transactions   415
Case Illustration—Hillsburg Hardware, Part I   416
Summary   424
Essential Terms   424
Review Questions   425
Multiple Choice Questions from CPA Examinations   426
Discussion Questions and Problems   428
Case   434
Integrated Case Application—Pinnacle Manufacturing: Part II   435
Internet Problem 13-1: Electronic Funds Transfer   436

14 **AUDIT SAMPLING FOR TESTS OF CONTROLS AND SUBSTANTIVE TESTS OF TRANSACTIONS   437**
Learning Objectives   437
Representative Samples   438
Statistical versus Nonstatistical Sampling and Probabilistic versus Nonprobabilistic Sample Selection   439
Nonprobabilistic Sample Selection Methods   440
Probabilistic Sample Selection Methods   441
Sampling for Exception Rates   443
Application of Nonstatistical Audit Sampling   444
Statistical Audit Sampling   453
Sampling Distribution   453
Application of Attributes Sampling   454
Case Illustration—Hillsburg Hardware, Part II   458
Essential Terms   465

Review Questions 466

Multiple Choice Questions from CPA Examinations 468

Discussion Questions and Problems 469

Case 473

Integrated Case Application—Pinnacle Manufacturing: Part III 474

15 COMPLETING THE TESTS IN THE SALES AND COLLECTION CYCLE: ACCOUNTS RECEIVABLE 475

Learning Objectives 475

Methodology for Designing Tests of Details of Balances 476

Designing Tests of Details of Balances 482

Confirmation of Accounts Receivable 488

Case Illustration—Hillsburg Hardware, Part III 493

Essential Terms 497

Review Questions 498

Multiple Choice Questions from CPA Examinations 499

Discussion Questions and Problems 500

Case 506

Integrated Case Application—Pinnacle Manufacturing: Part IV 507

Internet Problem 15-1: Revenue Recognition 512

16 AUDIT SAMPLING FOR TESTS OF DETAILS OF BALANCES 513

Learning Objectives 513

Comparisons of Audit Sampling for Tests of Details of Balances and for Tests of Controls and Substantive Tests of Transactions 514

Nonstatistical Sampling 514

Monetary Unit Sampling 522

Variables Sampling 533

Illustration Using Difference Estimation 538

Appendix A: Formulas for Monetary Unit Sampling 545

Essential Terms 546

Review Questions 547

Multiple Choice Questions from CPA Examinations 548

Discussion Questions and Problems 549

Cases 554

PART IV Application of the Audit Process to Other Cycles

17 AUDIT OF THE PAYROLL AND PERSONNEL CYCLE 557

Learning Objectives 557

Accounts and Transactions in the Payroll and Personnel Cycle 558

Business Functions in the Cycle and Related Documents and Records 558

Methodology for Designing Tests of Controls and Substantive Tests of Transactions 562

Methodology for Designing Tests of Details of Balances 567

Summary   570
Essential Terms   571
Review Questions   571
Multiple Choice Questions from CPA Examinations   572
Discussion Questions and Problems   573
Case   579

18   AUDIT OF THE ACQUISITION AND PAYMENT CYCLE: TESTS OF CONTROLS, SUBSTANTIVE TESTS OF TRANSACTIONS, AND ACCOUNTS PAYABLE   581

Learning Objectives   581
Accounts and Classes of Transactions in the Acquisition and Payment Cycle   582
Business Functions in the Cycle and Related Documents and Records   583
Methodology for Designing Tests of Controls and Substantive Tests of Transactions   586
Methodology for Designing Tests of Details of Balances for Accounts Payable   592
Summary   599
Essential Terms   600
Review Questions   601
Multiple Choice Questions from CPA Examinations   602
Discussion Questions and Problems   603
Cases   610

19   COMPLETING THE TESTS IN THE ACQUISITION AND PAYMENT CYCLE: VERIFICATION OF SELECTED ACCOUNTS   613

Learning Objectives   613
Types of Other Accounts in the Acquisition and Payment Cycle   614
Audit of Property, Plant, and Equipment   615
Audit of Prepaid Expenses   622
Audit of Accrued Liabilities   627
Audit of Income and Expense Accounts   628
Summary   634
Essential Terms   634
Review Questions   634
Multiple Choice Questions from CPA Examinations   635
Discussion Questions and Problems   637
Cases   640

20   AUDIT OF THE INVENTORY AND WAREHOUSING CYCLE   645

Learning Objectives   645
Business Functions in the Cycle and Related Documents and Records   646
Parts of the Audit of Inventory   649
Audit of Cost Accounting   650
Analytical Procedures   653
Methodology for Designing Tests of Details of Balances   653

Physical Observation of Inventory   655
Audit of Pricing and Compilation   659
Integration of the Tests   662
Summary   663
Essential Terms   664
Review Questions   664
Multiple Choice Questions from CPA Examinations   665
Discussion Questions and Problems   667
Cases   673

21   AUDIT OF THE CAPITAL ACQUISITION AND REPAYMENT CYCLE   677

Learning Objectives   677
Accounts in the Cycle   678
Notes Payable   680
Owners' Equity   685
Summary   691
Essential Terms   691
Review Questions   691
Multiple Choice Questions from CPA Examinations   692
Discussion Questions and Problems   693

22   AUDIT OF CASH BALANCES   699

Learning Objectives   699
Cash in the Bank and Transaction Cycles   700
Types of Cash Accounts   702
Audit of the General Cash Account   703
Fraud-Oriented Procedures   710
Audit of the Imprest Payroll Bank Account   715
Audit of Imprest Petty Cash   715
Summary   716
Essential Terms   716
Review Questions   716
Multiple Choice Questions from CPA Examinations   718
Discussion Questions and Problems   719
Case   723

PART V   Completing the Audit

23   COMPLETING THE AUDIT   727

Learning Objectives   727
Review for Contingent Liabilities and Commitments   728
Review for Subsequent Events   733
Final Evidence Accumulation   735
Evaluate Results   738
Issue the Audit Report   741

Communicate with the Audit Committee and Management 742

Subsequent Discovery of Facts 743

Essential Terms 745

Review Questions 745

Multiple Choice Questions from CPA Examinations 747

Discussion Questions and Problems 748

Cases 752

Internet Problem 23-1: Subsequent Events 755

PART VI Other Assurance and Nonassurance Services

24 **OTHER AUDIT, ATTESTATION SERVICES, AND COMPILATION ENGAGEMENTS 757**

Learning Objectives 757

Review and Compilation Services 758

Review of Interim Financial Information for Public Companies 762

Other Audits or Limited Assurance Engagements 763

Attestation Engagements 769

Prospective Financial Statements 772

Reporting on Internal Control 775

Agreed-Upon Procedures Engagements 777

Summary 779

Essential Terms 780

Review Questions 781

Multiple Choice Questions from CPA Examinations 782

Discussion Questions and Problems 785

25 **INTERNAL AND GOVERNMENTAL FINANCIAL AUDITING AND OPERATIONAL AUDITING 791**

Learning Objectives 791

Internal Financial Auditing 792

Governmental Financial Auditing 794

Operational Auditing 797

Summary 807

Essential Terms 807

Review Questions 808

Multiple Choice Questions from CPA, IIA, and CMA Examinations 809

Cases 811

INDEX 817

PREFACE

The eighth edition of *Auditing: An Integrated Approach* contains numerous changes and revisions, but the objectives and emphasis remain essentially the same.

The book is an introduction to auditing for students who have not had significant experience in auditing. It is intended for either a one-quarter or one-semester course at the undergraduate or graduate level. This book is also appropriate for introductory professional development courses for CPA firms, internal auditors, and government auditors.

The primary emphasis in this text is on the auditor's decision-making process. We believe that the most fundamental concepts in auditing relate to determining the nature and amount of evidence the auditor should accumulate after considering the unique circumstances of each engagement. If a student of auditing understands the objectives to be accomplished in a given audit area, the circumstances of the engagement, and the decisions to be made, he or she should be able to determine the appropriate evidence to gather and how to evaluate the evidence obtained.

Thus, as the title of this book reflects, our purpose is to integrate the most important concepts of auditing as well as certain practical aspects in a logical manner to assist students in understanding audit decision making and evidence accumulation. For example, internal control is integrated into each of the chapters dealing with a particular functional area and is related to tests of controls and substantive tests of transactions; tests of controls and substantive tests of transactions are, in turn, related to the tests of details of financial statement balances for the area; and audit sampling is applied to the accumulation of audit evidence rather than treated as a separate topic.

MOST IMPORTANT CHANGES IN THE EIGHTH EDITION

New Contributing Authors and Internet Information

The two most important changes in this edition are (1) bringing in two contributing authors and (2) adding a faculty member to manage the Internet site (www.prenhall.com/arens). The two contributing authors are Randy Elder (Syracuse University) and Mark Beasley (North Carolina State University), who have joined the team to enhance current coverage in all aspects of this book, but especially technology. Both will become coauthors in the ninth edition. Steve Glover (Brigham Young University) has added numerous in-text Internet references to current events, companies, and professional standards. In addition, he has provided Internet-based case/homework assignments.

Updates to Include Information Technology

Every chapter contains extensive changes to reflect the role that information technology (IT) plays in all accounting systems, whether those systems are relatively small or complex. The chapter on auditing in an IT environment has been completely rewritten to address how current technologies impact the auditing process at most companies.

Chapter 1 on Assurance Services

This new chapter explores various types of assurance services, including *CPA WebTrust*, and ElderCare services. This provides an introduction to the demand for all types of assurance services, including audit services. A later chapter highlights *CPA WebTrust* in even greater detail.

Internet Updates to Assist Faculty

Three times a year, adopters of the Eighth Edition will receive summaries of the **most recent changes to professional standards and summaries** of major issues affecting the auditing profession. This will help instructors easily stay abreast of emerging issues.

Editing and Updating

All chapters have been revised for clarity and technical updates with special emphasis on technology.

ORGANIZATION

The text is divided into six parts.

Part I, The Auditing Profession (Chapters 1–5)   This book begins with a study of the demand for audit and assurance services. Much of Chapter 1 is completely new material that emphasizes new assurance services being offered by CPA firms such as *CPA WebTrust* and ElderCare Plus. Chapter 2 covers the CPA profession including organization of CPA firms, the AICPA, and the SEC. In Chapter 3, there is a detailed discussion of audit reports. It emphasizes the conditions affecting the type of report the auditor must issue and the type of audit report applicable to each condition under varying levels of materiality. Chapter 4 explains ethical dilemmas, professional ethics, and the AICPA *Code of Professional Conduct*. Chapter 5 ends this part with an investigation of auditors' legal liability.

Part II, The Audit Process (Chapters 6–12)   The first two of these chapters deal with auditors' and managements' responsibilities, audit objectives, and general concepts of evidence accumulation. In addition, Chapter 7 emphasizes analytical procedures as an audit tool. Chapter 8 deals with planning the engagement and the preparation of audit working papers. Chapter 9 introduces materiality and risk and shows their effect on the audit. The study of internal control and assessment of control risk are discussed in Chapter 10, which emphasizes a proper methodology for obtaining an understanding of the five components of internal control. Chapter 11, The Impact of Information Technology on the Audit Process, is completely new and addresses the most important effects of information technology on internal controls in businesses, risks the auditor must consider, and audit evidence changes. This chapter also addresses such issues as microcomputer uses by auditors, auditing network environments, database management systems, and outsourced computer service centers. Chapter 12 summarizes Chapters 6 through 11 and integrates them with the remainder of the text.

Part III, Application of the Audit Process to the Sales and Collection Cycle (Chapters 13–16)   These chapters apply the concepts from Part II to the audit of sales, cash receipts, and the related income statement and balance sheet accounts. The appropriate audit procedures for accounts in the sales and collection cycle are related to internal control and audit objectives for tests of controls, substantive tests of transactions, and tests of details of balances. Students learn to apply audit sampling to the audit of sales, cash receipts, and accounts receivable.

In response to an increased emphasis on nonstatistical sampling by practitioners, Chapters 14 and 16 now emphasize nonstatistical sampling rather than statistical methods. Chapter 14 begins with a general discussion of audit sampling for tests of controls and substantive tests of transactions. Similarly, Chapter 16 begins with general sampling concepts for tests of details of balances. The next topic in each chapter is extensive coverage of nonstatistical sampling. The last part of each chapter covers statistical sampling techniques.

Part IV, Application of the Audit Process to Other Cycles (Chapters 17–22) Each of these chapters deals with a specific transaction cycle or part of a transaction cycle in much the same manner as Chapters 13 through 16 cover the sales and collection cycle. Each chapter in Part IV is meant to demonstrate the relationship of internal control, tests of controls, and substantive tests of transactions for each broad category of transactions to the related balance sheet and income statement accounts. Cash in the bank is studied late in the text to demonstrate how the audit of cash balances is related to most other audit areas.

Part V, Completing the Audit (Chapter 23) This part includes only one chapter, which deals with summarizing all audit tests, reviewing working papers, and all other aspects of completing an audit.

Part VI, Other Assurance and Nonassurance Services (Chapters 24 and 25) The last two chapters deal with various types of engagements and reports, other than the audit of financial statements using generally accepted accounting principles. Topics covered include review and compilation services, other audit engagements, attestation engagements, agreed-upon procedures engagements, internal financial auditing, governmental financial auditing, and operational auditing.

SUPPLEMENTS

Service to the Instructor

The Prentice Hall Accounting and Taxation Hotline 1-800-227-1816 Prentice Hall's unique Accounting and Taxation Hotline is your direct link to satisfying all your adoption needs! By calling our toll-free telephone number, you can receive information on Prentice Hall's Accounting and Tax texts and supplements. The Hotline will also process your orders and keep you up-to-date on the upcoming Prentice Hall Accounting Seminars for Educators (PHASE) in your area.

Supplements Available for Faculty and/or Students' Use

Instructor's Resource Manual This integrated source assists the instructor in teaching the course. The features include instructions for assignments, as well as helpful suggestions provided by the text authors on how to effectively teach each chapter. To enhance and simplify course planning, chapter Learning Objectives are integrated throughout the problem material. This helpful manual also includes enlarged Transparency Masters on key text tables and figures as well as additional exhibits to enhance learning.

Solutions Manual This comprehensive resource provides detailed solutions to all the end-of-chapter review questions, multiple choice questions, and cases.

Test Item File—prepared by David Kerr of Texas A&M University The Test Item File contains more than 2,500 test items, including true/false, multiple-choice, exercises/problems, critical thinking/essay, questions adapted from CPA examinations, and questions on the chapter opening vignettes. Each test item in this effective testing tool includes a difficulty level and has been content-reviewed for clarity and checked for accuracy.

Prentice Hall Custom Test—by Engineering Software Associates (ESA), Inc. Available on Windows platform and Macintosh on request, this easy-to-use computerized testing program is available on 3.5" diskettes. This user-friendly program allows you to create an exam, as well as evaluate and track student results. The PH Custom Test also provides on-line testing capabilities. Test material is adapted from the Test Item File.

A Database of PowerPoint Slides   A variety of PowerPoint slides are available for each chapter of the text. This computerized supplement provides the instructor with an interactive presentation that outlines the chapter material and reinforces text concepts using colorful graphics and charts. Instructors have the flexibility to customize the existing slides to meet their courses' needs.

Supplements for the Student

Auditing Cases—by Frank A. Buckless, Mark S. Beasley, Steven M. Glover, and Douglas F. Prawitt   This collection of 28 auditing cases addresses most major activities performed during the conduct of an audit, from client acceptance to issuance of an audit report. Many of the cases are based on actual companies, some of which were engaged in financial reporting fraud. Several cases involve students working with realistic audit evidence and preparing and evaluating audit working papers. Some cases expose students to assurance and other value-added services.

The Auditor: An Instructional Novella—by James K. Loebbecke   The purpose of this 120-page paperback is to teach students about various aspects of a typical career in public accounting that students will most likely encounter during their own careers. The novella forms a single, on-going, fictional case study of 14 situations that trace the professional life of Jack Butler, CPA.

Career Paths in Accounting—CD-ROM   Winner of the New Media INVISION Gold Award in Education, this CD-ROM provides students with a dynamic, interactive job-searching tool. Included are workshops in career planning, resume writing, and interviewing skills. Students can learn the latest market trends and facts as well as the skills required to get the right job. In addition, the CD-ROM provides the student with salary information, video clips describing specific jobs, and profiles of practitioners in the field.

The Audit: Its Environment and Application—by Gregory C. Yost   This hands-on text is designed to simulate elements of the actual audit process, the accounting profession, the public accounting firm, and the client. Used as a stand alone or as a supplement to a traditional text, this text requires students to identify and resolve issues associated with the auditing practice. An Instructor's Guide is also available.

The Lakeside Company: Case Studies in the Life-Cycle of an Audit, Eighth Edition, prepared by John Trussel, Hood College, and Joe Ben Hoyle, University of Richmond
An efficient and effective Practice Set that guides the student through the life cycle of an audit from beginning to end. The cases are designed to create a realistic view of how an auditor organizes and carries out an audit. An Instructor's Solutions Manual is also available.

ACKNOWLEDGMENTS

We acknowledge the American Institute of Certified Public Accountants for permission to quote extensively from statements on auditing standards, the *Code of Professional Conduct,* Accounting Principles Board Opinions, Uniform CPA Examinations, and other publications. The willingness of this major accounting organization to permit the use of its materials is a significant contribution to the book.

The continuing generous support of the PricewaterhouseCoopers Foundation is acknowledged, particularly in regard to the word processing, editing, and moral support of this text.

We gratefully acknowledge the contributions of the following reviewers for their suggestions and support: Sherri Anderson, Sonoma State University; Stephen K. Asare, University of Florida; Brian Ballou, Auburn University; William E. Bealing, Jr., James Madison University; Stanley F. Biggs, University of Connecticut; Joseph V. Calmie, Thomas Nelson Community College; Eric Carlsen, Kean College of New Jersey; Freddie Choo, San Francisco State University; Frank Daroca, Loyola Marymount University; Barb Esteves, University of Michigan at Flint; William L. Felix, University of Arizona; David S. Gelb, Seton Hall, University; Charles L. Holley, Virginia Commonwealth University; Gary L. Holstrum, University of South Florida; C. Randy Howard, Montana State University at Billings; Rita P. Hull, Virginia Commonwealth University; James Jiambalvo, University of Washington; David S. Kerr, Texas A & M University; Dennis Lee Kimmell, University of Akron; William R. Kinney, Jr., University of Texas at Austin; W. Robert Knechel, University of Florida; Heidi H. Meier, Cleveland State University; Alfred R. Michenzi, Loyola College in Maryland; Charles R. (Tad) Miller, California Polytechnic State University; Lawrence C. Mohrweis, Northern Arizona University; Frederick L. Neumann, University of Illinois; Kristine N. Palmer, Longwood College; Vicki S. Peden, Cal Poly—Pomona; Philip H. Siegel, Long Island University—CW Post; Robert R. Tucker, University of Illinois; D. Dewey Ward, Michigan State University; Robert J. Warth, Rochester Institute of Technology; and Jeanne H. Yamamura, University of Nevada, Reno.

A special recognition goes to Carol Borsum for her editorial, production, and moral support throughout the last three editions. Her concern for quality is beyond the ordinary. Thanks also to Mary Jo Mercer for excellence in word processing and final review and to Steve Borsum for his final review of several chapters.

We especially thank Annie Todd, Executive Editor, of Prentice Hall who is both a dedicated book publisher and a good friend. We also thank the other members of the Prentice Hall book team for their hard work and dedication, including Kathryn Sheehan, Assistant Editor; Fran Toepfer, Editorial Assistant; Beth Toland, Executive Marketing Manager; Sondra Greenfield, Associate Managing Editor; P. J. Boardman, Editor-in-Chief; Pat Smythe, Design Manager; and Paul Smolenski, Senior Manufacturing Supervisor.

A.A.A
J.K.L

PART I
(Chapters 1–5)

THE AUDITING PROFESSION

These first five chapters provide background for performing financial audits, which is our primary focus. This background will help you understand why auditors perform audits the way they do.

This book begins with a description of assurance services, including auditing, and the role of certified public accounting (CPA) firms and other organizations in doing audits. The chapters in Part I emphasize the regulation and control of CPA firms through auditing and ethical standards as well as the legal responsibilities of auditors. We also present a detailed discussion of audit reports, which are the final products of audits.

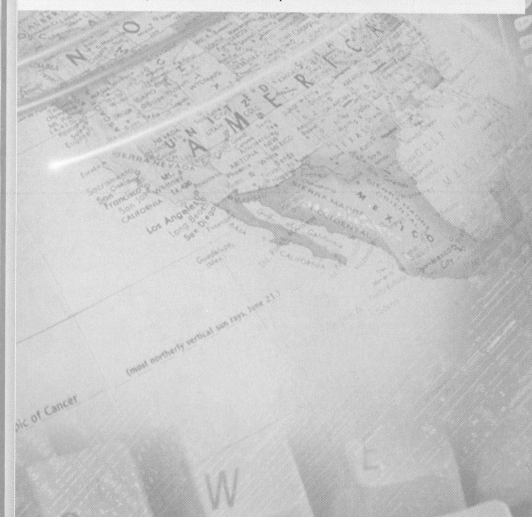

THE DEMAND FOR AUDIT AND ASSURANCE SERVICES

ALL THAT GLITTERS ISN'T GOLD

Gold! Just as the discovery of gold at Sutter's Mill started the 1849 gold rush in California, the announcement of a major gold discovery in Indonesia in 1993 sent Bre-X Minerals, Ltd., shares soaring on the Toronto stock exchange. The discovery had been billed as the "gold discovery of the century," and fights emerged over who had the rights to mine the gold.

Plenty of intrigue surrounded the gold find. Fire destroyed all the geologists' records of the find, and the exploration manager mysteriously plunged from a helicopter in an alleged suicide just before the announcement that the gold discovery appeared to be a fraud. Allegedly, the gold samples on which the original discovery was based had been "salted" with gold, and the samples had been destroyed, preventing independent verification. However, a separate, independent analysis of the discovery by another company indicated insignificant amounts of gold, resulting in a 90-percent decline in the value of Bre-X shares.

Source: William C. Symonds and Michael Shari, "After Bre-X, the Glow is Gone," *Business Week* (April 14, 1997), pp. 38–39.

LEARNING OBJECTIVES

After studying this chapter, you should be able to

1-1 Describe assurance services and distinguish audit services from other assurance and nonassurance services provided by CPAs.

1-2 Explain the importance of auditing in reducing information risk.

1-3 List the causes of information risk, and explain how this risk may be reduced.

1-4 Describe auditing.

1-5 Distinguish between auditing and accounting.

1-6 Differentiate the three main types of audits.

1-7 Identify the primary types of auditors.

1-8 Describe the requirements for becoming a CPA.

Each chapter's opening vignette illustrates important auditing principles based on realistic situations. Some vignettes are based on public information about the audits of real companies, whereas others are fictitious. Any resemblance in the latter vignettes to real firms, companies, or individuals is unintended and purely coincidental.

As the Bre-X case indicates, investors need independent assurances about financial information and other measures of company performance. Certified public accountants (CPAs) provide assurances about financial and nonfinancial statement information, including audits of historical financial statements. Auditors are valued because of their technical knowledge and independence, and they also assist companies in improving operations and internal controls. Auditors often make suggestions that improve profitability by reducing costs, including the reduction of errors and fraud, and by improving operational efficiency.

This book examines providing assurance services, especially auditing, in today's business environment. This chapter starts by defining assurance services and highlighting the relationship of audit services to other assurance and nonassurance services provided by CPAs.

ASSURANCE SERVICES

OBJECTIVE 1-1
Describe assurance services and distinguish audit services from other assurance and nonassurance services provided by CPAs.

Assurance services are independent professional services that improve the quality of information for decision makers. Individuals who are responsible for making business decisions seek assurance services to help improve the reliability and relevance of the information used as the basis for their decisions. Assurance services are valued because the assurance provider is independent and perceived as being unbiased with respect to the information examined.

Assurance services can be performed by CPAs or by a variety of other professionals. For example, Consumers Union is a nonprofit organization that tests a wide variety of products used by consumers and reports their evaluations of the quality of the products tested in *Consumer Reports*. The information provided in *Consumer Reports* is intended to help consumers make intelligent decisions about the products they buy. The information provided in *Consumer Reports* is considered more reliable by many consumers than information provided by the product manufacturers because Consumers Union is independent of the product manufacturers. Other examples of assurances provided by firms other than CPAs include the Nielsen television ratings and Arbitron radio ratings.

The need for assurance is not new. CPAs have provided many assurance services for years, particularly assurances about historical financial statement information. CPA firms have also performed assurance services related to lotteries and contests to provide assurance that winners were determined in an unbiased fashion in accordance with contest rules. More recently, CPAs have been expanding the types of assurance services they perform to include engagements that provide assurance about other types of information, such as assurance about company financial forecasts and assurance about web site controls. The demand for assurance services is expected to grow as the demand for forward-looking information increases and as more real-time information becomes available through the Internet.

Attestation Services

One category of assurance services provided by CPAs is attestation services. An **attestation service** is a type of assurance service in which the CPA firm issues a written communication that expresses a conclusion about the reliability of a written assertion of another party. There are three categories of attestation services: audit of historical financial statements, review of historical financial statements, and other attestation services.

Audit of Historical Financial Statements An **audit of historical financial statements** is a form of attestation service in which the auditor issues a written report expressing an opinion about whether the financial statements are in material conformity with generally accepted accounting principles. Audits represent the predominant form of assurance performed by CPA firms.

When presenting information in the form of financial statements, the client makes various assertions about its financial condition and results of operations. External users who rely on those financial statements to make business decisions look to the auditor's report as an indication of the statements' reliability. They value the auditor's assurance because of the auditor's independence from the client and knowledge of financial statement reporting matters.

Publicly traded companies in the United States are required to have audits under the federal securities acts. Auditor reports can be found in any public company's annual financial report, and most companies' audited financial statements can be accessed over the Internet from the Securities and Exchange Commission's (SEC's) EDGAR database. Even before enactment of the federal securities acts, many public companies voluntarily contracted for audits to provide assurance to investors and to facilitate access to capital. Many privately held companies also have annual financial statement audits to obtain financing from banks and other financial institutions. Government and not-for-profit entities often have audits to meet the requirements of lenders or funding sources.

Review of Historical Financial Statements A **review of historical financial statements** is another type of attestation service performed by CPAs. Many nonpublic companies want to provide assurance on their financial statements, without incurring the cost of an audit. Whereas an audit provides a high level of assurance, a review service provides a moderate amount of assurance on the financial statements, and less evidence is necessary to support this level of assurance. A review is often adequate to meet users' needs and can be provided by the CPA firm at a much lower fee than an audit.

Other Attestation Services CPAs provide numerous other attestation services. Many of these services are a natural extension of the audit of historical financial statements, as users seek independent assurances about other types of information. For example, banks often require debtors to engage CPAs to provide assurance about the debtor's compliance with certain financial covenant provisions stated in the loan agreement. CPAs also provide assurance about the effectiveness of a client's internal controls over financial reporting. The information about internal controls is closely related to the financial statements, but it is also forward-looking because effective internal controls reduce the likelihood of future misstatements in the financial statements. CPAs also can attest to the information in a client's forecasted financial statements, which are often used to obtain financing. Attestation services are discussed further in Chapter 24.

Other Assurance Services

Most of the other assurance services that CPAs provide do not meet the formal definition of attestation services. They are similar to attestation services in that the CPA must be independent and must provide assurance about information used by decision makers. They differ in that the CPA is not required to issue a written report, and the assurance does not have to be about the reliability of another party's written assertion about compliance with specified criteria. Rather, in these other assurance services engagements, the assurance is about the reliability and relevance of information, which may or may not have been asserted by another party. The common feature of all assurance services, including audits and attestation services, is the focus on improving the quality of information used by decision makers.

"AND THE OSCAR GOES TO ..."
"THERE SHE IS, MISS AMERICA ..."
"WELCOME TO THE NEW YORK STATE LOTTERY ..."

You probably recognize these statements from the Academy Awards, the Miss America Pageant, and the New York State Lottery drawing. What you may not recognize is what these well-known events have to do with assurance services. Each event is observed by CPAs from a major accounting firm to assure viewers that the contests were fairly conducted. So when you become a member of a CPA firm, you might not win an Oscar—but you could be on the Oscars!

Elliott
Committee
Report[1]

Users of traditional services provided by CPAs have expressed a desire for assurance about other information outside the scope of historical financial information. Because of this demand for other forms of assurance, the American Institute of Certified Public Accountants (AICPA) formed the Special Committee on Assurance Services (commonly called the Elliott Committee). The Elliott Committee was charged with researching and developing new assurance services opportunities for CPAs to provide to businesses and individual clients who need relevant and reliable information for critical decision making. The Elliott Committee initially released its findings in early 1997, reporting in a paperless format made available only on the AICPA's web page. The committee chose the electronic form of reporting to allow the report to be a "living document" that could evolve to meet the changing information demands of the business community.

CPAs have numerous opportunities to perform other assurance services engagements. The demand for assurance on other types of information is expected to grow substantially with new types of risks faced by businesses and increases in the amount of available information sources. However, one important difference between attestation services and other assurance services is the potential competition faced by CPA firms when performing other assurance services. Audits and many types of attestation services are limited by regulation to licensed CPAs, but the market for other forms of assurance is open to non-CPA competitors. For example, assisting clients in the preparation of customer surveys and evaluation of the reliability and relevance of information developed from those surveys is one potential assurance service that can be provided by CPAs. In the market for those services, CPAs will likely face competition from market research firms. One competitive advantage that CPA firms have in the market for assurance services is their reputation for competence and independence.

Assurance Services on Information Technology One of the major factors affecting the demand for other assurance services is the growth of the Internet and electronic commerce. Concerns over privacy and security of information on the Internet has slowed the potential growth of electronic commerce. In addition, the volume of real-time information available on the Internet is shifting the need for assurance from historical information at a point in time, such as financial statements, to assurances about the reliability of processes generating information in a real-time format. For example, many business functions, such as ordering and making payments, are conducted over the Internet and directly between computers using electronic data interchange (EDI). As transactions and information are shared on-line and in real-time, there is even greater demand for assurances about computer controls surrounding information transacted electronically and the security of the information related to the transactions. CPAs can help provide assurance about these functions. Two examples of assurance services related to information technology are assurances over web site controls and assurances about information system reliability.

CPA
WebTrust

- *CPA WebTrust services.* To respond to the growing need for assurance resulting from the explosion of business transacted over the Internet, the AICPA created the *CPA WebTrust* assurance service. CPA firms that are licensed by the AICPA to perform this service provide assurance to users of web sites through the CPA's electronic *WebTrust* seal affixed to the web site. This seal assures the user that the web site owner has met established criteria related to business practices, transaction integrity, and information processes. *WebTrust* is an attestation service, and the *WebTrust* seal is a symbolic representation of the CPA's report on management's assertions about its disclosure of electronic commerce practices.
- *Information system reliability services.* In these engagements, CPAs provide assurance that an information system has been designed and operated to produce reliable data, including tests of the system to determine whether the system protects against

[1]To illustrate or emphasize text material, the authors have identified interesting company or organization web sites on the Internet. Internet links are noted by icons in the margins, and a brief description and hot link for each site can be found at Prentice Hall's Companion Web Site (CW site), www.prenhall.com/arens.

potential causes of data defects. Whereas the *WebTrust* assurance service is primarily designed to provide assurance to third-party users of a web site, information systems reliability services might be performed by CPAs to provide assurance to management, the board of directors, or third parties about the reliability of information systems used to generate real-time information.

Assurance Services on Other Types of Information The AICPA Special Committee on Assurance Services has identified a number of other services designed to enhance the relevance of information. Examples of these services include defining business performance measures, defining and developing measures of quality for services to the elderly ("ElderCare Plus"), developing other health care performance measures, and developing comprehensive profiles of risk. The following is a description of the first two of these services:

- *Business performance measurement services.* Investors, creditors, boards of directors, and managers often need more comprehensive information to evaluate an entity's performance than historical financial statements provide. These comprehensive performance measures are often called a balanced scorecard. Using a balanced scorecard, the board of directors and managers define an entity's strategic objectives and goals, such as increased customer satisfaction, unit sales and revenue growth, and increased shareholder value. To help the entity achieve these goals, the board of directors and managers implement performance measurement systems. CPAs can provide assurance about whether financial and nonfinancial information being reported from the entity's performance measurement system is reliable and whether the performance measures being used are accurately leading the entity toward meeting its strategic goals and objectives.
- *ElderCare Plus.* As the U.S. population ages, more and more elderly persons require assistance to live in their own homes or require institutional care. These individuals and their family members are increasingly concerned about the quality of care and related services. This emerging trend offers CPAs an opportunity to provide assurances to these elderly individuals and their families that care is being provided at an acceptable level. Such services might include periodic reporting to family members about the degree to which caregivers are complying with the contracted level of care or supervising the investments and accounting for the elderly individual's estate. Due to the varying types of care services provided, ElderCare Plus is an example of an assurance service that may require the expertise of other professionals. In these engagements, the CPA serves as the coordinator and assurer of the quality of services provided to the elderly individual.

There are practically no limits to the types of assurances that CPAs can provide. Examples of other assurance service opportunities for CPAs are included in Table 1-1 (p. 6).

Nonassurance Services Provided by CPAs

CPA firms perform numerous other services that generally fall outside the scope of assurance services. Three specific examples of nonassurance services CPAs often provide include accounting and bookkeeping services, tax services, and management consulting services.

Some overlap exists between management consulting and assurance services. The primary purpose of a management consulting engagement is to generate a recommendation to management, whereas the primary purpose of an assurance services engagement is to improve the quality of information. Although the quality of information is often an important criterion in a consulting engagement, this goal is normally not the primary purpose. For example, a CPA may be engaged to design and install a new information technology system for a client as a consulting engagement. The purpose of that engagement is to install the new system, with the goal of improved information being a by-product of that engagement. Occasionally, consulting engagements and assurance services overlap when improving the quality of information for decision makers is a primary goal.

CPA firm revenues from management consulting services have increased significantly in recent years. Many large CPA firms have departments involved exclusively in performing management consulting services. Management consulting services are often called management advisory services (MAS).

Professional
Services Firms

TABLE 1-1   Other Assurance Services Examples

Other Assurance Services	These Services Involve
Controls over and risks related to investments, including policies related to derivatives	Assessing the processes surrounding a company's investment activities to identify risks and to determine the effectiveness of those processes in meeting the company's investment objectives
Mystery shopping	Performing anonymous shopping to assess sales personnel interactions with customers and procedures performed by sales personnel
Assessment of risks of accumulation, distribution, and storage of digital information	Assessing physical and on-line security risks and related controls surrounding data and other information stored electronically, including the adequacy of back-up and off-site storage
Fraud and illegal acts risk assessment	Developing fraud risk profiles and assessing the adequacy of company systems and policies in preventing and detecting fraud and illegal acts
Compliance with trading policies and procedures	Examining transactions between trading partners to ensure that the handling of the transactions complies with the terms of the trading agreement or contract, including the identification of risks surrounding the trade arrangement
Compliance with entertainment royalty agreements	Assessing whether royalties paid to artists, authors, and others are in accordance with royalty agreement provisions
ISO 9000 certifications	Certifying a company's compliance with ISO 9000 quality control standards, which help ensure company products are of high quality
Annual environmental audit	Assessing whether company policies effectively ensure the company's compliance with environmental standards and laws

Source: AICPA Special Committee on Assurance Services.

Figure 1-1 reflects the relationship between assurance and nonassurance services. Audits, reviews, and other attestation services are all examples of attestation services, which fall under the scope of assurance services. Some of the new assurance services identified by the AICPA, such as *CPA WebTrust*, are also attestation services. In contrast, most management consulting services, accounting and bookkeeping services, and tax services fall outside the scope of assurance services, although there is some common area of overlap between consulting and assurance services.

FIGURE 1-1   Relationships among Assurance Services, Attestation Services, and Nonassurance Services

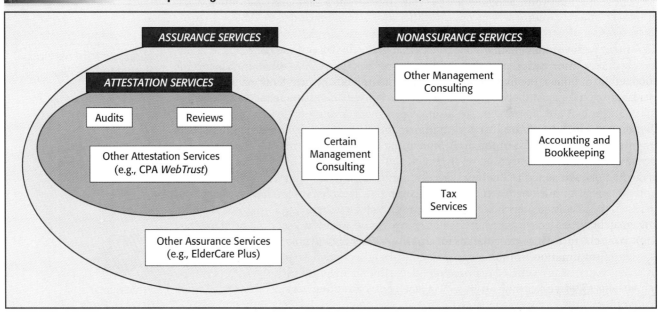

This book emphasizes the audit of historical financial statements by CPA firms. Because of the need for reliance on the financial statements by external users, there is a well-defined set of standards for the audit of historical financial statements. Also, the ability to issue opinions on financial statements is restricted to licensed CPAs. Many of the skills and concepts necessary to perform an audit of historical financial statements are useful in the performance of other assurance services.

OBJECTIVE 1-2
Explain the importance of auditing in reducing information risk.

To illustrate the need for auditing, consider the decision of a bank manager in making a loan to a business. This decision will be based on such factors as previous financial relationships with the business and the financial condition of the business as reflected by its financial statements. If the bank makes the loan, it will charge a rate of interest determined primarily by three factors:

1. *Risk-free interest rate.* This is approximately the rate the bank could earn by investing in U.S. treasury notes for the same length of time as the business loan.
2. *Business risk for the customer.* This risk reflects the possibility that the business will not be able to repay its loan because of economic or business conditions such as a recession, poor management decisions, or unexpected competition in the industry.
3. *Information risk.* **Information risk** reflects the possibility that the information upon which the business risk decision was made was inaccurate. A likely cause of the information risk is the possibility of inaccurate financial statements.

Auditing has no effect on either the risk-free interest rate or business risk, but it can have a significant effect on information risk. If the bank manager is satisfied that there is minimal information risk because a borrower's financial statements are audited, the risk is substantially reduced and the overall interest rate to the borrower can be reduced. The reduction of information risk can have a significant effect on the borrower's ability to obtain capital at a reasonable cost. For example, assume a large company has total interest-bearing debt of approximately $10 billion. If the interest rate on that debt is reduced by only 1 percent, the annual savings in interest is $100 million.

As society becomes more complex, decision makers are more likely to receive unreliable information. There are several reasons for this: remoteness of information, biases and motives of the provider, voluminous data, and the existence of complex exchange transactions.

Causes of Information Risk

OBJECTIVE 1-3
List the causes of information risk, and explain how this risk may be reduced.

Remoteness of Information In the modern world, it is virtually impossible for a decision maker to have much firsthand knowledge about the organization with which he or she does business. Information provided by others must be relied upon. When information is obtained from others, the likelihood of it being intentionally or unintentionally misstated increases.

Biases and Motives of the Provider If information is provided by someone whose goals are inconsistent with those of the decision maker, the information may be biased in favor of the provider. The reason could be an honest optimism about future events or an intentional emphasis designed to influence users in a certain manner. In either case, the result is a misstatement of information. For example, in a lending decision in which the borrower provides financial statements to the lender, there is considerable likelihood that the borrower will bias the statements to increase the chance of obtaining a loan. The misstatement could be in the form of outright incorrect dollar amounts or inadequate or incomplete disclosures of information.

Voluminous Data As organizations become larger, so does the volume of their exchange transactions. This increases the likelihood that improperly recorded information will be included in the records—perhaps buried in a large amount of other information. For example, if a large government agency overpays a vendor's invoice by $200, there is a fairly good chance that it will not be uncovered unless the agency has instituted reasonably complex procedures to find this type of misstatement. If many minor misstatements remain undiscovered, the combined total could be significant.

Complex Exchange Transactions In the past few decades, exchange transactions between organizations have become increasingly complex and therefore more difficult to record properly. For example, the correct accounting treatment of the acquisition of one entity by another poses relatively difficult and important accounting problems. Other examples include properly combining and disclosing the results of operations of subsidiaries in different industries and properly disclosing derivative financial instruments under Financial Accounting Standards Board Statement No. 133 (SFAS 133).

CAPITAL COSTS TO SHRINK

According to a recent article in *Accounting Today*, corporate America is paying too much for new capital, and independent auditors are part of the solution. Robert Elliott, a senior partner with KPMG, believes the cost of capital could shrink significantly in the next 5 to 10 years as a result of advances in technology, streamlined regulations, and broader audit coverage.

Elliott uses a hypothetical example to illustrate his prediction. Assuming a cost of capital of 13 percent, he estimates this rate is composed of the following:

- 5.5 percent risk-free interest rate
- 3.5 percent economic risk premium *(business risk)*
- 4 percent information cost *(information risk)*

According to Elliott's example, information risk comprises approximately 30 percent of the cost of capital. Elliott believes the following factors will drastically reduce information risk in the next 5 to 10 years:

- Technological advances will drastically decrease the cost of providing relevant and timely information to investors.
- As more companies go "on-line," the risk of investors obtaining outdated information decreases.
- New accounting and auditing standards already require better disclosures about segment operations, risks, and uncertainties. New rules may require data on nonfinancial performance and forward-looking information.
- Auditors will find more efficient ways to audit, such as continuous auditing of computerized control systems, which may provide new levels of assurance.

Elliott predicts that if and when all of the preceding factors materialize, the cost of capital in his hypothetical example could be reduced from 13 percent to 11.5 percent. The entire reduction would result from reduced information risk.

Source: Adapted from *Accounting Today* (December 11, 1995), p. 16.

Reducing Information Risk

Business managers and financial statement users may conclude that the best way to deal with information risk is simply to have it remain reasonably high. A small company may find it less expensive to pay higher interest costs than to increase the costs of reducing information risk.

For larger businesses, it is usually practical to incur costs to reduce information risk. There are three main ways to do so.

User Verifies Information The user may go to the business premises to examine records and obtain information about the reliability of the statements. Normally, this is impractical because of costs. In addition, it would be economically inefficient for all users to verify the information individually. Nevertheless, some users perform their own verification. For example, the Internal Revenue Service (IRS) does considerable verification of businesses and individuals to determine whether tax returns filed reflect the actual tax due the federal government. Similarly, if a business intends to purchase another business, it is common for the purchaser to use a special audit team to independently verify and evaluate key information of the prospective business.

User Shares Information Risk with Management There is considerable legal precedent indicating that management is responsible for providing reliable information to users. If users rely on inaccurate financial statements and as a result incur a financial loss, there is a basis for a lawsuit against management. A difficulty with sharing information risk with management is that users may not be able to collect on losses. If a company is unable to re-pay a loan because of bankruptcy, it is unlikely that management will have sufficient funds to repay users.

Audited Financial Statements Are Provided The most common way for users to obtain reliable information is to have an independent audit performed. The audited information is then used in the decision-making process on the assumption that it is reasonably complete, accurate, and unbiased.

Typically, management engages the auditor to provide assurances to users that the financial statements are reliable. If the financial statements are ultimately determined to be incorrect, the auditor can be sued by both the users and management. Auditors obviously have considerable legal responsibility for their work.

NATURE OF AUDITING

OBJECTIVE 1-4
Describe auditing.

So far, we have discussed the importance of audits of financial statements and their relation to other attestation and assurance services offered by CPA firms. We now examine auditing more specifically using the following definition:

> **Auditing** is the accumulation and evaluation of evidence about information to determine and report on the degree of correspondence between the information and established criteria. Auditing should be done by a competent, independent person.

This definition of the auditing process is considerably broader than the definition of an audit of historical financial statements and encompasses many attestation and assurance service activities. The definition also includes several key words and phrases. For ease of understanding, the terms are discussed in a different order than they occur in the description.

Information and Established Criteria

To do an audit, there must be information in a *verifiable form* and some standards (*criteria*) by which the auditor can evaluate the information. Information can and does take many forms. Auditors routinely perform audits of quantifiable information, including companies' financial statements and individuals' federal income tax returns. Auditors also perform audits of more subjective information, such as the effectiveness of computer systems and the efficiency of manufacturing operations.

The criteria for evaluating information also vary depending on the information being audited. For example, in the audit of historical financial statements by CPA firms, the criteria are usually generally accepted accounting principles. To illustrate, this means that in the audit of General Motors' financial statements, the CPA firm determines whether

General Motors' financial statements have been prepared in accordance with generally accepted accounting principles. For the audit of tax returns by the IRS, the criteria are found in the Internal Revenue Code. In the audit of General Motors' corporate tax return by the IRS, the internal revenue agent would use the Internal Revenue Code as the criteria for correctness, not generally accepted accounting principles.

For more subjective information, such as auditing the effectiveness of computer operations, it is more difficult to establish criteria. Typically, auditors and the entities being audited agree on the criteria well before the audit starts. For a computer application, for example, the criteria might include the absence of input or output errors.

Accumulating and Evaluating Evidence

Evidence is any information used by the auditor to determine whether the information being audited is stated in accordance with the established criteria. Evidence takes many different forms, including oral testimony of the auditee (client), written communication with outsiders, and observations by the auditor. It is important to obtain a sufficient quality and volume of evidence to satisfy the purpose of the audit. Determining the types and amount of evidence necessary and evaluating whether the information corresponds to the established criteria is a critical part of every audit. It is the primary subject of this book.

Competent, Independent Person

The auditor must be qualified to understand the criteria used and must be *competent* to know the types and amount of evidence to accumulate to reach the proper conclusion after the evidence has been examined. The auditor must also have an *independent mental attitude*. The competence of the individual performing the audit is of little value if he or she is biased in the accumulation and evaluation of evidence.

Auditors reporting on company financial statements are often called **independent auditors**. Even though an auditor of published financial statements is paid a fee by a company, he or she is normally sufficiently independent to conduct audits that can be relied on by users. Although absolute independence is impossible, auditors strive to maintain a high level of independence to keep the confidence of users relying on their reports. Although internal auditors work for the company, they usually report directly to top management to help maintain independence from the operating units being audited.

Reporting

The final stage in the auditing process is preparing the **audit report,** which is the communication of the auditor's findings to users. Reports differ in nature, but all must inform readers of the degree of correspondence between information and established criteria.

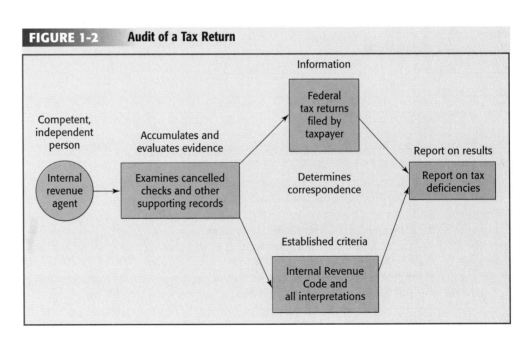

FIGURE 1-2   Audit of a Tax Return

Reports also differ in form and can vary from the highly technical type usually associated with financial statement audits to a simple oral report in the case of an operational audit of a small department's effectiveness.

Figure 1-2 (p. 10) summarizes the important ideas in the description of auditing by illustrating an audit of an individual's tax return by an internal revenue agent. The objective is to determine whether the tax return was prepared in a manner consistent with the requirements of the federal Internal Revenue Code. To accomplish the objective, the agent examines supporting records provided by the taxpayer and from other sources, such as the taxpayer's employer. After completing the audit, the internal revenue agent will issue a report to the taxpayer assessing additional taxes, advising that a refund is due, or stating that there is no change in the status of the tax return.

DISTINCTION BETWEEN AUDITING AND ACCOUNTING

OBJECTIVE 1-5
Distinguish between auditing and accounting.

Many financial statement users and members of the general public confuse auditing with accounting. The confusion results because most auditing is usually concerned with accounting information, and many auditors have considerable expertise in accounting matters. The confusion is increased by giving the title "certified public accountant" to many individuals who perform audits.

Accounting is the recording, classifying, and summarizing of economic events in a logical manner for the purpose of providing financial information for decision making. The function of accounting is to provide certain types of quantitative information that management and others can use to make decisions. To provide relevant information, accountants must have a thorough understanding of the principles and rules that provide the basis for preparing the accounting information. In addition, accountants must develop a system to make sure that the entity's economic events are properly recorded on a timely basis and at a reasonable cost.

In auditing accounting data, the concern is with determining whether recorded information properly reflects the economic events that occurred during the accounting period. Because accounting rules are the criteria for evaluating whether the accounting information is properly recorded, any auditor involved with these data must also thoroughly understand those rules. In the context of the audit of financial statements, the rules are generally accepted accounting principles. Throughout this text, the assumption is made that the reader has already studied generally accepted accounting principles.

In addition to understanding accounting, the auditor must possess expertise in the accumulation and interpretation of audit evidence. It is this expertise that distinguishes auditors from accountants. Determining the proper audit procedures, deciding the number and types of items to test, and evaluating the results are problems unique to the auditor.

TYPES OF AUDITS

OBJECTIVE 1-6
Differentiate the three main types of audits.

CPAs perform three primary types of audits: financial statement audits, operational audits, and compliance audits. The latter two services are often called audit activities, even though they are most similar to assurance and attestation services. We now examine each of the three types of audits in more detail.

Financial Statement Audits

A **financial statement audit** is conducted to determine whether the overall financial statements (the information being verified) are stated in accordance with specified criteria. Normally, the criteria are generally accepted accounting principles, although it is also common to conduct audits of financial statements prepared using the cash basis or some other basis of accounting appropriate for the organization. The financial statements most often included are the statement of financial position, income statement, and statement of cash flows, including accompanying footnotes.

Operational Audits

An **operational audit** is a review of any part of an organization's operating procedures and methods for the purpose of evaluating *efficiency* and *effectiveness*. At the completion of an operational audit, management normally expects recommendations for improving operations. An example of an operational audit is evaluating the efficiency and accuracy of processing payroll transactions in a newly installed computer system. Another example, where most accountants would feel less qualified, is evaluating the efficiency, accuracy, and customer satisfaction in processing the distribution of letters and packages by a company such as Federal Express.

Because of the many different areas in which operational effectiveness can be evaluated, it is impossible to characterize the conduct of a typical operational audit. In one organization, the auditor might evaluate the relevancy and sufficiency of the information used by management in making decisions to acquire new fixed assets, whereas in a different organization, the auditor might evaluate the efficiency of the information flow in processing sales. In operational auditing, the reviews are not limited to accounting. They can include the evaluation of organization structure, computer operations, production methods, marketing, and any other area in which the auditor is qualified.

The conduct of an operational audit and the reported results are less easily defined than for either of the other two types of audits. Efficiency and effectiveness of operations are far more difficult to evaluate objectively than compliance or the presentation of financial statements in accordance with generally accepted accounting principles. In addition, establishing criteria for evaluating the information in an operational audit is an extremely subjective matter. In this sense, operational auditing is more like management consulting than what is generally regarded as auditing. Operational auditing has increased in importance in the past decade. It is discussed in greater depth in Chapter 25.

Compliance Audits

The purpose of a **compliance audit** is to determine whether the auditee is following specific procedures, rules, or regulations set by some higher authority. A compliance audit for a private business could include determining whether accounting personnel are following the procedures prescribed by the company controller, reviewing wage rates for compliance with minimum wage laws, or examining contractual agreements with bankers and other lenders to be sure the company is complying with legal requirements. In the audit of governmental units such as school districts, there is considerable compliance auditing because of the extensive regulation by higher government authorities. In virtually every private and not-for-profit organization, there are prescribed policies, contractual agreements, and legal requirements that may call for compliance auditing.

Results of compliance audits are typically reported to someone within the organizational unit being audited rather than to a broad spectrum of users. Management, as opposed to outside users, is the primary group concerned with the extent of compliance with certain prescribed procedures and regulations. Therefore, a significant portion of work of this type is done by auditors employed by the organizational units themselves. There are

TABLE 1-2	Examples of the Three Types of Audits			
Type of Audit	**Example**	**Information**	**Established Criteria**	**Available Evidence**
Financial Statement Audit	Annual audit of General Motors' financial statements	General Motors' financial statements	Generally accepted accounting principles	Documents, records, and outside sources of evidence
Operational Audit	Evaluate whether the computerized payroll processing for subsidiary H is operating efficiently and effectively	Number of payroll records processed in a month, costs of the department, and number of errors made	Company standards for efficiency and effectiveness in payroll department	Error reports, payroll records, and payroll processing costs
Compliance Audit	Determine whether bank requirements for loan continuation have been met	Company records	Loan agreement provisions	Financial statements and calculations by the auditor

exceptions, however. When an organization wants to determine whether individuals or organizations are complying with its requirements, the auditor is employed by the organization issuing the requirements. An example is the auditing of taxpayers for compliance with the federal tax laws, in which case the auditor is employed by the government to audit the taxpayers' tax returns. Compliance audits for federally funded grant programs are widely performed by CPAs. These are discussed in detail in Chapter 25.

Table 1-2 (p. 12) summarizes the three types of audits and includes an example of each type and an illustration of three of the key parts of the definition of auditing applied to each type of audit.

TYPES OF AUDITORS

OBJECTIVE 1-7
Identify the primary types of auditors.

Several types of auditors are in practice today. The most common are certified public accounting firms, general accounting office auditors, internal revenue agents, and internal auditors.

Certified Public Accounting Firms

Certified public accounting firms are responsible for auditing the published historical financial statements of all publicly traded companies, most other reasonably large companies, and many smaller companies and noncommercial organizations. Because of the widespread use of audited financial statements in the U.S. economy, as well as businesspersons' and other users' familiarity with these statements, it is common to use the terms *auditor* and *CPA firm* synonymously, even though several different types of auditors exist. The title *certified public accounting firm* reflects the fact that auditors who express audit opinions on financial statements must be licensed as CPAs. CPA firms are often called *external auditors* or *independent auditors* to distinguish them from internal auditors.

General Accounting Office Auditors

The United States General Accounting Office (GAO) is a nonpartisan agency in the legislative branch of the federal government. A **general accounting office auditor** is an auditor working for the GAO. The GAO, which is headed by the Comptroller General, reports to and is responsible solely to Congress. The audit staff's primary responsibility is to perform the audit function for Congress.

Types of Auditors

Many of the GAO's audit responsibilities are the same as those of a CPA firm. Much of the financial information prepared by various government agencies is audited by the GAO before it is submitted to Congress. Because the authority for expenditures and receipts of governmental agencies is defined by law, there is considerable emphasis on compliance in these audits.

An increasing portion of the GAO's audit efforts has been devoted to evaluating the *operational efficiency and effectiveness* of various federal programs. An example is the evaluation of the computer operations of a governmental unit. The auditor can review and evaluate any aspect of the computer system but is likely to emphasize the adequacy of the equipment, the efficiency of the operations, the adequacy and usefulness of the output, and similar matters, with the objective of identifying means of providing the same services at a lower cost.

Because of the immense size of many federal agencies and the similarity of their operations, the GAO has made significant advances in developing better methods of auditing through the widespread use of highly sophisticated statistical sampling and computer risk assessment techniques.

In many states, experience as a GAO auditor fulfills the experience requirement for becoming a CPA. In those states, if an individual passes the CPA examination and fulfills the experience stipulations for becoming a GAO auditor, he or she may then obtain a CPA certificate.

As a result of their great responsibility for auditing the expenditures of the federal government, their use of advanced auditing concepts, their eligibility to be CPAs, and their opportunities for performing operational audits, GAO auditors are highly regarded in the auditing profession.

Internal Revenue Agents

The IRS, under the direction of the Commissioner of Internal Revenue, is responsible for enforcing the *federal tax laws* as they have been defined by Congress and interpreted by the courts. A major responsibility of the IRS is to audit the taxpayers' returns to determine whether they have complied with the tax laws. The auditors who perform these examinations are called **internal revenue agents.** These audits are solely compliance audits.

It might seem that the audit of returns for compliance with the federal tax laws would be a simple and straightforward problem, but nothing could be farther from the truth. The tax laws are highly complicated, and there are hundreds of volumes of interpretations. The tax returns being audited vary from the simple returns of individuals who work for only one employer and take the standard tax deduction to the highly complex returns of multinational corporations. Taxation problems involve individual taxpayers, gift taxes, estate taxes, corporate taxes, trusts, and so on. An auditor involved in any of these areas must have considerable tax knowledge and auditing skills to conduct an effective audit.

Internal Auditors

Internal auditors are employed by individual companies to audit for management much as the GAO does for Congress. The internal audit group in some large firms can include more than 100 people and typically reports directly to the president, another high executive officer, or even the audit committee of the board of directors.

Internal auditors' responsibilities vary considerably, depending on the employer. Some internal audit staffs consist of only one or two employees who may spend most of their time doing routine compliance auditing. Other internal audit staffs consist of numerous employees who have diverse responsibilities, including many outside the accounting area. Many internal auditors are involved in operational auditing or have expertise in evaluating computer systems.

To operate effectively, an internal auditor must be independent of the line functions in an organization, but he or she cannot be independent of the entity as long as an employer-employee relationship exists. Internal auditors provide management with valuable information for making decisions concerning effective operation of its business. Users from outside the entity are unlikely to want to rely on information verified solely by internal auditors because of their lack of independence. This lack of independence is the major difference between internal auditors and CPA firms.

In many states, internal audit experience can be used to fulfill the experience requirement for becoming a CPA. Many internal auditors pursue certification as a certified internal auditor (CIA), and some internal auditors pursue both the CPA and CIA designation.

CERTIFIED PUBLIC ACCOUNTANT

> **OBJECTIVE 1-8**
> Describe the requirements for becoming a CPA.

Use of the title **certified public accountant** (CPA) is regulated by state law through the licensing departments of each state. Within any state, the regulations usually differ for becoming a CPA and retaining a license to practice after the designation has been initially achieved. To become a CPA, three requirements must be met. These are summarized in Figure 1-3.

For a person planning to become a CPA, it is essential to know the requirements in the state where he or she plans to obtain and maintain the CPA designation. The best source of that information is the State Board of Accountancy for the state in which the person plans to be certified. It is possible to transfer the CPA designation from one state to another, but additional requirements often must be met for formal education, practice experience, or continuing education.

Most young professionals who want to become CPAs start their careers working for a CPA firm. After they become CPAs, many leave the firm to work in industry, government, or education. These people may continue to be CPAs but often give up their right to practice as independent auditors. CPAs who practice as independent auditors must meet defined continuing education and licensing requirements to maintain their right to practice in most states. Therefore, it is common for accountants to be CPAs who do not practice as independent auditors.

CPA Information
and Requirements

FIGURE 1-3   Three Requirements for Becoming a CPA

Educational Requirement	Uniform CPA Examination Requirement	Experience Requirement

Normally, an undergraduate degree with a major in accounting, including a minimum number of accounting credits. Some states require 150 semester credits (225 quarter credits) before taking the examination; others mandate fewer credits before taking the examination, but require 150 semester credits before receiving the certificate.	Two-day examination offered in May and November. Examination sections are as follows:
	  Auditing—$4\frac{1}{2}$ hours
	  Accounting and Reporting—$3\frac{1}{2}$ hours
	  Financial Accounting and Reporting—$4\frac{1}{2}$ hours
	  Business Law and Professional Responsibilities—3 hours
	All parts except accounting and reporting include at least 20 percent essay and problems. Some states also require a separate ethics examination.
		Varies widely from no experience to 2 years, including auditing. Some states include experience working for governmental units or in internal auditing.

Individuals wanting more information about the CPA examination will find the booklet *Information for Uniform CPA Examination Candidates* useful. The AICPA also publishes selected examination questions with unofficial answers that are indexed to the content specification outlines of the examination. Ordering information, as well as other information for CPA candidates, can be found at the AICPA web site (www.aicpa.org).

Some of the questions and problems at the end of the chapters in this book have been taken from past CPA examinations. They are designated "AICPA" or "AICPA adapted."

CPA EXAMINATION CHANGES ARE COMING

The AICPA board of examiners has set a target date of 2001 to have the Uniform CPA Examination totally or partially computerized. A computerized examination could be offered more frequently than the current written examination, which is given twice each year.

The AICPA made the Uniform CPA Examination nondisclosed, effective with the May 1996 examination. A nondisclosed examination means that questions from the examination are not made available to anyone. The nondisclosed examination allows questions to be reused, resulting in a consistent level of testing and enhanced reliability. Nondisclosure of questions will also facilitate the development of the large question bank necessary to offer a computerized examination. Although the AICPA no longer releases the complete examination text with unofficial answers following each CPA examination, the AICPA does publish selected questions and an outline of the examination content.

Source: *Journal of Accountancy* (January 1998), pp. 61–64.

SUMMARY

This chapter discussed audit and assurance services and described the relationships among audits, attestation services, and assurance services. The market for assurance services is expected to grow with increases in technology and information. Audits are valuable because they reduce information risk, which lowers the cost of obtaining capital. This chapter also defined auditing and described different types of audits and auditors.

Accounting—the recording, classifying, and summarizing of economic events in a logical manner for the purpose of providing financial information for decision making

Assurance services—independent professional services that improve the quality of information for decision makers

Attestation service—a type of assurance service in which the CPA firm issues a written communication that expresses a conclusion about the reliability of a written assertion of another party

Audit of historical financial statements—a form of attestation service in which the auditor issues a written report stating whether the financial statements are in material conformity with generally accepted accounting principles

Auditing—the accumulation and evaluation of evidence about information to determine and report on the degree of correspondence between the information and established criteria

Audit report—the communication of audit findings to users

Certified public accountant—a person who has met state regulatory requirements, including passing the uniform CPA examination, and has thus been certified; a CPA may have as his or her primary responsibility the performance of the audit function on published historical financial statements of commercial and noncommercial financial entities

Compliance audit—(1) a review of an organization's financial records performed to determine whether the organization is following specific procedures, rules, or regulations set by some higher authority; (2) an audit performed to determine whether an entity that receives financial assistance from the federal government has complied with specific laws and regulations

Evidence—any information used by the auditor to determine whether the information being audited is stated in accordance with established criteria

Financial statement audit—an audit conducted to determine whether the overall financial statements of an entity are stated in accordance with specified criteria (usually generally accepted accounting principles)

General accounting office auditor—an auditor working for the United States General Accounting Office (GAO); the GAO reports to and is responsible solely to Congress

Independent auditors—certified public accountants or accounting firms that perform audits of commercial and noncommercial financial entities

Information risk—the risk that information upon which a business decision is made is inaccurate

Internal auditors—auditors employed by a company to audit for the company's board of directors and management

Internal revenue agents—auditors who work for the Internal Revenue Service (IRS) and conduct examinations of taxpayers' returns

Operational audit—a review of any part of an organization's operating procedures and methods for the purpose of evaluating efficiency and effectiveness

Review of historical financial statements—a form of attestation in which a CPA firm issues a written report that provides less assurance than an audit as to whether the financial statements are in material conformity with generally accepted accounting principles

REVIEW QUESTIONS

1-1 (Objective 1-1) Explain the relationships among audit services, attestation services, and assurance services, and give examples of each.

1-2 (Objective 1-2) Discuss the major factors in today's society that have made the need for independent audits much greater than it was 50 years ago.

1-3 (Objective 1-2) Distinguish among the following three risks: risk-free interest rate, business risk, and information risk. Which one or ones does the auditor reduce by performing an audit?

1-4 (Objective 1-3) Identify the major causes of information risk and identify the three main ways information risk can be reduced. What are the advantages and disadvantages of each?

1-5 (Objective 1-4) Explain what is meant by determining the degree of correspondence between information and established criteria. What are the information and established criteria for the audit of Jones Company's tax return by an internal revenue agent? What are they for the audit of Jones Company's financial statements by a CPA firm?

1-6 (Objectives 1-4, 1-7) Describe the nature of the evidence the internal revenue agent will use in the audit of Jones Company's tax return.

1-7 (Objective 1-5) In the conduct of audits of financial statements, it would be a serious breach of responsibility if the auditor did not thoroughly understand accounting.

However, many competent accountants do not have an understanding of the auditing process. What causes this difference?

1-8 (Objective 1-6)   What are the differences and similarities in audits of financial statements, compliance audits, and operational audits?

1-9 (Objectives 1-6, 1-7)   List five examples of specific operational audits that could be conducted by an internal auditor in a manufacturing company.

1-10 (Objective 1-7)   What are the major differences in the scope of the audit responsibilities for CPAs, GAO auditors, IRS agents, and internal auditors?

1-11 (Objective 1-8)   Identify the four parts of the Uniform CPA Examination.

MULTIPLE CHOICE QUESTIONS FROM CPA EXAMINATIONS

1-12 (Objectives 1-1, 1-2, 1-4)   The following questions deal with audits by CPA firms. Choose the best response.

a. Which of the following best describes why an independent auditor is asked to express an opinion on the fair presentation of financial statements?
   (1) It is difficult to prepare financial statements that fairly present a company's financial position, operations, and cash flows without the expertise of an independent auditor.
   (2) It is management's responsibility to seek available independent aid in the appraisal of the financial information shown in its financial statements.
   (3) The opinion of an independent party is needed because a company may not be objective with respect to its own financial statements.
   (4) It is a customary courtesy that all stockholders of a company receive an independent report on management's stewardship of the affairs of the business.

b. Independent auditing can best be described as
   (1) a branch of accounting.
   (2) a discipline that attests to the results of accounting and other functional operations and data.
   (3) a professional activity that measures and communicates financial and business data.
   (4) a regulatory function that prevents the issuance of improper financial information.

c. Which of the following professional services would be considered an attestation engagement?
   (1) A consulting service engagement to provide computer processing advice to a client.
   (2) An engagement to report on statutory requirements.
   (3) An income tax engagement to prepare federal and state tax returns.
   (4) The compilation of financial statements from a client's financial records.

d. In performing an attestation engagement, a CPA typically
   (1) supplies litigation support services.
   (2) assesses control risk at a low level.
   (3) expresses a conclusion about an assertion.
   (4) provides management consulting advice.

1-13 (Objectives 1-6, 1-7)   The following questions deal with types of audits and auditors. Choose the best response.

a. Operational audits generally have been conducted by internal auditors and governmental audit agencies but may be performed by certified public accountants. A primary purpose of an operational audit is to provide
   (1) a means of assurance that internal accounting controls are functioning as planned.

(2) a measure of management performance in meeting organizational goals.

(3) the results of internal examinations of financial and accounting matters to a company's top-level management.

(4) aid to the independent auditor, who is conducting the audit of the financial statements.

b. In comparison to the external auditor, an internal auditor is more likely to be concerned with

(1) internal administrative control.

(2) cost accounting procedures.

(3) operational auditing.

(4) internal control.

c. Which of the following best describes the operational audit?

(1) It requires the constant review by internal auditors of the administrative controls as they relate to the operations of the company.

(2) It concentrates on implementing financial and accounting control in a newly organized company.

(3) It attempts and is designed to verify the fair presentation of a company's results of operations.

(4) It concentrates on seeking aspects of operations in which waste could be reduced by the introduction of controls.

d. Compliance auditing often extends beyond audits leading to the expression of opinions on the fairness of financial presentation and includes audits of efficiency, economy, effectiveness, as well as

(1) accuracy.

(2) evaluation.

(3) adherence to specific rules or procedures.

(4) internal control.

DISCUSSION QUESTIONS AND PROBLEMS

1-14 (Objective 1-1) The list below indicates various audit, attestation, and assurance engagements involving auditors.

1. An auditor's report on whether the financial statements are fairly presented in accordance with GAAP.

2. An electronic seal indicating that an electronic seller observes certain practices.

3. A report indicating whether a governmental entity has complied with certain government regulations.

4. A report on the examination of a financial forecast.

5. An evaluation of risk for investment securities.

6. A review report that provides moderate assurance about whether financial statements are fairly stated in accordance with GAAP.

7. A report on compliance with a royalty agreement.

Required

a. Explain or use a diagram to indicate the relationships among audit services, attestation services, and assurance services.

b. For each of the services listed above, indicate the type of service from the list that follows.

(1) An audit of historical financial statements.

(2) An attestation service other than an audit service.

(3) An assurance service that is not an attestation service.

1-15 (Objective 1-2) Vial-tek has an existing loan in the amount of $1.5 million with an annual interest rate of 9.5%. The company provides an internal company-prepared financial statement to the bank under the loan agreement. Two competing banks have offered to replace Vial-tek's existing loan agreement with a new one. First National Bank has offered to loan Vial-tek $1.5 million at a rate of 8.5% but would require Vial-tek to provide financial statements that have been reviewed by a CPA firm. City First Bank has offered to loan Vial-tek $1.5 million at a rate of 7.5% but would require Vial-tek to provide financial statements that have been audited by a CPA firm. The controller of Vial-tek approached a CPA firm and was given an estimated cost of $12,000 to perform a review, and $20,000 to perform an audit.

Required

    a. Explain why the interest rate for the loan that requires a review report is lower than that for the loan that did not require a review. Explain why the interest rate for the loan that requires an audit report is lower than the interest rate for the other two loans.

    b. Calculate Vial-tek's annual costs under each loan agreement, including interest and costs for the CPA firm's services. Indicate whether Vial-tek should keep its existing loan, accept the offer from First National Bank, or accept the offer from City First Bank.

    c. Discuss why Vial-tek may desire to have an audit performed, ignoring the potential reduction in interest costs.

1-16 (Objectives 1-1, 1-2, 1-3) Consumers Union is a nonprofit organization that provides information and counsel on consumer goods and services. A major part of its function is the testing of different brands of consumer products that are purchased on the open market and then reporting the results of the tests in *Consumer Reports,* a monthly publication. Examples of the types of products it tests are middle-sized automobiles, residential dehumidifiers, canned tuna, and boys' jeans.

Required

    a. In what ways are the services provided by Consumers Union similar to assurance services provided by CPA firms?

    b. Compare the concept of information risk introduced in this chapter with the information risk problem faced by a buyer of an automobile.

    c. Compare the four causes of information risk faced by users of financial statements as discussed in this chapter with those faced by a buyer of an automobile.

    d. Compare the three ways users of financial statements can reduce information risk with those available to a buyer of an automobile.

1-17 (Objective 1-4) Fred Oatly is the loan officer of the National Bank of Dallas. National has a loan of $260,000 outstanding to Regional Delivery Service, a company specializing in delivering products of all types on behalf of smaller companies. National's collateral on the loan consists of 35 small delivery trucks with an average original cost of $17,000.

Oatly is concerned about the collectibility of the outstanding loan and whether the trucks still exist. He therefore engages Susan Virms, CPA, to count the trucks, using registration information held by Oatly. She was engaged because she spends most of her time auditing used automobile and truck dealerships and has extensive specialized knowledge about used trucks. Oatly requests that Virms issue a report stating the following:

1. Which of the 35 trucks is parked in Regional's parking lot on the night of June 30, 1999.
2. Whether all of the trucks are owned by Regional Delivery Service.
3. The condition of each truck, using the guidelines of poor, good, and excellent.
4. The fair market value of each truck, using the current "blue book" for trucks, which states the approximate wholesale prices of all used truck models, and also using the poor, good, and excellent condition guidelines.

Required

    a. For each of the following parts of the definition of auditing, state which part of the preceding narrative fits the definition:

       (1) Information

       (2) Established criteria

(3) Accumulating and evaluating evidence

(4) Competent, independent person

(5) Reporting results

b. Identify the greatest difficulties Virms is likely to have doing this audit.

1-18 (Objective 1-7) Five college seniors with majors in accounting are discussing alternative career plans. The first senior plans to become an internal revenue agent because his primary interest is income taxes. He believes the background in tax auditing will provide him with better exposure to income taxes than will any other available career choice. The second senior has decided to go to work for a CPA firm for at least 5 years, possibly as a permanent career. She believes the variety of experience in auditing and related fields offers a better alternative than any other available choice. The third senior has decided on a career in internal auditing with a large industrial company because of the many different aspects of the organization with which internal auditors become involved. The fourth senior plans to become an auditor for the GAO because she believes that this career will provide excellent experience in computer risk assessment techniques. The fifth senior plans to pursue some aspect of auditing as a career but has not decided on the type of organization to enter. He is especially interested in an opportunity to continue to grow professionally, but meaningful and interesting employment is also an important consideration.

Required

a. What are the major advantages and disadvantages of each of the four types of auditing careers?

b. What other types of auditing careers are available to those who are qualified?

1-19 (Objectives 1-6, 1-7) In the normal course of performing their responsibilities, auditors often conduct audits or reviews of the following:

1. Federal income tax returns of an officer of the corporation to determine whether he or she has included all taxable income in his/her return. *IRS / Compliance*
2. Disbursements of a branch of the federal government for a special research project to determine whether it would have been possible to accomplish the same research results at a lower cost to the taxpayers. *GAO / Operational*
3. Computer operations of a corporation to evaluate whether the computer center is being operated as efficiently as possible. *Internal or CPA/ Operational*
4. Annual statements for the use of management. *CPA or Interal auditor/Fin St.*
5. Operations of the IRS to determine whether the internal revenue agents are using their time efficiently in conducting audits. *GAO/operational*
6. Statements for bankers and other creditors when the client is too small to have an audit staff. *CPA / F. stat.*
7. Financial statements of a branch of the federal government to make sure that the statements present fairly the actual disbursements made during a period of time. *GAO FIN.St.*
8. Federal income tax returns of a corporation to determine whether the tax laws have been followed. *IRS / Compliance*
9. Financial statements for use by stockholders when there is an internal audit staff. *CPA/ FIN St.*
10. A bond indenture agreement to make sure a company is following all requirements of the contract. *Internal auditor or CPA / compliance*
11. The computer operations of a large corporation to evaluate whether the internal controls are likely to prevent misstatements in accounting and operating data. *I.Aor CPA/Fin. St.*
12. Disbursements of a branch of the federal government for a special research project to determine whether the expenditures were consistent with the legislative bill that authorized the project. *GAO/compliance*

Required

a. For these 12 examples, state the most likely type of auditor (CPA, GAO, IRS, or internal) to perform each.

b. In each example, state the type of audit (financial statement audit, operational audit, or compliance audit).

1-20 (Objectives 1-6, 1-7)   A large conglomerate is considering acquiring a medium-sized manufacturing company in a closely related industry. A major consideration by the management of the conglomerate in deciding whether to pursue the merger is the operational efficiency of the company. Management has decided to obtain a detailed report based on an intensive investigation of the operational efficiency of the sales department, production department, and research and development department.

Required
    a. Whom should the conglomerate engage to conduct the operational audit?
    b. What major problems are the auditors likely to encounter in conducting the investigation and writing the report?

INTERNET PROBLEM 1-1: ASSURANCE SERVICES

Reference Prentice Hall's Companion Web Site (CW site).[2] Estimates are that the introduction of new assurance services could double or even triple the CPA profession's $7 billion accounting and auditing income. But the new opportunities will not come easily. New services must be identified, new competencies developed, and barriers overcome. To help the profession move forward, the AICPA formed the Special Committee on Assurance Services. This problem requires students to use the Internet to (1) research assurance services recommended by the committee, (2) examine components of assurance service business plans, and (3) identify and describe competencies needed by assurance providers in the upcoming decade.

[2]Internet problems can be found at Prentice Hall's Companion Web Site (CW site), www.prenhall.com/arens.

THE CPA PROFESSION

GOOD AUDITING INCLUDES GOOD CLIENT SERVICE

"It had been a good week," thought Jeanine Wilson, as she drove out of the parking lot of Solberg Paints on Friday afternoon. Just a few months earlier, she graduated from State University and sat for the CPA examination. Still, Jeanine did not think her transition to professional life had been all that smooth, and she was surprised at how much there still was to learn. But she had made great progress on the Solberg job.

John Hernandez was the audit senior on the Solberg Paints audit, and he had a reputation as a patient teacher and supervisor. Jeanine was not disappointed. At the start of the engagement, John told her, "Don't be afraid to ask questions. If you see anything that seems unusual, let's discuss it. And most importantly, if you have any ideas that will help the client, bring them up. The client expects us to deliver more than an audit report."

"I'd say I delivered," thought Jeanine. She found an error in the way the company had calculated LIFO inventory that was going to save the client a significant amount of taxes. But her biggest contribution almost did not happen. Jeanine read as much as she could about paint manufacturers and learned about some new production control methods that seemed like they could apply to Solberg. She was afraid to bring it up, thinking that she couldn't possibly know anything that the client didn't already know, but John encouraged her to discuss it with the client. The result was that the client was about to engage Jeanine's firm in a consulting engagement to improve their production processes.

Friday was the last day of field work on the audit, and the partner, Bill Marlow, was at the client's office to complete his review of the audit files. Jeanine was surprised to hear him say to her, "What are you doing on the 15th? We're going to meet with the client to discuss our audit findings. You've made a real contribution on this audit, and I'd like you to be there." Jeanine tried not to show her excitement too much, but she couldn't hide the smile on her face. "Yes, it *had* been a good week."

LEARNING OBJECTIVES

After studying this chapter, you should be able to

2-1 Describe the nature of CPA firms, what they do, and their structure.

2-2 Describe the key functions performed by the AICPA.

2-3 Use generally accepted auditing standards as a basis for further study.

2-4 Identify quality control standards and practices within the accounting profession.

2-5 Summarize the role of the Securities and Exchange Commission in accounting and auditing.

A s the opening vignette demonstrates, audit professionals and CPA firms are valued advisors to their clients. We learned in the first chapter that auditing plays an important role in society by reducing information risk and facilitating access to capital. This chapter describes the organization of CPA firms, the types of services they provide, and the standards and regulatory agencies that influence auditor performance.

CERTIFIED PUBLIC ACCOUNTING FIRMS

OBJECTIVE 2-1
Describe the nature of CPA firms, what they do, and their structure.

In Chapter 1, we learned that CPA firms are one of the four main types of auditors. Except for certain governmental organizations, the audits of all general use financial statements in the United States are done by CPA firms. The legal right to perform audits is granted to CPA firms by regulation of each state. CPA firms also provide many other services to their clients, such as tax and consulting services.

More than 40,000 CPA firms exist in the United States, ranging in size from 1 person to more than 30,000 partners and staff. *Accounting Today* annually publishes a list of the 100 largest accounting firms. Most of the largest accounting firms are CPA firms, although the list includes a few companies such as H&R Block Tax Services. Data for selected firms are included in Table 2-1. Four size categories are used to describe CPA firms: Big Five international firms, national firms, regional and large local firms, and small local firms.

TABLE 2-1	Revenue and Other Data for the Largest CPA Firms in the United States					
1997 Size by Revenue	Firm*	Net Revenue—U.S. Only (in $ millions)	Partners	Professionals	U.S. Offices	Percentage of Total Revenue from Accounting and Auditing/Taxes/Management Consulting Services
			BIG FIVE			
1	Andersen Worldwide	$5,445.0	1,673	32,319	95	20/14/66
2	PricewaterhouseCoopers	$4,844.5	2,439	26,404	211	37/21/42
3	Ernst & Young	$4,416.0	2,172	17,845	89	36/23/41
4	Deloitte & Touche	$3,600.0	1,719	16,426	106	35/20/45
5	KPMG	$3,000.0	1,600	13,400	130	41/25/34
			NATIONAL			
6	Grant Thornton	$289.0	278	1,979	48	42/30/28
7	McGladrey & Pullen	$270.1	381	1,883	64	45/32/23
8	BDO Seidman	$240.0	299	1,171	42	51/26/23
			REGIONAL			
9	Crowe, Chizek & Co.	$97.4	93	830	10	32/18/50
10	Baird Kurtz & Dobson	$90.0	124	567	20	47/30/23
11	Plante & Moran	$86.9	117	704	14	57/23/20
12	Clifton Gunderson & Co.	$74.8	115	508	42	56/32/12
13	Moss Adams	$72.0	94	451	16	47/37/16
			LARGE LOCAL			
50	Follmer, Rudzewicz & Co.	$18.3	12	148	2	39/28/33
75	Kaufman Rossin & Co.	$13.8	14	64	2	54/32/14

*Rankings reflect merger of Price Waterhouse and Coopers & Lybrand to form PricewaterhouseCoopers. Information for PricewaterhouseCoopers is based on separately reported information for Price Waterhouse and Coopers & Lybrand.
Source: *Accounting Today* (March 16–April 5, 1998), pp. 18–20.

- *Big Five international firms.* The five largest CPA firms in the United States are called the "Big Five" international CPA firms. They are the first five firms listed in Table 2-1. Before 1998, there were six large international firms. In 1998, Price Waterhouse and Coopers & Lybrand merged to form PricewaterhouseCoopers, resulting in the Big Five. These five firms have offices in cities throughout the United States and in many cities throughout the world. The Big Five firms audit nearly all of the largest companies both in the United States and worldwide, and many smaller companies as well.

- *National firms.* Three CPA firms in the United States are called national firms because they have offices in most major cities. These are firms 6 through 8 in Table 2-1. These firms are large but considerably smaller than the Big Five. The national firms perform the same services as the Big Five firms and compete directly with them for clients. Each national firm is affiliated with firms in other countries and therefore has an international capability.

Big Five, National, and Regional Firms

- *Regional and large local firms.* There are only approximately 100 CPA firms with professional staffs of more than 50 people. Some have only one office and serve clients primarily within commuting distance. Others have several offices in a state or region and serve a larger radius of clients. For example, Table 2-1 shows that the largest regional firms are not dramatically smaller than the three national firms. Regional and large local firms compete for clients with other CPA firms, including national and Big Five firms. Many of the regional and large local firms are affiliated with associations of CPA firms to share resources for such things as technical information and continuing education. Many of these firms also have international affiliations.

- *Small local firms.* More than 95 percent of all CPA firms have fewer than 25 professionals in a single-office firm. They perform audits and related services primarily for smaller businesses and not-for-profit entities, although some have one or two clients with public ownership. Many small local firms do not perform audits and primarily provide accounting and tax services to their clients.

ACTIVITIES OF CPA FIRMS

As we saw in Chapter 1, CPA firms provide audit services and have expanded their scope of services to provide additional attestation and assurance services. Additional services commonly provided by CPA firms include accounting and bookkeeping services, tax services, and management consulting services. CPA firms continue to develop new products and services, including specialties in financial planning and business valuation.

- *Accounting and bookkeeping services.* Many small clients with limited accounting staff rely on CPA firms to prepare their financial statements. Some small clients lack the personnel or expertise to prepare even their own journals and ledgers. Thus, CPA firms perform a variety of accounting and bookkeeping services to meet the needs of these clients. In many cases in which the financial statements are to be given to a third party, a review or even an audit is also performed. When neither of these is done, the financial statements are accompanied by a type of report by the CPA firm called a compilation report, which provides no assurance to third parties. Table 2-1 shows that attestation services and accounting and bookkeeping services account for approximately one-third to one-half of the revenue for most large CPA firms.

- *Tax services.* CPA firms prepare corporate and individual tax returns for both audit and nonaudit clients. In addition, estate tax, gift tax, tax planning, and other aspects of tax services are provided by most CPA firms. Tax services are now performed by almost every CPA firm, and for many small firms, such services are far more important to their practice than auditing. Table 2-1 shows that revenue from taxes for larger firms ranges from 14 percent to 37 percent. Many small firms receive a much larger portion of their revenue from tax services.

- *Management consulting services.* Most CPA firms provide certain services that enable their clients to operate their businesses more effectively. These services are called management consulting or management advisory services. These services range from simple suggestions for improving the client's accounting system to advice in marketing strategies, computer installations, and actuarial benefit consulting. Many large CPA firms have departments involved exclusively in management consulting services with little interaction with the audit or tax staff. Revenue from management consulting services has increased significantly in recent years. Table 2-1 shows that management consulting services now provide the largest share of revenues for most of the Big Five firms.

STRUCTURE OF CPA FIRMS

CPA firms vary in the nature and range of services offered, which will affect the organization and structure of the firms. Three main factors influence the organizational structure of all firms:

1. *The need for independence from clients.* Independence permits auditors to remain unbiased in drawing conclusions about the financial statements.
2. *The importance of a structure to encourage competence.* Competence permits auditors to conduct audits and perform other services efficiently and effectively.
3. *The increased litigation risk faced by auditors.* In the last decade, firms have experienced increases in litigation-related costs. Some organizational structures afford a degree of protection to individual firm members.

Organizational Structures

Six organizational structures are available to CPA firms. Except for the proprietorship, each structure results in an entity separate from the CPA personally, which helps promote auditor independence. The last four organizational structures provide some protection from litigation loss.

Proprietorship Only firms with one owner can operate in this form. Traditionally, all one-owner firms were organized as proprietorships, but in recent years, most of them have changed to organizational forms with more limited liability because of litigation risks.

General Partnership This form of organization is the same as a proprietorship, except that it applies to multiple owners. Until recently, all CPA firms were organized as general partnerships or proprietorships.

General Corporation The advantage of a corporation is that shareholders are liable only to the extent of their investment in the corporation. Most CPA firms do not organize as general corporations because they are prohibited by law from doing so in most states.

Professional Corporation A professional corporation (PC) provides professional services and is owned by one or more shareholders. PC laws and the resulting liability protection vary significantly from state to state. PC laws in some states offer personal liability protection similar to that of general corporations, whereas the protection in other states is minimal. This variation makes it difficult for a CPA firm with clients in different states to operate as a PC.

Limited Liability Company A limited liability company (LLC) combines the most favorable attributes of a general corporation and a general partnership. An LLC is structured and taxed like a general partnership, but its owners have limited personal liability similar to that of a general corporation.

The accounting profession has lobbied recently to enact LLC laws in more states. Currently, nearly all of the states have LLC laws, and many of them allow accounting firms to operate as LLCs.

Limited Liability Partnership A limited liability partnership (LLP) is owned by one or more partners. It is structured and taxed like a general partnership, but the personal liability protection of an LLP is less than that of a general corporation or an LLC. Partners of an LLP are personally liable for the partnership's debts and obligations, their own acts, and acts of others under their supervision. Partners are not personally liable for liabilities arising from negligent acts of other partners and employees not under their supervision. It is not surprising that all of the Big Five firms and many smaller firms now operate as LLPs.

most likely "popular" now

Hierarchy of a Typical CPA Firm

The organizational hierarchy in a typical CPA firm includes partners or shareholders, managers, supervisors, seniors or in-charge auditors, and assistants. A new employee usually starts as an assistant and spends 2 or 3 years in each classification before achieving partner status. The titles of the positions vary from firm to firm, but the structure is similar in all. When we refer in this text to the *auditor*, we mean the person performing some aspect of an audit. It is common to have one or more auditors from each level on larger engagements.

AICPA's "Just for Students"

Table 2-2 summarizes the experience and responsibilities of each classification level within CPA firms. As indicated in the table, advancement in CPA firms is fairly rapid, with evolving duties and responsibilities. In addition, audit staff members usually gain diversity of experience across client engagements. Because of advances in computer and audit technology, beginning assistants on the audit are rapidly given greater responsibility and challenges.

The hierarchical nature of CPA firms helps promote competence. Individuals at each level of the audit supervise and review the work of others at the level just below them in the organizational structure. For example, a new staff assistant is supervised directly by the senior or in-charge auditor. The staff assistant's work is then reviewed by the in-charge, as well as by the manager and partner.

To promote competence and to better serve their clients, many CPA firms have also organized along industry specialization lines. Auditors at each staff level may specialize in the performance of audits of certain industries, such as financial institutions. By specializing along industry lines, auditors gain a greater understanding of the client's business. To facilitate a total service approach, industry specialization groups may cross functional lines. For example, a health care specialization group may include auditors, tax professionals, and consultants specializing in health care.

TABLE 2-2	Staff Levels and Responsibilities	
Staff Level	**Average Experience**	**Typical Responsibilities**
Staff Assistant	0–2 years	Performs most of the detailed audit work.
Senior or in-charge auditor	2–5 years	Coordinates and is responsible for the audit field work, including supervising and reviewing staff work.
Manager	5–10 years	Helps the in-charge plan and manage the audit, reviews the in-charge's work, and manages relations with the client. A manager may be responsible for more than one engagement at the same time.
Partner	10+ years	Reviews the overall audit work and is involved in significant audit decisions. A partner is an owner of the firm, and therefore has the ultimate responsibility for conducting the audit and serving the client.

OBJECTIVE 2-2
Describe the key functions performed by the AICPA.

UcSec
↓
Sop

CPA firms provide oversight of individual firm members, but more formal regulatory bodies also exist. Although CPAs are licensed by the state in which they practice, the most important influence on CPAs is exerted by their national professional organization, the American Institute of Certified Public Accountants (**AICPA**). Membership in the AICPA is restricted to CPAs and currently exceeds 330,000, but not all members are practicing as independent auditors. Many members formerly worked for CPA firms but are currently working in government, industry, and education. AICPA membership is not required of CPAs. Because it is a voluntary organization, not all CPAs are members of the AICPA.

The AICPA sets professional requirements for CPAs, conducts research, and publishes materials on many different subjects related to accounting, auditing, attestation and assurance services, management consulting services, and taxes. The AICPA is also an advocate for the accounting profession. Initiatives undertaken by the AICPA to promote CPA services include national advertising campaigns, development of specialist certifications, and the efforts of the Special Committee on Assurance Services to develop and promote new assurance services. We will now examine the main functions of the AICPA.

VISION FOR THE FUTURE

The AICPA has established the CPA Vision Project to provide a core purpose and vision for the CPA profession in the year 2011 and beyond. The core purpose of the CPA Vision Project is "CPAs . . . making sense of a changing and complex world."

The CPA Vision Project has identified five core values, core competencies, core services, and issues for the future. The top five highest rated issues for the future are as follows:

CPA Vision
Project

- The future success of the CPA profession relies a great deal on public perceptions of CPAs' abilities and roles.
- CPAs must become market driven and not dependent on regulations to keep them in business.
- The market demands less audit and accounting and more value-adding consulting services.
- Specialization is critical for the future of the CPA profession.
- The market demands that CPAs be conversant in global business practices and strategies.

Establishing Standards and Rules

The AICPA is empowered to set standards (guidelines) and rules that all members and other practicing CPAs must follow. The requirements are set by committees made up of AICPA members. There are four major areas in which the AICPA has authority to set standards and make rules.

1. *Auditing standards.* The Auditing Standards Board (ASB) is responsible for issuing pronouncements on auditing matters. They are called **Statements on Auditing Standards** (SASs). The ASB and its predecessor organizations have been responsible for a considerable portion of the existing auditing literature. The SASs are examined later in this chapter and discussed throughout the text.
2. *Compilation and review standards.* The Accounting and Review Services Committee is responsible for issuing pronouncements of the CPA's responsibilities when the CPA is associated with financial statements of privately owned companies that are not audited. They are called Statements on Standards for Accounting and Review Services (SSARS). SSARS 1, issued in December 1978, supersedes preceding statements on auditing standards for unaudited financial statements. It covers two specific types of services: (1) situations in which the accountant assists a client in preparing financial statements without giving any assurance about them (compilation services) and

(2) situations in which the accountant performs inquiry and analytical procedures that provide a reasonable basis for expressing limited assurances that there are no material modifications that should be made to the statements (review services).

3. *Other attestation standards.* In 1986, the AICPA issued its Statement on Standards for Attestation Engagements. The purpose of that statement is twofold. First, it provides a framework to be followed by standard-setting bodies within the AICPA in developing detailed standards on specific types of attestation services. Second, it provides a framework for guidance to practitioners when no such specific standards exist. Both generally accepted auditing standards and compilation and review standards are consistent with the broader attestation standards. An example of a specific standard on other attestation services that has been issued under the broader attestation standards is the Statement on Standards for Accountant's Services on Prospective Financial Information. This standard is studied in Chapter 24.

4. *Code of Professional Conduct.* The AICPA Committee on Professional Ethics sets rules of conduct that CPAs are required to meet. These rules apply to all services performed by CPAs and provide a framework for the technical standards. The rules and their relationships to ethical conduct are the subject of Chapter 4.

Other AICPA Functions

The AICPA supports research by its own research staff and provides grants to others. It also publishes a variety of materials, including journals such as *The Journal of Accountancy*, industry audit guides for several industries, periodic updates of the *Codification of Statements on Auditing Standards*, and the *Code of Professional Conduct*.

The AICPA is responsible for both writing and grading the CPA examination. Approximately 60,000 candidates take the examination each time it is offered. The content and other information about the examination were discussed in Chapter 1.

The extensive and ever-changing body of knowledge in accounting, auditing, attestation and assurance services, management consulting services, and taxes is such that continuous study is required for CPAs to stay current. The AICPA provides to its members a considerable number of seminars and education aids in a variety of subject matters. An example is a 2-day seminar entitled "Professional and Legal Liability of the CPA."

GENERALLY ACCEPTED AUDITING STANDARDS

As noted in the previous section, setting auditing standards is one of the functions of the AICPA. Auditing standards are general guidelines to aid auditors in fulfilling their professional responsibilities in the audit of historical financial statements. They include consideration of professional qualities such as competence and independence, reporting requirements, and evidence.

OBJECTIVE 2-3
Use generally accepted auditing standards as a basis for further study.

The broadest guidelines available are the 10 **generally accepted auditing standards (GAAS)**. Developed by the AICPA in 1947, they have, with minimal changes, remained the same. These standards are not sufficiently specific to provide any meaningful guide to practitioners, but they do represent a framework upon which the AICPA can provide interpretations. These 10 standards are stated in their entirety in Table 2-3 (p. 30).

There are three categories for the 10 generally accepted auditing standards: general standards, standards of field work, and reporting standards. The standards for each category are summarized in Figure 2-1 (p. 30).

General Standards

The general standards stress the important personal qualities that the auditor should possess.

Adequate Technical Training and Proficiency The first general standard is normally interpreted as requiring the auditor to have formal education in auditing and accounting, adequate practical experience for the work being performed, and continuing professional education. Recent court cases clearly demonstrate that auditors must be technically qualified and experienced in those industries in which their audit clients are engaged.

TABLE 2-3	Generally Accepted Auditing Standards

GENERAL STANDARDS

1. The audit is to be performed by a person or persons having adequate technical training and proficiency as an auditor.
2. In all matters relating to the assignment, an independence in mental attitude is to be maintained by the auditor or auditors.
3. Due professional care is to be exercised in the planning and performance of the audit and the preparation of the report.

STANDARDS OF FIELD WORK

1. The work is to be adequately planned and assistants, if any, are to be properly supervised.
2. A sufficient understanding of internal control is to be obtained to plan the audit and to determine the nature, timing, and extent of tests to be performed.
3. Sufficient competent evidential matter is to be obtained through inspection, observation, inquiries, and confirmations to afford a reasonable basis for an opinion regarding the financial statements under audit.

STANDARDS OF REPORTING

1. The report shall state whether the financial statements are presented in accordance with generally accepted accounting principles.
2. The report shall identify those circumstances in which such principles have not been consistently observed in the current period in relation to the preceding period.
3. Informative disclosures in the financial statements are to be regarded as reasonably adequate unless otherwise stated in the report.
4. The report shall either contain an expression of opinion regarding the financial statements, taken as a whole, or an assertion to the effect that an opinion cannot be expressed. When an overall opinion cannot be expressed, the reasons therefor should be stated. In all cases where an auditor's name is associated with financial statements, the report should contain a clear-cut indication of the character of the auditor's work, if any, and the degree of responsibility the auditor is taking.

FIGURE 2-1	Summary of Generally Accepted Auditing Standards

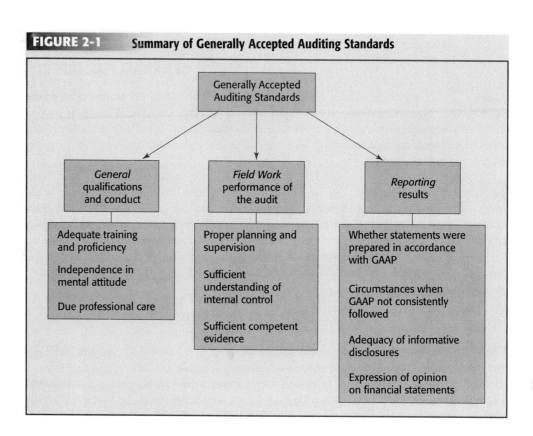

In any case in which the CPA or the CPA's assistants are not qualified to perform the work, a professional obligation exists to acquire the requisite knowledge and skills, suggest someone else who is qualified to perform the work, or decline the engagement.

Independence in Mental Attitude The importance of independence was stressed in Chapter 1 under the definition of auditing. The *Code of Professional Conduct* and SASs stress the need for independence. CPA firms are required to follow several practices to increase the likelihood of independence of all personnel. For example, there arc established procedures on larger audits when there is a dispute between management and the auditors. Specific methods to ensure that auditors maintain their independence are studied in Chapter 4.

Due Professional Care The third general standard involves due care in the performance of all aspects of auditing. Simply stated, this means that the auditor is a professional responsible for fulfilling his or her duties diligently and carefully. As an illustration, due care includes consideration of the completeness of the working papers, the sufficiency of the audit evidence, and the appropriateness of the audit report. As a professional, the auditor must avoid negligence and bad faith, but the auditor is not expected to make perfect judgments in every instance.

The standards of field work concern evidence accumulation and other activities during the actual conduct of the audit.

Standards of Field Work

Adequate Planning and Supervision The first standard deals with ascertaining that the engagement is sufficiently planned to ensure an adequate audit and proper supervision of assistants. Supervision is essential in auditing because a considerable portion of the field work is done by less experienced staff members.

Understand the Client's Internal Control One of the most widely accepted concepts in the theory and practice of auditing is the importance of the client's system of internal control to generate reliable financial information. If the auditor is convinced that the client has an excellent system of internal control, one that includes adequate internal controls for providing reliable data and for safeguarding assets and records, the amount of audit evidence to be accumulated can be significantly less than when controls are not adequate. In some instances, internal control may be so inadequate as to preclude conducting an effective audit.

Sufficient Competent Evidence The decisions about how much and what types of evidence to accumulate for a given set of circumstances are ones requiring professional judgment. A major portion of this book is concerned with the study of evidence accumulation and the circumstances affecting the amount and types needed.

The four reporting standards require the auditor to prepare a report on the financial statements taken as a whole, including informative disclosures. The reporting standards require that the report state whether the statements are presented in accordance with generally accepted accounting principles and also identify any circumstances in which generally accepted accounting principles have not been consistently applied in the current year compared with the previous one.

Standards of Reporting

express opinion

STATEMENTS ON AUDITING STANDARDS

The 10 generally accepted auditing standards are too general to provide meaningful guidance to auditors. More specific guidance is found in the SASs issued by the Auditing Standards Board of the AICPA. SASs interpret the 10 generally accepted auditing standards and are the most authoritative references available to auditors. These statements have the status of GAAS and are often referred to as auditing standards or GAAS, even though they are not part of the 10 generally accepted auditing standards. This book follows common practice and refers to these interpretations as auditing standards or SASs. Generally accepted auditing standards and SASs are regarded as *authoritative* literature, and every member who performs audits of historical financial statements is required to follow them under the AICPA *Code of Professional Conduct.*

SASs are successors to the statements on auditing procedure of the AICPA. SAS 1 is a codification of 54 previous statements on auditing procedure dating from 1939 to 1972, whereas subsequent SASs are new pronouncements. New statements are issued when an auditing problem arises of sufficient importance to warrant an official interpretation by the AICPA. At this writing, SAS 87 was the last one issued and incorporated into the text materials. Readers should be alert to subsequent standards that influence auditing requirements.

All SASs are given two classification numbers: an SAS and an AU number. For example, the Statement on Auditing Standards, *The Relationship of Generally Accepted Auditing Standards to Quality Control Standards,* is SAS 25 and AU 161. The SAS number identifies the order in which it was issued in relation to other SASs; the AU number identifies its location in the AICPA codification of all SASs. For example, AUs beginning with a "2" are always interpretations of the general standards. Those beginning with a "3" are related to field work standards, and those beginning with a "4," "5," or "6" deal with reporting standards. Both classification systems are used in practice.

Although GAAS and the SASs are the authoritative auditing guidelines for members of the profession, they provide less direction to auditors than might be assumed. There are almost no specific audit procedures required by the standards, and there are no specific requirements for auditors' decisions, such as determining sample size, selecting sample items from the population for testing, or evaluating results. Many practitioners believe that the standards should provide more clearly defined guidelines for determining the extent of evidence to be accumulated. Such specificity would eliminate some difficult audit decisions and provide a line of defense for a CPA firm charged with conducting an inadequate audit. However, highly specific requirements could turn auditing into mechanistic evidence gathering, devoid of professional judgment. From the point of view of both the profession and the users of auditing services, there is probably greater harm in defining authoritative guidelines too specifically than too broadly.

GAAS and the SASs should be looked on by practitioners as *minimum standards* of performance rather than as maximum standards or ideals. Any professional auditor who seeks means of reducing the scope of the audit by relying only on the standards, rather than evaluating the substance of the situation, fails to satisfy the spirit of the standards. At the same time, the existence of auditing standards does not mean the auditor must always follow them blindly. If an auditor believes that the requirement of a standard is impractical or impossible to perform, the auditor is justified in following an alternative course of action. Similarly, if the issue in question is immaterial in amount, it is also unnecessary to follow the standard. However, the burden of justifying departures from the standards falls on the auditor.

IFAC

When auditors desire more specific guidelines, they must turn to less authoritative sources, including textbooks, journals, and technical publications. Materials published by the AICPA, mentioned earlier in this chapter, such as the *Journal of Accountancy* and industry audit guides, are useful in furnishing assistance on specific questions. There is further study of the standards and frequent reference to the SASs throughout the text.

INTERNATIONAL STANDARDS— DEVELOPING HARMONY	International Standards on Auditing (ISAs) are issued by the International Auditing Practice Committee of the International Federation of Accountants (IFAC). IFAC is the worldwide organization for the accountancy profession, with 143 member organizations in 103 countries, representing more than 2 million accountants. The ISAs are generally similar to U.S. GAAS, although there are some differences. There is an interest and trend toward *harmonization,* which means developing uniform accounting and auditing standards throughout the world.

In 1978, the AICPA established the Quality Control Standards Committee and gave it responsibility to help CPA firms develop and implement quality control standards. For a CPA firm, **quality control** comprises the methods used to ensure that the firm meets its professional responsibilities to clients and others. These methods include the organizational structure of the CPA firm and the procedures the firm establishes. For example, a CPA firm might have an organizational structure that ensures the technical review of every engagement by a partner who has expertise in the client's industry.

OBJECTIVE 2-4
Identify quality control standards and practices within the accounting profession.

Quality control is closely related to but distinct from GAAS. A CPA firm must ensure that generally accepted auditing standards are followed on every audit. Quality controls are the procedures used by the CPA firm that help it meet those standards consistently on every engagement. Quality controls are therefore established for the entire CPA firm, whereas GAAS are applicable to individual engagements.

SAS 25 (AU 161) requires a CPA firm to establish quality control policies and procedures. The standard recognizes that a quality control system can provide only reasonable assurance, not a guarantee, that GAAS are followed.

Elements of Quality Control

The AICPA has not set specific quality control procedures for CPA firms. Procedures should depend on such things as the size of the firm, the number of practice offices, and the nature of the practice. For example, the quality control procedures of a 150-office international firm with many complex multinational clients should differ considerably from those of a 5-person firm specializing in small audits in one or two industries.

The Quality Control Standards Committee identified nine elements of quality control that firms should consider in setting up their own policies and procedures. In May 1996, the Auditing Standards Board reduced these nine elements to five, effective January 1, 1997. The five elements of quality control are listed in Table 2-4 (p. 34) with a brief description of the requirement for each element and an example of a quality control procedure that a firm might use to satisfy the requirement.

Division of CPA Firms

The AICPA has established a **division of CPA firms** and created two sections: the SEC Practice Section and the Private Companies Practice Section (The AICPA Alliance for CPA Firms). The intent is to improve the quality of practice by CPA firms consistent with AICPA quality control standards. Each practice section has membership requirements and the authority to impose sanctions for noncompliance by members. A firm can choose to belong to one section, both sections, or neither. However, if a member CPA firm audits one or more publicly held companies, it is required to belong to the SEC Practice Section.

The following are requirements for belonging to the SEC Practice Section (the first three are also requirements of the Private Companies Practice Section and are considered by many to be the most critical requirements):

- *Adherence to quality control standards.* The CPA firm must agree to and adhere to the quality control standards set forth in the preceding section.
- *Mandatory peer review.* Each firm must have a periodic review of its quality controls and auditing and accounting practices by another qualified CPA firm.
- *Continuing education.* Every professional in the firm is required to have 120 hours of continuing professional education in every 3-year period.
- *Partner rotation.* The assignment of a new audit partner to be in charge of each SEC engagement is required if another audit partner has been in charge of the engagement for a period of 7 consecutive years. The incumbent partner is prohibited from returning to partner-in-charge status on the engagement for a minimum of 2 years. Very small firms may be exempted from this requirement.
- *Concurring partner review.* All audits of publicly held companies must have a review by a partner other than the engagement partner, who must concur with the audit report before it can be issued.

TABLE 2-4	Five Elements of Quality Control	
Element	**Summary of Requirements**	**Example of a Procedure**
Independence, integrity, and objectivity	All personnel on engagements should maintain independence in fact and in appearance, perform all professional responsibilities with integrity, and maintain objectivity in performing their professional responsibilities.	Each partner and employee must answer an "independence questionnaire" annually, dealing with such things as stock ownership and membership on boards of directors.
Personnel management	Policies and procedures should be established to provide the firm with reasonable assurance that • All new personnel should be qualified to perform their work competently. • Work is assigned to personnel who have adequate technical training and proficiency. • All personnel should participate in continuing professional education and professional development activities that enable them to fulfill their assigned responsibilities. • Personnel selected for advancement have the qualifications necessary for the fulfillment of their assigned responsibilities.	Each professional must be evaluated on every engagement using the firm's individual engagement evaluation report.
Acceptance and continuation of clients and engagements	Policies and procedures should be established for deciding whether to accept or continue a client relationship. These policies and procedures should minimize the risk of associating with a client whose management lacks integrity. The firm should also only undertake engagements that can be completed with professional competence.	A client evaluation form, dealing with such matters as predecessor auditor comments and evaluation of management, must be prepared for every new client before acceptance.
Engagement performance	Policies and procedures should exist to ensure that the work performed by engagement personnel meets applicable professional standards, regulatory requirements, and the firm's standards of quality.	The firm's director of accounting and auditing is available for consultation and must approve all engagements before their completion.
Monitoring	Policies and procedures should exist to ensure that the other four quality control elements are being effectively applied.	The quality control partner must test the quality control procedures at least annually to ensure the firm is in compliance.

• *Proscription of certain services.* The CPA firm must refrain from performing certain types of management consulting services for audit clients that are publicly held. These services include psychological testing, public opinion polls, merger and acquisition assistance for a finder's fee, executive recruitment, and actuarial services to insurance companies.
• *Reporting on disagreements.* An auditor is required to report to the audit committee or board of directors of each SEC audit client on the nature of major disagreements with management about accounting, disclosure, or auditing matters.
• *Reporting on management consulting services performed.* An auditor is required to report to the audit committee or board of directors of each SEC audit client the types of management consulting services performed for the client during the audit year and the total fees received for such services.

The Public Oversight Board (POB) is an independent body that monitors and reports on the self-regulatory programs of the SEC Practice Section. The POB has significantly influenced the practice of public accounting in such areas as legal liability and the auditor's responsibility for the detection of fraud through the recommendations contained in the POB's annual report.

Peer Review

Peer review is the review, by CPAs, of a CPA firm's compliance with its quality control system. The purpose of a peer review is to determine and report whether the CPA firm being reviewed has developed adequate policies and procedures for the five elements of quality control and follows them in practice. Unless a firm has a peer review, all members of the CPA firm lose their eligibility for AICPA membership.

CPA firms that are members of the SEC Practice Section (SECPS) or Private Companies Practice Section (PCPS) must be reviewed at least once every 3 years. Peer reviews of SECPS member firms are administered under the peer review program of the POB. Peer reviews of PCPS member firms are administered through the state CPA societies under the overall direction of the AICPA peer review board. Typically, the review is done by a CPA firm selected by the firm being reviewed. Another option is to request the AICPA or state society to send a review team. After the review is completed, the reviewers issue a report stating their conclusions and recommendations. Only firms satisfactorily passing an SECPS or PCPS peer review can be members of the two practice sections. Approximately 1,300 firms are enrolled in the SECPS peer review program, whereas more than 7,200 PCPS member firms participate in the AICPA peer review program.

AICPA member firms who are not members of the SECPS or PCPS are also required to have peer reviews (formerly called quality reviews) every 3 years. This type of peer review has the same objective as a peer review of an SECPS or PCPS member, but it is typically less extensive in the review of the implementation of the firm's quality control system. These peer reviews are also administered through the state CPA societies under the overall direction of the AICPA peer review board. Currently, approximately 32,000 firms are enrolled in this part of the AICPA peer review program.

Peer reviews can be beneficial to the profession and individual firms. By helping firms meet quality control standards, the profession gains from improved practitioner performance and higher-quality audits. A firm having a peer review can also gain if it improves the firm's practice and thereby enhances its reputation and effectiveness and reduces the likelihood of lawsuits. Of course, these reviews are costly. There is always a trade-off between cost and benefit. Figure 2-2 summarizes the relationships among GAAS, quality control, division of CPA firms, and peer review.

> Have clients that have to follow SEC regulat. (Public)

> CPA's on 7 yrs, off ≥ 2 yrs so there is a more objective view.

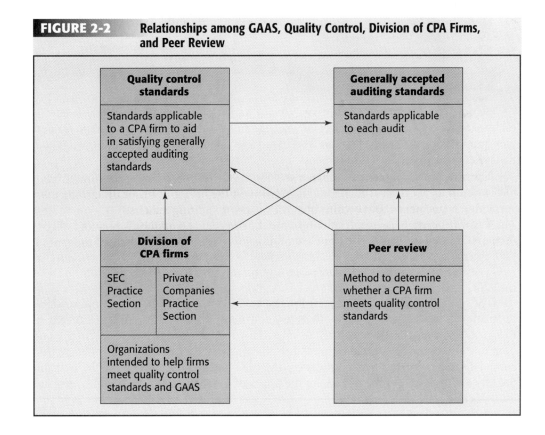

FIGURE 2-2 Relationships among GAAS, Quality Control, Division of CPA Firms, and Peer Review

Quality control standards	Generally accepted auditing standards
Standards applicable to a CPA firm to aid in satisfying generally accepted auditing standards	Standards applicable to each audit

Division of CPA firms	Peer review
SEC Practice Section / Private Companies Practice Section	Method to determine whether a CPA firm meets quality control standards
Organizations intended to help firms meet quality control standards and GAAS	

SECURITIES AND EXCHANGE COMMISSION

OBJECTIVE 2-5

Summarize the role of the Securities and Exchange Commission in accounting and auditing.

SEC

The overall purpose of the **Securities and Exchange Commission (SEC)**, an agency of the federal government, is to assist in providing investors with reliable information upon which to make investment decisions. To this end, the Securities Act of 1933 requires most companies planning to issue *new securities* to the public to submit a registration statement to the SEC for approval. The Securities Exchange Act of 1934 provides additional protection by requiring the same companies and others to file detailed annual reports with the commission. The commission examines these statements for completeness and adequacy before permitting the company to sell its securities through the securities exchanges.

Although the SEC requires considerable information that is not of direct interest to CPAs, the securities acts of 1933 and 1934 require financial statements, accompanied by the opinion of an independent public accountant, as part of a registration statement and subsequent reports.

Of special interest to auditors are several specific reports that are subject to the reporting provisions of the securities acts. The most important of these are as follows:

- *Forms S-1 to S-16.* These forms must be completed and registered with the SEC when a company plans to issue new securities to the public. The S-1 form is the general form used when there is no specifically prescribed form. The others are specialized forms. For example, S-10 is for restrictions of landholders' royalty interests in gas and oil. All "S" forms apply to the Securities Act of 1933.
- *Form 8-K.* This report is filed at the end of any month in which significant events have occurred that are of interest to public investors. Such events include the acquisition or sale of a subsidiary, a change in officers or directors, an addition of a new product line, or a change in auditors.
- *Form 10-K.* This report must be filed annually within 90 days after the close of each fiscal year. Extensive detailed financial information, including audited financial statements, is contained in this report.
- *Form 10-Q.* This report must be filed quarterly for all publicly held companies. It contains certain financial information and requires auditor involvement when there is a change in accounting principles.

Because large CPA firms usually have clients that must file one or more of these reports each year, and the rules and regulations affecting filings with the SEC are extremely complex, most CPA firms have specialists who spend a large portion of their time ensuring that their clients satisfy all SEC requirements.

The SEC has considerable influence in setting generally accepted accounting principles and disclosure requirements for financial statements as a result of its authority for specifying reporting requirements considered necessary for fair disclosure to investors. The SEC has power to establish rules for any CPA associated with audited financial statements submitted to the commission. Even though the commission has taken the position that accounting principles and auditing standards should be set by the profession, the SEC's attitude is generally considered in any major change proposed by the FASB or the ASB.

The SEC requirements of greatest interest to CPAs are set forth in the commission's Regulation S-X, Accounting Series Releases, and Accounting and Auditing Enforcement Releases. These publications constitute important regulations, as well as decisions and opinions on accounting and auditing issues affecting any CPA dealing with publicly held companies. Some of the major influences the SEC has had on auditors in the past few decades are discussed in the text under the topics of independence, legal liability, and audit reporting.

This chapter discussed the nature of the CPA profession and the activities of CPA firms. Because CPA firms play an important social role, the AICPA and other organizations provide mechanisms to increase the likelihood of appropriate audit quality and professional conduct. These are summarized in Figure 2-3. Shaded circles in the figure indicate items discussed in this or the last chapter. The AICPA *Code of Professional Conduct* provides a standard of conduct for practitioners and is discussed in Chapter 4. The potential for legal liability is also a significant influence on auditor conduct and is discussed in Chapter 5.

FIGURE 2-3	**Ways the Profession and Society Encourage CPAs to Conduct Themselves at a High Level**

AICPA—American Institute of Certified Public Accountants, a voluntary organization of CPAs that sets professional requirements, conducts research, and publishes materials relevant to accounting, auditing, management consulting services, and taxes

Division of CPA firms—a division of the AICPA established for CPA firms and consisting of two sections: the SEC Practice Section and the Private Companies Practice Section; the division was established to improve the quality of practice by CPA firms consistent with AICPA quality control standards

Generally accepted auditing standards (GAAS)—10 auditing standards, developed by the AICPA, consisting of general standards, standards of field work, and standards of reporting, along with interpretations; often called auditing standards

Peer review—the review by CPAs of a CPA firm's compliance with its quality control system

Quality control—methods used by a CPA firm to ensure that the firm meets its professional responsibilities to clients and others

Securities and Exchange Commission (SEC)—a federal agency that oversees the orderly conduct of the securities markets; the SEC assists in providing investors in public corporations with reliable information upon which to make investment decisions

Statements on Auditing Standards—pronouncements issued by the AICPA to interpret generally accepted auditing standards

2-1 (Objective 2-1) State the four major types of services CPAs perform, and explain each.

2-2 (Objectives 2-1, 2-4) What major characteristics of the organization and conduct of CPA firms permit them to fulfill their social function competently and independently?

2-3 (Objective 2-2) What roles are played by the American Institute of Certified Public Accountants for its members?

2-4 (Objective 2-2) What are the purposes of the AICPA *Statement on Standards for Attestation Engagements*?

2-5 (Objective 2-3) Distinguish between generally accepted auditing standards and generally accepted accounting principles, and give two examples of each.

2-6 (Objective 2-3) The first standard of field work requires the performance of the audit by a person or persons having adequate technical training and proficiency as an auditor. What are the various ways in which auditors can fulfill the requirement of the standard?

2-7 (Objective 2-3) Generally accepted auditing standards have been criticized by different sources for failing to provide useful guidelines for conducting an audit. The critics believe the standards should be more specific to enable practitioners to improve the quality of their performance. As the standards are now stated, some critics believe that they provide little more than an excuse to conduct inadequate audits. Evaluate this criticism of the 10 generally accepted auditing standards.

2-8 (Objective 2-4) What is meant by the term quality control as it relates to a CPA firm?

2-9 (Objective 2-4) The following is an example of a CPA firm's quality control procedure requirement: "Any person being considered for employment by the firm must have completed a basic auditing course and have been interviewed and approved by an audit partner of the firm before he or she can be hired for the audit staff." Which element of quality control does this procedure affect and what is the purpose of the requirement?

2-10 (Objective 2-4) State what is meant by the term peer review. What are the implications of peer review for the profession?

2-11 (Objective 2-4) What are the two sections of practice to which CPA firms may belong? What are the primary purposes of the sections?

2-12 (Objective 2-5) Describe the role of the Securities and Exchange Commission in society and discuss its relationship with and influence on the practice of auditing.

MULTIPLE CHOICE QUESTIONS FROM CPA EXAMINATIONS

2-13 (Objective 2-3) The following questions deal with generally accepted auditing standards. Choose the best response.

    a. The first general standard, which states in part that the audit is to be performed by a person or persons having adequate technical training, requires that an auditor have
    (1) education and experience in the field of auditing.
    (2) ability in the planning and supervision of the audit work.
    (3) proficiency in business and financial matters.
    (4) knowledge in the areas of financial accounting.

    b. Which of the following best describes what is meant by generally accepted auditing standards?
    (1) Acts to be performed by the auditor.
    (2) Measures of the quality of the auditor's performance.
    (3) Procedures to be used to gather evidence to support financial statements.
    (4) Audit objectives generally determined on audit engagements.

c. The general group of the generally accepted auditing standards includes a requirement that
   (1) field work be adequately planned and supervised.
   (2) the auditor's report state whether or not the financial statements conform to generally accepted accounting principles.
   (3) due professional care be exercised by the auditor.
   (4) informative disclosures in the financial statements be reasonably adequate.

d. What is the general character of the three generally accepted auditing standards classified as standards of field work?
   (1) The competence, independence, and professional care of persons performing the audit.
   (2) Criteria for the content of the auditor's report on financial statements and related footnote disclosures.
   (3) The criteria of audit planning and evidence gathering.
   (4) The need to maintain an independence in mental attitude in all matters pertaining to the audit.

2-14 (Objective 2-4) The following questions concern quality control standards. Choose the best response.

a. A CPA firm is reasonably assured of meeting its responsibility to provide services that conform with professional standards by
   (1) adhering to generally accepted auditing standards.
   (2) having an appropriate system of quality control.
   (3) joining professional societies that enforce ethical conduct.
   (4) maintaining an attitude of independence in its engagements.

b. Which of the following are elements of a CPA firm's quality control that should be considered in establishing its quality control policies and procedures?

	Personnel Management	Monitoring	Engagement Performance
(1)	Yes	Yes	No
(2)	Yes	Yes	Yes
(3)	No	Yes	Yes
(4)	Yes	No	Yes

c. Which of the following is an element of a CPA firm's quality control system that should be considered in establishing its quality control policies and procedures?
   (1) Complying with laws and regulations.
   (2) Using statistical sampling techniques.
   (3) Managing personnel.
   (4) Considering audit risk and materiality.

DISCUSSION QUESTIONS AND PROBLEMS

2-15 (Objective 2-4) The following comments summarize the beliefs of some practitioners about quality control and peer review.

Quality control and peer review are quasi-governmental methods of regulating the profession. There are two effects of such regulation. First, it gives a competitive advantage to national CPA firms because they already need formal structures to administer their complex organizations. Quality control requirements do not significantly affect their structure. Smaller firms now need a more costly organizational structure, which has proven unnecessary because of existing partner involvement on engagements. The major advantage smaller CPA firms have traditionally had is a simple and efficient organizational structure. Now that advantage has been eliminated because of quality control requirements. Second, quality control and peer review are not needed to regulate the profession. The first four elements of quality control have always existed, at least informally, for quality firms. Three things already provide sufficient assurance that informal quality control elements are followed without peer review. They are competitive pressures to do quality work, legal liability for inadequate performance, and a code of professional conduct requiring that CPA firms follow generally accepted auditing standards.

Required

a. State the pros and cons of those comments.
b. Evaluate whether quality control requirements and peer reviews are worth their cost.

2-16 (Objective 2-4) For each of the following procedures taken from the quality control manual of a medium-sized regional CPA firm, identify the applicable element of quality control from Table 2-4 on page 34.

Required

a. Appropriate accounting and auditing research requires adequate technical reference library facilities. Each practice office must maintain minimal facilities, including industry audit guides, to help ensure an awareness of problems unique to specific industries. In addition, a more extensive library is maintained in the office of the director of accounting and auditing.
b. Each audit engagement of the firm is directed by a partner and, in most instances, a manager of the firm. On every engagement, an attempt is made to maintain continuity of at least a portion of the personnel.
c. When prospective employees are interviewed by campus recruiters and are deemed to possess the potential for employment, they will be further screened by a practice office interview pursuant to the firm procedure for practice office visitation. Practice office partners make the final hiring decisions pursuant to the guidelines established by the director of personnel.
d. At all stages of any engagement, an effort is made to involve professional staff at appropriate levels in the accounting and auditing decisions. Various approvals of the manager or senior accountant are obtained throughout the audit.
e. No employee will have any direct or indirect financial interest, association, or relationship (for example, a close relative serving a client in a decision-making capacity) not otherwise disclosed, that might be adverse to the firm's best interest.
f. Each office of the firm shall be visited at least annually by review persons selected by the director of accounting and auditing. Procedures to be undertaken by the reviewers are illustrated by the office review program.
g. Existing clients of the firm are reviewed on a continuing basis by the engagement partner. Termination may result if circumstances indicate that there is reason to question the integrity of management or our independence, or if accounting and auditing differences of opinion cannot be reconciled. Doubts concerning whether the client-auditor relationship should be continued must be promptly discussed with the director of accounting and auditing.
h. Individual partners submit the nominations of those persons whom they wish to be considered for partner. To become a partner, an individual must have exhibited a high degree of technical competence; must possess integrity, motivation, and judgment; and must have a desire to help the firm progress through the efficient dispatch of the job responsibilities to which he or she is assigned.
i. Through our continuing employee evaluation and counseling program and through the quality control review procedures as established by the firm, educational needs are reviewed and formal staff training programs modified to accommodate changing needs. At the conclusion of practice office reviews, apparent accounting and auditing deficiencies are summarized and reported to the firm's director of personnel.

2-17 (Objectives 2-3, 2-5) The Mobile Home Manufacturing Company is audited by Rossi and Montgomery, CPAs. Mobile Home has decided to issue stock to the public and wants Rossi and Montgomery to perform all the audit work necessary to satisfy the requirements for filing with the SEC. The CPA firm has never had a client go public before.

Required

a. What are the ethical implications of Rossi and Montgomery's accepting the engagement?

b. List the additional problems confronting the auditors when they file with the SEC as compared with dealing with a regular audit client.

2-18 (Objective 2-3) Ray, the owner of a small company, asked Holmes, a CPA, to conduct an audit of the company's records. Ray told Holmes that an audit was to be completed in time to submit audited financial statements to a bank as part of a loan application. Holmes immediately accepted the engagement and agreed to provide an auditor's report within 3 weeks. Ray agreed to pay Holmes a fixed fee plus a bonus if the loan was granted.

Holmes hired two accounting students to conduct the audit and spent several hours telling them exactly what to do. Holmes told the students not to spend time reviewing the controls but instead to concentrate on proving the mathematical accuracy of the ledger accounts and summarizing the data in the accounting records that support Ray's financial statements. The students followed Holmes's instructions and after 2 weeks gave Holmes the financial statements, which did not include footnotes. Holmes reviewed the statements and prepared an unqualified auditor's report. The report did not refer to generally accepted accounting principles nor to the consistent application of such principles.

Required

Briefly describe each of the 10 generally accepted auditing standards and indicate how the action(s) of Holmes resulted in a failure to comply with each standard.

Organize your answer as follows:*

Brief Description of GAAS	Holmes' Actions Resulting in Failure to Comply with GAAS

*AICPA adapted.

INTERNET PROBLEM 2-1: CPA VISION PROJECT

Reference the CW site. The CPA Vision Project is all about helping the "CPA profession stay on top of the change curve." With input from CPAs across the nation, the CPA Vision Project has created a comprehensive and integrated vision of the profession's future. This problem requires students to use the Internet (1) to research the CPA Vision Statement, (2) to research the eight forces impacting the profession, and (3) to answer the question, "What is meant by moving up the economic value chain and how are CPAs going to accomplish this?"

AUDIT REPORTS

3

THE AUDIT REPORT WAS TIMELY, BUT AT WHAT COST?

Halvorson & Co., CPAs was hired as the auditor for Machinetron, Inc., a company that manufactured high-precision, computer-operated lathes. The owner, Al Trent, thought that Machinetron was ready to become a public company, and he hired Halvorson to conduct the upcoming audit and assist in the preparation of the registration statement for a securities offering.

Because Machinetron's machines were large and complex, they were expensive. Each sale was negotiated individually by Trent, and the sales often transpired over several months. As a result, improper recording of one or two machines could represent a material misstatement of the financial statements.

The engagement partner in charge of the Machinetron audit was Bob Lehman, who had significant experience auditing manufacturing companies. He recognized the risk for improper recording of sales, and he insisted that his staff confirm all receivables at year-end directly with customers. Lehman conducted his review of the Machinetron working papers the same day that Trent wanted to make the company's registration statement for the initial public stock offering effective. Lehman saw that a receivable for a major sale at year-end was supported by a telegram, rather than the usual written confirmation reply. Apparently, relations with this customer were "touchy," and Trent had discouraged the audit staff from communicating with the customer.

At the end of the day, there was a meeting in Machinetron's office. It was attended by Lehman, Trent, the underwriter of the stock offering, and the company's attorney. Lehman indicated that a better form of confirmation would be required to support the receivable. After hearing this, Trent blew his stack. Machinetron's attorney stepped in and calmed Trent down. He offered to write a letter to Halvorson & Co. stating that in his opinion, a telegram had legal substance as a valid confirmation reply. Lehman, feeling tremendous pressure, accepted this proposal and signed off on an unqualified audit opinion.

Six months after the stock offering, Machinetron issued a statement indicating that its revenues for the prior year had been overstated as a result of improperly recorded sales, including the sale supported by the telegram confirmation. The subsequent SEC investigation uncovered that the telegram had been sent by Trent, not the customer. Halvorson & Co. recalled their unqualified audit report, but this was too late to prevent the harm done to investors. Halvorson & Co. was forced to pay substantial damages, and Bob Lehman was forbidden to practice before the SEC. He subsequently left public accounting.

LEARNING OBJECTIVES

After studying this chapter, you should be able to

3-1 Describe the parts of the standard unqualified audit report.

3-2 Specify the conditions required to issue the standard unqualified audit report.

3-3 Describe the five circumstances when an unqualified report with an explanatory paragraph or modified wording is appropriate.

3-4 Identify the types of audit reports that can be issued when an unqualified opinion is not justified.

3-5 Explain how materiality affects audit reporting decisions.

3-6 Draft appropriately modified audit reports under a variety of circumstances.

3-7 Determine the appropriate audit report for a given audit situation.

eports are essential to audit and assurance engagements because they communicate the auditor's findings. Users of financial statements rely on the auditor's report to provide assurance on the company's financial statements. As the vignette at the beginning of this chapter illustrates, the auditor is likely to be held responsible if an incorrect audit report is issued.

The audit report is the final step in the entire audit process. The reason for studying it now is to permit reference to different audit reports as evidence accumulation is studied throughout this text. These evidence concepts are more meaningful after you understand the form and content of the final product of the audit. We begin by describing the content of the standard auditor's report.

STANDARD UNQUALIFIED AUDIT REPORT

The fourth standard of reporting requires that the audit report should contain a clear-cut indication of the character of the auditor's work and the degree of responsibility taken for the financial statements. To enable users to understand the audit report, professional standards provide uniform wording for the auditor's report.

An example of the auditor's **standard unqualified audit report** is included in Figure 3-1. Different auditors may vary the wording or presentation slightly, but the meaning will be the same. The seven parts of the audit report are described next.

Parts of Standard Unqualified Audit Report

OBJECTIVE 3-1
Describe the parts of the standard unqualified audit report.

The seven parts of the standard unqualified audit report are labeled in bold letters in the margin beside Figure 3-1.

1. *Report title.* Auditing standards require that the report be titled and that the title include the word *independent.* For example, appropriate titles would be "independent auditor's report," "report of independent auditor," or "independent accountant's opinion." The requirement that the title include the word *independent* is intended to convey to users that the audit was unbiased in all aspects.

2. *Audit report address.* The report is usually addressed to the company, its stockholders, or the board of directors. In recent years, it has become customary to address the report to the stockholders to indicate that the auditor is independent of the company and the board of directors.

3. *Introductory paragraph.* The first paragraph of the report does three things: First, it makes the simple statement that the CPA firm has done an *audit.* This is intended to distinguish the report from a compilation or review report. The scope paragraph (see part 4) clarifies what is meant by an audit.

Second, it lists the financial statements that were audited, including the balance sheet dates and the accounting periods for the income statement and statement of cash flows. The wording of the financial statements in the report should be identical to those used by management on the financial statements. Notice that the report in Figure 3-1 is on comparative financial statements. Therefore, a report on both years' statements is needed.

Third, the introductory paragraph states that the statements are the responsibility of management and that the auditor's responsibility is to express an opinion on the statements based on an audit. The purpose of these statements is to communicate that management is responsible for selecting the appropriate generally accepted accounting principles and making the measurement decisions and disclosures in applying those principles and to clarify the respective roles of management and the auditor.

4. *Scope paragraph.* The scope paragraph is a factual statement about what the auditor did in the audit. This paragraph first states that the auditor followed generally accepted auditing standards. The remainder briefly describes important aspects of an audit.

The scope paragraph states that the audit is designed to obtain *reasonable assurance* about whether the statements are free of **material misstatement.** The inclusion of the word *material* conveys that auditors are responsible only to search for significant misstatements,

ANDERSON and ZINDER, P.C.
Certified Public Accountants
Suite 100
Park Plaza East
Denver, Colorado 80110
303/359-0800

Independent Auditor's Report   **Report Title**

To the Stockholders   **Audit Report Address**
General Ring Corporation

We have audited the accompanying balance sheets of General Ring Corporation as of December 31,   **Introductory Paragraph**
1999 and 1998, and the related statements of income, retained earnings, and cash flows for the   **(Factual Statement)**
years then ended. These financial statements are the responsibility of the Company's management.
Our responsibility is to express an opinion on these financial statements based on our audits.

We conducted our audits in accordance with generally accepted auditing standards. Those standards   **Scope Paragraph**
require that we plan and perform the audit to obtain reasonable assurance about whether the   **(Factual Statement)**
financial statements are free of material misstatement. An audit includes examining, on a test basis,
evidence supporting the amounts and disclosures in the financial statements. An audit also includes
assessing the accounting principles used and significant estimates made by management, as well as
evaluating the overall financial statement presentation. We believe that our audits provide a
reasonable basis for our opinion.

In our opinion, the financial statements referred to above present fairly, in all material respects, the   **Opinion Paragraph**
financial position of General Ring Corporation as of December 31, 1999 and 1998 and the results of   **(Conclusions)**
its operations and its cash flows for the years then ended in conformity with generally accepted
accounting principles.

ANDERSON AND ZINDER, P.C., CPAs   **Name of CPA Firm**

March 5, 2000   **Audit Report Date (Date Audit**
                                                              Field Work Is Completed)

[handwritten annotation: refer to → GAAS & GAAP auditor has to know both]

not minor misstatements that do not affect users' decisions. The use of the term *reasonable assurance* is intended to indicate that an audit cannot be expected to completely eliminate the possibility that a material misstatement will exist in the financial statements. In other words, an audit provides a high level of assurance, but it is not a guarantee.

Audit Report Search

The remainder of the scope paragraph discusses the audit evidence accumulated and states that the auditor believes that the evidence accumulated was appropriate for the circumstances to express the opinion presented. The words *test basis* indicate that sampling was used rather than an audit of every transaction and amount on the statements. Whereas the introductory paragraph of the report states that management is responsible for the preparation and content of the financial statements, the scope paragraph states that the auditor evaluates the appropriateness of those accounting principles, estimates, and financial statement disclosures and presentations given.

5. *Opinion paragraph.* The final paragraph in the standard report states the auditor's conclusions based on the results of the audit. This part of the report is so important that often the entire audit report is referred to simply as the *auditor's opinion.* The opinion paragraph is stated as an opinion rather than as a statement of absolute fact or a guarantee. The intent is to indicate that the conclusions are based on professional judgment. The phrase *in*

our opinion indicates that there may be some information risk associated with the financial statements, even though the statements have been audited.

The opinion paragraph is directly related to the first and fourth generally accepted auditing reporting standards listed on page 30. The auditor is required to state an opinion about the financial statements taken as a whole, including a conclusion about whether the company followed generally accepted accounting principles.

One of the controversial parts of the auditor's report is the meaning of the term *present fairly*. Does this mean that if generally accepted accounting principles are followed, the financial statements are presented fairly, or something more? Occasionally, the courts have concluded that auditors are responsible for looking beyond generally accepted accounting principles to determine whether users might be misled, even if those principles are followed. Most auditors believe that financial statements are "presented fairly" when the statements are in accordance with generally accepted accounting principles but that it is also necessary to examine the substance of transactions and balances for possible misinformation.

6. *Name of CPA firm.* The name identifies the CPA firm or practitioner who performed the audit. Typically, the firm's name is used because the entire CPA firm has the legal and professional responsibility to ensure that the quality of the audit meets professional standards.

7. *Audit report date.* The appropriate date for the report is the one on which the auditor has completed the most important auditing procedures in the field. This date is important to users because it indicates the last day of the auditor's responsibility for the review of significant events that occurred after the date of the financial statements. For example, if the balance sheet is dated December 31, 1998, and the audit report is dated March 6, 1999, this indicates that the auditor has searched for material unrecorded transactions and events that occurred up to March 6, 1999.

Conditions for Standard Unqualified Audit Report

OBJECTIVE 3-2
Specify the conditions required to issue the standard unqualified audit report.

The standard unqualified audit report is issued when the following conditions have been met:

1. All statements—balance sheet, income statement, statement of retained earnings, and statement of cash flows—are included in the financial statements.
2. The three general standards have been followed in all respects on the engagement.
3. Sufficient evidence has been accumulated, and the auditor has conducted the engagement in a manner that enables him or her to conclude that the three standards of field work have been met.
4. The financial statements are presented in accordance with generally accepted accounting principles. This also means that adequate disclosures have been included in the footnotes and other parts of the financial statements.
5. There are no circumstances requiring the addition of an explanatory paragraph or modification of the wording of the report.

When these conditions are met, the standard unqualified audit report, as shown in Figure 3-1, is issued. The standard unqualified audit report is sometimes called a clean opinion because there are no circumstances requiring a qualification or modification of the auditor's opinion. The standard unqualified report is the most common audit opinion. Sometimes circumstances beyond the client's or auditor's control prevent the issuance of a clean opinion. However, in most cases, companies make the appropriate changes to their accounting records to avoid a qualification or modification by the auditor.

If any of the five requirements for the standard unqualified audit report are not met, the standard unqualified report cannot be issued. Figure 3-2 indicates the categories of audit reports that can be issued by the auditor. The departures from a standard unqualified report are considered increasingly severe as one moves down the figure. Financial statement users would normally be much more concerned about a disclaimer or adverse opinion than an unqualified report with an explanatory paragraph. These other categories of audit reports are discussed in the following sections.

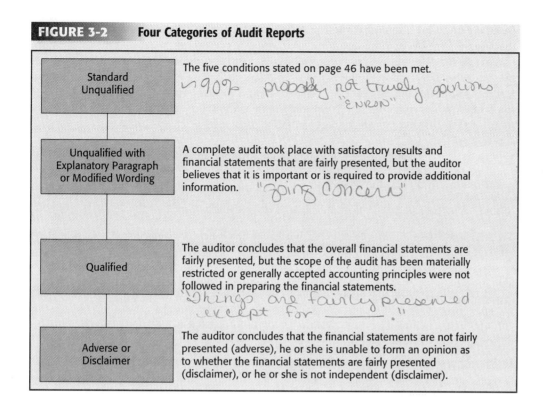

FIGURE 3-2   Four Categories of Audit Reports

Standard Unqualified	The five conditions stated on page 46 have been met. *~90% probably not truely opinions "ENRON"*
Unqualified with Explanatory Paragraph or Modified Wording	A complete audit took place with satisfactory results and financial statements that are fairly presented, but the auditor believes that it is important or is required to provide additional information. *"going concern"*
Qualified	The auditor concludes that the overall financial statements are fairly presented, but the scope of the audit has been materially restricted or generally accepted accounting principles were not followed in preparing the financial statements. *"Things are fairly presented except for ____."*
Adverse or Disclaimer	The auditor concludes that the financial statements are not fairly presented (adverse), he or she is unable to form an opinion as to whether the financial statements are fairly presented (disclaimer), or he or she is not independent (disclaimer).

UNQUALIFIED AUDIT REPORT WITH EXPLANATORY PARAGRAPH OR MODIFIED WORDING

In certain situations, an unqualified audit report is issued, but the wording deviates from the standard unqualified report. The **unqualified audit report with explanatory paragraph or modified wording** meets the criteria of a complete audit with satisfactory results and financial statements that are fairly presented, but the auditor believes it is important or is required to provide additional information. In a qualified, adverse, or disclaimer report, the auditor either has not performed a satisfactory audit, is not satisfied that the financial statements are fairly presented, or is not independent.

The following are the most important causes of the addition of an explanatory paragraph or a modification in the wording of the standard unqualified report:

- Lack of consistent application of generally accepted accounting principles
- Substantial doubt about going concern
- Auditor agrees with a departure from promulgated accounting principles
- Emphasis of a matter
- Reports involving other auditors

The first four reports all require an explanatory paragraph. In each case, the three standard report paragraphs are included without modification and a separate explanatory paragraph follows the opinion paragraph.

Only reports involving the use of other auditors use a modified wording report. This report contains three paragraphs and all three paragraphs are modified.

*disclaimer
① not independent
② scope of audit was too limited to actually audit*

The second reporting standard requires the auditor to call attention to circumstances in which accounting principles have not been consistently observed in the current period in relation to the preceding period. Generally accepted accounting principles require that changes in accounting principles or their method of application be to a preferable

Lack of Consistent Application of GAAP

principle and that the nature and impact of the change be adequately disclosed. When a material change occurs, the auditor should modify the report by adding an explanatory paragraph after the opinion paragraph that discusses the nature of the change and points the reader to the footnote that discusses the change. The materiality of a change is evaluated based on the current year effect of the change. An explanatory paragraph is required for both voluntary changes and required changes due to a new accounting pronouncement. Figure 3-3 presents such an explanatory paragraph.

FIGURE 3-3	Explanatory Paragraph Because of Change in Accounting Principle

<table>
<tr><td rowspan="3" style="text-align:right">Fourth Paragraph—
Explanatory Paragraph</td><td>INDEPENDENT AUDITOR'S REPORT</td></tr>
<tr><td>(Same introductory, scope, and opinion paragraphs as the standard report)</td></tr>
<tr><td>As discussed in Note 8 to the financial statements, the Company changed its method of computing depreciation in 1998.</td></tr>
</table>

It is implicit in the explanatory paragraph in Figure 3-3 that the auditor concurs with the appropriateness of the change in accounting principles. If the auditor does not so concur, the change is considered a violation of generally accepted accounting principles and his or her opinion must be qualified.

Consistency versus Comparability The auditor must be able to distinguish between changes that affect consistency and those that may affect comparability but do not affect consistency. The following are examples of changes that affect consistency and therefore require an explanatory paragraph if they are material:

1. Changes in accounting principles, such as a change from FIFO to LIFO inventory valuation
2. Changes in reporting entities, such as the inclusion of an additional company in combined financial statements
3. Corrections of errors involving principles, by changing from an accounting principle that is not generally acceptable to one that is generally acceptable, including correction of the resulting error

Changes that affect comparability but not consistency and therefore need not be included in the audit report include the following:

1. Changes in an estimate, such as a decrease in the life of an asset for depreciation purposes
2. Error corrections not involving principles, such as a previous year's mathematical error
3. Variations in format and presentation of financial information
4. Changes because of substantially different transactions or events, such as new endeavors in research and development or the sale of a subsidiary

Items that materially affect the comparability of financial statements generally require disclosure in the footnotes. A qualified audit report for inadequate disclosure may be required if the client refuses to properly disclose the items.

Substantial Doubt about Going Concern

Even though the purpose of an audit is not to evaluate the financial health of the business, the auditor has a responsibility to evaluate whether the company is likely to continue as a going concern. SAS 59 (AU 341) addresses this problem under the heading *The Auditor's Consideration of an Entity's Ability to Continue as a Going Concern*. For example, the existence of one or more of the following factors causes uncertainty about the ability of a company to continue as a going concern:

1. Significant recurring operating losses or working capital deficiencies
2. Inability of the company to pay its obligations as they come due

3. Loss of major customers, the occurrence of uninsured catastrophes such as an earthquake or flood, or unusual labor difficulties
4. Legal proceedings, legislation, or similar matters that have occurred that might jeopardize the entity's ability to operate

The auditor's concern in such situations is the possibility that the client may not be able to continue its operations or meet its obligations for a reasonable period. For this purpose, a reasonable period is considered not to exceed 1 year from the date of the financial statements being audited.

When the auditor concludes that there is substantial doubt about the entity's ability to continue as a going concern, an unqualified opinion with an explanatory paragraph is required, regardless of the disclosures in the financial statements. Figure 3-4 provides an example in which there is substantial doubt about going concern.

FIGURE 3-4   **Explanatory Paragraph Because of Substantial Doubt about Going Concern**

INDEPENDENT AUDITOR'S REPORT

(Same introductory, scope, and opinion paragraphs as the standard report)

The accompanying financial statements have been prepared assuming that Fairfax Company will continue as a going concern. As discussed in Note 11 to the financial statements, Fairfax Company has suffered recurring losses from operations and has a net capital deficiency that raise substantial doubt about the company's ability to continue as a going concern. Management's plans in regard to these matters are also described in Note 11. The financial statements do not include any adjustments that might result from the outcome of this uncertainty.

Fourth Paragraph— Explanatory Paragraph

SAS 59 permits but does not require a disclaimer of opinion when there is substantial doubt about going concern. The criteria for issuing a disclaimer of opinion instead of adding an explanatory paragraph are not stated in the standards and this type of opinion is rarely issued in practice. An example for which a disclaimer might be issued is when a regulatory agency, such as the Environmental Protection Agency, is considering a severe sanction against a company and, if the proceedings result in an unfavorable outcome, the company will be forced to liquidate.

Auditor Agrees with a Departure from a Promulgated Principle

Rule 203 of the AICPA *Code of Professional Conduct* states that in unusual situations, a departure from an accounting principle promulgated by a body designated by the AICPA to establish accounting principles may not require a qualified or adverse opinion. However, to justify an unqualified opinion, the auditor must be satisfied and must state and explain, in a separate paragraph or paragraphs in the audit report, that adhering to the principle would have produced a misleading result in that situation.

Emphasis of a Matter

Under certain circumstances, the CPA may want to emphasize specific matters regarding the financial statements, even though he or she intends to express an unqualified opinion. Normally, such explanatory information should be included in a separate paragraph in the report. The following are examples of explanatory information the auditor may think should be expressed: the existence of significant related party transactions, important events occurring subsequent to the balance sheet date, the description of accounting matters affecting the comparability of the financial statements with those of the preceding year, and material uncertainties disclosed in the footnotes.

Reports Involving Other Auditors

When the CPA relies on a different CPA firm to perform part of the audit, which is common when the client has several widespread branches or subdivisions, the principal CPA firm has three alternatives. Only the second is an unqualified report with modified wording.

1. Make No Reference in the Audit Report When no reference is made to the other auditor, a standard unqualified opinion is given unless other circumstances require a departure. This approach is typically followed when the other auditor audited an immaterial portion of the statements, the other auditor is well known or closely supervised by the principal auditor, or the principal auditor has thoroughly reviewed the other auditor's work. The other auditor is still responsible for his or her own report and work in the event of a lawsuit or SEC action.

2. Make Reference in the Report (Modified Wording Report) This type of report is called a shared opinion or report. A shared unqualified report is appropriate when it is impractical to review the work of the other auditor or when the portion of the financial statements audited by the other CPA is material in relation to the whole. An example of a shared report that should not be interpreted as a qualification is shown in Figure 3-5. Notice that the report does *not* include a separate paragraph that discusses the shared responsibility, but does so in the introductory paragraph and refers to the other auditor in the scope and opinion paragraphs. The portions of the financial statements audited by the other auditor can be stated as percentages or absolute amounts.

3. Qualify the Opinion The principal auditor may conclude that a qualified opinion is required. A qualified opinion or disclaimer, depending on materiality, is required if the principal auditor is not willing to assume any responsibility for the work of the other auditor. The principal auditor may also decide that a qualification is required in the overall report if the other auditor qualified his or her portion of the audit. Qualified opinions and disclaimers are discussed in a later section.

DEPARTURES FROM AN UNQUALIFIED AUDIT REPORT

OBJECTIVE 3-4
Identify the types of audit reports that can be issued when an unqualified opinion is not justified.

It is essential that auditors and readers of audit reports understand the circumstances when an unqualified report is inappropriate and the type of audit report issued in each circumstance. In the study of audit reports that depart from an unqualified report, there are three closely related topics: the conditions requiring a departure from an unqualified opinion, the types of opinions other than unqualified, and materiality.

First, the three conditions requiring a departure are briefly summarized. Each is discussed in greater depth later in the chapter.

1. The Scope of the Audit Has Been Restricted (Scope Limitation) When the auditor has not accumulated sufficient evidence to conclude whether financial statements are stated in accordance with GAAP, a scope restriction exists. There are two major causes of scope restrictions: restrictions imposed by the client and those caused by circumstances beyond either the client's or auditor's control. An example of a client restriction is management's refusal to permit the auditor to confirm material receivables or to physically examine inventory. An example of a restriction caused by circumstances is when the engagement is not agreed on until after the client's year-end. It may not be possible to physically observe inventories, confirm receivables, or perform other important procedures after the balance sheet date.

2. The Financial Statements Have Not Been Prepared in Accordance with Generally Accepted Accounting Principles (GAAP Departure) For example, if the client insists on using replacement costs for fixed assets or values inventory at selling price rather than historical cost, a departure from the unqualified report is required. When generally accepted accounting principles are referred to in this context, consideration of the adequacy of all informative disclosures, including footnotes, is especially important.

FIGURE 3-5   **Unqualified Shared Report**

INDEPENDENT AUDITOR'S REPORT

Stockholders and Board of Directors
Washington Felp
Midland, Texas

We have audited the accompanying consolidated balance sheets of Washington Felp as of July 31, 1999 and 1998, and the related consolidated statements of income, retained earnings, and cash flows for the years then ended. These financial statements are the responsibility of the Company's management. Our responsibility is to express an opinion on these financial statements based on our audits. We did not audit the financial statements of Stewart Pane and Lighting, a consolidated subsidiary in which the Company had an equity interest of 84% as of July 31, 1999, which statements reflect total assets of $2,420,000 and $2,237,000 as of July 31, 1999 and 1998, respectively, and total revenues of $3,458,000 and $3,121,000 for the years then ended. Those statements were audited by other auditors whose report has been furnished to us, and our opinion, insofar as it relates to the amounts included for Stewart Pane and Lighting, is based solely on the report of the other auditors.

Introductory Paragraph– Modified Wording

We conducted our audits in accordance with generally accepted auditing standards. Those standards require that we plan and perform the audit to obtain reasonable assurance about whether the financial statements are free of material misstatement. An audit includes examining, on a test basis, evidence supporting the amounts and disclosures in the financial statements. An audit also includes assessing the accounting principles used and significant estimates made by management, as well as evaluating the overall financial statement presentation. We believe that our audits and the report of other auditors provide a reasonable basis for our opinion.

Scope Paragraph– Modified Wording

In our opinion, based on our audits and the report of other auditors, the consolidated financial statements referred to above present fairly, in all material respects, the financial position of Washington Felp as of July 31, 1999 and 1998, and the results of its operations and its cash flows for the years then ended in conformity with generally accepted accounting principles.

Opinion Paragraph– Modified Wording

September 16, 1999
Farn, Ross, & Co.
Certified Public Accountants
Dallas, Texas

---

3. The Auditor Is Not Independent Independence ordinarily is determined by Rule 101 of the rules of the *Code of Professional Conduct.*

When any of the three conditions requiring a departure from an unqualified report exists and is material, a report other than an unqualified report must be issued. Three main types of audit reports are issued under these conditions: qualified opinion, adverse opinion, and disclaimer of opinion.

A **qualified opinion** report can result from a limitation on the scope of the audit or failure to follow generally accepted accounting principles. A qualified opinion report can be used *only when the auditor concludes that the overall financial statements are fairly stated.* A disclaimer or an adverse report must be used if the auditor believes that the condition being reported on is highly material. Therefore, the qualified opinion is considered the least severe type of departure from an unqualified report.

Qualified Opinion

A qualified report can take the form of a *qualification of both the scope and the opinion* or of the *opinion alone.* A scope and opinion qualification can be issued only when the auditor has been unable to accumulate all of the evidence required by generally accepted auditing standards. Therefore, this type of qualification is used when the auditor's scope has been restricted by the client or when circumstances exist that prevent the auditor from conducting a complete audit. The use of a qualification of the opinion alone is restricted to situations in which the financial statements are not stated in accordance with GAAP.

When an auditor issues a qualified report, he or she must use the term *except for* in the opinion paragraph. The implication is that the auditor is satisfied that the overall financial statements are correctly stated "except for" a specific aspect of them. Examples of this qualification are given later in this chapter. It is unacceptable to use the phrase *except for* with any other type of audit opinion.

Adverse Opinion

An **adverse opinion** is used only when the auditor believes that the overall financial statements are so *materially misstated or misleading* that they do not present fairly the financial position or results of operations and cash flows in conformity with GAAP. The adverse opinion report can arise only when the auditor has knowledge, after an adequate investigation, of the absence of conformity. This is uncommon and thus the adverse opinion is rarely used.

Disclaimer of Opinion

A **disclaimer of opinion** is issued when the auditor has been *unable to satisfy himself or herself* that the overall financial statements are fairly presented. The necessity for disclaiming an opinion may arise because of a *severe limitation on the scope* of the audit or a *nonindependent relationship* under the *Code of Professional Conduct* between the auditor and the client. Either of these situations prevents the auditor from expressing an opinion on the financial statements as a whole. The auditor also has the option to issue a disclaimer of opinion for a going concern problem.

The disclaimer is distinguished from an adverse opinion in that it can arise only from a *lack of knowledge* by the auditor, whereas to express an adverse opinion, the auditor must have knowledge that the financial statements are not fairly stated. Both disclaimers and adverse opinions are used only when the condition is highly material.

MATERIALITY

OBJECTIVE 3-5

Explain how materiality affects audit reporting decisions.

Materiality is an essential consideration in determining the appropriate type of report for a given set of circumstances. For example, if a misstatement is immaterial relative to the financial statements of the entity for the current period, it is appropriate to issue an unqualified report. A common instance is the immediate expensing of office supplies rather than carrying the unused portion in inventory because the amount is insignificant.

The situation is totally different when the amounts are of such significance that the financial statements are materially affected as a whole. In these circumstances, it is necessary to issue a disclaimer of opinion or an adverse opinion, depending on the nature of the misstatement. In situations of lesser materiality, a qualified opinion is appropriate.

Levels of Materiality

The common definition of materiality as it applies to accounting and therefore to audit reporting is as follows:

> A misstatement in the financial statements can be considered material if knowledge of the misstatement would affect a decision of a reasonable user of the statements.

In applying this definition, three levels of materiality are used for determining the type of opinion to issue.

Amounts Are Immaterial When a misstatement in the financial statements exists but is unlikely to affect the decisions of a reasonable user, it is considered to be immaterial. An unqualified opinion is therefore appropriate. For example, assume that management recorded unexpired insurance as an asset in the previous year and decides to expense it in the current year to reduce record-keeping costs. Management has failed to follow GAAP, but if the amounts are small, the misstatement would be immaterial and a standard unqualified audit report would be appropriate.

Amounts Are Material but Do Not Overshadow the Financial Statements as a Whole The second level of materiality exists when a misstatement in the financial statements would affect a user's decision, but the overall statements are still fairly stated and therefore useful. For example, knowledge of a large misstatement in fixed assets might affect a user's willingness to loan money to a company if the assets were the collateral. A misstatement of inventory does not mean that cash, accounts receivable, and other elements of the financial statements, or the financial statements as a whole, are materially incorrect.

To make materiality decisions when a condition requiring a departure from an unqualified report exists, the auditor must evaluate all effects on the financial statements. Assume that the auditor is unable to satisfy himself or herself whether inventory is fairly stated in deciding on the appropriate type of opinion. Because of the effect of a misstatement in inventory on other accounts and on totals in the statements, the auditor needs to consider the materiality of the combined effect on inventory, total current assets, total working capital, total assets, income taxes, income taxes payable, total current liabilities, cost of goods sold, net income before taxes, and net income after taxes.

When the auditor concludes that a misstatement is material but does not overshadow the financial statements as a whole, a qualified opinion (using "except for") is appropriate.

Amounts Are So Material or So Pervasive That Overall Fairness of the Statements Is in Question The highest level of materiality exists when users are likely to make incorrect decisions if they rely on the overall financial statements. To return to the previous example, if inventory is the largest balance on the financial statements, a large misstatement would probably be so material that the auditor's report should indicate the financial statements taken as a whole cannot be considered fairly stated. When the highest level of materiality exists, the auditor must issue either a disclaimer of opinion or an adverse opinion, depending on which conditions exist.

When determining whether an exception is highly material, the extent to which the exception affects different parts of the financial statements must be considered. This is called pervasiveness. A misclassification between cash and accounts receivable affects only those two accounts and is therefore not pervasive. On the other hand, failure to record a material sale is highly pervasive because it affects sales, accounts receivable, income tax expense, accrued income taxes, and retained earnings, which in turn affect current assets, total assets, current liabilities, total liabilities, owners' equity, gross margin, and operating income.

As misstatements become more pervasive, the likelihood of issuing an adverse opinion rather than a qualified opinion increases. For example, suppose the auditor decides a misclassification between cash and accounts receivable should result in a qualified opinion because it is material; the failure to record a sale of the same dollar amount may result in an adverse opinion because of pervasiveness.

Regardless of the amount involved, a disclaimer of opinion must be issued if the auditor is determined to lack independence under the rules of the *Code of Professional Conduct.* This harsh requirement reflects the importance of independence to auditors. Any deviation from the independence rule is therefore considered highly material. Table 3-1 (p. 54) summarizes the relationship between materiality and the type of opinion to be issued.

| TABLE 3-1 | Relationship of Materiality to Type of Opinion |

Materiality Level	Significance in Terms of Reasonable Users' Decisions	Type of Opinion
Immaterial	Users' decisions are unlikely to be affected.	Unqualified
Material	Users' decisions are likely to be affected only if the information in question is important to the specific decisions being made. The overall financial statements are presented fairly.	Qualified
Highly material	Most or all users' decisions based on the financial statements are likely to be significantly affected.	Disclaimer or Adverse

Note: Lack of independence requires a disclaimer regardless of materiality.

[handwritten annotations: "Things are in a shamble & it is a mess OR client would not allow certain audit steps to be performed" and "...fairly presented except for..."]

Materiality Decisions

In concept, the effect of materiality on the type of opinion to issue is straightforward. In application, deciding on actual materiality in a given situation is a difficult judgment. There are no simple, well-defined guidelines that enable auditors to decide when something is immaterial, material, or highly material. The evaluation of materiality also depends on whether the situation involves a failure to follow GAAP or a scope limitation.

Materiality Decisions—Non-GAAP Condition When a client has failed to follow GAAP, the audit report will be unqualified, qualified opinion only, or adverse, depending on the materiality of the departure. Several aspects of materiality must be considered.

Dollar Amounts Compared with a Base The primary concern in measuring materiality when a client has failed to follow GAAP is usually the total dollar misstatement in the accounts involved, compared with some base. A $10,000 misstatement might be material for a small company, but not for a larger one. Therefore, misstatements must be compared with some measurement base before a decision can be made about the materiality of the failure to follow GAAP. Common bases include net income, total assets, current assets, and working capital.

For example, assume that the auditor believes there is a $100,000 overstatement of inventory because of the client's failure to follow GAAP. Also assume recorded inventory of $1,000,000, current assets of $3,000,000, and net income before taxes of $2,000,000. In this case, the auditor must evaluate the materiality of a misstatement of inventory of 10 percent, current assets of 3.3 percent, and net income before taxes of 5 percent.

To evaluate overall materiality, the auditor must also combine all unadjusted misstatements and judge whether there may be individually immaterial misstatements that, when combined, significantly affect the statements. In the inventory example just given, assume the auditor believes there is also an overstatement of $150,000 in accounts receivable. The total effect on current assets is now 8.3 percent ($250,000 divided by $3,000,000) and on net income before taxes is 12.5 percent ($250,000 divided by $2,000,000).

When comparing potential misstatements with a base, the auditor must carefully consider all accounts affected by a misstatement (pervasiveness). For example, it is important not to overlook the effect of an understatement of inventory on cost of goods sold, income before taxes, income tax expense, and accrued income taxes payable.

Measurability The dollar amount of some misstatements cannot be accurately measured. For example, a client's unwillingness to disclose an existing lawsuit or the acquisition of a new company subsequent to the balance sheet date is difficult if not impossible to measure in terms of dollar amounts. The materiality question the auditor must evaluate in such situations is the effect on statement users of the failure to make the disclosure.

Nature of the Item The decision of a user may also be affected by the kind of misstatement in the statement. The following may affect the user's decision and therefore the auditor's opinion in a different way than most misstatements.

1. Transactions are illegal or fraudulent.
2. An item may materially affect some future period even though it is immaterial when only the current period is considered.
3. An item has a "psychic" effect (for example, small profit versus small loss or cash balance versus overdraft).
4. An item may be important in terms of possible consequences arising from contractual obligations (for example, the effect of failure to comply with a debt restriction may result in a material loan being called).

Materiality Decisions—Scope Limitations Condition When there is a scope limitation in an audit, the audit report will be unqualified, qualified scope and opinion, or disclaimer, depending on the materiality of the scope limitation. The auditor will consider the same three factors included in the previous discussion about materiality decisions for failure to follow GAAP, but they will be considered differently. The size of *potential* misstatements, rather than known misstatements, is important in determining whether an unqualified report, a qualified report, or a disclaimer of opinion is appropriate for a scope limitation. For example, if recorded accounts payable of $400,000 was not audited, the auditor must evaluate the potential misstatement in accounts payable and decide how materially the financial statements could be affected. The pervasiveness of these potential misstatements must also be considered.

It is typically more difficult to evaluate the materiality of potential misstatements resulting from a scope limitation than for failure to follow GAAP. Misstatements resulting from failure to follow GAAP are known. Those resulting from scope limitations must usually be subjectively measured in terms of potential or likely misstatements. For example, a recorded accounts payable of $400,000 might be understated by more than $1 million, which may affect several totals, including gross margin, net earnings, and total assets.

DISCUSSION OF CONDITIONS REQUIRING A DEPARTURE

You should now understand the relationships among the conditions requiring a departure from an unqualified report, the major types of reports other than unqualified, and the three levels of materiality. This part of the chapter examines the conditions requiring a departure from an unqualified report in greater detail and shows examples of reports.

OBJECTIVE 3-6
Draft appropriately modified audit reports under a variety of circumstances.

Auditor's Scope Has Been Restricted

Two major categories of scope restrictions exist: those caused by a client and those caused by conditions beyond the control of either the client or the auditor. The effect on the auditor's report is the same for either, but the interpretation of materiality is likely to be different. When there is a scope restriction, the appropriate response is to issue an unqualified report, a qualification of scope and opinion, or a disclaimer of opinion, depending on materiality.

For client-imposed restrictions, the auditor should be concerned about the possibility that management is trying to prevent discovery of misstated information. In such cases, the AICPA has encouraged a disclaimer of opinion when materiality is in question. When restrictions result from conditions beyond the client's control, a qualification of scope and opinion is more likely.

Two restrictions occasionally imposed by clients on the auditor's scope relate to the observation of physical inventory and the confirmation of accounts receivable, but other restrictions may also occur. Reasons for client-imposed scope restrictions may be a desire to save audit fees and, in the case of confirming receivables, to prevent possible conflicts between the client and customer when amounts differ. A qualified or disclaimer of opinion resulting from a client restriction requires a qualifying paragraph preceding the opinion to describe the restriction. In the case of disclaimer, the scope paragraph is excluded from the report in its entirety.

The most common case in which conditions beyond the client's and auditor's control cause a scope restriction is an engagement agreed on after the client's balance sheet date. The confirmation of accounts receivable, physical examination of inventory, and other important procedures may be impossible under those circumstances. When the auditor cannot perform procedures he or she considers desirable but can be satisfied with alternative procedures that the information being verified is fairly stated, an unqualified report is appropriate. If alternative procedures cannot be performed, a scope qualification and, depending on the materiality, either an opinion qualification or a disclaimer of opinion is necessary.

For example, the report in Figure 3-6 would be appropriate for an audit in which the amounts were material but not pervasive and the auditor could not obtain audited financial statements supporting an investment in a foreign affiliate and could not satisfy himself or herself by alternate procedures. The entire introductory paragraph and most of the second paragraph are omitted because they use standard wording.

FIGURE 3-6	Qualified Scope and Opinion Report Due to Scope Restriction

INDEPENDENT AUDITOR'S REPORT

(Same introductory paragraph as standard report)

Scope Paragraph— Qualified
Except as discussed in the following paragraph, we conducted our audit . . . (remainder is the same as the scope paragraph in the standard report)

Third Paragraph— Added
We were unable to obtain audited financial statements supporting the Company's investment in a foreign affiliate stated at $475,000, or its equity in earnings of that affiliate of $365,000, which is included in net income, as described in Note X to the financial statements. Because of the nature of the Company's records, we were unable to satisfy ourselves as to the carrying value of the investment or the equity in its earnings by means of other auditing procedures.

Opinion Paragraph— Qualified
In our opinion, except for the effects of such adjustments, if any, as might have been determined to be necessary had we been able to examine evidence regarding the foreign affiliate investment and earnings, the financial statements referred to above present fairly, in all material respects, the financial position of Laughlin Corporation as of December 31, 1999, and the results of its operations and its cash flows for the year then ended in conformity with generally accepted accounting principles.

When the amounts are so material that a disclaimer of opinion rather than a qualified opinion is required, the auditor uses only three paragraphs. The first (introductory) paragraph is modified slightly to say "We were engaged to audit. . . ." The second paragraph is the same as the third paragraph in Figure 3-6. The scope paragraph is deleted and the final (opinion) paragraph is changed to a disclaimer. The reason for deleting the scope paragraph is to avoid stating anything that might lead readers to believe that other parts of the financial statements were audited and therefore might be fairly stated. Figure 3-7 shows the audit report assuming the auditor had concluded that the facts in Figure 3-6 required a disclaimer rather than a qualified opinion.

Statements Are Not in Conformity with GAAP

When the auditor knows that the financial statements may be misleading because they were not prepared in conformity with GAAP, he or she must issue a qualified or an adverse opinion, depending on the materiality of the item in question. The opinion must clearly state the nature of the deviation from accepted principles and the amount of the misstatement,

FIGURE 3-7   Disclaimer of Opinion Due to Scope Restriction

INDEPENDENT AUDITOR'S REPORT

We were engaged to audit . . . (remainder is the same as the introductory paragraph in the standard report)

(Same wording as that used for the third paragraph in Figure 3-6)

Because we were unable to obtain audited financial statements supporting the Company's investment in a foreign affiliate and we were unable to satisfy ourselves as to the carrying value of the investment or the equity in its earnings by means of other auditing procedures, the scope of our work was not sufficient to enable us to express, and we do not express, an opinion on these financial statements.

*Introductory Paragraph–
Modification of Standard Report*

Second Paragraph–Added

Opinion Paragraph–Disclaimer

Note: In a disclaimer due to a scope restriction, the scope paragraph is omitted entirely.

if it is known. Figure 3-8 shows an example of a qualified opinion when a client did not capitalize leases as required by GAAP. The first and second paragraphs are omitted because they include standard wording.

FIGURE 3-8   Qualified Opinion Report Due to Non-GAAP

INDEPENDENT AUDITOR'S REPORT

(Same introductory and scope paragraphs as the standard report)

The Company has excluded from property and debt in the accompanying balance sheet certain lease obligations that, in our opinion, should be capitalized to conform with generally accepted accounting principles. If these lease obligations were capitalized, property would be increased by $4,600,000, long-term debt by $4,200,000, and retained earnings by $400,000 as of December 31, 1999, and net income and earnings per share would be increased by $400,000 and $1.75, respectively, for the year then ended.

In our opinion, except for the effects of not capitalizing lease obligations, as discussed in the preceding paragraph, the financial statements referred to above present fairly, in all material respects, the financial position of Ajax Company as of December 31, 1999, and the results of its operations and its cash flows for the year then ended in conformity with generally accepted accounting principles.

Third Paragraph–Added

Opinion Paragraph–Qualified

When the amounts are so material or pervasive that an adverse opinion is required, the scope would still be unqualified, and the qualifying paragraph could remain the same, but the opinion paragraph might be as shown in Figure 3-9.

When the client fails to include information that is necessary for the fair presentation of financial statements in the body of the statements or in the related footnotes, it is the

FASB

FIGURE 3-9   Adverse Opinion Due to Non-GAAP

INDEPENDENT AUDITOR'S REPORT

(Same introductory and scope paragraphs as the standard report)

(Same third paragraph as that used for the third paragraph in Figure 3-8)

In our opinion, because of the effects of the matters discussed in the preceding paragraph, the financial statements referred to above do not present fairly, in conformity with generally accepted accounting principles, the financial position of Ajax Company as of December 31, 1999, or the results of its operations and its cash flows for the year then ended.

Third Paragraph–Added

Opinion Paragraph–Adverse

---

auditor's responsibility to present the information in the audit report and to issue a qualified or an adverse opinion. It is common to put this type of qualification in an added paragraph preceding the opinion (the scope paragraph will remain unqualified) and to refer to the added paragraph in the opinion paragraph. Figure 3-10 shows an example of an audit report in which the auditor considered the financial statement disclosure inadequate.

FIGURE 3-10   **Qualified Opinion Due to Inadequate Disclosure**

INDEPENDENT AUDITOR'S REPORT

(Same introductory and scope paragraphs as the standard report)

Third Paragraph—Added   On January 15, 1999, the company issued debentures in the amount of $3,600,000 for the purpose of financing plant expansion. The debenture agreement restricts the payment of future cash dividends to earnings after December 31, 1999. In our opinion, disclosure of this information is required to conform with generally accepted accounting principles.

Opinion Paragraph—Qualified   In our opinion, except for the omission of the information discussed in the preceding paragraph, the financial statements referred to above present fairly . . . (remainder is the same as the opinion in the standard report)

Rule 203 Reports Determining whether statements are in accordance with GAAP can be difficult. Rule 203, from the *Code of Professional Conduct*, permits a departure from accounting research bulletins, Accounting Principles Board opinions, and FASB statements when the auditor believes that adherence to these would result in misleading statements.

Rule 203—Accounting Principles A member shall not (1) express an opinion or state affirmatively that financial statements or other financial data of any entity are presented in conformity with generally accepted accounting principles or (2) state that he or she is not aware of any material modifications that should be made to such statements or data in order for them to be in conformity with generally accepted accounting principles, if such statements or data contain any departure from an accounting principle promulgated by bodies designated by Council to establish such principles that has a material effect on the statements or data taken as a whole. If, however, the statements or data contain such a departure and the member can demonstrate that due to unusual circumstances the financial statements or data would otherwise have been misleading, the member can comply with the rule by describing the departure, its approximate effects, if practicable, and the reasons why compliance with the principle would result in a misleading statement.

When the auditor decides that adherence to GAAP would result in misleading statements, there should be a complete explanation in a third paragraph. The paragraph should fully explain the departure and why GAAP would have resulted in misleading statements. The opinion paragraph should then be unqualified except for the reference to the third paragraph. As discussed earlier in the chapter, this is called an unqualified audit report with an explanatory paragraph.

Lack of Statement of Cash Flows The client's unwillingness to include a statement of cash flows is specifically addressed in SAS 58 (AU 508). When the statement is omitted, there must be a third paragraph stating the omission and an "except for" opinion qualification.

Auditor Is Not Independent

If the auditor has not fulfilled the independence requirements specified by the *Code of Professional Conduct*, a disclaimer of opinion is required even though all the audit procedures considered necessary in the circumstances were performed. The wording in Figure 3-11 is recommended when the auditor is not independent.

FIGURE 3-11 Disclaimer Due to Lack of Independence

We are not independent with respect to XYZ Company, and the accompanying balance sheet as of December 31, 1999, and the related statements of income, retained earnings, and cash flows for the year then ended were not audited by us. Accordingly, we do not express an opinion on them.

Note: When the auditor lacks independence, no report title is included.

The lack of independence overrides any other scope limitations. Therefore, no other reason for disclaiming an opinion should be cited. There should be no mention in the report of the performance of any audit procedures. It is an example of a one-paragraph audit report.

Table 3-2 summarizes the appropriate audit report for each condition requiring a departure from an unqualified report at each level of materiality.

TABLE 3-2 Audit Report for Each Condition Requiring a Departure from an Unqualified Report at Different Levels of Materiality

Condition Requiring a Departure	Level of Materiality		
	Immaterial	Material, But Does Not Overshadow Financial Statements as a Whole	So Material That Overall Fairness Is in Question
Scope restricted by client or conditions	Unqualified report	Qualified scope, additional paragraph, and qualified opinion (except for)	Disclaimer of opinion
Financial statements not prepared in accordance with GAAP*	Unqualified report	Additional paragraph and qualified opinion (except for)	Adverse opinion
The auditor is not independent		Disclaimer of opinion (regardless of materiality)	

*If the auditor can demonstrate that GAAP would be misleading, a report with modified wording would be appropriate.

AUDITOR'S DECISION PROCESS FOR AUDIT REPORTS

Auditors use a well-defined process for deciding the appropriate audit report in a given set of circumstances. The auditor must first assess whether any conditions exist requiring a departure from a standard unqualified report. If any conditions exist, the auditor must then assess the materiality of the condition and determine the appropriate type of report.

> **OBJECTIVE 3-7**
> Determine the appropriate audit report for a given audit situation.

Determine Whether Any Condition Exists Requiring a Departure from a Standard Unqualified Report The most important of these conditions are identified in Table 3-3 (p. 60). Auditors identify these conditions as they perform the audit and include information about any condition in the working papers as discussion items for audit reporting. If none of these conditions exist, which is the case in most audits, the auditor issues a standard unqualified audit report.

Decide the Materiality for Each Condition When a condition requiring a departure from a standard unqualified opinion exists, the auditor evaluates the potential effect on the financial statements. For departures from GAAP or scope restrictions, the auditor must

TABLE 3-3	Audit Report for Each Condition Requiring a Departure from a Standard Unqualified Report at Different Levels of Materiality

Condition Requiring an Unqualified Report with Modified Wording or Explanatory Paragraph	Level of Materiality	
	Immaterial	Material
Accounting principles not consistently applied*	Unqualified *st.*	Unqualified report, explanatory paragraph
Substantial doubt about going concern†	Unqualified *st.*	Unqualified report, explanatory paragraph
Justified departure from GAAP or other accounting principle	Unqualified *st.*	Unqualified report, explanatory paragraph
Emphasis of a matter	Unqualified *st.*	Unqualified report, explanatory paragraph
Use of another auditor	Unqualified *st.*	Unqualified report, modified wording

(handwritten annotation: "90% are opinions" with arrow pointing to Immaterial column)

Condition Requiring a Departure from Unqualified Report	Level of Materiality		
	Immaterial	Material, But Does Not Overshadow Financial Statements as a Whole	So Material That Overall Fairness Is in Question
Scope restricted by client or conditions	Unqualified	Qualified scope, additional paragraph, and qualified opinion (except for)	Disclaimer
Financial statements not prepared in accordance with GAAP‡	Unqualified	Additional paragraph and qualified opinion (except for)	Adverse
The auditor is not independent		Disclaimer, regardless of materiality	

*If the auditor does not concur with the appropriateness of the change, the condition is considered a violation of GAAP.
†The auditor has the option of issuing a disclaimer of opinion.
‡If the auditor can demonstrate that GAAP would be misleading, a report with modified wording would be appropriate.

decide among immaterial, material, and highly material. All other conditions, except for lack of auditor independence, require only a distinction between immaterial and material. The materiality decision is a difficult one, requiring considerable judgment. For example, assume that there is a scope limitation in auditing inventory. It is difficult to assess the potential misstatement of an account that the auditor does not audit.

Decide the Appropriate Type of Report for the Condition, Given the Materiality Level After making the first two decisions, it is easy to decide the appropriate type of opinion by using a decision aid. An example of such an aid is Table 3-3. For example, assume that the auditor concludes that there is a departure from GAAP and it is material, but not highly material. Table 3-3 shows that the appropriate audit report is a qualified opinion with an additional paragraph discussing the departure. The introductory and scope paragraphs will be included using standard wording.

Write the Audit Report Most CPA firms have computer templates that include precise wording for different circumstances to help the auditor write the audit report. Also, one or more partners in most CPA firms have special expertise in writing audit reports. These partners typically write or review all audit reports before they are issued.

More Than One Condition Requiring a Departure or Modification

Auditors often encounter situations involving more than one of the conditions requiring a departure from an unqualified report or modification of the standard unqualified report. In these circumstances, the auditor should modify his or her opinion for each condition unless one has the effect of neutralizing the others. For example, if there is a scope limitation and a situation in which the auditor is not independent, the scope limitation should not be revealed. The following situations are examples when more than one modification should be included in the report:

- The auditor is not independent and the auditor knows that the company has not followed generally accepted accounting principles.
- There is a scope limitation and there is substantial doubt about the company's ability to continue as a going concern.
- There is a substantial doubt about the company's ability to continue as a going concern, and information about the causes of the uncertainties is not adequately disclosed in a footnote.
- There is a deviation in the statements' preparation in accordance with GAAP, and another accounting principle was applied on a basis that was not consistent with that of the preceding year.

Many readers interpret the number of paragraphs in the report as an important "signal" as to whether the financial statements are correct. A three-paragraph report ordinarily indicates that there are no exceptions in the audit. However, three-paragraph reports are also issued when a disclaimer of opinion is issued due to a scope limitation, or for an unqualified shared report involving other auditors. More than three paragraphs indicates some type of qualification or required explanation.

Number of Paragraphs in the Report

An additional paragraph is added before the opinion for a qualified opinion, an adverse opinion, and a disclaimer of opinion for a scope limitation. This results in a four-paragraph report, except for the disclaimer of opinion for a scope limitation. A disclaimer due to a scope limitation results in a three-paragraph report because the scope paragraph is omitted. A disclaimer due to a lack of independence is a one-paragraph report.

When an unqualified opinion with explanatory paragraph is issued, an explanatory paragraph usually follows the opinion. No explanatory paragraph is required for an unqualified shared report involving other auditors, but the wording in all three paragraphs is modified.

Table 3-4 summarizes the types of reports issued for the audit of financial statements, the number of paragraphs for each type, the standard wording paragraphs modified, and the location of the additional paragraph. The table excludes a disclaimer for a lack of independence, which is a special one-paragraph report.

TABLE 3-4	Number of Paragraphs, Standard Wording Paragraphs Modified, and Location of Additional Paragraph for Audit Reports		
Type of Report	Number of Paragraphs	Standard Wording Paragraphs Modified	Location of Additional Paragraph
Standard unqualified	3	None	None
Unqualified with explanatory paragraph	4	None	After opinion
Unqualified shared report with other auditors	3	All three paragraphs	None
Qualified—opinion only	4	Opinion only	Before opinion
Qualified—scope and opinion	4	Scope and opinion	Before opinion
Disclaimer—scope limitation	3	Introductory and opinion paragraphs modified; scope paragraph eliminated	Before opinion
Adverse	4	Opinion only	Before opinion

This chapter described the four categories of audit reports and the auditor's decision process in choosing the appropriate audit report to issue. The conditions necessary to issue the auditor's standard unqualified audit report and the content of that report were discussed. In some circumstances, an explanatory paragraph or modification of the unqualified report is required. When there is a material departure from GAAP or a material limitation on the scope of the audit, an unqualified report cannot be issued. The appropriate report to issue in these circumstances depends on whether the situation involves a GAAP departure or a scope limitation, as well as the level of materiality.

ESSENTIAL TERMS

Adverse opinion—a report issued when the auditor believes the financial statements are so materially misstated or misleading as a whole that they do not present fairly the entity's financial position or the results of its operations and cash flows in conformity with GAAP

Disclaimer of opinion—a report issued when the auditor has not been able to become satisfied that the overall financial statements are fairly presented or the auditor is not independent

Material misstatement—a misstatement in the financial statements, knowledge of which would affect a decision of a reasonable user of the statements

Qualified opinion—a report issued when the auditor believes that the overall financial statements are fairly stated but that either the scope of the audit was limited or the financial data indicated a failure to follow GAAP

Standard unqualified audit report—the report a CPA issues when all auditing conditions have been met, no significant misstatements have been discovered and left uncorrected, and it is the auditor's opinion that the financial statements are fairly stated in accordance with GAAP

Unqualified audit report with explanatory paragraph or modified wording—an unqualified report in which the financial statements are fairly presented, but the auditor believes it is important, or is required, to provide additional information

REVIEW QUESTIONS

3-1 (Objective 3-1)   Explain why auditors' reports are important to users of financial statements and why it is desirable to have standard wording.

3-2 (Objective 3-1)   List the seven parts of a standard unqualified audit report and explain the meaning of each part. How do the parts compare with those found in a qualified report?

3-3 (Objective 3-1)   What are the purposes of the scope paragraph in the auditor's report? Identify the most important information included in the scope paragraph.

3-4 (Objective 3-1)   What are the purposes of the opinion paragraph in the auditor's report? Identify the most important information included in the opinion paragraph.

3-5 (Objective 3-1)   On February 17, 2000, a CPA completed the field work on the financial statements for the Buckheizer Corporation for the year ended December 31, 1999. The audit is satisfactory in all respects except for the existence of a change in accounting principles from FIFO to LIFO inventory valuation, which results in an explanatory paragraph to consistency. On February 26, the auditor completed the tax return and the pencil draft of the financial statements. The final audit report was completed, attached to the financial statements, and delivered to the client on March 7. What is the appropriate date on the auditor's report?

3-6 (Objective 3-2)   What five circumstances are required for a standard unqualified report to be issued?

3-7 (Objectives 3-3, 3-6)   What type of opinion should an auditor issue when the financial statements are not in accordance with GAAP because such adherence would result in misleading statements?

3-8 (Objectives 3-3, 3-4)   Distinguish between an unqualified report with an explanatory paragraph or modified wording and a qualified report. Give examples when an explanatory paragraph or modified wording should be used in an unqualified opinion.

3-9 (Objective 3-3)   Describe what is meant by reports involving the use of other auditors. What are the three options available to the principal auditor and when should each be used?

3-10 (Objective 3-3)   The client has restated the prior-year statements because of a change from LIFO to FIFO. How should this be reflected in the auditor's report?

3-11 (Objective 3-3)   Distinguish between changes that affect consistency and those that may affect comparability but not consistency. Give an example of each.

3-12 (Objective 3-4)   List the three conditions that require a departure from an unqualified opinion and give one specific example of each of those conditions.

3-13 (Objective 3-4)   Distinguish between a qualified opinion, an adverse opinion, and a disclaimer of opinion, and explain the circumstances under which each is appropriate.

3-14 (Objective 3-5)   Define *materiality* as it is used in audit reporting. What conditions will affect the auditor's determination of materiality?

3-15 (Objective 3-5)   Explain how materiality differs for failure to follow GAAP and for lack of independence.

3-16 (Objective 3-6)   How does the auditor's opinion differ between scope limitations caused by client restrictions and limitations resulting from conditions beyond the client's control? Under which of these two would the auditor be most likely to issue a disclaimer of opinion? Explain.

3-17 (Objective 3-4)   Distinguish between a report qualified as to opinion only and one with both a scope and opinion qualification.

3-18 (Objectives 3-5, 3-6)   Identify the three alternative opinions that may be appropriate when the client's financial statements are not in accordance with GAAP. Under what circumstance is each appropriate?

3-19 (Objectives 3-4, 3-6)   Discuss why the AICPA has such strict requirements on audit opinions when the auditor is not independent.

3-20 (Objective 3-7)   When an auditor discovers more than one condition that requires departure from or modification of the standard unqualified report, what should the auditor's report include?

MULTIPLE CHOICE QUESTIONS FROM CPA EXAMINATIONS

3-21 (Objectives 3-1, 3-2, 3-3)   The following questions concern unqualified audit reports. Choose the best response.

a. An auditor's unqualified report
   (1) implies only that items disclosed in the financial statements and footnotes are properly presented and takes no position on the adequacy of disclosure.
   (2) implies that disclosure is adequate in the financial statements and footnotes.
   (3) explicitly states that disclosure is adequate in the financial statements and footnotes.
   (4) explicitly states that all material items have been disclosed in conformity with generally accepted accounting principles.

b. The date of the CPA's opinion on the financial statements of his or her client should be the date of the
   (1) closing of the client's books.
   (2) receipt of the client's letter of representation.
   (3) completion of all important audit procedures.
   (4) submission of the report to the client.

c. If a principal auditor decides that he or she will refer in his report to the audit of another auditor, he or she is required to disclose the
   (1) name of the other auditor.
   (2) nature of his inquiry into the other auditor's professional standing and extent of his review of the other auditor's work.
   (3) portion of the financial statements audited by the other auditor.
   (4) reasons why he or she is unwilling to assume responsibility for the other auditor's work.

d. An entity changed from the straight-line method to the declining-balance method of depreciation for all newly acquired assets. This change has no material effect on the current year's financial statements but is reasonably certain to have a substantial effect in later years. If the change is disclosed in the notes to the financial statements, the auditor should issue a report with a(n)
   (1) qualified opinion.
   (2) unqualified opinion with explanatory paragraph.
   (3) unqualified opinion.
   (4) qualified opinion with explanatory paragraph regarding consistency.

3-22 (Objectives 3-4, 3-5, 3-6)   The following questions concern audit reports other than unqualified audit reports with standard wording. Choose the best response.

a. A CPA will issue an adverse auditor's opinion if
   (1) the scope of his or her audit is limited by the client.
   (2) his or her exception to the fairness of presentation is so material that an "except for" opinion is not justified.
   (3) he or she did not perform sufficient auditing procedures to form an opinion on the financial statements taken as a whole.
   (4) major uncertainties exist concerning the company's future.

b. An auditor will express an "except for" opinion if
   (1) the client refuses to provide for a probable federal income tax deficiency that is highly material.
   (2) there is a high degree of uncertainty associated with the client company's future.
   (3) he or she did not perform procedures sufficient to form an opinion on the consistency of application of generally accepted accounting principles.
   (4) he or she is basing his or her opinion in part upon work done by another auditor.

c. Under which of the following sets of circumstances should an auditor issue a qualified opinion?
   (1) The financial statements contain a departure from generally accepted accounting principles, the effect of which is material.
   (2) The principal auditor decides to make reference to the report of another auditor who audited a subsidiary.
   (3) There has been a material change between periods in the method of the application of accounting principles.
   (4) There are significant uncertainties affecting the financial statements.

3-23 (Objective 3-1)   A careful reading of an unqualified report indicates several important phrases. Explain why each of the following phrases or clauses is used rather than the alternative provided.

  a. "In our opinion, the financial statements present fairly" rather than "The financial statements present fairly."
  b. "We conducted our audit in accordance with generally accepted auditing standards" rather than "Our audit was performed to detect material misstatements in the financial statements."
  c. "The financial statements referred to above present fairly in all material respects the financial position" rather than "The financial statements mentioned above are correctly stated."
  d. "In conformity with generally accepted accounting principles" rather than "are properly stated to represent the true economic conditions."
  e. "Brown & Phillips, CPAs (firm name)," rather than "James E. Brown, CPA (individual partner's name)."

3-24 (Objectives 3-1, 3-2, 3-3, 3-5, 3-6)   Roscoe, CPA, has completed the audit of the financial statements of Excelsior Corporation as of and for the year ended December 31, 1999. Roscoe also audited and reported on the Excelsior financial statements for the prior year. Roscoe drafted the following report for 1999.

> We have audited the balance sheet and statements of income and retained earnings of Excelsior Corporation as of December 31, 1999. We conducted our audit in accordance with generally accepted accounting standards. Those standards require that we plan and perform the audit to obtain reasonable assurance about whether the financial statements are free of misstatement.
>
> We believe that our audits provide a reasonable basis for our opinion.
>
> In our opinion, the financial statements referred to above present fairly the financial position of Excelsior Corporation as of December 31, 1999, and the results of its operations for the year then ended in conformity with generally accepted auditing standards, applied on a basis consistent with those of the preceding year.
>
> Roscoe, CPA
(Signed)

Other Information
  - Excelsior is presenting comparative financial statements.
  - Excelsior does not wish to present a statement of cash flows for either year.
  - During 1999, Excelsior changed its method of accounting for long-term construction contracts and properly reflected the effect of the change in the current year's financial statements and restated the prior year's statements. Roscoe is satisfied with Excelsior's justification for making the change. The change is discussed in footnote 12.
  - Roscoe was unable to perform normal accounts receivable confirmation procedures, but alternative procedures were used to satisfy Roscoe as to the existence of the receivables.
  - Excelsior Corporation is the defendant in a litigation, the outcome of which is highly uncertain. If the case is settled in favor of the plaintiff, Excelsior will be required to pay a substantial amount of cash, which might require the sale of certain fixed assets. The litigation and the possible effects have been properly disclosed in footnote 11.
  - Excelsior issued debentures on January 31, 1998, in the amount of $10,000,000. The funds obtained from the issuance were used to finance the expansion of plant facilities. The debenture agreement restricts the payment of future cash dividends to earnings after December 31, 2003. Excelsior declined to disclose this essential data in the footnotes to the financial statements.

Required

a. Identify and explain any items included in "Other Information" that need not be part of the auditor's report.

b. Explain the deficiencies in Roscoe's report as drafted.*

3-25 (Objectives 3-3, 3-4, 3-5, 3-6, 3-7)   For the following independent situations, assume that you are the audit partner on the engagement:

1. During your audit of Debold Batteries, you conclude that there is a possibility that inventory is materially overstated. The client refuses to allow you to expand the scope of your audit sufficiently to verify whether the balance is actually misstated.

2. You are auditing Woodcolt Linen Services for the first time. Woodcolt has been in business for several years but has never had an audit before. After the audit is completed, you conclude that the current year balance sheet is stated correctly in accordance with GAAP. The client did not authorize you to do test work for any of the previous years.

3. You were engaged to audit the Cutter Steel Company's financial statements after the close of the corporation's fiscal year. Because you were not engaged until after the balance sheet date, you were not able to physically observe inventory, which is highly material. On the completion of your audit, you are satisfied that Cutter's financial statements are presented fairly, including inventory about which you were able to satisfy yourself by the use of alternative audit procedures.

4. Four weeks after the year-end date, a major customer of Prince Construction Co. declared bankruptcy. Because the customer had confirmed the balance due to Prince at the balance sheet date, management refuses to charge off the account or otherwise disclose the information. The receivable represents approximately 10 percent of accounts receivable and 20 percent of net earnings before taxes.

5. You complete the audit of Johnson Department Store, and in your opinion, the financial statements are fairly presented. On the last day of the field work, you discover that one of your supervisors assigned to the audit had a material investment in Johnson.

6. Auto Delivery Company has a fleet of several delivery trucks. In the past, Auto Delivery had followed the policy of purchasing all equipment. In the current year they decided to lease the trucks. The method of accounting for the trucks is therefore changed to lease capitalization. This change in policy is fully disclosed in footnotes.

Required

For each situation, do the following:

a. Identify which of the conditions requiring a modification of or a deviation from an unqualified standard report is applicable.

b. State the level of materiality as immaterial, material, or highly material. If you cannot decide the level of materiality, state the additional information needed to make a decision.

c. Given your answers in parts a and b, state the type of audit report that should be issued. If you have not decided on one level of materiality in part b, state the appropriate report for each alternative materiality level.

3-26 (Objectives 3-3, 3-4, 3-5, 3-6, 3-7)   For the following independent situations, assume that you are the audit partner on the engagement:

1. Kieko Corporation has prepared financial statements but has decided to exclude the statement of cash flows. Management explains to you that the users of their financial statements find this statement confusing and prefer not to have it included.

2. Jet Stream Airlines has been audited by your firm for 10 years. In the past 3 years their financial condition has steadily declined. In the current year, for the first time, the current ratio is below 2.1, which is the minimum requirement specified in Jet Stream's major loan agreement. You now have reservations about the ability of Jet Stream to continue in operation for the next year.

*AICPA adapted.

3. Approximately 20 percent of the audit of Fur Farms, Inc., was performed by a different CPA firm, selected by you. You have reviewed their working papers and believe they did an excellent job on their portion of the audit. Nevertheless, you are unwilling to take complete responsibility for their work.

4. The controller of Fair City Hotels Co. will not allow you to confirm the receivable balance from two of its major customers. The amounts of the receivables are material in relation to Fair City's financial statements. You are unable to satisfy yourself as to the receivable balances by alternative procedures.

5. In the last 3 months of the current year, Oil Refining Company decided to change direction and go significantly into the oil drilling business. Management recognizes that this business is exceptionally risky and could jeopardize the success of its existing refining business, but there are significant potential rewards. During the short period of operation in drilling, the company has had three dry wells and no successes. The facts are adequately disclosed in footnotes.

6. Your client, Auto Rental Company, has changed from straight line to sum-of-the-years' digits depreciation. The effect on this year's income is immaterial, but the effect in future years is likely to be material. The facts are adequately disclosed in footnotes.

Required

For each situation, do the following:

    a. Identify which of the conditions requiring a modification of or a deviation from an unqualified standard report is applicable.

    b. State the level of materiality as immaterial, material, or highly material. If you cannot decide the level of materiality, state the additional information needed to make a decision.

    c. Given your answers in parts a and b, state the appropriate audit report from the following alternatives (if you have not decided on one level of materiality in part b, state the appropriate report for each alternative materiality level):

        (1) Unqualified—standard wording
        (2) Unqualified—explanatory paragraph
        (3) Unqualified—modified wording
        (4) Qualified opinion only—except for
        (5) Qualified scope and opinion
        (6) Disclaimer
        (7) Adverse

3-27 (Objectives 3-3, 3-4, 3-5, 3-6, 3-7)   The following are independent situations for which you will recommend an appropriate audit report:

1. Subsequent to the date of the financial statements as part of his post–balance sheet date audit procedures, a CPA learned that a recent fire caused heavy damage to one of a client's two plants; the loss will not be reimbursed by insurance. The newspapers described the event in detail. The financial statements and appended notes as prepared by the client did not disclose the loss caused by the fire.

2. A CPA is engaged in the audit of the financial statements of a large manufacturing company with branch offices in many widely separated cities. The CPA was not able to count the substantial undeposited cash receipts at the close of business on the last day of the fiscal year at all branch offices.

    As an alternative to this auditing procedure used to verify the accurate cutoff of cash receipts, the CPA observed that deposits in transit as shown on the year-end bank reconciliation appeared as credits on the bank statement on the first business day of the new year. He was satisfied as to the cutoff of cash receipts by the use of the alternative procedure.

3. On January 2, 1999, the Retail Auto Parts Company received a notice from its primary supplier that effective immediately, all wholesale prices would be increased 10 percent.

On the basis of the notice, Retail Auto Parts revalued its December 31, 1998, inventory to reflect the higher costs. The inventory constituted a material proportion of total assets; however, the effect of the revaluation was material to current assets but not to total assets or net income. The increase in valuation is adequately disclosed in the footnotes.

4. During 1999, the research staff of Scientific Research Corporation devoted its entire efforts toward developing a new pollution-control device. All costs that could be attributed directly to the project were accounted for as deferred charges and classified on the balance sheet at December 31, 1999, as a noncurrent asset. In the course of his audit of the corporation's 1999 financial statements, Anthony, CPA, found persuasive evidence that the research conducted to date would probably result in a marketable product. The deferred research charges are significantly material in relation to both income and total assets.

5. For the past 5 years a CPA has audited the financial statements of a manufacturing company. During this period, the audit scope was limited by the client as to the observation of the annual physical inventory. Because the CPA considered the inventories to be material and he was not able to satisfy himself by other auditing procedures, he was unable to express an unqualified opinion on the financial statements in each of the five years.

The CPA was allowed to observe physical inventories for the current year ended December 31, 1999, because the client's banker would no longer accept the audit reports. In the interest of economy, the client requested the CPA to not extend his audit procedures to the inventory as of January 1, 1999.

6. During the course of his audit of the financial statements of a corporation for the purpose of expressing an opinion on the statements, a CPA is refused permission to inspect the minute books containing the significant decisions from the board of directors meetings. The corporation secretary instead offers to give the CPA a certified copy of all resolutions and actions involving accounting matters.

7. A CPA has completed his audit of the financial statements of a bus company for the year ended December 31, 1999. Prior to 1999, the company had been depreciating its buses over a 10-year period. During 1999, the company determined that a more realistic estimated life for its buses was 12 years and computed the 1999 depreciation on the basis of the revised estimate. The CPA has satisfied himself that the 12-year life is reasonable.

The company has adequately disclosed the change in estimated useful lives of its buses and the effect of the change on 1999 income in a note to the financial statements.

Required

For each situation, do the following:

a. Identify which of the conditions requiring a deviation from or modification of an unqualified standard report is applicable.

b. State the level of materiality as immaterial, material, or highly material. If you cannot decide the level of materiality, state the additional information needed to make a decision.

c. Given your answers in parts a and b, state the appropriate audit report from the following alternatives (if you have not decided on one level of materiality in part b, state the appropriate report for each alternative materiality level):

(1) Unqualified—standard wording
(2) Unqualified—explanatory paragraph
(3) Unqualified—modified wording
(4) Qualified opinion only—except for
(5) Qualified scope and opinion
(6) Disclaimer
(7) Adverse*

*AICPA adapted.

3-28 (Objective 3-3) Various types of "accounting changes" can affect the second reporting standard of the generally accepted auditing standards. This standard reads, "The report shall identify those circumstances in which such principles have not been consistently observed in the current period in relation to the preceding period."

Assume that the following list describes changes that have a material effect on a client's financial statements for the current year.

1. A change from the completed-contract method to the percentage-of-completion method of accounting for long-term construction contracts.
2. A change in the estimated useful life of previously recorded fixed assets based on newly acquired information.
3. Correction of a mathematical error in inventory pricing made in a prior period.
4. A change from prime costing to full absorption costing for inventory valuation.
5. A change from presentation of statements of individual companies to presentation of consolidated statements.
6. A change from deferring and amortizing preproduction costs to recording such costs as an expense when incurred because future benefits of the costs have become doubtful. The new accounting method was adopted in recognition of the change in estimated future benefits.
7. A change to including the employer share of FICA taxes as "retirement benefits" on the income statement from including it with "other taxes."
8. A change from the FIFO method of inventory pricing to the LIFO method of inventory pricing.

Required

Identify the type of change described in each item above, and state whether any modification is required in the auditor's report *as it relates to the second standard of reporting*. Organize your answer sheet as shown below. For example, a change from the LIFO method of inventory pricing to the FIFO method of inventory pricing would appear as shown.

Assume that each item is material.*

Item No.	Type of Change	Should Auditor's Report Be Modified?
Example	An accounting change from one generally accepted accounting principle to another generally accepted accounting principle	Yes

3-29 (Objective 3-3) The following is the first paragraph of an audit report of a publicly held company, modified for the most current audit reporting standards.

REPORT OF INDEPENDENT, CERTIFIED PUBLIC ACCOUNTANTS

To the Board of Directors and Stockholders, Farmers Group, Inc.

We have audited the consolidated balance sheets of Farmers Group, Inc., as of December 31, 1999 and 1998, and the related consolidated statements of income, stockholders' equity, and cash flows for each of the three years ended December 31, 1999. These financial statements are the responsibility of Farmers Group, Inc.'s management. Our responsibility is to express an opinion on these financial statements based on our audits. We did not audit the financial statements of Farmers New World Life Insurance Company, The Ohio State Life Insurance Company, and Investors Guaranty Life Insurance Company as of December 31, 1999 and 1998, and the related combined statements of income, stockholders' equity, and cash flows for each of the three years in the period ended December 31, 1999,

*AICPA adapted.

which statements reflect assets constituting $26.2 million in 1999 and $26.2 million in 1998, and net income of $3.92 million, $2.43 million, and $1.68 million in 1999, 1998, and 1997, respectively, of the related consolidated totals. These statements were audited by other auditors whose report has been furnished to us, and our opinion, insofar as it relates to the amounts included for the above named three companies, is based solely on the report of the other auditors.

Required

    a. Should the audit opinion in this case be unqualified, qualified, a disclaimer, or adverse?

    b. Assuming that the audit was completed on March 9, 2000, write the opinion paragraph for this audit report.

3-30 (Objective 3-6)   The following is an audit report, except for the opinion paragraph, of Tri-Nation Coin Investments.

INDEPENDENT AUDITOR'S REPORT

To the Board of Directors and Stockholders, Tri-Nation Coin Investments, Philadelphia, Pennsylvania

We have audited the accompanying consolidated balance sheet of Tri-Nation Coin Investments and subsidiaries as of July 31, 1999, and the related statements of income, stockholders' equity, and cash flows for the year then ended and the related schedules listed in the accompanying index. These financial statements are the responsibility of the Company's management. Our responsibility is to express an opinion on these financial statements based on our audits.

The company had significant deficiencies in internal control, including the lack of detailed records and certain supporting data, which were not available for our audit. Therefore, we were not able to obtain sufficient evidence in order to form an opinion on the accompanying financial statements including whether the inventory at July 31, 1999 ($670,490) was stated at lower of cost or market, or whether the deferred subscription revenue ($90,260) is an adequate estimate for the applicable liability, as discussed in Notes 5 and 12, respectively.

Required

Write the auditor's opinion to accompany this portion of the audit report. Where is the opinion located in this audit report?

3-31 (Objectives 3-4, 3-5, 3-6)   The following two paragraphs were taken from the California First Bank audit report, modified for changes in current reporting standards.

INDEPENDENT ACCOUNTANT'S REPORT

To the Shareholders and Board of Directors of California First Bank

We have audited the accompanying consolidated balance sheets of California First Bank (a California chartered state bank, and a 76.5% owned subsidiary of The Bank of Tokyo, Ltd.) and subsidiaries as of December 31, 1998 and 1997, and the related consolidated statements of income, changes in shareholders' equity, and cash flows for each of the three years in the period ended December 31, 1998. These financial statements are the responsibility of the Company's management. Our responsibility is to express an opinion on these financial statements based on our audits.

As explained in Note 2 to the financial statements, the Bank has charged goodwill and certain other intangible assets acquired in two separate acquisitions directly to shareholders' equity. Under generally accepted accounting principles, these intangibles should have been recorded as assets and amortized to income over future periods.

Required

    a. Which condition requiring a departure from an unqualified opinion exists for the portion of the foregoing report?

b. Should the opinion be unqualified, qualified, disclaimer, or adverse?

c. Assuming a standard wording scope paragraph, write the opinion paragraph for this audit situation.

3-32 (Objectives 3-1, 3-2, 3-3) The following tentative auditor's report was drafted by a staff accountant and submitted to a partner in the accounting firm of Better & Best, CPAs:

AUDIT REPORT

To the Audit Committee of American Widgets, Inc.

We have examined the consolidated balance sheets of American Widgets, Inc., and subsidiaries as of December 31, 1998 and 1997, and the related consolidated statements of income, retained earnings, and cash flows for the years then ended. These financial statements are the responsibility of the Company's management. Our responsibility is to express an opinion on these financial statements based on our audits.

Our audits were made in accordance with generally accepted auditing standards as we considered necessary in the circumstances. Other auditors audited the financial statements of certain subsidiaries and have furnished us with reports thereon containing no exceptions. Our opinion expressed herein, insofar as it relates to the amounts included for those subsidiaries, is based solely upon the reports of the other auditors.

As fully discussed in Note 7 to the financial statements, in 1998, the company extended the use of the last-in, first-out (LIFO) method of accounting to include all inventories. In examining inventories, we engaged Dr. Irwin Same (Nobel Prize winner 1996) to test check the technical requirements and specifications of certain items of equipment manufactured by the company.

In our opinion, the financial statements referred to above present fairly the financial position of American Widgets, Inc., as of December 31, 1998, and the results of operations for the years then ended, in conformity with generally accepted accounting principles.

> To be signed by
> Better & Best, CPAs
>
> March 1, 1999

Required

Identify deficiencies in the staff accountant's tentative report that constitute departures from the generally accepted standards of reporting.*

CASE

3-33 (Objectives 3-1, 3-2, 3-4, 3-6) Following are the auditor's report and the complete financial statements of the Young Manufacturing Corporation for the year ended January 31, 1999. The audit was conducted by John Smith, an individual practitioner who has audited the corporation's financial statements and has reported on them for many years.

Required

List and discuss the deficiencies of the auditor's report prepared by John Smith. Your discussion should include justifications that the matters you cited are deficiencies. (Do not check the additions in the statements. Assume that the additions are correct.)*

*AICPA adapted.

To: Mr. Paul Young, President   January 31, 1999
    Young Manufacturing Corporation

I have audited the balance sheet of the Young Manufacturing Corporation and the related statements of income and retained earnings.

These statements present fairly the financial position and results of operations in conformity with generally accepted principles of accounting applied on a consistent basis. My audit was made in accordance with generally accepted auditing standards and, accordingly, included such tests of the accounting records and such other auditing procedures as I considered necessary in the circumstances.

(Signed) John Smith

YOUNG MANUFACTURING CORPORATION
Statements of Condition January 31, 1999 and 1998

	1999	1998
Assets		
Current assets:		
Cash	$ 43,822	$ 51,862
Accounts receivable, pledged—less allowances for doubtful accounts of $3,800 in 1999 and $3,000 in 1998 (see note)	65,298	46,922
Inventories, pledged—at average cost, not in excess of replacement cost	148,910	118,264
Other current assets	6,280	5,192
Total current assets	264,310	222,240
Fixed assets:		
Land—at cost	38,900	62,300
Buildings—at cost, less accumulated depreciation of $50,800 in 1999 and $53,400 in 1998	174,400	150,200
Machinery and equipment—at cost, less accumulated depreciation of $30,500 in 1999 and $25,640 in 1998	98,540	78,560
Total fixed assets	311,840	291,060
Total assets	$576,150	$513,300
Liabilities and Stockholders' Equity		
Current liabilities:		
Accounts payable	$ 27,926	$ 48,161
Other liabilities	68,743	64,513
Current portion of long-term mortgage payable	3,600	3,600
Income taxes payable	46,840	30,866
Total current liabilities	147,109	147,140
Long-term liabilities:		
Mortgage payable	90,400	94,000
Total liabilities	237,509	241,140
Stockholders' equity:		
Capital stock, par value $100, 1,000 shares authorized, issued and outstanding	100,000	100,000
Retained earnings	238,641	172,160
Total stockholders' equity	338,641	272,160
Total liabilities and stockholders' equity	$576,150	$513,300

YOUNG MANUFACTURING CORPORATION
Income Statements for the Years Ended January 31, 1999 and 1998

	1999	1998
Income:		
Sales	$884,932	$682,131
Other income	3,872	2,851
Total	888,804	684,982
Costs and expenses:		
Costs of goods sold	463,570	353,842
Selling expenses	241,698	201,986
Administrative expenses	72,154	66,582
Provision for income taxes	45,876	19,940
Other expenses	12,582	13,649
Total	835,880	655,999
Net income	$ 52,924	$ 28,983

INTERNET PROBLEM 3-1: RESEARCH ANNUAL REPORTS

Reference the CW site. The U.S. Securities and Exchange Commission (SEC) is an independent, nonpartisan, quasi-judicial regulatory agency with responsibility for administering the federal securities laws. Publicly traded companies must file electronically a variety of forms or reports with the SEC (for example, annual financial statements). The SEC makes most of these electronic documents available via the Internet with their "EDGAR Database of Corporate Information." EDGAR stands for electronic data gathering, analysis, and retrieval system. The primary purpose for EDGAR is to increase the efficiency and fairness of the securities market for the benefit of investors, corporations, and the economy by accelerating the receipt, acceptance, dissemination, and analysis of time-sensitive corporate information filed with the agency. This problem requires students to use the EDGAR site (1) to research the definitions of SEC filings (for example, 10-K, 8-K) and (2) to use several companies' 10-K reports to classify types of audit opinions issued.

PROFESSIONAL ETHICS

CPAs ARE HELD TO THE HIGHEST ETHICAL STANDARDS

Steve Smith stared blankly at the empty chair across from him at staff training school. Yesterday, that chair had been occupied by Bruce Tucker. Steve had gone to school with Bruce and had been a little surprised when Bruce received an offer from the firm. Bruce was a nice enough guy, but he hadn't been an ace in the classroom. The buzz at coffee that morning was that the firm discovered that Bruce had lied about his grade point average on his resume and that there were other inconsistencies on his resume as well. The word was that Bruce had been summarily dismissed from the firm.

"Wow!" thought Steve. He had known students who cheated and others who padded expense reports from their interview trips. He thought that these actions were wrong, but he hadn't given them much further thought. His thoughts were interrupted by the voice of Tom Conigliaro, the training session leader. "We'll start this morning with a discussion of the firm's ethical requirements. The public depends on us, and we are held to the highest ethical standards of any profession."

LEARNING OBJECTIVES

After studying this chapter, you should be able to

4-1 Distinguish ethical from unethical behavior in personal and professional contexts.

4-2 Resolve ethical dilemmas using an ethical framework.

4-3 Explain the importance of ethical conduct for the accounting profession.

4-4 Describe the purpose and content of the AICPA *Code of Professional Conduct.*

4-5 Apply the AICPA *Code* rules and interpretations on independence and explain their importance.

4-6 Understand the requirements of other rules under the AICPA *Code.*

4-7 Describe the enforcement mechanisms for the rules of conduct.

In preceding chapters, audit reports and the demand for audit and other assurance services were discussed. The value of the audit report and the demand for audit services depends on public confidence in the independence and integrity of CPAs. As the example involving Bruce Tucker indicates, CPAs are held to the highest ethical standards. This chapter discusses ethics and the ethical requirements for CPAs under the AICPA *Code of Professional Conduct*. We begin the chapter with a discussion of general ethical principles and their application to the CPA profession.

WHAT ARE ETHICS?

OBJECTIVE 4-1
Distinguish ethical from unethical behavior in personal and professional contexts.

Ethics can be defined broadly as a set of moral principles or values. Each of us has such a set of values, although we may or may not have considered them explicitly. Philosophers, religious organizations, and other groups have defined in various ways ideal sets of moral principles or values. Examples of prescribed sets of moral principles or values at the implementation level include laws and regulations, church doctrine, codes of business ethics for professional groups such as CPAs, and codes of conduct within individual organizations.

An example of a prescribed set of principles is included in Figure 4-1. These principles were developed by the Josephson Institute of Ethics, a nonprofit membership organization for the improvement of the ethical quality of society.

It is common for people to differ in their moral principles and values and the relative importance they attach to these principles. These differences reflect life experiences, successes and failures, as well as the influences of parents, teachers, and friends.

Need for Ethics

Ethical behavior is necessary for a society to function in an orderly manner. It can be argued that ethics is the glue that holds a society together. Imagine, for example, what would happen if we couldn't depend on the people we deal with to be honest. If parents, teachers, employers, siblings, co-workers, and friends all consistently lied, it would be almost impossible for effective communication to occur.

The need for ethics in society is sufficiently important that many commonly held ethical values are incorporated into laws. However, many of the ethical values found in Figure 4-1 cannot be incorporated into laws because of the judgmental nature of certain values. That does not imply, however, that the principles are less important for an orderly society.

Why People Act Unethically

Most people define *unethical behavior* as conduct that differs from what they believe would have been appropriate given the circumstances. Each of us decides for ourselves what we

FIGURE 4-1	Illustrative Prescribed Ethical Principles

The following are the six core ethical values that the Josephson Institute associates with ethical behavior:

Trustworthiness includes honesty, integrity, reliability, and loyalty. Honesty requires a good faith intent to convey the truth. Integrity means that the person acts according to conscience, regardless of the situation. Reliability means making all reasonable efforts to fulfill commitments. Loyalty is a responsibility to promote and protect the interests of certain people and organizations.

Respect includes notions such as civility, courtesy, dignity, tolerance, and acceptance. A respectful person treats others with consideration and accepts individual differences and beliefs without prejudice.

Responsibility means being accountable for one's actions and exercising restraint. Responsibility also

means pursuing excellence and leading by example, including perseverance and engaging in continuous improvement.

Fairness and justice include issues of equality, impartiality, proportionality, openness, and due process. Fair treatment means that similar situations are handled consistently.

Caring means being genuinely concerned for the welfare of others and includes acting altruistically and showing benevolence.

Citizenship includes obeying laws and performing one's fair share to make society work, including such activities as voting, serving on juries, and conserving resources.

consider unethical behavior, both for ourselves and others. It is important to understand what causes people to act in a manner that we decide is unethical.

There are two primary reasons why people act unethically: the person's ethical standards are different from those of society as a whole, or the person chooses to act selfishly. In many instances, both reasons exist.

Person's Ethical Standards Differ from General Society Extreme examples of people whose behavior violates almost everyone's ethical standards are drug dealers, bank robbers, and larcenists. Most people who commit such acts feel no remorse when they are apprehended because their ethical standards differ from those of society as a whole.

There are also many far less extreme examples when others violate our ethical values. When people cheat on their tax returns, treat other people with hostility, lie on employment applications, or perform below their competence level as employees, most of us regard that as unethical behavior. If the other person has decided that this behavior is ethical and acceptable, there is a conflict of ethical values that is unlikely to be resolved.

The Person Chooses to Act Selfishly The following example illustrates the difference between ethical standards that differ from general society's and acting selfishly. Person A finds a briefcase in an airport containing important papers and $1,000. He tosses the briefcase and keeps the money. He brags to his family and friends about his good fortune. Person A's values probably differ from most of society's. Person B faces the same situation but responds differently. He keeps the money but leaves the briefcase in a conspicuous place. He tells nobody and spends the money on a new wardrobe. It is likely that Person B has violated his own ethical standards, but he decided that the money was too important to pass up. He has chosen to act selfishly.

A considerable portion of unethical behavior results from selfish behavior. Political scandals result from the desire for political power; cheating on tax returns and expense reports is motivated by financial greed; performing below one's competence and cheating on tests typically arise from laziness. In each case, the person knows that the behavior is inappropriate but chooses to do it anyway because of the personal sacrifice needed to act ethically.

ETHICAL DILEMMAS

OBJECTIVE 4-2
Resolve ethical dilemmas using an ethical framework.

An **ethical dilemma** is a situation a person faces in which a decision must be made about the appropriate behavior. A simple example of an ethical dilemma is finding a diamond ring, which necessitates deciding whether to attempt to find the owner or to keep it. A far more difficult ethical dilemma to resolve is the following one, taken from *Easier Said Than Done*, a publication dealing with ethical issues. It is the type of case that might be used in an ethics course.

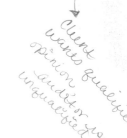
client wants qualified opinion auditor is unqualified

- In Europe, a woman was near death from a special kind of cancer. There was one drug that the doctors thought might save her. It was a form of radium that a druggist in the same town had recently discovered. The drug was expensive to make, but the druggist was charging ten times what the drug cost him to make. He paid $200 for the radium and charged $2,000 for a small dose of the drug. The sick woman's husband, Heinz, went to everyone he knew to borrow the money, but he could only get together about $1,000, which is half of what it cost. He told the druggist that his wife was dying and asked him to sell it cheaper or let him pay later. But the druggist said: "No, I discovered the drug and I'm going to make money from it." So Heinz got desperate and broke into the man's store to steal the drug for his wife. Should the husband have done that?[1]

[1]Norman Sprinthall and Richard C. Sprinthall, "Value and Moral Development," *Easier Said Than Done* (Vol. 1, No. 1, Winter 1988); p. 17.

Auditors, accountants, and other businesspeople face many ethical dilemmas in their business careers. Dealing with a client who threatens to seek a new auditor unless an unqualified opinion is issued presents a serious ethical dilemma if an unqualified opinion is inappropriate. Deciding whether to confront a supervisor who has materially overstated departmental revenues as a means of receiving a larger bonus is a difficult ethical dilemma. Continuing to be a part of the management of a company that harasses and mistreats employees or treats customers dishonestly is a moral dilemma, especially if the person has a family to support and the job market is tight.

Rationalizing Unethical Behavior

There are alternative ways to resolve ethical dilemmas, but care must be taken to avoid methods that are rationalizations of unethical behavior. The following are rationalization methods commonly employed that can easily result in unethical conduct.

Everybody Does It The argument that it is acceptable behavior to falsify tax returns, cheat on exams, or sell defective products is commonly based on the rationalization that everyone else is doing it and therefore it is acceptable.

If It's Legal, It's Ethical Using the argument that all legal behavior is ethical relies heavily on the perfection of laws. Under this philosophy, one would have no obligation to return a lost object unless the other person could prove that it was his or hers.

Likelihood of Discovery and Consequences This philosophy relies on evaluating the likelihood that someone else will discover the behavior. Typically, the person also assesses the severity of the penalty (consequences) if there is a discovery. An example is deciding whether to correct an unintentional overbilling to a customer when the customer has already paid the full billing. If the seller believes that the customer will detect the error and respond by not buying in the future, the seller will inform the customer now; otherwise, he will wait to see if the customer complains.

Resolving Ethical Dilemmas

In recent years, formal frameworks have been developed to help people resolve ethical dilemmas. The purpose of such a framework is in identifying the ethical issues and deciding on an appropriate course of action using the person's own values. The six-step approach that follows is intended to be a relatively simple approach to resolving ethical dilemmas:

1. Obtain the relevant facts.
2. Identify the ethical issues from the facts.
3. Determine who is affected by the outcome of the dilemma and how each person or group is affected.
4. Identify the alternatives available to the person who must resolve the dilemma.
5. Identify the likely consequence of each alternative.
6. Decide the appropriate action.

An illustration is used to demonstrate how a person might use this six-step approach to resolve an ethical dilemma.

Ethical Dilemma

Bryan Longview has been working 6 months as a staff assistant for Barton & Barton CPAs. Currently he is assigned to the audit of Reyon Manufacturing Company under the supervision of Charles Dickerson, an experienced audit senior. There are three auditors assigned to the audit, including Bryan, Charles, and a more experienced assistant, Martha Mills. During lunch on the first day, Charles says, "It will be necessary for us to work a few extra hours on our own time to make sure we come in on budget. This audit isn't very profitable anyway, and we don't want to hurt our firm by going over budget. We can accomplish this easily by coming in a half hour early, taking a short lunch break, and working an hour or so after normal quitting time. We just won't write that time down on our time report." Bryan recalls reading in the firm's policy manual that working hours and not charging for them on the time report is a violation of Barton & Barton's employment policy. He also knows that seniors are paid bonuses, instead of overtime, whereas staff are paid for overtime but get no bonuses. Later, when discussing the issue with Martha, she says, "Charles does this on all of his jobs. He is likely to be our firm's next audit manager. The partners think he's great because his jobs always come in under budget. He rewards us by giving us good engagement evaluations, especially under the cooperative attitude category. Several of the other audit seniors follow the same practice."

Relevant Facts There are three key facts in this situation that deal with the ethical issue and how the issue will likely be resolved:

1. The staff person has been informed that he will work hours without recording them as hours worked.
2. Firm policy prohibits this practice.
3. Another staff person has stated that this is common practice in the firm.

Ethical Issue The ethical issue in this situation is not difficult to identify.

- Is it ethical for Bryan to work hours and not record them as hours worked in this situation?

Who Is Affected and How Is Each Affected? There are typically more people affected in situations in which ethical dilemmas occur than would normally be expected. The following are the key persons involved in this situation:

Who	How Affected
Bryan	Being asked to violate firm policy.
	Hours of work will be affected.
	Pay will be affected.
	Performance evaluations may be affected.
	Attitude about firm may be affected.
Martha	Same as Bryan.
Charles	Success on engagement and in firm may be affected.
	Hours of work will be affected.
Barton & Barton	Stated firm policy is being violated.
	May result in underbilling clients in the current and future engagements.
	May affect firm's ability to realistically budget engagements and bill clients.
	May affect the firm's ability to motivate and retain employees.
Staff assigned to Reyon Manufacturing in the future	May result in unrealistic time budgets.
	May result in unfavorable time performance evaluations.
	May result in pressures to continue practice of not charging for hours worked.
Other staff in firm	Following the practice on this engagement may motivate others to follow the same practice on other engagements.

Bryan's Available Alternatives
- Refuse to work the additional hours.
- Perform in the manner requested.
- Inform Charles that he will not work the additional hours or will charge the additional hours to the engagement.
- Talk to a manager or partner about Charles's request.
- Refuse to work on the engagement.
- Quit working for the firm.

Each of these options includes a potential consequence, the worst likely one being termination by the firm.

Consequences of Each Alternative In deciding the consequences of each alternative, it is essential to evaluate both the short- and long-term effects. There is a natural tendency to emphasize the short term because those consequences will occur quickly, even when the long-term consequences may be more important. For example, consider the potential consequences if Bryan decides to work the additional hours and not report them. In the short term, he will likely get good evaluations for cooperation and perhaps a salary increase. In the longer term, what will be the effect of not reporting the hours this time when other ethical conflicts arise? Consider the following similar ethical dilemmas Bryan might face in his career as he advances:

- A supervisor asks Bryan to work 3 unreported hours daily and 15 unreported hours each weekend.
- A supervisor asks Bryan to initial certain audit procedures as having been performed when they were not.
- Bryan concludes that he cannot be promoted to manager unless he persuades assistants to work hours that they do not record.
- Management informs Bryan, who is now a partner, that either the company gets an unqualified opinion for a $40,000 audit fee or the company will change auditors.
- Management informs Bryan that the audit fee will be increased $25,000 if Bryan can find a plausible way to increase earnings by $1 million.

Appropriate Action Only Bryan can decide the appropriate option to select in the circumstances after considering his ethical values and the likely consequences of each option. At one extreme, Bryan could decide that the only relevant consequence is the potential impact on his career. Most of us would conclude that Bryan is an unethical person if he follows that course. At the other extreme, Bryan can decide to refuse to work for a firm that permits even one supervisor to violate firm policies. Many people would consider such an extreme reaction naive.

SOME ETHICAL VIOLATIONS ARE MORE SEVERE THAN OTHERS

Bryan Longview's ethical dilemma involved a situation in which he was asked to work without recording the time, which is sometimes called kitchen-tabling. One of the concerns with kitchen-tabling is that it can lead to a more severe problem known as premature signoff, in which a staff person signs off as having completed work without performing the necessary procedures.

Tom Holton had far too busy a social life to work overtime. To make certain that work did not interfere with his social life, he would test only part of the assigned sample. For example, if he was asked to test 25 cash disbursement transactions, he would test the first 15 but indicate that he had tested all 25. A supervisor, curious about Tom's amazing ability to beat the time budget, decided to carefully review Tom's work. When the firm discovered that Tom was signing off procedures without completing them, he was dismissed *that day*—no counseling out, no 2 weeks' notice.

SPECIAL NEED FOR ETHICAL CONDUCT IN PROFESSIONS

OBJECTIVE 4-3
Explain the importance of ethical conduct for the accounting profession.

Our society has attached a special meaning to the term *professional*. A professional is expected to conduct himself or herself at a higher level than most other members of society. For example, when the press reports that a physician, clergyperson, U.S. senator, or CPA has been indicted for a crime, most people feel more disappointment than when the same thing happens to people who are not labeled as professionals.

The term *professional* means a responsibility for conduct that extends beyond satisfying the person's responsibilities to himself or herself and beyond the requirements of our society's laws and regulations. A CPA, as a professional, recognizes a responsibility to the public, to the client, and to fellow practitioners, including honorable behavior, even if that means personal sacrifice.

The underlying reason for a high level of professional conduct by any profession is the need for *public confidence* in the quality of service by the profession, regardless of the individual providing it. For the CPA, it is essential that the client and external financial statement users have confidence in the quality of audits and other services. If users of services do not have confidence in physicians, judges, or CPAs, the ability of those professionals to serve clients and the public effectively is diminished.

It is not practical for users to evaluate the quality of the performance of most professional services because of their *complexity*. A patient cannot be expected to evaluate whether an operation was properly performed. A financial statement user cannot be expected to evaluate audit performance. Most users have neither the competence nor the time for such an evaluation. Public confidence in the quality of professional services is enhanced when the profession encourages high standards of performance and conduct on the part of all practitioners.

In recent years, increased competition has made it more difficult for CPAs and many other professionals to conduct themselves in a professional manner. Increased competition sometimes has the effect of making CPA firms more concerned about keeping clients and maintaining a reasonable profit than with providing high-quality audits for users. Because of the increased competition, many CPA firms have implemented philosophies and practices that are often called improved business practices. These include such things as improved recruiting and personnel practices, better office management, and more effective advertising and other promotional methods. CPA firms are also attempting to provide more efficient audits through the use of computers and more effective audit planning. These changes are desirable, as long as they do not interfere with the conduct of CPAs as professionals.

Difference between CPA Firms and Other Professionals

CPA firms have a different relationship with users of financial statements than most other professionals have with the users of their services. Attorneys, for example, are typically engaged and paid by a client and have primary responsibility to be an advocate for that client. CPA firms are engaged and paid by the company issuing the financial statements, but the primary beneficiaries of the audit are statement users. Often, the auditor does not know or have contact with the statement users but has frequent meetings and ongoing relationships with client personnel.

It is essential that users regard CPA firms as competent and unbiased. If users were to believe that CPA firms do not perform a valuable service (reduce information risk), the value of CPA firms' audit and other attestation reports would be reduced and the demand for audits would thereby also be reduced. Therefore, there is considerable incentive for CPA firms to conduct themselves at a high professional level.

Ways CPAs Are Encouraged to Conduct Themselves Professionally

As first discussed in Chapter 2, there are several ways in which the CPA profession and society encourage CPAs to conduct themselves appropriately and to do high-quality audits and related services. Figure 4-2 (p. 82) shows the most important ways. Several items already discussed include GAAS and their interpretations, the CPA examination, quality control, peer review requirements, SEC, division of CPA firms, and continuing education. The ability of individuals separately or together to sue CPA firms also exerts considerable influence on the way in which practitioners conduct themselves and audits. Legal liability is studied in Chapter 5. The AICPA *Code of Professional Conduct* also has a significant influence on practitioners. It is meant to provide a standard of conduct for CPAs. The AICPA *Code* and related issues of professional conduct are the content of the remainder of this chapter. For this reason, the *Code of Professional Conduct* oval is shaded in Figure 4-2.

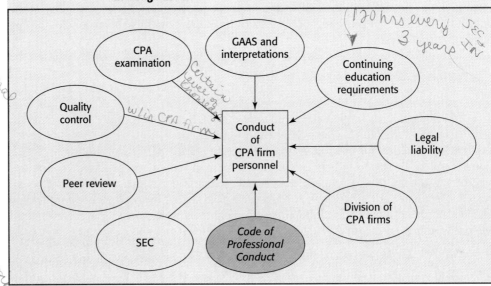

FIGURE 4-2   **Ways the Profession and Society Encourage CPAs to Conduct Themselves at a High Level**

CODE OF PROFESSIONAL CONDUCT

OBJECTIVE 4-4

Describe the purpose and content of the AICPA *Code of Professional Conduct.*

The AICPA *Code of Professional Conduct* provides both general standards of ideal conduct and specific enforceable rules of conduct. There are four parts to the code: principles, rules of conduct, interpretations of the rules of conduct, and ethical rulings. The parts are listed in order of increasing specificity; the principles provide ideal standards of conduct, whereas ethical rulings are highly specific. The four parts are summarized in Figure 4-3 and discussed on pages 83–86.

FIGURE 4-3   **Code of Professional Conduct**

Principles	Ideal standards of ethical conduct stated in philosophical terms.
	They are not enforceable.
Rules of conduct	Minimum standards of ethical conduct stated as specific rules.
	They are enforceable.
Interpretations of the rules of conduct	Interpretations of the rules of conduct by the AICPA Division of Professional Ethics.
	They are not enforceable, but a practitioner must justify departure.
Ethical rulings	Published explanations and answers to questions about the rules of conduct submitted to the AICPA by practitioners and others interested in ethical requirements.
	They are not enforceable, but a practitioner must justify departure.

A few definitions, taken from the AICPA *Code of Professional Conduct,* must be understood to minimize misinterpretation of the rules.

- *Client.* Any person or entity, other than the member's employer, that engages a member or a member's firm to perform professional services.
- *Firm.* A form of organization permitted by state law or regulation whose characteristics conform to resolutions of Council that is engaged in the practice of public accounting, including the individual owners thereof.
- *Institute.* The American Institute of Certified Public Accountants.
- *Member.* A member, associate member, or international associate of the American Institute of Certified Public Accountants.
- *Practice of public accounting.* The practice of public accounting consists of the performance for a client, by a member or a member's firm, while holding out as CPA(s), of the professional services of accounting, tax, personal financial planning, litigation support services, and those professional services for which standards are promulgated by bodies designated by Council.

AICPA Code

The section of the AICPA *Code* dealing with principles of professional conduct contains a general discussion of certain characteristics required of a CPA. The principles section consists of two main parts: six ethical principles and a discussion of those principles. The ethical principles are listed as follows. Discussions throughout this chapter include ideas taken from the principles section.

Principles of Professional Conduct

Ethical Principles

1. **Responsibilities** In carrying out their responsibilities as professionals, members should exercise sensitive professional and moral judgments in all their activities.
2. **The Public Interest** Members should accept the obligation to act in a way that will serve the public interest, honor the public trust, and demonstrate commitment to professionalism.
3. **Integrity** To maintain and broaden public confidence, members should perform all professional responsibilities with the highest sense of integrity.
4. **Objectivity and Independence** A member should maintain objectivity and be free of conflicts of interest in discharging professional responsibilities. A member in public practice should be independent in fact and appearance when providing auditing and other attestation services.
5. **Due Care** A member should observe the profession's technical and ethical standards, strive continually to improve competence and the quality of services, and discharge professional responsibility to the best of the member's ability.
6. **Scope and Nature of Services** A member in public practice should observe the principles of the *Code of Professional Conduct* in determining the scope and nature of services to be provided.

The first five of these principles are equally applicable to all members of the AICPA, regardless of whether they practice in a CPA firm, work as accountants in business or government, are involved in some other aspect of business, or are in education. One exception is the last sentence of objectivity and independence. It applies only to members in public practice, and then only when they are providing attestation services such as audits. The sixth principle, scope and nature of services, applies only to members in public practice. That principle addresses whether a practitioner should provide a certain service, such as providing personnel consulting when an audit client is hiring a controller. Providing such a service could create a loss of independence if the CPA firm recommends a controller who is hired and performs incompetently.

A careful examination of these six principles will likely lead us to conclude that they are applicable to any professional, not just CPAs. For example, physicians should exercise sensitive professional and moral judgment, act in the public interest, act with integrity, be objective and avoid conflicts of interest, follow due care, and evaluate the appropriateness of the nature of medical services provided. One difference between auditors and other

TABLE 4-1   **Summary of Rules of Conduct**

RULES OF CONDUCT		APPLICABILITY		SUMMARY OF RULES
Number	**Topic**	**All Members**	**Members in Public Practice**	
101	Independence		x	A member in public practice shall be independent in the performance of professional services as required by standards promulgated by bodies designated by Council.
102	Integrity and objectivity	x		In performing any professional service, a member shall maintain objectivity and integrity, shall be free of conflicts of interest, and shall not knowingly misrepresent facts or subordinate his or her judgment to others.
201	General standards	x		For all services, a member shall comply with the following professional standards and interpretations thereof by bodies designated by Council: (1) undertake only those professional services that the member can reasonably expect to complete with professional competence, (2) exercise due professional care, (3) adequately plan and supervise all engagements, and (4) obtain sufficient relevant data to afford a reasonable basis for all conclusions or recommendations.
202	Compliance with standards	x		A member who performs auditing, review, compilation, management consulting, tax, or other professional services shall comply with standards promulgated by bodies designated by Council.
203	Accounting principles	x		A member shall follow the professional audit reporting standards promulgated by bodies designated by Council in issuing reports about entities' compliance with generally accepted accounting principles.
301	Confidential client information		x	A member in public practice shall not disclose any confidential client information without the specific consent of the client, except for the four specific situations included in Rule 301.
302	Contingent fees		x	A member in public practice shall not perform for a contingent fee any professional service if the member also performs for the client an audit, review, or certain compilations of financial statements, or an examination of prospective financial statements. A member in public practice should also not prepare an original or amended tax return or claim for a tax refund for a contingent fee for any client.
501	Acts discreditable	x		A member shall not commit an act discreditable to the profession.
502	Advertising and other forms of solicitation		x	A member in public practice shall not seek to obtain clients by advertising or other forms of solicitation in a manner that is false, misleading, or deceptive. Solicitation by the use of coercion, overreaching, or harassing conduct is prohibited.
503	Commissions and referral fees		x	A member in public practice shall not receive or pay a commission or referral fee for any client if the member also performs for the client an audit, review, or certain compilations of financial statements, or an examination of prospective financial statements. For nonprohibited commissions or referral fees, a member must disclose the existence of such fees to the client.
505	Form of organization and name		x	A member may practice public accounting only in a form of organization permitted by state law or regulation whose characteristics conform to resolutions of Council and shall not practice public accounting under a firm name that is misleading.

professionals, as discussed earlier, is that most professionals need not be concerned about remaining independent.

This part of the *Code* includes the explicit rules that must be followed by every CPA in the practice of public accounting.[2] A summary of the rules of conduct is included in Table 4-1 (p. 84). Those individuals holding the CPA certificate but not actually practicing public accounting must follow most, but not all, of the requirements. Because the section on rules of conduct is the only enforceable part of the code, it is stated in more precise language than the section on principles. Because of their enforceability, many practitioners refer to the rules as the AICPA *Code of Professional Conduct*.

Rules of Conduct

The difference between the standards of conduct set by the *principles* and those set by the *rules of conduct* is shown in Figure 4-4. When practitioners conduct themselves at the minimum level in Figure 4-4, that does not imply unsatisfactory conduct. The profession has presumably set the standards sufficiently high to make the minimum conduct satisfactory.

At what level do practitioners conduct themselves in practice? As in any profession, the level varies among practitioners. Most practitioners conduct themselves at a high level. Unfortunately, a few conduct themselves below the minimum level set by the profession. The activities designed to encourage CPAs to conduct themselves at a high level described in Figure 4-2 (p. 82) help minimize the extent of any substandard practice.

The need for published interpretations of the rules of conduct arises when there are frequent questions from practitioners about a specific rule. The Division of Professional Ethics of the AICPA prepares each interpretation based on a consensus of a committee made up principally of public accounting practitioners. Before interpretations are finalized, they are sent to a large number of key people in the profession for comment. Interpretations are not officially enforceable, but a departure from the interpretations would be difficult if not impossible for a practitioner to justify in a disciplinary hearing. The most important interpretations are discussed as a part of each section of the rules.

Interpretation of Rules of Conduct

Rulings are explanations by the executive committee of the professional ethics division of *specific factual circumstances*. A large number of ethical rulings are published in the expanded version of the AICPA *Code of Professional Conduct*. The following is an example (Rule 101—Independence; Ruling No. 16):

Ethical Rulings

- *Question*—A member serves on the board of directors of a nonprofit social club. Would the independence of the member's firm be considered to be impaired with respect to the club?

[2]The AICPA *Code of Professional Conduct* is applicable to every CPA who is a member of the AICPA. Each state also has rules of conduct that are required for licensing by the state. Many states follow the AICPA rules, but some have somewhat different requirements.

FIGURE 4-4	Standards of Conduct

Ideal conduct by practitioners — Principles

Minimum level of conduct by practitioners — Rules of conduct

Substandard conduct

- *Answer*—Independence of the member's firm would be considered to be impaired because the board of directors has the ultimate responsibility for the affairs of the club. The exception in the interpretations was intended primarily to cover those situations in which a member lends his or her name to some worthwhile cause without assuming important administrative or financial responsibilities.

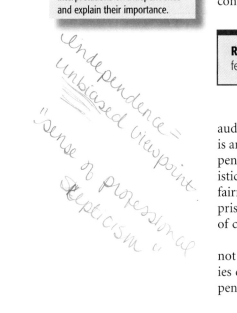

Applicability of the Rules of Conduct

The rules of conduct contained in the AICPA *Code of Professional Conduct* apply to all AICPA members for all services provided whether or not the member is in the practice of public accounting, unless it is specifically stated otherwise in the code. Table 4-1 indicates whether the rule applies to all members or only to members in public practice.

Each of the rules apply to attestation services and *unless stated otherwise*, each rule also applies to all services provided by CPA firms such as taxes and management services. There are only two rules that exempt certain nonattestation services:

1. Rule 101—Independence. This rule requires independence only when the AICPA has established independence requirements through its rule-setting bodies, such as the Auditing Standards Board. The AICPA requires independence only for attestation engagements. For example, a CPA firm can perform management services for a company in which the partners own stock. Of course, if the CPA firm also did an audit, that would violate the independence requirements for attestation services.
2. Rule 203—Accounting Principles. This rule applies only to issuing an audit opinion or review service opinion on financial statements.

It would be a violation of the rules if someone did something on behalf of a member that would have been a violation if the member had done it. An example is a banker who puts in a newsletter that Johnson and Able CPA firm has the best tax department in the state and consistently gets large refunds for its tax clients. That is likely to create false or unjustified expectations and is a violation of Rule 502. A member is also responsible for compliance with the rules by employees, partners, and shareholders.

The specific rules of conduct are discussed in the following sections. We begin by discussing the rules on independence.

INDEPENDENCE

OBJECTIVE 4-5
Apply the AICPA *Code* rules and interpretations on independence and explain their importance.

The value of auditing depends heavily on the public's perception of the independence of auditors. It is not surprising that independence is the first subject addressed in the rules of conduct.

> **Rule 101–Independence** A member in public practice shall be independent in the performance of professional services as required by standards promulgated by bodies designated by Council.

Independence in auditing means taking an *unbiased viewpoint* in the performance of audit tests, the evaluation of the results, and the issuance of the audit report. If the auditor is an advocate for the client, a banker, or anyone else, he or she cannot be considered independent. Independence must certainly be regarded as the auditor's most critical characteristic. The reason that many diverse users are willing to rely on the CPA's reports as to the fairness of financial statements is their expectation of an unbiased viewpoint. It is not surprising that independence is included as a generally accepted auditing standard and a rule of conduct.

CPA firms are required to be independent for certain services that they provide, but not for others. The last phrase in Rule 101, "as required by standards promulgated by bodies designated by Council" is a convenient way for the AICPA to include or exclude independence requirements for different types of services. For example, the Auditing Standards

Board requires that auditors of historical financial statements be independent. Rule 101 therefore applies to audits. Independence is also required for other types of attestations, such as review services and audits of prospective financial statements. However, a CPA firm can do tax returns and provide management services without being independent. Rule 101 does not apply to those types of services.

Not only is it essential for auditors to maintain an independent attitude in fulfilling their responsibilities, but it is also important that the users of financial statements have confidence in that independence. These two objectives are often identified as **independence in fact** and **independence in appearance**. Independence in fact exists when the auditor is actually able to maintain an unbiased attitude throughout the audit, whereas independence in appearance is the result of others' interpretations of this independence. If auditors are independent in fact, but users believe them to be advocates for the client, most of the value of the audit function will be lost.

Although it is possible to take the extreme position that anything affecting either independence in fact or in appearance must be eliminated to ensure a high level of respect in the community, it is doubtful whether this would solve as many problems as it would create. The difficulty with this position is that it is likely to significantly restrict the services offered to clients, the freedom of CPAs to practice in the traditional manner, and the ability of CPA firms to hire competent staff. At this point it will be helpful to examine some conflicts of independence that have arisen within the profession, evaluate their significance, and determine how the profession has resolved them. The profession deals with most independence issues through Interpretations of the Rules of Conduct. There are more interpretations for independence than for any of the other rules.

Do not own stock in what you audit

Financial Interests

Interpretations of Rule 101 prohibit CPAs in public accounting from owning *any stock or other direct investment* in audit clients because it is potentially damaging to actual audit independence, and it certainly is likely to affect the users' perceptions of the auditors' independence. *Indirect investments,* such as ownership of stock in a client's company by an auditor's grandparent, are also prohibited, but *only if the amount is material* to the auditor. The ownership of stock rule is more complex than it appears at first glance. A more detailed examination of that requirement is included to aid in understanding and to show the complexity of one of the rules. There are three important distinctions in the rules as they relate to independence and stock ownership.

Partners or Shareholders versus Nonpartners or Nonshareholders Rule 101 applies to partners and shareholders for all clients of a CPA firm. The rule applies to nonpartners or nonshareholders only *when they are involved in the engagement or when the engagement is performed by staff in the same office.* For example, a staff member in a national CPA firm could own stock in a client corporation and not violate Rule 101 if he or she was never involved in the engagement, but as soon as the staff member became a partner he or she would have to dispose of the stock or the CPA firm must stop doing the audit.

Some CPA firms do not permit any ownership by staff of client's stock regardless of which office serves the client. These firms have decided to have higher requirements than the minimums set by the rules of conduct.

Direct versus Indirect Financial Interest The ownership of stock or other equity shares by members or their immediate family is called a **direct financial interest**. For example, if either a partner or the partner's spouse had a partnership interest in a company, the CPA firm would be prohibited by Rule 101 from expressing an opinion on the financial statements of that company.

An **indirect financial interest** exists when there is a close, but not a direct, ownership relationship between the auditor and the client. An example of indirect ownership occurs when a CPA firm audits a mutual fund which owns stock that an audit partner also has in his or her personal portfolio. Another example is the ownership of a stock by a member's grandparent.

Material or Immaterial *Materiality* affects whether ownership is a violation of Rule 101 only for *indirect* ownership. Materiality must be considered in relation to the member person's wealth and income. For example, if a mutual fund client has a large portion of its ownership in the XY Company and a firm partner has a significant amount of her personal wealth invested in XY Company, a violation of the code exists.

Related Financial Interest Issues

Several interpretations of Rule 101 deal with specific aspects of financial relationships between CPA firm personnel and clients. These are summarized in this section.

Former Practitioners In most situations, the interpretations permit former partners or shareholders who left the firm due to such things as retirement or the sale of their ownership interest to have relationships with clients of the firm of the type that are normally a violation of Rule 101, without affecting a firm's independence. A violation by the firm would occur if the former partner was held out as an associate of the firm or took part in activities that are likely to cause other parties to believe the person was still active in the firm. Examples include participation in the CPA firm's business activities, the use of the CPA firm's office space when the former partner has significant influence over a client of the firm, or the receipt of benefits from the former CPA firm that are dependent on the firm's profitability.

Normal Lending Procedures Generally, loans between a CPA firm or its members and an audit client are prohibited because it is a financial relationship. There are several exceptions to the rule, however, including automobile loans, loans fully collateralized by cash deposits at the same financial institution, and unpaid credit card balances not exceeding $5,000 in total. It is also acceptable to accept a financial institution as a client even if members of the CPA firm have existing home mortgages, other fully collateralized secured loans, and immaterial loans with the institution. No new loans would be permitted, however. Both the restrictions and exceptions are reasonable ones, considering the trade-off between independence and the need to permit CPAs to function as business people and individuals.

Financial Interests of Next of Kin The financial interests of a spouse, dependent children, or relatives living with or supported by a member are ordinarily treated as if they were the financial interests of the member. For example, if the spouse of a partner of a CPA firm owned any stock in an audit client, Rule 101 would be violated. The interpretations provide two other examples in which a violation is presumed but may be offset by other circumstances such as infrequent contact or geographical separation. The first is when close kin such as nondependent children, brothers and sisters, grandparents, parents-in-law, or spouses of these kin have a significant financial interest, investment, or business relationship with an audit client of a member. The second is when any of these close kin have an important executive position such as director, chief executive, or financial officer with a client. Imagine the difficulty a CPA firm faces if it has an opportunity to accept a new audit client where the father of a young audit partner is chief executive officer and has material ownership in the potential client. Presumably, the partners of the CPA firm would discuss the matter and may contact the AICPA Ethics Division to decide whether to accept the client.

Joint Investor or Investee Relationship with Client Assume, for example, that a CPA firm partner owns stock in a nonaudit client, Jackson Company. Frank Company, which is an audit client, also owns stock in Jackson Company. This may be a violation of Rule 101. The interpretations prohibit the partners from owning any stock in Jackson Company or similar financial relationships if the investment in Jackson by Frank Company is material. The interpretation defines materiality for investee–investor relationships as either 5 percent of Frank's total assets or 5 percent of Frank's operating income before taxes, whichever is more restrictive. This is an illustration of an interpretation leaving little, if any, room for practitioners to make judgments.

Director, Officer, Management, or Employee of a Company If a CPA is a member of the board of directors or an officer of a client company, his or her ability to make independent evaluations of the fair presentation of financial statements would be affected. Even if holding one of these positions did not actually affect the auditor's independence, the frequent involvement with management and the decisions it makes is likely to affect how statement users would perceive the CPA's independence. To eliminate this possibility, interpretations prohibit the CPA from being a director or officer of an audit client company. Similarly, the auditor cannot be an underwriter, voting trustee, promoter, or trustee of a client's pension fund, or act in any other capacity of management, or be an employee of the company.

Interpretations permit members to do audits and be *honorary* directors or trustees for not-for-profit organizations, such as charitable and religious organizations, as long as the position is purely honorary. To illustrate, it is common for a partner of the CPA firm doing the audit of a city's United Fund drive to also be an honorary director, along with many other civic leaders. The CPA cannot vote or participate in any management functions.

When there is a lawsuit or intent to start a lawsuit between a CPA firm and its client, the ability of the CPA firm and client to remain objective is questionable. The interpretations regard such litigation as a violation of Rule 101 for the current audit. For example, if management sues a CPA firm claiming a deficiency in the previous audit, the CPA firm is not considered independent for the current year's audit. Similarly, if the CPA firm sues management for fraudulent financial reporting or deceit, independence is lost.

Litigation between CPA Firm and Client

Litigation by the client related to tax or other nonaudit services, or litigation against both the client and the CPA firm by another party, would not usually impair independence. The key consideration in all such suits is the likely effect on the ability of client, management, and CPA firm personnel to remain objective and comment freely.

If a CPA records transactions in the journals for the client, posts monthly totals to the general ledger, makes adjusting entries, and subsequently does an audit, there is some question as to whether the CPA can be independent in his or her audit role. The interpretations *permit a CPA firm to do both bookkeeping and auditing for the same client*. The AICPA's conclusion is presumably based on a comparison of the effect on independence of having both bookkeeping and auditing services performed by the same CPA firm with the additional cost of having a different CPA firm do the audit. There are three important requirements that the auditor must satisfy before it is acceptable to do bookkeeping and auditing for the client:

Bookkeeping and Other Services

1. The client must accept full responsibility for the financial statements. The client must be sufficiently knowledgeable about the enterprise's activities and financial condition and the applicable accounting principles so that the client can reasonably accept such responsibility, including the fairness of valuation and presentation and the adequacy of disclosure. When necessary, the CPA must discuss accounting matters with the client to be sure that the client has the required degree of understanding.
2. The CPA must not assume the role of employee or of management conducting the operations of an enterprise. For example, the CPA shall not consummate transactions, have custody of assets, or exercise authority on behalf of the client. The client must prepare the source documents on all transactions in sufficient detail to identify clearly the nature and amount of such transactions and maintain accounting control over data processed by the CPA, such as control totals and document counts.
3. The CPA, in making an audit of financial statements prepared from books and records that the CPA has maintained completely or in part, must conform to GAAS. The fact that the CPA has processed or maintained certain records does not eliminate the need to make sufficient audit tests.

The first two requirements are often difficult to satisfy for a smaller company whose owner may have little knowledge of or interest in accounting or processing transactions.

For SEC clients, *the SEC prohibits the performance of bookkeeping services and auditing by the same CPA firm.* Most SEC clients are larger and are more likely to have an accounting staff. Therefore, this prohibition causes few difficulties.

In addition to bookkeeping, CPA firms offer many other services to attest clients that may potentially impair independence. Such activities are permissible as long as the member does not perform management functions or make management decisions. For example, a CPA can provide investment advisory services to an attest client. However, independence would be considered impaired if the CPA had discretionary authority over a client's investments or took custody of the client's assets.

Internal Auditing and Extended Audit Services

In recent years, many CPA firms have begun providing internal auditing and other extended auditing services to their clients. For example, a manufacturing client may engage its CPA firm to perform an operational review of the company's production processes to determine whether products are being produced efficiently. Such services do not impair independence, as long as the CPA or his or her firm does not act or appear to act in a capacity equivalent to a member of client management or as an employee. The client must remain responsible for the internal audit function. This includes determining the scope of internal audit activities, evaluating the adequacy of procedures, and evaluating the findings and results arising from internal audit activities, including those performed by the AICPA member.

Engagement and Payment of Audit Fees by Management

Can an auditor be truly independent in fact and appearance if the payment of fees is dependent upon the management of the audited entity? There is probably no satisfactory answer to this question, but it does demonstrate the difficulty of obtaining an atmosphere of complete independence of auditors. The alternative to engagement of the CPA and payment of audit fees by management would probably be the use of either government or quasi-government auditors. All things considered, it is questionable whether the audit function would be performed better or more cheaply by the public sector.

Unpaid Fees

Under Rule 101 and its rulings and interpretations, independence is considered impaired if billed or unbilled fees remain unpaid for professional services provided more than 1 year before the date of the report. Such unpaid fees are deemed to be a loan from the auditor to the client and are therefore a violation of Rule 101. Unpaid fees from a client in bankruptcy do not violate Rule 101.

Independence Standards Board

Several factors, including increased competition and the increased importance of management consulting services, have increased concerns about the independence of external auditors. The **Independence Standards Board** (ISB), a private-sector body, was formed in 1997 to provide a conceptual framework for independence issues related to audits of public companies. In addition to promulgating standards, the ISB provides consultation to auditors and their SEC clients on questions about independence standards.

The ISB was established under an agreement between the SEC and the AICPA. The ISB is funded by the SEC Practice Section (SECPS) of the AICPA, and actions of the Board carry presumptive weight by the SEC. However, the ISB is an autonomous private-sector body and operates independently of the SEC and AICPA.

Independence Standards Board Standard No. 1, *Independence Discussions with Audit Committees,* was issued in January 1999. The standard requires auditors intending to be independent of companies reporting to the SEC to disclose in writing to the audit committee or board of directors all relationships between the auditing firm and the company that in the auditor's professional judgment may reasonably be thought to bear on independence. The auditing firm must also confirm in the letter that in its professional judgment, the firm is independent of the company. The auditor is also required to discuss the auditing firm's independence with the audit committee.

Independence Standards Board

Audit Committee

An **audit committee** is a selected number of members of a company's board of directors whose responsibilities include helping auditors remain independent of management. Most audit committees are made up of three to five or sometimes as many as seven directors who are not a part of company management.

A typical audit committee decides such things as which CPA firm to retain and the scope of services the CPA firm is to perform. It meets periodically with the CPA firm to discuss audit progress and findings, and helps resolve conflicts between the CPA firm and management. Audit committees for larger companies are looked upon with favor by most auditors, users, and management. The requirement of an audit committee would be costly for smaller companies.

An audit committee is required for all companies listed on the New York Stock Exchange. The AICPA rules of conduct and the SEC do not require audit committees.

Shopping for Accounting Principles

Both management and representatives of management, such as investment bankers, often consult with other accountants on the application of accounting principles. Although consultation with other accountants is an appropriate practice, it can lead to a loss of independence in certain circumstances. For example, suppose one CPA firm replaces the existing auditors on the strength of accounting advice offered but later finds facts and circumstances that require the CPA firm to change its stance. It may be difficult for the new CPA firm to remain independent in such a situation. SAS 50 (AU 625) sets forth requirements that must be followed when a CPA firm is requested to provide a written or oral opinion on the application of accounting principles or the type of audit opinion that would be issued for a specific or hypothetical transaction of an audit client of another CPA firm. The purpose of the requirement is to minimize the likelihood of management following the practice commonly called opinion shopping and the potential threat to independence of the kind described previously. Primary among the requirements is that the consulted CPA firm should communicate with the entity's existing auditors to ascertain all the available facts relevant to forming a professional judgment on the matters the firm has been requested to report on.

Approval of Auditor by Stockholders

Although not required by the AICPA or SEC, an increasing number of companies require stockholders to approve the selection of a new CPA firm or continuation of the existing one. Stockholders are usually a more objective group than management. However, it is questionable whether they are in a position to evaluate the performance of previous or potential auditors.

TEST YOUR KNOWLEDGE OF REAL SITUATIONS

Periodically, the *Journal of Accountancy* publishes questions on ethics topics that have been raised by AICPA members. This set deals with Rule 101—Independence.

Questions (Answers on p. 92)
1. A CPA's spouse is on the board of directors of one of the CPA firm's audit clients. The CPA is *not* an owner of the firm. If the CPA does not participate on the audit engagement, would the firm's independence be impaired?
   ❏ Yes ❏ No
2. A CPA's spouse is on the board of directors of one of the CPA firm's audit clients. The CPA *is* an owner of the firm. If the CPA does not participate on the audit engagement, would the firm's independence be impaired?
   ❏ Yes ❏ No
3. A one-office CPA firm employs an independent contractor for part-time tax preparation during "busy season." The independent contractor is the controller of one of the firm's audit clients but does not perform any tax services related to his or her employer. Is the firm's independence impaired?
   ❏ Yes ❏ No

OTHER RULES OF CONDUCT

Although independence is critical to public confidence in CPAs, it is also important that auditors adhere to the other rules of conduct listed in Table 4-1 on page 84. We begin by discussing the rules for integrity and objectivity.

Integrity and Objectivity

OBJECTIVE 4-6
Understand the requirements of other rules under the AICPA *Code*.

Integrity means impartiality in performing all services. Rule 102 on integrity and objectivity is presented below:

> **Rule 102—Integrity and Objectivity** In the performance of any professional service, a member shall maintain objectivity and integrity, shall be free of conflicts of interest, and shall not knowingly misrepresent facts or subordinate his or her judgment to others.

To illustrate the meaning of integrity and objectivity, assume that an auditor believes that accounts receivable may not be collectible but accepts management's opinion without an independent evaluation of collectibility. The auditor has subordinated his or her judgment and thereby lacks objectivity. Now assume that a CPA is preparing the tax return for a client and, as a client advocate, encourages the client to take a deduction on the returns that he or she believes is valid, but for which there is some but not complete support. This would not be a violation of either objectivity or integrity because it is acceptable for the CPA to be a client advocate in tax and management services. If the CPA encourages the client to take a deduction for which there is no support but has little chance of discovery by the IRS, a violation has occurred. That is a misrepresentation of the facts; therefore, the integrity of the CPA has been impaired.

Audit staff members should not subordinate their judgment to supervisors on the audit engagement. Staff auditors are responsible for their own judgments documented in the working papers and should not change those conclusions at the request of supervisors on the engagement, unless the staff auditor agrees with the supervisor's conclusion. In rare instances where the staff member does not agree with a conclusion involving a significant matter, the staff member should document the reasons for the disagreement as a way of disassociating himself or herself from the resolution of the matter.

Freedom from conflicts of interest means the absence of relationships that might interfere with objectivity or integrity. For example, it would be inappropriate for an auditor who is also an attorney to represent a client in legal matters. The attorney is an advocate for the client, whereas the auditor must be impartial.

An interpretation of Rule 102 states that apparent conflicts of interest may not be a violation of the rules of conduct if the information is disclosed to the member's client or employer. For example, if a partner of a CPA firm recommends that a client have its insurance coverage evaluated by an insurance agency that is owned by the partner's spouse, a conflict of interest may appear to exist. No violation of Rule 102 would occur if the partner informed the client's management of the relationship and management proceeded with the evaluation with that knowledge. The interpretation makes it clear that the independence requirements under Rule 101 cannot be eliminated by these disclosures.

The next three standards of the *Code* relate to the auditor's adherence with the requirements of technical standards. The following are the requirements of the technical standards:

Technical Standards

Rule 201—General Standards A member shall comply with the following standards and with any interpretations thereof by bodies designated by Council.

A. *Professional competence.* Undertake only those professional services that the member or the member's firm can reasonably expect to be completed with professional competence.
B. *Due professional care.* Exercise due professional care in the performance of professional services.
C. *Planning and supervision.* Adequately plan and supervise the performance of professional services.
D. *Sufficient relevant data.* Obtain sufficient relevant data to afford a reasonable basis for conclusions or recommendations in relation to any professional services performed.

Rule 202—Compliance with Standards A member who performs auditing, review, compilation, management consulting, tax, or other professional services shall comply with standards promulgated by bodies designated by Council.

Rule 203—Accounting Principles A member shall not (1) express an opinion or state affirmatively that the financial statements or other financial data of any entity are presented in conformity with generally accepted accounting principles or (2) state that he or she is not aware of any material modifications that should be made to such statements or data in order for them to be in conformity with generally accepted accounting principles, if such statements or data contain any departure from an accounting principle promulgated by bodies designated by Council to establish such principles that has a material effect on the statements or data taken as a whole. If, however, the statements or data contain such a departure and the member can demonstrate that due to unusual circumstances the financial statements or data would otherwise have been misleading, the member can comply with the rule by describing the departure, its approximate effects, if practicable, and the reasons why compliance with the principle would result in a misleading statement.

The primary purpose of the requirements of Rules 201 to 203 is to provide support for the ASB and FASB and other technical standard-setting bodies. For example, notice that requirements A and B of Rule 201 are the same in substance as general auditing standards 1 and 3, and C and D of Rule 201 have the same intent as field work standards 1 and 3. The only difference is that Rule 201 is stated in terms that apply to all types of services, whereas auditing standards apply only to audits. Rule 202 makes it clear that when a practitioner violates an auditing standard, the rules of conduct are also automatically violated.

Confidentiality

It is essential that practitioners not disclose confidential information obtained in any type of engagement without the consent of the client. The following are the specific requirements of Rule 301 related to **confidential client information:**

Rule 301—Confidential Client Information A member in public practice shall not disclose any confidential client information without the specific consent of the client.

This rule shall not be construed (1) to relieve a member of his or her professional obligations under Rules 202 and 203, (2) to affect in any way the member's obligation to comply with a validly issued and enforceable subpoena or summons, or to prohibit a member's compliance with applicable laws and government regulations, (3) to prohibit review of a member's professional practice under AICPA or state CPA society or Board of Accountancy authorization, or (4) to preclude a member from initiating a complaint with, or responding to any inquiry made by, the professional ethics division or trial board of the Institute or a duly constituted investigative or disciplinary body of a state CPA society or Board of Accountancy.

Members of any of the bodies identified in (4) above and members involved with professional practice reviews identified in (3) above shall not use to their own advantage or disclose any member's confidential client information that comes to their attention in carrying out those activities. This prohibition shall not restrict members' exchange of information in connection with the investigative or disciplinary proceedings described in (4) above or the professional practice reviews described in (3) above.

Need for Confidentiality During an audit or other type of engagement, practitioners obtain a considerable amount of information of a confidential nature, including officers' salaries, product pricing and advertising plans, and product cost data. If auditors divulged this information to outsiders or to client employees who have been denied access to the information, their relationship with management would be seriously strained, and in extreme cases, the client could be harmed. The confidentiality requirement applies to all services provided by CPA firms, including tax and management services.

Ordinarily, the CPA's working papers can be provided to someone else only with the express permission of the client. This is the case even if a CPA sells his or her practice to another CPA firm or is willing to permit a successor auditor to examine the working papers prepared for a former client. Permission is not required from the client, however, if the working papers are subpoenaed by a court or are used as part of an authorized peer review program with other CPA firms. If the working papers are subpoenaed, the client should be informed immediately. The client and its legal counsel may wish to challenge the subpoena.

Exceptions to Confidentiality As stated in the second paragraph of Rule 301, there are four exceptions to the confidentiality requirements. All four exceptions concern responsibilities that are more important than maintaining confidential relations with the client.

1. *Obligations related to technical standards.* Suppose that 3 months after an unqualified audit report was issued, the auditor discovers that the financial statements were materially misstated. When the chief executive officer is confronted, he responds that even though he agrees that the financial statements are misstated, confidentiality prevents the CPA from informing anyone. The previous example is similar to an actual legal case, *Yale Express.* Disagreements during the *Yale Express* case resulted in AU 561, which deals with auditors' responsibilities when subsequent facts show that an inappropriate audit report has been issued. (AU 561 is discussed in Chapter 23.) Exception (1) in Rule 301 makes it clear that the auditor's responsibility to discharge professional standards is greater than that for confidentiality. In such a case, a revised, correct audit report must be issued. Note, however, that the conflict seldom occurs.

2. *Subpoena or summons.* Legally, information is called **privileged information** if legal proceedings cannot require a person to provide the information, even if there is a subpoena. Information communicated by a client to an attorney or by a patient to a physician is privileged. *Information obtained by a CPA from a client generally is not*

privileged. Exception (2) of Rule 301 is therefore needed to put CPA firms in compliance with the law.

There have been considerable discussion and disagreement among CPAs, attorneys, and legislators about the need for privileged communication between CPAs and clients. Most CPAs and businesspeople dealing with CPAs support legislation protecting privileged communication. In fact, a number of states have statutes that provide some level of privilege to accountant–client communication. Of course, these statutes would apply only to litigation in state courts and would have no bearing on federal court suits.

3. *Peer review.* When a CPA or CPA firm conducts a peer review of the quality controls of another CPA firm, it is normal practice to examine several sets of working papers. If the peer review is authorized by the AICPA, state CPA society, or state Board of Accountancy, client permission to examine the working papers is not needed. Requiring permission from each client may restrict access of the peer reviewers and would be a time burden on all concerned. Naturally, the peer reviewers must keep the information obtained confidential and cannot use the information for other purposes.

4. *Response to ethics division.* If a practitioner is charged with inadequate technical performance by the AICPA Ethics Division trial board under any of Rules 201 to 203, the board members are likely to want to examine working papers. Exception (4) in Rule 301 prevents a CPA firm from denying the inquirers access to working papers by saying that they are confidential information. Similarly, a CPA firm that observes substandard working papers of another CPA firm cannot use confidentiality as the reason for not initiating a complaint of substandard performance against the firm.

Contingent Fees

To help CPAs maintain objectivity in conducting audits or other attestation services, basing fees on the outcome of the engagement is prohibited. The following are the requirements of Rule 302 related to contingent fees:

Rule 302–Contingent Fees A member in public practice shall not

(1) Perform for a contingent fee any professional services for, or receive such a fee from, a client for whom the member or member's firm performs:
  (a) an audit or review of a financial statement; or
  (b) a compilation of a financial statement when the member expects, or reasonably might expect, that a third party will use the financial statement and the member's compilation report does not disclose a lack of independence; or
  (c) an examination of prospective financial information;

or

(2) Prepare an original or amended tax return or claim for a tax refund for a contingent fee for any client.

The prohibition in (1) above applies during the period in which the member or the member's firm is engaged to perform any of the services listed above and the period covered by any historical financial statements involved in any such listed services.

Except as stated in the next sentence, a contingent fee is a fee established for the performance of any service pursuant to an arrangement in which no fee will be charged unless a specified finding or result is attained, or in which the amount of the fee is otherwise dependent upon the finding or result of such service. Solely for purposes of this rule, fees are not regarded as being contingent if fixed by courts or other public authorities, or, in tax matters, if determined based on the results of judicial proceedings or the findings of governmental agencies.

A member's fees may vary depending, for example, on the complexity of services rendered.

To illustrate the need for a rule on contingent fees, suppose a CPA firm was permitted to charge a fee of $5,000 if an unqualified opinion was provided, but only $2,500 if the opinion was qualified. Such an agreement may tempt a practitioner to issue the wrong opinion and would be a violation of Rule 302. It is also a violation of Rule 302 for members to prepare an original or amended tax return, or a claim for tax refunds for a contingent fee.

An agreement between the AICPA and the Federal Trade Commission eliminated the restrictions on contingent fees *for nonattestation services, unless the CPA firm is also performing attestation services* for the same client. The agreement also permits the AICPA to prohibit tax return preparation on a contingent fee basis. Under the agreement, for example, it is *not* a violation for a CPA to charge fees as an expert witness determined by the amount awarded to the plaintiff or to base consulting fees on a percentage of a bond issue *if the CPA firm does not also do an audit or other attestation for the same client.*

The reason for the agreement was a contention by the Federal Trade Commission that contingent fee restrictions reduce competition and therefore are not in the public interest. After considerable negotiation, the AICPA agreed to restrict the contingent fee prohibition only to attestation services clients and for tax return preparation. The Federal Trade Commission agreed to allow the AICPA to prohibit contingent fees for attestation services and tax return preparation because of the importance of independence and objectivity.

Discreditable Acts

Because of the special need for CPAs to conduct themselves in a professional manner, the *Code* has a specific rule prohibiting acts discreditable to the profession.

> **Rule 501—Acts Discreditable** A member shall not commit an act discreditable to the profession.

A discreditable act is not well defined in the rules or interpretations. The following are some of the requirements contained in the interpretations.

1. *Retention of client records.* It is an act discreditable to retain a client's records after a demand is made for them. Assume, for example, that a client did not pay an audit fee and the partners of the CPA firm therefore refused to return client-owned records. The partners have violated Rule 501.
2. *Discrimination and harassment in employment practices.* A member is presumed to have committed an act discreditable whenever the member is found to have violated any federal, state, or local antidiscrimination laws.
3. *Standards on government audits and requirements of government bodies and agencies.* Audits of government units and federal grant recipients must be done in compliance with government auditing standards, in addition to GAAS. Both the government auditing standards and GAAS must be followed unless the audit report discloses the reasons for not following such requirements. When a member accepts an engagement that involves reporting to a regulatory agency such as the SEC, the member must follow the additional requirements of the regulatory agency, in addition to GAAS. If the additional requirements are not followed, the reasons should be noted in the report.
4. *Solicitation or disclosure of CPA examination questions and answers.* As noted in Chapter 1, the Uniform CPA examination became nondisclosed effective with the May 1996 examination. It is an act discreditable to solicit or disclose questions from the May 1996 or later examinations without the permission of the AICPA.

Do excessive drinking, rowdy behavior, or other acts that many people would consider unprofessional constitute a discreditable act? Probably not. Determining what constitutes professional behavior continues to be the responsibility of each professional.

For guidance as to what constitutes a discreditable act, the AICPA bylaws provide clearer guidelines than the AICPA *Code of Professional Conduct*. The bylaws state that membership in the AICPA can be terminated without a hearing for judgment of conviction for any of the following four crimes: (1) a crime punishable by imprisonment for more than 1 year; (2) the willful failure to file any income tax return that the CPA, as an individual taxpayer, is required by law to file; (3) the filing of a false or fraudulent income tax return on the CPA's or client's behalf; or (4) the willful aiding in the preparation and presentation of a false and fraudulent income tax return of a client. Observe that three of these deal with income tax matters of the member or a client.

To encourage CPAs to conduct themselves professionally, the rules also prohibit advertising or solicitation that is false, misleading, or deceptive.

> **Rule 502—Advertising and Other Forms of Solicitation** A member in public practice shall not seek to obtain clients by advertising or other forms of solicitation in a manner that is false, misleading, or deceptive. Solicitation by the use of coercion, over-reaching, or harassing conduct is prohibited.

Solicitation consists of the various means that CPA firms use to engage new clients, other than accepting new clients who approach the firm. Examples include taking prospective clients to lunch to explain the CPA's services, offering seminars on current tax law changes to potential clients, and advertisements in the Yellow Pages of a phone book. The last example is advertising, which is only one form of solicitation. Advertising is the use of various media, such as magazines and radio, to communicate favorable information about the CPA firm's services.

Until 1978, advertising in any form was prohibited. Now, solicitation or advertising that is not *false or deceptive* is acceptable. This change in the rules of conduct is similar to that for other professions. Advertising is now acceptable within most professions.

The Federal Trade Commission prohibits the AICPA from restricting its membership from advertising and other forms of solicitation. The agreement discussed earlier *prohibits the AICPA from preventing* any of the following practices, as long as there are no falsehoods or deceptions:

- In-person solicitation of prospective clients
- Self-laudatory advertising
- Comparative advertising
- Testimonial or endorsement advertising
- Advertising that some members may believe is "undignified" or lacking in "good taste"
- Using trade names, such as "Suburban Tax Services"
- Offering clients a discount for referring a prospective client

Starting in the late 1970s, the federal government has pressured the AICPA to eliminate rules of conduct that restricted competition among CPA firms. Until then, the AICPA prohibited direct solicitation of clients, advertising, competitive bidding, contingent fees, commissions for obtaining client services, and referral fees. Now, all six of these activities are permitted for nonattestation clients and only the last three are prohibited for attestation services clients.

The effect of these changes has been an increased emphasis on marketing and more competitive pricing of services. Many CPA firms have developed sophisticated advertising for national journals read by business people and for local newspapers. It is common for CPA firms to identify potential clients being serviced by other CPA firms and make formal and informal presentations to convince management to change CPA firms. Price bidding for audits and other services is now common and often highly competitive. As a result of these changes, some companies now change auditors more often than previously to reduce audit cost. Most practitioners believe audits are less profitable than previously.

Has the quality of audits become endangered by these changes? The existing legal exposure of CPAs, peer review requirements, and the potential for interference by the SEC and government has kept audit quality high. In the opinion of the authors, the changes in the rules have caused greater competition in the profession, but not so much that high-quality, efficiently run CPA firms have been significantly harmed. However, for this to continue to be so, CPA firms need to be on guard so that increasing competitive pressures do not cause auditors to reduce quality below an acceptable level.

Commissions and Referral Fees

Restrictions on commissions and referral fees are similar to the rules on contingent fees. CPAs are generally prohibited from receiving commissions or referral fees for a client who is receiving attestation services from the CPA firm. Commissions and referrals are permissible for other clients, but they must be disclosed.

> **Rule 503—Commissions and Referral Fees**
>
> A. *Prohibited commissions.* A member in public practice shall not for a commission recommend or refer to a client any product or service, or for a commission recommend or refer any product or service to be supplied by a client, or receive a commission, when the member or the member's firm also performs for that client:
>   (a) an audit or review of a financial statement; or
>   (b) a compilation of a financial statement when the member expects, or reasonably might expect, that a third party will use the financial statement and the member's compilation report does not disclose a lack of independence; or
>   (c) an examination of prospective financial information.
>
> This prohibition applies during the period in which the member is engaged to perform any of the services listed above and the period covered by any historical financial statements involved in such listed services.
>
> B. *Disclosure of permitted commissions.* A member in public practice who is not prohibited by this rule from performing services for or receiving a commission and who is paid or expects to be paid a commission shall disclose that fact to any person or entity to whom the member recommends or refers a product or service to which the commission relates.
> C. *Referral fees.* Any member who accepts a referral fee for recommending or referring any service of a CPA to any person or entity or who pays a referral fee to obtain a client shall disclose such acceptance or payment to the client.

The rule for commissions and referral fees means that a CPA firm does not violate AICPA Rules of Conduct if it sells such things as real estate, securities, and entire firms on a commission basis *if the transaction does not involve a client who is receiving attestation services from the same CPA firm.* This rule enables CPA firms to profit by providing many services to nonattestation services clients that were previously prohibited.

The reason for the AICPA continuing to prohibit commissions for any attestation service client is the need to ensure that the CPA firm is independent. This requirement and the reasons for it are the same as those discussed under contingent fees.

The rationale for the AICPA's less restrictive enforcement of Rule 503 than before is the same as that discussed for contingent fees. The Federal Trade Commission contends that restrictions reduce competition and therefore are not in the public interest.

It is essential to understand that the Board of Accountancy in the state in which the firm is licensed may have more restrictive rules than the AICPA's. The CPA firm must follow the more restrictive requirements if different rules exist.

Form of Organization and Name

The organizational structure of CPA firms was first discussed in Chapter 2. The rules of conduct restrict the permissible forms of organization and prohibit a member from practicing under a firm name that is misleading.

> **Rule 505—Form of Organization and Name** A member may practice public accounting only in a form of organization permitted by state law or regulation whose characteristics conform to resolutions of Council.
>
> A member shall not practice public accounting under a firm name that is misleading. Names of one or more past owners may be included in the firm name of a successor organization. Also, an owner surviving the death or withdrawal of all other owners may continue to practice under a name which includes the name of past owners for up to two years after becoming a sole practitioner.
>
> A firm may not designate itself as "Members of the American Institute of Certified Public Accountants" unless all of its owners are members of the Institute.

Rule 505 permits practitioners to organize in any of six forms, as long as they are permitted by state law: proprietorship, general partnership, general corporation, professional corporation (PC), limited liability company (LLC), or limited liability partnership (LLP). Each of these forms of organization was discussed in Chapter 2 (pp. 26–27).

Prior to April 1994, all owners of a CPA firm had to be CPAs who were qualified to practice. Ownership of CPA firms by non-CPAs is now allowed under the following conditions:

- The CPAs must own a majority of the firm's financial interests and voting rights.
- A CPA must have ultimate responsibility for all financial statement attest, compilation, and other services provided by the firm that are governed by Statements on Auditing Standards or Statements on Standards for Accounting and Review Services.
- Owners must at all times own their equity in their own right.
- The following rules apply to all non-CPA owners:

1. They must actively provide services to the firm's clients as their principal occupation.
2. They cannot hold themselves out as CPAs but may use any title permitted by state law such as principal, owner, officer, member, or shareholder.
3. They cannot assume ultimate responsibility for any financial statement attest or compilation engagement.
4. They are not eligible for AICPA membership but must abide by the AICPA *Code of Professional Conduct.*
5. New non-CPA owners must have a bachelor's degree. Beginning in 2010, they must also meet the AICPA 150-hour education requirement.
6. They must meet the same continuing professional education requirements as AICPA members.

A recent development has been the acquisition of CPA firms by corporate entities such as American Express. In such instances, the CPA firm may form a subsidiary to provide attest services to clients. These alternative practice structures are permissible, but an AICPA Council resolution makes it clear that to protect the public interest, CPAs have the same responsibility for the conduct of their attest work as they have for traditional practice structures.

A CPA firm may use any name as long as it is not misleading. Most firms use the name of one or more of the owners. It is not unusual for a firm name to include the names of five or more owners. A CPA firm can use a trade name, although this is unusual in practice. Names such as Marshall Audit Co. or Chicago Tax Specialists are permissible if they are not misleading.

ENFORCEMENT

OBJECTIVE 4-7
Describe the enforcement mechanisms for the rules of conduct.

Failure to follow the rules of conduct can result in *expulsion* from the AICPA. This by itself would not prevent a CPA from practicing public accounting, but it would certainly be a weighty social sanction. All expulsions from the AICPA for a violation of the rules are published in the *CPA Newsletter,* a publication that is sent to all AICPA members.

In addition to the rules of conduct, the AICPA bylaws provide for automatic suspension or expulsion from the AICPA for conviction of a crime punishable by imprisonment for more than one year for various tax-related crimes.

Action by AICPA Professional Ethics Division

The AICPA Professional Ethics Division is responsible for investigating other violations of the code and deciding disciplinary action. The division's investigations result from information obtained primarily from complaints of practitioners or other individuals, state societies of CPAs, or governmental agencies.

There are two primary levels of disciplinary action. For less serious, and probably unintentional violations, the Division limits the discipline to a requirement of remedial or corrective action. An example is the unintentional failure to make sure that a small audit client included all disclosures in its financial statements, which would violate Rule 203 of the rules of conduct. The Division would likely require the member to attend a specified number of hours of continuing education courses to improve technical competence. The second level of disciplinary action is action before the Joint Trial Board. This board has authority to *suspend or expel members from the AICPA* for various violations of professional ethics. Typically, action by the board also results in publication in the *CPA Newsletter* of the name and address of the person suspended or expelled and reasons for the action.

Action by a State Board of Accountancy

Even more important than expulsion from the AICPA is the existence of rules of conduct, similar to the AICPA's, that have been enacted by the Board of Accountancy of each of the 50 states. Because each state grants the individual practitioner a license to practice as a CPA, a significant breach of a state Board of Accountancy's code of conduct can result in the *loss of the CPA certificate and the license to practice.* Although it rarely happens, the loss removes the practitioner from public accounting. Most states adopt the AICPA Rules of Conduct, but several have more restrictive codes. For example, some states have retained restrictions on advertising and other forms of solicitation. In recent years, an increasing number of states have adopted more restrictive codes of conduct than the AICPA's.

IT'S ALL A MATTER OF TRUST

Today's business environment clearly is different from that of 20 years ago. When the AICPA and most state CPA societies changed their conduct codes in the late 1970s to permit direct uninvited solicitations of clients, CPAs found themselves in a far more competitive business climate than ever before.

Public practitioners today must be particularly concerned with the efficiency and the effectiveness of their work. One can't cut corners and hope to prosper; one can't act unprofessionally and expect to survive. Maintaining skills throughout a career, exercising due professional care, following the promulgated standards for whatever kind of work is being done, and acting professionally in all endeavors are a practitioner's keys to success.

The bottom line is dedication to professional excellence. The *Code of Professional Conduct* calls for members to "observe the profession's technical and ethical standards, strive continually to improve competence and the quality of services, and discharge professional responsibility to the best of the member's ability." That's not a lofty ideal; it's what is needed to ensure public trust in the profession.

Source: Michael A. Pearson, "Doing the Right Thing," *Journal of Accountancy* (June 1995), p. 86.

SUMMARY

The demand for audit and other assurance services provided by CPA firms depends on public confidence in the profession. This chapter discussed the role of ethics in society and the unique ethical responsibilities of CPAs.

The professional activities of CPAs are governed by the AICPA *Code of Professional Conduct.* Foremost of all ethical responsibilities of CPAs is the need for independence. The rules of conduct and interpretations provide guidance on permissible financial and other interests to help CPAs maintain independence. Other rules of conduct are also designed to maintain public confidence in the profession. The ethical responsibilities of CPAs are enforced by the AICPA for members and by state boards of accountancy for licensed CPAs.

Audit committee—selected members of a client's board of directors, whose responsibilities include helping auditors to remain independent of management

Confidential client information—client information that may not be disclosed without the specific consent of the client except under authoritative professional or legal investigation

Direct financial interest—the ownership of stock or other equity shares by members or their immediate family

Ethical dilemma—a situation in which a decision must be made about the appropriate behavior

Ethics—a set of moral principles or values

Independence in appearance—the auditor's ability to maintain an unbiased viewpoint *in the eyes of others*

Independence in fact—the auditor's ability to take an unbiased viewpoint in the performance of professional services

Independence Standards Board—an autonomous private-sector body established under an agreement between the SEC and the AICPA to provide a conceptual framework for independence issues related to audits of public companies

Indirect financial interest—a close, but not direct, ownership relationship between the auditor and the client; an example is the ownership of stock by a member's grandparent

Privileged information—client information that the professional cannot be legally required to provide; information that an accountant obtains from a client is confidential but not privileged

4-1 (Objective 4-1) What are the six core ethical values described by the Josephson Institute? What are some other sources of ethical values?

4-2 (Objective 4-2) Describe an ethical dilemma. How does a person resolve an ethical dilemma?

4-3 (Objective 4-3) Why is there a special need for ethical behavior by professionals? Why do the ethical requirements of the CPA profession differ from other professions?

4-4 (Objective 4-4) List the four parts of the *Code of Professional Conduct,* and state the purpose of each.

4-5 (Objective 4-5) Distinguish between independence in fact and independence in appearance. State three activities that may not affect independence in fact but are likely to affect independence in appearance.

4-6 (Objective 4-5) Why is an auditor's independence so essential?

4-7 (Objective 4-5) Explain how the rules concerning stock ownership apply to partners and nonpartners. Give an example of when stock ownership would be prohibited for each.

4-8 (Objectives 4-5, 4-6) What is the profession's position regarding providing management advisory services for an audit client?

4-9 (Objective 4-5) Many people believe that a CPA cannot be truly independent when payment of fees is dependent on the management of the client. Explain two approaches that could reduce this appearance of lack of independence.

4-10 (Objective 4-6) After accepting an engagement, a CPA discovers that the client's industry is more technical than he realized and that he is not competent in certain areas of the operation. What are the CPA's options?

4-11 (Objective 4-6) Assume that an auditor makes an agreement with a client that the audit fee will be contingent upon the number of days required to complete the engagement. Is this a violation of the *Code of Professional Conduct?* What is the essence of the rule of professional ethics dealing with contingent fees, and what are the reasons for the rule?

4-12 (Objective 4-6) The auditor's working papers usually can be provided to someone else only with the permission of the client. Give three exceptions to this general rule.

4-13 (Objective 4-6) Identify and explain factors that should keep the quality of audits high even though advertising and competitive bidding are allowed.

4-14 (Objective 4-6) Summarize the restrictions on advertising by CPA firms in the rules of conduct and interpretations.

4-15 (Objective 4-6) What is the purpose of the AICPA's *Code of Professional Conduct* restriction on commissions as stated in Rule 503?

4-16 (Objective 4-6) State the allowable forms of organization a CPA firm may assume.

4-17 (Objective 4-7) Distinguish between the effect on a CPA firm's practice of enforcing the rules of conduct by the AICPA versus a state Board of Accountancy.

MULTIPLE CHOICE QUESTIONS FROM CPA EXAMINATIONS

4-18 (Objective 4-5) The following questions concern independence and the *Code of Professional Conduct* or GAAS. Choose the best response.

    a. What is the meaning of the generally accepted auditing standard that requires the auditor be independent?

      (1) The auditor must be without bias with respect to the client under audit.

      (2) The auditor must adopt a critical attitude during the audit.

      (3) The auditor's sole obligation is to third parties.

      (4) The auditor may have a direct ownership interest in his client's business if it is not material.

    b. The independent audit is important to readers of financial statements because it

      (1) determines the future stewardship of the management of the company whose financial statements are audited.

      (2) measures and communicates financial and business data included in financial statements.

      (3) involves the objective examination of and reporting on management-prepared statements.

      (4) reports on the accuracy of all information in the financial statements.

    c. An auditor strives to achieve independence in appearance to

      (1) maintain public confidence in the profession.

      (2) become independent in fact.

      (3) comply with the generally accepted auditing standards of field work.

      (4) maintain an unbiased mental attitude.

4-19 (Objective 4-6) The following questions concern possible violations of the AICPA *Code of Professional Conduct*. Choose the best response.

    a. In which one of the following situations would a CPA be in violation of the AICPA *Code of Professional Conduct* in determining his or her audit fee?

      (1) A fee based on whether the CPA's report on the client's financial statements results in the approval of a bank loan.

      (2) A fee based on the outcome of a bankruptcy proceeding.

      (3) A fee based on the nature of the service rendered and the CPA's expertise instead of the actual time spent on the engagement.

      (4) A fee based on the fee charged by the prior auditor.

    b. The AICPA *Code of Professional Conduct* states that a CPA shall not disclose any confidential information obtained in the course of a professional engagement except with the consent of his client. In which one of the situations given below would disclosure by a CPA be in violation of the code?

      (1) Disclosing confidential information in order to properly discharge the CPA's responsibilities in accordance with the profession's standards.

      (2) Disclosing confidential information in compliance with a subpoena issued by a court.

(3) Disclosing confidential information to another accountant interested in purchasing the CPA's practice. ✓

(4) Disclosing confidential information during an AICPA authorized peer review.

c. A CPA's retention of client records as a means of enforcing payment of an overdue audit fee is an action that is

(1) not addressed by the AICPA *Code of Professional Conduct.*

(2) acceptable if sanctioned by the state laws.

(3) prohibited under the AICPA rules of conduct. ✓

(4) a violation of generally accepted auditing standards.

DISCUSSION QUESTIONS AND PROBLEMS

4-20 (Objectives 4-5, 4-6)   Each of the following situations involves a possible violation of the AICPA's *Code of Professional Conduct.* For each situation, state the applicable section of the rules of conduct and whether it is a violation.

a. John Brown is a CPA, but not a partner, with three years of professional experience with Lyle and Lyle, CPAs, a one-office CPA firm. He owns 25 shares of stock in an audit client of the firm, but he does not take part in the audit of the client and the amount of stock is not material in relation to his total wealth.

b. In preparing the personal tax returns for a client, Phyllis Allen, CPA, observed that the deductions for contributions and interest were unusually large. When she asked the client for back-up information to support the deductions, she was told, "Ask me no questions, and I will tell you no lies." Allen completed the return on the basis of the information acquired from the client.

c. A client requests assistance of J. Bacon, CPA, in the installation of a computer system for maintaining production records. Bacon had no experience in this type of work and no knowledge of the client's production records, so he obtained assistance from a computer consultant. The consultant is not in the practice of public accounting, but Bacon is confident of his professional skills. Because of the highly technical nature of the work, Bacon is not able to review the consultant's work.

d. Five small Chicago CPA firms have become involved in an information project by taking part in an interfirm working paper review program. Under the program, each firm designates two partners to review the working papers, including the tax returns and the financial statements of another CPA firm taking part in the program. At the end of each review, the auditors who prepared the working papers and the reviewers have a conference to discuss the strengths and weaknesses of the audit. They do not obtain the authorization from the audit client before the review takes place.

e. James Thurgood, CPA, stayed longer than he should have at the annual Christmas party of Thurgood and Thurgood, CPAs. On his way home he drove through a red light and was stopped by a policeman, who observed that he was intoxicated. In a jury trial, Thurgood was found guilty of driving under the influence of alcohol. Because this was not his first offense, he was sentenced to 30 days in jail and his driver's license was revoked for 1 year.

f. Bill Wendal, CPA, set up a casualty and fire insurance agency to complement his auditing and tax services. He does not use his own name on anything pertaining to the insurance agency and has a highly competent manager, Frank Jones, who runs it. Wendal often requests Jones to review the adequacy of a client's insurance with management if it seems underinsured. He believes that he provides a valuable service to clients by informing them when they are underinsured.

g. Rankin, CPA, provides tax services, management advisory services, and bookkeeping services and conducts audits for the same client. Because the firm is small, the same person often provides all the services.

4-21 (Objectives 4-5, 4-6) Each of the following situations involves possible violations of the AICPA's *Code of Professional Conduct*. For each situation, state whether it is a violation of the code. In those cases in which it is a violation, explain the nature of the violation and the rationale for the existing rule.

   a. Ralph Williams is the partner on the audit of a nonprofit charitable organization. He is also a member of the board of directors, but this position is honorary and does not involve performing a management function.

   b. Pickens and Perkins, CPAs, are incorporated to practice public accounting. The only shareholders in the corporation are existing employees of the organization, including partners, staff members who are CPAs, staff members who are not CPAs, and administrative personnel.

   c. Fenn and Company, CPAs, has time available on a computer that it uses primarily for its own record keeping. Aware that the computer facilities of Delta Equipment Company, one of Fenn's audit clients, are inadequate for company needs, Fenn maintains on its computer certain routine accounting records for Delta.

   d. Godette, CPA, has a law practice. Godette has recommended one of his clients to Doyle, CPA. Doyle has agreed to pay Godette 10 percent of the fee for services rendered by Doyle to Godette's client.

   e. Theresa Barnes, CPA, has an audit client, Smith, Inc., which uses another CPA for management services work. Barnes sends her firm's literature covering its management services capabilities to Smith on a monthly basis, unsolicited.

   f. A bank issued a notice to its depositors that it was being audited and requested them to comply with the CPA's effort to obtain a confirmation on the deposit balances. The bank printed the name and address of the CPA in the notice. The CPA has knowledge of the notice.

   g. Myron Jones, CPA, is a member of a national CPA firm. His business card includes his name, the firm's name, address, and telephone number, and the word *consultant*.

   h. Gutowski, a practicing CPA, has written a tax article that is being published in a professional publication. The publication wishes to inform its readers about Gutowski's background. The information, which Gutowski has approved, includes his academic degrees, other articles he has had published in professional journals, and a statement that he is a tax expert.

   i. Poust, CPA, has sold his public accounting practice, which includes bookkeeping, tax services, and auditing, to Lyons, CPA. Poust obtained permission from all audit clients for audit-related working papers before making them available to Lyons. He did not get permission before releasing tax- and management services-related working papers.

   j. Murphy and Company, CPAs, is the principal auditor of the consolidated financial statements of Lowe, Inc., and subsidiaries. Lowe accounts for approximately 98 percent of consolidated assets and consolidated net income. The two subsidiaries are audited by Trotman and Company, CPAs, a firm with an excellent professional reputation. Murphy insists on auditing the two subsidiaries because he deems this necessary to warrant the expression of an opinion.*

4-22 (Objective 4-5) The New York Stock Exchange now requires all its member firms to have audit committees.

Required
   a. Describe an audit committee.
   b. What are the typical functions performed by an audit committee?
   c. Explain how an audit committee can help an auditor be more independent.
   d. Some critics of audit committees believe that they bias companies in favor of larger and perhaps more expensive CPA firms. These critics contend that a primary concern of audit committee members is to reduce their exposure to legal liability. The

*AICPA adapted.

committees will therefore recommend larger, more prestigious CPA firms, even if the cost is somewhat higher, to minimize the potential criticism of selecting an unqualified firm. Evaluate these comments.

4-23 (Objective 4-6) In recent years, there have been changes in the *Code of Professional Conduct* to permit advertising, competitive bidding, and offers of employment to employees of other firms.

Required
    a. Identify the likely effects on relations between competing CPA firms and other effects on the practice of auditing resulting from these changes.
    b. Identify the likely costs and benefits to audit clients and users of financial statements resulting from these changes.
    c. Make a subjective judgment about whether you believe that the rule changes have been beneficial or detrimental to each of the following groups:
       (1) Large CPA firms
       (2) Small CPA firms
       (3) Young professionals beginning their career with a CPA firm
       (4) Companies obtaining audits
       (5) Users of financial statements

4-24 (Objective 4-5) The following relate to auditors' independence:

Required
    a. Why is independence so essential for auditors?
    b. Compare the importance of independence of CPAs with that of other professionals, such as attorneys.
    c. Explain the difference between independence in appearance and in fact.
    d. Assume that a partner of a CPA firm owns two shares of stock of a large audit client. The ownership is an insignificant part of his total wealth.
       (1) Has he violated the *Code of Professional Conduct*?
       (2) Explain whether the ownership is likely to affect the partner's independence in fact.
       (3) Explain the reason for the strict requirements about stock ownership in the rules of conduct.
    e. Discuss how each of the following could affect independence in fact and independence in appearance, and evaluate the social consequence of prohibiting auditors from doing each one.
       (1) Ownership of stock in a client company
       (2) Having bookkeeping services for an audit client performed by the same person who does the audit
       (3) Recommending adjusting entries to the client's financial statements and preparing financial statements, including footnotes, for the client
       (4) Having management services for an audit client performed by individuals in a department that is separate from the audit department
       (5) Having the annual audit performed by the same audit team, except for assistants, for 5 years in a row
       (6) Having the annual audit performed by the same CPA firm for 10 years in a row
       (7) Having management select the CPA firm
    f. Which of (1) through (7) above are prohibited by the AICPA *Code of Professional Conduct*? Which are prohibited by the SEC?

4-25 (Objective 4-5) Marie Janes encounters the following situations in doing the audit of a large auto dealership. Janes is not a partner.

  1. The sales manager tells her that there is a sale (at a substantial discount) on new cars that is limited to long-established customers of the dealership. Because her firm has been doing the audit for several years, the sales manager has decided that Janes should also be eligible for the discount.

2. The auto dealership has an executive lunchroom that is available free to employees above a certain level. The controller informs Janes that she can also eat there any time.
3. Janes is invited to and attends the company's annual Christmas party. When presents are handed out, she is surprised to find her name included. The present has a value of approximately $200.

Required

a. Assuming Janes accepts the offer or gift in each situation, has she violated the rules of conduct?
b. Discuss what Janes should do in each situation.

CASES

4-26 (Objective 4-6) Gilbert and Bradley formed a corporation called Financial Services, Inc., each partner taking 50 percent of the authorized common stock. Gilbert is a CPA and a member of the American Institute of CPAs. Bradley is a CPCU (Chartered Property Casualty Underwriter). The corporation performs auditing and tax services under Gilbert's direction and insurance services under Bradley's supervision. The opening of the corporation's office was announced by a 3-inch, two-column "card" in the local newspaper.

One of the corporation's first audit clients was the Grandtime Company. Grandtime had total assets of $600,000 and total liabilities of $270,000. In the course of his audit, Gilbert found that Grandtime's building with a book value of $240,000 was pledged as security for a 10-year term note in the amount of $200,000. The client's statements did not mention that the building was pledged as security for the note. However, as the failure to disclose the lien did not affect either the value of the assets or the amount of the liabilities and his audit was satisfactory in all other respects, Gilbert rendered an unqualified opinion on Grandtime's financial statements. About 2 months after the date of his opinion, Gilbert learned that an insurance company was planning to loan Grandtime $150,000 in the form of a first mortgage note on the building. Realizing that the insurance company was unaware of the existing lien on the building, Gilbert had Bradley notify the insurance company of the fact that Grandtime's building was pledged as security for the term note.

Shortly after the events just described, Gilbert was charged with a violation of professional ethics.

Required

Identify and discuss the ethical implications of those acts by Gilbert that were in violation of the AICPA *Code of Professional Conduct*.*

4-27 (Objectives 4-5, 4-6) The following are situations that may violate the *Code of Professional Conduct*. Assume, in each case, that the CPA is a partner.

1. Able, CPA, owns a substantial limited partnership interest in an apartment building. Frederick Marshall is a 100 percent owner in Marshall Marine Co. Marshall also owns a substantial interest in the same limited partnership as Able. Able does the audit of Marshall Marine Co.
2. Baker, CPA, approaches a new audit client and tells the president that he has an idea that could result in a substantial tax refund in the prior year's tax return by application of a technical provision in the tax law that the client had overlooked. Baker adds that the fee will be 50 percent of the tax refund after it has been resolved by the Internal Revenue Service. The client agrees to the proposal.
3. Contel, CPA, advertises in the local paper that his firm does the audit of 14 of the 36 largest savings and loans in the city. The advertisement also states that the average audit fee, as a percentage of total assets for the savings and loans he audits, is lower than any other CPA firm's in the city.

*AICPA adapted.

4. Davis, CPA, sets up a small loan company specializing in loans to business executives and small companies. Davis does not spend much time in the business because he spends full time with his CPA practice. No employees of Davis's CPA firm are involved in the small loan company.

5. Elbert, CPA, owns a material amount of stock in a mutual fund investment company, which in turn owns stock in Elbert's largest audit client. Reading the investment company's most recent financial report, Elbert is surprised to learn that the company's ownership in his client has increased dramatically.

6. Finigan, CPA, does the audit, tax return, bookkeeping, and management services work for Gilligan Construction Company. Mildred Gilligan follows the practice of calling Finigan before she makes any major business decision to determine the effect on her company's taxes and the financial statements. Finigan attends continuing education courses in the construction industry to make sure that she is technically competent and knowledgeable about the industry. Finigan normally attends board of directors meetings and accompanies Gilligan when she is seeking loans. Mildred Gilligan often jokingly introduces Finigan with this statement, "I have my three business partners—my banker, the government, and my CPA, but Finny's the only one that is on my side."

Required

Discuss whether the facts in any of the situations indicate violations of the *Code of Professional Conduct*. If so, identify the nature of the violation(s).

4-28 (Objectives 4-2, 4-6)   Barbara Whitley had great expectations about her future as she sat in her graduation ceremony in May 1999. She was about to receive her Master of Accountancy degree, and next week she would begin her career on the audit staff of Green, Thresher & Co., CPAs.

Things looked a little different to Barbara in February 2000. She was working on the audit of Delancey Fabrics, a textile manufacturer with a calendar year-end. The pressure was enormous. Everyone on the audit team was putting in 70-hour weeks and it still looked as if the audit wouldn't be done on time. Barbara was doing work in the property area, vouching additions for the year. The audit program indicated that a sample of all items over $10,000 should be selected, plus a judgmental sample of smaller items. When Barbara went to take the sample, Jack Bean, the senior, had left the client's office and couldn't answer her questions about the appropriate size of the judgmental sample. Barbara forged ahead with her own judgment and selected 50 smaller items. Her basis for doing this was that there were about 250 such items, so 50 was a reasonably good proportion of such additions.

Barbara audited the additions with the following results: the items over $10,000 contained no misstatements; however, the 50 small items contained a large number of misstatements. In fact, when Barbara projected them to all such additions, the amount seemed quite significant.

A couple of days later, Jack Bean returned to the client's office. Barbara brought her work to Jack in order to apprise him of the problems she found, and got the following response:

> "My God, Barbara, why did you do this? You were only supposed to look at the items over $10,000 plus 5 or 10 little ones. You've wasted a whole day on that work, and we can't afford to spend any more time on it. I want you to throw away the schedules where you tested the last 40 small items and forget you ever did them."

When Barbara asked about the possible audit adjustment regarding the small items, none of which arose from the first 10 items, Jack responded, "Don't worry, it's not material anyway. You just forget it; it's my concern, not yours."

Required

   a. In what way is this an ethical dilemma for Barbara?
   b. Use the six-step approach discussed in the book to resolve the ethical dilemma.

4-29 (Objectives 4-1, 4-2, 4-3)   In 1995, Arnold Diaz was a bright, upcoming audit manager in the South Florida office of a national public accounting firm. He was an excellent technician and a good "people person." Arnold also was able to bring new business into the firm as the result of his contacts in the rapidly growing Hispanic business community.

Arnold was assigned a new client in 1996, XYZ Securities, Inc., a privately held broker–dealer in the secondary market for U.S. government securities. Neither Arnold nor anyone else in the South Florida office had broker–dealer audit experience. However, the AICPA and Arnold's firm had audit aids for the industry, which Arnold used to get started.

Arnold was promoted to partner in 1996. Although this was a great step forward for him (he was a new staff assistant in 1987), Arnold was also under a great deal of pressure. Upon making partner, he was required to contribute capital to the firm. He also thought he must maintain a special image with his firm, with his clients, and within the Hispanic community. To accomplish this, Arnold maintained an impressive wardrobe, bought a Lexus and a small speedboat, and traded up to a nicer house. He also entertained freely. Arnold financed much of this higher living with credit cards. He had six American Express and banking cards and ran up a balance of about $40,000.

After the audit was completed and before the 1997 audit was to begin, Arnold contacted Jack Oakes, the CFO of XYZ Securities, with a question. Arnold had noticed an anomaly in the financial statements that he couldn't understand and asked Oakes for an explanation. Oakes's reply was as follows:

> "Arnold, the 1996 financial statements were materially misstated and you guys just blew it. I thought you might realize this and call me, so here's my advice to you. Keep your mouth shut. We'll make up the loss we covered up last year, this year, and nobody will ever know the difference. If you blow the whistle on us, your firm will know you screwed up, and your career as the star in the office will be down the tubes."

Arnold said he'd think about this and get back to Oakes the next day. When Arnold called Oakes, he had decided to go along with him. After all, it would only be a "shift" of a loss between two adjacent years. XYZ is a private company and no one would be hurt or know the difference. In reality, only he was the person exposed to any harm in this situation, and he had to protect himself, didn't he?

When Arnold went to XYZ to plan for the 1997 audit, he asked Oakes how things were going and Oakes assured him they were fine. He then said to Oakes,

> "Jack, you guys are in the money business, maybe you can give me some advice. I've run up some debts and I need to refinance them. How should I go about it?"

After some discussions, Oakes volunteered a "plan." Oakes would give Arnold a check for $15,000. XYZ would request its bank to put $60,000 in an account in Arnold's name and guarantee the loan security on it. Arnold would pay back the $15,000 and have $45,000 of refinancing. Arnold thought the plan was great and obtained Oakes's check for $15,000.

During 1997 through 1999, three things happened. First, Arnold incurred more debts, and went back to the well at XYZ. By the end of 1999, he had "borrowed" a total of $125,000. Second, the company continued to lose money in various "off-the-books" investment schemes. These losses were covered up by falsifying the results of normal operations. Third, the audit team, under Arnold's leadership, "failed to find" the fraud and issued unqualified opinions.

In 1998, Oakes had a tax audit of his personal 1997 return. He asked Arnold's firm to handle it, and the job was assigned to Bob Smith, a tax manager. In reviewing Oakes's records, Smith found a $15,000 check payable from Oakes to Diaz. Smith asked to see Diaz and inquired about the check. Arnold somewhat broke down and confided in Smith about his problems. Smith responded by saying,

> "Don't worry Arnold, I understand. And believe me, I'll never tell a soul."

In 2000, XYZ's continuing losses caused it to be unable to deliver nonexistent securities when requested by a customer. This led to an investigation and bankruptcy by XYZ.

Losses totaled in the millions. Arnold's firm was held liable, and Arnold was found guilty of conspiracy to defraud. He is still in prison today.

Required

a. Try to put yourself in Arnold's shoes. What would you have done (be honest with yourself now) when told of the material misstatement in mid-1997?
b. What do you think of Bob Smith's actions to help Arnold?
c. Where does one draw the line between ethical and unethical behavior?

4-30 (Objective 4-2) Frank Dorrance, a senior audit manager for Bright and Lorren, CPAs, has recently been informed that the firm plans to promote him to partner within the next year or two if he continues to perform at the same high-quality level as in the past. Frank excels at dealing effectively with all people, including client personnel, professional staff, partners, and potential clients. He has recently built a bigger home for entertaining and has joined the city's most prestigious golf and tennis club. He is excited about his future with the firm.

Frank has recently been assigned to the audit of Machine International, a large wholesale company that ships goods throughout the world. It is one of Bright and Lorren's most prestigious clients. During the audit, Frank determines that Machine International uses a method of revenue recognition called "bill and hold" that has recently been questioned by the SEC. After considerable research, Frank concludes that the method of revenue recognition is not appropriate for Machine International. In discussing the matter with the engagement partner, she concludes that the accounting method has been used for more than 10 years by the client and is appropriate, especially considering that the client does not file with the SEC. The partner is certain the firm would lose the client if the revenue recognition method is found inappropriate. Frank argues that the revenue recognition method was appropriate in prior years, but the SEC ruling makes it inappropriate in the current year. Frank recognizes the partner's responsibility to make the final decision, but he feels strongly enough to state that he plans to follow the requirements of SAS 22 (AU 311) and include a statement in the working papers that he disagrees with the partner's decision. The partner informs Frank that she is unwilling to permit such a statement because of the potential legal implications. However, she is willing to write a letter to Frank stating that she takes full responsibility for making the final decision if a legal dispute ever arises. She concludes by saying, "Frank, partners must act like partners, not like loose cannons trying to make life difficult for their partners. You have some growing up to do before I would feel comfortable with you as a partner."

Required

Use the six-step approach discussed in the book to resolve the ethical dilemma.

INTERNET PROBLEM 4-1: AICPA *CODE OF PROFESSIONAL CONDUCT*—ETHICS RULINGS AND CASE

Reference the CW site. Imagine a CPA has provided extensive advisory services for a client. In that connection, the member has attended board meetings; interpreted financial statements, forecasts, and other analyses; counseled on potential expansion plans; and counseled on banking relationships. Would the independence of the member be considered to be impaired under these circumstances? The answer to many such questions can be found in Ethics Rulings associated with the AICPA *Code of Professional Conduct*. This problem requires students to use the Internet to (1) research ethics rulings in the *Code* and (2) answer questions and cases associated with another CPA ethics site.

LEGAL LIABILITY

5

IT TAKES THE NET PROFIT FROM MANY AUDITS TO OFFSET THE COST OF ONE LAWSUIT

Orange & Rankle, a CPA firm in San Jose, audited a small high-tech client that developed software. A significant portion of the client's capital was provided by a syndicate of 40 limited partners. The owners of these interests were knowledgeable business and professional people, including several lawyers.

Orange & Rankle audited the company for 4 consecutive years, from its inception, for an average annual fee of approximately $13,000. The audits were well done by competent auditors. It was clear to the firm and to others who subsequently reviewed the audits that they complied with generally accepted auditing standards in every way.

In the middle of the fifth year of the company's existence, it became apparent that the marketing plan it had developed was overly optimistic and the company was going to require additional capital or make a significant strategy change. The limited partners were polled and refused to provide the capital. The company folded its tent and filed bankruptcy. The limited partners lost their investment in the company. They subsequently filed a lawsuit against all parties involved in the enterprise, including the auditors.

Over the next several years, the auditors proceeded through the process of preparing to defend themselves in the lawsuit. They went through complete discovery, hired an expert witness on auditing-related issues, filed motions, and so forth. They attempted a settlement at various times, but the plaintiffs would not agree to a reasonable amount. Finally, during the second day of trial, the plaintiffs settled for a nominal amount.

It was clear that the plaintiffs knew the auditors bore no fault but kept them in the suit anyway. The total *out-of-pocket* cost to the audit firm was $1 million, not to mention personnel time, possible damage to their reputation, and general stress and strain. Thus, the cost of this suit, in which the auditors were completely innocent, was more than 75 times the average annual audit fee earned from this client.

LEARNING OBJECTIVES

After studying this chapter, you should be able to

5-1 Understand the litigious environment in which CPAs practice.

5-2 Explain why the failure of financial statement users to differentiate among business failure, audit failure, and audit risk has resulted in lawsuits.

5-3 Use the primary legal concepts and terms concerning accountants' liability as a basis for studying legal liability of auditors.

5-4 Describe accountants' liability to clients and related defenses.

5-5 Describe accountants' liability to third parties under common law and related defenses.

5-6 Describe accountants' civil liability under the federal securities laws and related defenses.

5-7 Specify what constitutes criminal liability for accountants.

5-8 Describe what the profession and the individual CPA can do and what is being done to reduce the threat of litigation.

This chapter on legal liability and the preceding chapter on professional ethics highlight the environment in which CPAs operate. We focus on these chapters now to provide an overview of the importance of protecting the profession's reputation as being one that is viewed as highly ethical and to highlight consequences accountants face when others believe they have failed to live up to that ethical standard. Legal liability and its consequences for the profession are serious. This chapter highlights ways CPAs can be held liable for the professional services they provide.

As the auditors at Orange & Rankle in the opening vignette learned the hard way, legal liability and its consequences are significant for CPAs. It is estimated that the profession's aggregate liability exposure exceeds $30 billion. Although firms have insurance to help alleviate the impact of assessed damages, the premiums are high and the policies available to the firms have large deductible amounts. The deductibles are such that the large firms are essentially self-insured for losses of many millions of dollars.

Legal liability can have serious consequences. One large national accounting firm, Laventhol & Horwath, filed for bankruptcy because of a large number of malpractice suits with large damage amounts facing the firm. Another large national firm, Panell Kerr Forster, closed or sold about 90 percent of its offices and reorganized its remaining offices as individual professional corporations partially because of litigation it faced.

Accountants' liability also affects the profession in human terms. For example, a study completed in 1994 indicated that of partners and managers leaving the six largest auditing firms in recent years, 29 percent were influenced by the threat of litigation, and 46 percent were influenced by the effect of ongoing litigation costs on future profits.

This chapter focuses on legal liability for CPAs both on a conceptual level and in terms of specific legal suits that have been filed against CPAs. It also highlights actions available to the profession and individual practitioners to minimize liability while still meeting society's needs.

CHANGED LEGAL ENVIRONMENT

OBJECTIVE 5-1
Understand the litigious environment in which CPAs practice.

Professionals have always had a duty to provide a reasonable level of care while performing work for those they serve. Audit professionals have a responsibility under common law to fulfill implied or expressed contracts with clients. They are liable to their clients for negligence and/or breach of contract should they fail to provide the services or not exercise due care in their performance. Auditors may also be held liable under common law in certain circumstances to parties other than their clients. Although the criteria for legal actions against auditors by third parties vary by state, the most common view is that the auditor owes a duty of care to third parties who are part of a limited group of persons whose reliance is "foreseen" by the auditor. Some states, including New York, take a more restrictive view of when auditors may be liable to third parties. A few states take a far broader view, extending the duty of due care to all persons whose reliance was "foreseeable." In addition to common law, auditors may be held liable to third parties under statutory law. Both the Securities Act of 1933 and the Securities Exchange Act of 1934 contain sections that serve as a basis for actions against auditors. Finally, in rare cases auditors have also been held liable for criminal acts. A criminal conviction against an auditor can result when it is demonstrated that the auditor intended to deceive or harm others.

Despite efforts to address legal liability of CPAs, both the number of lawsuits and size of awards to plaintiffs remain high, including suits involving third parties under both common law and the federal securities acts. There are no simple reasons for this trend, but the following are major factors:

- There is growing awareness of the responsibilities of public accountants by users of financial statements.
- There is an increased consciousness on the part of the Securities and Exchange Commission (SEC) regarding its responsibility for protecting investors' interests.

Stanford's Securities
Class Action
Clearinghouse

- Auditing and accounting are more complex because of factors such as the increasing size of business, the globalization of business, and the intricacies of business operations.
- Society accepts lawsuits by injured parties against anyone who might be able to provide compensation, regardless of who was at fault, coupled with the joint and several liability doctrine. This is often called the *deep-pocket* concept of liability.
- Large civil court judgments against CPA firms have been awarded in a few cases, which has encouraged attorneys to provide legal services on a contingent-fee basis. This arrangement offers the injured party a potential gain when the suit is successful, but minimal loss when it is unsuccessful.
- Many CPA firms are willing to settle their legal problems out of court in an attempt to avoid costly legal fees and adverse publicity rather than resolving them through the judicial process.
- Courts have difficulty in understanding and interpreting technical accounting and auditing matters.

AICPA's Assurance
Service Liability

Litigation costs for accountants and others caused great concern in Congress and in society in general during the last several years. It was recognized that all members of society bear these costs. As a result, legislation was introduced to attempt to control litigation costs, both by discouraging nonmeritorious lawsuits and by bringing damages more in line with relative fault. In December 1995, a law was passed bringing significant relief to accountants in the area of federal securities litigation and laws providing relief at the state level were signed into effect in November 1998. Nevertheless, accountants' liability is still onerous and a major consideration in the conduct of a CPA firm's professional practice.

DISTINCTION AMONG BUSINESS FAILURE, AUDIT FAILURE, AND AUDIT RISK

Many accounting and legal professionals believe that a major cause of lawsuits against CPA firms is the lack of understanding by financial statement users of the difference between a business failure and an audit failure and between an audit failure and audit risk. We will now examine these terms and the ways in which not understanding them can lead to lawsuits against auditors.

> **OBJECTIVE 5-2**
> Explain why the failure of financial statement users to differentiate among business failure, audit failure, and audit risk has resulted in lawsuits.

A **business failure** occurs when a business is unable to repay its lenders or meet the expectations of its investors because of economic or business conditions, such as a recession, poor management decisions, or unexpected competition in the industry. The extreme case of business failure is filing for bankruptcy. **Audit failure** occurs when the auditor issues an erroneous audit opinion as the result of an underlying failure to comply with the requirements of generally accepted auditing standards (GAAS). An example is assigning unqualified assistants to perform audit tasks who then fail to find material misstatements that qualified auditors would discover. **Audit risk** represents the risk that the auditor will conclude that the financial statements are fairly stated and an unqualified opinion can be issued when, in fact, they are materially misstated. Because auditors are able to gather evidence only on a test basis and detecting well-concealed frauds can be extremely difficult, there is always some risk that the auditor will not uncover a material fraud even though the auditor complied with GAAS.

Most accounting professionals agree that in most cases when an audit has failed to uncover material misstatements and the wrong type of audit opinion is issued, a legitimate question may be raised whether the auditor exercised due care. If the auditor failed to use due care in the conduct of the audit, there is an audit failure. In such cases, the law often allows parties who suffered losses as a result of the auditor's breach of a duty of care owed to them to recover some or all of the losses proximately caused by the audit failure. It is difficult in practice to determine when the auditor has failed to use due care because of the complexity of auditing. It is also difficult to determine who has a right to expect the benefits of an audit because of legal traditions. Nevertheless, an auditor's failure to follow due care often may be expected to result in liability and, when appropriate, damages against the CPA firm.

As highlighted by the lawsuit against Orange & Rankle in the opening vignette, the difficulty arises when there has been a business failure, but not an audit failure. For example, when a company goes bankrupt or cannot pay its debts, it is common for statement users to claim that there was an audit failure, especially when the most recently issued auditor's opinion indicates that the financial statements were fairly stated. Even worse, if there is a business failure and the financial statements are later determined to have been misstated, users may claim that the auditor was negligent even if the audit was conducted in accordance with GAAS. This conflict between statement users and auditors often arises because of what is called the *expectation gap* between users and auditors. Most auditors believe that the conduct of the audit in accordance with GAAS is all that can be expected of auditors. Many users believe that auditors guarantee the accuracy of financial statements, and some users even believe that the auditor guarantees the financial viability of the business. Fortunately for the profession, courts continue to support the auditor's view. Unfortunately, the expectation gap often results in unwarranted lawsuits. Perhaps the profession has a responsibility to educate statement users about the role of auditors and the difference between business failure, audit failure, and audit risk. Realistically, however, auditors must recognize that, in part, the claims of audit failure may also result from the hope of those who suffer a business loss to recover from any source, regardless of who is at fault.

LEGAL CONCEPTS AFFECTING LIABILITY

OBJECTIVE 5-3
Use the primary legal concepts and terms concerning accountants' liability as a basis for studying legal liability of auditors.

The CPA is responsible for every aspect of his or her public accounting work, including auditing, taxes, management advisory services, and accounting and bookkeeping services. For example, if a CPA negligently failed to properly prepare and file a client's tax return, the CPA can be held liable for any penalties and interest that the client was required to pay plus the tax preparation fee charged. In some states, the court can also assess punitive damages.

Most of the major lawsuits against CPA firms have dealt with audited or unaudited financial statements. The discussion in this chapter is restricted primarily to those two aspects of public accounting. Several legal concepts apply to lawsuits against CPAs. These are the prudent person concept, liability for the acts of others, and the lack of privileged communication.

Prudent Person Concept

There is agreement within the profession and the courts that the auditor is not a guarantor or insurer of financial statements. The auditor is expected only to conduct the audit with due care. Even then, the auditor cannot be expected to be perfect.

The standard of due care to which the auditor is expected to be held is often called the **prudent person concept.** It is expressed in *Cooley on Torts* as follows:

- Every man who offers his service to another and is employed assumes the duty to exercise in the employment such skill as he possesses with reasonable care and diligence. In all these employments where peculiar skill is prerequisite, if one offers his service, he is understood as holding himself out to the public as possessing the degree of skill commonly possessed by others in the same employment, and, if his pretentions are unfounded, he commits a species of fraud upon every man who employs him in reliance on his public profession. But no man, whether skilled or unskilled, undertakes that the task he assumes shall be performed successfully, and without fault or error. *He undertakes for good faith and integrity, but not for infallibility,* and he is liable to his employer for negligence, bad faith, or dishonesty, but not for losses consequent upon pure errors of judgment.

Liability for the Acts of Others

Generally, the partners, or shareholders in the case of a professional corporation, are jointly liable for the civil actions against any owner. However, if the firm operates as a limited liability partnership (LLP), a limited liability company (LLC), a general corporation, or a professional corporation with limited liability, the liability for one owner's actions does not extend to another owner's *personal* assets, unless the other owner was directly involved in the actions of the owner causing the liability. Of course, the firm's assets are all subject to the damages that arise.

The partners may also be liable for the work of others on whom they rely under the laws of agency. The three groups an auditor is most likely to rely on are *employees, other CPA firms* engaged to do part of the work, and *specialists* called upon to provide technical information. For example, if an employee performs improperly in doing an audit, the partners can be held liable for the employee's performance.

CPAs do not have the right under common law to withhold information from the courts on the grounds that the information is privileged. As stated in Chapter 4, information in an auditor's working papers can be subpoenaed by a court. Confidential discussions between the client and auditor cannot be withheld from the courts.

Lack of Privileged Communication

A number of states have statutes that permit privileged communication between the client and auditor. Even then, the intent at the time of the communication must have been for the communication to remain confidential. A CPA can refuse to testify in a state with privileged communications statutes. The privilege does not extend to federal courts.

The material in the rest of the chapter can be covered more effectively if the most common legal terms affecting CPAs' liability are understood. Table 5-1 (p. 116) defines many of the terms that will be used throughout the remainder of this chapter.

The distinction between joint and several liability and separate and proportionate liability, which are both defined in Table 5-1, is an extremely significant one, as the amounts will vary greatly between these two bases for assessing damages. Generally, these damage approaches apply in cases of liability to third parties under common law and under the federal securities laws. When lawsuits are filed in state court, the state laws will determine which approach to damages applies. When lawsuits are brought under the federal securities laws, the separate and proportionate approach will apply except where it can be shown that the CPA defendant has actual knowledge of fraud or has participated in fraud, in which case joint and several liability would apply. It should be noted that under the federal statutes, the amount of damages under separate and proportionate liability can be increased to 150 percent of the amount determined to be proportionate to the CPA's degree of fault, where the main defendant is insolvent.

The main focus of this chapter is on the four sources of auditor's **legal liability.** These four areas of liability are classified as (1) liability to clients, (2) liability to third parties under common law, (3) liability to third parties under the federal securities laws, and (4) criminal liability. Figure 5-1 provides examples of each of these classifications of liability. Next, each of these liability classifications is examined in more detail.

FIGURE 5-1   Four Major Sources of Auditors' Legal Liability

Source of Liability	Example of Potential Claim
Client—liability to client under common law	Client sues auditor for not discovering a material fraud during the audit.
Third party—liability to third parties under common law	Bank sues auditor for not discovering that a borrower's financial statements are partially misstated.
Liability under federal securities laws	Combined group of stockholders sues auditor for not discovering materially misstated financialstatements.
Criminal liability	Federal government prosecutes auditor for knowingly issuing an incorrect audit report.

LIABILITY TO CLIENTS

The most common source of lawsuits against CPAs is from clients. The suits vary widely, including such claims as failure to complete a nonaudit engagement on the agreed-upon date, inappropriate withdrawal from an audit, failure to discover a defalcation (theft of assets),

OBJECTIVE 5-4
Describe accountants' liability to clients and related defenses.

[handwritten: ★ Know terms]

| TABLE 5-1 | Legal Terms Affecting CPAs' Liability |

Legal Term	Description
Terms Related to Negligence and Fraud	
Ordinary Negligence	Absence of reasonable care that can be expected of a person in a set of circumstances. For auditors, it is in terms of what other competent auditors would have done in the same situation.
Gross Negligence	Lack of even slight care, tantamount to reckless behavior, that can be expected of a person. Some states do not distinguish between ordinary and gross negligence.
Constructive Fraud *[handwritten: — like gross neg., but NO intent to deceive]*	Existence of extreme or unusual negligence even though there was no intent to deceive or do harm. Constructive fraud is also termed *recklessness.* Recklessness in the case of an audit would be present if the auditor knew he or she had not done an adequate audit but still issued an opinion, even though he or she had no intention of deceiving statement users.
Fraud	Occurs when a misstatement is made and there is both the knowledge of its falsity and the intent to deceive.
Terms Related to Contract Law	
Breach of Contract	Failure of one or both parties in a contract to fulfill the requirements of the contract. An example is the failure of a CPA firm to deliver a tax return on the agreed-upon date. Parties who have a relationship that is established by a contract are said to have *privity of contract.*
Third-Party Beneficiary	A third party who does not have privity of contract but is known to the contracting parties and is intended to have certain rights and benefits under the contract. A common example is a bank that has a large loan outstanding at the balance sheet date and requires an audit as a part of its loan agreement. *[handwritten: John Q Public]*
Other Terms	
Common Law	Laws that have been developed through court decisions rather than through government statutes.
Statutory Law	Laws that have been passed by the U.S. Congress and other governmental units. The securities acts of 1933 and 1934 are important statutory laws affecting auditors.
Joint and Several Liability	The assessment against a defendant of the full loss suffered by a plaintiff, regardless of the extent to which other parties shared in the wrongdoing. For example, if management intentionally mis states financial statements, an auditor can be assessed the entire loss to shareholders if the company is bankrupt and management is unable to pay.
Separate and Proportionate Liability *[handwritten: Now CPA's ↑ have to prove guilt]*	The assessment against a defendant of that portion of the damage caused by the defendant's negligence. For example, if the courts determine that an auditor's negligence in conducting an audit was the cause of 30 percent of a loss to a defendant, only 30 percent of the aggregate damage would be assessed to the CPA firm.

and breaching the confidentiality requirements of CPAs. Typically, the amount of these lawsuits is relatively small, and they do not receive the publicity often given to other types of suits. The *Fund of Funds* case, in which the court awarded the company $80 million in a suit against a CPA firm for breach of confidentiality requirements, is a notable exception.

A typical lawsuit involves a claim that the auditor did not discover an employee defalcation as a result of negligence in the conduct of the audit. The lawsuit can be for breach of contract, a tort action for negligence, or both. Tort actions can be based on ordinary negligence, gross negligence, or fraud. Tort actions are common because the amounts recoverable under them are normally larger than under breach of contract.

The principal issue in cases involving alleged negligence is usually the level of care required. Although it is generally agreed that nobody is perfect, not even a professional, in most instances, any significant error or mistake in judgment will create at least a presumption of negligence that the professional will have to rebut. In the auditing environment, failure to meet GAAS is often conclusive evidence of negligence. A typical example of an audit case raising the question of negligent performance by a CPA firm is the case of *Cenco*

Incorporated v. *Seidman & Seidman*. The case, which is described in more detail in Figure 5-2, involved alleged negligence by the auditor in failing to find a fraud. In the legal suit by Cenco's new management, the auditor was able to successfully argue that it was not negligent and that the deceitful actions on the part of the old management team prevented the auditor from uncovering the fraud. The reader should remember from the study of GAAS in Chapter 2 that determining whether there is a violation is highly subjective.

The question of level of care becomes more difficult in the environment of an unaudited review or compilation of financial statements in which there are fewer accepted standards to evaluate performance. A widely known example of a lawsuit dealing with the failure to uncover fraud in unaudited financial statements is described in Figure 5-3 (p. 118). Although the CPA was never engaged to conduct an audit for the 1136 Tenants Corporation, the CPA was found liable for failing to detect an embezzlement scheme conducted by one of the client's managers. One of the reasons for this outcome was the lack of a clear understanding between the client and the CPA as to the exact nature of the services to be performed by the CPA. As noted in Figure 5-3, *engagement letters* between the client and the CPA firm developed as a result of this case. Now, CPA firms and clients typically sign engagement letters to formalize their agreements about the services to be provided, fees, and timing. There can be *privity of contract* (recall that was defined in Table 5-1) without a written agreement, but an engagement letter defines the contract more clearly.

The CPA firm normally uses one or a combination of four defenses when there are legal claims by clients: lack of duty to perform the service, nonnegligent performance, contributory negligence, and absence of causal connection.

Auditor's Defenses against Client Suits

Lack of Duty The **lack of duty to perform** the service means that the CPA firm claims that there was no implied or expressed contract. For example, the CPA firm might claim that misstatements were not uncovered because the firm did a review service, not an audit. A common way for a CPA firm to demonstrate a lack of duty to perform is by use of an engagement letter. Many litigation experts believe that a well-written engagement letter is one of the most important ways in which CPA firms can reduce the likelihood of adverse legal actions.

Nonnegligent Performance For **nonnegligent performance** in an audit, the CPA firm claims that the audit was performed in accordance with GAAS. Even if there were undiscovered misstatements, the auditor is not responsible if the audit was conducted properly.

FIGURE 5-2   *Cenco Incorporated* v. *Seidman & Seidman* (1982)—Liability to Clients

Between 1970 and 1975 Cenco's managerial employees, ultimately including top management, were involved in a massive fraud to inflate the value of the company's inventory. This in turn enabled the company to borrow money at a lower interest rate and to obtain higher fire insurance settlements than were proper. After the fraud was discovered by an employee of Cenco and reported to the SEC, a class action suit was filed by stockholders against Cenco, its management, and its auditors. The CPA firm settled out of court on the class action suit by paying $3.5 million.

By now, new management was operating Cenco. They brought a second suit against the CPA firm on behalf of Cenco for breach of contract, professional negligence, and fraud. The primary defense used by the CPA firm was that a diligent attempt was made on the part of the auditors to follow up any indications of fraud, but the combined efforts of a large number of Cenco's management prevented them from uncovering the fraud. The CPA firm argued that the wrongdoings of management were a valid defense against the charges.

The Seventh Circuit Court of Appeals concluded that the CPA firm was not responsible in this case. The wrongdoings of Cenco's management were considered an appropriate defense against the charges of breach of contract, negligence, and fraud, even though the management no longer worked for the company. Considering management's involvement, the CPA firm was not considered negligent.

know →
about
unaudited
financial
statements

FIGURE 5-3 1136 Tenants v. Max Rothenberg and Company (1967)—Liability to Clients

The *1136 Tenants* case was a civil case concerning a CPA's failure to uncover fraud as a part of unaudited financial statements. The tenants recovered approximately $235,000.

A CPA firm was engaged by a real estate management agent for $600 per year to prepare financial statements, a tax return, and a schedule showing the apportionment of real estate taxes for the 1136 Tenants Corporation, a cooperative apartment house. The statements were sent periodically to the tenants. The statements included the words *unaudited,* and there was a cover letter stating that "The statement was prepared from the books and records of the cooperative and no independent verifications were taken thereon."

During the period of the engagement, from 1963 to 1965, the manager of the management firm embezzled significant funds from the tenants of the cooperative. The tenants sued the CPA firm for negligence and breach of contract for failure to find the fraud.

There were two central issues in the case. Was the CPA firm engaged to do an audit instead of only write-up work, and was there negligence on the part of the CPA firm? The court answered yes on both counts. The reasoning for the court's conclusion that an audit had taken place was the performance of "some audit procedures" by the CPA firm, including the preparation of a worksheet entitled "missing invoices." Had the CPA followed up on these, the fraud would likely have been uncovered. Most important, the court concluded that even if the engagement had not been considered an audit, the CPA had a duty to follow up on any potential significant exceptions uncovered during an engagement.

Two developments resulted from the *1136 Tenants* case and similar lawsuits concerning unaudited financial statements:

- Engagement letters between the client and CPA firm have been strongly recommended by the AICPA for all engagements, but especially for unaudited engagements. The letter should clearly define the intent of the engagement, the CPA's responsibilities, and any restrictions imposed on the CPA.
- The Accounting and Review Services Committee was formed as a major committee of the AICPA to set forth guidelines for unaudited financial statements of nonpublic companies. They issued their first pronouncement in 1979. The Auditing Standards Board has eliminated all references to unaudited statements for nonpublic companies in SASs, to avoid confusion between audited and unaudited engagements.

spell it out →

SSARS (private companies)
(public companies-SAS71)

The prudent person concept discussed earlier establishes in law that the CPA firm is not expected to be infallible. Similarly, SAS 47 (AU 312) and SAS 82 (AU 312) make it clear that an audit in accordance with GAAS is subject to limitations and cannot be relied on for complete assurance that all misstatements will be found. Requiring auditors to discover all material misstatements would, in essence, make them insurers or guarantors of the accuracy of the financial statements. The courts do not require that.

Contributory Negligence A defense of **contributory negligence** exists when the client's own actions either resulted in the loss that is the basis for damages or interfered with the conduct of the audit in such a way that prevented the auditor from discovering the cause of the loss. As an example of the first circumstance, suppose a client claims that a CPA firm was negligent in not uncovering an employee's theft of cash. If the CPA firm had notified the client (preferably in writing) of a weakness in internal control that would have prevented the theft but management did not correct it, the CPA firm would have a defense of contributory negligence. As an example of the second circumstance, suppose a CPA firm failed to determine that certain accounts receivable were uncollectible and, in reviewing collectibility, were lied to and given false documents by the credit manager. In this circumstance, assuming the audit of accounts receivable was done in accordance with GAAS, a defense of contributory negligence would exist.

Absence of Causal Connection To succeed in an action against the auditor, the client must be able to show that there is a close causal connection between the auditor's breach of the standard of due care and the damages suffered by the client. For example, assume that an auditor failed to complete an audit on the agreed-upon date. The client alleges that this caused a bank not to renew an outstanding loan, which caused damages. A potential auditor defense is that the bank refused to renew the loan for other reasons, such as the weakening financial condition of the client. This defense is called an **absence of causal connection**.

LIABILITY TO THIRD PARTIES UNDER COMMON LAW

In addition to being sued by clients under common law, CPAs may be liable to third parties under common law. Third parties include actual and potential stockholders, vendors, bankers and other creditors, employees, and customers. A CPA firm may be liable to third parties if a loss was incurred by the claimant due to reliance on misleading financial statements. A typical suit might occur when a bank is unable to collect a major loan from an insolvent customer. The bank can claim that misleading audited financial statements were relied on in making the loan and that the CPA firm should be held responsible because it failed to perform the audit with due care.

OBJECTIVE 5-5
Describe accountants' liability to third parties under common law and related defenses.

The leading precedent-setting auditing case in third-party liability is a 1931 case, *Ultramares Corporation* v. *Touche*. It established the traditional common law approach known as the *Ultramares doctrine.* Take a look at the case, which is summarized in Figure 5-4.

Ultramares Doctrine

FIGURE 5-4	***Ultramares Corporation* v. *Touche* (1931)—Liability to Third Parties**

The creditors of an insolvent corporation (Ultramares) relied on the audited financials and subsequently sued the accountants, alleging that they were guilty of negligence and fraudulent misrepresentation. The accounts receivable had been falsified by adding to approximately $650,000 in accounts receivable another item of over $700,000. The creditors alleged that careful investigation would have shown the $700,000 to be fraudulent. The accounts payable contained similar discrepancies.

The court held that the accountants had been negligent but ruled that accountants would not be liable to third parties for honest blunders beyond the bounds of the original contract unless they were primary beneficiaries. The court held that only one who enters into a contract with an accountant for services can sue if those services are rendered negligently.

In this case, the court held that although the accountants were negligent, they were not liable to the creditors because the creditors were not deemed to be *primary beneficiaries.* In this context, a primary beneficiary is one about whom the auditor was informed before conducting the audit (a *known third party*). The key aspect of the *Ultramares* case was that the creditors lacked *privity of contract* with the auditor. This case established a precedent, commonly called the *Ultramares* doctrine, that ordinary negligence is insufficient for liability to third parties because of the lack of *privity of contract* between the third party and the auditor, unless the third party is a *primary beneficiary.* However, in a subsequent trial of the *Ultramares* case, the court pointed out that had there been fraud or gross negligence on the part of the auditor, the auditor could be held liable to more general third parties.

In recent years, many courts have broadened the *Ultramares* doctrine to allow recovery by third parties in more circumstances than previously by introducing the concept of foreseen users. Generally, a **foreseen user** is a member of a limited class of users whom the auditor is aware will rely on the financial statements. For example, a bank that has loans outstanding to a client at the balance sheet date may be a foreseen user. Under this concept, a foreseen user would be treated the same as a known third party.

Foreseen Users

Although the concept of foreseen users may seem straightforward, its application is not and has developed differently in different jurisdictions. At present, three approaches have emerged: the *Credit Alliance* approach, the *Restatement of Torts* approach, and the *Foreseeable User* approach.

Credit Alliance *Credit Alliance* v. *Arthur Andersen & Co.* (1986) was a case in New York in which a lender brought suit against the auditor of one of its borrowers, alleging that it relied on the financial statements of the borrower, who was in default, in granting the loan. The New York State Court of Appeals reversed a lower court's decision that prevented the defendant auditor from using absence of privity as a defense. In so doing, the appellate court upheld the basic concept of privity established by *Ultramares,* and stated that to be liable (1) an auditor must know and intend that his or her work product would be used by the plaintiff third party for a specific purpose, and (2) the knowledge and intent must be evidenced by the auditor's conduct. At present, 11 states (Arkansas, California, Idaho, Illinois, Kansas, Montana, Nebraska, New Jersey, New York, Pennsylvania, and Utah) follow some variation of this approach.

Restatement of Torts The approach followed by most states is to apply the rule cited in the *Restatement of Torts,* an authoritative compendium of legal principles. The *Restatement Rule* is that foreseen users must be members of a *reasonably limited and identifiable group of users* that have relied on the CPA's work, such as creditors, even though those persons were not specifically known to the CPA at the time the work was done. A leading case supporting the application of this rule is *Rusch Factors* v. *Levin,* presented in Figure 5-5.

FIGURE 5-5	*Rusch Factors* v. *Levin* (1968)—Liability to Third Parties

The plaintiff, a lender, asked the defendant auditor to audit the financial statements of a company seeking a loan. The auditor issued an unqualified opinion on the financial statements, indicating that the company was solvent when, in fact, it was insolvent. The plaintiff loaned the company money, suffered a subsequent loss, and sued the auditor for recovery.

The auditor's defense in the case was based on the absence of privity on the part of Rusch Factors. The court found in favor of this plaintiff. Although the court could have found in favor of Rusch Factors under *Ultramares* in that it was a primary beneficiary, it chose to rely on the *Restatement of Torts,* stating that the auditor should be liable for ordinary negligence in audits where the financial statements are relied on by *actually foreseen and limited classes of persons.*

Foreseeable User The broadest interpretation of the rights of third-party beneficiaries is to use the concept of **foreseeable users**. Under this concept, any users that the auditor should have reasonably been able to foresee as being likely users of financial statements have the same rights as those with privity of contract. These users are often called an unlimited class. Although a significant number of states have followed this approach in the past, there are now only two that use it, Mississippi and Wisconsin.

There has been confusion caused by differing views of liability to third parties under common law, but the movement is clearly away from the foreseeable user approach, and thus from three approaches to two. And there may be some movement from the *Restatement of Torts* approach toward *Credit Alliance.* For example, in New Jersey, where the foreseeable user approach had been followed by the courts, the legislature recently adopted a strict privity standard. And in *Bily* v. *Arthur Young* (1992), the California Supreme Court reversed a lower court decision against Arthur Young, clearly upholding the *Restatement* doctrine. In its decision, the Court stated that "an auditor owes no general duty of care regarding the conduct of an audit to persons other than the client," and reasoned that the potential liability to auditors under the foreseeable user doctrine would be distinctly out of proportion to fault.

Auditor Defenses against Third-Party Suits	Three of the four defenses available to auditors in suits by clients are also available in third-party lawsuits. Contributory negligence is ordinarily not available because a third party is not in a position to contribute to misstated financial statements.

The preferred defense in third-party suits is nonnegligent performance. If the auditor conducted the audit in accordance with GAAS, the other defenses are unnecessary. On the other hand, nonnegligent performance is difficult to demonstrate to a court, especially if it is a jury trial and the jury is made up of laypeople.

A lack of duty defense in third-party suits contends lack of privity of contract. The extent to which privity of contract is an appropriate defense and the nature of their defense depends heavily on the judicial jurisdiction. As has been shown, for example, there would be significant differences between New York, Florida, and Wisconsin in the nature of this defense.

Absence of causal connection in third-party suits often means nonreliance on the financial statements by the user. For example, assume that the auditor can demonstrate that a lender relied on an ongoing banking relationship with a customer, rather than the financial statements, in making a loan. The fact that the auditor was negligent in the conduct of the audit would not be relevant in that situation. Of course, it is difficult to prove nonreliance on the financial statements. And, losses can be caused by other factors, such as market behavior.

CIVIL LIABILITY UNDER THE FEDERAL SECURITIES LAWS

Although there has been some growth in actions brought against accountants by their clients and third parties under common law, the greatest growth in CPA liability litigation has been under the federal securities laws.

The emphasis on federal remedies has resulted primarily from the availability of class action litigation and the relative ease of obtaining massive recovery from defendants. In addition, several sections of the securities laws impose rather strict liability standards on CPAs. Federal courts are often likely to favor plaintiffs in lawsuits in which there are strict standards. However, this may change in light of recent tort reform legislation.

The **Securities Act of 1933** deals with the information in registration statements and prospectuses. It concerns only the reporting requirements for companies issuing new securities. The only parties who can recover from auditors under the 1933 act are original purchasers of securities. The amount of the potential recovery is the original purchase price less the value of the securities at the time of the suit. If the securities have been sold, users can recover the amount of the loss incurred.

The Securities Act of 1933 imposes an unusual burden on the auditor. Section 11 of the 1933 act defines the rights of third parties and auditors. These are summarized as follows:

- Any third party who purchased securities described in the registration statement may sue the auditor for material misrepresentations or omissions in audited financial statements included in the registration statement.
- The third-party user does not have the burden of proof that he or she relied on the financial statements or that the auditor was negligent or fraudulent in doing the audit. The user must only prove that the audited financial statements contained a material misrepresentation or omission.
- The auditor has the burden of demonstrating as a defense that (1) an adequate audit (that is, a "reasonable investigation") was conducted in the circumstances or (2) all or a portion of the plaintiff's loss was caused by factors other than the misleading financial statements. The 1933 act is the only common or statutory law where the burden of proof is on the defendant.

Furthermore, the auditor has responsibility for making sure that the financial statements were fairly stated beyond the date of issuance, up to the date the registration statement became effective, which could be several months later. For example, assume that the audit report date for December 31, 1999, financial statements is February 10, 2000, but the registration statement is dated November 1, 2000. In a typical audit, the auditor must review transactions through the audit report date, February 10, 2000. In statements filed under the 1933 act, the auditor is responsible to review transactions through the registration statement date, November 1, 2000.

Securities Act of 1933

1933 & 1934 Acts

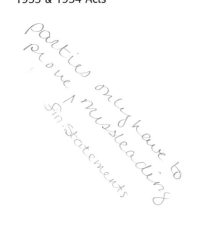

Parties only have to prove 1 misleading fin. statements

Although the burden may appear harsh to auditors, there have been few cases tried under the 1933 act. The most significant one is *Escott et al. v. Bar Chris Construction Corporation* (1968). As noted in Figure 5-6, the CPA firm was held liable for a lack of due diligence required under the 1933 act when performing its review of events occurring subsequent to the balance sheet date. Two significant results occurred directly because of this case:

1. Statements on Auditing Standards were changed to require greater emphasis on procedures that the auditor must perform regarding subsequent events, SAS 1 (AU 560). This change is a good example of the effect that the SEC has on the audits of all companies.
2. A greater emphasis began to be placed on the importance of the audit staff understanding the client's business and industry.

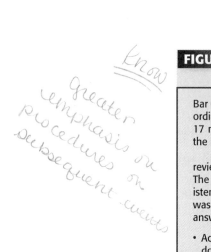

Handwritten margin note: know — greater emphasis on procedures on subsequent events

---

FIGURE 5-6   *Escott et al. v. Bar Chris Construction Corporation (1968)–Securities Act of 1933*

Bar Chris filed an S-1 registration statement with the SEC in 1961 for the issuance of convertible subordinated debentures, thereby subjecting the company to the Securities Act of 1933. Approximately 17 months later, Bar Chris filed for bankruptcy. The purchasers of the debentures filed suit against the CPA firm under the 1933 act.

The most significant issue of the case, especially to audit staff personnel, was the matter of the review for events subsequent to the balance sheet, called an S-1 review for registration statements. The courts concluded that the CPA firm's written audit program was in conformity with GAAS in existence at that time. However, they were highly critical of the auditor conducting the review, who was inexperienced in audits of construction companies, for the failure to appropriately follow up on answers by management. The following is an important part of the court's opinion in the case:

- Accountants should not be held to a higher standard than that recognized in their profession. I do not do so here. Richard's review did not come up to that written standard. He did not take the steps which the CPA firm's written program prescribed. He did not spend an adequate amount of time on a task of this magnitude. *Most important of all, he was too easily satisfied with glib answers to his inquiries.* This is not to say that he should have made a complete audit. But there were enough danger signals in the materials which he did examine to require some further investigation on his part. . . . It is not always sufficient merely to ask questions. (Italics were added and the name used in the case was changed.)

The CPA firm was found liable in the case on the grounds that they had not established due diligence required under the 1933 securities act.

Securities Exchange Act of 1934

The liability of auditors under the **Securities Exchange Act of 1934** often centers on the audited financial statements issued to the public in annual reports or submitted to the SEC as a part of annual Form 10-K reports. → *annual report filed w/SEC*

Every company with securities traded on national and over-the-counter exchanges is required to submit audited statements annually. Obviously, a much larger number of statements fall under the 1934 act than under the 1933 act.

In addition to annual audited financial statements, there is potential legal exposure to auditors for quarterly information (Form 10-Q) or other reporting information filed with the SEC, such as an unusual event filed in a Form 8-K. *significant Δs* The auditor is frequently involved in reviewing the information in these other reports; therefore, there may be legal responsibility. However, few cases have involved auditors for reports other than annual reports.

Rule 10b-5 of the Securities Exchange Act of 1934

The principal focus on CPA liability litigation under the 1934 act has been Rule 10b-5, a section of the federal Securities Exchange Act of 1934, which appears in the rules and regulations of the Securities and Exchange Commission. Rule 10b-5 states the following:

- It shall be unlawful for any person directly or indirectly, by the use of any means or instrumentality of interstate commerce, or of the mails or of any facility of any national securities exchange, (a) to employ any device, scheme, or artifice to defraud, (b) to make any untrue statement of a material fact or omit to state a material fact necessary in order to make the statements made, in the light of the circumstances under which they were made, not misleading, or (c) to engage in any act, practice, or course of business which operates or would operate as a fraud or deceit upon any person in connection with the purchase or sale of any security.

Section 10 and Rule 10b-5 are often called the antifraud provisions of the 1934 Act because they were designed primarily to thwart the commission of fraud by persons selling securities. Numerous federal court decisions have clarified that Rule 10b-5 applies not only to direct sellers but also to accountants, underwriters, and others. Generally, accountants can be held liable under Section 10 and Rule 10b-5 if they intentionally or recklessly misrepresent information intended for third-party use.

In 1976, in *Hochfelder* v. *Ernst & Ernst*, a leading securities law case as well as CPA liabilities case, the U.S. Supreme Court ruled that knowledge and intent to deceive are required before CPAs could be held liable for violation of Rule 10b-5. A summary of *Hochfelder* is included in Figure 5-7.

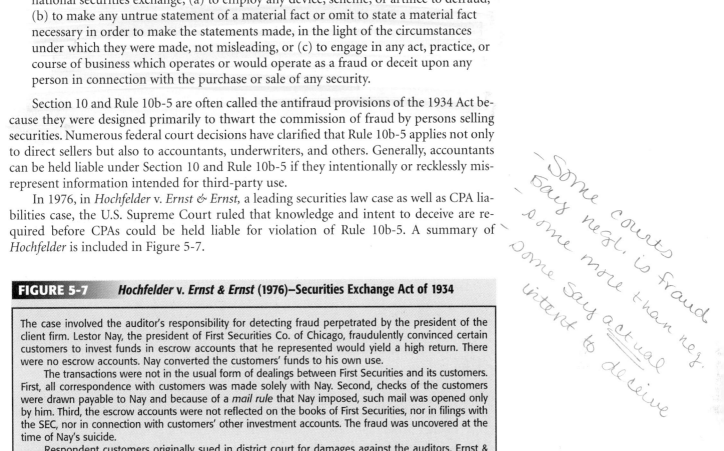

FIGURE 5-7   *Hochfelder v. Ernst & Ernst* (1976)–Securities Exchange Act of 1934

The case involved the auditor's responsibility for detecting fraud perpetrated by the president of the client firm. Lestor Nay, the president of First Securities Co. of Chicago, fraudulently convinced certain customers to invest funds in escrow accounts that he represented would yield a high return. There were no escrow accounts. Nay converted the customers' funds to his own use.

The transactions were not in the usual form of dealings between First Securities and its customers. First, all correspondence with customers was made solely with Nay. Second, checks of the customers were drawn payable to Nay and because of a *mail rule* that Nay imposed, such mail was opened only by him. Third, the escrow accounts were not reflected on the books of First Securities, nor in filings with the SEC, nor in connection with customers' other investment accounts. The fraud was uncovered at the time of Nay's suicide.

Respondent customers originally sued in district court for damages against the auditors, Ernst & Ernst, as aiders and abettors under section 10b-5. They alleged that Ernst & Ernst failed to conduct a proper audit that should have led them to discover the "mail rule" and the fraud. No allegations were made as to Ernst & Ernst's fraudulent and intentional conduct. The action was based solely on a claim that Ernst & Ernst failed to conduct a proper audit. The district court dismissed the action but did not resolve the issue of whether a cause of action could be based merely on allegations of negligence.

The court of appeals reversed the district court. The appeals court held that one who breaches a duty of inquiry and disclosure owed another is liable in damages for aiding and abetting a third party's violation of Rule 10b-5 if the fraud would have been discovered or prevented had the breach not occurred. The court reasoned that Ernst & Ernst had a common law and statutory duty of inquiry into the adequacy of First Securities' internal control because it had contracted to audit First Securities and to prepare for filing with the commission the annual report of its financial condition.

The U.S. Supreme Court reversed the court of appeals, concluding that the interpretation of Rule 10b-5 required the "intent to deceive, manipulate or defraud." Justice Powell wrote in the Court's opinion that:

• When a statute speaks so specifically in terms of manipulation and deception, and of implementing devices and contrivances—the commonly understood terminology of intentional wrongdoing—and when its history reflects no more expansive intent, we are quite unwilling to extend the scope of the statute to negligent conduct.

The Court pointed out that in certain areas of the law, recklessness is considered to be a form of intentional conduct for purposes of imposing liability. This left open the possibility that reckless behavior may be sufficient for liability under Rule 10b-5.

Many auditors believed the *Hochfelder* case would significantly reduce auditors' exposure to liability. However, suits have subsequently been brought under Rule 10b-5. In earlier suits, the knowledge and deceit standard was more easily met by plaintiffs in cases in which the auditor knew all the relevant facts but made poor judgments. In such a situation, the courts emphasized that the CPAs had requisite knowledge. The *Solitron Devices* case, described in Figure 5-8, is an example of that reasoning. In that case, the court of appeals

*Some courts is fraud
say negl. is
some more than neg.
some say actual
intent to deceive*

" White paper" is a position paper.

Solitron was a manufacturer of electronic devices, with its stock issued on the American Stock Exchange. It was involved in government contracts that subjected it to assessments on excess profits as determined by the Renegotiations Board. When the board determined that profits were excessive, management admitted that profits had been intentionally overstated to aid in acquiring new companies. It was subsequently shown in court, through an audit by another CPA firm, that earnings had been materially overstated by more than 30 percent in two different years, by overstating inventory.

A jury trial found the auditor responsible for reckless behavior in the conduct of the audit. The trial judge overturned the jury verdict on the grounds that the CPA firm could not be held liable for damages under Rule 10b-5 unless there was proof that the CPA firm *had actual knowledge* of the misstatement. Reckless behavior was not sufficient for damages.

On appeal, the Second Circuit Court of Appeals concluded that there had been sufficient evidence for the jury to conclude that the CPA firm had knowledge of the fraud. It therefore overturned the trial judge's findings and affirmed the original jury's guilty verdict.

The court of appeals also stated that proof of recklessness may meet the requirement of intent in Rule 10b-5, but that it need not address whether there was sufficient recklessness in this case because the CPA firm had knowledge of the misstatement.

ruled that reckless behavior on the part of the auditor was sufficient to hold the auditor liable for violation of Rule 10b-5. However, in two more recent suits, *Worlds of Wonder* and *Software Toolworks,* two key Ninth Circuit decisions stated that poor judgment isn't proof of fraud. This view appears now to be winning in the courts. In a third case, *McLean* v. *Alexander,* the appellate court ruled that the auditors—who were at most guilty of negligence, but not of bad-faith recklessness—were not liable under Rule 10b-5.

It is clear from the previous discussion that Rule 10b-5 continues to be a basis for lawsuits against auditors, even though *Hochfelder* has limited the liability somewhat.

Auditor Defenses— 1934 Act

The same three defenses available to auditors in common law suits by third parties are also available for suits under the 1934 Act. These are nonnegligent performance, lack of duty, and absence of causal connection.

As discussed in this section, the use of the lack of duty defense in response to actions under Rule 10b-5 has had varying degrees of success, depending on the jurisdiction. In the *Hochfelder* case, that defense was successful. In other cases, negligent or reckless behavior resulted in liability. Continued court interpretations are likely to clarify this unresolved issue.

SEC Sanctions

Closely related to auditors' liability is the SEC's authority to sanction. The SEC has the power in certain circumstances to sanction or suspend practitioners from doing audits for SEC companies. Rule 2(e) of the SEC's *Rules of Practice* says:

• The commission may deny, temporarily or permanently, the privilege of appearing or practicing before it in any way to any person who is found by the commission . . . (1) not to possess the requisite qualifications to represent others, or (2) to be lacking in character or integrity or to have engaged in unethical or improper professional conduct.

The SEC has temporarily suspended a number of individual CPAs from doing any audits of SEC clients in recent years. It has similarly prohibited a number of CPA firms from accepting any new SEC clients for a period, such as 6 months. At times, the SEC has required an extensive review of a major CPA firm's practices by another CPA firm. In some cases, individual CPAs and their firms have been required to participate in continuing education programs and to make changes in their practice. Sanctions such as these are published by the SEC and are often reported in the business press, making them a significant embarrassment to those involved.

In 1970, Congress passed legislation aimed at preventing organized crime from invading legitimate business enterprises. One of the elements of that legislation is the **Racketeer Influenced and Corrupt Organization Act** (*RICO*). That act allows an injured party to seek treble (triple) damages and recovery of legal fees in cases where it can be demonstrated that the defendant was engaged in a "pattern of racketeering activity." The statute states that a pattern of racketeering activity means at least two acts of racketeering activity within a 10-year period. In interpreting these requirements, the courts have generally focused on the continuity and relatedness of the acts to determine whether a pattern exists. Prior to 1993, the case law applying RICO to accountants was mixed. Some courts made it clear that a complaint must allege extensive participation by the auditor in the enterprise's affairs beyond conducting an annual audit, while others held that the issuance of a materially false audit report would constitute an act of racketeering activity. Legislation has been considered by the U.S. Congress to clarify the applicability of the act. However, from the auditor's point of view, the issue was essentially resolved by the U.S. Supreme Court. In a 1993 decision, the court ruled that outside professionals such as accountants who do not help run corrupt businesses cannot be sued under the provisions of RICO.

Racketeer Influenced and Corrupt Organization Act

Another significant congressional action affecting both CPA firms and their clients was the passage of the **Foreign Corrupt Practices Act of 1977.** The act makes it illegal to offer a bribe to an official of a foreign country for the purpose of exerting influence and obtaining or retaining business. The prohibition against payments to foreign officials is applicable to all U.S. domestic firms, regardless of whether they are publicly or privately held, and to foreign companies filing with the SEC.

Apart from the bribery provisions that affect all companies, the law also requires SEC registrants under the Securities Exchange Act of 1934 to meet additional requirements. These include the maintenance of reasonably complete and accurate records and an adequate system of internal control. The law significantly affects all SEC companies, but the unanswered question to the profession at this time is how it affects auditors.

The act may affect auditors through their responsibility to review and evaluate systems of internal control as a part of doing the audit. Most auditors believe that they are not currently required to do a review of internal control thorough enough to judge whether their clients meet the requirements of the Foreign Corrupt Practices Act.

To date, there have been no legal cases affecting auditors' legal responsibilities under the Foreign Corrupt Practices Act. But there is considerable disagreement about auditors' responsibilities under the law. There is likely to be ongoing discussion, and perhaps litigation, to resolve the issue.

Foreign Corrupt Practices Act of 1977

CRIMINAL LIABILITY

OBJECTIVE 5-7
Specify what constitutes criminal liability for accountants.

A fourth way CPAs can be held liable is under **criminal liability for accountants.** CPAs can be found guilty for criminal action under both federal and state laws. The most likely statutes to be used under state law are the Uniform Securities Acts, which are similar to parts of the SEC rules. The 1933 and 1934 securities acts, as well as the Federal Mail Fraud Statute and the Federal False Statements Statute, are the most relevant federal laws affecting auditors. All make it a criminal offense to defraud another person through *knowingly being involved* with false financial statements.

Unfortunately, there have been several criminal cases of notoriety involving CPAs. Although these are not great in absolute number, they have the effect of damaging the integrity of the profession, and reducing the profession's ability to attract and retain outstanding people. On the positive side, criminal actions encourage practitioners to use extreme care and exercise good faith in their activities.

The leading case of criminal action against CPAs is *United States* v. *Simon,* which occurred in 1969. Take a look at this case, which is summarized in Figure 5-9 on page 126. In this case, three auditors were prosecuted for filing false financial statements of a client with the government and held to be criminally liable. As noted in Figure 5-9, the consequences for these three men were significant. Simon has been followed by three additional major criminal cases. In *United States* v. *Natelli* (1975), two auditors were convicted of criminal liability under the 1934 Act for certifying financial statements of National Student Marketing Corporation that contained inadequate disclosures pertaining to accounts receivable.

FIGURE 5-9	*United States* v. *Simon* (1969)—Criminal Liability

The case was a criminal one concerning three auditors prosecuted for filing false statements with a government agency and violation of the 1934 Securities Exchange Act. The CPA firm had already settled out of court for civil liability issues for over $2 million after the audit client, Continental Vending Corporation, filed for bankruptcy.

The main issue of the trial was the reporting of transactions between Continental and its affiliate, Valley Commercial Corporation. Before the audit was complete, the auditors had learned that Valley was not in a position to repay its debt, and it was accordingly arranged that collateral would be posted. The president of Continental Vending, Roth, and members of his family transferred their equity in certain securities to Continental's counsel, as trustee to secure Roth's debt to Valley and Valley's debt to Continental. Note 2 included with the financial statements read as follows:

- The amount receivable from Valley Commercial Corp. (an affiliated company of which Mr. Harold Roth is an officer, director, and stockholder) bears interest at 12 percent a year. Such amount, less the balance of the notes payable to that company, is secured by the assignment to the Company of Valley's equity in certain marketable securities. As of February 15, 1963, the amount of such equity at current market quotations exceeded the net amount receivable.

The government contended that this note was inadequate and should have disclosed that the amount receivable from Valley was uncollectible at September 30, 1962, because Valley had loaned approximately the same amount to Roth, who was unable to pay. The note should also have stated that approximately 80 percent of the securities Roth had pledged was stock and convertible debentures of Continental Vending. The defendants called eight expert independent accountants as witnesses. They testified generally that, except for the misstatement with respect to netting, the treatment of the Valley receivable in note 2 was in no way inconsistent with generally accepted accounting principles or generally accepted auditing standards. Specifically, they testified that neither generally accepted accounting principles nor generally accepted auditing standards required disclosure of the makeup of the collateral or of the increase in the receivables after the closing date of the balance sheet, although three of the eight stated that in light of hindsight they would have preferred that the makeup of the collateral be disclosed. The witnesses also testified that the disclosure of the Roth borrowings from Valley was not required, and seven of the eight were of the opinion that such disclosure would be inappropriate.

The defendants asked for two instructions, which, in substance, would have told the jury that a defendant could be found guilty only if, according to generally accepted accounting principles, the statements as a whole did not fairly present the financial condition of Continental at September 30, 1962, and then only if this departure from accepted standards was due to willful disregard of those standards with knowledge of the falsity of the statements and an intent to deceive.

The judge declined to give those instructions and instead said that the critical test was whether the *statements were fairly presented and, if not, whether the defendants had acted in good faith.* Proof of compliance with generally accepted standards was "evidence which may be very persuasive but not necessarily conclusive that he acted in good faith, and that the facts as certified were not materially false or misleading."

The appeals court upheld the earlier conviction of the three auditors with the comment that even without satisfactory showing of motive, "the government produced sufficient evidence of criminal intent. Its burden was not to show that the defendants were wicked men . . . but rather that they had certified a statement knowing it to be false."

The effect on the three men was significant. The total fine was $17,000, but far more important, they lost their CPA certificates under Rule 501 of the *Code of Professional Conduct* (acts discreditable) and were forced to leave the profession. They were ultimately pardoned by President Nixon.

In *United States* v. *Weiner* (1975), three auditors were convicted of securities fraud in connection with their audit of Equity Funding Corporation of America. Equity Funding was a financial conglomerate whose financial statements had been overstated through a massive fraud by management. The fraud was so extensive and the audit work so poor that the court concluded that the auditors must have been aware of the fraud and were therefore guilty of knowing complicity.

In *ESM Government Securities* v. *Alexander Grant & Co.* (1986), it was revealed by management to the partner in charge of the audit of ESM that the previous year's audited financial statements contained a material misstatement. Rather than complying with professional and firm standards in such circumstances, the partner agreed to say nothing in the hope that management would work its way out of the problem during the current year. Instead, the situation worsened, eventually to the point where losses exceeded $300 million. The partner was convicted of criminal charges for his role in sustaining the fraud and was sentenced to a 12-year prison term.

Several critical lessons can be learned from these four cases:

- An investigation of the integrity of management is an important part of deciding on the acceptability of clients and the extent of work to perform. SAS 7 (AU 315) gives guidance to auditors in investigating new clients, which will be discussed in a subsequent chapter.
- The auditor can be found criminally guilty in the conduct of an audit even if the person's background indicates integrity in his or her personal and professional life. The criminal liability can extend to partners and staff.
- Independence in appearance and fact by all individuals on the engagement is essential, especially in a defense involving criminal actions. SAS 1 (AU 220) requires a firm to implement policies to help assure independence in fact and in appearance.
- Transactions with related parties require special scrutiny because of the potential for misstatement. SAS 45 (AU 334) gives guidance in auditing related party transactions.
- Generally accepted accounting principles cannot be relied on exclusively in deciding whether financial statements are fairly presented. The substance of the statements, considering all facts, is required. The SEC preferability requirement provides guidelines in selecting accounting principles.
- Good documentation may be just as important in the auditor's defense of criminal charges as in a civil suit.
- The potential consequences of the auditor knowingly committing a wrongful act are so severe that it is unlikely that the potential benefits could ever justify the actions.

THE PROFESSION'S RESPONSE TO LEGAL LIABILITY

The AICPA and the profession as a whole can do a number of things to reduce the practitioner's exposure to lawsuits. The AICPA's division of firms into the SEC Practice Section and the Private Companies Practice Section is one positive step in recognizing additional responsibility that the public demands of professionals. Some of the others are discussed briefly.

OBJECTIVE 5-8
Describe what the profession and the individual CPA can do and what is being done to reduce the threat of litigation.

- *Research in auditing.* Continued research is important in finding better ways to do such things as uncover unintentional material misstatements or fraud, communicate audit results to statement users, and make sure that auditors are independent. Significant research already takes place through the AICPA, CPA firms, and universities.
- *Standard and rule setting.* The AICPA must constantly set standards and revise them to meet the changing needs of auditing. New statements on auditing standards, revisions of the *Code of Professional Conduct,* and other pronouncements must be issued as society's needs change and as new technology arises from experience and research.
- *Set requirements to protect auditors.* The AICPA can help protect its members by setting certain requirements that better practitioners already follow. Naturally, these requirements should not be in conflict with meeting users' needs. An example of an auditor-set standard is the SAS 85 (AU 333) requirement of a written letter of representation from management in all audits.

- *Establish peer review requirements.* The periodic examination of a firm's practices and procedures is a way to educate practitioners and identify firms not meeting the standards of the profession.
- *Oppose lawsuits.* CPA firms must continue to oppose unwarranted lawsuits even if, in the short run, the costs of winning are greater than the costs of settling. The AICPA has aided practitioners in fighting an unwarranted expansion of legal liability for accountants by filing briefs as "a friend of the court" known as *amicus curiae* briefs.
- *Education of users.* Investors and others who read financial statements must be educated as to the meaning of the auditor's opinion and the extent and nature of the auditor's work. Users must be educated to understand that auditors do not test 100 percent of all records and do not guarantee the accuracy of the financial records or the future prosperity of the company. It is also important to educate users to understand that accounting and auditing are arts, not sciences, and that perfection and precision are not achievable.
- *Sanction members for improper conduct and performance.* One characteristic of a profession is its responsibility for policing its own membership. The AICPA has made progress toward dealing with the problems of inadequate CPA performance, but more rigorous review of alleged failures is still needed.
- *Lobby for changes in laws.* The year 1995 brought with it a major victory in the accounting profession's long efforts to obtain changes in federal laws concerning accountants' liability. As indicated at the beginning of this chapter, the **Private Securities Litigation Reform Act** (the Reform Act) was passed and significantly reduced potential damages in securities-related litigation. This law was the culmination of many years of effort by the Coalition to Eliminate Abusive Securities Suits, formed by the Big Five accounting firms and 180 industrial and commercial companies. The focus of their efforts was to have separate and proportionate liability replace joint and several liability, to require that plaintiffs pay a prevailing defendant's legal fees if the court determines that the lawsuit was without merit, and to allow accounting firms to practice in different organizational forms, including limited liability organizations. They were successful in regard to the first and last of these objectives. The Reform Act, however, applied only to federal courts, and lawyers began taking their cases to state courts, which the act did not cover. Fortunately, in November 1998, the loophole was closed with the issuance of the Securities Litigation Uniform Standards Act of 1998. The 1998 law says, "Any covered class action brought into any state court involving a covered security . . . shall be removable to the federal district court . . ." The profession believes that this new law will force potential plaintiffs to adhere to the spirit of the Reform Act.

Private Securities Litigation
Reform Act of 1995

1998 Litigation Reform Act

PROTECTING INDIVIDUAL CPAs FROM LEGAL LIABILITY

Practicing auditors may also take specific action to minimize their liability. Some of the more common actions are:

- *Deal only with clients possessing integrity.* There is an increased likelihood of having legal problems when a client lacks integrity in dealing with customers, employees, units of government, and others. A CPA firm needs procedures to evaluate the integrity of clients and should dissociate itself from clients found lacking.
- *Hire qualified personnel and train and supervise them properly.* A considerable portion of most audits is done by young professionals with relatively little experience. Given the high degree of risk CPA firms have in doing audits, it is important that these young professionals be qualified and well trained. Supervision of their work by experienced and qualified professionals is also essential.
- *Follow the standards of the profession.* A firm must implement procedures to ensure that all firm members understand and follow the SASs, FASB opinions, rules of conduct, and other professional guidelines.

- *Maintain independence.* Independence is more than merely financial. Independence in fact requires an attitude of responsibility separate from the client's interest. Much litigation has arisen from a too willing acceptance by an auditor of a client's representation or of a client's pressures. The auditor must maintain an attitude of *healthy skepticism.*
- *Understand the client's business.* The lack of knowledge of industry practices and client operations has been a major factor in auditors failing to uncover misstatements in several cases. It is important that the audit team be educated in these areas.
- *Perform quality audits.* Quality audits require that auditors obtain appropriate evidence and make appropriate judgments about the evidence. It is essential, for example, that the auditor evaluate a client's internal controls and modify the evidence to reflect the findings. Improved auditing reduces the likelihood of misstatements and the likelihood of lawsuits.
- *Document the work properly.* The preparation of good working papers helps the auditor organize and perform quality audits. Quality working papers are essential if an auditor has to defend an audit in court.
- *Obtain an engagement letter and a representation letter.* These two letters are essential in defining the respective obligations of the client and the auditor. They are helpful especially in lawsuits between the client and auditor, but also in third-party lawsuits.
- *Maintain confidential relations.* Auditors are under an ethical and sometimes legal obligation not to disclose client matters to outsiders.
- *Carry adequate insurance.* It is essential for a CPA firm to have adequate insurance protection in the event of a lawsuit. Although insurance rates have risen considerably in the past few years as a result of increasing litigation, professional liability insurance is still available for all CPAs.
- *Seek legal counsel.* When serious problems occur during an audit, a CPA would be wise to consult experienced counsel. In the event of a potential or actual lawsuit, the auditor should immediately seek an experienced attorney.
- *Choose a form of organization with limited liability.* As discussed in Chapter 2, many CPA firms now operate as professional corporations, limited liability companies, or limited liability partnerships in order to provide some personal liability protection to owners.
- *Exercise professional skepticism.* As highlighted in the material presented in the box below, auditors are often liable when they are presented with information indicating a problem that they fail to recognize. Auditors need to strive to maintain a healthy level of skepticism, one that keeps them alert to potential misstatements, so that they can recognize misstatements when they exist.

LESSONS LEARNED FROM AUDITOR LITIGATION

In considering the advisability of the laws being considered in reform of accountants' liability, it is useful to consider actual experiences with past accountants' litigation. Accordingly, a review was conducted of 23 cases of alleged audit failure with which I have been involved as a litigation consultant and expert witness. Of these 23 cases, 6 were clearly without merit and should not have been brought on equitable grounds. Of the 17 that were with merit, 13 did, in fact, represent a real audit failure. In considering the nature of the failure in each case, it was observed that the evidence that would lead the auditor to identify the misstatement that existed was usually there. In other words, the problem was not any inadequacy in the audit process as presented by professional standards; it was a *lack of professional skepticism* on the part of the auditor. The auditor had evidence in his or her possession that indicated the problem, but did not see it as such.

Source: Presentation by James K. Loebbecke at the Forum on Responsibilities and Liabilities of Accountants and Auditors, United Nations Conference on Trade and Development, March 16, 1995.

This chapter provides insight into the environment in which CPAs operate by highlighting the significance of the legal liability facing the CPA profession. No reasonable CPA would want to eliminate the profession's legal responsibility for fraudulent or incompetent performance. It is certainly in the profession's best interest to maintain public trust in the competent performance of the auditing profession, while avoiding liability for cases involving strictly business failure and not audit failure. To more effectively avoid legal liability, CPAs need to have an adequate understanding of how they can be held liable to their clients or third parties. Knowledge about how CPAs are liable to clients under common law, to third parties under common law, to third parties under federal securities laws, and for criminal liability provides auditors an awareness of issues that may subject them to greater liability. CPAs can protect themselves from legal liability in numerous ways, and the profession has worked diligently to identify ways to help CPAs reduce the profession's potential exposure. Fortunately, recent litigation reform efforts have been successful that are designed to limit abusive securities class action suits against CPAs. It is necessary for the profession and society to determine a reasonable trade-off between the degree of responsibility the auditor should take for fair presentation and the audit cost to society. CPAs, Congress, the SEC, and the courts will all continue to have a major influence in shaping the final solution.

ESSENTIAL TERMS

Absence of causal connection—an auditor's legal defense under which the auditor contends that the damages claimed by the client were not brought about by any act of the auditor

Audit failure—a situation in which the auditor issues an erroneous audit opinion as the result of an underlying failure to comply with the requirements of generally accepted auditing standards

Audit risk—the risk that the auditor will conclude that the financial statements are fairly stated and an unqualified opinion can therefore be issued when, in fact, they are materially misstated

Business failure—the situation when a business is unable to repay its lenders, or meet the expectations of its investors, because of economic or business conditions

Contributory negligence—an auditor's legal defense under which the auditor claims that the client failed to perform certain obligations and that it is the client's failure to perform those obligations that brought about the claimed damages

Criminal liability for accountants—defrauding a person through knowing involvement with false financial statements

Foreign Corrupt Practices Act of 1977—a federal statute that makes it illegal to offer a bribe to an official of a foreign country for the purpose of exerting influence and obtaining or retaining business, and that requires U.S. companies to maintain reasonably complete and accurate records and an adequate system of internal control

Foreseeable users—an unlimited class of users that the auditor should have reasonably been able to foresee as being likely users of financial statements

Foreseen user—a member of a limited class of users whom the auditor is aware will rely on the financial statements

Lack of duty to perform—an auditor's legal defense under which the auditor claims that no contract existed with the client; therefore no duty existed to perform the disputed service

Legal liability—the professional's obligation under the law to provide a reasonable level of care while performing work for those he or she serves

Nonnegligent performance—an auditor's legal defense under which the auditor claims that the audit was performed in accordance with generally accepted auditing standards

Private Securities Litigation Reform Act—a federal law passed in 1995 that significantly reduced potential damages in securities-related litigation

Prudent person concept—the legal concept that a person has a duty to exercise reasonable care and diligence in the performance of his or her obligations to another

Racketeer Influenced and Corrupt Organization Act (RICO)—a 1970 federal statute designed to discourage fraud, extortion, and other racketeering activities, under which an injured party may recover treble damages and legal fees; a 1993 Supreme Court ruling ruled that CPA firms are ordinarily exempt from this statute

Securities Act of 1933—a federal statute dealing with companies that register and sell securities to the public; under the statute, third parties who are original purchasers of securities may recover damages from the auditor if the financial statements are misstated unless the auditor proves that the audit was adequate or that the third party's loss was caused by factors other than misleading financial statements

Securities Exchange Act of 1934—a federal statute dealing with companies that trade securities on national and over-the-counter exchanges; auditors are involved because the annual reporting requirements include audited financial statements

Ultramares **doctrine**—a common-law approach to third-party liability, established in 1931 in the case of *Ultramares Corporation* v. *Touche,* in which ordinary negligence is insufficient for liability to third parties, because of the lack of *privity of contract* between the third party and the auditor, unless the third party is a *primary beneficiary*

REVIEW QUESTIONS

5-1 (Objective 5-1) State several factors that have affected the incidence of lawsuits against CPAs in recent years.

5-2 (Objective 5-1) Lawsuits against CPA firms have increased dramatically in the past decade. State your opinion of the positive and negative effects of the increased litigation on CPAs and on society as a whole.

5-3 (Objective 5-2) Distinguish between business failure and audit risk. Why is business failure a concern to auditors?

5-4 (Objective 5-3) How does the prudent person concept affect the liability of the auditor?

5-5 (Objective 5-3) Distinguish between "fraud" and "constructive fraud."

5-6 (Objectives 5-1, 5-8) Discuss why many CPA firms have willingly settled lawsuits out of court. What are the implications to the profession?

5-7 (Objective 5-4) A common type of lawsuit against CPAs is for the failure to detect a fraud. State the auditor's responsibility for such discovery. Give authoritative support for your answer.

5-8 (Objectives 5-3, 5-4) What is meant by contributory negligence? Under what conditions will this likely be a successful defense?

5-9 (Objective 5-4) Explain how an engagement letter might affect an auditor's liability to clients under common law.

5-10 (Objectives 5-4, 5-5) Compare and contrast traditional auditors' legal responsibilities to clients and third-party users under common law. How has that law changed in recent years?

5-11 (Objective 5-5) Is the auditor's liability affected if the third party was unknown rather than known? Explain.

5-12 (Objective 5-6) Contrast the auditor's liability under the Securities Act of 1933 with that under the Securities Exchange Act of 1934.

5-13 (Objectives 5-4, 5-5, 5-6, 5-7) Distinguish between the auditor's potential liability to the client, liability to third parties under common law, civil liability under the securities laws, and criminal liability. Describe one situation for each type of liability in which the auditor could be held legally responsible.

5-14 (Objective 5-6) What sanctions does the SEC have against a CPA firm?

5-15 (Objective 5-8) In what ways can the profession positively respond and reduce liability in auditing?

5-16 (Objectives 5-4, 5-5) The following questions concern CPA firms' liability under common law. Choose the best response.

a. Sharp, CPA, was engaged by Peters & Sons, a partnership, to give an opinion on the financial statements that were to be submitted to several prospective partners as part of a planned expansion of the firm. Sharp's fee was fixed on a per diem basis. After a period of intensive work, Sharp completed about half of the necessary field work. Then, because of unanticipated demands on his time by other clients, Sharp was forced to abandon the work. The planned expansion of the firm failed to materialize because the prospective partners lost interest when the audit report was not promptly available. Sharp offered to complete the task at a later date. This offer was refused. Peters & Sons suffered damages of $4,000 as a result. Under the circumstances, what is the probable outcome of a lawsuit between Sharp and Peters & Sons?
   (1) Sharp will be compensated for the reasonable value of the services actually performed.
   (2) Peters & Sons will recover damages for breach of contract.
   (3) Peters & Sons will recover both punitive damages and damages for breach of contract.
   (4) Neither Sharp nor Peters & Sons will recover against the other.

b. Magnus Enterprises engaged a CPA firm to perform the annual audit of its financial statements. Which of the following is a correct statement with respect to the CPA firm's liability to Magnus for negligence?
   (1) Such liability cannot be varied by agreement of the parties.
   (2) The CPA firm will be liable for any fraudulent scheme it does not detect.
   (3) The CPA firm will not be liable if it can show that it exercised the ordinary care and skill of a reasonable person in the conduct of its own affairs.
   (4) The CPA firm not only must exercise reasonable care in what it does but also must possess at least that degree of accounting knowledge and skill expected of a CPA.

c. Martin Corporation orally engaged Humm & Dawson to audit its year-end financial statements. The engagement was to be completed within 2 months after the close of Martin's fiscal year for a fixed fee of $15,000. Under these circumstances, what obligation is assumed by Humm & Dawson?
   (1) None. The contract is unenforceable because it is not in writing.
   (2) An implied promise to exercise reasonable standards of competence and care.
   (3) An implied obligation to take extraordinary steps to discover all defalcations.
   (4) The obligation of an insurer of its work, which is liable without fault.

d. If a CPA firm is being sued for common law fraud by a third party based on materially false financial statements, which of the following is the best defense the accountants could assert?
   (1) Lack of privity.
   (2) Nonnegligent performance.
   (3) A disclaimer contained in the engagement letter.
   (4) Contributory negligence on the part of the client.

5-17 (Objectives 5-5, 5-6, 5-7) The following questions deal with important cases in accountants' liability. Choose the best response.

a. The most significant aspect of the *Continental Vending* (*United States* v. *Simon*) case was that it
   (1) created a more general awareness of the auditor's exposure to criminal prosecution.
   (2) extended the auditor's responsibility for financial statements of subsidiaries.
   (3) extended the auditor's responsibility for events after the end of the audit period.
   (4) defined the auditor's common-law responsibilities to third parties.

b. The *1136 Tenants* case was important chiefly because of its emphasis on the legal liability of the CPA when associated with
   (1) an SEC engagement.
   (2) unaudited financial statements.
   (3) an audit resulting in a disclaimer of opinion.
   (4) letters for underwriters.

5-18 (Objective 5-6)   The following questions deal with liability under the 1933 and 1934 Securities Acts. Choose the best response.

a. Major, Major, & Sharpe, CPAs, are the auditors of MacLain Industries. In connection with the public offering of $10 million of MacLain securities, Major expressed an unqualified opinion as to the financial statements. Subsequent to the offering, certain misstatements were revealed. Major has been sued by the purchasers of the stock offered pursuant to the registration statement that included the financial statements audited by Major. In the ensuing lawsuit by the MacLain investors, Major will be able to avoid liability if
   (1) the misstatements were caused primarily by MacLain.
   (2) it can be shown that at least some of the investors did *not* actually read the audited financial statements.
   (3) it can prove due diligence in the audit of the financial statements of MacLain.
   (4) MacLain had expressly assumed any liability in connection with the public offering.

b. Donalds & Company, CPAs, audited the financial statements included in the annual report submitted by Markum Securities, Inc., to the SEC. The audit was improper in several respects. Markum is now insolvent and unable to satisfy the claims of its customers. The customers have instituted legal action against Donalds based on Section 10b and Rule 10b-5 of the Securities Exchange Act of 1934. Which of the following is likely to be Donalds's best defense?
   (1) They did *not* intentionally certify false financial statements.
   (2) Section 10b does *not* apply to them.
   (3) They were *not* in privity of contract with the creditors.
   (4) Their engagement letter specifically disclaimed any liability to any party that resulted from Markum's fraudulent conduct.

c. Josephs & Paul is a growing medium-sized partnership of CPAs. One of the firm's major clients is considering offering its stock to the public. This will be the firm's first client to go public. Which of the following is true with respect to this engagement?
   (1) If the client is a service corporation, the Securities Act of 1933 will not apply.
   (2) If the client is not going to be listed on an organized exchange, the Securities Exchange Act of 1934 will not apply.
   (3) The Securities Act of 1933 imposes important additional potential liability on Josephs & Paul.
   (4) As long as Josephs & Paul engages exclusively in intrastate business, the federal securities laws will not apply.

DISCUSSION QUESTIONS AND PROBLEMS

5-19 (Objectives 5-4, 5-5)   Verna Cosden & Co., a medium-sized CPA firm, was engaged to audit Joslin Supply Company. Several staff were involved in the audit, all of whom had attended the firm's in-house training program on effective auditing methods. Throughout the audit, Cosden spent most of her time in the field planning the audit, supervising the staff, and reviewing their work.

A significant part of the audit entailed verifying the physical count, cost, and summarization of inventory. Inventory was highly significant to the financial statements and Cosden knew the inventory was pledged as collateral for a large loan to East City National

Bank. In reviewing Joslin's inventory count procedures, Cosden told the president she believed the method of counting inventory at different locations on different days was highly undesirable. The president stated that it was impractical to count all inventory on the same day because of personnel shortages and customer preference. After considerable discussion, Cosden agreed to permit the practice if the president would sign a statement that no other method was practical. The CPA firm had at least one person at each site to audit the inventory count procedures and actual count. There were more than 40 locations.

Eighteen months later, Cosden found out that the worst had happened. Management below the president's level had conspired to materially overstate inventory, as a means of covering up obsolete inventory and inventory losses resulting from mismanagement. The misstatement occurred by physically transporting inventory at night to other locations after it had been counted in a given location. The accounting records were inadequate to uncover these illegal transfers.

Both Joslin Supply Company and East City National Bank sued Verna Cosden & Co.

Required

Answer the following questions, setting forth reasons for any conclusions stated:

    a. What defense should Cosden & Co. use in the suit by Joslin?
    b. What defense should Cosden & Co. use in the suit by East City National Bank?
    c. Is Cosden likely to be successful in her defenses?
    d. Would the issues or outcome be significantly different if the suit was brought under the Securities Exchange Act of 1934?

5-20 (Objective 5-5)   The CPA firm of Bigelow, Barton, and Brown was expanding rapidly. Consequently, it hired several junior accountants, including a man named Small. The partners of the firm eventually became dissatisfied with Small's production and warned him they would be forced to discharge him unless his output increased significantly.

At that time, Small was engaged in audits of several clients. He decided that to avoid being fired, he would reduce or omit some of the standard auditing procedures listed in audit programs prepared by the partners. One of the CPA firm's clients, Newell Corporation, was in serious financial difficulty and had adjusted several of the accounts being audited by Small to appear financially sound. Small prepared fictitious working papers in his home at night to support purported completion of auditing procedures assigned to him, although he in fact did not examine the adjusting entries. The CPA firm rendered an unqualified opinion on Newell's financial statements, which were grossly misstated. Several creditors, relying on the audited financial statements, subsequently extended large sums of money to Newell Corporation.

Required

Would the CPA firm be liable to the creditors who extended the money because of their reliance on the erroneous financial statements if Newell Corporation should fail to pay them? Explain.*

5-21 (Objectives 5-3, 5-5)   Watts and Williams, a firm of CPAs, audited the accounts of Sampson Skins, Inc., a corporation that imports and deals in fine furs. Upon completion of the audit, the auditors supplied Sampson Skins with 20 copies of the certified balance sheet. The firm knew in a general way that Sampson Skins wanted that number of copies of the auditor's report to furnish to banks and other potential lenders.

The balance sheet in question was misstated by approximately $800,000. Instead of having a $600,000 net worth, the corporation was insolvent. The management of Sampson Skins had doctored the books to avoid bankruptcy. The assets had been overstated by $500,000 of fictitious and nonexisting accounts receivable and $300,000 of nonexisting skins listed as inventory when in fact Sampson Skins had only empty boxes. The audit failed to detect these fraudulent entries. Martinson, relying on the certified balance sheet, loaned Sampson Skins $200,000. He seeks to recover his loss from Watts and Williams.

*AICPA adapted.

Required

State whether each of the following is true or false and give your reasons:

a. If Martinson alleges and proves negligence on the part of Watts and Williams, he will be able to recover his loss.

b. If Martinson alleges and proves constructive fraud (that is, gross negligence on the part of Watts and Williams) he will be able to recover his loss.

c. Martinson does not have a contract with Watts and Williams.

d. Unless actual fraud on the part of Watts and Williams could be shown, Martinson could not recover.

e. Martinson is a third-party beneficiary of the contract Watts and Williams made with Sampson Skins.*

5-22 (Objectives 5-4, 5-5, 5-7)   Donald Sharpe recently joined the CPA firm of Spark, Watts, and Wilcox. He quickly established a reputation for thoroughness and a steadfast dedication to following prescribed auditing procedures to the letter. On his third audit for the firm, Sharpe examined the underlying documentation of 200 disbursements as a test of acquisitions, receiving, vouchers payable, and cash disbursement procedures. In the process, he found 12 disbursements for the acquisition of materials with no receiving reports in the documentation. He noted the exceptions in his working papers and called them to the attention of the in-charge accountant. Relying on prior experience with the client, the in-charge accountant disregarded Sharpe's comments, and nothing further was done about the exceptions.

Subsequently, it was learned that one of the client's purchasing agents and a member of its accounting department were engaged in a fraudulent scheme whereby they diverted the receipt of materials to a public warehouse while sending the invoices to the client. When the client discovered the fraud, the conspirators had obtained approximately $70,000, $50,000 of which was recovered after the completion of the audit.

Required

Discuss the legal implications and liabilities to Spark, Watts, and Wilcox as a result of the facts just described.*

5-23 (Objectives 5-3, 5-4, 5-5)   In confirming accounts receivable on December 31, 1999, the auditor found 15 discrepancies between the customer's records and the recorded amounts in the accounts receivable master file. A copy of all confirmations that had exceptions was turned over to the company controller to investigate the reason for the difference. He, in turn, had the bookkeeper perform the analysis. The bookkeeper analyzed each exception, determined its cause, and prepared an elaborate working paper explaining each difference. Most of the differences in the bookkeeper's report indicated that the exceptions were caused by timing differences in the client's and customer's records. The auditor reviewed the working paper and concluded that there were no material exceptions in accounts receivable.

Two years subsequent to the audit, it was determined that the bookkeeper had stolen thousands of dollars in the past 3 years by taking cash and overstating accounts receivable. In a lawsuit by the client against the CPA, an examination of the auditor's December 31, 1999, accounts receivable working papers, which were subpoenaed by the court, indicated that one of the explanations in the bookkeeper's analysis of the exceptions was fictitious. The analysis stated the exception was caused by a sales allowance granted to the customer for defective merchandise the day before the end of the year. The difference was actually caused by the bookkeeper's theft.

Required

a. What are the legal issues involved in this situation? What should the auditor use as a defense in the event that he is sued?

b. What was the CPA's deficiency in conducting the audit of accounts receivable?

*AICPA adapted.

5-24 (Objectives 5-4, 5-5, 5-7)   Smith, CPA, is the auditor for Juniper Manufacturing Corporation, a privately owned company that has a June 30 fiscal year. Juniper arranged for a substantial bank loan that was dependent on the bank's receiving, by September 30, audited financial statements that showed a current ratio of at least 2 to 1. On September 25, just before the audit report was to be issued, Smith received an anonymous letter on Juniper's stationery indicating that a 5-year lease by Juniper, as lessee, of a factory building accounted for in the financial statements as an operating lease was, in fact, a capital lease. The letter stated that there was a secret written agreement with the lessor modifying the lease and creating a capital lease.

Smith confronted the president of Juniper, who admitted that a secret agreement existed but said it was necessary to treat the lease as an operating lease to meet the current ratio requirement of the pending loan and that nobody would ever discover the secret agreement with the lessor. The president said that if Smith did not issue his report by September 30, Juniper would sue Smith for substantial damages that would result from not getting the loan. Under this pressure and because the working papers contained a copy of the 5-year lease agreement that supported the operating lease treatment, Smith issued his report with an unqualified opinion on September 29.

Despite the fact that the loan was received, Juniper went bankrupt within 2 years. The bank is suing Smith to recover its losses on the loan and the lessor is suing Smith to recover uncollected rents.

Required

Answer the following questions, setting forth reasons for any conclusions stated:

    a. Is Smith liable to the bank?

    b. Is Smith liable to the lessor?

    c. Is there potential for criminal action against Smith?*

5-25 (Objective 5-4)   Ward & East, CPAs, were the auditors of Southern Development, Inc., a real estate company that owned several shopping centers. It was Southern's practice to let each shopping center manager negotiate that center's leases; they thought that such an arrangement resulted in much better leases because a local person did the negotiating.

Two of the center managers were killed in a plane accident returning home from a company meeting at the head office in Phoenix. In both cases, the new managers appointed to take their places discovered kickback schemes in operation; the managers had negotiated lower rents than normal in return for kickbacks from the tenants.

Southern brought in a new CPA firm, Jasper & Co., to investigate the extent of the fraud at those two locations and the possibility of similar frauds at other centers. Jasper & Co. completed their investigation and found that four locations were involved quite independently of each other and that the total loss over 5 years was more than $1,000,000. Southern sued Ward & East for negligence for $1,000,000 plus interest.

Required

What defense would Ward & East use? What would they have to prove?

5-26 (Objective 5-6)   Gordon & Groton, CPAs, were the auditors of Bank & Company, a brokerage firm and member of a national stock exchange. Gordon & Groton audited and reported on the financial statements of Bank, which were filed with the Securities and Exchange Commission.

Several of Bank's customers were swindled by a fraudulent scheme perpetrated by Bank's president, who owned 90 percent of the voting stock of the company. The facts establish that Gordon & Groton were negligent but not reckless or grossly negligent in the conduct of the audit, and neither participated in the fraudulent scheme or knew of its existence.

The customers are suing Gordon & Groton under the antifraud provisions of Section 10(b) and Rule 10b-5 of the Securities Exchange Act of 1934 for aiding and abetting the

*AICPA adapted.

fraudulent scheme of the president. The customers' suit for fraud is predicated exclusively on the nonfeasance of the auditors in failing to conduct a proper audit, thereby failing to discover the fraudulent scheme.

Required

Answer the following questions, setting forth reasons for any conclusions stated:

   a. What is the probable outcome of the lawsuit?
   b. What other theory of liability might the customers have asserted?*

5-27 (Objective 5-5)   Sarah Robertson, CPA, had been the auditor of Majestic Co. for several years. As she and her staff prepared for the audit for the year ended December 31, 1999, Herb Majestic told her that he needed a large bank loan to "tide him over" until sales picked up as expected in late 2000.

In the course of the audit, Robertson discovered that the financial situation at Majestic was worse than Majestic had revealed and that the company was technically bankrupt. She discussed the situation with Majestic, who pointed out that the bank loan would "be his solution"—he was sure he would get it as long as the financial statements didn't look too bad.

Robertson stated that she believed the statements would have to include a going concern note. Majestic said that such a note really wasn't needed because the bank loan was so certain and that inclusion of such a note would certainly cause the management of the bank to change its mind about the loan.

Robertson finally acquiesced and the audited statements were issued without the note. The company received the loan, but things did not improve as Majestic thought they would and the company filed for bankruptcy in August 2000.

The bank sued Sarah Robertson for fraud.

Required

Indicate whether or not you think the bank would succeed. Support your answer.

CASES

5-28 (Objectives 5-5, 5-6)   *Part 1.* Whitlow & Company is a brokerage firm registered under the Securities Exchange Act of 1934. The act requires such a brokerage firm to file audited financial statements with the SEC annually. Mitchell & Moss, Whitlow's CPAs, performed the annual audit for the year ended December 31, 1999, and rendered an unqualified opinion, which was filed with the SEC along with Whitlow's financial statements. During 1999, Charles, the president of Whitlow & Company, engaged in a huge embezzlement scheme that eventually bankrupted the firm. As a result, substantial losses were suffered by customers and shareholders of Whitlow & Company, including Thaxton, who had recently purchased several shares of stock of Whitlow & Company after reviewing the company's 1999 audit report. Mitchell & Moss's audit was deficient; if they had complied with GAAS, the embezzlement would have been discovered. However, Mitchell & Moss had no knowledge of the embezzlement, nor could their conduct be categorized as reckless.

Required

Answer the following questions, setting forth reasons for any conclusions stated:

   a. What liability to Thaxton, if any, does Mitchell & Moss have under the Securities Exchange Act of 1934?
   b. What theory or theories of liability, if any, are available to Whitlow & Company's customers and shareholders under common law?

Part 2. Jackson is a sophisticated investor. As such, she was initially a member of a small group that was going to participate in a private placement of $1 million of common stock of Clarion Corporation. Numerous meetings were held among management and the

---

*AICPA adapted.

investor group. Detailed financial and other information was supplied to the participants. Upon the eve of completion of the placement, it was aborted when one major investor withdrew. Clarion then decided to offer $2.5 million of Clarion common stock to the public pursuant to the registration requirements of the Securities Act of 1933. Jackson subscribed to $300,000 of the Clarion public stock offering. Nine months later, Clarion's earnings dropped significantly and as a result the stock dropped 20 percent beneath the offering price. In addition, the Dow Jones Industrial Average was down 10 percent from the time of the offering.

Jackson has sold her shares at a loss of $60,000 and seeks to hold all parties liable who participated in the public offering, including Clarion's CPA firm of Allen, Dunn, and Rose. Although the audit was performed in conformity with GAAS, there were some relatively minor misstatements. The financial statements of Clarion Corporation, which were part of the registration statement, contained minor misleading facts. It is believed by Clarion and Allen, Dunn, and Rose that Jackson's asserted claim is without merit.

Required

Answer the following questions, setting forth reasons for any conclusions stated:

    a. If Jackson sues under the Securities Act of 1933, what will be the basis of her claim?

    b. What are the probable defenses that might be asserted by Allen, Dunn, and Rose in light of these facts?*

5-29 (Objectives 5-3, 5-5) Western Leasing Incorporated (WSI) was a leasing company headquartered in San Diego that leased equipment to construction companies, restaurants, gas stations, and medical and dental practices. WSI grew rapidly and by the late 1990s had a portfolio of more than $100 million of gross lease receivables. WSI obtained its financing from its primary banker, First National Bank. The line of credit obtained by First National was secured by WSI's lease receivables. To maintain its credit line, WSI was required to maintain positive earnings and a positive net worth and to provide First National with annual audited financial statements. WSI engaged the accounting firm of Sinclair & Lewis as its auditors. Through the year ended December 31, 1998, Sinclair & Lewis had audited WSI for 10 consecutive years. Each audit had resulted in an unqualified opinion.

In June of 1999, WSI's president, Wally Vernon, became seriously ill and was forced to take sudden retirement. The Maxwell family, who owned all of the stock of WSI but were not actively involved in management other than holding two seats on the board, hired a consultant to consider Vernon's replacement. The consultant advised the Maxwells that first, an outsider should be brought in as the new CEO, and second, that he perceived that there were serious problems at WSI.

As its next step, the Maxwells hired Bob Riddell as WSI's new CEO. Riddell promptly informed the Maxwells that he believed there were a number of serious problems at WSI, including the quality of the lease portfolio. He requested that Sinclair & Lewis be brought in to do a June 30 special audit. This was done, and to Sinclair & Lewis and the Maxwell's unpleasant surprise, it was discovered that WSI's lease receivable loss reserves were understated by approximately $16 million. This amount resulted in a violation of the company's lending agreement. This default eventually resulted in WSI's filing for bankruptcy, with eventual losses to the Maxwells in excess of $10 million. The Maxwells sued Sinclair & Lewis for breach of contract, claiming that they failed to properly conduct their audits of WSI, for at least the period 1993 through 1998, the period during which, the Maxwells and Riddell concluded, Vernon and other management personnel made misrepresentations to Sinclair & Lewis about the condition of many leases, misrepresentations that Sinclair & Lewis failed to find.

During the discovery portion of the litigation, the Maxwells' attorney deposed Harold Raines, the Sinclair & Lewis manager on the WSI audit. The following questions and answers are excerpted from that deposition.

*AICPA adapted.

Q. How long were you associated with the WSI audit, Mr. Raines?

A. Ever since we did it. I started as staff auditor on the job and worked my way up to manager.

Q. Have you ever been to a training program on auditing leasing companies?

A. No sir, WSI was so small, I guess the partners in our firm didn't think it was necessary. Besides, when you get right down to it, all audits are about the same. I don't think there is anything special about a leasing company audit.

Q. Have you ever read the AICPA Industry Audit Guide for Commercial Finance Companies?

A. I may have; I don't recall.

Q. What were the higher risk areas in the audit?

A. I'm not sure that I looked at it that way. We have a standard audit program where we try to do the appropriate things in all areas of the audit. Saying that one area is riskier than another doesn't make sense.

Q. How did you audit the lease loss reserve account?

A. We did several things:

- We asked for and received a delinquency list that showed all leases past due.
- We tested the completeness of the list by pulling a sample of lease cards and seeing that those we selected were on the delinquency list if they were overdue.
- We discussed the large delinquent leases with Mr. Vernon and obtained his estimate of the potential losses. We added those up and compared them to the loss reserve balance to judge its reasonableness.

Q. When you added the potential losses for December 31, 1998, what did they total in relation to the balance in the loss reserve account?

A. They were significantly less than the reserve account balance. As I recall, the reserve account balance was about $3 million and the sum of the potential losses was only about $2.7 million.

Q. And you believe that indicates that the overall loss reserve was adequate to cover all losses?

A. Well, yes. But more important, WSI thought it was. They said so in their representation letter to us that we obtained at the end of the audit.

Q. As I understand it, in the closing conference for the audit, Mr. Vernon told you that ABC Manufacturing, one of their largest customers, had filed bankruptcy at about year end, yet that lease wasn't on the delinquency list. Didn't that cause you concern that the delinquency list might not be complete?

A. No, not really. After all, Mr. Vernon volunteered the information. Also, when I weighed 10 years of good experience with Mr. Vernon against that one incident, I certainly felt he was as trustworthy as ever.

Required

    a. Analyze Raines's responses to the questions posed in terms of possible violations by Sinclair & Lewis of GAAS.

    b. Assuming Sinclair & Lewis did fail to comply with GAAS in its audit of WSI, what should its responsibility be for damages relative to the responsibility of the other parties involved?

INTERNET PROBLEM 5-1: SEC ENFORCEMENT

Reference the CW site. The SEC's Enforcement Division posts Litigation Releases, which are descriptions of SEC civil and selected criminal suits in the federal courts proceedings. This problem requires students to use the Internet to look up and answer questions associated with litigation releases.

PART II
(Chapters 6–12)

THE AUDIT PROCESS

Part II presents the audit process in a manner that will enable you to apply the concepts developed in these chapters to any audit area. It is essential to understand the material in these chapters because the information will be used extensively in almost all chapters throughout the rest of the book. We also highlight the importance of audit planning.

Chapters 6 and 7 deal with auditors' and managements' responsibilities, audit objectives, and general concepts of evidence accumulation. The next four chapters study various aspects of audit planning in depth. Chapter 12 summarizes and integrates audit planning and audit evidence. You will use these planning concepts throughout the rest of the book.

AUDIT RESPONSIBILITIES AND OBJECTIVES

6

not expect to memorize everything

WHERE WERE THE AUDITORS?

Barry Minkow was a true "whiz kid." He started ZZZZ Best Company, a high-flying carpet cleaning company specializing in insurance restoration contracts, at the age of 16. In 1982, when Minkow started the business, it was run out of his garage, but a mere 5 years later he had taken the company public and it had sales of $50 million and earnings of more than $5 million. The market value of Minkow's stock in ZZZZ Best exceeded $100 million.

As it turned out, Minkow's genius lay not in business, but in deception. Instead of being a solid operation company, ZZZZ Best was an illusion. There were no large restoration jobs and no real revenues and profits. They were only on paper and supported by an effective network of methods to deceive shareholders, the SEC, and the reputable professionals who served the company, including its auditors. Many, including members of Congress, asked, "How could this happen? Where were the auditors?"

When ZZZZ Best first started to grow, Minkow ran into the common problem of needing credit. He devised a scheme with an insurance adjuster to validate nonexistent jobs to potential creditors. Minkow could then get large sums of cash or credit despite not doing any real work. The scam was broadened when ZZZZ Best started needing audits. To fool the auditors, the co-conspirator insurance adjuster was kept busy running a company that generated false contracts for ZZZZ Best. When the auditors tried to check on those contracts, the adjuster confirmed them. Minkow even went so far as taking auditors to real work sites, sites that weren't actually his. He even leased a partially completed building and hired subcontractors to perform work on the site, all for the sake of a visit by the auditors.

As incredible as the ZZZZ Best story may seem, when asked about it, most knowledgeable observers would answer: "It's not the first time, and it won't be the last." It is also not the last time people will ask, "Where were the auditors?"

Before beginning the study of how to conduct an audit, it is necessary to understand the overall objectives of the audit, the auditor's responsibilities in conducting the audit, and the specific objectives the auditor tries to accomplish. Without an understanding of these topics, planning and accumulating audit evidence during the audit has no relevance. Figure 6-1 (bottom of this page) summarizes the five topics that provide keys to understanding evidence accumulation. These are the steps used to develop specific audit objectives.

OBJECTIVE OF CONDUCTING AN AUDIT OF FINANCIAL STATEMENTS

OBJECTIVE 6-1
Explain the objective of conducting an audit of financial statements.

SAS 1 (AU 110) states

> The objective of the ordinary audit of financial statements by the independent auditor is the expression of an opinion on the fairness with which they present fairly, in all material respects, financial position, results of operations, and its cash flows in conformity with generally accepted accounting principles.

That section of the SAS appropriately emphasizes issuing an opinion on *financial statements*. The only reason auditors accumulate evidence is to enable them to reach conclusions about whether financial statements are fairly stated in all material respects and to issue an appropriate audit report.

When, on the basis of adequate evidence, the auditor concludes that the financial statements are unlikely to mislead a prudent user, the auditor gives an audit opinion on their fair presentation and associates his or her name with the statements. If facts subsequent to their issuance indicate that the statements were actually not fairly presented, the auditor is likely to have to demonstrate to the courts or regulatory agencies that he or she conducted the audit in a proper manner and drew reasonable conclusions. Although not an insurer or a guarantor of the fairness of the presentations in the statements, the auditor has

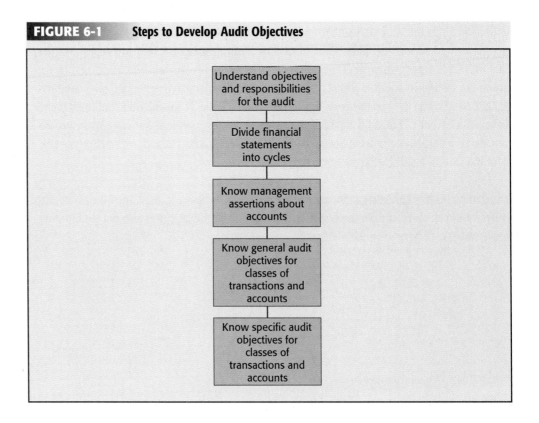

FIGURE 6-1   Steps to Develop Audit Objectives

considerable responsibility for notifying users whether the statements are properly stated. If the auditor believes that the statements are not fairly presented or is unable to reach a conclusion because of insufficient evidence or prevailing conditions, the auditor has the responsibility for notifying the users through the auditor's report.

MANAGEMENT'S RESPONSIBILITIES

> **OBJECTIVE 6-2**
> Distinguish management's responsibilities for preparing financial statements from the auditor's responsibilities for verifying those financial statements.

The responsibility for adopting sound accounting policies, maintaining adequate internal control, and making fair representations in the financial statements *rests with management* rather than with the auditor. Because they operate the business daily, a company's management knows more about the company's transactions and related assets, liabilities, and equity than the auditor does. In contrast, the auditor's knowledge of these matters and internal control is limited to that acquired during the audit.

In recent years, the annual reports of many public companies have included a statement about management's responsibilities and relationship with the CPA firm. Figure 6-2 (p. 144) presents a report of management for the Boeing Company as a part of their annual report. Read the report carefully to determine what management states about its responsibilities.

Management's responsibility for the fairness of the representations (assertions) in the financial statements carries with it the privilege of determining which disclosures it considers necessary. Although management has the responsibility for the preparation of the financial statements and the accompanying footnotes, it is acceptable for an auditor to draft the financial statements for the client or to offer suggestions for clarification. In the event that management insists on financial statement disclosure that the auditor finds unacceptable, the auditor can either issue an adverse or qualified opinion or withdraw from the engagement.

AUDITOR'S RESPONSIBILITIES

> **OBJECTIVE 6-3**
> Explain the auditor's responsibility for discovering material misstatements.

SAS 1 (AU 110) states

> The auditor has a responsibility to plan and perform the audit to obtain reasonable assurance about whether the financial statements are free of material misstatement, whether caused by error or fraud. Because of the nature of audit evidence and the characteristics of fraud, the auditor is able to obtain reasonable, but not absolute, assurance that material misstatements are detected. The auditor has no responsibility to plan and perform the audit to obtain reasonable assurance that misstatements, whether caused by errors or fraud, that are not material to the financial statements are detected.

This paragraph and the related discussion in the standards includes several important terms and phrases.

Material versus Immaterial Misstatements Misstatements are usually considered material if the combined uncorrected errors and fraud in the financial statements would likely have changed or influenced the decisions of a reasonable person using the statements. Although it is extremely difficult to quantify a measure of materiality, auditors are responsible for obtaining reasonable assurance that this materiality threshold has been satisfied. It would be extremely costly (and probably impossible) for auditors to have responsibility for finding all immaterial errors and fraud.

Reasonable Assurance Assurance is a measure of the level of certainty that the auditor has obtained at the completion of the audit. Reasonable assurance is not defined in the literature, but it is presumably less than certainty or absolute assurance and more than a low level of assurance. The concept of reasonable, but not absolute, assurance indicates that the auditor is not an insurer or guarantor of the correctness of the financial statements.

FIGURE 6-2	The Boeing Company's Report of Management

1997 ANNUAL REPORT

REPORT OF MANAGEMENT

To the Shareholders of the Boeing Company:

The accompanying consolidated financial statements of The Boeing Company and subsidiaries have been prepared by management who are responsible for their integrity and objectivity. The statements have been prepared in conformity with generally accepted accounting principles and include amounts based on management's best estimates and judgments. Financial information elsewhere in this Annual Report is consistent with that in the financial statements.

Management has established and maintains a system of internal control designed to provide reasonable assurance that errors or fraud that could be material to the financial statements are prevented or would be detected within a timely period. The system of internal control includes widely communicated statements of policies and business practices which are designed to require all employees to maintain high ethical standards in the conduct of Company affairs. The internal controls are augmented by organizational arrangements that provide for appropriate delegation of authority and division of responsibility and by a program of internal audit with management follow-up.

The financial statements have been audited by Deloitte & Touche LLP, independent certified public accountants. Their audit was conducted in accordance with generally accepted auditing standards and included a review of internal controls and selective tests of transactions. The Independent Auditors' Report appears below.

The Audit Committee of the Board of Directors, composed entirely of outside directors, meets periodically with the independent certified public accountants, management and internal auditors to review accounting, auditing, internal accounting controls, litigation and financial reporting matters. The independent certified public accountants and the internal auditors have free access to this committee without management present.

Philip M. Condit	B.E. Givan	Gary W. Beil
Chairman of the Board and Chief Executive Officer	Senior Vice President and Chief Financial Officer	Vice President and Controller

There are several reasons why the auditor is responsible for reasonable but not absolute assurance. First, most audit evidence results from testing a sample of a population such as accounts receivable or inventory. Sampling inevitably includes some risk of not uncovering a material misstatement. Also, the areas to be tested; the type, extent, and timing of those tests; and the evaluation of test results require significant auditor judgment. Even with good faith and integrity, auditors can make mistakes and errors in judgment. Second, accounting presentations contain complex estimates, which inherently involve uncertainty and can be affected by future events. As a result, the auditor has to rely on evidence that is persuasive, but not convincing. Third, fraudulently prepared financial statements are often extremely difficult, if not impossible, for the auditor to detect, especially when there is collusion among management.

If the auditor were responsible for making certain that all the assertions in the statements were correct, evidence requirements and the resulting cost of the audit function would increase to such an extent that audits would not be economically practical. Even then, auditors would be unlikely to uncover all material misstatements in every audit. The auditor's best defense when material misstatements are not uncovered in the audit is that the audit was conducted in accordance with generally accepted auditing standards.

Errors versus Fraud SAS 82 (AU 316) distinguishes between two types of misstatements: errors and fraud. Either type of misstatement can be material or immaterial. An **error** is an *unintentional* misstatement of the financial statements, whereas **fraud** is *intentional.* Two examples of errors are a mistake in extending prices times quantity on a sales invoice and overlooking older raw materials in determining the lower of cost or market for inventory.

For fraud, there is a distinction between **misappropriation of assets**, often called defalcation or employee fraud, and **fraudulent financial reporting**, often called management fraud. An example of misappropriation of assets is a clerk taking cash at the time a sale is made and not entering the sale in the cash register. An example of fraudulent financial reporting is the intentional overstatement of sales near the balance sheet date to increase reported earnings.

Professional Skepticism SAS 1 (AU 230) requires that an audit be designed to provide reasonable assurance of detecting *both* material errors and fraud in the financial statements. To accomplish this, the audit must be planned and performed with an *attitude of professional skepticism* in all aspects of the engagement. Professional skepticism is an attitude that includes a questioning mind and a critical assessment of audit evidence. The auditor should not assume that management is dishonest, but the possibility of dishonesty must be considered. The auditor also should not assume that management is unquestionably honest.

Auditors spend a great portion of their time planning and performing audits to detect the unintentional mistakes made by management and employees. Auditors find a variety of errors resulting from such things as mistakes in calculation, omissions, misunderstanding and misapplication of accounting standards, and incorrect summarizations and descriptions. Most of the remainder of this book deals with how the auditor plans and performs audits for detecting both errors and fraud.

Auditor's Responsibilities for Detecting Material Errors

Auditing standards make no distinction between the auditor's responsibilities for searching for errors and fraud, whether from fraudulent financial reporting or misappropriation of assets. For both errors and fraud, the auditor must obtain reasonable assurance about whether the statements are free of material misstatements.

Auditor's Responsibilities for Detecting Material Fraud

The standards also recognize that it is often more difficult to detect fraud than errors because management or the employees perpetrating the fraud *attempt to conceal the fraud.* The difficulty of detection does not change the auditor's responsibility to properly plan and perform the audit.

An important part of planning every audit is to assess the risk of errors and fraud. The discussion that follows deals only with the risk assessment requirements for fraud outlined in SAS 82.

In making a risk assessment for fraud, it is useful to keep in mind that fraud typically includes two characteristics. The auditor's risk assessment for fraud focuses on both of these two characteristics, which are as follows:

Certified Fraud Examiners

1. *Pressure or incentive to commit the fraud.* Often, this pressure is a desire for direct financial gain in the case of misappropriation of assets or an indirect gain in the case of fraudulent financial reporting. The gain in the second case may be, for example, an increase in the market value of company shares held by management.
2. *Perceived opportunity to commit the fraud.* Even though there is an incentive to commit fraud, it is unlikely to occur unless the individual or individuals involved believe they can do so without being detected.

Fraud Resulting from Fraudulent Financial Reporting versus Misappropriation of Assets There is an important difference between fraudulent financial reporting and misappropriation of assets. Fraudulent financial reporting harms users by providing incorrect financial statement information for their decision making. When assets are misappropriated, stockholders, creditors, and others are harmed because assets are no longer available to their rightful owners. Both types of fraud are potentially harmful to users.

Typically, fraudulent financial reporting is committed by management, sometimes without the knowledge of employees. Management is in a position to make accounting and reporting decisions without employees' knowledge. An example is the decision to omit an important footnote about pending litigation.

Usually, but not always, theft of assets is perpetrated by employees and not by management, and the amounts are often immaterial. However, there are well-known examples of extremely material misappropriation of assets by employees and management.

An important concept for misappropriation of assets is the distinction between the theft of assets and misstatements arising from the theft of assets. To illustrate, following are three situations involving the theft of assets:

1. Assets were taken and the theft was covered by overstating assets. For example, cash collected from a customer was stolen, and the account receivable for the customer's account was not credited. The misstatement has not been discovered.
2. Assets were taken and the theft was covered by understating revenues or overstating expenses. For example, cash from a cash sale was stolen, and the transaction was not recorded. The misstatement has not been discovered.
3. Assets were taken, but the misappropriation was discovered. The income statement and related footnotes clearly describe the misappropriation.

In all three situations, there has been a misappropriation of assets, but the financial statements are misstated only in situations 1 and 2. In situation 1, the balance sheet is misstated, whereas in situation 2, revenues or expenses are misstated.

Assessing Risks of Fraud

An important part of SAS 82 is the requirement that auditors specifically assess the risk of material misstatement due to fraud. The risk factors for fraudulent financial reporting are different than those for misappropriation of assets because the nature of the fraud is different.

For fraudulent financial reporting, three categories of risk factors are identified in SAS 82. For each category, the standard includes examples of these risk factors to provide guidance to practitioners. The three categories of risk factors and examples for each category are included in Table 6-1 (p. 147).

KPMG Fraud
Survey

The risk factors that auditors assess for misappropriation of assets are somewhat different than those for fraudulent financial reporting. The two categories of risk factors for misappropriation of assets and examples for each category are shown in Table 6-2 (p. 147).

For both fraudulent financial reporting and misappropriation of assets, the auditor must also do the following:

• Make inquiries of management about their assessment of the likelihood of fraud and whether they have knowledge of fraud that has occurred.
• Evaluate the risk of fraud as the audit proceeds. Often, the auditor's perception of the likelihood of fraud changes as he or she performs audit procedures and makes inquiries of management throughout the audit. For example, important missing documents or records may affect the auditor's assessment of the likelihood of fraud.

Evaluating Risk Factors and Modifying Evidence or Taking Other Action After the auditor has identified risk factors indicating a higher than normal potential for fraud, the

TABLE 6-1   The Three SAS 82 Categories of Risk Factors for Fraudulent Financial Reporting and Three Examples of Each

CATEGORY 1 **Management's Characteristics and Influence over the Control Environment**	CATEGORY 2 **Industry Conditions**	CATEGORY 3 **Operating Characteristics and Financial Stability**
These pertain to management's abilities, pressures, style, and attitude relating to internal control and the financial reporting process.	*These involve the economic and regulatory environment in which the entity operates.*	*These pertain to the nature and complexity of the entity and its transactions, financial condition, and profitability*

Examples of Risk Factors

Category 1:
- A motivation for management to engage in fraudulent financial reporting, such as an excessive interest by management to maintain or increase the entity's stock price or earnings trend through the use of unusually aggressive accounting practices
- A failure by management to display and communicate an appropriate attitude regarding internal control and the financial reporting process, such as domination of management by a single person or small group without compensating controls
- High turnover of senior management, counsel, or board members

Category 2:
- New accounting, statutory, or regulatory requirements that could impair the financial stability or profitability of the entity
- Declining industry with increasing business failures and significant declines in customer demand
- Rapid changes in the industry, such as high vulnerability to rapidly changing technology or rapid product obsolescence

Category 3:
- Significant pressure to obtain additional capital necessary to stay competitive considering the financial position of the entity
- Significant, unusual, or highly complex transactions, especially those close to year-end, that pose difficult "substance over form" questions
- Overly complex organizational structure involving numerous or unusual legal entities, managerial lines of authority, or contractual arrangements without apparent business purpose

auditor must decide the potential for fraud and what to do about it. These decisions are complex and require considerable professional judgment. SAS 82 provides guidance to help the auditor make these decisions. In concept, the process is the same for errors, fraudulent financial reporting, and misappropriation of assets. The specific effects will, of course, depend on the circumstances.

The box on page 148 highlights key findings from a recent study of financial statement fraud committed by U.S. public companies between 1987 and 1997.

TABLE 6-2   The Two SAS 82 Categories of Risk Factors for Misappropriation of Assets and Three Examples of Each

CATEGORY 1 **Susceptibility of Assets to Misappropriation**	CATEGORY 2 **Controls**
These pertain to the nature of an entity's assets and the degree to which they are subject to theft.	*These involve the lack of controls designed to prevent or detect misappropriations of assets.*

Examples of Risk Factors

Category 1:
- Large amounts of cash on hand or processed
- Easily convertible assets, such as bearer bonds, diamonds, or computer chips
- Fixed asset characteristics, such as small size, marketability, or lack of ownership identification

Category 2:
- Lack of appropriate management oversight, such as inadequate supervision or monitoring of remote locations
- Inadequate record keeping with respect to assets susceptible to misappropriation
- Lack of timely and appropriate documentation for transactions, such as credits for merchandise returns

The two most common techniques used by management to misstate financial statement information involve improper revenue recognition and overstatements of assets. According to a study commissioned by the Committee of Sponsoring Organizations of the Treadway Commission (COSO), 50 percent of U.S. companies committing financial statement fraud between 1987 and 1997 recorded revenues prematurely or created fictitious revenue transactions. In addition to these revenue and receivable overstatements, 50 percent of the fraud companies overstated assets by overvaluing existing assets, recording fictitious assets or assets not owned, or capitalizing items that should have been expensed. Assets typically overstated included inventory, net accounts receivable due to understated allowances for doubtful accounts, and property, plant, and equipment. Only 18 percent of the fraud companies understated expenses or liabilities. Most of the financial statement fraud instances involved intentionally misstating financial information, with only 12 percent of the fraud cases involving misappropriation of company assets.

The median fraud was $4.1 million, which is relatively large given that the median company had total assets of $15.7 million. Eighty-three percent of the fraud cases were perpetrated by the chief executive officer (CEO) and/or the chief financial officer (CFO). These individuals allegedly engaged in the fraud to avoid reporting a pre-tax loss, to maintain requirements to continue trading company stock on one of the national stock exchanges, or to increase stock prices. The motivation to commit the fraud was high because, on average, company officers and members of the board of directors owned 32 percent of the company stock.

Consequences of the fraud were significant. More than 50 percent of the companies filed for bankruptcy or were under a substantially different form of ownership following the fraud period. Many of the individuals involved were forced to resign or were terminated as a result of the fraud. In some cases, those involved were jailed. Additionally, both the companies and individuals faced lawsuits filed by shareholders and the SEC.

Source: *Fraudulent Financial Reporting: 1987–1997, An Analysis of U.S. Public Companies,* Committee of Sponsoring Organizations of the Treadway Commission, New York, 1999.

Auditor's Responsibilities for Discovering Illegal Acts

Illegal acts are defined in SAS 54 (AU 317) as violations of laws or government regulations *other than fraud.* Two examples of illegal acts are a violation of federal tax laws and a violation of the federal environmental protection laws.

Forensic Accounting and Fraud Information Sites

Direct-Effect Illegal Acts Certain violations of laws and regulations have a direct financial effect on specific account balances in the financial statements. For example, a violation of federal tax laws directly affects income tax expense and income taxes payable. The auditor's responsibilities under SAS 54 for these direct-effect illegal acts is the same as for errors and fraud. On each audit, therefore, the auditor will normally evaluate whether or not there is evidence available to indicate material violations of federal or state tax laws. This might be done by discussions with client personnel and examination of reports issued by the Internal Revenue Service after they have completed an examination of the client's tax return.

Indirect-Effect Illegal Acts Most illegal acts affect the financial statements only indirectly. For example, if the company violates environmental protection laws, there is an effect on the financial statements only if there is a fine or sanction. Potential material fines and sanctions indirectly affect financial statements by creating the need to disclose a contingent liability for the potential amount that might ultimately be paid. This is called an indirect-effect illegal act. Other examples of illegal acts that are likely to have only an indirect effect are violations of insider securities trading regulations, civil rights laws, and federal employee safety requirements.

Auditing standards clearly state that the auditor provides *no assurance* that indirect-effect illegal acts will be detected. Auditors lack legal expertise, and the frequent indirect relationship between illegal acts and the financial statements makes it impractical for auditors to assume responsibility for discovering those illegal acts.

There are three levels of responsibility that the auditor has for finding and reporting illegal acts.

Evidence Accumulation When There Is No Reason to Believe Indirect-Effect Illegal Acts Exist Many audit procedures normally performed on audits to search for errors and fraud may also uncover illegal acts. Examples include reading the minutes of the board of directors and inquiring of the client's attorneys about litigation. The auditor should also inquire of management about policies they have established to prevent illegal acts and whether management knows of any laws or regulations that the company has violated. Other than these procedures, the auditor should not search for indirect-effect illegal acts unless there is reason to believe they may exist.

Evidence Accumulation and Other Actions When There Is Reason to Believe Direct- or Indirect-Effect Illegal Acts May Exist The auditor may find indications of possible illegal acts in a variety of ways. For example, the minutes may indicate that an investigation by a government agency is in process or the auditor may have identified unusually large payments to consultants or government officials.

When the auditor believes that an illegal act may have occurred, it is necessary to take several actions: First, the auditor should inquire of management at a level above those likely to be involved in the potential illegal act. Second, the auditor should consult with the client's legal counsel or other specialist who is knowledgeable about the potential illegal act. Third, the auditor should consider accumulating additional evidence to determine whether there actually is an illegal act. All three of these actions are intended to provide the auditor with information about whether the suspected illegal act actually exists.

Actions When the Auditor Knows of an Illegal Act The first course of action when an illegal act has been identified is to consider the effects on the financial statements, including the adequacy of disclosures. These effects may be complex and difficult to resolve. For example, a violation of civil rights laws could involve significant fines, but it could also result in the loss of customers or key employees, which could materially affect future revenues and expenses. If the auditor concludes that the disclosures relative to an illegal act are inadequate, the auditor should modify the audit report accordingly.

The auditor should also consider the effect of such illegal acts on its relationship with management. If management knew of the illegal act and failed to inform the auditor, it is questionable whether management can be believed in other discussions.

The auditor should communicate with the audit committee or others of equivalent authority to make sure that they know of the illegal act. The communication can be oral or written. If it is oral, the nature of the communication and discussion should be documented in the working papers. If the client either refuses to accept the auditor's modified report or fails to take appropriate remedial action concerning the illegal act, the auditor may find it necessary to withdraw from the engagement. If the client is publicly held, the auditor must also report the matter directly to the SEC. Such decisions are complex and normally involve consultation by the auditor with the auditor's legal counsel.

FINANCIAL STATEMENT CYCLES

Audits are performed by dividing the financial statements into smaller segments or components. The division makes the audit more manageable and aids in the assignment of

OBJECTIVE 6-4

Classify transactions and account balances into financial statement cycles and identify benefits of a cycle approach to segmenting the audit.

tasks to different members of the audit team. For example, most auditors treat fixed assets and notes payable as different segments. Each segment is audited separately but not on a completely independent basis. (For example, the audit of fixed assets may reveal an unrecorded note payable.) After the audit of each segment is completed, including interrelationships with other segments, the results are combined. A conclusion can then be reached about the financial statements taken as a whole.

There are different ways of segmenting an audit. One approach would be to treat every account balance on the statements as a separate segment. Segmenting that way is usually inefficient. It would result in the independent audit of such closely related accounts as inventory and cost of goods sold.

Cycle Approach to Segmenting an Audit

A more common way to divide an audit is to keep closely related types (or classes) of transactions and account balances in the same segment. This is called the **cycle approach**. For example, sales, sales returns, cash receipts, and charge-offs of uncollectible accounts are the four classes of transactions that cause accounts receivable to increase and decrease. Therefore, they are all part of the sales and collection cycle. Similarly, payroll transactions and accrued payroll are a part of the payroll and personnel cycle.

The logic of using the cycle approach can be seen by thinking about the way transactions are recorded in journals and summarized in the general ledger and financial statements. Figure 6-3 shows that flow. To the extent that it is practical, the cycle approach combines transactions recorded in different journals with the general ledger balances that result from those transactions.

The cycles used in this text follow and are then explained in detail. Observe that each of these cycles is so important that it is part of the title of one or more chapters in the remainder of this book.

- Sales and collection cycle
- Acquisition and payment cycle
- Payroll and personnel cycle
- Inventory and warehousing cycle
- Capital acquisition and repayment cycle

*[margin flowchart:]*
Understand objectives and responsibilities for the audit
↓
Divide financial statements into cycles
↓
Know management assertions about accounts
↓
Know general audit objectives for classes of transactions and accounts
↓
Know specific audit objectives for classes of transactions and accounts

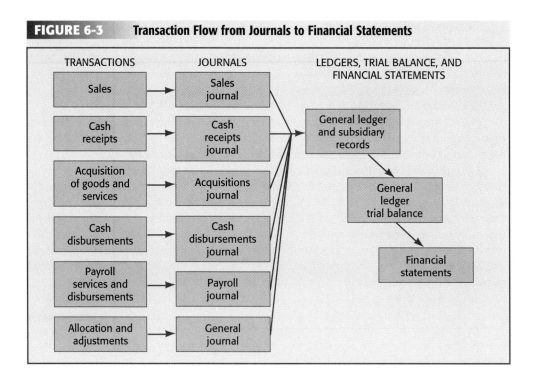

FIGURE 6-3 **Transaction Flow from Journals to Financial Statements**

To illustrate the application of cycles to audits, Figure 6-4 (p. 152) presents the December 31, 1999, trial balance for Hillsburg Hardware Company. A trial balance is used to prepare financial statements and is a primary focus of every audit. The letter representing a cycle is shown for each account in the left column beside the account name. Observe that each account has at least one cycle associated with it and only cash and inventory are a part of two or more cycles.

The cycles used in this text are shown again in Table 6-3 (p. 153). The accounts for Hillsburg Hardware Co. are summarized in Table 6-3, by cycle, and include the related journals and financial statements in which the accounts appear.

The following observations expand the information contained in Table 6-3:

- All general ledger accounts and journals for Hillsburg Hardware Co. are included at least once. For a different company, the number and titles of journals and general ledger accounts would differ, but all would be included.
- Some journals and general ledger accounts are included in more than one cycle. When that occurs, it means that the journal is used to record transactions from more than one cycle and indicates a tie-in between the cycles. The most important general ledger account included in and affecting several cycles is general cash (cash in bank). General cash connects most cycles.
- The capital acquisition and repayment cycle is closely related to the acquisition and payment cycle. The acquisition of goods and services includes the purchase of inventory, supplies, and general services in performing the main business operations. Transactions in the capital acquisition and repayment cycle are related to financing the business, such as issuing stock or debt, paying dividends, and repayment of debt. The same three journals are used to record transactions for both cycles, and the transactions are similar. There are two reasons for treating capital acquisition and repayment separately from the acquisition of goods and services. First, the transactions are related to financing a company rather than to its operations. Second, most capital acquisition and repayment cycle accounts involve few transactions, but each is often highly material and therefore should be audited extensively. Considering both reasons, it is more convenient to separate the two cycles.
- The inventory and warehousing cycle is closely related to all other cycles, especially for a manufacturing company. The cost of inventory includes raw materials (acquisition and payment cycle), direct labor (payroll and personnel cycle), and manufacturing overhead (acquisition and payment and payroll and personnel cycles). The sale of finished goods involves the sales and collection cycle. Because inventory is material for most manufacturing companies, it is common to borrow money using inventory as security. In those cases, the capital acquisition and repayment cycle is also related to inventory and warehousing.

Relationships among Cycles

Figure 6-5 on page 154 illustrates the relationships of the cycles. In addition to the five cycles, general cash is also shown. Each cycle is studied in detail in later chapters.

Figure 6-5 shows that cycles have no beginning or end except at the origin and final disposition of a company. A company begins by obtaining capital, usually in the form of cash. In a manufacturing company, cash is used to acquire raw materials, fixed assets, and related goods and services to produce inventory (acquisition and payment cycle). Cash is also used to acquire labor for the same reason (payroll and personnel cycle). Acquisition and payment and payroll and personnel are similar in nature, but the functions are sufficiently different to justify separate cycles. The combined result of these two cycles is inventory (inventory and warehousing cycle). At a subsequent point, the inventory is sold and billings and collections result (sales and collection cycle). The cash generated is used to pay dividends and interest and to start the cycles again. The cycles interrelate in much the same way in a service company, where there will be no inventory, but there may be unbilled receivables.

FIGURE 6-4   Hillsburg Hardware Co. Adjusted Trial Balance

HILLSBURG HARDWARE CO.
TRIAL BALANCE
December 31, 1999

		Debit	Credit
S,A,P,C	Cash in bank	$ 41,378	
S	Trade accounts receivable	1,009,800	
S	Allowance for uncollectible accounts		$ 62,000
S	Other accounts receivable	47,251	
A,I	Inventories	1,493,231	
A	Prepaid expenses	21,578	
A	Land	172,821	
A	Buildings	1,625,000	
A	Delivery equipment	187,917	
A	Furniture and fixtures	127,321	
A	Accumulated depreciation		1,596,006
A	Trade accounts payable		235,999
C	Notes payable		208,981
P	Accrued payroll		67,489
P	Accrued payroll taxes		5,983
C	Accrued interest		7,478
C	Dividends payable		95,000
A	Estimated income tax		39,772
C	Long-term notes payable		1,206,000
A	Deferred tax		36,912
A	Other accrued payables		41,499
C	Capital stock		250,000
C	Capital in excess of par value		175,000
C	Retained earnings		596,354
S	Sales		7,216,389
S	Sales returns and allowances	62,083	
I	Cost of goods sold	5,162,038	
P	Salaries and commissions	386,900	
P	Sales payroll taxes	71,100	
A	Travel and entertainment—selling	55,517	
A	Advertising	130,563	
A	Sales and promotional literature	16,081	
A	Sales meetings and training	46,224	
A	Miscellaneous sales expense	34,052	
P	Executive and office salaries	276,198	
P	Administrative payroll taxes	34,115	
A	Travel and entertainment—administrative	28,080	
A	Stationery and supplies	38,128	
A	Postage	12,221	
A	Telephone and telegraph	36,115	
A	Dues and memberships	3,013	
A	Rent	15,607	
A	Legal fees and retainers	14,153	
A	Auditing	20,142	
A	Depreciation—office building and equipment	72,604	
S	Bad debt expense	166,154	
A	Insurance	36,134	
A	Office repairs and maintenance	57,196	
A	Miscellaneous office expense	47,180	
A	Miscellaneous general expense	26,192	
A	Gain on sale of assets		35,987
A	Income taxes	87,330	
C	Interest expense	120,432	
C	Dividends	95,000	
		$11,876,849	$ 11,876,849

Note: Letters in the left-hand column refer to the following transaction cycles.

 S = Sales and collection
 A = Acquisition and payment
 P = Payroll and personnel
 I = Inventory and warehousing
 C = Capital acquisition and repayment

TABLE 6-3	Cycles Applied to Hillsburg Hardware Co.		
		General Ledger Accounts Included in the Cycle (See Figure 6-4)	
Cycle	**Journals Included in the Cycle (See Figure 6-3)**	**Balance Sheet**	**Income Statement**
Sales and collection	Sales journal Cash receipts journal General journal	Cash in bank Trade accounts receivable Other accounts receivable Allowance for uncollectible accounts	Sales Sales returns and allowances Bad debt expense
Acquisition and payment	Acquisitions journal Cash disbursements journal General journal	Cash in bank Inventories Prepaid expenses Land Buildings Delivery equipment Furniture and fixtures Accumulated depreciation Trade accounts payable Other accrued payables Estimated income tax Deferred tax	Advertising[S] Travel and entertainment[S] Sales meetings and training[S] Sales and promotional literature[S] Miscellaneous sales expense[S] Travel and entertainment[A] Stationery and supplies[A] Postage[A] Telephone and telegraph[A] Dues and memberships[A] Taxes[A] Depreciation—office building and equipment[A] Rent[A] Legal fees and retainers[A] Auditing[A] Insurance[A] Office repairs and maintenance expense[A] Miscellaneous office expense[A] Miscellaneous general expense[A] Gain on sale of assets Income taxes
Payroll and personnel	Payroll journal General journal	Cash in bank Accrued payroll Accrued payroll taxes	Salaries and commissions[S] Sales payroll taxes[S] Executive and office salaries[A] Administrative payroll taxes[A]
Inventory and warehousing	Acquisitions journal Sales journal General journal	Inventories	Cost of goods sold
Capital acquisition and repayment	Acquisitions journal Cash disbursements journal General journal	Cash in bank Notes payable Long-term notes payable Accrued interest Capital stock Capital in excess of par value Retained earnings Dividends Dividends payable	Interest expense

S = Selling expense; A = general and administrative expense.

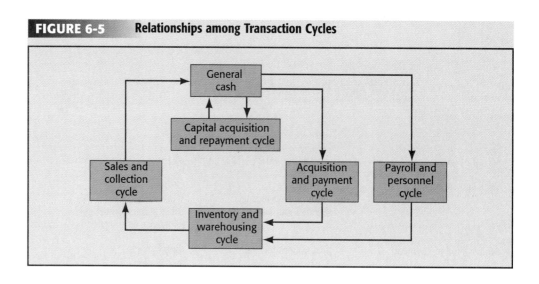

FIGURE 6-5 Relationships among Transaction Cycles

Transaction cycles are of major importance in the conduct of the audit. For the most part, auditors treat each cycle separately during the audit. Although care should be taken to interrelate different cycles at different times, the auditor must treat the cycles somewhat independently to manage complex audits effectively.

SETTING AUDIT OBJECTIVES

Auditors conduct audits consistently with the cycle approach by performing audit tests of the transactions making up ending balances and also by performing audit tests of the account balances themselves. Figure 6-6 illustrates this important concept by showing the four classes of transactions that determine the ending balance in accounts receivable. Assume that the beginning balance of $96 was audited in the prior year and is therefore considered reliable. If the auditor could be completely sure that each of the four classes of transactions

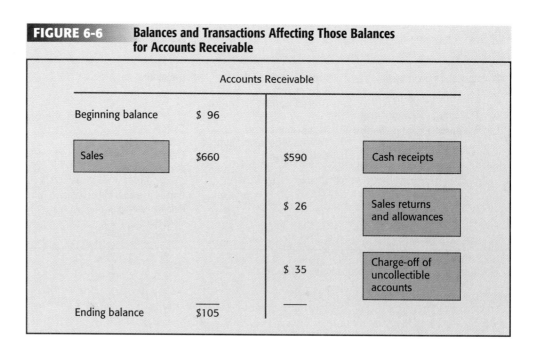

FIGURE 6-6 Balances and Transactions Affecting Those Balances for Accounts Receivable

Accounts Receivable			
Beginning balance	$ 96		
Sales	$660	$590	Cash receipts
		$ 26	Sales returns and allowances
		$ 35	Charge-off of uncollectible accounts
Ending balance	$105		

was correctly stated, the auditor could also be sure that the ending balance of $105 was correctly stated. But it may be impractical for the auditor to obtain complete assurance about the correctness of each class of transactions resulting in less than complete assurance about the ending balance in accounts receivable. In such a case, overall assurance can be increased by auditing the ending balance of accounts receivable. Auditors have found that, generally, the most efficient way to conduct audits is to *obtain some combination of assurance for each class of transactions and for the ending balance in the related account.*

For any given class of transactions, there are several audit objectives that must be met before the auditor can conclude that the transactions are properly recorded. They are called **transaction-related audit objectives** in the remainder of this book. For example, there are specific sales transaction-related audit objectives and specific sales returns and allowances transaction-related audit objectives.

Similarly, there are several audit objectives that must be met for each account balance. They are called **balance-related audit objectives**. For example, there are specific accounts receivable balance-related audit objectives and specific accounts payable balance-related audit objectives. It will be shown later that the transaction-related and balance-related audit objectives are somewhat different but closely related. Throughout the remainder of this text, the term *audit objectives* refers to both transaction-related and balance-related audit objectives.

Before examining audit objectives in more detail, it is necessary to understand management assertions. These are studied next.

Management assertions are implied or expressed representations by management about classes of transactions and the related accounts in the financial statements. As an illustration, the management of Hillsburg Hardware Co. asserts that cash of $41,378 (see Figure 6-4) was present in the company's bank accounts or on the premises as of the balance sheet date. Unless otherwise disclosed in the financial statements, management also asserts that the cash was unrestricted and available for normal use. Similar assertions exist for each asset, liability, owners' equity, revenue, and expense item in the financial statements. These assertions apply to both classes of transactions and account balances.

Management assertions are directly related to generally accepted accounting principles (GAAP). These assertions are part of the *criteria that management uses to record and disclose accounting information in financial statements.* Return to the definition of auditing in Chapter 1. It states, in part, that auditing is a comparison of information (financial statements) to established criteria (assertions established according to GAAP). Auditors must therefore understand the assertions to do adequate audits.

SAS 31 (AU 326) classifies assertions into five broad categories:

1. Existence or occurrence
2. Completeness
3. Valuation or allocation
4. Rights and obligations
5. Presentation and disclosure

Assertions about Existence or Occurrence Assertions about existence deal with whether assets, obligations, and equities included in the balance sheet actually existed on the balance sheet date. Assertions about occurrence concern whether recorded transactions included in the financial statements actually occurred during the accounting period. For example, management asserts that merchandise inventory included in the balance sheet exists and is available for sale at the balance sheet date. Similarly, management asserts that recorded sales transactions represent exchanges of goods or services that actually took place.

Assertions about Completeness These management assertions state that all transactions and accounts that should be presented in the financial statements are included. For example, management asserts that all sales of goods and services are recorded and included in the

Management Assertions

OBJECTIVE 6-6
Distinguish among the five categories of management assertions about financial information

Understand objectives and responsibilities for the audit

Divide financial statements into cycles

Know management assertions about accounts

Know general audit objectives for classes of transactions and accounts

Know specific audit objectives for classes of transactions and accounts

Phar-Mor
Accounting Fraud

financial statements. Similarly, management asserts that notes payable in the balance sheet include all such obligations of the entity.

The completeness assertion deals with matters opposite from those of the existence or occurrence assertion. The completeness assertion is concerned with the possibility of omitting items from the financial statements that should have been included, whereas the existence or occurrence assertion is concerned with inclusion of amounts that should not have been included. Thus, violations of the existence assertion relate to account overstatements, whereas violations of the completeness assertion relate to account understatements.

The recording of a sale that did not take place would be a violation of the occurrence assertion, whereas the failure to record a sale that did occur would be a violation of the completeness assertion.

Assertions about Valuation or Allocation These assertions deal with whether asset, liability, equity, revenue, and expense accounts have been included in the financial statements at appropriate amounts. For example, management asserts that property is recorded at historical cost and that such cost is systematically allocated to appropriate accounting periods through depreciation. Similarly, management asserts that trade accounts receivable included in the balance sheet are stated at net realizable value.

Assertions about Rights and Obligations These management assertions deal with whether assets are the rights of the entity and liabilities are the obligations of the entity at a given date. For example, management asserts that assets are owned by the company or that amounts capitalized for leases in the balance sheet represent the cost of the entity's rights to leased property and that the corresponding lease liability represents an obligation of the entity.

Assertions about Presentation and Disclosure These assertions deal with whether components of the financial statements are properly combined or separated, described, and disclosed. For example, management asserts that obligations classified as long-term liabilities in the balance sheet will not mature within 1 year. Similarly, management asserts that amounts presented as extraordinary items in the income statement are properly classified and described.

TRANSACTION-RELATED AUDIT OBJECTIVES

OBJECTIVE 6-7
Link the six general transaction-related audit objectives to the five management assertions.

The auditor's transaction-related audit objectives follow and are closely related to management assertions. That is not surprising because the auditor's primary responsibility is to determine whether management assertions about financial statements are justified.

These transaction-related audit objectives are intended to provide a *framework* to help the auditor accumulate sufficient competent evidence required by the third standard of field work and decide the proper evidence to accumulate for classes of transactions given the circumstances of the engagement. The objectives remain the same from audit to audit, but the evidence varies, depending on the circumstances.

A distinction must be made between general transaction-related audit objectives and specific transaction-related audit objectives for each class of transactions. The general transaction-related audit objectives discussed here are applicable to every class of transactions but are stated in broad terms. Specific transaction-related audit objectives are also applied to each class of transactions but are stated in terms tailored to a class of transactions such as sales transactions. Once you know the general transaction-related audit objectives, they can be used to develop specific transaction-related audit objectives for each class of transactions being audited. The six general transaction-related audit objectives are discussed next.

General Transaction-Related Audit Objectives

Existence—Recorded Transactions Exist This objective deals with whether recorded transactions have actually occurred. Inclusion of a sale in the sales journal when no sale occurred violates the existence objective. This objective is the auditor's counterpart to the management assertion of existence or occurrence.

Completeness—Existing Transactions Are Recorded This objective deals with whether all transactions that should be included in the journals have actually been included. Failure to include a sale in the sales journal and general ledger when a sale occurred violates the completeness objective. The objective is the counterpart to the management assertion of completeness.

The existence and completeness objectives emphasize opposite audit concerns; existence deals with potential overstatement and completeness with unrecorded transactions (understatement).

Accuracy—Recorded Transactions Are Stated at the Correct Amounts This objective deals with the accuracy of information for accounting transactions. For sales transactions, there would be a violation of the accuracy objective if the quantity of goods shipped was different from the quantity billed, the wrong selling price was used for billing, extension or adding errors occurred in billing, or the wrong amount was included in the sales journal. Accuracy is one part of the valuation or allocation assertion.

It is important to distinguish between accuracy and existence or completeness. For example, if a recorded sales transaction should not have been recorded because the shipment was on consignment, the existence objective has been violated, even if the amount of the invoice was accurately calculated. If the recorded sale was for a valid shipment but the amount was calculated incorrectly, there is a violation of the accuracy objective but not of existence. The same relationship exists between completeness and accuracy.

Classification—Transactions Included in the Client's Journals Are Properly Classified Examples of misclassifications for sales are including cash sales as credit sales, recording a sale of operating fixed assets as revenue, and misclassifying commercial sales as residential sales. Classification is also a part of the valuation or allocation assertion.

Timing—Transactions Are Recorded on the Correct Dates A timing error occurs if transactions are not recorded on the dates the transactions took place. A sales transaction, for example, should be recorded on the date of shipment. Timing is also a part of the valuation or allocation assertion.

Posting and Summarization—Recorded Transactions Are Properly Included in the Master Files and Are Correctly Summarized This objective deals with the accuracy of the transfer of information from recorded transactions in journals to subsidiary records and the general ledger. For example, if a sales transaction is recorded in the wrong customer's record or at the wrong amount in the master file, it is a violation of this objective. Posting and summarization is also a part of the valuation or allocation assertion.

Because the posting of transactions from journals to subsidiary records, the general ledger, and other related master files is typically accomplished automatically by computerized accounting systems, the risk of random human error in posting is minimal. Once the auditor can establish that the computer is functioning properly, there is a reduced concern about posting process errors.

The general transaction-related audit objectives must be applied to each material type (class) of transaction in the audit. Such transactions typically include sales, cash receipts, acquisitions of goods and services, payroll, and so on. Table 6-4 on page 158 summarizes the six transaction-related audit objectives. It includes the general form of the objectives, the application of the objectives to sales transactions, and the assertions. Notice that only three assertions are associated with transaction-related audit objectives. This shows that two of the assertions are not satisfied by performing transactions-related audit tests.

Understand objectives and responsibilities for the audit

Divide financial statements into cycles

Know management assertions about accounts

Know general audit objectives for classes of transactions and accounts

Know specific audit objectives for classes of transactions and accounts

Specific Transaction-Related Audit Objectives

TABLE 6-4 Transaction-Related Audit Objectives and Management Assertions for Sales Transactions

Management Assertions	General Transaction-Related Audit Objectives	Specific Sales Transaction-Related Audit Objectives
Existence or occurrence	Existence	Recorded sales are for shipments made to nonfictitious customers.
Completeness	Completeness	Existing sales transactions are recorded.
Valuation or allocation	Accuracy	Recorded sales are for the amount of goods shipped and are correctly billed and recorded.
	Classification	Sales transactions are properly classified.
	Timing	Sales are recorded on the correct dates.
	Posting and summarization	Sales transactions are properly included in the master file and are correctly summarized.
Rights and obligations	N/A	N/A
Presentation and disclosure	N/A	N/A

BALANCE-RELATED AUDIT OBJECTIVES

OBJECTIVE 6-8

Link the nine general balance-related audit objectives to the five management assertions.

Balance-related audit objectives are similar to the transaction-related audit objectives just discussed. They also follow from management assertions and they provide a framework to help the auditor accumulate sufficient competent evidence. There are also both general and specific balance-related audit objectives.

There are two differences between balance-related and transaction-related audit objectives. First, as the terms imply, balance-related audit objectives are applied to account balances, whereas transaction-related audit objectives are applied to classes of transactions such as sales transactions and cash disbursements transactions. Second, there are more audit objectives for account balances than for classes of transactions. There are nine balance-related audit objectives compared to six transaction-related audit objectives.

Because of the way audits are done, balance-related audit objectives are almost *always* applied to the ending balance in balance sheet accounts, such as accounts receivable, inventory, and notes payable. However, some balance-related objectives are applied to certain income statement accounts. These usually involve nonroutine transactions and unpredictable expenses, such as legal expense or repairs and maintenance. Other income statement accounts are closely related to balance sheet accounts and are tested simultaneously, such as depreciation expense with accumulated depreciation and interest expense with notes payable.

When using the balance-related audit objectives as a framework for auditing account balances, the auditor accumulates evidence to verify detail that supports the account balance, rather than verifying the account balance itself. For example, in auditing accounts receivable, the auditor obtains a listing of the accounts receivable master file from the client that agrees to the general ledger balance (see page 482 for an illustration). The accounts receivable balance-related audit objectives are applied to the customer accounts in that listing.

Following is a brief discussion of the nine general balance-related audit objectives. Throughout the discussion, there is reference to a supporting schedule, which refers to a client-provided working paper such as the accounts receivable listing just described.

Existence—Amounts Included Exist This objective deals with whether the amounts included in the financial statements should actually be included. For example, inclusion of an account receivable from a customer in the accounts receivable trial balance when there is no receivable from that customer violates the existence objective. This objective is the auditor's counterpart to the management assertion of existence or occurrence.

Completeness—Existing Amounts Are Included This objective deals with whether all amounts that should be included have actually been included. Failure to include an account receivable from a customer in the accounts receivable trial balance when a receivable exists violates the completeness objective. This objective is the counterpart to the management assertion of completeness.

The existence and completeness objectives emphasize opposite audit concerns; existence deals with potential overstatement and completeness with unrecorded transactions and amounts (understatement).

Accuracy—Amounts Included Are Stated at the Correct Amounts The accuracy objective refers to amounts being included at the correct arithmetic amount. An inventory item on a client's inventory listing could be wrong because the number of units of inventory on hand was misstated, the unit price was wrong, or the total was incorrectly extended. Each of these violates the accuracy objective. Accuracy is one part of the valuation or allocation assertion.

Classification—Amounts Included in the Client's Listing Are Properly Classified Classification involves determining whether items on a client's listing are included in the correct accounts. For example, on the accounts receivable listing, receivables must be separated into short-term and long-term, and amounts due from affiliates, officers, and directors must be classified separately from amounts due from customers. Classification is also a part of the valuation or allocation assertion.

Cutoff—Transactions Near the Balance Sheet Date Are Recorded in the Proper Period In testing for cutoff, the objective is to determine whether transactions are recorded in the proper period. The transactions that are most likely to be misstated are those recorded near the end of the accounting period. It is proper to think of cutoff tests as a part of verifying either the balance sheet accounts or the related transactions, but for convenience auditors usually perform them as a part of auditing balance sheet accounts. Cutoff is also a part of the valuation or allocation assertion.

Detail Tie-In—Details in the Account Balance Agree with Related Master File Amounts, Foot to the Total in the Account Balance, and Agree with the Total in the General Ledger Account balances on financial statements are supported by details in master files and schedules prepared by clients. The detail tie-in objective is concerned that the details on lists are accurately prepared, correctly added, and agree with the general ledger. For example, individual accounts receivable on a listing of accounts receivable should be the same in the accounts receivable master file and the total should equal the general ledger control account. Detail tie-in is also a part of the valuation or allocation assertion.

Realizable Value—Assets Are Included at the Amounts Estimated to Be Realized This objective concerns whether an account balance has been reduced for declines from historical cost to net realizable value. Examples when the objective applies are considering the adequacy of the allowance for uncollectible accounts receivable and write-downs of inventory for obsolescence. The objective applies only to asset accounts and is also a part of the valuation or allocation assertion.

Rights and Obligations In addition to existing, most assets must be owned before it is acceptable to include them in the financial statements. Similarly, liabilities must belong to the entity. Rights are always associated with assets and obligations with liabilities. This objective is the auditor's counterpart to the management assertion of rights and obligations.

Presentation and Disclosure—Account Balances and Related Disclosure Requirements Are Properly Presented in the Financial Statements In fulfilling the presentation and disclosure objective, the auditor tests to make certain that all balance sheet and income statement accounts and related information are correctly set forth in the financial statements and properly described in the body and footnotes of the statements. This objective has its counterpart in the management assertion of presentation and disclosure.

Presentation and disclosure is closely related to, but distinct from, classification. Accounting information for balance-related audit objectives is correctly classified if all information on a detailed schedule supporting an account balance is summarized in the appropriate accounts. The information is correctly disclosed if those account balances and related footnote information are properly combined, described, and presented in the financial statements. For example, if a long-term note receivable is included on an accounts receivable listing, there is a violation of the classification objective. If the long-term note receivable is correctly classified but combined with accounts receivable on the financial statements, there is a violation of the presentation and disclosure objective.

Specific Balance-Related Audit Objectives

After the general balance-related audit objectives are understood, specific balance-related audit objectives for each account balance on the financial statements can be developed. There should be at least one specific balance-related audit objective for each general balance-related audit objective unless the auditor believes that the general balance-related audit objective is not relevant or is unimportant in the circumstances. There may be more than one specific balance-related audit objective for a general balance-related audit objective. For example, specific balance-related audit objectives for rights and obligations of the inventory of Hillsburg Hardware Co. could include (1) the company has title to all inventory items listed and (2) inventory is not pledged as collateral unless it is disclosed.

Relationships among Management Assertions and Balance-Related Audit Objectives

The reason there are more general balance-related audit objectives than management assertions is to provide additional guidance to auditors in deciding what evidence to accumulate. Table 6-5 illustrates this by showing the relationships among management assertions, the general balance-related audit objectives, and specific balance-related audit objectives as applied to inventory for Hillsburg Hardware Co. Notice that there is a one-to-one relationship between assertions and objectives, except for the valuation or allocation assertion. The valuation or allocation assertion has multiple objectives because of the complexity of valuation issues and the need to provide auditors with additional guidance.

HOW AUDIT OBJECTIVES ARE MET

The auditor must obtain sufficient competent audit evidence to support all management assertions in the financial statements. As stated earlier, this is done by accumulating evidence in support of some appropriate combination of transaction-related audit objectives and balance-related audit objectives. A comparison of Tables 6-4 and 6-5 shows a significant overlap between the two types of audit objectives. The only assertions that must be addressed through balance-related audit objectives, rather than some combination of balance- and transaction-related audit objectives, are rights and obligations and presentation and disclosure.

TABLE 6-5	**Hillsburg Hardware Co.: Management Assertions and Balance-Related Audit Objectives Applied to Inventory**	

Management Assertions	General Balance-Related Audit Objectives	Specific Balance-Related Audit Objectives Applied to Inventory
Existence or occurrence	Existence	All recorded inventory exists at the balance sheet date.
Completeness	Completeness	All existing inventory has been counted and included in the inventory summary.
Valuation or allocation	Accuracy	Inventory quantities on the client's perpetual records agree with items physically on hand. Prices used to value inventories are materially correct. Extensions of price times quantity are correct and details are correctly added.
	Classification	Inventory items are properly classified as to raw materials, work in process, and finished goods.
	Cutoff	Purchase cutoff at year-end is proper. Sales cutoff at year-end is proper.
	Detail tie-in	Total of inventory items agrees with general ledger.
	Realizable value	Inventories have been written down where net realizable value is impaired.
Rights and obligations	Rights and obligations	The company has title to all inventory items listed. Inventories are not pledged as collateral.
Presentation and disclosure	Presentation and disclosure	Major categories of inventories and their bases of valuation are disclosed. The pledge or assignment of any inventories is disclosed.

The auditor plans the appropriate combination of audit objectives and the evidence that must be accumulated to meet them by following an audit process. An audit process is a well-defined methodology for organizing an audit to ensure that the evidence gathered is both sufficient and competent and that all appropriate audit objectives are both specified and met. The audit process described in this text has four specific phases. These are shown in Figure 6-7 (p. 162). The remainder of this chapter provides a brief introduction to each of the four **phases of the audit process**.

For any given audit, there are many ways in which an auditor can accumulate evidence to meet the overall audit objectives. Two overriding considerations affect the approach the auditor selects: *sufficient competent evidence must be accumulated to meet the auditor's professional responsibility,* and *the cost of accumulating the evidence should be minimized.* The first consideration is the most important, but cost minimization is necessary if CPA firms are to be competitive and profitable. If there were no concern for controlling costs, evidence decision making would be easy. Auditors would keep adding evidence, without concern for efficiency, until they were sufficiently certain that there were no material misstatements.

Concern for sufficient competent evidence and cost control necessitates planning the engagement. The plan should result in an effective audit approach at a reasonable cost. Planning and designing an audit approach can be broken down into several parts. Two are addressed briefly here. Others are discussed in later chapters.

Plan and Design an Audit Approach (Phase I)

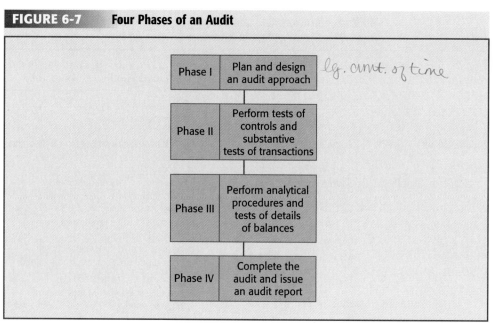

FIGURE 6-7   Four Phases of an Audit

Phase I	Plan and design an audit approach
Phase II	Perform tests of controls and substantive tests of transactions
Phase III	Perform analytical procedures and tests of details of balances
Phase IV	Complete the audit and issue an audit report

lg. amt. of time

permanent files

Obtaining Knowledge of the Client's Business To interpret adequately the meaning of information obtained throughout the audit, an understanding of the client's business and industry is essential. Unique aspects of different businesses are reflected in the financial statements. An audit of a life insurance company could not be performed with due care without an understanding of the unique characteristics of that business. Imagine attempting to audit a client in the bridge construction industry without understanding the construction business and the percentage-of-completion method of accounting. A reasonable understanding of the client's business and industry is required by SAS 22 (AU 311).

whole chapter

Understanding Internal Control and Assessing Control Risk It was pointed out in Chapter 2 that the ability of the client's internal controls to generate reliable financial information and safeguard assets and records is one of the most important and widely accepted concepts in the theory and practice of auditing. If the client has excellent internal controls, the amount of audit evidence to be accumulated can be significantly less than for internal controls that are not adequate.

To adequately plan the appropriate audit evidence, generally accepted auditing standards *require* the auditor to gain an understanding of internal control. This understanding is obtained by reviewing organization charts and procedural manuals, by discussions with client personnel, by completing internal control questionnaires and flowcharts, and by observing client activities.

After gaining an understanding of internal control, the auditor is in a position to evaluate how effective it should be in preventing and detecting errors and fraud. This evaluation involves identifying specific controls that reduce the likelihood that errors and fraud will occur and not be detected and corrected on a timely basis. This process is called assessing control risk.

Perform Tests of Controls and Substantive Tests of Transactions (Phase II)

When the auditor has reduced assessed control risk based on the identification of controls, he or she may then reduce the extent to which the accuracy of the financial statement information directly related to those controls must be supported through the accumulation of evidence. However, to justify reducing planned assessed control risk, the auditor must test the effectiveness of the controls. The procedures involved in this type of testing are commonly referred to as **tests of controls**. For example, assume that the client's internal controls require the verification by an independent clerk of all unit selling prices on sales before sales invoices are mailed to customers. This control is directly related to the accuracy transaction-related audit objective for sales. One possible test of the effectiveness of this control is for the auditor to examine a sample of the clerk's initials that he or she was required to put on each duplicate sales invoice after verifying the unit selling price.

Auditors also evaluate the client's recording of transactions by verifying the monetary amounts of transactions. This is called **substantive tests of transactions**. An example is for the auditor to compare the unit selling price on a duplicate sales invoice with the approved price list as a test of the accuracy objective for sales transactions. Like the test of control in the previous paragraph, this test satisfies the accuracy transaction-related audit objective for sales. Often, auditors perform tests of controls and substantive tests of transactions at the same time.

There are two general categories of phase III procedures: analytical procedures and tests of details of balances. **Analytical procedures** use comparisons and relationships to assess whether account balances or other data appear reasonable. An example of an analytical procedure that would provide some assurance for the accuracy objective for both sales transactions (transaction-related audit objective) and accounts receivable (balance-related audit objective) is to examine sales transactions in the sales journal for unusually large amounts and to compare total monthly sales with prior years. If a company is consistently using incorrect sales prices, significant differences are likely.

Tests of details of balances are specific procedures intended to test for monetary misstatements in the balances in the financial statements. An example related to the accuracy objective for accounts receivable (balance-related audit objective) is direct written communication with the client's customers. Tests of details of ending balances are essential to the conduct of the audit because most of the evidence is obtained from a source independent of the client and therefore considered to be of high quality.

There is a close relationship among the general review of the client's circumstances, results of understanding internal control and assessing control risk, analytical procedures, and the tests of details of the financial statement account balances. If the auditor has obtained a reasonable level of assurance for any given audit objective through performing tests of controls, substantive tests of transactions, and analytical procedures, the tests of details for that objective can be significantly reduced. In most instances, however, some tests of details of significant financial statement account balances are necessary.

Perform Analytical Procedures and Tests of Details of Balances (Phase III)

After the auditor has completed all procedures for each audit objective and for each financial statement account, it is necessary to combine the information obtained to reach an *overall conclusion* as to whether the financial statements are fairly presented. This is a highly subjective process that relies heavily on the auditor's professional judgment. In practice, the auditor continuously combines the information obtained as he or she proceeds through the audit. The final combination is a summation at the completion of the engagement. When the audit is completed, the CPA must issue an audit report to accompany the client's published financial statements. The report must meet well-defined technical requirements that are affected by the scope of the audit and the nature of the findings. These reports have already been studied in Chapter 3.

Complete the Audit and Issue an Audit Report (Phase IV)

SUMMARY

This chapter discussed the objectives of the audit and the way the auditor subdivides an audit to result in specific audit objectives. The auditor then accumulates evidence to obtain assurance that each audit objective has been satisfied. The illustration on meeting the accuracy objectives for sales transactions and accounts receivable shows that the auditor can obtain assurance by accumulating evidence using tests of controls, substantive tests of transactions, analytical procedures, and tests of details of balances. In some audits, there is more emphasis on certain of these tests such as analytical procedures and tests of controls, whereas on others, there is emphasis on substantive tests of transactions and tests of details of balances.

Analytical procedures—use of comparisons and relationships to assess whether account balances or other data appear reasonable

Balance-related audit objectives—nine audit objectives that must be met before the auditor can conclude that any given account balance is fairly stated; the general balance-related audit objectives are existence, completeness, accuracy, classification, cutoff, detail tie-in, realizable value, rights and obligations, and presentation and disclosure

Cycle approach—a method of dividing an audit by keeping closely related types of transactions and account balances in the same segment

Error—an unintentional misstatement of the financial statements

Fraud—an intentional misstatement of the financial statements

Fraudulent financial reporting—intentional misstatements or omissions of amounts or disclosures in financial statements to deceive users

Illegal acts—violations of laws or government regulations other than fraud

Management assertions—implied or expressed representations by management about classes of transactions and related accounts in the financial statements

Misappropriation of assets—a fraud involving the theft of an entity's assets

Phases of the audit process—the four aspects of a complete audit: (1) plan and design an audit approach, (2) perform tests of controls and substantive tests of transactions, (3) perform analytical procedures and tests of details of balances, and (4) complete the audit and issue the audit report

Substantive tests of transactions—audit procedures testing for monetary misstatements to determine whether the six transaction-related audit objectives have been satisfied for each class of transactions

Tests of controls—audit procedures to test the effectiveness of controls in support of a reduced assessed control risk

Tests of details of balances—audit procedures testing for monetary misstatements to determine whether the nine balance-related audit objectives have been satisfied for each significant account balance

Transaction-related audit objectives—six audit objectives that must be met before the auditor can conclude that the total for any given class of transactions is fairly stated; the general transaction-related audit objectives are existence, completeness, accuracy, classification, timing, and posting and summarization

REVIEW QUESTIONS

6-1 (Objective 6-1)   State the objective of the ordinary audit of financial statements. In general terms, how do auditors meet that objective?

6-2 (Objectives 6-2, 6-3)   Distinguish between management's and the auditor's responsibility for the financial statements being audited.

6-3 (Objective 6-3)   Distinguish between the terms errors and fraud. What is the auditor's responsibility for finding each?

6-4 (Objective 6-3)   Distinguish between fraudulent financial reporting and misappropriation of assets. Discuss the likely difference between these two types of fraud on the fair presentation of financial statements.

6-5 (Objective 6-3)   "It is well accepted in auditing that throughout the conduct of the ordinary audit, it is essential to obtain large amounts of information from management and to rely heavily on management's judgments. After all, the financial statements are management's representations, and the primary responsibility for their fair presentation rests with management, not the auditor. For example, it is extremely difficult, if not impossible, for the auditor to evaluate the obsolescence of inventory as well as management can in a highly complex business. Similarly, the collectibility of accounts receivable and the continued usefulness of machinery and equipment is heavily dependent on management's willingness to provide truthful responses to questions." Reconcile the auditor's responsibility for discovering material misrepresentations by management with these comments.

6-6 (Objective 6-3)   List two major characteristics that are useful in predicting the likelihood of fraudulent financial reporting in an audit. For each of the characteristics, state two things that the auditor can do to evaluate its significance in the engagement.

6-7 (Objective 6-4)   Describe what is meant by the cycle approach to auditing. What are the advantages of dividing the audit into different cycles?

6-8 (Objective 6-4)   Identify the cycle to which each of the following general ledger accounts would ordinarily be assigned: sales, accounts payable, retained earnings, accounts receivable, inventory, and repairs and maintenance.

6-9 (Objectives 6-4, 6-5)   Why are sales, sales returns and allowances, bad debts, cash discounts, accounts receivable, and allowance for uncollectible accounts all included in the same cycle?

6-10 (Objective 6-6)   Define what is meant by a management assertion about financial statements. Identify the five broad categories of management assertions.

6-11 (Objectives 6-6, 6-7)   Distinguish between the general audit objectives and management assertions. Why are the general audit objectives more useful to auditors?

6-12 (Objective 6-7)   An acquisition of a repair service by a construction company is recorded on the wrong date. Which transaction-related audit objective has been violated? Which transaction-related audit objective has been violated if the acquisition had been capitalized as a fixed asset rather than expensed?

6-13 (Objective 6-8)   Distinguish between the existence and completeness balance-related audit objectives. State the effect on the financial statements (overstatement or understatement) of a violation of each in the audit of accounts receivable.

6-14 (Objectives 6-7, 6-8)   What are specific audit objectives? Explain their relationship to the general audit objectives.

6-15 (Objectives 6-6, 6-8)   Identify the management assertion and general balance-related audit objective for the specific balance-related audit objective: All recorded fixed assets exist at the balance sheet date.

6-16 (Objectives 6-6, 6-8)   Explain how management assertions, general balance-related audit objectives, and specific balance-related audit objectives are developed for an account balance such as accounts receivable.

6-17 (Objective 6-9)   Identify the four phases of the audit. What is the relationship of the four phases to the objective of the audit of financial statements?

MULTIPLE CHOICE QUESTIONS FROM CPA EXAMINATIONS

6-18 (Objective 6-1)   The following questions concern the reasons auditors do audits. Choose the best response.

a. Which of the following *best* describes the reason why an independent auditor reports on financial statements?
   (1) A misappropriation of assets may exist, and it is more likely to be detected by independent auditors.
   (2) Different interests may exist between the company preparing the statements and the persons using the statements.
   (3) A misstatement of account balances may exist and is generally corrected as the result of the independent auditor's work.
   (4) Poorly designed internal controls may be in existence.

b. An independent audit aids in the communication of economic data because the audit
   (1) confirms the accuracy of management's financial representations.
   (2) lends credibility to the financial statements.
   (3) guarantees that financial data are fairly presented.

(4) assures the readers of financial statements that any fraudulent activity has been corrected.

c. The major reason an independent auditor gathers audit evidence is to
  √(1) form an opinion on the financial statements.
  (2) detect fraud.
  (3) evaluate management.
  (4) assess control risk.

6-19 (Objective 6-3)   The following questions deal with errors and fraud. Choose the best response.

a. An independent auditor has the responsibility to design the audit to provide reasonable assurance of detecting errors and fraud that might have a material effect on the financial statements. Which of the following, if material, would be a fraud as defined in *Codification of Statements on Auditing Standards?*
  √(1) Misappropriation of an asset or groups of assets.
  (2) Clerical mistakes in the accounting data underlying the financial statements.
  (3) Mistakes in the application of accounting principles.
  (4) Misinterpretation of facts that existed when the financial statements were prepared.

b. What assurance does the auditor provide that errors, fraud, and direct-effect illegal acts that are material to the financial statements will be detected?

	Errors	Fraud	Direct-Effect Illegal Acts
(1)	Limited	Negative	Limited
√(2)	Reasonable	Reasonable	Reasonable
(3)	Limited	Limited	Reasonable
(4)	Reasonable	Limited	Limited

6-20 (Objectives 6-2, 6-3, 6-6)   The following are miscellaneous questions from this chapter. Choose the best response.

a. An auditor most likely would analyze inventory turnover rates to obtain evidence concerning management's assertions about
  (1) existence or occurrence.
  (2) rights and obligations.
  √(3) valuation or allocation.
  (4) presentation and disclosure.

b. The audit client's board of directors and audit committee refused to take any action with respect to an immaterial illegal act that was brought to their attention by the auditor. Because of their failure to act, the auditor withdrew from the engagement. The auditor's decision to withdraw was primarily because of doubts concerning
  (1) inadequate financial statement disclosures.
  (2) compliance with the Foreign Corrupt Practices Act of 1977.
  (3) scope limitations resulting from their inaction.
  √(4) reliance on management's representations.

c. The primary responsibility for the adequacy of disclosure in the financial statements and footnotes rests with the
  (1) partner assigned to the engagement.
  (2) auditor in charge of field work.
  (3) staff member who drafts the statements and footnotes.
  √(4) client.

6-21 (Objectives 6-2, 6-3)   The following two reports are taken from the same page of a published annual report. (The first two paragraphs of a standard unqualified report have been omitted.)

Pg. 6 - 5 manual

REPORT OF MANAGEMENT

To Our Stockholders

Management is responsible for the preparation, integrity, and objectivity of the consolidated financial statements and related notes. To meet these responsibilities, management maintains a system of internal controls intended to insure that key employees adhere to the highest standards of personal and professional integrity. Although no cost-effective internal control system will preclude all errors and fraud, we believe the established system of internal controls provides reasonable assurance that the assets are safeguarded, transactions are recorded in accordance with management's policies, and the financial information is reliable.

The consolidated financial statements of Columbia/HCA Healthcare Corporation have been prepared in conformity with generally accepted accounting principles and include amounts based upon our best estimates and judgments. These financial statements have been audited and reported on by our independent auditors, Ernst & Young LLP, in accordance with generally accepted auditing standards.

The Audit Committee of the Board of Directors, consisting entirely of outside directors, meets regularly with management, internal auditors, and Ernst & Young LLP, and reviews audit plans and results as well as management's actions taken in discharging responsibilities for accounting, financial reporting and internal control. Ernst & Young LLP and the internal auditors have direct and confidential access to the Audit Committee at all times to discuss the results of their examinations.

Kenneth C. Donahey
Senior Vice President and Controller

REPORT OF INDEPENDENT AUDITORS

To the Board of Directors and Stockholders
Columbia/HCA Healthcare Corporation

(First two paragraphs of standard unqualified report have been omitted.)

In our opinion, the financial statements referred to above present fairly, in all material respects, the consolidated financial position of Columbia/HCA Healthcare Corporation at December 31, 1997 and 1996, and the consolidated results of their operations and their cash flows for each of the three years in the period ended December 31, 1997 in conformity with generally accepted accounting principles.

As explained in Note 11 to the Consolidated Financial Statements, effective January 1, 1997, the Company changed its method of accounting for start-up costs.

ERNST & YOUNG LLP
February 12, 1998

Required
   a. What are the purposes of the two reports and who was responsible for writing each?
   b. What information does the report of management provide to users of financial statements?

c. Explain the purpose of the audit committee as described in the third paragraph of management's report. What is the relevance of the phrase "consisting entirely of outside directors"?

d. Is the audit report a standard wording unqualified, qualified—except for, or something else? Explain your answer.

e. How long after the balance sheet date did the CPA firm complete the audit field work?

6-22 (Objectives 6-1, 6-3) Often, questions have been raised "regarding the responsibility of the independent auditor for the discovery of fraud (including misappropriation of assets and fraudulent financial reporting), and concerning the proper course of conduct of the independent auditor when his or her audit discloses specific circumstances that arouse suspicion as to the existence of fraud."

Required

a. What are (1) the function and (2) the responsibilities of the independent auditor in the audit of financial statements? Discuss fully, but in this part do not include fraud in the discussion.

b. What are the responsibilities of the independent auditor for the detection of fraud? Discuss fully.

c. What is the independent auditor's proper course of conduct when his or her audit discloses specific circumstances that arouse his or her suspicion as to the existence of fraud?*

6-23 (Objectives 6-2, 6-3) A competent auditor has done a conscientious job of conducting an audit, but because of a clever fraud by management, a material fraud is included in the financial statements. The fraud, which is an overstatement of inventory, took place over several years, and it covered up the fact that the company's financial position was rapidly declining. The fraud was accidentally discovered in the latest audit by an unusually capable audit senior, and the SEC was immediately informed. Subsequent investigation indicated that the company was actually near bankruptcy, and the value of the stock dropped from $26 per share to $1 in less than 1 month. Among the losing stockholders were pension funds, university endowment funds, retired couples, and widows. The individuals responsible for perpetrating the fraud were also bankrupt.

After making an extensive investigation of the audit performance in previous years, the SEC was satisfied that the auditor had done a high-quality audit and had followed generally accepted auditing standards in every respect. The commission concluded that it would be unreasonable to expect auditors to uncover this type of fraud.

Required

State your opinion as to who should bear the loss of the fraudulent financial reporting. Include in your discussion a list of potential bearers of the loss, and state why you believe they should or should not bear the loss.

6-24 (Objective 6-4) The following are the classes of transactions and the titles of the journals used for Phillips Equipment Rental Co.

Classes of Transactions	Titles of Journals
Purchase returns	Cash receipts journal
Rental revenue	Cash disbursements journal
Charge-off of uncollectible accounts	Acquisitions journal
Acquisition of goods and services (except payroll)	Revenue journal
Rental allowances	Payroll journal
Adjusting entries (for payroll)	Adjustments journal
Payroll service and payments	
Cash disbursements (except payroll)	
Cash receipts	

*AICPA adapted.

a. Identify one financial statement balance that is likely to be affected by each of the nine classes of transactions.

b. For each class of transactions, identify the journal that is likely to be used to record the transactions.

c. Identify the transaction cycle that is likely to be affected by each of the nine classes of transactions.

d. Explain how total rental revenue, as cited on the financial statements of Phillips Equipment Rental Co., is accumulated in journals and is summarized on the financial statements. Assume that there are several adjusting entries for rental revenue at the balance sheet date.

6-25 (Objective 6-4)   The following general ledger accounts are included in the trial balance for an audit client, Jones Wholesale Stationery Store.

Income tax expense	Allowance for doubtful accounts
Income tax payable	Inventory
Accounts receivable	Property tax expense
Advertising expense	Interest expense
Traveling expense	Depreciation expense—furniture and
Accounts payable	equipment
Bonds payable	Retained earnings
Common stock	Sales
Unexpired insurance	Salaries, office and general
Furniture and equipment	Telephone and telegraph expense
Cash	Bad debt expense
Notes receivable—trade	Insurance expense
Purchases	Interest receivable
Sales salaries expense	Interest income
Accumulated depreciation of	Accrued sales salaries
furniture and equipment	Rent expense
Notes payable	Prepaid interest expense
	Property tax payable

Required

a. Identify the accounts in the trial balance that are likely to be included in each transaction cycle. Some accounts will be included in more than one cycle. Use the format that follows.

Cycle	Balance Sheet Accounts	Income Statement Accounts
Sales and collection		
Acquisition and payment		
Payroll and personnel		
Inventory and warehousing		
Capital acquisition and repayment		

b. How would the general ledger accounts in the trial balance most likely differ if the company were a retail store rather than a wholesale company? How would they differ for a hospital or a government unit?

6-26 (Objectives 6-6, 6-8)   The following are specific balance-related audit objectives applied to the audit of accounts receivable (a through h) and management assertions (1 through 5). The list referred to in the specific balance-related audit objectives is the list of the accounts receivable from each customer at the balance sheet date.

Specific Balance-Related Audit Objective

a. There are no unrecorded receivables.
b. Receivables have not been sold or discounted.
c. Uncollectible accounts have been provided for.
d. Receivables that have become uncollectible have been written off.
e. All accounts on the list are expected to be collected within 1 year.
f. Any agreement or condition that restricts the nature of trade receivables is known and disclosed.
g. All accounts on the list arose from the normal course of business and are not due from related parties.
h. Sales cutoff at year-end is proper.

Management Assertion

1. Existence or occurrence
2. Completeness
3. Valuation or allocation
4. Rights and obligations
5. Presentation and disclosure

Required

For each specific balance-related audit objective, identify the appropriate management assertion. (*Hint:* See Table 6-5.)

6-27 (Objectives 6-6, 6-7) The following are specific transaction-related audit objectives applied to the audit of cash disbursement transactions (a through f), management assertions (1 through 5), and general transaction-related audit objectives (6 through 11).

Specific Transaction-Related Audit Objective

a. Recorded cash disbursement transactions are for the amount of goods or services received and are correctly recorded.
b. Cash disbursement transactions are properly included in the accounts payable master file and are correctly summarized.
c. Recorded cash disbursements are for goods and services actually received.
d. Cash disbursement transactions are properly classified.
e. Existing cash disbursement transactions are recorded.
f. Cash disbursement transactions are recorded on the correct dates.

Management Assertion

1. Existence or occurrence
2. Completeness
3. Valuation or allocation
4. Rights and obligations
5. Presentation and disclosure

General Transaction-Related Audit Objective

6. Existence
7. Completeness
8. Accuracy
9. Classification
10. Timing
11. Posting and summarization

Required

a. Explain the differences among management assertions, general transaction-related audit objectives, and specific transaction-related audit objectives and their relationships to each other.

b. For each specific transaction-related audit objective, identify the appropriate management assertion.

c. For each specific transaction-related audit objective, identify the appropriate general transaction-related audit objective.

6-28 (Objective 6-8) The following are two specific balance-related audit objectives in the audit of accounts payable. The list referred to is the list of accounts payable taken from the accounts payable master file. The total of the list equals the accounts payable balance on the general ledger.

1. All accounts payable included on the list represent amounts due to valid vendors.
2. There are no unrecorded accounts payable.

Required

    a. Explain the difference between these two specific balance-related audit objectives.

    b. Which of these two specific balance-related audit objectives applies to the general balance-related audit objective of existence, and which one applies to completeness?

    c. For the audit of accounts payable, which of these two specific balance-related audit objectives would usually be more important? Explain.

6-29 (Objective 6-8) The following are 9 general balance-related audit objectives for the audit of any balance sheet account (1 through 9) and 11 specific balance-related audit objectives for the audit of property, plant, and equipment (a through k).

General Balance-Related Audit Objective

1. Existence
2. Completeness
3. Accuracy
4. Classification
5. Cutoff
6. Detail tie-in
7. Realizable value
8. Rights and obligations
9. Presentation and disclosure

Specific Balance-Related Audit Objective

a. There are no unrecorded fixed assets in use.
b. The company has valid title to the assets owned.
c. Details of property, plant, and equipment agree with the general ledger.
d. Fixed assets physically exist and are being used for the purpose intended.
e. Property, plant, and equipment are recorded at the correct amount.
f. The company has a contractual right for use of assets leased.
g. Liens or other encumbrances on property, plant, and equipment items are known and disclosed.
h. Cash disbursements and/or accrual cutoff for property, plant, and equipment items are proper.
i. Expense accounts do not contain amounts that should have been capitalized.
j. Depreciation is determined in accordance with an acceptable method and is materially correct as computed.
k. Fixed asset accounts have been properly adjusted for declines in historical cost.

Required

    a. What are the purposes of the general balance-related audit objectives and the specific balance-related audit objectives? Explain the relationship between these two sets of objectives.

    b. For each general balance-related audit objective, identify one or more specific balance-related audit objectives. No letter can be used for more than one general balance-related audit objective.

6-30 (Objectives 6-1, 6-3) Rene Ritter opened a small grocery and related-products convenience store in 1976 with money she had saved working as an A&P store manager. She named it Ritter Dairy and Fruits. Because of the excellent location and her fine management skills, Ritter Dairy and Fruits grew to three locations by 1981. By that time, she needed additional capital. She obtained financing through a local bank at 2 percent above prime, under the condition that she submit quarterly financial statements reviewed by a CPA firm approved by the bank. After interviewing several firms, she decided to use the firm of Gonzalez & Fineberg CPAs, after obtaining approval from the bank.

In 1985, the company had grown to 6 stores and Rene developed a business plan to add another 10 stores in the next several years. Ritter's capital needs had also grown so Rene decided to add two business partners who both had considerable capital and some expertise in convenience stores. After further discussions with the bank and continued conversations with the future business partners, she decided to have an annual audit and quarterly reviews done by Gonzalez & Fineberg even though the additional cost was almost $5,000 annually. The bank agreed to reduce the interest rate on the $3,000,000 of loans to 1 percent above prime.

By 1990, things were going smoothly with the two business partners heavily involved in day-to-day operations and the company adding two new stores each year. The company was growing steadily and was more profitable than they had expected. By the end of 1991, one of the business partners, Fred Worm, had taken over responsibility for accounting and finance operations, as well as some marketing. Annually Gonzalez & Fineberg did an in-depth review of the accounting system, including internal controls, and reported their conclusions and recommendations to the board of directors. Specialists in the firm provided tax and other consulting advice. The other partner, Ben Gold, managed most of the stores and was primarily responsible for building new stores. Rene was president and managed four stores.

In 1995, the three partners decided to go public to enable them to add more stores and modernize existing ones. The public offering was a major success, resulting in $25 million in new capital and nearly 1,000 shareholders. Ritter Dairy and Fruits added stores rapidly under the three managers, and the company remained highly profitable under the leadership of Ritter, Worm, and Gold.

Rene retired in 1998 after a highly successful career. During the retirement celebration, she thanked her business partners, employees, and customers. She also added a special thanks to the bank management for their outstanding service and to Gonzalez & Fineburg for being partners in the best and most professional sense of the word. She mentioned their integrity, commitment, high-quality service in performing their audits and reviews, and considerable tax and business advice for more than two decades.

Required

   a. Explain why the bank imposed a requirement of a quarterly review of the financial statements as a condition of obtaining the loan at 2 percent above prime. Also explain why the bank didn't require an audit and why the bank demanded the right to approve which CPA firm was engaged.
   b. Explain why Ritter Dairy and Fruits agreed to have an audit performed rather than a review, considering the additional annual cost of $5,000.
   c. What did Rene mean when she referred to Gonzalez & Fineberg as partners? Does the CPA firm have an independence problem?
   d. What benefit does Gonzalez & Fineberg provide to stockholders, creditors, and management in performing the audit and other services?
   e. What are the responsibilities of the CPA firm to stockholders, creditors, management, and other users?

Reference the CW site. Chapter 1 of the text includes a brief description of the new assurance service known as ElderCare Plus. The AICPA has developed a business plan for ElderCare Plus. This problem requires students to use the Internet to (1) identify possible performance criteria associated with a client living in a long-term care facility, (2) determine in what form and to whom CPAs would report findings, and (3) identify what assertions would be tested and how.

AUDIT EVIDENCE

7

SOMETIMES THE MOST IMPORTANT EVIDENCE IS NOT FOUND IN THE ACCOUNTING RECORDS

Crenshaw Properties was a real estate developer that specialized in self-storage facilities that it sold to limited partner investors. Crenshaw's role was to identify projects, serve as general partner with a small investment, and raise capital from pension funds. Crenshaw had an extensive network of people who marketed these investments on a commission basis. As general partner, Crenshaw earned significant fees for related activities, including promotional fees, investment management fees, and real estate commissions.

As long as the investments were successful, Crenshaw prospered. Because the investments were reasonably long-term, the underlying investors did not pay careful attention to them. However, in the mid-1980s, the market for self-storage units in many parts of the country became oversaturated. Occupancy rates, rental rates, and market values declined.

Ralph Smalley, of Hambusch, Robinson & Co., did the annual audit of Crenshaw. As part of the audit, Smalley obtained financial statements for all of the partnerships in which Crenshaw was the general partner. He traced amounts back to the original partnership documents and determined that amounts agreed with partnership records. Smalley also determined that they were mathematically accurate. The purpose of doing these tests was to determine that the partnership assets, at original cost, exceeded liabilities, including the mortgage on the property and loans from investors. Under the law, Crenshaw, as general partner, was liable for any deficiency.

Every year, Smalley concluded that there were no significant deficiencies in partnership net assets for which Crenshaw would be liable. What Smalley failed to recognize in the late 1980s, however, was that current market prices had declined significantly because cash flows were lower than those projected in the original partnership offering documents. In fact, Crenshaw went bankrupt in 1989, and Hambusch, Robinson & Co. was named in a suit to recover damages filed by the bankruptcy trustee.

LEARNING OBJECTIVES

After studying this chapter, you should be able to

7-1 Contrast audit evidence with evidence used by other professions.

7-2 Identify the four audit evidence decisions that are needed to create an audit program.

7-3 Specify the characteristics that determine the persuasiveness of evidence.

7-4 Identify and apply the seven types of evidence used in auditing.

7-5 State the purposes of analytical procedures and the timing of each purpose.

7-6 Select the most appropriate analytical procedure from among the five major types.

7-7 Explain the benefits of using statistical techniques and computer software for analytical procedures.

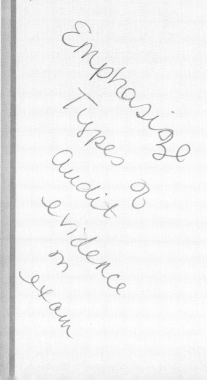

Emphasize Types of audit evidence on exam

The foundation of any audit is the evidence gathered and evaluated by the auditor. The auditor must have the knowledge and skill to accumulate sufficient competent evidence on every audit to meet the standards of the profession. As described in the opening vignette, Ralph Smalley learned the effect of not accumulating the appropriate evidence after being sued over his audit of Crenshaw Properties. This chapter deals with the types of evidence decisions auditors make, the evidence available to auditors, and the use of that evidence in performing audits.

NATURE OF EVIDENCE

OBJECTIVE 7-1
Contrast audit evidence with evidence used by other professions.

Evidence was defined in Chapter 1 as any *information used by the auditor* to determine whether the information being audited is stated in accordance with the established criteria. The information varies greatly in the extent to which it persuades the auditor whether financial statements are stated in accordance with generally accepted accounting principles. Evidence includes information that is highly persuasive, such as the auditor's count of marketable securities, and less persuasive information, such as responses to questions of client employees.

Audit Evidence Contrasted with Legal and Scientific Evidence

The use of evidence is not unique to auditors. Evidence is also used extensively by scientists, lawyers, and historians.

Through television, most people are familiar with the use of evidence in legal cases dealing with the guilt or innocence of a party charged with a crime such as robbery. In legal cases, there are well-defined rules of evidence enforced by a judge for the protection of the innocent. It is common, for example, for legal evidence to be judged inadmissible on the grounds that it is irrelevant, prejudicial, or based on hearsay.

Similarly, in scientific experiments, the scientist obtains evidence to draw conclusions about a theory. Assume, for example, that a medical scientist is evaluating a new medicine that may provide relief for asthma sufferers. The scientist will gather evidence from a large number of controlled experiments over an extended period to determine the effectiveness of the medicine.

The auditor also gathers evidence to draw conclusions. Different evidence is used by auditors than by scientists and in cases of law, and it is used in different ways, but in all three cases, evidence is used to reach conclusions. Table 7-1 illustrates key characteristics of evidence from the perspective of a scientist doing an experiment, an attorney prosecuting an accused thief, and an auditor of financial statements. There are six bases of comparison. Note the similarities and differences among the three professions.

AUDIT EVIDENCE DECISIONS

OBJECTIVE 7-2
Identify the four audit evidence decisions that are needed to create an audit program.

A major decision facing every auditor is determining the *appropriate types and amounts* of evidence to accumulate to be satisfied that the components of the client's financial statements and the overall statements are fairly stated. This judgment is important because of the prohibitive cost of examining and evaluating all available evidence. For example, in an audit of financial statements of most organizations, it is impossible for the CPA to examine the contents of all computer files or available evidence such as cancelled checks, vendors' invoices, customer orders, payroll time cards, and the many other types of documents and records.

The auditor's *decisions* on evidence accumulation can be broken down into the following four subdecisions:

1. Which audit procedures to use
2. What sample size to select for a given procedure
3. Which items to select from the population
4. When to perform the procedures

TABLE 7-1   **Characteristics of Evidence for a Scientific Experiment, Legal Case, and Audit of Financial Statements**

Basis of Comparison	Scientific Experiment Involving Testing a Medicine	Legal Case Involving an Accused Thief	Audit of Financial Statements
Use of the evidence	Determine effects of using the medicine	Decide guilt or innocence of accused	Determine whether statements are fairly presented
Nature of evidence used	Results of repeated experiments	Direct evidence and testimony by witnesses and parties involved	Various types of audit evidence generated by the auditor, third parties, and the client
Party or parties evaluating evidence	Scientist	Jury and judge	Auditor
Certainty of conclusions from evidence	Vary from uncertain to near certainty	Requires guilt beyond a reasonable doubt	High level of assurance
Nature of conclusions	Recommend or not recommend use of medicine	Innocence or guilt of party	Issue one of several alternative types of audit reports
Typical consequences of incorrect conclusions from evidence	Society uses ineffective or harmful medicine	Guilty party is not penalized or innocent party found guilty	Statement users make incorrect decisions and auditor may be sued

An **audit procedure** is the detailed instruction for the collection of a type of audit evidence that is to be obtained at some time during the audit. In designing audit procedures, it is common to spell them out in sufficiently specific terms to permit their use as instructions during the audit. For example, the following is an audit procedure for the verification of cash disbursements:

Audit Procedures

- Obtain the cash disbursements journal and compare the payor name, amount, and date on the cancelled check with the cash disbursements journal.

Once an audit procedure is selected, it is possible to vary the sample size from one to all the items in the population being tested. In the audit procedure above, suppose 6,600 checks are recorded in the cash disbursements journal. The auditor might select a sample size of 200 checks for comparison with the cash disbursements journal. The decision of how many items to test must be made by the auditor for each audit procedure. The sample size for any given procedure is likely to vary from audit to audit.

Sample Size

After the sample size has been determined for an audit procedure, it is still necessary to decide which items in the population to test. If the auditor decides, for example, to select 200 cancelled checks from a population of 6,600 for comparison with the cash disbursements journal, several different methods can be used to select the specific checks to be examined. The auditor could (1) select a week and examine the first 200 checks, (2) select the 200 checks with the largest amounts, (3) select the checks randomly, or (4) select those checks that the auditor thinks are most likely to be in error. Or a combination of these methods could be used.

Items to Select

An audit of financial statements usually covers a period such as a year, and an audit is usually not completed until several weeks or months after the end of the period. The timing of audit procedures can therefore vary from early in the accounting period to long after it has ended. In part, the timing decision is affected by when the client needs the audit to be completed. In the audit of financial statements, the client normally wants the audit completed 1 to 3 months after year-end. The SEC requires that all public companies file audited

Timing

financial statements with the SEC within 3 months of the companies' fiscal year-end. However, timing is also influenced by when the auditor believes the audit evidence will be most effective and when audit staff is available. For example, auditors often prefer to do counts of inventory as close to the balance sheet date as possible.

Audit procedures often incorporate sample size, items to select, and timing into the procedure. The following is a modification of the audit procedure previously used to include all four audit evidence decisions. (Italics identify the timing, items to select, and sample size decisions).

- Obtain the *October* cash disbursements journal and compare the payee name, amount, and date on the cancelled check with the cash disbursements journal for a *randomly selected sample of 40* check numbers.

Audit Program

Auditors Sharing Audit Programs

The list of audit procedures for an audit area or an entire audit is called an **audit program**. The audit program always includes a list of the audit procedures. It usually also includes sample sizes, items to select, and the timing of the tests. Normally, there is an audit program, including several audit procedures, for each component of the audit. Therefore, there will be an audit program for accounts receivable, for sales, and so on. An example of an audit program that includes audit procedures, sample size, items to select, and timing is given on page 377 in Table 12-4. The right side of the audit program also includes the balance-related audit objectives for each procedure, as studied in Chapter 6.

Most auditors use computers to facilitate the preparation of audit programs. The simplest computer application involves typing the audit program on a word processor and saving it from one year to the next to facilitate changes and updating. A more sophisticated application involves the use of a specialized program designed to help the auditor think through the planning considerations of the audit and select appropriate procedures from an "audit procedures data base."

PERSUASIVENESS OF EVIDENCE

OBJECTIVE 7-3
Specify the characteristics that determine the persuasiveness of evidence.

The third standard of field work that was introduced in Chapter 2 requires the auditor to accumulate *sufficient competent evidence to support the opinion issued.* Because of the nature of audit evidence and the cost considerations of doing an audit, it is unlikely that the auditor will be completely convinced that the opinion is correct. However, the auditor must be persuaded that his or her opinion is correct with a high level of assurance. By combining all evidence from the entire audit, the auditor is able to decide when he or she is persuaded to issue an audit report.

The two determinants of the **persuasiveness of evidence** are *competence* and *sufficiency,* which are taken directly from the third standard of field work.

Competence

Competence of evidence refers to the degree to which evidence can be considered believable or worthy of trust. If evidence is considered highly competent, it is a great help in persuading the auditor that financial statements are fairly stated. For example, if an auditor counted the inventory, that evidence would be more competent than if management gave the auditor its own figures. Most auditors, as well as the authors of this text, use the term **reliability of evidence** as being synonymous with competence.

Competence of evidence deals only with the audit procedures selected. Competence cannot be improved by selecting a larger sample size or different population items. It can be improved only by selecting audit procedures that contain a higher quality of one or more of the following seven characteristics of competent evidence.

Relevance Evidence must *pertain to or be relevant to the audit objective* that the auditor is testing before it can be reliable. For example, assume that the auditor is concerned that a client is failing to bill customers for shipments (completeness objective). If the auditor selected a sample of duplicate sales invoices and traced each to related shipping documents, the evidence would *not be relevant* for the completeness objective and therefore would not be considered reliable evidence for that objective. A relevant procedure would be to trace a sample of shipping documents to related duplicate sales invoices to determine whether each had been billed. The second audit procedure is relevant and the first is not because the shipment of goods is the normal criterion used for determining whether a sale has occurred and should have been billed. By tracing from shipping documents to duplicate sales invoices, the auditor can determine whether shipments have been billed to customers. When the auditor traces from duplicate sales invoices to shipping documents, it is impossible to find unbilled shipments.

Relevance can be considered only in terms of specific audit objectives. Evidence may be relevant to one audit objective but not to a different one. In the previous example, when the auditor traced from the duplicate sales invoices to related shipping documents, the evidence was relevant to the existence objective. Most evidence is relevant to more than one, but not all, audit objectives.

Independence of Provider Evidence obtained from a source outside the entity is more reliable than that obtained from within. For example, external evidence such as communications from banks, attorneys, or customers is generally considered more reliable than answers obtained from inquiries of the client. Similarly, documents that originate from outside the client's organization are considered more reliable than are those that originate within the company and have never left the client's organization. An example of the former is an insurance policy and the latter a purchase requisition.

Effectiveness of Client's Internal Controls When a client's internal controls are effective, evidence obtained is more reliable than when they are weak. For example, if internal controls over sales and billing are effective, the auditor could obtain more competent evidence from sales invoices and shipping documents than if the controls were inadequate.

Auditor's Direct Knowledge Evidence obtained directly by the auditor through physical examination, observation, computation, and inspection is more competent than information obtained indirectly. For example, if the auditor calculates the gross margin as a percentage of sales and compares it with previous periods, the evidence would be more reliable than if the auditor relied on the calculations of the controller.

Qualifications of Individuals Providing the Information Although the source of information is independent, the evidence will not be reliable unless the individual providing it is qualified to do so. Therefore, communications from attorneys and bank confirmations are typically more highly regarded than accounts receivable confirmations from persons not familiar with the business world. Also, evidence obtained directly by the auditor may not be reliable if he or she lacks the qualifications to evaluate the evidence. For example, examination of an inventory of diamonds by an auditor not trained to distinguish between diamonds and glass would not provide reliable evidence of the existence of diamonds.

Degree of Objectivity Objective evidence is more reliable than evidence that requires considerable judgment to determine whether it is correct. Examples of objective evidence include confirmation of accounts receivable and bank balances, the physical count of securities and cash, and adding (footing) a list of accounts payable to determine whether it agrees with the balance in the general ledger. Examples of subjective evidence include a letter written by a client's attorney discussing the likely outcome of outstanding lawsuits against the client, observation of obsolescence of inventory during physical examination, and inquiries of the credit manager about the collectibility of noncurrent accounts receivable. When the reliability of subjective evidence is being evaluated, the qualifications of the person providing the evidence are important.

Timeliness The timeliness of audit evidence can refer either to when it is accumulated or to the period covered by the audit. Evidence is usually more reliable for balance sheet accounts when it is obtained as close to the balance sheet date as possible. For example, the auditor's count of marketable securities on the balance sheet date would be more reliable than a count 2 months earlier. For income statement accounts, evidence is more reliable if there is a sample from the entire period under audit rather than from only a part of the period. For example, a random sample of sales transactions for the entire year would be more reliable than a sample from only the first 6 months.

Sufficiency

The *quantity* of evidence obtained determines its sufficiency. **Sufficiency of evidence** is measured primarily by the sample size the auditor selects. For a given audit procedure, the evidence obtained from a sample of 200 would ordinarily be more sufficient than from a sample of 100.

Several factors determine the appropriate sample size in audits. The two most important ones are the auditor's expectation of misstatements and the effectiveness of the client's internal controls. To illustrate, assume in the audit of Jones Computer Parts Co. that the auditor concludes that there is a high likelihood of obsolete inventory because of the nature of the client's industry. The auditor would sample more inventory items for obsolescence in an audit such as this than one where the likelihood of obsolescence was low. Similarly, if the auditor concludes that a client has effective rather than ineffective internal controls over recording fixed assets, a smaller sample size in the audit of acquisitions of fixed assets is warranted.

In addition to sample size, the individual items tested affect the sufficiency of evidence. Samples containing population items with large dollar values, items with a high likelihood of misstatement, and items that are representative of the population are usually considered sufficient. In contrast, most auditors would usually consider samples insufficient that contain only the largest dollar items from the population unless these items make up a large portion of the total population amount.

Combined Effect

The persuasiveness of evidence can be evaluated only after considering the combination of competence and sufficiency, including the effects of the factors influencing competence and sufficiency. A large sample of evidence provided by an independent party is not persuasive unless it is relevant to the audit objective being tested. A large sample of evidence that is relevant but not objective is also not persuasive. Similarly, a small sample of only one or two pieces of highly competent evidence also typically lacks persuasiveness. The auditor must evaluate the degree to which both competence and sufficiency, including all factors influencing them, have been met when determining the persuasiveness of evidence.

There are direct relationships among the four evidence decisions and the two qualities that determine the persuasiveness of evidence. Table 7-2 shows those relationships.

TABLE 7-2	Relationships among Evidence Decisions and Persuasiveness
Audit Evidence Decisions	**Qualities Affecting Persuasiveness of Evidence**

Audit procedures and timing	Competence
	   Relevance
	   Independence of provider
	   Effectiveness of internal controls
	   Auditor's direct knowledge
	   Qualifications of provider
	   Objectivity of evidence
	   Timeliness
	      When procedures are performed
	      Portion of period audited

Sample size and items to select	Sufficiency
	   Adequate sample size
	   Selecting appropriate population items

To illustrate the relationships shown in Table 7-2, assume an auditor is verifying inventory that is a major item in the financial statements. Generally accepted auditing standards require that the auditor be reasonably persuaded that inventory is not materially misstated. The auditor must therefore obtain a sufficient amount of competent evidence about inventory. This means deciding which procedures to use for auditing inventory to satisfy the competency requirements, as well as determining the appropriate sample size and items to select from the population to satisfy the sufficiency requirement. The combination of these four evidence decisions must result in sufficiently persuasive evidence to satisfy the auditor that inventory is materially correct. The audit program section for inventory will reflect these decisions. In practice, the auditor applies the four evidence decisions to specific audit objectives in deciding sufficient competent evidence.

In making decisions about evidence for a given audit, both persuasiveness and cost must be considered. It is rare when only one type of evidence is available for verifying information. The persuasiveness and cost of all alternatives should be considered before selecting the best type or types. The auditor's goal is to obtain a sufficient amount of competent evidence at the lowest possible total cost. However, cost is never an adequate justification for omitting a necessary procedure or not gathering an adequate sample size.

Persuasiveness and Cost

KNOW

TYPES OF AUDIT EVIDENCE

In deciding which audit procedures to use, the auditor can choose from seven broad categories of evidence. These categories, called *types of evidence*, are listed below and defined and discussed in this section.

OBJECTIVE 7-4
Identify and apply the seven types of evidence used in auditing.

1. Physical examination
2. Confirmation
3. Documentation
4. Observation
5. Inquiries of the client
6. Reperformance
7. Analytical procedures

Before beginning the study of types of evidence, it is useful to show the relationships among auditing standards, which were studied in Chapter 2, types of evidence, and the four evidence decisions discussed earlier in this chapter. These relationships are shown in Figure 7-1 (p. 182).

Notice that the standards are general, whereas audit procedures are specific. Types of evidence are broader than procedures and narrower than the standards. Every audit procedure obtains one or more types of evidence.

Physical examination is the inspection or count by the auditor of a *tangible asset*. This type of evidence is most often associated with inventory and cash, but it is also applicable to the verification of securities, notes receivable, and tangible fixed assets. The distinction between the physical examination of assets, such as marketable securities and cash, and the examination of documents, such as cancelled checks and sales documents, is important for auditing purposes. If the object being examined, such as a sales invoice, has no inherent value, the evidence is called documentation. For example, before a check is signed, it is a document; after it is signed, it becomes an asset; and when it is cancelled, it becomes a document again. Technically, physical examination of the check can occur only while the check is an asset.

Physical examination, which is a direct means of verifying that an asset actually exists (existence objective), is regarded as one of the most reliable and useful types of audit evidence. Generally, physical examination is an objective means of ascertaining both the quantity and the description of the asset. In some cases, it is also a useful method for

Physical Examination

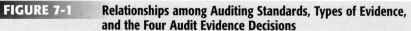

FIGURE 7-1 Relationships among Auditing Standards, Types of Evidence, and the Four Audit Evidence Decisions

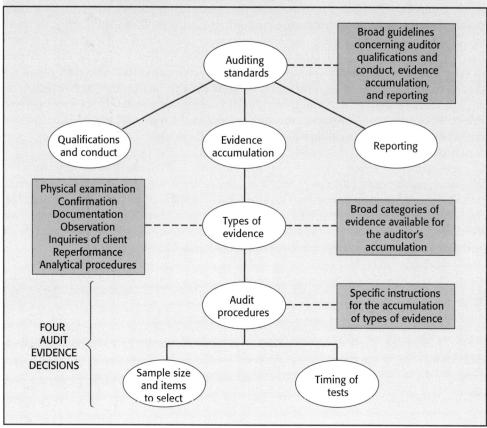

evaluating an asset's condition or quality. However, physical examination is not sufficient evidence to verify that existing assets are owned by the client (rights and obligations objective), and in many cases the auditor is not qualified to judge qualitative factors such as obsolescence or authenticity (net realizable value objective). Also, proper valuation for financial statement purposes usually cannot be determined by physical examination (accuracy objective).

Confirmation

Confirmation describes the *receipt* of a *written or oral response* from an *independent third party* verifying the accuracy of information that was *requested by the auditor*. The request is made to the client, and the client asks the independent third party to respond directly to the auditor. Because confirmations come from sources independent of the client, they are a highly regarded and often used type of evidence. However, confirmations are relatively costly to obtain and may cause some inconvenience to those asked to supply them. Therefore, they are not used in every instance in which they are applicable. Because of the high reliability of confirmations, auditors typically obtain written responses rather than oral ones when it is practical. Written confirmations are easier for supervisors to review, and they provide better support if it is necessary to demonstrate that a confirmation was received.

Whether or not confirmations should be used depends on the reliability needs of the situation as well as the alternative evidence available. Traditionally, confirmations are seldom used in the audit of fixed asset additions because these can be verified adequately by documentation and physical examination. Similarly, confirmations are ordinarily not used to verify individual transactions between organizations, such as sales transactions, because the auditor can use documents for that purpose. Naturally, there are exceptions. Assume the auditor determines that there are two extraordinarily large sales transactions recorded 3 days before year-end. Confirmation of these two transactions may be appropriate.

SAS 67 (AU 330) identifies three common types of confirmations used by auditors. The first type is a positive confirmation with a request for information to be supplied by the recipient. A positive confirmation means that the recipient is requested to return the confirmation in all circumstances. When the auditor does not receive a response to a positive confirmation, it is common to send a second or third request and in some cases even request the client to contact the independent third party and ask for a response to the auditor. If other efforts fail or are considered too costly, the auditor may be able to use different evidence to satisfy the audit objective. This evidence is called alternative procedures. The second is a positive confirmation with the information to be confirmed included on the form. This type of confirmation is considered less reliable than the first one because the recipient may sign the confirmation and return it without carefully examining the information. Research shows that the response rate for the first type is lower because it requires more effort by the recipient to complete the form. The third type is a negative confirmation. A negative confirmation means that the recipient is requested to respond only when the information is incorrect. Because confirmations are considered significant evidence only when returned, negatives are considered less competent than positive confirmations.

When practical and reasonable, the confirmation of a sample of accounts receivable is *required* of CPAs. This requirement, imposed by SAS 67, exists because accounts receivable usually represent a significant balance on the financial statements, and confirmations are a highly reliable type of evidence.

Although confirmation is not required for any account other than accounts receivable, this type of evidence is useful in verifying many types of information. The major types of information that are often confirmed, along with the source of the confirmation, are indicated in Table 7-3.

TABLE 7-3	Information Often Confirmed
Information	**Source**
Assets	
Cash in bank	Bank
Accounts receivable	Customer
Notes receivable	Maker
Owned inventory out on consignment	Consignee
Inventory held in public warehouses	Public warehouse
Cash surrender value of life insurance	Insurance company
Liabilities	
Accounts payable	Creditor
Notes payable	Lender
Advances from customers	Customer
Mortgages payable	Mortgagor
Bonds payable	Bondholder
Owners' Equity	
Shares outstanding	Registrar and transfer agent
Other Information	
Insurance coverage	Insurance company
Contingent liabilities	Bank, lender, and client's legal counsel
Bond indenture agreements	Bondholder
Collateral held by creditors	Creditor

To be considered reliable evidence, confirmations must be controlled by the auditor from the time they are prepared until they are returned. If the client controls the preparation of the confirmation, does the mailing, or receives the responses, the auditor has lost control and with it independence; thus, the reliability of the evidence is reduced.

Documentation

Documentation is the auditor's examination of the *client's documents and records* to substantiate the information that is or should be included in the financial statements. The documents examined by the auditor are the records used by the client to provide information for conducting its business in an organized manner. Because each transaction in the client's organization is normally supported by at least one document, there is a large volume of this type of evidence available. For example, the client often retains a customer order, a shipping document, and a duplicate sales invoice for each sales transaction. These same documents are useful evidence for verification by the auditor of the accuracy of the client's records for sales transactions. Documentation is a form of evidence widely used in every audit because it is usually readily available to the auditor at a relatively low cost. Sometimes it is the only reasonable type of evidence available.

Documents can be conveniently classified as internal and external. An **internal document** is one that has been prepared and used within the client's organization and is retained without ever going to an outside party such as a customer or a vendor. Examples of internal documents include duplicate sales invoices, employees' time reports, and inventory receiving reports. An **external document** is one that has been in the hands of someone outside the client's organization who is a party to the transaction being documented, but which is either currently in the hands of the client or readily accessible. In some cases, external documents originate outside the client's organization and end up in the hands of the client. Examples of this type of external document are vendors' invoices, cancelled notes payable, and insurance policies. Other documents, such as cancelled checks, originate with the client, go to an outsider, and are finally returned to the client.

The primary determinant of the auditor's willingness to accept a document as reliable evidence is whether it is internal or external and, when internal, whether it was created and processed under conditions of good internal control. Internal documents created and processed under conditions of weak internal control may not constitute reliable evidence.

Because external documents have been in the hands of both the client and another party to the transaction, there is some indication that both members are in agreement about the information and the conditions stated on the document. Therefore, external documents are considered more reliable evidence than internal ones. Some external documents have exceptional reliability because they are prepared with considerable care and often have been reviewed by attorneys or other qualified experts. Examples include title papers to property such as land, insurance policies, indenture agreements, and contracts.

When auditors use documentation to support recorded transactions or amounts, it is often called **vouching.** To vouch recorded acquisition transactions, the auditor might, for example, trace from the acquisitions journal to supporting vendors' invoices and receiving reports and thereby satisfy the existence objective. If the auditor traces from receiving reports to the acquisitions journal to satisfy the completeness objective, it would not be appropriate to call it vouching.

E-Commerce Information Sites

It is common in many companies for a considerable portion of clients' documentation to be available only in electronic form. For example, some companies use Electronic Data Interchange (EDI) to transact business electronically and complete purchase, shipping, billing, cash receipt, and cash disbursement transactions entirely by the exchange of electronic messages. Companies also use image processing systems to convert traditional documents into electronic images to facilitate storage and reference. Typically, the traditional documents are not retained.

Both written and electronic information, such as records of electronic transfers, are valid and useful. SAS 80 recognizes these changes in the nature of documentary audit evidence.

Observation is the use of the senses to assess certain activities. Throughout the audit, there are many opportunities to exercise sight, hearing, touch, and smell to evaluate a wide range of items. For example, the auditor may tour the plant to obtain a general impression of the client's facilities, observe whether equipment is rusty to evaluate whether it is obsolete, and watch individuals perform accounting tasks to determine whether the person assigned a responsibility is performing it. Observation is rarely sufficient by itself because there is a risk that the client personnel involved in those activities are aware of the auditor's presence. Therefore, they may perform their responsibilities in accordance with company policy but resume normal activities once the auditor is not in sight. It is necessary to follow up initial impressions with other kinds of corroborative evidence. Nevertheless, observation is useful in most parts of the audit.

Observation

Inquiry is the obtaining of *written* or *oral* information from the client in response to questions from the auditor. Although considerable evidence is obtained from the client through inquiry, it usually cannot be regarded as conclusive because it is not from an independent source and may be biased in the client's favor. Therefore, when the auditor obtains evidence through inquiry, it is normally necessary to obtain further corroborating evidence through other procedures. As an illustration, when the auditor wants to obtain information about the client's method of recording and controlling accounting transactions, he or she usually begins by asking the client how the internal controls operate. Later, the auditor performs audit tests using documentation and observation to determine whether the transactions are recorded (completeness objective) and authorized (existence objective) in the manner stated.

Inquiries of the Client

As the word implies, **reperformance** involves rechecking a sample of the computations and transfers of information made by the client during the period under audit. Rechecking of computations consists of testing the client's arithmetical accuracy. It includes such procedures as extending sales invoices and inventory, adding journals and subsidiary records, and checking the calculation of depreciation expense and prepaid expenses. Rechecking of transfers of information consists of tracing amounts to be confident that when the same information is included in more than one place, it is recorded at the same amount each time. For example, the auditor normally makes limited tests to ascertain that the information in the sales journal has been included for the proper customer and at the correct amount in the subsidiary accounts receivable records and is accurately summarized in the general ledger. A considerable portion of auditors' reperformance is done by computer-assisted audit software.

Reperformance

Analytical procedures use comparisons and relationships to assess whether account balances or other data appear reasonable. An example is comparing the gross margin percent in the current year with the preceding year's. For certain audit objectives or small account balances, analytical procedures may be the only evidence needed. For other accounts, other types of evidence may be reduced when analytical procedures indicate that an account balance appears reasonable. In some cases, analytical procedures are also used to isolate accounts or transactions that should be investigated more extensively to help in deciding whether additional verification is needed. An example is comparison of the current period's total repair expense with previous years' and investigation of the difference, if it is significant, to determine the cause of the increase or decrease.

Analytical Procedures

The Auditing Standards Board has concluded that analytical procedures are so important that they are *required during the planning and completion phases on all audits.* Because analytical procedures are an important part of planning audits, performing tests of each cycle, and completing audits, their use is studied more extensively at the end of this chapter and in most remaining chapters of this book.

The characteristics discussed earlier in the chapter for determining the competence of evidence are related to the seven types of evidence in Table 7-4 on page 186. Note that two of the characteristics that determine the competency of evidence—relevance and

Competence of Types of Evidence

TABLE 7-4   Competence of Types of Evidence

	Criteria to Determine Competence				
Type of Evidence	**Independence of Provider**	**Effectiveness of Client's Internal Controls**	**Auditor's Direct Knowledge**	**Qualifications of Provider**	**Objectivity of Evidence**
Physical examination	High (auditor does)	Varies	High	Normally high (auditor does)	High
Confirmation	High	Not applicable	Low	Varies—usually high	High
Documentation	Varies—external more independent than internal	Varies	Low	Varies	High
Observation	High (auditor does)	Varies	High	Normally high (auditor does)	Medium
Inquiries of client	Low (client provides)	Not applicable	Low	Varies	Varies—low to high
Reperformance	High (auditor does)	Varies	High	High (auditor does)	High
Analytical procedures	High/low (auditor does/ client responds)	Varies	Low	Normally high (auditor does/ client responds)	Varies—usually low

Evidence Defined for Jurors

timeliness—are not included in Table 7-4. Each of the seven types of evidence included in the table has the potential to be both relevant and timely, depending on its source and when the evidence is obtained. Several other observations are apparent from a study of Table 7-4.

First, the effectiveness of the client's internal controls has a significant impact on the competence of most types of evidence. For example, internal documentation from a company with effective internal control is more reliable because the documents are more likely to be accurate. Similarly, analytical procedures will not be competent evidence if the controls that produced the data provide inaccurate information.

Second, both physical examination and reperformance are likely to be highly reliable if the internal controls are effective, but their use differs considerably. These two types of evidence effectively illustrate that equally reliable evidence may be completely different.

Third, a specific type of evidence is rarely sufficient by itself to provide competent evidence to satisfy any audit objective. It is apparent from examining Table 7-4 that observation, inquiries of client, and analytical procedures are examples of this.

Cost of Types of Evidence

The two most expensive types of evidence are physical examination and confirmation. Physical examination is costly because it normally requires the auditor's presence when the client is counting the asset, often on the balance sheet date. For example, physical examination of inventory can result in several auditors traveling to widely separated geographical locations. Confirmation is costly because the auditor must follow careful procedures in the confirmation preparation, mailing, and receipt, and in the follow-up of nonresponses and exceptions.

Documentation and analytical procedures are moderately costly. If client personnel locate documents for the auditor and organize them for convenient use, documentation usually has a fairly low cost. When auditors must find those documents themselves, documentation can be extremely costly. Even under ideal circumstances, information and data on documents are sometimes complex and require interpretation and analysis. For example, it

TABLE 7-5   Types of Evidence and Four Evidence Decisions for a Balance-Related Audit Objective for Inventory*

Type of Evidence	Evidence Decisions			
	Audit Procedure	Sample Size	Items to Select	Timing
Observation	Observe client's personnel counting inventory to determine whether they are properly following instructions	All count teams	Not applicable	Balance sheet date
Physical examination	Count a sample of inventory and compare quantity and description to client's counts	120 items	40 items with large dollar value, plus 80 randomly selected	Balance sheet date
Documentation	Compare quantity on client's perpetual records to quantity on client's counts	70 items	30 items with large dollar value, plus 40 randomly selected	Balance sheet date

*Balance-related audit objective: Inventory quantities on the client's perpetual records agree with items physically on hand.

is usually time-consuming to read and evaluate a client's contracts, lease agreements, and minutes of the board of directors meetings. Analytical procedures require the auditor to decide which analytical procedures to use, make the calculations, and evaluate the results. Doing so often takes considerable time.

The three least expensive types of evidence are observation, inquiries of the client, and reperformance. Observation is normally done concurrently with other audit procedures. An auditor can easily observe whether client personnel are following appropriate inventory counting procedures at the same time he or she counts a sample of inventory (physical examination). Inquiries of clients are done extensively on every audit and normally have a low cost. Certain inquiries may be costly, such as obtaining written statements from the client documenting discussions throughout the audit. Reperformance is usually low cost because it involves simple calculations and tracing that can be done at the auditor's convenience. Often, the auditor's computer software is used to perform many of these tests.

Application of Types of Evidence to the Four Evidence Decisions

An application of three types of evidence to the four evidence decisions for one balance-related audit objective—inventory quantities on the client's perpetual records agree with items physically on hand—is shown in Table 7-5. First, examine column 3 in Table 6-5 on page 161. These are the balance-related audit objectives for the audit of inventory for Hillsburg Hardware Co. The overall objective is to obtain persuasive evidence at minimum cost that inventory is materially correct. The auditor must therefore decide which audit procedures to use to satisfy each balance-related audit objective, what the sample size should be for each procedure, which items from the population to include in the sample, and when to perform each procedure.

For the objective "inventory quantities on the client's perpetual records agree with items physically on hand," the auditor selected the three types of evidence included in Table 7-5. He or she decided that the other four types of evidence studied in this chapter were not relevant or necessary for this objective. Only one audit procedure is included for each type of evidence and illustrative decisions for sample size, items to select, and timing are shown for each procedure.

Terms Used in Audit Procedures

As stated earlier, audit procedures are the detailed steps, usually written in the form of instructions, for the accumulation of the seven types of audit evidence. They should be sufficiently clear to enable members of the audit team to understand what is to be done.

| TABLE 7-6 | Terms, Audit Procedures, and Types of Evidence |

Term and Definition	Illustrative Audit Procedure	Type of Evidence
Examine—A reasonably detailed study of a document or record to determine specific facts about it.	*Examine* a sample of vendors' invoices to determine whether the goods or services received are reasonable and of the type normally used by the client's business.	Documentation
Scan—A less detailed examination of a document or record to determine whether there is something unusual warranting further investigation.	*Scan* the sales journal, looking for large and unusual transactions.	Analytical procedures
Read—An examination of written information to determine facts pertinent to the audit.	*Read* the minutes of a board of directors meeting and summarize all information that is pertinent to the financial statements in a working paper.	Documentation
Compute—A calculation done by the auditor independent of the client.	*Compute* the inventory turnover ratios and compare with those of previous years as a test of inventory obsolescence.	Analytical procedures
Recompute—A calculation done to determine whether a client's calculation is correct.	*Recompute* the unit sales price times the number of units for a sample of duplicate sales invoices and compare the totals with the calculations.	Reperformance
Foot—Addition of a column of numbers to determine whether the total is the same as the client's.	*Foot* the sales journal for a 1-month period and compare all totals with the general ledger.	Reperformance
Trace—An instruction normally associated with documentation or reperformance. The instruction should state what the auditor is tracing and where it is being traced from and to. Often, an audit procedure that includes the term *trace* will also include a second instruction, such as *compare* or *recalculate*.	*Trace* a sample of sales transactions from the sales journal to sales invoices and *compare* customer name, date, and the total dollar value of the sale. *Trace* postings from the sales journal to the general ledger accounts.	Documentation Reperformance
Compare—A comparison of information in two different locations. The instruction should state which information is being compared in as much detail as practical.	Select a sample of sales invoices and *compare* the unit selling price as stated on the invoice to the list of unit selling prices authorized by management.	Documentation
Count—A determination of assets on hand at a given time. This term should be associated only with the type of evidence defined as physical examination.	*Count* petty cash on hand at the balance sheet date.	Physical examination
Observe—The act of observation should be associated with the type of evidence defined as observation.	*Observe* whether the two inventory count teams independently count and record inventory costs.	Observation
Inquire—The act of inquiry should be associated with the type of evidence defined as inquiry.	*Inquire* of management whether there is any obsolete inventory on hand at the balance sheet date.	Inquiries of client
Vouch—The use of documents to verify recorded transactions or amounts.	*Vouch* a sample of recorded acquisition transactions to vendors' invoices and receiving reports.	Documentation

Several different terms are commonly used to describe audit procedures. These are presented and defined in Table 7-6 above. To help you understand each term, an illustrative audit procedure and the type of evidence that it is associated with are shown.

ANALYTICAL PROCEDURES

One of the seven types of evidence discussed in the previous section was analytical procedures. Because of the importance of this topic and increased emphasis on analytical procedures in practice, this section expands on the subject. Analytical procedures are defined by

SAS 56 (AU 329) as *evaluations of financial information made by a study of plausible relationships among financial and nonfinancial data . . . involving comparisons of recorded amounts to expectations developed by the auditor.* This definition is more formal than the description of analytical procedures used earlier in the chapter, but they say essentially the same thing. In both cases, analytical procedures use comparisons and relationships to assess whether account balances or other data appear reasonable. The emphasis in the SAS 56 definition is on expectations developed by the auditor. For example, the auditor might compare current year recorded commissions expense to total recorded sales multiplied by the average commission rate as a test of the overall reasonableness of recorded commissions. For this analytical procedure to be relevant and reliable, the auditor has likely concluded that recorded sales are correctly stated, all sales earn a commission, and there is an average actual commission rate that is readily determinable.

OBJECTIVE 7-5
State the purposes of analytical procedures and the timing of each purpose.

Generally, an auditor considers knowledge and experience about a client company obtained in prior years as a starting point for planning the audit for the current year. By conducting analytical procedures in which the current year's unaudited information is compared with prior years' audited information, changes are highlighted. These changes can represent important trends or specific events, all of which will influence audit planning. For example, a decline in gross margin percentages over time may indicate increasing competition in the company's market area, and the need to consider inventory pricing more carefully during the audit. Similarly, an increase in the balance in fixed assets may indicate a significant acquisition that must be reviewed.

Understanding the Client's Industry and Business

On-Line Industry Information

Analytical procedures are often useful as an indication that the client company is encountering severe financial difficulty. The likelihood of financial failure must be considered by the auditor in the assessment of audit-related risks, as well as in connection with management's use of the going concern assumption in preparing the financial statements. Certain analytical procedures can be helpful in that regard. For example, if a higher than normal ratio of long-term debt to net worth is combined with a lower than average ratio of profits to total assets, a relatively high risk of financial failure may be indicated. Not only would such conditions affect the audit plan, they may indicate that substantial doubt exists about the entity's ability to continue as a going concern, which would require a report modification, as discussed in Chapter 3.

Assessment of the Entity's Ability to Continue as a Going Concern

Significant unexpected differences between the current year's unaudited financial data and other data used in comparisons are commonly called **unusual fluctuations**. Unusual fluctuations occur when significant differences are not expected but do exist or when significant differences are expected but do not exist. In either case, one of the possible reasons for an unusual fluctuation is the presence of an accounting misstatement. Thus, if the unusual fluctuation is large, the auditor must determine the reason for it and must be satisfied that the cause is a valid economic event and not a misstatement. For example, in comparing the ratio of the allowance for uncollectible accounts receivable to gross accounts receivable with that of the previous year, suppose that the ratio had decreased while, at the same time, accounts receivable turnover also decreased. The combination of these two pieces of information would indicate a possible understatement of the allowance. This aspect of analytical procedures is often called *attention directing* because it results in more detailed procedures in the specific audit areas where misstatements might be found.

Indication of the Presence of Possible Misstatements in the Financial Statements

When an analytical procedure reveals no unusual fluctuations, the implication is that the possibility of a material misstatement is minimized. In that case, the analytical procedure constitutes substantive evidence in support of the fair statement of the related account balances, and it is possible to perform fewer detailed tests in connection with those accounts. For example, if analytical procedures results of a small account balance such as prepaid insurance are favorable, no detailed tests may be necessary. In other cases, certain audit procedures can be eliminated, sample sizes can be reduced, or the timing of the procedures can be moved farther away from the balance sheet date.

Reduction of Detailed Audit Tests

Analytical procedures are usually inexpensive compared with tests of details. Therefore, most auditors prefer to replace tests of details with analytical procedures when possible. To illustrate, it may be far less expensive to calculate and review sales and accounts receivable ratios than to confirm accounts receivable. If it is possible to reduce or replace confirmations by doing analytical procedures, considerable cost savings can occur.

The extent to which analytical procedures provide useful substantive evidence depends on their reliability in the circumstances. For some audit objectives and in some circumstances, they may be the most effective procedure to apply. These audit objectives might include proper classification of transactions, completeness of recording transactions, and accuracy of management's judgments and estimates in certain areas, such as the allowance for uncollectible accounts. For other audit objectives and circumstances, analytical procedures may be considered attention directing at best, and not relied on for gathering substantive evidence. An example is determining the existence of sales transactions. The factors that determine when analytical procedures are effective are discussed in a later section of this chapter.

Timing

Analytical procedures may be performed at any of three times during an engagement. Some analytical procedures are *required* to be performed in the *planning phase* to assist in determining the nature, extent, and timing of work to be performed. Performance of analytical procedures during planning helps the auditor identify significant matters requiring special consideration later in the engagement. For example, the calculation of inventory turnover before inventory price tests are done may indicate the need for special care during those tests.

Analytical procedures done in the planning phase typically use data aggregated at a high level and the sophistication, extent, and timing of the procedures vary among clients. For some clients, the comparison of prior year and current year account balances using the unaudited trial balance may be sufficient. For other clients, the procedures might involve extensive analysis of quarterly financial statements based on the auditor's judgment.

Analytical procedures are often done *during the testing phase* of the audit in conjunction with other audit procedures. For example, the prepaid portion of each insurance policy might be compared with the same policy for the previous year as a part of doing tests of prepaid insurance.

Analytical procedures are also *required* to be done *during the completion phase* of the audit. Such tests are useful at that point as a final review for material misstatements or financial problems, and to help the auditor take a final "objective look" at the financial statements that have been audited. It is common for a partner to do the analytical procedures during the final review of working papers and financial statements. Typically, a partner has a good understanding of the client and its business because of ongoing relationships. Knowledge about the client's business combined with effective analytical procedures is a way to identify possible oversights in an audit.

The purposes of analytical procedures for each of the three different phases when they are performed are shown in Figure 7-2. The shaded boxes in the figure indicate that a purpose is applicable for a phase. In addition, several purposes are indicated as being the primary purpose. Notice that purposes vary for different phases. Analytical procedures are performed during the planning phase for all four purposes, whereas the other two phases are used primarily to determine appropriate audit evidence and to reach conclusions about the fair presentation of financial statements.

FIVE TYPES OF ANALYTICAL PROCEDURES

The usefulness of analytical procedures as audit evidence depends significantly on the auditor developing an *expectation* of what a recorded account balance or ratio based on account balances *should be*, regardless of the type of analytical procedures used. Auditors develop an expectation of an account balance or ratio by considering information from prior

FIGURE 7-2   Timing and Purposes of Analytical Procedures

Purpose	Phase		
	(Required) Planning Phase	Testing Phase	(Required) Completion Phase
Understand client's industry and business	Primary purpose		
Assess going concern	Secondary purpose		Secondary purpose
Indicate possible misstatements (attention directing)	Primary purpose	Secondary purpose	Primary purpose
Reduce detailed tests	Secondary purpose	Primary purpose	

periods, industry trends, client-prepared budgeted expectations, and nonfinancial information. The auditor typically compares the client's balances and ratios with expected balances and ratios using one or more of the following types of analytical procedures:

• Compare client and industry data.
• Compare client data with similar prior-period data.
• Compare client data with client-determined expected results.
• Compare client data with auditor-determined expected results.
• Compare client data with expected results, using nonfinancial data.

Suppose that you are doing an audit and obtain the following information about the client and the average company in the client's industry:

Compare Client and Industry Data

	Client		Industry	
	1999	1998	1999	1998
Inventory turnover	3.4	3.5	3.9	3.4
Gross margin percent	26.3%	26.4%	27.3%	26.2%

If we look only at client information for the two ratios shown, the company appears to be stable with no apparent indication of difficulties. However, if the auditor uses industry data to develop expectations about the two ratios for 1999, the auditor would expect both ratios for the client to increase. Although these two ratios by themselves may not indicate significant problems, the example illustrates how developing expectations using industry data may provide useful information about the client's performance. For example, the company may have lost market share, its pricing may not be competitive, it may have incurred abnormal costs, or it may have obsolete items in inventory.

Dun & Bradstreet, Robert Morris Associates, and other publishers accumulate financial information for thousands of companies and compile the data for different lines of business. Many CPA firms purchase these publications for use as a basis for industry comparisons in their audits.

The most important benefits of industry comparisons are as an aid to understanding the client's business and as an indication of the likelihood of financial failure. The ratios in Robert Morris Associates, for example, are primarily of a type that bankers and other credit executives use in evaluating whether a company will be able to repay a loan. That same information is useful to auditors in assessing the relative strength of the client's capital structure, its borrowing capacity, and the likelihood of financial failure.

A major weakness in using industry ratios for auditing is the difference between the nature of the client's financial information and that of the firms making up the industry totals. Because the industry data are broad averages, the comparisons may not be meaningful. Often, the client's line of business is not the same as the industry standards. In addition, different companies follow different accounting methods, and this affects the comparability of data. If most companies in the industry use FIFO inventory valuation and straight-line depreciation, and the audit client uses LIFO and double-declining-balance depreciation, comparisons may not be meaningful. This does not mean that industry comparisons should not be made. Rather, it is an indication of the need for care in interpreting the results.

USING ANALYTICAL PROCEDURES EFFECTIVELY

According to a recent article in the *Journal of Accountancy,* auditors often face potentially serious judgment problems while performing analytical procedures. An auditor can encounter judgment problems when he or she:

- Allows unaudited account balances or ratios to unduly influence expectations of what current balances should be.
- Does not fully consider the pattern reflected by several unusual fluctuations when trying to explain what caused them.
- Places reliance on management's explanations about unusual fluctuations without first developing independent explanations.

The authors of the article offer the following recommendations to auditors performing analytical procedures:

- Compare unaudited balances with independent expectations of what those balances should be.
- Examine patterns of discrepancies, rather than analyze each discrepancy on its own.
- Identify reasonable explanations for unexpected fluctuations from knowledge of the client and industry *before* inquiring of the client's management.
- Evaluate management's explanations carefully, including considering how each explanation affects all account balances in question.

Source: Timothy B. Bell and Arnold M. Wright, "When Judgment Counts," *Journal of Accountancy* (November 1997), pp. 73–77.

Compare Client Data with Similar Prior-Period Data

Suppose that the gross margin percent for a company has been between 26 and 27 percent for each of the past 4 years but is 23 percent in the current year. This decline in gross margin should be a concern to the auditor if there is no expectation of a decline. The cause of the decline could be a change in economic conditions. However, it could also be caused by misstatements in the financial statements, such as sales or purchase cutoff errors, unrecorded sales, overstated accounts payable, or inventory costing errors. The auditor should determine the cause of the decline in gross margin and consider the effect, if any, on evidence accumulation.

There are a wide variety of analytical procedures in which client data are compared with similar data from one or more prior periods. The following are common examples.

Compare the Current Year's Balance with That for the Preceding Year One of the easiest ways to make this test is to include the preceding year's adjusted trial balance results in a separate column of the current year's trial balance worksheet. The auditor can easily compare the current year's and previous year's balance to decide early in the audit whether an account should receive more than the normal amount of attention because of a significant change in the balance. For example, if the auditor observes a substantial increase in supplies expense, the auditor should determine whether the cause was an increased use of supplies, an error in the account due to a misclassification, or a misstatement of supplies inventory.

Microsoft's Investor Relations Site

Compare the Detail of a Total Balance with Similar Detail for the Preceding Year If there have been no significant changes in the client's operations in the current year, much of the detail making up the totals in the financial statements should also remain unchanged. By briefly comparing the detail of the current period with similar detail of the preceding period, it is often possible to isolate information that needs further examination. Comparison of details may take the form of details over time or details at a point in time. A common example of the former is comparing the monthly totals for the current and preceding year for sales, repairs, and other accounts. An example of the latter is comparing the details of loans payable at the end of the current year with those at the end of the preceding year. In each of these examples, the auditor should first develop an expectation of a change or lack thereof before making the comparison.

Compute Ratios and Percentage Relationships for Comparison with Previous Years The comparison of totals or details with previous years as described in the two preceding paragraphs has two shortcomings. First, it fails to consider growth or decline in business activity. Second, relationships of data to other data, such as sales to cost of goods sold, are ignored. Ratio and percentage relationships overcome both shortcomings. The example discussed earlier about the decline in gross margin is a common percentage relationship used by auditors.

A few types of ratios and internal comparisons are included in Table 7-7 to show the widespread use of ratio analysis. In all cases, the comparisons should be with calculations made in previous years for the same client. There are many potential ratios and comparisons available for use by an auditor. Subsequent chapters dealing with specific audit areas describe other examples.

Many of the ratios and percentages used for comparison with previous years are the same ones used for comparison with industry data. For example, it is useful to compare

TABLE 7-7	Internal Comparisons and Relationships
Ratio or Comparison	**Possible Misstatement**
Raw material turnover for a manufacturing company	Misstatement of inventory or cost of goods sold or obsolescence of raw material inventory
Sales commissions divided by net sales	Misstatement of sales commissions
Sales returns and allowances divided by gross sales	Misclassified sales returns and allowances or unrecorded returns or allowances subsequent to year-end
Cash surrender value of life insurance (current year) divided by cash surrender value of life insurance (preceding year)	Failure to record the change in cash surrender value or an error in recording the change
Each of the individual manufacturing expenses as a percentage of total manufacturing expense	Significant misstatement of individual expenses within a total

current year gross margin with industry averages and previous years. The same can be said for most of the ratios described in Appendix A (begins on p. 196).

There are also numerous potential comparisons of current- and prior-period data beyond those normally available from industry data. For example, the percent of each expense category to total sales can be compared with that of previous years. Similarly, in a multiunit operation (for example, a retail chain), internal comparisons for each unit can be made with previous periods.

Compare Client Data with Client-Determined Expected Results

Most companies prepare **budgets** for various aspects of their operations and financial results. Because budgets represent the client's expectations for the period, an investigation of the most significant areas in which differences exist between budgeted and actual results may indicate potential misstatements. The absence of differences may also indicate that misstatements are unlikely. It is common, for example, in the audit of local, state, and federal governmental units to use this type of analytical procedure.

When client data are compared with budgets, there are two special concerns. First, the auditor must evaluate whether the budgets were realistic plans. In some organizations, budgets are prepared with little thought or care and therefore are not realistic expectations. Such information has little value as audit evidence. The second concern is the possibility that current financial information was changed by client personnel to conform to the budget. If that has occurred, the auditor will find no differences in comparing actual data with budgeted data even if there are misstatements in the financial statements. Discussing budget procedures with client personnel is used to satisfy the first concern. Assessment of control risk and detailed audit tests of actual data are usually done to minimize the likelihood of the latter concern.

Compare Client Data with Auditor-Determined Expected Results

A second common type of comparison of client data with expected results occurs when the *auditor calculates the expected balance for comparison with the actual balance*. In this type of analytical procedure, the auditor makes an estimate of what an account balance should be by relating it to some other balance sheet or income statement account or accounts or by making a projection based on some historical trend. An example of calculating an expected value based on relationships of accounts is the independent calculation of interest expense on long-term notes payable by multiplying the ending monthly balance in notes payable by the average monthly interest rate (see Figure 7-3). An example of using an historical trend would be when the moving average of the allowance for uncollectible accounts receivable as a percent of gross accounts receivable is applied to the balance of gross accounts receivable at the end of the audit year to determine an expected value for the current allowance.

Compare Client Data with Expected Results Using Nonfinancial Data

Suppose that in auditing a hotel, you can determine the number of rooms, room rate for each room, and occupancy rate. Using those data, it is relatively easy to estimate total revenue from rooms to compare with recorded revenue. The same approach can sometimes be used to estimate such accounts as tuition revenue at universities (average tuition times enrollment), factory payroll (total hours worked times wage rate), and cost of materials sold (units sold times materials cost per unit).

The major concern in using nonfinancial data is the accuracy of the data. In the previous illustration, it is not appropriate to use an estimated calculation of hotel revenue as audit evidence unless the auditor is satisfied with the reasonableness of the count of the number of rooms, room rate, and occupancy rate. It would be more difficult for the auditor to evaluate the accuracy of the occupancy rate than the other two items.

USING STATISTICAL TECHNIQUES AND COMPUTER SOFTWARE

The use of statistical techniques is desirable to make analytical procedures more relevant. Many auditors use computer software to make statistical and nonstatistical calculations easier. These two auditors' tools are discussed briefly.

Hillsburg Hardware Co.
Overall Test of Interest Expense
12/31/99

Schedule __N-3__   Date
Prepared by __TM__ 3/6/00
Approved by __JW__ 3/12/00

Interest expense per general ledger   120,432[1]

Computation of estimate:

  Short-term loans:

    Balance outstanding at month-end: [2]

Jan.	147,500
Feb.	159,200
Mar.	170,600
Apr.	170,800
May	130,200
June	93,700
July	70,000
Aug.	–0–
Sept.	–0–
Oct.	42,700
Nov.	126,300
Dec.	209,000
Total	1,320,000

    Average (÷12) 110,000 @ 12.5%[3] 13,750

  Long-term loans:

Beginning balance	1,326,000[2]
Ending balance	1,206,000[2]
	2,532,000

    Average (÷2) 1,266,000 @ 8.5%[4] 107,610

    Estimated total interest expense   121,360

    Differences   (928)[5]

<u>Legend and Comments</u>
[1] Agrees with general ledger and working trial balance.
[2] Obtained from general ledger.
[3] Estimated based on examination of several notes throughout the
    year with rates ranging from 12% to 13%.
[4] Agrees with permanent file schedule of long-term debt.
[5] Difference not significant. Indicates that interest expense per books is reasonable.

Several statistical techniques that aid in interpreting results can be applied to analytical procedures. The advantages of using statistical techniques are the ability to make more sophisticated calculations and their objectivity.

The most common statistical technique for analytical procedures is regression analysis. Regression analysis is used to evaluate the reasonableness of a recorded balance by relating (regressing) the total to other relevant information. For example, the auditor might conclude that total selling expenses should be related to total sales, the previous year's selling expenses, and the number of salespeople. The auditor would then use regression analysis to statistically determine an estimated value of selling expenses for comparison with

Statistical Techniques

OBJECTIVE 7-7
Explain the benefits of using statistical techniques and computer software for analytical procedures.

recorded values. Regression analysis and other statistical methods commonly used for analytical procedures can be found in several advanced texts dealing with statistical sampling techniques for auditing.

Auditor's Computer Software

As is discussed in a later chapter, computer-based audit software is being used by auditors in a wide variety of ways. One feature common to all such software is the ability to input the client's general ledger into the auditor's computer system. Adjusting entries and financial statements are thereby computerized to save time. The general ledger information for the client is saved and carried forward in the auditor's computerized data file year after year. The existence of current and previous years' general ledger information on the auditor's computer files permits extensive and inexpensive computerized analytical calculations. The analytical information can also be shown in different forms such as graphs and charts to help interpret the data.

A major benefit of computerized analytical procedures is the ease of updating the calculations when adjusting entries to the client's statements are made. If there are several adjusting entries to the clients' records, the analytical procedures calculations can be quickly revised. For example, a change in inventory and cost of goods sold affects a large number of ratios. All affected ratios would be revised at almost no cost with computer software.

APPENDIX A: COMMON FINANCIAL RATIOS

No testing on Ratios)

Auditors' analytical procedures often include the use of general financial ratios during planning and final review of the audited financial statements. These are useful for understanding the most recent events and financial status of the business and for viewing the statements from the perspective of a user. The general financial analysis may be effective for identifying possible problem areas for additional analysis and audit testing, as well as business problem areas for which the auditor can provide other assistance. This appendix presents a number of widely used general financial ratios.

SHORT-TERM DEBT-PAYING ABILITY

$$\text{Current ratio} = \frac{\text{current assets}}{\text{current liabilities}}$$

$$\text{Quick ratio} = \frac{\text{cash} + \text{marketable securities} + \text{net accounts receivable}}{\text{current liabilities}}$$

$$\text{Cash ratio} = \frac{\text{cash} + \text{marketable securities}}{\text{current liabilities}}$$

Many companies follow an operating cycle whereby production inputs are obtained and converted into finished goods, and then sold and converted into cash. This requires an investment in working capital; that is, funds are needed to finance inventories and accounts receivable. A majority of these funds come from trade creditors, and the balance will arise from initial capitalization, bank borrowings, and positive net cash flow from operations.

At any given time, the company will attain a net working capital position. This is the excess of current assets over current liabilities, and is also measured by the current ratio. Presumably, if net working capital is positive (that is, the current ratio is greater than 1.0), the company has sufficient available assets to pay its immediate debts; the greater the excess (the larger the ratio), the better able the company is in this regard. Thus, companies with a comfortable net working capital position are considered preferred customers by their bankers and trade creditors and are given favorable treatment. Companies with inadequate net working capital will be in danger of not being able to obtain credit.

However, this is a somewhat simplistic view. The current assets of companies will differ in terms of both valuation and liquidity, and these aspects will affect a company's ability to meet its current obligations. One way to examine this problem is to restrict the analysis to the most available and objective current assets. Thus, the quick ratio eliminates inventories from the computation and the cash ratio further eliminates accounts receivable. Usually, if the cash ratio is greater than 1.0, the company has excellent short-term debt-paying ability. In some cases, it is appropriate to state marketable securities at market value rather than cost in computing these ratios.

SHORT-TERM LIQUIDITY

If a company does not have sufficient cash and cashlike items to meet its obligations, the key to its debt-paying ability will be the length of time it takes the company to convert less liquid current assets into cash. This is measured by the short-term liquidity ratios.

The two turnover ratios—accounts receivable and inventory—are especially useful to auditors. Trends in the accounts receivable turnover ratio are often used in assessing the reasonableness of the allowance for uncollectible accounts. Trends in the inventory turnover ratio are used in identifying a potential inventory obsolescence problem.

$$\text{Average accounts receivable turnover} = \frac{\text{net sales}}{\text{average gross receivables}}$$

$$\text{Average days to collect} = \frac{\text{average gross receivables} \times 360}{\text{net sales}}$$

$$\text{Average inventory turnover} = \frac{\text{cost of goods sold}}{\text{average inventory}}$$

$$\text{Average days to sell} = \frac{\text{average inventory} \times 360}{\text{cost of goods sold}}$$

$$\text{Average days to convert inventory to cash} = \text{average days to sell} + \text{average days to collect}$$

When the short-term liquidity ratios (and the current ratio) are used to examine a company's performance over time or to compare performance among companies, differences in inventory accounting methods, fiscal year-ends, and cash–credit sales mix can have a significant effect. With regard to inventories, many companies have adopted the LIFO method. This can cause inventory values to differ significantly from FIFO values. When companies with different valuation methods are being compared, the company's LIFO value inventory can be adjusted to FIFO to obtain a better comparison.

When companies have different fiscal year-ends, such that one is on a natural business year and the other is not, the simple average gross receivables and inventory figures for the former will be lower. This will tend to cause the natural business year company to appear more liquid than it really is. If this is a problem, an averaging computation with quarterly data can be used.

Finally, the use of net sales per the financial statements in the receivables liquidity ratios can be a problem when a significant portion of sales is for cash. This will be somewhat mitigated when the proportions are fairly constant among periods or companies for which comparisons are being made.

ABILITY TO MEET LONG-TERM DEBT OBLIGATIONS AND PREFERRED DIVIDENDS

$$\text{Debt to equity ratio} = \frac{\text{total liabilities}}{\text{total equity}}$$

$$\text{Tangible net assets to equity ratio} = \frac{\text{total equity} - \text{intangible assets}}{\text{total equity}}$$

$$\text{Times interest earned} = \frac{\text{operating income}}{\text{interest expense}}$$

$$\text{Times interest and preferred dividends earned} = \frac{\text{operating income}}{\text{interest expense} + [\text{preferred dividends}/(1 - \text{tax rate})]}$$

A company's long-run solvency depends on the success of its operations and on its ability to raise capital for expansion or even survival over periods of temporary difficulty. From another point of view, common shareholders will benefit from the leverage obtained from borrowed capital that earns a positive net return.

A key measure in evaluating this long-term structure and capacity is the debt-to-equity ratio. If this ratio is too high, it may indicate that the company has used up its borrowing capacity and has no cushion for future events. If it is too low, it may mean that available leverage is not being used to the owners' benefit. If the ratio is trending up, it may mean that earnings are too low to support the needs of the enterprise. And if it is trending down, it may mean that the company is doing well and setting the stage for future expansion.

The tangible net assets-to-equity ratio indicates the current quality of the company's equity by removing assets such as goodwill whose realization is wholly dependent on future operations. This ratio can be used to interpret better the debt-to-equity ratio.

Lenders are generally concerned about a company's ability to meet interest payments as well as its ability to repay principal amounts. The latter will be appraised by evaluating the company's long-term prospects as well as its net asset position. The realizable value of assets will be important in this regard and may involve specific assets that collateralize the debt.

The ability to make interest payments is more a function of the company's ability to generate positive cash flows from operations in the short run, as well as over time. Thus, times interest earned shows how comfortably the company should be able to make interest (and preferred dividend) payments, assuming that earnings trends are stable.

OPERATING AND PERFORMANCE RATIOS

The key to remedying many financial ills is to improve operations. Therefore, all creditors and investors are interested in the results of operations of a business enterprise, and it is not surprising that a number of operating and performance ratios are in use. The most widely used operating and performance ratio is earnings per share, which is an integral part of the basic financial statements for most companies. Several additional ratios can be calculated and will give further insights into operations.

The first of these is the efficiency ratio. This shows the relative volume of business generated from the company's operating asset base. In other words, it shows whether sufficient revenues are being generated to justify the assets employed. When the efficiency ratio is low, there is an indication that additional volume should be sought before more assets are obtained. When the ratio is high, it may be an indication that assets are reaching the end of their useful lives and an investment in additional assets will soon be necessary.

The second ratio is the gross margin percentage. This ratio represents the percentage of sales revenue that exceeds variable costs. When this ratio is low, it is a sign that product costs are too high in comparison with selling prices.

The third ratio is the profit margin ratio. This shows the portion of sales that exceeds cost (both variable and fixed). When there is a weakness in this ratio, it is generally an indication that either (1) gross margins (revenues in excess of variable costs) are too low or (2) volume is too low with respect to fixed costs.

$$\text{Efficiency ratio} = \frac{\text{net sales}}{\text{tangible operating assets}}$$

$$\text{Gross margin percentage} = \frac{\text{net sales} - \text{cost of goods sold}}{\text{net sales}}$$

$$\text{Profit margin ratio} = \frac{\text{operating income}}{\text{net sales}}$$

$$\text{Profitability ratio} = \frac{\text{operating income}}{\text{tangible operating assets}}$$

$$\text{Return on total assets ratio} = \frac{\text{income before interest} + \text{taxes}}{\text{total assets}}$$

$$\text{Return on common equity ratio} = \frac{\text{income before taxes} - [\text{preferred dividends}/(1 - \text{tax rate})]}{\text{common equity}}$$

Leverage ratios (computed separately for each source of capital other than common equity, for example, short-term debt, long-term debt, deferred taxes) =

$$\frac{(\text{RTA} \times \text{amount of source}) - \text{cost attributable to source}}{\text{common equity}}$$

$$\text{Book value per common share} = \frac{\text{common equity}}{\text{common shares}}$$

Two ratios that indicate the adequacy of earnings relative to the asset base are the profitability ratio and the return on total assets ratio. In effect, these ratios show the efficiency and profit margin ratios combined.

An important perspective on the earnings of the company is what kind of return is provided to the owners. This is reflected in the return (before taxes) on common equity. If this ratio is below prevailing long-term interest rates or returns on alternative investments, owners will perceive that they should convert the company's assets to some other use, or perhaps liquidate, unless return can be improved.

An interesting supplemental analysis is provided through leverage analysis. Here, the proportionate share of assets for each source of capital is multiplied times the company's return on total assets. This determines the return on each source of capital. The result is compared with the cost of each source of capital (for example, interest expense), and a net contribution by capital source is derived. If this amount is positive for a capital source, it may be an indication that additional capital should be sought. If the leverage is negative from a capital source, recapitalization alternatives and/or earnings improvements should be investigated. It is also helpful to use this leverage analysis when considering the debt-to-equity ratio.

The final operating and performance ratio is book value per common share. This shows the combined effect of equity transactions over time.

The use of operating and performance ratios is subject to the same accounting inconsistencies mentioned for the liquidity ratios previously identified. The usefulness of these ratios in making comparisons over time or among companies may be affected by the classification of operating versus nonoperating items, inventory methods, depreciation methods, amortization of goodwill, research and development costs, and off-balance-sheet financing.

Observe that earning per share (EPS) is not included in the ratios discussed. Although EPS is extremely relevant for comparing the success of a given company over time, it is one of the few ratios that is irrelevant for comparison between companies. The cause of the irrelevancy is the ability of a company to arbitrarily change the number of shares outstanding through stock dividends and splits.

ILLUSTRATION

Computation of the various ratios is illustrated using the 1999 financial statements of Hillsburg Hardware Co. The financial statements appear in Figure 7-4 and were prepared from the trial balance in Figure 6-4 on page 152. The ratio computations for Hillsburg are

---

FIGURE 7-4   Hillsburg Hardware Co. Financial Statements

HILLSBURG HARDWARE CO.
BALANCE SHEET
December 31, 1999
(in thousands)

Assets
Current assets

Cash	$ 41		
Trade accounts receivable (net)	948		
Other accounts receivable	47		
Inventories	1,493		
Prepaid expenses	21		
Total current assets		2,550	
Property, plant, and equipment			
Land	173		
Buildings	1,625		
Delivery equipment	188		
Furniture and fixtures	127		
Less: Accumulated depreciation	(1,596)		
Total property, plant, and equipment		517	
Total assets			$3,067

Liabilities and Stockholders' Equity
Current liabilities

Trade accounts payable	$ 236		
Notes payable	209		
Accrued payroll	67		
Accrued payroll tax	6		
Accrued interest and dividends payable	102		
Estimated income tax	39		
Total current liabilities		659	
Long-term liabilities			
Notes payable	1,206		
Deferred tax	37		
Other accrued payables	41		
Total long-term liabilities		1,284	
Stockholders' equity			
Capital stock	250		
Capital in excess of par value	175		
Retained earnings	699		
Total stockholders' equity		1,124	
Total liabilities and stockholders' equity			$3,067

FIGURE 7-4   Hillsburg Hardware Co. Financial Statements [cont'd]

HILLSBURG HARDWARE CO.
COMBINED STATEMENT OF
INCOME AND RETAINED EARNINGS
for Year Ending December 31, 1999
(in thousands)

Sales		$7,216	
Less: Returns and allowances		62	
Net sales			7,154
Cost of goods sold			5,162
Gross profit			1,992
Selling expense			
Salaries and commissions	387		
Sales payroll taxes	71		
Travel and entertainment	56		
Advertising	131		
Sales and promotional literature	16		
Sales meetings and training	46		
Miscellaneous sales expense	34		
Total selling expense		741	
Administrative expense			
Executive and office salaries	276		
Administrative payroll taxes	34		
Travel and entertainment	28		
Stationery and supplies	38		
Postage	12		
Telephone and telegraph	36		
Dues and memberships	3		
Rent	16		
Legal fees and retainers	14		
Auditing	20		
Depreciation—office building and equipment	73		
Bad debt expense	166		
Insurance	36		
Office repairs and maintenance	57		
Miscellaneous office expense	47		
Miscellaneous general expense	26		
Total administrative expense		882	
Total selling and administrative expense			1,623
Earnings from operations			369
Other income and expense			
Interest expense		120	
Gain on sale of assets		(36)	84
Earnings before income taxes			285
Income taxes			87
Net income			198
Retained earnings at January 1, 1999			596
			794
Dividends			(95)
Retained earnings at December 31, 1999			$ 699

shown in Figure 7-5. The following simplifying assumptions were made for the ratio computations:

- Assumes that average receivables and inventories for the year are not significantly different from the year-end balances.
- Assumes that there is no preferred stock and the tax rate is 34 percent.
- Assumes that there are 250,000 common shares with a market value of $12 per share.

FIGURE 7-5   Hillsburg Hardware Co. Ratio Computations

$$\text{Current ratio} = \frac{2,550}{659} = 3.9$$

$$\text{Quick ratio} = \frac{41 + 948 + 47}{659} = 1.6$$

$$\text{Cash ratio} = \frac{41}{659} = .06$$

$$\text{Accounts receivable turnover} = \frac{7,154}{948 + 62} = 7.1$$

$$\text{Days to collect} = \frac{(948 + 62) \times 360}{7,154} = 50.8 \text{ days}$$

$$\text{Inventory turnover} = \frac{5,162}{1,493} = 3.5$$

$$\text{Days to sell} = \frac{1,493 \times 360}{5,162} = 104.1 \text{ days}$$

$$\text{Days to convert to cash} = 50.8 + 104.1 = 154.9 \text{ days}$$

$$\text{Debt to equity} = \frac{1,284 + 659}{1,124} = 1.7$$

$$\text{Tangible net assets to equity} = \frac{1,124}{1,124} = 1.0$$

$$\text{Times interest earned} = \frac{369}{120} = 3.1$$

$$\text{Times interest and preferred dividends earned} = \frac{369}{120 + [0/(1 - .34)]} = 3.1$$

$$\text{Efficiency ratio} = \frac{7,154}{3,067} = 2.3$$

$$\text{Gross margin percentage} = \frac{7,154 - 5,162}{7,154} = 27.8\%$$

$$\text{Profit margin ratio} = \frac{369}{7,154} = .05$$

$$\text{Profitability ratio} = \frac{369}{3,067} = .12$$

$$\text{Return on total assets} = \frac{369 + 36}{3,067} = .13$$

$$\text{Return on common equity} = \frac{285 - [0/(1 - .34)]}{1,124} = .25$$

FIGURE 7-5   Hillsburg Hardware Co. Ratio Computations [cont'd]

Leverage ratios:

$$\text{Current liabilities} = \frac{(.13 \times 659) - 0}{1,124} = .08$$

$$\text{Notes payable} = \frac{(.13 \times 1,206) - 120}{} = .03$$

$$\text{Book value per common share} = \frac{1,124}{250} = 4.50$$

ESSENTIAL TERMS

Analytical procedures—use of comparisons and relationships to assess whether account balances or other data appear reasonable

Audit procedure—detailed instruction for the collection of a type of audit evidence

Audit program—list of audit procedures for an audit area or an entire audit; the audit program always includes audit procedures and may also include sample sizes, items to select, and timing of the tests

Budgets—written records of the client's expectations for the period; a comparison of budgets with actual results may indicate whether or not misstatements are likely

Competence of evidence—the degree to which evidence can be considered believable or worthy of trust; evidence is competent when it is obtained (1) from a relevant source, (2) from an independent provider, (3) from a client with effective internal controls, (4) from the auditor's direct knowledge, (5) from qualified providers such as law firms and banks, (6) from objective sources, and (7) in a timely manner

Confirmation—the auditor's receipt of a written or oral response from an independent third party verifying the accuracy of information requested

Documentation—the auditor's examination of the client's documents and records to substantiate the information that is or should be included in the financial statements

External document—a document, such as a vendor's invoice, that has been used by an outside party to the transaction being documented, and that the client now has or can easily obtain

Inquiry—the obtaining of written or oral information from the client in response to specific questions during the audit

Internal document—a document, such as an employee time report, that is prepared and used within the client's organization

Observation—the use of the senses to assess certain activities

Persuasiveness of evidence—the degree to which the auditor is convinced that the evidence supports the audit opinion; the two determinants of persuasiveness are the competence and sufficiency of the evidence

Physical examination—the auditor's inspection or count of a tangible asset

Reliability of evidence— see *competence of evidence*

Reperformance—the rechecking of a sample of the computations and transfers of information made by the client during the period under audit

Sufficiency of evidence—the quantity of evidence; appropriate sample size

Unusual fluctuations—significant unexpected differences indicated by analytical procedures between the current year's unaudited financial data and other data used in comparisons

Vouching—the use of documentation to support recorded transactions or amounts

7-1 (Objective 7-1)   Discuss the similarities and differences between evidence in a legal case and evidence in an audit of financial statements.

7-2 (Objective 7-2)   List the four major evidence decisions that must be made on every audit.

7-3 (Objective 7-2)   Describe what is meant by an audit procedure. Why is it important for audit procedures to be carefully worded?

7-4 (Objective 7-2)   Describe what is meant by an audit program for accounts receivable. What four things should be included in an audit program?

7-5 (Objective 7-3)   State the third standard of field work. Explain the meaning of each of the major phrases of the standard.

7-6 (Objective 7-3)   Explain why the auditor can be persuaded only with a reasonable level of assurance, rather than convinced, that the financial statements are correct.

7-7 (Objective 7-3)   Identify the two factors that determine the persuasiveness of evidence. How are these two factors related to audit procedures, sample size, items to select, and timing?

7-8 (Objective 7-3)   Identify the seven characteristics that determine the competence of evidence. For each characteristic, provide one example of a type of evidence that is likely to be competent.

7-9 (Objective 7-4)   List the seven types of audit evidence included in this chapter and give two examples of each.

7-10 (Objective 7-4)   What are the four characteristics of the definition of a confirmation? Distinguish between a confirmation and external documentation.

7-11 (Objective 7-4)   Distinguish between internal documentation and external documentation as audit evidence and give three examples of each.

7-12 (Objectives 7-4, 7-5)   Explain the importance of analytical procedures as evidence in determining the fair presentation of the financial statements.

7-13 (Objectives 7-4, 7-5)   Identify the most important reasons for performing analytical procedures.

7-14 (Objectives 7-5, 7-6)   Your client, Harper Company, has a contractual commitment as a part of a bond indenture to maintain a current ratio of 2.0. If the ratio falls below that level on the balance sheet date, the entire bond becomes payable immediately. In the current year, the client's financial statements show that the ratio has dropped from 2.6 to 2.05 over the past year. How should this situation affect your audit plan?

7-15 (Objective 7-5)   Distinguish between attention-directing analytical procedures and those intended to eliminate or reduce detailed substantive procedures.

7-16 (Objective 7-5)   Explain why the statement "Analytical procedures are essential in every part of an audit, but these tests are rarely sufficient by themselves for any audit area" is correct or incorrect.

7-17 (Objective 7-6)   Gale Gordon, CPA, has found ratio and trend analysis relatively useless as a tool in conducting audits. For several engagements, he computed the industry ratios included in publications by Robert Morris Associates and compared them with industry standards. For most engagements, the client's business was significantly different from the industry data in the publication and the client would automatically explain away any discrepancies by attributing them to the unique nature of its operations. In cases in which the client had more than one branch in different industries, Gordon found the ratio analysis no help at all. How could Gordon improve the quality of his analytical procedures?

7-18 (Objective 7-6)   At the completion of every audit, Roger Morris, CPA, calculates a large number of ratios and trends for comparison with industry averages and prior-year calculations. He believes the calculations are worth the relatively small cost of doing them because they provide him with an excellent overview of the client's operations. If the ratios are out of line, Morris discusses the reasons with the client and often makes suggestions on how to bring the ratio back in line in the future. In some cases, these discussions with management have been the basis for management consulting engagements. Discuss the major strengths and shortcomings in Morris's use of ratio and trend analysis.

7-19 (Objective 7-6)   It is imperative that the auditor follow up on all material differences discovered through analytical procedures. What factors will affect such investigations?

MULTIPLE CHOICE QUESTIONS FROM CPA EXAMINATIONS

7-20 (Objectives 7-3, 7-4)   The following questions concern persuasiveness of evidence. Choose the best response.

a. Which of the following types of documentary evidence should the auditor consider to be the most reliable?
   (1) A sales invoice issued by the client and supported by a delivery receipt from an outside trucker.
   (2) Confirmation of an account payable balance mailed by and returned directly to the auditor.
   (3) A check, issued by the company and bearing the payee's endorsement, that is included with the bank statements mailed directly to the auditor.
   (4) A working paper prepared by the client's controller and reviewed by the client's treasurer.

b. The most reliable type of audit evidence that an auditor can obtain is
   (1) physical examination by the auditor.
   (2) calculations by the auditor from company records.
   (3) confirmations received directly from third parties.
   (4) external documents.

c. Audit evidence can come in different forms with different degrees of persuasiveness. Which of the following is the *least* persuasive type of evidence?
   (1) Vendor's invoice.
   (2) Bank statement obtained from the client.
   (3) Computations made by the auditor.
   (4) Prenumbered sales invoices.

d. Which of the following is the *least* persuasive documentation in support of an auditor's opinion?
   (1) Schedules of details of physical inventory counts conducted by the client.
   (2) Notation of inferences drawn from ratios and trends.
   (3) Notation of appraisers' conclusions documented in the auditor's working papers.
   (4) Lists of negative confirmation requests for which *no* response was received by the auditor.

7-21 (Objectives 7-4, 7-5, 7-6)   The following questions deal with analytical procedures. Choose the best response.

a. Analytical procedures are
   (1) statistical tests of financial information designed to identify areas requiring intensive investigation.
   (2) calculations of financial information made by a computer.
   (3) substantive tests of financial information made by a study and comparison of relationships among data.
   (4) diagnostic tests of financial information that may *not* be classified as evidential matter.

b. Significant unexpected fluctuations identified by analytical procedures will usually necessitate a(n)
   (1) consistency qualification.
   (2) understanding of the client's internal control.
   (3) explanation in the representation letter.
   (4) auditor investigation.

c. Which of the following situations has the best chance of being detected when a CPA compares 1999 revenues and expenses with the prior year and investigates all changes exceeding a fixed percentage?
   (1) An increase in property tax rates has not been recognized in the company's 1999 accrual.
   (2) The cashier began lapping accounts receivable in 1999.
   (3) Because of worsening economic conditions, the 1999 provision for uncollectible accounts was inadequate.
   (4) The company changed its capitalization policy for small tools in 1999.

d. Your analytical procedures and other tests of the Dey Company reveal that the firm's poor financial condition makes it unlikely that it will survive as a going concern. Assuming that the financial statements have otherwise been prepared in accordance with generally accepted accounting principles, what disclosure should you make of the company's precarious financial position?
   (1) You should issue a qualified opinion and, in a paragraph between the scope and opinion paragraphs of your report, direct the reader's attention to the poor financial condition of the company.
   (2) You should insist that a note to the financial statements clearly indicates that the company appears to be on the verge of bankruptcy.
   (3) You need not insist on any specific disclosure because the company's poor financial condition is clearly indicated by the financial statements themselves.
   (4) You should make sure there is adequate disclosure and appropriately modify your report because the company does not appear to have the ability to continue as a going concern.

DISCUSSION QUESTIONS AND PROBLEMS

7-22 (Objective 7-4) The following are examples of documentation typically obtained by auditors:

1. Vendors' invoices
2. General ledgers
3. Bank statements
4. Cancelled payroll checks
5. Payroll time cards
6. Purchase requisitions
7. Receiving reports (documents prepared when merchandise is received)
8. Minutes of the board of directors
9. Remittance advices
10. Signed W-4s (Employees' Withholding Exemption Certificates)
11. Signed lease agreements
12. Duplicate copies of bills of lading
13. Subsidiary accounts receivable records
14. Cancelled notes payable
15. Duplicate sales invoices
16. Articles of incorporation
17. Title insurance policies for real estate
18. Notes receivable

Required

    a. Classify each of the preceding items according to type of documentation: (1) internal or (2) external.

    b. Explain why external evidence is more reliable than internal evidence.

7-23 (Objective 7-4) The following are examples of audit procedures:

1. Review the accounts receivable with the credit manager to evaluate their collectibility. 5
2. Stand by the payroll time clock to determine whether any employee "punches in" more than one time. 4
3. Count inventory items and record the amount in the audit working papers. 1
4. Obtain a letter from the client's attorney addressed to the CPA firm stating that the attorney is not aware of any existing lawsuits. 2
5. Extend the cost of inventory times the quantity on an inventory listing to test whether it is accurate. 6
6. Obtain a letter from an insurance company to the CPA firm stating the amount of the fire insurance coverage on buildings and equipment. 2
7. Examine an insurance policy stating the amount of the fire insurance coverage on buildings and equipment. 3
8. Calculate the ratio of cost of goods sold to sales as a test of overall reasonableness of gross margin relative to the preceding year. 7
9. Obtain information about internal control by requesting the client to fill out a questionnaire. 5
10. Trace the total on the cash disbursements journal to the general ledger. 6
11. Watch employees count inventory to determine whether company procedures are being followed. 4
12. Examine a piece of equipment to make sure that a major acquisition was actually received and is in operation. 1
13. Calculate the ratio of sales commissions expense to sales as a test of sales commissions. 7
14. Examine corporate minutes to determine the authorization of the issue of bonds. 3
15. Obtain a letter from management stating that there are no unrecorded liabilities. 5
16. Review the total of repairs and maintenance for each month to determine whether any month's total was unusually large. 7
17. Compare a duplicate sales invoice with the sales journal for customer name and amount. 3
18. Add the sales journal entries to determine whether they were correctly totaled. 6
19. Make a petty cash count to make sure that the amount of the petty cash fund is intact. 1
20. Obtain a written statement from a bank stating that the client has $15,671 on deposit and liabilities of $50,000 on a demand note. 2

Required

Classify each of the preceding items according to the seven types of audit evidence: (1) physical examination, (2) confirmation, (3) documentation, (4) observation, (5) inquiries of the client, (6) reperformance, and (7) analytical procedures.

7-24 (Objective 7-4) List two examples of audit evidence the auditor can use in support of each of the following:

    a. Recorded amount of entries in the acquisitions journal
    b. Physical existence of inventory
    c. Accuracy of accounts receivable
    d. Ownership of fixed assets
    e. Liability for accounts payable
    f. Obsolescence of inventory
    g. Existence of petty cash

7-25 (Objectives 7-4, 7-5)   Seven different types of evidence were discussed. The following questions concern the reliability (competence) of that evidence:

    a. Explain why confirmations are normally more reliable evidence than inquiries of the client.

    b. Describe a situation in which confirmation would be considered highly reliable and another in which it would not be reliable.

    c. Under what circumstances is the physical observation of inventory considered relatively unreliable evidence?

    d. Explain why reperformance tests are highly reliable but of relatively limited use.

    e. Give three examples of relatively reliable documentation and three examples of less reliable documentation. What characteristics distinguish the two?

    f. Give several examples in which the qualifications of the respondent or the qualifications of the auditor affect the reliability of the evidence.

    g. Explain why analytical procedures are important evidence even though they are relatively unreliable by themselves.

7-26 (Objectives 7-3, 7-4, 7-6)   In an audit of financial statements, an auditor must judge the competence of the audit evidence obtained.

Required

    a. In the course of his or her audit, the auditor asks many questions of client officers and employees.

      (1) Describe the factors the auditor should consider in evaluating oral evidence provided by client officers and employees.

      (2) Discuss the competence and limitations of oral evidence.

    b. An audit may include computation of various balance sheet and operating ratios for comparison with previous years and industry averages. Discuss the competence and limitations of ratio analysis.*

7-27 (Objective 7-4)   As auditor of the Star Manufacturing Company, you have obtained

    a. A trial balance taken from the books of Star one month before year-end:

	Dr. (Cr.)
Cash in bank	$ 87,000
Trade accounts receivable	345,000
Notes receivable	125,000
Inventories	317,000
Land	66,000
Buildings, net	350,000
Furniture, fixtures, and equipment, net	325,000
Trade accounts payable	(235,000)
Mortgages payable	(400,000)
Capital stock	(300,000)
Retained earnings	(510,000)
Sales	(3,130,000)
Cost of sales	2,300,000
General and administrative expenses	622,000
Legal and professional fees	3,000
Interest expense	35,000

    b. There are no inventories consigned either in or out.

    c. All notes receivable are due from outsiders and held by Star.

*AICPA adapted.

Required

Which accounts should be confirmed with outside sources? Briefly describe from whom they should be confirmed and the information that should be confirmed. Organize your answer in the following format:*

Account Name	From Whom Confirmed	Information to Be Confirmed

7-28 (Objective 7-4) The following audit procedures were performed in the audit of inventory to satisfy specific balance-related audit objectives as discussed in Chapter 6. The audit procedures assume that the auditor has obtained the inventory count sheets that list the client's inventory. The general balance-related audit objectives from Chapter 6 are also included.

Audit Procedures

1. Test extend unit prices times quantity on the inventory list, test foot the list, and compare the total to the general ledger.
2. Trace selected quantities from the inventory list to the physical inventory to make sure that it exists and the quantities are the same.
3. Question operating personnel about the possibility of obsolete or slow-moving inventory.
4. Select a sample of quantities of inventory in the factory warehouse and trace each item to the inventory count sheets to determine if it has been included and if the quantity and description are correct.
5. Compare the quantities on hand and unit prices on this year's inventory count sheets with those in the preceding year as a test for large differences.
6. Examine sales invoices and contracts with customers to determine whether any goods are out on consignment with customers. Similarly, examine vendors' invoices and contracts with vendors to determine whether any goods on the inventory listing are owned by vendors.
7. Send letters directly to third parties who hold the client's inventory and request that they respond directly to the auditors.

General Balance-Related Audit Objectives

Existence
Completeness
Accuracy
Classification
Cutoff
Detail tie-in
Realizable value
Rights and obligations
Presentation and disclosure

Required

a. Identify the type of audit evidence used for each audit procedure.
b. Identify the general balance-related audit objective or objectives satisfied by each audit procedure.

7-29 (Objective 7-4) Audit procedures differ from, but are related to, types of evidence. The following questions relate to types of evidence and audit procedures.

*AICPA adapted.

Required

    a. What is an audit procedure?

    b. Why should audit procedures be specific and carefully written?

    c. For each of the following types of evidence, carefully write one audit procedure for the audit of accounts receivable.

Type of Evidence	Audit Procedure
(1) Confirmation	
(2) Documentation	
(3) Inquiries of the client	
(4) Reperformance	
(5) Analytical procedures	

7-30 (Objectives 7-3, 7-4) The following are nine situations, each containing two means of accumulating evidence.

1. Confirm receivables with consumers versus confirming accounts receivable with business organizations.
2. Physically examine 3-inch steel plates versus examining electronic parts.
3. Examine duplicate sales invoices when several competent people are checking each other's work versus examining documents prepared by a competent person in a one-person staff.
4. Physically examine inventory of parts for the number of units on hand versus examining them for the likelihood of inventory being obsolete.
5. Discuss the likelihood and amount of loss in a lawsuit against the client with client's in-house legal counsel versus discussion with the CPA firm's own legal counsel.
6. Confirm the oil and gas reserves with a geologist specializing in oil and gas versus confirming a bank balance.
7. Confirm a bank balance versus examining the client's bank statements.
8. Physically count the client's inventory held by an independent party versus confirming the count with an independent party.
9. Obtain a physical inventory count from the company president versus physically counting the client's inventory.

Required

    a. Identify the seven factors that determine the competence of evidence.

    b. For each of the nine situations, state whether the first or second type of evidence is more reliable.

    c. For each situation, state which of the seven factors affected the competence of the evidence.

7-31 (Objective 7-4) Following are 10 audit procedures with words missing and a list of several terms commonly used in audit procedures.

Audit Procedures

obsev. 1. ____J____ whether the accounts receivable bookkeeper is prohibited from handling cash.

anal, proc 2. ____D____ the ratio of cost of goods sold to sales and compare the ratio to previous years.

Re perf. 3. ____F____ the sales journal and ____G____ the total to the general ledger.

anal. proc 4. ____B____ the sales journal, looking for large and unusual transactions requiring investigation.

5. _____k_____ of management whether all accounting employees are required to take annual vacations.

6. _____L_____ the balance in the bank account directly with the East State Bank.

7. _____I_____ all marketable securities as of the balance sheet date to determine whether they equal the total on the client's list.

8. _____A_____ a sample of duplicate sales invoices to determine if the controller's approval is included and _____H_____ each duplicate sales invoice to the sales journal for agreement of name and amount.

9. _____e_____ the unit selling price times quantity on the duplicate sales invoice and compare the total to the amount on the duplicate sales invoice.

10. _____G_____ the agreement between Johnson Wholesale Company and the client to determine whether the shipment is a sale or a consignment.

Terms

a. Examine	g. Trace
b. Scan	h. Compare
c. Read	i. Count
d. Compute	j. Observe
e. Recompute	k. Inquire
f. Foot	l. Confirm

Required

a. For each of the 12 blanks in procedures 1 through 10, identify the most appropriate term. No term can be used more than once.

b. For each of the procedures 1 through 10, identify the type of evidence that is being used.

7-32 (Objectives 7-4, 7-5) In auditing the financial statements of a manufacturing company that were prepared using information technology, the CPA has found that the traditional audit trail has been obscured. As a result, the CPA may place increased emphasis on analytical procedures of the data under audit. These tests, which are also applied in auditing visibly posted accounting records, include the computation of ratios that are compared with prior year ratios or with industrywide norms. Examples of analytical procedures are the computation of the rate of inventory turnover and the computation of the number of days in receivables.

Required

a. Discuss the advantages to the CPA of the use of analytical procedures in an audit.

b. In addition to the computations given above, list ratios that an auditor may compute during an audit on balance sheet accounts and related income accounts. For each ratio listed, name the two (or more) accounts used in its computation.

c. When an auditor discovers that there has been a significant change in a ratio when compared with the preceding year's, he or she considers the possible reasons for the change. Give the possible reasons for the following significant changes in ratios:

(1) The rate of inventory turnover (ratio of cost of sales and average inventory) has decreased from the preceding year's rate.

(2) The number of days' sales in receivables (ratio of average daily accounts receivable and sales) has increased over the prior year.*

*AICPA adapted.

7-33 (Objective 7-6)   Your comparison of the gross margin percentage for Jones Drugs for the years 1996 through 1999 indicates a significant decline. This is shown by the following information:

	1999	1998	1997	1996
Sales (thousands)	$14,211	$12,916	$11,462	$10,351
CGS (thousands)	9,223	8,266	7,313	6,573
Gross margin	$4,988	$4,650	$4,149	$3,778
Percentage	35.1	36.0	36.2	36.5

A discussion with Marilyn Adams, the controller, brings to light two possible explanations. She informs you that the industry gross profit percentage in the retail drug industry declined fairly steadily for 3 years, which accounts for part of the decline. A second factor was the declining percentage of the total volume resulting from the pharmacy part of the business. The pharmacy sales represent the most profitable portion of the business, yet the competition from discount drugstores prevents it from expanding as fast as the nondrug items such as magazines, candy, and many other items sold. Adams feels strongly that these two factors are the cause of the decline.

The following additional information is obtained from independent sources and the client's records as a means of investigating the controller's explanations:

	Jones Drugs ($ in thousands)				Industry Gross Profit Percentage for Retailers of Drugs and Related Products
	Drug Sales	Nondrug Sales	Drug Cost of Goods Sold	Nondrug Cost of Goods Sold	
1999	$5,126	$9,085	$3,045	$6,178	32.7
1998	5,051	7,865	2,919	5,347	32.9
1997	4,821	6,641	2,791	4,522	33.0
1996	4,619	5,732	2,665	3,908	33.2

Required
   a. Evaluate the explanation provided by Adams. Show calculations to support your conclusions.
   b. Which specific aspects of the client's financial statements require intensive investigation in this audit?

7-34 (Objective 7-6)   In the audit of the Worldwide Wholesale Company, you performed extensive ratio and trend analysis. No material exceptions were discovered except for the following:

1. Commission expense as a percentage of sales has stayed constant for several years but has increased significantly in the current year. Commission rates have not changed.
2. The rate of inventory turnover has steadily decreased for 4 years.
3. Inventory as a percentage of current assets has steadily increased for 4 years.
4. The number of days' sales in accounts receivable has steadily increased for 3 years.
5. Allowance for uncollectible accounts as a percentage of accounts receivable has steadily decreased for 3 years.
6. The absolute amounts of depreciation expense and depreciation expense as a percentage of gross fixed assets are significantly smaller than in the preceding year.

Required
   a. Evaluate the potential significance of each of the exceptions just listed for the fair presentation of financial statements.
   b. State the follow-up procedures you would use to determine the possibility of material misstatements.

7-35 (Objective 7-6)   As part of the analytical procedures of Mahogany Products, Inc., you perform calculations of the following ratios:

Ratio	Industry Averages		Mahogany Products	
	1999	**1998**	**1999**	**1998**
1. Current ratio	3.30	3.80	2.20	2.60
2. Days to collect receivables	87.00	93.00	67.00	60.00
3. Days to sell inventory	126.00	121.00	93.00	89.00
4. Purchases divided by accounts payable	11.70	11.60	8.50	8.60
5. Inventory divided by current assets	.56	.51	.49	.48
6. Operating income divided by tangible assets	.08	.06	.14	.12
7. Operating income divided by net sales	.06	.06	.04	.04
8. Gross margin percentage	.21	.27	.21	.19
9. Earnings per share	$14.27	$13.91	$2.09	$1.93

Required

For each of the preceding ratios:

    a. State whether there is a need to investigate the results further and, if so, the reason for further investigation.

    b. State the approach you would use in the investigation.

    c. Explain how the operations of Mahogany Products appear to differ from those of the industry.

7-36 (Objective 7-6)   Below are the auditor's calculations of several key ratios for Cragston Star Products. The primary purpose of this information is to assess the risk of financial failure, but any other relevant conclusions are also desirable.

Ratio	1999	1998	1997	1996	1995
Current ratio	2.08	2.26	2.51	2.43	2.50
Quick ratio	.97	1.34	1.82	1.76	1.64
Earnings before taxes divided by interest expense	3.50	3.20	4.10	5.30	7.10
Accounts receivable turnover	4.20	5.50	4.10	5.40	5.60
Days to collect receivables	108.20	83.10	105.20	80.60	71.60
Inventory turnover	2.03	1.84	2.68	3.34	3.36
Days to sell inventory	172.60	195.10	133.90	107.80	108.30
Net sales divided by tangible assets	.68	.64	.73	.69	.67
Operating income divided by net sales	.13	.14	:16	.15	.14
Operating income divided by tangible assets	.09	.09	.12	.10	.09
Net income divided by common equity	.05	.06	.10	.10	.11
Earnings per share	$4.30	$4.26	$4.49	$4.26	$4.14

Required

    a. What major conclusions can be drawn from this information about the company's future?

    b. What additional information would be helpful in your assessment of this company's financial condition?

    c. Based on the ratios above, which aspects of the company do you believe should receive special emphasis in the audit?

7-37 (Objectives 7-6, 7-7) Solomon is a highly successful, closely held Boston, Massachusetts, company that manufactures and assembles automobile specialty parts that are sold in auto parts stores in the East. Sales and profits have expanded rapidly in the past few years, and the prospects for future years are every bit as encouraging. In fact, the Solomon brothers are currently considering either selling out to a large company or going public to obtain additional capital.

The company originated in 1964 when Frank Solomon decided to manufacture tooled parts. In 1979 the company changed over to the auto parts business. Fortunately, it has never been necessary to expand the facilities, but space problems have recently become severe and expanded facilities will be necessary. Land and building costs in Boston are currently extremely inflated.

Management has always relied on you for help in its problems because the treasurer is sales-oriented and has little background in the controllership function. Salaries of all officers have been fairly modest in order to reinvest earnings in future growth. In fact, the company is oriented toward long-run wealth of the brothers more than toward short-run profit. The brothers have all of their personal wealth invested in the firm.

A major reason for the success of Solomon has been the small but excellent sales force. The sales policy is to sell to small auto shops at high prices. This policy is responsible for fairly high credit losses, but the profit margin is high and the results have been highly successful. The firm has every intention of continuing this policy in the future.

Your firm has been auditing Solomon since 1974, and you have been on the job for the past 3 years. The client has excellent internal controls and has always been cooperative. In recent years, the client has attempted to keep net income at a high level because of borrowing needs and future sellout possibilities. Overall, the client has always been pleasant to deal with and willing to help in any way possible. There have never been any major audit adjustments, and an unqualified opinion has always been issued.

In the current year, you have completed the tests of the sales and collection area. The tests of controls and substantive tests of transactions for sales and sales returns and allowances were excellent, and an extensive confirmation yielded no material misstatements. You have carefully reviewed the cutoff for sales and for sales returns and allowances and find these to be excellent. All recorded bad debts appear reasonable, and a review of the aged trial balance indicates that conditions seem about the same as in past years.

Required
  a. Evaluate the information in the case to provide assistance to management for improved operation of its business. Prepare the supporting analysis using an electronic spreadsheet program (instructor option).
  b. Do you agree that sales, accounts receivable, and allowance for doubtful accounts are probably correctly stated? Show calculations to support your conclusion.

	12-31-99 (Current Year)	12-31-98	12-31-97	12-31-96
Balance Sheet				
Cash	$ 49,615	$ 39,453	$ 51,811	$ 48,291
Accounts receivable	2,366,938	2,094,052	1,756,321	1,351,470
Allowance for doubtful accounts	(250,000)	(240,000)	(220,000)	(200,000)
Inventory	2,771,833	2,585,820	2,146,389	1,650,959
Current assets	4,938,386	4,479,325	3,734,521	2,850,720
Fixed assets	3,760,531	3,744,590	3,498,930	3,132,133
Total assets	$8,698,917	$8,223,915	$7,233,451	$5,982,853
Current liabilities	$2,253,422	$2,286,433	$1,951,830	$1,625,811
Long-term liabilities	4,711,073	4,525,310	4,191,699	3,550,481
Owners' equity	1,734,422	1,412,172	1,089,922	806,561
Total liabilities and owners' equity	$8,698,917	$8,223,915	$7,233,451	$5,982,853
Income Statement Information				
Sales	$6,740,652	$6,165,411	$5,313,752	$4,251,837
Sales returns and allowances	(207,831)	(186,354)	(158,367)	(121,821)
Sales discounts allowed	(74,147)	(63,655)	(52,183)	(42,451)
Bad debts	(248,839)	(245,625)	(216,151)	(196,521)
Net sales	$6,209,835	$5,669,777	$4,887,051	$3,891,044
Gross margin	$1,415,926	$1,360,911	$1,230,640	$1,062,543
Net income after taxes	$335,166	$322,250	$283,361	$257,829
Aged Accounts Receivable				
0–30 days	$ 942,086	$ 881,232	$ 808,569	$ 674,014
31–60 days	792,742	697,308	561,429	407,271
61–120 days	452,258	368,929	280,962	202,634
>120 days	179,852	146,583	105,361	67,551
Total	$2,366,938	$2,094,052	$1,756,321	$1,351,470

INTERNET PROBLEM 7-1: ANALYTICAL PROCEDURES—INDUSTRY COMPARISONS

Reference the CW site. This problem requires students to use the Internet to research and compare several key financial ratios and seasonal patterns between a hypothetical audit client, SmartClothes, and The Gap, Inc.

AUDIT PLANNING AND DOCUMENTATION

8

AN AUDITOR WHO DOES NOT UNDERSTAND A CLIENT'S BUSINESS TAKES A GREAT RISK

Art Myers, of Myers & Co., CPAs, got an opportunity to break into the health care market when his physician, Dr. Gary Nettles, approached him about auditing Brookside Health Associates, a new health maintenance organization (HMO) that Gary and his associates had started. Brookside's business was to provide medical services to companies for a monthly membership fee per employee.

When Brookside was formed, its owners hired Michael Sullivan to be the chief financial officer, even though he had no HMO experience. Just before the end of Brookside's first fiscal year, Art met with Michael to plan Brookside's initial audit. Neither Art nor Michael had any direct experience with an HMO (nor did anyone else in Myers & Co.), but they both read articles and other literature about the subject, including the *AICPA Healthcare Audit Guide* and the AICPA's *Audit Risk Alert* for the healthcare industry.

A specific area of focus at the planning meeting was how to estimate the liability for medical services rendered but not yet billed to the HMO. This liability is called incurred but not recorded (IBNR) and was new to both Art and Michael. Art agreed to investigate how to calculate this and get back to Michael.

Art's approach was to contact a friend of his who audited an HMO in another state. His friend, who had only one HMO client, sent Art information that included a formula for estimating the IBNR liability. The formula was based on historical data and made sense to Art. He gave the formula to Michael, who applied it using the 12 months of data available from the initial year of operations. During the audit, Myers & Co. determined the formula was applied accurately.

Shortly after the completion of Brookside's second year of operations, Michael Sullivan had some personal problems that required him to move to another city. Brookside replaced Michael with Bart Chemers, primarily because Bart had previously worked for an HMO.

When Bart saw how the IBNR liability was estimated, he questioned the formula used and made an in-depth investigation of the situation. He determined that the formula was significantly underestimating the IBNR liability, that the liability was materially understated in the previously audited financial statements, and that as a result, the rates negotiated in contracts with participants were much lower than they should have been. This finding led to a change in auditors and a sizable monetary settlement by Myers & Co.

LEARNING OBJECTIVES

After studying this chapter, you should be able to

8-1 Discuss why adequate audit planning is essential.

8-2 Preplan the audit.

8-3 Obtain appropriate background information about an audit client.

8-4 Obtain information about an audit client's legal obligations.

8-5 Discuss the nature and purposes of preliminary analytical procedures.

8-6 Understand the purposes of audit working papers.

8-7 Prepare organized audit working papers.

A rt Myers realized too late the importance of proper audit planning, given his experience in the audit of Brookside Health Associates. Good planning includes determining all of the background information necessary to design an effective audit approach. This chapter explains planning in detail, including documenting the auditor's planning, accumulating evidence, and writing conclusions in the auditor's working papers.

PLANNING

OBJECTIVE 8-1

Discuss why adequate audit planning is essential.

The first generally accepted auditing standard of field work requires adequate planning.

> The work is to be adequately planned, and assistants, if any, are to be properly supervised.

There are three main reasons why the auditor should properly plan engagements: to enable the auditor to obtain sufficient competent evidence for the circumstances, to help keep audit costs reasonable, and to avoid misunderstandings with the client. Obtaining sufficient competent evidence is essential if the CPA firm is to minimize legal liability and maintain a good reputation in the business community. Keeping costs reasonable helps the firm remain competitive and thereby retain or expand its client base, assuming the firm has a reputation for doing high-quality work. Avoiding misunderstandings with the client is important for good client relations and for facilitating high-quality work at reasonable cost. For example, suppose that the auditor informs the client that the audit will be completed before June 30 but is unable to finish it until August because of inadequate scheduling of staff. The client is likely to be upset with the CPA firm and may even sue for breach of contract.

Figure 8-1 presents the seven major parts of audit planning. Each of the first six parts is intended to help the auditor develop the last part, an effective and efficient overall audit plan and audit program. The first four parts of the planning phase of an audit are studied in this chapter. The last three are studied separately in later chapters.

Before beginning the discussion of the first four parts of the planning phase, it is useful to briefly introduce two risk terms: *acceptable audit risk* and *inherent risk*. These two risks have a significant effect on the conduct and cost of audits. Much of the early planning on audits deals with obtaining information to help auditors assess these risks.

Acceptable audit risk is a measure of how willing the auditor is to accept that the financial statements may be materially misstated after the audit is completed and an unqualified opinion has been issued. When the auditor decides on a lower acceptable audit risk, it means that the auditor wants to be more certain that the financial statements are *not* materially misstated. Zero risk would be certainty, and a 100 percent risk would be complete uncertainty.

When the auditor decides that a lower acceptable audit risk on an audit is appropriate, there are three potential actions, where all three, two, or just one can be done, depending on the auditor's judgment.

1. More evidence is required to increase audit assurance that there are no material misstatements. It is difficult to implement increased evidence accumulation because acceptable audit risk applies to the entire audit. It is expensive and often impractical to increase evidence in every part of an audit.
2. The engagement may require more experienced staff. CPA firms should staff all engagements with qualified staff, but for low acceptable audit risk clients, special care is appropriate in staffing.
3. The engagement will be reviewed more carefully than usual. CPA firms need to be sure that the working papers that document the auditor's planning, evidence accumulation and conclusions, and other matters in the audit are adequately reviewed. When acceptable audit risk is low, there is often more extensive review, including a review by personnel who were not assigned to the engagement.

FIGURE 8-1   **Planning an Audit and Designing an Audit Approach**

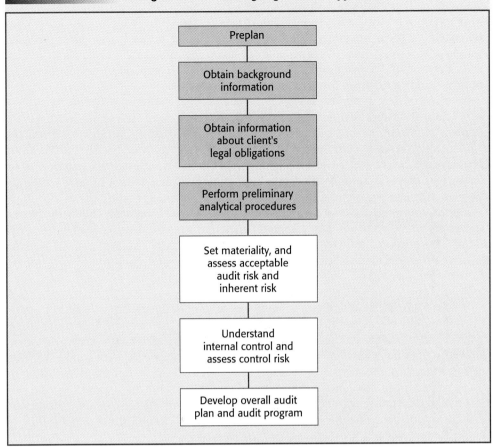

Inherent risk is a measure of the auditor's assessment of the likelihood that there are material misstatements in an account balance before considering the effectiveness of internal control. If, for example, the auditor concludes that there is a high likelihood of material misstatement in an account such as accounts receivable, the auditor would conclude that inherent risk for accounts receivable is high.

When the auditor concludes that there is a high inherent risk for an account or a class of transactions, the same three potential effects are appropriate as for the lower acceptable audit risk. However, it is easier and more common to implement increased evidence accumulation for inherent risk than it is for acceptable audit risk because inherent risk can usually be isolated to one or two accounts. For example, if inherent risk is high only for accounts receivable, the auditor can restrict the evidence expansion to the audit of accounts receivable.

Internal control is supposed to find the problem

cash is more tricky (no) frand Checks

PREPLAN THE AUDIT

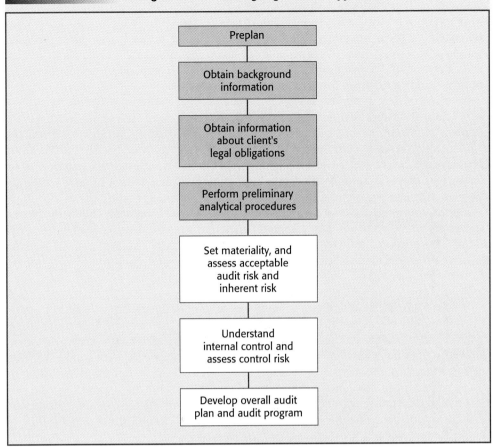

OBJECTIVE 8-2
Preplan the audit.

Preplanning the audit involves three things, all of which should be done early in the audit. First, the auditor decides whether to accept a new client or continue serving an existing one. This is typically done by an experienced auditor who is in a position to make important decisions. The auditor wants to make that decision early, before incurring any significant costs that cannot be recovered. Second, the auditor identifies why the client wants or needs an audit. This information is likely to affect the remaining parts of the planning process. Finally, the auditor obtains an understanding with the client about the terms of the engagement to avoid misunderstandings.

Client Acceptance and Continuance

Even though obtaining and retaining clients is not easy in a competitive profession such as public accounting, a CPA firm must use care in deciding which clients are acceptable. The firm's legal and professional responsibilities are such that clients who lack integrity or argue constantly about the proper conduct of the audit and fees can cause more problems than they are worth. Some CPA firms now refuse any clients in certain high-risk industries, such as savings and loans, health, and casualty insurance companies, and may even discontinue auditing existing clients in those industries.

Preplan
Obtain background information
Obtain information about client's legal obligations
Perform preliminary analytical procedures
Set materiality, and assess acceptable audit risk and inherent risk
Understand internal control and assess control risk
Develop overall audit plan and audit program

Private Investigator Directory

New Client Investigation Before accepting a new client, most CPA firms investigate the company to determine its acceptability. To the extent possible, the prospective client's standing in the business community, financial stability, and relations with its previous CPA firm should be evaluated. For example, many CPA firms use considerable caution in accepting new clients in newly formed, rapidly growing businesses. Many of these businesses fail financially and expose the CPA firm to significant potential liability.

For prospective clients that have previously been audited by another CPA firm, the new (successor) auditor is *required* by SAS 84 (AU 315) to communicate with the predecessor auditor. The purpose of the requirement is to help the successor auditor evaluate whether to accept the engagement. The communication may, for example, inform the successor auditor that the client lacks integrity or that there have been disputes over accounting principles, audit procedures, or fees.

The burden of initiating the communication rests with the successor auditor. The predecessor auditor is required to respond to the request for information. However, because of the confidentiality requirement in the *Code of Professional Conduct,* the predecessor auditor must obtain permission from the client before the communication can be made. In the event that legal problems or disputes arise between the client and the predecessor, the latter's response can be limited to stating that no information will be provided. The successor should seriously consider the desirability of accepting a prospective engagement, without considerable other investigation, if a client will not permit the communication or the predecessor will not provide a comprehensive response.

Even when a prospective client has been audited by another CPA firm, other investigations are often made. Sources of information include local attorneys, other CPAs, banks, and other businesses. In some cases, the auditor may hire a professional investigator to obtain information about the reputation and background of the key members of management. More extensive investigation is appropriate when there has been no previous auditor, when a predecessor auditor will not provide the desired information, or if any indication of problems arises from the communication.

Many practitioners take advantage of the Internet as a search tool to learn more about the potential new client and its key operations by studying available client web sites and by using search engines for other sites that discuss the potential client. In addition, they use database search tools, Lexis/Nexis, Dow Jones News Retrieval, Disclosure, and the SEC's EDGAR Database. This information is useful in the client acceptance decision and throughout the audit if the client is accepted.

Continuing Clients Many CPA firms evaluate existing clients annually to determine whether there are reasons for not continuing to do the audit. Previous conflicts over such things as the appropriate scope of the audit, the type of opinion to issue, or fees may cause the auditor to discontinue association. The auditor may also determine that the client lacks integrity and therefore should no longer be a client. If the client files a lawsuit against a CPA firm or vice versa, the firm cannot do the audit. Similarly, if there are unpaid fees for services performed more than 1 year previously, the CPA firm cannot do the current year audit. To do an audit in either of these circumstances violates the AICPA *Code of Professional Conduct* rules on independence.

Even if none of the previously discussed conditions exist, the CPA firm may decide not to continue doing audits for a client because of excessive risk. For example, a CPA firm might decide that there is considerable risk of a regulatory conflict between a governmental agency and a client, which could result in financial failure of the client and ultimately lawsuits against the CPA firm. Even if the engagement is profitable, the risk may exceed the short-term benefits of doing the audit.

Investigation of new clients and reevaluation of existing ones is an essential part of deciding acceptable audit risk. Assume a potential client in a reasonably risky industry, where management has a reputation of integrity, but is also known to take aggressive financial risks. If the CPA firm decides that acceptable audit risk is extremely low, it may choose not to accept the engagement. If the CPA firm concludes that acceptable audit risk is low but the client is still acceptable, it is likely to affect the fee proposed to the client. Audits with a low acceptable audit risk will normally result in higher audit costs, which should be reflected in higher audit fees.

Identify Client's Reasons for Audit

Two major factors affecting acceptable audit risk are the likely statement users and their intended uses of the statements. The auditor is likely to accumulate more evidence when the statements are to be used extensively. This is often the case for publicly held companies, those with extensive indebtedness, and companies that are to be sold in the near future.

The most likely uses of the statements can be determined from previous experience with the client and discussion with management. Throughout the engagement, the auditor may get additional information about why the client is having an audit and the likely uses of the financial statements. This information may affect the auditor's assessment of acceptable audit risk.

Obtain an Understanding with the Client

A clear understanding of the terms of the engagement should exist between the client and the CPA firm. SAS 83 (AU 310) requires that auditors must document their understanding of an engagement in the working papers, including the engagement's objectives, the responsibilities of the auditor and management, and the engagement's limitations. This is typically done with an **engagement letter**, even though one is not required.

The engagement letter is an agreement between the CPA firm and the client for the conduct of the audit and related services. It should specify whether the auditor will perform an audit, a review, or a compilation, plus any other services such as tax returns or management consulting. It should also state any restrictions to be imposed on the auditor's work, deadlines for completing the audit, assistance to be provided by the client's personnel in obtaining records and documents, and schedules to be prepared for the auditor. It often includes an agreement on fees. The engagement letter is also a means of informing the client that the auditor cannot guarantee that all acts of fraud will be discovered.

On-Line Engagement Letter

The engagement letter does not affect the CPA firm's responsibility to external users of audited financial statements, but it can affect legal responsibilities to the client. For example, if the client sued the CPA firm for failing to find a material misstatement, one defense a CPA firm could use would be a signed engagement letter stating that a review service, rather than an audit, was agreed upon.

Engagement letter information is important in planning the audit principally because it affects the timing of the tests and the total amount of time the audit and other services will take. If the deadline for submitting the audit report is soon after the balance sheet date, a significant portion of the audit must be done before the end of the year. When the auditor is preparing tax returns and a management letter, or if client assistance is not available, arrangements must be made to extend the amount of time for the engagement. Client-imposed restrictions on the audit could affect the procedures performed and possibly even the type of audit opinion issued. An example of an engagement letter for the audit of Hillsburg Hardware Co. is given in Figure 8-2 (p. 222).

Select Staff for the Engagement

Assigning the appropriate staff to the engagement is important to meet generally accepted auditing standards and to promote audit efficiency. The first general standard states:

The audit is to be performed by a person or persons having adequate technical training and proficiency as an auditor.

FIGURE 8-2   **Engagement Letter**

BERGER AND ANTHONY, CPAs
Gary, Indiana 46405

June 14, 1999

Mr. Rick Chulick, President
Hillsburg Hardware Co.
2146 Willow St.
Gary, Indiana 46405

Dear Mr. Chulick:

This will confirm our understanding of the arrangements for our audit of the financial statements of Hillsburg Hardware Co. for the year ending December 31, 1999.

We will audit the company's financial statements for the year ending December 31, 1999, for the purpose of expressing an opinion on the fairness with which they present, in all material respects, the financial position, results of operations, and cash flows in conformity with generally accepted accounting principles.

We will conduct our audit in accordance with generally accepted auditing standards. Those standards require that we obtain reasonable, rather than absolute, assurance that the financial statements are free of material misstatement, whether caused by error or fraud. Accordingly, a material misstatement may remain undetected. Also, an audit is not designed to detect error or fraud that is immaterial to the financial statements; therefore, the audit will not necessarily detect misstatements less than this materiality level that might exist because of error, fraudulent financial reporting, or misappropriation of assets. If, for any reason, we are unable to complete the audit or are unable to form or have not formed an opinion, we may decline to express an opinion or decline to issue a report as a result of the engagement.

Although an audit includes obtaining an understanding of internal control sufficient to plan the audit and to determine the nature, timing, and extent of audit procedures to be performed, it is not designed to provide assurance on internal control or to identify reportable conditions. However, we are responsible for ensuring that the audit committee is aware of any reportable conditions that come to our attention.

The financial statements are the responsibility of the company's management. Management is also responsible for (1) establishing and maintaining effective internal control over financial reports, (2) identifying and ensuring the company complies with the laws and regulations applicable to its activities, (3) making all financial records and related information available to us, and (4) providing to us at the conclusion of the engagement a representation letter that, among other things, will confirm management's responsibility for the preparation of the financial statements in conformity with generally accepted accounting principles, the availability of financial records and related data, the completeness and availability of all minutes of the board and committee meetings, and, to the best of its knowledge and belief, the absence of fraud involving management or those employees who have a significant role in the entity's internal control.

The timing of our audit and the assistance to be supplied by your personnel, including the preparation of schedules and analyses of accounts, is described on a separate attachment. Timely completion of this work will facilitate the completion of our audit.

As part of our engagement for the year ending December 31, 1999, we will also prepare the federal and state income tax returns for Hillsburg Hardware Co.

Our fees will be billed as work progresses and are based on the amount of time required at various levels of responsibility, plus actual out-of-pocket expenses. Invoices are payable upon presentation. We will notify you immediately of any circumstances we encounter that could significantly affect our initial estimate of total fees of $21,000.

If this letter correctly expresses your understanding, please sign the enclosed copy and return it to us. We appreciate the opportunity to serve you.

Yours very truly:

Joe Anthony

Joe Anthony
Partner

Accepted:

By: *Rick Chulick*
Date: 6-21-99

Staff must therefore be assigned with that standard in mind. On larger engagements, there are likely to be one or more partners and staff at several experience levels doing the audit. Specialists in such technical areas as statistical sampling and computer risk assessment may also be assigned. On smaller audits there may be only one or two staff members.

A major consideration affecting staffing is the need for continuity from year to year. An inexperienced staff assistant is likely to become the most experienced nonpartner on the engagement within a few years. Continuity helps the CPA firm maintain familiarity with the technical requirements and closer interpersonal relations with client personnel.

Another consideration is that the persons assigned be familiar with the client's industry. This is discussed shortly.

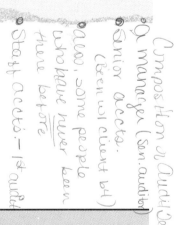

MANY CPA FIRMS REORGANIZE TO FOCUS ON INDUSTRIES

A high level of knowledge of a client's industry and business is so critical to conducting quality audits and providing value-added tax and consulting services that many CPA firms have reorganized to focus on industry lines. For example, KPMG has reorganized their entire practice around the following lines of business: Financial Services; Health Care and Life Sciences; Manufacturing, Retailing and Distribution; Information, Communications and Entertainment; and Public Services. Reorganizing along industry lines may help CPA firms such as KPMG better understand their clients' businesses and provide additional value-added services.

To illustrate the importance of assigning appropriate staff to engagements, consider a computer manufacturing client with extensive inventory of computers and computer parts. Inherent risk for inventory has been assessed as high. It is essential for the staff person doing the inventory portion of the audit to be experienced in auditing inventory. In addition, he or she should have a good understanding of the computer manufacturing industry.

OBTAIN BACKGROUND INFORMATION

Obtain Knowledge of Client's Industry and Business

KPMG's Business Measurement Process

Preplan

Obtain background information

Obtain information about client's legal obligations

Perform preliminary analytical procedures

Set materiality, and assess acceptable audit risk and inherent risk

Understand internal control and assess control risk

Develop overall audit plan and audit program

An extensive understanding of the client's business and industry and knowledge about the company's operations are essential for doing an adequate audit. Most of this information is obtained at the client's premises, especially for a new client.

There are three primary reasons for obtaining a good understanding of the client's industry. First, many industries have unique accounting requirements that the auditor must understand to evaluate whether the client's financial statements are in accordance with generally accepted accounting principles. For example, if an auditor is doing an audit of a city, the auditor must understand governmental accounting and auditing requirements. There are also unique accounting requirements for construction companies, railroads, not-for-profit organizations, financial institutions, and many other organizations.

Second, the auditor can often identify risks in the industry that may affect the auditor's assessment of acceptable audit risk, or even whether auditing companies in the industry is advisable. As stated earlier, certain industries are more risky than others, such as the savings and loan and health insurance industries.

Finally, there are inherent risks that are typically common to all clients in certain industries. Understanding those risks aids the auditor in identifying the client's inherent risks. Examples include potential inventory obsolescence inherent risk in the fashion clothes industry, accounts receivable collection inherent risk in the consumer loan industry, and reserve for loss inherent risk in the casualty insurance industry.

Knowledge of the client's industry can be obtained in different ways. These include discussions with the auditor who was responsible for the engagement in previous years and auditors currently on similar engagements, as well as conferences with the client's personnel. AICPA industry audit guides, textbooks, and technical magazines are available for the auditor to study in most major industries. Some auditors follow the practice of subscribing to specialized journals for those industries to which they devote a large amount of time. Considerable knowledge can also be obtained by participating actively in industry associations and training programs.

Knowledge about the client's business that differentiates it from other companies in its industry is also needed. That knowledge will help the auditor more effectively assess acceptable audit risk and inherent risk and will also be useful in designing analytical procedures.

Companies filing with the SEC are required under SFAS 131 to disclose segment information for different lines of business in the financial statements. SAS 21 (AU 435) provides guidelines for auditing the segment information. Auditors must have sufficient knowledge of a company's business to enable them to evaluate whether there are segments requiring separate disclosure. Because SAS 21 requires audit testing of the segment information, it is important for the auditor to identify the segments early.

The auditor's permanent files often include the history of the company, a list of the major lines of business, and a record of the most important accounting policies in previous years. Study of this information and discussions with the client's personnel aid in understanding the business.

Tour the Plant and Offices

A tour of the client's facilities is helpful in obtaining a better understanding of the client's business and operations because it provides an opportunity to observe operations firsthand and to meet key personnel. The actual viewing of the physical facilities aids in understanding physical safeguards over assets and in interpreting accounting data by providing a frame of reference in which to visualize such assets as inventory in process and factory equipment. Knowledge of the physical layout also facilitates getting answers to questions later in the audit. The tour may also help the auditor identify inherent risks. For example, if the auditor observes unused equipment and potentially unsalable inventory, it will affect the assessment of inherent risks for equipment and inventory. Discussions with nonaccounting employees during the tour and throughout the audit are useful in maintaining a broad perspective.

Industry Trends and Information

Identify Related Parties

Transactions with related parties are important to auditors because generally accepted accounting principles require that they be *disclosed in the financial statements* if they are material. Transactions with a related party are not arm's length transactions. Therefore, there is a risk that they were not valued at the same amount as they would have been if the transactions had been with an independent third party. The disclosure requirements include the nature of the related party relationship; a description of transactions, including dollar amounts; and amounts due from and to related parties. Most auditors assess inherent risk as high for related parties and related party transactions, both because of the accounting disclosure requirements and the lack of independence between the parties involved in the transactions.

A **related party** is defined in SAS 45 (AU 334) as an affiliated company, a principal owner of the client company, or any other party with which the client deals where one of the parties can influence the management or operating policies of the other. A **related party transaction** is any transaction between the client and a related party. Common examples include sales or purchase transactions between a parent company and its subsidiary, exchanges of equipment between two companies owned by the same person, and loans to officers. A less common example is the exercise of significant management influence on an audit client by its most important customer.

Because material related party transactions must be disclosed, it is important that all related parties be *identified and included in the permanent files* early in the engagement. Finding undisclosed related party transactions is thereby enhanced. Common ways of identifying related parties include inquiry of management, review of SEC filings, and examination of stockholders' listings to identify principal stockholders.

Evaluate Need for Outside Specialists

When the auditor encounters situations requiring specialized knowledge, it may be necessary to consult a specialist. SAS 73 (AU 336) establishes the requirements for selecting specialists and reviewing their work. Examples include using a diamond expert in evaluating the replacement cost of diamonds and an actuary for determining the appropriateness of the recorded value of insurance loss reserves. Another common use of specialists is consulting with attorneys on the legal interpretation of contracts and titles. In the previously discussed example of a large inventory of computers and computer parts, the CPA firm may decide to engage a specialist if no one within the firm is qualified to evaluate whether the inventory is obsolete.

The auditor should have a sufficient understanding of the client's business to recognize the need for a specialist. The auditor should evaluate the specialist's professional qualifications and understand the objectives and scope of the specialist's work. The auditor should also consider the specialist's relationship to the client, including circumstances that might impair the specialist's objectivity.

OBTAIN INFORMATION ABOUT CLIENT'S LEGAL OBLIGATIONS

OBJECTIVE 8-4
Obtain information about an audit client's legal obligations.

Three closely related types of legal documents and records should be examined early in the engagement: corporate charter and bylaws, minutes of board of directors' and stockholders' meetings, and contracts. Some information, such as contracts, must be disclosed in the financial statements. Other information, such as authorizations in the board of directors' minutes, is useful in other parts of the audit. Early knowledge of these legal documents and records enables auditors to interpret related evidence throughout the engagement and to make sure there is proper disclosure in the financial statements.

Corporate Charter and Bylaws

The **corporate charter** is granted by the state in which the company is incorporated and is the legal document necessary for recognizing a corporation as a separate entity. It includes the exact name of the corporation, the date of incorporation, the kinds and amounts of capital stock the corporation is authorized to issue, and the types of business activities the corporation is authorized to conduct. In specifying the kinds of capital stock, there is also included such information as the voting rights of each class of stock, par or stated value of the stock, preferences and conditions necessary for dividends, and prior rights in liquidation.

The **bylaws** include the rules and procedures adopted by the stockholders of the corporation. They specify such things as the fiscal year of the corporation, the frequency of stockholder meetings, the method of voting for directors, and the duties and powers of the corporate officers.

The auditor must understand the requirements of the corporate charter and the bylaws to determine whether the financial statements are properly presented. The correct disclosure of the stockholders' equity, including the proper payment of dividends, depends heavily on these requirements.

Minutes of Meetings

The **corporate minutes** are the official record of the meetings of the board of directors and stockholders. They include summaries of the most important topics discussed at these meetings and the decisions made by the directors and stockholders. The auditor should read the minutes to obtain information that is relevant to performing the audit. There are two categories of relevant information in minutes: authorizations and discussions by the board of directors affecting inherent risk.

Common authorizations in the minutes include compensation of officers, new contracts and agreements, acquisitions of property, loans, and dividend payments. While reading the minutes, the auditor should identify relevant authorizations and include the information in the working papers by making an abstract of the minutes or by obtaining a copy and underlining significant portions. Some time before the audit is completed, there must be a follow-up of this information to be sure that management has complied with actions taken by the stockholders and the board of directors. As an illustration, the authorized compensation of officers should be traced to each individual officer's payroll record as a test of whether the correct total compensation was paid. Similarly, the auditor should compare the authorizations of loans with notes payable to make certain that these liabilities are recorded.

Information included in the minutes affecting the auditor's assessment of inherent risk is likely to involve more general discussions. To illustrate, assume that the minutes state that the board of directors discussed two topics: changes in its industry that affect the usefulness of existing machinery and equipment and a possible lawsuit by the Environmental Protection Agency for chemical seepage at a plant in Pennsylvania. The first discussion is likely to affect the inherent risk of obsolete equipment and the second one the inherent risk of an illegal act.

Contracts

Clients become involved in different types of contracts that are of interest to the auditor. These can include such diverse items as long-term notes and bonds payable, stock options, pension plans, contracts with vendors for future delivery of supplies, government contracts for completion and delivery of manufactured products, royalty agreements, union contracts, and leases.

Most contracts are of primary interest in individual parts of the audit and, in practice, receive special attention during the different phases of the detailed tests. For example, the provisions of a pension plan would receive substantial emphasis as a part of the audit of the unfunded liability for pensions. The auditor should review and abstract the documents early in the engagement to gain a better perspective of the organization and to become familiar with potential problem areas. Later these documents can be examined more carefully as a part of the tests of individual audit areas.

The existence of contracts often affects the auditor's assessed inherent risks. To illustrate, assume that the auditor determines early in the audit that the client has signed several sales contracts with severe nonperformance clauses committing the company to deliver specified quantities of its product at agreed-upon prices during the current and next 5 years. The inherent risks for total sales, liabilities for penalties, and sales commitment disclosures are likely to be assessed as high in this situation.

PERFORM PRELIMINARY ANALYTICAL PROCEDURES

As discussed in Chapter 7, auditors are required to perform analytical procedures while planning the audit to assist in determining the nature, timing, and extent of auditing procedures. Analytical procedures performed during the planning phase enhance the auditor's understanding of the client's business and events occurring since the prior year's audit. Planning analytical procedures also help the auditor identify areas that may represent specific risks of material misstatements warranting further attention.

Analytical procedures used in planning are often based on aggregate, companywide data. For some clients, reviewing changes in account balances on the trial balance may be sufficient for planning purposes. Table 8-1 (p. 228) presents key financial ratios for Hillsburg Hardware Co. that auditors might consider during audit planning, along with comparative industry information. Hillsburg is a small wholesale distributor of hardware to independent, high-quality hardware stores in the midwestern part of the United States. The company is a niche provider in the overall hardware market, which is recently becoming dominated by huge hardware and building supply national chains. The following discussion indicates how the auditor might use this ratio information in gaining an understanding of the client and identifying potential audit risk areas.

The profitability measures indicate that Hillsburg is performing fairly well, despite the increased competition from larger national chains. Several of the profitability measures, such as the efficiency ratio and return on assets, have improved in the current year and are above industry averages. Although lower than the industry averages, the liquidity measures indicate that the company is in good financial condition and the leverage ratios indicate additional borrowing capacity. Because Hillsburg's market consists of smaller, independent

OBJECTIVE 8-5
Discuss the nature and purposes of preliminary analytical procedures.

- Preplan
- Obtain background information
- Obtain information about client's legal obligations
- Perform preliminary analytical procedures
- Set materiality, and assess acceptable audit risk and inherent risk
- Understand internal control and assess control risk
- Develop overall audit plan and audit program

TABLE 8-1   Examples of Planning Analytical Procedures

Selected Ratios	Hillsburg 12/31/99	Industry 12/31/99	Hillsburg 12/31/98	Industry 12/31/98
Short-Term Debt-Paying Ability				
Current ratio	3.90	5.20	4.40	5.10
Quick ratio	1.60	3.10	1.40	3.00
Cash ratio	0.06	0.22	0.02	0.20
Short-Term Liquidity				
Accounts receivable turnover	7.10	12.15	6.97	12.25
Days to collect accounts receivable	50.80	29.63	51.60	29.38
Inventory turnover	3.50	5.20	3.00	4.90
Days to sell inventory	104.10	69.23	120.00	73.47
Days to convert inventory to cash	154.90	98.86	171.60	102.85
Ability to Meet Long-Term Obligations and Preferred Dividends				
Debt to equity	1.70	2.51	1.40	2.53
Tangible net assets to equity	1.00	0.95	1.00	0.94
Times interest earned	3.10	5.50	2.60	5.60
Times interest and preferred dividends earned	3.10	4.90	2.60	5.00
Operating and Performance Ratios				
Efficiency ratio	2.30	2.10	2.13	2.15
Gross margin percentage	27.80	31.00	27.70	32.00
Profit margin ratio	0.05	0.07	0.05	0.08
Profitability ratio	0.12	0.10	0.10	0.10
Return on assets	0.13	0.09	0.10	0.09
Return on common equity	0.25	0.37	0.20	0.35
Leverage ratios—current liabilities	0.08	0.15	0.06	0.14
Leverage ratio—notes payable	0.03	0.08	0.01	0.07
Book value per common share	4.50	2.30	4.10	2.20

hardware stores, the company holds more inventory and takes longer to collect receivables than the industry average.

In identifying areas of specific risk, the auditor would likely focus on the liquidity ratios. Inventory and accounts receivable turnover have improved but are still lower than industry averages. The collectibility of accounts receivable and inventory obsolescence will likely warrant attention in the current year's audit. These areas also likely received additional attention during the prior year's audit. The improvement in the turnover ratios suggests that testing in these areas probably will not need to be expanded compared to the prior year.

SUMMARY OF THE PURPOSES OF AUDIT PLANNING

There are several purposes of the planning procedures discussed in this section. A major purpose is to provide information to aid the auditor in assessing acceptable audit risk and inherent risk. These assessments will affect the auditor's client acceptance or continuation decision, the proposed audit fee, and the auditor's evidence decisions. A second purpose is to obtain information that requires follow-up during the audit. Doing so is one step in obtaining sufficient competent evidence. Examples include identifying approvals in the minutes of such items as dividends and officers' salaries, and searching for the names of related parties to help the auditor determine whether related party transactions exist. Other purposes include staffing the engagement and obtaining an engagement letter.

Keep in mind that there are three additional parts of audit planning, each of which is discussed in subsequent chapters: set materiality and assess acceptable audit risk and inherent risk (Chapter 9), understand internal control and assess control risk (Chapter 10), and develop an overall audit plan and audit program (Chapter 12). Figure 8-3 below summarizes the four major parts of audit planning discussed in this section and the key components of each part, with a brief illustration of how a CPA firm applied each component to a continuing client, Hillsburg Hardware Co.

FIGURE 8-3 Key Parts of Planning: Preplan, Obtain Background Information, Obtain Information about Client's Legal Obligations, and Perform Preliminary Analytical Procedures Applied to Hillsburg Hardware Co.

MAJOR PART OF PLANNING	SUBPARTS OF PLANNING	APPLICATION TO HILLSBURG HARDWARE CO.
Preplan	New client acceptance and continuance	Hillsburg is a continuing audit client. No circumstances were identified in the continuation review to cause discontinuance.
	Identify client's reasons for audit	There are two primary reasons. Audit is required by bank due to large notes payable outstanding and management desires an audit for the assurance it provides.
	Obtain an understanding with the client	(See Figure 8-2, p. 222) Obtained an engagement letter before starting field work.
	Staff the engagement	Partner—Joe Anthony Senior—Fran Moore Assistant—One person to be named later
Obtain background information	Obtain knowledge of client's industry and business	Fran Moore discussed with Chulick and updated permanent files.
	Tour the plant and offices	Done by Fran Moore and assistant on the first day of field work. Fran made notes of significant observations for later follow-up.
	Identify related parties	Fran Moore reviewed information in permanent file with owner and controller and updated file.
	Evaluate need for outside specialists	Because of the noncomplexity of the audit, no specialists are considered necessary.
Obtain information about client's legal obligations	Corporate charter and bylaws	Fran Moore discussed with owner and controller. There were no changes.
	Minutes of meetings	Fran Moore read all minutes. She had a copy made for the working papers and identified items requiring follow-up during the audit and two inherent risks.
	Contracts	Fran Moore briefly reviewed all continuing contracts for changes and summarized all new contracts that were relevant to the audit.
Perform preliminary analytical procedures		Fran Moore compared 12-31-99 unaudited balances to the prior year. She calculated key ratios and compared them with prior years and industry averages. All significant differences were identified for follow-up.

WORKING PAPERS

OBJECTIVE 8-6
Understand the purposes of audit working papers.

"Audit documentation"

Planning is the beginning of the evidence accumulation process. Given that adequate planning is required by the second standard of field work, auditors document their planning activities in working papers to provide evidence that planning was adequately performed. In addition to planning, working papers document the audit evidence accumulated during the audit and the auditor's conclusions. According to SAS 41 (AU 339), **working papers** are the *records kept by the auditor of the procedures applied, the tests performed, the information obtained, and the pertinent conclusions reached in the engagement.* Working papers should include all the information the auditor considers necessary to conduct the audit adequately and to provide support for the audit report. Increasingly, working papers are maintained in computerized files.

Purposes of Working Papers

The overall objective of working papers is to aid the auditor in providing reasonable assurance that an adequate audit was conducted in accordance with generally accepted auditing standards. More specifically, the working papers, as they pertain to the current year's audit, provide a basis for planning the audit, a record of the evidence accumulated and the results of the tests, data for determining the proper type of audit report, and a basis for review by supervisors and partners.

If the auditor is to plan the current year's audit adequately, the necessary reference information must be available in the working papers. The papers include such diverse planning information as descriptive information about internal control, a time budget for individual audit areas, the audit program, and the results of the preceding year's audit.

The working papers are the primary means of documenting that an adequate audit was conducted in accordance with GAAS. If the need arises, the auditor must be able to demonstrate to regulatory agencies and courts that the audit was well planned and adequately supervised; the evidence accumulated was competent, sufficient, and timely; and the audit report was proper, considering the results of the audit.

The working papers provide an important source of information to assist the auditor in deciding the appropriate audit report to issue in a given set of circumstances. The data in the papers are useful for evaluating the adequacy of audit scope and the fairness of the financial statements. In addition, the working papers contain information needed to assist the client in the preparation of the financial statements.

The working papers are the primary frame of reference used by supervisory personnel to evaluate whether sufficient competent evidence was accumulated to justify the audit report.

In addition to the purposes directly related to the audit report, the working papers have other uses. They often serve as the basis for preparing tax returns, filings with the SEC, and other reports. They are a source of information for issuing communications to the audit committee and management concerning various matters such as internal control weaknesses or operations recommendations. Working papers are also a useful frame of reference for training personnel and as an aid in planning and coordinating subsequent audits.

Ownership of Working Papers

The working papers prepared during the engagement, including those prepared by the client for the auditor, are the *property of the auditor.* The only time anyone else, including the client, has a legal right to examine the papers is when they are subpoenaed by a court as legal evidence. At the completion of the engagement, working papers and computer files are retained on the CPA's premises for future reference. Many firms follow the practice of microfilming hard copy working papers after several years to reduce storage costs.

Confidentiality of Working Papers

The need to maintain a confidential relationship with the client is expressed in Rule 301 of the *Code of Professional Conduct,* which states (see top of p. 231)

• A member shall not disclose any confidential information obtained in the course of a professional engagement except with the consent of the client.

During the course of the audit, auditors obtain a considerable amount of information of a confidential nature, including officers' salaries, product pricing and advertising plans, and product cost data. If auditors divulged this information to outsiders or to client employees who have been denied access, their relationship with management would be seriously strained. Furthermore, having access to the working papers would give employees an opportunity to alter information on them. For these reasons, care must be taken to protect the working papers at all times.

Ordinarily, the working papers can be provided to someone else only with the express permission of the client. This is the case even if a CPA sells his or her practice to another CPA firm. Permission is not required from the client, however, if the working papers are subpoenaed by a court or are used as part of an AICPA or state society approved peer review program with other CPA firms.

THE BURDEN OF PROOF

Jury studies conducted by a professional liability insurance company in California show jurors consider CPAs experts in documentation. Therefore, when practitioners are faced with a liability suit and have fallen short of that expectation, they are likely to be judged negligent. On the other hand, even an informal note documenting a brief telephone conversation can sway a jury in the CPA's favor. Legally, the burden of proof rests with the plaintiff, but as a practical matter, the burden to document falls on the CPA.

Source: Excerpted from an article by Ric Rosario, "Making Documentation Pay Off," *Journal of Accountancy* (February 1995), p. 70.

Contents and Organization

Each CPA firm establishes its own approach to preparing and organizing working papers, and the beginning auditor must adopt his or her firm's approach. The emphasis in this text is on the general concepts common to all working papers.

Figure 8-4 (p. 232) illustrates the contents and organization of a typical set of papers. They contain virtually everything involved in the audit. There is a definite logic to the type of working papers prepared for an audit and the way they are arranged in the files, even though different firms may follow somewhat different approaches. In the figure, the working papers start with more general information, such as corporate data in the permanent files, and end with the financial statements and audit report. In between are the working papers supporting the auditor's tests.

> **OBJECTIVE 8-7**
> Prepare organized audit working papers.

Permanent Files

Permanent files are intended to contain data of a *historical or continuing nature* pertinent to the current audit. These files provide a convenient source of information about the audit that is of continuing interest from year to year. The permanent files typically include the following:

• *Extracts or copies of such company documents of continuing importance as the articles of incorporation, bylaws, bond indentures, and contracts.* The contracts are pension plans, leases, stock options, and so on. Each of these documents is of significance to the auditor for as many years as it is in effect.
• *Analyses, from previous years, of accounts that have continuing importance to the auditor.* These include accounts such as long-term debt, stockholders' equity accounts, goodwill, and fixed assets. Having this information in the permanent files enables the auditor to concentrate on analyzing only the changes in the current year's balance while retaining the results of previous years' audits in a form accessible for review.

FIGURE 8-4   Working Paper Contents and Organization

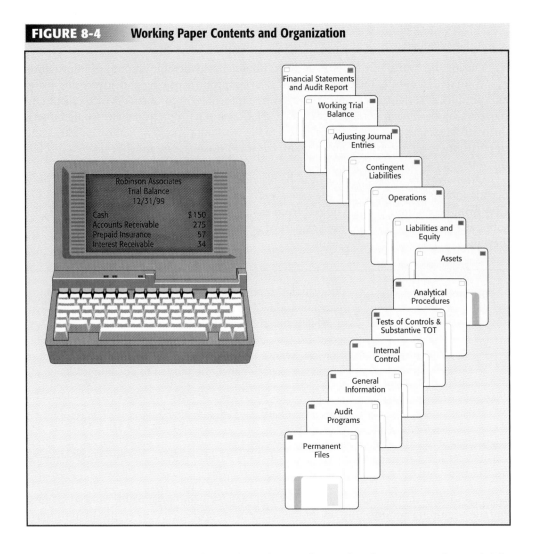

- *Information related to the understanding of internal control and assessment of control risk.* This includes organization charts, flowcharts, questionnaires, and other internal control information, including enumeration of controls and weaknesses in the system.
- *The results of analytical procedures from previous years' audits.* Among these data are ratios and percentages computed by the auditor and the total balance or the balance by month for selected accounts. This information is useful in helping the auditor decide whether there are unusual changes in the current year's account balances that should be investigated more extensively.

Analytical procedures and the understanding of internal control and assessment of control risk are included in the current period working papers rather than in the permanent file by many CPA firms.

Current Files

The **current files** include all working papers applicable to the year under audit. There is one set of permanent files for the client and a set of current files for each year's audit. The types of information included in the current file are briefly discussed in the sections that follow.

Audit Program The audit program is ordinarily maintained in a separate file to improve the coordination and integration of all parts of the audit, although some firms also include a copy of the audit program for each audit section with that section's working papers. As the audit progresses, each auditor initials the program for the audit procedures performed and indicates the date of completion. The inclusion in the working papers of a well-designed audit program completed in a conscientious manner is evidence of a high-quality audit.

General Information Some working papers include current period information that is of a general nature rather than designed to support specific financial statement amounts. This includes such items as audit planning memos, abstracts or copies of minutes of the board of directors' meetings, abstracts of contracts or agreements not included in the permanent files, notes on discussions with the client, working paper review comments, and general conclusions. Documentation of the assessment of control risk may also be included.

Working Trial Balance Because the basis for preparing the financial statements is the general ledger, the amounts included in that record are the focal point of the audit. As early as possible after the balance sheet date, the auditor obtains or prepares a listing of the general ledger accounts and their year-end balances. This schedule is the **working trial balance**. Software programs enable the auditor to download the client's ending general ledger balances into a working trial balance file.

The technique used by many firms is to have the auditor's working trial balance in the same format as the financial statements. Each line item on the trial balance is supported by a **lead schedule**, containing the detailed accounts from the general ledger making up the line item total. Each detailed account on the lead schedule is, in turn, supported by appropriate schedules supporting the audit work performed and the conclusions reached. As an example, the relationship between cash as it is stated on the financial statements, the working trial balance, the lead schedule for cash, and the supporting working papers is presented in Figure 8-5 (p. 234). As the figure indicates, cash on the financial statements is the same as on the working trial balance and the total of the detail on the cash lead schedule. Initially, figures for the lead schedule were taken from the general ledger. The audit work performed resulted in an adjustment to cash that would be evidenced in the detail schedules and reflected on the lead schedule, the working trial balance, and the financial statements.

Adjusting and Reclassification Entries When the auditor discovers material misstatements in the accounting records, the financial statements must be corrected. For example, if the client failed to properly reduce inventory for obsolete raw materials, an adjusting entry can be made by the auditor to reflect the realizable value of the inventory. Even though adjusting entries discovered in the audit are typically prepared by the auditor, they must be approved by the client because management has primary responsibility for the fair presentation of the statements. Figure 8-5 illustrates an adjustment of the general cash account for $90.

Reclassification entries are frequently made in the statements to present accounting information properly, even when the general ledger balances are correct. A common example is the reclassification for financial statement purposes of material credit balances in accounts receivable to accounts payable. Because the balance in accounts receivable on the general ledger reflects the accounts receivable properly from the point of view of operating the company on a day-to-day basis, the reclassification entry is not included in the client's general ledger.

Only those adjusting and reclassification entries that significantly affect the fair presentation of financial statements must be made. The determination of when a misstatement should be adjusted is based on materiality. The auditor should keep in mind that several immaterial misstatements that are not adjusted could result in a material overall misstatement when they are combined. It is common for auditors to summarize all entries that have not been recorded on a separate working paper as a means of determining their cumulative effect.

Supporting Schedule Working Papers The largest portion of working papers includes the detailed **supporting schedule working papers** prepared by the client or the auditors in support of specific amounts on the financial statements. Many different types of schedules are used. Use of the appropriate type for a given aspect of the audit is necessary to

FIGURE 8-5 Relationship of Working Papers to Financial Statements

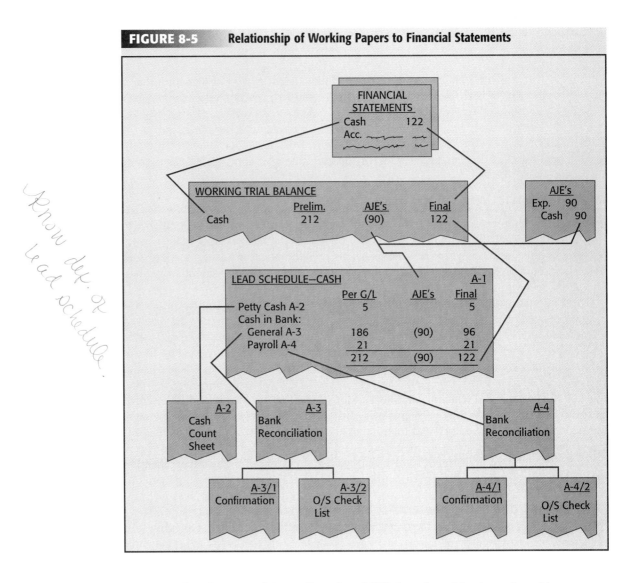

document the adequacy of the audit and to fulfill the other objectives of working papers. Following are the major types of supporting schedules:

- *Analysis.* An analysis is designed to show the *activity in a general ledger account* during the entire period under audit, tying together the beginning and ending balances. This type of schedule is normally used for accounts such as marketable securities; notes receivable; allowance for doubtful accounts; property, plant, and equipment; long-term debt; and all equity accounts. The common characteristic of these accounts is the significance of the activity in the account during the year. In most cases, the working papers for analysis have cross-references to other working papers.
- *Trial balance or list.* This type of schedule consists of the *details that make up a year-end balance* of a general ledger account. It differs from an analysis in that it includes only those items constituting the end-of-the-period balance. Common examples include trial balances or lists in support of trade accounts receivable, trade accounts payable, repair and maintenance expense, legal expense, and miscellaneous income. An example is included in Figure 8-6.
- *Reconciliation of amounts.* A reconciliation *supports a specific amount* and is normally expected to tie the amount recorded in the client's records to another source of information. Examples include the reconciliation of bank balances with bank statements,

FIGURE 8-6 **Common Characteristics of Proper Working Papers**

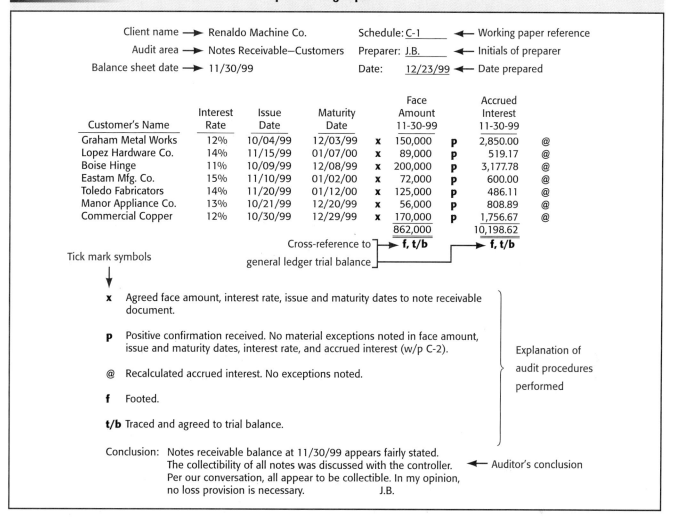

Client name → Renaldo Machine Co. Schedule: C-1 ← Working paper reference
Audit area → Notes Receivable—Customers Preparer: J.B. ← Initials of preparer
Balance sheet date → 11/30/99 Date: 12/23/99 ← Date prepared

Customer's Name	Interest Rate	Issue Date	Maturity Date		Face Amount 11-30-99		Accrued Interest 11-30-99	
Graham Metal Works	12%	10/04/99	12/03/99	x	150,000	p	2,850.00	@
Lopez Hardware Co.	14%	11/15/99	01/07/00	x	89,000	p	519.17	@
Boise Hinge	11%	10/09/99	12/08/99	x	200,000	p	3,177.78	@
Eastam Mfg. Co.	15%	11/10/99	01/02/00	x	72,000	p	600.00	@
Toledo Fabricators	14%	11/20/99	01/12/00	x	125,000	p	486.11	@
Manor Appliance Co.	13%	10/21/99	12/20/99	x	56,000	p	808.89	@
Commercial Copper	12%	10/30/99	12/29/99	x	170,000	p	1,756.67	@
					862,000		10,198.62	

Cross-reference to → **f, t/b** → **f, t/b**
general ledger trial balance

Tick mark symbols ↓

x Agreed face amount, interest rate, issue and maturity dates to note receivable document.

p Positive confirmation received. No material exceptions noted in face amount, issue and maturity dates, interest rate, and accrued interest (w/p C-2).

@ Recalculated accrued interest. No exceptions noted.

f Footed.

t/b Traced and agreed to trial balance.

Explanation of audit procedures performed

Conclusion: Notes receivable balance at 11/30/99 appears fairly stated. The collectibility of all notes was discussed with the controller. Per our conversation, all appear to be collectible. In my opinion, no loss provision is necessary. J.B. ← Auditor's conclusion

the reconciliation of subsidiary accounts receivable balances with confirmations from customers, and the reconciliation of accounts payable balances with vendors' statements. An example is included on page 706.

• *Tests of reasonableness.* A test of reasonableness schedule, as the name implies, contains information that enables the auditor to evaluate whether the client's balance appears to include a misstatement considering the circumstances in the engagement. Frequently, auditors test depreciation expense, the provision for federal income taxes, and the allowance for doubtful accounts by tests of reasonableness. These tests are primarily analytical procedures.

• *Summary of procedures.* Another type of schedule *summarizes the results* of a specific audit procedure performed. Examples are the summary of the results of accounts receivable confirmation and the summary of inventory observations.

• *Examination of supporting documents.* A number of special-purpose schedules are designed to *show detailed tests performed,* such as examination of documents during tests of controls and substantive tests of transactions or cutoffs. These schedules show no totals, and they do not tie in to the general ledger because they document only the tests performed and the results found. However, the schedules must state a definite positive or negative conclusion about the objective of the test.

• *Informational.* This type of schedule contains information as opposed to audit evidence. These schedules include information for tax returns and SEC Form 10-K data and data such as time budgets and the client's working hours, which are helpful in administration of the engagement.

- *Outside documentation.* Much of the content of the working papers consists of the outside documentation gathered by auditors, such as confirmation replies and copies of client agreements. Although not "schedules" in the real sense, these are indexed and interfiled, and procedures are indicated on them in the same manner as on the other schedules.

Preparation of Working Papers

The proper preparation of schedules to document the audit evidence accumulated, the results found, and the conclusions reached is an important part of the audit. Read the following insert about Rhonda and imagine yourself in her position several years after completing an audit.

WILL IT STAND UP IN COURT?

Rhonda McMillan had been the in-charge auditor on the audit of Blaine Construction Company in 1993. Now she is sitting here, in 1999, in a room full of attorneys who are asking her questions about the 1993 audit. Blaine was sold to another company in 1994 at a purchase price that was based primarily on the 1993 audited financial statements. Several of the large construction contracts showed a profit in 1993 using the percentage of completion method, but they ultimately resulted in large losses for the buyer. Because Rhonda's firm audited the 1993 financial statements, the buyer is trying to make the case that Rhonda's firm failed in their audit of contract costs and revenues.

The buyer's attorney is taking Rhonda's deposition and is asking her about the audit work she did on contracts. Referring to the working papers, his examination goes something like this:

ATTORNEY	Do you recognize this exhibit, and if you do, would you please identify it for us?
RHONDA	Yes, this is the summary of contracts in progress at the end of 1993.
ATTORNEY	Did you prepare this document?
RHONDA	I believe the client prepared it, but I audited it. My initials are right here in the upper right-hand corner.
ATTORNEY	When did you do this audit work?
RHONDA	I'm not sure, I forgot to date this one. But it must have been about the second week in March, because that's when we did the field work.
ATTORNEY	Now I'd like to turn your attention to this tick mark next to the Baldwin contract. You see where it shows Baldwin, and then the red sort of cross-like mark?
RHONDA	Yes.
ATTORNEY	In the explanation for that tick mark it says: "Discussed status of job with Elton Burgess. Job is going according to schedule and he believes that the expected profit will be earned." Now my question is, Ms. McMillan, what exactly was the nature and content of your discussion with Mr. Burgess?
RHONDA	Other than what is in the explanation to this tick mark, I have no idea. I mean, this all took place 5 years ago. I only worked on the engagement that 1 year, and I can hardly even remember that.

Although the design depends on the objectives involved, working papers should possess certain characteristics:

- Each working paper should be properly identified with such information as the client's name, the period covered, a description of the contents, the initials of the preparer, the date of preparation, and an index code.

- Working papers should be indexed and cross-referenced to aid in organizing and filing. One type of indexing is illustrated in Figure 8-5 (p. 234). The lead schedule for cash has been indexed as A-1, and the individual general ledger accounts making up the total cash on the financial statements are indexed as A-2 through A-4. The final indexing is for the schedules supporting A-3 and A-4.
- Completed working papers must clearly indicate the audit work performed. This is accomplished in three ways: by a written statement in the form of a memorandum, by initialing the audit procedures in the audit program, and by notations directly on the working paper schedules. Notations on working papers are accomplished by the use of **tick marks**, which are symbols written adjacent to the detail on the body of the schedule. These notations must be clearly explained at the bottom of the working paper.
- Each working paper should include sufficient information to fulfill the objectives for which it was designed. If the auditor is to prepare working papers properly, the auditor must be aware of his or her goals. For example, if a working paper is designed to list the detail and show the verification of support of a balance sheet account, such as prepaid insurance, it is essential that the detail on the working paper reconcile with the trial balance.
- The conclusions that were reached about the segment of the audit under consideration should be plainly stated.

The common characteristics of proper working paper preparation are indicated in Figure 8-6 (p. 235).

CPA FIRMS USE COMPUTER-AUTOMATED WORKING PAPERS

Many CPA firms use their own computers to produce some or all of their working papers. Most large firms develop their own software. Smaller firms usually buy commercial working paper software. An example of such software is ACE (Automated Client Engagement). Using ACE, an auditor can prepare a trial balance, lead schedules, supporting working papers, and financial statements, as well as perform ratio analysis. Tick marks and other items, such as reviewer notes, can be entered directly on the computer screen. In addition, data can be imported from and exported to other applications. Examples include downloading a client's general ledger into ACE and exporting tax information to a commercial tax preparation package.

SUMMARY OF WORKING PAPERS

Working papers are an essential part of every audit for effectively planning the audit, providing a record of the evidence accumulated and the results of the tests, deciding the proper type of audit report, and reviewing the work of assistants. CPA firms establish their own policies and approaches for working paper preparation to make sure that these objectives are met. High-quality CPA firms make sure that working papers are properly prepared and are appropriate for the circumstances in the audit.

Acceptable audit risk—a measure of how willing the auditor is to accept that the financial statements may be materially misstated after the audit is completed and an unqualified opinion has been issued

Bylaws—the rules and procedures adopted by a corporation's stockholders, including the corporation's fiscal year and the duties and powers of its officers

Corporate charter—a legal document granted by the state in which a company is incorporated that recognizes a corporation as a separate entity; it includes the name of the corporation, the date of incorporation, capital stock the corporation is authorized to issue, and the types of business activities the corporation is authorized to conduct

Corporate minutes—the official record of the meetings of a corporation's board of directors and stockholders, in which corporate issues such as the declaration of dividends and the approval of contracts are documented

Current files—all working papers applicable to the year under audit

Engagement letter—an agreement between the CPA firm and the client as to the terms of the engagement for the conduct of the audit and related services

Inherent risk—a measure of the auditor's assessment of the likelihood that there are material misstatements in a segment before considering the effectiveness of internal control

Lead schedule—a working paper that contains the detailed accounts from the general ledger making up a line item total in the working trial balance

Permanent files—auditors' working papers that contain data of a *historical or continuing nature* pertinent to the current audit such as copies of articles of incorporation, bylaws, bond indentures, and contracts

Preplanning the audit—involves deciding whether to accept or continue doing the audit for the client, identifying the client's reasons for the audit, obtaining an engagement letter, and selecting staff for the engagement

Related party—affiliated company, principal owner of the client company, or any other party with which the client deals where one of the parties can influence the management or operating policies of the other

Related party transaction—any transaction between the client and a related party

Supporting schedule working papers—detailed schedules prepared by the client or the auditor in support of specific amounts on the financial statements

Tick marks—symbols used on a working paper that provide additional information or details of audit procedures performed

Working papers—the records kept by the auditor of the procedures applied, the tests performed, the information obtained, and the pertinent conclusions reached in the engagement

Working trial balance—a listing of the general ledger accounts and their year-end balances

REVIEW QUESTIONS

8-1 (Objective 8-1)   What benefits does the auditor derive from planning audits?

8-2 (Objective 8-1)   Identify the seven major steps in planning audits.

8-3 (Objective 8-2)   What are the responsibilities of the successor and predecessor auditors when a company is changing auditors?

8-4 (Objective 8-2)   What factors should an auditor consider prior to accepting an engagement? Explain.

8-5 (Objective 8-2)   What is the purpose of an engagement letter? What subjects should be covered in such a letter?

8-6 (Objective 8-3)   List the four types of information the auditor should obtain or review as a part of gaining background information for the audit, and provide one specific example of how the information will be useful in conducting an audit.

8-7 (Objective 8-3)   When a CPA has accepted an engagement from a new client who is a manufacturer, it is customary for the CPA to tour the client's plant facilities. Discuss the ways in which the CPA's observations made during the course of the plant tour will be of help as he or she plans and conducts the audit.

8-8 (Objective 8-3) An auditor often tries to acquire background knowledge of the client's industry as an aid to his or her audit work. How does the acquisition of this knowledge aid the auditor in distinguishing between obsolete and current inventory?

8-9 (Objective 8-3) Define what is meant by a related party. What are the auditor's responsibilities for related parties and related party transactions?

8-10 (Objective 8-6) Jennifer Bailey is an experienced senior auditor who is in charge of several important audits for a medium-sized firm. Her philosophy of conducting audits is to ignore all previous years' and permanent working papers until near the end of the audit as a means of keeping from prejudicing herself. She believes that this enables her to perform the audit in a more independent manner because it eliminates the tendency of simply doing the same things in the current audit that were done on previous audits. Near the end of the audit, Bailey reviews the working papers from the preceding year, evaluates the significance of any items she has overlooked, and modifies her evidence if she considers it necessary. Evaluate Bailey's approach to conducting an audit.

8-11 (Objective 8-4) Your firm has performed the audit of the Rogers Company for several years and you have been assigned the audit responsibility for the current audit. How would your review of the corporate charter and bylaws for this audit differ from that of the audit of a client who was audited by a different CPA firm in the preceding year?

8-12 (Objective 8-4) For the audit of Radline Manufacturing Company, the audit partner asks you to carefully read the new mortgage contract with the First National Bank and abstract all pertinent information. List the information in a mortgage that is likely to be relevant to the auditor.

8-13 (Objective 8-4) Identify two types of information in the client's minutes of the board of directors' meetings that are likely to be relevant to the auditor. Explain why it is important to read the minutes early in the engagement.

8-14 (Objective 8-6) List the purposes of working papers and explain why each purpose is important.

8-15 (Objective 8-7) Explain why it is important for working papers to include each of the following: identification of the name of the client, period covered, description of the contents, initials of the preparer, date of the preparation, and an index code.

8-16 (Objective 8-7) Define what is meant by a permanent file of working papers, and list several types of information typically included. Why does the auditor not include the contents of the permanent file with the current year's working papers?

8-17 (Objective 8-7) Distinguish between the following types of current period supporting schedules and state the purpose of each: analysis, trial balance, and tests of reasonableness.

8-18 (Objective 8-7) Why is it essential that the auditor not leave questions or exceptions in the working papers without an adequate explanation?

8-19 (Objective 8-7) Define what is meant by a tick mark. What is its purpose?

8-20 (Objective 8-7) Who owns the working papers? Under what circumstances can they be used by other people?

8-21 (Objective 8-7) A CPA sells his auditing practice to another CPA firm and includes all working papers as a part of the purchase price. Under what circumstances is this a violation of the *Code of Professional Conduct?*

8-22 (Objectives 8-1, 8-3)   The following questions concern the planning of the engagement. Select the best response.

   a. Which of the following is an effective audit planning procedure that helps prevent misunderstandings and inefficient use of audit personnel?

     (1) Arrange to make copies, for inclusion in the working papers, of those client-supporting documents examined by the auditor.

     (2) Arrange to provide the client with copies of the audit programs to be used during the audit.

     (3) Arrange a preliminary conference with the client to discuss audit objectives, fees, timing, and other information.

     (4) Arrange to have the auditor prepare and post any necessary adjusting or reclassification entries prior to final closing.

   b. An auditor is planning an audit engagement for a new client in a business with which he is unfamiliar. Which of the following would be the most useful source of information during the preliminary planning stage, when the auditor is trying to obtain a general understanding of audit problems that might be encountered?

     (1) Client manuals of accounts and charts of accounts.

     (2) AICPA Industry Audit Guides.

     (3) Prior-year working papers of the predecessor auditor.

     (4) Latest annual and interim financial statements issued by the client.

8-23 (Objective 8-2)   The following questions pertain to the predecessor/successor auditor relationship. Choose the best response.

   a. When approached to perform an audit for the first time, the CPA should make inquiries of the predecessor auditor. This is a necessary procedure because the predecessor may be able to provide the successor with information that will assist the successor in determining whether

     (1) the predecessor's work should be used.

     (2) the company follows the policy of rotating its auditors.

     (3) in the predecessor's opinion internal control of the company has been satisfactory.

     (4) the engagement should be accepted.

   b. Hawkins requested permission to communicate with the predecessor auditor and review certain portions of the predecessor's working papers. The prospective client's refusal to permit this will bear directly on Hawkins' decision concerning the

     (1) adequacy of the preplanned audit program.

     (2) ability to establish consistency in application of accounting principles between years.

     (3) apparent scope limitation.

     (4) integrity of management.

   c. What is the responsibility of a successor auditor with respect to communicating with the predecessor auditor in connection with a prospective new audit client?

     (1) The successor auditor has *no* responsibility to contact the predecessor auditor.

     (2) The successor auditor should obtain permission from the prospective client to contact the predecessor auditor.

     (3) The successor auditor should contact the predecessor regardless of whether the prospective client authorizes contact.

     (4) The successor auditor need *not* contact the predecessor if the successor is aware of all available relevant facts.

8-24 (Objectives 8-6, 8-7)   The following questions concern working papers. Choose the best response.

   a. Which of the following is *not* a primary purpose of audit working papers?

     (1) To coordinate the audit.

(2) To assist in preparation of the audit report.

(3) To support the financial statements.

(4) To provide evidence of the audit work performed.

b. During an audit engagement, pertinent data are compiled and included in the audit working papers. The working papers primarily are considered to be

(1) a client-owned record of conclusions reached by the auditors who performed the engagement.

(2) evidence supporting financial statements.

(3) support for the auditor's representations as to compliance with generally accepted auditing standards.

(4) a record to be used as a basis for the following year's engagement.

c. Although the quantity, type, and content of working papers will vary with the circumstances, the working papers generally would include the

(1) copies of those client records examined by the auditor during the course of the engagement.

(2) evaluation of the efficiency and competence of the audit staff assistants by the partner responsible for the audit.

(3) auditor's comments concerning the efficiency and competence of client management personnel.

(4) auditing procedures followed and the testing performed in obtaining evidential matter.

8-25 (Objective 8-5)   The following questions concern the use of analytical procedures during the planning phase of an audit. Select the best response.

a. Analytical procedures used in planning an audit should focus on identifying

(1) material weaknesses of internal control.

(2) the predictability of financial data from individual transactions.

(3) the various assertions that are embodied in the financial statements.

(4) areas that may represent specific risks relevant to the audit.

b. A basic premise underlying the application of analytical procedures is that

(1) the study of financial ratios is an acceptable alternative to the investigation of unusual fluctuations.

(2) statistical tests of financial information may lead to the discovery of material misstatements in the financial statements.

(3) plausible relationships among data may reasonably be expected to exist and continue in the absence of known conditions to the contrary.

(4) these procedures *cannot* replace tests of controls, substantive tests of transactions, and tests of details of balances.

DISCUSSION QUESTIONS AND PROBLEMS

8-26 (Objectives 8-2, 8-3, 8-4)   In late spring, you are advised of a new assignment as in-charge accountant of your CPA firm's recurring annual audit of a major client, the Lancer Company. You are given the engagement letter for the audit covering the current calendar year and a list of personnel assigned to this engagement. It is your responsibility to plan and supervise the field work for the engagement.

Required
Discuss the necessary preparation and planning for the Lancer Company annual audit before beginning field work at the client's office. In your discussion, include the sources you should consult, the type of information you should seek, the preliminary plans and preparation you should make for the field work, and any actions you should take relative to the staff assigned to the engagement.*

*AICPA adapted.

8-27 (Objective 8-3)   Generally accepted accounting principles set certain requirements for disclosure of related parties and related party transactions. Similarly, the SASs set requirements for the audit of related parties and related party transactions. For this problem, you are expected to research appropriate SFASs and SASs.

Required

    a. Define *related party* as used for generally accepted accounting principles and explain the disclosure requirements for related parties and related party transactions.

    b. Explain why disclosure of related party transactions is relevant information for decision makers.

    c. List the most important related parties who are likely to be involved in related party transactions.

    d. List several different types of related party transactions that could take place in a company.

    e. Discuss ways the auditor can determine the existence of related parties and related party transactions.

    f. For each type of related party transaction, discuss different ways the auditor can evaluate whether they are recorded on an arm's-length basis, assuming that the auditor knows the transactions exist.

    g. Assume that you know the material related party transactions occurred and were transacted at significantly less favorable terms than ordinarily occur when business is done with independent parties. The client refuses to disclose these facts in the financial statements. What are your responsibilities?

8-28 (Objective 8-4)   The minutes of the board of directors of the Marygold Catalog Company for the year ended December 31, 1999 were provided to you.

MEETING OF FEBRUARY 16, 1999

Ruth Jackson, chairman of the board, called the meeting to order at 4:00 PM. The following directors were in attendance:

John Aronson	Licorine Phillips
Fred Brick	Lucille Renolds
Oron Carlson	J. T. Smith
Homer Jackson	Raymond Werd
Ruth Jackson	Ronald Wilder

The minutes of the meeting of October 11, 1998 were read and approved.

Homer Jackson, president, discussed the new marketing plan for wider distribution of catalogs in the southwestern U.S. market. He made a motion for approval of increased expenditures of approximately $50,000 for distribution costs that was seconded by Wilder and unanimously passed.

The unresolved dispute with the Internal Revenue Service over the tax treatment of leased office buildings was discussed with Cecil Makay, attorney. In Mr. Makay's opinion, the matter would not be resolved for several months and may result in an unfavorable settlement.

J. T. Smith moved that the computer equipment that was no longer being used in the Kingston office, because of new equipment acquired in 1998, be donated to the Kingston vocational school for use in their repair and training program. John Aronson seconded the motion and it unanimously passed.

Annual cash dividends were unanimously approved as being payable April 30, 1999, for stockholders of record April 15, 1999, as follows:

Class A common—$10 per share
Class B common—$5 per share

Officers' bonuses for the year ended December 31, 1998, were approved for payment March 1, 1999, as follows:

Homer Jackson—President	$26,000
Lucille Renolds—Vice president	12,000
Ronald Wilder—Controller	12,000
Fred Brick—Secretary-treasurer	9,000

Meeting adjourned 6:30 PM

Fred Brick, Secretary

MEETING OF SEPTEMBER 15, 1999

Ruth Jackson, chairman of the board, called the meeting to order at 4:00 PM. The following directors were in attendance:

John Aronson	Licorine Phillips
Fred Brick	Lucille Renolds
Oron Carlson	J. T. Smith
Homer Jackson	Raymond Werd
Ruth Jackson	Ronald Wilder

The minutes of the meeting of February 16, 1999, were read and approved.

Homer Jackson, president, discussed the improved sales and financial condition for 1999. He was pleased with the results of the catalog distribution and cost control for the company. No action was taken.

The nominations for officers were made as follows:

President	—Homer Jackson
Vice president	—Lucille Renolds
Controller	—Ronald Wilder
Secretary-treasurer	—Fred Brick

The nominees were elected by unanimous voice vote.

Salary increases of 6 percent, exclusive of bonuses, were recommended for all officers for the year 2000. Homer Jackson moved that such salary increases be approved, seconded by J. T. Smith, and unanimously approved.

	SALARY	
	1999	2000
Homer Jackson, President	$90,000	$95,000
Lucille Renolds, Vice president	60,000	63,600
Ronald Wilder, Controller	60,000	63,600
Fred Brick, Secretary-treasurer	40,000	42,000

Ronald Wilder moved that the company consider adopting a pension/profit-sharing plan for all employees as a way to provide greater incentive for employees to stay with the company. Considerable discussion ensued. It was agreed without adoption that Wilder should discuss the legal and tax implications with attorney Cecil Makay and a CPA firm reputed to be knowledgeable about pension and profit-sharing plans, Able and Better, CPAs.

Ronald Wilder discussed expenditure of $58,000 for acquisition of a new computer for the Kingston office to replace equipment that was purchased in 1998 and has proven ineffective. A settlement has been tentatively reached to return the equipment for a refund of $21,000. Wilder moved that both transactions be approved, seconded by Jackson, and unanimously adopted.

Fred Brick moved that a loan of $36,000, from the Kingston Federal Bank and Trust, be approved. The interest is floating at 2 percent above prime. The collateral is to be the new computer equipment being installed in the Kingston office. A checking account, with a minimum balance of $2,000 at all times until the loan is repaid, must be opened and maintained if the loan is granted. Seconded by Phillips and unanimously approved.

Lucille Renolds, chair of the audit committee, moved that the CPA firm of Moss and Lawson be selected again for the company's annual audit and related tax work for the year ended December 31, 1999. Seconded by Aronson and unanimously approved.

Meeting adjourned 6:40 PM.

Fred Brick, Secretary

Required

    a. How do you, as the auditor, know that all minutes has been made available to you?

    b. Read the minutes of the meetings of February 16 and September 15. Use the following format to list and explain information that is relevant for the 1999 audit:

Information Relevant to 1999 Audit	Audit Action Required
1.	
2.	

    c. Read the minutes of the meeting of February 16, 1999. Did any of that information pertain to the December 31, 1998 audit? Explain what the auditor should have done during the December 31, 1998, audit with respect to 1999 minutes.

8-29 (Objectives 8-4, 8-5) You are engaged in the annual audit of the financial statements of Maulack Company, a medium-sized wholesale company that manufactures light fixtures. The company has 25 stockholders. During your review of the minutes, you observe that the president's salary has been increased substantially over the preceding year by action of the board of directors. His present salary is much greater than salaries paid to presidents of companies of comparable size and is clearly excessive. You determine that the method of computing the president's salary was changed for the year under audit. In previous years, the president's salary was consistently based on sales. In the latest year, however, his salary was based on net income before income taxes. The Maulack Company is in a cyclical industry and would have had an extremely profitable year except that the increase in the president's salary siphoned off much of the income that would have accrued to the stockholders. The president is a substantial stockholder.

Required

    a. What is the implication of this condition on the fair presentation of the financial statements?

    b. Discuss your responsibility for disclosing this situation.

    c. Discuss the effect, if any, that the situation has on your auditor's opinion as to

        (1) the fairness of the presentation of the financial statements.

        (2) the consistency of the application of accounting principles.*

8-30 (Objectives 8-6, 8-7) The preparation of working papers is an integral part of a CPA's audit of financial statements. On a recurring engagement, a CPA reviews audit programs and working papers from the prior audit while planning the current audit to determine their usefulness for the current engagement.

Required

    a. What are the purposes or functions of audit working papers?

*AICPA adapted.

b. What records may be included in audit working papers?

c. What factors affect the CPA's judgment of the type and content of the working papers for an engagement?*

8-31 (**Objectives 8-6, 8-7**)   Do the following with regard to the working paper for the Vandervoort Company shown below.

a. List the deficiencies in the working paper.

b. For each deficiency, state how the working paper could be improved.

c. Prepare an improved working paper, using an electronic spreadsheet software program. Include an indication of the audit work done as well as the analysis of the client data. (Instructor's option.)

	Vandervoort Company **A/C # 110–Notes Receivable** **12-31-99**						**Schedule** N-1 **Date**	
							Prepared by JD 1-21-00	
							Approved by PP 2-15-00	

	APEX CO.		**AJAX, INC.**		**J.J. CO.**		**P. SMITH**		**MARTIN- PETERSON**		**TENT CO.**			
Date made	6/15/98		11/21/98		11/1/98		7/26/99		5/12/98		9/3/99			
Date due	6/15/00		Demand		$200/mo.		$1,000/mo.		Demand		$400/mo.			
Paid to date	None		Paid		12/31/99		9/30/99		Paid		11/30/99			
Face amount	$5,000	x	$3,591	x	$13,180	x	$25,000	x	$2,100	x	$12,000	x		
Interest rate	5%		5%		5%		5%		5%		6%			
Value of security	None		None		$24,000		$50,000		None		$10,000			
Note Receivable:														
12/31/98 bal.	$4,000	py	$3,591	py	$12,780	py	$0		$2,100	py	$ 0			
Additions							25,000				12,000			
Payments	(1,000)	x	(3,591)	x	(2,400)	x	(5,000)	x	(2,100)	x	(1,600)	x		
12/31/99 bal.	$3,000		$0		$10,380		$20,000		$ 0		$10,400		TOTALS	
Current	$3,000		–		$ 2,400		$12,000		–		$ 4,800		$22,200	tb
Long-term	–		–		7,980		8,000		–		5,600		21,580	tb
Total end. bal.	$3,000	@	$0		$10,380	@	$20,000	@	$ 0		$10,400	@	$43,780	tb
Interest Receivable:														
12/31/98 bal.	$104	py	$0	py	$24	py	$0		$0	py	$0		$128	
Interest earned	175	x	102	x	577	x	468	x	105	x	162	x	1,589	#
Interest received	0		(102)	x	(601)	x	(200)	x	(105)	x	(108)	x	(1,116)	
12/31/99 bal.	$ 279		$ 0		$ 0		$ 268		$ 0		$ 54		$ 601	a/r

x	Tested
py	Agrees with prior year's working papers.
tb	Agrees with working trial balance.
#	Agrees with miscellaneous income analysis in operations w/p.
a/r	Agrees with A/R lead schedule.

*AICPA adapted.

8-32 (Objectives 8-2, 8-4)   Winston Black was an audit partner in the firm of Henson, Davis & Company. He was in the process of reviewing the working papers for the audit of a new client, McMullan Resources. McMullan was in the business of heavy construction. Black was conducting his first review after the field work was substantially complete. Normally, he would have done an initial review during the planning phase as required by his firm's policies; however, he had been overwhelmed by an emergency with his largest and most important client. He rationalized not reviewing audit planning information because (1) the audit was being overseen by Sarah Beale, a manager in whom he had confidence, and (2) he could "recover" from any problems during his end-of-audit review.

Now, Black found that he was confronted with a couple of problems. First, he found that the firm may have accepted McMullan without complying with its new client acceptance procedures. McMullan came to Henson, Davis on a recommendation from a friend of Black's. Black got "credit" for the new business, which was important to him because it would affect his compensation from the firm. Because Black was busy, he told Beale to conduct a new client acceptance review and let him know if there were any problems. He never heard from Beale and assumed everything was okay. In reviewing Beale's preaudit planning documentation, he saw a check mark in the box "Contact prior auditors" but found no details indicating what was done. When he asked Beale about this, she responded with the following:

"I called Gardner Smith [the responsible partner with McMullan's prior audit firm] and left a phone mail message for him. He never returned my call. I talked to Ted McMullan about the change, and he told me that he informed Gardner about the change and that Gardner said, "Fine, I'll help in any way I can." Ted said Gardner sent over copies of analyses of fixed assets and equity accounts, which Ted gave to me. I asked Ted why they replaced Gardner's firm, and he told me it was over the tax contingency issue and the size of their fee. Other than that, Ted said the relationship was fine."

The tax contingency issue that Beale referred to was a situation in which McMullan had entered into litigation with a bank from which it had received a loan. The result of the litigation was that the bank forgave several hundred thousand dollars in debt. This was a windfall to McMullan, and they recorded it as a gain, taking the position that it was non-taxable. The prior auditors disputed this position and insisted that a contingent tax liability existed that required disclosure. This upset McMullan, but they agreed in order to receive an unqualified opinion. Before hiring Henson, Davis as their new auditors, McMullan requested that Henson, Davis review the situation. Henson, Davis believed the contingency was remote and agreed to the elimination of the disclosure.

The second problem involved a long-term contract with a customer in Montreal. Under GAAP, McMullan was required to recognize income on this contract using the percentage-of-completion method. The contract was partially completed as of year-end and had a material effect on the financial statements. When Black went to review the copy of the contract in the working papers, he found three things. First, there was a contract summary that set out its major features. Second, there was a copy of the contract written in French. Third, there was a signed confirmation confirming the terms and status of the contract. The space requesting information about any contract disputes was left blank, indicating no such problems.

Black's concern about the contract was that to recognize income in accordance with GAAP, the contract had to be enforceable. Often, contracts contain a cancellation clause that might mitigate enforceability. Because he was not able to read French, Black couldn't tell whether the contract contained such a clause. When he asked Beale about this, she responded that she had asked the company's vice-president for the Canadian division about the contract and he told her that it was their standard contract. The company's standard contract did have a cancellation clause in it, but it required mutual agreement and could not be cancelled unilaterally by the buyer.

Required

a. Evaluate and discuss whether Henson, Davis & Company complied with generally accepted auditing standards in their acceptance of McMullan Resources as a new client. What can they do at this point in the engagement to resolve deficiencies if they exist?

b. Evaluate and discuss whether sufficient audit work has been done with regard to McMullan's Montreal contract. If not, what more should be done?

c. Evaluate and discuss whether Black and Beale conducted themselves in accordance with generally accepted auditing standards.

INTERNET PROBLEM 8-1: INDUSTRY RESEARCH AND CLIENT ACCEPTANCE

Reference the CW site. The vignette at the beginning of Chapter 6 in the text contains a brief description of the ZZZZ Best fraud. One area in which the auditors were criticized in that audit was the auditors' lack of industry knowledge. With hindsight, it appeared that the fraud should have been easily detected because ZZZZ Best's large restoration contracts were in excess of $7 million, whereas the largest restoration jobs on record in the insurance restoration industry were less than $3 million. This problem requires students to use the Internet to research industry data to determine the reasonableness of reported unit sales.

MATERIALITY AND RISK

EXPLAIN TO ME ONE MORE TIME THAT YOU DID A GOOD JOB, BUT THE COMPANY WENT BROKE

Maxwell Spencer is a senior partner in his firm, and one of his regular duties is to attend the firm's annual training session for newly hired auditors. He loves doing this because it gives him a chance to share his many years of experience with inexperienced people who have bright and receptive minds. He covers several topics formally during the day and then sits around and "shoots the breeze" with participants during the evening hours. Here we listen to what he is saying.

Suppose you are a retired 72-year-old man. You and your wife, Minnie, live on your retirement fund, which you elected to manage yourself, rather than receive income from an annuity. You decide that your years in business prepared you with the ability to earn a better return than the annuity would provide.

So when you retired and got your bundle, you called your broker and discussed with him what you should do with it. He tells you the most important thing is to protect your principal and recommends that you buy bonds. You settle on three issues that your broker and his firm believe are good ones, with solid balance sheets: (1) a utility company, (2) a fast-growing alternative energy company, and (3) a major county in Southern California. Now all you have to do is sit back and clip your coupons.

Ah, but the best made plans of mice and men. . . . First, the utility company goes broke, and you can look forward to recovering only a few cents on the dollar over several years. Then, the alternative energy company fails, and you might get something back—eventually. Finally, the county has a scandal and has to default on all of its outstanding bonds. A recovery plan is initiated, but don't hold your breath. Your best strategy is to apply for a job at McDonald's. They hire older people, don't they?

Now what could the auditors of these three entities ever say to you about how they planned and conducted their audits and decided to issue an unqualified opinion that would justify that opinion in your mind? You don't care about business failure versus audit failure, or risk assessment and reliability of audit evidence or any of that technical mumbo jumbo. The auditors were supposed to be there for you when you needed them, and they weren't. And materiality? Anything that would have indicated a problem is material to you.

The message is, folks, that it's a lot easier to sweat over doing a tough audit right than it is to justify your judgments and decisions after it's too late. And God help you if you think that a harmed investor will ever see things from your point of view.

LEARNING OBJECTIVES

After studying this chapter, you should be able to

9-1 Apply the concept of materiality to the audit.

9-2 Make a preliminary judgment about what amounts to consider material.

9-3 Allocate preliminary materiality to segments of the audit during planning.

9-4 Use materiality to evaluate audit findings.

9-5 Define risk in auditing.

9-6 Describe the audit risk model and its components.

9-7 Consider the impact of business risk on acceptable audit risk.

9-8 Consider the impact of several factors on the assessment of inherent risk.

9-9 Discuss risk for segments and measurement difficulties.

9-10 Discuss how materiality and risk are related and integrated into the audit process.

The scope paragraph in auditors' reports includes two important phrases that are directly related to materiality and risk. These phrases are emphasized in italic print in the following two sentences of a standard scope paragraph.

- We conducted our audits in accordance with generally accepted auditing standards. Those standards require that we plan and perform the audit to obtain reasonable assurance about whether the financial statements are free of material misstatement.

The phrase *obtain reasonable assurance* is intended to inform users that auditors do not guarantee or ensure the fair presentation of the financial statements. The phrase communicates that there is some *risk* that the financial statements are not fairly stated even when the opinion is unqualified.

The phrase *free of material misstatement* is intended to inform users that the auditor's responsibility is limited to *material* financial information. Materiality is important because it is impractical for auditors to provide assurances on immaterial amounts.

Thus, materiality and risk are fundamental concepts that are important to planning the audit and designing the audit approach. This chapter shows how these concepts fit into the planning phase of the audit.

There is a close relationship between this chapter and Chapters 6 and 8. Chapter 6 discussed the auditor's responsibilities, transaction cycles, and audit objectives. In this chapter, both materiality and risk are applied to the concepts studied in these topics. The first part of Chapter 8 dealt with planning the audit, primarily the first four parts, which are shown in the margin below. This chapter deals with the fifth part, which is shaded in the margin. A considerable amount of the information that auditors acquire and document during the first four parts of planning is used when the auditor decides materiality and assesses risks.

MATERIALITY

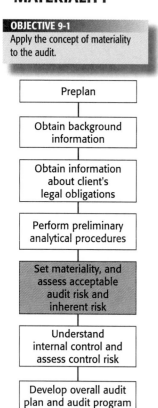

OBJECTIVE 9-1
Apply the concept of materiality to the audit.

Preplan

Obtain background information

Obtain information about client's legal obligations

Perform preliminary analytical procedures

Set materiality, and assess acceptable audit risk and inherent risk

Understand internal control and assess control risk

Develop overall audit plan and audit program

As was shown in Chapter 3, materiality is a major consideration in determining the appropriate audit report to issue. The concepts of materiality discussed in this chapter are directly related to those in Chapter 3.

FASB 2 has defined **materiality** as

- The magnitude of an omission or misstatement of accounting information that, in the light of surrounding circumstances, makes it *probable* that the judgment of a reasonable person relying on the information would have been changed or influenced by the omission or misstatement. [italics added]

The auditor's responsibility is to determine whether financial statements are materially misstated. If the auditor determines that there is a material misstatement, he or she will bring it to the client's attention so that a correction can be made. If the client refuses to correct the statements, a qualified or an adverse opinion must be issued, depending on how material the misstatement is. Therefore, auditors must have a thorough knowledge of the application of materiality.

A careful reading of the FASB definition reveals the difficulty that auditors have in applying materiality in practice. The definition emphasizes reasonable users who rely on the statements to make decisions. Therefore, auditors must have knowledge of the likely users of their clients' statements and the decisions that are being made. For example, if an auditor knows that financial statements will be relied on in a buy–sell agreement for the entire business, the amount that the auditor considers material may be smaller than for an otherwise similar audit. In practice, auditors may not know who all users are or what decisions will be made.

There are five closely related steps in applying materiality. They are shown in Figure 9-1 and discussed in the next few sections of this chapter. The steps start with setting a preliminary judgment about materiality and allocating this estimate to the segments of the

FIGURE 9-1   Steps in Applying Materiality

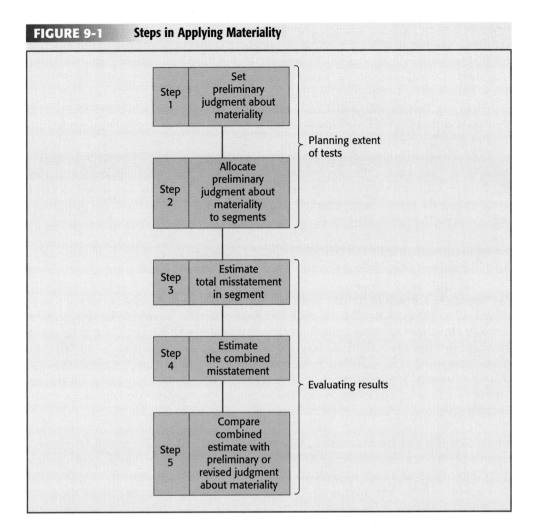

audit. As shown in the first bracket in Figure 9-1, these two steps are done as part of planning and are the primary topics of the discussion of materiality in this chapter. Estimation of the amount of misstatements in each segment takes place throughout the audit. The final two steps are done near the end of the audit during the engagement completion phase. These three steps are shown in the second bracket in Figure 9-1 and are done as part of evaluating the results of audit tests.

SET PRELIMINARY JUDGMENT ABOUT MATERIALITY

OBJECTIVE 9-2
Make a preliminary judgment about what amounts to consider material.

Ideally, an auditor decides early in the audit the combined amount of misstatements in the financial statements that would be considered material. SAS 47 (AU 312) defines the amount as the **preliminary judgment about materiality**. This judgment need not be quantified but often is. It is called a preliminary judgment about materiality because it is a professional judgment and may change during the engagement if circumstances change.

The preliminary judgment about materiality (step 1 in Figure 9-1) is thus the maximum amount by which the auditor believes the statements could be misstated and still *not* affect the decisions of reasonable users. (Conceptually, this would be an amount that is $1 less than materiality as defined by the FASB. Preliminary materiality is defined in this manner as a convenience in application.) This judgment is one of the most important decisions the auditor makes. It requires considerable professional judgment.

The reason for setting a preliminary judgment about materiality is to help the auditor plan the appropriate evidence to accumulate. If the auditor sets a low dollar amount, more evidence is required than for a high amount. Examine the financial statements of Hillsburg Hardware Co. on pages 200–201. What do you think is the combined amount of misstatements that would affect decisions of reasonable users? Do you believe that a $100 misstatement would affect users' decisions? If so, the amount of evidence required for the audit is likely to be beyond that for which the management of Hillsburg Hardware would be willing to pay. Do you believe that a $1 million misstatement would be material? Most experienced auditors would say that amount is far too large as a combined materiality amount in these circumstances.

The auditor will often change the preliminary judgment about materiality during the audit. When that is done, the new judgment is called a **revised judgment about materiality**. Reasons for using a revised judgment can include a change in one of the factors used to determine the preliminary judgment or a decision by the auditor that the preliminary judgment was too large or too small.

Factors Affecting Judgment

Several factors affect setting a preliminary judgment about materiality for a given set of financial statements. The most important of these are discussed below.

Materiality Is a Relative Rather Than an Absolute Concept A misstatement of a given magnitude might be material for a small company, whereas the same dollar misstatement could be immaterial for a large one. For example, a total misstatement of $1 million would be extremely material for Hillsburg Hardware Co. because, as shown on pages 200–201, total assets are about $3 million and net income before taxes is about $285,000. A misstatement of this amount would be immaterial for a company such as IBM, which has total assets and net income of several billion dollars. Hence, it is impossible to establish any dollar-value guidelines for a preliminary judgment about materiality applicable to all audit clients.

Bases Are Needed for Evaluating Materiality Because materiality is relative, it is necessary to have bases for establishing whether misstatements are material. *Net income before taxes* is normally the primary base for deciding what is material because it is regarded as a critical item of information for users. Some firms use a different primary base because net income often fluctuates considerably from year to year and therefore does not provide a stable base. Examples of other primary bases used by firms are net sales, gross profit, and total assets. In addition to establishing a primary base, it also is important to decide whether the misstatements could materially affect the reasonableness of other possible bases such as current assets, total assets, current liabilities, and owners' equity.

Assume that for a given company, an auditor decided that a misstatement of income before taxes of $100,000 or more would be material, but a misstatement of $250,000 or more would be material for current assets. It would be inappropriate for the auditor to use a preliminary judgment about materiality of $250,000 for both income before taxes and current assets. The auditor must therefore plan to find all misstatements affecting income before taxes that exceed the preliminary judgment about materiality of $100,000. Because most misstatements affect both the income statement and balance sheet, the auditor will not be greatly concerned about the possibility of misstatement of current assets exceeding $250,000 and will use a materiality level of $100,000 for most tests. However, some misstatements, such as misclassifying a long-term asset as a current one, affect only the balance sheet. The auditor will therefore also need to plan the audit with the $250,000 preliminary judgment about materiality for certain tests of current assets.

Qualitative Factors Also Affect Materiality Certain types of misstatements are likely to be more important to users than others, even if the dollar amounts are the same. For example:

• Amounts involving fraud are usually considered more important than unintentional errors of equal dollar amounts because fraud reflects on the honesty and reliability of the management or other personnel involved. To illustrate, most users would consider an intentional misstatement of inventory as being more important than clerical errors in inventory of the same dollar amount.

- Misstatements that are otherwise minor may be material if there are possible consequences arising from contractual obligations. An example is when net working capital included in the financial statements is only a few hundred dollars more than the required minimum in a loan agreement. If the correct net working capital were less than the required minimum putting the loan in default, the current and noncurrent liability classifications would be materially affected.
- Misstatements that are otherwise immaterial may be material if they affect a trend in earnings. For example, if reported income has increased 3 percent annually for the past 5 years but income for the current year has declined 1 percent, that change of trend may be material. Similarly, a misstatement that would cause a loss to be reported as a profit would be of concern.

The FASB and AICPA are currently unwilling to provide specific materiality guidelines to practitioners. The concern is that such guidelines might be applied without considering all the complexities that should affect the auditor's final decision. Therefore, this chapter provides illustrative guidelines to show the application of materiality. They are intended only to help you better understand the concept of applying materiality in practice. The guidelines are stated in Figure 9-2 in the form of a policy guideline for a CPA firm. Notice that the guidelines are formulas using one or more bases and a range of percentages. Guidelines such as the ones presented require considerable professional judgment.

Illustrative Guidelines

FIGURE 9-2   Illustrative Materiality Guidelines

BERGER AND ANTHONY, CPAs
Gary, Indiana 46405

POLICY STATEMENT   Charles G. Berger
No. 32 IC   Joe Anthony
Title: Materiality Guidelines

Professional judgment is to be used at all times in setting and applying materiality guidelines. As a general guideline, the following policies are to be applied:

1. The combined total of misstatements in the financial statements exceeding 10 percent is normally considered material. A combined total of less than 5 percent is presumed to be immaterial in the absence of qualitative factors. Combined misstatements between 5 percent and 10 percent require the greatest amount of professional judgment to determine their materiality.

2. The 5 percent to 10 percent must be measured in relation to the appropriate base. Many times there is more than one base to which misstatements should be compared. The following guides are recommended in selecting the appropriate base:
   a. *Income statement.* Combined misstatements in the income statement should ordinarily be measured at 5 percent to 10 percent of operating income before taxes. A guideline of 5 percent to 10 percent may be inappropriate in a year in which income is unusually large or small. When operating income in a given year is not considered representative, it is desirable to substitute as a base a more representative income measure. For example, average operating income for a 3-year period may be used as the base.
   b. *Balance sheet.* Combined misstatements in the balance sheet should originally be evaluated for current assets, current liabilities, and total assets. For current assets and current liabilities, the guidelines should be between 5 percent and 10 percent, applied in the same way as for the income statement. For total assets, the guidelines should be between 3 percent and 6 percent, applied in the same way as for the income statement.

3. Qualitative factors should be carefully evaluated on all audits. In many instances, they are more important than the guidelines applied to the income statement and balance sheet. The intended uses of the financial statements and the nature of the information in the statements, including footnotes, must be carefully evaluated.

Using the illustrative guideliness in Figure 9-2, we will now present a preliminary judgment about materiality for Hillsburg Hardware Co. The guidelines are as follows:

	Preliminary Judgment about Materiality (Rounded)			
	Minimum		Maximum	
	Percentage	Dollar Amount	Percentage	Dollar Amount
Earnings from operations	5	$ 19,000	10	$ 37,000
Current assets	5	128,000	10	255,000
Total assets	3	92,000	6	184,000
Current liabilities	5	33,000	10	66,000

If the auditor for Hillsburg Hardware decides that the general guidelines are reasonable, the first step is to evaluate whether any qualitative factors significantly affect the materiality judgment. If not, the auditor must decide that if combined misstatements of operating income before taxes were less than $19,000, the statements would be considered fairly stated. If the combined misstatements exceeded $37,000, the statements would not be considered fairly stated. If the misstatements were between $19,000 and $37,000, a more careful consideration of all facts would be required. The auditor then applies the same process to the other three bases.

ALLOCATE PRELIMINARY JUDGMENT ABOUT MATERIALITY TO SEGMENTS (TOLERABLE MISSTATEMENT)

OBJECTIVE 9-3
Allocate preliminary materiality to segments of the audit during planning.

The **allocation of the preliminary judgment about materiality** to segments (step 2 in Figure 9-1) is necessary because evidence is accumulated by segments rather than for the financial statements as a whole. If auditors have a preliminary judgment about materiality for each segment, it helps them decide the appropriate audit evidence to accumulate. For example, an auditor is likely to accumulate more evidence for an accounts receivable balance of $1,000,000 when a misstatement of $50,000 in accounts receivable is considered material than if $300,000 were material.

Most practitioners allocate materiality to balance sheet rather than income statement accounts. Most income statement misstatements have an equal effect on the balance sheet because of the double-entry bookkeeping system. Therefore, the auditor can allocate materiality to either income statement or balance sheet accounts. Because there are fewer balance sheet than income statement accounts in most audits and most audit procedures focus on balance sheet accounts, allocating materiality to balance sheet accounts is the most appropriate alternative.

When auditors allocate the preliminary judgment about materiality to account balances, the materiality allocated to any given account balance is referred to in SAS 39 (AU 350) as **tolerable misstatement**. For example, if an auditor decides to allocate $100,000 of a total preliminary judgment about materiality of $200,000 to accounts receivable, tolerable misstatement for accounts receivable is $100,000. This means that the auditor is willing to consider accounts receivable fairly stated if it is misstated by $100,000 or less.

There are three major difficulties in allocating materiality to balance sheet accounts (segments): auditors expect certain accounts to have more misstatements than others, both overstatements and understatements must be considered, and relative audit costs affect the allocation. All three of these difficulties are considered in the allocation in Figure 9-3.

Allocation Illustrated

Figure 9-3 illustrates the allocation approach followed by the senior, Fran Moore, for the audit of Hillsburg Hardware Co. It summarizes the balance sheet from page 200, combining certain accounts, and shows the allocation of total materiality of $37,000 (10 percent of

FIGURE 9-3	Tolerable Misstatement Allocated to Hillsburg Hardware Co.	
	Balance 12-31-99 (in Thousands)	Tolerable Misstatement (in Thousands)
Cash	$ 41	$ 1 (a)
Trade accounts receivable	948	22 (b)
Inventories	1,493	22 (b)
Other current assets	68	5 (c)
Property, plant, and equipment	517	4 (d)
Total assets	$3,067	
Trade accounts payable	$ 236	9 (e)
Notes payable—total	1,415	0 (a)
Accrued payroll and payroll tax	73	5 (c)
Accrued interest and dividends payable	102	0 (a)
Other liabilities	117	6 (c)
Capital stock and capital in excess of par	425	0 (a)
Retained earnings	699	NA (f)
Total liabilities and equity	$3,067	$74 (2 × $37)

NA = Not applicable.
(a) Zero or small tolerable misstatement because account can be completely audited at low cost and no misstatements are expected.
(b) Large tolerable misstatement because account is large and requires extensive sampling to audit the account.
(c) Large tolerable misstatement as a percent of account because account can be verified at extremely low cost, probably with analytical procedures, if tolerable misstatement is large.
(d) Small tolerable misstatement as a percent of account balance because most of the balance is in land and buildings, which is unchanged from the prior year and need not be audited.
(e) Moderately large tolerable misstatement because a relatively large number of misstatements are expected.
(f) Not applicable—retained earnings is a residual account that is affected by the net amount of the misstatements in the other accounts.

earnings from operations). The allocation approach followed by Moore for Hillsburg Hardware Co. is to use judgment in the allocation, subject to two arbitrary requirements established by Berger and Anthony, CPAs: tolerable misstatement for any account cannot exceed 60 percent of the preliminary judgment (60 percent of $37,000 = $22,000, rounded), and the sum of all tolerable misstatements cannot exceed twice the preliminary judgment about materiality (2 × $37,000 = $74,000).

The reason for the first requirement is to keep the auditor from allocating all of total materiality to one account. If, for example, all of the preliminary judgment of $37,000 is allocated to trade accounts receivable, a $37,000 misstatement in that account would be acceptable. However, it may not be acceptable to have such a large misstatement in one account, and even if it is acceptable, it would not allow for any misstatements in other accounts.

There are two reasons for permitting the sum of the tolerable misstatement to exceed overall materiality. First, it is unlikely that all accounts will be misstated by the full amount of tolerable misstatement. If, for example, other current assets have a tolerable misstatement of $5,000 but no misstatements are found in auditing those accounts, it means that the auditor, after the fact, could have allocated zero or a small tolerable misstatement to other current assets. It is common for auditors to find fewer misstatements than tolerable misstatement. Second, some accounts are likely to be overstated, whereas others are likely to be understated, resulting in a net amount that is likely to be less than overall materiality.

Notice in the allocation that the auditor is concerned about the combined effect on operating income of the misstatement of each balance sheet account. An overstatement of an asset account will therefore have the same effect on the income statement as an understatement of a liability account. In contrast, a misclassification in the balance sheet, such as a classification of a note payable as an account payable, will have no effect on operating income. The materiality of items not affecting the income statement must be considered separately.

Figure 9-3 also includes the rationale that Fran Moore followed in deciding tolerable misstatement for each account. For example, she concluded that it was unnecessary to assign any tolerable misstatement to notes payable, even though it is as large as inventories. If she had assigned $11,000 to each of those two accounts, more evidence would have been required in inventories, but the confirmation of the balance in notes payable would still have been required. It was therefore more efficient to allocate $22,000 to inventories and none to notes payable. Similarly, she allocated $5,000 to other current assets and accrued payroll and payroll tax, both of which are large compared with the recorded account balance. Moore did so because she believes that these accounts can be verified within $5,000 by using only analytical procedures, which are low cost. If tolerable misstatement were set lower, she would have to use more costly audit procedures such as documentation and confirmation.

In practice, it is often difficult to predict in advance which accounts are most likely to be misstated and whether misstatements are likely to be overstatements or understatements. Similarly, the relative costs of auditing different account balances often cannot be determined. It is therefore a difficult professional judgment to allocate the preliminary judgment about materiality to accounts. Accordingly, many accounting firms have developed rigorous guidelines and sophisticated statistical methods for doing so.

To summarize, the purpose of allocating the preliminary judgment about materiality to balance sheet accounts is to help the auditor decide the appropriate evidence to accumulate for each account. An aim of the allocation should be to minimize audit costs. Regardless of how the allocation is done, when the auditor has completed the audit, he or she must be confident that the combined misstatements in all accounts are less than or equal to the preliminary (or revised) judgment about materiality.

ESTIMATE MISSTATEMENT AND COMPARE WITH PRELIMINARY JUDGMENT

OBJECTIVE 9-4
Use materiality to evaluate audit findings.

The first two steps in applying materiality involve planning, whereas the last three (steps 3, 4, and 5 in Figure 9-1) result from performing audit tests. The last three steps are discussed in greater detail in later chapters. This section only shows their relationship to the first two.

When the auditor performs audit procedures for each segment of the audit, a worksheet is kept of all misstatements found. For example, assume that the auditor finds six client misstatements in a sample of 200 in testing inventory costs. These misstatements are used to estimate the *total* misstatements in inventory (step 3). The total is called an estimate or often a "projection" because only a sample, rather than the entire population, was audited. Estimation of projected misstatement is required by SAS 39 (AU 350). The projected misstatement amounts for each account are combined on the worksheet (step 4), and then the combined misstatement is compared with materiality (step 5).

Table 9-1 is used to illustrate the last three steps in applying materiality. For simplicity, only three accounts are included. The estimated misstatements are calculated based on actual audit tests. Assume, for example, that in auditing inventory, the auditor found $3,500 of net overstatement amounts in a sample of $50,000 of the total population of $450,000. One way to calculate the estimate of the misstatements is to make a direct projection from the sample to the population and add an estimate for sampling error. The calculation of the **direct projection estimate of misstatement** is:

$$\frac{\text{Net misstatements in the sample (\$3,500)}}{\text{Total sampled (\$50,000)}} \times \begin{array}{c}\text{Total recorded} \\ \text{population value} \\ \text{(\$450,000)}\end{array} = \begin{array}{c}\text{Direct projection} \\ \text{estimate of} \\ \text{misstatement} \\ \text{(\$31,500)}\end{array}$$

The direct projection for accounts receivable of $12,000 is not illustrated.

The estimate for **sampling error** results because the auditor has sampled only a portion of the population (this is discussed in detail in Chapter 14 and 16). In this simplified

TABLE 9-1	Illustration of Comparison of Estimated Total Misstatement to Preliminary Judgment about Materiality			
		Estimated Misstatement Amount		
Account	**Tolerable Misstatement**	**Direct Projection**	**Sampling Error**	**Total**
Cash	$ 4,000	$ 0	$ NA	$ 0
Accounts receivable	20,000	12,000	6,000	18,000
Inventory	36,000	31,500	15,750	47,250
Total estimated misstatement amount		$43,500	$16,800	$60,300
Preliminary judgment about materiality	$50,000			

NA = Not applicable.
Cash audited 100 percent.

example, the estimate for sampling error is assumed to be 50 percent of the direct projection of the misstatement amounts for the accounts where sampling was used (accounts receivable and inventory).

In combining the misstatements in Table 9-1, observe that the direct projection misstatements for the three accounts add to $43,500. However, the total sampling error is less than the sum of the individual sampling errors. This is because sampling error represents the maximum misstatement in account details not audited. It is unlikely that this maximum misstatement amount would exist in all accounts subjected to sampling. Thus, sampling methodology provides for determining a combined sampling error that takes this into consideration. Again, this is discussed in detail in Chapters 14 and 16.

Table 9-1 shows that total estimated misstatement of $60,300 exceeds the preliminary judgment about materiality of $50,000. Furthermore, the major area of difficulty is inventory, where estimated misstatement of $47,250 is significantly greater than tolerable misstatement of $36,000. Because the estimated combined misstatement exceeds the preliminary judgment, the financial statements are not acceptable. The auditor can either determine whether the estimated misstatement actually exceeds $50,000 by performing additional audit procedures or require the client to make an adjustment for estimated misstatements. If additional audit procedures are performed, they would be concentrated in the inventory area.

If the estimated net overstatement amount for inventory had been $28,000 ($18,000 plus $10,000 sampling error), the auditor probably would not need to expand audit tests because it would have met both the tests of tolerable misstatement ($36,000) and the preliminary judgment about materiality ($18,000 + $28,000 = $46,000 < $50,000). In fact, there would be some leeway with that amount because the results of cash and accounts receivable procedures indicate that those accounts are well within their tolerable misstatement limits. If the auditor were to approach the audit of the accounts in a sequential manner, the findings of the audit of the earlier accounts can be used to revise the tolerable misstatement established for other accounts. For example, in the illustration, if the auditor had audited cash and accounts receivable before inventories, tolerable misstatement for inventories could be increased.

Set preliminary judgment about materiality

Allocate preliminary judgment about materiality to segments

Estimate total misstatement in segment

Estimate the combined misstatement

Compare combined estimate with preliminary or revised judgment about materiality

RISK

There is a close relationship between materiality and risk. In the example in Table 9-1, the auditor estimated a $6,000 sampling error for accounts receivable, which was used to calculate the total estimated misstatement of $18,000 for comparison to tolerable misstatement of $20,000. The $6,000 sampling error *includes a risk* resulting from sampling. This is only one of several kinds of risks auditors must address.

OBJECTIVE 9-5
Define risk in auditing.

As we saw in Chapter 8, auditors accept some level of **risk** or uncertainty in performing the audit function. The auditor recognizes, for example, that there is uncertainty about the competence of evidence, uncertainty about the effectiveness of a client's internal controls, and uncertainty about whether the financial statements are fairly stated when the audit is completed.

An effective auditor recognizes that risks exist and deals with those risks in an appropriate manner. Most risks auditors encounter are difficult to measure and require careful thought to respond to appropriately. For example, assume the auditor determines that the client's industry is undergoing significant technological changes that affect both the client and the client's customers. This change may affect the obsolescence of the client's inventory, collectibility of accounts receivable, and perhaps even the ability of the client's business to continue. Responding to these risks properly is critical to achieving a high-quality audit.

Illustration Concerning Risks and Evidence

Before discussing the audit risk model, an illustration for a hypothetical company is provided in Table 9-2 as a frame of reference for the discussion. The table first shows that there are differences among cycles in the frequency and size of expected misstatements (A). For example, there are almost no misstatements expected in payroll and

TABLE 9-2	Illustration of Differing Evidence among Cycles				
		Sales and Collection Cycle	Acquisition and Payment Cycle	Payroll and Personnel Cycle	Inventory and Warehousing Cycle	Capital Acquisition and Repayment Cycle
A	Auditor's assessment of expectation of material misstatement before considering internal control (inherent risk)	Expect some misstatements (medium)	Expect many misstatements (high)	Expect few misstatements (low)	Expect many misstatements (high)	Expect few misstatements (low)
B	Auditor's assessment of effectiveness of internal controls to prevent or detect material misstatements (control risk)	Medium effectiveness (medium)	High effectiveness (low)	High effectiveness (low)	Low effectiveness (high)	Medium effectiveness (medium)
C	Auditor's willingness to permit material misstatements to exist after completing the audit (acceptable audit risk)	Low willingness (low)	Low willingness (low)	Low willingness (low)	Low willingness (low)	Low willingness (low)
D	Extent of evidence the auditor plans to accumulate (planned detection risk)	Medium level (medium)	Medium level (medium)	Low level (high)	High level (low)	Medium level (medium)

personnel but many in inventory and warehousing. The reason may be that the payroll transactions are highly routine, whereas there may be considerable complexities in recording inventory. Similarly, internal control is believed to differ in effectiveness among the five cycles (B). For example, internal controls in payroll and personnel are considered highly effective, whereas those in inventory and warehousing are considered ineffective. Finally, the auditor has decided on a low willingness that material misstatements exist after the audit is complete for all five cycles (C). It is common for auditors to want an equally low likelihood of misstatements for each cycle after the audit is finished to permit the issuance of an unqualified opinion.

The previous considerations (A, B, C) affect the auditor's decision about the appropriate extent of evidence to accumulate (D). For example, because the auditor expects few misstatements in payroll and personnel (A) and internal controls are effective (B), the auditor plans for less evidence (D) than for inventory and warehousing. Notice that the auditor has the same level of willingness to accept material misstatements after the audit is finished for all five cycles, but a different extent of evidence is needed for various cycles. The difference is caused by differences in the auditor's expectations of misstatements and assessment of internal control.

Audit Risk Model for Planning

OBJECTIVE 9-6
Describe the audit risk model and its components.

The primary way that auditors deal with risk in planning audit evidence is through the application of the **audit risk model**. The source of the audit risk model is the professional literature in SAS 39 (AU 350) on audit sampling and SAS 47 (AU 312) on materiality and risk. A thorough understanding of the model is essential to effective audit planning and to the study of the remaining chapters of this book.

The audit risk model is used primarily for planning purposes in deciding how much evidence to accumulate in each cycle. It is usually stated as follows:

$$PDR = \frac{AAR}{IR \times CR}$$

where:

$$PDR = \text{planned detection risk}$$

$$AAR = \text{acceptable audit risk}$$

$$IR = \text{inherent risk}$$

$$CR = \text{control risk}$$

A numerical example is provided for discussion, even though it is not practical to measure as precisely as these numbers imply. The numbers used are for the inventory and warehousing cycle in Table 9-2.

$$IR = 100\%$$

$$CR = 100\%$$

$$AAR = 5\%$$

$$PDR = \frac{.05}{1.0 \times 1.0} = .05 \text{ or } 5\%$$

TYPES OF RISKS

The four risks in the audit risk model are sufficiently important to merit detailed discussion. All four risks are discussed briefly in this section to provide an overview of the risks. Acceptable audit risk and inherent risk are then discussed in greater detail later in this chapter. Control risk is studied in detail in Chapter 10.

Planned Detection Risk

Planned detection risk is a measure of the risk that audit evidence for a segment will fail to detect misstatements exceeding a tolerable amount, should such misstatements exist. There are two key points about planned detection risk. First, it is dependent on the other three factors in the model. Planned detection risk will change only if the auditor changes one of the other factors. Second, it determines the amount of substantive evidence that the auditor plans to accumulate, inversely with the size of planned detection risk. If planned detection risk is reduced, the auditor needs to accumulate more evidence to achieve the reduced planned risk. For example, in Table 9-2 (D), planned detection risk is low for inventory and warehousing, which causes planned evidence to be high. The opposite is true for payroll and personnel.

The planned detection risk of .05 in the previous numerical example means the auditor plans to accumulate evidence until the risk of misstatements exceeding tolerable misstatement is reduced to 5 percent. If control risk had been .50 instead of 1.0, planned detection risk would be .10 and planned evidence could therefore be reduced.

Inherent Risk

As stated in Chapter 8, **inherent risk** is a measure of the auditor's assessment of the likelihood that there are material misstatements (errors or fraud) in a segment before considering the effectiveness of internal control. Inherent risk is the susceptibility of the financial statements to material misstatement, assuming no internal controls. If the auditor concludes that there is a high likelihood of misstatement, ignoring internal controls, the auditor would conclude that inherent risk is high. Internal controls are ignored in setting inherent risk because they are considered separately in the audit risk model as control risk. In Table 9-2 inherent risk (A) has been assessed high for inventory and warehousing and lower for payroll and personnel and capital acquisition and repayment. The assessment was likely based on discussions with management, knowledge of the company, and results in audits of previous years.

The relationship of inherent risk to planned detection risk and planned evidence is that inherent risk is inversely related to planned detection risk and directly related to evidence. Inherent risk for inventory and warehousing in Table 9-2 is high, and in the numerical example 1.0, which will result in a lower planned detection risk and more planned evidence than would be necessary had inherent risk been lower. Inherent risk is examined in greater detail later in the chapter.

In addition to increasing audit evidence for a higher inherent risk in a given audit area, it is also common to assign more experienced staff to that area and review the completed working papers more thoroughly. For example, if inherent risk for inventory obsolescence is extremely high, it makes sense for the CPA firm to have an experienced staff person perform more extensive tests for inventory obsolescence and to have the audit results more carefully reviewed.

Control Risk

Control risk is a measure of the auditor's assessment of the likelihood that misstatements exceeding a tolerable amount in a segment will not be prevented or detected by the client's internal controls. Control risk represents (1) an assessment of whether a client's internal controls are effective for preventing or detecting misstatements, and (2) the auditor's intention to make that assessment at a level below the maximum (100 percent) as part of the audit plan. For example, assume that the auditor concludes that internal controls are completely ineffective to prevent or detect misstatements. That is the likely conclusion for inventory and warehousing in Table 9-2 (B). The auditor would therefore assign a high, perhaps 100 percent, risk factor to control risk. The more effective the internal controls, the lower the risk factor that *could* be assigned to control risk.

The audit risk model shows the close relationship between inherent and control risks. For example, an inherent risk of 40 percent and a control risk of 60 percent affect planned detection risk and planned evidence the same as an inherent risk of 60 percent and a control risk of 40 percent. In both cases, multiplying IR by CR results in a denominator in the audit risk model of 24 percent. The combination of inherent risk and control risk can be thought of as the *expectation of misstatements after considering the effect of internal control.*

Inherent risk is the expectation of misstatements before considering the effect of internal control.

As with inherent risk, the relationship between control risk and planned detection risk is inverse, whereas the relationship between control risk and substantive evidence is direct. For example, if the auditor concludes that internal controls are effective, planned detection risk can be increased and evidence therefore decreased. The auditor can increase planned detection risk when controls are effective because effective internal controls reduce the likelihood of misstatements in the financial statements.

Before auditors can set control risk less than 100 percent, they must obtain an understanding of internal control, evaluate how well it should function based on the understanding, and test the internal controls for effectiveness. The first of these is the *understanding* requirement that relates to all audits. The latter two are the *assessment of control risk* steps that are required when the auditor *chooses* to assess control risk below maximum.

Understanding internal control, assessing control risk, and evaluating their impact on evidence requirements are so important that the entire next chapter is devoted to that topic. However, it should be noted here that if the auditor elects not to assess control risk below maximum, control risk must be set at 100 percent regardless of the actual effectiveness of the underlying controls. Use of the audit risk model in this circumstance then causes the auditor to control acceptable audit risk entirely through a low level of planned detection risk (assuming that inherent risk is high).

Acceptable Audit Risk

As stated in Chapter 8, **acceptable audit risk** is a measure of how willing the auditor is to accept that the financial statements may be materially misstated after the audit is completed and an unqualified opinion has been issued. When the auditor decides on a lower acceptable audit risk, it means the auditor wants to be more certain that the financial statements are *not* materially misstated. Zero risk would be certainty, and a 100 percent risk would be complete uncertainty. Complete assurance (zero risk) of the accuracy of the financial statements is not economically practical. It has already been established in Chapter 6 that the auditor cannot guarantee the complete absence of material misstatements.

Often, auditors refer to the terms **audit assurance, overall assurance,** or **level of assurance** instead of acceptable audit risk. Audit assurance or any of the equivalent terms is the complement of acceptable audit risk, that is, one minus acceptable audit risk. For example, acceptable audit risk of 2 percent is the same as audit assurance of 98 percent.

The concept of acceptable audit risk can be more easily understood by thinking in terms of a large number of audits, say, 10,000. What portion of these audits could include material misstatements without having an adverse effect on society? Certainly, the portion would be below 10 percent. It is probably much closer to 1 or one-half of 1 percent or perhaps even one-tenth of 1 percent. If an auditor believes that the appropriate percentage is 1 percent, then acceptable audit risk should be set at 1 percent, or perhaps lower, based on the specific circumstances.

Using the audit risk model, there is a direct relationship between acceptable audit risk and planned detection risk, and an inverse relationship between acceptable audit risk and planned evidence. For example, if the auditor decides to reduce acceptable audit risk, planned detection risk is thereby reduced and planned evidence must be increased. As stated in Chapter 8, auditors also often assign more experienced staff or review the working papers more extensively for a client with lower acceptable audit risk.

FACTORS AFFECTING ACCEPTABLE AUDIT RISK

Auditors must decide the appropriate acceptable audit risk for an audit, preferably during audit planning. First, auditors decide business risk and use business risk to modify acceptable audit risk.

Impact of Business Risk on Acceptable Audit Risk

OBJECTIVE 9-7
Consider the impact of business risk on acceptable audit risk.

Business risk is the risk that the auditor or audit firm will suffer harm because of a client relationship, even though the audit report rendered for the client was correct. For example, if a client declares bankruptcy after an audit is completed, the likelihood of a lawsuit against the CPA firm is reasonably high even if the quality of the audit was good.

Auditors disagree about whether business risk should be considered in planning the audit. Opponents of modifying evidence for business risk contend that auditors do not provide audit opinions for different levels of assurance and therefore should not provide more or less assurance because of business risk. Proponents contend that it is appropriate for auditors to accumulate additional evidence, assign more experienced personnel, and review the audit more thoroughly on audits where legal exposure is high, as long as the assurance level is not decreased below a reasonably high level when there is low business risk.

When auditors modify evidence for business risk, it is done by control of acceptable audit risk. The authors believe that a reasonably low acceptable audit risk is always desirable, but in some circumstances an even lower risk is needed because of business risk factors. Research has indicated that several factors affect business risk and therefore acceptable audit risk. Only three of those are discussed here: the degree to which external users rely on the statements, the likelihood that a client will have financial difficulties after the audit report is issued, and the integrity of management.

The Degree to Which External Users Rely on the Statements When external users place heavy reliance on the financial statements, it is appropriate that acceptable audit risk be decreased. When the statements are heavily relied on, a great social harm could result if a significant misstatement were to remain undetected in the financial statements. The cost of additional evidence can be more easily justified when the loss to users from material misstatements is substantial. Several factors are good indicators of the degree to which statements are relied on by external users:

SEC EDGAR

- *Client's size.* Generally speaking, the larger a client's operations, the more widely the statements will be used. The client's size, measured by total assets or total revenues, will have an effect on the acceptable audit risk.
- *Distribution of ownership.* The statements of publicly held corporations are normally relied on by many more users than those of closely held corporations. For these companies, the interested parties include the SEC, financial analysts, and the general public. The availability of the SEC's EDGAR Internet web site allows for easy downloading of financial statement information for publicly traded companies. Therefore, distribution of these financial statements is potentially increasing as a result of technology.
- *Nature and amount of liabilities.* When statements include a large amount of liabilities, they are more likely to be used extensively by actual and potential creditors than when there are few liabilities.

The Likelihood That a Client Will Have Financial Difficulties after the Audit Report Is Issued If a client is forced to file for bankruptcy or suffers a significant loss after completion of the audit, there is a greater chance of the auditor being required to defend the quality of the audit than if the client were under no financial strain. There is a natural tendency for those who lose money in a bankruptcy or because of a stock price reversal to file suit against the auditor. This can result from the honest belief that the auditor failed to conduct an adequate audit or from the users' desire to recover part of their loss regardless of the adequacy of the audit work.

In situations in which the auditor believes the chance of financial failure or loss is high and there is a corresponding increase in business risk for the auditor, acceptable audit risk should be reduced. If a subsequent challenge does occur, the auditor will then be in a better position to defend the audit results successfully. The total audit evidence and costs will increase, but this is justifiable because of the additional risk of lawsuits that the auditor faces.

It is difficult for an auditor to predict financial failure before it occurs, but certain factors are good indicators of its increased probability:

- *Liquidity position.* If a client is constantly short of cash and working capital, it indicates a future problem in paying bills. The auditor must assess the likelihood and significance of a steadily declining liquidity position.
- *Profits (losses) in previous years.* When a company has rapidly declining profits or increasing losses for several years, the auditor should recognize the future solvency problems that the client is likely to encounter. It is also important to consider the changing profits relative to the balance remaining in retained earnings.
- *Method of financing growth.* The more a client relies on debt as a means of financing, the greater the risk of financial difficulty if the client's operations become less successful. It is also important to evaluate whether fixed assets are being financed with short- or long-term loans. Large amounts of required cash outflows during a short time can force a company into bankruptcy.
- *Nature of the client's operations.* Certain types of businesses are inherently riskier than others. For example, other things being equal, a start-up technology company dependent on one product is much more likely to go bankrupt than a diversified food manufacturer.
- *Competence of management.* Competent management is constantly alert for potential financial difficulties and modifies its operating methods to minimize the effects of short-run problems. The ability of management must be assessed as a part of the evaluation of the likelihood of bankruptcy.

The Auditor's Evaluation of Management's Integrity As discussed in Chapter 8 as a part of new client investigation and continuing client evaluation, if a client has questionable integrity, the auditor is likely to assess acceptable audit risk lower. Companies with low integrity often conduct their business affairs in a manner that results in conflicts with their stockholders, regulators, and customers. In turn, these conflicts often reflect on the users' perceived quality of the audit and can result in lawsuits and other disagreements. An obvious example of a situation in which management's integrity is questionable is prior criminal convictions of key management personnel. Other examples of questionable integrity might include frequent disagreements with previous auditors, the Internal Revenue Service, and the SEC. Frequent turnover of key financial and internal audit personnel and ongoing conflicts with labor unions and employees may also indicate integrity problems.

To assess acceptable audit risk, the auditor must first assess each of the factors affecting acceptable audit risk. Table 9-3 illustrates the methods used by auditors to assess each of the three factors already discussed. It is easy to see after examining Table 9-3 that the

Assessing Acceptable Audit Risk

TABLE 9-3	Methods Practitioners Use to Assess Acceptable Audit Risk
Factors	**Methods Used to Assess Acceptable Audit Risk**
External users reliance on financial statements	• Examine the financial statements, including footnotes. • Read minutes of board of directors meetings to determine future plans. • Examine Form 10K for a publicly held company. • Discuss financing plans with management.
Likelihood of financial difficulties	• Analyze the financial statements for financial difficulties using ratios and other analytical procedures. • Examine historical and projected cash flow statements for the nature of cash inflows and outflows.
Management integrity	Follow the procedures discussed in Chapter 8 for client acceptance and continuance.

assessment of each of the factors is highly subjective, which means that the overall assessment is also highly subjective. A typical evaluation of acceptable audit risk is high, medium, or low, where a low acceptable audit risk assessment means a "risky" client requiring more extensive evidence, assignment of more experienced personnel, and/or a more extensive review of working papers. As the audit progresses, additional information about the client is obtained and acceptable audit risk may be modified.

ASSESSING ACCEPTABLE AUDIT RISK IN PRACTICE	Henry Rinsk, of Links, Rinsk and Rodman, CPAs, is the partner responsible for the audit of Hungry Food Restaurants, a chain of nine Midwestern family restaurants. The firm has audited Hungry Food for 10 years and has always found management competent, cooperative, and easy to deal with. Hungry Food is family-owned with a business succession plan in place; it is profitable, is liquid, and has little debt. Management has a reputation in the community for high integrity and good relationships with employees, customers, and suppliers. After meeting with the other partners as part of the firm's annual client continuation meeting, Henry recommends that acceptable audit risk for Hungry Food be assessed at high. For Links, Rinsk and Rodman, this means no expansion of evidence, a "standard" review of working papers, and a "standard" assignment of personnel to the engagement.

FACTORS AFFECTING INHERENT RISK

OBJECTIVE 9-8
Consider the impact of several factors on the assessment of inherent risk.

The inclusion of inherent risk in the audit risk model is one of the most important concepts in auditing. It implies that auditors should attempt to predict where misstatements are most and least likely in the financial statement segments. This information affects the total amount of evidence that the auditor is required to accumulate and influences how the auditor's efforts to gather the evidence are allocated among the segments of the audit.

At the start of the audit, there is not much that can be done about changing inherent risk. Instead, the auditor must *assess the factors* that make up the risk and *modify audit evidence* to take them into consideration. The auditor should consider several major factors when assessing inherent risk:

- Nature of the client's business
- Factors related to misstatements arising from fraudulent financial reporting
- Results of previous audits
- Initial versus repeat engagement
- Related parties
- Nonroutine transactions
- Judgment required to correctly record account balances and transactions
- Susceptibility of assets to misappropriation
- Makeup of the population

Nature of the Client's Business

Inherent risk for certain accounts is affected by the nature of the client's business. For example, there is a greater likelihood of obsolete inventory for an electronics manufacturer than for a steel fabricator. Inherent risk is most likely to vary from business to business for accounts such as inventory, accounts and loans receivable, and property, plant, and equipment. The nature of the client's business should have little or no effect on inherent risk for accounts such as cash, notes, and mortgages payable. Information gained while obtaining knowledge about the client's industry and business, as discussed in Chapter 8, is useful for assessing this factor.

There was a discussion in Chapter 6 of the auditor's responsibilities under SAS 82 to assess the risk of fraud arising from fraudulent financial reporting and misappropriation of assets. The three categories of risk factors for fraudulent financial reporting are summarized in Table 6-1, page 147, including examples. These three categories are as follows:

1. Management's characteristics and influence over the control environment
2. Industry conditions
3. Operating characteristics and financial stability

Factors Related to Misstatements Arising from Fraudulent Financial Reporting

It is difficult in concept and practice to separate these three categories of factors into acceptable audit risk, inherent risk, or control risk. For example, management that lacks integrity and is motivated to misstate financial statements (management characteristics) is one of the factors in acceptable audit risk, but it also increases the likelihood of misstatement, which is an inherent risk. Similarly, it will be shown in Chapter 10 that several of the risk factors influencing management characteristics are a part of the control environment. An example is the attitude, actions, and policies that reflect the overall attitudes of top management about integrity, ethical values, and commitment to competence.

To satisfy the requirements of SAS 82, it is more important for the auditor to assess the risks and to respond to them than it is to identify them as acceptable audit risk, inherent risk, or control risk.

Misstatements found in the previous year's audit have a high likelihood of occurring again in the current year's audit. This is because many types of misstatements are systemic in nature, and organizations are often slow in making changes to eliminate them. Therefore, an auditor would be negligent if the results of the preceding year's audit were ignored during the development of the current year's audit program. For example, if the auditor found a significant number of misstatements in pricing inventory, inherent risk would likely be high, and extensive testing would have to be done in the current audit as a means of determining whether the deficiency in the client's system had been corrected. If, however, the auditor has found no misstatements for the past several years in conducting tests of an audit area, the auditor is justified in reducing inherent risk, provided that changes in relevant circumstances have not occurred.

Results of Previous Audits

Auditors gain experience and knowledge about the likelihood of misstatements after auditing a client for several years. The lack of previous years' audit results would cause most auditors to use a larger inherent risk for initial audits than for repeat engagements in which no material misstatements had been found. Most auditors set a high inherent risk in the first year of an audit and reduce it in subsequent years as they gain experience.

Initial versus Repeat Engagement

Transactions between parent and subsidiary companies and those between management and the corporate entity are examples of related-party transactions as defined by SFAS 57. Because these transactions do not occur between two independent parties dealing at "arm's

Related Parties

length," a greater likelihood exists that they might be misstated, causing an increase in inherent risk. Determining the existence of related parties was discussed in Chapter 8.

Nonroutine Transactions

Transactions that are unusual for the client are more likely to be incorrectly recorded by the client than routine transactions because the client lacks experience in recording them. Examples include fire losses, major property acquisitions, and lease agreements. Knowledge of the client's business and review of minutes of meetings, as discussed in Chapter 8, are useful to learn about nonroutine transactions.

Judgment Required to Correctly Record Account Balances and Transactions

Many account balances require estimates and a great deal of management judgment. Examples are allowance for uncollectible accounts receivable, obsolete inventory, liability for warranty payments, and bank loan loss reserves. Similarly, transactions for major repairs or partial replacement of assets are examples where considerable judgment is needed to correctly record the information.

Susceptibility of Assets to Misappropriation

The auditor should be concerned about the risk of possible defalcation in situations in which it is relatively easy to convert company assets to personal use. Such is the case when currency, marketable securities, or highly marketable inventory are not closely controlled. When the likelihood of defalcation is high, inherent risk is increased.

Makeup of the Population

Often, the individual items making up the total population also affect the auditor's expectation of material misstatement. For example, most auditors would use a higher inherent risk for accounts receivable where most accounts are significantly overdue than where most accounts are current. Transactions with affiliated companies, amounts due from officers, cash disbursements made payable to cash, and accounts receivable outstanding for several months are examples of situations requiring a higher inherent risk and therefore greater investigation because there is usually a greater likelihood of misstatement than for more typical transactions.

Assessing Inherent Risk

Center for Excellence in Financial Management

The auditor must evaluate the information affecting inherent risk and decide on an appropriate inherent risk factor for each cycle, account, and many times for each audit objective. Some factors, such as the integrity of management, will affect many or perhaps all cycles, whereas others, such as nonroutine transactions, will affect only specific accounts or audit objectives. Although the profession has not established standards or guidelines for setting inherent risk, the authors believe that auditors are generally conservative in making such assessments. Most auditors would probably set inherent risk at well above 50 percent, even in the best of circumstances, and at 100 percent when there is any reasonable possibility of significant misstatements. For example, assume that in the audit of inventory the auditor notes that (1) a large number of misstatements were found in the previous year and (2) inventory turnover has slowed in the current year. Many auditors would probably set inherent risk at relatively high level (some would use 100 percent) for each audit objective for inventory in this situation.

Obtain Information to Assess Inherent Risk

Auditors begin their assessments of inherent risk during the planning phase and update the assessments throughout the audit. A considerable portion of Chapter 8 dealt with information that is relevant to inherent risk assessment during the planning phase. For example, the discussion of obtaining knowledge about the client's business and industry, touring the client's plant and offices, and identifying related parties all pertain directly to inherent risk assessment. As the auditor performs the wide variety of tests on an audit, additional information is obtained that often affects the original assessment.

Relationship of Risks to Evidence and Factors Influencing Risks

Figure 9-4 summarizes the factors that determine each of the risks, the effect of the three component risks on the determination of planned detection risk, and the relationship of all four risks to planned audit evidence. "D" in the figure indicates a direct relationship between a component risk and planned detection risk or planned evidence. "I" indicates an

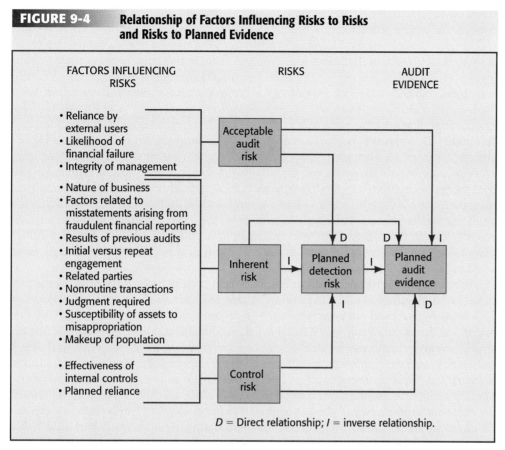

FIGURE 9-4 Relationship of Factors Influencing Risks to Risks and Risks to Planned Evidence

FACTORS INFLUENCING RISKS | RISKS | AUDIT EVIDENCE

- Reliance by external users
- Likelihood of financial failure
- Integrity of management

Acceptable audit risk

- Nature of business
- Factors related to misstatements arising from fraudulent financial reporting
- Results of previous audits
- Initial versus repeat engagement
- Related parties
- Nonroutine transactions
- Judgment required
- Susceptibility of assets to misappropriation
- Makeup of population

Inherent risk

Planned detection risk

Planned audit evidence

- Effectiveness of internal controls
- Planned reliance

Control risk

D = Direct relationship; I = inverse relationship.

inverse relationship. For example, an increase in acceptable audit risk results in an increase in planned detection risk (D) and a decrease in planned audit evidence (I). Compare Figure 9-4 to Table 9-2 on page 258 and observe that these two illustrations include the same concepts. In addition to affecting planned audit evidence, acceptable audit risk can also affect the selection of personnel assigned to the audit and the extent of the review of the completed audit.

OTHER MATERIALITY AND RISK CONSIDERATIONS

The use of materiality and risk in practice involves applying both concepts to segments of the audit and audit objectives. There are also measurement difficulties that practitioners must resolve. These are discussed in this section.

Both control risk and inherent risk are typically set for each cycle, each account, and often even each audit objective, not for the overall audit, and are likely to vary from cycle to cycle, account to account, and objective to objective on the same audit. Internal controls may be more effective for inventory-related accounts than for those related to fixed assets. Control risk would therefore also be different for different accounts depending on the effectiveness of the controls. Factors affecting inherent risk, such as susceptibility to defalcation and routineness of the transactions, are also likely to differ from account to account. For that reason, it is normal to have inherent risk vary for different accounts in the same audit unless there is some strong overriding factor of concern, such as management integrity.

Acceptable audit risk is ordinarily set by the auditor during planning and held constant for each major cycle and account. Auditors normally use the same acceptable audit risk for each segment because the factors affecting acceptable audit risk are related to the entire audit, not individual accounts. For example, the extent to which financial statements are

Audit Risk for Segments

OBJECTIVE 9-9
Discuss risk for segments and measurement difficulties.

relied on for external users' decisions is usually related to the overall financial statements, not just one or two accounts.

In some cases, however, a *lower* acceptable audit risk may be more appropriate for one account than for others. In the previous example, even though the auditor decided to use a medium acceptable audit risk for the audit as a whole, the auditor might decide to reduce acceptable audit risk to low for inventory if inventory is used as collateral for a short-term loan.

Some auditors use the same acceptable audit risk for each segment as overall acceptable audit risk, whereas others use a higher acceptable audit risk for each segment. The argument for using a higher acceptable audit risk for each segment is the effect of the interactions of the various accounts and transactions making up the financial statements and the synergy of multiple tests. Stated differently, if all individual segments of the audit are completed at an acceptable audit risk of a given level, the auditor can be assured that the audit risk for the financial statements as a whole will be lower. Other auditors use the same acceptable audit risk for segments as overall acceptable audit risk because of the difficulties of measurement. The latter approach is followed in the illustrations in this and subsequent chapters, but either approach is acceptable.

Because control risk and inherent risk vary from cycle to cycle, account to account, or objective to objective, planned detection risk and required audit evidence will also vary. This conclusion should not be surprising. The circumstances of each engagement are different, and the extent of evidence needed will depend on the unique circumstances. For example, inventory might require extensive testing on an engagement because of weak internal controls and concern about obsolescence resulting from technological changes in the industry. On the same engagement, accounts receivable may require little testing because of effective internal controls, fast collection of receivables, excellent relationships between the client and customers, and good audit results in previous years. Similarly, for a given audit of inventory, an auditor may assess that there is a higher inherent risk of a realizable value misstatement because of the higher potential for obsolescence, but a low inherent risk of a classification misstatement because there is only purchased inventory.

Relating Tolerable Misstatement and Risks to Balance-Related Audit Objectives

Although it is common in practice to assess inherent and control risks for each balance-related audit objective, it is not common to allocate materiality to objectives. Auditors are able to effectively associate most risks with different objectives. It is reasonably easy to determine the relationship between a risk and one or two objectives. For example, obsolescence in inventory would be unlikely to affect any objective other than realizable value. It is more difficult to decide how much of the materiality allocated to a given account should in turn be allocated to one or two objectives. Most auditors do not attempt to do so.

Measurement Limitations

One major limitation in the application of the audit risk model is the difficulty of measuring the components of the model. Despite the auditor's best efforts in planning, the assessments of acceptable audit risk, inherent risk, and control risk and therefore planned detection risk are highly subjective and are approximations of reality at best. Imagine, for example, attempting to precisely assess inherent risk by determining the impact of factors such as the misstatements discovered in prior years' audits and technology changes in the client's industry.

To offset this measurement problem, many auditors use broad and subjective measurement terms, such as *low, medium,* and *high.* Table 9-4 shows how auditors can use the information to decide on the appropriate amount of evidence to accumulate. For example, in situation 1, the auditor has decided to accept a high audit risk for an account or objective. The auditor has concluded that there is a low risk of misstatement in the financial statements and that internal controls are effective. Therefore, a high planned detection risk is appropriate. As a result, a low level of evidence is needed. Situation 3 is at the opposite extreme. If both inherent and control risks are high and the auditor wants a low audit risk, considerable evidence is required. The other three situations fall between the two extremes.

TABLE 9-4	Relationships of Risk to Evidence				
Situation	Acceptable Audit Risk	Inherent Risk	Control Risk	Planned Detection Risk	Amount of Evidence Required
1	High	Low	Low	High	Low
2	Low	Low	Low	Medium	Medium
3	Low	High	High	Low	High
4	Medium	Medium	Medium	Medium	Medium
5	High	Low	Medium	Medium	Medium

It is equally difficult to measure the amount of evidence implied by a given planned detection risk. A typical audit program that is intended to reduce detection risk to the planned level is a combination of several audit procedures, each using a different type of evidence that is applied to different audit objectives. Auditor's measurement methods are too imprecise to permit an accurate quantitative measure of the combined evidence. Instead, auditors subjectively evaluate whether sufficient evidence has been planned to satisfy a planned detection risk of low, medium, or high. Presumably, measurement methods are sufficient to permit an auditor to know that more evidence is needed to satisfy a low planned detection risk than for medium or high. Considerable professional judgment is needed to decide how much more.

In applying the audit risk model, auditors are concerned about both overauditing and underauditing, but most auditors are more concerned about the latter. Underauditing exposes the CPA firm to legal liability and loss of professional reputation.

Because of the concern to avoid underauditing, auditors typically assess risks conservatively. For example, an auditor might not assess either control risk or inherent risk below .5 even when the likelihood of misstatement is low. In these audits, a low risk might be .5, medium .8, and high 1.0, if the risks are quantified.

Practicing auditors develop various types of worksheets to aid in relating the considerations affecting audit evidence to the appropriate evidence to accumulate. One such worksheet is included in Figure 9-5 on page 270 for the audit of accounts receivable for Hillsburg Hardware Co. The nine balance-related audit objectives introduced in Chapter 6 are included in the columns at the top of the worksheet. Rows one and two are acceptable audit risk and inherent risk, which were studied in this chapter. Tolerable misstatement is included at the bottom of the worksheet. The engagement in-charge, Fran Moore, made the following decisions in the audit of Hillsburg Hardware Co.:

Tests of Details of Balances Evidence Planning Worksheet

- *Tolerable misstatement.* The preliminary judgment about materiality was set at $37,000 (approximately 10 percent of earnings from operations of $369,000). She allocated $22,000 to the audit of accounts receivable (see p. 255).
- *Acceptable audit risk.* Fran assessed acceptable audit risk as high because of the good financial condition of the company, high management integrity, and the relatively few users of the financial statements.
- *Inherent risk.* Fran assessed inherent risk as low for all balance-related audit objectives except realizable value. In past years, there have been audit adjustments to the allowance for uncollectible accounts because it was found to be understated.

Planned detection risk would be approximately the same for each balance-related audit objective in the audit of accounts receivable for Hillsburg Hardware Co. if the only three factors the auditor needs to consider are acceptable audit risk, inherent risk, and tolerable misstatement. The evidence planning worksheet shows that other factors must be considered before making the final evidence decisions. These are studied in subsequent chapters and will be integrated into the evidence planning worksheet at that time.

Relationship of Risk and Materiality and Audit Evidence

OBJECTIVE 9-10
Discuss how materiality and risk are related and integrated into the audit process.

The concepts of materiality and risk in auditing are closely related and inseparable. Risk is a measure of uncertainty, whereas materiality is a measure of magnitude or size. Taken together, they measure the uncertainty of amounts of a given magnitude. For example, the statement that the auditor plans to accumulate evidence such that there is only a 5 percent risk (acceptable audit risk) of failing to uncover misstatements exceeding tolerable misstatements of $22,000 (materiality) is a precise and meaningful statement. If the statement eliminates either the risk or materiality portion, it would be meaningless. A 5 percent risk without a specific materiality measure could imply that a $100 or $1 million misstatement is acceptable. A $22,000 overstatement without a specific risk could imply that a 1 percent or 80 percent risk is acceptable.

The relationships between tolerable misstatement and the four risks to planned audit evidence are shown in Figure 9-6 (p. 271). This figure expands Figure 9-4 to include

---

FIGURE 9-5 Evidence Planning Worksheet to Decide Tests of Details of Balances for Hillsburg Hardware Co.– Accounts Receivable

	Detail tie-in	Existence	Completeness	Accuracy	Classification	Cutoff	Realizable value	Rights	Presentation and disclosure
Acceptable audit risk	High	High	High	High	High	High	High	High	High
Inherent risk	Low	Low	Low	Low	Low	Low	Medium	Low	Low
Control risk—Sales									
Control risk—Cash receipts									
Control risk—Additional controls									
Substantive tests of transactions—Sales									
Substantive tests of transactions—Cash receipts									
Analytical procedures									
Planned detection risk for tests of details of balances									
Planned audit evidence for tests of details of balances									

Tolerable misstatement $22,000

FIGURE 9-6   Relationship of Tolerable Misstatement and Risks to Planned Evidence

TOLERABLE MISSTATEMENT AND RISKS

PLANNED AUDIT EVIDENCE

Acceptable audit risk

Inherent risk

Planned detection risk

Planned audit evidence

Control risk

Tolerable misstatement

D = Direct relationship; *I* = inverse relationship.

tolerable misstatement. Observe that tolerable misstatement does not affect any of the four risks and the risks have no effect on tolerable misstatement, but together they determine the planned evidence.

EVALUATING RESULTS

After the auditor plans the engagement and accumulates audit evidence, results can also be stated in terms of the evaluation version of the audit risk model. The audit risk model for evaluating audit results is stated in SAS 47 as:

$$AcAR = IR \times CR \times AcDR$$

where:

AcAR = Achieved audit risk. A measure of the risk the auditor has taken that an account in the financial statements is materially misstated after the auditor has accumulated audit evidence.

IR = Inherent risk. It is the same inherent risk factor discussed in planning unless it has been revised as a result of new information.

CR = Control risk. It is also the same control risk discussed previously unless it has been revised during the audit.

AcDR = Achieved detection risk. A measure of the risk that audit evidence for a segment did not detect misstatements exceeding a tolerable amount, if such misstatements existed. The auditor can reduce achieved detection risk only by accumulating substantive evidence.

Research subsequent to the issuance of SAS 47 has shown that it is *not appropriate to use this evaluation formula* in the way it is stated in SAS 47. The research indicates that using the formula can result in an understatement of achieved audit risk.

Even though it is not appropriate to use the formula to calculate achieved audit risk, the relationships in the formula are valid and should be used in practice. The formula shows that there are three ways to reduce achieved audit risk to an acceptable level:

1. *Reduce inherent risk.* Because inherent risk is assessed by the auditor based on the client's circumstances, this assessment is done during planning and is typically not changed unless new facts are uncovered as the audit progresses.
2. *Reduce control risk.* Assessed control risk is affected by the client's internal controls and the auditor's tests of those controls. Auditors can reduce control risk by more extensive tests of controls if the client has effective controls.
3. *Reduce achieved detection risk by increasing substantive audit tests.* Auditors reduce achieved detection risk by accumulating evidence using analytical procedures, substantive tests of transactions, and tests of details of balances. Additional audit procedures, assuming that they are effective, and larger sample sizes both reduce achieved detection risk.

Subjectively combining these three factors to achieve an acceptably low audit risk requires considerable professional judgment. Some firms develop sophisticated approaches to help their auditors make those judgments, whereas other firms leave those decisions to each audit team.

Figure 9-7 graphically shows both the planning and evaluating results versions of the audit risk model. The right side of the figure shows that accumulating more substantive evidence reduces achieved detection risk. A lower achieved detection risk along with lower inherent and control risk reduce achieved audit risk.

Revising Risks and Evidence

As already stated, the audit risk model is primarily a *planning* model and is therefore of limited use in evaluating results. Great care must be used in revising the risk factors when the actual results are not as favorable as planned.

FIGURE 9-7   Audit Risk Models for Planning Evidence and Evaluating Results

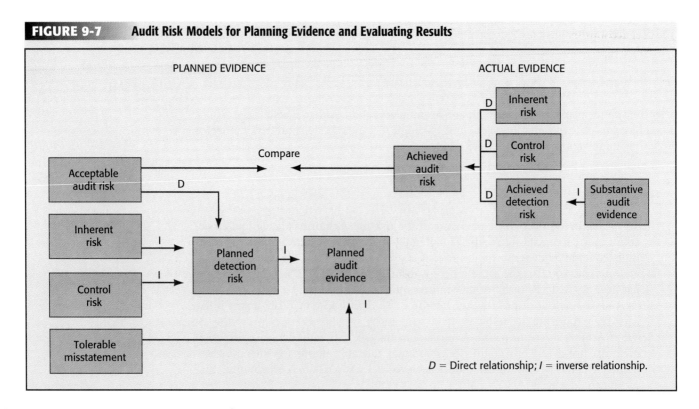

No difficulties occur when the auditor accumulates planned evidence and concludes that the assessment of each of the risks was reasonable or better than originally thought. The auditor will conclude that sufficient competent evidence has been collected for that account or cycle.

Special care must be exercised when the auditor decides, on the basis of accumulated evidence, that the original assessment of control risk or inherent risk was understated or acceptable audit risk was overstated. In such a circumstance, the auditor should follow a two-step approach. First, the auditor must revise the original assessment of the appropriate risk. It would violate due care to leave the original assessment unchanged if the auditor knows it is inappropriate. Second, the auditor should consider the effect of the revision on evidence requirements, *without use of the audit risk model*. Research in auditing has shown that if a revised risk is used in the audit risk model to determine a revised planned detection risk, there is a danger of not increasing the evidence sufficiently. Instead, the auditor should carefully evaluate the implications of the revision of the risk and modify evidence appropriately, outside of the audit risk model. An example is used to illustrate revision of a factor in the audit risk model. Assume that the auditor confirms accounts receivable and, based on the misstatements found, concludes that the original control risk assessment as low was inappropriate. The auditor should revise the estimate of control risk upward and carefully consider the effect of the revision on the additional evidence needed in the sales and collection cycle. That should be done without recalculating planned detection risk.

ESSENTIAL TERMS

Acceptable audit risk—a measure of how willing the auditor is to accept that the financial statements may be materially misstated after the audit is completed and an unqualified audit opinion has been issued; see also *audit assurance*

Allocation of the preliminary judgment about materiality—the process of assigning to each balance sheet account the misstatement amount to be considered material for that account based on the auditor's preliminary judgment

Audit assurance—a complement to acceptable audit risk; an acceptable audit risk of 2 percent is the same as audit assurance of 98 percent; also called *overall assurance* and *level of assurance*

Audit risk model—a formal model reflecting the relationships between acceptable audit risk (AAR), inherent risk (IR), control risk (CR), and planned detection risk (PDR); $PDR = AAR/(IR \times CR)$

Business risk—risk that the auditor or audit firm will suffer harm because of a client relationship, even though the audit report rendered for the client was correct

Control risk—a measure of the auditor's assessment of the likelihood that misstatements exceeding a tolerable amount in a segment will not be prevented or detected by the client's internal controls

Direct projection estimate of misstatement—estimate of likely misstatement in a population based on a sample, excluding sampling risk, and calculated as net misstatements in the sample, divided by the total sampled, multiplied by the total recorded population value

Inherent risk—a measure of the auditor's assessment of the likelihood that there are material misstatements in a segment before considering the effectiveness of internal control

Materiality—the magnitude of an omission or misstatement of accounting information that, in the light of surrounding circumstances, makes it *probable* that the judgment of a reasonable person relying on the information would have been changed or influenced by the omission or misstatement

Planned detection risk—a measure of the risk that audit evidence for a segment will fail to detect misstatements exceeding a tolerable amount, should such misstatements exist; $PDR = AAR/(IR \times CR)$

Preliminary judgment about materiality—the maximum amount by which the auditor believes that the statements could be misstated and still *not* affect the decisions of reasonable users; used in audit planning

Revised judgment about materiality—a change in the auditor's preliminary judgment made when the auditor determines that the preliminary judgment was too large or too small

Risk—the acceptance by auditors that there is some level of uncertainty in performing the audit function

Sampling error—results because the auditor has sampled only a portion of the population

Tolerable misstatement—the materiality allocated to any given account balance; used in audit planning

9-1 (Objective 9-1)   Chapter 8 introduced the seven parts of the planning phase of an audit. Which part is the evaluation of materiality and risk?

9-2 (Objective 9-1)   Define the meaning of the term materiality as it is used in accounting and auditing. What is the relationship between materiality and the phrase *obtain reasonable assurance* used in the auditor's report?

9-3 (Objectives 9-1, 9-2)   Explain why materiality is important but difficult to apply in practice.

9-4 (Objective 9-2)   What is meant by setting a preliminary judgment about materiality? Identify the most important factors affecting the preliminary judgment.

9-5 (Objective 9-2)   What is meant by using bases for setting a preliminary judgment about materiality? How would those bases differ for the audit of a manufacturing company and a government unit such as a school district?

9-6 (Objective 9-2)   Assume that Rosanne Madden, CPA, is using 5 percent of net income before taxes, current assets, or current liabilities as her major guidelines for evaluating materiality. What qualitative factors should she also consider in deciding whether misstatements may be material?

9-7 (Objectives 9-2, 9-3)   Distinguish between the terms tolerable misstatement and preliminary judgment about materiality. How are they related to each other?

9-8 (Objective 9-3)   Assume a company with the following balance sheet accounts:

Account	Amount
Cash	$10,000
Fixed assets	60,000
	$70,000
Long-term loans	$30,000
M. Johnson, proprietor	40,000
	$70,000

You are concerned only about overstatements of owner's equity. Set tolerable misstatement for the three relevant accounts such that the preliminary judgment about materiality does not exceed $5,000. Justify your answer.

9-9 (Objective 9-4)   Explain what is meant by making an estimate of the total misstatement in a segment and in the overall financial statements. Why is it important to make these estimates? What is done with them?

9-10 (Objective 9-2)   How would the conduct of an audit of a medium-sized company be affected by the company's being a small part of a large conglomerate as compared with it being a separate entity?

9-11 (Objective 9-6)   Define the audit risk model and explain each term in the model.

9-12 (Objective 9-6)   What is meant by planned detection risk? What is the effect on the amount of evidence the auditor must accumulate when planned detection risk is increased from medium to high?

9-13 (Objective 9-6)   Explain the causes of an increased or decreased planned detection risk.

9-14 (Objectives 9-6, 9-8)   Define what is meant by inherent risk. Identify four factors that make for *high* inherent risk in audits.

9-15 (Objective 9-8)   Explain why inherent risk is set for segments rather than for the overall audit. What is the effect on the amount of evidence the auditor must accumulate when inherent risk is increased from medium to high for a segment? Compare your answer with the one for 9-12.

9-16 (Objective 9-8)   Explain the effect of extensive misstatements found in the prior year's audit on inherent risk, planned detection risk, and planned audit evidence.

9-17 (Objectives 9-6, 9-7)   Explain what is meant by the term acceptable audit risk. What is its relevance to evidence accumulation?

9-18 (Objective 9-7)   Explain the relationship between acceptable audit risk and the legal liability of auditors.

9-19 (Objective 9-7)   State the three categories of factors that affect acceptable audit risk and list the factors that the auditor can use to indicate the degree to which each category exists.

9-20 (Objective 9-9)   Auditors have not been successful in measuring the components of the audit risk model. How is it possible to use the model in a meaningful way without a precise way of measuring the risk?

9-21 (Objective 9-10)   Explain the circumstances when the auditor should revise the components of the audit risk model and the effect of the revisions on planned detection risk and planned evidence.

MULTIPLE CHOICE QUESTIONS FROM CPA EXAMINATIONS

9-22 (Objectives 9-1, 9-2)   The following questions deal with materiality. Choose the best response.

a. Which one of the following statements is correct concerning the concept of materiality?
   (1) Materiality is determined by reference to guidelines established by the AICPA.
   (2) Materiality depends only on the dollar amount of an item relative to other items in the financial statements.
   (3) Materiality depends on the nature of an item rather than the dollar amount.
   (4) Materiality is a matter of professional judgment.

b. The concept of materiality will be least important to the CPA in determining the
   (1) scope of the audit of specific accounts.
   (2) specific transactions that should be reviewed.
   (3) effects of audit exceptions upon the opinion.
   (4) effects of the CPA's direct financial interest in a client upon his or her independence.

9-23 (Objectives 9-1, 9-6, 9-8)   The following questions concern materiality and risk. Choose the best response.

a. Edison Corporation has a few large accounts receivable that total $1,400,000. Victor Corporation has a great number of small accounts receivable that also total $1,400,000. The importance of a misstatement in any one account is therefore greater for Edison than for Victor. This is an example of the auditor's concept of
   (1) materiality.
   (2) comparative analysis.
   (3) reasonable assurance.
   (4) relative risk.

b. Which of the following elements ultimately determines the specific auditing procedures that are necessary in the circumstances to afford a reasonable basis for an opinion?
   (1) Auditor judgment
   (2) Materiality
   (3) Inherent risk
   (4) Reasonable assurance

c. Which of the following *best* describes the element of inherent risk that underlies the application of generally accepted auditing standards, specifically the standards of field work and reporting?
   (1) Cash audit work may have to be carried out in a more conclusive manner than inventory audit work.
   (2) Intercompany transactions are usually subject to less detailed scrutiny than arm's-length transactions with outside parties.
   (3) Inventories may require more attention by the auditor on an engagement for a merchandising enterprise than on an engagement for a public utility.
   (4) The scope of the audit need *not* be expanded if misstatements that arouse suspicion of fraud are of relatively insignificant amounts.

9-24 (Objectives 9-1, 9-2, 9-5, 9-6, 9-8)   The following questions deal with materiality and risk. Choose the best response.

   a. Which of the following statements is *not* correct about materiality?
      (1) The concept of materiality recognizes that some matters are important for fair presentation of financial statements in conformity with GAAP, whereas other matters are *not* important.
      (2) An auditor considers materiality for planning purposes in terms of the largest aggregate level of misstatements that could be material to any one of the financial statements.
      (3) Materiality judgments are made in light of surrounding circumstances and necessarily involve both quantitative and qualitative judgments.
      (4) An auditor's consideration of materiality is influenced by the auditor's perception of the needs of a reasonable person who will rely on the financial statements.
   b. Inherent risk and control risk differ from planned detection risk in that they
      (1) arise from the misapplication of auditing procedures.
      (2) may be assessed in either quantitative or nonquantitative terms.
      (3) exist independently of the financial statement audit.
      (4) can be changed at the auditor's discretion.
   c. In considering materiality for planning purposes, an auditor believes that misstatements aggregating $10,000 would have a material effect on an entity's income statement but that misstatements would have to aggregate $20,000 to materially affect the balance sheet. Ordinarily, it would be appropriate to design auditing procedures that would be expected to detect misstatements that aggregate.
      (1) $10,000
      (2) $15,000
      (3) $20,000
      (4) $30,000

DISCUSSION QUESTIONS AND PROBLEMS

9-25 (Objectives 9-2, 9-3, 9-4)   You are evaluating audit results for current assets in the audit of Quicky Plumbing Co. You set the preliminary judgment about materiality for current assets at $12,500 for overstatements and at $20,000 for understatements. The preliminary and actual estimates are shown on the following page.

| | Tolerable Misstatement | | Estimate of Total Misstatement | |
	Overstatements	Understatements	Overstatements	Understatements
Account				
Cash	$ 2,000	$ 3,000	$ 2,000	$ 0
Accounts receivable	12,000	18,000	4,000	19,000
Inventory	8,000	14,000	3,000	10,000
Prepaid expenses	3,000	5,000	2,000	1,000
Total	$25,000	$40,000	$11,000	$30,000

Required

a. Justify a lower preliminary judgment about materiality for overstatements than understatements in this situation.

b. Explain why the totals of the tolerable misstatements exceed the preliminary judgments about materiality for both understatements and overstatements.

c. Explain how it is possible that three of the estimates of total misstatement have both an overstatement and an understatement.

d. Assume that you are not concerned whether the estimate of misstatement exceeds tolerable misstatement for individual accounts if the total estimate is less than the preliminary judgment.

   (1) Given the audit results, should you be more concerned about the existence of material overstatements or understatements at this point in the audit of Quicky Plumbing Co.?

   (2) Which account or accounts would you be most concerned about in (1)? Explain.

e. Assume that the estimate of total overstatement amount for each account is less than tolerable misstatement but that the total overstatement estimate exceeds the preliminary judgment of materiality.

   (1) Explain why this would occur.

   (2) Explain what the auditor should do.

9-26 (Objectives 9-2, 9-3, 9-4) On pages 278–279 are statements of earnings and financial position for Wexler Industries.

Required

a. Use professional judgment in deciding on the preliminary judgment about materiality for earnings, current assets, current liabilities, and total assets. Your conclusions should be stated in terms of percentages and dollars.

b. Assume that you define materiality for this audit as a combined misstatement of earnings from continuing operations before income taxes of 5 percent. Also assume that you believe there is an equal likelihood of a misstatement of every account in the financial statements and each misstatement is likely to result in an overstatement of earnings. Allocate materiality to these financial statements as you consider appropriate.

c. As discussed in part b, net earnings from continuing operations *before* income taxes was used as a base for calculating materiality for the Wexler Industries audit. Discuss why most auditors use *before* tax net earnings instead of *after* tax net earnings when calculating materiality based on the income statement.

d. Now, assume that you have decided to allocate 75 percent of your preliminary judgment to accounts receivable, inventories, and accounts payable because you believe all other accounts have a low inherent and control risk. How does this affect evidence accumulation on the audit?

e. Assume that you complete the audit and conclude that your preliminary judgment about materiality for current assets, current liabilities, and total assets has been met. The actual estimate of misstatements in *earnings* exceeds your preliminary judgment. What should you do?

Consolidated Statements of Earnings
Wexler Industries

	For the 53 Weeks Ended April 3, 2000*	For the 52 Weeks Ended March 28, 1999	For the 52 Weeks Ended March 29, 1998
Revenue			
Net sales	$8,351,149	$6,601,255	$5,959,587
Other income	59,675	43,186	52,418
	8,410,824	6,644,441	6,012,005
Costs and expenses			
Cost of sales	5,197,375	4,005,548	3,675,369
Marketing, general, and administrative expenses	2,590,080	2,119,590	1,828,169
Provision for loss on restructured operations	64,100	—	—
Interest expense	141,662	46,737	38,546
	7,993,217	6,171,875	5,542,084
Earnings from continuing operations before income taxes	417,607	472,566	469,921
Income taxes	(196,700)	(217,200)	(214,100)
Earnings from continuing operations	220,907	255,366	255,821
Provision for loss on discontinued operations, net of income taxes	(20,700)	—	—
Net earnings	$ 200,207	$ 255,366	$ 255,821

*All dollar amounts are expressed in thousands.

Consolidated Statements of Financial Position
Wexler Industries

Assets	April 3, 2000*	March 28, 1999
Current assets		
Cash	$ 39,683	$ 37,566
Temporary investments, including time deposits of $65,361 in 2000		
and $181,589 in 1999 (at cost, which approximates market)	123,421	271,639
Receivables, less allowances of $16,808 in 2000 and $17,616 in 1999	899,752	759,001
Inventories		
Finished product	680,974	550,407
Raw materials and supplies	443,175	353,795
	1,124,149	904,202
Deferred income tax benefits	9,633	10,468
Prepaid expenses	57,468	35,911
Current assets	2,254,106	2,018,787
Land, buildings, and equipment, at cost, less accumulated depreciation	1,393,902	1,004,455
Investments in affiliated companies and sundry assets	112,938	83,455
Goodwill and other intangible assets	99,791	23,145
Total	$3,860,737	$3,129,842

Liabilities and Stockholders' Equity		
Current liabilities		
Notes payable	$ 280,238	$ 113,411
Current portion of long-term debt	64,594	12,336
Accounts and drafts payable	359,511	380,395
Accrued salaries, wages, and vacations	112,200	63,557
Accrued income taxes	76,479	89,151
Other accrued liabilities	321,871	269,672
Current liabilities	1,214,893	928,522
Long-term debt	730,987	390,687
Other noncurrent liabilities	146,687	80,586
Deferred income taxes	142,344	119,715
Stockholders' equity		
Common stock issued, 51,017,755 shares in 2000 and 50,992,410 in 1999	51,018	50,992
Additional paid-in capital	149,177	148,584
Cumulative foreign currency translation adjustment	(76,572)	—
Retained earnings	1,554,170	1,462,723
Common stock held in treasury, at cost, 1,566,598 shares	(51,967)	(51,967)
Stockholders' equity	1,625,826	1,610,332
Total	$3,860,737	$3,129,842

*All dollar amounts are expressed in thousands.

9-27 (Objectives 9-2, 9-3, 9-4, 9-6, 9-7, 9-8, 9-10)   The following are concepts discussed in this chapter:

1. Preliminary judgment about materiality
2. Estimate of the combined misstatements
3. Acceptable audit risk
4. Tolerable misstatement
5. Inherent risk
6. Estimated total misstatement in a segment
7. Control risk
8. Planned detection risk

Required

    a. Identify which items are *audit planning decisions* requiring professional judgment.

    b. Identify which items are *audit conclusions* resulting from application of audit procedures and requiring professional judgment.

    c. Under what circumstances is it acceptable to change those items in part a, after the audit is started? Which items can be changed after the audit is 95 percent completed?

9-28 (Objectives 9-6, 9-7)   Describe what is meant by acceptable audit risk. Explain why each of the following statements is true:

    a. A CPA firm should attempt to achieve the same audit risk for all audit clients when circumstances are similar.

    b. A CPA firm should decrease acceptable audit risk for audit clients when external users rely heavily on the statements.

    c. A CPA firm should decrease acceptable audit risk for audit clients when there is a reasonably high likelihood of a client's filing bankruptcy.

    d. Different CPA firms should attempt to achieve reasonably similar audit risks for clients with similar circumstances.

9-29 (Objectives 9-5, 9-6, 9-7, 9-8)   State whether each of the following statements is true or false, and give your reasons:

    a. The audit evidence accumulated for every client should be approximately the same, regardless of the circumstances.

    b. If acceptable audit risk is the same for two different clients, the audit evidence for the two clients should be approximately the same.

    c. If acceptable audit risk, inherent risk, and control risk are approximately the same for two different clients, the audit evidence for the two clients should be approximately the same.

9-30 (Objectives 9-6, 9-7, 9-8)   The following questions deal with the use of the audit risk model.

    a. Assume that the auditor is doing a first-year municipal audit of Redwood City, Missouri, and concludes that the internal controls are not likely to be effective.

      (1) Explain why the auditor is likely to set both inherent and control risks at 100 percent for most segments.

      (2) Assuming (1), explain the relationship of acceptable audit risk to planned detection risk.

      (3) Assuming (1), explain the effect of planned detection risk on evidence accumulation compared with its effect if planned detection risk were larger.

    b. Assume that the auditor is doing the third-year municipal audit of Redwood City, Missouri, and concludes that internal controls are effective and inherent risk is low.

      (1) Explain why the auditor is likely to set inherent and control risks for material segments at a higher level than, say, 40 percent, even when the two risks are low.

      (2) For the audit of fixed asset accounts, assume inherent and control risks of 50 percent each, and an acceptable audit risk of 5 percent. Calculate planned detection risk.

      (3) For (2), explain the effect of planned detection risk on evidence accumulation compared with its effect if planned detection risk were smaller.

    c. Assume that the auditor is doing the fifth-year municipal audit of Redwood City, Missouri, and concludes that acceptable audit risk can be set high, and inherent and control risks should be set low.

      (1) What circumstances would result in these conclusions?

      (2) For the audit of repairs and maintenance, inherent and control risk are set at 20 percent each. Acceptable audit risk is 5 percent. Calculate planned detection risk.

      (3) How much evidence should be accumulated in this situation?

9-31 (Objective 9-6) Following are six situations that involve the audit risk model as it is used for planning audit evidence requirements. Numbers are used only to help you understand the relationships among factors in the risk model.

			Situation			
Risk	**1**	**2**	**3**	**4**	**5**	**6**
Acceptable audit risk	5%	5%	5%	5%	1%	1%
Inherent risk	100%	40%	60%	20%	100%	40%
Control risk	100%	60%	40%	30%	100%	60%
Planned detection risk	—	—	—	—	—	—

Required

  a. Explain what each of the four risks mean.

  b. Calculate planned detection risk for each situation.

  c. Using your knowledge of the relationships among the foregoing factors, state the effect on planned detection risk (increase or decrease) of changing each of the following factors while the other two remain constant.

    (1) A decrease in acceptable audit risk

    (2) A decrease in control risk

    (3) A decrease in inherent risk

    (4) An increase in control risk and a decrease in inherent risk of the same amount

  d. Which situation requires the greatest amount of evidence and which requires the least?

9-32 (Objectives 9-6, 9-9) Following are six situations that involve the audit risk model as it is used for planning audit evidence requirements in the audit of inventory.

			Situation			
Risk	**1**	**2**	**3**	**4**	**5**	**6**
Acceptable audit risk	High	High	Low	Low	High	Medium
Inherent risk	Low	High	High	Low	Medium	Medium
Control risk	Low	Low	High	High	Medium	Medium
Planned detection risk	—	—	—	—	—	—
Planned evidence	—	—	—	—	—	—

Required

  a. Explain what low, medium, and high mean for each of the four risks and planned evidence.

  b. Fill in the blanks for planned detection risk and planned evidence using the terms *low, medium,* or *high.*

  c. Using your knowledge of the relationships among the foregoing factors, state the effect on planned evidence (increase or decrease) of changing each of the following five factors, while the other three remain constant.

    (1) An increase in acceptable audit risk

    (2) An increase in control risk

    (3) An increase in planned detection risk

    (4) An increase in inherent risk

    (5) An increase in inherent risk and a decrease in control risk of the same amount

9-33 (Objectives 9-6, 9-10) Using the audit risk model, state the effect on control risk, inherent risk, acceptable audit risk, and planned evidence for each of the following independent events. In each of the events a to j, circle one letter for each of the three independent variables and planned evidence: I = increase, D = decrease, N = no effect, and C = cannot determine from the information provided.

   a. The client's management materially increased long-term contractual debt:
   Control risk   I D N C   Acceptable audit risk   I D N C
   Inherent risk   I D N C   Planned evidence   I D N C

   b. The company changed from a privately held company to a publicly held company:
   Control risk   I D N C   Acceptable audit risk   I D N C
   Inherent risk   I D N C   Planned evidence   I D N C

   c. The auditor decided to set assessed control risk below maximum (it was previously assessed at maximum):
   Control risk   I D N C   Acceptable audit risk   I D N C
   Inherent risk   I D N C   Planned evidence   I D N C

   d. The account balance increased materially from the preceding year without apparent reason:
   Control risk   I D N C   Acceptable audit risk   I D N C
   Inherent risk   I D N C   Planned evidence   I D N C

   e. You determined through the planning phase that working capital, debt to equity ratio, and other indicators of financial condition had improved during the past year:
   Control risk   I D N C   Acceptable audit risk   I D N C
   Inherent risk   I D N C   Planned evidence   I D N C

   f. This is the second year of the engagement, and there were few misstatements found in the previous year's audit. The auditor also decided to increase reliance on internal control:
   Control risk   I D N C   Acceptable audit risk   I D N C
   Inherent risk   I D N C   Planned evidence   I D N C

   g. About halfway through the audit, you discover that the client is constructing its own building during idle periods, using factory personnel. This is the first time the client has done this, and it is being done at your recommendation:
   Control risk   I D N C   Acceptable audit risk   I D N C
   Inherent risk   I D N C   Planned evidence   I D N C

   h. In discussions with management, you conclude that management is planning to sell the business in the next few months. Because of the planned changes, several key accounting personnel quit several months ago for alternative employment. You also observe that the gross margin percent has significantly increased compared with that of the preceding year:
   Control risk   I D N C   Acceptable audit risk   I D N C
   Inherent risk   I D N C   Planned evidence   I D N C

   i. There has been a change in several key management personnel. You believe that management is somewhat lacking in personal integrity, compared with the previous management. You believe it is still appropriate to do the audit:
   Control risk   I D N C   Acceptable audit risk   I D N C
   Inherent risk   I D N C   Planned evidence   I D N C

   j. In auditing inventory, you obtain an understanding of internal control and perform tests of controls. You find it significantly improved compared with that of the preceding year. You also observe that because of technology changes in the industry, the client's inventory may be somewhat obsolete:
   Control risk   I D N C   Acceptable audit risk   I D N C
   Inherent risk   I D N C   Planned evidence   I D N C

9-34 (Objectives 9-6, 9-7, 9-8) In the audit of Whirland Chemical Company, a large pub-licly traded company, you have been assigned the responsibility for obtaining background information for the audit. Your firm is auditing the client for the first time in the current year as a result of a dispute between Whirland and the previous auditor over the proper val-uation of work-in-process inventory and the inclusion in sales of inventory that has not been delivered but has for practical purposes been completed and sold.

Whirland Chemical has been highly successful in its field in the past two decades, pri-marily because of many successful mergers negotiated by Bert Randolph, the president and chairman of the board. Even though the industry as a whole has suffered dramatic setbacks in recent years, Whirland continues to prosper, as evidenced by its constantly increasing earnings and growth. Only in the last 2 years have the company's profits turned downward. Randolph has a reputation for having been able to hire an aggressive group of young exec-utives by the use of relatively low salaries combined with an unusually generous profit-sharing plan.

A major difficulty you face in the new audit is the lack of highly sophisticated ac-counting records for a company the size of Whirland. Randolph believes that profits come primarily from intelligent and aggressive action based on forecasts, not by relying on his-torical data that come after the fact. Most of the forecast data are generated by the sales and production department rather than by the accounting department. The personnel in the accounting department do seem competent but somewhat overworked and underpaid rel-ative to other employees. One of the recent changes that will potentially improve the record keeping is the installation of sophisticated computer equipment. All the accounting records are not computerized yet, but such major areas as inventory and sales are included in the new system. Most of the computer time is being reserved for production and marketing be-cause these areas are more essential to operations than the record-keeping function.

The first 6 months' financial statements for the current year include a profit of ap-proximately only 10 percent less than the first 6 months of the preceding year, which is somewhat surprising, considering the reduced volume and the disposal of a segment of the business, Mercury Supply Co. The disposal of this segment was considered necessary be-cause it had become increasingly unprofitable over the past 4 years. At the time of its ac-quisition from Roger Randolph, who is a brother of Bert Randolph, the company was highly profitable and it was considered a highly desirable purchase. The major customer of Mercury Supply Co. was the Mercury Corporation, which is owned by Roger Randolph. Gradually, the market for its products declined as the Mercury Corporation began diversi-fying and phasing out its primary products in favor of more profitable business. Even though Mercury Corporation is no longer buying from Mercury Supply Co., it compen-sates for it by buying a large volume of other products from Whirland Chemical.

The only major difficulty Whirland faces right now, according to financial analysts, is underfinancing. There is an excessive amount of current debt and long-term debt because of the depressed capital markets. Management is reluctant to obtain equity capital at this point because the increased number of shares would decrease the earnings per share even more than 10 percent. At the present time, Randolph is negotiating with several cash-rich companies in the hope of being able to merge with them as a means of overcoming the cap-ital problems.

Required
  a. List the major concerns you should have in the audit of Whirland Company and ex-plain why they are potential problems.
  b. State the appropriate approach to investigating the significance of each item you listed in a.

9-35 (Objectives 9-2, 9-3, 9-6, 9-7, 9-8)   Pamela Albright is the manager of the audit of Stanton Enterprises, a public company that manufactures formed steel subassemblies for other manufacturers. Albright is planning the 1999 audit and is considering an appropriate amount for planning materiality, what tolerable misstatement should be allocated to the financial statement accounts, and the appropriate inherent risks. Summary financial statement information is shown in Figure 9-8 (p. 285). Additional relevant planning information is summarized below:

1. Stanton has been a client for 4 years, and Albright's firm has always had a good relationship with the Company. Management and the accounting people have always been cooperative, honest, and positive about the audit and financial reporting. No material misstatements were found in the prior year's audit. Albright's firm has monitored the relationship carefully, because when the audit was obtained, Leonard Stanton, the CEO, had the reputation of being a "high-flyer" and had been through bankruptcy at an earlier time in his career.

2. Stanton runs the Company in an autocratic way, primarily because of a somewhat controlling personality. He believes that it is his job to make all the tough decisions. He delegates responsibility to others but is not always willing to delegate a commensurate amount of authority.

3. The industry in which Stanton participates has been in a favorable cycle the past few years and that trend is continuing in the current year. Industry profits are reasonably favorable, and there are no competitive or other apparent threats on the horizon.

4. Internal controls for Stanton are evaluated as reasonably effective for all cycles but not unusually strong. Although Stanton supports the idea of control, Albright has been disappointed that management has continually rejected Albright's recommendation to establish an internal audit function.

5. Stanton has a contract with its employees that if earnings before taxes, interest expense, and pension cost exceeds $7.8 million for the year, an additional contribution must be made to the pension fund equal to 5 percent of the excess.

Required

a. You are to play the role of Pamela Albright in the 12-31-99 audit of Stanton Enterprises. Make a preliminary judgment of materiality and allocate tolerable misstatement to financial statement accounts. Prepare a working paper showing your calculations. (Instructor option: prepare the working paper using an electronic spreadsheet.)

b. Make an acceptable audit risk decision for the current year as high, medium, or low, and support your answer.

c. Perform analytical procedures for Stanton Enterprises that will help you identify accounts that may require additional evidence in the current year's audit. Document the analytical procedures you perform and your conclusions. (Instructor option: use an electronic spreadsheet to calculate analytical procedures.)

d. The evidence planning worksheet to decide tests of details of balances for Stanton's accounts receivable is shown in Figure 9-9 (p. 286). Use the information in the case and your conclusions in parts a–c to complete the following rows of the evidence planning worksheet: Acceptable audit risk, Inherent risk, and Analytical procedures. Also fill in tolerable misstatement for accounts receivable at the bottom of the worksheet. Make any assumptions you believe are reasonable and appropriate and document them.

FIGURE 9-8   Stanton Enterprises Summary Financial Statements

Balance Sheet

	Preliminary 12-31-99	Audited 12-31-98
Cash	$ 243,689	$ 133,981
Trade accounts receivable	3,544,009	2,224,921
Allowance for uncollectible accounts	(120,000)	(215,000)
Inventories	4,520,902	3,888,400
Prepaid expenses	29,500	24,700
Total current assets	8,218,100	6,057,002
Property, plant, and equipment:		
At cost	12,945,255	9,922,534
Less accumulated depreciation	(4,382,990)	(3,775,911)
Total prop., plant, and equipment	8,562,265	6,146,623
Goodwill	1,200,000	345,000
Total assets	$17,980,365	$12,548,625
Accounts payable	$ 2,141,552	$ 2,526,789
Bank loan payable	150,000	–
Accrued liabilities	723,600	598,020
Federal income taxes payable	1,200,000	1,759,000
Current portion of long-term debt	240,000	240,000
Total current liabilities	4,455,152	5,123,809
Long-term debt	960,000	1,200,000
Stockholders' equity:		
Common stock	1,250,000	1,000,000
Additional paid-in capital	2,469,921	1,333,801
Retained earnings	8,845,292	3,891,015
Total stockholders' equity	12,565,213	6,224,816
Total liabilities and stockholders' equity	$17,980,365	$12,548,625

Combined Statement of Income and Retained Earnings

	Preliminary 12-31-99	Audited 12-31-98
Sales	$43,994,931	$32,258,015
Cost of goods sold	24,197,212	19,032,229
Gross profit	19,797,719	13,225,786
Selling, general, and administrative expenses	10,592,221	8,900,432
Pension cost	1,117,845	865,030
Interest expense	83,376	104,220
Total operating expenses	11,793,442	9,869,682
Income before taxes	8,004,277	3,356,104
Income tax expense	1,800,000	1,141,000
Net income	6,204,277	2,215,104
Beginning retained earnings	3,891,015	2,675,911
	10,095,292	4,891,015
Dividends declared	(1,250,000)	1,000,000
Ending retained earnings	$ 8,845,292	$ 3,891,015

FIGURE 9-9 **Stanton Enterprises Evidence Planning Worksheet to Decide Tests of Details of Balances for Accounts Receivable**

	Detail tie-in	Existence	Completeness	Accuracy	Classification	Cutoff	Realizable value	Rights	Presentation and disclosure
Acceptable audit risk									
Inherent risk									
Control risk—Sales									
Control risk—Cash receipts									
Control risk—Additional controls									
Substantive tests of transactions—Sales									
Substantive tests of transactions—Cash receipts									
Analytical procedures									
Planned detection risk for tests of details of balances									
Planned audit evidence for tests of details of balances									

Tolerable misstatement _____

INTERNET PROBLEM 9-1: MATERIALITY AND TOLERABLE MISSTATEMENT

Reference the CW site. This problem requires students to apply specific materiality and tolerable misstatement guidelines to actual financial statements obtained from the Internet. This problem also asks students to research the recommendations of the Big Five's Audit Materiality Task Force.

INTERNAL CONTROL AND CONTROL RISK

GOOD INTERNAL CONTROL PREVENTS MORE DEFALCATIONS THAN GOOD AUDITORS FIND

Shortly after its tenth consecutive audit of the Foundation for Youth Bible Studies (FYBS), Able & Co. was informed that FYBS's general ledger accountant was found to have embezzled $2 million during the past 4 years. FYBS wanted to know how this could have occurred without Able discovering it. Able responded that he would have to know how the fraud was carried out to answer the question.

The FYBS's camp facility was in a different state than its home office. Funds were collected from campers and sent in the form of a cashier's check to the general ledger accountant who was supposed to forward the check to the home office cash receipts clerk. The general ledger accountant recorded the revenue using the information on the cashier's check. No record of the source or amount of the cash receipts was maintained at the FYBS camp, which allowed her to occasionally pocket some of the checks. Obviously, she did not record the revenue for these defalcations.

When the auditors gained an understanding of internal control at FYBS, they regularly interviewed employees about how the system functioned. During the course of those discussions, they were never told about the procedure for transmitting funds from the camp. It was not clear that anyone in the home office, other than the embezzler, was aware of it. Fortunately, Able & Co.'s audit report contained a qualification that they could verify only those revenues that were actually recorded. Given the qualification in the audit report and the conduct of their audit, Able & Co. was not held responsible for the loss. They helped FYBS implement new controls to prevent a similar occurrence, but nevertheless, FYBS changed auditors.

LEARNING OBJECTIVES

After studying this chapter, you should be able to

10-1 Contrast management's need for internal control with the auditor's need to consider internal control when designing an audit.

10-2 Explain the five components of internal control.

10-3 Explain methods used to obtain an understanding of internal control.

10-4 Assess control risk by linking strengths and weaknesses of internal control to transaction-related audit objectives.

10-5 Describe the process of designing and performing tests of controls.

As the third chapter dealing with planning the audit, Chapter 10 shows why and how effective internal controls can reduce planned audit evidence. To support the assessment of the control risk component of the audit risk model studied in Chapter 9, auditors must obtain an understanding of internal control and gather related evidence to support that assessment. The shaded part of the chart included in the margin shows where obtaining an understanding of internal control and assessing control risk fit into planning the audit. As the example in the opening vignette involving FYBS demonstrates, weaknesses in internal control can result in material misstatements or fraud.

To effectively assess internal controls for the purpose of reducing planned audit evidence, auditors need to understand key internal control and control risk concepts. Accordingly, this chapter focuses on the objectives of internal control, the components of internal control, and the auditor's methodology for fulfilling the requirements of the second standard of field work. We start by examining both the auditor's and the client's objectives for internal control.

CLIENT AND AUDITOR CONCERNS

OBJECTIVE 10-1

Contrast management's need for internal control with the auditor's need to consider internal control when designing an audit.

A system of internal control consists of policies and procedures designed to provide management with reasonable assurance that the company achieves its objectives and goals. These policies and procedures are often called controls, and collectively they comprise the entity's **internal control**. An understanding of internal control, especially those controls related to the reliability of financial reporting, are important to the auditor's purposes. We will first look at an overview of several key concepts related to internal control before examining both client and auditor concerns about internal control.

Key Concepts

Three key concepts underlie the study of internal control and assessment of control risk.

Management's Responsibility Management, not the auditor, must establish and maintain the entity's controls. This concept is consistent with the requirement that management, not the auditor, is responsible for the preparation of financial statements in accordance with GAAP.

Reasonable Assurance A company should develop internal controls that provide reasonable, but not absolute, assurance that the financial statements are fairly stated. Internal controls are developed by management after considering both the costs and benefits of the controls. Management is often unwilling to implement an ideal system because the costs may be too high. For example, it is unreasonable to expect management of a small company to hire several additional accounting personnel to make small improvements in the reliability of accounting data. It is often less expensive to have auditors do more extensive auditing than to incur higher internal control costs.*

Preplan

Obtain background information

Obtain information about client's legal obligations

Perform preliminary analytical procedures

Set materiality, and assess acceptable audit risk and inherent risk

Understand internal control and assess control risk

Develop overall audit plan and audit program

Inherent Limitations Internal controls can never be regarded as completely effective, regardless of the care followed in their design and implementation. Even if systems personnel could design an ideal system, its effectiveness depends on the competency and dependability of the people using it. For example, assume that a procedure for counting inventory is carefully developed and requires two employees to count independently. If neither of the employees understands the instructions or if both are careless in doing the counts, the inventory count is likely to be wrong. Even if the count is right, management might override the procedure and instruct an employee to increase the count of quantities to improve reported earnings. Similarly, the employees might decide to overstate the counts

---

*Because the Foreign Corrupt Practices Act requires public companies to have an effective accounting system, public companies must evaluate whether their records meet legal requirements even if it is less expensive to have auditors uncover misstatements.

intentionally to cover up a theft of inventory by one or both of them. An act of two or more employees to steal assets or misstate records is called **collusion**.

The 1992 study on internal control titled *Internal Control—Integrated Framework* by the Committee of Sponsoring Organizations of the Treadway Commission (COSO) and SAS 78 provide an extensive description of internal control. The client concerns discussed in this section are taken primarily from SAS 78 and the *COSO Report.*

Management typically has the following three concerns, or broad objectives, in designing an effective control system.

Reliability of Financial Reporting As discussed in Chapter 6, management is responsible for preparing financial statements for investors, creditors, and other users. Management has both a legal and professional responsibility to be sure that the information is fairly prepared in accordance with reporting requirements such as GAAP.

Efficiency and Effectiveness of Operations Controls within an organization are meant to encourage efficient and effective use of its resources, including personnel, to optimize the company's goals. An important part of these controls is accurate information for internal decision making. A variety of information is used for making critical business decisions. For example, the price to charge for products is based in part on information about the cost of making the products.

Another important part of effectiveness and efficiency is safeguarding assets and records. The physical assets of a company can be stolen, misused, or accidentally destroyed unless they are protected by adequate controls. The same is true of nonphysical assets such as accounts receivable, important documents (confidential government contracts), and records (general ledger and journals). Safeguarding certain assets and records has become increasingly important since the advent of computer systems. Large amounts of information stored on computer media can be destroyed if care is not taken to protect them. Safeguarding of accounting records also affects the reliability of financial reporting.

Compliance with Applicable Laws and Regulations Organizations are required to follow many laws and regulations. Some are only indirectly related to accounting. Examples include environmental protection and civil rights laws. Others are closely related to accounting, such as income tax regulations and fraud.

One important law affecting all companies subject to the Securities and Exchange Act of 1934 is the Foreign Corrupt Practices Act of 1977. This law, which amended the securities acts, requires that a company maintain "proper record-keeping systems." A proper record-keeping system is one that allows the preparation of reliable external financial statements and prevents off-the-books slush funds and payment of bribes.

Knowledge about a client's internal control is sufficiently important to the audit process to merit a separate generally accepted auditing standard. Recall that the second GAAS field work standard states, "A sufficient understanding of internal control is to be obtained to plan the audit and to determine the nature, timing, and extent of tests to be performed." Auditors are primarily concerned about controls related to the reliability of financial reporting and controls over classes of transactions.

Controls Related to the Reliability of Financial Reporting To comply with the second standard of field work, the auditor is interested primarily in controls that relate to the first of management's internal control concerns: reliability of financial reporting. This is the area that directly affects the financial statements and their related assertions and therefore affects the auditor's objective of determining that the financial statements are fairly stated. The financial statements are not likely to correctly reflect GAAP if the controls affecting the reliability of financial reporting are inadequate. On the other hand, the statements can be fairly stated even if the company's controls do not promote efficiency and effectiveness in its operations.

KPMG
Fraud Survey

As stated in Chapter 6, auditors have significant responsibility for the discovery of material fraudulent financial reporting and misappropriation of assets (fraud) and direct-effects illegal acts. Auditors are therefore also concerned with a client's internal control over the safeguarding of assets and compliance with applicable laws and regulations if they affect the fairness of the financial statements. Internal controls, if properly designed and implemented, can be effective in preventing or detecting fraud. The results of a recent fraud survey by KPMG (see p. 291) indicate that about half of the typical frauds are detected by internal controls.

It has already been stated that auditors should emphasize controls concerned with the reliability of data for *external reporting purposes,* but controls affecting internal management information, such as budgets and internal performance reports, should not be completely ignored. These types of information are often important sources of evidence in helping the auditor decide whether the financial statements are fairly presented. If the controls over these internal reports are considered inadequate, the value of the reports as evidence diminishes.

Controls over Classes of Transactions The primary emphasis by auditors is on internal control over classes of transactions rather than account balances. The reason is that the accuracy of the output of the accounting system (account balances) is heavily dependent on the accuracy of the inputs and processing (transactions). For example, if products sold, units shipped, or unit selling prices are wrong in billing customers for sales, both sales and accounts receivable will be misstated. If controls are adequate to make sure billings, cash receipts, sales returns and allowances, and charge-offs are correct, the ending balance in accounts receivable is likely to be correct.

When gaining an understanding of internal control and assessing control risk, auditors are primarily concerned with the transaction-related audit objectives discussed in Chapter 6. These objectives were discussed in detail on pages 156–157. Table 10-1 illustrates the development of transaction-related audit objectives for sales transactions.

While gaining an understanding of internal control and assessing control risk, the auditor does not, however, ignore internal control over account balances. For example, transaction-related audit objectives typically have no effect on three balance-related audit objectives: realizable value, rights and obligations, and presentation and disclosure. The auditor is likely to evaluate separately whether management has implemented internal controls for each of these three balance-related audit objectives.

Because of the inherent limitations of internal controls and because auditors cannot obtain more than reasonable assurance of their effectiveness, there is almost always some

TABLE 10-1 Sales Transaction-Related Audit Objectives	
Transaction-Related Audit Objectives—General Form	**Sales Transaction-Related Audit Objectives**
Recorded transactions exist (existence).	Recorded sales are for shipments made to existing customers.
Existing transactions are recorded (completeness).	Existing sales transactions are recorded.
Recorded transactions are stated at the correct amounts (accuracy).	Recorded sales are for the amount of goods shipped and are correctly billed and recorded.
Transactions are properly classified (classification).	Sales transactions are properly classified.
Transactions are recorded on the correct dates (timing).	Sales are recorded on the correct dates.
Recorded transactions are properly included in the master files and correctly summarized (posting and summarization).	Sales transactions are properly included in the master files and are correctly summarized.

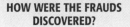

HOW WERE THE FRAUDS DISCOVERED?

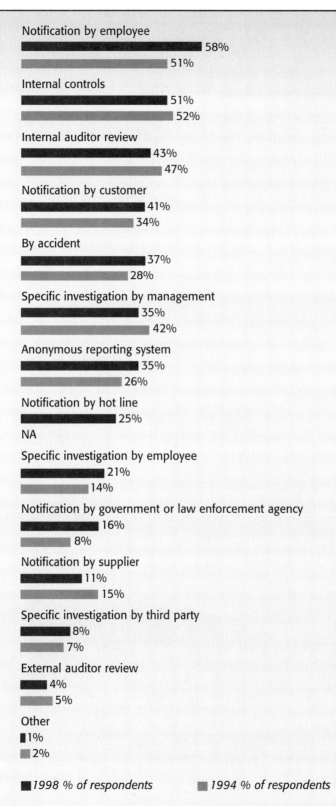

Notification by employee
58%
51%

Internal controls
51%
52%

Internal auditor review
43%
47%

Notification by customer
41%
34%

By accident
37%
28%

Specific investigation by management
35%
42%

Anonymous reporting system
35%
26%

Notification by hot line
25%
NA

Specific investigation by employee
21%
14%

Notification by government or law enforcement agency
16%
8%

Notification by supplier
11%
15%

Specific investigation by third party
8%
7%

External auditor review
4%
5%

Other
1%
2%

■ *1998 % of respondents*   ■ *1994 % of respondents*

Source: KPMG's *1998 Fraud Survey* of 5,000 U.S. companies and organizations.

level of control risk greater than zero. Therefore, even with the most effectively designed internal controls, the auditor must obtain audit evidence beyond testing the controls for every material financial statement account.

COMPONENTS OF INTERNAL CONTROL

OBJECTIVE 10-2
Explain the five components of internal control.

Internal control includes five categories of controls that management designs and implements to provide reasonable assurance that management's control objectives will be met. These are called the components of internal control and are (1) the control environment, (2) risk assessment, (3) control activities, (4) information and communication, and (5) monitoring. Figure 10-1 shows that the control environment is the umbrella for the other four components. Without an effective control environment, the other four components are unlikely to result in effective internal control, regardless of their quality.

Each of the categories contain many controls. The auditor is concerned primarily with those designed to prevent or detect material misstatements in the financial statements. Those aspects are the focus of the remainder of this chapter.

FIGURE 10-1	**Five Components of Internal Control**

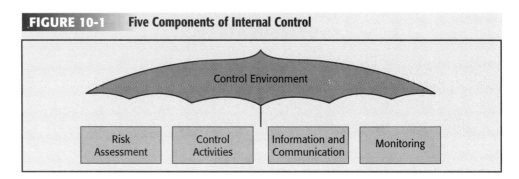

The Control Environment

The essence of an effectively controlled organization lies in the attitude of its management. If top management believes that control is important, others in the organization will sense that and respond by conscientiously observing the controls established. On the other hand, if it is clear to members of the organization that control is not an important concern to top management and it is given lip service rather than meaningful support, it is almost certain that management's control objectives will not be effectively achieved.

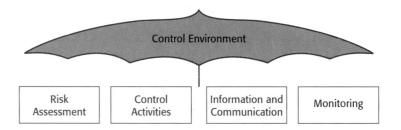

The **control environment** consists of the actions, policies, and procedures that reflect the overall attitudes of top management, directors, and owners of an entity about internal control and its importance to the entity. For the purpose of understanding and assessing the control environment, the following are the most important subcomponents the auditor should consider.

Integrity and Ethical Values Integrity and ethical values are the product of the entity's ethical and behavioral standards and how they are communicated and reinforced in practice. They include management's actions to remove or reduce incentives and temptations that might prompt personnel to engage in dishonest, illegal, or unethical acts. They also include the communication of entity values and behavioral standards to personnel through policy statements and codes of conduct and by example.

Commitment to Competence Competence is the knowledge and skills necessary to accomplish tasks that define the individual's job. Commitment to competence includes management's consideration of the competence levels for specific jobs and how those levels translate into requisite skills and knowledge.

Board of Directors or Audit Committee Participation An effective board of directors is independent of management, and its members are involved in and scrutinize management's activities. The board delegates responsibility for internal control to management and is charged with providing regular independent assessments of management-established internal control. In addition, an active and objective board can often effectively reduce the likelihood that management overrides existing controls. To assist the board in its oversight, the board often creates an audit committee that is charged with oversight responsibility for the financial reporting process. The audit committee is also responsible for maintaining ongoing communication with both external and internal auditors. This allows the auditors and directors to discuss matters that might relate to such things as the integrity or actions of management. The audit committee's independence from management and knowledge of financial reporting issues are considered important determinants in their ability to effectively evaluate internal controls and financial statements prepared by management. In fact, the New York Stock Exchange requires and the American Stock Exchange recommends that listed companies have an audit committee composed entirely of outside directors. The NASDAQ market requires only that a majority of the audit committee positions are held by outside directors. Many privately held companies also create effective audit committees, recognizing the importance of effective financial reporting and internal control oversight.

Audit Committee
Best Practices

AUDIT COMMITTEE EFFECTIVENESS	An abundance of accounting scandals, such as the alleged recording of millions of dollars in bogus revenues at Cendant Corporation, suggest that audit committees are not always effectively doing their jobs. Investor activists attack such committees for lacking independence or financial expertise to uncover most financial reporting failures. They note that audit committees sometimes fall short because a chief executive picks members who are willing to go with the flow. Audit committees need independent directors with sophisticated financial backgrounds. In response to these concerns, the Securities and Exchange Commission created a blue ribbon committee to study the effectiveness of audit committees. That committee issued a report in 1999 titled *Report and Recommendations of the Blue Ribbon Committee on Improving the Effectiveness of Corporate Audit Committees*. The report contains 10 recommendations designed to (1) strengthen the independence of the audit committee, (2) make the audit committee more effective, and (3) address mechanisms for accountability among the audit committee, the outside auditors, and management.

Sources: "Scandals Signal Laxity of Audit Panels," *The Wall Street Journal* (July 17, 1998), B1. *Report and Recommendations of the Blue Ribbon Committee on Improving the Effectiveness of Corporate Audit Committees*, New York Stock Exchange and the National Association of Securities Dealers, 1999.

Management's Philosophy and Operating Style Management, through its activities, provides clear signals to employees about the importance of internal control. For example, does management take significant risks, or are they risk averse? Are profit plans and budget data set as "best possible" plans or "most likely" targets? Can management be described as "fat and bureaucratic," "lean and mean," dominated by one or a few individuals, or is it "just right"? Understanding these and similar aspects of management's philosophy and operating style gives the auditor a sense of management's attitude about internal control.

National Association of Corporate Directors

Organizational Structure The entity's organizational structure defines the existing lines of responsibility and authority. By understanding the client's organizational structure, the auditor can learn the management and functional elements of the business and perceive how controls are implemented.

Assignment of Authority and Responsibility In addition to the informal aspects of communication already mentioned, formal methods of communication about authority and responsibility and similar control-related matters are equally important. These might include such methods as memoranda from top management about the importance of control and control-related matters, formal organizational and operating plans, and employee job descriptions and related policies.

Human Resource Policies and Practices The most important aspect of internal control is personnel. If employees are competent and trustworthy, other controls can be absent and reliable financial statements will still result. Honest, efficient people are able to perform at a high level even when there are few other controls to support them. Even if there are numerous other controls, incompetent or dishonest people can reduce the system to a shambles. Even though personnel may be competent and trustworthy, people have certain innate shortcomings. For example, they can become bored or dissatisfied, personal problems can disrupt their performance, or their goals may change.

a lot has to do w/ compensation

Because of the importance of competent, trustworthy personnel in providing effective control, the methods by which persons are hired, evaluated, trained, promoted, and compensated are an important part of internal control.

The auditor obtains information about each of the subcomponents of the control environment. The auditor then uses this understanding as a basis for assessing management's and the directors' attitude and awareness about the importance of control. For example, the auditor might determine the nature of a client's budgeting system as a part of understanding the design of the control environment. The operation of the budgeting system might then be evaluated in part by inquiry of budgeting personnel to determine budgeting procedures and follow-up of differences between budget and actual. The auditor might also examine client schedules comparing actual results to budgeted amounts.

Risk Assessment

Deloitte & Touche *Perspectives on Risk*

Risk assessment for financial reporting is *management's* identification and analysis of risks relevant to the preparation of financial statements in conformity with GAAP. For example, if a company frequently sells products at a price below inventory cost because of rapid technology changes, it is essential for the company to incorporate adequate controls to overcome the risk of overstating inventory.

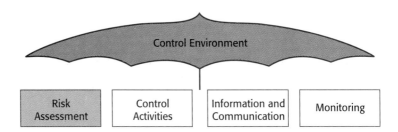

All entities, regardless of size, structure, nature, or industry, face a variety of risks from external and internal sources that must be managed. Because economic, industry, regulatory, and operating conditions constantly change, management is challenged with developing mechanisms to identify and deal with risks associated with change. Internal control under one set of conditions will not necessarily be effective under another.

Identifying and analyzing risk is an ongoing process and a critical component of effective internal control. Management must focus on risks at all levels of the organization and take necessary actions to manage them. An important first step is for management to identify factors that may increase risk. Failure to meet prior objectives, quality of personnel, geographic dispersion of company operations, significance and complexity of core business processes, introduction of new information technologies, and entrance of new competitors all represent examples of factors that may lead to increased risk. Once a risk is identified, management estimates the significance of that risk, assesses the likelihood of the risk occurring, and develops specific actions that need to be taken to reduce the risk to an acceptable level. Of course, there is no cost-beneficial way to eliminate risk. However, management must assess how much risk is prudently acceptable and strive to maintain risk within this level.

Management's risk assessment differs from but is closely related to the auditor's risk assessment discussed in Chapter 9. Management assesses risks as a part of designing and operating internal controls to minimize errors and fraud. Auditors assess risks to decide the evidence needed in the audit. If management effectively assesses and responds to risks, the auditor will typically accumulate less evidence than when management fails to identify or respond to significant risks.

The auditor obtains knowledge about management's risk assessment process by determining how management identifies risks relevant to financial reporting, evaluating their significance and likelihood of occurrence, and deciding the actions needed to address the risks. Questionnaires and discussions with management are the most common ways to obtain this understanding.

Control activities are the policies and procedures, in addition to those included in the other four components, that help ensure that necessary actions are taken to address risks in the achievement of the entity's objectives. There are potentially many such control activities in any entity. SAS 78 and the *COSO Report* note that control activities generally relate to policies and procedures that pertain to (1) segregation of duties, (2) information processing, (3) physical controls, and (4) performance reviews. The development of control activities related to these types of policies and procedures generally falls into the following five types of specific control activities, which are discussed next:

Control Activities

1. Adequate separation of duties
2. Proper authorization of transactions and activities
3. Adequate documents and records
4. Physical control over assets and records
5. Independent checks on performance

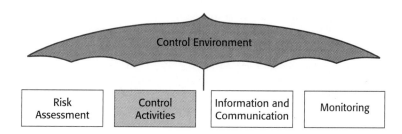

Adequate Separation of Duties Four general guidelines for adequate **separation of duties** to prevent both fraud and errors are of special significance to auditors.

Separation of the Custody of Assets from Accounting The reason for not permitting a person who has temporary or permanent custody of an asset to account for that asset is to protect the company against defalcation. When one person performs both functions, there is an increased risk of that person disposing of the asset for personal gain and adjusting the records to relieve himself or herself of responsibility. If the cashier, for example, receives cash and is responsible for data entry for cash receipts and sales, it is possible for the cashier to take the cash received from a customer and adjust the customer's account by failing to record a sale or by recording a fictitious credit to the account.

Separation of the Authorization of Transactions from the Custody of Related Assets If possible, it is desirable to prevent persons who authorize transactions from having control over the related asset. For example, the same person should not authorize the payment of a vendor's invoice and also sign the check in payment of the bill. The authorization of a transaction and the handling of the related asset by the same person increase the possibility of defalcation within the organization.

Separation of Operational Responsibility from Record-Keeping Responsibility If each department or division in an organization were responsible for preparing its own records and reports, there would be a tendency to bias the results to improve its reported performance. To ensure unbiased information, record keeping is typically included in a separate department under the controller.

Separation of IT Duties from Duties of Key Users Outside IT The use of computers to process and manage information is called **information technology (IT)**. As the level of complexity of IT systems increases, often the segregation of authorization, record keeping, and custody is blurred. For example, sales agents may enter customer orders on-line. The computer authorizes those sales based on its comparison of customer credit limits to the master file and posts all approved sales in the sales cycle journals. Therefore, the computer plays a significant role in the authorization and record keeping of sales transactions. To compensate for these potential overlaps of duties, it is important for companies to separate major IT-related functions from key user department functions. In this example, responsibility for designing and controlling accounting software programs that contain the sales authorization and posting controls should be under the authority of IT, whereas the ability to update information in the master file of customer credit limits should reside in the company's credit department outside the IT function.

Naturally, the extent of separation of duties depends heavily on the size of the organization. In many small companies, it is not practical to segregate the duties to the extent suggested. In these cases, audit evidence may require modification.

Proper Authorization of Transactions and Activities Every transaction must be properly authorized if controls are to be satisfactory. If any person in an organization could acquire or expend assets at will, complete chaos would result. Authorization can be either *general* or *specific*. **General authorization** means that management establishes policies for the organization to follow. Subordinates are instructed to implement these general authorizations by approving all transactions within the limits set by the policy. Examples of general authorization are the issuance of fixed price lists for the sale of products, credit limits for customers, and fixed reorder points for making acquisitions.

Specific authorization applies to individual transactions. Management is often unwilling to establish a general policy of authorization for some transactions. Instead, it prefers to make authorizations on a case-by-case basis. An example is the authorization of a sales transaction by the sales manager for a used-car company.

There is also a distinction between authorization and approval. Authorization is a policy decision for either a general class of transactions or specific transactions. Approval is the implementation of management's general authorization decisions. For example, assume that management sets a policy authorizing the ordering of inventory when less than a 3-week supply is on hand. That is a general authorization. When a department orders inventory, the clerk responsible for maintaining the perpetual record approves the order to indicate that the authorization policy has been met. In other cases, the computer performs the general approval of transactions. The comparison of quantities of inventory on hand to a master file of reorder points may be performed by the computer, and the computer may use that comparison to decide whether to submit purchase orders to authorized suppliers in the vendor master file. In that case, the computer is performing the general approval function using preauthorized information contained in the master files. The authorization in this case is performed by purchasing department personnel when they authorize changes to reorder points and vendors in the inventory and vendor master files, respectively.

Adequate Documents and Records Documents and records are the physical objects upon which transactions are entered and summarized. They include such diverse items as sales invoices, purchase orders, subsidiary records, sales journals, and employee time cards. Many of these documents and records are maintained in the form of computer files until they are printed out for specific purposes. Both documents of original entry and records upon which transactions are entered are important, but the inadequacy of documents typically causes greater control problems.

Documents perform the function of transmitting information throughout the client's organization and between different organizations. The documents must be adequate to provide reasonable assurance that all assets are properly controlled and all transactions are correctly recorded. For example, if the receiving department fills out a receiving report when material is obtained, the accounts payable department can verify the quantity and description on the vendor's invoice by comparing it with the information on the receiving report.

Certain relevant principles dictate the proper design and use of documents and records. Documents and records should be

- Prenumbered consecutively to facilitate control over missing documents and as an aid in locating documents when they are needed at a later date (significantly affects the transaction-related audit objective of completeness).
- Prepared at the time a transaction takes place, or as soon as possible thereafter. When there is a longer time interval, records are less credible and the chance for misstatement increases (affects the transaction-related audit objective of timing).
- Sufficiently simple to ensure that they are clearly understood.
- Designed for multiple use, when possible, to minimize the number of different forms. For example, a properly designed and used shipping document can be the basis for releasing goods from storage to the shipping department, informing billing of the quantity of goods to bill to the customer and the appropriate billing date, and updating the perpetual inventory records.
- Constructed in a manner that encourages correct preparation. This can be done by providing internal checks within the form or record. For example, a document might include instructions for proper routing, blank spaces for authorizations and approvals, and designated column spaces for numerical data.

When data related to transactions are entered on-line into the computer, the design of the input screen is important to minimize errors and to improve efficiencies in the input process. For example, automatic prompts that provide instructional messages assist input personnel in identifying information needed for input. Automatic cursor movement to the next desired cell of information requested helps guide the input process in a systematic and organized way, which increases input accuracy and completeness. Input screen controls often validate information entered. For example, a general ledger account code entered may be automatically rejected when the account number does not match the chart of accounts master file. Other input screen controls automatically assign sequential document numbers and prevent the input clerk from changing that sequence number.

A control closely related to documents and records is the **chart of accounts**, which classifies transactions into individual balance sheet and income statement accounts. The chart of accounts is an important control because it provides the framework for determining the information presented to management and other financial statement users. The chart of accounts is helpful in preventing classification errors if it accurately and precisely describes which type of transactions should be in each account.

The procedures for proper record keeping should be spelled out in systems manuals to encourage consistent application. The manuals should provide sufficient information to facilitate adequate record keeping and maintain proper control over assets. Many software applications contain Help screens, which assist in the proper use of accounting software.

Physical Control over Assets and Records To maintain adequate internal control, it is essential to protect assets and records. If assets are left unprotected, they can be stolen. If records are not adequately protected, they can be stolen, damaged, or lost. In the event of such an occurrence, the accounting process and normal operations could be seriously disrupted. When a company is highly computerized, it is especially important to protect its computer equipment, programs, and data files. The equipment and programs are expensive and essential to operations. The data files are the records of the company and, if damaged, could be costly or even impossible to reconstruct.

The most important type of protective measure for safeguarding assets and records is the use of physical precautions. An example is the use of storerooms for inventory to guard against theft. When the storeroom is under the control of a competent employee, there is further assurance that obsolescence is minimized. Fireproof safes and safety deposit vaults for the protection of assets such as currency and securities are other important physical safeguards.

There are three categories of controls related to safeguarding IT equipment, programs, and data files. As with other types of assets, physical controls are used to protect the computer facilities. Examples are locks on doors to the computer room and terminals, proper control of environmental conditions such as temperature and humidity where the computer resides, adequate storage space for software and data files to protect them from loss, and proper fire-extinguishing systems. Access controls deal with ensuring that only authorized people can use the equipment and have access to software and data files. An example is an on-line access password system. Back-up and recovery procedures are steps an organization can take in the event of a loss of equipment, programs, or data. For example, a back-up copy of programs and critical data files stored in a safe remote location is a common back-up control.

Independent Checks on Performance The last category of control activities is the careful and continuous review of the other four, often called **independent checks** or internal verification. The need for independent checks arises because internal control tends to change over time unless there is a mechanism for frequent review. Personnel are likely to forget or intentionally fail to follow procedures, or they may become careless unless someone observes and evaluates their performance. In addition, both fraudulent and unintentional misstatements are possible, regardless of the quality of the controls.

An essential characteristic of the persons performing internal verification procedures is independence from the individuals originally responsible for preparing the data. The least expensive means of internal verification is the separation of duties in the manner previously discussed. For example, when the bank reconciliation is performed by a person independent of the accounting records and handling of cash, there is an opportunity for verification without incurring significant additional costs.

Computerized accounting systems can be designed so that many internal verification procedures can be automated as part of the system. For example, the computer will prevent the processing of payment on a vendor invoice if there is no matched purchase order number or receiving report number for that invoice recorded in the system.

Auditors obtain an understanding of the control environment and risk assessment in a similar manner for most audits, but obtaining an understanding of control activities varies considerably. For smaller clients, it is common to identify few or even no control activities because controls are often ineffective because of limited personnel. In that case, the auditor sets a high assessed control risk. For clients with extensive controls that the auditor believes to be excellent, it is often appropriate to identify many controls during the understanding phase. In other audits, the auditor may identify a limited number of controls during this phase and then identify additional controls later in the process. The extent to which controls are identified is a matter of audit judgment. A methodology for identifying controls is studied later in the chapter.

The purpose of an entity's accounting **information and communication** system is to identify, assemble, classify, analyze, record, and report the entity's transactions and to maintain accountability for the related assets. An accounting information and communication system has several subcomponents, typically made up of classes of transactions such as sales, sales returns, cash receipts, acquisitions, and so on. For each class of transactions, the accounting system must satisfy all of the six transaction-related audit objectives identified earlier in the chapter (p. 290). For example, the sales accounting system should be designed to ensure that all shipments of goods by a company are correctly recorded as sales (completeness and accuracy objectives) and reflected in the financial statements in the proper period (timing objective). The system must also avoid duplicate recording of sales and recording a sale if a shipment did not occur (existence objective).

For a small company with active involvement by the owner, a simple computerized accounting system that involves primarily one honest competent accountant may provide an adequate accounting information system. A larger company requires a more complex system that includes carefully defined responsibilities and written procedures.

To understand the design of the accounting information system, the auditor determines (1) the major classes of transactions of the entity; (2) how those transactions are initiated; (3) what accounting records exist and their nature; (4) how transactions are processed from initiation to completion, including the extent and nature of computer use; and (5) the nature and details of the financial reporting process followed. Typically, this is accomplished and documented by a narrative description of the system or by a flowchart. (These are described later in the chapter.) The operation of the accounting information system is often determined by tracing one or a few transactions through the system (called a **transaction walk-through**).

Monitoring activities deal with ongoing or periodic assessment of the quality of internal control performance by management to determine that controls are operating as intended and that they are modified as appropriate for changes in conditions. Information for

internal audit staff would be in charge of.

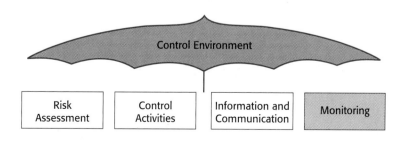

assessment and modification comes from a variety of sources, including studies of existing internal controls, internal auditor reports, exception reporting on control activities, reports by regulators such as bank regulatory agencies, feedback from operating personnel, and complaints from customers about billing charges.

The most important things the auditor needs to know about monitoring are the major types of monitoring activities a company uses and how these activities are used to modify internal controls when necessary. Discussion with management is the most common way to obtain this understanding.

For many companies, especially larger ones, an internal audit department is essential for effective monitoring. For an internal audit function to be effective, it is essential that the internal audit staff be independent of both the operating and accounting departments and

UC Irvine's Department
of Internal Control

TABLE 10-2	Components of Internal Control	
Internal Control		
Components	**Description of Component**	**Further Subdivision (if applicable)**
Control environment	Actions, policies, and procedures that reflect the overall attitude of top management, directors, and owners of an entity about internal control and its importance	Subcomponents of the control environment: • Integrity and ethical values • Commitment to competence • Board of directors or audit committee participation • Management's philosophy and operating style • Organizational structure • Assignment of authority and responsibility • Human resource policies and practices
Risk assessment	Management's identification and analysis of risks relevant to the preparation of financial statements in accordance with GAAP	Risk assessment processes: • Identify factors affecting risks. • Assess significance of risks and likelihood of occurrence. • Determine actions necessary to manage risks. Management assertions that must be satisfied: • Existence or occurrence • Completeness • Valuation or allocation • Rights and obligations • Presentation and disclosure
Control activities	Policies and procedures that management has established to meet its objectives for financial reporting	Types of specific control activities: • Adequate separation of duties • Proper authorization of transactions and activities • Adequate documents and records • Physical control over assets and records • Independent checks on performance
Information and communication	Methods used to identify, assemble, classify, record, and report an entity's transactions and to maintain accountability for related assets	Transaction-related audit objectives that must be satisfied: • Existence • Completeness • Accuracy • Classification • Timing • Posting and summarization
Monitoring	Management's ongoing and periodic assessment of the quality of internal control performance to determine whether controls are operating as intended and modified when needed	Not applicable

that it report directly to a high level of authority within the organization, either top management or the audit committee of the board of directors.

In addition to its role in monitoring an entity's internal control, an adequate internal audit staff can reduce external audit costs by providing direct assistance to the external auditor. SAS 65 (AU 322) defines the way internal auditors affect the external auditor's evidence accumulation. If the external auditor obtains evidence that supports the competence, integrity, and objectivity of internal auditors, the external auditor can rely on the internal auditor's work in a number of ways.

A company's size has a significant effect on the nature of internal control and the specific controls that are placed in operation. Obviously, it is more difficult to establish adequate separation of duties in a small company. It would also be unreasonable to expect a small firm to have internal auditors. However, if the various subcomponents of internal control are examined, it becomes apparent that most are applicable to both large and small companies. Even though it may not be common to formalize policies in manuals, it is certainly possible for a small company to have (1) competent, trustworthy personnel with clear lines of authority; (2) proper procedures for authorization, execution, and recording of transactions; (3) adequate documents, records, and reports; (4) physical controls over assets and records; and, to a limited degree, (5) independent checks on performance.

How the Size of the Business Affects the Components of Internal Control

A major control available in a small company is the knowledge and concern of the top operating person, who is often an owner-manager. A personal interest in the organization and a close relationship with personnel make careful evaluation of the competence of the employees and the effectiveness of the overall system possible. For example, internal control can be significantly strengthened if the owner conscientiously performs such duties as signing all checks after carefully reviewing supporting documents, reviewing bank reconciliations, examining accounts receivable statements sent to customers, approving credit, examining all correspondence from customers and vendors, and approving bad debts.

The five components of internal control discussed in the preceding sections are summarized in Table 10-2 (p. 300).

PROCEDURES TO OBTAIN AN UNDERSTANDING OF INTERNAL CONTROL

Now that the various components of internal control have been discussed, we turn our attention to considering these components when obtaining an understanding of internal control and assessing control risk. The procedures used to gather evidence about design and placement in operation during the understanding phase are called **procedures to obtain an understanding**. Auditors obtain information about internal control and use that information as a basis for audit planning. Figure 10-2 shows how the auditor's consideration of internal control affects substantive testing of account balances. The auditor considers internal control by first obtaining an understanding of internal control, which is then used to initially assess control risk. When the auditor's control risk assessment is below maximum, the auditor performs tests of controls. Once the results of the tests of controls are known, the auditor considers how those results affect planned detection risk and substantive testing. The remainder of this chapter deals with ways that practitioners implement the first three parts of Figure 10-2.

> **OBJECTIVE 10-3**
> Explain methods used to obtain an understanding of internal control.

FIGURE 10-2   Process of Understanding Internal Control and Assessing Control Risk

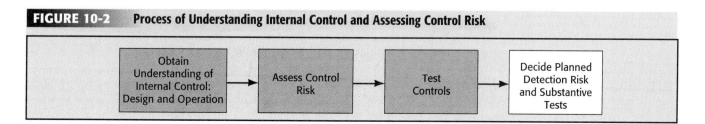

In practice, the procedures used to gain an understanding of internal control and assess control risk vary considerably from client to client. For smaller clients, many auditors obtain a level of understanding sufficient only to assess whether the statements are auditable, evaluate the control environment for management's attitude toward internal control and financial reporting, and determine the adequacy of the client's accounting system. Often, for efficiency, internal controls are ignored, control risk is assumed to be maximum, and detection risk is therefore low. For many larger clients, especially for repeat engagements, the auditor sets a low assessed control risk for most parts of the audit before the audit starts.

Reasons for Understanding Internal Control Sufficiently to Plan the Audit

SAS 55 (as amended by SAS 78, AU 319) *requires the auditor to obtain an understanding of internal control for every audit.* The extent of that understanding must, at a minimum, be sufficient to adequately plan the audit, in terms of four specific planning matters.

Auditability The auditor must obtain information about the integrity of management and the nature and extent of the accounting records to be satisfied that sufficient, competent evidence is available to support the financial statement balances.

Potential Material Misstatements The understanding should allow the auditor to identify the types of potential errors and fraud that might affect the financial statements and to assess the risk that such misstatements might occur in amounts that are material to the financial statements.

Detection Risk Control risk in the planning form of the audit risk model directly affects planned detection risk for each audit objective [PDR = AAR ÷ (IR × CR)]. Information about internal control is used to assess control risk for each objective, which affects planned detection risk and planned audit evidence.

Design of Tests The information obtained should allow the auditor to design effective tests of the financial statement balances. Such tests include tests for monetary correctness of both transactions and balances, and analytical procedures.

A common approach used by auditors is to (1) obtain an understanding of the control environment, risk assessment procedures, accounting information and communication system, and monitoring methods at a fairly detailed level; (2) identify specific controls that will reduce control risk and make an assessment of control risk; and (3) test the controls for effectiveness. The auditor can conclude that control risk is low only after all three steps are completed. The three steps just discussed are now explained in more detail to illustrate further how gaining an understanding of a client's internal controls and assessing control risk are done.

Procedures to Determine Design and Placement in Operation

The auditor's task in obtaining an understanding of internal control is to find out about each of the five components of internal control. In obtaining that understanding, the auditor should consider two aspects: (1) the *design* of the various controls within each component and (2) whether they have been *placed in operation*. The following are procedures to determine the design and placement in operation.

Update and Evaluate Auditor's Previous Experience with the Entity Most audits of a company are done annually by the same CPA firm. Except for initial engagements, the auditor begins the audit with a great deal of information developed in prior years about the client's internal control. Because systems and controls usually do not change frequently, this information can be updated and carried forward to the current year's audit.

Make Inquiries of Client Personnel A logical starting place for updating information carried forward from the previous audit, or for obtaining information initially, is with appropriate client personnel. Inquiries of client personnel at the management, supervisory, and staff level will usually be conducted as part of obtaining an understanding of internal control.

Read Client's Policy and Systems Manuals To design, implement, and maintain internal controls, an entity must have extensive documentation of its own. This includes policy manuals and documents (such as a corporate code of conduct) and systems manuals and documents (such as an accounting manual and an organization chart). This information is read by the auditor and discussed with company personnel to ensure that it is properly interpreted and understood.

Examine Documents and Records The five components of internal control all involve the creation of many documents and records. These will have been presented to some degree in the policy and systems manuals. By examining completed documents, records, and computer files, the auditor can bring the contents of the manuals to life and better understand them. Examination of the documents and records also provides evidence that the control policies and procedures have been placed in operation.

Observe Entity Activities and Operations In addition to examining completed documents and records, the auditor can observe client personnel in the process of preparing them and carrying out their normal accounting and control activities. This further enhances understanding and knowledge that controls have been placed in operation.

Observation, documentation, and inquiry can be conveniently and effectively combined in the form of the transaction walk-through mentioned earlier. With that procedure, the auditor selects one or a few documents for the initiation of a transaction type and traces it (them) through the entire accounting process. At each stage of processing, the auditor makes inquiries and observes current activities, in addition to examining completed documentation for the transaction or transactions selected.

Three commonly used methods of documenting the understanding of internal control are narratives, flowcharts, and internal control questionnaires. These may be used separately or in combination, as discussed in the following sections.

Documentation of the Understanding

Narrative A **narrative** is a written description of a client's internal controls. A proper narrative of an accounting system and related controls includes four characteristics:

1. *The origin of every document and record in the system.* For example, the description should state where customer orders come from and how sales invoices are generated.
2. *All processing that takes place.* For example, if sales amounts are determined by a computer program that multiplies quantities shipped by standard prices contained in price master files, that should be described.
3. *The disposition of every document and record in the system.* The filing of documents, sending them to customers, or destroying them should be shown.
4. *An indication of the controls relevant to the assessment of control risk.* These typically include separation of duties (such as separating recording cash from handling cash), authorizations and approvals (such as credit approvals), and internal verification (such as comparison of unit selling price to sales contracts).

Flowchart An internal control **flowchart** is a symbolic, diagrammatic representation of the client's documents and their sequential flow in the organization. An adequate flowchart includes the same four characteristics identified for narratives.

Flowcharting is advantageous primarily because it can provide a concise overview of the client's system, which is useful to the auditor as an analytical tool in evaluation. A well-prepared flowchart aids in identifying inadequacies by facilitating a clear understanding of how the system operates. For most uses, it is superior to narratives as a method of communicating the characteristics of a system, especially to show adequate separation of

Flowchart Software

duties. It is easier to follow a diagram than to read a description. It is also usually easier to update a flowchart than a narrative.

It would be unusual to use both a narrative and a flowchart to describe the same system because both are intended to describe the flow of documents and records in an accounting system. Sometimes, a combination of a narrative and flowchart is used. The decision to use one or the other or a combination of the two is dependent on two factors: (1) the relative ease of understanding by current- and subsequent-year auditors and (2) the

FIGURE 10-3	Partial Internal Control Questionnaire for Sales

Client _Hillsburg Hardware Co._ ————————— Audit Date _12/31/99_

Auditor _MSW_   Date Completed _9/30/99_   Reviewed by _9R_   Date Completed _10/1/99_

Objective (shaded) and Question	Answer			Remarks
	Yes	No	N/A	
Sales				
A. Recorded sales are for shipments actually made to existing customers.				
1. Is the recording of sales supported by authorized shipping documents and approved customer orders?	✓			_Pam Dilley examines underlying documentation._
2. Is customers' credit approved by a responsible official and is access to change credit limit master files restricted?	✓			_By Chulick, the president_
3. Is a prenumbered written shipping order required for any merchandise to leave the premises?	✓			
B. Existing sales transactions are recorded.				
1. Is a record of shipments maintained?	✓			
2. Is the shipping document controlled from the office in a manner that helps ensure that all shipments are billed?	✓			
3. Are shipping documents prenumbered and accounted for?	✓			
4. Are sales invoices prenumbered and accounted for?		✓		_Prenumbered but not accounted for. Additional substantive testing required._
C. Recorded sales are for the amount of goods shipped and are correctly billed and recorded.				
1. Is there independent comparison of the quantity on the shipping documents to the sales invoices?	✓			_By Pam Dilley, controlled by Chulick_
2. Is an authorized price list used and is access to change the price master file restricted?	✓			
3. Are monthly statements sent to customers?	✓			
D. Recorded sales transactions are properly classified.				
1. Is there independent comparison of recorded sales to the chart of accounts?			✓	_All sales are on account and there is only one sales account._
E. Sales are recorded on the correct dates.				
1. Is there independent comparison of dates on shipping documents to dates recorded?		✓		_There is a weakness in the system and additional substantive testing required._
F. Sales transactions are properly included in the master files and correctly summarized.				
1. Are journals independently footed and traced to the general ledger and printout of master file?		✓		_Examined for reasonableness by Chulick._
2. Is there a comparison of customer names on shipping documents to posting in the printout of the master file?	✓			_By Pam Dilley_

relative cost of preparation. Several flowcharting software packages can be downloaded at no charge from the Internet.

Internal Control Questionnaire An **internal control questionnaire** asks a series of questions about the controls in each audit area as a means of indicating to the auditor aspects of internal control that may be inadequate. In most instances, it is designed to require a "yes" or a "no" response, with "no" responses indicating potential internal control deficiencies.

The primary advantage of using a questionnaire is the ability to thoroughly cover each audit area reasonably quickly at the beginning of the audit. The primary disadvantage is that individual parts of the client's systems are examined without providing an overall view. In addition, a standard questionnaire is often inapplicable to some audit clients, especially smaller ones.

Figure 10-3 (p. 304) illustrates part of an internal control questionnaire for the sales and collection cycle of Hillsburg Hardware Co. The questionnaire is also designed for use with the six transaction-related audit objectives. Notice that each objective (A through F) is a transaction-related audit objective as it applies to sales transactions (see shaded portions). The same is true for all other audit areas.

The use of both questionnaires and flowcharts is highly desirable for understanding the client's internal control. Flowcharts provide an overview of the system, and questionnaires are useful checklists to remind the auditor of many different types of internal controls that should exist. When properly used, a combination of these two approaches should provide the auditor with an excellent description of the system.

It is often desirable to use the client's narratives or flowcharts and have the client fill out the internal control questionnaire. When understandable and reliable narratives, flowcharts, and questionnaires are not available from a client, which is often the case, the auditor must prepare them. Many auditors rely on electronic auditing tools including industry-specific checklists and industry-specific flowcharting templates that can be completed and viewed electronically, to assist them in the audit. Once completed in that form, these electronic workpapers can be shared with others on the audit team through the use of groupware software.

ASSESS CONTROL RISK

Now that the auditor's procedures for gaining an understanding of internal control have been discussed, the chapter now focuses on how the auditor uses that information to assess control risk. Once the auditor obtains an understanding of internal control sufficient for audit planning, he or she must make an initial assessment of control risk. Four specific assessments must be made to arrive at the initial assessment.

> **OBJECTIVE 10-4**
> Assess control risk by linking strengths and weaknesses of internal control to transaction-related audit objectives.

Assess Whether the Financial Statements Are Auditable The first assessment is whether the entity is auditable. Two primary factors determine auditability: the integrity of management and the adequacy of accounting records. Many audit procedures rely to some extent on the representations of management. For example, it is difficult for the auditor to evaluate whether inventory is obsolete without an honest assessment by management. If management lacks integrity, management may provide false representations, causing the auditor to rely on unreliable evidence.

The accounting records serve as a direct source of audit evidence for most audit objectives. If the accounting records are deficient, necessary audit evidence may not be available. For example, if the client has not kept duplicate sales invoices and vendors' invoices, it would usually be impractical to do an audit. Unless the auditor can identify an alternative source of reliable evidence or appropriate records can be constructed for the auditor's use, the only recourse may be to consider the entity unauditable.

In complex IT environments, much of the transaction information is translated strictly in electronic form without generating a visible audit trail of documents and records. In that case, the company is generally still auditable; however, the auditor must assess whether he or she has the necessary skills to gather evidence that is in electronic form and can assign personnel with adequate IT training and experience.

When the auditor concludes that the entity is not auditable, he or she discusses the circumstances with the client (usually at the highest level) and either withdraws from the engagement or issues a disclaimer form of audit report.

Determine Assessed Control Risk Supported by the Understanding Obtained After obtaining an understanding of internal control, the auditor makes an initial **assessment of control risk**. This assessment is a measure of the auditor's expectation that internal controls *will neither prevent material misstatements* from occurring *nor detect and correct them* if they have occurred.

The initial assessment is generally made for each transaction-related audit objective for each major type of transaction. For example, the auditor makes an assessment of the existence objective for sales and a separate assessment of the completeness objective. There are different ways to express this expectation. Some auditors use a subjective expression such as *high, moderate,* or *low*. Others use numerical probabilities such as *1.0, 0.6,* or *0.2*.

The initial assessment usually starts with consideration of the control environment. If the attitude of management is that control is unimportant, it is doubtful that detailed control activities will be reliable. The best course of action in that case is to assume that control risk for all transaction-related audit objectives is at the maximum (such as high or 1.0). On the other hand, if management's attitude is positive, the auditor then considers the specific policies and procedures within the subcomponents of the control environment and those of the four other components of internal control. The controls within all five components are used as a basis for an assessment below the maximum.

There are two important considerations about the initial assessment: First, the auditor does not have to make the initial assessment in a formal, detailed manner. In many audits, such as audits of smaller companies, the auditor assumes that the control risk is at the maximum whether or not it actually is. The auditor's reason for taking this approach is that he or she has concluded that it is more economical to more extensively audit the financial statement balances than to test related internal controls.

Second, even though the auditor believes control risk is low, assessed control risk is limited to that level supported by the evidence obtained. For example, suppose that the auditor believes that control risk for unrecorded sales is low but has gathered little evidence in support of controls for the completeness transaction-related audit objective. The auditor's assessment of control risk for unrecorded sales must be either moderate or high. It could be low only if additional evidence was obtained in support of the pertinent controls.

Assess Whether It Is Likely That a Lower Assessed Control Risk Could Be Supported When the auditor believes that actual control risk may be significantly lower than the initial assessment, he or she may decide to support a lower assessed control risk. The most likely case in which this occurs is when the auditor has identified a limited number of controls during the understanding phase. Based on the results of the initial assessment, the auditor now believes that additional controls can be identified and tested to further reduce assessed control risk.

Determine the Appropriate Assessed Control Risk After the auditor completes the initial assessment and considers whether a lower assessed control risk is likely, he or she is in a position to decide which assessed control risk should be used: either a level already supported in the initial assessment or a lower level. The decision about which level to use is essentially an economic one, recognizing the trade-off between the costs of testing relevant controls and the costs of substantive tests that would be avoided by reducing assessed control risk. Assume, for example, that for the existence and accuracy transaction-related audit objectives for sales, the auditor believes that the cost of confirming accounts receivable could be reduced by $5,000 by incurring $2,000 to support a lower assessed control risk. It would be cost-effective to incur the $2,000 additional cost.

The auditor typically assesses control risk for transaction-related audit objectives for each major type of transaction in each transaction cycle. For example, in the sales and collection cycle, the types of transactions usually involve sales, sales returns and allowances, cash receipts, and the provision for and write-off of uncollectible accounts. The first step in the assessment is to identify the transaction-related audit objectives to which the assessment applies. This is done by applying the transaction-related audit objectives introduced earlier, which are stated in general form, to each major type of transaction for the entity.

Identify Transaction-Related Audit Objectives

The next step is to identify the specific controls that contribute to accomplishing each transaction-related audit objective. The auditor identifies pertinent controls by proceeding through the descriptive information about the client's system. Those policies, procedures, and activities that in his or her judgment provide control over the transactions involved are identified. In doing this, it is often helpful to refer back to the types of controls that might exist, and ask whether they do exist. For example: Is there adequate separation of duties and how is it achieved? Are the documents used well designed? Are prenumbered documents properly accounted for? Are key master files properly restricted from unauthorized access?

Identify Specific Controls

In making this analysis, it is not necessary to consider every control. The auditor should identify and include controls that are expected to have the greatest effect on meeting the transaction-related audit objectives. These are often called key controls. The reason for including only key controls is that they will be sufficient to achieve the transaction-related audit objectives and should provide audit efficiency.

An **internal control weakness** is the *absence of adequate controls,* which increases the risk of misstatements existing in the financial statements. If, in the auditor's judgment, controls are inadequate to satisfy one of the transaction-related audit objectives, expectation of such a misstatement occurring increases. For example, if payroll accounting personnel have the ability to modify items in the payroll master file, the auditor may conclude that there is a weakness in internal control.

Identify and Evaluate Weaknesses

A four-step approach can be used for identifying significant weaknesses.

Identify Existing Controls Because weaknesses are the absence of adequate controls, the auditor must first know which controls exist. The methods for identifying existing controls have already been discussed.

Identify the Absence of Key Controls Internal control questionnaires, narratives, and flowcharts are useful to identify areas in which key controls are lacking and in which the likelihood of misstatements is thereby increased. When control risk is assessed as moderate or high, there is usually an absence of controls.

Determine Potential Material Misstatements That Could Result This step is intended to identify specific misstatements that are likely to result because of the absence of controls. The importance of a weakness is proportionate to the magnitude of the misstatements that are likely to result from it.

Consider the Possibility of Compensating Controls A compensating control is one elsewhere in the system that offsets a weakness. A common example in a smaller company is active involvement of the owner. When a compensating control exists, the weakness is no longer a concern because the potential for misstatement has been sufficiently reduced.

Figure 10-4 shows the documentation of weaknesses for the sales and collection cycle of Airtight Machine Company. The fifth column shows the effect of the weakness on the auditor's planned audit program.

FIGURE 10-4 **Weaknesses in Internal Control**

Client _Airtight Machine Company_   Schedule _P-3_

Weaknesses in Internal Control   Prepared by _JR_

Cycle _Sales and Collection_   Period _12/31/99_

Weakness	Compensating Control	Potential Misstatement	Materiality	Effect on Audit Evidence
1. The accounts receivable clerk approves credit memos and has access to cash.	The owner reviews all credit memos after they are recorded. He knows all customers.	N/A	N/A	N/A
2. There is no internal verification of the key entry of customer number, quantities, prices, extensions, and related information for sales invoices and credit memos.*	None	Clerical errors in billings to customers, posting to master file, and account classification.	Potentially material	Increase substantive tests of transactions for sales to 125 transactions.

*Included in the reportable conditions letter.

The Control Risk Matrix

Many auditors use a **control risk matrix** to assist in the control risk–assessment process. Most controls affect more than one transaction-related audit objective, and often several different controls affect a given transaction-related audit objective. These complexities make a control risk matrix a useful way to help assess control risk. The auditor uses the control risk matrix to identify both controls and weaknesses and to assess control risk.

Figure 10-5 (p. 309) illustrates the use of a control risk matrix for sales transactions of Airtight Machine Company. In constructing the matrix, the transaction-related audit objectives for sales were listed as column headings, and pertinent controls that were identified were listed as headings for the rows. In addition, where significant weaknesses were identified, they were also entered as row headings below the listing of key controls. The body of the matrix was then used to show how the controls contribute to the accomplishment of the transaction-related audit objectives and how weaknesses affect the objectives. In this illustration, a *C* was entered in each cell where a control partially or fully satisfied an objective, and a *W* was entered to show the affect of the weaknesses.

Assess Control Risk

Once the auditor identifies controls and weaknesses and relates them to transaction-related audit objectives, he or she can assess control risk. Again, the control risk matrix is a useful tool for that purpose. Referring to Figure 10-5, the auditor assessed control risk for Airtight's sales by reviewing each column for pertinent controls and weaknesses and asking, "What is the likelihood that a material misstatement of the type to be controlled would not be prevented or detected and corrected by these controls, and what is the affect of the weaknesses?" If the likelihood is high, then control risk is high, and so forth.

Once a preliminary assessment of control risk is made for sales and cash receipts, the auditor can complete the three control risk rows of the evidence planning worksheet that was introduced in Chapter 9 on page 270. If tests of controls results do not support the preliminary assessment of control risk, the auditor must modify the worksheet accordingly.

INTERNAL CONTROL	Recorded sales are for shipments made to existing customers (existence).	Existing sales transactions are recorded (completeness).	Recorded sales are for the amount of goods shipped and are correctly billed and recorded (accuracy).	Recorded sales are properly classified (classification).	Sales are recorded on the correct dates (timing).	Sales transactions are properly included in the accounts receivable master file and correctly summarized (posting and summarization).
SALES TRANSACTION-RELATED AUDIT OBJECTIVES						
Credit is approved automatically by the computer for customers included in the credit master file before shipment occurs.	C					
Sales are supported by authorized shipping documents and approved customer orders, which are attached to the duplicate sales invoice, and the shipping document number and approved customer order number must be entered at the time of sales input.	C					
Separation of duties among billing, recording sales, and handling cash receipts.	C	C				C
Unit selling prices are obtained from the price list master file of approved prices.			C			
Shipping documents are forwarded to billing daily and billed the subsequent day.		C			C	
Shipping documents and duplicate sales invoice numbers are issued in numerical order by the computer, accounted for weekly, and traced to the sales journal.		C			C	
Shipping documents are batched daily by quantity shipped.	C	C	C		C	C
Once the batch of sales transactions is entered, the computer automatically posts transactions to the accounts receivable subsidiary records and to the general ledger.						C
Statements are mailed to all customers each month.	C		C			C
The input screen for entering sales transactions limits account coding to the default general ledger account numbers for sales, sales returns, and accounts receivable.				C		
Sales journal is reviewed monthly for reasonableness of total and compared with the general ledger for sales and sales returns.						C
Lack of internal verification of the key entry of customer number, quantities, prices, extensions, and related information for sales invoices and credit memos.			W	W		W
Assessed control risk	low	low	mod	mod	low	mod

ILLUSTRATIVE KEY CONTROLS (rows above) — *WEAKNESSES* (lack of internal verification row)

C = The control partially or fully satisfies the sales transaction-related audit objective; *W* = weakness identified in Figure 10-4.

Alternatively, the auditor can wait until tests of controls are done to complete the three control risk rows of the worksheet. An evidence planning worksheet for Hillsburg Hardware with the three rows for control risk completed is illustrated in Figure 14-7 on page 465.

Communicate Reportable Conditions and Related Matters

During the course of obtaining an understanding of internal control and assessing control risk, auditors obtain information that is of interest to the audit committee in fulfilling its responsibilities. Generally, such information concerns significant deficiencies in the design or operation of internal control. Such matters are called **reportable conditions** in SAS 60 (AU 325).

Audit Committee Communications Reportable conditions should be communicated to the audit committee as a part of every audit. If the client does not have an audit committee, the communication should go to the person or persons in the organization who have overall responsibility for internal control, such as the board of directors or the owner-manager.

FIGURE 10-6 Reportable Conditions Letter

JOHNSON AND SEYGROVES
Certified Public Accountants
2016 Village Boulevard
Troy, Michigan 48801

February 12, 2000

Board of Directors
Airtight Machine Company
1729 Athens Street
Troy, MI 48801

In planning and performing our audit of the financial statements of Airtight Machine Company for the year ended December 31, 1999, we considered its internal control in order to determine our auditing procedures for the purpose of expressing our opinion on the financial statements and not to provide assurance on internal control. However, we noted certain matters involving internal control and its operation that we consider to be a reportable condition under standards established by the American Institute of Certified Public Accountants. Reportable conditions involve matters coming to our attention relating to significant deficiencies in the design or operation of internal control that, in our judgment, could adversely affect the organization's ability to record, process, summarize, and report financial data consistent with the assertions of management in the financial statements.

The matter noted is that there is a lack of independent verification of the key entry of the customer's name, product number, quantity shipped, prices used, and the related mathematical extensions on sales invoices and credit memos. As a consequence, errors in these activities could occur and remain uncorrected, adversely affecting both recorded net sales and accounts receivable. This deficiency is significant because of the large size of the average sale of Airtight Machine Company.

This report is intended solely for the information and use of the board of directors, management, and others in Airtight Machine Company.

Very truly yours,
Johnson and Seygroves

Johnson and Seygroves, CPAs

The form of communication would typically be a letter, although oral communication, documented in the working papers, is also allowable under professional standards. An illustrative reportable conditions letter is shown in Figure 10-6 (p. 310).

Management Letters In addition to reportable conditions, auditors often observe less significant internal control–related matters, as well as opportunities for the client to make operational improvements. These types of matters should also be communicated to the client. The form of communication is often a separate letter for that purpose, called a **management letter**. Although management letters are not required by auditing standards, auditors generally prepare them as a value-added service of the audit.

have to have been engaged by the company to do.

OBJECTIVE 10-5
Describe the process of designing and performing tests of controls.

This chapter has examined how auditors link the strengths and weaknesses of internal control to transaction-related audit objectives to assess control risk for each objective. This section of the chapter now discusses how auditors test those controls that are used to support a control risk assessment below maximum. For example, each key control in Figure 10-5 (p. 309) that the auditor intends to rely on to support a control risk of moderate or low must be supported by sufficient tests of controls.

Assessing control risk requires the auditor to consider the design of controls to evaluate whether they should be effective in meeting transaction-related audit objectives. Some evidence will have been gathered in support of the design of the controls, as well as evidence that they have been placed in operation, during the understanding phase. To use specific controls as a basis for reducing assessed control risk, however, specific evidence must be obtained about their *operating effectiveness* throughout all, or at least most, of the period under audit. The procedures to test effectiveness of controls in support of a reduced assessed control risk are called **tests of controls**.

When the results of tests of controls support the design of controls as expected, the auditor proceeds to use the same assessed control risk. If, however, the tests of controls indicate that the controls did not operate effectively, the assessed control risk must be reconsidered. For example, the tests may indicate that the application of a control was curtailed midway through the year or that the person applying it made frequent misstatements. In such situations, the auditor uses a higher assessed control risk, unless additional controls for the same transaction-related audit objectives are identified and found to be effective.

other than a dollar amount

Four types of procedures are used to support the operation of internal controls. They are as follows.

Procedures for Tests of Controls

Make Inquiries of Appropriate Client Personnel Although inquiry is not generally a strong source of evidence about the effective operation of controls, it is an appropriate form of evidence. For example, the auditor may determine that unauthorized personnel are not allowed access to computer files by making inquiries of the person who controls the computer library and of the person who controls on-line access security password rights assignments.

Examine Documents, Records, and Reports Many controls leave a clear trail of documentary evidence. Suppose, for example, that when a customer order is received, it is used to create a customer sales order, which is approved for credit. (See the first and second key controls in Figure 10-5.) The customer order is attached to the sales order as authorization for further processing. The auditor examines the documents to make sure that they are complete and properly matched and that required signatures or initials are present.

Observe Control-Related Activities Other types of control-related activities do not leave an evidential trail. For example, separation of duties relies on specific persons performing specific tasks, and there is typically no documentation of the separate performance. (See the third key control in Figure 10-5.) For controls that leave no documentary evidence, the auditor generally observes them being applied at various points during the year.

Reperform Client Procedures There are also control-related activities for which there are related documents and records, but their content is insufficient for the auditor's purpose of assessing whether controls are operating effectively. For example, assume that prices on sales invoices are to be verified with a standard price list by client personnel as an internal verification procedure, but no indication of performance is entered on the sales invoices. (See the fourth key control in Figure 10-5.) In these cases, it is common for the auditor to actually reperform the control activity to see whether the proper results were obtained. For this example, the auditor can reperform the procedure by tracing the sales prices to the authorized price list in effect at the date of the transaction. If no misstatements are found, the auditor can conclude that the procedure is operating as intended.

Extent of Procedures

The extent to which tests of controls are applied depends on the desired assessed level of control risk. If the auditor wants a lower assessed control risk, more extensive tests of controls are applied, both in terms of the number of controls tested and the extent of the tests for each control. For example, if the auditor wants to use a low assessed control risk, a larger sample size for documentation, observation, and reperformance procedures should be applied.

Reliance on Evidence from Prior Year's Audit If evidence was obtained in the prior year's audit that indicates that a key control was operating effectively and the auditor determines that it is still in place, the extent of the tests of that control may be reduced somewhat in the current year. For example, in such circumstances, the auditor might use a reduced sample size in testing a control that leaves documentary evidence, or certain tests might be rotated among areas across 2 years or more.

Testing Less Than the Entire Audit Period Ideally, tests of controls should be applied to transactions and controls for the entire period under audit. However, it is not always practical to do so. When less than the entire period is tested, the auditor should determine whether changes in controls occurred in the period not tested and obtain evidence about the nature and extent of any changes.

In many instances, accounting software contains internal controls automatically performed by the computer. One advantage of having the computer perform the controls is that once the computer is programmed correctly, the computer processes that control systematically until the program is later changed. In such an environment, the auditor may be able to reduce the extent of testing of computer-performed controls if the auditor determines that there is a low risk of unauthorized changes being made to the software program and underlying master files of data used to process that control. The auditor will need to retest the control if the software is changed or if controls over access to the master file are weak.

Relationship of Tests of Controls to Procedures to Obtain an Understanding

There is a significant overlap between tests of controls and procedures to obtain an understanding. Both include inquiry, documentation, and observation. There are two primary differences in the application of these common procedures between phases. First, in obtaining an understanding, the procedures are applied to all the controls identified as part of the understanding of internal control. Tests of controls, on the other hand, are applied only when the assessed control risk is below the maximum, and then only to the key controls.

Second, procedures to obtain an understanding are performed only on one or a few transactions or, in the case of observations, at a single point in time. Tests of controls are performed on larger samples of transactions (perhaps 20 to 100), and often observations are made at more than one point in time.

For key controls, tests of controls other than reperformance are essentially an *extension* of related procedures to obtain an understanding. Therefore, when auditors plan from the beginning of the audit to obtain a low assessed control risk, they will combine both types of procedures and perform them simultaneously.

Table 10-3 illustrates this concept in more detail. When only the required minimum understanding of internal control is planned, the auditor will conduct a transaction walk-through. In so doing, the auditor determines that the audit documentation is complete and accurate and observes that the control-related activities described are in operation.

When control risk is assessed below maximum, not only is a transaction walk-through performed, but a larger sample of documents is examined for indications of the effectiveness of the operation of controls. (The determination of appropriate sample size is discussed in Chapters 14 and 16.) Similarly, when observations are made, they will be more extensive and often at several points in time. Also, the auditors will do reperformance for some controls.

TABLE 10-3	Relationship of Assessed Control Risk and Extent of Procedures	
	Assessed Control Risk	
Type of Procedure	**High Level: Obtaining an Understanding Only**	**Lower Level: Tests of Controls**
Inquiry	Yes—extensive	Yes—some
Documentation	Yes—with transaction walk-through	Yes—using sampling
Observation	Yes—with transaction walk-through	Yes—at multiple times
Reperformance	No	Yes—using sampling

DECIDE PLANNED DETECTION RISK AND DESIGN SUBSTANTIVE TESTS

We've focused on how auditors assess control risk for each transaction-related audit objective and support control risk assessments that are below the maximum with specific tests of controls. The auditor uses the results of the control risk assessment process and tests of controls to determine the planned detection risk and related substantive tests. The auditor does this by linking the control risk assessments to the balance-related audit objectives for the accounts affected by the major transaction types. The appropriate level of detection risk for each balance-related audit objective is then determined using the audit risk model. The relationship of transaction-related audit objectives to balance-related audit objectives and the selection and design of audit procedures for substantive tests of financial statement balances are discussed and illustrated in Chapter 12.

SUMMARY

This chapter highlighted how effective internal controls can reduce planned audit evidence. To use the strengths of a client's internal control to reduce planned audit evidence, the auditor must first obtain an understanding of each of the five components of internal control. Knowledge about the design of the client's control environment, risk assessment, control activities, information and communication, and monitoring activities and information about whether internal control components have been placed in operation assist the auditor in assessing the level of control risk for each transaction-related audit objective.

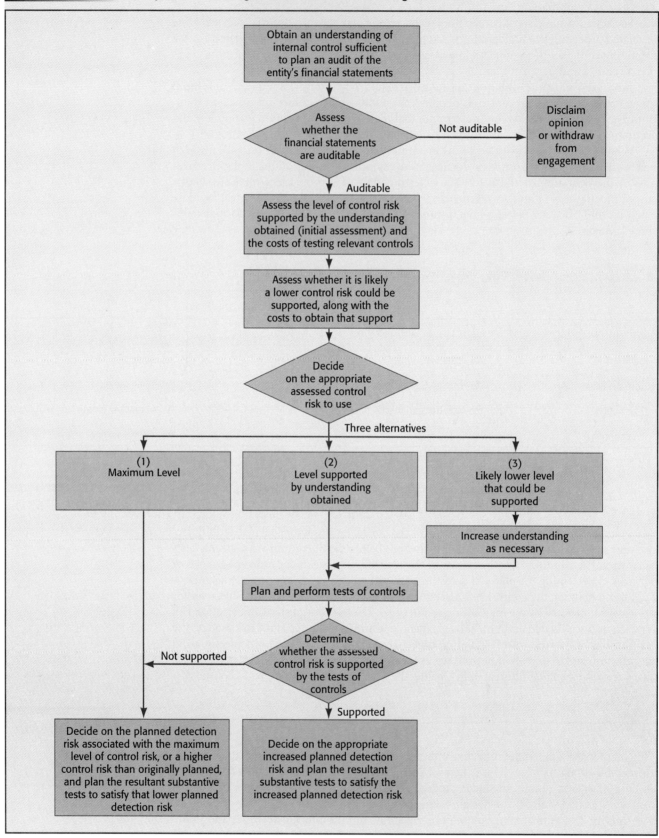

When internal control components support a control risk assessment below the maximum level, the auditor must perform tests of controls to assess the operating effectiveness of those controls. When the results of tests of controls support the control risk assessment below maximum, the auditor is able to reduce planned substantive testing for related accounts. This entire process is summarized in Figure 10-7 (p. 314).

ESSENTIAL TERMS

Assessment of control risk—a measure of the auditor's expectation that internal controls will neither prevent material misstatements from occurring, nor detect and correct them if they have occurred; control risk is assessed for each transaction-related audit objective in a cycle or class of transactions

Chart of accounts—a listing of all the entity's accounts, which classifies transactions into individual balance sheet and income statement accounts

Collusion—a cooperative effort among employees to defraud a business of cash, inventory, or other assets

Control activities—policies and procedures, in addition to those included in the other four components of internal control, that help ensure that necessary actions are taken to address risks in the achievement of the entity's objectives; they typically include the following five specific control activities: (1) adequate separation of duties, (2) proper authorization of transactions and activities, (3) adequate documents and records, (4) physical control over assets and records, and (5) independent checks on performance

Control environment—the actions, policies, and procedures that reflect the overall attitudes of top management, directors, and owners of an entity about internal control and its importance to the entity

Control risk matrix—a methodology used to help the auditor assess control risk by matching key internal controls and internal control weaknesses with transaction-related audit objectives

Flowchart—a diagrammatic representation of the client's documents and records and the sequence in which they are processed

General authorization—companywide policies for the approval of all transactions within stated limits

Independent checks—internal control activities designed for the continuous internal verification of other controls

Information and communication—the set of manual and/or computerized procedures that identifies, assembles, classifies, analyzes, records, and reports an entity's transactions and maintains accountability for the related assets

Information technology (IT)—use of computers to process and manage information

Internal control—a process designed to provide reasonable assurance regarding the achievement of management's objectives in the following categories: (1) reliability of financial reporting, (2) effectiveness and efficiency of operations, and (3) compliance with applicable laws and regulations

Internal control questionnaire—a series of questions about the controls in each audit area used as a means of indicating to the auditor aspects of internal control that may be inadequate

Internal control weakness—the absence of adequate controls; an internal control weakness increases the risk of misstatements in the financial statements

Management letter—an optional letter written by the auditor to a client's management containing the auditor's recommendations for improving any aspect of the client's business

Monitoring—management's ongoing and periodic assessment of the quality of internal control performance to determine that controls are operating as intended and modified when needed

Narrative—a written description of a client's internal controls, including the origin, processing, and disposition of documents and records, and the relevant control procedures

Procedures to obtain an understanding—procedures used by the auditor to gather evidence about the design and placement in operation of specific controls

Reportable conditions—significant deficiencies in the design or operation of internal control

Risk assessment—management's identification and analysis of risks relevant to the preparation of financial statements in accordance with generally accepted accounting principles

Separation of duties—segregation of the following activities in an organization: (1) custody of assets from accounting, (2) authorization from custody of assets, (3) operational responsibility from record keeping, and (4) IT duties from outside users of IT

Specific authorization—case-by-case approval of transactions not covered by companywide policies

Tests of controls—audit procedures to test the operating effectiveness of controls in support of reduced assessed control risk

Transaction walk-through—the tracing of selected transactions through the accounting system to determine that controls are in place

10-1 (Objective 10-1) Chapter 8 introduced the seven parts of the planning phase of audits. Which part is understanding internal control and assessing control risk? What parts precede and follow that understanding and assessing?

10-2 (Objective 10-1) Compare management's concerns about internal control with those of the auditor.

10-3 (Objective 10-1) Often, management is more concerned about internal controls that promote operational efficiency than about those that result in reliable financial data. How can the independent auditor persuade management to devote more attention to controls affecting the reliability of accounting information when management has this attitude?

10-4 (Objectives 10-1, 10-4) State the six transaction-related audit objectives.

10-5 (Objective 10-2) What is meant by the control environment? What are the factors the auditor must evaluate to understand it?

10-6 (Objective 10-2) What is the relationship among the five components of internal control?

10-7 (Objective 10-2) List the types of specific control activities and provide one specific illustration of a control in the sales area for each control activity.

10-8 (Objective 10-2) The separation of operational responsibility from record keeping is meant to prevent different types of misstatements than the separation of the custody of assets from accounting. Explain the difference in the purposes of these two types of separation of duties.

10-9 (Objective 10-2) Distinguish between general and specific authorization of transactions and give one example of each type.

10-10 (Objective 10-2) For each of the following, give an example of a physical control the client can use to protect the asset or record:

1. Petty cash
2. Cash received by retail clerks
3. Accounts receivable records
4. Raw material inventory
5. Perishable tools
6. Manufacturing equipment
7. Marketable securities

10-11 (Objective 10-2) Explain what is meant by independent checks on performance and give five specific examples.

10-12 (Objectives 10-3, 10-4) Distinguish between obtaining an understanding of internal control and assessing control risk. Also explain the methodology the auditor uses for each of them.

10-13 (Objective 10-4) Define what is meant by a control and a weakness in internal control. Give two examples of each in the sales and collection cycle.

10-14 (Objectives 10-2, 10-4) Frank James, a highly competent employee of Brinkwater Sales Corporation, had been responsible for accounting-related matters for two decades. His devotion to the firm and his duties had always been exceptional, and over the years, he had been given increased responsibility. Both the president of Brinkwater and the partner of an independent CPA firm in charge of the audit were shocked and dismayed to discover that James had embezzled more than $500,000 over a 10-year period by not recording billings in the sales journal and subsequently diverting the cash receipts. What major factors permitted the defalcation to take place?

10-15 (Objective 10-3) Jeanne Maier, CPA, believes that it is appropriate to obtain an understanding of internal control about halfway through the audit, after she is familiar with the client's operations and the way the system actually works. She has found through experience that filling out internal control questionnaires and flowcharts early in the engagement is not beneficial because the system rarely functions the way it is supposed to. Later in the engagement, the auditor can prepare flowcharts and questionnaires with relative ease because of the knowledge already obtained on the audit. Evaluate her approach.

10-16 (Objective 10-3) Distinguish between the objectives of an internal control questionnaire and the objectives of a flowchart for documenting information about a client's internal control. State the advantages and disadvantages of each of these two methods.

10-17 (Objective 10-4) Explain what is meant by reportable conditions as they relate to internal control. What should the auditor do with reportable conditions?

10-18 (Objective 10-4) Examine the control risk matrix in Figure 10-5 (p. 309). Explain the purpose of the matrix. Also explain the meaning and effect of an assessment of control risk of low compared with one of medium.

10-19 (Objectives 10-4, 10-5) Explain what is meant by tests of controls. Write one examination of documents test of control and one reperformance test of control for the following internal control: hours on time cards are re-added by an independent payroll clerk and initialed to indicate performance.

MULTIPLE CHOICE QUESTIONS FROM CPA EXAMINATIONS

10-20 (Objectives 10-1, 10-3) The following are general questions about internal control. Choose the best response.

   a. When considering internal control, an auditor must be aware of the concept of reasonable assurance, which recognizes that the
      (1) employment of competent personnel provides assurance that management's control objectives will be achieved.
      (2) establishment and maintenance of internal control is an important responsibility of the management and not of the auditor.
      (3) cost of internal control should not exceed the benefits expected to be derived therefrom.
      (4) separation of incompatible functions is necessary to ascertain that the internal control is effective.
   b. When an auditor issues an unqualified opinion, it is implied that the
      (1) entity has not violated provisions of the Foreign Corrupt Practices Act.
      (2) likelihood of fraud is minimal.
      (3) financial records are sufficiently reliable to permit the preparation of financial statements.
      (4) entity's internal control conforms with criteria established by its audit committee.
   c. Which of the following statements about the auditor's responsibility for internal control is correct?
      (1) The auditor must gain an understanding of internal controls in every audit given that the auditor's opinion on the financial statements addresses assurance obtained about internal controls.
      (2) The nature and extent of procedures performed to gain an understanding of internal controls and to test controls are essentially the same.
      (3) Even when controls are adequately designed and placed in operation, the auditor can assess control at maximum and not perform tests of controls when substantive tests are less costly to perform.
      (4) The second standard of field work requires that the auditor obtain evidence in every audit that internal controls are operating effectively on a consistent basis throughout the year.

d. What is the independent auditor's principal purpose for obtaining an understanding of internal control and assessing control risk?
(1) To comply with generally accepted accounting principles.
(2) To obtain a measure of assurance of management's efficiency.
(3) To maintain a state of independence in mental attitude during the audit.
(4) To determine the nature, timing, and extent of subsequent audit work.

10-21 (Objective 10-4) The following questions deal with weaknesses of internal control. Choose the best response.

a. In general, a significant internal control weakness may be defined as a condition under which material misstatements would ordinarily not be detected within a timely period by
(1) an auditor during the typical obtaining of an understanding of internal control and assessment of control risk.
(2) a controller when reconciling accounts in the general ledger.
(3) employees in the normal course of performing their assigned functions.
(4) the chief financial officer when reviewing interim financial statements.

b. Which of the following statements with respect to required auditor communication of reportable conditions is correct?
(1) Such communication is required to be in writing.
(2) Such communication must include a description of all weaknesses.
(3) Such communication is the principal reason for testing and evaluating internal controls.
(4) Such communication is incidental to the auditor's understanding of internal control and assessment of control risk.

c. The auditor who becomes aware of a reportable condition is required to communicate this to the
(1) audit committee.
(2) senior management and board of directors.
(3) board of directors and internal auditors.
(4) internal auditors and senior management.

10-22 (Objective 10-4) The following questions deal with assessing control risk. Choose the best response.

a. The ultimate purpose of assessing control risk is to contribute to the auditor's evaluation of the
(1) factors that raise doubts about the auditability of the financial statements.
(2) operating effectiveness of internal controls.
(3) risk that material misstatements exist in the financial statements.
(4) possibility that the nature and extent of substantive tests may be reduced.

b. An auditor uses assessed control risk to
(1) evaluate the effectiveness of the entity's internal controls.
(2) identify transactions and account balances where inherent risk is at the maximum.
(3) indicate whether materiality thresholds for planning and evaluation purposes are sufficiently high.
(4) determine the acceptable level of detection risk for financial statement assertions.

c. On the basis of audit evidence gathered and evaluated, an auditor decides to increase assessed control risk from that originally planned. To achieve an audit risk level (AcAR) that is substantially the same as the planned audit risk level (AAR), the auditor would
(1) increase inherent risk.
(2) increase materiality levels.
(3) decrease substantive testing.
(4) decrease planned detection risk.

d. Which of the following statements about tests of controls is incorrect? Tests of controls

(1) are often performed because they can be more efficiently performed than substantive tests of transactions.

(2) provide persuasive evidence that a material misstatement exists when the auditor determines that the control is not being consistently applied.

(3) are often based on the same types of audit techniques used to gain an understanding of internal controls, except the extent of testing is generally greater when testing controls.

(4) allow a reduction in the extent of substantive testing, as long as the results of the tests of controls are equal to or better than what the auditor expects.

DISCUSSION QUESTIONS AND PROBLEMS

10-23 (Objectives 10-2, 10-4, 10-5)   Each of the following internal controls has been taken from a standard internal control questionnaire used by a CPA firm for assessing control risk in the payroll and personnel cycle.

1. Approval of department head or foreman on time cards is required before preparing payroll.
2. All prenumbered time cards are accounted for before beginning data entry for preparation of checks.
3. The payroll accounting software application will not accept data input for an employee number not contained in the employee master file.
4. Persons preparing the payroll do not perform other payroll duties (timekeeping, distribution of checks) or have access to payroll data master files or cash.
5. The computer calculates gross and net pay based on hours inputted and information in employee master files, and payroll accounting personnel double-check the mathematical accuracy on a test basis.
6. All voided and spoiled payroll checks are properly mutilated and retained.
7. Personnel requires an investigation of an employment application from new employees. Investigation includes checking the employee's background, former employers, and references.
8. Written termination notices, with properly documented reasons for termination, and approval of an appropriate official are required.
9. All checks not distributed to employees are returned to the treasurer for safekeeping.
10. On-line ability to add employees or change pay rates to the payroll master file is restricted via passwords to certain human resource personnel.

Required

a. For each internal control, identify the type(s) of specific control activity (activities) to which it applies (such as adequate documents and records or physical control over assets and records).

b. For each internal control, identify the transaction-related audit objective(s) to which it applies.

c. For each internal control, identify a specific misstatement that is likely to be prevented if the control exists and is effective.

d. For each control, list a specific misstatement that could result from the absence of the control.

e. For each control, identify one audit test that the auditor could use to uncover misstatements resulting from the absence of the control.

10-24 (Objectives 10-2, 10-4)   The following are misstatements that have occurred in Fresh Foods Grocery Store, a retail and wholesale grocery company.

1. The incorrect price was used on sales invoices for billing shipments to customers because the wrong price was entered into the computer master file of prices.

2. A vendor's invoice was paid twice for the same shipment. The second payment arose because the vendor sent a duplicate copy of the original 2 weeks after the payment was due.

3. Employees in the receiving department took sides of beef for their personal use. When a shipment of meat was received, the receiving department filled out a receiving report and forwarded it to the accounting department for the amount of goods actually received. At that time, two sides of beef were put in an employee's pickup truck rather than in the storage freezer.

4. During the physical count of inventory of the retail grocery, one counter wrote down the wrong description of several products and miscounted the quantity.

5. A salesperson sold an entire carload of lamb at a price below cost because she did not know the cost of lamb had increased in the past week.

6. On the last day of the year, a truckload of beef was set aside for shipment but was not shipped. Because it was still on hand the inventory was counted. The shipping document was dated the last day of the year, so it was also included as a current-year sale.

7. A vendor invoice was paid even though no merchandise was ever received. The accounts payable software application does not require the input of a valid receiving report number before payment can be made.

8. An accounts payable clerk processed payments to himself by adding a fictitious vendor address to the approved vendor master file.

Required

a. For each misstatement, identify one or more types of controls that were absent.

b. For each misstatement, identify the transaction-related audit objectives that have not been met.

c. For each misstatement, suggest a control to correct the deficiency.

10-25 (Objective 10-2) The division of the following duties is meant to provide the best possible controls for the Meridian Paint Company, a small wholesale store.

†1. Assemble supporting documents for general and payroll cash disbursements.
†2. Sign general cash disbursement checks.
†3. Input information to prepare checks for signature, record checks in the cash disbursements journal, and update the appropriate master files.
†4. Mail checks to suppliers and deliver checks to employees.
5. Cancel supporting documents to prevent their reuse.
†6. Approve credit for customers included in the customer credit master file.
†7. Input shipping and billing information to bill customers, record invoices in the sales journal, and update the accounts receivable master file.
†8. Open the mail and prepare a prelisting of cash receipts.
†9. Enter cash receipts data to prepare the cash receipts journal and update the accounts receivable master file.
†10. Prepare daily cash deposits.
†11. Deliver daily cash deposits to the bank.
†12. Assemble the payroll time cards and input the data to prepare payroll checks and update the payroll journal and payroll master files.
†13. Sign payroll checks.
14. Update the general ledger at the end of each month and review all accounts for unexpected balances.
15. Reconcile the accounts receivable master file with the control account and review accounts outstanding more than 90 days.
16. Prepare monthly statements for customers by printing the accounts receivable master file; then mail the statements to customers.
17. Reconcile the monthly statements from vendors with the accounts payable master file.
18. Reconcile the bank account.

Required

You are to divide the accounting-related duties 1 through 18 among Robert Smith, James Cooper, and Bill Miller. All of the responsibilities marked with a dagger are assumed to take about the same amount of time and must be divided equally between Smith and Cooper. Both employees are equally competent. Miller, who is president of the company, is not willing to perform any functions designated by a dagger and will perform only a maximum of two of the other functions.*

10-26 (Objectives 10-1, 10-2, 10-4)   Recently, while eating lunch with your family at a local cafeteria, you observe a practice that is somewhat unusual. As you reach the end of the cafeteria line, an adding machine operator asks how many persons are in your party. He then totals the food purchases on the trays for all of your family and writes the number of persons included in the group on the adding machine tape. He hands you the tape and asks you to pay when you finish eating. Near the end of the meal, you decide you want a piece of pie and coffee so you return to the line, select your food, and again go through the line. The adding machine operator goes through the same procedures, but this time he staples the second tape to the original and returns it to you.

When you leave the cafeteria, you hand the stapled adding machine tapes to the cash register operator, who totals the two tapes, takes your money, and puts the tapes on a spindle.

Required

   a. What internal controls has the cafeteria instituted for its operations?
   b. How can the manager of the cafeteria evaluate the effectiveness of the controls?
   c. How do these controls differ from those used by most cafeterias?
   d. What are the costs and benefits of the cafeteria's system?

10-27 (Objectives 10-1, 10-3)   Lew Pherson and Vera Collier are friends who are employed by different CPA firms. One day during lunch they are discussing the importance of internal control in determining the amount of audit evidence required for an engagement. Pherson expresses the view that internal control must be evaluated carefully in all companies, regardless of their size, in a similar manner. His CPA firm requires a standard internal control questionnaire on every audit as well as a flowchart of every transaction area. In addition, he says the firm requires a careful evaluation of the system and a modification in the evidence accumulated based on the controls and weaknesses in the system.

Collier responds by saying she believes that internal control cannot be adequate in many of the small companies she audits; therefore, she simply ignores internal control and acts under the assumption of inadequate controls. She goes on to say, "Why should I spend a lot of time obtaining an understanding of internal control and assessing control risk when I know it has all kinds of weaknesses before I start? I would rather spend the time it takes to fill out all those forms in testing whether the statements are correct."

Required

   a. Express in general terms the most important difference between the nature of the potential controls available for large and small companies.
   b. Criticize the positions taken by Pherson and Collier, and express your own opinion about the similarities and differences that should exist in understanding internal control and assessing control risk for different-sized companies.

10-28 (Objective 10-4)   The following are partial descriptions of internal controls for companies engaged in the manufacturing business:

   1. When Mr. Clark orders materials for his machine-rebuilding plant, he sends a duplicate purchase order to the receiving department. During the delivery of materials, Mr. Smith, the receiving clerk, records the receipt of shipment on this purchase order. After recording, Mr. Smith sends the purchase order to the accounting department, where it is used to record materials purchased and accounts payable. The materials are transported to the storage area by forklifts. The additional purchased quantities are recorded on storage records.

*AICPA adapted.

2. Every day, hundreds of employees clock in using time cards at Generous Motors Corporation. The timekeepers collect these cards once a week and deliver them to the computer department. There, the data on these time cards are entered into the computer. The information entered into the computer is used in the preparation of the labor cost distribution records, the payroll journal, and the payroll checks. The treasurer, Mrs. Webber, compares the payroll journal with the payroll checks, signs the checks, and returns them to Mr. Strode, the supervisor of the computer department. The payroll checks are distributed to the employees by Mr. Strode.

3. The smallest branch of Connor Cosmetics in South Bend employs Mary Cooper, the branch manager, and her sales assistant, Janet Hendrix. The branch uses a bank account in South Bend to pay expenses. The account is kept in the name of "Connor Cosmetics—Special Account." To pay expenses, checks must be signed by Mary Cooper or by the treasurer of Connor Cosmetics, John Winters. Cooper receives the cancelled checks and bank statements. She reconciles the branch account herself and files cancelled checks and bank statements in her records. She also periodically prepares reports of cash disbursements and sends them to the home office.

Required

    a. List the weaknesses in internal control for each of the above. To identify the weaknesses, use the methodology that was discussed in this chapter.

    b. For each weakness, state the type(s) of misstatement(s) that is (are) likely to result. Be as specific as possible.

    c. How would you improve internal controls for each of the three companies?*

10-29 (Objective 10-4) The Art Appreciation Society operates a museum for the benefit and enjoyment of the community.

When the museum is open to the public, two clerks who are positioned at the entrance collect a $5.00 admission fee from each nonmember patron. Members of the Art Appreciation Society are permitted to enter free of charge upon presentation of their membership cards.

At the end of each day, one of the clerks delivers the proceeds to the treasurer. The treasurer counts the cash in the presence of the clerk and places it in a safe. Each Friday afternoon, the treasurer and one of the clerks deliver all cash held in the safe to the bank and receive an authenticated deposit slip that provides the basis for the weekly entry in the accounting records.

The Art Appreciation Society board of directors has identified a need to improve its internal controls over cash admission fees. The board has determined that the cost of installing turnstiles, sales booths, or otherwise altering the physical layout of the museum will greatly exceed any benefits.

However, the board has agreed that the sale of admission tickets must be an integral part of its improvement efforts.

Smith has been asked by the board of directors of the Art Appreciation Society to review the internal control over cash admission fees and provide suggestions for improvements.

Required

Indicate weaknesses in the existing internal controls over cash admission fees that Smith should identify, and recommend one improvement for each of the weaknesses identified. To identify the weaknesses, use the methodology that was discussed in this chapter. Organize the answer as indicated in the following illustrative example:*

Weakness	Recommendation
1. There is no basis for establishing the documentation of the number of paying patrons.	1. Prenumbered admission tickets should be issued upon payment of the admission fee.

*AICPA adapted.

10-30 (Objective 10-4)   Anthony, CPA, prepared the flowchart below, which portrays the raw materials purchasing function of one of Anthony's clients, Medium-Sized Manufacturing Company, from the preparation of initial documents through the vouching of invoices for payment in accounts payable. Assume that all documents are prenumbered.

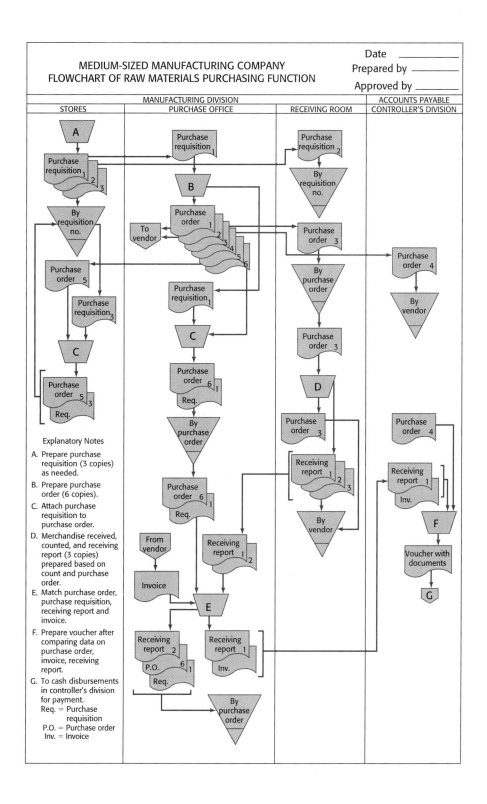

Required

Identify the weaknesses of internal control that can be determined from the flowchart. Use the methodology discussed in this chapter. Include internal control weaknesses resulting from activities performed or not performed.*

CASE

10-31 (Objective 10-4) The following is the description of sales and cash receipts for the Lady's Fashion Fair, a retail store dealing in expensive women's clothing. Sales are for cash or credit, using the store's own billing rather than credit cards.

Each salesclerk has her own sales book with prenumbered, three-copy, multicolored sales slips attached, but perforated. Only a central cash register is used. It is operated by the store supervisor, who has been employed for 10 years by Alice Olson, the store owner. The cash register is at the store entrance to control theft of clothes.

Salesclerks prepare the sales invoices in triplicate. The original and the second copy are given to the cashier. The third copy is retained by the salesclerk in the sales book. When the sale is for cash, the customer pays the salesclerk, who marks all three copies "paid" and presents the money to the cashier with the invoice copies.

All clothing is put into boxes or packages by the supervisor after comparing the clothing to the description on the invoice and the price on the sales tag. She also rechecks the clerk's calculations. Any corrections are approved by the salesclerk. The clerk changes her sales book at that time.

A credit sale is approved by the supervisor from an approved credit list after the salesclerk prepares the three-part invoice. Next, the supervisor enters the sale in her cash register as a credit or cash sale. The second copy of the invoice, which has been validated by the cash register, is given to the customer.

At the end of the day, the supervisor recaps the sales and cash and compares the totals to the cash register tape. The supervisor deposits the cash at the end of each day in the bank's lock box. The cashier's copies of the invoices are sent to the accounts receivable clerk along with a summary of the day's receipts. The bank mails the deposit slip directly to the accounts receivable clerk.

Each clerk summarizes her sales each day on a daily summary form, which is used in part to calculate employees' sales commissions. Marge, the accountant, who is prohibited from handling cash, receives the supervisor's summary and the clerk's daily summary form. Daily, she puts all sales invoice information into the firm's computer, which provides a complete printout of all input and summaries. The accounting summary includes sales by salesclerk, cash sales, credit sales, and total sales. Marge compares this output with the supervisor's and salesclerks' summaries and reconciles all differences.

The computer updates accounts receivable, inventory, and general ledger master files. After the update procedure has been run on the computer, Marge's assistant files all sales invoices by customer number. A list of the invoice numbers in numerical sequence is included in the sales printout.

The mail is opened each morning by a secretary in the owner's office. All correspondence and complaints are given to the owner. The secretary prepares a prelist of cash receipts. He totals the list, prepares a deposit slip, and deposits the cash daily. A copy of the prelist, the deposit slip, and all remittances returned with the cash receipts are given to Marge. She uses this list and the remittances to record cash receipts and update accounts receivable, again by computer. She reconciles the total receipts on the prelist to the deposit slip and to her printout. At the same time, she compares the deposit slip received from the bank for cash sales to the cash receipts journal.

Marge prepares a weekly aged trial balance of accounts receivable by use of the computer. A separate listing of all unpaid bills over 60 days is also automatically prepared.

*AICPA adapted.

These are given to Mrs. Olson, who acts as her own credit collector. She also approves all charge-offs of uncollectible items and forwards the list to Marge, who writes them off.

Each month Marge prepares and mails statements to customers. Complaints and disagreements from customers are directed to Mrs. Olson, who resolves them and informs Marge in writing of any write-downs or misstatements that require correction.

The computer system also automatically totals the journals and posts the totals to the general ledger. A general ledger trial balance is printed out, from which Marge prepares financial statements. Marge also prepares a monthly bank reconciliation and reconciles the general ledger to the aged accounts receivable trial balance.

Because of the importance of inventory control, Marge prints out the inventory perpetual totals monthly, on the last day of each month. Salesclerks count all inventory after store hours on the last day of each month for comparison with the perpetuals. An inventory shortages report is provided to Mrs. Olson. The perpetuals are adjusted by Marge after Mrs. Olson has approved the adjustments.

Required

a. For each sales transaction-related audit objective, identify one or more existing controls.

b. For each cash receipts transaction-related audit objective, identify one or more existing controls.

c. Identify weaknesses of internal control for sales and cash receipts.

INTEGRATED CASE APPLICATION—PINNACLE MANUFACTURING: PART I

10-32 (Objective 10-4) This case study is presented in four parts. Each part deals with the material in the chapter in which that part appears. However, the parts are connected in such a way that in completing all four, you will gain a better understanding of how the parts of the audit are interrelated and integrated by the audit process. The parts appear in the following locations:

Part I—Understand internal control and assess control risk for the acquisition and payment cycle, Chapter 10, pages 325–327.

Part II—Design tests of controls and substantive tests of transactions, Chapter 13, pages 435–436.

Part III—Determine sample sizes using audit sampling and evaluate results, Chapter 14, page 474.

Part IV—Design, perform, and evaluate results for tests of details of balances, Chapter 15, pages 507–512.

Background Information

Pinnacle Manufacturing is a medium-sized manufacturing company with a December 31, 1999 year-end. You have been assigned the responsibility of auditing the acquisition and payment cycle and one related balance sheet account, accounts payable. The general approach to be taken will be to reduce assessed control risk to a low level, if possible, for the two main types of transactions affecting accounts payable: acquisitions and cash disbursements. The following are furnished as background information:

Figure 10-8 (p. 326)—A summary of key information from the audit of the acquisition and payment cycle and accounts payable in the prior year's audit.

Figure 10-9 (p. 327)—A flowchart description of the accounting system and internal controls for the acquisition and payment cycle.

Part I

The purpose of Part I is to obtain an understanding of internal control and assess control risk for Pinnacle Manufacturing's acquisition and cash disbursement transactions.

Required

Study Figures 10-8 and 10-9 to gain an understanding of Pinnacle's internal control for the acquisition and payment cycle. Assess control risk as high, medium, or low on an objective-by-objective basis for the acquisition and payment cycle's internal controls, considering both internal controls and weaknesses. You should use a matrix similar to the one in Figure 10-5 (p. 309) for the assessment. There should be one matrix for acquisitions and a separate one for cash disbursements. The source of the internal controls and weaknesses is the information in Figure 10-9.

FIGURE 10-8 **Information for Audit of Accounts Payable—Previous Year**

Accounts payable, 12-31-98

Number of accounts	52
Total accounts payable	$163,892.27
Range of individual balances	$27.83–$14,819.62
Tolerable misstatement for accounts payable	$6,500

Transactions, 1998
Acquisitions:

Number of acquisitions	3,800
Total acquisitions	$2,933,812

Cash disbursements:

Number of disbursements	2,600
Total cash disbursements	$3,017,112

Results of audit procedures—tests of controls and substantive tests of transactions for acquisitions (sample size of 100):

Purchase order not approved	2
Purchase quantities, prices, and/or extensions not correct	1
Transactions charged to wrong general ledger account	1
Transactions recorded in wrong period	1
No other exceptions	

Results of audit procedures—cash disbursements (sample size of 100):

Cash disbursement recorded in wrong period	1
No other exceptions	

Results of audit procedures—accounts payable
50 percent of vendors' balances were verified; combined net understatement amounts were projected to the population as follows:

Three cutoff misstatements	$4,873.28
One difference in amounts due to disputes and discounts	$1,103.12

No adjustment was necessary because the total projected misstatement was not material.

FIGURE 10-9 Pinnacle Manufacturing—Acquisition and Payment Cycle

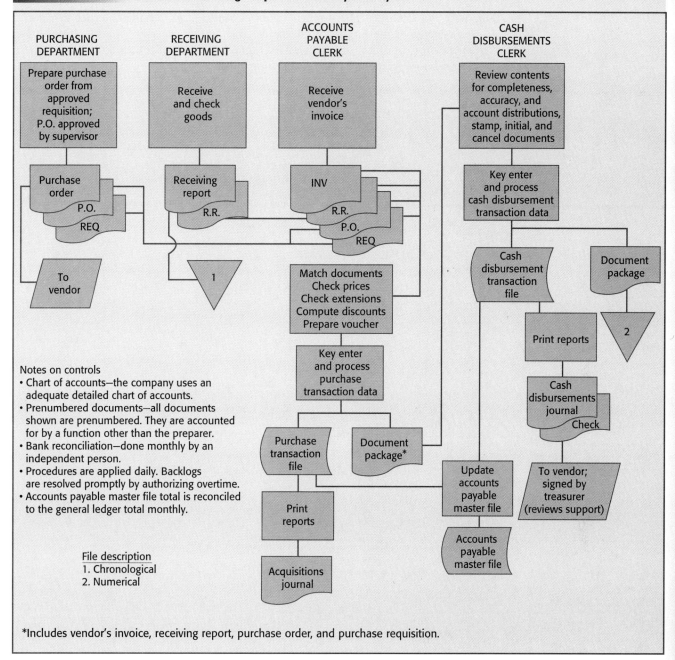

PURCHASING DEPARTMENT

Prepare purchase order from approved requisition; P.O. approved by supervisor

Purchase order
P.O.
REQ

To vendor

RECEIVING DEPARTMENT

Receive and check goods

Receiving report
R.R.

1

ACCOUNTS PAYABLE CLERK

Receive vendor's invoice

INV
R.R.
P.O.
REQ

Match documents
Check prices
Check extensions
Compute discounts
Prepare voucher

Key enter and process purchase transaction data

Purchase transaction file

Document package*

Print reports

Acquisitions journal

CASH DISBURSEMENTS CLERK

Review contents for completeness, accuracy, and account distributions, stamp, initial, and cancel documents

Key enter and process cash disbursement transaction data

Cash disbursement transaction file

Document package

2

Print reports

Cash disbursements journal
Check

Update accounts payable master file

Accounts payable master file

To vendor; signed by treasurer (reviews support)

Notes on controls
• Chart of accounts—the company uses an adequate detailed chart of accounts.
• Prenumbered documents—all documents shown are prenumbered. They are accounted for by a function other than the preparer.
• Bank reconciliation—done monthly by an independent person.
• Procedures are applied daily. Backlogs are resolved promptly by authorizing overtime.
• Accounts payable master file total is reconciled to the general ledger total monthly.

File description
1. Chronological
2. Numerical

*Includes vendor's invoice, receiving report, purchase order, and purchase requisition.

Reference the CW site. The problem requires students to use the Internet to research (1) the purpose of the Business Roundtable (BR), and (2) specific issues within the BR's Statement on Corporate Governance (for example, board of directors function with respect to risk management, controls, and compliance).

THE IMPACT OF INFORMATION TECHNOLOGY ON THE AUDIT PROCESS

JUST BECAUSE THE COMPUTER DID THE WORK DOESN'T MEAN IT'S RIGHT

Foster Wellman's audit client, Manion's Department Stores Inc., installed a software program that processed and aged customer accounts receivable. The aging, which indicated how long the customers' accounts were outstanding, was useful to Foster when evaluating the collectibility of those accounts.

Because Foster did not know whether the aging totals were computed correctly, he decided to test Manion's aging by using his own firm's audit software to recalculate the aging, using an electronic copy of Manion's accounts receivable data file. He reasoned that if the aging produced by his audit software was in reasonable agreement with Manion's aging, he would have evidence that Manion's aging was correct.

Foster was shocked when he found a material difference between his and Manion's calculated aging. Manion's manager of the information technology (IT) function, Rudy Rose, investigated the discrepancy and discovered that programmer errors had resulted in design flaws in Manion's software used to calculate the aging. This outcome caused Foster to substantially increase the amount of his testing of the year-end balance of the allowance for uncollectible accounts.

LEARNING OBJECTIVES

After studying this chapter, you should be able to

11-1 Describe how IT improves internal control.

11-2 Identify risks that arise from using an IT-based accounting system.

11-3 Explain how specific types of general controls and application controls reduce risks associated with using IT-based accounting systems.

11-4 Describe how the strength of general controls affects the auditor's testing of application controls.

11-5 Use test data, parallel simulation, and embedded audit module approaches when auditing through the computer.

11-6 Identify issues for environments involving microcomputers, networks, database management systems, and outsourced computer service centers.

In Chapter 10, the components of internal control and how the auditor obtains an understanding of internal control and assesses control risk were discussed. We now turn our attention to how the client's integration of information technology (IT) into the accounting system affects risks and internal control. The use of IT can enhance internal control by adding new control procedures performed by the computer and by replacing manual controls subject to human error. Although enhancing internal control, reliance on IT can introduce new risks, which the client can manage through the implementation of controls specific to IT environments. This chapter highlights risks specific to IT environments, identifies controls that can be implemented to address those risks, and highlights how IT-related controls affect the audit process.

Auditors must be careful in assessing internal control when clients have technology-based accounting systems before they can accept the reliability of any computer-generated output. As shown in the chapter vignette, Manion's overreliance on the accuracy of the computer-produced accounts receivable aging highlights a risk associated with the use of computer-generated information. A common assumption is that "the information is correct because the computer produced it." Too often, reliance is placed on the untested accuracy of computer-generated output because auditors fail to remember that computers perform only what they are programmed to do. Auditors must understand and test computer-based controls before concluding that computer-generated information is reliable. We begin by focusing on how IT can enhance internal control.

HOW INFORMATION TECHNOLOGIES ENHANCE INTERNAL CONTROL

OBJECTIVE 11-1
Describe how IT improves internal control.

Most entities, including small, family-owned businesses, rely on IT to record and process business transactions. As a result of explosive advancements in IT, even relatively simple businesses use personal computers with purchased accounting software for their accounting processes to replace inefficient and less effective manual accounting systems. As businesses grow and evolve, they often upgrade their IT systems to handle continually increasing information needs. The use of complex network environments and centralized IT functions are common in businesses today.

Enhancements to internal control resulting from the integration of IT into accounting systems include the following:

- *Computer controls replace manual controls.* The obvious benefits of IT, such as the ability to handle tremendous volumes of complex business transactions cost effectively, cause organizations to use IT throughout their financial reporting processes. One advantage of IT is the ability to improve internal controls by incorporating computer-performed controls in day-to-day transaction processing activities. Replacing manual procedures with programmed controls that apply checks and balances to each processed transaction can reduce human error that is likely to occur in traditional manual environments. A well-controlled IT system offers greater potential for reducing misstatements because computers process information consistently. Examples of internal controls performed by computers that once were processed by employees are comparing customer and product numbers with master files and comparing sales transaction amounts with preprogrammed credit limits.
- *Higher-quality information is available.* Once management is confident about the reliability of information produced by IT, management's use of the information offers further potential for improved management decisions. First, complex IT environments are usually administered effectively because the complexity requires effective organization, procedures, and documentation. Second, IT systems typically provide management with more and higher-quality information faster than most manual systems.

Although IT can enhance a company's internal control, it can also affect a company's overall control risk. Many risks associated with manual systems are reduced and in some cases eliminated. However, new risks specific to IT environments are created and can lead to substantial losses if ignored. For example, the inability to retrieve important information because of IT systems failure or use of unreliable information because of processing errors produced by that technology could paralyze organizations. These risks increase the likelihood of material misstatements in financial statements that must be considered by management and the auditor. The following highlights key risks specific to IT environments:

- *Reliance on the functioning capabilities of hardware and software.* Without proper physical protection, hardware or software may not function. Therefore, it is critical to physically protect hardware, software, and related data from physical damage that might result from inappropriate use, sabotage, or environmental damage (such as fire, heat, humidity, water).
- *Visibility of audit trail.* Because much of the information is entered directly into the computer, the use of IT often reduces or even eliminates source documents and records that allow the organization to trace accounting information. These documents and records are called the audit trail. Because of the loss of the audit trail, other controls must be put into place to replace the traditional ability to compare output information with hard copy data.
- *Reduced human involvement.* In many IT environments, employees who deal with the initial processing of transactions never see the final results. Therefore, they are less able to identify processing misstatements. Even if they see the final output, it is often difficult to recognize misstatements because the results are often highly summarized. Also, employees tend to regard output generated through the use of technology as "correct" because a computer produced it.
- *Systematic versus random errors.* As organizations replace manual procedures with technology-based procedures, the risk of random errors decreases. However, the risk of systematic error increases because of the uniformity of computer processing. Once procedures are programmed into computer software, the computer processes information consistently for all transactions until the programmed procedures are changed. Unfortunately, flaws in software programming and changes to that software affect the reliability of computer processing, often resulting in many significant misstatements. This risk is heightened if the system is not programmed to recognize unusual transactions or when transaction audit trails are inadequate.
- *Unauthorized access.* IT-based accounting systems often allow on-line access to data in master files and other records stored in electronic form. Because on-line access can occur from many remote access points, there is potential for illegitimate access. Without proper on-line restrictions such as passwords and user IDs, unauthorized activity may be initiated through the computer, resulting in improper changes in software programs and master files. Also, confidential information may be improperly obtained.
- *Loss of data.* Much of the underlying data in an IT environment is stored in centralized electronic files. When data are centralized, there is an increased risk of loss or destruction of entire data files with severe ramifications. There is potential for misstated financial statements, and in certain cases, the organization may incur serious business interruptions.
- *Reduced segregation of duties.* As organizations convert from manual to computer processes, computers perform many duties that were traditionally segregated, such as authorization and record keeping. Therefore, combining activities from different parts of the organization into one IT function centralizes responsibilities that were traditionally divided. IT personnel with access to software and master files may be able to steal assets unless key duties are appropriately segregated within the IT function.

- *Lack of traditional authorization.* It is common in advanced IT systems for certain types of transactions to be initiated automatically by the computer. Examples include calculating interest on savings accounts and ordering inventory when prespecified order levels are reached. Therefore, proper authorization depends on software procedures and the accuracy of master files used in making the authorization decision.
- *Need for IT experience.* Even when companies purchase relatively simple computer systems that include purchased software, personnel with knowledge and experience to install, maintain, and use the system is essential. As the use of IT systems increases in organizations, the need for qualified IT specialists often arises. Many companies create an entire function of IT personnel that includes programmers, operators, network supervisors, librarians, data entry clerks, quality assurance specialists, and database administrators. The reliability of an IT system and the information it generates often depends on the ability of the organization to employ personnel or hire consultants with appropriate technology knowledge and experience.

INTERNAL CONTROLS SPECIFIC TO INFORMATION TECHNOLOGY

OBJECTIVE 11-3
Explain how specific types of general controls and application controls reduce risks associated with using IT-based accounting systems.

To address many of the risks associated with greater reliance on IT, organizations often implement controls specific to the IT function. Auditing standards describe two broad control groupings for IT systems: general controls and application controls.

General controls relate to all aspects of the IT function, including administration; software acquisition and maintenance; physical and on-line security over access to hardware, software, and related data; back-up planning in the event of unexpected emergencies; and hardware controls.

Application controls apply to the processing of individual transactions, such as controls over the processing of sales or cash receipts. Therefore, application controls are specific to certain software applications and typically do not affect all IT functions. Processing controls must therefore be evaluated for every audit area (account or class of transactions) affected by an application in which the auditor plans to reduce assessed control risk.

As shown in Figure 11-1, general controls are designed to protect all application controls to ensure that those controls are effective. Strong general controls mitigate the types of risks identified in the boxes outside the general controls oval in Figure 11-1.

Table 11-1 describes six categories of general controls and three categories of application controls, with specific examples of each category. The next two sections discuss each of the categories of general and application controls in more detail.

General Controls

Similar to the effect that the control environment has on other components of internal control discussed in the last chapter, the six categories of general controls have an overriding effect on all IT functions. Auditors typically evaluate general controls early in the audit because of the impact of general controls on application controls. We now examine each category of general controls in more detail.

IFAC Guidelines
for IT

Administration of the IT Function As reliance on IT in business increases, managing and administrating the IT function becomes more important. Management must allocate sufficient resources to support technology.

The attitude about the importance of IT within an organization is often dictated by the attitude of the board of directors and senior management. Their oversight, resource allocation, and involvement in key IT decisions provide a strong signal about the importance of the function. In complex environments, management often establishes IT steering committees to help monitor the organization's technology needs. In less complex organizations, the board may rely on regular reporting by a Chief Information Officer (CIO) or other senior IT manager to keep management informed.

FIGURE 11-1   Relationship between General and Application Controls

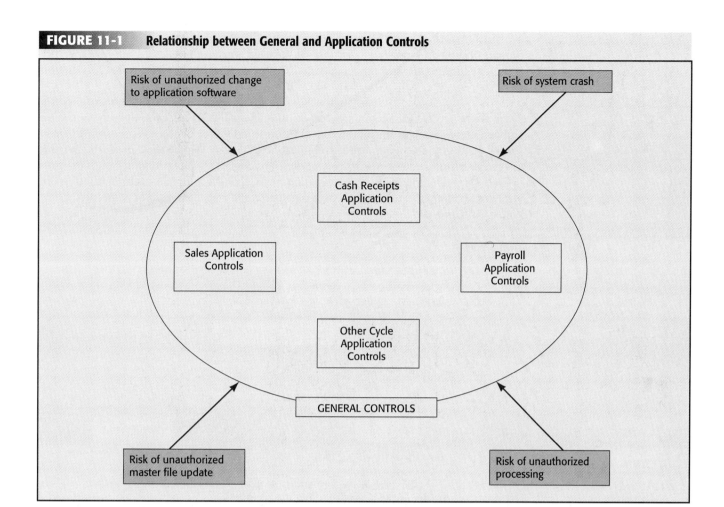

TABLE 11-1   Categories of General and Application Controls

Control Type	Category of Control	Example of Control
General Controls	Administration of the IT function	Chief information officer or IT manager reports to senior management and board.
	Segregation of IT duties	Responsibility for programming, operations, and data control are separated.
	Systems development	Teams of users, systems analysts, and programmers develop and thoroughly test software.
	Physical and on-line security	Access to hardware is restricted, and passwords and user IDs limit access to software and data files.
	Back-up and contingency planning	Written back-up plans are prepared and tested regularly throughout the year.
	Hardware controls	Memory failure or hard drive failure causes error messages on the monitor.
Application Controls	Input controls	Preformatted screens prompt data input personnel for information to be entered.
	Processing controls	Reasonableness tests review unit-selling prices used to process a sale.
	Output controls	The sales department performs postprocessing review of sales transactions.

In contrast, when technology functions are delegated exclusively to lower level employees or outside consultants, an implied message is given that IT may not be a high priority. The result is often an understaffed, underfunded, and poorly controlled IT function.

Segregation of IT Duties To respond to the risk of combining traditional custody, authorization, and record-keeping responsibilities under the IT function, well-controlled organizations respond by segregating key duties within IT. One concern is preventing IT personnel from authorizing and recording transactions to cover the theft of assets. Another concern is minimizing errors. To reduce these concerns, software programming, computer operations (including security surrounding physical and on-line access to hardware, software, and data files), and controls over data entry and output should be segregated as depicted in Figure 11-2.

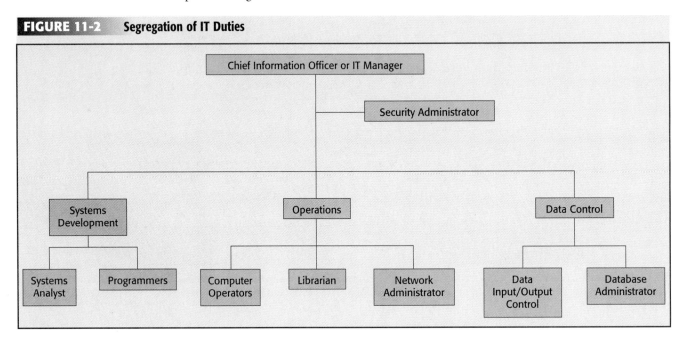

FIGURE 11-2   Segregation of IT Duties

Ideally, responsibilities for IT management, systems development, operations, and data control should be separated as follows:

- *IT management.* Oversight of the IT function is generally the responsibility of the CIO or IT manager. This individual is responsible for the oversight of all IT functions to ensure that activities are carried out consistently with the IT strategic plan. In addition to the CIO, a security administrator monitors both physical and on-line access to hardware, software, and data files and performs follow-up investigative procedures for detected security breaches.
- *Systems development.* Development and changes to IT systems are generally coordinated by a systems analyst who is responsible for the overall design of each application system and serves as the liaison between IT personnel responsible for programming the application and personnel outside the IT function who will be the primary system users (such as accounts receivable personnel). Programmers develop special flowcharts for the application, prepare computer instructions, test programs, and document the results based on direction from the systems analyst. Programmers should not have access to input data or computer operation because understanding the program logic can easily be used for personal benefit. Access to copies of actual programs used to produce accounting information and access to data should be restricted so that programmers are not able to implement software programming changes without proper authorization. Instead, programmers should be allowed to work only with test copies of programs and data.

- *Operations.* The day-to-day operations of the computer are the responsibility of computer operators who are responsible for executing jobs in accordance with the job schedule established by the CIO and for monitoring computer consoles for messages about computer efficiency and malfunctions. A librarian is responsible for maintaining computer programs, transaction files, and other important computer records and documentation. The librarian maintains control over these programs and records by releasing them to operators only as indicated on the job schedule. The librarian releases a test copy to programmers only on approval by senior management. In networked environments, the network administrator is responsible for planning, implementing, and maintaining a network of servers that link users to various applications and data files.
- *Data control.* Data input/output control personnel independently verify the quality of input and the reasonableness of output. For organizations that use databases to store information shared by accounting and other functions, database administrators are responsible for the operation and access security of shared databases.

Naturally, the extent of segregation of duties depends on the organization's size and complexity. In many small companies, it is not practical to segregate the duties to the extent described here.

Systems Development To increase confidence that tested software continues to process information as intended, management must design and implement internal controls designed to reduce the risk of unauthorized software changes. These internal controls are called systems development methodology procedures.

A key to successful software purchase decisions or to in-house programming of software is to involve a team of both IT and non-IT personnel, including key users of the software and internal auditors. This combination of personnel increases the likelihood that information needs as well as software design and implementation problems are properly addressed. A team approach usually results in more effective systems and better acceptance by key users.

Whether software is purchased or developed internally, extensive testing of the software with realistic data is critical. The purpose is to ensure that the new software is compatible with existing hardware and software components and to determine whether the hardware and software can handle realistic volumes of transactions. Two typical test strategies companies use are pilot testing and parallel testing. **Pilot testing** involves implementing a system in one part of the organization, while other locations continue to rely on the old system. **Parallel testing** involves operating the old and new systems simultaneously in all locations.

Once successfully tested, the software supporting the new system is transferred from the programming staff to the librarian. Controls over this transfer process are critical to be certain that only approved changes are implemented. The librarian should accept the new or modified software only when proper documentation of the systems development is provided. In addition, to avoid implementation problems, conversion should be scheduled during off-peak time periods when reliance on the system is reduced.

Physical and On-Line Security Strong physical controls over computers and on-line restrictions to software and related data files decrease the risk that unauthorized changes are made to software programs and data files. Security plans should be in writing and continually monitored. Following is a brief description of typical physical controls and on-line access controls:

- *Physical controls.* Physical control over computer equipment begins with restricting access to hardware, software, and back-up data files on magnetic tapes or disks, CDs, and floppy disks. Examples of ways to restrict unauthorized use include keypad entrances, badge-entry systems, security cameras, and security personnel. For higher levels of security, physical and on-line access is granted only after employee fingerprints are read or employee retinas are scanned and matched with an approved database. Other physical controls include monitoring of cooling and humidity to ensure that the equipment functions properly. Readily available fire extinguishing equipment reduces potential damage from fire.

- *On-line access controls.* Appropriately enforced user IDs and passwords to access software and related data files reduce the likelihood that unauthorized changes are made to software applications and data files. The operating systems of many computers provide user ID and password control features. In more advanced IT systems, separate add-on security software packages can be installed to strengthen security.

**Disaster Recovery
Plan Example**

Back-Up and Contingency Planning Disasters such as power failures, fire, excessive heat or humidity, water damage, or even sabotage have serious consequences to businesses using IT. To address such risks, organizations develop detailed back-up and contingency plans. One key to a back-up and contingency plan is to make sure that all critical copies of software and data files are backed up and stored off premises. Fire and bombproof underground vaults are often used to store these back-up copies. Also, the plans should identify alternative hardware to process company data.

For smaller IT systems, replacement computers and servers can be purchased and used with back-up copies of software and data files. In more advanced systems, organizations install battery backups for temporary power outages and have gasoline generators on-site, and they may also contract for back-up facilities.

Hardware Controls Controls that are built into computer equipment by the manufacturer to detect and report equipment failures are called **hardware controls**. Independent auditors are more concerned with the client's methods of handling the errors identified by the computer than with the adequacy of the hardware controls in the system. Regardless of the quality of hardware controls, output will remain uncorrected unless the client's organization has made provisions for handling machine errors.

Application Controls

Application controls are designed for each software application and are intended to help a company satisfy the six transaction-related audit objectives discussed in previous chapters. Although some application controls affect one or only a few transaction-related audit objectives, most controls prevent or detect several types of misstatements. Although the objectives for input, processing, and output controls are the same, the procedures for meeting the objectives vary considerably. We will now discuss these three types of application controls.

Input Controls Controls designed by an organization to ensure that the information being processed by the computer is authorized, accurate, and complete are called **input controls**. Input controls are critical because a large portion of errors in IT systems result from errors in entering data. Errors in input result in output errors regardless of the quality of the information processing. Typical controls found in manual systems continue to be important. Examples include management's written authorization of transactions, adequate preparation of input source documents, and competent personnel. Other controls are specific to IT. Examples include adequately designed input screens with preformatted prompts for transaction information, pull-down menu lists of available software options, and computer performed validation tests of input accuracy, such as the validation of customer numbers against the customer master files. Also, immediate error correction procedures and accumulation of errors in an error file for subsequent follow-up by data input personnel provide for early detection and correction of input errors.

For IT environments that group similar transactions together into batches, the use of financial batch totals, hash totals, and record count totals help increase the accuracy and completeness of input. Batch input controls are described in Table 11-2.

TABLE 11-2   Batch Input Controls

Control	Definition	Examples
Financial total	Summary total of field amounts for all records in a batch that represent a meaningful total such as dollars or amounts	The total of dollars of all vendor invoices to be paid
Hash total	Summary total of codes from all records in a batch that do not represent a meaningful total	The total of all vendor account numbers for vendor invoices to be paid
Record count	Summary total of physical records in a batch	The total number of vendor invoices to be processed

Processing Controls Controls that prevent and detect errors when transaction data are processed are called **processing controls**. Even though strong general controls, especially controls related to systems development and security, provide some of the best control for minimizing errors, application processing controls are often embedded in software to prevent, detect, and correct processing errors. Table 11-3 includes examples of processing controls.

TABLE 11-3   Processing Controls

Type of Processing Control	Description	Example
Validation test	Ensures the use of the correct master file, database, and programs in processing	Does the internal label on the payroll master file tape match the file label indicated in the application software?
Sequence test	Determines that data submitted for processing is in the correct order	Has the file of payroll input transactions been sorted in departmental order before processing?
Arithmetic accuracy test	Checks the accuracy of processed data	Does the sum of net pay plus withholdings equal gross pay for the entire payroll?
Data reasonableness test	Determines whether data exceeds prespecified amounts	Does employee's gross pay exceed 60 hours or $999 for the week?
Completeness test	Determines that every field in a record has been completed	Is employee number, name, number of regular hours, number of overtime hours, department number, etc., included for each employee?

Output Controls Controls that focus on detecting errors after processing is completed rather than on preventing errors are called **output controls**. The most important output control is review of the data for reasonableness by someone knowledgeable about the output. Users can often identify errors because they know the approximate correct amounts. In addition, reconciliation of computer-produced output to manual control totals and comparisons of the number of units processed to the number of units submitted for processing help identify errors in output. In some cases, sample comparisons of transaction output to input source documents are performed. Similarly, verification of dates and times of processing may help identify out-of-sequence processing. For sensitive output, such as payroll checks automatically generated by computer, control is enhanced by requiring the presentation of proper employee identification before distribution of checks. Also, access to sensitive output viewed on computer screens can be restricted by using passwords and user IDs.

IMPACT OF INFORMATION TECHNOLOGY ON THE AUDIT PROCESS

OBJECTIVE 11-4
Describe how the strength of general controls affects the auditor's testing of application controls.

The last section provided an overview of general controls and application controls. An auditor must be knowledgeable about these controls because he or she is responsible for gaining an understanding of internal control, including general and application controls, regardless of whether the client's use of IT is simple or complex. Also, knowledge about general controls increases the auditor's ability to rely on effective application controls to reduce control risk for transaction-related audit objectives. This section highlights how general and application controls affect the audit process.

Effect of General Controls on Control Risk

ISACA

Most auditors evaluate the effectiveness of general controls before evaluating application controls. If general controls are ineffective, there is potential for material misstatement in each computer-based accounting application, regardless of the quality of application controls. For example, if duties are inadequately segregated such that computer operators are also programmers and have access to computer programs and files, the auditor should be concerned about the potential for fictitious transactions or unauthorized data and omissions in accounts such as sales, purchases, and salaries. Similarly, if the auditor observes that data files are inadequately safeguarded, he or she may conclude that there is a significant risk of loss of data because the general controls affect each application. In this situation, audit testing to satisfy the completeness objective may need to be expanded in several areas such as cash receipts, cash disbursements, and sales.

On the other hand, if good general controls are in place, there is an increased likelihood of placing greater reliance on application controls. Auditors can therefore test specific application controls for operating effectiveness and rely on the results to reduce substantive testing. This use of effective general and application controls can result in significant audit efficiencies.

One challenge, however, in IT environments is the effect of changes in software on the auditor's reliance on controls. When the client changes the software, the auditor must evaluate whether additional testing is needed. If general controls are effective, the auditor will be able to easily identify when software changes are made. In environments where general controls are weak, there is greater likelihood of unidentified changes in application software. As a result, auditors must consider performing tests of application control operating effectiveness on a continual basis throughout the year when general controls are weak.

Auditors typically obtain information about general and application controls through interviews with IT personnel and key users; examination of system documentation such as flowcharts, user manuals, program change requests, and testing results; and review of detailed questionnaires completed by IT staff. In most cases, it is desirable to use several approaches in understanding internal control because each offers different information. Interviews with the chief information officer and systems analysts provide useful information about the operation of the entire IT function, the extent of software development and hardware changes made to key accounting application software, and an overview of planned changes. Reviews of program change requests and system test results are useful in identifying program changes in application software. Questionnaires are useful to identify specific internal controls.

Effect of IT Controls on Control Risk and Substantive Tests

Recall from the last chapter that auditors relate strengths and weaknesses in internal control to specific transaction-related audit objectives. Based on those strengths and weaknesses, the auditor assesses control risk for each transaction-related audit objective. That same approach is used in IT environments, but now the auditor may be able to rely on application controls performed by the computer to reduce control risk.

Auditors do not normally link strengths and weaknesses in general controls to specific transaction-related audit objectives. Like the control environment discussed in Chapter 10, general controls affect transaction-related audit objectives in several cycles. If the general controls are ineffective, the auditor's ability to rely on application controls to reduce control risk is reduced. Conversely, if general controls are effective, it increases the auditor's ability to rely on application controls to reduce control risk.

Auditors identify both manual and computer-performed application controls and weaknesses for each transaction-related audit objective using a control risk matrix in much the same manner as discussed in the last chapter. For example, the computer's comparison of inputted employee identification numbers with the employee master file might reduce control risk for the existence objective for payroll expense by preventing payments to fictitious employees.

Similar to the discussion in the last chapter, when the auditor identifies specific application controls that can be used to reduce control risk, the auditor can reduce substantive testing. In addition, effective application controls performed by the computer are likely to be more consistent than manually performed controls because of the absence of random human errors. Also, the auditor may be able to reduce tests of controls audit costs by using the audit firm's software to test the controls. These factors, when combined, often lead to extremely effective and efficient audits.

The impact of general controls and application controls on audits is likely to vary depending on the level of complexity in the IT environment. The next two sections highlight issues in auditing clients with relatively simple IT environments and ones with more complex environments.

Auditing in Less Complex IT Environments

Many organizations use IT to process business transactions and design those systems so that source documents are retrievable in readable form and can be traced easily through the accounting system to output. In those instances, many of the traditional source documents such as customer purchase orders, shipping and receiving records, and sales and vendor invoices are maintained. The related accounting software also produces printed journals and ledgers that allow the auditor to trace individual transactions through the accounting records. In addition, internal controls often include client comparison of computer-produced records with source documents.

In these situations, the use of IT does not significantly impact the audit trail. Typically, the auditor obtains an understanding of internal control and performs tests of controls, substantive tests of transactions, and account balance verification procedures in the same manner as if the accounting system were entirely manual. The auditor is still responsible for gaining an understanding of general and application computer controls because such knowledge is useful in identifying risks that may affect the financial statements. However, the auditor does not typically perform tests of computer controls. This approach to auditing is often called **auditing around the computer** because the auditor is not using computer controls to reduce assessed control risk. Instead, the auditor uses non-IT controls to support reduced control risk assessment in a manner similar to that presented in the last chapter.

Auditing in More Complex IT Environments

OBJECTIVE 11-5
Use test data, parallel simulation, and embedded audit module approaches when auditing through the computer.

As organizations expand their use of IT, internal controls are often embedded in applications that are visible only in electronic form. When traditional source documents such as invoices, purchase orders, billing records, and accounting records such as sales journals, inventory listings, and accounts receivable subsidiary records are only in electronic form rather than hard copy, the auditor must change his or her approach to auditing. This approach to the audit is often called **auditing through the computer**. Table 11-4 (p. 340) contains examples that highlight differences in auditing around the computer and auditing through the computer.

There are three categories of testing strategies when auditing through the computer: the test data approach, parallel simulation, and the embedded audit module approach.

Test Data Approach The **test data approach** involves processing the auditor's test data using the client's computer system and the client's application program to determine whether the computer-performed controls correctly process the test data. Because the auditor designs the test data, the auditor is able to identify which test items should be accepted or

TABLE 11-4 Examples of Auditing around and through the Computer

Internal Control	Auditing around the Computer Approach	Auditing through the Computer Approach
Credit is approved for sales on account.	Select a sample of sales transactions from the sales journal and obtain the related customer sales order to determine that the credit manager's initials are present, indicating approval of sales on account.	Obtain a copy of the client's sales application program and related credit limit master file and process a test data sample of sales transactions to determine whether the application software properly rejects those test sales transactions that exceed the customer's credit limit amount and accepts all other transactions.
Payroll is processed only for individuals currently employed.	Select a sample of payroll disbursements from the payroll journal and verify by reviewing human resource department files that the payee is currently employed.	Create a test data file of valid and invalid employee ID numbers and process that file using a controlled copy of the client's payroll application program to determine that all invalid employee ID numbers are rejected and that all valid employee ID numbers are accepted.
Column totals for the cash disbursements journal are subtotaled automatically by the computer.	Obtain a printout of the cash disbursements journal and manually foot each column to verify the accuracy of the printed column totals.	Obtain an electronic copy of the cash disbursements journal transactions and use generalized audit software to verify the accuracy of the column totals.

rejected by the client's system. The auditor compares the output generated by the system from the test data to the auditor's expected output to assess the effectiveness of the application program's internal controls. Figure 11-3 illustrates the use of the test data approach.

When using the test data approach, there are three main auditor considerations:

1. *Test data should include all relevant conditions that the auditor wants tested.* The auditor should design test data to test the key computer-based controls the auditor intends to rely on to reduce control risk. The auditor's test data should contain realistic data items that are likely to be a part of the client's normal processing, including both valid and invalid transactions.

   For example, assume the client's payroll application contains a limit check that disallows a payroll transaction that exceeds 80 hours per week. To test this control, the auditor can prepare payroll transactions with 79, 80, and 81 hours for each sampled week and process them through the client's system in a manner shown in Figure 11-3. If the limit check control is operating effectively, the client's system should reject the transaction for 81 hours and the client's error listing should report the 81-hour transaction error.

2. *Application programs tested by the auditor's test data must be the same as those the client used throughout the year.* One approach is to run the test data on a surprise basis, possibly at random times throughout the year, even though doing so is costly and time-consuming. Another method is to rely on the client's general controls in the librarian and systems development functions for assurance that the program tested is the one used in normal processing.

3. *Test data must be eliminated from the client's records.* If testing of the client's software involves processing test data while simultaneously processing actual client transactions, the auditor must eliminate test data in client master files once testing is complete. It is not appropriate to permit fictitious transactions to remain permanently in the client's master file. To remove the fictitious transactions, the auditor submits additional input that reverses the effect of those transactions.

Because of the complexities of many clients' application software programs, auditors who plan to use the test data approach often obtain assistance from a computer audit specialist. Many larger accounting firms have staff dedicated to assisting in testing client application controls.

FIGURE 11-3 Test Data Approach

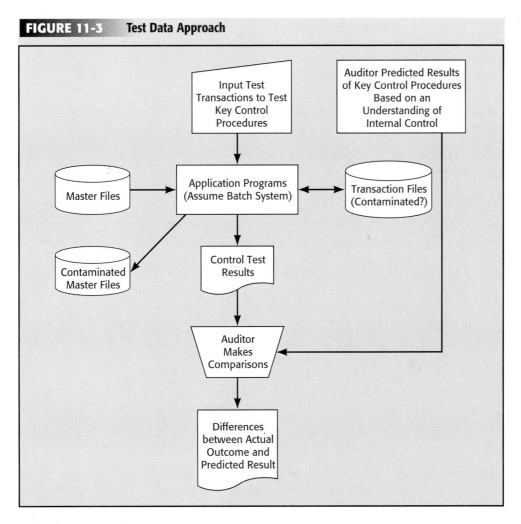

Parallel Simulation A variety of software is available to assist auditors in determining the effectiveness of controls in software and to obtain evidence about account balances that are in an electronic format. The auditor uses auditor-controlled software to perform parallel operations to the client's software by using the same data files. Whether testing controls or ending balances, the auditor compares his or her output to output from the client's software to test the effectiveness of the client's software. The lack of differences in output indicates effectively functioning client software, whereas differences indicate potential weaknesses. Because the auditor's software is designed to parallel an operation performed by the client's software, this testing strategy is called **parallel simulation** testing.

A tool commonly used by auditors to perform parallel simulation testing is **generalized audit software (GAS)**, which is software designed specifically for use by auditors. These off-the-shelf purchased audit software programs are normally Windows-based and can be easily operated on an auditor's desktop or laptop computer. Examples are ACL Software and Interactive Data Extraction and Analysis (IDEA) software. The auditor obtains copies of client databases or master files in machine-readable form and uses the generalized audit software to perform a variety of tests of the client's electronic data. Some auditors use spreadsheet software to perform basic parallel simulation tests. Others may develop their own customized audit software. Figure 11-4 (p. 342) depicts a typical parallel simulation.

ACL
IDEA

There are two advantages of generalized audit software. First, it is relatively easy to train audit staff in its use even if they have had little audit-related IT training. Second, generalized audit software can be applied to a wide variety of clients with minimal customization.

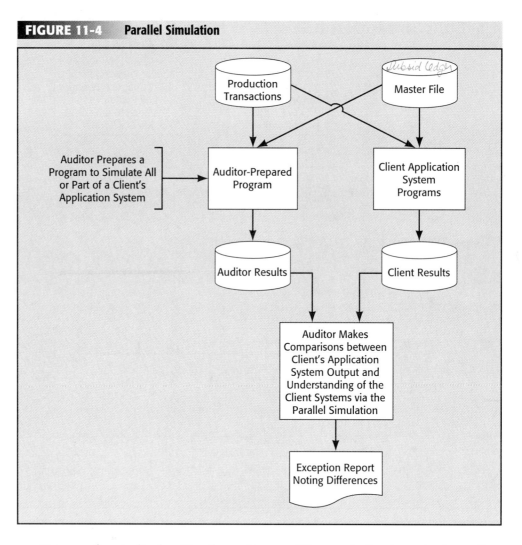

FIGURE 11-4　**Parallel Simulation**

One use of generalized audit software is to test IT controls. For example, the auditor can obtain copies of a client's customer credit limit master file and input file of customer orders and instruct the auditor's computer to list transactions that fall below the customer's authorized credit limit. The auditor can then reconcile the audit software output tests to the client's recorded transactions to verify the accuracy and completeness of the client's files. A second use of generalized audit software is for the auditor to verify the client's account balances. For example, the auditor can use the software to add the master file of customer accounts receivable to determine whether the total agrees with the general ledger balance. A significant benefit of generalized audit software is the ability to perform audit tests much faster and in more detail than using traditional manual procedures. Table 11-5 highlights other common uses of generalized audit software.

Embedded Audit Module Approach When using the **embedded audit module approach**, an auditor inserts an audit module in the client's application system to capture transactions with characteristics that are of specific interest to the auditor. For example, the auditor might capture all purchases exceeding a set dollar amount so that he or she can examine all large transactions processed through the acquisition and payment cycle. When the auditor uses an embedded audit module approach, he or she is able to continuously audit transactions by identifying actual transactions processed by the client. An important advantage is the auditor's ability to test continuously, compared with the test data and parallel simulation approaches, which are done at points in time. Another advantage of embedded audit modules is the ability to identify all unusual transactions for auditor

TABLE 11-5	Common Uses of Generalized Audit Software	
Uses	**Description**	**Examples**
Verify extensions and footings.	Verify the accuracy of the client's computations by calculating information independently.	Foot accounts receivable trial balance.
Examine records for quality, completeness, consistency, and correctness.	Scan all records using specified criteria.	Review payroll files for terminated employees.
Compare data on separate files.	Determine that information in two or more data files agrees.	Compare changes in accounts receivable balances between two dates using sales and cash receipts in transaction files.
Summarize or resequence data and perform analyses.	Change or aggregate data.	Resequence inventory items by location to facilitate physical observation.
Select audit samples.	Select samples from machine-readable data.	Randomly select accounts receivable for confirmation.
Print confirmation requests.	Print data for sample items selected for confirmation testing.	Print customer name, address, and account balance information from master files.
Compare data obtained through other audit procedures with company records.	Compare machine-readable data with audit evidence gathered manually, which is converted to machine-readable form.	Compare confirmation responses with accounts receivable master files.

evaluation. In some cases, these unusual transactions are copied to a separate data file, which is processed by an auditor-designed software program to duplicate the function performed by the client's system. The computer then compares the client's output with the auditor's output. Discrepancies are printed on an exception report for auditor follow-up. In this case, the embedded audit module permits the auditor to perform a real-time parallel simulation test.

An auditor may use one or a combination of the test data, parallel simulation, and embedded audit module approaches. Auditors typically use test data to perform tests of controls and substantive tests of transactions. Parallel simulation is often used for substantive testing, such as recalculating transaction amounts and footing master file subsidiary records of account balances. Auditors use the embedded audit module approach to identify unusual transactions for substantive testing.

ISSUES FOR DIFFERENT IT ENVIRONMENTS

OBJECTIVE 11-6
Identify issues for environments involving microcomputers, networks, database management systems, and outsourced computer service centers.

Much of the material presented in this chapter thus far addresses the effect of IT on the audit process for organizations that centralize the IT function. Although all organizations need a strong general control environment regardless of the structure of their IT function, some general control issues vary depending on the IT environment. The next four sections highlight IT issues for clients who use microcomputers, networks, database management systems, and outsourced computer service centers.

Issues for Microcomputer Environments

Microcomputers are widely used in most businesses regardless of the organization's size. They usually play an important role for even small businesses in processing or analyzing accounting data through the use of purchased or tailored accounting and electronic spreadsheet software.

General controls in smaller companies are usually less effective than in more complex IT environments. Often, there are no dedicated IT personnel or the client relies on periodic involvement of IT consultants to assist in installing and maintaining hardware and software. Also, the responsibility of the IT function is often assigned to user departments, such as in the accounting department, where the hardware physically resides. However, even in these IT environments, controls over software acquisition, physical and on-line access security, and back-up planning are important.

Often, auditors of clients that use microcomputers in less sophisticated general control environments do most of their auditing around the computer. These systems often produce sufficient audit trails that permit the auditor to reconcile input source documentation to output.

However, even in less sophisticated IT environments, there are situations in which computer controls can be relied on. For example, software programs in microcomputers can be loaded on the computer's hard drive in a format that does not permit changes by client personnel. The risk of unauthorized changes in the software is therefore low. Before relying on controls built into that software, the auditor must have confidence in the software vendor's reputation for quality.

A concern in a microcomputer environment is access to master files by unauthorized people. For example, the usefulness of comparing customer sales orders and customer accounts receivable balances with the master file of credit limits depends on the accuracy of customer credit limits. Unlike sophisticated IT environments, microcomputers often lack data file password protection. Without such protection, a user may be able to enter changes that make the control useless. An example is raising a customer credit limit high enough to avoid rejection. In such situations, appropriate segregation of duties between personnel with access to master files and responsibilities for processing in such situations is critical. In addition, regular owner-manager review of transaction output increases internal control.

Another risk with microcomputers is the loss of data and programs because of computer viruses, which can infect other programs and the entire system. Certain viruses can damage disk files or shut down an entire network of computers. Regularly updated virus protection software that continually screens for virus infections enhances controls.

Issues for Network Environments

The explosive use of networks that link equipment such as microcomputers, midrange computers, mainframes, workstations, servers, and printers is changing the IT function for many businesses. **Local area networks (LANs)** link equipment within a single or small cluster of buildings and are used only for intracompany purposes. A common use of LANs is to transfer data and programs from one computer or workstation to another using network system software to allow all of the devices to function together. **Wide area networks (WANs)** link equipment in larger geographic regions, including global operations.

In network environments, the application software and data files used to process transactions reside on servers, which are devices to manipulate data. Access to the application from microcomputers or workstations is managed by network server software. Companies often have several servers.

For many large client network environments, most of the general controls discussed in this chapter apply because the IT support and user involvement is centralized. For other companies, the network environment often presents control changes that the auditor must consider in planning the audit. Many organizations decentralize their network's servers, which often increases control risk because of a lack of security and overall management supervision of network operations. Also, many network environments lack standardized equipment and procedures. Organizations that need fast communication and easy access to data often create networks outside the control of the IT function. Responsibility for purchasing equipment and software, maintenance, administration, and physical security often resides with key user groups rather than with a centralized IT function, which often leads to lack of adequate controls. Also, network-related software often lacks the security features, including segregation of duties, typically available in traditionally centralized environments because of the ready access to software and data by multiple users.

When clients have accounting applications processed in a network environment, the auditor's understanding of internal control should include knowledge of the network configuration, including the location of servers, workstations, and computers linked to one another, and knowledge of network software used to manage the system. Auditors should also know about controls over access and changes to application programs and data files located on servers.

Issues for Database Management Systems

Auditors often encounter accounting applications that use database management systems to process transactions and maintain data files. **Database management systems** allow clients to create databases that contain information that can be shared in multiple applications. In nondatabase environments, each application contains its own data file, whereas in database management systems, many applications share files. Clients implement database management systems to reduce data redundancy, improve control over data, and provide better information for decision making by integrating information throughout functions and departments. For example, customer data, such as the customer's name and address, can be shared in the sales, credit, accounting, marketing, and shipping functions, resulting in significant cost reductions. Companies often integrate database management systems across the entire organization. Such programs are called enterprise software.

Controls often improve when data is centralized in a database management system by eliminating the redundant data files. However, database management systems also can create internal control risks. For example, there are risks associated with multiple users, including individuals outside of accounting, accessing and updating data files. Without proper database administration and access control, risks of unauthorized, inaccurate, and incomplete data files increase. Also, the centralization of data into a single file increases the importance of proper backup of data information on a regular basis.

Auditors of clients using database management systems should understand the clients' planning, organization, and policies and procedures to determine how well the systems are managed.

Issues when Clients Outsource IT

Many clients outsource some or all of their IT needs to an independent computer **service center** rather than maintain an internal IT center. Many smaller companies outsource their payroll function because payroll is reasonably standard from company to company and there are reliable providers of payroll services. Like all outsourcing decisions, companies decide whether to outsource IT on a cost-benefit basis.

When outsourcing to a computer service center, the client submits input data, which the service center processes for a fee and returns the agreed-upon output and the original input. For payroll, the company submits time cards, pay rates, and W-4s to the service center. The service center returns payroll checks, journals, and input data each week, and W-2s at the end of each year. The service center is responsible for designing the computer system and providing adequate controls to ensure that the processing is reliable.

The auditor faces a difficulty when obtaining an understanding of the client's internal controls because many of the controls reside at the service center and the auditor cannot assume that the controls are adequate simply because it is an independent enterprise. Auditing standards require the auditor to consider the need to understand and test the service center's controls if the service center application involves processing significant financial data.

The extent of obtaining an understanding and testing the service center's controls should be based on the same criteria that the auditor follows in evaluating a client's internal controls. The depth of the understanding depends on the complexity of the system and the extent to which the auditor intends to reduce assessed control risk to reduce substantive audit tests. If the auditor concludes that active involvement at the service center is the only way to conduct the audit, it may be necessary to obtain an understanding of internal controls at the service center and test controls using test data and other tests of controls.

In recent years, it has become increasingly common to have one independent auditor obtain an understanding and test internal controls of the service center for use by all customers and their independent auditors. The purpose of this independent assessment is to provide service center customers with a reasonable level of assurance of the adequacy of the service center's general and application controls and to eliminate the need for redundant audits by customers' auditors. If the service center has many customers and each requires an understanding of the service center's internal control by its own independent auditor, the inconvenience and cost to the service center can be substantial. When the service center's independent auditor completes the understanding and testing of service center controls, a special report is issued, indicating the scope of the audit and the conclusions. It is then the responsibility of the customer's auditor to decide the extent to which he or she wants to rely on the service center's audit report. SAS 70 (AU 324) contains guidance for both the customer's and the service center's auditors.

SUMMARY

This chapter studied the impact of IT on the audit process. Even when a client's use of IT leads to enhanced internal control, the use of IT-based accounting systems introduces new risks typically not associated with traditional manual systems. Well-managed companies recognize these new risks and respond by implementing effective general and application controls in the IT system to reduce the impact of those risks on financial reporting. The auditor must be knowledgeable about these risks and obtain an understanding of the client's general and application controls to effectively plan an audit. Obtaining knowledge about general controls provides a basis for the auditor to rely on application controls. Some of the auditor's tests of controls can be performed by the computer, often as a way to achieve more effective and efficient audits. Reliance on general and application controls to reduce control risk is likely to change when clients use microcomputers, networks, database management systems, and outsourced computer service centers instead of centralized IT systems.

ESSENTIAL TERMS

Application controls—controls related to a specific use of IT, such as the inputting, processing, and output of sales or cash receipts

Auditing around the computer—auditing without relying on and testing controls embedded in computer application programs, which is acceptable when the auditor has access to source documents in a readable form that can be reconciled to detailed listings of output

Auditing through the computer—auditing by testing computer-performed internal controls and account balances electronically, generally because strong general controls exist

Database management systems—hardware and software systems that allow clients to establish and maintain databases shared by multiple applications

Embedded audit module approach—a method of auditing transactions processed by IT whereby the auditor embeds a module in the client's application system to capture transactions with characteristics that are of interest to the auditor; the auditor is then able to analyze the captured transactions on a real-time, continuous basis as client transactions are processed

General controls—controls that relate to all parts of the IT function

Generalized audit software (GAS)—computer programs used by auditors that provide data retrieval, data manipulation, and reporting capabilities specifically oriented to the needs of auditors

Hardware controls—controls built into the computer equipment by the manufacturer to detect and report equipment failure

Input controls—controls designed by an organization to ensure that the information to be processed by the computer is authorized, accurate, and complete

Local area networks (LANs)—networks that connect computer equipment, data files, software, and peripheral equipment within a local area, such as a single building or a small cluster of buildings for intracompany use

Output controls—controls designed to ensure that computer-generated data are valid, accurate, complete, and distributed only to authorized people

Parallel simulation—an audit testing strategy that involves the auditor's use of audit software, either purchased or programmed by the auditor, to replicate some part of a client's application system

Parallel testing—a company's computer testing strategy that involves operating the old and new system simultaneously

Pilot testing—a company's computer testing strategy that involves implementing a new system in just one part of the organization, while maintaining the old system at other locations

Processing controls—controls designed to ensure that data input into the system are accurately and completely processed

Service center—an organization that provides IT services for companies on an outsourcing basis

Test data approach—a method of auditing an IT system that uses the auditor's test data to determine whether the client's computer program can correctly process valid and invalid transactions

Wide area networks (WANs)—networks that connect computer equipment, databases, software, and peripheral equipment that reside in many geographic locations, such as client offices located around the world

REVIEW QUESTIONS

11-1 (Objective 11-1) Explain how client internal controls can be enhanced through the proper installation of IT.

11-2 (Objective 11-2) Identify risks for accounting systems that rely heavily on IT functions.

11-3 (Objective 11-2) Define what is meant by an *audit trail* and explain how it can be affected by the client's integration of IT.

11-4 (Objective 11-2) Distinguish between random error resulting from manual processing and systematic error resulting from IT processing and give an example of each category of error.

11-5 (Objective 11-2) Identify the traditionally segregated duties in noncomplex IT environments and explain how increases in the complexity of the IT function affect that segregation.

11-6 (Objective 11-3) Distinguish between general controls and application controls and give two examples of each.

11-7 (Objective 11-3) Identify the typical duties within an IT function and describe how those duties should be segregated among IT personnel.

11-8 (Objective 11-4) Explain how the strength of general controls affects the auditor's tests of application controls.

11-9 (Objective 11-4) Explain the relationship between application controls and transaction-related audit objectives.

11-10 (Objective 11-4) Explain what is meant by auditing around the computer and describe what must be present for this strategy to be effective when auditing clients that use IT to process accounting information.

11-11 (Objective 11-5) Explain what is meant by the test data approach. What are the major difficulties with using this approach? Define parallel simulation with audit software and provide an example of how it could be used to test a client's payroll system.

11-12 (Objective 11-6) Describe risks that are associated with purchasing software to be installed on microcomputer hard drives. What precautions can clients take to reduce those risks?

11-13 (Objective 11-6) Compare the risks associated with network environments to those associated with centralized IT functions.

11-14 (Objective 11-6) How does the use of a database management system affect risks?

11-15 (Objective 11-6) Explain why it is unacceptable for an auditor to assume that an independent computer service center is providing reliable accounting information to an audit client. What can the auditor do to test the service center's internal controls?

11-16 (Objectives 11-1, 11-4) The following questions concern the characteristics of IT systems. Choose the best response.

    a. An IT system is designed to ensure that management possesses the information it needs to carry out its functions through the integrated actions of
        (1) data gathering, analysis, and reporting functions.
        (2) a computer-based information retrieval and decision-making system.
        (3) statistical and analytical procedures functions.
        (4) production-budgeting and sales-forecasting activities.

    b. Which of the following conditions would *not* normally cause the auditor to question whether material misstatements exist?
        (1) Bookkeeping errors are listed on an IT-generated error listing.
        (2) Differences exist between control accounts and supporting master files.
        (3) Transactions are not supported by proper documentation.
        (4) Differences are disclosed by confirmations.

    c. As the strength of general IT controls weakens, the auditor is most likely to
        (1) reduce testing of application controls performed by the computer.
        (2) increase testing of general IT controls to conclude whether they are operating effectively.
        (3) expand testing of application controls used to reduce control risk to cover greater portions of the fiscal year under audit.
        (4) ignore gaining knowledge about the design of general IT controls and whether they have been placed in operation.

    d. Which of the following is an example of an application control?
        (1) The client uses access security software to limit access to each of the accounting applications.
        (2) Employees are assigned a user ID and password that must be changed every quarter.
        (3) The sales system automatically computes the total sale amount and posts the total to the sales journal master file.
        (4) Systems programmers are restricted from performing applications programming functions.

11-17 (Objectives 11-2, 11-4) The following questions concern auditing complex IT systems. Choose the best response.

    a. Which of the following client IT systems generally can be audited without examining or directly testing the computer programs of the system?
        (1) A system that performs relatively uncomplicated processes and produces detailed output.
        (2) A system that affects a number of essential master files and produces limited output.
        (3) A system that updates a few essential master files and produces no printed output other than final balances.
        (4) A system that performs relatively complicated processing and produces little detailed output.

    b. Which of the following is true of generalized audit software programs?
        (1) They can be used only in auditing on-line computer systems.
        (2) They can be used on any computer without modification.
        (3) They each have their own characteristics that the auditor must carefully consider before using in a given audit situation.
        (4) They enable the auditor to perform all manual tests of control procedures less expensively.

c. Assume that an auditor estimates that 10,000 checks were issued during the accounting period. If an IT application control that performs a limit check for each check request is to be subjected to the auditor's test data approach, the sample should include
   (1) approximately 1,000 test items.
   (2) a number of test items determined by the auditor to be sufficient under the circumstances.
   (3) a number of test items determined by the auditor's reference to the appropriate sampling tables.
   (4) one transaction.

d. An auditor will use the test data approach to gain certain assurances with respect to the
   (1) input data.
   (2) machine capacity.
   (3) procedures contained within the program.
   (4) degree of data entry accuracy.

11-18 (Objectives 11-2, 11-3)   The following are misstatements that can occur in the sales and collection cycle.

1. A customer order was filled and shipped to a former customer that had already filed bankruptcy.
2. The sales manager approved the price of goods ordered by a customer, but he wrote down the wrong price.
3. Several remittance advices were batched together for inputting. The cash receipts clerk stopped for coffee, set them on a box, and failed to deliver them to the data input personnel.
4. A customer number on a sales invoice was transposed and, as a result, charged to the wrong customer. By the time the error was found, the original customer was no longer in business.
5. A former computer operator, who is now a programmer, entered information for a fictitious sales return and ran it through the computer system at night. When the money came in, he took it and deposited it in his own account.
6. A computer operator picked up a computer-based data file for sales of the wrong week and processed them through the system a second time.
7. For a sale, a data entry operator erroneously failed to enter the information for the salesman's department. As a result, the salesman received no commission for that sale.
8. A nonexistent part number was included in the description of goods on a shipping document. Therefore, no charge was made for those goods.

Required
   a. Identify the transaction-related audit objective(s) to which the misstatement pertains.
   b. Identify one computer-based control that would have likely prevented each misstatement.

11-19 (Objectives 11-2, 11-3)   You are doing the audit of Phelps College, a private school with approximately 2,500 students. With your firm's consultation, they have instituted an IT system that separates the responsibilities of the computer operator, systems analyst, librarian, programmer, and data control group by having a different person do each function. Now, a budget reduction is necessary and one of the five people must be laid off. You are requested to give the college advice as to how the five functions could be performed with reduced personnel and minimal negative effects on internal control. The amount of time the functions take is not relevant because all five people also perform nonaccounting functions.

Required

a. Divide the five functions among four people in such a way as to maintain the best possible control system.

b. Assume that economic times become worse for Phelps College and they must terminate employment of another person. Divide the five functions among three people in such a way as to maintain the best possible internal control. Again, the amount of time each function takes should not be a consideration in your decision.

c. Assume that economic times become so severe for Phelps College that only two people can be employed to perform IT functions. Divide the five functions between two people in such a way as to maintain the best possible control system.

d. If the five functions were performed by one person, would internal controls be so inadequate that an audit could not be performed? Discuss.

11-20 (Objectives 11-2, 11-3, 11-4, 11-5)   The Meyers Pharmaceutical Company has the following system for billing and recording accounts receivable:

1. An incoming customer's purchase order is received in the order department by a clerk who prepares a prenumbered company sales order form on which the pertinent information, such as the customer's name and address, customer's account number, and quantity and items ordered, is inserted. After the sales order form has been prepared, the customer's purchase order is stapled to it.

2. The sales order form is then passed to the credit department for credit approval. Rough approximations of the billing values of the orders are made in the credit department for those accounts on which credit limitations are imposed. After investigation, approval of credit is noted on the form.

3. Next the sales order form is passed to the billing department, where a clerk key-enters the sales order information onto a data file, including unit sales prices obtained from an approved price list. The data file is used to prepare sales invoices.

   The billing application automatically accumulates daily totals of customer account numbers and invoice amounts to provide "hash" totals and control amounts. These totals, which are inserted in a daily record book, serve as predetermined batch totals for verification of computer inputs. The billing is done on prenumbered, continuous, carbon-interleaved forms that have the following designations:

   (a) Customer's copy
   (b) Sales department copy, for information purposes
   (c) File copy
   (d) Shipping department copy, which serves as a shipping order

   Bills of lading are also prepared as carbon copy by-products of the invoicing procedure.

4. The shipping department copy of the invoice and the bills of lading are then sent to the shipping department. After the order has been shipped, copies of the bill of lading are returned to the billing department. The shipping department copy of the invoice is filed in the shipping department.

5. In the billing department, one copy of the bill of lading is attached to the customer's copy of the invoice and both are mailed to the customer. The other copy of the bill of lading, together with the sales order form, is then stapled to the invoice file copy and filed in invoice numerical order.

6. The data file is updated for shipments that are different from those billed earlier. After these changes are made, the file is used to prepare a sales journal in sales invoice order

and to update the accounts receivable master file. Daily totals are printed to match the control totals prepared earlier. These totals are compared with the "hash" and control totals by an independent person.

Required

    a. Identify the important controls and related sales transaction–related audit objectives.

    b. List the procedures that a CPA would use in his or her audit of sales transactions to test the identified controls and the substantive aspects of the sales transactions.

11-21 (Objective 11-5) The following are audit procedures taken from a CPA firm's audit program for acquisitions and cash disbursements:

    1. Foot the list of accounts payable and trace the balance to the general ledger. *test of details of bal.*

    2. Select a sample of accounts payable for confirmation, emphasizing vendors with a large balance and those that the client transacts with frequently, but include several with small and zero balances. *test of det. of bal.*

    3. Compare all transactions recorded for 4 days before and after the balance sheet date with related receiving reports and vendors' invoices to determine the appropriate recording period. *test of det. of bal (cutoff + A/P bal)*

    4. Examine a random sample of 100 acquisition transactions to determine whether each was authorized by an appropriate official and paid within the discount period to obtain the maximum cash discount. *Test of control*

    5. Compare the total of each account payable outstanding, including zero balances, with those in the preceding year and examine vendors' statements for any total with a difference in excess of $500. *test of det. of bal.*

    6. Compare the unit cost on a random sample of 100 vendors' invoices with catalogs or other price lists and investigate any with a difference of more than 3 percent. *Subs. test of trans.*

Required

    a. For each audit procedure, identify whether it is a test of control, a substantive test of transactions, or a test of details of balances.

    b. Explain how generalized audit software could be used, at least in part, to perform some or all of each audit procedure. Assume all information is in both machine- and nonmachine-readable form. Also, identify audit procedures or parts of procedures to which the general audit software is not likely to be applicable. Use the following format:

Procedure	Data File or Files Needed	Kind of Test or Tests the Auditor Can Perform Using GAS	Procedure for which GAS is Likely to Be Inappropriate

11-22 (Objectives 11-1, 11-2, 11-3, 11-4, 11-5) You are conducting an audit of sales for the James Department Store, a retail chain store with a computer-based sales system in which computer-based cash registers are integrated directly with accounts receivable, sales, perpetual inventory records, and sales commission expense. At the time of sale, the sales-clerks key-enter the following information directly into the cash register:

    • Product number
    • Quantity sold
    • Unit selling price
    • Store code number
    • Salesclerk number
    • Date of sale
    • Cash sale or credit sale
    • Customer account number for all credit sales

The total amount of the sale, including sales tax, is automatically computed by the system and indicated on the cash register's visual display. The only printed information for cash sales is the cash register receipt, which is given to the customer. For credit sales, a credit slip is prepared and one copy is retained by the clerk and submitted daily to the accounting department.

A summary of sales is printed out daily in the accounting department. The summary includes daily and monthly totals by salesclerks for each store as well as totals for each of 93 categories of merchandise by store. Perpetual inventory and accounts receivable records are updated daily on magnetic tape, but supporting records are limited primarily to machine-readable records.

Required

 a. What major problems does the auditor face in verifying sales and accounts receivable?

 b. How can the concept of test data be used in the audit? Explain the difficulties the auditor would have to overcome in using test data.

 c. How can generalized audit software be used in this audit? List several tests that can be conducted by using this approach.

 d. The client would also like to reduce the time it takes to key-enter the information into the cash register. Suggest several ways in which this could be accomplished, considering the information now being key-entered manually.

11-23 (Objective 11-5) A CPA's client, Boos & Baumkirchner, Inc., is a medium-size manufacturer of products for the leisure-time activities market (camping equipment, scuba gear, bows and arrows, and so forth). During the past year, a computer system was installed and inventory records of finished goods and parts were converted to computer processing. The inventory master file is maintained on a disk. Each record of the file contains the following information:

- Item or part number
- Description
- Size
- Unit-of-measure code
- Quantity on hand
- Cost per unit
- Total value of inventory on hand at cost
- Date of last sale or usage
- Quantity used or sold this year
- Economic order quantity
- Code number of major vendor
- Code number of secondary vendor

In preparation for year-end inventory, the client has two identical sets of preprinted inventory count cards. One set is for the client's inventory counts, and the other is for the CPA's use to make audit test counts. The following information is on each card:

- Item or part number
- Description
- Size
- Unit-of-measure code

In taking the year-end inventory, the client's personnel will write the actual counted quantity on the face of each card. When all counts are complete, the counted quantity will be entered into the system. The cards will be processed against the inventory database, and quantity-on-hand figures will be adjusted to reflect the actual count. A computer-generated edit listing will be prepared to show any missing inventory count cards and all quantity adjustments of more than $100 in value. These items will be investigated by client personnel, and all required adjustments will be made. When adjustments have been completed, the final year-end balances will be computed and posted to the general ledger.

The CPA has available generalized audit software that will run on the client's computer and can process both card and disk files.

a. In general and without regard to the facts in this case, discuss the nature of generalized audit software and list the various types and uses.

b. List and describe at least five ways generalized audit software can be used to assist in all aspects of the audit of the inventory of Boos & Baumkirchner, Inc. (For example, the software can be used to read the disk inventory master file and list items and parts with a high unit cost or total value. Such items can be included in the test counts to increase the dollar coverage of the audit verification.)*

11-24 (Objectives 11-2, 11-3)   One of the firm's audit partners, Alice Goodwin, just had lunch with a good friend, Sara Hitchcock, who is President of Granger Container Corporation. Granger Container Corp. is a fast-growing company that has been in business for only a few years. During lunch, Sara asked Alice for some advice and direction on how Granger Container should structure its systems development process within the Information Systems Department. Sara noted that because Granger has experienced such tremendous growth, the systems development process has evolved into its current state without much direction. Given Granger Container's current size, Sara questions whether their current processes are reasonable. Sara's concern is magnified by the fact that she has little understanding of information systems processes. Alice told Sara about your information systems evaluation experience and agreed to have you look at Granger Container's current systems development procedures. Sara gave Alice the following summary of the current processes.

Eric Winecoff is the Information Systems Manager at Granger Container and has been at the company for 3 years. Before becoming an employee, Eric provided software consulting services for Granger Container. Granger Container purchased a basic software package from Eric's former employer. Granger Container has the capability to make extensive modifications to the purchased software to adapt the software to Granger Container's specific business needs.

Program change requests are initiated by either the operations staff (two employees) or the programming staff (two employees), depending on the nature of the change. All change requests are discussed in Eric's office with the initiating staff. Based on that discussion, Eric provides a verbal approval or denial of the requested change. For approved projects, he encourages the programmers to visit with him from time to time to discuss progress on the projects. Eric's long and varied experience with this particular software is helpful in the evaluation of work performed, and he is able to make substantive suggestions for improvement. Eric has complete faith in his programmers. He believes that if he controlled their activities too carefully, he would stifle their creativity.

Upon completion of the technical programming, Eric reviews the programs and related systems flowcharts. Eric only rarely identifies last minute changes before granting his final approval for implementation. One evening a week is set aside in the computer room for program debugging and testing.

The programmers stay late on those evenings so that they can load the programs themselves. To speed up the coding, debugging, and testing process, the programmers work with the actual production program. As a safeguard, however, testing is performed on copies of the data files. The original data files are locked carefully in the file storage room. Eric is the only person who has access to the room.

When program changes are tested to the satisfaction of the programmers, Eric reviews the test results. If he approves the test results, he personally takes care of all the necessary communications and documentation. This involves preparing a short narrative description of the change, usually no longer than a paragraph. A copy of the narrative is sent to the user. Another copy is filed with the systems documentation. When the narrative is complete, Eric instructs operations to resume normal production with the new program.

*AICPA adapted.

Required

    a. Describe strengths in Granger Container's systems development and program change processes.

    b. Describe weaknesses in Granger Container's systems development and program change processes.

    c. Provide recommendations for how Granger Container could improve their processes.

11-25 (Objective 11-4)   Following are 10 key internal controls in the payroll cycle for Gilman Stores, Inc.

Key Controls:

1. To input hours worked, payroll accounting personnel input the employee's social security number. The system does not allow input of hours worked for invalid employee numbers.

2. The system automatically computes pay at time and a half once hours worked exceed 80 in a 2-week pay period.

3. The system accumulates totals each pay period of employee checks processed and debits the payroll expense general ledger account for the total amount.

4. Each pay period, payroll accounting clerks count the number of time cards submitted by department heads for processing and compare that total with the number of checks printed by the system to ensure that each time card has a check.

5. For factory personnel, the payroll system matches employee ID numbers with ID numbers listed on job costing tickets as direct labor per the cost accounting system. The purpose of the reconciliation is to verify that the amount paid to each employee matches the amount charged to production during the time period.

6. The system generates a listing by employee name of checks processed. Department heads review these listings to ensure that each employee actually worked during the pay period.

7. The payroll application is programmed so that only human resource personnel are able to add employee names to the employee master files.

8. On a test basis, payroll accounting personnel obtain a listing of pay rates and withholding information for a sample of employees from human resources to recalculate gross and net pay.

9. Input menus distinguish executive payroll, administrative payroll, and factory payroll.

10. The system automatically rejects processing an employee's pay if inputted hours exceed 160 hours for a 2-week pay period.

Required

For each control,

    a. Identify whether the control is an application control performed by the computer (AC) or a manual control performed by Gilman employees (MC).

    b. Identify the related transaction-related audit objective that is affected by the control.

11-26 (Objectives 11-2, 11-3)   Your new audit client, Hardwood Lumber Company, has a computerized accounting system for all financial statement cycles. During planning, you visited with the Information Systems Vice President and learned that personnel in Information Systems are assigned to one of four departments: systems programming, applications programming, operations, or data control. Job tasks are specific to the individual and no responsibilities overlap with other departments. Hardwood Lumber relies on the operating system software to restrict on-line access to individuals. The operating system allows an employee with "READ" capabilities to only view the contents of the program or file. "CHANGE" allows the employee to update the contents of the program or file. "RUN" allows the employee to use a program to process data. Programmers, both systems and applications, are restricted to a READ-only access to all live application software program files but have READ and CHANGE capabilities for test copies of those software program files. Operators have READ and RUN capabilities for live application programs. Data control clerks have CHANGE access to data files only and no access to software program files. The person in charge of operations maintains access to the operating software security features and is responsible for assigning access rights to individuals. The computer room is locked and requires a card-key to access the room. Only operations staff have a card-key to access the room. Security cameras monitor access to the room. A TV screen is in the Information Systems Vice President's office to allow periodic monitoring of access. The TV presents the live picture and no tape record is maintained. The librarian, who is in the operations department, is responsible for maintaining the library of program tapes and files. The librarian has READ and CHANGE access rights to program tapes and files. The files, when not being used, are stored in shelves located in a room adjacent to the computer room. They are filed numerically based on the tape label physically attached on the outside of the tape cartridge to allow for easy identification by operators as they access tapes from the shelves for processing.

Required

What recommendations for change can you suggest to improve Hardwood's Information Systems function?

CASE

11-27 (Objectives 11-2, 11-3)   The Information Systems (IS) department at Jacobsons Inc. consists of eight employees, including the IS Manager, Melinda Cullen. Melinda is responsible for the day-to-day oversight of the IS function and reports to Jacobsons' chief operating officer (COO). The COO is a senior vice president responsible for the overall retail operations. The COO reports directly to the president and chief executive officer. The COO attends board of director meetings to provide an update of key operating performance issues. Because Melinda takes an active role in managing the IS department, the COO rarely discusses IS issues with the board or CEO. Melinda and the COO identify hardware and software needs and are authorized to approve those purchases.

In addition to Melinda, the IS department is composed of seven other individuals: three programmers, three operators, and one data control clerk. Melinda has been employed by Jacobsons for 12 years, working her way up through various positions in the department. Fortunately, she has been able to retain a fairly stable staff and has experienced minimal turnover. All IS personnel have been employed in their current positions since mid-1997. When hiring personnel, Melinda performs extensive background checks on prospective employees, including reference, credit, and criminal checks. Melinda has developed a trust with each employee and, as a result, delegates extensively to each individual. This is especially beneficial because Melinda spends most of her time working with user departments in a systems analyst role, identifying changes needed to existing applications. She conducts weekly IS departmental meetings on Tuesday mornings. Each staff member attends, including night operators, to discuss issues affecting the performance of the department.

The three programmers are responsible for maintaining and updating systems and application software. The lead programmer is responsible for assigning duties among the programming staff. All three programmers have extensive experience with the operating, utility, security, and library software as well as all of Jacobsons' application software packages. Programming assignments are made based on who is least busy among the programming staff at the time. This method of management keeps all programmers familiar with most software packages in use at Jacobsons and keeps programmers excited about the job tasks because of the variety of assignments they receive. Melinda encourages each programmer to take continuing education courses to keep current with the latest technical developments. In addition to programming responsibilities, the programming staff maintains the library of programs and data tapes, which is located in a locked room nearby. The programming staff maintains extensive logs of tape use and of changes made to program files.

The three operators consist of a day operator and two night operators. Most of the applications are based on on-line inputting from various user departments for batch processing overnight. Thus, the heaviest volume of processing occurs during the night shift, although there is some daytime processing of payroll and general ledger applications. All operators are responsible for monitoring the operation of the equipment and correcting system-caused errors. In addition, they perform routine monthly back-up procedures. The computer operators have programming experience with the program language used in application programs. Occasionally, when a small change is identified for an application program, Melinda asks the day shift operator to implement that change to avoid overburdening the programming staff. Operators follow the production schedule prepared by Melinda, who consults with user departments to develop the schedule. The day shift operator reviews the Job Processed Log (which chronologically details the jobs processed) generated at the end of the previous night shift for deviations from the schedule, and the lead night shift operator reviews the Job Processed Log generated at the end of the previous day shift for deviations from the schedule. If jobs processed reconcile to the job schedule, the Job Processed Log is discarded. When there are deviations, the operator performing the review leaves a copy for Melinda, highlighting the deviation. Before performing batch processing jobs, the operators generate an Input Listing Report that summarizes the number of on-line input entries submitted during the day for processing. This number is recorded and then later compared by the operators with the computer output generated after batch processing and file updating occur. This provides a check figure of the number of transactions processed. When the numbers agree, the output is submitted to the data control clerk. When the numbers disagree, the operators identify the error and resubmit the application for processing.

The data control clerk collates all computer output, including output reports and exception listings. The data control clerk reviews exception reports and prepares correction forms for reprocessing. Examples of changes that the data control clerk might make include corrections for inputting errors (i.e., amounts accidentally transposed) and preparation of Change Request Forms for changes to existing master files (i.e., revising sales price lists and inventory product numbers in the sales master file and adding new employee names, addresses, and social security numbers to the payroll master file). After all corrections are made, the data control clerk distributes all computer output to the various user departments. User departments have high regard for the IS staff. Output reports are reconciled to input reports by users on a test basis quarterly.

Required

You are the senior auditor assigned to the audit of Jacobsons. The audit partner has asked you to assist in performing the IS general controls review. The partner has asked you to review this narrative information and respond to the following questions:

1. What strengths and weaknesses exist in the lines of reporting from IS to senior management? If you note any weaknesses, provide recommendations that can be included in the management letter.
2. What is your assessment of how Melinda Cullen fulfills her IS management responsibilities? What tasks performed by her do you believe strengthen the department? Which of her tasks cause you concern? What changes in her day-to-day responsibilities would you make?
3. What is your assessment of the programming function at Jacobsons? What are the strengths? What are the weaknesses? Make recommendations for improvement.

4. What is your assessment of the IS operations function at Jacobsons? What are the strengths? What are the weaknesses? Make recommendations for improvement.
5. What is your assessment of the data control function at Jacobsons? What are the strengths? What are the weaknesses? Make recommendations for improvement.
6. Make recommendations for improving controls over the involvement of users.

INTERNET PROBLEM 11-1: COBIT

Reference the CW site. The mission of COBIT is to research, develop, publicize, and promote an authoritative, up-to-date, international set of generally accepted information technology control objectives for day-to-day use by business managers and auditors. The second edition of COBIT, released by the COBIT Steering Committee and the ISACA, is available on-line. This problem requires students to use the Internet to research COBIT and address control-related questions.

OVERALL AUDIT PLAN AND AUDIT PROGRAM

HOW MUCH AND WHAT KIND OF TESTING WILL GET THE JOB DONE?

Terry Holland and Al Baker have known each other for years, and it seems like the debate they are having has been going on that long as well. Terry is a partner in the Southern California office of a national accounting firm. Al is an auditing professor at a nearby university. They get together once a month faithfully for lunch, and the conversation always gets around to auditing theory versus practice. Following is their most recent conversation:

PROFESSOR AL: A shortcoming of GAAS is that it offers too many choices of approaches. An auditor can do an audit with virtually no testing of detailed transactions by relying on observation, inquiry, analytical procedures, and tests of details of balances involving only large items. In a highly competitive market like we have now, I am concerned that firms will take the lowest cost approach instead of being concerned enough about quality.   There is already evidence that this is happening by CPA firms shifting away from large sample sizes.

PARTNER TERRY: Auditors must understand internal control on all audits and where control risk is reduced below the maximum, some tests of controls and substantive tests of transactions are always done to support that reduction. Detailed cutoff tests are always performed and it is appropriate to concentrate on larger items in tests of details of balances. We only take this efficient approach on the clients that don't present any real risks. Where risks are high, we pull out all the stops and do a lot of detailed testing.

PROFESSOR AL: That sounds fine, but there are certain things that only detailed testing will find. I'm thinking specifically about misappropriation of assets. I'm sure your clients expect you to find it, but analytical procedures and tests of large items at year-end won't get that job done. What about that?

PARTNER TERRY: Well, Al, our clients also tell us they want our opinion on their financial statements at as low a cost as possible. If we went looking for misappropriation of assets in every audit, our costs would go through the roof. And I'll tell you, the best way for the client to deal with fraud is to have good controls. We focus our attention on giving them good recommendations for improving their controls. It's "value-added" and they appreciate that.

PROFESSOR AL: I'm not convinced. I'm sure your clients would appreciate it a lot more if you actually found that John Bookkeeper was dipping his fingers into the till, but I'm also concerned about the reduction in testing to search for errors as well as fraud. It seems to me you guys are taking the requirements of GAAS and figuring out how to audit so efficiently that you're not allowing any slack in the process. I think you're creeping more and more toward being an insurer rather than an assurer of the financial statements.

PARTNER TERRY: What do you mean, Al? I don't understand your theory at all.

PROFESSOR AL: Well, you guys are counting on most of your clients not having misstated financial statements, doing minimal audit work at relatively high fees, and then banking on the fact that you'll be able to absorb the cost of any damages you suffer from bad audit opinions.

PARTNER TERRY: Oh come on, Al, sitting in this ivory tower of yours has turned you into a cynic. I hope you don't talk to your students this way. Auditors do a terrific job, and there are lots of incentives for high quality. We want people to come into the profession with a positive attitude. Let's talk about something else. Say, I believe it's your turn to pay.

LEARNING OBJECTIVES

After studying this chapter, you should be able to

12-1 Use the five types of audit tests to determine whether financial statements are fairly stated.

12-2 Select the appropriate types of audit tests.

12-3 Understand the concept of evidence mix and how it should be varied in different circumstances.

12-4 Design an audit program.

12-5 Compare and contrast transaction-related audit objectives and balance-related audit objectives.

12-6 Integrate the four phases of the audit process.

This chapter deals with the seventh and last step in the planning phase of an audit. It is a critical step because it results in the entire audit program the auditor plans to follow in the audit, including all audit procedures, sample sizes, items to select, and timing. This chapter's opening vignette deals with the importance of making the correct decisions in forming the overall audit plan and developing the detailed audit program, considering both the effectiveness of evidence and the efficiency of the audit process.

The first part of this chapter discusses the overall audit plan, which means selecting a mix of five types of tests that will result in an effective and efficient audit. This topic includes discussion of the trade-offs among the types of tests and consideration of the cost of each type of test. After the auditor decides the most cost-effective mix of the types of tests, a detailed audit program can be designed. This topic is covered later in the chapter. Because the material in this chapter is the final step in phase I, the planning phase, the relationship of phase I to the other three phases of the audit is discussed at the end of this chapter.

TYPES OF TESTS

OBJECTIVE 12-1
Use the five types of audit tests to determine whether financial statements are fairly stated.

In developing an overall audit plan, auditors have five **types of tests** they can use to determine whether financial statements are fairly stated. These tests are included in Figure 12-1, which shows the relationship of each type of test to the audit risk model. All five of these tests were introduced in earlier chapters and are now discussed in more detail, including the relationships among the five types of tests. All audit procedures fall into one, and sometimes more than one, of these five categories.

As shown in Figure 12-1, procedures to gain an understanding and tests of controls reduce control risk, whereas analytical procedures and tests of details of balances are used to satisfy planned detection risk. Substantive tests of transactions affect both control risk and planned detection risk because they are used to test the effectiveness of internal controls and the dollar amounts of transactions.

Procedures to Obtain an Understanding of Internal Control

Procedures to obtain an understanding of internal control were studied in Chapter 10. During this part of an audit, the auditor must focus attention on both the *design* and the *operation* of aspects of internal control to the extent necessary to effectively plan the rest of the audit. After appropriately documenting internal controls, it is critical that a system walk-through be completed to ensure that the described controls have actually been put into place. Five types of audit procedures that relate to the auditor's understanding of internal control were identified in Chapter 10.

- Update and evaluate the auditor's previous experience with the entity.
- Make inquiries of client personnel.

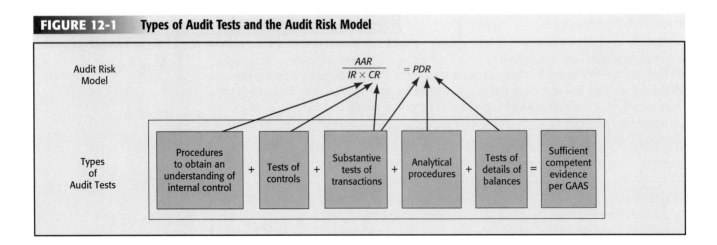

FIGURE 12-1   Types of Audit Tests and the Audit Risk Model

- Read client's policy and systems manuals.
- Examine documents and records.
- Observe entity activities and operations.

A major use of the auditor's understanding of internal control is to assess control risk for each transaction-related audit objective. Examples are assessing the accuracy objective for sales transactions as low and the existence objective as moderate. When the auditor believes control policies and procedures are effectively designed and when it is efficient to do so, he or she will elect to assess control risk at a level that reflects that evaluation. In making this risk assessment, however, assessed control risk must be limited to the level supported by evidence. The procedures used to obtain such evidence are called **tests of controls**.

Tests of controls are performed to determine the appropriateness of the design and operating effectiveness of specific internal controls. These tests include the following types of procedures:

- Make inquiries of appropriate client personnel.
- Examine documents, records, and reports.
- Observe control-related activities.
- Reperform client procedures.

The first two procedures are the same as those used to obtain an understanding of internal control. A system walk-through performed as part of procedures to gain an understanding is used to determine whether controls are in place and is normally applied to one or a few transactions. Tests of controls are used to determine whether those controls are effective and usually involve testing a sample of transactions. For example, the auditor may select one sales transaction for a system walk-through of the credit approval process. As part of the walk-through, the auditor would follow the credit approval process from initiation of the sales transaction through the granting of credit. In tests of controls, the auditor might examine a sample of sales transactions from throughout the year to determine whether credit was granted before the shipment of goods as a test of the operating effectiveness of the credit approval process. For some objectives, procedures to gain an understanding may provide sufficient evidential matter to support a reduced level of control risk. The amount of additional evidence required for tests of controls depends on the extent of evidence obtained in gaining the understanding and on the planned reduction in control risk.

The role of tests of controls in the audit of the sales and collection cycle is shown in Figure 12-2 (p. 362). Procedures to gain an understanding of internal control and tests of controls are combined in Figure 12-2 because they are essentially the same. For simplicity, two assumptions are made. First, only sales and cash receipts transactions and three general ledger balances make up the sales and collection cycle. Second, the beginning balances in cash and accounts receivable were audited in the previous year and are considered correct. If the auditor verifies that sales and cash receipts transactions are correctly recorded in the accounting records and posted to the general ledger, he or she can conclude that the ending balances in accounts receivable and sales are correct. (Cash disbursements transactions will have to be audited before the auditor can reach a conclusion about the ending balance in the cash account.) One way the auditor can verify this is to perform tests of controls. If controls are in place over sales and cash receipts transactions, the auditor can perform tests of controls to determine whether the six transaction-related audit objectives are being met for the cycle. Substantive tests of transactions, which are studied in the next section, also affect audit assurance for sales and cash receipts transactions.

To illustrate typical tests of controls, it is useful to return to the control risk matrix for Airtight Machine Company in Figure 10-5 (p. 309). For each of the 11 controls included in Figure 10-5, Table 12-1 (p. 363) identifies a test of control that might be performed to test its effectiveness.

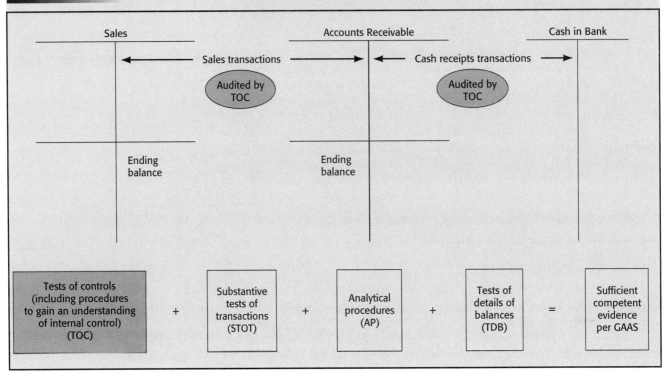

Substantive Tests of Transactions

innocent error or fraud

Substantive tests are procedures designed to test for dollar misstatements directly affecting the correctness of financial statement balances. Such misstatements (often termed *monetary misstatements*) are a clear indication of the misstatement of the accounts. There are three types of substantive tests: substantive tests of transactions, analytical procedures, and tests of details of balances.

The purpose of **substantive tests of transactions** is to determine whether all six transaction-related audit objectives have been satisfied for each class of transactions. For example, the auditor performs substantive tests of transactions to test whether recorded transactions exist and existing transactions are recorded. The auditor also performs these tests to determine whether recorded sales transactions are accurately recorded, recorded in the appropriate time period, correctly classified, and accurately summarized and posted to the general ledger and master files. If the auditor is confident that transactions were correctly recorded in the journals and correctly posted, he or she can be confident that general ledger totals are correct.

The role of substantive tests of transactions in the audit of the sales and collection cycle is illustrated in Figure 12-3 (p. 364). In comparing Figure 12-3 with Figure 12-2 above, observe that both tests of controls and substantive tests of transactions are performed for transactions in the cycle, not on the ending account balances. The auditor verifies the recording and summarizing of sales and cash receipts transactions by performing substantive tests of transactions. In this example, there is one set of tests for sales and another for cash receipts.

Tests of controls can be performed separately from all other tests, but for efficiency, they are often done at the same time as substantive tests of transactions. For example, tests of controls involving documentation and reperformance usually are applied to the same transactions tested for monetary misstatements. In fact, reperformance always simultaneously provides evidence about both controls and monetary correctness. In the remainder

TABLE 12-1   Illustration of Tests of Controls

Illustrative Key Controls	Typical Tests of Controls
Credit is approved automatically by the computer for customers included in the credit master file before shipment occurs.	Examine a sample of sales invoices and compare customer order to authorized credit limit (reperformance).
Sales are supported by authorized shipping documents and approved customer orders, which are attached to the duplicate sales invoice, and the shipping document number and approved customer order number must be entered at the time of sales input.	Examine a sample of duplicate sales invoices to determine that each one is supported by an attached authorized shipping document and approved customer order (documentation).
Separation of duties between billing, recording sales, and handling cash receipts.	Observe whether personnel responsible for handling cash have no accounting responsibilities and inquire as to their duties (observation and inquiry).
Unit selling prices are obtained from the price list master file of approved prices.	Examine a sample of sales invoices and agree prices to authorized computer price list. Review changes to price file throughout the year for proper approval (reperformance and documentation).
Shipping documents are forwarded to billing daily and billed the subsequent day.	Observe whether shipping documents are forwarded daily to billing and observe when they are billed (observation).
Shipping documents and duplicate sales invoice numbers are issued in numerical order by the computer, accounted for weekly, and traced to the sales journal.	Account for a sequence of sales invoices and shipping documents and trace each to the sales journal (documentation and reperformance).
Shipping documents are batched daily by quantity shipped.	Examine a sample of daily batches, recalculate the shipping quantities, and trace totals to reconciliation with input reports (reperformance).
Once the batch of sales transactions is entered, the computer automatically posts transactions to the accounts receivable subsidiary records and to the general ledger.	Use audit software to trace postings from the batch of sales transactions to the subsidiary records and general ledger.
Statements are mailed to all customers each month.	Observe whether statements are mailed for 1 month and inquire about who is responsible for mailing the statements (observation and inquiry).
The input screen for entering sales transactions limits account coding for the default general ledger account numbers for sales, sales returns, and accounts receivable.	Examine a sample of sales invoices to determine whether each one has an account number and that the account number is correct (documentation and reperformance).
Sales journal is reviewed monthly for reasonableness of total and compared with the general ledger for sales and sales returns.	Use audit software to recalculate the sales journal for 1 month and trace the total to the general ledger (reperformance).

of this book, it is assumed that tests of controls and substantive tests of transactions are done at the same time.

Analytical Procedures

As discussed in Chapter 7, **analytical procedures** involve comparisons of recorded amounts to expectations developed by the auditor. They often involve the calculation of ratios by the auditor for comparison with the previous years' ratios and other related data.

The two most important purposes of analytical procedures in the audit of account balances are to (1) indicate the presence of possible misstatements in the financial statements

FIGURE 12-3 **Role of Substantive Tests of Transactions in the Audit of the Sales and Collection Cycle**

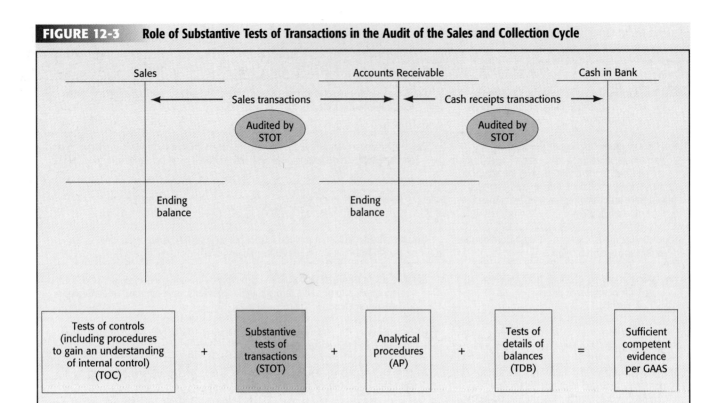

FIGURE 12-4 **Role of Analytical Procedures in the Audit of the Sales and Collection Cycle**

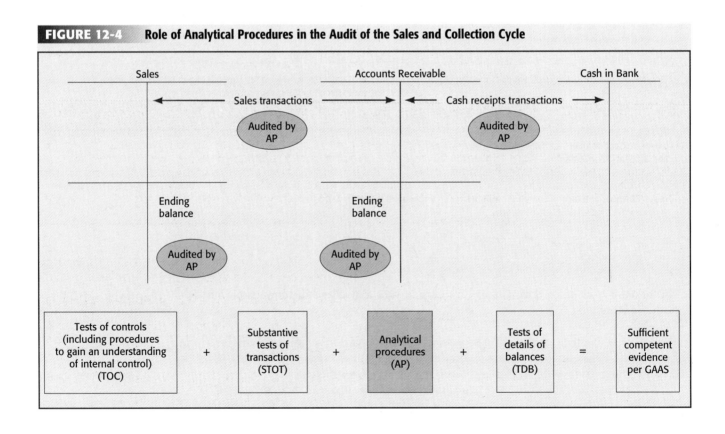

and (2) reduce tests of details of balances. There is typically a difference in the analytical procedures done during planning and those done in the testing phase. Even if, for example, the gross margin is calculated during planning, it is probably done using interim data. Later, during the tests of the ending balances, the auditor will recalculate the ratio using full-year data. If the auditor believes that analytical procedures include a reasonable possibility of misstatement, additional analytical procedures may be performed or the auditor may decide to modify tests of details of balances.

When the auditor develops expectations using analytical procedures and concludes that the client's ending balances in certain accounts appear reasonable, certain tests of details of balances audit procedures may be eliminated or sample sizes may be reduced. The SASs state that analytical procedures can be used as substantive tests.

Figure 12-4 (p. 364) illustrates the role of analytical procedures in the audit of the sales and collection cycle. Observe that the auditor performs analytical procedures on sales and cash receipts transactions, as well as on the ending balances of the accounts in the cycle.

a company a going concern?

Tests of details of balances focus on the ending general ledger balances for both balance sheet and income statement accounts, but the primary emphasis in most tests of details of balances is on the balance sheet. Examples include confirmation of customer balances for accounts receivable, physical examination of inventory, and examination of vendors' statements for accounts payable. These tests of ending balances are essential because the evidence is usually obtained from a source independent of the client and thus is considered highly reliable.

Tests of Details of Balances

Examine Figure 12-5 to see the role of tests of details of balances in the audit of the sales and collection cycle. Detailed tests of the ending balances are performed for sales and accounts receivable. These include audit procedures such as confirmation of account receivable balances and sales cutoff tests. The extent of these tests depends on the results of tests of controls, substantive tests of transactions, and analytical procedures for these accounts.

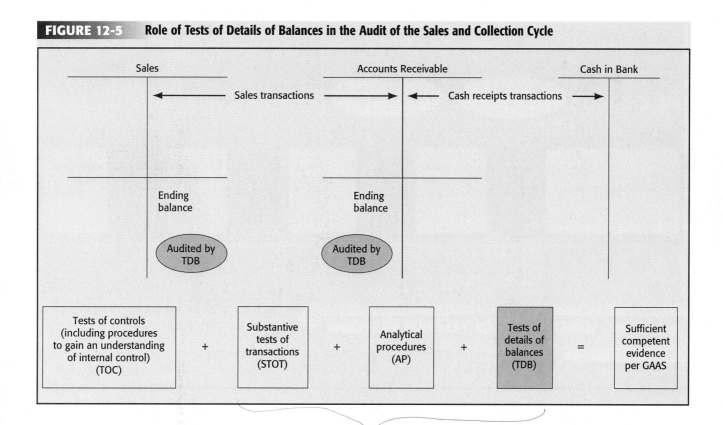

FIGURE 12-5 Role of Tests of Details of Balances in the Audit of the Sales and Collection Cycle

all substantive tests

Tests of details of balances have the objective of establishing the monetary correctness of the accounts they relate to and therefore are substantive tests. For example, confirmations test for monetary misstatements and are therefore substantive. Similarly, counts of inventory and cash on hand are also substantive tests.

Summary of Types of Tests

Figure 12-6 summarizes how the five types of audit tests are used to obtain audit assurance in the audit of the sales and collection cycle. Observe that this figure combines the concepts included in Figures 12-2 through 12-5. Procedures to gain an understanding of internal control and tests of controls evaluate whether controls over transactions in the cycle are sufficiently effective to reduce control risk and thereby reduce substantive testing. Substantive tests of transactions emphasize the verification of transactions recorded in the journals and then posted in the general ledger. Analytical procedures emphasize the overall reasonableness of transactions and the general ledger balances. Tests of details of balances emphasize the ending balances in the general ledger. By combining the types of audit tests shown in Figure 12-6, the auditor obtains a higher overall assurance for transactions and accounts in the sales and collection cycle than the assurance obtained from any one test. To increase overall assurance for the cycle, the auditor can increase the assurance obtained from any one of the tests.

FIGURE 12-6   **Roles of All Audit Tests in the Audit of the Sales and Collection Cycle**

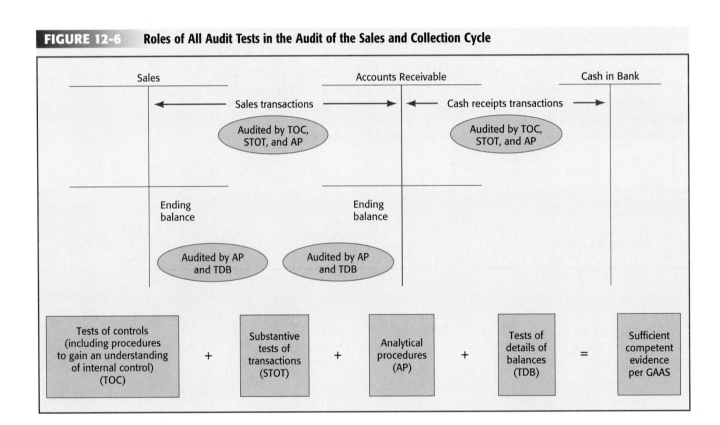

SELECTING WHICH TYPES OF TESTS TO PERFORM

OBJECTIVE 12-2
Select the appropriate types of audit tests.

Typically, auditors use all five types of tests when performing an audit, but certain types are emphasized, depending on the circumstances. Factors such as the availability of the seven types of evidence, the cost of each type of test, the effectiveness of internal controls, and the existence of inherent risks all affect the mix of the types of tests the auditor selects.

Each of the five types of tests involves only certain types of evidence (confirmation, documentation, and so forth). Table 12-2 summarizes the relationship between types of tests and types of evidence. Several observations about Table 12-2 follow:

- Procedures to obtain an understanding of internal control and tests of controls involve only observation, documentation, inquiry, and reperformance. Substantive tests of transactions involve only the last three of these types of evidence.
- More types of evidence are obtained by using tests of details of balances than by using any other type of test. Only tests of details of balances involve confirmation and physical examination.
- Inquiries of clients are made with every type of test.
- Documentation and reperformance are used for every type of test except analytical procedures.

TABLE 12-2	Relationship between Types of Tests and Evidence

Type of Test	Type of Evidence						
	Physical Examination	Confirmation	Documentation	Observation	Inquiries of the Client	Reperformance	Analytical Procedures
Procedures to obtain an understanding of internal control			√	√	√	√	
Tests of controls			√	√	√	√	
Substantive tests of transactions			√		√	√	
Analytical procedures					√		√
Tests of details of balances	√	√	√		√	√	

In deciding which type of test to select for obtaining sufficient competent evidence, the cost of the evidence is one important consideration. The types of tests are listed in order of increasing cost as follows:

- Analytical procedures
- Procedures to obtain an understanding of internal control and tests of controls
- Substantive tests of transactions
- Tests of details of balances

The reason analytical procedures are least costly is the relative ease of making calculations and comparisons. Often, considerable information about potential misstatements can be obtained by simply comparing two or three numbers. Auditors often calculate these ratios using computer software at almost no cost.

Tests of controls are also low in cost because the auditor is making inquiries and observations and examining such things as initials on documents and outward indications of other controls. Often, tests of controls can be done on a large number of items in a few minutes. Auditors often take advantage of computerized audit technologies to test controls embedded in clients' computerized accounting systems. For example, many computerized accounts receivable systems automatically authorize sales to existing customers by comparing the proposed sales amount and current balance with the customer's credit limit. The auditor can test this control using audit software.

Substantive tests of transactions are more expensive than tests of controls that do not include reperformance because recalculations and tracings are often required. In a computerized environment, however, the auditor can often perform substantive tests of transactions quickly for a large number of transactions.

Tests of details of balances are almost always considerably more costly than any of the other types of procedures. It is costly to send confirmations and to count assets. Because of the high cost of tests of details of balances, auditors usually try to plan the audit to minimize their use.

Naturally, the cost of each type of evidence varies in different situations. For example, the cost of an auditor's test-counting inventory (a substantive test of the details of the inventory balance) often depends on the nature and dollar value of the inventory, its location, and the number of different items.

Relationship between Tests of Controls and Substantive Tests

To better understand the nature of tests of controls and substantive tests, an examination of how they differ is useful. An exception in a test of control is only an *indication* of the likelihood of misstatements affecting the dollar value of the financial statements, whereas an exception in a substantive test of transactions or a test of details of balances *is* a financial statement misstatement. Exceptions in tests of controls are often called *control test deviations*. Thus, control test deviations are significant only if they occur with sufficient frequency to cause the auditor to believe there may be material dollar misstatements in the statements. Substantive tests of transactions or tests of details of balances should then be performed to determine whether dollar misstatements have actually occurred.

As an illustration, assume that the client's controls require an independent clerk to verify the quantity, price, and extension of each sales invoice, after which the clerk must initial the duplicate invoice to indicate performance. A test of control audit procedure would be to examine a sample of duplicate sales invoices for the initials of the person who verified the quantitative data. If a significant number of documents do not have a signature, the auditor should follow up with substantive tests. This can be done by extending the tests of the duplicate sales invoices to include verifying prices, extensions, and footings (substantive tests of transactions) or by increasing the sample size for the confirmation of accounts receivable (substantive test of details of balances). Of course, even though the control is not operating effectively, the invoices may still be correct. This will be the case if the person originally preparing the sales invoices did a conscientious and competent job.

On the other hand, if no or only a few documents have missing initials, the control would be considered effective and the auditor could therefore reduce substantive tests of transactions and tests of details of balances. Some substantive tests are still necessary to provide the auditor assurance that the initials were not written without the clerk performing the control procedures or performing them carelessly. Because of the need to complete some reperformance tests, many auditors prefer to perform them as a part of the original tests of controls. Others prefer to reperform, in the form of a substantive test, only when there is indication of the need to do so.

Relationship between Analytical Procedures and Substantive Tests

Similar to the relationships discussed in the previous section, analytical procedures also provide only an indication of the likelihood of misstatements affecting the dollar value of the financial statements. Unusual fluctuations in the relationships of an account to other accounts or to nonfinancial information provide an indication of an increased likelihood that material misstatements exist without necessarily providing direct evidence of a material misstatement. When unusual analytical procedure fluctuations are identified, substantive tests of transactions or tests of details of balances should be performed to determine whether dollar misstatements have actually occurred. If the auditor performs analytical procedures and believes that the likelihood of material misstatement is small, other substantive tests can be reduced.

As explained in Chapter 10, there is a trade-off between tests of controls and substantive tests. The auditor makes a decision during planning whether to assess control risk below the maximum. Tests of controls must be performed to determine whether the assessed control risk is supported. If it is, planned detection risk in the audit risk model is increased, and planned substantive tests can therefore be reduced. Figure 12-7 shows the relationship between substantive tests and control risk assessment (including tests of controls) at differing levels of internal control effectiveness.

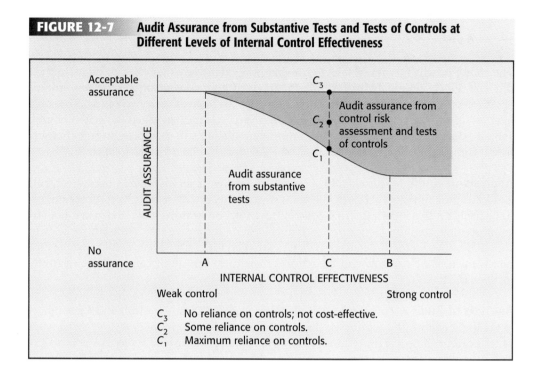

FIGURE 12-7 Audit Assurance from Substantive Tests and Tests of Controls at Different Levels of Internal Control Effectiveness

The shaded area in Figure 12-7 is the maximum assurance obtainable from control risk assessment and tests of controls. For example, at any point to the left of point A, assessed control risk is 1.0 because the auditor evaluates internal controls as ineffective. Any point to the right of point B results in no further reduction of control risk because the CPA firm has established a minimum assessed control risk it will permit. Notice in Figure 12-7 that regardless of the level of audit assurance obtained from control risk assessment and tests of controls, some substantive procedures are always required.

After the auditor decides the effectiveness of the client's internal controls, it is appropriate to select any point within the shaded area of Figure 12-7 consistent with the assessed control risk the auditor decides to support. To illustrate, assume that the auditor contends that internal control effectiveness is at point C. Tests of controls at the C_1 level would provide the minimum control risk, given the internal controls. The auditor could choose to perform no tests of controls (point C_3), which would support a control risk of 1.0. Any point between the two, such as C_2, would also be appropriate. If C_2 is selected, the audit assurance from tests of controls is $C_3 - C_2$ and from substantive tests is $C - C_2$. The auditor will likely select C_1, C_2, or C_3 based on the relative cost of tests of controls and substantive tests.

SAS 80 (AU 326) provides guidance for auditors of entities that transmit, process, maintain, or access significant information electronically. Examples of electronic evidence include records of electronic fund transfers and purchase orders transmitted through electronic data interchange (EDI) or image processing systems. SAS 80 recognizes that in instances in which a significant amount of audit evidence is in electronic form, it may not be practical or possible to reduce detection risk to an acceptable level by performing only substantive tests. For example, the potential for improper initiation or alteration of information may be greater if information is produced, maintained, or accessed only in electronic form. In these circumstances, the auditor should perform tests of controls to gather evidence to support an assessed level of control risk below maximum for certain financial statement assertions. Although some substantive tests are still required, the auditor can significantly reduce substantive tests if the tests of controls results support an assessed control risk below the maximum.

EVIDENCE MIX

good part to re-read

OBJECTIVE 12-3
Understand the concept of evidence mix and how it should be varied in different circumstances.

The choice of which types of tests to use and how extensively they need to be performed can vary widely among audits for differing levels of internal control effectiveness and inherent risks. There can also be variations from cycle to cycle within a given audit. The combination of the five types of tests used for any given cycle is often called the **evidence mix**. Table 12-3 shows the evidence mix for four different audits. In each case, assume that sufficient competent evidence was accumulated. An analysis of each audit follows.

Analysis of Audit 1 This client is a large company with sophisticated internal controls and low inherent risk. Therefore, the auditor performs extensive tests of controls and relies heavily on the client's internal controls to reduce substantive tests. Extensive analytical procedures are also performed to reduce other substantive tests. Substantive tests of transactions and tests of details of balances are therefore minimized. Because of the emphasis on tests of controls and analytical procedures, this audit can be done relatively inexpensively.

Analysis of Audit 2 This company is medium sized, with some controls and a few inherent risks. Therefore, the auditor has decided to do a medium amount of testing for all types of tests except analytical procedures, which will be done extensively. There will be more extensive testing done where there are specific inherent risks.

Analysis of Audit 3 This company is medium sized but has few effective controls and significant inherent risks. Management has decided that it is not cost-effective to have better internal controls. No tests of controls are done because reliance on internal controls is inappropriate when controls are insufficient. The emphasis is on tests of details of balances and substantive tests of transactions, but some analytical procedures are also done. Analytical procedures are usually performed to reduce other substantive tests because they

TABLE 12-3   **Variations in Evidence Mix**

	Procedures to Obtain an Understanding of Internal Control	Tests of Controls	Substantive Tests of Transactions	Analytical Procedures	Tests of Details of Balances
Audit 1	E	E	S	E	S
Audit 2	M	M	M	E	M
Audit 3	M	N	E	M	E
Audit 4	M	M	E	E	E

E = Extensive amount of testing; M = medium amount of testing; S = small amount of testing; N = no testing.

provide evidence about the likelihood of material misstatements. The auditor already expects to find material misstatements in the account balances, so additional analytical procedures are not cost-effective. The cost of the audit is likely to be relatively high because of the amount of detailed substantive testing.

Analysis of Audit 4 The original plan on this audit was to follow the approach used in Audit 2. However, the auditor found extensive control test deviations and significant misstatements while performing substantive tests of transactions and analytical procedures. Therefore, the auditor concluded that the internal controls were not effective. Extensive tests of details of balances are performed to offset the unacceptable results of the other tests. The costs of this audit are higher because tests of controls and substantive tests of transactions were performed but could not be used to reduce tests of details of balances.

DESIGN OF THE AUDIT PROGRAM

OBJECTIVE 12-4
Design an audit program.

After the auditor determines the appropriate emphasis on each of the five types of tests, he or she must design the specific audit procedures for each type. The audit procedures, when combined, form the audit program. This part of the chapter focuses on designing audit procedures to satisfy transaction-related and balance-related audit objectives.

The audit program for most audits is designed in three parts: tests of controls and substantive tests of transactions, analytical procedures, and tests of details of balances. There will likely be a separate set of subaudit programs for each transaction cycle. An example in the sales and collection cycle might be tests of controls and substantive tests of transactions audit programs for sales and cash receipts; an analytical procedures audit program for the entire cycle; and tests of details of balances audit programs for cash, accounts receivable, bad debt expense, allowance for uncollectible accounts, and miscellaneous accounts receivable.

Auditors Sharing
Audit Programs

Tests of Controls and Substantive Tests of Transactions

The tests of controls and substantive tests of transactions audit program normally includes a descriptive section documenting the understanding obtained about internal control. It is also likely to include a description of the procedures performed to obtain an understanding of internal control and assessed control risk. Both of these affect the tests of controls and substantive tests of transactions audit program. The methodology to design these tests is shown in Figure 12-8 (p. 372). The first three steps in the figure were described in Chapter 10. The audit procedures include both tests of controls and substantive tests of transactions and vary depending on assessed control risk. When controls are effective and assessed control risk is low, there will be heavy emphasis on tests of controls. Some substantive tests of transactions will also be included. If control risk is assessed at 1.0, only substantive tests of transactions will be used. The procedures already performed in obtaining an understanding of internal control will affect both tests of controls and substantive tests of transactions.

Audit Procedures The approach to designing tests of controls and substantive tests of transactions emphasizes satisfying the transaction-related audit objectives developed in Chapter 6. A four-step approach is followed when the auditor plans to reduce assessed control risk.

1. Apply the transaction-related audit objectives to the class of transactions being tested, such as sales.
2. Identify key controls that should reduce control risk for each transaction-related audit objective.
3. For all internal controls used to reduce the initial assessment of control risk below maximum (key controls), develop appropriate tests of controls.
4. For the potential types of misstatements related to each transaction-related audit objective, design appropriate substantive tests of transactions, considering weaknesses in internal control and expected results of the tests of controls in step 3.

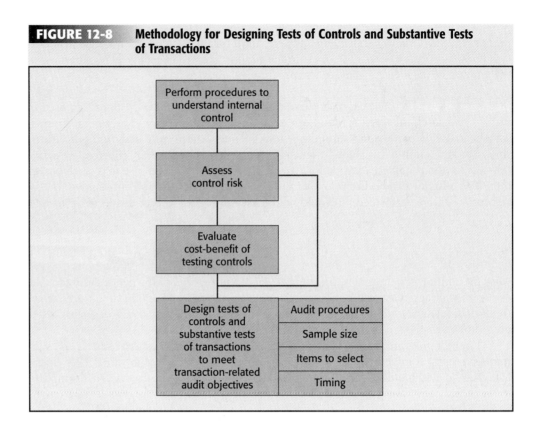

FIGURE 12-8 **Methodology for Designing Tests of Controls and Substantive Tests of Transactions**

Perform procedures to understand internal control

Assess control risk

Evaluate cost-benefit of testing controls

Design tests of controls and substantive tests of transactions to meet transaction-related audit objectives

Audit procedures

Sample size

Items to select

Timing

This four-step approach to designing tests of controls and substantive tests of transactions is summarized in Figure 12-9 (p. 373). The approach in Figure 12-9 is illustrated in several chapters in the text. For example, see Table 13-2 on page 406 for an application of the four-step procedure for the audit of sales transactions. Each of the steps corresponds to a column in Table 13-2.

Analytical Procedures

Because they are relatively inexpensive, many auditors perform extensive analytical procedures on all audits. As stated in Chapter 7, analytical procedures are performed at three different stages of the audit: (1) in the planning stage to help the auditor determine the other evidence needed to satisfy acceptable audit risk; (2) during the audit, especially during substantive testing; and (3) near the end of the audit as a final test of reasonableness. Analytical procedures performed during substantive testing, such as for the audit of accounts receivable, are typically more focused and extensive than those done as part of planning. For example, during planning, the auditor might calculate the gross margin percentage for total sales. During substantive testing of accounts receivable, the auditor might calculate gross margin percentage by month or by line of business, or possibly both. Analytical procedures calculated using monthly amounts will typically be more effective in detecting misstatements than those calculated using annual amounts, and comparisons by line of business will usually be more effective than companywide comparisons. If sales and accounts receivable are based on predictable relationships with nonfinancial data, the auditor often uses that information for analytical procedures. For example, if revenue billings are based on the number of hours professionals charge to clients, such as in law firms and other organizations that provide services, the auditor can estimate total revenue by multiplying hours billed by average billing rate.

FIGURE 12-9 **Four-Step Approach to Designing Tests of Controls and Substantive Tests of Transactions**

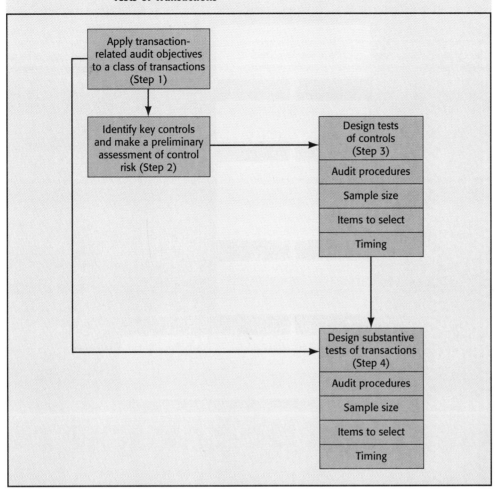

When the auditor plans to use analytical procedures as a part of the assurance gained through substantive testing, it is important that the data used in the calculations be considered sufficiently reliable. This is important for all data, especially nonfinancial data. For example, if the auditor used hours billed and the average billing rate to estimate total revenue, he or she must be confident that both of these are reasonably reliable numbers.

The methodology for designing tests of details of balances audit procedures is oriented to the balance-related audit objectives developed in Chapter 6 (pp. 158–160). For example, if the auditor is verifying accounts receivable, the planned audit procedures must be sufficient to satisfy each of the balance-related audit objectives. In planning tests of details of balances audit procedures to satisfy these objectives, many auditors follow a methodology such as the one shown in Figure 12-10 (p. 374) for accounts receivable. The design of these procedures is normally the most difficult part of the entire planning process. Designing such procedures is subjective and requires considerable professional judgment.

A discussion of the key decisions in designing tests of details of balances audit procedures as shown in Figure 12-10 follows.

**Tests of Details
of Balances**

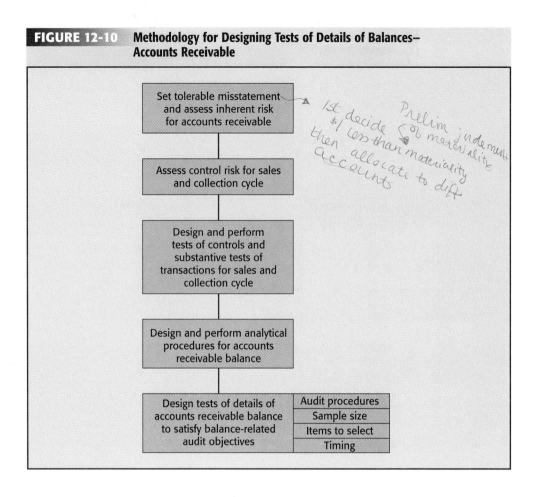

FIGURE 12-10 Methodology for Designing Tests of Details of Balances—Accounts Receivable

Set tolerable misstatement and assess inherent risk for accounts receivable

[handwritten note: 1st decide $ materiality $/ less than materiality then allocate to diff accounts. Prelim judgment materiality]

Assess control risk for sales and collection cycle

Design and perform tests of controls and substantive tests of transactions for sales and collection cycle

Design and perform analytical procedures for accounts receivable balance

Design tests of details of accounts receivable balance to satisfy balance-related audit objectives

Audit procedures
Sample size
Items to select
Timing

Set Tolerable Misstatement and Assess Inherent Risk for Accounts Receivable Setting the preliminary judgment about materiality for the audit as a whole and allocating the total to account balances (tolerable misstatement) are auditor decisions that were discussed in Chapter 9. After the preliminary judgment about materiality is made, tolerable misstatement is set for each significant balance. A lower tolerable misstatement would result in more testing of details than a higher amount. Some auditors may allocate tolerable misstatement to individual balance-related audit objectives, but most do not.

Inherent risk is assessed by identifying any aspect of the client's history, environment, or operations that indicates a high likelihood of misstatement in the current year's financial statements. Considerations affecting inherent risk that were discussed in Chapter 9 applied to accounts receivable include make-up of accounts receivable, nature of the client's business, initial engagement, and so on. An account balance for which inherent risk has been assessed as high would result in more evidence accumulation than for an account with low inherent risk.

Inherent risk also can be extended to individual balance-related audit objectives. For example, because of adverse economic conditions in the client's industry, the auditor may conclude that there is a high risk of uncollectible accounts receivable (realizable value objective). Inherent risk could still be low for all other objectives.

Assess Control Risk for the Sales and Collection Cycle Control risk is evaluated in the manner discussed in Chapter 10 and in earlier parts of this chapter. That methodology would be applied to both sales and cash receipts in the audit of accounts receivable. Effective controls reduce control risk and therefore the evidence required for substantive tests of transactions and tests of details of balances; inadequate controls increase the substantive evidence needed.

Design and Perform Tests of Controls and Substantive Tests of Transactions for the Sales and Collection Cycle The methodology for designing tests of controls and substantive tests of transactions was discussed earlier in this section and is illustrated in subsequent chapters. The tests are designed with the expectation that certain results will be obtained. These predicted results affect the design of tests of details of balances.

Design and Perform Analytical Procedures for Accounts Receivable Balance As discussed earlier, the auditor performs analytical procedures for an account such as accounts receivable for two purposes: (1) to identify possible misstatements in the account balance and (2) to reduce detailed audit tests. The results of analytical procedures directly affect the extent of tests of details of balances, as discussed in the following section.

Design Tests of Details of Accounts Receivable Balance to Satisfy Balance-Related Audit Objectives The planned tests of details of balances include audit procedures, sample size, items to select, and timing. Procedures must be selected and designed for each account and each balance-related audit objective within each account. The balance-related audit objectives for accounts receivable are shown on page 476.

A difficulty the auditor faces in designing tests of details of balances is the need to predict the outcome of the tests of controls, substantive tests of transactions, and analytical procedures before they are performed. This is necessary because the auditor should design tests of details of balances during the planning phase, but the appropriate design depends on the outcome of the other tests. In planning tests of details of balances, the auditor usually predicts that there will be few or no exceptions in tests of controls, substantive tests of transactions, and analytical procedures, unless there are reasons to believe otherwise. If the results of the tests of controls, substantive tests of transactions, and analytical procedures are *not* consistent with the predictions, the tests of details of balances will need to be changed as the audit progresses.

The discussion about the approach to designing tests of details of balances applied to accounts receivable is summarized in Figure 12-11 (p. 376). The light shading on the left side of the figure is the design of tests of controls and substantive tests of transactions as presented in Figure 12-9. The figure shows that the tests of controls and substantive tests of transactions affect the design of the tests of details of balances. The darker shading on the right side of the figure shows the design of tests of details of balances and the factors affecting that decision.

One of the most difficult parts of auditing is properly applying the factors that affect tests of details of balances. Each of the factors is subjective, requiring considerable professional judgment. The impact of each factor on tests of details of balances is equally subjective. For example, if inherent risk is reduced from medium to low, there is agreement that tests of details of balances can be reduced. Deciding the specific effect on audit procedures, sample size, timing, and items to select is a difficult decision.

Level of Disaggregation of Planning Activities

The various planning activities discussed in Chapters 6 through 12 are applied at different levels of disaggregation, depending on the nature of the activity. Figure 12-12 (p. 377) shows the primary planning activities and the levels of disaggregation normally applied. These levels of disaggregation range from the overall audit to the balance-related audit objective for each account. For example, when the auditor obtains background information about the client's business and industry, it pertains to the overall audit. As the audit progresses, the information will first be used in assessing acceptable audit risk and assessing inherent risk and later is likely to affect tests of details of balances.

Illustrative Audit Program

City Audit
Program Guides

SAS 77 (AU 311) requires the auditor to use a written audit program. Table 12-4 (p. 378) shows the tests of details of balances segment of an audit program for accounts receivable. The format used relates the audit procedures to the balance-related audit objectives. Notice that most procedures satisfy more than one objective. Also, more than one audit procedure is used for each objective. Audit procedures can be added or deleted as the auditor considers necessary. Sample size, items to select, and timing can also be changed for most procedures.

The audit program in Table 12-4 was developed after consideration of all the factors affecting tests of details of balances and is based on several assumptions about inherent risk, control risk, and the results of tests of controls, substantive tests of transactions, and analytical procedures. As indicated, if those assumptions are materially incorrect, the planned audit program will require revision. For example, analytical procedures could indicate potential misstatements for several balance-related audit objectives, tests of controls results could indicate weak internal controls, or new facts could cause the auditor to change inherent risk.

Audit programs are often computerized. The simplest form of this application is to type the audit program on a word processor and save it from one year to the next to facilitate changes and updating. A more sophisticated use is to have a special-use program that helps the auditor think through the planning considerations of the audit and select appropriate procedures from an audit procedures database. These are then formulated into an audit program.

PLANNING ACTIVITY	LEVEL OF DISAGGREGATION				
	Overall Audit	Cycle	Account	Transaction-Related Audit Objective	Balance-Related Audit Objective
Preplan audit.	P				
Obtain background information.	P				
Obtain information about client's legal obligations.	P				
Understand internal control. Control environment Risk assessment Control activities Information and communication Monitoring	P	P P P P			
Identify key internal controls.				P	
Identify internal control weaknesses.				P	
Design tests of controls.				P	
Design substantive tests of transactions.				P	
Assess control risk.				P	
Assess inherent risk.			P		P
Assess acceptable audit risk.	P				
Set preliminary judgment about materiality.	P				
Set tolerable misstatement.			P		
Design analytical procedures.			P		P
Design tests of details of balances.					P

P = Primary level to which planning activity is applied.

Example: DO NOT memorize

Tests of Details of Balances Audit Procedures	Sample Size for Each Audit Procedure	Items to Select from the Population	Timing of the Test	Accounts Receivable Balance-Related Audit Objectives								
				Detail tie-in	Existence	Completeness	Accuracy	Classification	Cutoff	Realizable value	Rights	Presentation and disclosure
1. Obtain an aged list of receivables: trace accounts to the master file, foot schedule, and trace to general ledger.	Trace 20 items; foot 2 pages and all subtotals	Random	I	x								
2. Obtain an analysis of the allowance for doubtful accounts and bad debt expense: test accuracy, examine authorization for write-offs, and trace to general ledger.	All	All	Y	x	x	x	x			x		
3. Obtain direct confirmation of accounts receivable and perform alternative procedures for nonresponses.	100	30 largest 70 random	I		x		x	x	x		x	
4. Review accounts receivable control account for the period. Investigate the nature of and review support for any large or unusual entries or any entries not arising from normal journal sources. Also investigate any significant increases or decreases in sales toward year-end.	NA	NA	Y		x		x	x	x		x	x
5. Review receivables for any that have been assigned or discounted.	All	All	Y								x	x
6. Investigate collectibility of account balances.	NA	NA	Y							x		
7. Review lists of balances for amounts due from related parties or employees, credit balances, and unusual items, as well as notes receivable due after 1 year.	All	All	Y		x			x				x
8. Determine that proper cutoff procedures were applied at the balance sheet date to ensure that sales, cash receipts, and credit memos have been recorded in the correct period.	30 transactions for sales and cash receipts; 10 for credit memos	50% before and 50% after year-end	Y						x			

I = Interim; *Y* = year-end; *NA* = not applicable.

Most large CPA firms develop their own standard audit programs, whereas smaller firms often purchase similar audit programs from outside organizations. Standard audit programs are normally computerized and can easily be modified to meet the circumstances of individual audit engagements. One example of standard audit programs available for purchase is the AICPA's *Audit Program Generator (APG)*. *APG* contains audit programs, as well as general and industry-specific checklists, that auditors can use and modify for individual engagements.

Standard audit programs, whether developed internally or purchased from an outside organization, can dramatically increase audit efficiency if they are used properly. They should *not* be used, however, as a substitute for an auditor's professional judgment. Because each audit is different, it is usually necessary to add, modify, or delete steps within a standard audit program to accumulate sufficient and competent evidence.

It has already been shown that tests of details of balances must be designed to satisfy balance-related audit objectives for each account and the extent of these tests can be reduced when transaction-related audit objectives have been satisfied by tests of controls or substantive tests of transactions. Therefore, it is important to understand how each transaction-related audit objective relates to each balance-related audit objective. A general presentation of these relationships is shown in Table 12-5 (p. 380). The major implication of Table 12-5 is that even when all transaction-related audit objectives are met, the auditor will still rely primarily on substantive tests of balances to meet the following balance-related audit objectives: realizable value, rights and obligations, and presentation and disclosure. Some substantive tests of balances are also likely for the other balance-related audit objectives, depending on the results of the tests of controls and substantive tests of transactions.

Relationship of Transaction-Related Audit Objectives to Balance-Related Audit Objectives

OBJECTIVE 12-5
Compare and contrast transaction-related audit objectives and balance-related audit objectives.

SUMMARY OF THE AUDIT PROCESS

The four **phases of the audit process** were introduced at the end of Chapter 6. Considerable portions of Chapters 7 through 12 have discussed the seven steps in phase I. Figure 12-13 (p. 381) shows the four phases for the entire audit process. Table 12-6 (p. 382) shows the timing of the tests in each phase for an audit with a December 31 balance sheet date.

OBJECTIVE 12-6
Integrate the four phases of the audit process.

Phase I: Plan and Design an Audit Approach

Chapters 7 through 12 have emphasized various aspects of planning the audit. At the end of phase I, the auditor should have a well-defined audit plan and a specific audit program for the entire audit.

Information obtained during preplanning, obtaining background information, obtaining information about the client's legal obligations, and performing preliminary analytical procedures (first four boxes in Figure 12-13) is used primarily to assess inherent risk and acceptable audit risk. Assessments of materiality, acceptable audit risk, inherent risk, and control risk are used to develop an overall audit plan and audit program.

Phase II: Perform Tests of Controls and Substantive Tests of Transactions

Performance of the tests of controls and substantive tests of transactions occurs during this phase. The objectives of phase II are to (1) obtain evidence in support of the specific controls that contribute to the auditor's assessed control risk (that is, where it is reduced below the maximum) and (2) to obtain evidence in support of the monetary correctness of transactions. The former objective is met by performing tests of controls, and the latter by

TABLE 12-5   Relationship of Transaction-Related Audit Objectives to Balance-Related Audit Objectives

Transaction-Related Audit Objective	Balance-Related Audit Objective	Nature of Relationship	Explanation
Existence	Existence or completeness	Direct	There is a direct relationship of the existence transaction-related audit objective to the existence balance-related audit objective if a class of transactions increases the related account balance (e.g., sales transactions increase accounts receivable). There is a direct relationship of the existence transaction-related audit objective to the completeness balance-related audit objective if a class of transactions decreases the related account balance (e.g., cash receipts transactions decrease accounts receivable).
Completeness	Completeness or existence	Direct	See comments above for existence objective.
Accuracy	Accuracy	Direct	–
Classification	Classification	Direct	–
Timing	Cutoff	Direct	–
Posting and summarization	Detail tie-in	Direct	–
	Realizable value	None	Few internal controls over realizable value are related to classes of transactions but the credit approval process affects the extent of tests.
	Rights and obligations	None	Few internal controls over rights and obligations are related to classes of transactions.
	Presentation and disclosure	None	Internal controls provide little assurance that proper presentations and disclosures will be made and there are no relevant substantive tests of transactions.

performing substantive tests of transactions. Many of both types of tests are conducted simultaneously on the same transactions. When controls are not considered effective or when control deviations are discovered, substantive tests can be expanded in this phase or in phase III.

Because the results of tests of controls and substantive tests of transactions are a major determinant of the extent of tests of details of balances, they are often performed 2 or 3 months before the balance sheet date. This helps the auditor plan for contingencies, revise the audit program for unexpected results, and complete the audit as soon as possible after the balance sheet date.

For computerized accounting systems, auditors often perform tests of controls and substantive tests of transactions throughout the year to determine whether the computer programs have been changed without the auditor's knowledge. This approach is often called continuous auditing.

Phase III: Perform Analytical Procedures and Tests of Details of Balances

The objective of phase III is to obtain sufficient additional evidence to determine whether the ending balances and footnotes in financial statements are fairly stated. The nature and extent of the work will depend heavily on the findings of the two previous phases.

There are two general categories of phase III procedures: analytical procedures and tests of details of balances. Analytical procedures are those that assess the overall

FIGURE 12-13 **Summary of the Audit Process**

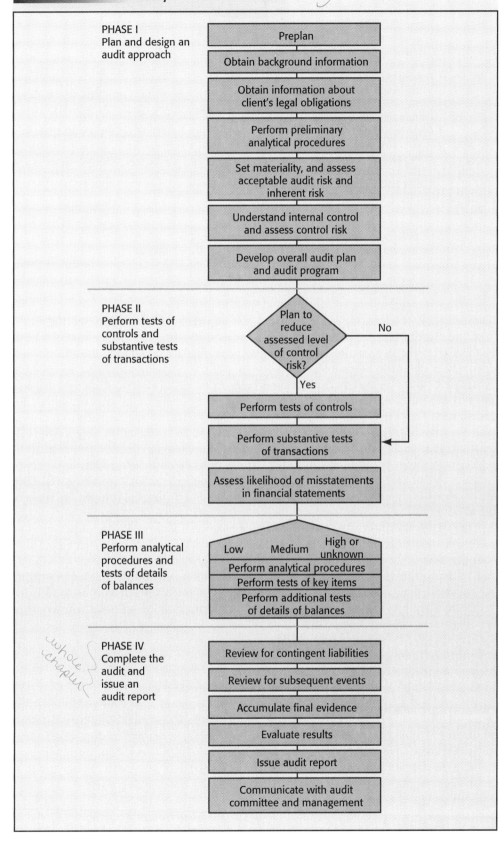

PHASE I
Plan and design an audit approach

- Preplan
- Obtain background information
- Obtain information about client's legal obligations
- Perform preliminary analytical procedures
- Set materiality, and assess acceptable audit risk and inherent risk
- Understand internal control and assess control risk
- Develop overall audit plan and audit program

PHASE II
Perform tests of controls and substantive tests of transactions

- Plan to reduce assessed level of control risk? — No
- Yes
- Perform tests of controls
- Perform substantive tests of transactions
- Assess likelihood of misstatements in financial statements

PHASE III
Perform analytical procedures and tests of details of balances

- Low   Medium   High or unknown
- Perform analytical procedures
- Perform tests of key items
- Perform additional tests of details of balances

PHASE IV
Complete the audit and issue an audit report

whole chapter

- Review for contingent liabilities
- Review for subsequent events
- Accumulate final evidence
- Evaluate results
- Issue audit report
- Communicate with audit committee and management

Important page *whole chapters*

TABLE 12-6	Timing of Tests		
Phase I	Plan and design audit approach. Update understanding of internal control. Update audit program. Perform preliminary analytical procedures.	8-30-99	
Phase II	Perform tests of controls and substantive tests of transactions for first 9 months of the year.	9-30-99	
Phase III	Confirm accounts receivable. Observe inventory.	10-31-99	
	Count cash. Perform cutoff tests. Request various other confirmations.	12-31-99	Balance sheet date
	Perform analytical procedures, complete tests of controls and substantive tests of transactions, and complete most tests of details of balances.	1-7-00	Books closed
Phase IV	Summarize results, review for contingent liabilities, review for subsequent events, accumulate final evidence (including analytical procedures), and finalize audit.	3-8-00	Last date of field work
	Issue audit report.	3-15-00	*date on audit report*

reasonableness of transactions and balances. Tests of details of balances are specific procedures intended to test for monetary misstatements in the balances in the financial statements. Certain key transactions and amounts are so important that each one must be audited. Other items can be sampled.

Table 12-6 shows analytical procedures being done both before and after the balance sheet date. Because of their low cost, it is common to use analytical procedures when they are relevant. They are often done early with preliminary data before year-end as a means of planning and directing other audit tests to specific areas. But the greatest benefit from calculating ratios and making comparisons occurs after the client has finished preparing its financial statements. Ideally, these analytical procedures are done before tests of details of balances so that they can then be used to determine how extensively to test balances. They are also used as a part of performing tests of balances and during the completion phase of the audit.

Table 12-6 also shows that tests of details of balances are normally done last. On some audits, all are done after the balance sheet date. When clients want to issue statements soon after the balance sheet date, however, the more time-consuming tests of details of balances will be done at interim dates before year-end with additional work being done to "bring up" the audited interim-date balances to year-end. Substantive tests of balances performed before year-end provide less assurance and are not normally done unless internal controls are effective.

Phase IV: Complete the Audit and Issue an Audit Report

After the first three phases are completed, it is necessary to accumulate some additional evidence for the financial statements, summarize the results, issue the audit report, and perform other forms of communication. This phase has several parts.

Review for Contingent Liabilities Contingent liabilities are potential liabilities that must be disclosed in the client's footnotes. Auditors must make sure that the disclosure is adequate. A considerable portion of the search for contingent liabilities is done during the first three phases, but additional testing is done during phase IV. Contingent liabilities are studied in Chapter 23.

Review for Subsequent Events Occasionally, events occurring subsequent to the balance sheet date but before the issuance of the financial statements and auditor's report will have an effect on the information presented in the financial statements. Specific review procedures are designed to bring to the auditor's attention any subsequent events that may require recognition in the financial statements. Review for subsequent events is also studied in Chapter 23.

Accumulate Final Evidence In addition to the evidence obtained for each cycle during phases I and II and for each account during phase III, it is also necessary to gather evidence for the financial statements as a whole during the completion phase. This evidence includes performing final analytical procedures, evaluating the going concern assumption, obtaining a client representation letter, and reading information in the annual report to make sure that it is consistent with the financial statements.

Issue Audit Report The type of audit report issued depends on the evidence accumulated and the audit findings. The appropriate reports for differing circumstances were studied in Chapter 3.

Communicate with Audit Committee and Management The auditor is required to communicate reportable conditions to the audit committee or senior management. The SASs also require the auditor to communicate certain other matters to the audit committee or a similarly designated body upon completion of the audit or sooner. Although not required, auditors often also make suggestions to management to improve business performance.

ESSENTIAL TERMS

Analytical procedures—use of comparisons and relationships to assess whether account balances or other data appear reasonable

Evidence mix—the combination of the five types of tests to obtain sufficient competent evidence for a cycle; there are likely to be variations in the mix from cycle to cycle depending on the circumstances of the audit

Phases of the audit process—the four aspects of a complete audit: (1) plan and design an audit approach, (2) perform tests of controls and substantive tests of transactions, (3) perform analytical procedures and tests of details of balances, and (4) complete the audit and issue the audit report

Procedures to obtain an understanding of internal control—procedures used by the auditor to gather evidence about the design and placement in operation of specific controls

Substantive tests—audit procedures designed to test for dollar (monetary) misstatements of financial statement balances

Substantive tests of transactions—audit procedures testing for monetary misstatements to determine whether the six transaction-related audit objectives have been satisfied for each class of transactions

Tests of controls—audit procedures to test the effectiveness of controls in support of a reduced assessed control risk

Tests of details of balances—audit procedures testing for monetary misstatements to determine whether the nine balance-related audit objectives have been satisfied for each significant account balance

Types of tests—the five categories of audit tests auditors use to determine whether financial statements are fairly stated: procedures to obtain an understanding of internal control, tests of controls, substantive tests of transactions, analytical procedures, and tests of details of balances

---

REVIEW QUESTIONS

12-1 (Objective 12-1) What are the five types of tests auditors use to determine whether financial statements are fairly stated? Identify which tests are performed to reduce control risk and which tests are performed to reduce planned detection risk.

12-2 (Objective 12-1) What is the purpose of tests of controls? Identify specific accounts on the financial statements that are affected by performing tests of controls for the acquisition and payment cycle.

12-3 (Objective 12-1) Distinguish between a test of control and a substantive test of transactions. Give two examples of each.

12-4 (Objectives 12-1, 12-4) State a test of control audit procedure to test the effectiveness of the following control: approved wage rates are used in calculating employees' earnings. State a substantive test of transactions audit procedure to determine whether approved wage rates are actually used in calculating employees' earnings.

12-5 (Objective 12-1) A considerable portion of the tests of controls and substantive tests of transactions are performed simultaneously as a matter of audit convenience. But the substantive tests of transactions procedures and sample size, in part, depend on the results of the tests of controls. How can the auditor resolve this apparent inconsistency?

12-6 (Objectives 12-2, 12-3) Evaluate the following statement: "Tests of sales and cash receipts transactions are such an essential part of every audit that I like to perform them as near the end of the audit as possible. By that time I have a fairly good understanding of the client's business and its internal controls because confirmations, cutoff tests, and other procedures have already been completed."

12-7 (Objectives 12-1, 12-2) Explain how the calculation and comparison to previous years of the gross margin percentage and the ratio of accounts receivable to sales is related to the confirmation of accounts receivable and other tests of the accuracy of accounts receivable.

12-8 (Objective 12-1) Distinguish between substantive tests of transactions and tests of details of balances. Give one example of each for the acquisition and payment cycle.

12-9 (Objective 12-3) Assume that the client's internal controls over the recording and classifying of fixed asset additions are considered weak because the individual responsible for recording new acquisitions has inadequate technical training and limited experience in accounting. How would this situation affect the evidence you should accumulate in auditing fixed assets as compared with another audit in which the controls are excellent? Be as specific as possible.

12-10 (Objective 12-2) For each of the seven types of evidence discussed in Chapter 7, identify whether it is applicable for procedures to obtain an understanding of internal control, tests of controls, substantive tests of transactions, analytical procedures, and tests of details of balances.

12-11 (Objective 12-2) Rank the following types of tests from most costly to least costly: analytical procedures, tests of details of balances, procedures to obtain an understanding of internal control and tests of controls, and substantive tests of transactions.

12-12 (Objective 12-2) In Figure 12-7, explain the difference among C_3, C_2, and C_1. Explain the circumstances under which it would be a good decision to obtain audit assurance from substantive tests at point C_1. Do the same for points C_2 and C_3.

12-13 (Objective 12-2) The following are three decision factors related to assessed control risk: effectiveness of internal controls, cost-effectiveness of a reduced assessed control risk, and results of tests of controls. Identify the combination of conditions for these three factors that is required before reduced substantive testing is permitted.

12-14 (Objective 12-3) Table 12-3 illustrates variations in the emphasis on different types of audit tests. What are the benefits to the auditor of identifying the best mix of tests?

12-15 (Objective 12-4) State the four-step approach to designing tests of controls and substantive tests of transactions.

12-16 (Objective 12-4) Explain the relationship between the methodology for designing tests of controls and substantive tests of transactions in Figure 12-8 to the methodology for designing tests of details of balances in Figure 12-10.

12-17 (Objective 12-4) Why is it desirable to design tests of details of balances before performing tests of controls and substantive tests of transactions? State the assumptions that the auditor must make in doing that. What does the auditor do if the assumptions are wrong?

12-18 (Objective 12-4) Explain the relationship between tolerable misstatement, inherent risk, and control risk to planned tests of details of balances.

12-19 (Objective 12-4) List the nine balance-related audit objectives in the verification of the ending balance in inventory, and provide one useful audit procedure for each of the objectives.

12-20 (Objective 12-6) Why do auditors often consider it desirable to perform audit tests throughout the year rather than wait until year-end? List several examples of evidence that can be accumulated before year-end.

MULTIPLE CHOICE QUESTIONS FROM CPA EXAMINATIONS

12-21 (Objective 12-1) The following questions concern types of audit tests. Choose the best response.

    a. The auditor looks for an indication on duplicate sales invoices to see whether the invoices have been verified. This is an example of
        (1) a test of details of balances.
        (2) a test of control.
        (3) a substantive test of transactions.
        (4) both a test of control and a substantive test of transactions.

    b. Analytical procedures may be classified as being primarily
        (1) tests of controls.
        (2) substantive tests.
        (3) tests of ratios.
        (4) tests of details of balances.

    c. To support the auditor's initial assessment of control risk below maximum, the auditor performs procedures to determine that internal controls are operating effectively. Which of the following audit procedures is the auditor performing?
        (1) Tests of details of balances.
        (2) Substantive tests of transactions.
        (3) Tests of controls.
        (4) Tests of trends and ratios.

    d. The auditor faces a risk that the audit will not detect material misstatements that occur in the accounting process. To minimize this risk, the auditor relies primarily on
        (1) substantive tests.
        (2) tests of controls.
        (3) internal control.
        (4) statistical analysis.

12-22 (Objective 12-1) The following questions deal with tests of controls. Choose the best response.

    a. Which of the following statements about tests of controls is most accurate?
        (1) Auditing procedures cannot concurrently provide both evidence of the effectiveness of internal control procedures and evidence required for substantive tests.
        (2) Tests of controls include observations of the proper segregation of duties.
        (3) Test of controls provide direct evidence about monetary misstatements in transactions.
        (4) Tests of controls ordinarily should be performed as of the balance sheet date or during the period subsequent to that date.

b. Which of the following would be *least* likely to be included in an auditor's tests of controls?
   (1) Documentation.
   (2) Observation.
   (3) Inquiry.
   (4) Confirmation.

c. The two phases of the auditor's involvement with internal control are sometimes called "understanding and assessment" and "tests of controls." In the tests of controls phase, the auditor attempts to obtain
   (1) a reasonable degree of assurance that the client's internal controls are operating effectively on a consistent basis throughout the year.
   (2) sufficient, competent evidential matter to afford a reasonable basis for the auditor's opinion.
   (3) assurances that informative disclosures in the financial statements are reasonably adequate.
   (4) knowledge and understanding of the client's prescribed procedures and methods.

d. Which of the following is ordinarily considered a test of control audit procedure?
   (1) Send confirmation letters to banks.
   (2) Count and list cash on hand.
   (3) Examine signatures on checks.
   (4) Prepare reconciliations of bank accounts as of the balance sheet date.

12-23 (Objectives 12-4, 12-6) The following questions concern the sequence and timing of audit tests. Choose the best response.

a. A conceptually logical approach to the auditor's evaluation of internal control consists of the following four steps:
   I. Determine the internal controls that should prevent or detect errors and fraud.
   II. Identify weaknesses to determine their effect on the nature, timing, or extent of auditing procedures to be applied and suggestions to be made to the client.
   III. Determine whether the necessary procedures are prescribed and are being followed satisfactorily.
   IV. Consider the types of errors and fraud that could occur.
   What should be the order in which these four steps are performed?
   (1) I, II, III, and IV.
   (2) I, III, IV, and II.
   (3) III, IV, I, and II.
   (4) IV, I, III, and II.

b. The sequence of steps in gathering evidence as the basis of the auditor's opinion is:
   (1) substantive tests, initial assessment of control risk, and tests of controls.
   (2) initial assessment of control risk, substantive tests, and tests of controls.
   (3) initial assessment of control risk, tests of controls, and substantive tests.
   (4) tests of controls, initial assessment of control risk, and substantive tests.

DISCUSSION QUESTIONS AND PROBLEMS

12-24 (Objectives 12-1, 12-2) The following are 11 audit procedures taken from an audit program:

1. Foot the accounts payable trial balance and compare the total with the general ledger.
2. Examine vendors' invoices to verify the ending balance in accounts payable.
3. Compare the balance in payroll tax expense with previous years. The comparison takes the increase in payroll tax rates into account.

4. Discuss the duties of the cash disbursements clerk with him and observe whether he has responsibility for handling cash or preparing the bank reconciliation.
5. Confirm accounts payable balances directly with vendors.
6. Account for a sequence of checks in the cash disbursements journal to determine whether any have been omitted.
7. Examine the internal auditor's initials on monthly bank reconciliations as an indication of whether they have been reviewed.
8. Examine vendors' invoices and other documentation in support of recorded transactions in the acquisitions journal.
9. Multiply the commission rate by total sales and compare the result with commission expense.
10. Examine vendors' invoices and other supporting documents to determine whether large amounts in the repair and maintenance account should be capitalized.
11. Examine the initials on vendors' invoices that indicate internal verification of pricing, extending, and footing by a clerk.

Required
    a. Indicate whether each procedure is a test of control, substantive test of transactions, analytical procedure, or a test of details of balances.
    b. Identify the type of evidence for each procedure.

12-25 (Objectives 12-1, 12-2, 12-5) The following are audit procedures from different transaction cycles:

1. Foot and cross-foot the cash disbursements journal and trace the balance to the general ledger.
2. Select a sample of entries in the acquisitions journal and trace each one to a related vendor's invoice to determine whether one exists.
3. Compute inventory turnover for each major product and compare with previous years.
4. Confirm a sample of notes payable balances, interest rates, and collateral with lenders.
5. Foot the accounts payable trial balance and compare the balance with the general ledger.
6. Examine documentation for acquisition transactions before and after the balance sheet date to determine whether they are recorded in the proper period.
7. Inquire of the credit manager whether each account receivable on the aged trial balance is collectible.

Required
    a. For each audit procedure, identify the transaction cycle being audited.
    b. For each audit procedure, identify the type of evidence.
    c. For each audit procedure, identify whether it is a test of control or a substantive test.
    d. For each substantive audit procedure, identify whether it is a substantive test of transactions, a test of details of balances, or an analytical procedure.
    e. For each test of control or substantive test of transactions procedure, identify the transaction-related audit objective or objectives being satisfied.
    f. For each analytical procedure or test of details of balances procedure, identify the balance-related audit objective or objectives being satisfied.

12-26 (Objective 12-1) For each of the following controls, identify whether the control leaves an audit trail. Also identify a test of control audit procedure the auditor can use to test the effectiveness of the control.

    a. An accounting clerk accounts for all shipping documents on a monthly basis and initials the monthly shipping log.
    b. Bank reconciliations are prepared by the controller, who does not have access to cash receipts.
    c. As employees check in daily by using time clocks, a supervisor observes to make certain that no individual "punches in" more than one time card.

d. Vendors' invoices are approved by the controller after she examines the purchase order and receiving report attached to each invoice.

e. The cashier, who has no access to accounting records, prepares the deposit slip and delivers the deposit directly to the bank daily.

f. An accounting clerk verifies the price, extensions, and footings of all sales invoices in excess of $300 and initials the duplicate sales invoice when he has completed the procedure.

g. All mail is opened and cash is prelisted daily by the president's secretary, who has no other responsibility for handling assets or recording accounting data.

12-27 (Objectives 12-1, 12-4, 12-5) The following are independent internal controls commonly found in the acquisition and payment cycle. Each control is to be considered independently.

1. At the end of each month, an accounting clerk accounts for all prenumbered receiving reports (documents evidencing the receipt of goods) issued during the month, and he traces each one to the related vendor's invoice and acquisitions journal entry. The clerk's tests do not include testing quantity or description of the merchandise received.

2. The cash disbursements clerk is prohibited from handling cash. The bank account is reconciled by another person even though the clerk has sufficient expertise and time to do it.

3. Before a check is prepared to pay for acquisitions by the accounts payable department, the related purchase order and receiving report are attached to the vendor's invoice being paid. A clerk compares the quantity on the invoice with the receiving report and purchase order, compares the price with the purchase order, recomputes the extensions, re-adds the total, and examines the account number indicated on the invoice to determine whether it is properly classified. He indicates his performance of these procedures by initialing the invoice.

4. Before a check is signed by the controller, she examines the supporting documentation accompanying the check. At that time, she initials each vendor's invoice to indicate her approval.

5. After the controller signs the checks, her secretary writes the check number and the date the check was issued on each of the supporting documents to prevent their reuse.

Required

a. For each of the internal controls, state the transaction-related audit objective(s) the control is meant to fulfill.

b. For each control, list one test of control the auditor could perform to test the effectiveness of the control.

c. For each control, list one substantive test the auditor could perform to determine whether financial misstatements are actually taking place.

12-28 (Objectives 12-1, 12-4, 12-5) The following internal controls for the acquisition and payment cycle were selected from a standard internal control questionnaire.

1. Vendors' invoices are recalculated before payment.
2. Approved price lists are used for acquisitions.
3. Prenumbered receiving reports are prepared as support for acquisitions and numerically accounted for.
4. Dates on receiving reports are compared with vendors' invoices before entry into the acquisitions journal.
5. The accounts payable master file is updated, balanced, and reconciled to the general ledger monthly.
6. Account classifications are reviewed by someone other than the preparer.
7. All checks are signed by the owner or manager.
8. The check signer compares data on supporting documents with checks.

9. All supporting documents are cancelled after the checks are signed.
10. Checks are mailed by the owner or manager or a person under her supervision after signing.

Required

    a. For each control, identify which element of the five categories of control activities is applicable (separation of duties, proper authorization, adequate documents or records, physical control over assets and records, or independent checks on performance).

    b. For each control, state which transaction-related audit objective(s) is (are) applicable.

    c. For each control, write an audit procedure that could be used to test the control for effectiveness.

    d. For each control, identify a likely misstatement, assuming that the control does not exist or is not functioning.

    e. For each likely misstatement, identify a substantive audit procedure to determine whether the misstatement exists.

12-29 (Objectives 12-4, 12-6) Jennifer Schaefer, CPA, follows the philosophy of performing interim tests of controls and substantive tests of transactions on every December 31 audit as a means of keeping overtime to a minimum. Typically, the interim tests are performed some time between August and November.

Required

    a. Evaluate her decision to perform interim tests of controls and substantive tests of transactions.

    b. Under what circumstances is it acceptable for her to perform no additional tests of controls and substantive tests of transactions work as a part of the year-end audit tests?

    c. If she decides to perform no additional testing, what is the effect on other tests she performs during the remainder of the engagement?

12-30 (Objectives 12-3, 12-4) Following are several decisions that the auditor must make in an audit. Letters indicate alternative conclusions that could be made:

Decisions	Alternative Conclusions
1. Determine whether it is cost-effective to perform tests of controls.	A. It is cost-effective B. It is not cost-effective
2. Perform substantive tests of details of balances.	C. Perform reduced tests D. Perform expanded tests
3. Complete initial assessment of control risk.	E. Controls are effective F. Controls are ineffective
4. Perform tests of controls.	G. Controls are effective H. Controls are ineffective

Required

    a. Identify the sequence in which the auditor should make decisions 1–4 above.

    b. For the audit of the sales and collection cycle and accounts receivable, an auditor reached the following conclusions: A, D, E, H. Put the letters in the appropriate sequence and evaluate whether the auditor's logic was reasonable. Explain your answer.

c. For the audit of inventory and related inventory cost records, an auditor reached the following conclusions: B, C, E, G. Put the letters in the appropriate sequence and evaluate whether the auditor used good professional judgment. Explain your answer.

d. For the audit of property, plant, and equipment and related acquisition records, an auditor reached the following conclusions; A, C, F, G. Put the letters in the appropriate sequence and evaluate whether the auditor used good professional judgment. Explain your answer.

e. For the audit of payroll expenses and related liabilities, an auditor recorded the following conclusions: D, F. Put the letters in the appropriate sequence and evaluate whether the auditor used good professional judgment. Explain your answer.

12-31 (Objective 12-3) The following are three situations in which the auditor is required to develop an audit strategy:

1. The client has inventory at approximately 50 locations in a three-state region. The inventory is difficult to count and can be observed only by traveling by automobile. The internal controls over acquisitions, cash disbursements, and perpetual records are considered effective. This is the fifth year that you have done the audit, and audit results in past years have always been excellent. The client is in excellent financial condition and is privately held.

2. This is the first year of an audit of a medium-sized company that is considering selling its business because of severe underfinancing. A review of the acquisition and payment cycle indicates that controls over cash disbursements are excellent, but controls over acquisitions cannot be considered effective. The client lacks receiving reports and a policy as to the proper timing to record acquisitions. When you review the general ledger, you observe that there are many large adjusting entries to correct accounts payable.

3. You are doing the audit of a small loan company with extensive receivables from customers. Controls over granting loans, collections, and loans outstanding are considered effective, and there is extensive follow-up of all outstanding loans weekly. You have recommended a computer system for the past 2 years, but management believes the cost is too great, given their low profitability. Collections are an ongoing problem because many of the customers have severe financial problems. Because of adverse economic conditions, loans receivable have significantly increased and collections are less than normal. In previous years, you have had relatively few adjusting entries.

Required

a. For audit 1, recommend an evidence mix for the five types of tests for the audit of inventory and cost of goods sold. Justify your answer. Include in your recommendations both tests of controls and substantive tests.

b. For audit 2, recommend an evidence mix for the audit of the acquisition and payment cycle, including accounts payable. Justify your answer.

c. For audit 3, recommend an evidence mix for the audit of outstanding loans. Justify your answer.

12-32 (Objectives 12-1, 12-4) Brad Jackson was assigned to the audit of a client that had not been audited by any CPA firm in the preceding year. In conducting the audit, he did no testing of the beginning balance of accounts receivable, inventory, or accounts payable on the grounds that the audit report is being limited to the ending balance sheet, the income statement, and the statement of cash flows. No comparative financial statements are to be issued.

Required

a. Explain the error in Jackson's reasoning.

b. Suggest an approach that Jackson can follow in verifying the beginning balance in accounts receivable.

c. Why does the same problem not exist in the verification of beginning balances on continuing audit engagements?

12-33 (Objective 12-3) Kim Bryan, a new staff auditor, is confused by the inconsistency of the three audit partners she has been assigned to on her first three audit engagements. On the first engagement, she spent a considerable amount of time in the audit of cash disbursements by examining cancelled checks and supporting documentation, but almost no testing was spent in the verification of fixed assets. On the second engagement, a different partner had her do less intensive tests in the cash disbursements area and take smaller sample sizes than in the first audit, even though the company was much larger. On her most recent engagement under a third audit partner, there was a thorough test of cash disbursement transactions, far beyond that of the other two audits, and an extensive verification of fixed assets. In fact, this partner insisted on a complete physical examination of all fixed assets recorded on the books. The total audit time on the most recent audit was longer than that of either of the first two audits despite the smaller size of the company. Bryan's conclusion is that the amount of evidence to accumulate depends on the audit partner in charge of the engagement.

Required

a. State several factors that could explain the difference in the amount of evidence accumulated in each of the three audit engagements as well as the total time spent.
b. What could the audit partners have done to help Bryan understand the difference in the audit emphasis on the three audits?
c. Explain how these three audits are useful in developing Bryan's professional judgment. How could the quality of her judgment have been improved on the audits?

12-34 (Objectives 12-4, 12-6) The following are parts of a typical audit for a company with a fiscal year-end of July 31.

1. Confirm accounts payable.
2. Do tests of controls and substantive tests of transactions for the acquisition and payment and payroll and personnel cycles.
3. Do other tests of details of balances for accounts payable.
4. Do tests for review of subsequent events.
5. Preplan the audit.
6. Issue the audit report.
7. Understand internal control and assess control risk.
8. Do analytical procedures for accounts payable.
9. Set acceptable audit risk and decide preliminary judgment about materiality and tolerable misstatement.

Required

a. Put parts 1 through 9 of the audit in the sequential order in which you would expect them to be performed in a typical audit.
b. Identify those parts that would frequently be done before July 31.

CASES

12-35 (Objectives 12-3, 12-4) Gale Brewer, CPA, has been the partner in charge of the audit of Merkle Manufacturing Company, a client listed on the Midwest Stock Exchange, for 13 years. Merkle has had excellent growth and profits in the past decade, primarily as a result of the excellent leadership provided by Bill Merkle and other competent executives.

Brewer has always enjoyed a close relationship with the company and prides himself on having made several constructive comments over the years that have aided in the success of the firm. Several times in the past few years, Brewer's CPA firm has considered rotating a different audit team on the engagement, but this has been strongly resisted by both Brewer and Merkle.

For the first few years of the audit, internal controls were inadequate and the accounting personnel had inadequate qualifications for their responsibilities. Extensive audit evidence was required during the audit, and numerous adjusting entries were necessary. However, because of Brewer's constant prodding, internal controls improved gradually and competent personnel were hired. In recent years, there were normally no audit adjustments required, and the extent of the evidence accumulation was gradually reduced. During the past 3 years, Brewer was able to devote less time to the audit because of the relative ease of conducting the audit and the cooperation obtained throughout the engagement.

In the current year's audit, Brewer decided that the total time budget for the engagement should be kept approximately the same as in recent years. The senior in charge of the audit, Phil Warren, was new on the job and highly competent, and he had the reputation of being able to cut time off the budget. The fact that Merkle had recently acquired a new division through merger would probably add to the time, but Warren's efficiency would probably compensate for it.

The interim tests of controls took somewhat longer than expected because of the use of several new assistants, a change in the accounting system to computerize the inventory and other accounting records, a change in accounting personnel, and the existence of a few more errors in the tests of the system. Neither Brewer nor Warren was concerned about the budget deficit, however, because they could easily make up the difference at year-end.

At year-end, Warren assigned the responsibility for inventory to an assistant who also had not been on the audit before but was competent and extremely fast at his work. Even though the total value of inventory increased, he reduced the size of the sample from that of other years because there had been few errors in the preceding year. He found several items in the sample that were overstated as a result of errors in pricing and obsolescence, but the combination of all of the errors in the sample was immaterial. He completed the tests in 25 percent less time than the preceding year. The entire audit was completed on schedule and in slightly less time than the preceding year. There were only a few adjusting entries for the year, and only two of them were material. Brewer was extremely pleased with the results and wrote a special letter to Warren and the inventory assistant complimenting them on the audit.

Six months later, Brewer received a telephone call from Merkle and was informed that the company was in serious financial trouble. Subsequent investigation revealed that the inventory had been significantly overstated. The major cause of the misstatement was the inclusion of obsolete items in inventory (especially in the new division), errors in pricing as a result of the new computer system, and the inclusion of nonexistent inventory in the final inventory listing. The new controller had intentionally overstated the inventory to compensate for the reduction in sales volume from the preceding year.

Required

    a. List the major deficiencies in the audit and state why they took place.

    b. What things should have been apparent to Brewer in the conduct of the audit?

    c. If Brewer's firm is sued by stockholders or creditors, what is the likely outcome?

12-36 (Objectives 12-3, 12-4) McClain Plastics has been an audit client of Belcor, Rich, Smith & Barnes, CPAs (BRS&B), for several years. McClain Plastics was started by Evers McClain, who owns 51 percent of the Company's stock. The balance is owned by about 200 stockholders who are investors with no operational responsibilities. McClain Plastics makes products that have plastic as their primary material. Some are made to order, but most products are made for inventory. An example of a McClain-manufactured product is a plastic chair pad that is used in a carpeted office. Another is a plastic bushing that is used with certain fastener systems.

McClain has grown from a small two-product company, when they first engaged BRS&B, to a successful diverse company. At the time Randall Sessions of BRS&B became manager of the audit, annual sales had grown to $20 million and profits to $1.9 million. Historically, the Company presented no unusual audit problems, and BRS&B had issued an unqualified opinion every year.

The audit approach BRS&B always used on the audit of McClain Plastics was a "substantive" audit approach. Under this approach, the in-charge auditor obtained an understanding of internal control, but control risk was assumed to be at the maximum (100 percent). Extensive analytical procedures were done on the income statement, and unusual fluctuations were investigated. Detailed audit procedures emphasized balance sheet accounts. The theory was that if the balance sheet accounts were correct at year-end and had been audited as of the beginning of the year, then retained earnings and the income statement must be correct.

Part I

In evaluating the audit approach for McClain for the current year's audit, Sessions believed that a substantive approach was certainly within the bounds of generally accepted auditing standards but was really only appropriate for the audits of small companies. In his judgment, McClain Plastics, with sales of $20 million and 46 employees, had reached the size where it was not economical, and probably not wise, to concentrate all the tests on the balance sheet. Therefore, he designed an audit program that emphasized identifying internal controls in all major transaction cycles and included tests of controls. The intended economic benefit of this "reducing control risk" approach was that the time spent testing controls would be more than offset by reduced tests of details of the balance sheet accounts.

In planning tests of inventories, Sessions used the audit risk model included in the Statements on Auditing Standards to determine the number of inventory items BRS&B would test at year-end. Because of the number of different products, features, sizes, and colors, McClain's inventory consisted of 2,450 different items. These were maintained on a perpetual inventory management system that used a relational database.

In using the audit risk model for inventories, Sessions believed that an audit risk of 5 percent was acceptable. He assessed inherent risk as high (100 percent) because inventory, by its nature, is subject to many types of misstatements. Based on his understanding of the relevant transaction cycles, Sessions believed that internal controls were good. He therefore assessed control risk as low (50 percent) before performing tests of controls. Sessions also planned to use analytical procedures for tests of inventory. These planned tests included comparing gross profit margins by month and reviewing for slow-moving items. Sessions believed that these tests would provide assurance of 40 percent. Substantive tests of details would include tests of inventory quantities, costs, and net realizable values at an interim date 2 months before year-end. Cutoff tests would be done at year-end. Inquiries and analytical procedures would be relied on for assurance about events between the interim audit date and fiscal year-end.

Required

a. Decide which of the following would likely be done under both a "reducing control risk" approach and a "substantive" approach:
   (1) Assess acceptable audit risk.
   (2) Assess inherent risk.
   (3) Obtain an understanding of internal control.
   (4) Assess control risk at less than 100 percent.

(5) Perform analytical procedures.

(6) Assess planned detection risk.

b. What advantages does the "reducing control risk" approach Sessions plans to use have over the "substantive" approach previously used in the audit of McClain Plastics?

c. What advantages does the "substantive" approach have over the "reducing control risk" approach?

Part II

The engagement partner agreed with Sessions's recommended approach. In planning the audit evidence for detailed inventory tests, the audit risk model was applied with the following results:

$$TDR = \frac{AAR}{IR \times CR \times APR}$$

where,

$$
\begin{aligned}
TDR &= \text{test of details risk} \\
AAR &= \text{acceptable audit risk} \\
IR &= \text{inherent risk} \\
CR &= \text{control risk} \\
APR &= \text{analytical procedures risk}
\end{aligned}
$$

Therefore, using Sessions's assessments and judgments as described previously,

$$TDR = \frac{.05}{1.0 \times .5 \times .6}$$

$$TDR = .17$$

Required

a. Explain what .17 means in this audit.

b. Calculate *TDR* assuming that Sessions had assessed control risk at 100 percent and all other risks as they are stated.

c. Explain the effect of your answer in requirement b on the planned audit procedures and sample size in the audit of inventory compared with the .17 calculated by Sessions.

Part III

Although the planning went well, the actual testing yielded some surprises. When conducting tests of controls over acquisitions and additions to the perpetual inventory, the staff person performing the tests found that the exception rates for several important controls were significantly higher than expected. As a result, the staff person considered internal control weak, supporting an 80 percent control risk rather than the 50 percent level used. Accordingly, the staff person "reworked" the audit risk model as follows:

$$TDR = \frac{.05}{1.0 \times .8 \times .6}$$

$$TDR = .10$$

A 10 percent test of details risk still seemed to the staff person to be in the "moderate" range, so he recommended no increase in planned sample size for substantive tests.

Required

Do you agree with the staff person's revised judgments about the effect of tests of controls on planned substantive tests? Explain the nature and basis of any disagreement.

PART III

(Chapters 13–16)

APPLICATION OF THE AUDIT PROCESS TO THE SALES AND COLLECTION CYCLE

To understand how auditing is done in practice, it is important to understand how auditing concepts are applied to specific auditing areas. The sales and collection cycle is the first area we look at for a detailed application of auditing concepts because this cycle is an important part of every audit and because it is reasonably straightforward. These four chapters apply the concepts you learned in Part II to the audit of sales, cash receipts, and the related income statement and balance sheet accounts in the cycle.

The objective of Chapter 13 is to help you learn the methodology for designing tests of controls and substantive tests of transactions audit procedures for sales, cash receipts, and the other classes of transactions in the sales and collection cycle. Chapter 14 deals with both nonstatistical and statistical sampling methods for tests of controls and substantive tests of transactions. Chapter 15 presents the methodology for designing audit procedures for the audit of account balances in the sales and collection cycle. Chapter 16 covers audit sampling, with a focus on sampling for test of details of balances.

AUDIT OF THE SALES AND COLLECTION CYCLE: TESTS OF CONTROLS AND SUBSTANTIVE TESTS OF TRANSACTIONS

13

THE CHOICE IS SIMPLE—RELY ON INTERNAL CONTROL OR RESIGN

City Finance is the largest client managed out of the Pittsburgh office of a Big Five firm. It is a financial services conglomerate with almost 1,000 offices in the United States and Canada, as well as correspondent offices overseas. The company's records contain more than a million accounts receivable and process millions of sales and other transactions annually.

The company's computer center is in a large environmentally controlled room that contains several large mainframe computers and a great deal of ancillary equipment. There are two complete on-line systems, one serving as a backup for the other, as systems failure would preclude operations in all of the company's branches.

The company has an unusual system of checks and balances in which branch office transaction records are reconciled to data processing controls daily, which, in turn, are reconciled to outside bank account records monthly. Whenever this reconciliation process indicates a significant out-of-balance condition, procedures are initiated to resolve the problem as quickly as possible. A large internal audit staff oversees any special investigative efforts that are required.

Because City Finance is a public company, it must file its report on Form 10-K with the Securities and Exchange Commission within 90 days after its fiscal year-end. In addition, the company likes to announce annual earnings and issue its annual report as soon after year-end as reasonably feasible. Under these circumstances, there is always a great deal of pressure on the CPA firm to complete the audit quickly.

A standard audit planning question is: "How much shall we rely on internal control?" In the case of the City Finance audit, there is only one possible answer: as much as we can. Otherwise, how could the audit possibly be completed to meet the reporting deadlines, let alone control audit cost to a reasonable level? Accordingly, the CPA firm conducts the audit with significant reliance on IT controls, reconciliation processes, and internal audit procedures. They test these controls extensively and perform many of their substantive procedures before year-end. In all honesty, if City Finance did not have excellent internal controls, the CPA firm would admit that an audit of the company just could not be done.

LEARNING OBJECTIVES

After studying this chapter, you should be able to

13-1 Identify the accounts and the classes of transactions in the sales and collection cycle.

13-2 Describe the business functions and the related documents and records in the sales and collection cycle.

13-3 Understand internal control and design and perform tests of controls and substantive tests of transactions for sales.

13-4 Apply the methodology for controls over sales transactions to controls over sales returns and allowances.

13-5 Understand internal control and design and perform tests of controls and substantive tests of transactions for cash receipts.

13-6 Apply the methodology for controls over the sales and collection cycle to write-offs of uncollectible accounts receivable.

13-7 Develop an integrated audit plan for the sales and collection cycle.

The circumstances of City Finance Company in the opening vignette illustrate an audit in which extensive reliance on internal controls in the sales and collection cycle will likely require the auditor to expand tests of controls and substantive tests of transactions. In other situations, the auditor is likely to rely far less on internal controls but, as was shown in Chapter 10, will still need to understand the internal controls over sales and cash receipts. It is important for auditors to know when they should rely extensively on internal controls and when they should not. This chapter studies assessing control risk and designing tests of controls and substantive tests of transactions for each of the classes of transactions in the sales and collection cycle.

For the most part, the audit of the sales and collection cycle can be performed independently of the audit of other cycles and subjectively combined with the other parts of the audit as the evidence accumulation process proceeds. Auditors must keep in mind that the concept of materiality requires them to consider the combination of misstatements in all parts of the audit before making a final judgment on the fair presentation in the financial statements. This is done by stopping at various times throughout the engagement and integrating the parts of the audit.

Before studying the process of assessing control risk and designing tests of controls and substantive tests of transaction for each class of transactions in detail, two related topics are covered. First, it is important to know the sales and collection cycle classes of transactions and account balances in a typical company. These were discussed earlier but are reviewed here. Second, because a considerable portion of the audit of transactions in the sales and collection cycle involves documents and records, it is essential to understand the typical documents and records used in the cycle.

ACCOUNTS AND CLASSES OF TRANSACTIONS IN THE SALES AND COLLECTION CYCLE

OBJECTIVE 13-1

Identify the accounts and the classes of transactions in the sales and collection cycle.

The overall objective in the audit of the sales and collection cycle is to evaluate whether the account balances affected by the cycle are fairly presented in accordance with generally accepted accounting principles. Typical accounts included in the sales and collection cycle are

FIGURE 13-1   **Accounts in the Sales and Collection Cycle**

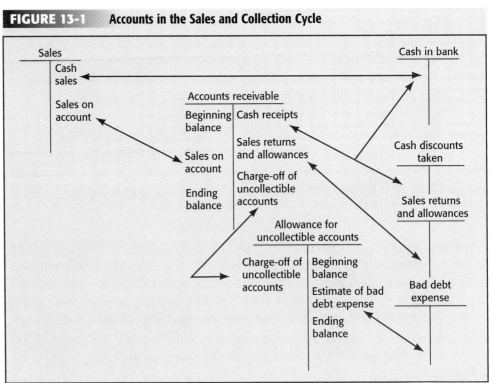

shown in Figure 13-1 with the use of T accounts. The nature of the accounts may vary, of course, depending on the industry and client involved. There are differences in account titles for a service industry, a retail company, and an insurance company, but the key concepts are the same. To provide a frame of reference for understanding the material in this chapter, a wholesale merchandising company is assumed.

Figure 13-1 shows the way accounting information flows through the various accounts in the sales and collection cycle. This figure shows that there are five **classes of transactions in the sales and collection cycle**.

1. Sales (cash and sales on account)
2. Cash receipts
3. Sales returns and allowances
4. Charge-off of uncollectible accounts
5. Estimate of bad debt expense

Figure 13-1 also shows that with the exception of cash sales, every transaction and amount ultimately is included in one of two balance sheet accounts, accounts receivable or allowance for uncollectible accounts. For simplicity, assume that the same internal controls exist for both cash and credit sales.

BUSINESS FUNCTIONS IN THE CYCLE AND RELATED DOCUMENTS AND RECORDS

The **sales and collection cycle** involves the decisions and processes necessary for the transfer of the ownership of goods and services to customers after they are made available for sale. It begins with a request by a customer and ends with the conversion of material or service into an account receivable, and ultimately into cash.

There are eight **business functions for the sales and collection cycle** shown in the third column of Table 13-1 (p. 400). They occur in every business in the recording of the five classes of transactions in the sales and collection cycle. Observe in Table 13-1 that the first four processes are for recording sales, whereas every other class of transactions includes only one business function. This section explains each of the eight business functions and describes typical documents and records for each function. These documents and records are shown in the fourth column of Table 13-1. It is essential to understand the business functions and documents and records in a business before assessing control risk and designing tests of controls and substantive tests of transactions.

The request for goods by a customer is the starting point for the entire cycle. Legally, it is an offer to buy goods under specified terms. The receipt of a customer order often results in the immediate creation of a sales order.

Customer Order A request for merchandise by a customer. It may be received by telephone, letter, a printed form that has been sent to prospective and existing customers, through salespeople, or through electronic submission of the customer order through the Internet or other network linkage between the supplier and the customer.

Sales Order A document for communicating the description, quantity, and related information for goods ordered by a customer. This is often used to indicate credit approval and authorization for shipment.

Before goods are shipped, a properly authorized person must *approve credit* to the customer for sales on account. Weak practices in credit approval often result in excessive bad debts and accounts receivable that may be uncollectible. An indication of credit approval on the sales order often serves as the approval to ship the goods. In some companies, the computer automatically approves a credit sale based on preapproved credit limits

OBJECTIVE 13-2

Describe the business functions and the related documents and records in the sales and collection cycle.

Processing Customer Orders

Government
E-Commerce Site

Granting Credit

Credit Rating Services

Classes of Transactions	Accounts	Business Functions	Documents and Records
Sales	Sales Accounts receivable	Processing customer orders	Customer order Sales order
		Granting credit	Customer order or sales order
		Shipping goods	Shipping document
		Billing customers and recording sales	Sales invoice Sales journal Summary sales report Accounts receivable master file Accounts receivable trial balance Monthly statements
Cash receipts	Cash in bank (debits from cash receipts) Accounts receivable	Processing and recording cash receipts	Remittance advice Prelisting of cash receipts Cash receipts journal
Sales returns and allowances	Sales returns and allowances Accounts receivable	Processing and recording sales returns and allowances	Credit memo Sales returns and allowances journal
Charge-off of uncollectible accounts	Accounts receivable Allowance for uncollectible accounts	Charging off uncollectible accounts receivable	Uncollectible account authorization form General journal
Bad debt expense	Bad debt expense Allowance for uncollectible accounts	Providing for bad debts	General journal

maintained in a customer master file. The computer allows the sale to proceed only when the proposed sales order total plus the existing customer balance is less than the credit limit in the master file.

Shipping Goods

This critical function is the first point in the cycle where company assets are given up. Most companies recognize sales when goods are shipped. A shipping document is prepared at the time of shipment; this can be done automatically by the computer based on sales order information. The shipping document, which is often a multicopy bill of lading, is essential to the proper billing of shipments to customers. Companies that maintain perpetual inventory records also update them based on shipping information.

Shipping Document A document prepared to initiate shipment of the goods, indicating the description of the merchandise, the quantity shipped, and other relevant data. The original is sent to the customer, and one or more copies are retained. It is also used as a signal to bill the customer. One type of shipping document is a bill of lading, which is a written contract between the carrier and seller of the receipt and shipment of goods. Often, bills of lading include only the number of boxes or pounds shipped, rather than complete details of quantity and description. Throughout the text, we assume that complete details are included on bills of lading. The computer operator informs the computer by a key entry that the goods described on the shipping document have been shipped.

The bill of lading is often transmitted electronically and automatically generates the related sales invoice as well as the entry in the sales journal. In addition, inventory items may contain bar codes that can be scanned when inventory is removed from the warehouse. This information is used to update the perpetual inventory records in the inventory master file.

Because the billing of customers is the means by which the customer is informed of the amount due for the goods, it must be done correctly and on a timely basis. The most important aspects of billing are making sure that all shipments made have been billed, that no shipment has been billed more than once, and that each one is billed for the proper amount. Billing at the proper amount is dependent on charging the customer for the quantity shipped at the authorized price. The authorized price includes consideration for freight charges, insurance, and terms of payments.

In most systems, billing of the customer includes preparation of a multicopy sales invoice and simultaneous updating of the sales transactions file, accounts receivable master file, and general ledger master file for sales and accounts receivable. This information is used to generate the sales journal and, along with cash receipts and miscellaneous credits, allows preparation of the accounts receivable trial balance.

Sales Invoice A document indicating the description and quantity of goods sold, the price, freight charges, insurance, terms, and other relevant data. The sales invoice is the method of indicating to the customer the amount of a sale and due date of a payment. The original is sent to the customer, and one or more copies are retained. Typically, the sales invoice is automatically prepared by the computer after the customer number, quantity, destination of goods shipped, and sales terms are entered. The computer calculates the invoice extensions and total sales amount using the information entered along with prices in the inventory master file.

Sales Journal A journal used to record sales transactions. A detailed sales journal includes each sales transaction. It usually indicates gross sales for different classifications, such as product lines, the entry to accounts receivable, and miscellaneous debits and credits. The sales journal can also include sales returns and allowances transactions. In a computerized environment, the sales journal is automatically updated as sales transactions occur.

Summary Sales Report A computer-generated document that summarizes sales for a period. The report typically includes information analyzed by key components such as salesperson, product, and territory.

Accounts Receivable Master File A file used to record individual sales, cash receipts, and sales returns and allowances for each customer and to maintain customer account balances. The master file is updated from the sales, sales returns and allowances, and cash receipts computer transaction files. The total of the individual account balances in the master file equals the total balance of accounts receivable in the general ledger. A printout of the accounts receivable master file shows, by customer, the beginning balance in accounts receivable, each sales transaction, sales returns and allowances, cash receipts, and the ending balance. The term *master file* is used in this book to refer to either the computer file or a printout of that file. It is also sometimes called the accounts receivable subsidiary ledger or subledger.

Accounts Receivable Trial Balance A list of the amount owed by each customer at a point in time. This is prepared directly from the accounts receivable master file. It is most often an *aged* trial balance, showing how old the accounts receivable components of each customer's balance are as of the report date.

Monthly Statement A document sent to each customer indicating the beginning balance of accounts receivable, the amount and date of each sale, cash payments received, credit memos issued, and the ending balance due. It is, in essence, a copy of the customer's portion of the accounts receivable master file.

The preceding four functions are necessary for getting the goods into the hands of customers, properly billing them, and reflecting the information in the accounting records. The result of these four functions is sales transactions. The remaining four functions involve the collection and recording of cash, sales returns and allowances, charge-off of uncollectible accounts, and providing for bad debt expense.

Processing and recording cash receipts includes receiving, depositing, and recording cash. Cash includes both currency and checks. The most important concern is the possibility of theft. Theft can occur before receipts are entered in the records or later. The most important consideration in the handling of cash receipts is that all cash must be deposited in the bank at the proper amount on a timely basis and recorded in the cash receipts transaction file, which is used to prepare the cash receipts journal and update the accounts receivable and general ledger master files. Remittance advices are important for this purpose.

Cash Management

Remittance Advice A document that accompanies the sales invoice mailed to the customer and can be returned to the seller with the cash payment. It is used to indicate the customer name, the sales invoice number, and the amount of the invoice when the payment is received. If the customer fails to include the remittance advice with his or her payment, it is common for the person opening the mail to prepare one at that time. A remittance advice is used to permit the immediate deposit of cash and to improve control over the custody of assets.

Prelisting of Cash Receipts A list prepared when cash is received by someone who has no responsibility for recording sales, accounts receivable, or cash, and who has no access to accounting records. It is used to verify whether cash received was recorded and deposited at the correct amounts and on a timely basis.

Cash Receipts Journal A journal used to record cash receipts from collections, cash sales, and all other cash receipts. It indicates total cash received, the credit to accounts receivable at the gross amount of the original sale, trade and cash discounts taken, and other debits and credits. The daily entries in the cash receipts journal are supported by remittance advices. The journal is generated for any time period from the cash receipts transactions included in the computer files.

LOCKBOX SYSTEMS AND ELECTRONIC FUNDS TRANSFER	Many companies engage a bank to assist in the processing of cash receipts from customers. Some companies use a lockbox system, whereby customers mail payments to an address maintained by bank personnel. The bank is responsible for opening all receipts, maintaining records of all payments by customers received at the lockbox address, and depositing receipts into the company's bank account on a timely basis. In other cases, receipts are submitted electronically from customers' bank accounts to a company bank account through the use of electronic funds transfer (EFT). For both lockbox systems and EFT, the bank provides information to the company to prepare the cash receipt entries in the company's accounting records. The use of both lockboxes and EFT allows for faster deposit of cash receipts into company bank accounts and often reduces risks associated with company personnel handling cash receipts.

Processing and Recording Sales Returns and Allowances

When a customer is dissatisfied with the goods, the seller often accepts the return of the goods or grants a reduction in the charges. The company normally prepares a receiving report for the returned goods and returns them to storage. Returns and allowances must be correctly and promptly recorded in the sales returns and allowances transaction file and the accounts receivable master file. Credit memos are normally issued for returns and allowances to aid in maintaining control and to facilitate record keeping.

Credit Memo A document indicating a reduction in the amount due from a customer because of returned goods or an allowance granted. It often takes the same general form as a sales invoice, but it supports reductions in accounts receivable rather than increases.

Sales Returns and Allowances Journal A journal used to record sales returns and allowances. It performs the same function as the sales journal. Many companies record these transactions in the sales journal rather than in a separate journal.

Regardless of the diligence of credit departments, it is not unusual if some customers do not pay their bills. When the company concludes that an amount is no longer collectible, it must be charged off. Typically, this occurs after a customer files bankruptcy or the account is turned over to a collection agency. Proper accounting requires an adjustment for these uncollectible accounts.

Uncollectible Account Authorization Form A document used internally to indicate authority to write an account receivable off as uncollectible.

The provision for bad debts must be sufficient to allow for the current period sales that the company will be unable to collect in the future. For most companies, the provision represents a residual, resulting from management's end-of-period adjustment of the allowance for uncollectible accounts.

METHODOLOGY FOR DESIGNING TESTS OF CONTROLS AND SUBSTANTIVE TESTS OF TRANSACTIONS FOR SALES

OBJECTIVE 13-3
Understand internal control and design and perform tests of controls and substantive tests of transactions for sales.

The account balances, classes of transactions, business functions, and related documents and records for the sales and collection cycle were described in earlier sections of this chapter. With this knowledge, it is now appropriate to study the design of tests of controls and substantive tests of transactions for each of the five classes of transactions in the cycle. This is the topic for the remainder of this chapter.

The methodology for obtaining an understanding of internal control and designing tests of controls and substantive tests of transactions for sales is shown in Figure 13-2. That methodology was studied in general terms in Chapters 10 and 12. It is applied specifically to sales in this section. The bottom box in Figure 13-2 shows the four evidence decisions

FIGURE 13-2 Methodology for Designing Tests of Controls and Substantive Tests of Transactions for Sales

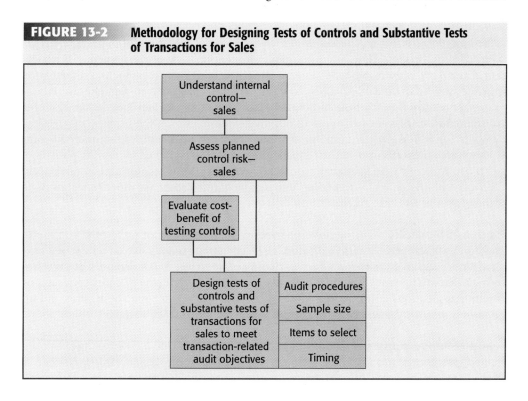

the auditor must make. This section deals with deciding the appropriate audit procedures. The following sections deal with each of the parts in Figure 13-2, starting with gaining an understanding of internal control for sales.

Understand Internal Control–Sales

Chapter 10 discussed how auditors obtain an understanding of internal control. A typical approach for sales is to study the client's flowcharts, prepare an internal control question-naire, and perform walk-through tests of sales. Figures 13-5 and 13-6 (p. 417) include an organization chart and a flowchart for the Hillsburg Hardware Co. that are used to demonstrate the design of tests of controls and substantive tests of transactions audit procedures.

Assess Planned Control Risk–Sales

The auditor uses the information obtained in understanding internal control to assess control risk. There are four essential steps to this assessment, all of which were discussed in Chapter 10.

1. First, the auditor needs a framework for assessing control risk. The framework for all classes of transactions is the six transaction-related audit objectives. For sales, these are shown for Hillsburg Hardware in Figure 13-7 on page 418. These six objectives are the same for every audit of sales.
2. Second, the auditor must identify the key internal controls and weaknesses for sales. These are also shown on page 418. The controls and weaknesses will be different for every audit.
3. After identifying the controls and weaknesses, the auditor associates them with the objectives. This is also shown on page 418 with *W*'s and *C*'s in appropriate columns.
4. Finally, the auditor assesses control risk for each objective by evaluating the controls and weaknesses for each objective. This step is critical because it affects the auditor's decisions about both tests of controls and substantive tests. It is a highly subjective decision. The bottom of page 418 shows the auditor's conclusions for Hillsburg Hardware.

We will now examine key control activities (see pp. 295–299) for sales. A knowledge of these control activities is important for identifying the key controls and weaknesses for sales, which was first discussed in Chapter 10.

Adequate Separation of Duties Proper separation of duties is useful to prevent various types of misstatements, both intentional and unintentional. To prevent fraud, it is important that anyone responsible for inputting sales and cash receipts transaction information into the computer be denied access to cash. It is also desirable to separate the credit-granting function from the sales function because credit checks are intended to offset the natural tendency of sales personnel to optimize volume even at the expense of high bad debt write-offs. It is equally desirable that personnel responsible for doing internal comparisons are independent of those entering the original data. For example, comparison of batch control totals with summary reports and comparison of accounts receivable master file totals with the general ledger balance should be done by someone independent of those who input sales and cash receipt transactions.

Proper Authorization The auditor is concerned about authorization at *three key points:* credit must be properly authorized before a sale takes place; goods should be shipped only after proper authorization; and prices, including basic terms, freight, and discounts, must be authorized. The first two controls are meant to prevent the loss of company assets by shipping to fictitious customers or those who will fail to pay for the goods. Price authorization is meant to ensure that the sale is billed at the price set by company policy.

Adequate Documents and Records Because each company has a unique system of originating, processing, and recording transactions, it may be difficult to evaluate whether its procedures are designed for maximum control; nevertheless, adequate record-keeping procedures must exist before most of the transaction-related audit objectives can be met. Some companies, for example, automatically prepare a multicopy prenumbered sales invoice at the time a customer order is received. Copies of this document are used to approve credit, authorize shipment, record the number of units shipped, and bill customers. Under this system, there is almost no chance of the failure to bill a customer if all invoices are accounted for periodically. Under a different system, in which the sales invoice is prepared only after a shipment has been made, the likelihood of failure to bill a customer is high unless some compensating control exists.

Prenumbered Documents An important characteristic of documents for sales is the use of prenumbering, which is meant to prevent both the *failure* to bill or record sales and the occurrence of *duplicate* billings and recordings. Of course, it does not do much good to have prenumbered documents unless they are properly accounted for. An example of the use of this control is the filing, by a billing clerk, of a copy of all shipping documents in sequential order after each shipment is billed, with someone else periodically accounting for all numbers and investigating the reason for any missing documents. Another example is to program the computer to prepare a listing of unused numbers at month's end with follow-up by appropriate personnel.

Mailing of Monthly Statements The mailing of monthly statements by someone who has no responsibility for handling cash or preparing the sales and accounts receivable records is a useful control because it encourages a response from customers if the balance is improperly stated. For maximum effectiveness, all disagreements about the balance in the account should be directed to a designated official who has no responsibility for handling cash or recording sales or accounts receivable.

Internal Verification Procedures The use of independent persons for checking the processing and recording of sales transactions is essential for fulfilling each of the six transaction-related audit objectives. Examples of these procedures include accounting for the numerical sequence of prenumbered documents, checking the accuracy of document preparation, and reviewing reports for unusual or incorrect items.

Evaluate Cost-Benefit of Testing Controls

After the auditor has identified the key internal controls and weaknesses and assessed control risk, it is appropriate to decide whether substantive tests will be reduced sufficiently to justify the cost of performing tests of controls. When practical, auditors make this decision before completing a matrix such as the one illustrated in Figure 13-7 on page 418. It makes little sense to incur the cost of identifying controls and assessing control risk below the maximum if there will be no reduction of substantive tests.

Design Tests of Controls for Sales

For each control the auditor plans to rely on to reduce assessed control risk, he or she must design one or more tests of controls to verify its effectiveness. In most audits, it is relatively easy to determine the nature of the test of the control from the nature of the control. For example, if the internal control is to initial customer orders after they have been approved for credit, the test of control is to examine the customer order for a proper initial.

The first three columns of Table 13-2 (p. 406) illustrate the design of tests of controls for sales. Column three in Table 13-2 shows one test of control for each key internal control in column two. Observe that Table 13-2 is organized by transaction-related audit objective. For example, the first key internal control for the existence objective is "recording of sales is supported by authorized shipping documents and approved customer orders." The test of control is to "examine copies of sales invoices for supporting bills of lading and customers' orders." For this test, the auditor should start with sales invoices and examine documents in support of the sales invoices rather than going in the opposite direction. If the auditor traced from shipping documents to sales invoices, it would be a test of completeness. Direction of tests is discussed further on pages 408–409.

TABLE 13-2   Summary of Transaction-Related Audit Objectives, Key Controls, Tests of Controls, and Substantive Tests of Transactions for Sales

Transaction-Related Audit Objective	Key Internal Control	Common Test of Control	Common Substantive Tests of Transactions
Recorded sales are for shipments actually made to existing customers (existence).	Recording of sales is supported by authorized shipping documents and approved customer orders. Credit is authorized before shipment takes place. Sales invoices are prenumbered and properly accounted for. Only customer numbers existing in the computer data files are accepted when they are entered. Monthly statements are sent to customers; complaints receive independent follow-up.	Examine copies of sales invoices for supporting bills of lading and customers' orders. Examine customer order for credit approval. Account for integrity of numerical sequence of sales invoices. Examine printouts of transactions rejected by the computer as having nonexistent customer numbers. Observe whether statements are mailed and examine customer correspondence files.	Review the sales journal, general ledger, and accounts receivable master file or trial balance for large or unusual items.* Trace sales journal entries to copies of sales orders, sales invoices, and shipping documents. Trace shipping documents to entry of shipments in perpetual inventory records. Trace credit entries in accounts receivable master file to existing source.
Existing sales transactions are recorded (completeness).	Shipping documents are prenumbered and accounted for. Sales invoices are prenumbered and accounted for. Shipping documents are matched with related sales invoices and customer orders.	Account for integrity of numerical sequence of shipping documents. Account for integrity of numerical sequence of sales invoices. Examine copies of shipping documents to determine that each has a related sales invoice and customer order.	Trace shipping documents to resultant sales invoices and entry into sales journal and accounts receivable master file.
Recorded sales are for the amount of goods shipped and are correctly billed and recorded (accuracy).	Determination of prices, terms, freight, and discounts is properly authorized. Invoice preparation is internally verified. Approved unit selling prices are entered into the computer and used for all sales. Batch totals are compared with computer summary reports.	Examine copies of sales invoices for proper authorization. Examine indication of internal verification on affected documents. Examine approved computer printout of unit selling prices. Examine file of batch totals for initials of data control clerk; compare totals with summary reports.	Recompute information on sales invoices. Trace entries in sales journal to sales invoices. Trace details on sales invoices to shipping documents, approved price lists, and customers' orders.
Sales transactions are properly classified (classification).	An adequate chart of accounts is used. Sales transactions are internally reviewed and verified.	Review chart of accounts for adequacy. Examine indication of internal verification on affected documents.	Examine documents supporting sales transactions for proper classification.
Sales are recorded on the correct dates (timing).	Procedures require billing and recording of sales on a daily basis as close to time of occurrence as possible. Sales are internally verified.	Examine documents for unbilled shipments and unrecorded sales. Examine indication of internal verification on affected documents.	Compare dates of recorded sales transactions with dates on shipping records.
Sales transactions are properly included in the accounts receivable master file and are correctly summarized (posting and summarization).	Regular monthly statements are sent to customers. Accounts receivable master file contents are internally verified. Accounts receivable master file or trial balance totals are compared with general ledger balance.	Observe whether statements are mailed. Examine indication of internal verification. Examine initials on general ledger account indicating comparison.	Foot journals and trace postings to general ledger and accounts receivable master file.

*This analytical procedure can also apply to other transaction-related audit objectives, including completeness, accuracy, and timing.

As shown in the third column of Table 13-2 for the existence and completeness objectives, a common test of control for sales is to account for a sequence of various types of documents. For example, accounting for the sequence of sales invoices selected from the sales journal and watching for omitted and duplicate numbers or invoices outside the normal sequence is a test that simultaneously provides evidence of both the existence and completeness objectives.

As an illustration, assume that the auditor selects sales invoices #18100 to #18199. The completeness objective will be partially satisfied if all 100 sales invoices are recorded. The existence objective will be satisfied if there is no duplicate recording of any of the invoice numbers.

The appropriate tests of controls for separation of duties are ordinarily restricted to the auditor's observations of activities and discussions with personnel. For example, it is possible to observe whether the billing clerk has access to cash when incoming mail is opened or cash is deposited. It is usually also necessary to ask personnel what their responsibilities are and if there are any circumstances where their responsibilities are different from the normal policy. For example, the employee responsible for billing customers may state that he or she does not have access to cash. Future discussion may bring out that when the cashier is on vacation, that person takes over the cashier's duties.

Several of the tests of controls in Table 13-2 can be performed using the computer. For example, one of the key internal controls to prevent fraudulent transactions is to include a list of existing customer numbers in the computer files. If a nonexistent customer number is entered into the computer, it is rejected. A test of control is for the auditor to attempt to enter nonexistent customer numbers into the computer to make sure that the computer control is in operation. Another test of control is for the auditor to enter existing customer numbers into the master file to determine that customer numbers are authorized, accurate, and complete.

Design Substantive Tests of Transactions for Sales

In deciding on substantive tests of transactions, some procedures are commonly used on every audit regardless of the circumstances, whereas others are dependent on the adequacy of the controls and the results of the tests of controls. In Table 13-2, the substantive tests of transactions in column four are related to the transaction-related audit objectives in the first column and are designed to determine whether any monetary misstatements for that objective exist in the transaction. The audit procedures used are affected by the internal controls and tests of controls for that objective. Materiality, results of the prior year, and the other factors discussed in Chapter 9 also affect the procedures used. Some of the audit procedures used when internal controls are inadequate are discussed in a later section.

Determining the proper substantive tests of transactions procedures for sales is relatively difficult because they vary considerably depending on the circumstances. In subsequent paragraphs, the procedures often *not* performed are emphasized because they are the ones requiring an audit decision. The substantive tests of transactions procedures are discussed in the order of the sales transaction-related audit objectives in Table 13-2. It should be noted that some procedures fulfill more than one objective.

Recorded Sales Exist For this objective, the auditor is concerned with the possibility of *three types of misstatements:* sales being included in the journals for which no shipment was made, sales recorded more than once, and shipments being made to nonexistent customers and recorded as sales. The first two types of misstatements can be intentional or unintentional. The last type is always intentional. The potential consequences are significant because they lead to an overstatement of assets and income.

There is an important difference between finding intentional and unintentional overstatements of sales. An unintentional overstatement normally also results in a clear overstatement of accounts receivable, which can often be easily found through confirmation procedures. For fraud, the perpetrator will attempt to conceal the overstatement, making it more difficult for auditors to find. Substantive tests of transactions may be necessary to discover overstated sales in these circumstances.

The appropriate substantive tests of transactions for testing the existence objective depend on where the auditor believes the misstatements are likely to take place. Many auditors do substantive tests of transactions for the existence objective only if they believe that a control weakness exists; therefore, the nature of the tests depends on the nature of the potential misstatement as follows.

Recorded Sale for Which There Was No Shipment The auditor can trace from selected entries in the sales journal to make sure that related copies of the shipping and other supporting documents exist. If the auditor is concerned about the possibility of a fictitious duplicate copy of a shipping document, it may be necessary to trace the amounts to the perpetual inventory records as a test of whether inventory was reduced.

Sale Recorded More Than Once Duplicate sales can be determined by reviewing a numerically sorted list of recorded sales transactions for duplicate numbers. The auditor can also test for the proper cancellation of shipping documents. Proper cancellation decreases the likelihood that a shipping document will be used to record another sale.

Shipment Made to Nonexistent Customers This type of fraud normally occurs only when the person recording sales is also in a position to authorize shipments. When internal controls are weak, it is difficult to detect fictitious shipments.

Another effective approach to detecting the three types of misstatements of sales transactions discussed previously is to trace the *credit* in the accounts receivable master file to its source. If the receivable was actually collected in cash or the goods were returned, there must originally have been a sale. If the credit was for a bad debt charge-off or a credit memo or if the account was still unpaid at the time of the audit, intensive follow-up by examining shipping and customer order documents is required because each of these could indicate an inappropriate sales transaction.

It should be kept in mind that *the ordinary audit is not primarily intended to detect fraud* unless the effect on the financial statements is material. The preceding substantive tests of transactions should be necessary only if the auditor is concerned about the occurrence of fraud because of inadequate controls.

Existing Sales Transactions Are Recorded In many audits, no substantive tests of transactions are made for the completeness objective on the grounds that overstatements of assets and income are a greater concern in the audit of sales transactions than their understatement. If controls are inadequate, which is likely if the client does no independent internal tracing from shipping documents to the sales journal, substantive tests are necessary.

An effective procedure to test for unbilled shipments is to trace selected shipping documents from a file in the shipping department to related duplicate sales invoices and the sales journal. To conduct a meaningful test using this procedure, the auditor must be confident that all shipping documents are included in the file. This can be done by accounting for a numerical sequence of the documents.

Direction of Tests It is important that auditors understand the difference between tracing from source documents to the journals and tracing from the journals back to source documents. The former is a test for *omitted transactions* (completeness objective), whereas the latter is a test for *nonexistent transactions* (existence objective).

In testing for the existence objective, the starting point is the journal. A sample of invoice numbers is selected *from* the journal and traced *to* duplicate sales invoices, shipping documents, and customer orders. In testing for the completeness objective, the likely starting point is the shipping document. A sample of shipping documents is selected and traced *to* duplicate sales invoices and the sales journal as a test of omissions.

When designing audit procedures for the existence and completeness objectives, the starting point for tracing the document is essential. This is called the *direction of tests*. For example, if the auditor is concerned about the existence objective but traces in the wrong direction (from shipping documents to the journals), a serious audit deficiency exists. The direction of tests is illustrated in Figure 13-3.

In testing for the other four transaction-related audit objectives, the direction of tests is usually not relevant. For example, the accuracy of sales transactions can be tested by tracing from a duplicate sales invoice to a shipping document or vice versa.

Sales Are Accurately Recorded The accurate recording of sales transactions concerns shipping the amount of goods ordered, accurately billing for the amount of goods shipped, and accurately recording the amount billed in the accounting records. Substantive tests to ensure that each of these aspects of accuracy is correct are ordinarily conducted in every audit.

Typical substantive tests of transactions include recomputing information in the accounting records to verify whether it is proper. A common approach is to start with entries in the sales journal and compare the total of selected transactions with accounts receivable master file entries and duplicate sales invoices. Prices on the duplicate sales invoices are normally compared with an approved price list, extensions and footings are recomputed, and the details listed on the invoices are compared with shipping records for description, quantity, and customer identification. Often, customer orders and sales orders are also examined for the same information.

The comparison of tests of controls and substantive tests of transactions for the accuracy objective is a good example of how audit time can be saved when effective internal controls exist. It is obvious that the test of control for this objective takes almost no time because it involves examining only an initial or other evidence of internal verification. Because the sample size for substantive tests of transactions can be reduced if this control is effective, a significant savings will result from performing the test of control because of its lower cost.

When sales invoices are automatically calculated and posted by a computer, the auditor may be able to reduce substantive tests of transactions for the accuracy objective. If the auditor determines that the computer is programmed accurately and the price list master file is authorized and correct, detailed invoice computations can be reduced or eliminated. In this case, the auditor focuses on determining that strong computer controls exist to ensure that the computer is properly programmed and has not been altered since it was last tested by the auditor.

Recorded Sales Are Properly Classified Charging the correct general ledger account is less of a problem in sales than in some other transaction cycles, but it is still of some concern. When there are cash and credit sales, it is important not to debit accounts receivable for a cash sale or to credit sales for collection of a receivable. It is also important not to classify sales of operating assets, such as buildings, as sales. For those companies using more

FIGURE 13-3   Direction of Tests for Sales

than one sales classification, such as companies issuing segmented earnings statements, proper classification is essential.

It is common to test sales for proper classification as part of testing for accuracy. The auditor examines supporting documents to determine the proper classification of a given transaction and compares this with the actual account to which it is charged.

Sales Are Recorded on the Correct Dates Sales should be billed and recorded as soon after shipment takes place as possible to prevent the unintentional omission of transactions from the records and to make sure that sales are recorded in the proper period. Timely recorded transactions are also less likely to contain misstatements. At the same time that substantive tests of transactions procedures for accuracy are being performed, it is common to compare the date on selected bills of lading or other shipping documents with the date on related duplicate sales invoices, the sales journal, and the accounts receivable master file. Significant differences indicate a potential cutoff problem.

Audit Software

Sales Transactions Are Properly Included in the Master File and Correctly Summarized The proper inclusion of all sales transactions in the accounts receivable master file is essential because the accuracy of these records affects the client's ability to collect outstanding receivables. Similarly, the sales journal must be correctly totaled and posted to the general ledger if the financial statements are to be correct. In most audits, it is common to perform some clerical accuracy tests such as footing the journals and tracing the totals and details to the general ledger and the master file to check whether there are intentional or unintentional misstatements in the processing of sales transactions. The extent of such tests is affected by the quality of the internal controls. Tracing from the sales journal to the master file is typically done as a part of fulfilling other transaction-related audit objectives, but footing the sales journal and tracing the totals to the general ledger is done as a separate procedure.

The distinction between posting and summarization and other transaction-related audit objectives is that posting and summarization includes footing journals, master file records, and ledgers and tracing from one to the other among these three. When footing and comparisons are restricted to these three records, the process is posting and summarization. In contrast, accuracy involves determining the monetary correctness of transactions and comparing amounts between documents or with journals and master file records. To illustrate, comparing a duplicate sales invoice with either the sales journal or master file entry is an accuracy objective procedure. Tracing an entry from the sales journal to the master file is a posting and summarization procedure.

Summary of Methodology for Sales

Figure 13-2 and Table 13-2 provide summaries of the previous discussion. Figure 13-2 (p. 403) shows the methodology for designing tests of controls and substantive tests of transactions for sales. Table 13-2 (p. 406) combines the four parts of the previous discussion.

Transaction-Related Audit Objectives (Column 1) The transaction-related audit objectives included in the table are derived from the framework developed in Chapters 6 and 10. Although certain internal controls satisfy more than one objective, it is desirable to consider each objective separately to facilitate a better assessment of control risk.

Key Internal Controls (Column 2) The internal controls for sales are designed to achieve the six transaction-related audit objectives discussed in Chapters 6 and 10. If the controls necessary to satisfy any one of the objectives are inadequate, the likelihood of misstatements related to that objective is increased, regardless of the controls for the other objectives. The methodology for determining existing controls was studied in Chapter 10.

The source of the controls in column 2 is the controls from a control risk matrix such as the one illustrated on page 418. A control will be included in more than one row in Table 13-2 if there is more than one C for that control on the control risk matrix.

Tests of Controls (Column 3) For each internal control in column 2, the auditor designs a test of control to verify its effectiveness. Observe that the tests of controls in Table 13-2 relate directly to the internal controls. For each control, there should be at least one test of control.

Substantive Tests of Transactions (Column 4) The purpose of these tests is to determine whether there are monetary misstatements in sales transactions. In Table 13-2, the substantive tests of transactions are related to the objectives in the first column.

It is essential to understand the relationships among the columns in Table 13-2. The first column includes the six transaction-related audit objectives. The general objectives are the same for any class of transactions, but the specific objectives vary for sales, cash receipts, or any other classes of transactions. Column 2 lists one or more illustrative internal controls *for each transaction-related audit objective.* It is essential that any given control be related to one or more specific objective(s). Next, each common test of control in column 3 relates *to a given internal control.* A test of control has no meaning unless it tests a specific control. The table contains at least one test of control in column 3 for each internal control in column 2. Finally, the common substantive tests of transactions in the table's last column are evidence to support *a specific transaction-related audit objective* in column 1. The substantive tests of transactions are not directly related to the key control or test of control columns, but the extent of substantive tests of transactions depends, in part, on which key controls exist and on results of the tests of controls.

Design and Performance Format Audit Procedures

The information presented in Table 13-2 is intended to help auditors design audit programs that satisfy the transaction-related audit objectives in a given set of circumstances. If certain objectives are important in a given audit or when the controls are different for different clients, the methodology helps the auditor design an effective and efficient audit program.

After the appropriate audit procedures for a given set of circumstances have been designed, they must be performed. It is likely to be inefficient to do the audit procedures as they are stated in the design format of Table 13-2. In converting from a **design format audit program** to a **performance format audit program**, procedures are combined. This will do the following:

- Eliminate duplicate procedures.
- Make sure that when a given document is examined, all procedures to be performed on that document are done at that time.
- Enable the auditor to do the procedures in the most effective order. For example, by footing the journal and reviewing the journal for unusual items first, the auditor gains a better perspective in doing the detailed tests.

The process of converting from a design to a performance format is illustrated for the Hillsburg Hardware case application at the end of this chapter. The design format is shown on pages 420–422. The performance format is on page 423.

SALES RETURNS AND ALLOWANCES

OBJECTIVE 13-4

Apply the methodology for controls over sales transactions to controls over sales returns and allowances.

The transaction-related audit objectives and the client's methods of controlling misstatements are essentially the same for processing credit memos as those described for sales, with two important differences. The first relates to *materiality.* In many instances, sales returns and allowances are so immaterial that they can be ignored in the audit altogether. The second major difference relates to *emphasis on objectives.* For sales returns and allowances, the primary emphasis is normally on testing the existence of recorded transactions as a means of uncovering any diversion of cash from the collection of accounts receivable that has been covered up by a fictitious sales return or allowance.

Although the emphasis for the audit of sales returns and allowances is often on testing the existence of recorded transactions, the *completeness* objective is especially important at year-end. Unrecorded sales returns and allowances can be material and can be used by a company's management to overstate net income.

Naturally, the other objectives should not be ignored. But because the objectives and methodology for auditing sales returns and allowances are essentially the same as for sales, we will not include a detailed study of the area. The reader should be able to apply the same logic to arrive at suitable controls, tests of controls, and substantive tests of transactions to verify the amounts.

<table>
<tr><td>SALES CAN BE RETURNED (AND COME BACK TO HAUNT YOU)</td><td>Late in 1993, Bausch & Lomb, Inc., informed its independent distributors that they would have to purchase up to 2 years' inventory of contact lenses. The lenses had to be purchased before December 24, when Bausch & Lomb closed its books. The distributors claimed that they had oral agreements with Bausch & Lomb that they would not have to pay for the lenses until they were sold. If these agreements existed, the shipments of lenses should not have been recognized as sales.

Ten months after the December sales, most of the lenses had not been sold and Bausch & Lomb had collected less than 15 percent of the accounts receivable from the sales. In October 1994, Bausch & Lomb agreed to take back three-quarters of the inventory that had been shipped the previous December, resulting in an unexpected charge to quarterly earnings.</td></tr>
</table>

Source: Mark Maremont, "Numbers Game at Bausch & Lomb?" *Business Week* (December 19, 1994), pp. 108–110.

METHODOLOGY FOR DESIGNING TESTS OF CONTROLS AND SUBSTANTIVE TESTS OF TRANSACTIONS FOR CASH RECEIPTS

OBJECTIVE 13-5
Understand internal control and design and perform tests of controls and substantive tests of transactions for cash receipts.

The same methodology used for designing tests of controls and substantive tests of transactions for sales is used for cash receipts. Similarly, cash receipts tests of controls and substantive tests of transactions audit procedures are developed around the same framework used for sales; that is, given the transaction-related audit objectives, key internal controls for each objective are determined, tests of control are developed for each control, and substantive tests of transactions for the monetary misstatements related to each objective are developed. As in all other audit areas, the tests of controls depend on the controls the auditor has identified and the extent they will be relied on to reduce assessed control risk.

Key internal controls, common tests of controls, and common substantive tests of transactions to satisfy each of the transaction-related audit objectives for cash receipts are listed in Table 13-3. Because this summary follows the same format as the previous one for sales, no further explanation of its meaning is necessary.

The detailed discussion of the internal controls, tests of controls, and substantive tests of transactions that was included for the audit of sales is not included for cash receipts. Instead, the audit procedures that are most likely to be misunderstood are explained in more detail.

An essential part of the auditor's responsibility in auditing cash receipts is identification of weaknesses in internal control that increase the likelihood of fraud. In expanding on Table 13-3, the emphasis will be on those audit procedures that are designed primarily for the discovery of fraud. Those procedures that are not discussed are omitted only because their purpose and the methodology for applying them should be apparent from their description.

Determine Whether Cash Received Was Recorded

The most difficult type of cash defalcation for the auditor to detect is that which occurs *before the cash is recorded* in the cash receipts journal or other cash listing, especially if the sale and cash receipt are recorded simultaneously. For example, if a grocery store clerk takes cash and intentionally fails to process the receipt of cash on the cash register, it is extremely difficult to discover the theft. To prevent this type of fraud, internal controls such as those

CASH RECEIPTS

TABLE 13-3	Summary of Transaction-Related Audit Objectives, Key Controls, Tests of Controls, and Substantive of Transactions for Cash Receipts		
Transaction-Related Audit Objective	Key Internal Control	Common Test of Control	Common Substantive Tests of Transactions
Recorded cash receipts are for funds actually received by the company (existence).	There is adequate separation of duties between handling cash and record keeping. Bank accounts are independently reconciled.	Observe separation of duties. Observe independent reconciliation of bank accounts.	Review the cash receipts journal, general ledger, and accounts receivable master file or trial balance for large and unusual amounts.* Trace from cash receipts journal to bank statements. Proof of cash receipts.
Cash received is recorded in the cash receipts journal (completeness).	There is adequate separation of duties between handling cash and record keeping. Remittance advices or prelistings of cash are used. Incoming checks are immediately endorsed. Cash receipts transactions are internally verified. Regular monthly statements are sent to customers.	Discuss with personnel and observe. Account for numerical sequence or examine prelistings. Observe immediate endorsement of incoming checks. Examine indication of internal verification. Observe whether monthly statements are being sent to customers.	Trace from remittances or prelisting to cash receipts journal.
Cash receipts are deposited and recorded at the amounts received (accuracy).	Same as previous objective. Cash discounts are approved. Bank accounts are reconciled on a regular basis. Batch totals are compared with computer summary reports.	Same as previous objective. Examine remittance advices for proper approval. Review monthly bank reconciliations. Examine file of batch totals for initials of data control clerk; compare totals with reports.	Same as previous objective. Proof of cash receipts. Examine remittance advices and sales invoices to determine whether discounts allowed are consistent with company policy.
Cash receipts transactions are properly classified (classification).	An adequate chart of accounts is used. Cash receipts transactions are internally reviewed and verified.	Review chart of accounts. Examine indication of internal verification.	Examine documents supporting cash receipts for proper classification.
Cash receipts are recorded on the correct dates (timing).	Procedures require recording of cash receipts on a daily basis. Cash receipts are internally verified.	Observe unrecorded cash at any point of time. Examine indication of internal verification.	Compare dates of deposits with dates in the cash receipts journal and prelisting of cash receipts.
Cash receipts are properly included in the accounts receivable master file and are correctly summarized (posting and summarization).	Regular monthly statements are sent to customers. Accounts receivable master file contents are internally verified. Accounts receivable master file or trial balance totals are compared with general ledger balances.	Observe whether statements are mailed. Examine indication of internal verification. Examine initials on general ledger account indicating comparison.	Foot journals and trace postings to general ledger and accounts receivable master file.

*This analytical procedure can also apply to other transaction-related audit objectives, including completeness, accuracy, and timing.

included in the second objective in Table 13-3 are implemented by many companies. The type of control will, of course, depend on the type of business. For example, the controls for a retail store in which the cash is received by the same person who sells the merchandise and rings up the cash receipts should be different from the controls for a company in which all receipts are received through the mail several weeks after the sales have taken place.

It is normal practice to trace from prenumbered remittance advices or prelists of cash receipts to the cash receipts journal and subsidiary accounts receivable records as a substantive test of the recording of actual cash received. This test will be effective only if a cash register tape or some other prelisting was prepared at the time cash was received.

Prepare Proof of Cash Receipts

A useful audit procedure to test whether all recorded cash receipts have been deposited in the bank account is a **proof of cash receipts**. In this test, the total cash receipts recorded in the cash receipts journal for a given period, such as a month, are reconciled with the actual deposits made to the bank during the same period. There may be a difference in the two as a result of deposits in transit and other items, but the amounts can be reconciled and compared. The procedure is not useful in discovering cash receipts that have not been recorded in the journals or time lags in making deposits, but it can help uncover recorded cash receipts that have not been deposited, unrecorded deposits, unrecorded loans, bank loans deposited directly into the bank account, and similar misstatements. This somewhat time-consuming procedure is ordinarily used only when the controls are weak. In rare instances in which controls are extremely weak, the period covered by the proof of cash receipts may be the entire year.

Test to Discover Lapping of Accounts Receivable

Lapping of accounts receivable is the postponement of entries for the collection of receivables to *conceal an existing cash shortage*. The defalcation is perpetrated by a person who handles cash receipts and then enters them into the computer system. He or she defers recording the cash receipts from one customer and covers the shortages with receipts of another. These in turn are covered from the receipts of a third customer a few days later. The employee must continue to cover the shortage through repeated lapping, replace the stolen money, or find another way to conceal the shortage.

This defalcation can be easily prevented by separation of duties and a mandatory vacation policy for employees who both handle cash and enter cash receipts into the system. It can be detected by comparing the name, amount, and dates shown on remittance advices with cash receipts journal entries and related duplicate deposit slips. Because the procedure is relatively time-consuming, it is ordinarily performed only when there is specific concern with defalcation because of a weakness in internal control.

AUDIT TESTS FOR UNCOLLECTIBLE ACCOUNTS

OBJECTIVE 13-6

Apply the methodology for controls over the sales and collection cycle to write-offs of uncollectible accounts receivable.

Existence of recorded write-offs is the most important transaction-related audit objective that the auditor should keep in mind in the verification of the write-off of individual uncollectible accounts. A major concern in testing accounts charged off as uncollectible is the possibility of the client covering up a defalcation by charging off accounts receivable that have already been collected. The major control for preventing this type of misstatement is proper authorization of the write-off of uncollectible accounts by a designated level of management only after a thorough investigation of the reason the customer has not paid.

Normally, verification of the accounts charged off takes relatively little time. A typical procedure is the examination of approvals by the appropriate persons. For a sample of accounts charged off, it is also usually necessary for the auditor to examine correspondence in the client's files establishing their uncollectibility. In some cases, the auditor will also examine credit reports such as those provided by Dun & Bradstreet. After the auditor has concluded that the accounts charged off by general journal entries are proper, selected items should be traced to the accounts receivable master file as a test of the records.

ADDITIONAL INTERNAL CONTROLS OVER ACCOUNT BALANCES

The preceding discussion emphasized internal controls, tests of controls, and substantive tests of transactions for the five classes of transactions that affect account balances in the sales and collection cycle. If the internal controls for these classes of transactions are determined to be effective and the related substantive tests of transactions support the conclusions, the likelihood of misstatements in the financial statements is reduced.

In addition, there may be internal controls directly related to account balances that have not been identified or tested as a part of tests of controls or substantive tests of transactions. For the sales and collection cycle, these are most likely to affect three balance-related audit objectives: realizable value, rights and obligations, and presentation and disclosure.

Realizable value is an essential balance-related audit objective for accounts receivable because collectibility of receivables is often a major financial statement item and has been an issue in a number of accountants' liability cases. Therefore, it is common for inherent risk to be high for the realizable value objective.

Several controls are common for the realizable value objective. One that has already been discussed is credit approval by an appropriate person. A second is the preparation of a periodic aged accounts receivable trial balance for review and follow-up by appropriate management personnel. A third control is a policy of charging off uncollectible accounts when they are no longer likely to be collected.

Rights and obligations and presentation and disclosure are rarely a significant problem for accounts receivable. Therefore, competent accounting personnel are typically sufficient controls for these two balance-related audit objectives.

EFFECT OF RESULTS OF TESTS OF CONTROLS AND SUBSTANTIVE TESTS OF TRANSACTIONS

The results of the tests of controls and substantive tests of transactions will have a significant effect on the remainder of the audit, especially on the substantive tests of details of balances. The parts of the audit most affected by the tests of controls and substantive tests of transactions for the sales and collection cycle are the balances in *accounts receivable, cash, bad debt expense,* and *allowance for doubtful accounts.* Furthermore, if the test results are unsatisfactory, it is necessary to do additional substantive testing for the propriety of sales, sales returns and allowances, charge-off of uncollectible accounts, and processing of cash receipts.

At the completion of the tests of controls and substantive tests of transactions, it is essential to *analyze each exception* to determine its cause and the implication of the exception on assessed control risk, which may affect the supported detection risk and thereby the remaining substantive tests. The methodology and implications of exceptions analysis are explained more fully in the next chapter.

The most significant effect of the results of the tests of controls and substantive tests of transactions in the sales and collection cycle is on the confirmation of accounts receivable. The type of confirmation, the size of the sample, and the timing of the test are all affected. The effect of the tests on accounts receivable, bad debt expense, and allowance for uncollectible accounts is considered in Chapter 15.

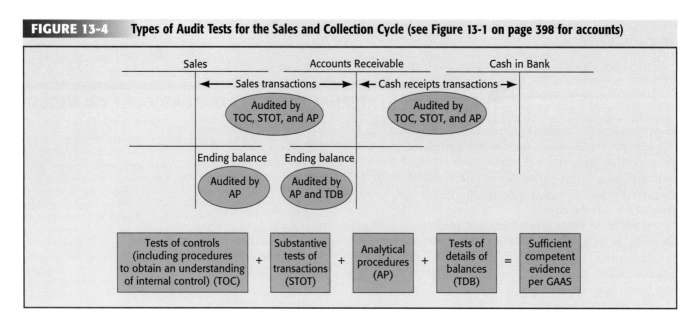

Figure 13-4 illustrates the major accounts in the sales and collection cycle and the types of audit tests used to audit these accounts. This figure was introduced in the last chapter and is presented here for further review.

CASE ILLUSTRATION—HILLSBURG HARDWARE, PART I

OBJECTIVE 13-7
Develop an integrated audit plan for the sales and collection cycle.

The concepts for testing the sales and collection cycle presented in this chapter are now illustrated for Hillsburg Hardware Co. The company's general ledger trial balance and financial statements were shown in Chapters 6 and 7. Additional information was included in other chapters. A study of this case is intended to illustrate a methodology for designing audit procedures and integrating different parts of the audit.

Hillsburg Hardware Co. is a small wholesale distributor of hardware to independent, high-quality hardware stores in the southeastern part of the United States. This is the fourth year of the audit of this client, and there have never been any significant misstatements discovered in the tests. During the current year, a major change has occurred. The controller left the firm and has been replaced by Erma Swanson. There has also been some turnover of other accounting personnel.

The overall assessment by management is that the accounting personnel are reasonably competent and highly trustworthy. The president, Rick Chulick, has been the chief operating officer for approximately 10 years. He is regarded as a highly competent, honest individual who does a conscientious job. The following information is provided from the auditor's files:

- *The organization chart and flowchart of internal control prepared for the audit.* This information is included in Figures 13-5 and 13-6. Sales returns and allowances for this client are too immaterial to include in the flowchart or to verify in the audit.
- *Internal controls and weaknesses, and assessment of control risk for sales and cash receipts.* An appropriate approach to identifying and documenting internal controls and weaknesses and assessing control risk is included for sales in Figure 13-7 (p. 418) and for cash receipts in Figure 13-8 (p. 419). There are several things the auditor, Fran Moore, did to complete each matrix. First, she identified internal controls from flowcharts, internal control questionnaires, and discussions with client personnel. Only flowcharts are available in the Hillsburg case. Second, she identified weaknesses using the same sources. Third, she decided which transaction-related audit objectives are affected by the internal controls and weaknesses. Finally, she assessed control risk using the information obtained in the preceding three steps. The use of the

FIGURE 13-5　Hillsburg Hardware Organization Chart: Personnel

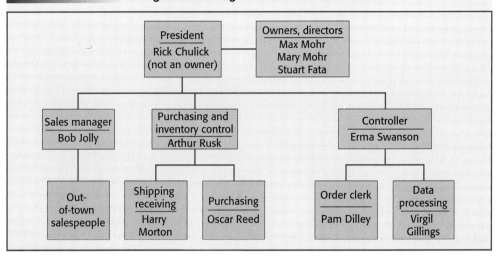

FIGURE 13-6　Hillsburg Hardware—Flowchart of Sales and Cash Receipts

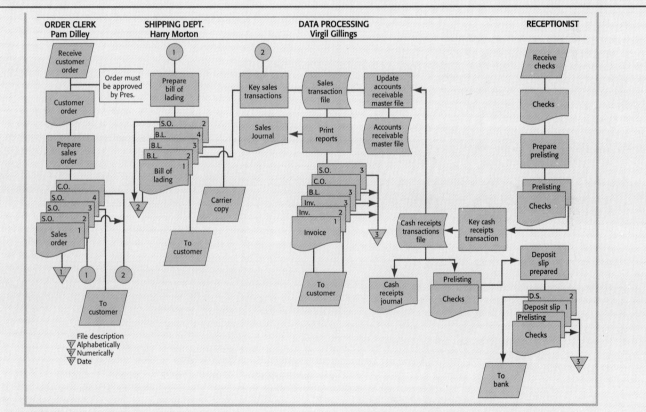

NOTES
1. All correspondence is sent to the president.
2. All sales order numbers are accounted for weekly by the controller.
3. All bills of lading numbers are accounted for weekly by the controller.
4. Sales amount recorded on sales invoice is based on standard price list. It is stored in the inventory master file and can be changed only with authorization of the controller.
5. Duplicate sales invoice is compared with bill of lading daily by Pam Dilley for descriptions and quantities and the sales invoice is reviewed for reasonableness of the extensions and footing. She initials a copy of the invoice before the original is mailed to the customer.
6. Sales are batched daily by Pam Dilley. The batch totals are compared with the sales journal weekly.
7. Statements are sent to customers monthly.
8. Accounts receivable master file total is compared with general ledger by the controller on a monthly basis.
9. Unpaid invoices are filed separately from paid invoices.
10. The receptionist stamps incoming checks with a restrictive endorsement immediately upon receipt.
11. There are no cash sales.
12. Deposits are made at least weekly.
13. Cash receipts are batched daily by the receptionist. The batch totals are compared with the cash receipts journal weekly.
14. The bank account is reconciled by the controller on a monthly basis.
15. All bad debt expense and charge-off of bad debts are approved by the president after being initiated by the controller.
16. Financial statements are printed monthly by the controller and reviewed by the president.
17. All errors are reviewed daily by the controller immediately after the updating run. Corrections are made the same day.

FIGURE 13-7 Control Risk Matrix for Hillsburg Hardware Co.–Sales

INTERNAL CONTROL	Recorded sales are for shipments actually made to nonfictitious customers (existence).	Existing sales transactions are recorded (completeness).	Recorded sales are for the amount of goods shipped and are correctly billed and recorded (accuracy).	Sales transactions are properly classified (classification).	Sales are recorded on the correct dates (timing).	Sales transactions are properly included in the accounts receivable master file and correctly summarized (posting and summarization).
	SALES TRANSACTION-RELATED AUDIT OBJECTIVES					
CONTROLS						
Dilley examines documents before bill is sent to customer (C1).	C		C			
Credit is approved by the president before shipment (C2).	C					
Bills of lading are accounted for weekly by the accountant to ensure that they are billed (C3).		C				
Batch totals are compared with computer summary reports (C4).	C	C	C			
The sales amount on the sales invoice is computed automatically using an approved price list stored in the inventory master file (C5).			C			
Accountant compares accounts receivable master file total with general ledger account (C6).						C
Monthly statements are sent to customers (C7).	C		C			C
WEAKNESSES						
There is a lack of internal verification for the possibility of sales invoices being recorded more than once (W1).	W					
There is a lack of control to test for timely recording (W2).					W	
Assessed control risk	Medium	Low	Low	Low*	High	Low

*Because there are no cash sales, classification is not a problem.

C = Control; W = weakness.

objective-by-objective matrix in Figures 13-7 and 13-8 is primarily to help Fran Moore effectively assess control risk.

- *Tests of control for each internal control.* The tests of controls for sales are included in the third column of Table 13-4 (p. 420) and for cash receipts in the same column in Table 13-5 (p. 421). The source of the internal controls is Figure 13-7 for sales and Figure 13-8 for cash receipts. Fran decided the appropriate tests for each control.

		CASH RECEIPTS TRANSACTION-RELATED AUDIT OBJECTIVES					
	INTERNAL CONTROL	Recorded cash receipts are for funds actually received by the company (existence).	Cash received is recorded in the cash receipts journal (completeness).	Cash receipts are deposited at the amount received (accuracy).	Cash receipts transactions are properly classified (classification).	Cash receipts are recorded on the correct dates (timing).	Cash receipts are properly included in the accounts receivable master file and are correctly summarized (posting and summarization).
CONTROLS	Accountant reconciles bank account (C1).	C		C			
	Checks are stamped with a restrictive endorsement (C2).		C				
	Statements are sent to customers monthly (C3).		C	C			
	Batch totals are compared with computer summary reports (C4).	C	C	C			
	Accountant compares accounts receivable master file total with general ledger account (C5).						C
WEAKNESSES	Prelisting of cash is not used to verify recorded cash receipts (W1).		W				
	Receptionist handles cash after it is returned from cash receipts (W2).		W				
	Data processor has access to cash receipts and maintains accounts receivable records (W3).		W				
	Cash receipts are not deposited daily (W4).					W	
	There is a lack of internal verification of classification of cash receipts (W5).				W		
	Assessed control risk	Low	High	Low	High	High	Medium

C = Control; W = weakness.

• *Substantive tests of transactions for each transaction-related audit objective.* The substantive tests of transactions are included in the last column of sales (Table 13-4) and cash receipts (Table 13-5). Fran decided the appropriate substantive tests of transactions for each objective after considering assessed control risk, planned tests of controls, and weaknesses of internal control for that objective.

Notice that the use of the objective-by-objective format in Tables 13-4 and 13-5 is to help Fran more effectively decide the appropriate substantive tests of transactions. She

Text continued on page 423.

TABLE 13-4	Internal Controls, Tests of Controls, and Substantive Tests of Transactions for Hillsburg Hardware Co.– Sales* (Design Format)				
Transaction-Related Audit Objective	**Existing Control†**	**Test of Control**	**Weakness**	**Substantive Tests of Transactions**
Recorded sales are for shipments actually made to existing customers.	Dilley examines documents before bill is sent to customer (C1). Credit is approved by the president before shipment (C2). Batch totals are compared with computer summary reports (C4). Monthly statements are sent to customers (C7).	Examine underlying documents for indication of internal verification by Pam Dilley (13b). Account for a sequence of sales invoices in the sales journal (12). Examine customer order for credit approval by Rick Chulick (13e). Examine file of batch totals for initials of data control clerk (8). Observe whether monthly statements are mailed (6).	There is a lack of internal verification for the possibility of sales invoices being recorded more than once (W1).	Review journals and master file for unusual transactions and amounts (1). Trace recorded sales from the sales journal to the file of supporting documents, which includes a duplicate sales invoice, bill of lading, sales order, and customer order (14).
Existing sales transactions are recorded.	Bills of lading are accounted for weekly by the accountant to ensure that they are billed (C3). Batch totals are compared with computer summary reports (C4).	Account for a sequence of shipping documents (10). Examine file of batch totals for initials of data control clerk (8).		Trace selected shipping documents to the sales journal to be sure that each one has been included (11).
Recorded sales are for the amount of goods shipped and are correctly billed and recorded.	Dilley examines documents before bill is sent to customer (C1). Credit is approved by president before shipment (C2). Batch totals are compared with computer summary reports (C4). The sales amount on the sales invoice is computed automatically using an approved price list stored in the inventory master file (C5). Monthly statements are sent to customers (C7).	Examine underlying documents for indication of internal verification by Dilley (13b). Examine customer order for credit approval by Chulick (13e). Examine file of batch totals for initials of data control clerk (8). Examine the approved price list in the inventory master file for accuracy and proper authorization (9). Observe whether monthly statements are mailed (6).		Trace selected sales invoice numbers from the sales journal to: (13) a. Duplicate sales invoice, and check for the total amount recorded in journal, date, customer name, and account classification. Check the pricing, extensions, and footings (13b). b. Bill of lading and test for customer name, product description, quantity, and date (13c). c. Duplicate sales order and test for customer name, product description, quantity, and date (13d). d. Customer order and test for customer name, product description, quantity, and date (13e).

TABLE 13-4

TABLE 13-4 Internal Controls, Tests of Controls, and Substantive Tests of Transactions for Hillsburg Hardware Co.– Sales* (Design Format) [continued]

Transaction-Related Audit Objective	Existing Control†	Test of Control	Weakness	Substantive Tests of Transactions
Sales transactions are properly classified.	None.			Examine duplicate sales invoice for proper account classification (13b).
Sales are recorded on the correct dates.	None.		There is a lack of control for test of timely recording (W2).	Compare dates on sales journal, duplicate sales invoice, and bill of lading (13b and 13c).
Sales transactions are properly included in the accounts receivable master file and are correctly summarized.	Accountant compares accounts receivable master file total with general ledger account (C6). Monthly statements are sent to customers (C7).	Observe whether accountant compares master file total with general ledger account (7). Observe whether monthly statements are mailed (6).		Trace selected sales invoice numbers from the sales journal to the accounts receivable master file, and test for amount, date, and invoice number (13a). Foot and crossfoot the sales journal and trace the totals to the general ledger (3).

*The procedures are summarized into a performance format in Figure 13-9. The number in parentheses after each test of control and substantive test of transactions refers to an audit procedure in Figure 13-9.
†Only the primary (key) control(s) for each transaction-related audit objective is (are) shown. Most objectives are also affected by one or more additional controls.

TABLE 13-5 Internal Controls, Tests of Controls, and Substantive Tests of Transactions for Hillsburg Hardware Co.– Cash Receipts* (Design Format)

Transaction-Related Audit Objective	Existing Control†	Test of Control	Weakness	Substantive Tests of Transactions
Recorded cash receipts are for funds actually received by the company.	Accountant reconciles bank account (C1). Batch totals are compared with computer summary reports (C4).	Observe whether accountant reconciles the bank account (4). Examine file of batch totals for initials of data control clerk (8).		Review the journals and master file for unusual transactions and amounts (1). Review the master file for miscellaneous credits (2). Prepare a proof of cash receipts (18). Trace cash receipt entries from the cash receipts journal to the bank statement, testing for dates and amounts of deposits (19).

[continued]

Transaction-Related Audit Objective	Existing Control†	Test of Control	Weakness	Substantive Tests of Transactions
Cash received is recorded in the cash receipts journal.	Checks are stamped with a restrictive endorsement (C2). Statements are sent to customers monthly (C3). Batch totals are compared with computer summary reports (C4).	Observe whether a restrictive endorsement is used on cash receipts (5). Observe whether monthly statements are mailed (6). Examine file of batch totals for initials of data control clerk (8).	Prelisting of cash is not used to verify recorded cash receipts (W1). Receptionist handles cash after it is returned from cash receipts (W2). Data processor has access to cash receipts and maintains accounts receivable records (W3).	Obtain the prelisting of cash receipts, and trace amounts to the cash receipts journal, testing for names, amounts, and dates (15). Compare the prelisting of cash receipts with the duplicate deposit slip, testing for names, amounts, and dates (16).
Cash receipts are deposited and recorded at the amounts received.	Accountant reconciles bank account (C1). Statements are sent to customers monthly (C3). Batch totals are compared with computer summary reports (C4).	Observe whether accountant reconciles the bank account (4). Observe whether monthly statements are mailed (6). Examine file of batch totals for initials of data control clerk (8).		The procedures for the existence objective also fulfill this objective.
Cash receipts transactions are properly classified.	None.		There is a lack of internal verification of classification of cash receipts (W5).	Examine prelisting for proper account classification (17).
Cash receipts are recorded on the correct dates.	None.		Cash receipts are not deposited daily (W4).	Trace the total from the cash receipts journal to the bank statement, testing for a delay in deposit (16).
Cash receipts are properly included in the accounts receivable master file and are correctly summarized.	Accountant compares accounts receivable master file total with general ledger account (C5).	Observe whether accountant compares master file total with general ledger account (7).		Trace selected entries from the cash receipts journal to entries in the accounts receivable master file, and test for dates and amounts (20). Trace selected credits from the accounts receivable master file to the cash receipts journal and test for dates and amounts (21). Foot and crossfoot the cash receipts journal and trace totals to the general ledger (3).

*The procedures are summarized into a performance format in Figure 13-9. The number in parentheses after each test of control and substantive test of transactions refers to an audit procedure in Figure 13-9.
†Only the primary (key) control(s) for each transaction-related audit objective is (are) shown. Most objectives are also affected by one or more additional controls.

could have decided tests of controls as easily by selecting tests of controls for each internal control included in Figures 13-7 and 13-8.

- *Tests of controls and substantive tests of transactions audit program in a performance format.* The tests of controls and substantive tests of transactions in Table 13-4 and Table 13-5 are combined into one audit program in Figure 13-9 below.

FIGURE 13-9   **Audit Program for Tests of Controls and Substantive Tests of Transactions for Sales and Cash Receipts for Hillsburg Hardware Co. (Performance Format)**

HILLSBURG HARDWARE CO.
Tests of Controls and Substantive Tests of Transactions Audit Procedures for Sales and Cash Receipts
(Sample size and the items in the sample are not included.)

General

1. Review journals and master file for unusual transactions and amounts.
2. Review the master file for miscellaneous credits.
3. Foot and crossfoot the sales and cash receipts journals, and trace the totals to the general ledger.
4. Observe whether accountant reconciles the bank account.
5. Observe whether a restrictive endorsement is used on cash receipts.
6. Observe whether monthly statements are mailed.
7. Observe whether accountant compares master file total with general ledger account.
8. Examine file of batch totals for initials of data control clerk.
9. Examine the approved price list in the inventory master file for accuracy and proper authorization.

Shipment of Goods

10. Account for a sequence of shipping documents.
11. Trace selected shipping documents to the sales journal to be sure that each one has been included.

Billing of Customers and Recording the Sales in the Records

12. Account for a sequence of sales invoices in the sales journal.
13. Trace selected sales invoice numbers from the sales journal to:
    a. accounts receivable master file and test for amount, date, and invoice number.
    b. duplicate sales invoice and check for the total amount recorded in the journal, date, customer name, and account classification. Check the pricing, extensions, and footings. Examine underlying documents for indication of internal verification by Pam Dilley.
    c. bill of lading and test for customer name, product description, quantity, and date.
    d. duplicate sales order and test for customer name, product description, quantity, date, and indication of internal verification by Pam Dilley.
    e. customer order and test for customer name, product description, quantity, date, and credit approval of Rick Chulick.
14. Trace recorded sales from the sales journal to the file of supporting documents, which includes a duplicate sales invoice, bill of lading, sales order, and customer order.

Processing Cash Receipts and Recording the Amounts in the Records

15. Obtain the prelisting of cash receipts, and trace amounts to the cash receipts journal, testing for names, amounts, and dates.
16. Compare the prelisting of cash receipts with the duplicate deposit slip, testing for names, amounts, and dates. Trace the total from the cash receipts journal to the bank statement, testing for a delay in deposit.
17. Examine prelisting for proper account classification.
18. Prepare a proof of cash receipts.
19. Trace cash receipt entries from the cash receipts journal to the bank statement, testing for dates and amounts of deposits.
20. Trace selected entries from the cash receipts journal to entries in the accounts receivable master file and test for dates and amounts.
21. Trace selected credits from the accounts receivable master file to the cash receipts journal and test for dates and amounts.

The cross-referencing of the numbers in parentheses shows that no procedures have been added to or deleted from Tables 13-4 and 13-5, and the wording is unchanged. The reasons that Fran prepared the performance format audit program were to eliminate audit procedures that were included more than once in Tables 13-4 and 13-5 and to include them in an order that permits audit assistants to complete the procedures as efficiently as possible. Sample size and the items for inclusion in the sample are not included here, but they are considered in an extension of the case in the next chapter.

- *Update the evidence planning worksheet.* After completing tests of controls and substantive tests of transactions, the auditor should complete rows three through seven of the evidence planning worksheet. The evidence planning worksheet for Hillsburg Hardware is shown in Figure 14-7 on page 465. Recall from Chapter 10 that the control risk rows could have been completed before the tests of controls were done and then modified if the test results were not satisfactory.

SUMMARY

This chapter deals with designing tests of controls and substantive tests of transactions for each of the five classes of transactions in the sales and collection cycle. The classes of transactions in the cycle are sales, cash receipts, sales returns and allowances, charge-off of uncollectible accounts receivable, and bad debt expense.

The methodology for designing tests of controls and substantive tests of transactions is, in concept, the same for each of the five classes of transactions and includes the following steps:

- Understand internal control.
- Assess planned control risk.
- Evaluate the cost-benefit of testing the controls.
- Design tests of controls and substantive tests of transactions to meet transaction-related audit objectives.

In designing tests of controls, the emphasis for each class of transactions is on testing internal controls that the auditor intends to rely on to reduce control risk. First, the auditor identifies internal controls, if any exist, for each transaction-related audit objective. After assessing control risk for each objective, the auditor then evaluates the cost-benefit of testing the controls. If it is cost-effective, the auditor designs tests of controls to determine the effectiveness of the existing controls.

The auditor also designs substantive tests of transactions for each class of transactions to determine whether the monetary amounts of transactions are correctly recorded. Like tests of controls, substantive tests of transactions are designed for each transaction-related audit objective.

After the auditor completes the design of tests of controls and substantive tests of transactions for each audit objective and each class of transactions, he or she organizes the audit procedures into a performance format audit program. The purpose of this audit program is to help the auditor complete the audit tests efficiently.

ESSENTIAL TERMS

Business functions for the sales and collection cycle—the key activities that an organization must complete to execute and record business transactions for sales, cash receipts, sales returns and allowances, charge-off of uncollectible accounts, and bad debt expense

Classes of transactions in the sales and collection cycle—the categories of transactions for the sales and collection cycle in a typical company: sales, cash receipts, sales returns and allowances, charge-off of uncollectible accounts, and bad debt expense

Design format audit program—the audit procedures resulting from the auditor's decisions about the appropriate audit procedures for each audit objective; this audit program is used to prepare a performance format audit program

Lapping of accounts receivable—the postponement of entries for the collection of receivables to *conceal an existing cash shortage*; a common type of defalcation

Performance format audit program—the audit procedures for a class of transactions organized in the format they will be performed; this audit program is prepared from a design format audit program

Proof of cash receipts—an audit procedure to test whether all recorded cash receipts have been deposited in the bank account by reconciling the total cash receipts recorded in the cash receipts journal for a given period with the actual deposits made to the bank

Sales and collection cycle—involves the decisions and processes necessary for the transfer of the ownership of goods and services to customers after they are made available for sale; it begins with a request by a customer and ends with the conversion of material or service into an account receivable, and ultimately into cash

---

REVIEW QUESTIONS

13-1 (Objective 13-2)   Describe the nature of the following documents and records and explain their use in the sales and collection cycle: bill of lading, sales invoice, credit memo, remittance advice, monthly statement to customers.

13-2 (Objective 13-2)   Explain the importance of proper credit approval for sales. What effect do adequate controls in the credit function have on the auditor's evidence accumulation?

13-3 (Objective 13-2)   Distinguish between bad debt expense and the charge-off of uncollectible accounts for a company using the allowance method for recording uncollectible accounts receivable. Explain why they are audited in completely different ways.

13-4 (Objective 13-3)   List the transaction-related audit objectives for the verification of sales transactions. For each objective, state one internal control that the client can use to reduce the likelihood of misstatements.

13-5 (Objective 13-3)   State one test of control and one substantive test of transactions that the auditor can use to verify the following sales transaction-related audit objective: Recorded sales are stated at the proper amount.

13-6 (Objective 13-3)   List the most important duties that should be segregated in the sales and collection cycle. Explain why it is desirable that each duty be segregated.

13-7 (Objective 13-3)   Explain how prenumbered shipping documents and sales invoices can be useful controls for preventing misstatements in sales.

13-8 (Objective 13-3)   What three types of authorizations are commonly used as internal controls for sales? For each authorization, state a substantive test that the auditor could use to verify whether the control was effective in preventing misstatements.

13-9 (Objective 13-3)   Explain the purpose of footing and crossfooting the sales journal and tracing the totals to the general ledger.

13-10 (Objective 13-4)   What is the difference between the auditor's approach in verifying sales returns and allowances and that for sales? Explain the reasons for the difference.

13-11 (Objective 13-5)   Explain why auditors usually emphasize the detection of fraud in the audit of cash. Is this consistent or inconsistent with the auditor's responsibility in the audit? Explain.

13-12 (Objective 13-5)   List the transaction-related audit objectives for the verification of cash receipts. For each objective, state one internal control that the client can use to reduce the likelihood of misstatements.

13-13 (Objective 13-5)   List several audit procedures that the auditor can use to determine whether all cash received was recorded.

13-14 (Objective 13-5)   Explain what is meant by a proof of cash receipts and state its purpose.

13-15 (Objective 13-5)   Explain what is meant by lapping, and discuss how the auditor can uncover it. Under what circumstances should the auditor make a special effort to uncover lapping?

13-16 (Objective 13-6)   What audit procedures are most likely to be used to verify accounts receivable charged off as uncollectible? State the purpose of each of these procedures.

13-17 (Objective 13-7)   State the relationship between the confirmation of accounts receivable and the results of the tests of controls and substantive tests of transactions.

13-18 (Objectives 13-3, 13-5)   Under what circumstances is it acceptable to perform tests of controls and substantive tests of transactions for sales and cash receipts at an interim date?

13-19 (Objective 13-3)   Diane Smith, CPA, performed tests of controls and substantive tests of transactions for sales for the month of March in an audit of the financial statements for the year ended December 31, 1999. Based on the excellent results of both the tests of controls and the substantive tests of transactions, she decided to significantly reduce her substantive tests of details of balances at year-end. Evaluate this decision.

MULTIPLE CHOICE QUESTIONS FROM CPA EXAMINATIONS

13-20 (Objectives 13-3, 13-4, 13-5, 13-6)   The following questions deal with internal controls in the sales and collection cycle. Choose the best response.

a. When a customer fails to include a remittance advice with a payment, it is common for the person opening the mail to prepare one. Consequently, mail should be opened by which of the following four company employees?
   (1) Credit manager.
   (2) Sales manager.
   (3) Accounts receivable clerk.
   (4) Receptionist.

b. A key internal control in the sales and collection cycle is the separation of duties between cash handling and record keeping. The objective most directly associated with this control is to verify that
   (1) cash receipts recorded in the cash receipts journal are reasonable.
   (2) cash receipts are properly classified.
   (3) recorded cash receipts result from legitimate transactions.
   (4) existing cash receipts are recorded.

c. An auditor tests a company's policy of obtaining credit approval before shipping goods to customers in support of management's financial statement assertion of
   (1) valuation or allocation.
   (2) completeness.
   (3) existence or occurrence.
   (4) rights and obligations.

d. Which of the following internal controls would most likely reduce charge-offs of uncollectible accounts receivable?
   (1) Employees responsible for authorizing sales and charge-offs of uncollectible accounts receivable are denied access to cash.
   (2) Shipping documents and sales invoices are matched by an employee who does not have the authority to charge-off uncollectible accounts receivable.
   (3) Employees involved in the credit-granting function are separated from the sales function.
   (4) Accounts receivable master file records are reconciled to the control account by an employee who is not involved in the credit-granting function.

13-21 (Objectives 13-3, 13-4)   For each of the following types of misstatements (parts a through d), select the control that should have prevented the misstatement:

a. A manufacturing company received a substantial sales return in the last month of the year, but the credit memorandum for the return was not prepared until after the auditors had completed their field work. The returned merchandise was included in the physical inventory.

    (1) Aged trial balance of accounts receivable is prepared.

    (2) Credit memoranda are prenumbered and all numbers are accounted for.

    (3) A reconciliation of the trial balance of customers' accounts with the general ledger control is prepared periodically.

    (4) Receiving reports are prepared for all materials received and such reports are accounted for on a regular basis.

b. The sales manager credited a salesman, Jack Smith, with sales that were actually "house account" sales. Later, Smith divided his excess sales commissions with the sales manager.

    (1) The summary sales entries are checked periodically by persons independent of sales functions.

    (2) Sales orders are reviewed and approved by persons independent of the sales department.

    (3) The internal auditor compares the sales commission statements with the cash disbursements record.

    (4) Sales orders are prenumbered, and all numbers are accounted for.

c. A sales invoice for $5,200 was computed correctly but, by mistake, was key entered as $2,500 to the sales journal and to the accounts receivable master file. The customer remitted only $2,500, the amount on his monthly statement.

    (1) Prelistings and predetermined totals are used to control postings.

    (2) Sales invoice serial numbers, prices, discounts, extensions, and footings are independently checked.

    (3) The customers' monthly statements are verified and mailed by a responsible person other than the bookkeeper who prepared them.

    (4) Unauthorized remittance deductions made by customers or other matters in dispute are investigated promptly by a person independent of the accounts receivable function.

d. Copies of sales invoices show different unit prices for apparently identical items.

    (1) All sales invoices are checked as to all details after their preparation.

    (2) Differences reported by customers are satisfactorily investigated.

    (3) Statistical sales data are compiled and reconciled with recorded sales.

    (4) All sales invoices are compared with the customers' purchase orders.

13-22 (Objectives 13-1, 13-3)   The following questions deal with audit evidence for the sales and collection cycle. Choose the best response.

a. Auditors sometimes use comparison of ratios as audit evidence. For example, an unexplained decrease in the ratio of gross profit to sales may suggest which of the following possibilities?

    (1) Unrecorded acquisitions.

    (2) Unrecorded sales.

    (3) Merchandise acquisitions being charged to selling and general expense.

    (4) Fictitious sales.

b. An auditor is performing substantive tests of transactions for sales. One step is to trace a sample of debit entries from the accounts receivable master file back to the supporting duplicate sales invoices. What would the auditor intend to establish by this step?

    (1) Sales invoices represent existing sales.

    (2) All sales have been recorded.

    (3) All sales invoices have been properly posted to customer accounts.

    (4) Debit entries in the accounts receivable master file are properly supported by sales invoices.

c. To verify that all sales transactions have been recorded, a substantive test of transactions should be completed on a representative sample drawn from
   (1) entries in the sales journal.
   (2) the billing clerk's file of sales orders.
   (3) a file of duplicate copies of sales invoices for which all prenumbered forms in the series have been accounted.
   (4) the shipping clerk's file of duplicate copies of bills of lading.

DISCUSSION QUESTIONS AND PROBLEMS

13-23 (Objectives 13-3, 13-4, 13-5, 13-7) Items 1 through 8 are selected questions of the type generally found in internal control questionnaires used by auditors to obtain an understanding of internal control in the sales and collection cycle. In using the questionnaire for a client, a "yes" response to a question indicates a possible internal control, whereas a "no" indicates a potential weakness.

1. Are sales invoices independently compared with customers' orders for prices, quantities, extensions, and footings?
2. Are sales orders, invoices, and credit memoranda issued and filed in numerical sequence and are the sequences accounted for periodically?
3. Are the selling and cash register functions independent of the cash receipts, shipping, delivery, and billing functions?
4. Are all C.O.D., scrap, equipment, and cash sales accounted for in the same manner as charge sales and is the record keeping independent of the collection procedure?
5. Is the collection function independent of and does it constitute a check on billing and recording sales?
6. Are accounts receivable master files balanced regularly to control accounts by an employee independent of billing functions?
7. Are cash receipts entered in books of original entry by persons independent of the mail-opening and receipts-listing functions?
8. Are receipts deposited intact daily on a timely basis?

Required
   a. For each of the questions above, state the transaction-related audit objectives being fulfilled if the control is in effect.
   b. For each control, list a test of control to test its effectiveness.
   c. For each of the questions above, identify the nature of the potential financial misstatements.
   d. For each of the potential misstatements in part c, list a substantive audit procedure to determine whether a material misstatement exists.

13-24 (Objectives 13-3, 13-5, 13-7) The following misstatements are included in the accounting records of the Joyce Manufacturing Company:

1. A sales invoice was misadded by $1,000 as a result of a key entry mistake.
2. A material sale was unintentionally recorded for the second time on the last day of the year. The sale had originally been recorded 2 days earlier.
3. Cash paid on accounts receivable was stolen by the mail clerk when the mail was opened.
4. Cash paid on accounts receivable that had been prelisted by a secretary was stolen by the bookkeeper who records cash receipts and accounts receivable. He failed to record the transactions.
5. A shipment to a customer was not billed because of the loss of the bill of lading.

6. Merchandise was shipped to a customer, but no bill of lading was prepared. Because billings are prepared from bills of lading, the customer was not billed.
7. A sale to a residential customer was unintentionally classified as a commercial sale.

Required

a. Identify whether each misstatement is an error or a fraud.
b. For each misstatement, state a control that should have prevented it from occurring on a continuing basis.
c. For each misstatement, state a substantive audit procedure that could uncover it.

13-25 (Objectives 13-3, 13-4, 13-5) The following are commonly performed tests of controls and substantive tests of transactions audit procedures in the sales and collection cycle:

1. Examine sales returns for approval by an authorized official.
2. Account for a sequence of shipping documents and examine each one to make sure that a duplicate sales invoice is attached.
3. Account for a sequence of sales invoices and examine each one to make sure that a duplicate copy of the shipping document is attached.
4. Compare the quantity and description of items on shipping documents with the related duplicate sales invoices.
5. Trace recorded sales in the sales journal to the related accounts receivable master file and compare the customer name, date, and amount for each one.
6. Review the prelisting in the cash receipts book to determine whether cash is prelisted daily.
7. Reconcile the recorded cash receipts on the prelisting with the cash receipts journal and the bank statement for a 1-month period.

Required

a. Identify whether each audit procedure is a test of control or a substantive test of transactions.
b. State which of the six transaction-related audit objectives each of the audit procedures fulfills.
c. Identify the type of evidence used for each audit procedure, such as confirmation and observation.

13-26 (Objectives 13-3, 13-7) The following are selected transaction-related audit objectives and audit procedures for sales transactions:

Transaction-Related Audit Objectives

1. Recorded sales exist.
2. Existing sales are recorded.
3. Sales transactions are properly included in the accounts receivable master file and are correctly summarized.

Procedures

1. Trace a sample of shipping documents to related duplicate sales invoices and the sales journal to make sure that the shipment was billed.
2. Examine a sample of duplicate sales invoices to determine whether each one has a shipping document attached.
3. Examine the sales journal for a sample of sales transactions to determine whether each one has a tick mark in the margin indicating that it has been compared with the accounts receivable master file for customer name, date, and amount.
4. Examine a sample of shipping documents to determine whether each one has a duplicate sales invoice number written on the bottom left corner.

5. Trace a sample of debit entries in the accounts receivable master file to the sales journal to determine whether the date, customer name, and amount are the same.
6. Trace a sample of duplicate sales invoices to related shipping documents filed in the shipping department to make sure that a shipment was made.

Required

    a. For each objective, identify at least one specific misstatement that could occur.
    b. Describe the differences between the purposes of the first and second objectives.
    c. For each audit procedure, identify it as a test of control or substantive test of transactions. (There are three of each.)
    d. For each objective, identify one test of control and one substantive test of transactions.
    e. For each test of control, state the internal control that is being tested. Also, identify or describe a misstatement that the client is trying to prevent by use of the control.

13-27 (Objectives 13-2, 13-3) The following sales procedures were encountered during the annual audit of Marvel Wholesale Distributing Company.

Customer orders are received by the sales order department. A clerk computes the approximate dollar amount of the order and sends it to the credit department for approval. Credit approval is stamped on the order and sent to the accounting department. A computer is then used to generate two copies of a sales invoice. The order is filed in the customer order file.

The customer copy of the sales invoice is held in a pending file awaiting notification that the order was shipped. The shipping copy of the sales invoice is routed through the warehouse, and the shipping department has authority for the respective departments to release and ship the merchandise. Shipping department personnel pack the order and manually prepare a three-copy bill of lading: the original copy is mailed to the customer, the second copy is sent with the shipment, and the other is filed in sequence in the bill of lading file. The sales invoice shipping copy is sent to the accounting department with any changes resulting from lack of available merchandise.

A clerk in accounting matches the received sales invoice shipping copy with the sales invoice customer copy from the pending file. Quantities on the two invoices are compared and prices are compared on an approved price list. The customer copy is then mailed to the customer, and the shipping copy is sent to the data processing department.

The data processing clerk in accounting enters the sales invoice data into the computer, which is used to prepare the sales journal and update the accounts receivable master file. She files the shipping copy in the sales invoice file in numerical sequence.

    a. To determine whether the internal controls operated effectively to minimize instances of failure to post invoices to customers' accounts receivable master file, the auditor would select a sample of transactions from the population represented by the
        (1) customer order file.
        (2) bill of lading file.
        (3) customers' accounts receivable master file.
        (4) sales invoice file.
    b. To determine whether the internal controls operated effectively to minimize instances of failure to invoice a shipment, the auditor would select a sample of transactions from the population represented by the
        (1) customer order file.
        (2) bill of lading file.
        (3) customers' accounts receivable master file.
        (4) sales invoice file.

c. To gather audit evidence that uncollected items in customers' accounts represented existing trade receivables, the auditor would select a sample of items from the population represented by the
  (1) customer order file.
  (2) bill of lading file.
  (3) customers' accounts receivable master file.
  (4) sales invoice file.*

13-28 (Objectives 13-3, 13-5) The following are common audit procedures for tests of sales and cash receipts.

1. Compare the quantity and description of items on duplicate sales invoices with related shipping documents.
2. Trace recorded cash receipts in the accounts receivable master file to the cash receipts journal and compare the customer name, date, and amount of each one.
3. Examine duplicate sales invoices for an indication that unit selling prices were compared to the approved price list.
4. Examine duplicate sales invoices to determine whether the account classification for sales has been included on the document.
5. Examine the sales journal for related-party transactions, notes receivable, and other unusual items.
6. Select a sample of customer orders and trace the document to related shipping documents, vendors' invoices, and the accounts receivable master file for comparison of name, date, and amount.
7. Perform a proof of cash receipts.
8. Examine a sample of remittance advices for approval of cash discounts.
9. Account for a numerical sequence of remittance advices and determine whether there is a cross-reference mark for each one, indicating that it has been recorded in the cash receipts journal.

Required
  a. Identify whether each audit procedure is a test of control or substantive test of transactions.
  b. State which transaction-related audit objective(s) each of the audit procedures fulfills.
  c. For each test of control in part a, state a substantive test that could be used to determine whether there was a monetary misstatement.

13-29 (Objective 13-5) Appliances Repair and Service Company bills all customers rather than collecting in cash when services are provided. All mail is opened by Tom Gyders, treasurer. Gyders, a CPA, is the most qualified person in the company who is in the office daily. Therefore, he can solve problems and respond to customers' needs quickly. Upon receipt of cash, he immediately prepares a listing of the cash and a duplicate deposit slip. Cash is deposited daily. Gyders uses the listing to enter the financial transactions in the computerized accounting records. He also contacts customers about uncollected accounts receivable. Because he is so knowledgeable about the business and each customer, he grants credit, authorizes all sales allowances, and charges off uncollectible accounts. The owner is extremely pleased with the efficiency of the company. He can run the business without spending much time there because of Gyders' effectiveness.

Imagine the owner's surprise when he discovers that Gyders has committed a major theft of the company's cash receipts. He did so by not recording sales, recording improper credits to recorded accounts receivable, and overstating receivables.

Required

a. Given that cash was prelisted, went only to the treasurer, and was deposited daily, what internal control deficiency permitted the fraud?

b. What are the benefits of a prelisting of cash? Who should prepare the prelisting and what duties should that person not perform?

c. Assume that an appropriate person, as discussed in part b, prepares a prelisting of cash. What is to prevent that person from taking the cash after it is prelisted but before it is deposited?

d. Who should deposit the cash, given your answer to part b?

13-30 (Objective 13-5) The receptionist at Jones Supply Co. prelists cash before making daily deposits. He gives the data processing clerk remittance advices, which she uses to enter the cash receipts transactions into the computerized accounting records. Monthly, the controller prepares a proof of cash receipts and prints out a copy of the cash receipts journal and compares it with the prelisting.

Required

a. Define a proof of cash receipts and state its purpose.

b. For each error or fraud listed below, state whether it is (i) likely to be uncovered by a proof of cash receipts, (ii) likely to be uncovered by a comparison of the prelisting to the cash receipts journal, (iii) likely to be uncovered by either a proof of cash receipts or a comparison of the prelisting to the cash receipts journal, or (iv) not likely to be uncovered by either a proof of cash receipts or a comparison of the prelisting to the cash receipts journal.

c. For those questions in part b that you answered (iv), identify an audit procedure that is likely to uncover the misstatement.

1. Cash was prelisted and correctly inputted to the computerized accounting records, but the bank credited the wrong amount to Jones's bank account.

2. The receptionist unintentionally failed to give the data processing clerk two remittance advices for which the cash had been prelisted.

3. The receptionist unintentionally threw away an unopened envelope that included a check and remittance advice.

4. The data processing clerk made a transposition error in entering the transaction into the computerized accounting records (she recorded a receipt as $4,621 rather than $6,421).

5. The data processing clerk recorded the cash received at the correct amount but credited the wrong customer's account.

6. The receptionist listed the cash receipts but afterward withheld a check for his own use and did not forward the remittance advice to the data processing clerk.

13-31 (Objective 13-5) You have been asked by the board of trustees of a local church to review its accounting procedures. As part of this review you have prepared the following comments about the collections made at weekly services and record keeping for members' pledges and contributions:

1. The church's board of trustees has delegated responsibility for financial management and audit of the financial records to the finance committee. This group prepares the annual budget and approves major cash disbursements but is not involved in collections or record keeping. No audit has been considered necessary in recent years because the same trusted employee has kept church records and served as financial secretary for 15 years.

2. The collection at the weekly service is taken by a team of ushers. The head usher counts the collection in the church office after each service. He then places the collection and a notation of the amount in the church safe. The next morning, the financial secretary opens the safe and recounts the collection. He withholds about $100 to meet cash expenditures during the coming week and deposits the remainder intact. To facilitate the deposit, members who contribute by check are asked to draw their checks to cash.

3. At their request, a few members are furnished prenumbered predated envelopes in which to insert their weekly contributions. The head usher removes the cash from the envelopes to be counted with the loose cash included in the collection and discards the envelopes. No record is maintained of issuance or return of the envelopes, and the envelope system is not encouraged.

4. Each member is asked to prepare a contribution pledge card annually. The pledge is regarded as a moral commitment by the member to contribute a stated weekly amount. Based on the amounts shown on the pledge cards, the financial secretary furnishes a letter to members, upon request, to support the tax deductibility of their contributions.

Required

Identify the weaknesses and recommend improvements in procedures for collections made at weekly services and record keeping for members' pledges and contributions.

Use the methodology for identifying weaknesses that was discussed in Chapter 10. Organize your answer sheets as follows:*

Weakness	Recommended Improvement

13-32 (Objectives 13-3, 13-5) The customer billing and cash receipts functions of the Robinson Company, a small paint manufacturer, are attended to by a receptionist, an accounts receivable clerk, and a cashier who also serves as a secretary. The company's paint products are sold to wholesalers and retail stores.

The following describes all the procedures performed by the employees of the Robinson Company pertaining to customer billings and cash receipts:

1. The mail is opened by the receptionist, who gives the customers' purchase orders to the accounts receivable clerk. Fifteen to twenty orders are received each day. Under instructions to expedite the shipment of orders, the accounts receivable clerk at once prepares a five-copy sales invoice form that is distributed as follows:
   (a) Copy 1 is the customer billing copy and is held by the accounts receivable clerk until notice of shipment is received.
   (b) Copy 2 is the accounts receivable department copy and is held for the ultimate updating of the accounting records.
   (c) Copies 3 and 4 are sent to the shipping department.
   (d) Copy 5 is sent to the storeroom as authority for the release of goods to the shipping department.

2. After the paint order has been moved from the storeroom to the shipping department, the shipping department prepares the bills of lading and labels the cartons. Sales invoice copy 4 is inserted in a carton as a packing slip. After the trucker has picked up the shipment, the customer's copy of the bill of lading and copy 3, on which are noted any undershipments, are returned to the accounts receivable clerk. The company does not "back order" in the event of undershipments; customers are expected to reorder the merchandise. The Robinson Company's copy of the bill of lading is filed by the shipping department.

3. When copy 3 and the customer's copy of the bill of lading are received by the accounts receivable clerk, copies 1 and 2 are completed by numbering them and inserting quantities shipped, unit prices, extensions, discounts, and totals. Copies 2 and 3 are stapled together.

*AICPA adapted.

4. The accounts receivable clerk then enters the sales transactions into the computerized accounting records from copy 2. Only the quantities, prices, discounts, and accounts are entered because the computer computes extensions and totals. These extensions and totals are then compared with copy 1. The accounts receivable clerk then mails copy 1 and the copy of the bill of lading to the customer. Copy 2 is then filed, along with staple-attached copy 3, in numerical order.

5. Because the Robinson Company is short of cash, the deposit of cash receipts is also expedited. The receptionist turns over all mail receipts and related correspondence to the accounts receivable clerk, who examines the checks and determines that the accompanying vouchers or correspondence contain enough detail to permit the entering of the transactions into the computer. The accounts receivable clerk then endorses the checks and gives them to the cashier, who prepares the daily deposit. No currency is received in the mail, and no paint is sold over the counter at the factory.

6. The accounts receivable clerk uses the vouchers or correspondence that accompanied the checks to enter the transactions into the computerized accounting records. The accounts receivable clerk is the one who corresponds with customers about unauthorized deductions for discounts, freight or advertising allowances, returns, and so forth, and prepares the appropriate credit memos. Disputed items of large amounts are turned over to the sales manager for settlement. Each month, the accounts receivable clerk prints out a trial balance of accounts receivable and compares the total with the general ledger control accounts for accounts receivable.

Required

a. Identify the internal control weaknesses in the Robinson Company's procedures related to customer billings and cash receipts and the accounting for these transactions. Use the methodology for identifying weaknesses that was discussed in Chapter 10.

b. For each weakness, identify the error or fraud that could result.

c. For each weakness, list one substantive audit procedure for testing the significance of the potential misstatement.*

CASE

13-33 (Objectives 13-3, 13-7) The Meyers Pharmaceutical Company, a drug manufacturer, has the following internal controls for billing and recording accounts receivable:

1. An incoming customer's purchase order is received in the order department by a clerk who prepares a prenumbered company sales order form in which is inserted the pertinent information, such as the customer's name and address, customer's account number, quantity, and items ordered. After the sales order form has been prepared, the customer's purchase order is stapled to it.

2. The sales order form is then passed to the credit department for credit approval. Rough approximations of the billing values of the orders are made in the credit department for those accounts on which credit limitations are imposed. After investigation, approval of credit is noted on the form.

3. Next, the sales order form is passed to the billing department, where a clerk uses a computer to generate the customer's invoice. It automatically cross-multiplies the number of items with the unit price, and adds the extended amounts for the total amount of the invoice. The billing clerk determines the unit prices for the items from a list of billing prices.

---

*AICPA adapted.

The computer automatically accumulates daily totals of customer account numbers and invoice amounts to provide "hash" totals and control amounts. These totals, which are inserted in a daily record book, serve as predetermined batch totals for verification of inputs into the computerized accounting records.

The billing is done on prenumbered, continuous, carbon-interleaved forms having the following designations:
(a) Customer's copy.
(b) Sales department copy, for information purposes.
(c) File copy.
(d) Shipping department copy, which serves as a shipping order. Bills of lading are also prepared as carbon copy by-products of the invoicing procedure.

4. The shipping department copy of the invoice and the bills of lading are then sent to the shipping department. After the order has been shipped, copies of the bill of lading are returned to the billing department. The shipping department copy of the invoice is filed in the shipping department.

5. In the billing department, one copy of the bill of lading is attached to the customer's copy of the invoice and both are mailed to the customer. The other copy of the bill of lading, together with the sales order form, is then stapled to the invoice file copy and filed in invoice numerical order.

6. As the computer is generating invoices, it is also storing the transactions on disk. This disk is then used to update the computerized accounting records. This update procedure is run daily, and a summary report is generated. Hard copy output of all journals and ledgers is prepared.

7. Periodically, an internal auditor traces a sample of sales orders all the way through the system to the journals and ledgers, testing both the procedures and dollar amounts. The procedures include comparing control totals with output, recalculating invoices and refooting journals, and tracing totals to the master file and general ledger.

Required
a. Flowchart the billing function as a means of understanding the system.
b. List the internal controls over sales for each of the six transaction-related audit objectives.
c. For each control, list a useful test of control to verify the effectiveness of the control.
d. For each transaction-related audit objective for sales, list appropriate substantive tests of transactions audit procedures, considering internal controls.
e. Combine the audit procedures from parts c and d into an efficient audit program for sales.

INTEGRATED CASE APPLICATION—PINNACLE MANUFACTURING: PART II

13-34 (Objective 13-7) In Part I of this case study (pp. 325–327), you obtained an understanding of internal control and made an initial assessment of control risk for each transaction-related audit objective for acquisition and cash disbursement transactions. The purpose of Part II is to continue the assessment of control risk by determining the appropriate tests of controls and substantive tests of transactions.

Assume that in Part I it was determined that the key internal controls are the following:

1. Segregation of the purchasing, receiving, and cash disbursement functions
2. Review of supportive documents and signing of checks by an independent, authorized person
3. Use of prenumbered checks, properly accounted for
4. Use of prenumbered purchase orders, properly accounted for
5. Use of prenumbered document package, properly accounted for
6. Internal verification of document package before check preparation
7. Independent monthly reconciliation of bank statement

For requirements a and b, you should follow a format similar to the one illustrated for sales in Table 13-2 (p. 406). You should prepare one matrix for acquisitions and a separate one for cash disbursements. Observe that the first column in each matrix should include the transaction-related audit objectives from the top row in the worksheet you prepared for Problem 10-32. Also, the key internal controls include only those seven from above, and the tests of controls include only those you developed in requirement a. The substantive tests of transactions procedures should be designed based on an assumption that the results of the tests of controls will be favorable.

Required

a. Design tests of controls audit procedures that will provide appropriate evidence for each of these controls. Do not include more than two tests of control for each internal control.

b. Although controls appear to be well designed and test of control deviations are not expected, last year's results indicate that misstatements may still exist. Therefore, you decide to perform substantive tests of transactions for acquisitions and cash disbursements. Design substantive tests of transactions for each transaction-related audit objective. Do not include more than two substantive tests of transactions for any objective. Use Tables 13-4 on pages 420 and 421 and 13-5 on pages 421 and 422 as frames of reference.

c. Combine the tests of controls and substantive tests of transactions designed in requirements a and b into a performance format. Include both tests of acquisitions and cash disbursements in the same audit program. Use Figure 13-9 on page 423 as a frame of reference for preparing the performance format audit program.

INTERNET PROBLEM 13-1: ELECTRONIC FUNDS TRANSFER

Reference the CW site. The Federal Electronic Commerce Program Office (FECPO) provides a "List of Best Practices." This problem requires students to use the Internet to research FECPO information to determine the costs, benefits, risks, and potential controls associated with electronic funds transfer.

AUDIT SAMPLING FOR TESTS OF CONTROLS AND SUBSTANTIVE TESTS OF TRANSACTIONS

14

LEARNING OBJECTIVES

After studying this chapter, you should be able to

14-1 Explain the concept of representative sampling.

14-2 Distinguish between statistical and nonstatistical sampling and between probabilistic and nonprobabilistic sample selection.

14-3 Select representative samples.

14-4 Define and describe audit sampling for exception rates.

14-5 Use nonstatistical sampling in tests of controls and substantive tests of transactions.

14-6 Define and describe attributes sampling and a sampling distribution.

14-7 Use attributes sampling in tests of controls and substantive tests of transactions.

14-8 Apply sampling concepts and methodology to the audit plan for the sales and collection cycle.

IF YOU ARE NOT GOING TO BELIEVE IT, DON'T USE IT

Brooks & Company, CPAs, uses random samples in performing audit tests whenever possible. They believe that this gives them the best chance of getting representative samples of their clients' accounting information. In the audit of Sensational Products, a random sample of 30 inventory items was taken from a population of 1,800 items in doing a test of unit and total costs. Only 1 of the 30 items was in error, but it was large. In investigating the error, Harold Davis, the audit staff person doing the test, was told by Sensational's controller that the error occurred while the regular inventory clerk was on vacation and was really only an "isolated error."

Harold knew that generally accepted auditing standards require that errors in random samples be projected to the entire population. In this case, such a projection would involve multiplying the error found by a factor of 60 (1,800 divided by 30). This would result in an audit adjustment or additional audit work. Harold knew that the client would not be happy about this because the adjustment would reduce an already "strained" net income figure and additional auditing would increase the audit fee. If the error was, in fact, an isolated one, it would not be significant enough to require an audit adjustment.

Harold decided to look at the situation in terms of the probability of the error being an isolated example. He calculated the chance to be about only 1 in 60 of including an isolated error in a sample of 30 from a population of 1,800. He then looked at accepting the client's representation about the uniqueness of the error as a bet. If he accepted the representation and didn't do the projection and act on it, he was in effect betting his career in a situation where the odds were 60 to 1 against him. It didn't take Harold long to recognize the wisdom of the professional standards and conclude that the projection should be done.

What items?
How many?

In the last chapter, we learned about designing tests of controls and substantive tests of transactions needed to perform an audit of the sales and collection cycle. Before these tests can be performed, the auditor needs to decide for each audit procedure the sample size and sample items to select from the population. When the auditor decides to select less than 100 percent of the population for testing for the purpose of making inferences about the population, it is called **audit sampling**. As demonstrated by Harold Davis of Brooks & Company in the chapter vignette, evaluating audit samples is an essential, and often challenging, part of the audit process. When is a sample size sufficiently large to evaluate a population? Does a given sample accurately represent the accounting information? This chapter discusses sampling issues for tests of controls and substantive tests of transactions. These sampling concepts are illustrated for the sales and collection cycle, but they are equally applicable to all other cycles.

REPRESENTATIVE SAMPLES

OBJECTIVE 14-1
Explain the concept of representative sampling.

When an auditor selects a sample from a population, the objective is to obtain a representative one. A **representative sample** is one in which the characteristics in the sample of audit interest are approximately the same as those of the population. This means that the sampled items are similar to the items not sampled. For example, assume that a client's internal controls require a clerk to attach a shipping document to every duplicate sales invoice, but the procedure is not followed exactly 3 percent of the time. If the auditor selects a sample of 100 duplicate sales invoices and finds three missing, the sample is highly representative. If two or four such items are found in the sample, the sample is reasonably representative. If no or many missing items are found, the sample is nonrepresentative.

In practice, auditors do not know whether a sample is representative, even after all testing is complete. However, auditors can increase the likelihood of a sample being representative by using care in its design, selection, and evaluation. Two things can cause a sample result to be nonrepresentative: nonsampling error and sampling error. The risk of these occurring is termed nonsampling risk and sampling risk. Both of these can be controlled.

Nonsampling risk (nonsampling error) occurs when audit tests do not uncover existing exceptions in the sample. The two causes of nonsampling error are the auditor's failure to recognize exceptions and inappropriate or ineffective audit procedures. An auditor might fail to recognize an exception because of exhaustion, boredom, or lack of understanding of what to look for. In the previous example in which three shipping documents were not attached to duplicate sales invoices, if the auditor concluded that no exceptions existed, there is a nonsampling error. An ineffective audit procedure for the exceptions in question would be to examine a sample of shipping documents and determine whether each is attached to a set of duplicate sales invoices, rather than to examine a sample of duplicate sales invoices. In this case, the auditor has done the test in the wrong direction by starting with the shipping document instead of the duplicate sales invoice. Careful design of audit procedures, proper instruction, supervision, and review are ways to control nonsampling risk.

Sampling risk (sampling error) is an inherent part of sampling that results from testing less than the entire population. Even with zero nonsampling error, there is always a chance that a sample is not reasonably representative. For example, if a population has a 3 percent exception rate, the auditor could select a sample of 100 items containing no or many exceptions.

There are two ways to control sampling risk: by adjusting sample size and by using an appropriate method of selecting sample items from the population. Increasing sample size will reduce sampling risk, and vice versa. At the extreme, a sample of all the items of a population will have a zero sampling risk. Using an appropriate sampling method will reasonably ensure representativeness. This does not eliminate or even reduce sampling risk, but it does allow the auditor to measure the risk associated with a given sample size in a reliable manner. Determining the appropriate sample size to reduce sampling risk to an appropriate level is a major topic of this chapter.

STATISTICAL VERSUS NONSTATISTICAL SAMPLING AND PROBABILISTIC VERSUS NONPROBABILISTIC SAMPLE SELECTION

Before discussing the methods of sample selection to obtain representative samples, it is useful to make two distinctions and discuss the terms involved: statistical versus nonstatistical sampling and probabilistic versus nonprobabilistic sample selection.

Audit sampling methods can be divided into two broad categories: statistical sampling and nonstatistical sampling. These categories have important similarities and differences. They are similar in that they both involve three steps: (1) plan the sample, (2) select the sample and perform the tests, and (3) evaluate the results. The purpose of planning the sample is to make sure that the audit tests are performed in a manner that provides the desired sampling risk and minimizes the likelihood of nonsampling error. Selecting the sample involves deciding how to select sample items from the population. Performing the tests is the examination of documents and doing other audit procedures. Evaluating the results involves drawing conclusions based on the audit tests. To illustrate, assume that an auditor selects a sample of 100 duplicate sales invoices from a population, tests each to determine whether a shipping document is attached, and determines that there are three exceptions. Deciding that a sample size of 100 is needed is a part of planning the sample. Deciding which 100 items to select from the population is a sample selection problem. Doing the audit procedure for each of the 100 items and determining that there were three exceptions constitutes performing the tests. Reaching conclusions about the likely exception rate in the total population when there is a sample exception rate of 3 percent is evaluating the results.

Statistical sampling differs from nonstatistical sampling in that, through the application of mathematical rules, it allows the quantification (measurement) of sampling risk in planning the sample (Step 1) and evaluating the results (Step 3). (You may remember calculating a statistical result at a 95 percent confidence level in a statistics course. The 95 percent confidence level provides a 5 percent sampling risk.)

In **nonstatistical sampling**, the auditor does not quantify sampling risk. Instead, the auditor selects those sample items that he or she believes will provide the most useful information in the circumstances. Conclusions are reached about populations on a judgmental basis. For that reason, the selection of nonprobabilistic samples is often termed judgmental sampling.

Both probabilistic and nonprobabilistic sample selection are a part of Step 2 in using auditing sampling, selecting sample items from the population. **Probabilistic sample selection** is a method of selecting a sample such that each population item has a known probability of being included in the sample and the sample is selected by a random process. To satisfy this definition, the auditor must use great care in selecting samples using one of several methods discussed shortly. **Nonprobabilistic sample selection** is a method of selecting a sample in which the auditor uses professional judgment rather than probabilistic methods to select sample items. There are also several nonprobabilistic sample selection methods.

It is equally acceptable under professional standards for auditors to use either statistical or nonstatistical sampling methods. However, it is essential that either method be applied with due care. All steps of the process must be followed carefully. When statistical sampling is used, the sample *must be a probabilistic one* and appropriate statistical evaluation methods must be used with the sample results to make the sampling risk computations.

It is also acceptable to make nonstatistical evaluations by using probabilistic selection. It is *never* acceptable, however, to evaluate a nonprobabilistic sample as if it were a statistical sample.

Three types of sample selection methods are commonly associated with nonstatistical audit sampling. All three methods are nonprobabilistic. Four types of sample selection

Statistical versus Nonstatistical Sampling

OBJECTIVE 14-2
Distinguish between statistical and nonstatistical sampling and between probabilistic and nonprobabilistic sample selection.

E & Y Statistical Sampling Services

Probabilistic versus Nonprobabilistic Sample Selection

Applying Statistical and Nonstatistical Sampling in Practice and Sample Selection Methods

methods are commonly associated with statistical audit sampling. All four methods are probabilistic.

Nonprobabilistic (judgmental) sample selection methods include the following:

1. Directed sample selection
2. Block sample selection
3. Haphazard sample selection

Probabilistic sample selection methods include the following:

1. Simple random sample selection
2. Systematic sample selection
3. Probability proportional to size sample selection
4. Stratified sample selection

We will now discuss each of these seven sample selection methods, starting with non-probabilistic methods.

NONPROBABILISTIC SAMPLE SELECTION METHODS

Nonprobabilistic sample selection methods are those that do not meet the technical requirements for probabilistic sample selection. Because these methods are not based on strict mathematical probabilities, the representativeness of the sample may be difficult to determine. The information content of the sample, including its representativeness, will be based on the knowledge and skill of the auditor in applying his or her judgment in the circumstances.

Directed Sample Selection

Directed sample selection is the selection of each item in the sample based on some judgmental criteria established by the auditor. The auditor does not rely on equal chances of selection, but rather, deliberately selects items according to the criteria. These criteria may relate to representativeness, or they may not. Commonly used criteria are the following.

Items Most Likely to Contain Misstatements Often, auditors are able to identify which population items are most likely to be misstated. Examples are receivables outstanding for a long time, purchases from and sales to officers and affiliated companies, and unusually large or complex transactions. These kinds of items can be efficiently investigated by the auditor, and the results can be applied to the population on a judgmental basis. The reasoning underlying the evaluation of such samples is often that, if none of the items selected contain misstatements, it is highly unlikely that a material misstatement exists in the population.

Items Containing Selected Population Characteristics The auditor may be able to describe the various types and sources of items that make up the population and design the sample to be representative by selecting one or more items of each type. For example, a sample of cash disbursements might include some from each month, each bank account or location, and each major type of acquisition.

Large Dollar Coverage A sample can often be selected to cover such a large portion of total population dollars that the risk of drawing an improper conclusion by not examining small items is not a concern. This is a practical approach on many audits, especially smaller ones. There are also statistical methods that are intended to accomplish the same effect.

Block Sample Selection

Block sample selection is the selection of several items in sequence. Once the first item in the block is selected, the remainder of the block is chosen automatically. One example of a block sample is the selection of a sequence of 100 sales transactions from the sales journal for the third week of March. A total sample of 100 could also be selected by taking 5 blocks of 20 items each, 10 blocks of 10, or 50 blocks of 2.

It is ordinarily acceptable to use block samples only if a reasonable number of blocks is used. If few blocks are used, the probability of obtaining a nonrepresentative sample is too great, considering the possibility of such things as employee turnover, changes in the accounting system, and the seasonal nature of many businesses.

Block sampling can also be used to supplement other samples when there is a high likelihood of misstatement for a known period. For example, selecting all 100 cash receipts from the third week of March may be appropriate if that is when the accounting clerk was on vacation and an inexperienced temporary employee processed the cash receipt transactions.

Haphazard sample selection is the selection of items without any bias on the part of the auditor. In such cases, the auditor selects population items without regard to their size, source, or other distinguishing characteristics.

Haphazard Sample Selection

The most serious shortcoming of haphazard sample selection is the difficulty of remaining completely unbiased in the selection. Because of the auditor's training and "cultural bias," certain population items are more likely than others to be included in the sample.

Although haphazard and block sample selection appear to be less logical than directed sample selection, they are often useful as audit tools and should not be ignored. In some situations, the cost of more complex sample selection methods outweighs the benefits obtained from using them. For example, assume that the auditor wants to trace credits from the accounts receivable master files to the cash receipts journal and other authorized sources as a test for fictitious credits in the master files. A haphazard or block approach is simpler and much less costly than other selection methods in this situation and would be used by many auditors. However, for most nonstatistical sampling applications involving tests of controls and substantive tests of transactions, auditors often prefer to use a probabilistic sample selection method to increase the likelihood of selecting a representative sample. Note that probabilistic selection is required for statistical sampling.

PROBABILISTIC SAMPLE SELECTION METHODS

As previously indicated, to measure sampling risk, statistical sampling requires a probabilistic sample. For probabilistic samples, the auditor uses no judgment about which sample items are selected, except to select which of the four selection methods to use.

A simple **random sample** is one in which every possible combination of elements in the population has an equal chance of constituting the sample. Simple random sampling is used to sample populations that are not segmented for audit purposes. For example, the auditor may wish to sample the client's cash disbursements for the year. A simple random sample of 60 items contained in the cash disbursements journal might be selected for that purpose. Appropriate auditing procedures would be applied to the 60 items selected, and conclusions would be drawn and applied to all cash disbursement transactions recorded for the year.

Simple Random Sample Selection

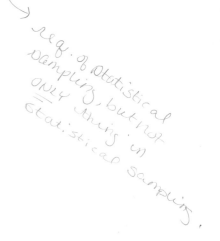

req. of statistical sampling, but not only prob, but this in statistical sampling

Random Number Tables When a simple random sample is obtained, a method must be used that ensures that all items in the population have an equal chance of selection. Suppose that in the above example, there were a total of 12,000 cash disbursement transactions for the year. A simple random sample of one transaction would be such that each of the 12,000 transactions would have an equal chance of being selected. This would be done by obtaining a random number between 1 and 12,000. If the number was 3,895, the auditor would select and test the 3,895th cash disbursement transaction recorded in the cash disbursements journal.

Random numbers are a series of digits that have equal probabilities of occurring over long runs and which have no discernable pattern. A **random number table** is a presentation of these random digits in table form with numbered rows and columns. The auditor chooses a random sample by first establishing a correspondence between the client's document numbers to be tested and the digits in the random number table. After selecting a random starting point, the auditor reads down the table and finds the first random number that falls within the sequence of the document numbers being tested. The process continues until the final sample item is selected.

Computer Generation of Random Numbers It is useful to understand the use of random number tables as a means of understanding the concept of selecting simple random samples. However, most random samples obtained by auditors are obtained by using computers. There are three main types: electronic spreadsheet programs, random number generators, and generalized audit software programs.

Used more often

The advantages of using computer programs in selecting random samples are time savings, reduced likelihood of auditor error in selecting the numbers, and automatic documentation. Because most auditors have access to a computer and to electronic spreadsheets or random number generator programs, auditors often prefer to use computer generation of random numbers over other probabilistic selection methods.

To illustrate computer generation of random numbers, Figure 14-1 on page 443 shows the input parameters and a printout from an electronic spreadsheet program, using the program's random number generator function. In the application illustrated, the auditor wishes to sample 50 items from a population of sales invoices numbered from 3689 to 9452. The program requires only input parameters by the auditor for a sample to be selected. It possesses great flexibility in the formatting of the numbers. For example, the program can generate random dates or ranges of sets of numbers (such as page and line numbers). It also provides output in both sorted and selection orders.

Random numbers may be obtained with replacement or without replacement. In replacement sampling, an element in the population can be included in the sample more than once, whereas in nonreplacement sampling, an element can be included only once. If the random number corresponding to an element is selected more than once in nonreplacement sampling, it is not included in the sample a second time. Although both selection approaches are consistent with sound statistical theory, auditors rarely use replacement sampling.

Systematic Sample Selection

In **systematic sample selection** (also called systematic sampling), the auditor calculates an interval and then methodically selects the items for the sample based on the size of the interval. The interval is determined by dividing the population size by the number of sample items desired. For example, if a population of sales invoices ranges from 652 to 3151 and the desired sample size is 125, the interval is 20 [(3,151 − 651)/125]. The auditor must now select a random number between 0 and 19 to determine the starting point for the sample. If the randomly selected number is 9, the first item in the sample is invoice number 661 (652 + 9). The remaining 124 items are 681 (661 + 20), 701 (681 + 20), and so on through item 3141.

The advantage of systematic selection is its ease of use. In most populations, a systematic sample can be drawn quickly, the approach automatically puts the numbers in sequence, and it is easy to develop the appropriate documentation.

A major problem with systematic selection is the possibility of bias. Because of the way systematic selection works, once the first item in the sample is selected, all other items are chosen automatically. This causes no problem if the characteristic of interest, such as a possible control deviation, is distributed randomly throughout the population; however, in some cases, characteristics of interest may not be randomly distributed. For example, if a control deviation occurred at a certain time of the month or with certain types of documents, a systematic sample could have a higher likelihood of failing to be representative than a simple random sample. Therefore, when systematic selection is used, possible patterns in the population data that could cause sample bias must be considered.

Probability Proportional to Size and Stratified Sample Selection

There are many situations in auditing when it is advantageous to select samples that emphasize population items that have larger recorded amounts. There are two ways to obtain such samples. The first is to take a sample where the probability of selecting any

FIGURE 14-1   Computer Generation of Random Numbers

Random Number Generation   ? X

Number of Variables: 1

Number of Random Numbers: 50   Cancel

Distribution: Uniform ▼   Help

Parameters

Between 3689 and 9452

Random Numbers Selected		Sorted in Ascending Order	
5890	5440	3773	5841
4269	9312	3787	5890
7127	8338	3876	6037
8871	9402	3924	6145
8787	5166	3951	6375
9213	9174	3997	6376
3773	3997	4058	6496
6037	7752	4117	6635
8664	8395	4269	6880
4488	9294	4488	7127
5101	6376	4635	7752
3951	5419	4833	8012
3876	8012	4955	8159
4635	5715	5019	8338
4955	8159	5101	8395
3787	4117	5166	8664
5332	4833	5332	8787
5666	4058	5419	8871
6880	5754	5440	8935
5749	6496	5666	9174
5832	6635	5715	9213
5738	5841	5738	9294
8935	9371	5749	9312
6375	3924	5754	9371
6145	5019	5832	9402

individual population item is proportional to its recorded amount. This method is called sampling with probability proportional to size (PPS). The second way of emphasizing larger items in the population is to divide the population into subpopulations by size and take larger samples of the larger subpopulations. This is called stratified sampling. The first of these methods is evaluated using monetary unit sampling and the second using variables sampling. These selection methods and their related evaluation methods are discussed in a later chapter.

SAMPLING FOR EXCEPTION RATES

Audit sampling for tests of controls and substantive tests of transactions is used to estimate the proportion of items in a population containing a characteristic or **attribute** of interest. This proportion is called the **occurrence rate** or **exception rate** and is the ratio of the items containing the specific attribute to the total number of population items. The occurrence

OBJECTIVE 14-4
Define and describe audit sampling for exception rates.

rate is usually expressed as a percentage. For example, an auditor might conclude that the exception rate for the internal verification of sales invoices is approximately 3 percent, meaning that invoices are not properly verified 3 percent of the time.

Auditors are interested in the occurrence of the following types of exceptions in populations of accounting data: (1) deviations from client's established controls, (2) monetary misstatements in populations of transaction data, and (3) monetary misstatements in populations of account balance details. Knowing the occurrence rate of such exceptions is particularly helpful for the first two types of exceptions, which relate to transactions. Therefore, auditors make extensive use of audit sampling that measures the occurrence or exception rate in performing tests of controls and substantive tests of transactions. With the third type of exception, the auditor usually needs to estimate the total dollar amount of the exceptions because a judgment must be made about whether the exceptions are material. When the auditor wants to know the total amount of a misstatement, he or she will use methods that measure dollars, not the exception or occurrence rate. This topic is studied in a later chapter.

The exception rate in a sample is intended to be an estimate of the exception rate in the entire population. It means that for a given sample, the sample exception rate is the auditor's "best estimate" of the population exception rate. The term *exception* should be understood to refer to both deviations from prescribed controls and situations when amounts are not monetarily correct, whether because of an unintentional accounting error or any other cause. The term *deviation* refers to the specific type of exception of a departure from prescribed controls.

Assume, for example, that the auditor wants to determine the percentage of duplicate sales invoices that do not have shipping documents attached. There is an actual, but unknown, percentage of missing shipping documents. The auditor will obtain a sample of duplicate sales invoices and determine what percentage of the invoices do not have shipping documents attached. The auditor will conclude that the sample exception rate is the best estimate of the population exception rate.

Because it is based on a sample, however, there is a significant likelihood that the sample exception rate and the actual population exception rate differ. This difference is called sampling error, a term that was first introduced in Chapter 9. The auditor is concerned with the estimate of the sampling error and the reliability of that estimate, called sampling risk, a term that was introduced earlier in this chapter. Assume that the auditor determines that there is a 3 percent sample exception rate and a sampling error of 1 percent with a sampling risk of 10 percent. The auditor can now state an interval estimate of the population exception rate as between 2 percent and 4 percent (3 percent ± 1) at a 10 percent risk of being wrong (and a 90 percent chance of being right).

In using audit sampling in auditing for exception rates, the auditor is primarily interested in knowing the *most* the exception rate might be, rather than the width of the confidence interval. Thus, the auditor focuses on the upper limit of the interval estimate. That limit is called the estimated or **computed upper exception rate (CUER)** in tests of controls and substantive tests of transactions. In the above example, the auditor might conclude that the CUER for missing shipping documents is 4 percent at a 5 percent sampling risk. This means that the auditor concludes that the exception rate in the population is no greater than 4 percent with a 5 percent risk of the exception rate exceeding 4 percent. Once the CUER is determined, the auditor can consider it in the context of the specific audit objectives. For example, in testing for missing shipping documents, the auditor must determine whether a 4 percent exception rate indicates an acceptable control risk for the existence objective.

APPLICATION OF NONSTATISTICAL AUDIT SAMPLING

OBJECTIVE 14-5
Use nonstatistical sampling in tests of controls and substantive tests of transactions.

We will now examine the application of nonstatistical audit sampling in testing transactions for control deviations and monetary misstatements. Statistical sampling is examined later in this chapter. Before doing so, the terminology from SAS 39 (AU 350) and other terminology are defined. The same terminology is used for statistical sampling. These are summarized in Table 14-1.

TABLE 14-1   Terms Used in Audit Sampling

Term	Definition
Terms Related to Planning	
Characteristic or attribute	The characteristic being tested in the application
Acceptable risk of assessing control risk too low (ARACR)	The risk that the auditor is willing to take of accepting a control as effective or a rate of monetary misstatements as tolerable, when the true population exception rate is greater than the tolerable exception rate
Tolerable exception rate (TER)	Exception rate that the auditor will permit in the population and still be willing to use the assessed control risk and/or the amount of monetary misstatements in the transactions established during planning
Estimated population exception rate (EPER)	Exception rate that the auditor expects to find in the population before testing begins _dev. @ time of planning_
Initial sample size	Sample size decided after considering the above factors in planning
Terms Related to Evaluating Results	
Exception	Exception from the attribute in a sample item
Sample exception rate (SER)	Number of exceptions in the sample divided by the sample size
Computed upper exception rate (CUER)	The highest estimated exception rate in the population at a given ARACR

Audit sampling is applied to tests of controls and substantive tests of transactions through a set of 14 well-defined steps. The steps are divided into three sections: plan the sample, select the sample and perform the audit procedures, and evaluate the results. It is important to follow these steps carefully as a means of ensuring that both the auditing and the sampling aspects of the process are properly applied. The steps provide an outline of the discussion that follows.

Plan the Sample

1. State the objectives of the audit test.
2. Decide whether audit sampling applies.
3. Define attributes and exception conditions.
4. Define the population.
5. Define the sampling unit.
6. Specify the tolerable exception rate.
7. Specify acceptable risk of assessing control risk too low.
8. Estimate the population exception rate.
9. Determine the initial sample size.

Select the Sample and Perform the Audit Procedures

10. Select the sample.
11. Perform the audit procedures.

Evaluate the Results

12. Generalize from the sample to the population.
13. Analyze exceptions.
14. Decide the acceptability of the population.

University Audit
Sampling Guide

The overall objectives of the test must be stated in terms of the transaction cycle being tested. Typically, the overall objectives of tests of controls and substantive tests of transactions are to test the application of controls and to determine whether the transactions contain monetary misstatements.

State the Objectives of the Audit Test

In the tests of the sales and collection cycle, the overall objectives are usually to test the effectiveness of internal controls over sales and cash receipts and to determine whether sales and cash receipts transactions contain monetary misstatements. The objectives of the audit test are normally decided as a part of designing the audit program, which was discussed for the sales and collection cycle in Chapter 13.

Decide Whether Audit Sampling Applies

Audit sampling applies whenever the auditor plans to reach conclusions about a population based on a sample. The auditor should examine the audit program and decide those audit procedures for which audit sampling applies. Assume the following partial audit program.

1. Review sales transactions for large and unusual amounts (analytical procedure).
2. Observe whether the duties of the accounts receivable clerk are separate from handling cash (test of control).
3. Examine a sample of duplicate sales invoices for
   a. credit approval by the credit manager (test of control).
   b. existence of an attached shipping document (test of control).
   c. inclusion of a chart of accounts number (test of control).
4. Select a sample of shipping documents and trace each to related duplicate sales invoices (test of control).
5. Compare the quantity on each duplicate sales invoice with the quantity on related shipping documents (substantive test of transactions).

Audit sampling is inappropriate for the first two procedures in this audit program. The first is an analytical procedure for which sampling is inappropriate. The second is an observation procedure for which no documentation exists to perform audit sampling. Audit sampling can be used for the remaining three procedures.

Define Attributes and Exception Conditions

When audit sampling is used, the auditor must carefully define the characteristics (attributes) being tested and the exception conditions. Unless a precise statement of what constitutes an attribute is made in advance, the staff person who performs the audit procedure will have no guidelines for identifying exceptions.

Attributes of interest and exception conditions come directly from the audit procedures for which the auditor has decided to use audit sampling. Table 14-2 shows five attributes of interest and exception conditions for each of the attributes from audit procedures three through five mentioned previously. Each of the five attributes will be verified for every item selected for the sample. The absence of the attribute for any sample item will be an exception for that attribute. It is important to note that both missing documents and immaterial misstatements result in exceptions unless the auditor specifically states otherwise in the exception conditions.

TABLE 14-2	Attributes Defined
Attribute *Yes*	**Exception Condition** *NO*
1. The duplicate sales invoice is approved for credit (procedure 3a).	Lack of initials indicating credit approval.
2. A copy of the shipping document is attached to the duplicate sales invoice (procedure 3b).	Shipping document is not attached to duplicate sales invoice.
3. The account number charged is included on the duplicate sales invoice (procedure 3c).	Account number is not included on duplicate sales invoice.
4. A duplicate sales invoice exists for each shipping document (procedure 4).	Duplicate sales invoice does not exist for shipping document.
5. The quantity on the sales invoice is the same as on the shipping document (procedure 5).	Quantity on the shipping document differs from that on the duplicate sales invoice.

The population represents the body of data about which the auditor wishes to generalize. The auditor can define the population to include whatever data are desired, but he or she must sample from the entire population as it has been defined. The auditor may generalize *only* about that population that has been sampled. For example, in performing tests of controls and substantive tests of sales transactions, the auditor generally defines the population as all recorded sales for the year. If the auditor samples from only 1 month's transactions, it is invalid to draw conclusions about the invoices for the entire year.

The auditor must carefully define the population in advance, consistent with the objectives of the audit tests. Furthermore, in some cases, it may be necessary to define more than one population for a given set of audit procedures. For example, if the auditor intends to trace from sales invoices to shipping documents (attribute 2 in Table 14-2) and from shipping documents to duplicate sales invoices (attributes 4 and 5 in Table 14-2), there are two populations (one population of shipping documents and another of duplicate sales invoices). It is also important to test the population for completeness and detail tie-in before a sample is selected to ensure that all population items will be properly subjected to sample selection.

The major consideration in defining the sampling unit is to make it consistent with the objectives of the audit tests. Thus, the definition of the population and the planned audit procedures usually dictate the appropriate sampling unit. For example, if the auditor wants to determine how often the client fails to fill a customer's order, the sampling unit must be defined as the customer's order. If, however, the objective is to determine whether the proper quantity of the goods described on the customer's order is correctly shipped and billed, it is possible to define the sampling unit as the customer's order, the shipping document, or the duplicate sales invoice.

Attribute 2 in Table 14-2 is a test for the existence of recorded sales. Therefore, the appropriate sampling unit is the duplicate sales invoice. However, it is impossible to test for attribute 2 if the sampling unit is the shipping document. The appropriate sampling unit for attribute 4 is the shipping document because this attribute tests that existing sales are recorded (completeness). Attribute 4 cannot be tested if the sampling unit is the duplicate sales invoice. Either the duplicate sales invoice or the shipping document is appropriate for attributes 1, 3, and 5 because these are all nondirectional tests.

The auditor could define the sampling unit in Table 14-2 as the duplicate sales invoice, examine the invoice for attributes 1 and 3, determine whether a shipping document is attached (attribute 2), and then perform the test for attribute 5. Attribute 4 would still have to be tested separately using a sample of shipping documents.

Establishing the **tolerable exception rate (TER)** requires professional judgment on the part of the auditor. TER represents the exception rate that the auditor will permit in the population and still be willing to use the assessed control risk and/or the amount of monetary misstatements in the transactions established during planning. For example, assume that the auditor decides that TER for attribute 1 in Table 14-2 is 6 percent. That means that the auditor has decided that even if 6 percent of the duplicate sales invoices are not approved for credit, the credit approval control is still effective in terms of the assessed control risk included in the audit plan.

TER is the result of an auditor's judgment. The suitable TER is a question of materiality and is therefore affected by both the definition and the importance of the attribute in the audit plan. For example, if only one internal control is used to support a low control risk assessment for an objective, TER will be lower for this attribute than if there are multiple controls used to support a low control risk assessment for the objective.

TER has a significant impact on sample size. A larger sample size is needed for a low TER than for a high TER. For example, a larger sample is required for a TER of 4 percent for attribute 1 in the previous example than for a TER of 6 percent.

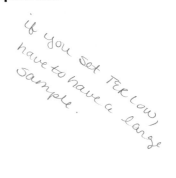
If you set TER low, have to have a large sample.

When a sample is taken, there is a risk that the quantitative conclusions about the population will be incorrect. This is always true unless 100 percent of the population is tested. As has already been stated, this is the case with both nonstatistical and statistical sampling.

For audit sampling in tests of controls and substantive tests of transactions, that risk is called the **acceptable risk of assessing control risk too low (ARACR)**. ARACR is the risk that the auditor is willing to take of accepting a control as effective (or a rate of monetary misstatements as tolerable) when the true population exception rate is greater than TER. ARACR is the auditor's measure of sampling risk. To illustrate, assume that TER is 6 percent, ARACR is 10 percent, and the true population exception rate is 8 percent. The control in this case is not acceptable because the true exception rate of 8 percent exceeds TER. The auditor, of course, does not know the true population exception rate. The ARACR of 10 percent means that the auditor is willing to take a 10 percent risk of concluding that the control is effective after all testing is completed, even when it is ineffective. If the auditor finds the control effective in this illustration, he or she will have overrelied on the system of internal control (used a lower assessed control risk than justified).

In choosing the appropriate ARACR in a situation, the auditor must use his or her best judgment. Because ARACR is a measure of the risk that the auditor is willing to take, the main consideration is the extent to which the auditor plans to reduce assessed control risk as a basis for the extent of tests of details of balances. The lower the assessed control risk, the lower will be the ARACR chosen and the planned extent of tests of details of balances. Referring to Figure 10-7 (p. 314), the most common situation in which audit sampling would be used for tests of controls and substantive tests of transactions is when the auditor decides to assess control risk at a lower level than can be supported by understanding internal control (alternative 3). If the auditor decides to assess control risk at maximum (alternative 1), tests of controls are not performed. If control risk is assessed below maximum, texts of controls must be performed. In some cases, this testing may have already been done as part of procedures to obtain an understanding of internal control.

For nonstatistical sampling, it is common for auditors to use ARACR of high, medium, or low instead of a percentage. A low ARACR implies that the tests of controls are important and would correspond to a low assessed control risk and reduced substantive tests of details of balances.

The auditor can establish different TER and ARACR levels for different attributes of an audit test. For example, it is common for auditors to use higher TER and ARACR levels for tests of credit approval than for tests of the existence of duplicate sales invoices and bills of lading. This is because the exceptions for the latter are likely to have a more direct impact on the correctness of the financial statements than the former.

Tables 14-3 and 14-4 present illustrative guidelines for establishing TER and ARACR. The guidelines should not be interpreted as representing broad professional standards; however, they are typical of the types of guidelines CPA firms issue to their staff.

TABLE 14-3	Guidelines for ARACR and TER for Nonstatistical Sampling: Tests of Controls

Factor	Judgment	Guideline

Assessed control risk. Consider:
    Nature, extent, and timing of substantive tests (extensive planned
        substantive tests relate to higher assessed control risk and vice versa)
    Quality of evidence available for tests of controls (a lower quality
        of evidence available results in a higher assessed control risk and vice versa).
	• Lowest assessed control risk
	• Moderate assessed control risk
	• Higher assessed control risk
	• 100% assessed control risk
		• ARACR of low
		• ARACR of medium
		• ARACR of high
		• ARACR is not applicable

Significance of the transactions and related account balances that the internal controls are intended to affect.	• Highly significant balances • Significant balances • Less significant balances	• TER of 4% • TER of 5% • TER of 6%

Note: The guidelines should recognize that there may be variations in ARACRs based on audit considerations. The guidelines above are the most conservative that should be followed.

TABLE 14-4   Guidelines for ARACR and TER for Nonstatistical Sampling: Substantive Tests of Transactions

Planned Reduction in Substantive Tests of Details of Balances	Results of Understanding Internal Control and Tests of Controls	ARACR for Substantive Tests of Transactions	TER for Substantive Tests of Transactions
Large	Excellent[1] Good Not good	High Medium Low	Percent or amount based on materiality considerations for related accounts
Moderate	Excellent[1] Good Not good	High Medium Medium–low	Percent or amount based on materiality considerations for related accounts
Small[2]	Excellent[1] Good Not good	High Medium–high Medium	Percent or amount based on materiality considerations for related accounts

Note: The guidelines should also recognize that there may be variations in ARACRs based on audit considerations. The guidelines above are the most conservative that should be followed.

[1]In this situation, both internal control and evidence about it are good. Substantive tests of transactions are least likely to be performed in this situation.

[2]In this situation, little emphasis is being placed on internal controls. Neither tests of controls nor substantive tests of transactions are likely in this situation.

An advance estimate of the population exception rate should be made to plan the appropriate sample size. If the **estimated population exception rate (EPER)** is low, a relatively small sample size will satisfy the auditor's tolerable exception rate. This is because a less precise estimate is required. In other words, to be more precise, an estimate of the population exception rate must be based on more data, that is, a larger sample.

It is common to use the results of the preceding year's audit to make this estimate. If prior-year results are not available or if they are considered unreliable, the auditor can take a small preliminary sample of the current year's population for this purpose. It is not critical that the estimate be precise because the current year's sample exception rate is ultimately used to estimate the population characteristics.

Note that if a preliminary sample is used, it can be included in the ultimate sample, as long as appropriate sample selection procedures are followed. For example, assume that an auditor takes a preliminary sample of 30 items to estimate the EPER that considers the entire population. Later, if the auditor decides that a total sample size of 100 is needed, only 70 additional items will need to be properly selected and tested.

Estimate the Population Exception Rate

Four factors determine the **initial sample size** for audit sampling: population size, TER, ARACR, and EPER. Population size is not nearly as significant a factor as the others and typically can be ignored.

An important characteristic of nonstatistical sampling compared with statistical methods is the need to decide the sample size using professional judgment for nonstatistical methods rather than by calculation using a statistical formula. Once the three major factors affecting sample size have been determined, the auditor can decide an initial sample size.

The initial sample size is called that because the exceptions in the actual sample must be evaluated before it is possible to know whether the sample is sufficiently large to achieve the objectives of the tests.

Determine the Initial Sample Size

least → most imp.
Pop. Siz → TER → AARCR → EPER

Sensitivity of Sample Size to a Change in the Factors To properly understand the concepts underlying sampling in auditing, it is helpful to understand the effect of changing any of the four factors that determine sample size while the other factors are held constant. Table 14-5 on page 450 illustrates the effect of increasing each of the four factors; a decrease will have the opposite effect.

TABLE 14-5	Effect on Sample Size of Changing Factors
Type of Change	**Effect on Initial Sample Size**
Increase acceptable risk of assessing control risk too low	Decrease
Increase tolerable exception rate	Decrease
Increase estimated population exception rate	Increase
Increase population size	Increase (minor effect)

A combination of two factors has the greatest effect on sample size: TER minus EPER. The difference is the *precision* of the planned sample estimate. A smaller precision, which is called a more precise estimate, requires a larger sample.

Select the Sample

After the auditor has computed the initial sample size for the audit sampling application, he or she must choose the items in the population to be included in the sample. The sample can be chosen by using any of the probabilistic or nonprobabilistic methods discussed earlier in this chapter. To minimize the possibility of the client altering the sample items, the auditor should not inform the client too far in advance of the sample items selected. The auditor should also control the sample after the client provides the documents.

Perform the Audit Procedures

The auditor performs the audit procedures by examining each item in the sample to determine whether it is consistent with the definition of the attribute and maintains a record of all the exceptions found. When audit procedures have been completed for a sampling application, there will be a sample size and number of exceptions for each attribute. Using the example from Table 14-2 on page 446, there may be a sample size of 125 and 2 exceptions for attribute 1, a sample size of 150 and 3 exceptions for attribute 2, and so on.

Generalize from the Sample to the Population

The **sample exception rate (SER)** can be easily calculated from the actual sample results. SER equals the actual number of exceptions divided by the actual sample size. Continuing the example in the previous paragraph, attribute 1 from Table 14-2 has an SER of 1.6 percent ($2 \div 125$) and attribute 2 has an SER of 2 percent ($3 \div 150$).

It is improper for the auditor to conclude that the population exception rate is exactly the same as the sample exception rate; the chance that they are exactly the same is too small. For nonstatistical methods, there are two ways to generalize from the sample to the population.

1. Add an estimate of sampling error to SER to arrive at a computed upper exception rate (CUER) for a given acceptable risk of assessing control risk too low. It is extremely difficult for auditors to make sampling error estimates using nonstatistical sampling because of the judgment required to do so; therefore, this approach is generally not used.

2. Subtract the sample exception rate from the tolerable exception rate, which is calculated sampling error (TER − SER = calculated sampling error), and evaluate whether calculated sampling error is sufficiently large to indicate the true population exception rate is acceptable. Most auditors using nonstatistical sampling follow this approach. For example, if an auditor takes a sample of 100 items for an attribute and finds no exceptions (SER = 0) and TER is 5 percent, calculated sampling error is 5 percent (TER of 5 percent − SER of 0 = 5 percent). On the other hand, if there had been four exceptions, calculated sampling error would have been 1 percent (TER of 5 percent − SER of 4 percent). It is much more likely that the true population exception rate is less than or equal to the tolerable exception rate in the first case than in the second one. Therefore, most auditors would probably find the population acceptable based on the first sample result and not acceptable based on the second.

In addition, the auditor's consideration of whether sampling error is sufficiently large will depend on sample size. For example, if the sample size in the previous example had been only 20 items, the auditor would have been much less confident that finding no exceptions was an indication that the true population exception rate does not exceed TER.

Note that under this approach, the auditor does not make an estimate of the computed upper exception rate.

Analyze Exceptions

In addition to determining the SER for each attribute and evaluating whether the true but unknown exception rate is likely to exceed the tolerable exception rate, it is necessary to analyze individual exceptions to determine the breakdown in the internal controls that caused them. Exceptions could be caused by carelessness of employees, misunderstood instructions, intentional failure to perform procedures, or many other factors. The nature of an exception and its cause have a significant effect on the qualitative evaluation of the system. For example, if all the exceptions in the tests of internal verification of sales invoices occurred while the person normally responsible for performing the tests was on vacation, this would affect the auditor's evaluation of the internal controls and the subsequent investigation.

Decide the Acceptability of the Population

It was shown under generalizing from the sample to the population that most auditors subtract SER from TER when they use nonstatistical sampling and evaluate whether the difference, which is calculated sampling error, is sufficiently large. If the auditor concludes that the difference is sufficiently large, the control being tested can be used to reduce assessed control risk as planned, provided a careful analysis of the cause of exceptions does not indicate the possibility of other significant problems with internal controls.

When the auditor concludes that TER − SER is too small to conclude that the population is acceptable, the auditor must take specific action. Four courses of action can be followed.

Revise TER or ARACR This alternative should be followed only when the auditor has concluded that the original specifications were too conservative. Relaxing either TER or ARACR may be difficult to defend if the auditor is ever subject to review by a court or a commission. If these requirements are changed, it should be done on the basis of careful thought.

Expand the Sample Size An increase in the sample size has the effect of decreasing the sampling error if the actual sample exception rate does not increase. Of course, SER may also increase or decrease if additional items are selected.

Revise Assessed Control Risk If the results of the tests of controls and substantive tests of transactions do not support the planned assessed control risk, the auditor should revise assessed control risk upward. The effect of the revision is likely to increase substantive tests of transactions and tests of details of balances. For example, if tests of controls of internal verification procedures for verifying prices, extensions, and quantities on sales invoices indicate that those procedures are not being followed, the auditor should increase substantive tests of transactions for the accuracy of sales. If the substantive tests of transactions results are unacceptable, the auditor must increase tests of details of balances for accounts receivable.

The decision whether to increase sample size until sampling error is sufficiently small or to revise assessed control risk must be made on the basis of cost versus benefit. If the sample is not expanded, it is necessary to revise assessed control risk upward and therefore perform additional substantive tests. The cost of additional tests of controls must be compared with that of additional substantive tests. If an expanded sample still continues to produce unacceptable results, additional substantive tests will still be necessary.

If the original test performed is to test transactions for monetary misstatements and an exception rate higher than that assumed is indicated, the response would generally be the same as for tests of controls.

Communicate with the Audit Committee or Management This action is desirable, in combination with one of the other three just described, regardless of the nature of the exceptions. When the auditor determines that the internal controls are not operating effectively, management should be informed. If there is a significant deficiency in the design or operation of internal control, SAS 60 (AU 325) requires the auditor to communicate this reportable condition to the audit committee.

In some instances, it may be acceptable to limit the action to writing a letter to management when TER minus SER is too small. This occurs if the auditor has no intention of reducing the assessed control risk or has already carried out sufficient procedures to his or her own satisfaction as a part of substantive tests of transactions.

Adequate Documentation

It is important that the auditor retain adequate records of the procedures performed, the methods used to select the sample and perform the tests, the results found in the tests, and the conclusions drawn. This is necessary as a means of evaluating the combined results of all tests and as a basis for defending the audit if the need arises. Documentation is equally important for statistical or nonstatistical sampling. An example of the type of documentation commonly found in practice is included in the case illustration for Hillsburg Hardware at the end of this chapter.

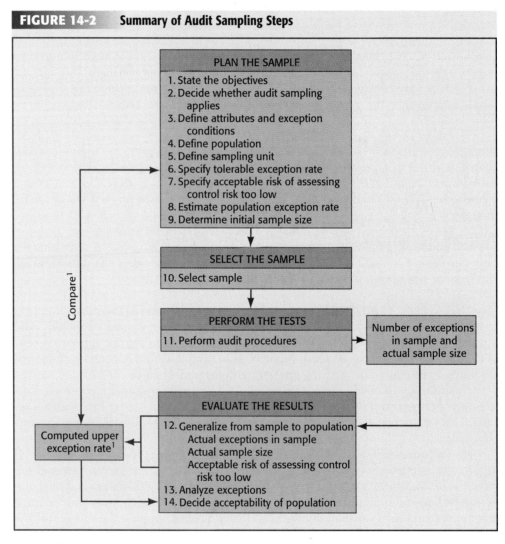

FIGURE 14-2   Summary of Audit Sampling Steps

[1]Many auditors using nonstatistical methods calculate tolerable exception rate minus sample exception rate and evaluate whether the difference is sufficiently large.

All of the steps involved in nonstatistical sampling are summarized in Figure 14-2 (p. 452). Although this figure deals with nonstatistical sampling, the 14 steps in the figure also apply to statistical sampling, which is studied in the next section.

STATISTICAL AUDIT SAMPLING

The statistical sampling method most commonly used for tests of controls and substantive tests of transactions is **attributes sampling**. When the term *attributes sampling* is used in this text, it refers to attributes statistical sampling. Both attributes sampling and nonstatistical sampling have attributes, which are the characteristics being tested for in the population, but attributes sampling is a statistical method.

There are far more similarities than differences in applying attributes sampling instead of nonstatistical sampling to tests of controls and substantive tests of transactions. All 14 steps discussed are used for both approaches, and the terminology is essentially the same. The important differences are the calculation of planned sample sizes using tables developed from statistical probability distributions and the calculation of estimated upper exception rates using similar tables. The quantification of these calculations is an extremely important difference to those auditors who prefer statistical to nonstatistical sampling. Before applying attributes sampling using the same 14 steps already discussed, we will discuss sampling distributions.

SAMPLING DISTRIBUTION

Statistical inferences are based on sampling distributions. A **sampling distribution** is a frequency distribution of the results of all possible samples of a specified size that could be obtained from a population containing some specific parameters. The existence of a sampling distribution allows the auditor to make probability statements about the likely degree of representativeness of any sample that is a member of that distribution.

Attributes sampling is based on the binomial distribution. The binomial distribution is a distribution of all possible samples where the items in the population each have one of two possible states, for example, yes/no, black/white, or control deviation/no control deviation.

Assume that a population of sales invoices exists, 5 percent of which have no shipping documents attached as required by the client's internal controls. If the auditor takes a sample of 50 sales invoices, how many will he or she find that have no shipping documents? The sample could contain no exceptions, or it might contain six or seven. A binomial-based sampling distribution would tell us the probability of each possible number of exceptions occurring. The sampling distribution for the example population is shown in Table 14-6 (p. 454). This distribution shows that, with a sample of 50 items from a very large population with an exception rate of 5 percent, the likelihood of obtaining a sample with at least one exception is 92.31 percent $(1 - .0769)$. (Because the probability of no exceptions is 7.69%, the probability of more than 0 is 92.31%.)

There is a unique sampling distribution for each population exception rate and sample size. The distribution for a sample size of 100 from a population with a 5 percent exception rate is different from the previous one, as is the distribution for a sample of 50 from a population with a 3 percent exception rate.

In actual audit situations, auditors do not take repeated samples from known populations. They take one sample from an unknown population and get a specific number of exceptions in that sample. But knowledge about sampling distributions enables auditors to make statistical statements about the population. For example, if the auditor selects a sample of 50 sales invoices to test for attached shipping documents and finds one exception, the auditor could examine the probability table in Table 14-6 and know there is a 20.25 percent probability that the sample came from a population with a 5 percent exception rate,

TABLE 14-6	Probability of Each Exception Rate—5% Population Exception Rate and Sample Size of 50		
Number of Exceptions	Percentage of Exception	Probability	Cumulative Probability
0	0	.0769	.0769
1	2	.2025	.2794
2	4	.2611	.5405
3	6	.2199	.7604
4	8	.1360	.8964
5	10	.0656	.9620
6	12	.0260	.9880
7	14	.0120	1.0000

and a 79.75 percent $(1 - .2025)$ probability that the sample was taken from a population having some other exception rate. It is also possible to state by examining the cumulative probabilities column in Table 14-6 that there is a 27.94 percent probability that the sample came from a population with *more* than a 5 percent exception rate, and a 72.06 percent $(1 - .2794)$ probability that the sample was taken from a population having an exception rate of 5 percent or less. Because it is similarly possible to calculate the probability distributions for other population exception rates, these can be examined in the aggregate to draw more specific statistical conclusions about the unknown population being sampled. These sampling distributions are the basis for the tables used by auditors for attributes sampling.

APPLICATION OF ATTRIBUTES SAMPLING

OBJECTIVE 14-7
Use attributes sampling in tests of controls and substantive tests of transactions.

As already stated, the 14 steps discussed for nonstatistical sampling are equally applicable to attributes sampling. This section focuses on the differences between the two.

Plan the Sample

1. *State the objectives of the audit test.* Same for attributes and nonstatistical sampling.
2. *Decide whether audit sampling applies.* Same for attributes and nonstatistical sampling.
3. *Define attributes and exception conditions.* Same for attributes and nonstatistical sampling.
4. *Define the population.* Same for attributes and nonstatistical sampling.
5. *Define the sampling unit.* Same for attributes and nonstatistical sampling.
6. *Specify the tolerable exception rate.* Same for attributes and nonstatistical sampling.
7. *Specify acceptable risk of assessing control risk too low.*

The concepts of specifying this risk are the same for both statistical and nonstatistical sampling, but the method of quantification is usually different. For nonstatistical sampling, most auditors use low, medium, or high acceptable risk, whereas auditors using attributes sampling assign a specific amount such as 10 percent or 5 percent risk. The reason for the difference is the need to quantify risk when auditors plan to determine sample size and evaluate results statistically.

8. *Estimate the population exception rate.* Same for attributes and nonstatistical sampling.
9. *Determine the initial sample size.*

Four factors determine the initial sample size for both statistical and nonstatistical sampling: population size, TER, ARACR, and EPER. The difference is that special computer programs or tables developed from statistical formulas are used to determine the sample size for attributes sampling. Tables are used to illustrate determining the sample size. Determining binomial probabilities using computers is not discussed because the software required is complex.

Other Industries Using Sampling

The two tables that make up Table 14-7 (p. 456) are taken from the AICPA *Audit Sampling Guide.* They are the same, except that the first one is for a 5 percent ARACR and the second one a 10 percent ARACR. These tables are "one-sided tables," which means that they represent the *upper* exception rate for a given ARACR.

Use of the Tables Use of the tables to determine initial sample size involves four steps:

1. Select the table corresponding to the ARACR.
2. Locate the TER at the top of the table.
3. Locate the EPER in the far left column.
4. Read down the appropriate TER column until it intersects with the appropriate EPER row. The number at the intersection is the initial sample size.

To illustrate, assume that an auditor is willing to reduce assessed control risk for credit approval if the rate of missing credit approvals in the population (attribute 1 in Table 14-2) does not exceed 6 percent (TER), at a 5 percent ARACR. On the basis of past experience, EPER is set at 2 percent. Use the 5 percent ARACR table, locate the 6 percent TER column, and read down to where the column intersects with the 2 percent EPER row. The initial sample size is determined to be 127.

Is 127 a large enough sample size for this audit? It is not possible to say until after the tests have been performed. If the actual exception rate in the sample turns out to be greater than 2 percent, the auditor will be unsure of the effectiveness of the internal controls. The reasons for this will become apparent as we proceed.

Effect of Population Size In the preceding discussion, the size of the population was ignored in determining the initial sample size. It may seem strange to some readers, but statistical theory proves that in most types of populations to which attributes sampling applies, the population size is a minor consideration in determining sample size. This is true because representativeness is ensured by the sample selection process more than by sample size. Once a sample is obtained that includes a good cross section of items, additional items are not needed. Because most auditors use attributes sampling for reasonably large populations, the reduction of sample size for smaller populations is ignored here.

Select the Sample and Perform the Audit Procedures

10. *Select the sample.* The only difference in sample selection for statistical and nonstatistical sampling is the requirement that probabilistic methods must be used for statistical sampling. Either simple random or systematic sampling is used for attributes sampling.
11. *Perform the audit procedures.* Same for attributes and nonstatistical sampling.

Evaluate the Results

12. *Generalize from the sample to the population.* For attributes sampling, the auditor calculates an upper precision limit (CUER) at a specified ARACR, again using special computer programs or tables developed from statistical formulas. To illustrate the calculations, tables such as the one for a 5 percent ARACR in Table 14-8 (p. 457) are used. These tables are consistent with those used to determine the initial sample size but are in a form more convenient for sample evaluation.

TABLE 14-7 Determining Sample Size for Attributes Sampling

5 PERCENT ARACR *tolerate 5% error when done w/ Stat. work* (handwritten)

Estimated Population Exception Rate (in Percentage)	Tolerable Exception Rate (in Percentage)										
	2	3	4	5	6	7	8	9	10	15	20
0.00	149	99	74	59	49	42	36	32	29	19	14
0.25	236	157	117	93	78	66	58	51	46	30	22
0.50	*	157	117	93	78	66	58	51	46	30	22
0.75	*	208	117	93	78	66	58	51	46	30	22
1.00	*	*	156	93	78	66	58	51	46	30	22
1.25	*	*	156	124	78	66	58	51	46	30	22
1.50	*	*	192	124	103	66	58	51	46	30	22
1.75	*	*	227	153	103	88	77	51	46	30	22
2.00	*	*	*	181	127	88	77	68	46	30	22
2.25	*	*	*	208	127	88	77	68	61	30	22
2.50	*	*	*	*	150	109	77	68	61	30	22
2.75	*	*	*	*	173	109	95	68	61	30	22
3.00	*	*	*	*	195	129	95	84	61	30	22
3.25	*	*	*	*	*	148	112	84	61	30	22
3.50	*	*	*	*	*	167	112	84	76	40	22
3.75	*	*	*	*	*	185	129	100	76	40	22
4.00	*	*	*	*	*	*	146	100	89	40	22
5.00	*	*	*	*	*	*	*	158	116	40	30
6.00	*	*	*	*	*	*	*	*	179	50	30
7.00	*	*	*	*	*	*	*	*	*	68	37

10 PERCENT ARACR *tolerate 10% error when doing Stat. work* (handwritten)

Estimated Population Exception Rate (in Percentage)	2	3	4	5	6	7	8	9	10	15	20
0.00	114	76	57	45	38	32	28	25	22	15	11
0.25	194	129	96	77	64	55	48	42	38	25	18
0.50	194	129	96	77	64	55	48	42	38	25	18
0.75	265	129	96	77	64	55	48	42	38	25	18
1.00	*	176	96	77	64	55	48	42	38	25	18
1.25	*	221	132	77	64	55	48	42	38	25	18
1.50	*	*	132	105	64	55	48	42	38	25	18
1.75	*	*	166	105	88	55	48	42	38	25	18
2.00	*	*	198	132	88	75	48	42	38	25	18
2.25	*	*	*	132	88	75	65	42	38	25	18
2.50	*	*	*	158	110	75	65	58	38	25	18
2.75	*	*	*	209	132	94	65	58	52	25	18
3.00	*	*	*	*	132	94	65	58	52	25	18
3.25	*	*	*	*	153	113	82	58	52	25	18
3.50	*	*	*	*	194	113	82	73	52	25	18
3.75	*	*	*	*	*	131	98	73	52	25	18
4.00	*	*	*	*	*	149	98	73	65	25	18
4.50	*	*	*	*	*	218	130	87	65	34	18
5.00	*	*	*	*	*	*	160	115	78	34	18
5.50	*	*	*	*	*	*	*	142	103	34	18
6.00	*	*	*	*	*	*	*	182	116	45	25
7.00	*	*	*	*	*	*	*	*	199	52	25
7.50	*	*	*	*	*	*	*	*	*	52	25
8.00	*	*	*	*	*	*	*	*	*	60	25
8.50	*	*	*	*	*	*	*	*	*	68	32

*Sample is too large to be cost-effective for most audit applications.
Notes: 1. This table assumes a large population. 2. Sample sizes are the same in certain columns even when estimated population exception rates differ, because of the method of constructing the tables. Sample sizes are calculated for attributes sampling by using the expected number of exceptions in the population, but auditors can deal more conveniently with estimated population exception rates. For example, in the 15 percent column for tolerable exception rate, at an ARACR of 5 percent, the initial sample size for most EPERs is 30. One exception, divided by a sample size of 30, is 3.3 percent. Therefore, for all EPERs greater than zero but less than 3.3 percent, the initial sample size is the same.

TABLE 14-8   Evaluating Sample Results Using Attributes Sampling

(handwritten note at top right: 95% sure Rate is ↓ rate or lower in true popul.)

5 PERCENT ARACR

Sample Size	Actual Number of Exceptions Found										
	0	1	2	3	4	5	6	7	8	9	10
25	11.3	17.6	*	*	*	*	*	*	*	*	*
30	9.5	14.9	19.5	*	*	*	*	*	*	*	*
35	8.2	12.9	16.9	*	*	*	*	*	*	*	*
40	7.2	11.3	14.9	18.3	*	*	*	*	*	*	*
45	6.4	10.1	13.3	16.3	19.2	*	*	*	*	*	*
50	5.8	9.1	12.1	14.8	17.4	19.9	*	*	*	*	*
55	5.3	8.3	11.0	13.5	15.9	18.1	*	*	*	*	*
60	4.9	7.7	10.1	12.4	14.6	16.7	18.8	*	*	*	*
65	4.5	7.1	9.4	11.5	13.5	15.5	17.4	19.3	*	*	*
70	4.2	6.6	8.7	10.7	12.6	14.4	16.2	18.0	19.7	*	*
75	3.9	6.2	8.2	10.0	11.8	13.5	15.2	16.9	18.4	20.0	*
80	3.7	5.8	7.7	9.4	11.1	12.7	14.3	15.8	17.3	18.8	*
90	3.3	5.2	6.8	8.4	9.9	11.3	12.7	14.1	15.5	16.8	18.1
100	3.0	4.7	6.2	7.6	8.9	10.2	11.5	12.7	14.0	15.2	16.4
125	2.4	3.7	4.9	6.1	7.2	8.2	9.3	10.3	11.3	12.2	13.2
150	2.0	3.1	4.1	5.1	6.0	6.9	7.7	8.6	9.4	10.2	11.0
200	1.5	2.3	3.1	3.8	4.5	5.2	5.8	6.5	7.1	7.7	8.3

(handwritten annotation near column 6-7: (CUER) as perc.)

10 PERCENT ARACR

Sample Size	Actual Number of Exceptions Found										
	0	1	2	3	4	5	6	7	8	9	10
20	10.9	18.1	*	*	*	*	*	*	*	*	*
25	8.8	14.7	19.9	*	*	*	*	*	*	*	*
30	7.4	12.4	16.8	*	*	*	*	*	*	*	*
35	6.4	10.7	14.5	18.1	*	*	*	*	*	*	*
40	5.6	9.4	12.8	15.9	19.0	*	*	*	*	*	*
45	5.0	8.4	11.4	14.2	17.0	19.6	*	*	*	*	*
50	4.5	7.6	10.3	12.9	15.4	17.8	*	*	*	*	*
55	4.1	6.9	9.4	11.7	14.0	16.2	18.4	*	*	*	*
60	3.8	6.3	8.6	10.8	12.9	14.9	16.9	18.8	*	*	*
70	3.2	5.4	7.4	9.3	11.1	12.8	14.6	16.2	17.9	19.5	*
80	2.8	4.8	6.5	8.3	9.7	11.3	12.8	14.3	15.7	17.2	18.6
90	2.5	4.3	5.8	7.3	8.7	10.1	11.4	12.7	14.0	15.3	16.6
100	2.3	3.8	5.2	6.6	7.8	9.1	10.3	11.5	12.7	13.8	15.0
120	1.9	3.2	4.4	5.5	6.6	7.6	8.6	9.6	10.6	11.6	12.5
160	1.4	2.4	3.3	4.1	4.9	5.7	6.5	7.2	8.0	8.7	9.5
200	1.1	1.9	2.6	3.3	4.0	4.6	5.2	5.8	6.4	7.0	7.6

(handwritten annotation near column 7: CUER as perc.)

*More than 20 percent.

Note: This table presents computed upper exception rates as percentages. Table assumes a large population.

(handwritten note on right margin: Computed upper exception rate – net perception rate high. CUER ≤ TER. If CUER ≤ TER stating by)

Audit Software
and Statistical Sampling

Use of the Tables Use of tables to compute CUER involves four steps:

1. Select the table corresponding to the ARACR. This ARACR should be the same as the ARACR used for determining the initial sample size.
2. Locate the actual number of exceptions found in the audit tests at the top of the table.
3. Locate the actual sample size in the far left column.
4. Read down the appropriate actual number of exceptions column until it intersects with the appropriate sample size row. The number at the intersection is the CUER.

To illustrate the use of the evaluation table, assume an actual sample size of 125 and 2 exceptions in attribute 1. Using an ARACR of 5 percent, CUER equals 4.9 percent. Stated another way, the result is that the CUER for attribute 1 is 4.9 percent at a 5 percent ARACR. Does this mean that if 100 percent of the population were tested, the true exception rate would be 4.9 percent? No, the true exception rate is unknown. The result means that if the auditor concludes that the true exception rate does not exceed 4.9 percent, there is a 95 percent chance that the conclusion is right and a 5 percent chance that it is wrong.

It is possible to have a sample size that is not equal to those provided for in the attributes sampling evaluation tables. When this occurs, it is common to interpolate.

These tables assume a very large (infinite) population size, which results in a more conservative CUER than for smaller populations. Because the effect of population size on sample size is typically very small, it is ignored.

13. *Analyze exceptions.* Same for attributes and nonstatistical sampling.
14. *Decide the acceptability of the population.*

The methodology for deciding the acceptability of the population is essentially the same for attributes and nonstatistical sampling. For attributes sampling, the auditor compares CUER with TER for each attribute.

Before the population can be considered acceptable, the CUER determined on the basis of the actual sample results must be *less than or equal to* TER when both are based on ARACR. In the example just given, in which the auditor has specified that he or she would accept a 6 percent population exception rate at a 5 percent ARACR and the CUER was 4.9 percent, the requirements of the sample have been met. In this case, the control being tested can be used to reduce assessed control risk as planned, provided a careful analysis of the cause of exceptions does not indicate the possibility of a significant problem in an aspect of the control not previously considered.

When the CUER is greater than the TER, it is necessary to take specific action. The four courses of action discussed for nonstatistical sampling are equally applicable to attributes sampling.

Need for Professional Judgment

A criticism occasionally leveled against statistical sampling is that it reduces the use of professional judgment. A comparison of the 14 steps discussed in this chapter for nonstatistical and attributes sampling shows how unwarranted this criticism is. For proper application of attributes sampling, it is necessary to use professional judgment in most of the steps. For example, selection of the initial sample size depends primarily on the TER, ARACR, and EPER. Choosing the first two requires the exercise of high-level professional judgment; the latter requires a careful estimate. Similarly, the final evaluation of the adequacy of the entire application of attributes sampling, including the adequacy of the sample size, must also be based on high-level professional judgment.

CASE ILLUSTRATION—HILLSBURG HARDWARE, PART II

To illustrate the concepts discussed in this chapter, the Hillsburg Hardware Co. case from Chapter 13 is extended to include determination of sample size, selection of items for testing, and the conclusions drawn on the basis of the results of the tests using attributes

TABLE 14-9   Audit Procedures

Procedure	Comment
Shipment of Goods	
10. Account for a sequence of shipping documents.	It is possible to do this by selecting a random sample and accounting for all shipping documents selected. This requires a separate set of random numbers because the sampling unit is different from that used for the other tests.
11. Trace selected shipping documents to the sales journal to be sure that each one has been included.	No exceptions are expected, and a 6 percent TER is considered acceptable at an ARACR of 10 percent. A sample size of 38 is selected using Table 14-7 on page 456. The shipping documents are traced to the sales journal. This is done for all 38 items. There are no exceptions for either test. The results are considered acceptable. There is no further information about this portion of the tests in this illustration.
Billing of Customers and Recording the Sales in the Records	
12. Account for a sequence of sales invoices in the sales journal.	The audit procedures for billing and recording sales (procedures 12 to 14) are the only ones tested by using attributes sampling for this case illustration. The attributes sampling data sheet includes each of these procedures as attributes. For audit procedure 12, a random sample of sales invoices is a test of the sequence of sales invoices.

13. Trace selected sales invoice numbers from the sales journal to
   a. accounts receivable master file and test for amount, date, and invoice number.
   b. duplicate sales invoice and check for the total amount recorded in the journal, date, customer name, and account classification. Check the pricing, extensions, and footings. Examine underlying documents for indication of internal verification by Pam Dilley.
   c. bill of lading and test for customer name, product description, quantity, and date.
   d. duplicate sales order and test for customer name, product description, quantity, date, and indication of internal verification by Pam Dilley.
   e. customer order and test for customer name, product description, quantity, date, and credit approval by Rick Chulick.	

14. Trace recorded sales from the sales journal to the file of supporting documents, which includes a duplicate sales invoice, bill of lading, sales order, and customer order.	

Note: Random selection and statistical sampling are not applicable for the nine general audit procedures in Figure 13-9. Advanced statistical techniques, such as regression analysis, could be applicable for analysis of the results of analytical procedures. Random selection could be used for procedure 3.

sampling (see p. 423). The only parts of the tests of the sales and collection cycle included here are tests of credit approval, shipment of goods, billing of customers, and recording the amounts in the records. It should be kept in mind that the procedures for Hillsburg Hardware Co. were developed specifically for that client and would probably not be applicable for a different audit. The audit procedures for these tests are repeated in Table 14-9 along with comments to indicate the relationship of each procedure to attributes sampling.

In applying attributes sampling to the procedures for Hillsburg Hardware Co. (see Figure 13-9 on p. 423), there are only two functions for which attributes sampling is being used: shipment of goods and billing of customers. Emphasis is placed on the billing of customers in the illustration because the duplicate sales invoice is the sampling unit for most of the audit procedures. To concentrate on the attributes sampling applications for the billing

OBJECTIVE 14-8

Apply sampling concepts and methodology to the audit plan for the sales and collection cycle.

function, comments about the shipping function are restricted to those shown adjacent to the list of audit procedures in the table. The reader should recognize, however, that the attributes sampling methodology followed for the shipping function would be essentially the same as the methodology illustrated for the billing function in the remainder of the case.

Objectives, Deciding Whether Audit Sampling Applies, Population, and Sampling Unit

Most auditors use some type of preprinted form to document each attributes sampling application. An example of a commonly used form is given in Figure 14-3. The top part of the form includes a definition of the objective, the population, and the sampling unit.

The note on the bottom of Table 14-9 (p. 459) indicates that audit sampling does not apply to audit procedures 1 through 9 in Figure 13-9. Audit sampling can be applied to audit procedures 10 through 14.

Define the Attributes of Interest

The attributes used in this application are taken directly from the audit program. The procedures that can be used as attributes for a specific application of attributes sampling depend on the definition of the sampling unit. In this case, all the procedures in the billing function can be included. The nine attributes used for this case are listed in Figure 14-3.

The definition of the attribute is a critical part of attributes sampling. The decision as to which attributes to combine and which ones to keep separate is the most important aspect of the definition. If all possible types of attributes, such as customer name, date, price, and quantity, are separated for each procedure, the large number of attributes makes the problem unmanageable. However, if all the procedures are combined into one or two attributes, greatly dissimilar exceptions are evaluated together. Somewhere in between is a reasonable compromise.

Establish TER, ARACR, EPER, and Determine Initial Sample Size

The TER for each attribute is decided on the basis of the auditor's judgment of what exception rate is material. The failure to record a sales invoice would be highly significant, especially considering this system; therefore, as indicated in Figure 14-3, the lowest TER (3 percent) is chosen for attribute 1. The incorrect billing of the customer represents potentially significant misstatements, but no misstatement is likely to be for the full amount of the invoice. As a result, a 4 percent TER is chosen for each of the attributes directly related to the billing of shipments and recording the amounts in the records. The last four attributes have higher TERs because they are of less importance for the audit.

An ARACR of 10 percent is chosen because the potential for reducing assessed control risk is limited even if the internal controls tested are proven effective, due to several internal control weaknesses.

The estimated population exception rate is based on previous years' results, modified upward slightly to account for the change in personnel. Initial sample size for each attribute is determined from Table 14-7 on the basis of the above considerations. This information is summarized for all attributes in Figure 14-3. For convenience in selection and evaluation, the auditor decided to select a sample of 75 for attribute 1, 100 for attributes 2 through 5, 65 for attributes 6 and 9, and 50 for the other two.

Select the Sample

The random selection for the Hillsburg case is straightforward except for the need for different sample sizes for different attributes. This problem can be overcome by selecting a random sample of 50 for use on all nine attributes followed by another sample of 15 for all attributes except attributes 7 and 8, an additional 10 for attribute 1, and 25 more for attributes 2 through 5. Figure 14-1 on page 443 illustrates the selection of the first sample of 50 items for Hillsburg Hardware using computer generation of random numbers.

Perform the Audit Procedures and Generalize to the Population

The audit procedures that are included in the audit program and summarized in the attributes sampling data sheet must be carefully performed for every item in the sample. As a means of documenting the tests and providing information for review, it is common to include a worksheet of the results. Some auditors prefer to include a worksheet containing a listing of all items in the sample; others prefer to limit the documentation to identifying the exceptions. This latter approach is followed in Figure 14-4 on page 462.

FIGURE 14-3   **Attributes Sampling Data Sheet: Attributes**

Client: Hillsburg Hardware   **Year-end:** 12/31/99
Audit Area: Tests of Controls and Substantive Tests of Transactions—   **Pop. size:** 5,764
Billing Function

Define the objective(s): Examine duplicate sales invoices and related documents to determine whether the system has functioned as intended and as described in the audit program.

Define the population precisely (including stratification, if any): Sales invoices for the period 1/1/99 to 12/31/99. First invoice number = 3689. Last invoice number = 9452.

Define the sampling unit, organization of population items, and random selection procedures: Sales invoice number, recorded in the sales journal sequentially; computer generation of random numbers.

Description of attributes	Planned Audit				Actual Results			
	EPER	TER	ARACR	Initial sample size	Sample size	Number of exceptions	Sample exception rate	CUER
1. Existence of the sales invoice number in the sales journal (procedure 12).	0	3	10	76				
2. Amount and other data in the master file agree with sales journal entry (procedure 13a).	1	4	10	96				
3. Amount and other data on the duplicate sales invoice agree with the sales journal entry (procedure 13b).	1	4	10	96				
4. Evidence that pricing, extensions, and footings are checked (initials and correct amount) (procedure 13b).	1	4	10	96				
5. Quantity and other data on the bill of lading agree with the duplicate sales invoice and sales journal (procedure 13c).	1	4	10	96				
6. Quantity and other data on the sales order agree with the duplicate sales invoice (procedure 13d).	1	6	10	64				
7. Quantity and other data on the customer order agree with the duplicate sales invoice (procedure 13e).	2	8	10	48				
8. Credit is approved by Rick Chulick (procedure 13e).	2	8	10	48				
9. The file of supporting documents includes a duplicate sales invoice, bill of lading, sales order, and customer order (procedure 14).	1	6	10	64				

Intended use of sampling results:

1. Effect on Audit Plan:

2. Recommendations to Management:

At the completion of the testing, the exceptions are tabulated to determine the number of exceptions in the sample for each attribute. This enables the auditor to compute the sample exception rate and determine the CUER from the tables. This information is summarized in Figure 14-5 (p. 463).

Analyze Exceptions

The final part of the application consists of analyzing the exceptions to determine their cause and drawing conclusions about each attribute tested. For every attribute for which CUER exceeds TER, it is essential that some conclusion concerning follow-up action be reached and documented. The exception analysis and conclusions reached are illustrated in Figure 14-6 (p. 464) and summarized at the bottom of the data sheet in Figure 14-5 (p. 463).

FIGURE 14-4   Inspection of Sample Items for Attributes

CLIENT: Hillsburg Hardware INSPECTION OF SAMPLE ITEMS FOR ATTRIBUTES YEAR-END: DECEMBER 31, 1999	Prepared by	MSW
	Date	2/3/00

Identity of Item Selected	Attributes								X = Exception		
Invoice no.	1	2	3	4	5	6	7	8	9	10	11
3787					X						
3924				X				X			
3990				X							
4058		X		X							
4117								X			
4222					X						
4488								X			
4635				X	X						
4955						X		X			
4969				X							
5101								X			
5166								X			
5419								X			
5832								X			
5890								X			
6157		X		X							
6229				X							
6376								X			
6635					X						
7127				X							
8338								X			
8871				X							
9174								X			
9371				X							
No. Exceptions	0	2	0	10	4	1	0	12	0		
Sample Size	75	100	100	100	100	65	50	50	65		

Update the Evidence Planning Worksheet

After completing tests of controls and substantive tests of transactions, the auditor should complete rows three through seven of the evidence planning worksheet. This worksheet is illustrated for Hillsburg Hardware in Figure 14-7 on page 465.

Recall that rows one and two were completed in an earlier chapter. Rows three through five document control risk for sales, cash receipts, and additional controls. The control risk assessments in Figure 14-7 are the same as the planned assessments in the control risk matrices for Hillsburg Hardware on pages 418 and 419, with the following modifications:

- Control risk is high for the accuracy objective for sales because of the unsatisfactory results for attribute 4 (procedure 13b).
- Control risk is high for the realizable value objective for sales based on the results for attribute 8 (procedure 13e).

FIGURE 14-5 **Attributes Sampling Data Sheet: Attributes**

Client: Hillsburg Hardware
Audit Area: Tests of Controls and Substantive Tests of Transactions—
Billing Function

Year-end: 12/31/99
Pop. size: 5,764

Define the objective(s): Examine duplicate sales invoices and related documents to determine whether the system has functioned as intended and as described in the audit program.

Define the population precisely (including stratification, if any): Sales invoices for the period 1/1/99 to 12/31/99. First invoice number = 3689. Last invoice number = 9452.

Define the sampling unit, organization of population items, and random selection procedures: Sales invoice number, recorded in the sales journal sequentially; computer generation of random numbers.

Description of attributes	Planned Audit				Actual Results			
	EPER	TER	ARACR	Initial sample size	Sample size	Number of exceptions	Sample exception rate	CUER
1. Existence of the sales invoice number in the sales journal (procedure 12).	0	3	10	76	75	0	0	3.0
2. Amount and other data in the master file agree with sales journal entry (procedure 13a).	1	4	10	96	100	2	2	5.2
3. Amount and other data on the sales invoice agree with the sales journal entry (procedure 13b).	1	4	10	96	100	0	0	2.3
4. Evidence that pricing extensions and footings are checked (initials and correct amount) (procedure 13b).	1	4	10	96	100	10	10	15.0
5. Quantity and other data on the bill of lading agree with the duplicate sales invoice and sales journal (procedure 13c).	1	4	10	96	100	4	4	7.8
6. Quantity and other data on the sales order agree with the duplicate sales invoice (procedure 13d).	1	6	10	64	65	1	1.5	5.9
7. Quantity and other data on the customer order agree with the duplicate sales invoice (procedure 13e).	2	8	10	48	50	0	0	4.5
8. Credit is approved by Rick Chulick (procedure 13e).	2	8	10	48	50	12	24	.20
9. The file of supporting documents includes a duplicate sales invoice, bill of lading, sales order, and customer order (procedure 14).	1	6	10	64	65	0	0	3.5

Intended use of sampling results:

1. Effect on Audit Plan: Controls tested through attributes 1, 3, 6, 7, and 9 can be viewed as operating effectively. Additional emphasis is needed in confirmation, allowance for uncollectible accounts, cutoff tests, and price tests due to results of tests for attributes 2, 4, 5, and 8.

2. Recommendations to Management: Each of the exceptions should be discussed with management. Specific recommendations are needed to correct the internal verification of sales invoices and to improve the approach to credit approvals.

- Recall that the existence (completeness) objective for cash receipts relates to the completeness (existence) objective for accounts receivable.

Finally, note in Figure 14-7 that all substantive tests of transactions results were satisfactory except for the accuracy and cutoff objectives for sales. The substantive tests of transactions results for the accuracy objective were only fair because of exceptions found for attribute 2 (procedure 13a). Results were unacceptable for the cutoff objective because of unsatisfactory results for attribute 5 (procedure 13c).

FIGURE 14-6 **Analysis of Exceptions**

CLIENT: Hillsburg Hardware
ANALYSIS OF EXCEPTIONS **Prepared by:** MSW
YEAR-END: December 31, 1999 **Date:** 2/3/00

Attribute	Number of exceptions	Nature of exceptions	Effect on the audit and other comments
2	2	Both errors were posted to the wrong account and were still outstanding after several months. The amounts were for $125\frac{00}{}$ and $395\frac{00}{}$.	Because the upper exception rate is greater than TER, additional substantive work is needed. Perform expanded confirmation procedures and review older uncollected balances thoroughly.
4	10	In 6 cases there were no initials for internal verification. In 2 cases the wrong price was used but the errors were under $10 in each case. In 1 case there was a pricing error of $1,000. In 1 case freight was not charged. (Three of the last 4 exceptions had initials for internal verification.)	As a result, have independent client personnel recheck a random sample of 500 duplicate sales invoices under our control. Also, expand the confirmation of accounts receivable.
5	4	In each case the date on the duplicate sales invoice was several days later than the shipping date.	Do extensive tests of the sales cutoff by comparing recorded sales with the shipping documents.
6	1	Just 106 items were shipped and billed though the sales order was for 112 items. The reason for the difference was an error in the perpetual inventory master file. The perpetuals indicated that 112 items were on hand, when there were actually 106. The system does not backorder for undershipments smaller than 25%.	No expansion of tests of controls or substantive tests. The system appears to be working effectively.
8	12	Credit was not approved. Four of these were for new customers. Discussed with Chulick, who stated his busy schedule did not permit approving all sales.	Expand the year-end procedures extensively in evaluating allowance for uncollectible accounts. This includes scheduling of cash receipts subsequent to year-end and for all outstanding accounts receivable to determine collectibility at year-end.

FIGURE 14-7 **Evidence Planning Worksheet to Decide Tests of Details of Balances for Hillsburg Hardware Co.– Accounts Receivable**

	Detail tie-in	Existence	Completeness	Accuracy	Classification	Cutoff	Realizable value	Rights	Presentation and disclosure
Acceptable audit risk	High	High	High	High	High	High	High	High	High
Inherent risk	Low	Low	Low	Low	Low	Low	Medium	Low	Low
Control risk—Sales	Low	Medium	Low	High	Low	High	High	Not applicable	Not applicable
Control risk—Cash receipts	Medium	High	Low	Low	High	High	Not applicable	Not applicable	Not applicable
Control risk—Additional controls	None	None	None	None	None	None	None	Low	Low
Substantive tests of transactions—Sales	Good results	Good results	Good results	Fair results	Good results	Unacceptable results	Not applicable	Not applicable	Not applicable
Substantive tests of transactions—Cash receipts	Good results	Good results	Good results	Good results	Good results	Good results	Not applicable	Not applicable	Not applicable
Analytical procedures									
Planned detection risk for tests of details of balances									
Planned audit evidence for tests of details of balances									

Tolerable misstatement $22,000

ESSENTIAL TERMS

Acceptable risk of assessing control risk too low (ARACR)—the risk that the auditor is willing to take of accepting a control as effective or a rate of monetary misstatements as tolerable, when the true population exception rate is greater than the tolerable exception rate

Attribute—the characteristic being tested for in the population

Attributes sampling—a statistical, probabilistic method of sample evaluation that results in an estimate of the proportion of items in a population containing a characteristic or attribute of interest.

Audit sampling—testing less than 100 percent of a population for the purpose of making inferences about that population

Block sample selection—a nonprobabilistic method of sample selection in which items are selected in measured sequences

Computed upper exception rate (CUER)—the upper limit of probable population exception rate; the highest exception rate in the population at a given ARACR

Directed sample selection—a nonprobabilistic method of sample selection in which each item in the sample is selected based on some judgmental criteria established by the auditor

Estimated population exception rate (EPER)—exception rate the auditor expects to find in the population before testing begins

Exception rate—the percentage of items in a population that include exceptions in prescribed controls or monetary correctness

Haphazard sample selection—a nonprobabilistic method of sample selection in which items are chosen without regard to their size, source, or other distinguishing characteristics

Initial sample size—sample size determined by professional judgment (nonstatistical sampling) or by statistical tables (attributes sampling)

Judgmental sampling—use of professional judgment rather than probabilistic methods to select sample items for audit tests

Nonprobabilistic sample selection—a method of sample selection in which the auditor uses professional judgment to select items from the population

Nonsampling risk—the risk that the auditor fails to identify existing exceptions in the sample; nonsampling risk (nonsampling error) is caused by failure to recognize exceptions and by inappropriate or ineffective audit procedures

Nonstatistical sampling—the auditor's use of professional judgment to select sample items, estimate the population values, and estimate sampling risk

Occurrence rate—the ratio of items in a population that contain a specific attribute to the total number of population items

Probabilistic sample selection—a method of selecting a sample such that each population item has a known probability of being included in the sample and the sample is selected by a random process

Random number table—a listing of independent random digits conveniently arranged in tabular form to facilitate the selection of random numbers with multiple digits

Random sample—a sample in which every possible combination of elements in the population has an equal chance of constituting the sample

Representative sample—a sample whose characteristics are the same as those of the population

Sample exception rate (SER)—number of exceptions in the sample divided by the sample size

Sampling distribution—a frequency distribution of the results of all possible samples of a specified size that could be obtained from a population containing some specific parameters

Sampling risk—the chance of exception inherent in tests of less than the entire population; sampling risk may be reduced by using an increased sample size and using an appropriate method of selecting sample items from the population

Statistical sampling—the use of mathematical measurement techniques to calculate formal statistical results and quantify sampling risk

Systematic sample selection—a probabilistic method of sampling in which the auditor calculates an interval (the population size divided by the number of sample items desired) and selects the items for the sample based on the size of the interval and a randomly selected starting point between zero and the length of the interval

Tolerable exception rate (TER)—the exception rate that the auditor will permit in the population and still be willing to use the assessed control risk and/or the amount of monetary misstatements in the transactions established during planning

REVIEW QUESTIONS

14-1 (Objective 14-1)   State what is meant by a representative sample and explain its importance in sampling audit populations.

14-2 (Objective 14-2)   Explain the major difference between statistical and nonstatistical sampling. What are the three main parts of statistical and nonstatistical methods?

14-3 (Objective 14-3)   Explain the difference between replacement sampling and nonreplacement sampling. Which method do auditors usually follow? Why?

14-4 (Objective 14-3)   What are the two types of simple random sample selection methods? Which of the two methods is used most often by auditors and why?

14-5 (Objective 14-3)   Describe systematic sample selection and explain how an auditor would select 35 numbers from a population of 1,750 items using this approach. What are the advantages and disadvantages of systematic sample selection?

14-6 (Objective 14-4) What is the purpose of using nonstatistical sampling for tests of controls and substantive tests of transactions?

14-7 (Objective 14-2) Explain what is meant by block sample selection and describe how an auditor could obtain five blocks of 20 sales invoices from a sales journal.

14-8 (Objective 14-5) Define each of the following terms:

a. Acceptable risk of assessing control risk too low (ARACR)

b. Computed upper exception rate (CUER)

c. Estimated population exception rate (EPER)

d. Sample exception rate (SER)

e. Tolerable exception rate (TER)

14-9 (Objective 14-5) Describe what is meant by a sampling unit. Explain why the sampling unit for verifying the existence of recorded sales differs from the sampling unit for testing for the possibility of omitted sales.

14-10 (Objective 14-5) Distinguish between the TER and the CUER. How is each determined?

14-11 (Objective 14-1) Distinguish between a sampling error and a nonsampling error. How can each be reduced?

14-12 (Objective 14-4) What is meant by an attribute in sampling for tests of controls and substantive tests of transactions? What is the source of the attributes that the auditor selects?

14-13 (Objective 14-4) Explain the difference between an attribute and an exception condition. State the exception condition for the audit procedure: the duplicate sales invoice has been initialed indicating the performance of internal verification.

14-14 (Objective 14-5) Identify the factors an auditor uses to decide the appropriate TER. Compare the sample size for a TER of 6 percent with that of 3 percent, all other factors being equal.

14-15 (Objective 14-5) Identify the factors an auditor uses to decide the appropriate ARACR. Compare the sample size for an ARACR of 10 percent with that of 5 percent, all other factors being equal.

14-16 (Objective 14-5) State the relationship between the following:

a. ARACR and sample size   c. TER and sample size

b. Population size and sample size   d. EPER and sample size

14-17 (Objective 14-7) Assume that the auditor has selected 100 sales invoices from a population of 100,000 to test for an indication of internal verification of pricing and extensions. Determine the CUER at a 5 percent ARACR if three exceptions existed in the sample using attributes sampling. Explain the meaning of the statistical results in auditing terms.

14-18 (Objective 14-5) Explain what is meant by analysis of exceptions and discuss its importance.

14-19 (Objective 14-5) When the CUER exceeds the TER, what courses of action are available to the auditor? Under what circumstances should each of these be followed?

14-20 (Objective 14-3) Distinguish between probabilistic selection and statistical measurement. State the circumstances under which one can be used without the other.

14-21 (Objective 14-7) List the major decisions that the auditor must make in using attributes sampling. State the most important considerations involved in making each decision.

14-22 (Objective 14-7) The following items apply to determining sample sizes using random sampling from large populations for attributes sampling. Select the most appropriate response for each question.

a. If all other factors specified in a sampling plan remain constant, changing the ARACR from 10 percent to 5 percent would cause the required sample size to

    (1) increase.   (3) decrease.

    (2) remain the same.   (4) become indeterminate.

b. If all other factors specified in a sampling plan remain constant, changing the TER from 8 percent to 12 percent would cause the required sample size to

    (1) increase.   (3) decrease.

    (2) remain the same.   (4) become indeterminate.

c. If an auditor wishes to select a random sample that must have a 10 percent ARACR and a TER of 10 percent, the size of the sample he or she must select will decrease as the estimate of the

    (1) population exception rate increases.   (3) population size increases.

    (2) population exception rate decreases.   (4) ARACR increases.

d. In planning a statistical sample for tests of controls, an auditor increases the expected population exception rate from the prior year's rate because of the results of the prior year's tests of controls. As a result, the auditor would most likely increase the planned

    (1) tolerable exception rate.

    (2) allowance for sampling risk.

    (3) acceptable risk of assessing control risk too low.

    (4) sample size.

14-23 (Objective 14-7) The following items concern determining exception rates using random sampling from large populations using attributes sampling. Select the best response.

a. From a random sample of items listed from a client's inventory count, an auditor estimates with a 90 percent confidence level that the CUER is between 4 percent and 6 percent. The auditor's major concern is that there is one chance in twenty that the true exception rate in the population is

    (1) more than 6 percent.   (3) more than 4 percent.

    (2) less than 6 percent.   (4) less than 4 percent.

b. If, from a random sample, an auditor can state with a 5 percent ARACR that the exception rate in the population does not exceed 20 percent, he or she can state that the exception rate does not exceed 25 percent with

    (1) 5 percent risk.

    (2) risk greater than 5 percent.

    (3) risk less than 5 percent.

    (4) This cannot be determined from the information provided.

c. As a result of tests of controls, an auditor assessed control risk too low and decreased substantive testing. This assessment occurred because the true deviation rate in the population was

    (1) less than the risk of assessing control risk too low, based on the auditor's sample.

    (2) less than the deviation rate in the auditor's sample.

    (3) more than the risk of assessing control risk too low, based on the auditor's sample.

    (4) more than the deviation rate in the auditor's sample.

14-24 (Objectives 14-1, 14-2) The following questions concern sampling risk. Choose the best response.

a. An advantage of statistical sampling over nonstatistical sampling is that statistical sampling helps an auditor

    (1) minimize the failure to detect errors and fraud.

(2) eliminate the risk of nonsampling errors.

(3) design more effective audit procedures.

(4) measure the sufficiency of evidential matter by quantifying sampling risk.

b. Which of the following is an element of sampling risk?

(1) Choosing an audit procedure that is inconsistent with the audit objective.

(2) Choosing a sample size that is too small to achieve the sampling objective.

(3) The auditor failing to detect an error on a document in the sample.

(4) Failing to perform audit procedures.

c. Which of the following best illustrates the concept of sampling risk?

(1) The documents related to the chosen sample may not be available to the auditor for inspection.

(2) An auditor may fail to recognize errors in the documents from the sample.

(3) A randomly chosen sample may not be representative of the population as a whole for the characteristic of interest.

(4) An auditor may select audit procedures that are not appropriate to achieve the specific objective.

DISCUSSION QUESTIONS AND PROBLEMS

14-25 (Objective 14-3)

a. In each of the following independent problems, design an unbiased random sampling plan, using an electronic spreadsheet or a random number generator program. The plan should include defining the sampling unit and establishing a numbering system for the population. After the plan has been designed, select the sample using the computer. Assume that the sample size is 50 for each of (1) through (4).

(1) Prenumbered sales invoices in a sales journal where the lowest invoice number is 1 and the highest is 6211.

(2) Prenumbered bills of lading where the lowest document number is 21926 and the highest is 28511.

(3) Accounts receivable on 10 pages with 60 lines per page except the last page, which has only 36 full lines. Each line has a customer name and an amount receivable.

(4) Prenumbered invoices in a sales journal where each month starts over with number 1. (Invoices for each month are designated by the month and document number.) There is a maximum of 20 pages per month with a total of 185 pages for the year. All pages have 75 invoices except for the last page for each month.

b. Using systematic sampling, select the first five sample items for populations (1) through (3) from part a, using the random starting points shown below. Recall that the sample size is 50 in each case.

(1) Invoice #67

(2) Bill of lading #22011

(3) Page 1, line #8

14-26 (Objectives 14-3, 14-5, 14-7) Lenter Supply Company is a medium-sized distributor of wholesale hardware supplies in the central Ohio area. It has been a client of yours for several years and has instituted excellent internal controls for sales at your recommendation.

In providing control over shipments, the client has prenumbered "warehouse removal slips" that are used for every sale. It is company policy never to remove goods from the warehouse without an authorized warehouse removal slip. After shipment, two copies of the warehouse removal slip are sent to billing for the computerized preparation of a sales invoice. One copy is stapled to the duplicate copy of a prenumbered sales invoice, and the other copy is filed numerically. In some cases, more than one warehouse removal slip is used for billing one sales invoice. The smallest warehouse removal slip number for the year is 14682 and the largest is 37521. The smallest sales invoice number is 47821 and the largest is 68507.

In the audit of sales, one of the major concerns is the effectiveness of the controls in ensuring that all shipments are billed. You have decided to use audit sampling in testing internal controls.

Required

    a. State an effective audit procedure for testing whether shipments have been billed. What is the sampling unit for the audit procedure?

    b. Assuming that you expect no exceptions in the sample but are willing to accept a TER of 3 percent, at a 10 percent ARACR, what is the appropriate sample size for the audit test? You may complete this requirement using attributes sampling.

    c. Design a random selection plan for selecting the sample from the population, using either systematic sampling or computer generation of random numbers. Use the sample size determined in part b. If you use systematic sampling, use a random starting point of 14825.

    d. Your supervisor suggests the possibility of performing other sales tests with the same sample as a means of efficiently using your audit time. List two other audit procedures that could conveniently be performed using the same sample and state the purpose of each of the procedures.

    e. Is it desirable to test the existence of sales with the random sample you have designed in part c? Why?

14-27 (Objective 14-7) The following is a partial audit program for the audit of cash receipts.

1. Review the cash receipts journal for large and unusual transactions.
2. Trace entries from the prelisting of cash receipts to the cash receipts journal to determine whether each is recorded.
3. Compare customer name, date, and amount on the prelisting with the cash receipts journal.
4. Examine the related remittance advice for entries selected from the prelisting to determine whether cash discounts were approved.
5. Trace entries from the prelisting to the deposit slip to determine whether each has been deposited.

Required

    a. Identify which audit procedures could be tested by using attributes sampling.

    b. What is the appropriate sampling unit for the tests in part a?

    c. List the attributes for testing in part a.

    d. Assume an ARACR of 5 percent and a TER of 8 percent for tests of controls and 6 percent for substantive tests of transactions. The EPER for tests of controls is 2 percent, and for substantive tests of transactions it is 1 percent. What is the initial sample size for each attribute?

14-28 (Objectives 14-5, 14-7) The following questions concern the determination of the proper sample size in audit sampling using the following table:

	1	2	3	4	5	6	7
ARACR (in percentage)	10	5	5	5	10	10	5
TER	6	6	5	6	20	20	2
EPER (in percentage)	2	2	2	2	8	2	0
Population size	1,000	100,000	6,000	1,000	500	500	1,000,000

Required

a. Assume that the initial sample size for column 1 was determined to be 90 items, using nonstatistical sampling. For each of columns 2 through 7, use your judgment to decide the appropriate nonstatistical sample size. In deciding each sample size, consider the effects of changes in each of the four factors (ARACR, TER, EPER, and population size) compared with column 1.

b. For each of the columns numbered 1 through 7, determine the initial sample size needed to satisfy the auditor's requirements using attributes sampling from the appropriate part of Table 14-7.

c. Using your understanding of the relationship between the following factors and sample size, state the effect on the initial sample size (increase or decrease) of changing each of the following factors while the other three are held constant:

   (1) An increase in ARACR   (3) An increase in the EPER

   (2) An increase in the TER   (4) An increase in the population size

d. Explain why there is such a large difference in the sample sizes for columns 3 and 6.

e. Compare your answers in part c with the results you determined in part a (nonstatistical sampling) or part b (attributes sampling). Which of the four factors appears to have the greatest effect on the initial sample size? Which one appears to have the least effect?

f. Why is the sample size called the initial sample size?

14-29 (Objectives 14-5, 14-7) The questions below relate to determining the CUER in audit sampling for tests of controls, using the following table:

	1	2	3	4	5	6	7	8
ARACR								
(in percentage)	10	5	5	5	5	5	5	5
Population size	5,000	5,000	5,000	50,000	500	900	5,000	500
Sample size	200	200	50	200	100	100	100	25
Number								
of exceptions	4	4	1	4	2	10	0	0

Required

a. Using nonstatistical sampling, calculate TER − SER for each of columns 1 through 8 and evaluate whether or not sampling error is large enough to accept the population. Assume that TER is 5 percent for each column.

b. For each of the columns 1 through 8, determine CUER using attributes sampling from the appropriate table.

c. Using your understanding of the relationship between the four factors above and the CUER, state the effect on the CUER (increase or decrease) of changing each of the following factors while the other three are held constant:

   (1) A decrease in the ARACR

   (2) A decrease in the population size

   (3) A decrease in the sample size

   (4) A decrease in the number of exceptions in the sample

d. Compare your answers in part c with the results you determined in part a (nonstatistical sampling) or part b (attributes sampling). Which of the factors appears to have the greatest effect on the CUER? Which one appears to have the least effect?

e. Why is it necessary to compare the CUER with the TER?

14-30 (Objective 14-7)   The following are auditor judgments and attributes sampling results for six populations. Assume large population sizes.

	1	2	3	4	5	6
EPER (in percentage)	2	0	3	1	1	8
TER (in percentage)	6	3	8	5	20	15
ARACR (in percentage)	5	5	10	5	10	10
Actual sample size	100	100	60	100	20	60
Actual number of exceptions in the sample	2	0	1	4	1	8

Required

    a. For each population, did the auditor select a smaller sample size than is indicated by using the attributes sampling tables in Table 14-7 for determining sample size? Evaluate selecting either a larger or smaller size than those determined in the tables.

    b. Calculate the SER and CUER for each population.

    c. For which of the six populations should the sample results be considered unacceptable? What options are available to the auditor?

    d. Why is analysis of the exceptions necessary even when the populations are considered acceptable?

    e. For the following terms, identify which is an audit decision, a nonstatistical estimate made by the auditor, a sample result, and a statistical conclusion about the population:

       (1) EPER

       (2) TER

       (3) ARACR

       (4) Actual sample size

       (5) Actual number of exceptions in the sample

       (6) SER

       (7) CUER

14-31 (Objective 14-5)   For the audit of the financial statements of Mercury Fifo Company, Stella Mason, CPA, has decided to apply nonstatistical audit sampling in the tests of controls and substantive tests of transactions for sales transactions. Based on her knowledge of Mercury's operations in the area of sales, she decides that the EPER is likely to be 3 percent and that she is willing to accept a 5 percent risk that the true population exception rate is not greater than 6 percent. Given this information, Mason selects a random sample of 150 sales invoices from the 5,000 generated during the year and examines them for exceptions. She notes the exceptions below in her working papers. There is no other documentation.

INVOICE NO.	COMMENT
5028	Sales invoice was originally footed incorrectly but was corrected by client before the bill was sent out.
6791	Voided sales invoice examined by auditor.
6810	Shipping document for a sale of merchandise could not be located.
7364	Sales invoice for $2,875 has not been collected and is 6 months past due.
7625	Client unable to locate the duplicate sales invoice.
8431	Invoice was dated 3 days later than the date entered in the sales journal.
8528	Customer order is not attached to the duplicate sales invoice.
8566	Billing is for $100 less than it should be due to an unintentional pricing error. No indication of internal verification is included on the invoice.
8780	Client unable to locate the duplicate sales invoice.
9169	Credit not authorized, but the sale was for only $7.65.
9974	Lack of indication of internal verification of price extensions and postings of sales invoice.

Required

   a. Which of the preceding should be defined as an exception?

   b. Explain why it is inappropriate to set a single acceptable TER and EPER for the combined exceptions.

   c. For each attribute in the population that is tested, calculate SER assuming a 5 percent ARACR for each attribute. (You must decide which attributes should be combined, which should be kept separate, and which exceptions are actual exceptions before you can calculate SER.)

   d. Calculate TER − SER for each attribute and evaluate whether sampling error is sufficiently large given the 5 percent ARACR. Assume TER is 6 percent for each attribute.

   e. State the appropriate analysis of exceptions for each of the exceptions in the sample, including additional procedures to be performed.

14-32 (Objectives 14-5, 14-7)   In performing tests of controls and substantive tests of transactions of sales for the Oakland Hardware Company, Ben Frentz, CPA, is concerned with the internal verification of pricing, extensions, and footings of sales invoices and the accuracy of the calculations. In testing sales using audit sampling, a separate attribute is used for the test of control (the existence of internal verification) and the substantive test of transactions (the accuracy of calculation). Because internal controls are considered good, Frentz uses a 10 percent ARACR, a zero EPER, and a 5 percent TER for both attributes; therefore, the initial sample size is 45 items, which Ben rounded up to 50.

In conducting the tests, the auditor finds three sample items for which there was no indication of internal verification on the sales invoice, but no sales invoices tested in the sample had a financial misstatement. You may complete the following requirements using either a nonstatistical sampling or an attributes sampling approach.

Required

   a. Estimate or determine the CUER for both the attributes, assuming a population of 5,000 sales invoices.

   b. Decide whether the control is acceptable and whether the substance of the transaction is acceptable.

   c. Discuss the most desirable course of action that the auditor should follow in deciding the effect of the CUER exceeding the TER.

   d. Which type of exception analysis is appropriate in this case?

CASE

14-33 (Objectives 14-4, 14-5, 14-7, 14-8)   For the audit of Carbald Supply Company, Carole Wever, CPA, is conducting a test of sales for 9 months of the year ended December 31, 1999. Included among her audit procedures are the following:

1. Foot and crossfoot the sales journal and trace the balance to the general ledger.
2. Review all sales transactions for reasonableness.
3. Select a sample of recorded sales from the sales journal and trace the customer name and amounts to duplicate sales invoices and the related shipping document.
4. Select a sample of shipping document numbers and perform the following tests:
   (a) Trace the shipping document to the related duplicate sales invoice.
   (b) Examine the duplicate sales invoice to determine whether copies of the shipping document, shipping order, and customer order are attached.
   (c) Examine the shipping order for an authorized credit approval.
   (d) Examine the duplicate sales invoice for an indication of internal verification of quantity, price, extensions, footings, and tracing the balance to the accounts receivable master file.

(e) Compare the price on the duplicate sales invoice with the approved price list and the quantity with the shipping document.

(f) Trace the balance in the duplicate sales invoice to the sales journal and accounts receivable master file for customer name, amount, and date.

Required

a. For which of these procedures could audit sampling for exceptions be conveniently used?

b. Considering the audit procedures Wever developed, what is the most appropriate sampling unit for conducting most of the audit sampling tests?

c. Set up a sampling data sheet using attributes or nonstatistical sampling. For all tests of controls, assume a TER rate of 5 percent and an EPER of 1 percent. For all substantive tests of transactions, use a 4 percent TER and a 0 percent EPER. Use a 10 percent ARACR for all tests.

INTEGRATED CASE APPLICATION—PINNACLE MANUFACTURING: PART III

 14-34 (Objectives 14-3, 14-5, 14-7, 14-8) In Part II of the Pinnacle Manufacturing integrated case application, a tests of controls and substantive tests of transactions audit program was designed for acquisitions and cash disbursements. In Part III, sample sizes will be determined by using nonstatistical or attributes sampling, and the results of the tests will be evaluated.

Required

a. Use the performance format audit program you prepared for acquisitions and cash disbursements from Problem 13-34 to prepare a sampling data sheet. Use Figure 14-3 on page 461 as a frame of reference for preparing the data sheet. Complete all parts of the data sheet except those parts that are blank in Figure 14-3. Use the following additional information to complete this requirement:

(1) Prepare only one sampling data sheet.

(2) Decide the appropriate sampling unit and select all audit procedures that are appropriate for that sampling unit from the performance format audit program you prepared in Problem 13-34. The following information is available to define the population on the sampling data sheet for the sampling unit selected:

Acquisitions Journal		Cash Disbursements Journal	
First voucher number	8672	First check number	6240
Last voucher number	13652	Last check number	9875

(3) Decide EPER, TER, and ARACR for each attribute. Base EPER on the prior year's results of tests of controls and substantive tests of transactions in Figure 10-8 on page 326. Use your judgment in deciding TER, considering the nature and importance of each attribute. Assume that assessed control risk is low for each procedure.

b. Design a random sampling plan using an electronic spreadsheet or systematic selection for the attribute with the largest sample size in requirement a. Document the design and the first 10 numbers selected under the sampling plan.

c. Assume that you performed all audit procedures included in Problem 13-34 using the sample sizes in requirement a. The only exceptions found when you performed the tests were one missing indication of internal verification on a vendor's invoice, one acquisition of inventory transaction recorded for $200 more than the amount stated in the vendor's invoice (the vendor was also overpaid by $200), and one vendor invoice recorded as an acquisition 18 days after the receipt of the goods. Complete the sampling data sheet prepared in part a. Use Figure 14-5 on page 463 as a frame of reference for completing the data sheet.

d. (Instructor Option) Develop the sampling data sheet, using an electronic spreadsheet.

COMPLETING THE TESTS IN THE SALES AND COLLECTION CYCLE: ACCOUNTS RECEIVABLE

LEARNING OBJECTIVES

After studying this chapter, you should be able to

15-1 Describe the methodology for designing tests of details of balances using the audit risk model.

15-2 Design and perform analytical procedures for accounts in the sales and collection cycle.

15-3 Design and perform tests of details of balances for accounts receivable for each balance-related audit objective.

15-4 Obtain and evaluate accounts receivable confirmations.

15-5 Design audit procedures for the audit of accounts receivable, using an evidence planning worksheet as a guide.

WHEN MORE ISN'T BETTER

On Susan Jackson's first audit assignment, she is asked to handle the confirmation of accounts receivable. She is excited because it was one of the areas in her auditing class that she was confident that she understood. The audit client is a retailer with a large number of customer accounts. In previous years, Susan's firm confirmed these accounts using negative confirmations. Last year, 200 negative confirmations were sent. Confirmations were sent 1 month before year-end. Those that were returned showed only timing differences; none represented a misstatement in the client's books.

The tentative audit plan for the current year is to do about the same as the prior year. Before the current year's planned confirmation date, Susan performs a review of internal controls over sales and cash receipts transactions. She discovers that a new system for sales transactions has been implemented, but the client is having considerable problems getting it to work properly. There are a significant number of misstatements in recording sales during the past few months. Susan's tests of controls and substantive tests of sales transactions also identify similar misstatements.

When Susan takes her findings to her supervisor and asks him what to do, he responds, "No problem, Susan. Just send 300 confirmation requests instead of the usual 200. And be sure you get a good random sample so we can get a good projection of the results." Susan is seriously bothered by this instruction. She recalls from her auditing class that negative confirmation requests aren't considered to be good evidence when there are weak controls. Because customers are asked to respond only when there are differences, the auditor cannot be confident of the correct value for each misstatement in the sample. If this is so, then the results of using negative confirmations will be misleading even if a request is sent to *every* account. Susan concludes that expanding the sample size is the wrong solution. When Susan talks with her supervisor about her point of view, this time he responds, "You are absolutely right. I spoke too quickly. We need to sit down and think about a better strategy to find out if accounts receivable is materially misstated."

SEC's Revenue
Recognition Concerns

In the last two chapters, we examined tests of controls and substantive tests of transactions for the sales and collection cycle. Both types of tests are a part of phase II of the audit process. We now move on to phase III and turn our attention to analytical procedures and tests of details of balances for the sales and collection cycle.

As was shown in the vignette introducing this chapter, it is essential for the auditor to select the appropriate evidence, given the conclusions that are reached in evaluating initial controls and performing tests of controls and substantive tests of transactions. Because reliable evidence is available, auditors do extensive analytical procedures and tests of details of balances in almost all audits to reduce detection risk for account balances to a reasonable level. To provide reasonable assurance that account balances are fairly stated, but to do so at a reasonable cost, the auditor must carefully design the most appropriate and cost-effective analytical procedures and tests of details of balances. This chapter examines designing analytical procedures and tests of details of balances for accounts receivable.

METHODOLOGY FOR DESIGNING TESTS OF DETAILS OF BALANCES

OBJECTIVE 15-1
Describe the methodology for designing tests of details of balances using the audit risk model.

Figure 15-1 shows the methodology that auditors follow in designing the appropriate tests of details of balances for accounts receivable. Notice that the second to the last step includes designing and performing analytical procedures. The methodology was introduced in Chapter 12 and is now applied to the audit of accounts receivable. The methodology shown in Figure 15-1 relates directly to the evidence planning worksheet first introduced in Chapter 9. The worksheet was partially completed in Chapter 9 for materiality and risk considerations (part of phase I) and was further completed as a part of the study of tests of controls and substantive tests of transactions in the last chapter (phase II). We will continue to complete the worksheet as we proceed through phase III in this chapter.

Deciding the appropriate tests of details of balances evidence is complicated because it must be decided on an objective-by-objective basis, and there are several interactions that affect the evidence decision. For example, the auditor must consider inherent risk, which may differ by objective, and results of substantive tests of sales and cash receipts, which also may vary by objective. The auditor must also consider the results of tests of controls and the related control risk assessment.

In designing tests of details of balances for accounts receivable, it is essential to satisfy each of the nine balance-related audit objectives first discussed in Chapter 6. It was shown in Chapter 6 that these nine general objectives are the same for all accounts. Specifically applied to accounts receivable, they are called **accounts receivable balance-related audit objectives** and are as follows:[1]

1. Accounts receivable in the aged trial balance agree with related master file amounts, and the total is correctly added and agrees with the general ledger (Detail tie-in).
2. Recorded accounts receivable exist (Existence).
3. Existing accounts receivable are included (Completeness).
4. Accounts receivable are accurate (Accuracy).
5. Accounts receivable are properly classified (Classification).
6. Cutoff for accounts receivable is correct (Cutoff).
7. Accounts receivable is stated at realizable value (Realizable value).
8. The client has rights to accounts receivable (Rights).
9. Accounts receivable presentation and disclosures are proper (Presentation and disclosure).

The columns in the evidence planning worksheet in Figure 15-7 (p. 495) include the balance-related audit objectives. The auditor uses the factors in the rows to aid in assessing

---

[1]Detail tie-in is included as the first objective here, compared with being objective six in Chapter 6, because tests for detail tie-in are normally done first.

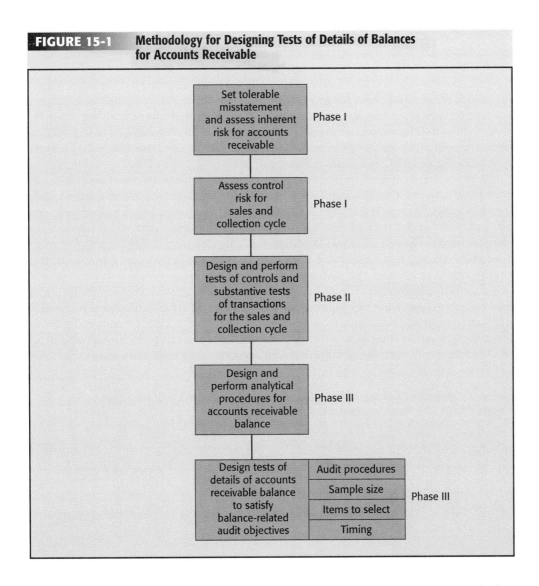

FIGURE 15-1 Methodology for Designing Tests of Details of Balances for Accounts Receivable

Set tolerable misstatement and assess inherent risk for accounts receivable	Phase I
Assess control risk for sales and collection cycle	Phase I
Design and perform tests of controls and substantive tests of transactions for the sales and collection cycle	Phase II
Design and perform analytical procedures for accounts receivable balance	Phase III
Design tests of details of accounts receivable balance to satisfy balance-related audit objectives — Audit procedures / Sample size / Items to select / Timing	Phase III

planned detection risk for accounts receivable, by objective. These factors were studied in earlier chapters.

It is important for students of auditing to understand the entire methodology for designing tests of details of balances for accounts receivable and all other accounts. The following discussion explains the methodology. Portions of the discussion are a review of information studied in earlier chapters, but they are intended to aid in understanding the relationship of each part of Figure 15-1 to designing tests of details of balances.

As studied in Chapter 9, the auditor first decides the preliminary judgment about materiality for the entire financial statements. Next, the auditor allocates the preliminary judgment amount to each significant balance sheet account, including accounts receivable. This allocation is called *setting tolerable misstatement*. Accounts receivable is typically one of the most material accounts in the financial statements for companies that sell on credit. Even if the accounts receivable balance is not large, the transactions in the sales and collection cycle that affect the balance in accounts receivable are almost certain to be highly significant.

Inherent risk is assessed for each objective for an account such as accounts receivable. For most audits, inherent risk for accounts receivable is moderate or low except for two objectives: accounts receivable is stated at realizable value and sales and sales returns and allowances cutoff is correct. It is difficult, because of the judgments involved, for clients to evaluate realizable value and correctly adjust the allowance for uncollectible accounts. It is relatively easy for

Set Tolerable Misstatement and Assess Inherent Risk (Phase I)

clients to intentionally misstate the allowance account because of the difficulty of the judgments. Similarly, it is common for clients to intentionally or unintentionally misstate cutoff.

Assess Control Risk for the Sales and Collection Cycle (Phase I)

Internal controls over sales and cash receipts and the related accounts receivable are at least reasonably effective for most companies because management is concerned with keeping accurate records as a means to good relations with customers. Auditors are often especially concerned with three aspects of internal controls: controls that prevent or detect defalcations, controls over cutoff, and controls related to the allowance for uncollectible accounts, such as the approval of credit sales before shipment.

We have already studied transaction-related audit objectives in the sales and collection cycle (see Chapter 13). The auditor must relate control risk for transaction-related audit objectives to balance-related audit objectives in deciding planned detection risk and planned evidence for tests of details of balances. For the most part, the relationship is straightforward. Figure 15-2 shows the relationship for the two primary classes of transactions in the sales and collection cycle. For example, assume that the auditor concluded that control risk for both sales and cash receipts transactions is low for the accuracy transaction-related audit objective. The auditor can therefore conclude that controls for the accuracy balance-related audit objective for accounts receivable are effective because the only transactions that affect accounts receivable are sales and cash receipts. Of course, if sales returns and allowances and charge-off of uncollectible accounts receivable are significant, assessed control risk must also be considered for these two classes of transactions.

FIGURE 15-2   **Relationship between Transaction-Related Audit Objectives for the Sales and Collection Cycle and Balance-Related Audit Objectives for Accounts Receivable**

CLASS OF TRANSACTIONS	TRANSACTION-RELATED AUDIT OBJECTIVES	Detail tie-in	Existence	Completeness	Accuracy	Classification	Cutoff	Realizable value	Rights	Presentation and disclosure
Sales	Existence		X							
	Completeness			X						
	Accuracy				X					
	Classification					X				
	Timing						X			
	Posting and summarization	X								
Cash receipts	Existence			X						
	Completeness		X							
	Accuracy				X					
	Classification					X				
	Timing						X			
	Posting and summarization	X								

ACCOUNTS RECEIVABLE BALANCE-RELATED AUDIT OBJECTIVES

Two aspects of the relationships in Figure 15-2 deserve special mention:

1. For sales, the existence transaction-related audit objective affects the existence balance-related audit objective, but for cash receipts the existence transaction-related audit objective affects the completeness balance-related audit objective. A similar relationship exists for the completeness transaction-related audit objective. The reason for this somewhat surprising conclusion is that an increase of sales increases accounts receivable, but an increase of cash receipts decreases accounts receivable. For example, recording a sale that did not occur violates the existence transaction-related audit objective and existence balance-related audit objective (both overstatements). Recording a cash receipt that did not occur violates the existence transaction-related audit objective, but it violates the completeness balance-related audit objective for accounts receivable because a receivable that is still outstanding is no longer included in the records.

2. Three accounts receivable balance-related audit objectives are not affected by assessed control risk for classes of transactions. These are realizable value, rights, and presentation and disclosure. When the auditor wants to reduce assessed control risk below the maximum for these three objectives, separate controls are identified and tested.

Figure 15-7 on page 495 includes three rows for assessed control risk: one for sales, one for cash receipts, and one for additional controls related to the accounts receivable balance. The source of each control risk for sales and cash receipts is the control risk matrix, assuming that the tests of controls results supported the original assessment. The auditor makes a separate assessment of control risk for objectives related only to the accounts receivable balance.

Designing audit procedures for tests of controls and substantive tests of transactions, deciding sample size, and evaluating the results of those tests were covered in the last two chapters. The results of the tests of controls determine whether assessed control risk for sales and cash receipts needs to be revised. The results of the substantive tests of transactions are used to determine the extent to which planned detection risk is satisfied for each accounts receivable balance-related audit objective. The evidence planning worksheet in Figure 15-7 shows three rows for control risk and two for substantive tests of transactions, one for sales, and the other for cash receipts.

As discussed in Chapter 7, analytical procedures are often done during three phases of the audit: during planning, when performing detailed tests, and as a part of completing the audit. This chapter covers those done during planning and when performing detailed tests for accounts in the sales and collection cycle.

Most analytical procedures performed during the detailed testing phase are done after the balance sheet date but before tests of details of balances. It makes little sense to perform extensive analytical procedures before the client has recorded all transactions for the year and finalized the financial statements.

Analytical procedures are done for the entire sales and collection cycle, not only for accounts receivable. This is done because of the close relationship between income statement and balance sheet accounts. If the auditor determines possible misstatement in sales or sales returns and allowances through analytical procedures, accounts receivable will likely be the offsetting misstatement.

Table 15-1 (p. 480) presents examples of the major types of ratios and comparisons for the sales and collection cycle and potential misstatements that may be indicated by the analytical procedures. Although Table 15-1 focuses on the comparison of current year results with previous years, the auditor also considers current year results compared to budgets and industry trends. It is important to observe in the "possible misstatement" column that both balance sheet and income statement accounts are affected. For example, when the auditor performs analytical procedures for sales, evidence is being obtained about both sales and accounts receivable.

Outsource Revenue Management

Design and Perform Tests of Controls and Substantive Tests of Transactions (Phase II)

Design and Perform Analytical Procedures (Phase III)

OBJECTIVE 15-2
Design and perform analytical procedures for accounts in the sales and collection cycle.

TABLE 15-1	Analytical Procedures for the Sales and Collection Cycle
Analytical Procedure	**Possible Misstatement**
Compare gross margin percentage with previous years (by product line).	Overstatement or understatement of sales and accounts receivable.
Compare sales by month (by product line) over time.	Overstatement or understatement of sales and accounts receivable.
Compare sales returns and allowances as a percentage of gross sales with previous years (by product line).	Overstatement or understatement of sales returns and allowances and accounts receivable.
Compare individual customer balances over a stated amount with previous years.	Misstatements in accounts receivable and related income statement accounts.
Compare bad debt expense as a percentage of gross sales with previous years.	Uncollectible accounts receivable that have not been provided for.
Compare number of days that accounts receivable are outstanding with previous years and related turnover of accounts receivable.	Overstatement or understatement of allowance for uncollectible accounts and bad debt expense; also may indicate fictitious accounts receivable.
Compare aging categories as a percentage of accounts receivable with previous years.	Overstatement or understatement of allowance for uncollectible accounts and bad debt expense.
Compare allowance for uncollectible accounts as a percentage of accounts receivable with previous years.	Overstatement or understatement of allowance for uncollectible accounts and bad debt expense.
Compare charge-off of uncollectible accounts as a percentage of total accounts receivable with previous years.	Overstatement or understatement of allowance for uncollectible accounts and bad debt expense.

In addition to the analytical procedures in Table 15-1, there should also be a review of accounts receivable for large and unusual amounts. Individual receivables that deserve special attention are large balances, accounts that have been outstanding for a long time, receivables from affiliated companies, officers, directors, and other related parties, and credit balances. The auditor should review the listing of accounts (aged trial balance) at the balance sheet date to determine which accounts should be investigated further.

The auditor's conclusion about analytical procedures for the sales and collection cycle is incorporated into the third row from the bottom on the evidence planning worksheet in Figure 15-7. Analytical procedures are substantive tests and therefore reduce the extent to which the auditor needs to test details of balances, if the analytical procedures' results are favorable.

When analytical procedures in the sales and collection cycle uncover unusual fluctuations, the auditor should make additional inquiries of management. Management's responses should be critically evaluated to determine whether they adequately explain the unusual fluctuations and whether they are supported by other corroborative evidence.

Design and Perform Tests of Details of Accounts Receivable Balance (Phase III)

The appropriate tests of details of balances depend on the factors incorporated into the evidence planning worksheet in Figure 15-7. The second row from the bottom shows planned detection risk for each accounts receivable balance-related audit objective. Planned detection risk for each objective is an auditor decision, decided by subjectively combining the conclusions reached about each of the factors listed above that row.

Combining the factors that determine planned detection risk is complex because the measurement for each factor is imprecise and the appropriate weight to be given each

Ron Stopps, CPA, is the auditor for Great Western Lumber Company, a wholesale wood milling company. Ron calculates the gross margin by three product lines and obtains industry information from published data as follows:

	1999 Gross Margin Percent		1998 Gross Margin Percent		1997 Gross Margin Percent	
	Great Western	Industry	Great Western	Industry	Great Western	Industry
Hardwood	36.3	32.4	36.4	32.5	36.0	32.3
Softwood	23.9	22.0	20.3	22.1	20.5	22.3
Plywood	40.3	50.1	44.2	54.3	45.4	55.6

In discussing the results, the controller states that Great Western has always had a higher gross margin on hardwood products than the industry because they focus on the markets where they are able to sell at higher prices instead of emphasizing volume. The opposite is true of plywood, for which they have a reasonably small number of customers, each of whom demands lower prices because of high volume. The controller states that competitive forces have caused reductions in plywood gross margin for both the industry and Great Western in 1998 and 1999. Great Western has traditionally had a somewhat lower gross margin for softwood than the industry until 1999, when gross margin went up significantly due to aggressive selling.

Stopps observed that most of what the controller said was reasonable given the facts. Hardwood gross margin for the industry was stable and approximately 3.5 percent to 4 percent lower than Great Western's every year. Industry gross margin for plywood has declined annually but is about 10 percent higher than Great Western's. Industry gross margin for softwood has been stable for the three years, but Great Western's has increased by a fairly large amount.

The change in Great Western's softwood gross margin from 20.3 percent to 23.9 percent is a concern to Stopps, so he goes through a three-step procedure:

1. Calculate the potential misstatement and evaluate the materiality of that amount. He calculates 23.9% − 20.3% × softwood sales and concludes the amount is potentially material.
2. Identify potential causes of the change.
   - Overstatement of sales
   - Overstatement of inventory (understatement of cost of goods sold)
   - Understatement of purchases (understatement of cost of goods sold)
   - Good results of aggressive selling
3. Indicate in the working papers a concern for the potential overstatement of sales and inventory, and understatement of purchases of softwood. This may require an expansion of other substantive audit tests.

factor is highly judgmental. Conversely, the relationship between each factor and planned detection risk is well established. For example, the auditor knows that a high inherent risk or control risk decreases planned detection risk and increases planned substantive tests, whereas good results of substantive tests of transactions increases planned detection risk and decreases other planned substantive tests.

The bottom row in Figure 15-7 shows the planned audit evidence for tests of details of balances for accounts receivable, by objective. As discussed in previous chapters, planned audit evidence is the complement of planned detection risk.

The conclusion that planned audit evidence for a given objective is high, medium, or low is implemented by the auditor deciding the appropriate audit procedures, sample size, items to select, and timing. The remainder of this chapter discusses deciding the specific audit procedures and timing decisions for auditing accounts receivable. Chapter 16 deals with sample size and selecting items from the population for testing.

DESIGNING TESTS OF DETAILS OF BALANCES

OBJECTIVE 15-3
Design and perform tests of details of balances for accounts receivable for each balance-related audit objective.

Tests of details of balances for all cycles are directed to balance sheet accounts, but income statement accounts are not ignored because they are verified as a by-product of the balance sheet tests. For example, if the auditor confirms accounts receivable balances and finds overstatements because of mistakes in billing customers, there are overstatements of both accounts receivable and sales.

Confirmation of accounts receivable is the most important test of details of accounts receivable. Confirmation is discussed briefly in studying the appropriate tests for each of the balance-related audit objectives, then separately in more detail later in this chapter.

The discussion of tests of details of balances for accounts receivable that follows assumes that the auditor has completed an evidence planning worksheet similar to the one in Figure 15-7 and has decided planned detection risk for tests of details for each balance-related audit objective. The audit procedures selected and their sample size will depend heavily on whether planned evidence for a given objective is low, medium, or high. The discussion focuses on accounts receivable balance-related audit objectives.

Accounts Receivable Are Correctly Added and Agree with the Master File and the General Ledger

Most tests of accounts receivable and the allowance for uncollectible accounts are based on the aged trial balance. An **aged trial balance** is a listing of the balances in the accounts receivable master file at the balance sheet date. It includes the individual customer balances outstanding and a breakdown of each balance by the time passed between the date of sale and the balance sheet date. An illustration of a typical aged trial balance is given in Figure 15-3 for Hillsburg Hardware. Notice that the total is the same as accounts receivable on the general ledger trial balance on page 152.

| FIGURE 15-3 | Aged Trial Balance for Hillsburg Hardware Co. |

Hillsburg Hardware Co.
Accounts Receivable
Aged Trial Balance
12/31/99

PBC

Schedule Prepared by Client — Approved by
Date 1/5/00

			Aging, Based on Invoice Date				
Account Number	Customer	Balance 12/31/99	0-30 days	31-60 days	61-90 days	91-120 days	over 120
01011	Adams Supply	7,329	4,511	2,818			
01044	Argonaut, Inc.	1,542	1,542				
01100	Atwater Brothers	10,519	10,519				
01191	Beekman Bearings	4,176	3,676		500		
01270	Brown and Phillips	3,000				3,000	
01301	Christopher Plumbing	789					789
09733	Travelers Equipment	2,976	2,976				
09742	Underhill Parts and Maintenance	8,963	8,963				
09810	UJW Co.	5,111	1,811		1,700	1,600	
09907	Zephyr Plastics	14,300	9,300	5,000			
		$1,009,800	$785,856	$128,466	$55,432	$34,446	$5,600

Testing the information on the aged trial balance for detail tie-in is a necessary audit procedure. It is ordinarily done before any other tests to assure the auditor that the population being tested agrees with the general ledger and accounts receivable master file. The total column and the columns depicting the aging must be test footed, and the total on the trial balance compared with the general ledger. In addition, a sample of individual balances should be traced to supporting documents such as duplicate sales invoices to verify the customer's name, balance, and proper aging. The extent of the testing for detail tie-in depends on the number of accounts involved, the degree to which the master file has been tested as a part of tests of controls and substantive tests of transactions, and the extent to which the schedule has been verified by an internal auditor or other independent person before it is given to the auditor. Audit software can be used to perform footing and cross-footing of the aged trial balance, as well as to recalculate the aging.

Audit Software

The most important test of details of balances for determining the existence of recorded accounts receivable is the confirmation of customers' balances. Confirmations were defined and discussed in detail in Chapter 7. When customers do not respond to confirmations, auditors also examine supporting documents to verify the shipment of goods and evidence of subsequent cash receipts to determine whether the accounts were collected. Normally, auditors do not examine shipping documents or evidence of subsequent cash receipts for any account in the sample that is confirmed, but these documents are used extensively as alternative evidence for nonresponses.

Recorded Accounts Receivable Exist

It is difficult to test for account balances omitted from the aged trial balance except by relying on the self-balancing nature of the accounts receivable master file. For example, if the client accidentally excluded an account receivable from the trial balance, the only likely way it would be discovered is by footing the accounts receivable trial balance and reconciling the balance with the control account in the general ledger.

Existing Accounts Receivable Are Included

If all sales to a customer are omitted from the sales journal, the understatement of accounts receivable is almost impossible to uncover by tests of details of balances. For example, auditors rarely send accounts receivable confirmations to customers with zero balances, in part because research shows that customers are unlikely to respond to requests that indicate their balances are understated. The understatement of sales and accounts receivable is best uncovered by substantive tests of transactions for shipments made but not recorded (completeness objective for tests of sales transactions) and by analytical procedures.

Confirmation of accounts selected from the trial balance is the most common test of details of balances for the accuracy of accounts receivable. When customers do not respond to confirmation requests, auditors examine supporting documents, in the same way as described for the existence objective. Tests of the debits and credits to individual customers' balances are done by examining supporting documentation for shipments and cash receipts.

Accounts Receivable Are Accurate

It is normally relatively easy to evaluate the classification of accounts receivable by reviewing the aged trial balance for material receivables from affiliates, officers, directors, or other related parties. If notes receivable or accounts that should not be classified as a current asset are included with the regular accounts, these should also be segregated. Finally, if credit balances in accounts receivable are significant, it is appropriate to reclassify them as accounts payable.

There is a close relationship between the classification objective as discussed here and the presentation and disclosure objective. Classification concerns determining whether the client has correctly separated different classifications of accounts receivable. Presentation and disclosure concerns making sure that the classifications are properly presented. For example, under the classification objective, the auditor determines whether receivables from related parties have been separated on the aged trial balance. Under the presentation and

Accounts Receivable Are Properly Classified

disclosure objective, the auditor determines whether related party transactions are correctly shown in the financial statements.

Cutoff for Accounts Receivable Is Correct

Cutoff misstatements exist when current period transactions are recorded in the subsequent period or subsequent period transactions are recorded in the current period. The objective of cutoff tests, regardless of the type of transaction, is to verify whether transactions near the end of the accounting period are recorded in the proper period. The cutoff objective is one of the most important in the cycle because misstatements in cutoff can significantly affect current period income. For example, the intentional or unintentional inclusion of several large, subsequent period sales in the current period or the exclusion of several current period sales returns and allowances can materially overstate net earnings.

In determining the reasonableness of cutoff, a threefold approach is needed: (1) decide on the appropriate *criteria for cutoff*, (2) evaluate whether the client has established *adequate procedures* to ensure a reasonable cutoff, and (3) *test* whether a reasonable cutoff was obtained. Cutoff misstatements can occur for *sales, sales returns and allowances,* and *cash receipts.*

Sales Cutoff The criterion used by most merchandising and manufacturing clients for determining when a sale takes place is the *shipment of goods,* but some companies record invoices at the time title passes. The passage of title can take place before shipment (as in the case of custom-manufactured goods), at the time of shipment, or subsequent to shipment. For the correct measurement of current period income, the method must be in accordance with generally accepted accounting principles (GAAP) and consistently applied.

The most important part of evaluating the client's method of obtaining a reliable cutoff is to determine the procedures in use. When a client issues prenumbered shipping documents sequentially, it is usually a simple matter to evaluate and test cutoff. Moreover, the segregation of duties between the shipping and the billing function also enhances the likelihood of recording transactions in the proper period. However, if shipments are made by company truck, if the shipping records are unnumbered, and if shipping and billing department personnel are not independent of each other, it may be difficult, if not impossible, to be assured of an accurate cutoff.

When the client's internal controls are adequate, the cutoff can usually be verified by obtaining the shipping document number for the last shipment made at the end of the period and comparing this number with current and subsequent period recorded sales. As an illustration, assume that the shipping document number for the last shipment in the current period is 1489. All recorded sales before the end of the period should bear a shipping document number preceding number 1490. There should also be no sales recorded in the subsequent period for a shipment with a bill of lading numbered 1489 or lower. This can easily be tested by comparing recorded sales with the related shipping documents for the last few days of the current period and the first few days of the subsequent period.

Sales Returns and Allowances Cutoff GAAP requires that sales returns and allowances be *matched with related sales* if the amounts are material. For example, if current period shipments are returned in the subsequent period, the proper treatment is to include the sales return in the current period. (The returned goods would be treated as current period inventory.) For most companies, however, sales returns and allowances are recorded in the *accounting period in which they occur,* under the assumption of approximately equal, offsetting amounts at the beginning and end of each accounting period. This is acceptable as long as the amounts are not significant.

When the auditor is confident that the client records all sales returns and allowances promptly, the cutoff tests are simple and straightforward. The auditor can examine supporting documentation for a sample of sales returns and allowances recorded during several weeks subsequent to the closing date to determine the date of the original sale. If the amounts recorded in the subsequent period are significantly different from unrecorded returns and allowances at the beginning of the period under audit, an adjustment must be

Most companies say made a sale when shipped.
OK until 12/31

Ex) Ret. Jan 10
Sale 12-15,
use Jan 10

considered. If the internal controls for recording sales returns and allowances are evaluated as ineffective, a larger sample is needed to verify cutoff.

Cash Receipts Cutoff For most audits, a proper cash receipts cutoff is *less important* than either the sales or the sales returns and allowances cutoff because the improper cutoff of cash affects only the cash and the accounts receivable balances, not earnings. Nevertheless, if the misstatement is material, it could affect the fair presentation of these accounts, especially when cash is a small or negative balance.

It is easy to test for a cash receipts cutoff misstatement (often called *holding the cash receipts book open*) by tracing recorded cash receipts to subsequent period bank deposits on the bank statement. If there is a delay of several days, this could indicate a cutoff misstatement.

The confirmation of accounts receivable may also be relied on to some degree to uncover cutoff misstatements for sales, sales returns and allowances, and cash receipts, especially when there is a long interval between the date the transaction took place and the recording date. However, when the interval is only a few days, mail delivery delays may cause confusion of a cutoff misstatement with a normal **timing difference**. For example, if a customer mails and records a check to a client for payment of an unpaid account on December 30 and the client receives and records the amount on January 2, the records of the two organizations will be different on December 31. This is not a cutoff misstatement, but a timing difference due to the delivery time. It may be difficult for the auditor to evaluate whether a cutoff misstatement or a timing difference occurred when a confirmation reply is the source of information. This type of situation requires additional investigation, such as inspection of underlying documents.

Tests of the **realizable value of accounts receivable** objective are for the purpose of evaluating the account, *allowance for uncollectible accounts*. GAAP requires that accounts receivable be stated at the amount that will ultimately be collected, which is gross accounts receivable less the allowance. The client's estimate of the total amount that is uncollectible is represented by the allowance for uncollectible accounts. Although it is not possible to predict the future precisely, it is necessary for the auditor to evaluate whether the allowance is reasonable, considering all available facts. To assist with this evaluation, the auditor often prepares a working paper which analyzes the allowance for uncollectible accounts. An illustration of this working paper for Hillsburg Hardware is shown in Figure 15-4 (p. 486).

Accounts Receivable Is Stated at Realizable Value

The starting point for the evaluation of the allowance for uncollectible accounts is to review the results of the tests of controls that are concerned with the client's credit policy. If the client's credit policy has remained unchanged and the results of the tests of credit policy and credit approval are consistent with those of the preceding year, the change in the balance in the allowance for uncollectible accounts should reflect only changes in economic conditions and sales volume. However, if the client's credit policy or the degree to which it correctly functions has significantly changed, great care must be taken to consider the effects of these changes as well.

A common way to evaluate the adequacy of the allowance is to carefully examine the noncurrent accounts on the aged trial balance to determine which ones have not been paid subsequent to the balance sheet date. The size and age of unpaid balances can then be compared with similar information from previous years to evaluate whether the amount of noncurrent receivables is increasing or decreasing over time. The examination of credit files, discussions with the credit manager, and review of the client's correspondence file may also provide insights into the collectibility of the accounts. These procedures are especially important if a few large balances are noncurrent and are not being paid on a regular basis.

There are two pitfalls in evaluating the allowance by reviewing individual noncurrent balances on the aged trial balance. First, the current accounts are ignored in establishing the adequacy of the allowance, even though some of these amounts will undoubtedly become uncollectible. Second, it is difficult to compare the results of the current year with those of previous years on such an unstructured basis. If the accounts

Analysis of Allowance for Uncollectible Accounts for Hillsburg Hardware Co.

Hillsburg Hardware Co.
Analysis of Allowance for Uncollectible Accounts
12/31/99

Schedule	B-4	Date
Prepared by	TW	1/8/00
Approved by	SB	1/10/00

A/R Category	A/R Balance 12/31/99		Estimated Allowance Percentage		Estimated Required Allowance
0-30 days	$ 785,856	√	3%	×	$23,576
31-60 days	128,466	√	6%	×	7,708
61-90 days	55,432	√	20%	×	11,086
91-120 days	34,446	√	35%	×	12,056
Over 120	5,600	√	60%	×	3,360
Total	$1,009,800				$57,786
Recorded Allowance					$62,000 TB

√ – Traced to aged accounts receivable trial balance.
× – Allowance percentages are consistent with prior year, and appear reasonable
     based on historical loss percentages documented in permanent file.
TB – Agreed to trial balance.

Conclusion: Recorded allowance appears adequate based on aging analysis.

are becoming progressively uncollectible over several years, this fact could be overlooked. A way to avoid these difficulties is to establish the history of bad debt charge-offs over a period of time as a frame of reference for evaluating the current year's allowance. As an example, if historically a certain percentage of the total of each age category becomes uncollectible, it is relatively easy to compute whether the allowance is properly stated. If 2 percent of current accounts, 10 percent of 30- to 90-day accounts, and 35 percent of all balances over 90 days ultimately become uncollectible, these percentages can easily be applied to the current year's aged trial balance totals, and the result can be compared with the balance in the allowance account. Of course, the auditor has to be careful to modify the calculations for changed conditions.

Bad Debt Expense   After the auditor is satisfied with the allowance for uncollectible accounts, it is easy to verify bad debt expense. Assume that (1) the beginning balance in the allowance account was verified as a part of the previous audit, (2) the uncollectible accounts charged off were verified as a part of the substantive tests of transactions, and (3) the ending balance in the allowance account has been verified by various means. Then bad debt expense is simply a residual balance that can be verified by a reperformance test.

The Client Has Rights to Accounts Receivable

The client's rights to accounts receivable ordinarily cause no audit problems because the receivables usually belong to the client, but in some cases, a portion of the receivables may have been pledged as collateral, assigned to someone else, factored, or sold at discount. Normally, the client's customers are not aware of the existence of such matters; therefore, the confirmation of receivables will not bring it to light. A review of the minutes, discussions with the client, confirmation with banks, the examination of debt contracts for evidence of accounts receivable pledged as collateral, and the examination of correspondence files are usually sufficient to uncover instances in which the client has limited rights to receivables.

Sears, Roebuck & Co. was enjoying a remarkable turnaround in earnings in 1996. However, most of the increase in profits was attributable to interest on credit card balances. In the early 1990s, Sears had added more than 17 million new credit card customers. However, many of these new customers were not good credit risks, and they tended to carry high balances. As a result, in 1997, Sears had to increase its allowance for credit card delinquencies to $393 million, a 44 percent increase.

Unfortunately, the delinquencies were only part of the problem. Many of these delinquent customers also filed for bankruptcy. In fact, by 1997 Sears was a creditor in more than one-third of all bankruptcies filed in the United States. Sears aggressively sought reaffirmation agreements with these customers, in which they pledged to continue making payments on their accounts. However, many of these agreements were not filed in the bankruptcy cases, which meant the company was collecting on unenforceable agreements for debt that no longer legally existed. As a result of a federal investigation, Sears was forced to pay a $60 million fine and set aside $475 million in reserves to cover complaints over its debt collection practices.

Sources: 1. De'Ann Weimer, "Put the Comeback on My Card," *Business Week* (November 10, 1997), pp. 118–119.
2. John McCormick, "The Sorry Side of Sears," *Newsweek* (February 22, 1999), pp. 36–39.

Accounts Receivable Presentation and Disclosures Are Proper

In addition to testing for the proper statement of the dollar amount in the general ledger, the auditor must also determine that information about the account balance resulting from the sales and collection cycle is properly presented and disclosed in the financial statements. The auditor must decide whether the client has properly combined amounts and disclosed related party information in the statements. To evaluate the adequacy of the presentation and disclosure, the auditor must have a thorough understanding of generally accepted accounting principles and presentation and disclosure requirements.

An important part of the evaluation involves deciding whether material amounts requiring separate disclosure have actually been separated in the statements. For example, receivables from officers and affiliated companies must be segregated from accounts receivable from customers if the amounts are material. Similarly, under SEC requirements, it is necessary to disclose sales and assets for different business segments separately. The proper aggregation of general ledger balances in the financial statements also requires combining account balances that are not relevant for external users of the statements. If all accounts included in the general ledger were disclosed separately on the statements, most statement users would be more confused than enlightened.

As a part of proper presentation and disclosure, the auditor is also required to evaluate the adequacy of the *footnotes*. One of the major lawsuits in the history of the profession, the *Continental Vending* case, revolved primarily around the adequacy of the footnote disclosure of a major receivable from an affiliated company. This case was discussed in Chapter 5 in the study of legal liability. The required footnote disclosure for accounts receivable includes information about the pledging, discounting, factoring, assignment of accounts receivable, and amounts due from related parties. Of course, to evaluate the adequacy of these disclosures, it is first necessary to know of their existence and to have complete information about their nature. As discussed in the previous section, this is generally obtained in other parts of the audit.

CONFIRMATION OF ACCOUNTS RECEIVABLE

In the preceding discussion of designing the tests of details of balances, you should have noticed the recurrence of confirmation issues. Confirmation is extremely important because, as discussed in Chapter 7, confirmations are highly reliable evidence. The primary purpose of accounts receivable confirmation is to satisfy the *existence, accuracy,* and *cutoff* objectives.

AICPA Requirements

Auditing standards require the confirmation of accounts receivable in normal circumstances, but SAS 67 (AU 330) permits an unqualified report even when accounts receivable are not confirmed in any of three circumstances:

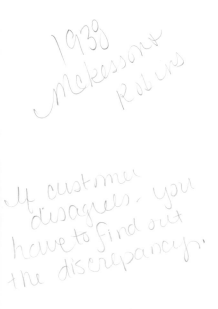

1. *Accounts receivable are immaterial.* This is common for certain companies such as discount stores with primarily cash or credit card sales.
2. *The auditor considers confirmations ineffective evidence because response rates will likely be inadequate or unreliable.* In certain industries, such as hospitals, response rates to confirmations are very low.
3. *The combined level of inherent risk and control risk is low and other substantive evidence can be accumulated to provide sufficient evidence.* If a client has effective internal controls and low inherent risk for the sales and collection cycle, the auditor should often be able to satisfy the evidence requirements by tests of controls, substantive tests of transactions, and analytical procedures.

If the auditor decides not to confirm accounts receivable, the justification for doing so must be documented in the working papers.

Although the remaining sections in this chapter refer specifically to the confirmation of accounts receivable from customers, the concepts apply equally to other receivables such as notes receivable, amounts due from officers, and employee advances. Confirmations are not required by auditing standards for any other accounts.

Confirmation Decisions

In performing confirmation procedures, the auditor must decide the type of confirmation to use, timing of the procedures, sample size, and individual items to select.

Type of Confirmation Two common types of confirmations are used for confirming accounts receivable: positive and negative. A **positive confirmation** is a communication addressed to the debtor requesting him or her to confirm directly whether the balance as stated on the confirmation request is correct or incorrect. Figure 15-5 (p. 489) illustrates a positive confirmation in the audit of Hillsburg Hardware Co. Notice that this confirmation is for one of the largest accounts on the aged trial balance in Figure 15-3 on page 482. A second type of positive confirmation, often called a **blank confirmation form**, does not state the amount on the confirmation but requests the recipient to fill in the balance or furnish other information. Because blank forms require the recipient to determine the information requested, they are considered more reliable than confirmations that include balance information. Blank forms are rarely used in practice because they often result in lower response rates.

An **invoice confirmation** is another type of positive confirmation in which an individual invoice is confirmed, rather than the customer's entire accounts receivable balance. Many customers use voucher systems that allow them to confirm individual invoices but not balance information. As a result, invoice confirmations may improve confirmation response rates. However, invoice confirmations have the disadvantage of not directly confirming ending balances.

A **negative confirmation** is also addressed to the debtor but requests a response only when the debtor disagrees with the stated amount. Figure 15-6 (p. 489) illustrates a negative confirmation in the audit of Hillsburg Hardware Co. that has been attached to a customer's monthly statement with a gummed label.

FIGURE 15-5 Positive Confirmation

HILLSBURG HARDWARE CO.
Gary, Indiana

January 5, 2000

Atwater Brothers
19 South Main Street
Middleton, Ohio 36947

To Whom It May Concern:

    In connection with an audit of our financial statements, please confirm directly to our auditors

BERGER & ANTHONY, CPAs
Gary, Indiana

the correctness of the balance of your account with us as of December 31, 1999, as shown below.
    This is not a request for payment; please do not send your remittance to our auditors. Your prompt attention to this request will be appreciated. An envelope is enclosed for your reply.

Erma Swanson

Erma Swanson, Controller

BERGER & ANTHONY, CPAs
Gary, Indiana

    The balance receivable from us of <u>$10,519</u> as of December 31, 1999, is correct except as noted below:

_____
_____
_____
_____
_____
_____

                                                         _____

Date _____   By _____

[handwritten marginal note: If pos. confirm's are not returned, have to check indiv "T" accts.]

FIGURE 15-6 Negative Confirmation

AUDITOR'S ACCOUNT CONFIRMATION

Please examine this statement carefully. If it does NOT agree with your records, please report any exceptions directly to our auditors

BERGER & ANTHONY, CPAs
Gary, Indiana

who are conducting an audit of our financial statements as of December 31, 1999. An addressed envelope is enclosed for your convenience in replying.

Do not send your remittance to our auditors.

A positive confirmation is *more reliable* evidence because the auditor can perform follow-up procedures if a response is not received from the debtor. With a negative confirmation, failure to reply must be regarded as a correct response, even though the debtor may have ignored the confirmation request.

Offsetting the reliability disadvantage, negative confirmations are *less expensive* to send than positive confirmations, and thus more can be distributed for the same total cost. Negative confirmations cost less because there are no second requests and no follow-up of nonresponses.

The determination of which type of confirmation to use is an auditor's decision, and it should be based on the facts in the audit. SAS 67 states that it is acceptable to use negative confirmations only when *all* of the following circumstances are present:

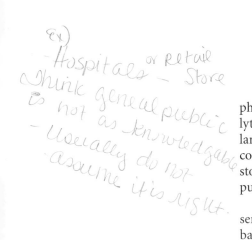

- Accounts receivable is made up of a large number of small accounts.
- Combined assessed control risk and inherent risk is low. The combined risk is unlikely to be low if either internal controls are ineffective or there is a high expectation of misstatements. For example, if prior years' audits indicate that there are often disputed or inaccurate accounts receivable, negative confirmations would be inappropriate.
- There is no reason to believe that the recipients of the confirmations are unlikely to give them consideration. For example, if the response rate to positive confirmations in prior years was extremely high or if there are high response rates on audits of similar clients, it is likely that recipients will give confirmations reasonable consideration.

Typically, when negative confirmations are used, the auditor puts considerable emphasis on the effectiveness of internal controls, substantive tests of transactions, and analytical procedures as evidence of the fairness of accounts receivable, and assumes that the large majority of the recipients will provide a conscientious reading and response to the confirmation request. Negative confirmations are often used for audits of hospitals, retail stores, banks, and other industries in which the receivables are due from the general public.

It is also common to use a combination of negative and positive confirmations by sending the latter to accounts with large balances and the former to those with small balances.

The discussion of confirmations to this point shows that there is a continuum for the type of confirmation decision, starting with using no confirmations in some circumstances, to using only negatives, to using both negatives and positives, to using only positives. The primary factors affecting the decision are the materiality of total accounts receivable, the number and size of individual accounts, control risk, inherent risk, the effectiveness of confirmations as audit evidence, and the availability of other audit evidence.

Timing The most reliable evidence from confirmations is obtained when they are sent as close to the balance sheet date as possible, as opposed to confirming the accounts several months before year-end. This permits the auditor to directly test the accounts receivable balance on the financial statements without making any inferences about the transactions taking place between the confirmation date and the balance sheet date. However, as a means of completing the audit on a timely basis, it is often necessary to confirm the accounts at an interim date. This is permissible if internal controls are adequate and can provide reasonable assurance that sales, cash receipts, and other credits are properly recorded between the date of the confirmation and the end of the accounting period. Other factors the auditor is likely to consider in making the decision are the materiality of accounts receivable and the auditor's exposure to lawsuits because of the possibility of client bankruptcy and similar risks.

If the decision is made to confirm accounts receivable before year-end, it may be necessary to test the transactions occurring between the confirmation date and the balance sheet date by examining such internal documents as duplicate sales invoices, shipping documents, and evidence of cash receipts, in addition to performing analytical procedures of the intervening period.

Sample Size The major factors affecting sample size for confirming accounts receivable fall into several categories and include the following:

- Tolerable misstatement
- Inherent risk (relative size of total accounts receivable, number of accounts, prior year results, and expected misstatements)
- Control risk
- Achieved detection risk from other substantive tests (extent and results of substantive tests of transactions, analytical procedures, and other tests of details)
- Type of confirmation (negatives normally require a larger sample size)

Selection of the Items for Testing Some type of *stratification* is desirable with most confirmations. A typical approach to stratification is to consider both the dollar size of individual accounts and the length of time an account has been outstanding as a basis for selecting the balances for confirmation. In most audits, the emphasis should be on confirming larger and older balances because these are most likely to include a significant misstatement. But it is also important to sample some items from every material segment of the population. In many cases, the auditor selects all accounts above a certain dollar amount and selects a random sample from the remainder.

When selecting a sample of accounts receivable for confirmation, the auditor should be careful to avoid being influenced by the client. If a client tries to discourage the auditor from sending confirmations to certain customers, the auditor should consider the possibility that the client is attempting to conceal fictitious or known misstatements of accounts receivable.

Maintaining Control

After the items for confirmation have been selected, the auditor must maintain control of the confirmations until they are returned from the customer. When the client assists by preparing the confirmations, enclosing them in envelopes, or putting stamps on the envelopes, close supervision by the auditor is required. A return address must be included on all envelopes to make sure that undelivered mail is received by the CPA firm. Similarly, self-addressed return envelopes accompanying the confirmations must be addressed for delivery to the CPA firm's office. It is even important to mail the confirmations *outside* the client's office. All of these steps are necessary to ensure independent communication between the auditor and the customer.

Follow-Up on Nonresponses

It is inappropriate to regard confirmations mailed but not returned by customers as significant audit evidence. For example, nonresponses to positive confirmations do not provide audit evidence. Similarly, for negative confirmations, the auditor should not conclude that the recipient received the confirmation request and verified the information requested. Negative confirmations do, however, provide some evidence of the existence assertion.

When positive confirmations are used, SAS 67 requires follow-up procedures for confirmations not returned by the customer. It is common to send second and sometimes even third requests for confirmations. Even with these efforts, some customers do not return the confirmation, so it is necessary to follow up with **alternative procedures.** The objective of alternative procedures is to determine by a means other than confirmation whether the non-confirmed account existed and was properly stated at the confirmation date. For any positive confirmation not returned, the following documentation can be examined to verify the existence and accuracy of individual sales transactions making up the ending balance in accounts receivable.

Fraud Case Study

Subsequent Cash Receipts Evidence of the receipt of cash subsequent to the confirmation date includes examining remittance advices, entries in the cash receipts records, or perhaps even subsequent credits in the accounts receivable master file. On the one hand, the examination of evidence of subsequent cash receipts is a highly useful alternative procedure because it is reasonable to assume that a customer would not make a payment unless it was an existing receivable. On the other hand, the fact of payment does not establish whether there was an obligation on the date of the confirmation. In addition, care should be taken to match each unpaid sales transaction with evidence of its subsequent payment as a test for disputes or disagreements over individual outstanding invoices.

Duplicate Sales Invoices These are useful in verifying the actual issuance of a sales invoice and the actual date of the billing.

Shipping Documents These are important in establishing whether the shipment was actually made and as a test of cutoff.

Correspondence with the Client Usually, the auditor does not need to review correspondence as a part of alternative procedures, but correspondence can be used to disclose disputed and questionable receivables not uncovered by other means.

The extent and nature of the alternative procedures depend primarily on the materiality of the nonresponses, the types of misstatements discovered in the confirmed responses, the subsequent cash receipts from the nonresponses, and the auditor's conclusions about internal control. It is normally desirable to account for all unconfirmed balances with alternative procedures even if the amounts are small, as a means of properly generalizing from the sample to the population. Another acceptable approach is to assume that nonresponses are 100 percent overstatement amounts.

Analysis of Differences

When the confirmation requests are returned by the customer, it is necessary to determine the reason for any reported differences. In many cases, they are caused by timing differences between the client's and the customer's records. It is important to distinguish between these and *exceptions*, which represent misstatements of the accounts receivable balance. The most commonly reported types of differences in confirmations follow.

Payment Has Already Been Made Reported differences typically arise when the customer has made a payment before the confirmation date, but the client has not received the payment in time for recording before the confirmation date. Such instances should be carefully investigated to determine the possibility of a cash receipts cutoff misstatement, lapping, or a theft of cash.

Goods Have Not Been Received These differences typically result because the client records the sale at the date of shipment and the customer records the acquisition when the goods are received. The time that the goods are in transit is often the cause of differences reported on confirmations. These should be investigated to determine the possibility of the customer not receiving the goods at all or the existence of a cutoff misstatement on the client's records.

The Goods Have Been Returned The client's failure to record a credit memo could result from timing differences or the improper recording of sales returns and allowances. Like other differences, these must be investigated.

Clerical Errors and Disputed Amounts The most likely types of reported differences in a client's records are when the customer states that there is an error in the price charged for the goods, the goods are damaged, the proper quantity of goods was not received, and so forth. These differences must be investigated to determine whether the client is in error and what the amount of the error is.

In most instances, the auditor will ask the client to reconcile the difference and, if necessary, will communicate with the customer to resolve any disagreements. Naturally, the auditor must carefully verify the client's conclusions on each significant difference.

Drawing Conclusions

When all differences have been resolved, including those discovered in performing alternative procedures, it is important to *reevaluate internal control*. Each client misstatement must be analyzed to determine whether it was consistent or inconsistent with the original assessed level of control risk. If a significant number of misstatements take place that are inconsistent with the assessment of control risk, it is necessary to revise the assessment and consider the effect of the revision on the audit.

It is also necessary to generalize from the sample to the entire population of accounts receivable. Even though the sum of the misstatements in the sample may not significantly affect the financial statements, the auditor must consider whether the population is likely to be materially misstated. This conclusion can be arrived at by using statistical sampling techniques or on a nonstatistical basis. Projection of misstatements was discussed in Chapter 9 and is further explained in Chapter 16.

The auditor should always evaluate the *qualitative* nature of the misstatements found in the sample, regardless of the dollar amount of the projected misstatement. Even if the projected misstatement is less than tolerable misstatement for accounts receivable, the misstatements found in a sample can be symptomatic of a more serious problem.

The final decision about accounts receivable and sales is whether sufficient evidence has been obtained through tests of controls and substantive tests of transactions, analytical procedures, cutoff procedures, confirmation, and other substantive tests to justify drawing conclusions about the correctness of the stated balance.

CASE ILLUSTRATION—HILLSBURG HARDWARE, PART III

The Hillsburg Hardware Co. case illustration from Chapters 13 and 14 continues here to include the determination of the tests of details of balances audit procedures in the sales and collection cycle. Table 15-2 (p. 494) includes comparative trial balance information for the sales and collection cycle for Hillsburg Hardware Co. Some of that information is used to illustrate several analytical procedures in Table 15-3 (p. 494). None of the analytical procedures indicated potential misstatements except the ratio of the allowance of uncollectible accounts to accounts receivable. The explanation at the bottom of Table 15-3 comments on the potential misstatement.

> **OBJECTIVE 15-5**
> Design audit procedures for the audit of accounts receivable, using an evidence planning worksheet as a guide.

Fran Moore prepared the evidence planning worksheet in Figure 15-7 on page 495 as an aid to help her decide the extent of planned tests of details of balances. The source of each of the rows are as follows:

- *Tolerable misstatement.* The preliminary judgment of materiality was set at $37,000 (approximately 10 percent of earnings from operations of $369,000). She allocated $22,000 to the audit of accounts receivable (see p. 255).
- *Acceptable audit risk.* Fran assessed acceptable audit risk as high because of the good financial condition of the company, its financial stability, and the relatively few users of the financial statements.
- *Inherent risk.* Fran assessed inherent risk as low for all objectives except realizable value. In past years, there have been audit adjustments to the allowance for uncollectible accounts because it was found to be understated.
- *Control risk.* Control risk assessments for each audit objective are the same as those in Figure 14-7 on page 465. Recall that results of tests of controls and substantive tests of transactions in Chapter 14 were consistent with the auditor's initial control risk assessments, except for the accuracy and realizable value objectives for sales.
- *Substantive tests of transactions results.* These results were also taken from Figure 14-7 on page 465. Recall from Chapter 14 that all results were acceptable except the accuracy and cutoff objectives for sales.
- *Analytical procedures.* See Tables 15-2 and 15-3.
- *Planned detection risk and planned audit evidence.* These two rows are decided for each objective based on the conclusions in the other rows.

Table 15-4 (p. 496) shows the tests of details audit program for accounts receivable, by objective, and for the allowance for uncollectible accounts. The audit program reflects the

TABLE 15-2 Comparative Information for Hillsburg Hardware Co.–Sales and Collection Cycle

	Amount				
	12-31-99 (in thousands)	Percent Change 1998–1999	12-31-98 (in thousands)	Percent Change 1997–1998	12-31-97 (in thousands)
Sales	$7,216	14.2%	$6,321	6.5%	$5,937
Sales returns and allowances	62	8.8	57	14.0	50
Gross margin	1,992	14.6	1,738	7.2	1,621
Accounts receivable	1,010	12.5	898	8.8	825
Allowance for uncollectible accounts	62	(19.5)	77	11.6	69
Bad debt expense	166	1.2	164	15.5	142
Total current assets	2,550	13.9	2,239	6.7	2,099
Total assets	3,067	(7.1)	3,301	8.0	3,057
Net earnings before taxes	285	(34.6)	436	9.8	397
Number of accounts receivable	258	16.7	221	5.7	209
Number of accounts receivable with balances over $5,000	37	15.6	32	6.7	30

TABLE 15-3 Analytical Procedures for Hillsburg Hardware Co.– Sales and Collection Cycle

	12-31-99	12-31-98	12-31-97
Gross margin/net sales	27.8%	27.7%	27.5%
Sales returns and allowances/gross sales	.9%	.9%	.8%
Bad debt expense/net sales	2.3%	2.6%	2.4%
Allowance for uncollectible accounts/ accounts receivable	6.1%	8.6%	8.4%
Number of days receivables outstanding	50.8	51.6	50.5
Net accounts receivable/total current assets	37.2%	36.7%	36.0%

Comment: Allowance as a percentage of accounts receivable has declined from 8.4% to 6.1%. Number of days receivables outstanding and economic conditions do not justify this change. Potential misstatement is approximately $23,000 ($1,010,000 × .084 − .061), which is greater than tolerable misstatement.

conclusions for planned audit evidence on the evidence planning worksheet in Figure 15-7. Table 15-5 (p. 497) shows the audit program in a performance format. The audit procedures are identical to those in Table 15-4 except for procedure 2, which is an analytical procedure. The numbers in parentheses are a cross reference between the two tables.

	Detail tie-in	Existence	Completeness	Accuracy	Classification	Cutoff	Realizable value	Rights	Presentation and disclosure
Acceptable audit risk	High	High	High	High	High	High	High	High	High
Inherent risk	Low	Low	Low	Low	Low	Low	Medium	Low	Low
Control risk—Sales	Low	Medium	Low	High	Low	High	High	Not applicable	Not applicable
Control risk—Cash receipts	Medium	High	Low	Low	High	High	Not applicable	Not applicable	Not applicable
Control risk—Additional controls	None	None	None	None	None	None	None	Low	Low
Substantive tests of transactions—Sales	Good results	Good results	Good results	Fair results	Good results	Un-acceptable results	Not applicable	Not applicable	Not applicable
Substantive tests of transactions—Cash receipts	Good results	Good results	Good results	Good results	Good results	Good results	Not applicable	Not applicable	Not applicable
Analytical procedures	Good results	Good results	Good results	Good results	Good results	Good results	Un-acceptable results	Not applicable	Not applicable
Planned detection risk for tests of details of balances	High	Medium	High	High	High	Low	Low	High	High
Planned audit evidence for tests of details of balances	Low	Medium	Low	Low	Low	High	High	Low	Low

Tolerable misstatement $22,000

Balance-Related Audit Objective	Audit Procedure
Accounts receivable in the aged trial balance agree with related master file amounts, and the total is correctly added and agrees with the general ledger (detail tie-in).	Trace 10 accounts from the trial balance to accounts on master file (6). Foot two pages of the trial balance, and total all pages (7). Trace the balance to the general ledger (8).
The accounts receivable on the aged trial balance exist (existence).	Confirm accounts receivable, using positive confirmations. Confirm all amounts over $5,000 and a nonstatistical sample of the remainder (10). Perform alternative procedures for all confirmations not returned on the first or second request (11). Review accounts receivable trial balance for large and unusual receivables (1).
Existing accounts receivable are included in the aged trial balance (completeness).	Trace 5 accounts from the accounts receivable master file to the aged trial balance (9).
Accounts receivable in the trial balance are accurate (accuracy).	Confirm accounts receivable, using positive confirmations. Confirm all amounts over $5,000 and a nonstatistical sample of the remainder (10). Perform alternative procedures for all confirmations not returned on the first or second request (11). Review accounts receivable trial balance for large and unusual receivables (1).
Accounts receivable on the aged trial balance are properly classified (classification).	Review the receivables listed on the aged trial balance for notes and related party receivables (3). Inquire of management whether there are any related party notes or long-term receivables included in the trial balance (4).
Transactions in the sales and collection cycle are recorded in the proper period (cutoff).	Select the last 20 sales transactions from the current year's sales journal and the first 20 from the subsequent year's and trace each to the related shipping documents, checking for the date of actual shipment and the correct recording (14). Review large sales returns and allowances before and after the balance sheet date to determine whether they are recorded in the correct period (15).
Accounts receivable is stated at realizable value (realizable value).	Trace 10 accounts from the aging schedule to the accounts receivable master file to test for the correct aging on the trial balance (6). Foot the aging columns on the trial balance and total the pages (7). Crossfoot the aging columns (7). Discuss with the credit manager the likelihood of collecting older accounts. Examine subsequent cash receipts and the credit file on all accounts over 90 days and evaluate whether the receivables are collectible (12). Evaluate whether the allowance is adequate after performing other audit procedures for collectibility of receivables (13).
The client has rights to accounts receivable on the trial balance (rights).	Review the minutes of the board of directors meetings for any indication of pledged or factored accounts receivable (5). Inquire of management whether any receivables are pledged or factored (5).
Accounts in the sales and collection cycle and related information are properly presented and disclosed (presentation and disclosure).	Review the minutes of the board of directors meetings for any indication of pledged or factored accounts receivable (5). Inquire of management whether any receivables are pledged or factored (5).

Note: The procedures are summarized into a performance format in Table 15-5 on page 497. The numbers in parentheses after the procedures refer to Table 15-5.

1. Review accounts receivable trial balance for large and unusual receivables.
2. Calculate analytical procedures indicated in carry-forward working papers (not included) and follow up on any significant changes from prior years.
3. Review the receivables listed on the aged trial balance for notes and related party receivables.
4. Inquire of management whether there are any related party, notes, or long-term receivables included in the trial balance.
5. Review the minutes of the board of directors meetings and inquire of management to determine whether any receivables are pledged or factored.
6. Trace 10 accounts from the trial balance to the accounts receivable master file for aging and the balance.
7. Foot 2 pages of the trial balance for aging columns and balance and total all pages and crossfoot the aging.
8. Trace the balance to the general ledger.
9. Trace 5 accounts from the accounts receivable master file to the aged trial balance.
10. Confirm accounts receivable, using positive confirmations. Confirm all amounts over $5,000 and a nonstatistical sample of the remainder.
11. Perform alternative procedures for all confirmations not returned on the first or second request.
12. Discuss with the credit manager the likelihood of collecting older accounts. Examine subsequent cash receipts and the credit file on all larger accounts over 90 days and evaluate whether the receivables are collectible.
13. Evaluate whether the allowance is adequate after performing other audit procedures for collectibility of receivables.
14. Select the last 20 sales transactions from the current year's sales journal and the first 20 from the subsequent year's and trace each to the related shipping documents, checking for the date of actual shipment and the correct recording.
15. Review large sales returns and allowances before and after the balance sheet date to determine whether they are recorded in the correct period.

ESSENTIAL TERMS

Accounts receivable balance-related audit objectives—the nine specific audit objectives used by the auditor to decide the appropriate audit evidence for accounts receivable

Aged trial balance—a listing of the balances in the accounts receivable master file at the balance sheet date broken down according to the amount of time passed between the date of sale and the balance sheet date

Alternative procedures—the follow-up of a positive confirmation not returned by the debtor with the use of documentation evidence to determine whether the recorded receivable exists and is collectible

Blank confirmation form—a letter, addressed to the debtor, requesting the recipient to fill in the amount of the accounts receivable balance; it is considered a positive confirmation

Cutoff misstatements—misstatements that take place as a result of current period transactions being recorded in a subsequent period, or subsequent period transactions being recorded in the current period

Invoice confirmation—a type of positive confirmation in which an individual invoice is confirmed, rather than the customer's entire accounts receivable balance

Negative confirmation—a letter, addressed to the debtor, requesting a response only if the recipient disagrees with the amount of the stated account balance

Positive confirmation—a letter, addressed to the debtor, requesting that the recipient indicate directly on the letter whether the stated account balance is correct or incorrect and, if incorrect, by what amount

Realizable value of accounts receivable—the amount of the outstanding balances in accounts receivable that will ultimately be collected

Timing difference—a reported difference in a confirmation from a debtor that is determined to be a timing difference between the client's and debtor's records and therefore not a misstatement

15-1 (Objective 15-1) Distinguish among tests of details of balances, tests of controls, and substantive tests of transactions for the sales and collection cycle. Explain how the tests of controls and substantive tests of transactions affect the tests of details of balances.

15-2 (Objective 15-1) Cynthia Roberts, CPA, expresses the following viewpoint: "I do not believe in performing tests of controls and substantive tests of transactions for the sales and collection cycle. As an alternative, I send a lot of negative confirmations on every audit at an interim date. If I find a lot of misstatements, I analyze them to determine their cause. If internal controls are inadequate, I send positive confirmations at year-end to evaluate the amount of misstatements. If the negative confirmations result in minimal misstatements, which is often the case, I have found that the internal controls are effective without bothering to perform tests of controls and substantive tests of transactions, and the AICPA's confirmation requirement has been satisfied at the same time. In my opinion, the best test of internal controls is to go directly to third parties." Evaluate her point of view.

15-3 (Objective 15-2) List five analytical procedures for the sales and collection cycle. For each test, describe a misstatement that could be identified.

15-4 (Objective 15-3) Identify the nine accounts receivable balance-related audit objectives. For each objective, list one audit procedure.

15-5 (Objective 15-3) Which of the nine accounts receivable balance-related audit objectives can be partially satisfied by confirmations with customers?

15-6 (Objective 15-3) State the purpose of footing the total column in the client's trial balance, tracing individual customer names and amounts to the accounts receivable master file, and tracing the total to the general ledger. Is it necessary to trace each amount to the master file? Why?

15-7 (Objective 15-3) Distinguish between accuracy tests of gross accounts receivable and tests of the realizable value of receivables.

15-8 (Objective 15-3) Explain why you agree or disagree with the following statement: "In most audits, it is more important to test carefully the cutoff for sales than for cash receipts." Describe how you perform each type of test, assuming the existence of prenumbered documents.

15-9 (Objective 15-4) Evaluate the following statement: "In many audits in which accounts receivable is material, the requirement of confirming customer balances is a waste of time and would not be performed by competent auditors if it were not required by the AICPA. When internal controls are excellent and there are a large number of small receivables from customers who do not recognize the function of confirmation, it is a meaningless procedure. Examples include well-run utilities and department stores. In these situations, tests of controls and substantive tests of transactions are far more effective than confirmations."

15-10 (Objective 15-4) Distinguish between a positive and a negative confirmation and state the circumstances in which each should be used. Why do CPA firms often use a combination of positive and negative confirmations on the same audit?

15-11 (Objective 15-4) Under what circumstances is it acceptable to confirm accounts receivable before the balance sheet date?

15-12 (Objective 15-4) State the most important factors affecting the sample size in confirmations of accounts receivable.

15-13 (Objective 15-4) In Chapter 14, one of the points brought out was the need to obtain a representative sample of the population. How can this concept be reconciled with the statement in this chapter that the emphasis should be on confirming larger and older balances because these are most likely to contain misstatements?

15-14 (Objective 15-4) Define what is meant by alternative procedures in the confirmation of accounts receivable and explain their purpose. Which alternative procedures are the most reliable? Why?

15-15 (Objective 15-4) Explain why the analysis of differences is important in the confirmation of accounts receivable, even if the misstatements in the sample are not material.

15-16 (Objective 15-4) State three types of differences that might be observed in the confirmation of accounts receivable that do not constitute misstatements. For each, state an audit procedure that would verify the difference.

15-17 (Objective 15-1) What is the relationship of each of the following to the sales and collection cycle: flowcharts, assessing control risk, tests of controls, and tests of details of balances?

15-18 (Objective 15-3) Describe GAAP requirements for proper recording of sales returns and allowances.

MULTIPLE CHOICE QUESTIONS FROM CPA EXAMINATIONS

15-19 (Objective 15-2) The following questions concern analytical procedures in the sales and collection cycle. Choose the best response.

a. As a result of analytical procedures, the independent auditor determines that the gross profit percentage has declined from 30 percent in the preceding year to 20 percent in the current year. The auditor should
   (1) express a qualified opinion due to inability of the client company to continue as a going concern.
   (2) evaluate management's performance in causing this decline.
   (3) require footnote disclosure.
   (4) consider the possibility of a misstatement in the financial statements.
b. Once a CPA has determined that accounts receivable have increased as a result of slow collections in a "tight money" environment, the CPA would be likely to
   (1) increase the balance in the allowance for bad debt account.
   (2) review the going concern ramifications.
   (3) review the credit and collection policy.
   (4) expand tests of collectibility.
c. In connection with his review of key ratios, the CPA notes that Pyzi had accounts receivable equal to 30 days' sales at December 31, 1998, and to 45 days' sales at December 31, 1999. Assuming that there had been no changes in economic conditions, clientele, or sales mix, this change most likely would indicate
   (1) a steady increase in sales in 1999.
   (2) an easing of credit policies in 1999.
   (3) a decrease in accounts receivable relative to sales in 1999.
   (4) a steady decrease in sales in 1999.

15-20 (Objective 15-4) The following questions deal with confirmation of accounts receivable. Choose the best response.

a. In connection with his audit of the Beke Supply Company for the year ended August 31, 1999, Derek Lowe, CPA, has mailed accounts receivable confirmations to three groups as follows:

Group Number	Type of Customer	Type of Confirmation
1	Wholesale	Positive
2	Current retail	Negative
3	Past-due retail	Positive

The confirmation responses from each group vary from 10 percent to 90 percent. The most likely response percentages are:

    (1) Group 1—90 percent, group 2—50 percent, group 3—10 percent
    (2) Group 1—90 percent, group 2—10 percent, group 3—50 percent
    (3) Group 1—50 percent, group 2—90 percent, group 3—10 percent
    (4) Group 1—10 percent, group 2—50 percent, group 3—90 percent

b. The negative form of accounts receivable confirmation request is useful *except* when

    (1) internal control surrounding accounts receivable is considered to be effective.
    (2) a large number of small balances are involved.
    (3) the auditor has reason to believe the persons receiving the requests are likely to give them consideration.
    (4) individual account balances are relatively large.

c. The return of a positive confirmation of accounts receivable without an exception attests to the

    (1) collectibility of the receivable balance.
    (2) accuracy of the receivable balance.
    (3) accuracy of the aging of accounts receivable.
    (4) accuracy of the allowance for uncollectible accounts.

d. In confirming a client's accounts receivable in prior years, an auditor found that there were many differences between the recorded account balances and the confirmation responses. These differences, which were not misstatements, required substantial time to resolve. In defining the sampling unit for the current year's audit, the auditor would most likely choose

    (1) individual overdue balances.
    (2) individual invoices.
    (3) small account balances.
    (4) large account balances.

15-21 (Objective 15-3) The following questions concern audit objectives and management assertions for accounts receivable. Choose the best response.

a. When evaluating the adequacy of the allowance for uncollectible accounts, an auditor reviews the entity's aging of receivables to support management's financial assertion of

    (1) existence or occurrence.
    (2) valuation or allocation.
    (3) completeness.
    (4) rights and obligations.

b. Which of the following audit procedures would best uncover an understatement of sales and accounts receivable?

    (1) Test a sample of sales transactions, selecting the sample from prenumbered shipping documents.
    (2) Test a sample of sales transactions, selecting the sample from sales invoices recorded in the sales journal.
    (3) Confirm accounts receivable.
    (4) Review the aged accounts receivable trial balance.

DISCUSSION QUESTIONS AND PROBLEMS

15-22 (Objective 15-3) The following are common tests of details of balances for the audit of accounts receivable.

1. Obtain a list of aged accounts receivable, foot the list, and trace the total to the general ledger.
2. Trace 35 accounts to the accounts receivable master file for name, amount, and age categories.

3. Examine and document cash receipts on accounts receivable for 20 days after the engagement date.
4. Request 25 positive and 65 negative confirmations of accounts receivable.
5. Perform alternative procedures on accounts not responding to second requests by examining subsequent cash receipts documentation and shipping reports or sales invoices.
6. Test the sales cutoff by tracing entries in the sales journal for 15 days before and after the balance sheet date to shipping documents, if available, and/or sales invoices.
7. Determine and disclose accounts pledged, discounted, sold, assigned, or guaranteed by others.
8. Evaluate the materiality of credit balances in the aged trial balance.

Required

For each audit procedure, identify the balance-related audit objective or objectives it partially or fully satisfies.

15-23 (Objective 15-3)   The following misstatements are sometimes found in the sales and collection cycle's account balances:

1. Cash received from collections of accounts receivable in the subsequent period is recorded as current period receipts.
2. The allowance for uncollectible accounts is inadequate because of the client's failure to reflect depressed economic conditions in the allowance.
3. Several accounts receivable are in dispute as a result of claims of defective merchandise.
4. The pledging of accounts receivable to the bank for a loan is not disclosed in the financial statements.
5. Goods shipped and included in the current period sales were returned in the subsequent period.
6. Several accounts receivable in the accounts receivable master file are not included in the aged trial balance.
7. One account receivable in the accounts receivable master file is included on the aged trial balance twice.
8. Long-term interest-bearing notes receivable from affiliated companies are included in accounts receivable.
9. The trial balance total does not equal the amount in the general ledger.

Required

   a. For each misstatement, identify the balance-related audit objective to which it pertains.
   b. For each misstatement, list an internal control that should prevent it.
   c. For each misstatement, list one test of details of balances audit procedure that the auditor can use to detect it.

15-24 (Objective 15-3)   The following are audit procedures in the sales and collection cycle.

1. Examine a sample of shipping documents to determine whether each has a sales invoice number included on it.
2. Discuss with the sales manager whether any sales allowances have been granted after the balance sheet date that may apply to the current period.
3. Add the columns on the aged trial balance and compare the total with the general ledger.
4. Observe whether the controller makes an independent comparison of the total in the general ledger with the trial balance of accounts receivable.
5. Compare the date on a sample of shipping documents throughout the year with related duplicate sales invoices and the accounts receivable master file.
6. Examine a sample of customer orders and see if each has a credit authorization.
7. Compare the date on a sample of shipping documents a few days before and after the balance sheet date with related sales journal transactions.

8. Compute the ratio of allowance for uncollectible accounts divided by accounts receivable and compare with previous years.
9. Examine a sample of noncash credits in the accounts receivable master file to determine if the internal auditor has initialed each indicating internal verification.

Required
a. For each procedure, identify the applicable type of audit evidence.
b. For each procedure, identify which of the following it is:
   (1) Test of control
   (2) Substantive test of transactions
   (3) Analytical procedure
   (4) Test of details of balances
c. For those procedures you identified as a test of control or substantive test of transactions, what transaction-related audit objective or objectives are being satisfied?
d. For those procedures you identified as a test of details of balances, what balance-related audit objective or objectives are being satisfied?

15-25 (Objective 15-3) The following are the nine balance-related audit objectives, seven tests of details of balances for accounts receivable, and seven tests of controls or substantive tests of transactions for the sales and collection cycle.

Balance-Related Audit Objective
Detail tie-in
Existence
Completeness
Accuracy
Classification
Cutoff
Realizable value
Rights
Presentation and disclosure

Test of Details of Balances, Test of Control, or Substantive Test of Transactions Audit Procedure
1. Confirm accounts receivable.
2. Review sales returns after the balance sheet date to determine whether any are applicable to the current year.
3. Compare dates on shipping documents and the sales journal throughout the year.
4. Perform alternative procedures for nonresponses to confirmation.
5. Examine sales transactions for related party or employee sales recorded as regular sales.
6. Examine duplicate sales invoices for consignment sales and other shipments for which title has not passed.
7. Trace a sample of accounts from the accounts receivable master file to the aged trial balance.
8. Trace recorded sales transactions to shipping documents to determine whether a document exists.
9. Examine the financial statements to determine whether all related parties, notes, and pledged receivables are properly presented.
10. Examine duplicate sales invoices for initials that indicate internal verification of extensions and footings.
11. Trace a sample of shipping documents to related sales invoice entries in the sales journal.
12. Compare amounts and dates on the aged trial balance and accounts receivable master file.

13. Trace from the sales journal to the accounts receivable master file to make sure the information is the same.

14. Inquire of management whether there are notes from related parties included with trade receivables.

Required

    a. Identify which procedures are tests of details of balances, which are tests of controls, and which are substantive tests of transactions.

    b. Identify one test of details and one test of control or substantive test of transactions that will partially satisfy each balance-related audit objective. (Tests of controls and substantive tests of transactions are not used for presentation and disclosure.) Each procedure must be used at least once.

15-26 (Objective 15-3) Niosoki Auto Parts sells new parts for foreign automobiles to auto dealers. Company policy requires that a prenumbered shipping document be issued for each sale. At the time of pickup or shipment, the shipping clerk writes the date on the shipping document. The last shipment made in the fiscal year ended August 31, 1999, was recorded on document 2167. Shipments are billed in the order that the billing clerk receives the shipping documents.

For late August and early September, shipping documents are billed on sales invoices as follows:

Shipping Document No.	Sales Invoice No.
2163	4332
2164	4326
2165	4327
2166	4330
2167	4331
2168	4328
2169	4329
2170	4333
2171	4335
2172	4334

The August and September sales journals have the following information included:

SALES JOURNAL—AUGUST 1999

Day of Month	Sales Invoice No.	Amount of Sale
30	4326	$ 726.11
30	4329	1,914.30
31	4327	419.83
31	4328	620.22
31	4330	47.74

SALES JOURNAL—SEPTEMBER 1999

Day of Month	Sales Invoice No.	Amount of Sale
1	4332	$4,641.31
1	4331	106.39
1	4333	852.06
2	4335	1,250.50
2	4334	646.58

Required

a. What are the GAAP requirements for a correct sales cutoff?
b. Which sales invoices, if any, are recorded in the wrong accounting period? Prepare an adjusting entry to correct the financial statement for the year ended August 31, 1999. Assume that the company uses a periodic inventory system (inventory and cost of sales do not need to be adjusted).
c. Assume that the shipping clerk accidentally wrote August 31 on shipping documents 2168 through 2172. Explain how that would affect the correctness of the financial statements. How would you, as an auditor, discover that error?
d. Describe, in general terms, the audit procedures you would follow in making sure that cutoff for sales is accurate at the balance sheet date.
e. Identify internal controls that would reduce the likelihood of cutoff misstatements. How would you test each control?

15-27 (Objective 15-4)   Dodge, CPA, is auditing the financial statements of a manufacturing company with a significant amount of trade accounts receivable. Dodge is satisfied that the accounts are properly summarized and classified and that allocations, reclassifications, and valuations are made in accordance with GAAP. Dodge is planning to use accounts receivable confirmation requests to satisfy the third standard of field work as to trade accounts receivable.

Required

a. Identify and describe the two forms of accounts receivable confirmation requests and indicate what factors Dodge will consider in determining when to use each.
b. Assume that Dodge has received a satisfactory response to the confirmation requests. Describe how Dodge could evaluate collectibility of the trade accounts receivable.
c. What are the implications to a CPA if during his or her audit of accounts receivable some of a client's trade customers do not respond to a request for positive confirmation of their accounts?
d. What auditing steps should a CPA perform if there is no response to a second request for a positive confirmation?*

15-28 (Objective 15-4)   You have been assigned to the confirmation of aged accounts receivable for the Blank Paper Company audit. You have tested the aged trial balance and selected the accounts for confirming. Before the confirmation requests are mailed, the controller asks to look at the accounts you intend to confirm to determine whether he will permit you to send them.

He reviews the list and informs you that he does not want you to confirm six of the accounts on your list. Two of them are credit balances, one is a zero balance, two of the other three have a fairly small balance, and the remaining balance is highly material. The reason he gives is that he feels the confirmations will upset these customers because "they are kind of hard to get along with." He does not want the credit balances confirmed because it may encourage the customer to ask for a refund.

In addition, the controller asks you to send an additional 20 confirmations to customers he has listed for you. He does this as a means of credit collection for "those stupid idiots who won't know the difference between a CPA and a credit collection agency."

Required

a. Is it acceptable for the controller to review the list of accounts you intend to confirm? Discuss.
b. Discuss the appropriateness of sending the twenty additional confirmations to the customers.
c. Assuming that the auditor complies with all the controller's requests, what is the effect on the auditor's opinion?

*AICPA adapted.

15-29 (Objective 15-4) You have been assigned to the first audit of the Chicago Company for the year ending March 31, 2000. Accounts receivable were confirmed on December 31, 1999, and at that date the receivables consisted of approximately 200 accounts with balances totaling $956,750. Seventy-five of these accounts with balances totaling $650,725 were selected for confirmation. All but 20 of the confirmation requests have been returned; 30 were signed without comments, 14 had minor differences that have been cleared satisfactorily, and 11 confirmations had the following comments:

1. We are sorry, but we cannot answer your request for confirmation of our account as the PDQ Company uses an accounts payable voucher system.
2. The balance of $1,050 was paid on December 23, 1999.
3. The balance of $7,750 was paid on January 5, 2000.
4. The balance noted above has been paid.
5. We do not owe you anything at December 31, 1999, as the goods, represented by your invoice dated December 30, 1999, number 25050, in the amount of $11,550, were received on January 5, 2000, on FOB destination terms.
6. An advance payment of $2,500 made by us in November 1999 should cover the two invoices totaling $1,350 shown on the statement attached.
7. We never received these goods.
8. We are contesting the propriety of this $12,525 charge. We think the charge is excessive.
9. Amount okay. As the goods have been shipped to us on consignment, we will remit payment upon selling the goods.
10. The $10,000, representing a deposit under a lease, will be applied against the rent due to us during 2001, the last year of the lease.
11. Your credit memo dated December 5, 1999, in the amount of $440 cancels the balance above.

Required

What steps would you take to satisfactorily clear each of the preceding 11 comments.*

15-30 (Objectives 15-2, 15-3, 15-4, 15-5) You have audited the financial statements of the Heft Company for several years. Internal controls for accounts receivable are satisfactory. The Heft Company is on a calendar-year basis. An interim audit, which included confirmation of the accounts receivable, was performed on August 31 and indicated that the accounting for cash, sales, sales returns and allowances, and receivables was reliable.

The company's sales are principally to manufacturing concerns. There are about 1,500 active trade accounts receivable of which about 35 percent represent 65 percent of the total dollar amount. The accounts receivable are maintained alphabetically in a master file of accounts receivable.

Shipping document data are keyed into a computerized system that simultaneously produces a sales invoice, sales journal, and an updated accounts receivable master file.

All cash receipts are in the form of customers' checks. Information for cash receipts is obtained from the remittance advice portions of the customers' checks. The computer operator compares the remittance advices with the list of checks that was prepared by another person when the mail was received. As for sales, a cash receipts journal and updated accounts receivable master file are simultaneously prepared after the cash receipts information is entered.

Summary totals are produced monthly by the computer operations department for updating the general ledger master file accounts such as cash, sales, and accounts receivable. An aged trial balance is prepared monthly.

Required

Prepare the additional audit procedures necessary for testing the balances in the sales and collection cycle. (Ignore bad debts and allowance for uncollectible accounts.)*

*AICPA adapted.

15-31 (Objective 15-4)   In the confirmation of accounts receivable for the Reliable Service Company, 85 positive and no negative confirmations were mailed to customers. This represents 35 percent of the dollar balance of the total accounts receivable. Second requests were sent for all nonresponses, but there were still 10 customers who did not respond. The decision was made to perform alternative procedures on the 10 unanswered confirmation requests. An assistant is requested to conduct the alternative procedures and report to the senior auditor after he has completed his tests on two accounts. He prepared the following information for the working papers:

1. Confirmation request no. 9
   Customer name—Jolene Milling Co.
   Balance—$3,621 at December 31, 1999
       Subsequent cash receipts per the accounts
           receivable master file:

	January 15, 2000—$1,837
	January 29, 2000—$1,263
	February 6, 2000—$1,429

2. Confirmation request no. 26
   Customer name—Rosenthal Repair Service
   Balance—$2,500 at December 31, 1999
       Subsequent cash receipts per the accounts
           receivable master file   February 9, 2000—$500
       Sales invoices per the accounts receivable
           master file (I examined the duplicate invoice)   September 1, 1999—$4,200

Required

a. If you were called on to evaluate the adequacy of the sample size, the type of confirmation used, and the percentage of accounts confirmed, what additional information would you need?

b. Discuss the need to send second requests and perform alternative procedures for nonresponses.

c. Evaluate the adequacy of the alternative procedures used for verifying the two nonresponses.

CASE

15-32 (Objectives 15-1, 15-3, 15-4, 15-5)   You are auditing the sales and collection cycle for the Smalltown Regional Hospital, a small not-for-profit hospital. The hospital has a reputation for excellent medical services and weak record keeping. The medical people have a tradition of doing all aspects of their job correctly, but because of a shortage of accounting personnel, there is not time for internal verification or careful performance. In previous years, your CPA firm has found quite a few misstatements in billings, cash receipts, and accounts receivable. As in all hospitals, the two largest assets are accounts receivable and property, plant, and equipment.

The hospital has several large loans payable to local banks, and the two banks have told management that they are reluctant to extend more credit, especially considering the modern hospital that is being built in a nearby city. In the past, county taxes have made up deficits, but in the past year, the county has also been incurring deficits because of high unemployment.

In previous years, your response from patients to confirmation requests has been frustrating at best. The response rate has been extremely low, and those who did respond did not know the purpose of the confirmations or their correct outstanding balance. You have had the same experience in confirming receivables at other hospitals.

You conclude that control over cash is excellent and the likelihood of fraud is extremely small. You are less confident about unintentional errors in billing, recording sales, cash receipts, accounts receivable, and bad debts.

Required

    a. Identify the major factors affecting acceptable audit risk for this audit.

    b. What inherent risks are you concerned about?

    c. In this audit of the sales and collection cycle, which types of tests are you likely to emphasize?

    d. For each of the following, explain whether you plan to emphasize the tests and give reasons.

       (1) Tests of controls

       (2) Substantive tests of transactions

       (3) Analytical procedures

       (4) Tests of details of balances

INTEGRATED CASE APPLICATION— PINNACLE MANUFACTURING: PART IV

15-33 (Objectives 15-2, 15-3, 15-4, 15-5) Parts I (pp. 325–327), II (pp. 435–436), and III (p. 474) of this case study dealt with obtaining an understanding of internal control and assessing control risk for transactions affecting accounts payable of Pinnacle Manufacturing. In Part IV, we design analytical procedures and design and perform tests of details of balances for accounts payable.

Assume that your understanding of internal controls over acquisitions and cash disbursements and the related tests of controls and substantive tests of transactions support an assessment of a low control risk. Also assume that analytical procedures support the overall reasonableness of the balance. Accounts payable at December 31, 1999, are included in Figure 15-8 (p. 508).

Required

    a. List those relationships, ratios, and trends that you believe will provide useful information about the overall reasonableness of accounts payable.

    b. Prepare an audit program in a design format for tests of details of balances for accounts payable. Before preparing the audit program, you should review the Hillsburg Hardware Co. Case Illustration starting on page 493. You should prepare a matrix similar to the one in Figure 15-7 on page 495 for accounts payable. Assume that acceptable audit risk was assessed as high. Use your judgment to assess inherent risk for each objective. Assume that assessed control risk is low for all transaction-related audit objectives and analytical procedures results were satisfactory for those balance-related audit objectives where analytical procedures are relevant. The design format audit program should include audit procedures and sample size for each procedure.

    c. Prepare an audit program for accounts payable in a performance format, using the audit procedures and sample sizes from part b.

    d. Assume for requirement b that (1) assessed control risk had been high rather than low for each transaction-related audit objective, (2) inherent risk was high for each balance-related audit objective, and (3) analytical procedures indicated a high potential for misstatement. What would the effect have been on the audit procedures and sample sizes for part b?

    e. Confirmation requests were sent to the 20 vendors listed in Figure 15-9 (p. 509). Fourteen confirmation responses were returned indicating no difference between the vendor's and the company's records. Figure 15-10 (pp. 510–511) presents the six replies that indicate a difference between the vendor's balance and the company's records. The auditor's follow-up findings are indicated on each reply. Prepare a worksheet similar to the one illustrated in Figure 15-11 on page 512 to determine the misstatements, if any, for each difference. The exception for Fiberchem is analyzed as an illustration. Assume that Pinnacle Manufacturing took a complete physical inventory at December 31, 1999, and the auditor concluded that recorded

FIGURE 15-8 Pinnacle Manufacturing Trial Balance of Trade Accounts Payable December 31, 1999

Advent Sign Mfg. Co.	$ 2,500.00	M & A Milling	$ 4,662.00
Alder Insurance Co.	660.00	Midwest Electric Utility	3,698.15
American Computing Service	1,211.00	Midwest Gas Co.	2,442.10
Bauer and Adamson	86.00	Mobil Oil Co.	11,480.00
Bleyl & Sons	1,500.00	Monsanto Chemical	14,622.15
Central Steel Inc.	8,753.00	Nielsen Enterprises	437.56
Chelsea Development Co.	1,800.00	Norris Industries	9,120.00
Commercial Supply	3,250.00	Pacific Title Co.	320.00
Country Electric	980.00	Permaloy Manufacturing	3,290.00
Diamond Janitorial Service	750.00	Polein Drill and Bit	2,870.16
Dictaphone Corp.	675.00	Propec Inc.	510.00
Douglas Equipment	6,425.00	Rayno Sales and Service	1,917.80
Ellison, Robt. & Assoc.	346.10	Reames Construction	4,500.00
FMC Corp.	15,819.00	Remington Supply Co.	9,842.10
Fiberchem Inc.	6,315.80	Ritter Engineering Corp.	1,200.00
Fuller Travel	943.00	Roberts Bros. Service	189.73
GAFCO	5,750.00	S & S Truck Painting	819.00
Glade Specialties	1,000.00	Sanders, Geo. A. & Co.	346.00
Granger Supply Co.	4,250.00	Semco, Inc.	50.20
Hesco Services	719.62	Standard Oil Co.	12,816.27
Innes, Brush & Co. CPAs	1,500.00	Stationery Supply	619.12
J & L Plastics Corp.	1,412.00	Thermal Tape Co.	123.00
Judkins Co.	2,500.00	Todd Machinery, Inc.	6,888.12
Kazco. Mfg. Co.	1,627.30	Valco Sales	1,429.00
Kedman Company	19.27	Vermax Corp.	284.00
Koch Plumbing Contractors	2,750.00	Waco Electronics, Inc.	126.33
Kohler Products	10,483.23	Western Telephone Co.	2,369.62
Lakeshore Inc.	1,850.00	Williams Controls, Inc.	1,915.00
Landscape Services	420.00	Xerox Corp.	3,250.00
Lundberg Coatings, Inc.	2,733.10	Yates Supply Co.	919.70
		Total	$192,085.53

Other related information:

• The vendors with the greatest volume of transactions during the year are as follows:

Central Steel Inc.	Mobil Oil Co.
Commercial Supply	Monsanto Chemical
FMC Corp.	Norris Industries
Fiberchem Inc.	Remington Supply Co.
GAFCO	Standard Oil Co.

• Tolerable misstatement for accounts payable is $7,500.00.

inventory reflects all inventory on hand at the balance sheet date. Include the 14 balances confirmed without exception as one amount on the worksheet, and total the worksheet columns.

Use a computer with appropriate software to prepare this worksheet and analysis (instructor option).

f. Estimate the total misstatement in accounts payable based on the sample misstatements you identified in requirement e. The total misstatement should include likely misstatements in accounts payable not confirmed, and an estimate for sampling error. Use your judgment to estimate sampling error, considering the size of the population and the amounts tested. What is your conclusion about the fairness of the recorded balance in accounts payable for Pinnacle Manufacturing and your assessment of control risk as low for all transaction-related audit objectives?

FIGURE 15-9 **Pinnacle Manufacturing Sample of Accounts Payable Selected for Confirmation—December 31, 1999**

High-Volume Items	
1. Central Steel	$ 8,753.00
2. Commercial Supply	3,250.00
3. FMC	15,819.00
4. Fiberchem	6,315.80
5. GAFCO	5,750.00
6. Mobil Oil	11,480.00
7. Monsanto	14,622.15
8. Norris Industries	9,120.00
9. Remington Supply	9,842.10
10. Standard Oil	12,816.27
Other Material Items	
11. Kohler Products	10,483.23
Random Sample of Additional Items	
12. Advent Sign Mfg. Co.	2,500.00
13. Country Electric	980.00
14. Fuller Travel	943.00
15. J & L Plastics	1,412.00
16. M & A Milling	4,662.00
17. Permaloy Manufacturing	3,290.00
18. S & S Truck Painting	819.00
19. Todd Machinery	6,888.12
20. Western Telephone Co.	2,369.62
TOTAL TESTED	$132,115.29

FIGURE 15-10   Replies to Requests for Information

STATEMENT FROM FIBERCHEM

Pinnacle Manufacturing
Midvale, IL

Amounts due as of December 31, 1999:

Invoice No.	Date	Amount	Balance Due
8312	11-22-99	$2,217.92	$2,217.92
8469	12-02-99	2,540.11	4,758.03
8819	12-18-99	1,557.77	6,315.80(1)
9002	12-30-99	2,403.42(2)	8,719.22

Auditor's notes:
(1) Agrees with accounts payable listing.
(2) Goods received December 31, 1999. As a result of the New Year's Eve shut-
    down, recorded on January 2, 2000.

STATEMENT FROM MOBIL OIL

Pinnacle Manufacturing
Midvale, IL

Amounts due as of December 31, 1999:

Invoice No.	Date	Amount	Balance Due
DX10037	12-02-99	$2,870.00	$2,870.00
DX11926	12-09-99	2,870.00	5,740.00
DX12619	12-16-99	2,870.00	8,610.00
DX14777	12-23-99	2,870.00	11,480.00(1)
DX16908	12-30-99	2,870.00(2)	14,350.00

Auditor's notes:
(1) Agrees with accounts payable listing.
(2) Goods shipped FOB Pinnacle Manufacturing. Arrived on January 3, 2000.

STATEMENT FROM NORRIS INDUSTRIES

Pinnacle Manufacturing
Midvale, IL

Amounts due as of December 31, 1999:

Invoice No.	Date	Amount	Balance Due
14896	12-27-99	$9,120.00	$ 9,120.00(1)
15111	12-27-99	4,300.00(2)	13,420.00

Auditor's notes:
(1) Agrees with accounts payable listing.
(2) Goods shipped FOB Norris Industries' plant on December 21, 1999, arrived
    at Pinnacle Manufacturing on January 4, 2000.

[continued]

FIGURE 15-10   **Replies to Requests for Information** [continued]

STATEMENT FROM REMINGTON SUPPLY

Pinnacle Manufacturing
Midvale, IL

Amounts due as of December 31, 1999:

Invoice No.	Date	Amount	Balance Due
141702	11-11-99	$3,712.09(2)	$ 3,712.09
142619	11-19-99	1,984.80(1)	5,696.89
142811	12-04-99	2,320.00(2)	8,016.89
143600	12-21-99	3,810.01(2)	11,826.90
143918	12-26-99	3,707.00(3)	15,533.90

Auditor's notes:
(1) Paid by Pinnacle Manufacturing on December 28, 1999. Payment in transit at year-end.
(2) The total of these items of $9,842.10 agrees with accounts payable listing.
(3) Goods shipped FOB Remington Supply on December 26, 1999, arrived at Pinnacle Manufacturing on January 3, 2000.

STATEMENT FROM ADVENT SIGN MFG. CO.

Pinnacle Manufacturing
Midvale, IL

Amounts due as of December 31, 1999:

First progress billing per contract	$2,500.00(1)
Second progress billing per contract	1,500.00(2)
Total due	$4,000.00

Auditor's notes:
(1) Agrees with accounts payable listing.
(2) Progress payment due as of December 31, 1999, per contract for construction of new custom electric sign. Sign installation completed on January 15, 2000.

STATEMENT FROM FULLER TRAVEL

Pinnacle Manufacturing
Midvale, IL

Amounts due as of December 31, 1999:

Ticket No.	Date	Amount	Balance Due
843 601 102	12-04-99	$280.00(2)	$ 280.00
843 601 819	12-12-99	280.00(2)	560.00
843 602 222	12-21-99	383.00(1)	943.00
843 602 919	12-26-99	383.00(2)	1,326.00

Auditor's notes:
(1) Ticket not used and returned for credit. Credit given on January 2000 statement.
(2) The total of these items of $943.00 agrees with accounts payable listing.

Vendor	Balance per Books	Amount Confirmed by Vendor	Difference: Books Over (Under) Amount Confirmed	Timing Difference: No Misstatement	Misstatement in Accounts Payable DR (CR)	Misstatement in Related Accounts		Brief Explanation
						Balance Sheet Misstatement DR (CR)	Income Statement Misstatement DR (CR)	
Fiberchem	6,315.80	8,719.22	(2,403.42)		(2,403.42)		2,403.42	Unrecorded A/P: Dr Purchases Cr A/P

INTERNET PROBLEM 15-1: REVENUE RECOGNITION

Reference the CW site. In recent years, several high-profile incidents of improper revenue recognition attracted the attention of the business media and led to unflattering coverage. The SEC has also expressed concerns about the number of instances of improper revenue recognition identified by SEC staff. In response to the concerns about audit issues associated with revenue recognition, the AICPA put together a "tool kit" summarizing audit guidance in this area. This problem requires students to use the Internet to (1) identify deterrents to improper revenue recognition, (2) define a "bill and hold" sale, and (3) evaluate bill and hold transactions.

AUDIT SAMPLING FOR TESTS OF DETAILS OF BALANCES

16

BOTH STATISTICAL AND NONSTATISTICAL SAMPLING ARE ACCEPTABLE UNDER GAAS, BUT WHICHEVER IS USED, IT MUST BE DONE RIGHT

Bob Lake was the manager on the audit of Images, Inc., a specialty retailer that had shops throughout the Midwest. Images appealed to upscale working women and offered its own credit card. Images' accounting was done centrally. Transactions were captured on-line and sales and accounts receivable files were maintained on a database.

Bob Lake's firm encouraged the use of statistical sampling in its practice and provided a training program for the development of a statistical coordinator for each office. The coordinator in Bob's office was Barbara Ennis. Bob believed that sales transactions and accounts receivable confirmation tests should be done using statistical sampling and asked Barbara to help design and oversee the statistical aspects of this testing.

Barbara developed a program for the design of confirmation audit procedures as part of doing tests of details of balances for accounts receivable. Her work included determining sample sizes. She left the program with Bob to carry out, and said that she would be available to help evaluate the results after the tests were performed.

When all the confirmation replies were received or alternative procedures were completed several weeks later, Bob called Barbara to do the statistical evaluation. Much to his dismay, he found out that Barbara had left the firm, and worse, there was no statistically trained person to take her place. Bob was under a lot of pressure to get the job completed and decided to make the statistical calculations himself. Based on his calculations, he concluded that the potential misstatement was large, but not material, so Bob concluded the objectives of the confirmation tests had been met.

The next year Images, Inc.'s earnings declined sharply, partially because of large write-offs of accounts receivable. The stock price dropped sharply and a class action suit was filed, naming Bob's firm among the defendants. An outside expert was brought in to review the audit work papers. The expert redid all of Bob's work and found errors in the statistical calculations. The expert calculated that the misstatement in accounts receivable, based on the auditor's sample, was significantly more than a material amount. Bob's firm settled the suit for $3.5 million.

LEARNING OBJECTIVES

After studying this chapter, you should be able to

16-1 Differentiate audit sampling for tests of details of balances and for tests of controls and substantive tests of transactions.

16-2 Apply nonstatistical sampling to tests of details of balances.

16-3 Apply monetary unit sampling.

16-4 Describe variables sampling.

16-5 Use difference estimation in tests of details of balances.

In the last chapter, we moved into phase III of the audit process by examining analytical procedures and tests of details of balances for accounts receivable. We will now continue with phase III by determining sample size and items to select from the population for the audit of accounts receivable. Although the concepts discussed in this chapter deal with accounts receivable, they are applicable to the audit of many other account balances.

Both statistical and nonstatistical audit sampling are used extensively for tests of details of balances. Deciding which one to use depends primarily on the auditor's preference, experience, and knowledge about statistical sampling. Both topics are covered in this chapter.

As was demonstrated in the opening vignette, it is extremely important to correctly use the sampling method selected to avoid making wrong conclusions about a population. The study of this chapter is intended to help you make correct inferences about populations using either statistical or nonstatistical methods.

Before starting the study of this chapter, we suggest you refer to Figure 12-13 on page 380 to be sure you understand where we are in the audit process. Before determining sample size and items to select from the population in an audit, all items in phases I and II will have already been completed. The auditor will have also already completed the analytical procedures and designed the audit procedures for tests of details of balances, as studied in Chapter 15 (part of phase III). The auditor cannot perform the audit procedures for tests of details of balances until sample size and items to select from the population are decided.

COMPARISONS OF AUDIT SAMPLING FOR TESTS OF DETAILS OF BALANCES AND FOR TESTS OF CONTROLS AND SUBSTANTIVE TESTS OF TRANSACTIONS

OBJECTIVE 16-1
Differentiate audit sampling for tests of details of balances and for tests of controls and substantive tests of transactions.

Most of the sampling concepts discussed in Chapter 14 for tests of controls and substantive tests of transactions apply equally to sampling for tests of details of balances. In both cases, the auditor wants to make inferences about the entire population based on a sample. Both sampling and nonsampling risks are therefore important for tests of controls, substantive tests of transactions, and tests of details of balances. In dealing with sampling risk, it is acceptable to use either nonstatistical or statistical methods for all three types of tests.

The most important differences among tests of controls, substantive tests of transactions, and tests of details of balances is in what the auditor wants to measure. In tests of controls, the concern is testing the effectiveness of internal controls using tests of controls. When an auditor performs tests of controls, the purpose is to determine whether the exception rate in the population is sufficiently low to justify reducing assessed control risk to reduce substantive tests. In substantive tests of transactions, the auditor is concerned about both the effectiveness of controls and the monetary correctness of transactions in the accounting system. In tests of details of balances, the concern is determining whether the dollar amount of an account balance is materially misstated. Tests for the rate of occurrence, therefore, are seldom useful for tests of details of balances. Instead, auditors use sampling methods that provide results in *dollar* terms. There are three primary types of sampling methods used for calculating dollar misstatements in auditing: nonstatistical sampling, monetary unit sampling, and variables sampling. We will now examine each of these, starting with nonstatistical sampling.

NONSTATISTICAL SAMPLING

OBJECTIVE 16-2
Apply nonstatistical sampling to tests of details of balances.

There are 14 steps required in audit sampling for tests of details of balances. These steps parallel the 14 steps used for sampling for tests of controls and substantive tests of transactions, although there are a few differences because of the different objectives of the tests. Understanding the similarities and differences in the application of audit sampling for tests of details of balances compared to those for tests of controls and substantive tests of transactions is essential. The following are the 14 steps, with the steps for tests of controls and substantive tests of transactions included in the right column for comparison:

Steps—Audit Sampling for Tests of Details of Balances	**Steps—Audit Sampling for Tests of Controls and Substantive Tests of Transactions (see p. 445)**
Plan the Sample	*Plan the Sample*
1. State the objectives of the audit test.	1. State the objectives of the audit test.
2. Decide whether audit sampling applies.	2. Decide whether audit sampling applies.
3. Define misstatement conditions.	3. Define attributes and exception conditions.
4. Define the population.	4. Define the population.
5. Define the sampling unit.	5. Define the sampling unit.
6. Specify tolerable misstatement.	6. Specify the tolerable exception rate.
7. Specify acceptable risk of incorrect acceptance.	7. Specify acceptable risk of assessing control risk too low.
8. Estimate misstatements in the population.	8. Estimate the population exception rate.
9. Determine the initial sample size.	9. Determine the initial sample size.
Select the Sample and Perform the Audit Procedures	*Select the Sample and Perform the Audit Procedures*
10. Select the sample.	10. Select the sample.
11. Perform the audit procedures.	11. Perform the audit procedures.
Evaluate the Results	*Evaluate the Results*
12. Generalize from the sample to the population.	12. Generalize from the sample to the population.
13. Analyze the misstatements.	13. Analyze the exceptions.
14. Decide the acceptability of the population.	14. Decide the acceptability of the population.

State the Objectives of the Audit Test

When auditors sample for tests of details of balances, the objective is to determine whether the account balance being audited is fairly stated. The population of 40 accounts receivable in Table 16-1 (p. 516), totaling $207,295, is used as an illustration in applying nonstatistical sampling. The objective of the audit test will be to determine whether the total of $207,295 is materially misstated. Typically, materially misstated is defined in terms of tolerable misstatement.

Decide Whether Audit Sampling Applies

As stated in Chapter 14, "Audit sampling applies whenever the auditor plans to reach conclusions about a population based on a sample." Although it is common to sample in many accounts, there are situations when sampling does not apply. For the population in Table 16-1, the auditor may decide to audit only items over $5,000 and ignore all others because the total of the smaller ones is immaterial. In this case, the auditor has not sampled. Similarly, if the auditor is verifying fixed asset additions and there are many small additions and one extremely large purchase of a building, the auditor may decide to ignore the small items entirely. Again, the auditor has not sampled.

Define Misstatement Conditions

Audit sampling for tests of details of balances measures monetary misstatements in the population. Thus, the misstatement conditions are any conditions that represent a monetary misstatement in a sample item. In auditing accounts receivable, any client misstatement in a sample item is a misstatement.

TABLE 16-1	Illustrative Accounts Receivable Population		
Population Item	Recorded Amount	Population Item (cont.)	Recorded Amount (cont.)
1	$ 1,410	21	$ 4,865
2	9,130	22	770
3	660	23	2,305
4	3,355	24	2,665
5	5,725	25	1,000
6	8,210	26	6,225
7	580	27	3,675
8	44,110	28	6,250
9	825	29	1,890
10	1,155	30	27,705
11	2,270	31	935
12	50	32	5,595
13	5,785	33	930
14	940	34	4,045
15	1,820	35	9,480
16	3,380	36	360
17	530	37	1,145
18	955	38	6,400
19	4,490	39	100
20	17,140	40	8,435
			$207,295

Define the Population

The population is defined as the *recorded dollar population.* The auditor then evaluates whether the recorded population is overstated or understated. For example, the population of accounts receivable in Table 16-1 consists of 40 accounts totaling $207,295. Most accounting populations subject to audit would, of course, contain far more items totaling a much larger dollar amount.

Stratified Sampling For many populations, auditors subdivide the population into two or more subpopulations before applying audit sampling. Subdividing populations is called **stratified sampling**, where each subpopulation is a stratum. The purpose of stratification is to permit the auditor to emphasize certain population items and deemphasize others. In most audit sampling situations, including confirming accounts receivable, auditors want to emphasize the larger recorded dollar values; therefore, stratification is typically done on the basis of the size of recorded dollar values.

Examining the population in Table 16-1, there are different ways to stratify the population. Assume that the auditor decided to stratify as follows:

Stratum	Stratum Criteria	No. in Population	Dollars in Population
1	>$10,000	3	$ 88,955
2	$ 5,000−$10,000	10	71,235
3	<$ 5,000	27	47,105
		40	$207,295

Define the Sampling Unit

The sampling unit for nonstatistical audit sampling in tests of details of balances is almost always the item making up the account balance. For accounts receivable, it is usually the customer account balance, which is represented by the customer account name or number on the accounts receivable list.

Specify Tolerable Misstatement

Tolerable misstatement as it was discussed in Chapter 9 is used for determining sample size and evaluating results in nonstatistical sampling. The auditor starts with a preliminary judgment about materiality and uses that total in deciding tolerable misstatement for each account.

For all statistical and nonstatistical sampling applications, there is a risk that the quantitative conclusions about the population will be incorrect. This is always true unless 100 percent of the population is tested.

Specify Acceptable Risk of Incorrect Acceptance

Acceptable risk of incorrect acceptance (ARIA) is the risk that the auditor is willing to take of accepting a balance as correct when the true misstatement in the balance is greater than tolerable misstatement. It is a measure of the auditor's desired assurance for an account balance. If the auditor wants more assurance in auditing a balance, ARIA is set lower. ARIA is the equivalent term to acceptable risk of assessing control risk too low (ARACR) for tests of controls and substantive tests of transactions.

There is an inverse relationship between ARIA and required sample size. If, for example, the auditor decides to reduce ARIA from 10 percent to 5 percent, the required sample size would increase.

The primary factor affecting the auditor's decision about ARIA is assessed control risk in the audit risk model. When internal controls are effective, control risk can be reduced, permitting the auditor to increase ARIA. This, in turn, reduces the sample size required for the test of details of the related account balance.

Understanding how ARACR and ARIA affect evidence accumulation can be difficult. Earlier it was shown that tests of details of balances for monetary misstatements can be reduced if internal controls are found to be effective through assessing control risk and performing tests of controls. The effects of ARACR and ARIA are consistent with that conclusion. If the auditor concludes that internal controls may be effective, control risk can be reduced. A lower control risk requires a lower ARACR in testing the controls, which requires a larger sample size. If controls are found to be effective, control risk can remain low, which permits the auditor to increase ARIA (through use of the audit risk model), thereby requiring a smaller sample size in the related substantive tests of details of balances. The effect of ARACR and ARIA on substantive testing in the two different circumstances is shown in Figure 16-1 (p. 518).

Besides control risk, ARIA is also directly affected by acceptable audit risk and inversely by other substantive tests already performed or planned for the account balance. For example, if acceptable audit risk is reduced, ARIA should also be reduced. If analytical procedures were performed and indicate that the account balance is fairly stated, ARIA should be increased. Stated differently, the analytical procedures are evidence in support of the account balance; therefore, less evidence from the detailed test using sampling is required to achieve acceptable audit risk. The same conclusion is appropriate for the relationship among substantive tests of transactions, ARIA, and sample size for tests of details of balances. The various relationships affecting ARIA are summarized in Table 16-2 (p. 518).

Estimate Misstatements in the Population

The auditor typically makes this estimate based on prior experience with the client and by assessing inherent risk, considering the results of tests of controls, substantive tests of transactions, and analytical procedures already performed.

Determine the Initial Sample Size

Auditors using nonstatistical sampling determine the initial sample size judgmentally considering the factors discussed so far. Table 16-3 (p. 519) summarizes the primary factors that influence sample size for nonstatistical sampling and how sample size is affected.

When the auditor uses stratified sampling, the sample size must be allocated among the strata. Typically, auditors allocate a higher portion of the sample items to larger population items. For example, in the example from Table 16-1 on page 516, allocating a sample size of 15, the auditor might decide to select all three accounts from stratum one, and six each from strata two and three. Observe that audit sampling does not apply to stratum one because all population items are being audited.

Select the Sample

For nonstatistical sampling, auditing standards permit the auditor to use any of the selection methods discussed in Chapter 14. It is important for the auditor to use a method that will permit meaningful conclusions about the sample results.

FIGURE 16-1   Effect of ARACR and ARIA on Substantive Testing

*Assumes tests of controls results were satisfactory, which permits control risk to remain low.

TABLE 16-2   Relationship among Factors Affecting ARIA, Effect on ARIA, and Required Sample Size for Audit Sampling

Factor Affecting ARIA	Example	Effect on ARIA	Effect on Sample Size
Effectiveness of internal controls (control risk)	Internal controls are effective (reduced control risk).	Increase	Decrease
Substantive tests of transactions	No exceptions were found in substantive tests of transactions.	Increase	Decrease
Acceptable audit risk	Likelihood of bankruptcy is low (increased acceptable audit risk).	Increase	Decrease
Analytical procedures	Analytical procedures are performed with no indications of likely misstatements.	Increase	Decrease

For stratified sampling, the auditor selects samples independently from each stratum. For example, in stratum three in the previous example, the auditor will select six sample items from the 27 population items in that stratum.

Perform the Audit Procedures

To perform the audit procedures, the auditor applies the appropriate audit procedures to each item in the sample to determine whether it is correct or contains a misstatement. For example, in the confirmation of accounts receivable, the auditor will mail the sample of positive confirmations in the manner described in Chapter 15 and determine the amount

TABLE 16-3 — Factors Influencing Sample Sizes for Tests of Details of Balances

Factor	Conditions Leading to Smaller Sample Size	Conditions Leading to Larger Sample Size
Control risk (ARACR)–Affects acceptable risk of incorrect acceptance	Low control risk	High control risk
Results of other substantive tests related to the same assertion (including analytical procedures and other relevant substantive tests)–Affect acceptable risk of incorrect acceptance	Satisfactory results in other related substantive tests	Unsatisfactory results in other related substantive tests
Acceptable audit risk–Affects acceptable risk of incorrect acceptance	High acceptable audit risk	Low acceptable audit risk
Tolerable misstatement for a specific account	Larger tolerable misstatement	Smaller tolerable misstatement
Inherent risk–Affects estimated misstatements in the population	Low inherent risk	High inherent risk
Expected size and frequency of misstatements–Affect estimated misstatements in the population	Smaller misstatements or lower frequency	Larger misstatements or higher frequency
Dollar amount of population	Smaller account balance	Larger account balance
Number of items in the population	Almost no effect on sample size unless population is very small	Almost no effect on sample size unless population is very small

of misstatement in each account confirmed. For nonresponses, alternative procedures will be used to determine the misstatements. The auditor cannot expect meaningful results from using audit sampling unless the audit procedures are applied carefully.

Assume that the auditor sends first and second requests for confirmations and performs alternative procedures in the previous example. Assume also that the following conclusions are reached about the sample after reconciling all timing differences:

Stratum	Sample Size	Dollars Audited Recorded Value	Dollars Audited Audited Value	Client Misstatement
1	3	$ 88,955	$ 91,695	$(2,740)
2	6	43,995	43,024	971
3	6	13,105	10,947	2,158
	15	$146,055	$145,666	$ 389

Generalize from the Sample to the Population and Decide the Acceptability of the Population

The auditor must generalize from the sample to the population by (1) projecting misstatements from the sample results to the population and (2) considering sampling error and sampling risk (ARIA). For example, in the previous example does the auditor conclude that accounts receivable is overstated by $389? No, the auditor is interested in the *population* results, not those for the sample. It is therefore necessary to project from the sample to the population to estimate the population misstatement. The first step is to make a **point estimate**, which was first shown on page 256 in Chapter 9. There are different ways to calculate the point estimate, but a common way is to assume that misstatements in the unaudited population are proportional to the misstatements in the sample. That calculation must be done for each stratum and then totaled, rather than from the total misstatements in the sample. Thus, the point estimate of the misstatement from the preceding example is determined by using a weighted-average method, as shown on the following page.

Stratum	Client Misstatement ÷ Recorded Value of the Sample	×	Recorded Book Value for the Stratum	=	Point Estimate of Misstatement
1	$(2,740)/$88,955		$88,955		$(2,740)
2	$ 971 /$43,995		71,235		1,572
3	$ 2,158 /$13,105		47,105		7,757
Total					$ 6,589

The point estimate of the misstatement in the population is $6,589, indicating an overstatement. The point estimate, by itself, is not an adequate measure of the population misstatement, however, because of sampling error. In other words, because the estimate is based on a sample, it will be close to the true population misstatement, but it is unlikely that it is exactly the same. The auditor must consider the possibility that the true population misstatement is greater than the amount of misstatement that is tolerable in the circumstances whenever the point estimate is less than the tolerable misstatement amount. This must be done for both statistical and nonstatistical samples.

An auditor using nonstatistical sampling cannot formally measure sampling error and therefore must subjectively consider the possibility that the true population misstatement exceeds a tolerable amount. This is done by considering (1) the difference between the point estimate and tolerable misstatement, (2) the extent to which items in the population have been audited 100 percent, (3) whether misstatements tend to be offsetting or in only one direction, (4) the amounts of individual misstatements, and (5) the sample size. To continue the example, suppose that tolerable misstatement is $40,000. In that case, the auditor may conclude that there is little chance, given the point estimate of $6,589, that the true population misstatement exceeds the tolerable amount.

Suppose that tolerable misstatement is $12,000, only $5,411 greater than the point estimate. In that case, other factors would be considered. For example, if the larger items in the population were audited 100 percent (as was done here), any unidentified misstatements would be restricted to smaller items. If the misstatements tend to be offsetting and are relatively small in size, the auditor may conclude that the true population misstatement is likely to be less than the tolerable amount. Also, the larger the sample size, the more confident the auditor can be that the point estimate is close to the true population value. Therefore, the auditor would be more willing to accept that the true population misstatement is less than tolerable misstatement in this example where the sample size is considered large, than where it is considered moderate or small. However, if one or more of these other conditions is different, the chance of a misstatement in excess of the tolerable amount may be judged to be high and the recorded population unacceptable.

Even if the amount of likely misstatement is not considered material, the auditor must wait to make a final evaluation until the entire audit is completed. For example, the estimated total misstatement and estimated sampling error in accounts receivable must be combined with estimates of misstatements in all other parts of the audit to evaluate the effect of all misstatements on the financial statements as a whole.

Analyze the Misstatements

As for sampling for tests of controls and substantive tests of transactions, an evaluation of the nature and cause of each misstatement found is essential. For example, in confirming accounts receivable, suppose that all misstatements resulted from the client's failure to record returned goods. The auditor would determine why that type of misstatement occurred so often, the implications of the misstatements on other audit areas, the potential impact on the financial statements, and its effect on company operations.

An important part of misstatement analysis is deciding whether any modification of the audit risk model is needed. If the auditor concluded that the failure to record the returns discussed in the previous paragraph resulted from a breakdown of internal controls, it might be necessary to reassess control risk. That in turn would probably cause the auditor to reduce ARIA, which would increase planned sample size. As discussed in Chapter 9, revisions of the audit risk model must be done with extreme care because the model is intended primarily for planning, not evaluating results.

When the auditor concludes that the misstatement in a population may be larger than tolerable misstatement after considering sampling error, the population is not considered acceptable. There are several possible courses of action.

Take No Action Until Tests of Other Audit Areas Are Completed Ultimately, the auditor must evaluate whether the financial statements taken as a whole are materially misstated. If offsetting misstatements are found in other parts of the audit, such as in inventory, the auditor may conclude that the estimated misstatements in accounts receivable are acceptable. Of course, before the audit is finalized, the auditor must evaluate whether a misstatement in one account may make the financial statements misleading even if there are offsetting misstatements.

Perform Expanded Audit Tests in Specific Areas If an analysis of the misstatements indicates that most of the misstatements are of a specific type, it may be desirable to restrict the additional audit effort to the problem area. For example, if an analysis of the misstatements in confirmations indicates that most of the misstatements result from failure to record sales returns, an extended search could be made of returned goods to make sure that they have been recorded. However, great care must be taken to evaluate the cause of all misstatements in the sample before a conclusion is reached about the proper emphasis in the expanded tests. There may be more than one problem area.

When a problem area is analyzed and corrected by adjusting the client's records, the sample items that led to isolating the problem area can then be shown as "correct." The point estimate can now be recalculated without the misstatements that have been "corrected." Sampling error and the acceptability of the population will also have to be reconsidered with the new facts.

Increase the Sample Size When the auditor increases the sample size, sampling error is reduced if the rate of misstatements in the expanded sample, their dollar amount, and their direction are similar to those in the original sample. Therefore, increasing the sample size may satisfy the auditor's tolerable misstatement requirements.

Increasing the sample size enough to satisfy the auditor's tolerable misstatement standards is often costly, especially when the difference between tolerable misstatement and projected misstatement is small. Even if the sample size is increased, there is no assurance of a satisfactory result. If the number, amount, and direction of the misstatements in the extended sample are proportionately greater or more variable than in the original sample, the results are still likely to be unacceptable.

For tests such as accounts receivable confirmation and inventory observation, it is often difficult to increase the sample size because of the practical problem of "reopening" those procedures once the initial work is done. By the time the auditor discovers that the sample was not large enough, several weeks have usually passed.

Despite these difficulties, sometimes the auditor must increase the sample size after the original testing is completed. It is much more common to increase sample size in audit areas other than confirmations and inventory observation, but it is occasionally necessary to do so even for these two areas. When stratified sampling is used, increased samples usually focus on the strata containing larger amounts, unless misstatements appear to be concentrated in some other strata.

Adjust the Account Balance When the auditor concludes that an account balance is materially misstated, the client may be willing to adjust the book value based on the sample results. In the previous example, assume the client is willing to reduce book value by the amount of the point estimate ($6,589) to adjust for the estimate of the misstatement. The auditor's estimate of the misstatement is now zero, but it is still necessary to consider sampling error. Again, assuming a tolerable misstatement of $12,000, the auditor must now assess whether sampling error exceeds $12,000, not the $5,411 originally considered. If the auditor believes sampling error is $12,000 or less, accounts receivable is acceptable after the adjustment. If the auditor believes it is more than $12,000, adjusting the account balance is not a practical option.

Request the Client to Correct the Population In some cases, the client's records are so inadequate that a correction of the entire population is required before the audit can be completed. For example, in accounts receivable, the client may be asked to prepare the aging schedule again if the auditor concludes that it has significant misstatements. When the client changes the valuation of some items in the population, the results must be audited again.

Refuse to Give an Unqualified Opinion If the auditor believes that the recorded amount in an account is not fairly stated, it is necessary to follow at least one of the preceding alternatives or to qualify the audit report in an appropriate manner. If the auditor believes that there is a reasonable chance that the financial statements are materially misstated, it would be a serious breach of auditing standards to issue an unqualified opinion.

MONETARY UNIT SAMPLING

OBJECTIVE 16-3
Apply monetary unit sampling.

Now that we have discussed nonstatistical sampling, we will move on to statistical sampling, starting with monetary unit sampling. **Monetary unit sampling (MUS)** is an innovation in statistical sampling methodology that was developed specifically for use by auditors. It is now the most commonly used statistical method of sampling for tests of details of balances because it has the statistical simplicity of attributes sampling yet provides a statistical result expressed in dollars (or another appropriate currency). MUS is also called dollar unit sampling, cumulative monetary amount sampling, and sampling with probability proportional to size.[1]

Differences between MUS and Nonstatistical Sampling

There are far more similarities than differences in using MUS and nonstatistical sampling. All 14 of the steps must also be performed for MUS even though some are done differently. Understanding those differences, though, is the key to understanding MUS. The following discussion explains these differences in detail.

Audit Software

The Definition of the Sampling Unit Is an Individual Dollar A critical feature of MUS is the definition of the sampling unit as an individual dollar in an account balance. The name of the statistical method, monetary unit sampling, results from this distinctive feature. For example, in the population in Table 16-1 on page 516, the sampling unit is 1 dollar and the population size is 207,295 dollars, not the 40 physical units discussed earlier.

The result of the individual dollar being the sampling unit for MUS is its automatic emphasis on physical units with larger recorded balances. Because the sample is selected on the basis of individual dollars, an account with a large balance has a greater chance of being included than an account with a small balance. For example, in accounts receivable confirmation, an account with a $5,000 balance has a 10 times greater probability of selection than one with a $500 balance, as it contains 10 times as many dollar units. As a result, there is no need to use stratified sampling with MUS. Stratification occurs automatically.

---

[1]The currency in many countries will be called something other than "dollars." Thus, in Mexico, for instance, one might use "Peso Unit Sampling." This is why the more universal term, *monetary* unit sampling, has been adopted. We recognize the appropriateness of this term in this text but also refer to dollars as the sampling unit in most cases.

The Population Size Is the Recorded Dollar Population For example, the population of accounts receivable in Table 16-1 on page 516 consists of 207,295 dollars, which is the population size, not the 40 physical units. This definition of population size is consistent with the use of dollar units.

Because of the method of sample selection in MUS, which is discussed later, it is not possible to evaluate the likelihood of unrecorded items in the population. Assume, for example, that MUS is used to evaluate whether inventory is fairly stated. MUS cannot be used to evaluate whether certain inventory items exist but have not been counted. If the completeness objective is important in the audit test, and it usually is, that objective must be satisfied separately from the MUS tests.

Preliminary Judgment of Materiality Is Used for Each Account Instead of Tolerable Misstatement Another unique aspect of MUS is the use of the preliminary judgment about materiality, as discussed in Chapter 9, to directly determine the tolerable misstatement amount for the audit of each account. Other sampling techniques require the auditor to determine tolerable misstatement for each account by allocating the preliminary judgment about materiality. This is not required when MUS is used. For example, assume that the auditor decides that the preliminary judgment about materiality should be $60,000 for the financial statements as a whole. That materiality amount of $60,000, or a derivative of it, would be used as tolerable misstatement in all applications of MUS—inventory, accounts receivable, accounts payable, and so forth.

Sample Size Is Determined Using a Statistical Formula The information used and the calculation of the planned sample size are shown later.

A Formal Decision Rule Is Used for Deciding the Acceptability of the Population The decision rule used for MUS is similar to that used for nonstatistical sampling, but it is sufficiently different to merit discussion. The decision rule is illustrated after the calculation of the misstatement bounds is shown.

Sample Selection Is Done Using PPS Monetary unit samples are samples selected with **probability proportional to size sample selection (PPS)**. Such samples are samples of individual dollars in the population. Auditors cannot, however, audit individual dollars. Therefore, the auditor must determine the physical unit to perform the audits tests. For example, in Table 16-4 on page 524 the auditor will take a random sample of population items between 1 and 7,376 (individual dollars). However, to perform the audit procedures, the auditor must identify the population items between 1 and 12 (physical units). If the auditor selected the random number 3014, the physical unit associated with that number is 6.

PPS samples can be obtained by using computer software, random number tables, or systematic sampling techniques. An illustration of an accounts receivable population, including cumulative totals, is provided in Table 16-4 to demonstrate selecting a sample using computer software.

Assume that the auditor wants to select a PPS sample of four accounts from the population in Table 16-4. Because the sampling unit is defined as an individual dollar, the population size is 7,376, and four random numbers are needed from a computer program. Assume that the computer program generates the following random numbers: 6,586, 1,756, 850, and 6,499. The population physical unit items that contain these random dollars are determined by reference to the cumulative total column. They are items 11 (containing dollars 6,577 through 6,980), 4 (dollars 1,699 through 2,271), 2 (dollars 358 through 1,638), and 10 (dollars 5,751 through 6,576). These will be audited, and the result for each physical unit will be applied to the random dollar it contains.

The statistical methods used to evaluate monetary unit samples permit the inclusion of a physical unit in the sample more than once. That is, in the previous example, if the random numbers had been 6,586, 1,756, 856, and 6,599, the sample items would be 11, 4,

TABLE 16-4   Accounts Receivable Population

Population Item (Physical Unit)	Recorded Amount	Cumulative Total (Dollar Unit)
1	$ 357	$ 357
2	1,281	1,638
3	60	1,698
4	573	2,271
5	691	2,962
6	143	3,105
7	1,425	4,530
8	278	4,808
9	942	5,750
10	826	6,576
11	404	6,980
12	396	7,376

2, and 11. Item 11 would be audited once but would be treated as two sample items statistically, and the sample total would be four items because four monetary units were involved.

One problem using PPS selection is that population items with a zero recorded balance have no chance of being selected with PPS sample selection even though they could contain misstatements. Similarly, small balances that are significantly understated have little chance of being included in the sample. This problem can be overcome by doing specific audit tests for zero- and small-balance items, assuming that they are of concern.

Another problem is the inability to include negative balances, such as credit balances in accounts receivable, in the PPS (monetary unit) sample. It is possible to ignore negative balances for PPS selection and test those amounts by some other means. An alternative is to treat them as positive balances and add them to the total number of monetary units being tested; however, this complicates the evaluation process.

The Auditor Generalizes from the Sample to the Population Using MUS Techniques Regardless of the sampling method selected, the auditor must generalize from the sample to the population by (1) projecting misstatements from the sample results to the population and (2) determining the related sampling error. There are four important aspects in doing this using MUS:

1. Attributes sampling tables are used to calculate the results. Tables such as the one on page 457 can be used, replacing ARACR with ARIA.
2. The attributes results must be converted to dollars. MUS estimates the dollar misstatement in the population, not the percent of items in the population that are misstated. MUS accomplishes this by defining each population item as an individual dollar. Therefore, estimating the rate of population dollars that contain a misstatement is a way of estimating the total dollar misstatement.
3. The auditor must make an assumption about the percentage of misstatement for each population item that is misstated. This assumption enables the auditor to use the attributes sampling tables to estimate dollar misstatements.

4. The statistical results when MUS is used are called **misstatement bounds**. These misstatement bounds are estimates of the likely maximum overstatement (upper misstatement bound) and likely maximum understatement (lower misstatement bound) at a given ARIA. Both an upper misstatement bound and lower misstatement bound are calculated.

This final step, generalizing from the sample to the population, is an extremely important part of MUS. Generalization is different when the auditor finds no misstatements in the sample compared to when there are misstatements. Generalizing under these two situations is covered next.

Suppose that the auditor is confirming a population of accounts receivable for monetary correctness. The population totals $1,200,000, and a sample of 100 confirmations is obtained. Upon audit, no misstatements are uncovered in the sample. The auditor wants to determine the maximum amount of overstatement and understatement amounts that could exist in the population even when the sample contains no misstatements. These are the upper misstatement bound and the lower misstatement bound, respectively. Assuming an ARIA of 5 percent, and using the attributes sampling table on page 457, both the upper and lower bounds are determined by locating the intersection of the sample size (100) and the actual number of misstatements (0) in the same manner as for attributes sampling. The CUER of 3 percent on the table represents both the upper and lower bound, *expressed as a percent*. Because the sample misstatement rate was 0 percent, the 3 percent represents an estimate of sampling error.

Generalizing from the Sample to the Population When No Misstatements Are Found Using MUS

Thus, based on the sample results and the misstatement bounds from the table, the auditor can conclude with a 5 percent sampling risk that no more than 3 percent of the dollar units in the population are misstated. To convert this percent into *dollars,* the auditor must make an assumption about the average percent of misstatement for population dollars that contain a misstatement. This assumption significantly affects the misstatement bounds. To illustrate this, three sets of example assumptions are examined: (1) a 100 percent misstatement assumption for both overstatements and understatements, (2) a 10 percent misstatement assumption for both overstatements and understatements, and (3) a 20 percent misstatement assumption for overstatements and a 200 percent assumption for understatements.

Assumption 1 Overstatement amounts equal 100 percent; understatement amounts equal 100 percent; misstatement bounds at a 5 percent ARIA are

$$\text{Upper misstatement bound} = \$1,200,000 \times 3\% \times 100\% = \$36,000$$

$$\text{Lower misstatement bound} = \$1,200,000 \times 3\% \times 100\% = \$36,000$$

The assumption is that, on average, those population items that are misstated are misstated by the full dollar amount of the recorded value. Because the misstatement bound is 3 percent, the dollar value of the misstatement is not likely to exceed $36,000 (3 percent of the total recorded dollar units in the population). If all the amounts are overstated, there is an overstatement of $36,000. If they are all understated, there is an understatement of $36,000.

The assumption of 100 percent misstatements is extremely conservative, especially for overstatements. Assume that the actual population exception rate is 3 percent. The following two conditions both have to exist before the $36,000 properly reflects the true overstatement amount:

1. All amounts have to be overstatements. Offsetting amounts would have reduced the amount of the overstatement.
2. All population items misstated have to be 100 percent misstated. There could not, for example, be a misstatement such as a check written for $226 that was recorded at $262. This would be only a 13.7 percent misstatement (262 − 226 = 36 overstatement; 36/262 = 13.7%).

In the calculation of the misstatement bounds of $36,000 overstatement and understatement, the auditor did not calculate a point estimate and sampling error (called precision amount in MUS) in the manner discussed earlier in the chapter. This is because the tables used include both a point estimate and a precision amount to derive the upper exception rate. Even though the point estimate and precision amount are not calculated for MUS, they are implicit in the determination of misstatement bounds and can be determined from the tables. For example, in this illustration, the point estimate is zero and the statistical precision is $36,000.

Assumption 2 Overstatement amounts equal 10 percent; understatement amounts equal 10 percent; misstatement bounds at a 5 percent ARIA are

$$\text{Upper misstatement bound} = \$1,200,000 \times 3\% \times 10\% = \$3,600$$

$$\text{Lower misstatement bound} = \$1,200,000 \times 3\% \times 10\% = \$3,600$$

The assumption is that, on average, those items that are misstated are misstated by no more than 10 percent. If all items were misstated in one direction, the misstatement bounds would be +$3,600 and −$3,600. The change in assumption from 100 percent to 10 percent misstatements significantly affects the misstatement bounds. The effect is in direct proportion to the magnitude of the change.

Assumption 3 Overstatement amounts equal 20 percent; understatement amounts equal 200 percent; misstatement bounds at a 5 percent ARIA are

$$\text{Upper misstatement bound} = \$1,200,000 \times 3\% \times 20\% = \$7,200$$

$$\text{Lower misstatement bound} = \$1,200,000 \times 3\% \times 200\% = \$72,000$$

The justification for a larger percent for understatements is the potential for a larger misstatement in percentage terms. For example, an accounts receivable recorded at $20 that should have been recorded at $200 is understated by 900 percent $[(200 - 20)/20]$, whereas one that is recorded at $200 that should have been recorded at $20 is overstated by 90 percent $[(200 - 20)/200]$.

Items containing large understatement amounts may have a small recorded value as a result of those misstatements. As a consequence, because of the mechanics of MUS, few of them will have a chance of being selected in the sample. Because of this, some auditors select an additional sample of small items to supplement the monetary unit sample when understatement amounts are an important audit concern.

Appropriate Percent of Misstatement Assumption The appropriate assumption for the overall percent of misstatement in those population items containing a misstatement is an auditor's decision. The auditor must set these percentages based on professional judgment in the circumstances. In the absence of convincing information to the contrary, most auditors believe that it is desirable to assume a 100 percent amount for both overstatements and understatements unless there are misstatements in the sample results. This approach is considered highly conservative, but it is easier to justify than any other assumption. In fact, the reason upper and lower limits are called misstatement bounds when MUS is used, rather than maximum likely misstatement or the commonly used statistical term *confidence limit*, is because of widespread use of that conservative assumption. Unless stated otherwise, the 100 percent misstatement assumption is used in this chapter and problem materials.

Generalizing When Misstatements Are Found

In the preceding section, we assumed there were no misstatements in the sample. What happens, though, if misstatements are found? We will use the example from the preceding section but assume there are five misstatements instead of none. The misstatements are shown in Table 16-5 on the following page.

| | | | | Misstatement |
Customer No.	Recorded Accounts Receivable Amount	Audited Accounts Receivable Amount	Misstatement	÷ Recorded Amount
2073	$ 6,200	$ 6,100	$ 100	.016
5111	12,910	12,000	910	.07
5206	4,322	4,450	(128)	(.03)
7642	23,000	22,995	5	.0002
9816	8,947	2,947	6,000	.671

TABLE 16-5   Misstatements Found

The four aspects of generalizing from the sample to the population discussed earlier still apply, but their use is modified as follows:

1. *Overstatement and understatement amounts are dealt with separately and then combined.* First, initial upper and lower misstatement bounds are calculated separately for overstatement and understatement amounts. Next, a point estimate of overstatements and understatements is calculated. The point estimate of understatements is used to reduce the initial upper misstatement bound, and the point estimate of overstatements is used to reduce the initial lower misstatement bound. The method and rationale for these calculations will be illustrated by using the four overstatement and one understatement amounts in Table 16-5.

2. *A different misstatement assumption is made for each misstatement, including the zero misstatements.* When there were no misstatements in the sample, an assumption was required as to the average percent of misstatement for the population items misstated. The misstatement bounds were calculated showing several different assumptions. Now that misstatements have been found, sample information is available to use in determining the misstatement bounds. The misstatement assumption is still required, but it can be modified based on this actual misstatement data.

   Where misstatements are found, a 100 percent assumption for all misstatements is not only exceptionally conservative, it is inconsistent with the sample results. A common assumption in practice, and the one followed in this book, is that the actual sample misstatements are representative of the population misstatements. This assumption requires the auditor to calculate the percent that each sample item is misstated (misstatement ÷ recorded amount), and apply that percent to the population. The calculation of the percent for each misstatement is shown in the last column in Table 16-5. As is explained shortly, a misstatement assumption is still needed for the zero misstatement portion of the computed results. For this example, a 100 percent misstatement assumption is used for the zero misstatement portion for both overstatement and understatement misstatement bounds.

3. *The auditor must deal with layers of the computed upper exception rate (CUER) from the attributes sampling table.* The reason for doing so is that there is a different misstatement assumption for each misstatement. Layers are calculated by first determining the CUER from the table for each misstatement and then calculating each layer. Table 16-6 on page 528 shows the layers in the attributes sampling table for the example at hand. The layers were determined by reading across the table for a sample size of 100, from the 0 through 4 exception columns.

TABLE 16-6   **Percent Misstatement Bounds**

Number of Misstatements	Upper Precision Limit from Table	Increase in Precision Limit Resulting from Each Misstatement (Layers)
0	.03	.03
1	.047	.047-.03 .017
2	.062	.062-.047 .015
3	.076	.076-.062 .014
4	.089	.089-.076 .013

(handwritten: pg. 456)

4. *Misstatement assumptions must be associated with each layer.* The most common method of associating misstatement assumptions with layers is to be conservative by associating the largest dollar misstatement percents with the largest layers. Table 16-7 below shows the association. For example, the largest average misstatement was .671 for customer 9816. That misstatement is associated with the layer factor of .017, the largest layer where misstatements were found. The portion of the upper precision limit related to the zero misstatement layer has a misstatement assumption of 100 percent, which is still conservative. Table 16-7 shows the calculation of misstatement bounds before consideration of offsetting amounts. The upper misstatement bound was calculated as if there were no understatement amounts, and the lower misstatement bound was calculated as if there were no overstatement amounts.

Most MUS users believe that the approach just discussed is overly conservative when there are offsetting amounts. If an understatement amount is found, it is logical and reasonable that the bound for overstatement amounts should be lower than it would be had

TABLE 16-7   **Illustration of Calculating Initial Upper and Lower Misstatement Bounds**

Number of Misstatements	Upper Precision Limit Portion*	Recorded Value	Unit Misstatement Assumption	Misstatement Bound Portion (Columns 2 × 3 × 4)
Overstatements			*deces. order*	
0	.030	$1,200,000	1.0 *always 1*	$36,000
1	.017	1,200,000	.671	13,688
2	.015	1,200,000	.07	1,260
3	.014	1,200,000	.016	269
4	.013	1,200,000	.0002	3
Upper precision limit	.089			
Initial misstatement bound				$51,220
Understatements				
0	.030	$1,200,000	1.0	$36,000
1	.017	1,200,000	.03	612
Lower precision limit	.047			
Initial misstatement bound				$36,612

(handwritten above columns: 2, 3, 4 pg 527)

*ARIA of 5%. Sample size of 100.

no understatement amounts been found, and vice versa. The adjustment of bounds for off-setting amounts is made as follows: (1) a point estimate of misstatements is made for both overstatement and understatement amounts and (2) each bound is reduced by the opposite point estimate.

The point estimate for overstatements is calculated by multiplying the average overstatement amount in the dollar units audited times the recorded value. The same approach is used for calculating the point estimate for understatements. In the example, there is one understatement amount of 3 cents per dollar unit in a sample of 100. The understatement point estimate is therefore $360 (.03/100 × $1,200,000). Similarly, the overstatement point estimate is $9,086 [(.671 + .07 + .016 + .0002)/100 × $1,200,000].

Table 16-8 shows the adjustment of the bounds that follow from this procedure. The initial upper bound of $51,220 is reduced by the estimated most likely understatement amount of $360 to an adjusted bound of $50,860. The initial lower bound of $36,612 is reduced by the estimated most likely overstatement amount of $9,086 to an adjusted bound of $27,526. Thus, given the methodology and assumptions followed, the auditor concludes that there is a 5 percent risk that accounts receivable is overstated by more than $50,860, or understated by more than $27,526. It should be noted that if the misstatement assumptions are changed, the misstatement bounds will also change. The reader is advised that the method used to adjust the bounds for offsetting amounts is only one of several in current use. The method illustrated here is taken from Leslie, Teitlebaum, and Anderson.[2]

The seven steps followed in the calculation of the adjusted misstatement bounds for monetary unit sampling when there are offsetting amounts are shown in Table 16-9 (p. 530). The calculation of the adjusted upper misstatement bound for the four overstatement amounts in Table 16-5 is used to illustrate.

After the auditor calculates the misstatement bounds, he or she must decide whether the population is acceptable. To do that, a *decision rule* is needed. The decision rule for MUS is as follows: If *both* the lower misstatement bound (LMB) and upper misstatement bound (UMB) fall between the understatement and overstatement tolerable misstatement amounts, *accept* the conclusion that the book value is not misstated by a material amount. Otherwise conclude that the book value is misstated by a material amount.

Decide the Acceptability of the Population Using MUS

[2]D. A. Leslie, A. D. Teitlebaum, and R. J. Anderson, *Dollar Unit Sampling: A Practical Guide for Auditors,* Toronto, Copp, Clark and Pitman, 1979.

| TABLE 16-8 | Illustration of Calculating Adjusted Misstatement Bounds |

Number of Misstatements	Unit Misstatement Assumption	Sample Size	Recorded Population	Point Estimate	Bounds
Initial overstatement bound					$51,220
Understatement amount					
1	.03	100	$1,200,000	$ 360	(360)
Adjusted overstatement bound					$50,860
Initial understatement bound					$36,612
Overstatement amounts					
1	.671				
2	.07				
3	.016				
4	.0002				
Sum	.7572	100	$1,200,000	$9,086	(9,086)
Adjusted understatement bound					$27,526

TABLE 16-9   Summary of Steps to Calculate Adjusted Misstatement Bounds

Steps to Calculate Adjusted Misstatement Bounds	Calculation for Overstatements in Tables 16-5, 16-7, and 16-8
1. Determine misstatement for each sample item, keeping overstatements and understatements separate.	Table 16-5; 4 overstatements
2. Calculate misstatement per dollar unit in each sample item (misstatement/recorded amount).	Table 16-5; .016, .07, .0002, .671
3. Layer misstatements per dollar unit from highest to lowest, including the percent misstatement assumption for sample items not misstated.	Table 16-7; 1.0, .671, .07, .016, .0002
4. Determine upper precision limit from attributes sampling table and calculate the percent misstatement bound for each misstatement (layer).	Table 16-7; Total of 8.9% for 4 misstatements; calculate 5 layers
5. Calculate initial upper and lower misstatement bounds for each layer and total.	Table 16-7; Total of $51,220
6. Calculate point estimate for overstatements and understatements.	Table 16-8; $360 for understatements
7. Calculate adjusted upper and lower misstatement bounds.	Table 16-8; $50,860 adjusted overstatement

This decision rule is illustrated in Figure 16-2. The auditor should conclude that both the LMB and UMB for situations 1 and 2 fall completely within both the understatement and overstatement tolerable misstatement limits. Therefore, the conclusion that the population is not misstated by a material amount is accepted. For situations 3, 4, and 5, either LMB or UMB, or both, are outside tolerable misstatements. Therefore, the population book value is rejected.

Assume in the example being used that the auditor had set a tolerable misstatement amount for accounts receivable of $40,000 (overstatement or understatement). That means the auditor will accept the recorded value if he or she concludes that accounts receivable is

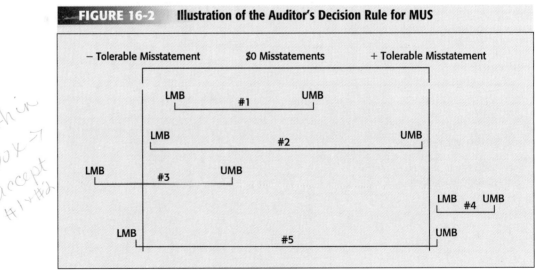

FIGURE 16-2   Illustration of the Auditor's Decision Rule for MUS

not overstated or understated by more than $40,000. As was previously shown, the auditor selected a sample of 100 items, found 5 misstatements, and calculated the lower bound to be $27,526 and the upper bound to be $50,860. Application of the decision rule leads the auditor to the conclusion that the population should not be accepted because the upper misstatement bound is more than tolerable misstatement of $40,000.

When one or both of the misstatement bounds lie outside the tolerable misstatement limits and the population is not considered acceptable, the auditor has several options. These are the same as for nonstatistical sampling and have already been discussed.

Determining sample size was discussed earlier as one of the steps in MUS, but the method of the calculation was deferred until you had an understanding of average misstatement assumptions. Because you now understand that concept, determining the sample size is covered in more depth. The method used to determine sample size for MUS is similar to that used for physical unit attributes sampling, using the attributes sampling tables. The five things that must be known or specified have already been discussed in this chapter. An example is used to illustrate determining sample size.

Materiality The preliminary judgment about materiality is normally the basis for the tolerable misstatement amount used. If misstatements in non-MUS tests are expected, tolerable misstatement would be materiality less those amounts. Tolerable misstatement may be different for overstatements or understatements. For this example, tolerable misstatement for both overstatements and understatements is $100,000.

Assumption of the Average Percent of Misstatement for Population Items That Contain a Misstatement Again, there may be a separate assumption for the upper and lower bounds. This is also an auditor judgment. It should be based on the auditor's knowledge of the client and past experience, and if less than 100 percent is used, the assumption must be clearly defensible. For this example, 50 percent is used for overstatements and 100 percent for understatements.

Acceptable Risk of Incorrect Acceptance ARIA is an auditor judgment and is often reached with the aid of the audit risk model. It is 5 percent for this example.

Recorded Population Value The dollar value of the population is taken from the client's records. For this example, it is $5 million.

Estimate the Population Exception Rate Normally, the estimate of the population exception rate for MUS is zero, as it is most appropriate to use MUS when no or only a few misstatements are expected. When misstatements are expected, the total dollar amount of expected population misstatements is estimated and then expressed as a percent of the population recorded value. In this example, $20,000 overstatement amount is expected. This is equivalent to a .4 percent exception rate. To be conservative, a .5 percent expected exception rate is used.

These assumptions are summarized as follows:

Tolerable misstatement (same for upper and lower)	$ 100,000
Average percent of misstatement assumption, overstatements	50%
Average percent of misstatement assumption, understatements	100%
ARIA	5%
Accounts receivable–recorded value	$5 million
Estimated misstatement in accounts receivable	$ 20,000

The sample size is calculated as follows:

	Upper Bound	Lower Bound
Tolerable misstatement	100,000	100,000
Average percent of misstatement assumption	÷ .50	÷ 1.00
	200,000	100,000
Recorded population value	÷ 5,000,000	÷ 5,000,000
Tolerable exception rate	4%	2%
Estimated population exception rate (EPER)	.5%	0
Sample size from the attributes table (p. 456) 5% ARACR, 4% and 2% TER, and .5% and 0% EPER	117	149

Because only one sample is taken for both overstatements and understatements, the *larger* of the two computed sample sizes is used, in this case 149 items. In auditing the sample, finding any understatement amounts will cause the lower bound to exceed the tolerable limit because the sample size is based on no expected misstatements. Conversely, several overstatement amounts might be found before the tolerable limit for the upper bound is exceeded. When the auditor is concerned about unexpectedly finding a misstatement that would cause the population to be rejected, he or she can guard against it by arbitrarily increasing sample size above the amount determined by the tables. For example, in this illustration, the auditor might use a sample size of 200 instead of 149.

Relationship of the Audit Risk Model to Sample Size for MUS The audit risk model for planning was shown in Chapter 9 and subsequent chapters as:

$$PDR = \frac{AAR}{IR \times CR} \quad \text{(see pp. 259–261 for description of the terms)}$$

It was shown in Chapter 15 that the auditor reduces detection risk to the planned level by performing substantive tests of transactions, analytical procedures, and tests of details of balances. MUS is used in performing tests of details of balances. Therefore, understanding the relationship of the three independent factors in the audit risk model plus analytical procedures and substantive tests of transactions to sample size for tests of details of balances is important.

Table 16-2 on page 518 shows that four of these five factors (control risk, substantive tests of transactions, acceptable audit risk, and analytical procedures) all affect ARIA. ARIA in turn determines the planned sample size. The other factor, inherent risk, affects the estimated population exception rate directly.

Audit Uses of Monetary Unit Sampling

MUS is appealing to auditors for at least four reasons. First, it automatically increases the likelihood of selecting high dollar items from the population being audited. Auditors make a practice of concentrating on these items because they generally represent the greatest risk of material misstatements. Stratified sampling can also be used for this purpose, but MUS is often easier to apply.

Second, MUS often reduces the cost of doing the audit testing because several sample items are tested at once. For example, if one large item makes up 10 percent of the total recorded dollar value of the population and the sample size is 100, the PPS sample selection method is likely to result in approximately 10 percent of the sample items from that one large population item. Naturally, that item needs to be audited only once, but it counts as a sample of 10. If the item is misstated, it is also counted as 10 misstatements. Larger population items may be eliminated from the sampled population by auditing them 100 percent and evaluating them separately if the auditor so desires.

Third, MUS is appealing because of its ease of application. Monetary unit samples can be evaluated by the application of simple tables. It is easy to teach and to supervise the use of MUS techniques. Firms that use MUS extensively use computer programs or special tables that streamline sample size determination and evaluation even further than shown here.

Finally, MUS provides a statistical conclusion rather than a nonstatistical one. Many auditors believe that statistical sampling aids them in making better and more defensible conclusions.

The primary disadvantage of MUS is twofold. First, the total misstatement bounds resulting when misstatements are found may be too high to be useful to the auditor. This is because these evaluation methods are inherently conservative when misstatements are found and often produce bounds far in excess of materiality. To overcome this problem, large samples may be required. Second, it may be cumbersome to select PPS samples from large populations without computer assistance.

For all these reasons, MUS is most commonly used when zero or few misstatements are expected, a dollar result is desired, and the population data are maintained on computer files.

VARIABLES SAMPLING

Variables sampling, like monetary unit sampling, is a statistical method used by auditors. Variables sampling and nonstatistical sampling for tests of details of balances have the same objective, which is to measure the true amount of misstatement in an account balance. As with nonstatistical sampling, when it is determined that the misstatement amount exceeds the tolerable amount, the population is rejected and additional actions are taken by the auditor.

OBJECTIVE 16-4
Describe variables sampling.

There are several sampling techniques that constitute the general class of methods called variables sampling. Those studied in this section are difference estimation, ratio estimation, and mean-per-unit estimation. These are discussed more later.

There are far more similarities than differences in using variables methods and nonstatistical sampling. All 14 of the steps discussed for nonstatistical sampling must be performed for variables methods and almost all of them are identical. This section focuses on the differences between variables and nonstatistical sampling following the assumption that you understand the material in the earlier part of this chapter on nonstatistical sampling.

Differences between Variables and Nonstatistical Sampling

To understand why and how auditors use variables sampling methods in auditing, it is important to understand sampling distributions and how they affect auditors' statistical conclusions. These are studied next.

Although auditors can assess the general nature of populations for the purpose of selecting the most appropriate sampling method, they do not know the mean value (average) or the distribution of the misstatement amounts or the audited values of the populations they are testing in audit engagements. The population characteristics must be *estimated* from samples. That, of course, is the purpose of the audit test. In this section, there is a discussion of sampling distributions, which are essential to drawing conclusions about populations on the basis of samples using variables sampling methods.

Sampling Distributions

Assume that an auditor, as an experiment, took thousands of repeated samples of equal size from a population of accounting data having a mean value of $\overline{X}$. For each sample, the auditor calculates the mean value of the items in the sample as follows:

$$\overline{x} = \frac{\Sigma x_j}{n}$$

where

$\overline{x}$ = mean value of the sample items

x_j = value of each individual sample item

n = sample size

After calculating $\overline{x}$ for each sample, the auditor plots them into a frequency distribution. As long as the sample size is sufficient, the frequency distribution of the sample means will appear much like that shown in Figure 16-3.

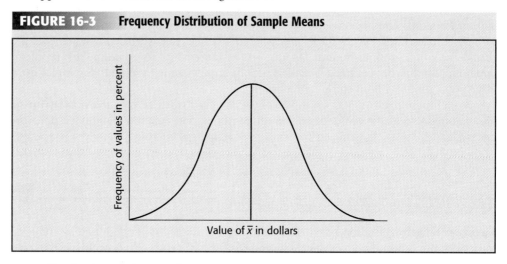

FIGURE 16-3   Frequency Distribution of Sample Means

A distribution of the sample means such as this is normal and has all the characteristics of the normal curve: (1) the curve is symmetrical, and (2) the sample means fall within known portions of the sampling distribution around th average or mean of those means, measured by the distance along the horizontal axis in   ns of standard deviations. Furthermore, the mean of the sample means (the midpo,   of the sampling distribution) is equal to the population mean and the standard deviat   of the sampling distribution is equal to SD/$\sqrt{n}$, where SD is the population standard deviation and n is the sample size.

To illustrate, assume a population with a mean of $40 and a standard deviation of $15 ($\overline{X}$ = $40 and SD = $15), from which we elected to take many random samples of 100 items each. The standard deviation of our sampling distribution would be $1.50 (SD/$\sqrt{n}$ = 15/$\sqrt{100}$ = 1.50). The reference to "standard deviation" of the population and to "standard deviation" of the sampling distribution is often confusing. To avoid confusion, the standard deviation of the distribution of the sample means is often called the standard error of the mean (SE). With this information, the tabulation of the sampling distribution can be made, as shown in Table 16-10.

To summarize, three things are important about the results of the experiment of taking a large number of samples from a known population:

1. The mean value of all the sample means is equal to the population mean ($\overline{X}$). A corollary is that the sample mean value ($\overline{x}$) with the highest frequency of occurrence is also equal to the population mean.
2. The shape of the frequency distribution of the sample means is that of a normal distribution (curve), as long as the sample size is sufficiently large, *regardless of the distribution of the population*. A graphic representation of this conclusion is shown in Figure 16-4.

TABLE 16-10	Calculated Sampling Distribution from a Population with a Known Mean and Standard Deviation			
(1) Number of Standard Errors of the Mean (Confidence Coefficient)	(2) Value [(1) × $1.50]	(3) Range Around $\overline{X}$ [$40 ± (2)]	(4) Percent of Sample Means Included in Range	
1	$1.50	$38.50 – $41.50	68.2	
2	$3.00	$37.00 – $43.00	95.4	
3	$4.50	$35.50 – $44.50	99.7	
		(taken from table for normal curve)		

3. The percentage of sample means between any two values of the sampling distribution is measurable. The percentage can be calculated by (1) determining the number of standard errors between any two values and (2) determining the percentage of sample means represented from a table for normal curves.

Naturally, when the auditor samples from a population in an actual audit situation, the auditor does not know the population's characteristics and there is ordinarily only one sample taken from the population. But the *knowledge of sampling distributions* enables auditors to draw statistical conclusions, or **statistical inferences**, about the population. For example, assume that the auditor takes a sample from a population and calculates $\overline{x}$ as $46 and SE at $9 (the way to calculate SE is shown later). We can now calculate a confidence interval of the population mean using the logic gained from the study of sampling distributions. It is as follows:

Statistical Inference

$$CI_{\overline{x}} = \hat{\overline{X}} \pm Z \cdot SE$$

where

$CI_{\overline{x}}$ = confidence interval for the population mean

$\hat{\overline{X}}$ = point estimate of the population mean

Z = confidence coefficient $\begin{cases} 1 = 68.2\% \text{ confidence level} \\ 2 = 95.4\% \text{ confidence level} \\ 3 = 99.7\% \text{ confidence level} \end{cases}$

SE = standard error of the mean

$Z \cdot SE$ = precision interval

FIGURE 16-4	Sampling Distribution for a Population Distribution

Sampling Distribution Simulation

For the example:

$$CI_{\bar{x}} = \$46 \pm 1(\$9) = \$46 \pm \$9 \text{ at a } 68.2\% \text{ confidence level}$$

$$CI_{\bar{x}} = \$46 \pm 2(\$9) = \$46 \pm \$18 \text{ at a } 95.4\% \text{ confidence level}$$

$$CI_{\bar{x}} = \$46 \pm 3(\$9) = \$46 \pm \$27 \text{ at a } 99.7\% \text{ confidence level}$$

The results can also be stated in terms of confidence limits ($CL_{\bar{x}}$). The upper confidence limit ($UCL_{\bar{x}}$) is $\hat{X} + Z \cdot SE$ ($\$46 + \$18 = \$64$ at a 95 percent confidence level) and a lower confidence limit ($LCL_{\bar{x}}$) is $\hat{X} - Z \cdot SE$ ($\$46 - \$18 = \$28$ at a 95 percent confidence level).

Graphically, the results are as follows:

The conclusion that the auditor will draw from a confidence interval using statistical inference can be stated in different ways, but care must be taken to avoid incorrect conclusions. The auditor must remember that the true population value is always unknown. There is always a possibility that the sample is not sufficiently representative of the population to provide a sample mean and/or standard deviation reasonably close to those of the population. The auditor can say, however, that the procedure used to obtain the sample and compute the confidence interval will provide an interval that will contain the true population mean value a given percent of the time. In other words, the auditor knows the reliability of the statistical inference process that is used to draw his or her conclusions.

Variables Methods

The statistical inference process just discussed is used for all the variables sampling methods. The main difference among the various methods is in the characteristic item and thus in the population being measured. The three variables methods are now discussed individually.

Difference Estimation **Difference estimation** is used to measure the estimated total misstatement amount in a population when there is both a recorded value and an audited value for each item in the sample. An example is to confirm a sample of accounts receivable and determine the difference (misstatement) between the client's recorded amount and the amount the auditor considers correct for each selected account. The auditor makes an estimate of the population misstatement based on the number of misstatements, average misstatement size, and individual misstatement size in the sample. The result is stated as a point estimate of the population misstatement plus or minus a computed precision interval at a stated confidence level. For example, in the earlier discussion of sampling distributions, assume the auditor was confirming a random sample of 100 from a population of 1,000 accounts receivable and concluded that the confidence limits of the mean of the misstatement for the population was between $28 and $64 at a 95 percent confidence level. The estimate of the total population misstatement can also be easily calculated as being between $28,000 and $64,000 at a 95 percent confidence level (1,000 × 28 and 1,000 × 64). If the auditor's tolerable misstatement is $100,000, the population is clearly acceptable. If it is $40,000, the population is not acceptable. An extended illustration using difference estimation is shown later in the chapter.

Difference estimation frequently results in smaller sample sizes than any other method, and it is relatively easy to use. For that reason, difference estimation is often the preferred variables method.

Ratio Estimation Ratio estimation is similar to difference estimation except that the point estimate of the population misstatement is determined by multiplying the portion of sample dollars misstated times the total recorded population book value. The calculation of confidence limits of the total misstatement can be made for ratio estimation with a calculation similar to the one shown for difference estimation. The ratio estimate results in even smaller sample sizes than difference estimation if the size of the misstatements in the population is proportionate to the recorded value of the population items. If the size of the individual misstatements is independent of the recorded value, the difference estimate results in smaller sample sizes.

Mean-per-Unit Estimation In **mean-per-unit estimation**, the auditor is concerned with the audited value rather than with the misstatement amount of each item in the sample. Except for the definition of what is being measured, the mean-per-unit estimate is calculated in exactly the same manner as the difference estimate. The point estimate of the audited value is the average audited value of items in the sample times the population size. The computed precision interval is calculated on the basis of the audited value of the sample items rather than the misstatements. When the auditor has computed the upper and lower confidence limits, a decision is made about the acceptability of the population by comparing these amounts with the recorded book value.

As discussed earlier, stratified sampling is a method of sampling in which all the elements in the total population are divided into two or more subpopulations. Each subpopulation is then independently tested. When auditors use stratified statistical sampling, the results are measured statistically. The calculations are made for each stratum. They are combined into one overall population estimate in terms of a confidence interval. Stratification is applicable to difference, ratio, and mean-per-unit estimation, but it is most commonly used with mean-per-unit estimation.

Stratified Statistical Methods

It was shown earlier that stratifying a population is not unique to statistical sampling, of course. Auditors have traditionally emphasized certain types of items when they are testing a population. For example, in confirming accounts receivable, it has been customary to place more emphasis on large accounts than on small ones. The major difference is that in statistical stratified sampling, the approach is more objective and better defined than it is under nonstatistical stratification methods.

Acceptable risk of incorrect acceptance was discussed earlier for nonstatistical sampling. For variables sampling, acceptable risk of incorrect rejection (ARIR) is also used. The distinctions between and uses of the two risks must be understood.

Sampling Risks

ARIA After an audit test is performed and statistical results are calculated, the auditor must conclude either that the population is not materially misstated or that it is materially misstated. ARIA is the statistical risk that the auditor has accepted a population that is actually materially misstated. ARIA is a serious concern to auditors because there are potential legal implications in concluding that an account balance is fairly stated when it is misstated by a material amount.

An account balance can be either overstated or understated, but not both; therefore, ARIA is a one-tailed statistical test. The confidence coefficients for ARIA are therefore different from the confidence level. (Confidence level = $1 - 2 \times$ ARIA; for example, if ARIA is 10 percent, the confidence level is 80 percent.) The confidence coefficients for various ARIAs are shown in Table 16-11 (p. 538) together with confidence coefficients for the confidence level and ARIR.

ARIR **Acceptable risk of incorrect rejection (ARIR)** is the statistical risk that the auditor has concluded that a population is materially misstated when it is not. The only time that ARIR affects the auditor's actions is when an auditor concludes that a population is not fairly stated. The most likely action when the auditor finds a balance not fairly stated is to

TABLE 16-11	Confidence Coefficient for Confidence Levels, ARIAs, and ARIRs		
Confidence Level (%)	ARIA (%)	ARIR (%)	Confidence Coefficient
99	.5	1	2.58
95	2.5	5	1.96
90	5	10	1.64
80	10	20	1.28
75	12.5	25	1.15
70	15	30	1.04
60	20	40	.84
50	25	50	.67
40	30	60	.52
30	35	70	.39
20	40	80	.25
10	45	90	.13
0	50	100	.0

increase the sample size or perform other tests. An increased sample size will usually lead the auditor to conclude that the balance was fairly stated if the account is not materially misstated.

ARIR is important only when there is a high cost to increasing the sample size or performing other tests. ARIA is always important. Confidence coefficients for ARIR are also shown in Table 16-11.

ARIA and ARIR are summarized in Table 16-12. It may seem from Table 16-12 that the auditor should attempt to minimize ARIA and ARIR. The way to accomplish that is by increasing the sample size, thus minimizing the risks. Because that is costly, having reasonable ARIA and ARIR is a more desirable goal.

TABLE 16-12	ARIA and ARIR	
	Actual State of the Population	
Actual Audit Decision	**Materially Misstated**	**Not Materially Misstated**
Conclude that the population is materially misstated	Correct conclusion— no risk	Incorrect conclusion— risk is ARIR
Conclude that the population is not materially misstated	Incorrect conclusion— risk is ARIA	Correct conclusion— no risk

ILLUSTRATION USING DIFFERENCE ESTIMATION

OBJECTIVE 16-5
Use difference estimation in tests of details of balances.

As previously discussed, several different types of variables sampling techniques may be applicable to auditing in different circumstances. One of these, difference estimation using hypothesis testing, has been selected as a means of illustrating the concepts and methodology of variables sampling. The reason for using difference estimation is its relative simplicity. When the method is considered reliable in a given set of circumstances, it is preferred to other variables sampling methods by most auditors.

In explaining difference estimation, the 14 steps in determining whether the account balance in the audit of accounts receivable is correctly stated are illustrated. These steps correspond to the ones used for nonstatistical sampling. Positive confirmations in the audit of Hart Lumber Company are used as a frame of reference to illustrate the use of difference estimation. There are 4,000 accounts receivable listed on the aged trial balance with a recorded value of $600,000. Internal controls are considered somewhat weak, and a large number of small misstatements in recorded amounts are expected in the audit. Total assets are $2,500,000, and net earnings before taxes are $400,000. Acceptable audit risk is reasonably high because of the limited users of the statements and the good financial health of Hart Lumber. Analytical procedures results indicated no significant problems.

The assumptions throughout are either that all confirmations were returned or that effective alternative procedures were carried out. Hence, the sample size is the number of positive confirmations mailed.

State the Objectives of the Audit Test The objective of the audit test in the Hart Lumber Company example is to determine whether accounts receivable before consideration of the allowance for uncollectible accounts is materially misstated.

Plan the Sample and Calculate the Sample Size Using Difference Estimation

Decide Whether Audit Sampling Applies Audit sampling applies in the confirmation of the accounts receivable because of the large number of accounts receivable.

Define Misstatement Conditions The misstatement condition is a client error determined in the confirmation of each account or alternative procedure.

Define the Population The population size is determined by count, as it was for attributes sampling. An accurate count is much more important in variables sampling because sample size and the computed precision limits are directly affected by population size. The population size for Hart Lumber's accounts receivable is 4,000.

Define the Sampling Unit The sampling unit is an account on the list of accounts receivable.

Specify Tolerable Misstatement The amount of misstatement the auditor is willing to accept is a materiality question. The auditor decides to accept a tolerable misstatement of $21,000 in the audit of Hart Lumber's accounts receivable.

Specify Acceptable Risk The auditor specifies two risks:

1. *Acceptable risk of incorrect acceptance (ARIA).* It is the risk of accepting accounts receivable as correct if it is actually misstated by more than $21,000. ARIA is affected by acceptable audit risk, results of tests of controls and substantive tests of transactions, analytical procedures, and the relative significance of accounts receivable in the financial statements. In Hart Lumber, an ARIA of 10 percent is used.
2. *Acceptable risk of incorrect rejection (ARIR).* It is the risk of rejecting accounts receivable as incorrect if it is not actually misstated by a material amount. ARIR is affected by the additional cost of resampling. Because it is fairly costly to confirm receivables a second time, an ARIR of 25 percent is used. For audit tests for which it is not costly to increase the sample size, a much higher ARIR is common.

After the auditor specifies the tolerable misstatement and ARIA, the hypothesis can be stated. The auditor's hypothesis for the audit of accounts receivable for Hart Lumber is: accounts receivable is not misstated by more than $21,000 at an ARIA of 10 percent.

Estimate Misstatements in the Population There are two parts of this estimate.

1. *Estimate an expected point estimate.* An advance estimate of the population point estimate is needed for difference estimation, much as the estimated population exception rate is needed for attributes sampling. The advance estimate is $1,500 (overstatement) for Hart Lumber, based on the previous year's audit tests.

2. *Make an advance population standard deviation estimate—variability of the population.* An advanced estimate of the variation in the misstatements in the population as measured by the population standard deviation is needed to determine the initial sample size. The calculation of the standard deviation is shown later. For Hart Lumber, it is estimated to be $20 based on the previous year's audit tests.

Calculate the Initial Sample Size The initial sample size for Hart Lumber can be now calculated from the following formula:

$$n = \left[\frac{SD^{\star}(Z_A + Z_R)N}{TM - E^{\star}} \right]^2$$

where

n = initial sample size

$SD^{\star}$ = advance estimate of the standard deviation

Z_A = confidence coefficient for ARIA (see Table 16-11)

Z_R = confidence coefficient for ARIR (see Table 16-11)

N = population size

TM = tolerable misstatement for the population (materiality)

$E^{\star}$ = estimated point estimate of the population misstatement

Applied to Hart Lumber, this equation yields

$$n = \left[\frac{20(1.28 + 1.15)4{,}000}{21{,}000 - 1{,}500} \right]^2 = (9.97)^2 = 100$$

Select the Sample and Perform the Procedures

Select the Sample Because a random sample (other than PPS) is required, the auditor must use one of the probabilistic sample selection methods discussed in Chapter 14 to select the 100 sample items for confirmation.

Perform the Audit Procedures The auditor must use care in confirming the accounts receivable and performing alternative procedures using the methods discussed in Chapter 15. For confirmations, a misstatement is the *difference* between the confirmation response and the client's balance after the reconciliation of all timing differences and customer errors. For example, if a customer returns a confirmation and states the correct balance is $887.12, and the balance in the client's records is $997.12, the difference of $110 is an overstatement amount if the auditor concludes that the client's records are incorrect. For nonresponses, the misstatements discovered by alternative procedures are treated identically to those discovered through confirmation. At the end of this step, there is a misstatement value for each item in the sample, many of which are likely to be zero. The misstatements for Hart Lumber are shown in Table 16-13.

Evaluate the Results

Generalize from the Sample to the Population In concept, nonstatistical and difference estimation do the same thing in generalizing from the sample to the population. Both methods are measuring the likely population misstatement based on the results of the sample. Difference estimation uses statistical measurement to compute confidence limits. The four steps discussed on pages 540–543 describe the calculation of the confidence limits for Hart Lumber Company. Steps 3 through 6 in Table 16-13 illustrate the calculations.

1. *Compute the point estimate of the total misstatement.* The point estimate is a direct extrapolation from the misstatements in the sample to the misstatements in the

TABLE 16-13	Calculation of Confidence Limits	
Step	**Statistical Formula**	**Illustration for Hart Lumber**
1. Take a random sample of size n.	n = sample size	100 accounts receivable are selected randomly from the aged trial balance containing 4,000 accounts.
2. Determine the value of each misstatement in the sample.		75 accounts are confirmed by customers, and 25 accounts are verified by alternative procedures. After reconciling timing differences and customer errors, the following 12 items were determined to be client errors (understatements):

<table>
<tr><td>1.</td><td>12.75</td><td>7.</td><td>(.87)</td></tr>
<tr><td>2.</td><td>(69.46)</td><td>8.</td><td>24.32</td></tr>
<tr><td>3.</td><td>85.28</td><td>9.</td><td>36.59</td></tr>
<tr><td>4.</td><td>100.00</td><td>10.</td><td>(102.16)</td></tr>
<tr><td>5.</td><td>(27.30)</td><td>11.</td><td>54.71</td></tr>
<tr><td>6.</td><td>41.06</td><td>12.</td><td>71.56</td></tr>
<tr><td></td><td></td><td></td><td>Sum = 226.48</td></tr>
</table>

Step	Statistical Formula	Illustration for Hart Lumber
3. Compute the point estimate of the total misstatement.	$$\bar{e} = \frac{\Sigma e_j}{n}$$ $$\hat{E} = N\bar{e} \text{ or } N\frac{\Sigma e_j}{n}$$ where $\bar{e}$ = average misstatement in the sample Σ = summation e_j = an individual misstatement in the sample n = sample size $\hat{E}$ = point estimate of the total misstatement N = population size	$$\bar{e} = \frac{226.48}{100} = 2.26$$ $$\hat{E} = \$4{,}000(2.26) = \$9{,}040$$ or $$\hat{E} = \$4{,}000\left(\frac{226.48}{100}\right) = \$9{,}040$$
4. Compute the population standard deviation of the misstatements from the sample.	$$SD = \sqrt{\frac{\Sigma(e_j) - n(\bar{e})^2}{n-1}}$$ where SD = standard deviation e_j = an individual misstatement in the sample n = sample size $\bar{e}$ = average misstatement in sample	

	e_j (rounded to nearest dollar)	$(e_j)^2$
1.	13	169
2.	(69)	4,761
3.	85	7,225
4.	100	10,000
5.	(27)	729
6.	41	1,681
7.	(1)	1
8.	24	576
9.	37	1,369
10.	(102)	10,404
11.	55	3,025
12.	72	5,184
	228	45,124

$$SD = \sqrt{\frac{45{,}124 - 100(2.26)^2}{99}}$$

$$SD = 21.2$$

[continued]

TABLE 16-13   Calculation of Confidence Limits [cont'd]

Step	Statistical Formula	Illustration for Hart Lumber
5. Compute the precision interval for the estimate of the total population misstatement at the desired confidence level.	$CPI = NZ_A \dfrac{SD}{\sqrt{n}} \sqrt{\dfrac{N-n}{N}}$ where CPI = computed precision interval N = population size Z_A = confidence coefficient for ARIA (see Table 16-11) SD = population standard deviation n = sample size $\sqrt{\dfrac{N-n}{N}}$ = finite correction factor	$CPI = \$4,000 \cdot 1.28 \cdot \dfrac{21.2}{\sqrt{100}} \sqrt{\dfrac{4,000-100}{4,000}}$ $= \$4,000 \cdot 1.28 \cdot \dfrac{21.2}{10} \cdot .99$ $= \$4,000 \cdot 1.28 \cdot 2.12 = \$10,800$
6. Compute the confidence limits at the CL desired.	$UCL = \hat{E} + CPI$ $LCL = \hat{E} - CPI$ where UCL = computed upper confidence limit LCL = computed lower confidence limit $\hat{E}$ = point estimate of the total misstatement CPI = computed precision interval at desired CL	$UCL = \$9,040 + \$10,800 = \$19,840$ $LCL = \$9,040 - \$10,800 = \$(1,760)$

population [termed projected misstatement in SAS 39 (AU 350)]. The calculation of the point estimate for Hart Lumber is shown in Table 16-13, step 3.

It is unlikely, of course, for the actual, but unknown, misstatement to be *exactly* the same as the point estimate. It is more realistic to estimate the misstatement in terms of a confidence interval determined by the point estimate plus and minus a computed precision interval. It should be apparent at this point that the calculation of the confidence interval is an essential part of variables sampling and that the process used to develop it depends on obtaining a representative sample.

2. *Compute an estimate of the population standard deviation.* The population standard deviation is a statistical measure of the variability in the values of the individual items in the population. If there is a large amount of variation in the values of population items, the standard deviation is larger than when the variation is small. For example, in the confirmation of accounts receivable, misstatements of $4, $14, and $26 have far less variation than the set $2, $275, and $812. Hence, the standard deviation is smaller in the first set.

The standard deviation has a significant effect on the computed precision interval. As might be expected, the ability to predict the value of a population is better when there is a small rather than a large amount of variation in the individual values of the population.

A reasonable estimate of the value of the population standard deviation is computed by the auditor using the standard statistical formula shown in Table 16-13, step 4. The size of the standard deviation estimate is determined solely by the characteristics of the auditor's sample results and is not affected by professional judgment.

3. *Compute the precision interval.* The precision interval is calculated by a statistical formula. The results are a dollar measure of the inability to predict the true population misstatement because the test was based on a sample rather than on the entire population. For the computed precision interval to have any meaning, it must be associated with ARIA. The formula to calculate the precision interval is shown in Table 16-13, step 5.

An examination of the formula in step 5 of Table 16-13 indicates the effect of changing each factor while the other factors remain constant is as follows:

Type of Change	*Effect on the Computed Precision Interval*
Increase ARIA	Decrease
Increase the point estimate of the misstatements	Increase
Increase the standard deviation	Increase
Increase the sample size	Decrease

4. *Compute the confidence limits.* The confidence limits, which define the confidence interval, are calculated by combining the point estimate of the total misstatements and the computed precision interval at the desired confidence level (point estimate ± computed precision interval). The formula to calculate the confidence limits is shown in Table 16-13, step 6.

   The lower and upper confidence limits for Hart Lumber are ($1,760) and $19,840, respectively. There is a 10 percent statistical risk that the population is understated by more than $1,760, and the same risk that it is overstated by more than $19,840. This is because an ARIA of 10 percent is equivalent to a confidence level of 80 percent.

Analyze the Misstatements There are no differences in analyzing misstatements for nonstatistical and statistical methods. The auditor must evaluate misstatements to determine the cause of each misstatement and decide whether modification of the audit risk model is needed.

Decide the Acceptability of the Population When a statistical method is used, a decision rule is needed to decide whether the population is acceptable. The decision rule is as follows: If the two-sided confidence interval for the misstatements is completely within the plus and minus tolerable misstatements, accept the hypothesis that the book value is not misstated by a material amount. Otherwise, accept the hypothesis that the book value is misstated by a material amount.

This decision rule is illustrated in Figure 16-5. The auditor should conclude that both the LCL and UCL for situations 1 and 2 fall completely within both the understatement and overstatement tolerable misstatement limits. Therefore, the conclusion that the population is not misstated by a material amount is accepted. For situations 3, 4, and 5, either

---

FIGURE 16-5   Illustration of the Auditor's Decision Rule for Difference Estimation

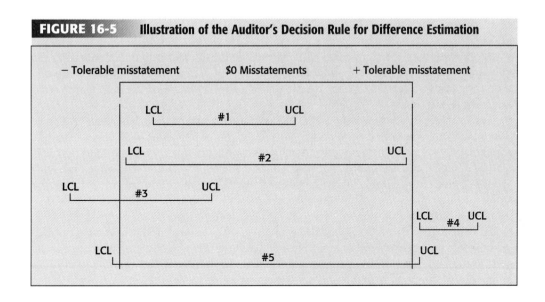

LCL or UCL, or both, are outside tolerable misstatements. Therefore, the population book value is rejected.

Application of the decision rule to Hart Lumber leads the auditor to the conclusion that the population should be accepted, because both confidence limits are within the tolerable misstatement range:

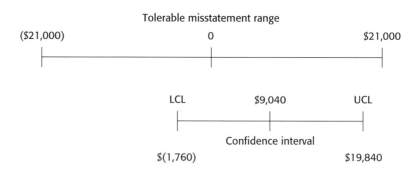

In accepting the population in this way, the auditor is taking a 10 percent chance of being wrong—that is, that the population is in fact misstated by a material amount. However, based on the auditor's planning judgments, this level of risk is appropriate.

Analysis Given that the actual standard deviation (21.2) was larger than the advanced estimate (20), and the actual point estimate $9,040 was larger than the advanced estimate ($1,500), it may seem surprising that the population was accepted. The reason is that the use of a reasonably small ARIR caused the sample size to be larger than if ARIR had been 100 percent. If ARIR had been 100 percent, which is common when the additional audit cost to increase the sample size is small, the required sample size would have been only 28:

$$\left[\frac{20(1.28 + 0)4,000}{21,000 - 1,500} \right]^2 = 28$$

Assuming a sample size of 28 and the same actual point estimate and standard deviation, the upper confidence limit would have been $29,559, and therefore, the population book value would have been rejected. One reason that auditors use ARIR is to reduce the likelihood of needing to increase the sample size if the standard deviation or point estimate is larger than was expected.

Action When a Hypothesis is Rejected

When one or both of the confidence limits lie outside the tolerable misstatement range, the population is not considered acceptable. The courses of action are the same as those discussed for nonstatistical sampling, except that a better estimate of the population misstatement is practical.

For example, in the Hart Lumber case, if the confidence level had been $9,040 ± $15,800, and the client had been willing to reduce the book value by $9,040, the results would be 0 ± $15,800. The new computed lower confidence limit would be an understatement of $15,800, and the upper confidence limit a $15,800 overstatement, which are both acceptable given the tolerable misstatement of $21,000. The minimum adjustment that the auditor could make and still have the population acceptable is $3,840 [($9,040 + $15,800) − $21,000].

However, the client may be unwilling to adjust the balance on the basis of a sample. Furthermore, if the computed precision interval exceeds tolerable misstatement, an adjustment to the books cannot be made that will satisfy the auditor. This would be the case in the previous example if tolerable misstatement was only $15,000.

Formulas for calculating misstatement bounds for MUS follow. Each formula is illustrated with the example that has already been shown in the text.

The following symbols are used:

$D(i)$ = maximum total population misstatement bound when i misstatements are found (D_o for overstatement amounts and D_u for understatement amounts)

Y = total population recorded dollars

$Pu(i)$ = upper precision limit from the one-sided attributes table for i misstatements

$E(i)$ = amount of a dollar unit misstatement number i [$E_o(i)$ for overstatement amount number i, and $E_u(i)$ for understatement amount number i]

M = assumed maximum amount of misstatement in any population dollar unit (M_o for overstatement amount and M_u for understatement amount)

MLE = estimated most likely misstatement (MLE_o for overstatement amount and MLE_u for understatement amount)

Σ = summation

n = sample size

Formula Where No Misstatements Are Found

$$D(0) = Y \cdot Pu(0) \cdot M$$

Illustration 100 percent misstatement assumption; 5 percent risk; sample size 100.

$$\text{Upper and lower bounds} = \$1,200,000 \times .03 \times 1 = \$36,000$$

Formula Where Misstatements Are Found (before Adjustment)

$$D(i) = Y \cdot [Pu(0) \cdot M] + Y \cdot [Pu(1) - Pu(0)] \cdot E(1) + Y \cdot [Pu(2) - Pu(1)] \cdot E(2) + \cdots + Y \cdot [Pu(i) - Pu(i - 1)] \cdot E(i)]$$

Illustration 100 percent misstatement assumption; four overstatement amounts and one understatement amount; misstatements are ordered from the largest dollar unit misstatement to the smallest; 5 percent risk; sample size 100. Therefore,

$$E_o(1) = .671$$

$$E_o(2) = .07$$

$$E_o(3) = .016$$

$$E_o(4) = .0002$$

$$E_u(1) = .03$$

The 5 percent risk bound for maximum total population overstatement amount (before adjustment) is as follows:

$$\begin{aligned}
D_o(4) &= [(1,200,000)(.03)(1.00)] + [(1,200,000)(.047 - .03)(.671)] \\
&\quad + [(1,200,000)(.062 - .047)(.07)] + [(1,200,000)(.076 - .062)(.016)] \\
&\quad + [(1,200,000)(.089 - .076)(.0002)] \\
&= 36,000 + 13,688 + 1,260 + 269 + 3 \\
&= 51,220
\end{aligned}$$

and the 5 percent risk bound for maximum total population understatement amount (before adjustment) is as follows:

$$D_u(1) = [(1,200,000)(.03)(1.00)] + [(1,200,000)(.047 - .03)(.03)]$$

$$= 36,000 + 612$$

$$= 36,612$$

Formula for Adjustment for Offsetting Amounts

$$D_o \text{ adjusted} = D_o(i) - MLE_u$$

$$D_u \text{ adjusted} = D_u(i) - MLE_o$$

where

$$MLE = \Sigma E(i) \cdot \frac{Y}{n}$$

Illustration

$$MLE_o = (.671 + .07 + .016 + .0002)(1,200,000/100)$$

$$= (.7572)(12,000)$$

$$= 9,086$$

$$MLE_u = (.03)(1,200,000/100)$$

$$= (.03)(12,000)$$

$$= 360$$

$$D_o \text{ adjusted} = 51,220 - 360$$

$$= 50,860$$

$$D_u \text{ adjusted} = 36,612 - 9,086$$

$$= 27,526$$

ESSENTIAL TERMS

Acceptable risk of incorrect acceptance (ARIA)—the risk that the auditor is willing to take of accepting a balance as correct when the true misstatement in the balance is equal to or greater than tolerable misstatement

Acceptable risk of incorrect rejection (ARIR)—the risk that the auditor is willing to take of rejecting a balance as incorrect when it is not misstated by a material amount

Difference estimation—a method of variables sampling in which the auditor estimates the population misstatement by multiplying the average misstatement in the sample by the total number of population items and also calculates sampling risk

Mean-per-unit estimation—a method of variables sampling in which the auditor estimates the audited value of a population by multiplying the average audited value of the sample times the population size and also calculates sampling risk

Misstatement bounds—an estimate of the largest likely overstatements and understatements in a population at a given ARIA, using monetary unit sampling

Monetary unit sampling (MUS)—a statistical sampling method that provides upper and lower misstatement bounds expressed in monetary amounts; also referred to as dollar unit sampling, cumulative monetary amount sampling, and sampling with probability proportional to size

Point estimate—a method of projecting from the sample to the population to estimate the population misstatement, commonly by assuming that misstatements in the unaudited population are proportional to the misstatements found in the sample

Probability proportion to size sample selection (PPS)—sample selection of individual dollars in a population by the use of random or systematic sample selection

Ratio estimation—a method of variables sampling in which the auditor estimates the population misstatement by multiplying the portion of sample dollars misstated by the total recorded population book value and also calculates sampling risk

Statistical inferences—statistical conclusions that the auditor draws from sample results based on knowledge of sampling distributions

Stratified sampling—a method of sampling in which all the elements in the total population are divided into two or more subpopulations that are independently tested and statistically measured

Variables sampling—sampling techniques for tests of details of balances that use the statistical inference process

REVIEW QUESTIONS

16-1 (Objective 16-1) What major difference between (a) tests of controls and substantive tests of transactions and (b) tests of details of balances makes attributes sampling inappropriate for tests of details of balances?

16-2 (Objective 16-2) Define stratified sampling and explain its importance in auditing. How could an auditor obtain a stratified sample of 30 items from each of three strata in the confirmation of accounts receivable?

16-3 (Objective 16-2) Distinguish between the point estimate of the total misstatements and the true value of the misstatements in the population. How can each be determined?

16-4 (Objective 16-2) Evaluate the following statement made by an auditor: "On every aspect of the audit where it is possible, I calculate the point estimate of the misstatements and evaluate whether the amount is material. If it is, I investigate the cause and continue to test the population until I determine whether there is a serious problem. The use of statistical sampling in this manner is a valuable audit tool."

16-5 (Objective 16-3) Define monetary unit sampling and explain its importance in auditing. How does it combine the features of attributes and variables sampling?

16-6 (Objectives 16-1, 16-2, 16-3, 16-4) Define what is meant by sampling risk. Does sampling risk apply to nonstatistical sampling, MUS, attributes sampling, and variables sampling? Explain.

16-7 (Objectives 16-1, 16-2) What are the major differences in the 14 steps used to do nonstatistical sampling for tests of details of balances versus for tests of controls and substantive tests of transactions?

16-8 (Objective 16-3) The 2,620 inventory items described in question 16-14 are listed on 44 inventory pages with 60 lines per page. There is a total for each page. The client's data are not in machine-readable form, and the CPA firm does not have a computer terminal available. Describe how a monetary unit sample can be selected in this situation.

16-9 (Objective 16-3) Explain how the auditor determines tolerable misstatement for MUS.

16-10 (Objective 16-2) Explain what is meant by acceptable risk of incorrect acceptance. What are the major audit factors affecting ARIA?

16-11 (Objective 16-4) Evaluate the following statement made by an auditor: "I took a random sample and derived a 90 percent confidence interval of $800,000 to $900,000. That means that the true population value will be between $800,000 and $900,000, 90 percent of the time."

16-12 (Objective 16-2) What is the relationship between ARIA and ARACR?

16-13 (Objective 16-3) What is meant by the "percent of misstatement assumption" for MUS in those population items that are misstated? Why is it common to use a 100 percent misstatement assumption when it is almost certain to be highly conservative?

16-14 (Objective 16-3) An auditor is determining the appropriate sample size for testing inventory valuation using MUS. The population has 2,620 inventory items valued at $12,625,000. The tolerable misstatement for both understatements and overstatements is $500,000 at a 10 percent ARIA. No misstatements are expected in the population. Calculate the preliminary sample size using a 100 percent average misstatement assumption.

16-15 (Objective 16-5)   Assume that a sample of 100 units was obtained in sampling the inventory in Question 16-14. Assume further that the following three misstatements were found:

Misstatement	Recorded Value	Audited Value
1	$ 897.16	$ 609.16
2	47.02	0
3	1,621.68	1,522.68

Calculate adjusted misstatement bounds for the population. Draw audit conclusions based on the results.

16-16 (Objective 16-3)   Why is it difficult to determine the appropriate sample size for MUS? How should the auditor determine the proper sample size?

16-17 (Objective 16-5)   What is meant by a decision rule using difference estimation? State the decision rule.

16-18 (Objective 16-2)   What alternative courses of action are appropriate when a population is rejected using nonstatistical sampling for tests of details of balances? When should each option be followed?

16-19 (Objective 16-4)   Define what is meant by the population standard deviation and explain its importance in variables sampling. What is the relationship between the population standard deviation and the required sample size?

16-20 (Objective 16-5)   In using difference estimation, an auditor took a random sample of 100 inventory items from a large population to test for proper pricing. Several of the inventory items were misstated, but the combined net amount of the sample misstatement was not material. In addition, a review of the individual misstatements indicated that no misstatement was by itself material. As a result, the auditor did not investigate the misstatements or make a statistical evaluation. Explain why this practice is improper.

16-21 (Objectives 16-3, 16-4)   Distinguish among difference estimation, ratio estimation, mean-per-unit estimation, and stratified mean-per-unit estimation. Give one example in which each could be used. When would MUS be preferable to any of these?

16-22 (Objective 16-4)   An essential step in difference estimation is the comparison of each computed confidence limit with tolerable misstatement. Why is this step so important, and what should the auditor do if one of the confidence limits is larger than the tolerable misstatement?

16-23 (Objective 16-4)   Explain why difference estimation is commonly used by auditors.

16-24 (Objectives 16-3, 16-4)   Give an example of the use of attributes sampling, MUS, and variables sampling in the form of an audit conclusion.

MULTIPLE CHOICE QUESTIONS FROM CPA EXAMINATIONS

16-25 (Objective 16-2)   The following questions refer to the use of stratified sampling in auditing. For each one, select the best response.

a. Mr. Murray decides to use stratified sampling. The reason for using stratified sampling rather than unrestricted random sampling is to
  (1) reduce as much as possible the degree of variability in the overall population.
  (2) give every element in the population an equal chance of being included in the sample.
  (3) allow the person selecting the sample to use his or her own judgment in deciding which elements should be included in the sample.
  (4) allow the auditor to emphasize larger items from the population.

b. In an audit of financial statements, a CPA will generally find stratified sampling techniques to be most applicable to
  (1) recomputing net wage and salary payments to employees.

(2) tracing hours worked from the payroll summary back to the individual time cards.

⌘ (3) confirming accounts receivable for residential customers at a large electric utility.

(4) reviewing supporting documentation for additions to plant and equipment.

c. From prior experience, a CPA is aware that the accounts receivable trial balance contains a few unusually large balances. In using statistical sampling, the CPA's best course of action is to

(1) eliminate any unusually large balances that appear in the sample.

(2) continue to draw new samples until no unusually large balances appear in the sample.

⍰ (3) stratify the accounts receivable population so that the unusually large balances are reviewed separately.

(4) increase the sample size to lessen the effect of the unusually large balances.

16-26 (Objectives 16-1, 16-2) The following apply to audit sampling. For each one, select the best response.

a. The auditor's failure to recognize a misstatement in an amount or a control deviation is described as a

(1) statistical error.

(2) sampling error.

(3) standard error of the mean.

⍰ (4) nonsampling error.

b. An auditor uses audit sampling to perform tests of controls in the acquisition and payment cycle. Those tests indicate that the related controls are operating effectively. The auditor plans to use audit sampling to perform tests of details of balances for accounts payable. The auditor's acceptable risk of incorrect acceptance (ARIA) for the tests of details of balances for accounts payable would most likely be

(1) the same as the ARACR for tests of controls.

⍰ (2) greater than the ARACR for tests of controls.

(3) less than the ARACR for tests of controls.

(4) totally independent from the ARACR used for tests of controls.

c. How should an auditor determine the tolerable misstatement required in establishing an audit sampling plan?

⍰ (1) By the materiality of an allowable margin of misstatement the auditor is willing to accept.

(2) By the amount of reliance the auditor will place on the results of the sample.

(3) By reliance on a table of random numbers.

(4) By the amount of risk the auditor is willing to take that material misstatements will occur in the accounting process.

DISCUSSION QUESTIONS AND PROBLEMS

16-27 (Objective 16-2) You are planning to use nonstatistical sampling to evaluate the results of accounts receivable confirmation for the Meridian Company. You have already performed tests of controls for sales, sales returns and allowances, and cash receipts, and they are considered excellent. Because of the quality of the controls, you decide to use an acceptable risk of incorrect acceptance of 10 percent. There are 3,000 accounts receivable with a gross value of $6,900,000. The accounts are similar in size and will be treated as a single stratum. An overstatement or understatement of more than $150,000 would be considered material.

Required

a. Calculate the required sample size. Assume your firm uses the following nonstatistical formula to determine sample size:

Sample size = (Book value of population/tolerable misstatement) × Assurance factor

Assurance factor:
5% ARIA = 3
10% ARIA = 2
20% ARIA = 1

b. Assume that instead of good results, poor results were obtained for tests of controls and substantive tests of transactions for sales, sales returns and allowances, and cash receipts. How would this affect your required sample size? How would you use this information in your sample size determination?

c. Regardless of your answer to part a, assume you decide to select a sample of 100 accounts for testing. Indicate how you would select the accounts for testing using systematic selection.

d. Assume a total book value of $230,000 for the 100 accounts selected for testing. You uncover three overstatements totaling $1,500 in the sample. Evaluate whether the population is fairly stated.

16-28 (Objective 16-3) The accounts receivable population for Jake's Bookbinding Company is shown below. This table is the same as Table 16-1 on page 516, except that cumulative amounts are included to assist you in completing the problem. The population is smaller than would ordinarily be the case for statistical sampling, but an entire population is useful to show how to select PPS samples.

Required
a. Select a random PPS sample of 10 items, using computer software.
b. Select a sample of 10 items using systematic PPS sampling using the same concepts discussed in Chapter 14 for systematic sampling. Use a starting point of 1857. Identify the physical units associated with the sample dollars. (Hint: the interval is 207, 295 ÷ 10.)
c. Which sample items will always be included in the systematic PPS sample regardless of the starting point? Will that also be true of random PPS sampling?
d. Which method is preferable in terms of ease of selection in this case?
e. Why would an auditor use MUS?

Population Item	Recorded Amount	Cumulative Amount	Population Item (cont.)	Recorded Amount (cont.)	Cumulative Amount (cont.)
1	$ 1,410	$ 1,410	21	$ 4,865	$117,385
2	9,130	10,540	22	770	118,155
3	660	11,200	23	2,305	120,460
4	3,355	14,555	24	2,665	123,125
5	5,725	20,280	25	1,000	124,125
6	8,210	28,490	26	6,225	130,350
7	580	29,070	27	3,675	134,025
8	44,110	73,180	28	6,250	140,275
9	825	74,005	29	1,890	142,165
10	1,155	75,160	30	27,705	169,870
11	2,270	77,430	31	935	170,805
12	50	77,480	32	5,595	176,400
13	5,785	83,265	33	930	177,330
14	940	84,205	34	4,045	181,375
15	1,820	86,025	35	9,480	190,855
16	3,380	89,405	36	360	191,215
17	530	89,935	37	1,145	192,360
18	955	90,890	38	6,400	198,760
19	4,490	95,380	39	100	198,860
20	17,140	112,520	40	8,435	207,295

16-29 (Objective 16-3)   In the audit of Price Seed Company for the year ended September 30, the auditor set a tolerable misstatement of $50,000 at an ARIA of 10 percent. A PPS sample of 100 was selected from an accounts receivable population that had a recorded balance of $1,975,000. The table below shows the differences uncovered in the confirmation process.

Accounts Receivable per Records	Accounts Receivable per Confirmation	Follow-Up Comments by Auditor
1. $2,728.00	$2,498.00	Pricing error on two invoices.
2. $5,125.00	-0-	Customer mailed check 9/26; company received check 10/3.
3. $3,890.00	$1,190.00	Merchandise returned 9/30 and counted in inventory; credit was issued 10/6.
4. $ 791.00	$ 815.00	Footing error on an invoice.
5. $ 548.00	$1,037.00	Goods were shipped 9/28; sale was recorded on 10/6.
6. $3,115.00	$3,190.00	Pricing error on a credit memorandum.
7. $1,540.00	-0-	Goods were shipped on 9/29; customer received goods 10/3; sale was recorded on 9/30.

Required

    a. Calculate the upper and lower misstatement bounds on the basis of the client misstatements in the sample.

    b. Is the population acceptable as stated? If not, what options are available to the auditor at this point? Which option should the auditor select? Explain.

16-30 (Objective 16-3)   You intend to use MUS as a part of the audit of several accounts for Roynpower Manufacturing Company. You have done the audit for the past several years, and there has rarely been an adjusting entry of any kind. Your audit tests of all tests of controls and substantive tests of transactions cycles were completed at an interim date, and control risk has been assessed as low. You therefore decide to use an ARIA of 10 percent and an EPER of 0 percent for all tests of details of balances. You also decide to use a 100 percent misstatement assumption for both overstatements and understatements.

You intend to use MUS in the audit of the three most material asset balance sheet account balances: accounts receivable, inventory, and marketable securities. You feel justified in using the same ARIA for each audit area because of the low assessed control risk.

The recorded balances and related information for the three accounts are as follows:

	Recorded Value
Accounts receivable	$ 3,600,000
Inventory	4,800,000
Marketable securities	1,600,000
	$10,000,000

Net earnings before taxes for Roynpower are $2,000,000. You decide that a combined misstatement of $100,000 is allowable for the client.

The audit approach to be followed will be to determine the total sample size needed for all three accounts. A sample will be selected from all $10 million, and the appropriate testing for a sample item will depend on whether the item is a receivable, inventory, or marketable security. The audit conclusions will pertain to the entire $10 million, and no conclusion will be made about the three individual accounts unless significant misstatements are found in the sample.

Required

    a. Evaluate the audit approach of testing all three account balances in one sample.

b. Calculate the required sample size for all three accounts.

c. Calculate the required sample size for each of the three accounts, assuming you decide that the tolerable misstatement in each account is $100,000. (Recall that tolerable misstatement equals preliminary judgment about materiality for MUS.)

d. Assume that you select the random sample using computer software. How would you identify which sample item in the population to audit for the number 4,627,871? What audit procedures would be performed?

e. Assume that you select a sample of 200 sample items for testing and you find one misstatement in inventory. The recorded value is $987.12, and the audit value is $887.12. Calculate the misstatement bounds for the three combined accounts and reach appropriate audit conclusions.

16-31 (Objectives 16-2, 16-3, 16-4, 16-5)   An audit partner is developing an office training program to familiarize her professional staff with audit sampling decision models applicable to the audit of dollar-value balances. She wishes to demonstrate the relationship of sample sizes to population size and estimated population exception rate and the auditor's specifications as to tolerable misstatement and ARIA. The partner prepared the following table to show comparative population characteristics and audit specifications of the two populations.

| | Characteristics of Population 1 Relative to Population 2 | | Audit Specifications as to a Sample from Population 1 Relative to a Sample from Population 2 | |
	Size	Estimated Population Exception Rate	Tolerable Misstatement	ARIA
Case 1	Equal	Equal	Equal	Lower
Case 2	Smaller	Smaller	Equal	Higher
Case 3	Larger	Equal	Equal	Lower
Case 4	Equal	Larger	Larger	Equal
Case 5	Larger	Equal	Smaller	Higher

Required

In items (1) through (5) you are to indicate for the specific case from the table the required sample size to be selected from population 1 relative to the sample from population 2.

(1) In case 1, the required sample size from population 1 is _____.

(2) In case 2, the required sample size from population 1 is _____.

(3) In case 3, the required sample size from population 1 is _____.

(4) In case 4, the required sample size from population 1 is _____.

(5) In case 5, the required sample size from population 1 is _____.

Your answer choice should be selected from the following responses:

a. Larger than the required sample size from population 2.

b. Equal to the required sample size from population 2.

c. Smaller than the required sample size from population 2.

d. Indeterminate relative to the required sample size from population 2.*

 16-32 (Objective 16-5)   In auditing the valuation of inventory, the auditor, Claire Butler, decided to use difference estimation. She decided to select an unrestricted random sample of 80 inventory items from a population of 1,840 that had a book value of $175,820.

*AICPA adapted.

Butler decided in advance that she was willing to accept a maximum misstatement in the population of $6,000 at an ARIA of 5 percent. There were eight misstatements in the sample, which were as follows:

	Audit Value	Book Value	Sample Misstatements
	$ 812.50	$ 740.50	$(72.00)
	12.50	78.20	65.70
	10.00	51.10	41.10
	25.40	61.50	36.10
	600.10	651.90	51.80
	.12	0	(.12)
	51.06	81.06	30.00
	83.11	104.22	21.11
Total	$1,594.79	$1,768.48	$173.69

Required

a. Calculate the point estimate, the computed precision interval, the confidence interval, and the confidence limits for the population. Label each calculation. Use a computer for this purpose (instructor's option).
b. Should Butler accept the book value of the population? Explain.
c. What options are available to her at this point?

16-33 (Objective 16-5) Marjorie Jorgenson, CPA, is verifying the accuracy of outstanding accounts payable for Marygold Hardware, a large single-location retail hardware store. There are 650 vendors listed on the outstanding accounts payable list. She has eliminated from the population 40 vendors that have large ending balances and will audit them separately. There are now 610 vendors.

She plans to do one of three tests for each item in the sample: examine a vendor's statement in the client's hands, obtain a confirmation when no statement is on hand, or extensively search for invoices when neither of the first two are obtained. There is no accounts payable master file available, and a large number of misstatements is expected. Marjorie has obtained facts or made audit judgments as follows:

ARIR	20%	ARIA	10%
Tolerable misstatement	$ 45,000	Expected misstatement	$20,000
Recorded book value	$600,000	Estimated standard deviation	$ 280

Required

a. Under what circumstances is it desirable to use difference estimation in the situation described? Under what circumstances would it be undesirable?
b. Calculate the required sample size for the audit tests of accounts payable using difference estimation, assuming that ARIR is ignored.
c. Assume that the auditor selects exactly the sample size calculated in part b. The point estimate calculated from the sample results is $21,000 and the estimated population standard deviation is 267. Is the population fairly stated as defined by the decision rule? Explain what causes the result to be acceptable or unacceptable.
d. Calculate the required sample size for the audit tests of accounts payable, assuming that the ARIR is considered.
e. Explain the reason for the large increase of the sample size resulting from including ARIR in determining sample size.
f. Marjorie Jorgenson calculates the required sample size using the formula without consideration of ARIR. After the sample size is determined, she increases the sample size by 25 percent. Marjorie believes that this does the same thing as using ARIR without having to bother to make the calculation. Is this approach appropriate? Evaluate the desirability of the approach.

16-34 (Objective 16-3) You are doing the audit of Peckinpah Tire and Parts, a wholesale auto parts company. You have decided to use monetary unit sampling (MUS) for the audit of accounts receivable and inventory. The following are the recorded balances:

Accounts receivable	**$12,000,000**
Inventory	**$23,000,000**

You have already made the following judgments:

Materiality for planning purposes	$800,000
Acceptable audit risk	5%
Inherent risk:	
Accounts receivable	80%
Inventory	100%
Assessed control risk:	
Accounts receivable	50%
Inventory	80%

Analytical procedures have been planned for inventory, but not for accounts receivable. The analytical procedures for inventory are expected to have a 60 percent chance of detecting a material misstatement should one exist.

You have concluded that it would be difficult to alter sample size for accounts receivable confirmation once confirmations are sent and replies are received. However, inventory tests could be reopened without great difficulty.

After discussions with the client, you believe that the accounts are in about the same condition this year as they were last year. Last year no misstatements were found in the confirmation of accounts receivable. Inventory tests revealed an overstatement amount of about 1 percent.

For requirements a–c, make any assumptions necessary in deciding the factors affecting sample size. If no table is available for the ARIA chosen, estimate sample size judgmentally.

Required
   a. Plan the sample size for the confirmation of accounts receivable using MUS.
   b. Plan the sample size for the test of pricing of inventories using MUS.
   c. Plan the combined sample size for both the confirmation of accounts receivable and the price tests of inventory using MUS.
   d. (Instructor's option) Using an electronic spreadsheet, generate a list of random dollars in generation order and in ascending order, for the sample of accounts receivable items determined in part a.

 16-35 (Objectives 16-2, 16-3) You have just completed the accounts receivable confirmation process in the audit of Danforth Paper Company, a paper supplier to retail shops and commercial users. Following are the data related to this process:

Accounts receivable recorded balance	$2,760,000
Number of accounts	7,320
A nonstatistical sample was taken as follows:	
All accounts over $10,000 (23 accounts)	$ 465,000
77 accounts under $10,000	$ 81,500
Tolerable misstatement for the confirmation test	$ 100,000
Inherent and control risk are both high	
No relevant analytical procedures were performed	

The following are the results of the confirmation procedures:

	Recorded Value	Audited Value
Items over $10,000	$465,000	$432,000
Items under $10,000	81,500	77,150
Individual misstatements for items under $10,000:		
Item 12	5,120	4,820
Item 19	485	385
Item 33	1,250	250
Item 35	3,975	3,875
Item 51	1,850	1,825
Item 59	4,200	3,780
Item 74	2,405	0

Required
  a. Evaluate the results of the nonstatistical sample. Consider both the direct implications of the misstatements found and the effect of using a sample.
  b. Assume that the sample was a PPS sample. Evaluate the results using monetary unit sampling.
  c. (Instructor's option) Do the above analyses using an electronic spreadsheet.

PART IV
(Chapters 17–22)

APPLICATION OF THE AUDIT PROCESS TO OTHER CYCLES

The chapters in Part IV apply auditing concepts first presented in Chapters 6 through 12, and then expanded in Chapters 13 through 16, to the other cycles in an audit. Although there are considerable similarities in auditing each cycle, there are also important differences that auditors need to understand.

Each of these chapters deals with a specific transaction cycle or part of a transaction cycle in much the same manner as Chapters 13 through 16 cover the sales and collection cycle. Each chapter in Part IV demonstrates the relationship of internal control, tests of controls, substantive tests of transactions, and analytical procedures to the related balance sheet and income statement accounts in the cycle and to tests of details of balances.

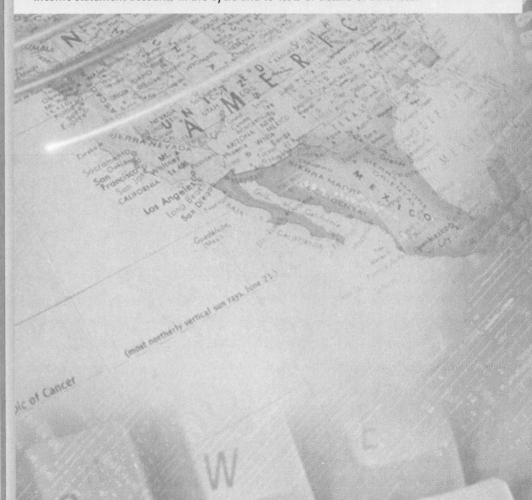

AUDIT OF THE PAYROLL AND PERSONNEL CYCLE

17

THE STAFF AUDITOR MUST NEVER "SIMPLY FOLLOW ORDERS"

Leslie Scott graduated with a Masters of Accountancy degree from a major university before joining the audit staff of a CPA firm. During her first "busy season," she was working on the audit of Sysco, Inc., a software development company. Her immediate supervisor on the Sysco audit was Bob Stith. Bob had been with the firm 3 years longer than Leslie, and worked on the Sysco audit the previous year. He was supervising Leslie's work on capitalized software development costs. In preparing herself, Leslie had read FASB Statement 86, and had a good understanding of the accounting rules concerning the capitalization of such costs. She understood, for example, that costs could not be capitalized until after technological feasibility was established either through detail program design or product design and the completion of a working model, confirmed by testing.

Bob Stith drafted an audit program for capitalized software development costs. He told Leslie to verify the payroll costs that were a significant part of the development cost and to talk to Jack Smart, Sysco's controller, about whether the projects with capitalized costs had reached the technological feasibility stage. Leslie tested the payroll costs and found no misstatements. She also made inquiries of Smart and was told that the appropriate stage was reached. Leslie documented Smart's representation in the working papers and went on to the next area assigned to her.

Later, Leslie began to have second thoughts. She understood that management's representations were a weak form of audit evidence and she was concerned about whether Jack Smart was the most knowledgeable person about the technical status of software projects. To resolve her concerns, she decided to talk to the responsible software engineers about one of the projects to confirm Smart's representations. She intended to clear this with Stith, but he was at another client's office that morning, so she proceeded on her own initiative. The engineer she talked to on the first project told her that he was almost finished with a working model, but hadn't tested it yet. She decided to inquire about another project and discovered the same thing. Leslie documented these findings on a working paper and planned to discuss the situation with Stith as soon as he returned to the job.

When Leslie (somewhat proud of herself) told Stith of her findings and showed him the working paper, he told her the following:

> "Listen, Leslie, I told you just to talk to Jack. You shouldn't do procedures that you're not instructed to do. I want you to destroy this working paper and don't record the wasted time. We're under a lot of time pressure and we can't bill Sysco for procedures that aren't necessary. Jack knows what he's talking about. There's nothing wrong with the capitalized software development costs. The fact that they have working products that they're selling indicates technological feasibility was reached."

Leslie was extremely distressed with this reaction from Stith, but followed his instructions. The following fall, the SEC conducted an investigation of Sysco and found, among other things, that they had overstated capitalized software development costs. The SEC brought an action against both the management of Sysco and their auditors.

LEARNING OBJECTIVES

After studying this chapter, you should be able to

17-1 Identify the accounts and transactions in the payroll and personnel cycle.

17-2 Describe the business functions and the related documents and records in the payroll and personnel cycle.

17-3 Understand internal control and design and perform tests of controls and substantive tests of transactions for the payroll and personnel cycle.

17-4 Design and perform analytical procedures for the payroll and personnel cycle.

17-5 Design and perform tests of details of balances for accounts in the payroll and personnel cycle.

The **payroll and personnel cycle** involves the employment and payment of all employees. Labor is an important consideration in the valuation of inventory in manufacturing, construction, and other industries. As the vignette involving Leslie Scott and the audit of Sysco, Inc., demonstrates, the improper valuation and allocation of labor can result in a material misstatement of net income. Payroll is also an area in which large amounts of company resources can be wasted because of inefficiency or stolen through fraud.

As with the sales and collection cycle, the audit of the payroll and personnel cycle includes obtaining an understanding of internal control, assessment of control risk, tests of controls and substantive tests of transactions, analytical procedures, and tests of details of balances. There are several important differences between the payroll and personnel cycle and other cycles in a typical audit.

- *There is only one class of transactions for payroll.* Most cycles include at least two classes of transactions. For example, the sales and collection cycle includes both sales and cash receipts transactions and often sales returns and charge-off of uncollectibles. Payroll has only one class because the receipt of services from employees and the payment for those services through payroll occurs within a short time period.
- *Transactions are far more significant than related balance sheet accounts.* Payroll-related accounts such as accrued payroll and withheld taxes are usually small compared to the total amount of transactions for the year.
- *Internal controls over payroll are effective for almost all companies, even small ones.* The reasons for effective controls are harsh federal and state penalties for errors in withholding and paying payroll taxes and employee morale problems if employees are not paid or are underpaid.

Because of these three characteristics, auditors typically emphasize tests of controls, substantive tests of transactions, and analytical procedures in the audit of payroll. Tests of details of balances often take only a few minutes. Before discussing the tests in the cycle, we review the transactions and account balances, as well as the documents and records used in the payroll and personnel cycle for a typical company.

ACCOUNTS AND TRANSACTIONS IN THE PAYROLL AND PERSONNEL CYCLE

OBJECTIVE 17-1
Identify the accounts and transactions in the payroll and personnel cycle.

The overall objective in the audit of the payroll and personnel cycle is to evaluate whether the account balances affected by the cycle are fairly stated in accordance with generally accepted accounting principles. Typical accounts in the payroll and personnel cycle are shown in Figure 17-1 with the use of T-accounts.

The way in which accounting information flows through the various accounts in the payroll and personnel cycle is illustrated by the T-accounts. In most systems, the accrued wages and salaries account is used only at the end of an accounting period. Throughout the period, expenses are charged when the employees are actually paid rather than when the labor costs are incurred. The accruals for labor are recorded by adjusting entries at the end of the period for any earned but unpaid labor costs.

BUSINESS FUNCTIONS IN THE CYCLE AND RELATED DOCUMENTS AND RECORDS

OBJECTIVE 17-2
Describe the business functions and the related documents and records in the payroll and personnel cycle.

The payroll and personnel cycle begins with the hiring of personnel and ends with payment to the employees for the services performed and to the government and other institutions for the withheld and accrued payroll taxes and benefits. In between, the cycle involves obtaining services from the employees consistent with the objectives of the company and accounting for the services in a proper manner.

FIGURE 17-1   Accounts in the Payroll and Personnel Cycle

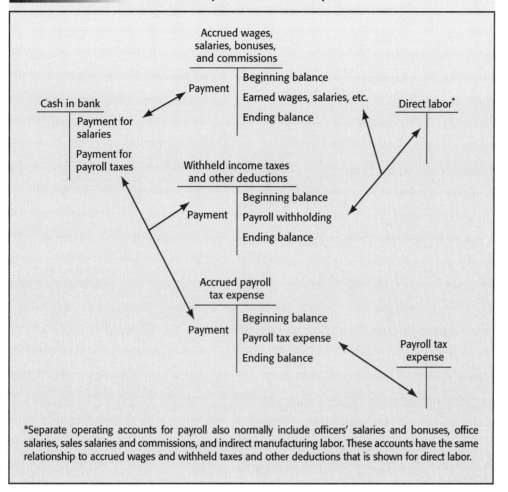

*Separate operating accounts for payroll also normally include officers' salaries and bonuses, office salaries, sales salaries and commissions, and indirect manufacturing labor. These accounts have the same relationship to accrued wages and withheld taxes and other deductions that is shown for direct labor.

Column 3 of Table 17-1 on page 560 identifies the four business functions in a typical payroll and personnel cycle. The table also shows the relationships among the business functions, classes of transactions, accounts, and documents and records. Understanding the business functions and documents and records is necessary before assessing control risk and designing tests of controls and substantive tests of transactions.

The personnel department provides an independent source for interviewing and hiring qualified personnel. The department is also an independent source of records for the internal verification of wage information, including additions and deletions from the payroll, and changes in wages and deductions.

Personnel and Employment

Personnel Records Records that include such data as the date of employment, personnel investigations, rates of pay, authorized deductions, performance evaluations, and termination of employment are called **personnel records**.

Deduction Authorization Form A form authorizing payroll deductions, including the number of exemptions for withholding of income taxes, 401(K) and other retirement savings plans, U.S. savings bonds, and union dues.

Rate Authorization Form A form authorizing the rate of pay. The source of the information is a labor contract, authorization by management, or in the case of officers, authorization from the board of directors.

TABLE 17-1 Classes of Transactions, Accounts, Business Functions, and Related Documents and Records for the Payroll and Personnel Cycle

Class of Transactions	Accounts	Business Functions	Documents and Records
Payroll	Payroll cash All payroll expense accounts All payroll withholding accounts All payroll accrual accounts	Personnel and employment	Personnel records Deduction authorization form Rate authorization
		Timekeeping and payroll preparation	Time card Job time ticket Summary payroll report Payroll journal Payroll master file
		Payment of payroll	Payroll check Payroll bank account reconciliation
		Preparation of payroll tax returns and payment of taxes	W-2 form Payroll tax returns

Timekeeping and Payroll Preparation

This function is of major importance in the audit of payroll because it directly affects payroll expense for the period. It includes the preparation of time cards by employees; the summarization and calculation of gross pay, deductions, and net pay; the preparation of payroll checks; and the preparation of payroll records. There must be adequate controls to prevent misstatements in each of these activities.

Time Card A **time card** is a document indicating the time the employee started and stopped working each day and the number of hours the employee worked. For many employees, the time card is prepared automatically by time clocks. Time cards are usually submitted weekly.

Job Time Ticket A document indicating jobs on which a factory employee worked during a given time period. This form is used only when an employee works on different jobs or in different departments.

Summary Payroll Report A computer-generated document that summarizes payroll for a period in various forms. One summary is the totals debited to each general ledger account for payroll charges. These will equal gross payroll for the period. Another common summary for a manufacturing company is the totals charged to various jobs in a job cost accounting system. Similarly, commissions earned by each salesperson may be summarized.

Payroll Journal A journal for recording payroll checks. It typically indicates gross pay, withholdings, and net pay. The payroll journal is generated for any time period from the payroll transactions included in the computer files. The details in the journal are also included in the payroll master file. Journal totals are posted to the general ledger by the computer.

Payroll Master File A **payroll master file** is used for recording each payroll transaction for each employee and maintaining total employee wages paid for the year to date. The record for each employee includes gross pay for each payroll period, deductions from gross pay, net pay, check number, and date. The master file is updated from payroll computer transaction files. The total of the individual employee earnings in the master file equals the total balance of gross payroll in various general ledger accounts.

Payment of Payroll

The actual signing and distribution of the checks must be properly handled to prevent their theft. Separate imprest payroll bank accounts are often used to prevent the payment of unauthorized payroll transactions.

Payroll Check A check written to the employee for services performed. The check is prepared as a part of the payroll preparation function, but the authorized signature makes the check an asset. The amount of the check is the gross pay less taxes and other deductions withheld. After the check is cashed and returned to the company from the bank, it is referred to as a cancelled check. It is now common for payroll to be directly deposited into employees' bank accounts.

Payroll Bank Account Reconciliation An important control is the independent reconciliation of the imprest payroll bank account. An **imprest payroll account** is a separate payroll account in which a small balance is maintained. A check for the exact amount of each net payroll is transferred from the general account to the imprest account immediately before the distribution of the payroll. The advantages of an imprest account are that it limits the client's exposure to payroll fraud, allows the delegation of payroll check-signing duties, separates routine payroll expenditures from irregular expenditures, and facilitates cash management. It also simplifies the reconciliation of the payroll bank account if it is done at the low point in the payment cycle.

Preparation of Payroll Tax Returns and Payment of Taxes

The timely preparation and mailing of payroll tax returns is required by federal and state payroll laws. Most computerized payroll systems include the preparation of payroll tax returns using the information on the payroll transaction and master files. The independent verification of the output by a competent individual is an important control to prevent misstatements and potential liability for taxes and penalties.

W-2 Form A form issued for each employee summarizing the earnings record for the calendar year. The information includes gross pay, income taxes withheld, and FICA withheld. The same information is also submitted to the Internal Revenue Service and state and local tax commissions when applicable. This information is prepared from the payroll master file and is normally prepared by the computer.

Payroll Outsourcing

Payroll Tax Returns Tax forms submitted to local, state, and federal units of government for the payment of withheld taxes and the employer's tax. The nature and due dates of the forms vary depending on the type of taxes. For example, federal withholding and social security payments are due weekly, monthly, or quarterly depending on the amount of withholding, and most state unemployment taxes are due quarterly. These forms are prepared from information on the payroll master file and are often prepared by the computer.

METHODOLOGY FOR DESIGNING TESTS OF CONTROLS AND SUBSTANTIVE TESTS OF TRANSACTIONS

OBJECTIVE 17-3
Understand internal control and design and perform tests of controls and substantive tests of transactions for the payroll and personnel cycle.

Now that you are familiar with the business functions and related documents and records in the payroll and personnel cycle, we can discuss the assessment of control risk and the design of tests of controls and substantive tests of transactions for the cycle. Figure 17-2 shows the methodology for designing tests of controls and substantive tests of transactions for the payroll and personnel cycle. It is the same methodology used in Chapter 13 for the sales and collection cycle.

Internal control for payroll is normally highly structured and well controlled, to control cash disbursed and to minimize employee complaints and dissatisfaction. Payroll checks and all related journals and payroll records are usually processed by computer. Because the processing of payroll is similar for most organizations and programs need to be modified annually for changes in withholding schedules, it is common to use an outside payroll service for the processing of payroll. The auditor can often rely on the internal controls of the service organization. SAS 70 indicates that this is appropriate if the service organization's auditor issues a report on the internal controls of the service organization.

It is usually not difficult to establish good control in the payroll and personnel cycle. For factory and office employees, there are usually a large number of relatively homogeneous, small amount transactions. There are fewer executive payroll transactions, but they are ordinarily consistent in timing, content, and amount. Because of relatively consistent payroll concerns from company to company, high-quality computer systems are available.

FIGURE 17-2 Methodology for Designing Tests of Controls and Substantive Tests of Transactions for the Payroll and Personnel Cycle

```
        Understand internal
            control—
       payroll and personnel
               │
         Assess planned
          control risk—
       payroll and personnel
               │
        Evaluate cost-benefit
         of testing controls
               │
   ┌───────────────────────┬──────────────────┐
   Design tests of controls │  Audit procedures │
    and substantive tests   ├──────────────────┤
      of transactions for   │    Sample size    │
     payroll and personnel  ├──────────────────┤
       to meet transaction- │  Items to select  │
      related audit objectives ├────────────────┤
                            │      Timing       │
```

Consequently, auditors seldom expect to find exceptions in testing payroll transactions. Occasionally, control test deviations occur, but most monetary misstatements are corrected by internal verification controls or in response to employee complaints.

Tests of controls and substantive tests of transactions procedures are the *most important* means of verifying account balances in the payroll and personnel cycle. These tests are emphasized because of the lack of independent third-party evidence, such as confirmation, for verifying accrued wages, withheld income taxes, accrued payroll taxes, and other balance sheet accounts. Furthermore, in most audits, the amounts in the balance sheet accounts are small and can be verified with relative ease if the auditor is confident that payroll transactions are correctly entered into the computer and payroll tax returns are properly prepared.

Even though the tests of controls and substantive tests of transactions are the most important part of testing payroll, the tests in this area are usually not extensive. In many audits, there is a minimal risk of material misstatements even though payroll is often a significant part of total expenses. There are three reasons for this: employees are likely to complain to management if they are underpaid, all payroll transactions are typically uniform and uncomplicated, and payroll transactions are extensively audited by federal and state governments for income tax withholding, social security, and unemployment taxes.

Following the same approach used in Chapter 13 for tests of sales and cash receipts transactions, the internal controls, tests of controls, and substantive tests of transactions for each transaction-related audit objective are summarized in Table 17-2. Again, the reader should recognize the following:

- Internal controls vary from company to company; therefore, the auditor must identify the controls and weaknesses for each organization.
- Controls the auditor intends to use for reducing assessed control risk must be tested with tests of controls.
- Substantive tests of transactions vary depending on the assessed control risk and the other considerations of the audit, such as the effect of payroll on inventory.
- Tests are not actually performed in the order given in Table 17-2 (p. 564). The tests of controls and substantive tests of transactions are combined when appropriate and are performed in as convenient a manner as possible, using a performance format audit program.

The purposes of many internal controls and the nature of the tests of controls and substantive tests of transactions are apparent for most tests from their description in Table 17-2. The section that follows discusses some of the key controls for the payroll and personnel cycle for the assessment of control risk.

Understand Internal Control–Payroll and Personnel Cycle

Payroll Link Software

Adequate Separation of Duties Separation of duties is important in the payroll and personnel cycle, especially to prevent overpayments and payments to nonexistent employees. The personnel department should be independent of the payroll function and is responsible for authorizing the addition and termination of employees, as well as changes in pay rates and deductions. Payroll processing should be separate from the custody of signed payroll checks.

Proper Authorization As noted earlier, the personnel department should be responsible for the authorization of additions and deletions of employees from the payroll. Pay rates and deductions should also be properly authorized. The hours worked by each employee, especially overtime, should be authorized by the employee's supervisor. Approval may be noted on all time cards or done on an exception basis for overtime hours only.

Adequate Documents and Records The appropriate documents and records will depend on the nature of the payroll system. For example, time cards or records are necessary for hourly employees but not for salaried employees. Some employees may be compensated

Transaction-Related Audit Objective	Key Internal Control	Common Test of Control	Common Substantive Tests of Transactions
Recorded payroll payments are for work actually performed by existing employees (existence).	Time cards are approved by supervisor. Time clock is used to record time. Adequate personnel files are maintained. Work is authorized. There is separation of duties among personnel, timekeeping, and payroll disbursements. Only employees existing in the computer data files are accepted when they are entered. Check is authorized before issuance.	Examine the cards for indication of approvals. Examine time cards. Review personnel policies. Examine personnel files. Review organization chart, discuss with employees, and observe duties being performed. Examine printouts of transactions rejected by the computer as having nonexistent employee numbers. Examine payroll records for indication of approval.	Review the payroll journal, general ledger, and payroll earnings records for large or unusual amounts.* Compare cancelled checks with payroll journal for name, amount, and date. Examine cancelled checks for proper endorsement. Compare cancelled checks with personnel records.
Existing payroll transactions are recorded (completeness).	Payroll checks are prenumbered and accounted for. Bank accounts are independently reconciled.	Account for a sequence of payroll checks. Discuss with employees and observe reconciliation.	Reconcile the disbursements in the payroll journal with the disbursements on the payroll bank statement. Prove the bank reconciliation.
Recorded payroll transactions are for the amount of time actually worked and at the proper pay rate; withholdings are properly calculated (accuracy).	Calculations and amounts are internally verified. Batch totals are compared with computer summary reports. Wage rate, salary, or commission rate is properly authorized. Withholdings, including amounts for insurance and payroll savings, are properly authorized.	Examine indication of internal verification. Examine file of batch totals for initials of data control clerk; compare totals to summary reports. Examine payroll records for indication of internal verification. Examine authorizations in personnel file.	Recompute hours worked from time cards. Compare pay rates with union contract, approval by board of directors, or other source. Recompute gross pay. Check withholdings by reference to tax tables and authorization forms in personnel file. Recompute net pay. Compare cancelled check with payroll journal for amount.
Payroll transactions are properly classified (classification).	An adequate chart of accounts is used. Account classifications are internally verified.	Review chart of accounts. Examine indication of internal verification.	Compare classification with chart of accounts or procedures manual. Review time card for employee department and job ticket for job assignment, and trace through to labor distribution.
Payroll transactions are recorded on the correct dates (timing).	Procedures require recording transactions as soon as possible after the payroll is paid. Dates are internally verified.	Examine procedures manual and observe when recording takes place. Examine indication of internal verification.	Compare date of recorded check in the payroll journal with date on cancelled check and time card. Compare date on check with date the check cleared the bank.
Payroll transactions are properly included in the payroll master file and are properly summarized (posting and summarization).	Payroll master file contents are internally verified. Payroll master file totals are compared with general ledger totals.	Examine indication of internal verification. Examine initialed summary total reports indicating that comparisons have been made.	Test clerical accuracy by footing the payroll journal and tracing postings to the general ledger and the payroll master file.

*This analytical procedure can also apply to other objectives, including completeness, accuracy, and timing.

based on piece rate or other incentive systems. For many companies, time records must be adequate to accumulate payroll costs by job or assignment. Prenumbered documents for recording time are less of a concern in the payroll area because the completeness of payroll is not normally a concern.

Physical Control Over Assets and Records Access to unsigned payroll checks should be restricted. Checks should be signed by a responsible employee, and payroll should be distributed by someone independent of the payroll and timekeeping functions. Any unclaimed checks should be returned for redeposit. If checks are signed by a signature machine, access to the machine should be restricted.

Independent Checks on Performance Payroll computations should be independently verified, including comparison of batch totals to summary reports. A member of management or other responsible employee should review the payroll output for any obvious misstatements or unusual amounts. When manufacturing labor affects inventory valuation or when it is necessary to accumulate costs by job, adequate controls are necessary to verify the proper assignment of costs.

Several additional concerns for the payroll and personnel cycle are discussed in the following sections. These relate to payroll tax and other withholdings, the allocation of payroll costs to inventory, and the potential for fraudulent payroll transactions.

Payroll taxes are an important consideration in many companies, both because the amounts are often material and because the potential liability for failure to file timely tax forms can be severe.

Payroll Tax Forms and Payments

Preparation of Payroll Tax Forms As a part of understanding internal control, the auditor should review the preparation of at least one of each type of payroll tax form that the client is responsible for filing. There is a potential liability for unpaid taxes, penalty, and interest if the client fails to prepare the tax forms properly. The payroll tax forms are for such taxes as federal income and FICA withholding, state and city income withholding, and federal and state unemployment.

A detailed reconciliation of the information on the tax forms and the payroll records may be necessary when the auditor believes that there is a reasonable chance that the tax returns may be improperly prepared. Indications of potential misstatements in the returns include the payment of penalties and interest in the past for improper payments, new personnel in the payroll department who are responsible for the preparation of the returns, the lack of internal verification of the information, and the existence of serious cash flow problems for the client.

Payment of the Payroll Taxes Withheld and Other Withholdings on a Timely Basis It is desirable to test whether the client has fulfilled its legal obligation in submitting payments for all payroll withholdings as a part of the payroll tests even though the payments are usually made from general cash disbursements. The withholdings of concern in these tests are such items as taxes, 401(K) and other retirement savings, union dues, insurance, and payroll savings. The auditor must first determine the client's requirements for submitting the payments. The requirements are determined by reference to such sources as tax laws, union contracts, and agreements with employees. After the auditor knows the requirements, it is easy to determine whether the client has paid the proper amount on a timely basis by comparing the subsequent cash disbursement with the payroll records.

Auditors often extend their procedures considerably in the audit of payroll under the following circumstances: when payroll significantly affects the valuation of inventory and when the auditor is concerned about the possibility of material fraudulent payroll transactions.

Inventory and Fraudulent Payroll Considerations

Relationship between Payroll and Inventory Valuation In audits in which payroll is a significant portion of inventory, a common occurrence for manufacturing and construction companies, the improper account classification of payroll can significantly affect asset valuation for accounts such as work in process, finished goods, or construction in process. For example, the overhead charged to inventory at the balance sheet date can be overstated if the salaries of administrative personnel are inadvertently or intentionally charged to indirect manufacturing overhead. Similarly, the valuation of inventory is affected if the direct labor cost of individual employees is improperly charged to the wrong job or process. When some jobs are billed on a cost-plus basis, revenue and the valuation of inventory are both affected by charging labor to incorrect jobs.

When labor is a material factor in inventory valuation, special emphasis should be placed on testing the internal controls over proper classification of payroll transactions. Consistency from period to period, which is essential for classification, can be tested by reviewing the chart of accounts and procedures manuals. It is also desirable to trace job tickets or other evidence of an employee's having worked on a job or process to the accounting records that affect inventory valuation. For example, if each employee must account for all of his or her time on a weekly basis by assigning it to individual job numbers, a useful test is to trace the recorded hours of several employees for a week to the related job-cost records to make sure each has been properly recorded. It may also be desirable to trace from the job-cost records to employee summaries as a test for nonexistent payroll charges being included in inventory.

Tests for Nonexistent Payroll Because auditors have significant responsibility for the detection of fraud, they must extend audit procedures when they become concerned about the possibility of material fraud. There are several ways in which employees can significantly defraud a company in the payroll area. This discussion is limited to tests for the two most common types: nonexistent employees and fraudulent hours.

The issuance of payroll checks to individuals who do not work for the company (nonexistent employees) often results from the continuance of an employee's check after his or her employment has been terminated. Usually, the person committing this type of defalcation is a payroll clerk, foreman, fellow employee, or perhaps the former employee. For example, under some systems a foreman could clock in daily for an employee and approve the time card at the end of the time period. If the foreman also distributes paychecks, considerable opportunity for defalcation exists.

Certain procedures can be performed on cancelled checks as a means of detecting defalcation. A procedure used on payroll audits is to compare the names on cancelled checks with time cards and other records for authorized signatures and reasonableness of the endorsements. It is also common to scan endorsements on cancelled checks for unusual or recurring second endorsements as an indication of a possible fraudulent check. The examination of checks that are recorded as voided is also desirable to make sure that they have not been fraudulently used.

A test for nonexistent employees is to trace selected transactions recorded in the payroll journal to the personnel department to determine whether the employees were actually employed during the payroll period. The endorsement on the cancelled check written out to an employee can be compared with the authorized signature on the employee's withholding authorization forms.

A procedure that tests for proper handling of terminated employees is to select several files from the personnel records for employees who were terminated in the current year to determine whether each received his or her termination pay in accordance with company policy. Continuing payments to terminated employees is tested by examining the payroll records in the subsequent period to ascertain that the employee is no longer being paid. Naturally, this procedure is not effective if the personnel department is not informed of terminations.

In some cases, the auditor may request a surprise payroll payoff. This is a procedure in which each employee must pick up and sign for his or her check or direct deposit payroll record in the presence of a supervisor and the auditor. Any checks that have not been claimed must be subject to an extensive investigation to determine whether an unclaimed check is fraudulent. Surprise payoff is often expensive and in some cases may even cause problems with a labor union, but it may be the only likely means of detecting a defalcation.

Fraudulent hours occur when an employee reports more time than was actually worked. Because of the lack of available evidence, it is usually difficult for an auditor to discover fraudulent hours. One procedure is to reconcile the total hours paid according to the payroll records with an independent record of the hours worked, such as those often maintained by production control. Similarly, it may be possible to observe an employee clocking in more than one time card under a buddy approach. However, it is ordinarily easier for the client to prevent this type of defalcation by adequate controls than for the auditor to detect it.

Assessing control risk and performing tests of controls and substantive tests of transactions are done during the first two phases of the audit. After completing these tests and assessing the likelihood of misstatement in financial statement accounts in the payroll and personnel cycle, the auditor will follow the methodology of designing tests of details of balances.

METHODOLOGY FOR DESIGNING TESTS OF DETAILS OF BALANCES

Figure 17-3 summarizes the methodology for deciding the appropriate tests of details of balances for payroll liability accounts. This methodology is the same as that followed in Chapter 15 for accounts receivable.

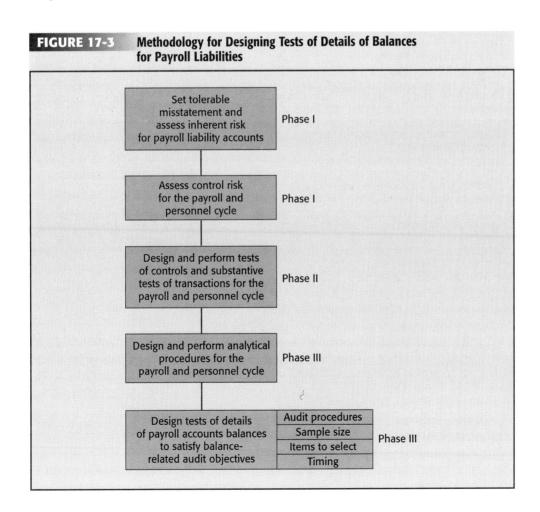

FIGURE 17-3 Methodology for Designing Tests of Details of Balances for Payroll Liabilities

Set Tolerable Misstatement and Assess Inherent Risk (Phase I)

Most companies have a large number of transactions involving payroll, often with large total amounts. However, balance sheet accounts are normally insignificant, except for labor charged to inventory.

Except for the potential for fraud, inherent risk is typically low for all balance-related audit objectives. There is inherent risk of payroll fraud because most transactions involve cash. The existence objective is therefore often considered to be important. Also, for manufacturing companies with significant labor charged to inventory, there is potential for misclassification between payroll expense and inventory or among categories of inventory.

Assess Control Risk and Perform Related Tests (Phases I and II)

Assessing control risk and the related tests of controls and substantive tests of transactions have been discussed extensively in earlier sections of the chapter and are not repeated here.

Perform Analytical Procedures (Phase III)

OBJECTIVE 17-4
Design and perform analytical procedures for the payroll and personnel cycle.

The use of analytical procedures is as important in the payroll and personnel cycle as it is in every other cycle. Table 17-3 illustrates analytical procedures for the balance sheet and income statement accounts in the payroll and personnel cycle. Most of the relationships included in Table 17-3 are highly predictable and are therefore useful for uncovering areas in which additional investigation is desirable.

TABLE 17-3   Analytical Procedures for the Payroll and Personnel Cycle

Analytical Procedure	Possible Misstatement
Compare payroll expense account balance with previous years (adjusted for pay rate increases and increases in volume).	Misstatement of payroll expense accounts
Compare direct labor as a percentage of sales with previous years.	Misstatement of direct labor and inventory
Compare commission expense as a percentage of sales with previous years.	Misstatement of commission expense and commission liability
Compare payroll tax expense as a percentage of salaries and wages with previous years (adjusted for changes in the tax rates).	Misstatement of payroll tax expense and payroll tax liability
Compare accrued payroll tax accounts with previous years.	Misstatement of accrued payroll taxes and payroll tax expense

Design and Perform Tests of Details of Balances for Liability and Expense Accounts (Phase III)

OBJECTIVE 17-5
Design and perform tests of details of balances for accounts in the payroll and personnel cycle.

The verification of the liability accounts associated with payroll, often termed **accrued payroll expenses**, ordinarily is straightforward if internal controls are operating effectively. When the auditor is satisfied that payroll transactions are being properly recorded in the payroll journal and the related payroll tax forms are being accurately prepared and promptly paid, the tests of details of balances should not be time-consuming.

The two major balance-related audit objectives in testing payroll liabilities are (1) accruals in the trial balance are stated at the correct amounts (accuracy) and (2) transactions in the payroll and personnel cycle are recorded in the proper period (cutoff). The primary concern in both objectives is to make sure that there are no understated or omitted accruals. The major liability accounts in the payroll and personnel cycle are now discussed.

Amounts Withheld from Employees' Pay Payroll taxes withheld but not yet disbursed can be tested by comparing the balance with the payroll journal, the payroll tax form prepared in the subsequent period, and the subsequent period cash disbursements. Other withheld items such as retirement savings, union dues, savings bonds, and insurance can be verified in the same manner. If internal controls are operating effectively, cutoff and accuracy can easily be tested at the same time by these procedures.

Accrued Salaries and Wages The accrual for salaries and wages arises whenever employees are not paid for the last few days or hours of earned wages until the subsequent period. Salaried personnel usually receive all of their pay except overtime on the last day of the month, but often, several days of wages for hourly employees are unpaid at the end of the year.

The correct cutoff and accuracy of accrued salaries and wages depends on company policy, which should be followed consistently from year to year. Some companies calculate the exact hours of pay that were earned in the current period and paid in the subsequent period, whereas others compute an approximate proportion. For example, if the subsequent payroll results from 3 days' employment during the current year and 2 days' employment during the subsequent year, the use of 60 percent of the subsequent period's gross pay as the accrual is an example of an approximation.

Once the auditor has determined the company's policy for accruing wages and knows that it is consistent with that of previous years, the appropriate audit procedure to test for cutoff and accuracy is to recalculate the client's accrual. The most likely misstatement of any significance in the balance is the failure to include the proper number of days of earned but unpaid wages.

Accrued Commissions The same concepts used in verifying accrued salaries and wages are applicable to accrued commissions, but the accrual is often more difficult to verify because companies often have several different types of agreements with salespeople and other commission employees. For example, some salespeople might be paid a commission every month and earn no salary, whereas others will get a monthly salary plus a commission paid quarterly. In some cases, the commission varies for different products and may not be paid until several months after the end of the year. In verifying accrued commissions, it is necessary first to determine the nature of the commission agreement and then test the calculations based on the agreement. It is important to compare the method of accruing commissions with that of previous years for purposes of consistency. If the amounts are material, the auditor may confirm the amount that is due directly with the employees.

Accrued Bonuses In many companies, the year-end unpaid bonuses to officers and employees are such a major item that the failure to record them would result in a material misstatement. The verification of the recorded accrual can usually be accomplished by comparing it with the amount authorized in the minutes of the board of directors.

Accrued Vacation Pay, Sick Pay, or Other Benefits The consistent accrual of these liabilities relative to those of the preceding year is the most important consideration in evaluating the fairness of the amounts. The company policy for recording the liability must first be determined, followed by the recalculation of the recorded amounts. The company policy should be in accordance with SFAS 43, which deals with compensated absences.

Accrued Payroll Taxes Payroll taxes such as FICA and state and federal unemployment taxes can be verified by examining tax forms prepared in the subsequent period to determine the amount that should have been recorded as a liability at the balance sheet date.

Tests of Details of Balances for Expense Accounts Several accounts in the income statement are affected by payroll transactions. The most important are officers' salaries and bonuses, office salaries, sales salaries and commissions, and direct manufacturing labor.

There is often a further breakdown of costs by division, product, or branch. Fringe benefits such as medical insurance may also be included in the expenses.

There should be relatively little additional testing of the income statement accounts in most audits beyond the analytical procedures, tests of controls, substantive tests of transactions, and related tests of liability accounts, which have already been discussed. Extensive additional testing should be necessary only when there are weaknesses in internal control, significant misstatements are discovered in the liability tests, or major unexplained variances are found in the analytical procedures. Nevertheless, some income statement accounts are often tested in the payroll and personnel cycle. These include officers' compensation, commissions, payroll tax expense, and total payroll.

Officers' Compensation It is common to verify whether the total compensation of officers is the amount authorized by the board of directors, because their salaries and bonuses must be included in the SEC's 10-K report and federal income tax return. Verification of officers' compensation is also warranted because some individuals may be in a position to pay themselves more than the authorized amount. The usual audit test is to obtain the authorized salary of each officer from the minutes of the board of directors meetings and compare it with the related earnings record.

Commissions Commission expense can be verified with relative ease if the commission rate is the same for each type of sale and the necessary sales information is available in the accounting records. The total commission expense can be verified by multiplying the commission rate for each type of sale by the amount of sales in that category. If the desired information is not available, it may be necessary to test the annual or monthly commission payments for selected salespeople and trace those to the total commission payments. When the auditor believes it is necessary to perform these tests, they are normally done in conjunction with tests of accrued liabilities.

Payroll Tax Expense Payroll tax expense for the year can be tested by first reconciling the total payroll on each payroll tax form with the total payroll for the entire year. Total payroll taxes can then be recomputed by multiplying the appropriate rate by the taxable payroll. The calculation is often time-consuming because the tax is usually applicable on only a portion of the payroll and the rate may change partway through the year if the taxpayer's financial statements are not on a calendar-year basis. On most audits, the calculation is costly and is not necessary unless analytical procedures indicate a problem that cannot be resolved through other procedures. When the auditor believes that the test is necessary, it is ordinarily done in conjunction with tests of payroll tax accruals.

Total Payroll A closely related test to the one for payroll taxes is the reconciliation of total payroll expense in the general ledger with the payroll tax returns and the W-2 forms. The objectives of the test are to determine whether payroll transactions were charged to a non-payroll account or not recorded in the payroll journal at all. These objectives are certainly relevant, but it is questionable whether the procedure is useful in uncovering the type of misstatement for which it was intended. Because the payroll tax records and the payroll are both usually prepared directly from the payroll master file, the misstatements, if any, are likely to be in both records. The procedure may be worthwhile in rare situations, but it is usually not necessary to perform it. Tests of controls and substantive tests of transactions are a better means of uncovering these two types of misstatements in most audits.

SUMMARY

This chapter described the audit of the payroll and personnel cycle. Figure 17-4 illustrates the major accounts in the payroll and personnel cycle and the types of audit tests used to audit these accounts. Emphasis is on tests of controls and substantive tests of transactions

FIGURE 17-4 Types of Audit Tests for the Payroll and Personnel Cycle (see Figure 17-1 on p. 559 for accounts)

because of the significance of transactions and the high quality of internal controls in most companies. Tests of details of balances are normally limited to analytical procedures and verification of accrued liabilities related to payroll.

Accrued payroll expenses—the liability accounts associated with payroll; these include accounts for accrued salaries and wages, accrued commissions, accrued bonuses, accrued benefits, and accrued payroll taxes

Imprest payroll account—a bank account to which the exact amount of payroll for the pay period is transferred by check from the employer's general cash account

Payroll and personnel cycle—the transaction cycle that begins with the hiring of personnel, includes obtaining and accounting for services from the employees, and ends with payment to the employees for the services performed and to the government and other institutions for withheld and accrued payroll taxes and benefits

Payroll master file—a computer file for recording each payroll transaction for each employee and maintaining total employee wages paid and related data for the year to date

Personnel records—records that include such data as the date of employment, personnel investigations, rates of pay, authorized deductions, performance evaluations, and termination of employment

Time card—a document indicating the time that the employee started and stopped working each day and the number of hours worked

17-1 (Objective 17-1)   Identify five general ledger accounts that are likely to be affected by the payroll and personnel cycle in most audits.

17-2 (Objectives 17-1, 17-3)   Explain the relationship between the payroll and personnel cycle and inventory valuation.

17-3 (Objective 17-3)   List five tests of controls that can be performed for the payroll and personnel cycle and state the purpose of each control being tested.

17-4 (Objective 17-3)   Explain why the percentage of total audit time in the cycle devoted to performing tests of controls and substantive tests of transactions is usually far greater for the payroll and personnel cycle than for the sales and collection cycle.

17-5 (Objectives 17-2, 17-3) Evaluate the following comment by an auditor: "My job is to determine whether the payroll records are fairly stated in accordance with generally accepted accounting principles, not to find out whether they are following proper hiring and termination procedures. When I conduct an audit of payroll I keep out of the personnel department and stick to the time cards, journals, and payroll checks. I don't care whom they hire and whom they fire, as long as they properly pay the ones they have."

17-6 (Objective 17-3) Distinguish between the following payroll audit procedures and state the purpose of each: (1) Trace a random sample of prenumbered time cards to the related payroll checks in the payroll register and compare the hours worked with the hours paid, and (2) trace a random sample of payroll checks from the payroll register to the related time cards and compare the hours worked with the hours paid. Which of these two procedures is typically more important in the audit of payroll? Why?

17-7 (Objective 17-5) In auditing payroll withholding and payroll tax expense, explain why emphasis should normally be on evaluating the adequacy of the payroll tax return preparation procedures rather than the payroll tax liability. If the preparation procedures are inadequate, explain the effect this will have on the remainder of the audit.

17-8 (Objective 17-4) List several analytical procedures for the payroll and personnel cycle and explain the type of misstatement that might be indicated when there is a significant difference in the comparison of the current year with previous years' results for each of the tests.

17-9 (Objective 17-3) Explain the circumstances under which an auditor should perform audit tests primarily designed to uncover fraud in the payroll and personnel cycle. List three audit procedures that are primarily for the detection of fraud and state the type of fraud the procedure is meant to uncover.

17-10 (Objective 17-2) Distinguish between a payroll master file, a W-2 form, and a payroll tax return. Explain the purpose of each.

17-11 (Objectives 17-2, 17-3) List the supporting documents and records the auditor will examine in a typical payroll audit in which the primary objective is to detect fraud.

17-12 (Objective 17-3) List five types of authorizations in the payroll and personnel cycle and state the type of misstatement that is likely to occur when each authorization is lacking.

17-13 (Objective 17-5) Explain why it is common to verify total officers' compensation even when the tests of controls and substantive tests of transactions results in payroll are excellent. What audit procedures can be used to verify officers' compensation?

17-14 (Objective 17-2) Explain what is meant by an imprest payroll account. What is its purpose as a control over payroll?

17-15 (Objective 17-3) List several audit procedures that the auditor can use to determine whether payroll transactions are recorded at the proper amount.

17-16 (Objective 17-3) Explain how audit sampling can be used to test the payroll and personnel cycle.

MULTIPLE CHOICE QUESTIONS FROM CPA EXAMINATIONS

17-17 (Objective 17-3) The following questions concern internal controls in the payroll and personnel cycle. Choose the best response.

    a. A factory foreman at Steblecki Corporation discharged an hourly worker but did *not* notify the payroll department. The foreman then forged the worker's signature on time cards and work tickets and, when giving out the checks, diverted the payroll checks drawn from the discharged worker to his own use. The most effective procedure for preventing this activity is to

        (1) require written authorization for all employees added to or removed from the payroll.

(2) have a paymaster who has *no* other payroll responsibility distribute the payroll checks.

(3) have someone other than persons who prepare or distribute the payroll obtain custody of unclaimed payroll checks.

(4) from time to time, rotate persons distributing the payroll.

b. The CPA reviews Pyzi's payroll procedures. An example of an internal control weakness is to assign to a department supervisor the responsibility for

(1) distributing payroll checks to subordinate employees.

(2) reviewing and approving time reports for subordinates.

(3) interviewing applicants for subordinate positions before hiring is done by the personnel department.

(4) initiating requests for salary adjustments for subordinate employees.

c. From the standpoint of good internal control, distributing payroll checks to employees is best handled by the

(1) accounting department.

(2) personnel department.

(3) treasurer's department.

(4) employee's departmental supervisor.

17-18 (Objective 17-3) The following questions concern audit testing of the payroll and personnel cycle. Choose the best response.

a. A computer operator perpetrated a theft by preparing erroneous W-2 forms. The operator's FICA withheld was overstated by $500, and the FICA withheld from all other employees was understated. Which of the following audit procedures would detect such a fraud?

(1) Multiplication of the applicable rate by the individual's gross taxable earnings.

(2) Using form W-4 and withholding charts to determine whether deductions authorized per pay period agree with amounts deducted per pay period.

(3) Footing and crossfooting of the payroll register followed by tracing postings to the general ledger.

(4) Vouching cancelled checks to federal tax form 941.

b. In the audit of which of the following types of profit-oriented enterprises would the auditor be most likely to place special emphasis on tests of controls for proper classifications of payroll transactions?

(1) A manufacturing organization.

(2) A retailing organization.

(3) A wholesaling organization.

(4) A service organization.

c. A common audit procedure in the audit of payroll transactions involves tracing selected items from the payroll journal to employee time cards that have been approved by supervisory personnel. This procedure is designed to provide evidence in support of the audit proposition that

(1) only proper employees worked and their pay was properly computed.

(2) jobs on which employees worked were charged with the appropriate labor cost.

(3) internal controls over payroll disbursements are operating effectively.

(4) all employees worked the number of hours for which their pay was computed.

DISCUSSION QUESTIONS AND PROBLEMS

17-19 (Objectives 17-2, 17-3) Items 1 through 9 are selected questions typically found in internal control questionnaires used by auditors to obtain an understanding of internal control in the payroll and personnel cycle. In using the questionnaire for a client, a "yes" response to a question indicates a possible internal control, whereas a "no" indicates a potential weakness.

1. Does an appropriate official authorize initial rates of pay and any subsequent changes in rates?
2. Are written notices required documenting reasons for termination?
3. Are formal records such as time cards used for keeping time?
4. Is approval by a department head or foreman required for all time cards before they are submitted for payment?
5. Does anyone verify pay rates, overtime hours, and computations of gross payroll before payroll checks are prepared?
6. Does an adequate means exist for identifying jobs or products, such as work orders, job numbers, or some similar identification provided to employees to ensure proper coding of time records?
7. Are employees paid by checks prepared by persons independent of timekeeping?
8. Are employees required to show identification to receive paychecks?
9. Is a continuing record maintained of all unclaimed wages?

Required

    a. For each of the questions, state the transaction-related audit objective(s) being fulfilled if the control is in effect.

    b. For each control, list a test of control to test its effectiveness.

    c. For each of the questions, identify the nature of the potential financial misstatement(s) if the control is not in effect.

    d. For each of the potential misstatements in part (c), list a substantive audit procedure for determining whether a material misstatement exists.

17-20 (Objectives 17-2, 17-3) Following are some of the tests of controls and substantive tests of transactions procedures often performed in the payroll and personnel cycle. (Each procedure is to be done on a sample basis.)

1. Reconcile the monthly payroll total for direct manufacturing labor with the labor cost distribution.
2. Examine the time card for the approval of a foreman.
3. Recompute hours on the time card and compare the total with the total hours for which the employee has been paid.
4. Compare the employee name, date, check number, and amounts on cancelled checks with the payroll journal.
5. Trace the hours from the employee time cards to job tickets to make sure that the total reconciles, and trace each job ticket to the job-cost record.
6. Account for a sequence of payroll checks in the payroll journal.
7. Select employees from the personnel file who have been terminated and determine whether their termination pay was in accordance with the union contract. As part of this procedure, examine two subsequent periods to determine whether the terminated employee is still being paid.

Required

    a. Identify whether each of the procedures is primarily a test of control or a substantive test of transactions.

    b. Identify the transaction-related audit objective(s) of each of the procedures.

17-21 (Objectives 17-2, 17-3) The following misstatements are included in the accounting records of Lathen Manufacturing Company.

1. Direct labor was unintentionally charged to job 620 instead of job 602 by the payroll clerk when he key-entered the labor distribution sheets. Job 602 was completed and the costs were expensed in the current year, whereas job 620 was included in work-in-process.
2. Joe Block and Frank Demery take turns "punching in" for each other every few days. The absent employee comes in at noon and tells his foreman that he had car trouble or some other problem. The foreman does not know that the employee is getting paid for the time.

3. The foreman submits a fraudulent time card for a former employee each week and delivers the related payroll check to the employee's house on the way home from work. They split the amount of the paycheck.
4. Employees often overlook recording their hours worked on job-cost tickets as required by the system. Many of the client's contracts are on a cost-plus basis.
5. The payroll clerk prepares a check to the same nonexistent person every week when he key-enters payroll transactions in the microcomputer system, which also records the amount in the payroll journal. He submits it along with all other payroll checks for signature. When the checks are returned to him for distribution, he takes the check and deposits it in a special bank account bearing that person's name.
6. In withholding payroll taxes from employees, the computer operator deducts $.50 extra federal income taxes from several employees each week and credits the amount to his own employee earnings record.
7. The payroll clerk manually prepares payroll checks but often forgets to record one or two checks in the computer-prepared payroll journal.

Required
  a. For each misstatement, state a control that should have prevented it from occurring on a continuing basis.
  b. For each misstatement, state a substantive audit procedure that could uncover it.

17-22 (Objectives 17-3, 17-4, 17-5) The following audit procedures are typical of those found in auditing the payroll and personnel cycle.

1. Examine evidence of double-checking payroll wage rates and calculations by an independent person.
2. Obtain a schedule of all payroll liabilities and trace to the general ledger.
3. Select a sample of 20 cancelled payroll checks and account for the numerical sequence.
4. Foot and crossfoot the payroll journal for two periods and trace totals to the general ledger.
5. For payroll liabilities, examine subsequent cash disbursements and supporting documents such as payroll tax returns, depository receipts, and tax receipts.
6. Select a sample of 20 cancelled payroll checks and trace to payroll journal entries for name, date, and amounts.
7. Compute direct labor, indirect labor, and commissions as a percentage of net sales and compare with prior years.
8. Examine owner approval of rates of pay and withholdings.
9. Compute payroll tax expense as a percentage of total wages, salaries, and commissions.
10. Discuss with management any payroll liabilities at the last engagement date that are not provided for currently.
11. Scan journals for all periods for unusual transactions to determine whether they are recorded properly.
12. Select a sample of 40 entries in the payroll journal and trace each to an approved time card.

Required
  a. Select the type of test for each audit procedure from the following:
    (1) Test of control
    (2) Substantive test of transactions
    (3) Analytical procedure
    (4) Test of details of balances
  b. For each test of control or substantive test of transactions, identify the applicable transaction-related audit objective(s).
  c. For each test of details of balances, identify the applicable balance-related audit objective(s).

17-23 (Objectives 17-3, 17-5)   The following are steps in the methodology for designing tests of controls, substantive tests of transactions, and tests of details of balances for the payroll and personnel cycle:

1. Design tests of details of balances for the payroll and personnel cycle.
2. Evaluate risk and materiality for payroll expense and liability accounts.
3. Evaluate the cost-benefit of assessing control risk as low for payroll.
4. Design and perform payroll- and personnel-related analytical procedures.
5. Identify controls and weaknesses in internal control for the payroll and personnel cycle.
6. Obtain an understanding of the payroll and personnel cycle internal controls.
7. Evaluate tests of controls and substantive tests of transactions results.
8. Design payroll and personnel cycle tests of controls and substantive tests of transactions.
9. Assess inherent risk for payroll-related accounts.

Required

    a. Identify (1) those steps that are tests of controls or substantive tests of transactions and (2) those that are tests of details of balances.

    b. Put steps that are tests of controls and substantive tests of transactions in the order of their performance in most audits.

    c. Put the tests of details of balances in their proper order.

17-24 (Objective 17-4)   In comparing total payroll tax expense with that of the preceding year, Merlin Brendin, CPA, observed a significant increase, even though the total number of employees had increased only from 175 to 195. To investigate the difference, he selected a large sample of payroll disbursement transactions and carefully tested the withholdings for each employee in the sample by referring to federal and state tax withholding schedules. In his test, he found no exceptions; therefore, he concluded that payroll tax expense was fairly stated.

Required

    a. Evaluate Brendin's approach to testing payroll tax expense.

    b. Discuss a more suitable approach for determining whether payroll tax expense was properly stated in the current year.

17-25 (Objective 17-5)   As part of the audit of McGree Plumbing and Heating, you have responsibility for testing the payroll and personnel cycle. Payroll is the largest single expense in the client's trial balance, and hourly wages make up most of the payroll total. A unique aspect of its business is the extensive overtime incurred by employees on some days. It is common for employees to work only 3 or 4 days during the week but to work long hours while they are on the job. McGree's management has found that this actually saves money, despite the large amount of overtime, because the union contract requires payment for all travel time. Because many of the employees' jobs require long travel times and extensive startup costs, this policy is supported by both McGree and the employees.

You have already carefully evaluated and tested the payroll and personnel cycle's internal control and concluded that it contains no significant weaknesses. Your tests included tests of the time cards, withholdings, pay rates, the filing of all required tax returns, payroll checks, and all other aspects of payroll.

As part of the year-end tests of payroll, you are responsible for verifying all accrued payroll as well as accrued and withheld payroll taxes. The accrued factory payroll includes the last 6 working days of the current year. The client has calculated accrued wages by taking 60 percent of the subsequent period's gross payroll and has recorded it as an adjusting entry to be reversed in the subsequent period.

Required

List all audit procedures you would follow in verifying accrued payroll, withheld payroll taxes, and accrued payroll taxes.

17-26 (Objective 17-3)   In the audit of Larnet Manufacturing Company, the auditor concluded that internal controls were inadequate because of the lack of segregation of duties.

As a result, the decision was made to have a surprise payroll payoff 1 month before the client's balance sheet date. Because the auditor had never been involved in a payroll payoff, she did not know how to proceed.

Required

    a. What is the purpose of a surprise payroll payoff?

    b. What other audit procedures can the auditor perform that may fulfill the same objectives?

    c. Discuss the procedures that the auditor should require the client to observe when the surprise payroll payoff is taking place.

    d. At the completion of the payroll payoff, there are often several unclaimed checks. What procedures should be followed for these?

17-27 (Objective 17-3) The Kowal Manufacturing Company employs about 50 production workers and has the following payroll procedures:

The factory foreman interviews applicants and on the basis of the interview either hires or rejects them. When the applicant is hired, he or she prepares a W-4 form (Employee's Withholding Exemption Certificate) and gives it to the foreman. The foreman writes the hourly rate of pay for the new employee in the corner of the W-4 form and then gives the form to a payroll clerk as notice that the worker has been employed. The foreman verbally advises the payroll department of rate adjustments.

A supply of blank time cards is kept in a box near the entrance to the factory. Each worker takes a time card on Monday morning, fills in his or her name, and notes in pencil his or her daily arrival and departure times. At the end of the week, the workers drop the time cards in a box near the door to the factory.

On Monday morning, the completed time cards are taken from the box by a payroll clerk. One of the payroll clerks then records the payroll transactions using a computer system, which records all information for the payroll journal that was calculated by the clerk and automatically updates the employees' earnings records and general ledger. Employees are automatically removed from the payroll when they fail to turn in a time card.

The payroll checks are manually signed by the chief accountant and given to the foreman. The foreman distributes the checks to the workers in the factory and arranges for the delivery of the checks to the workers who are absent. The payroll bank account is reconciled by the chief accountant, who also prepares the various quarterly and annual payroll tax reports.

Required

    a. List the most serious weaknesses in internal control and state the misstatements that are likely to result from the weaknesses. In your audit of Kowal's payroll, what will you emphasize in your audit tests? Explain.

    b. List your suggestions for improving the Kowal Manufacturing Company's internal controls for the factory hiring practices and payroll procedures.*

17-28 (Objectives 17-4, 17-5) During the first-year audit of Jones Wholesale Stationery, you observe that commissions amount to almost 25 percent of total sales, which is somewhat higher than in previous years. Further investigation reveals that the industry typically has larger sales commissions than Jones and that there is significant variation in rates depending on the product sold.

At the time a sale is made, the salesperson records his or her commission rate and the total amount of the commissions on the office copy of the sales invoice. When sales are entered into the computer system for the recording of sales, the debit to sales commission expense and credit to accrued sales commission are also recorded. As part of recording the sales and sales commission expense, the accounts receivable clerk verifies the prices, quantities, commission rates, and all calculations on the sales invoices. Both the accounts receivable and the salespersons' commission master files are updated when the sale and sales commission are recorded. On the fifteenth day after the end of the month, the salesperson is paid for the preceding month's sales commissions.

*AICPA adapted.

Required

    a. Develop an audit program to verify sales commission expense, assuming that no audit tests have been conducted in any audit area to this point.

    b. Develop an audit program to verify accrued sales commissions at the end of the year, assuming that the tests you designed in part a. (above) resulted in no significant misstatements.

17-29 (Objective 17-3) You are engaged to audit the financial statements of Henry Brown, a large independent contractor. All employees are paid in cash because Brown believes this arrangement reduces clerical expenses and is preferred by his employees.

    During the audit, you find in the petty cash fund approximately $200, of which $185 is stated to be unclaimed wages. Further investigation reveals that Brown has installed the procedure of putting any unclaimed wages in the petty cash fund so that the cash can be used for disbursements. When the claimant to the wages appears, he or she is paid from the petty cash fund. Brown contends that this procedure reduces the number of checks drawn to replenish the petty cash fund and centers the responsibility for all cash on hand in one person, inasmuch as the petty cash custodian distributes the pay envelopes.

Required

    a. Are Brown's internal controls over unclaimed wages adequate? Explain fully.

    b. Because Brown insists on paying salaries in cash, what procedures would you recommend to provide better internal control over unclaimed wages?*

17-30 (Objective 17-3) In many companies, labor costs represent a substantial percentage of total dollars expended in any one accounting period. One of the auditor's primary means of verifying payroll transactions is by a detailed payroll test.

    You are performing an annual audit of the Joplin Company, a medium-sized manufacturing company. You have selected a number of hourly employees for a detailed payroll test. The worksheet outline at the bottom of this page has been prepared.

Required

    a. What factors should the auditor consider in selecting his or her sample of employees to be included in any payroll test?

    b. Using the column numbers below as a reference, state the principal way(s) that the information for each heading would be verified.

    c. In addition to the payroll test, the auditor uses a number of other audit procedures in the verification of payroll transactions. List five additional procedures that may be used.*

Column Number	Heading
1	Employee number
2	Employee name
3	Job classification
	Hours worked
4	Straight time
5	Premium time
6	Hourly rate
7	Gross earnings
	Deductions
8	FICA withheld
9	Medicare withheld
10	FIT withheld
11	Union dues
12	Hospitalization
13	Amount of check
14	Check number
15	Account number charged
16	Description of account

*AICPA adapted.

17-31 (Objective 17-3) Roost and Briley, CPAs, are doing the audit of Leggert Lumber Co., an international wholesale lumber broker. Because of the nature of their business, payroll and telephone expense are the two largest expenses.

You are the in-charge auditor on the engagement responsible for writing the audit program for the payroll and personnel cycle. Leggert Lumber uses a computer service company to prepare weekly payroll checks, update earnings records, and prepare the weekly payroll journal for its 30 employees. The president maintains all personnel files, knows every employee extremely well, and is a full-time participant in the business.

All employees, except the president, check into the company building daily using a time clock. The president's secretary, Mary Clark, hands out the time cards daily, observes employees clocking in, collects the cards, and immediately returns them to the file. She goes through the same process when employees clock out on their way home.

At the end of each week, employees calculate their own hours. Clark rechecks those hours, and the president approves all time cards. Each Tuesday, Clark prepares a payroll input form for delivery to the computer service center. She files a copy of the form. The form has the following information for each employee:

Information	Source
Employee name	Time card
Social security number	Employee list
Hourly labor rate*	Wage rate list (approved by president)
Regular hours	Time card
Overtime hours	Time card
Special deductions*	Special form (prepared by employee)
W-4 information*	W-4 form
Termination of employment*	President

*Included on input form only for new employees, terminations, and changes.

The service center enters the information from the payroll input form into its computer, updates master files, and prints out payroll checks and a payroll register. The payroll register has the following headings:

Employee name	FICA taxes withheld
Social security number	Medicare withheld
Regular hours	Federal taxes withheld
Overtime hours	State taxes withheld
Regular payroll dollars	Other deductions
Overtime payroll dollars	Net pay
Gross payroll	Check number

A line is prepared for each employee and the journal is totaled.

Payroll checks and the journal are delivered to Clark, who compares the information on the journal with her payroll input form and initials the journal. She gives the checks to the president, who signs them and personally delivers them to employees.

Clark re-adds the journal and posts the totals to the ledger. Cancelled checks are mailed to the president, and he prepares a monthly bank reconciliation.

Required

a. Is there any loss of documentation because of the computer service center? Explain.

b. For each transaction-related audit objective for the payroll and personnel cycle, write appropriate tests of controls and substantive tests of transactions audit procedures. Consider both controls and weaknesses in writing your program. Label each procedure as either a test of control or a substantive test of transactions.

c. Rearrange your design format audit program in requirement b into a performance format audit program.

d. Prepare a sampling data sheet using either nonstatistical or attributes sampling, such as the ones shown in Chapter 14, for the audit program in part b. Set ARACR and other factors required for sampling as you consider appropriate. Do not assume that you actually performed any tests.

AUDIT OF THE ACQUISITION AND PAYMENT CYCLE: TESTS OF CONTROLS, SUBSTANTIVE TESTS OF TRANSACTIONS, AND ACCOUNTS PAYABLE

18

LEARNING OBJECTIVES

After studying this chapter, you should be able to

18-1 Identify the accounts and the classes of transactions in the acquisition and payment cycle.

18-2 Describe the business functions and the related documents and records in the acquisition and payment cycle.

18-3 Understand internal control and design and perform tests of controls and substantive tests of transactions for the acquisition and payment cycle.

18-4 Describe the methodology for designing tests of details of balances for accounts payable using the audit risk model.

18-5 Design and perform analytical procedures for accounts payable.

18-6 Design and perform tests of details of balances for accounts payable, including out-of-period liability tests.

18-7 Distinguish the reliability of vendors' invoices, vendors' statements, and confirmations of accounts payable as audit evidence.

FALSE PURCHASES CAMOUFLAGE OVERSTATED PROFITS

On November 25, 1992, Comptronix Corporation announced that members of its senior management team had overstated profits and that there would be material adjustments to the prior years' audited financial statements. In its subsequent investigation, the SEC determined that Comptronix's chief executive officer (CEO), chief operating officer (COO), and the controller/treasurer colluded to overstate assets and profits by recording fictitious sales, accounts receivable, and purchases of equipment on account.

To camouflage the fraud, the executives made it appear that collections from customers were received on the nonexistent receivables and that payments were made to fictitious accounts payable vendors. They even prepared cash disbursement checks to the phony vendors but retained the unendorsed checks and redeposited them into the company's disbursement account on which they had been drawn. These fraudulent disbursements were recorded in the accounting records as payments against the nonexistent accounts payable, which eliminated the phony liabilities.

The senior executives circumvented Comptronix's existing internal controls by bypassing the purchasing and receiving departments so that no one at Comptronix could discover the scheme. Comptronix employees usually created a fairly extensive paper trail for equipment purchases. Company internal controls over acquisition and cash disbursement transactions typically required a purchase order, receiving report, and vendor invoice before payment could be authorized by the COO or the controller/treasurer, who were both participants in the fraud. As a result, the executives were able to bypass controls related to cash disbursements and authorize payment for nonexistent purchases without creating any documents for the fictitious transactions.

The fraud scheme grossly exaggerated the company's performance by reporting profits when the company was actually incurring losses. On the day that the public announcement of the fraud

[continued]

FALSE PURCHASES CAMOUFLAGE OVERSTATED PROFITS [CONT'D]

was made, Comptronix's common stock price declined abruptly by 72 percent! The SEC ultimately charged all three executives with violating the anti-fraud provisions of the Securities Act of 1933 and the Securities Exchange Act of 1934. The SEC permanently barred the executives from serving as officers or directors of any public company, ordered them to repay bonuses and trading losses avoided, and imposed civil monetary penalties against them.

Source: *Accounting and Auditing Enforcement Release No. 543,* Commerce Clearing House, Inc. Chicago.

The third major transaction cycle discussed in this text is the **acquisition and payment cycle**. The acquisition of goods and services includes such items as the acquisition of raw materials, equipment, supplies, utilities, repairs and maintenance, and research and development. This chapter discusses assessing control risk and designing tests of controls and substantive tests of transactions for each of the classes of transactions in the acquisition and payment cycle. This chapter also covers performing tests of details of balances for accounts payable, the major balance sheet account in the cycle.

Before studying assessing control risk and designing tests of controls and substantive tests of transactions for each class of transactions, two related topics are covered. First, it is important to know the acquisition and payment cycle classes of transactions and account balances in a typical company. Second, because a considerable portion of the audit of transactions in the acquisition and payment cycle involves documents and records, it is essential to understand the typical documents and records used in the cycle. Then, if faced with auditing recorded transactions where documents such as purchase orders, receiving reports, and vendor invoices are missing—like the situation described in the Comptronix vignette—the auditor will be more likely to detect misstatements.

ACCOUNTS AND CLASSES OF TRANSACTIONS IN THE ACQUISITION AND PAYMENT CYCLE

OBJECTIVE 18-1

Identify the accounts and the classes of transactions in the acquisition and payment cycle.

The overall objective in the audit of the acquisition and payment cycle is to evaluate whether the accounts affected by the acquisitions of goods and services and the cash disbursements for those acquisitions are fairly presented in accordance with generally accepted accounting principles. Figure 18-1 shows the way accounting information flows through the various accounts in the acquisition and payment cycle. This figure shows that there are three classes of transactions included in the cycle:

1. Acquisitions of goods and services
2. Cash disbursements
3. Purchase returns and allowances and purchase discounts

Typical accounts included in the acquisition and payment cycle are shown by T-accounts in Figure 18-1. Note the large number of accounts affected by this cycle. To keep the illustration manageable, only the control accounts are shown for the three major categories of expenses used by most companies. For each control account, examples of the subsidiary expense accounts are also given. Because of the large number of accounts in the cycle, it is not surprising that it often takes more time to audit the acquisition and payment cycle than any other.

Figure 18-1 shows that every transaction is either debited or credited to accounts payable. Because many companies make acquisitions directly by check or through petty cash, the figure is an oversimplification. We assume that cash disbursement transactions are processed in the same manner as all others.

FIGURE 18-1   Accounts in the Acquisition and Payment Cycle

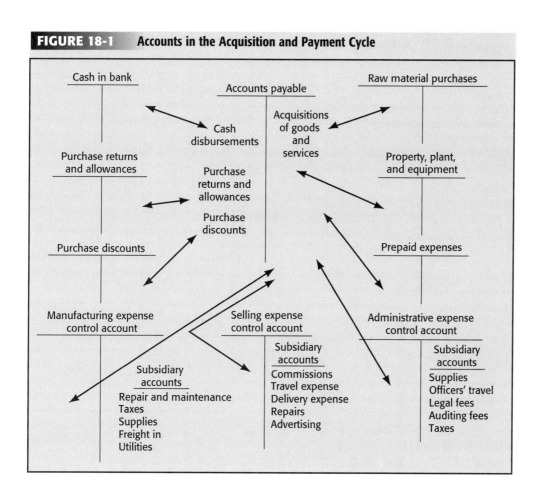

BUSINESS FUNCTIONS IN THE CYCLE
AND RELATED DOCUMENTS AND RECORDS

The acquisition and payment cycle involves the decisions and processes necessary for obtaining the goods and services for operating a business. The cycle typically begins with the initiation of a purchase requisition by an authorized employee who needs the goods or services and ends with payment for the benefits received. Although the discussion that follows deals with a small manufacturing company that makes tangible products for sale to third parties, the same principles apply to a service company, a government unit, or any other type of organization.

There are four business functions shown in the third column of Table 18-1 (p. 584). These functions occur in every business in the recording of the three classes of transactions in the acquisition and payment cycle. Observe that the first three business functions are for recording the acquisition of goods and services on account and the last process is for recording the cash disbursements for payments to vendors. Processing purchase returns and allowances and purchase discounts are also business functions in the cycle, but these are not separately shown on Table 18-1 because the amounts are not significant for most companies.

This section explains the four business functions in Table 18-1 and describes typical documents and records for each function. These documents and records are shown in the fourth column of Table 18-1. It is essential to understand the business functions and documents and records in a company before assessing control risk and designing test of controls and substantive tests of transactions.

OBJECTIVE 18-2
Describe the business functions and the related documents and records in the acquisition and payment cycle.

Classes of Transactions	Accounts	Business Functions	Documents and Records
Acquisitions	Inventory Property, plant, and equipment Prepaid expenses Leasehold improvements Accounts payable Manufacturing expenses Selling expenses Administrative expenses	Processing purchase orders	Purchase requisition Purchase order
		Receiving goods and services	Receiving report
		Recognizing the liability	Acquisitions journal Summary acquisitions report Vendor's invoice Debit memo Voucher Accounts payable master file Accounts payable trial balance Vendor's statement
Cash disbursements	Cash in bank (from cash disbursements) Accounts payable Purchase discounts	Processing and recording cash disbursements	Check Cash disbursements journal

Processing Purchase Orders

The request for goods or services by the client's personnel is the starting point for the cycle. The exact form of the request and the required approval depend on the nature of the goods and services and company policy.

Purchase Requisition A **purchase requisition** is a request for goods and services by an authorized employee. It may take the form of a request for such acquisitions as materials by a foreman or the storeroom supervisor, outside repairs by office or factory personnel, or insurance by the vice president in charge of property and equipment.

Purchase Order A **purchase order** is a document identifying the description, quantity, and related information for goods and services the company intends to purchase. This document is often used to indicate authorization to acquire goods and services. In many instances, companies submit purchase orders electronically to vendors who have made arrangements for electronic data interchange (EDI).

Receiving Goods and Services

The receipt by the company of goods or services from the vendor is a critical point in the cycle because it is the point at which most companies first recognize the acquisition and related liability on their records. When goods are received, adequate control requires examination for description, quantity, timely arrival, and condition. A **receiving report** is a document prepared at the time tangible goods are received that indicates the description of goods, the quantity received, the date received, and other relevant data. The receipt of goods and services in the normal course of business represents the date companies normally recognize the liability for an acquisition.

Recognizing the Liability

The proper recognition of the liability for the receipt of goods and services requires *prompt and accurate* recording. The initial recording has a significant effect on the recorded financial statements and the actual cash disbursement; therefore, great care must be taken to include only existing company acquisitions at the correct amounts.

Acquisitions Journal An acquisitions journal is used for recording acquisition transactions. A detailed acquisitions journal includes each acquisition transaction. It usually includes several classifications for the most significant types of acquisitions, such as the purchase of inventory, repairs and maintenance, supplies, the entry to accounts payable, and miscellaneous debits and credits. The acquisitions journal can also include acquisition returns and allowances transactions if a separate journal is not used. The acquisitions journal is generated for any time period from acquisition transactions included in the computer files. Details from the journal are posted to the accounts payable master file and journal totals are posted to the general ledger by the computer.

Summary Acquisitions Report This report is a computer-generated document that summarizes acquisitions for a period. The report typically includes information analyzed by key components such as account classification, type of inventory, and division.

Vendor's Invoice A **vendor's invoice** is a document that indicates such things as the description and quantity of goods and services received, price (including freight), cash discount terms, and date of the billing. It is an essential document because it specifies the amount of money owed to the vendor for an acquisition. For companies using EDI, the vendor invoice is transmitted electronically rather than in paper form.

Debit Memo A **debit memo** is a document indicating a reduction in the amount owed to a vendor because of returned goods or an allowance granted. It often takes the same general form as a vendor's invoice, but it supports reductions in accounts payable rather than increases.

Voucher This document is commonly used by organizations to establish a formal means of recording and controlling acquisitions. Vouchers include a cover sheet or folder for containing documents and a package of relevant documents such as the purchase order, copy of the packing slip, receiving report, and vendor's invoice. After payment, a copy of the check is added to the voucher package.

Accounts Payable Master File An **accounts payable master file** is used for recording individual acquisitions, cash disbursements, and acquisition returns and allowances for each vendor. The master file is updated from the acquisition, returns and allowances, and cash disbursement computer transaction files. The total of the individual account balances in the master file equals the total balance of accounts payable in the general ledger. A printout of the accounts payable master file shows, by vendor, the beginning balance in accounts payable, each acquisition, acquisition returns and allowances, cash disbursements, and the ending balance. Many companies do not maintain an accounts payable master file by vendor. These companies pay on the basis of individual vendor's invoices. Therefore, the total of unpaid vendor's invoices in the master file equals total accounts payable.

Accounts Payable Trial Balance An **accounts payable trial balance** lists the amount owed to each vendor or for each invoice or voucher at a point in time. It is prepared directly from the accounts payable master file.

Vendor's Statement A **vendor's statement** is prepared monthly by the vendor and indicates the beginning balance, acquisitions, returns and allowances, payments to the vendor, and ending balance. These balances and activities are the vendor's representations of the transactions for the period and not the client's. Except for disputed amounts and timing differences, the client's accounts payable master file should be the same as the vendor's statement.

For most companies, payment is made by computer-prepared checks from information included in the acquisition transactions file at the time goods and services are received. Checks are typically prepared in a multicopy format, with the original going to the payee, one copy

Processing and Recording Cash Disbursements

filed with the vendor's invoice and other supporting documents, and another filed numerically. In most cases, individual checks are recorded in a cash disbursements transactions file.

Check The document used to pay for the acquisition when payment is due. After the check is signed by an authorized person, it is an asset. Therefore, signed checks should be mailed by the signer or a person under his or her control. When cashed by the vendor and cleared by the client's bank, it is called a cancelled check. In some EDI arrangements, the company submits payments to the vendor electronically through an electronic funds transfer (EFT) between the company's bank and the vendor's bank.

Cash Disbursements Journal This journal is used for recording cash disbursement transactions. It is generated for any time period from the cash disbursement transactions included in the computer files. Details from the journal are posted to the accounts payable master file and journal totals are posted to the general ledger by the computer.

ARE COMPANIES THROWING MONEY AWAY?

Howard Schultz is the president of a Dallas-based accounts payable auditing firm. Mr. Schultz's firm specializes in analyzing acquisitions and cash disbursements for its clients. In an article written for *The Wall Street Journal*, Mr. Schultz states that auditors in his firm find that clients often overpay vendors.

Mr. Schultz notes that many of the errors are intrinsic to the process of buying and selling. For example, in many companies, the person or department placing the order is not the same party who pays the bill. When you combine this with the significant amount of price promotions and special allowances that vendors often offer on a limited-time-only basis, the odds increase of making payments that exceed the amounts actually due. To reduce losses from overpayments, Mr. Schultz suggests that companies reevaluate the purchasing and payment processes to improve communications. He also recommends that companies pay special attention to peaks and transitional periods when companies are more vulnerable to errors and that they track detected patterns of overpayments, such as repeated failure to take advantage of trade allowances or discounts for early payments. In addition to Mr. Schultz's recommendations, companies should consider taking advantage of technology to track many of these savings opportunities. For example, many accounts payable software packages provide opportunities for computer tracking of payment due dates. Using the dates entered, the computer issues payment automatically within the discount period. That takes the human tracking costs out of the equation and lets technology do the work. A win–win situation!

Source: Howard Schultz, "Washing Away the Sin of Overpayment," *The Wall Street Journal* (August 9, 1993), p. A.12.

METHODOLOGY FOR DESIGNING TESTS OF CONTROLS AND SUBSTANTIVE TESTS OF TRANSACTIONS

OBJECTIVE 18-3
Understand internal control and design and perform tests of controls and substantive tests of transactions for the acquisition and payment cycle.

In a typical audit, the most time-consuming accounts to verify by substantive tests of details of balances are accounts receivable, inventory, fixed assets, accounts payable, and expense accounts. Of these five, four are directly related to the acquisition and payment cycle. The net time saved can be dramatic if the auditor can reduce the tests of details of the account balances by using tests of controls and substantive tests of transactions to verify the effectiveness of internal controls for acquisitions and cash disbursements. Therefore, it should not be surprising that tests of controls and substantive tests of transactions for the acquisition and payment cycle receive a considerable amount of attention in well-conducted audits, especially when the client has effective internal controls.

Tests of controls and substantive tests of transactions for the acquisition and payment cycle are divided into two broad areas: tests of acquisitions and tests of payments.

Acquisition tests concern three of the four business functions discussed earlier in this chapter: processing purchase orders, receiving goods and services, and recognizing the liability. Tests of payments concern the fourth function, processing and recording cash disbursements.

Figure 18-2 shows the methodology for designing tests of controls and substantive tests of transactions for the acquisition and payment cycle. It is the same methodology used in earlier chapters. The following sections deal with each part of Figure 18-2, starting with understanding internal control.

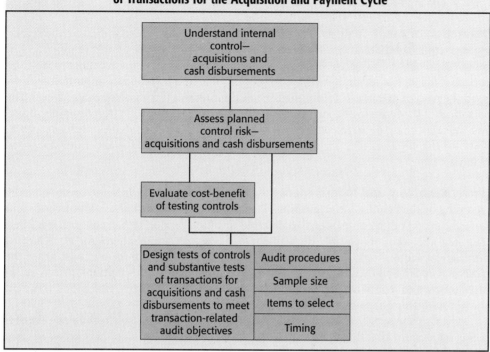

FIGURE 18-2 Methodology for Designing Tests of Controls and Substantive Tests of Transactions for the Acquisition and Payment Cycle

The auditor gains an understanding of internal control for the acquisition and payment cycle by studying the client's flowcharts, preparing internal control questionnaires, and performing walk-through tests for acquisitions and cash disbursements. The procedures for understanding internal control in the acquisition and payment cycle are similar to the procedures performed in other transaction cycles.

Understand Internal Control

There are key internal controls for each of the business functions described earlier in this chapter. Key internal controls are for the authorization of purchases, the separation of the custody of the received goods from other functions, the timely recording and independent review of transactions, and the authorization of payments to vendors. We now examine each of these key controls.

Assess Planned Control Risk

Authorization of Purchases Proper authorization for acquisitions is essential because it ensures that the goods and services acquired are for authorized company purposes and it avoids the acquisition of excessive or unnecessary items. Most companies permit general authorization for the acquisition of regular operating needs, such as inventory, at one level and acquisitions of capital assets or similar items at another. For example, acquisitions of fixed assets in excess of a specified dollar limit may require approval from the board of directors; items acquired relatively infrequently, such as insurance policies and long-term service contracts, are approved by certain officers; supplies and services costing less than a designated amount are approved by supervisors and department heads; and some types of raw materials and supplies are reordered automatically when they fall to a predetermined level, often by direct communication with vendors' computers.

After the purchase requisition for an acquisition has been approved, a purchase order to acquire the goods or services must be initiated. A purchase order is issued to a vendor for a specified item at a certain price to be delivered at or by a designated time. The purchase order is usually in writing and is a legal document that is an offer to buy.

It is common for companies to establish purchasing departments to ensure an adequate quality of goods and services at a minimum price. For good internal control, the purchasing department should not be responsible for authorizing the acquisition or receiving the goods. All purchase orders should be prenumbered and should include sufficient columns and spaces to minimize the likelihood of unintentional omissions on the form when goods are ordered.

Separation of Asset Custody from Other Functions Most companies have the receiving department initiate a receiving report as evidence of the receipt and examination of goods. One copy is normally sent to the storeroom and another to the accounts payable department for their information needs. To prevent theft and misuse, it is important that the goods be *physically controlled* from the time of their receipt until their use or disposal. The personnel in the receiving department should be independent of the storeroom personnel and the accounting department. Finally, the accounting records should transfer responsibility for the goods as they are transferred from receiving to storage and from storage to manufacturing.

Timely Recording and Independent Review of Transactions In some companies, the recording of the liability for acquisitions is made on the basis of the receipt of goods and services, and in other companies, it is deferred until the vendor's invoice is received. In either case, the accounts payable department typically has responsibility for verifying the propriety of acquisitions. This is done by comparing the details on the purchase order, the receiving report, and the vendor's invoice to determine that the descriptions, prices, quantities, terms, and freight on the vendor's invoice are correct. Typically, extensions, footings, and account distributions are also verified.

An important control in the accounts payable and information technology departments is to require that those personnel who record acquisitions do not have access to cash, marketable securities, and other assets. Adequate documents and records, proper procedures for record keeping, and independent checks on performance are also necessary controls in the accounts payable function.

Authorization of Payments The most important controls over cash disbursements include the signing of checks by an individual with proper authority, separation of responsibilities for signing the checks and performing the accounts payable function, and careful examination of the supporting documents by the check signer at the time the check is signed.

The checks should be prenumbered and printed on special paper that makes it difficult to alter the payee or amount. Care should be taken to provide physical control over blank, voided, and signed checks. It is also important to have a method of cancelling the supporting documents to prevent their reuse as support for another check at a later time. A common method is to write the check number on the supporting documents.

Evaluate Cost-Benefit of Testing Controls	After the auditor has identified the key internal controls and weaknesses and assessed control risk, it is appropriate to decide whether substantive tests will be reduced sufficiently to justify the cost of performing tests of controls. It makes little sense to incur the cost of identifying controls and assessing control risk below the maximum if there will be no reduction of substantive tests.
Design Tests of Controls and Substantive Tests of Transactions for Acquisitions	Key internal controls, common tests of controls, and common substantive tests of transactions for each transaction-related audit objective are summarized in Table 18-2. An assumption underlying the internal controls and audit procedures is the existence of a separate acquisitions journal for recording all acquisitions.

TABLE 18-2 Summary of Transaction-Related Audit Objectives, Key Controls, Tests of Controls, and Substantive Tests of Transactions for Acquisitions

Transaction-Related Audit Objective	Key Internal Control	Common Test of Control	Common Substantive Tests of Transactions
Recorded acquisitions are for goods and services received, consistent with the best interests of the client (existence).	Purchase requisition, purchase order, receiving report, and vendor's invoice are attached to the voucher.* Acquisitions are approved at the proper level. Computer accepts entry of purchases only from authorized vendors in the vendor master file. Documents are cancelled to prevent their reuse. Vendors' invoices, receiving reports, purchase orders, and purchase requisitions are internally verified.*	Examine documents in voucher package for existence. Examine indication of approval. Attempt to input transactions with valid and invalid vendors. Examine indication of cancellation. Examine indication of internal verification.	Review the acquisitions journal, general ledger, and accounts payable master file for large or unusual amounts.† Examine underlying documents for reasonableness and authenticity (vendors' invoices, receiving reports, purchase orders, and purchase requisitions).* Examine vendor master file for unusual vendors. Trace inventory acquisitions to inventory master file. Examine fixed assets acquired.
Existing acquisition transactions are recorded (completeness).	Purchase orders are prenumbered and accounted for. Receiving reports are prenumbered and accounted for.* Vouchers are prenumbered and accounted for.	Account for a sequence of purchase orders. Account for a sequence of receiving reports. Account for a sequence of vouchers.	Trace from a file of receiving reports to the acquisitions journal.* Trace from a file of vendors' invoices to the acquisitions journal.
Recorded acquisition transactions are accurate (accuracy).	Calculations and amounts are internally verified. Batch totals are compared with computer summary reports. Acquisitions are approved for prices and discounts.	Examine indication of internal verification. Examine file of batch totals for initials of data control clerk; compare totals to summary reports. Examine indication of approval.	Compare recorded transactions in the acquisitions journal with the vendor's invoice, receiving report, and other supporting documentation.* Recompute the clerical accuracy on the vendor's invoice, including discounts and freight.
Acquisition transactions are properly classified (classification).	An adequate chart of accounts is used. Account classifications are internally verified.	Examine procedures manual and chart of accounts. Examine indication of internal verification.	Compare classification with chart of accounts by reference to vendors' invoices.
Acquisition transactions are recorded on the correct dates (timing).	Procedures require recording transactions as soon as possible after the goods and services have been received. Dates are internally verified.	Examine procedures manual and observe whether unrecorded vendors' invoices exist. Examine indication of internal verification.	Compare dates of receiving reports and vendors' invoices with dates in the acquisitions journal.*
Acquisition transactions are properly included in the accounts payable and inventory master files, and are properly summarized (posting and summarization).	Accounts payable master file contents are internally verified. Accounts payable master file or trial balance totals are compared with general ledger balances.	Examine indication of internal verification. Examine initials on general ledger accounts indicating comparison.	Test clerical accuracy by footing the journals and tracing postings to general ledger and accounts payable and inventory master files.

*Receiving reports are used only for tangible goods and are therefore not used for services, such as utilities and repairs and maintenance. Often, vendors' invoices are the only documentation available.

†This analytical procedure can also apply to other objectives, including completeness, accuracy, and timing.

In studying Table 18-2, it is important to relate internal controls to transaction-related audit objectives, tests of controls to internal controls, and substantive tests of transactions to monetary misstatements that would be absent or present due to controls and weaknesses in the system. It should be kept in mind that a set of audit procedures for an audit engagement will vary with the internal controls and other circumstances.

If controls are operating effectively, significant audit efficiencies may be realized. Four of the six transaction-related audit objectives for acquisitions deserve special attention. A discussion of each of these objectives follows.

Recorded Acquisitions Are for Goods and Services Received, Consistent with the Best Interests of the Client (Existence)

If the auditor is satisfied that the controls are adequate for this objective, tests for improper and nonexistent transactions can be greatly reduced. Adequate controls are likely to prevent the client from including as a business expense or asset those transactions that primarily benefit management or other employees rather than the entity being audited. In some instances, improper transactions are obvious, such as the acquisition of unauthorized personal items by employees or the actual embezzlement of cash by recording a fraudulent acquisition in the acquisitions journal. In other instances, the propriety of a transaction is more difficult to evaluate, such as the payment of officers' memberships to country clubs, expense-paid vacations to foreign countries for members of management and their families, and management-approved illegal payments to officials of foreign countries. If the controls over improper or nonexistent transactions are inadequate, extensive examination of supporting documentation is necessary.

Existing Acquisitions Are Recorded (Completeness)

Failure to record the acquisition of goods and services received directly affects the balance in accounts payable and may result in an overstatement of net income and owners' equity. Because of this, auditors are usually very concerned with the completeness objective. In some instances, it may be difficult to perform tests of details to determine whether there are unrecorded transactions, and the auditor must rely on controls for this purpose. In addition, because the audit of accounts payable generally takes a considerable amount of audit time, effective internal controls, properly tested, can significantly reduce audit costs.

Acquisitions Are Accurately Recorded (Accuracy)

Because the accuracy of many asset, liability, and expense accounts depends on the correct recording of transactions in the acquisitions journal, the extent of tests of details of many balance sheet and expense accounts depends on the auditor's evaluation of the effectiveness of the internal controls over the accuracy of recorded acquisitions transactions. For example, if the auditor believes that the fixed assets are correctly recorded in the books of original entry, it is acceptable to vouch fewer current period acquisitions than if the controls are inadequate.

When a client uses perpetual inventory records, the tests of details of inventory can also be significantly reduced if the auditor believes that the perpetual records are accurate. The controls over the acquisitions included in the perpetual records are normally tested as a part of the tests of controls and substantive tests of transactions for acquisitions, and the controls over this objective play a key role in the audit. The inclusion of both quantity and unit costs in the inventory perpetual records permits a reduction in the tests of the physical count and the unit costs of inventory if the controls are operating effectively.

Acquisitions Are Correctly Classified (Classification)

The auditor can reduce the tests of details of certain individual accounts if he or she believes that internal controls are adequate to provide reasonable assurance of correct classification in the acquisitions journal. Although all accounts are affected to some degree by effective controls over classification, the two areas most affected are current period acquisitions of fixed assets and all expense accounts, such as repairs and maintenance, utilities, and advertising. Because performing documentation tests of current period fixed asset acquisitions and expense accounts for accuracy and classification are relatively time-consuming audit procedures, the saving in audit time can be significant.

The same format used in Table 18-2 for acquisitions is also used in Table 18-3 for cash disbursements. The assumption underlying these controls and audit procedures is the existence of separate cash disbursements and acquisitions journals. The comments made about the methodology and process for developing audit procedures for acquisitions apply equally to cash disbursements.

TABLE 18-3   Summary of Transaction-Related Audit Objectives, Key Controls, Tests of Controls, and Substantive Tests of Transactions for Cash Disbursements

Transaction-Related Audit Objective	Key Internal Control	Common Test of Control	Common Substantive Tests of Transactions
Recorded cash disbursements are for goods and services actually received (existence).	There is adequate segregation of duties between accounts payable and custody of signed checks. Supporting documentation is examined before signing of checks by an authorized person. Approval of payment on supporting documents at the time checks are signed.	Discuss with personnel and observe activities. Discuss with personnel and observe activities. Examine indication of approval.	Review the cash disbursements journal, general ledger, and accounts payable master file for large or unusual amounts.* Trace the cancelled check to the related acquisitions journal entry and examine for payee name and amount. Examine cancelled check for authorized signature, proper endorsement, and cancellation by the bank. Examine supporting documents as a part of the tests of acquisitions.
Existing cash disbursement transactions are recorded (completeness).	Checks are prenumbered and accounted for. The bank reconciliation is prepared monthly by an employee independent of recording cash disbursements or custody of assets.	Account for a sequence of checks. Examine bank reconciliations and observe their preparation.	Reconcile recorded cash disbursements with the cash disbursements on the bank statement (proof of cash disbursements).
Recorded cash disbursement transactions are accurate (accuracy).	Calculations and amounts are internally verified. The bank reconciliation is prepared monthly by an independent person.	Examine indication of internal verification. Examine bank reconciliations and observe their preparation.	Compare cancelled checks with the related acquisitions journal and cash disbursements journal entries. Recompute cash discounts. Prepare a proof of cash disbursements.
Cash disbursement transactions are properly classified (classification).	An adequate chart of accounts is used. Account classifications are internally verified.	Examine procedures manual and chart of accounts. Examine indication of internal verification.	Compare classification with chart of accounts by reference to vendors' invoices and acquisitions journal.
Cash disbursement transactions are recorded on the correct dates (timing).	Procedures require recording of transactions as soon as possible after the check has been signed. Dates are internally verified.	Examine procedures manual and observe whether unrecorded checks exist. Examine indication of internal verification.	Compare dates on cancelled checks with the cash disbursements journal. Compare dates on cancelled checks with the bank cancellation date.
Cash disbursement transactions are properly included in the accounts payable master file and are properly summarized (posting and summarization).	Accounts payable master file contents are internally verified. Accounts payable master file or trial balance totals are compared with general ledger balances.	Examine indication of internal verification. Examine initials on general ledger accounts indicating comparison.	Test clerical accuracy by footing journals and tracing postings to general ledger and accounts payable master file.

*This analytical procedure can also apply to other objectives, including completeness, accuracy, and timing.

Once the auditor has decided on procedures, the acquisitions and cash disbursements tests are typically performed concurrently. For example, for a transaction selected for examination from the acquisitions journal, the vendor's invoice and the receiving report are examined at the same time as the related cancelled check. Thus, the verification is done efficiently without reducing the effectiveness of the tests.

Attributes Sampling for Tests of Controls and Substantive Tests of Transactions

Because of the importance of tests of controls and substantive tests of transactions for acquisitions and cash disbursements, the use of attributes sampling is common in this audit area. The approach is similar to that used for the tests of controls and substantive tests of transactions for sales discussed in Chapter 14. With reference to the most essential transaction-related audit objectives presented earlier, however, it should be noted, that most of the important attributes in the acquisition and payment cycle have a direct monetary effect on the accounts. Furthermore, many of the types of errors and fraud that may be found represent a misstatement of earnings and are of significant concern to the auditor. For example, there may be inventory cutoff misstatements or an incorrect recording of an expense amount. Because of this, the tolerable exception rate selected by the auditor in tests of many of the attributes in this cycle is relatively low. Because the dollar amounts of individual transactions in the cycle cover a wide range, it is also common to segregate large and unusual items and to test them on a 100 percent basis.

METHODOLOGY FOR DESIGNING TESTS OF DETAILS OF BALANCES FOR ACCOUNTS PAYABLE

OBJECTIVE 18-4
Describe the methodology for designing tests of details of balances for accounts payable using the audit risk model.

Accounts Payable
News & Tips

Because all acquisition and payment cycle transactions typically flow through accounts payable, this account is critical to any audit of the acquisition and payment cycle. If tests of controls and related substantive tests of transactions show that controls are operating effectively, the auditor may be able to reduce analytical procedures and tests of details of balances for accounts payable. However, because accounts payable tend to be material for many companies, auditors almost always perform extensive analytical procedures and some tests of details of balances of that account. We now take a brief look at the audit of accounts payable and discuss substantive audit tests often performed for this account.

Accounts payable are *unpaid obligations* for goods and services received in the ordinary course of business. It is sometimes difficult to distinguish between accounts payable and accrued liabilities, but it is useful to define a liability as an account payable if the total amount of the obligation is *known and owed at the balance sheet date*. The accounts payable account therefore includes obligations for the acquisition of raw materials, equipment, utilities, repairs, and many other types of goods and services that were received before the end of the year. Most accounts payable can also be identified by the existence of vendors' invoices for the obligation. Accounts payable should also be distinguished from interest-bearing obligations. If an obligation includes the payment of interest, it should be recorded as a note payable, contract payable, mortgage payable, or bond payable.

The methodology for designing tests of details for accounts payable is summarized in Figure 18-3. This methodology is the same as that used for accounts receivable in Chapter 15.

Set Tolerable Misstatement and Assess Inherent Risk (Phase I)

Like accounts receivable, there are typically a large number of transactions affecting accounts payable, the balance is often made up of a large number of accounts, the balance is large, and it is relatively expensive to audit the account. For these reasons, auditors typically set tolerable misstatement for accounts payable relatively high. For the same reasons, the auditor also often assesses inherent risk as medium or high. Auditors are usually especially concerned about the completeness and the cutoff balance-related audit objectives for accounts payable because of the potential for understatements in the account balance.

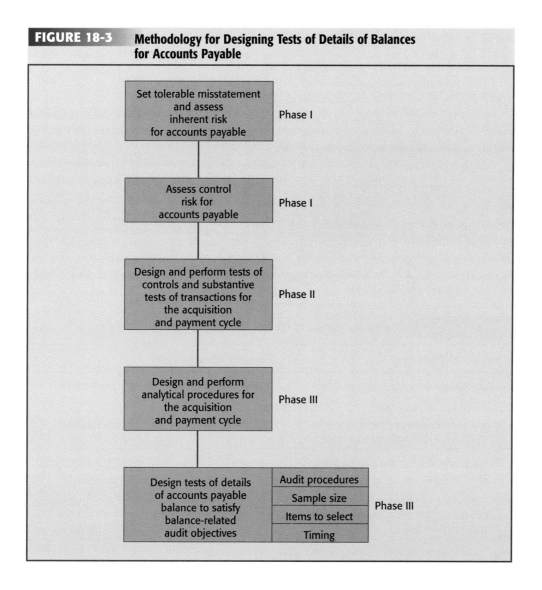

FIGURE 18-3 Methodology for Designing Tests of Details of Balances for Accounts Payable

Set tolerable misstatement and assess inherent risk for accounts payable — Phase I

Assess control risk for accounts payable — Phase I

Design and perform tests of controls and substantive tests of transactions for the acquisition and payment cycle — Phase II

Design and perform analytical procedures for the acquisition and payment cycle — Phase III

Design tests of details of accounts payable balance to satisfy balance-related audit objectives — Audit procedures / Sample size / Items to select / Timing — Phase III

(handwritten margin note: If A/P controls are weak, do most test of details of balances)

As shown in Figure 18-3, once the auditor sets tolerable misstatement and inherent risk for accounts payable, the auditor uses his or her understanding of internal control to assess control risk. The auditor's ultimate substantive tests depend on the relative effectiveness of internal controls related to accounts payable. Therefore, it is important to have an understanding of how these controls relate to accounts payable.

The effects of the client's internal controls on accounts payable tests can be illustrated by two examples. In the first, assume that the client has highly effective internal controls over recording and paying for acquisitions. The receipt of goods is promptly documented by prenumbered receiving reports; prenumbered vouchers are promptly and efficiently prepared and recorded in the acquisition transactions file and the accounts payable master file. Cash disbursements are also made promptly when due and immediately recorded in the cash disbursements transactions file and the accounts payable master file. On a monthly basis, individual accounts payable balances in the master file are reconciled with vendors' statements, and the computer automatically reconciles the master file total to the general ledger. Under these circumstances, the verification of accounts payable should require little audit effort once the auditor concludes that internal controls are operating effectively.

In the second example, assume that receiving reports are not used, the client defers recording acquisitions until cash disbursements are made, and because of a weak cash position, bills are often paid several months after their due date. When an auditor faces such

Assess Control Risk and Design and Perform Tests of Controls and Substantive Tests of Transactions (Phases I and II)

a situation, there is a high likelihood of an understatement of accounts payable; therefore, under these circumstances, extensive tests of details of accounts payable are necessary to determine whether accounts payable is properly stated on the balance sheet date.

The most important controls over accounts payable and the related tests of controls and substantive tests of transactions were discussed earlier in this chapter. In addition to those controls, it is important to have a monthly reconciliation of vendors' statements with recorded liabilities and the accounts payable master file with the general ledger. This should be done by an independent person or by the computer.

After assessing control risk, the auditor designs and performs tests of controls and substantive tests of transactions for the acquisitions and cash disbursements. These procedures were discussed in detail earlier in this chapter and are not repeated here.

Design and Perform Analytical Procedures (Phase III)

OBJECTIVE 18-5
Design and perform analytical procedures for accounts payable.

The use of analytical procedures is as important in the acquisition and payment cycle as it is in every other cycle, especially for uncovering misstatements in accounts payable. Table 18-4 illustrates analytical procedures for the balance sheet and income statement accounts in the acquisition and payment cycle that are useful for uncovering areas in which additional investigation is desirable.

TABLE 18-4	**Analytical Procedures for the Acquisition and Payment Cycle**
Analytical Procedure	**Possible Misstatement**
Compare acquisition-related expense account balances with prior years.	Misstatement of accounts payable and expenses.
Review list of accounts payable for unusual, nonvendor, and interest-bearing payables.	Classification misstatement for nontrade liabilities.
Compare individual accounts payable with previous years.	Unrecorded or nonexistent accounts, or misstatements.
Calculate ratios such as purchases divided by accounts payable, and accounts payable divided by current liabilities.	Unrecorded or nonexistent accounts, or misstatements.

One of the most important analytical procedures for uncovering misstatements of accounts payable is comparing current-year expense totals with prior years. For example, by comparing utilities expense with the prior year, the auditor may determine that the last utilities bill for the year was not recorded. Comparing expenses with prior years is an effective analytical procedure for accounts payable because expenses from year to year are typically relatively stable. Examples include rent, utilities, and other expenses billed on a regular basis.

Design and Perform Tests of Details of Accounts Payable Balance (Phase III)

OBJECTIVE 18-6
Design and perform tests of details of balances for accounts payable, including out-of-period liability tests.

The overall objective in the audit of accounts payable is to determine whether accounts payable is fairly stated and properly disclosed. Eight of the nine balance-related audit objectives discussed in Chapter 6 are applicable to accounts payable. Realizable value is not applicable to liabilities.

The auditor should recognize the difference in emphasis between the audit of liabilities and the audit of assets. When assets are being verified, attention is focused on making certain that the balance in the account is not overstated. The existence of recorded assets is constantly questioned and verified by confirmation, physical examination, and examination of supporting documents. The auditor should certainly not ignore the possibility of assets being understated, but the fact remains that the auditor is more concerned about the possibility of overstatement than understatement. The opposite approach is taken in verifying liability balances; that is, the main focus is on the discovery of understated or omitted liabilities.

The difference in emphasis in auditing assets and liabilities results directly from the *legal liability of CPAs*. If equity investors, creditors, and other users determine subsequent to the issuance of the audited financial statements that owners' equity was materially overstated, a lawsuit against the CPA firm is fairly likely. Because an overstatement of owners' equity can arise either from an overstatement of assets or from an understatement of liabilities, it is natural for CPAs to emphasize those two types of misstatements. The probability of a successful lawsuit against a CPA for failing to discover an understatement of owners' equity is far less likely.

Nevertheless, the auditing profession must avoid too much emphasis on protecting users from overstatements of owners' equity at the expense of ignoring understatements. If assets are consistently understated and liabilities are consistently overstated for large numbers of audited companies, the decision-making value of financial statement information is likely to decline. Therefore, even though it is natural for auditors to emphasize the possibility of overstating assets and understating liabilities, uncovering the opposite types of misstatements is also a significant responsibility.

The same balance-related audit objectives that were used as a frame of reference for verifying accounts receivable in Chapter 15 are also applicable to liabilities, with three minor modifications. The most obvious difference in verifying liabilities is the nonapplicability of the realizable value objective. The second difference is in the rights and obligations objective. For assets, the auditor is concerned with the client's rights to the use and disposal of the assets. For liabilities, the auditor is concerned with the client's obligations for the payment of the liability. If the client has no obligation to pay a liability, it should not be included as a liability. The third difference was discussed earlier: In auditing liabilities, the emphasis is on the search for understatements rather than for overstatements.

Table 18-5 (p. 596) includes the balance-related audit objectives and common tests of details of balances procedures for accounts payable. The actual audit procedures will vary considerably depending on the nature of the entity, the materiality of accounts payable, the nature and effectiveness of internal controls, and inherent risk.

Out-of-Period Liabilities Tests Because of the emphasis on understatements in liability accounts, *out-of-period liability tests* are important for accounts payable. The extent of tests to uncover unrecorded accounts payable, often called the *search for unrecorded accounts payable*, depends heavily on assessed control risk and the materiality of the potential balance in the account. The same audit procedures used to uncover unrecorded payables are applicable to the accuracy objective. The audit procedures that follow are typical tests.

Examine Underlying Documentation for Subsequent Cash Disbursements The purpose of this audit procedure is to uncover cash disbursements made in the subsequent accounting period that represent liabilities at the balance sheet date. The supporting documentation is examined to determine whether a cash disbursement was for a current period obligation. For example, if inventory was received before the balance sheet date, it will be so indicated on the receiving report. Often, documentation for cash disbursements made in the subsequent period are examined for several weeks, especially when the client does not pay bills on a timely basis. Any cash disbursement that is for a current period obligation should be traced to the accounts payable trial balance to make sure that it has been included as a liability.

Examine Underlying Documentation for Bills Not Paid Several Weeks after the Year-End This procedure is carried out in the same manner as the preceding one and serves the same purpose. The only difference is that it is done for unpaid obligations near the end of the audit field work rather than for obligations that have already been paid. For example, in an audit with a March 31 year-end, if the auditor examines the supporting documentation for checks paid until June 28, bills that are still unpaid at that date should be examined to determine whether they are obligations of the year ended March 31.

Balance-Related Audit Objective	Common Tests of Details of Balances Procedures	Comments
Accounts payable in the accounts payable list agree with related master file, and the total is correctly added and agrees with the general ledger (detail tie-in).	Re-add or use the computer to total the accounts payable list. Trace the total to the general ledger. Trace individual vendors' invoices to master file for names and amounts.	All pages need not ordinarily be footed if footing manually. Unless controls are weak, tracing to master file should be limited.
Accounts payable in the accounts payable list exist (existence).	Trace from accounts payable list to vendors' invoices and statements. Confirm accounts payable, emphasizing large and unusual amounts.	Ordinarily receives little attention because the primary concern is with understatements.
Existing accounts payable are included in the accounts payable list (completeness).	Perform out-of-period liability tests (see discussion).	These are essential audit tests for accounts payable.
Accounts payable in the accounts payable list are accurate (accuracy).	Perform same procedures as those used for existence objective and out-of-period liability tests.	Ordinarily, the emphasis in these procedures for accuracy is understatement rather than omission.
Accounts payable in the accounts payable list are properly classified (classification).	Review the list and master file for related parties, notes or other interest-bearing liabilities, long-term payables, and debit balances.	Knowledge of the client's business is essential for these tests.
Transactions in the acquisition and payment cycle are recorded in the proper period (cutoff).	Perform out-of-period liability tests (see discussion). Perform detailed tests as a part of physical observation of inventory (see discussion). Test for inventory in transit (see discussion).	These are essential audit tests for accounts payable. These are called *cutoff* tests.
The company has an obligation to pay the liabilities included in accounts payable (obligations).	Examine vendors' statements and confirm accounts payable.	Normally, not a concern in the audit of accounts payable because all accounts payable are obligations.
Accounts in the acquisition and payment cycle are properly presented and disclosed (presentation and disclosure).	Review statements to make sure material related parties, long-term, and interest-bearing liabilities are segregated.	Ordinarily not a problem.

Trace Receiving Reports Issued before Year-End to Related Vendors' Invoices All merchandise received before the year-end of the accounting period, indicated by the issuance of a receiving report, should be included as accounts payable. By tracing receiving reports issued at and before year-end to vendors' invoices and making sure that they are included in accounts payable, the auditor is testing for unrecorded obligations.

Trace Vendors' Statements That Show a Balance Due to the Accounts Payable Trial Balance If the client maintains a file of vendors' statements, any statement indicating a balance due can be traced to the listing to make sure that it is included as an account payable.

Send Confirmations to Vendors with Which the Client Does Business Although the use of confirmations for accounts payable is less common than for accounts receivable, it is often used to test for vendors omitted from the accounts payable list, omitted transactions, and misstated account balances. Sending confirmations to active vendors for which a balance has not been included in the accounts payable list is a useful means of searching for omitted amounts. This type of confirmation is commonly called zero balance confirmation. Additional discussion of confirmation of accounts payable is deferred until the end of this chapter.

Cutoff Tests Cutoff tests for accounts payable are intended to determine whether transactions recorded a few days before and after the balance sheet date are included in the correct period. The five out-of-period liability audit tests just discussed are directly related to cutoff for acquisitions, but they emphasize understatements. For the first three procedures, it is also appropriate to examine supporting documentation as a test of overstatement of accounts payable. For example, the third procedure is to trace receiving reports issued before year-end to related vendors' invoices in order to test for unrecorded accounts payable. To test for overstatement cutoff amounts, the auditor should trace receiving reports issued *after* year-end to related invoices to make sure that they are not recorded as accounts payable (unless they are inventory in transit, which is discussed shortly).

Because most cutoff tests have already been discussed, only two aspects are expanded on here: the examination of receiving reports and the determination of the amount of inventory in transit.

Relationship of Cutoff to Physical Observation of Inventory In determining that the accounts payable cutoff is correct, *it is essential that the cutoff tests be coordinated with the physical observation of inventory.* For example, assume that an inventory acquisition for $40,000 is received late in the afternoon of December 31, after the physical inventory is completed. If the acquisition is included in accounts payable and purchases but excluded from inventory, the result is an understatement of net earnings of $40,000. Conversely, if the acquisition is excluded from both inventory and accounts payable, there is a misstatement in the balance sheet but the income statement is correct. The only way the auditor will know which type of misstatement has occurred is to coordinate cutoff tests with the observation of inventory.

The cutoff information for acquisitions should be obtained *during the physical observation* of the inventory. At this time, the auditor should review the procedures in the receiving department to determine that all inventory received was counted, and the auditor should record in his or her working papers the last receiving report number of inventory included in the physical count. During the year-end field work, the auditor should then test the accounting records for cutoff. The auditor should trace receiving report numbers to the accounts payable records to verify that they are correctly included or excluded.

For example, assume that the last receiving report number representing inventory included in the physical count was 3167. The auditor should record this document number and subsequently trace it and several preceding numbers to their related vendors' invoices and to the accounts payable list or the accounts payable master file to determine that they are all included. Similarly, accounts payable for acquisitions recorded on receiving reports with numbers larger than 3167 should be excluded from accounts payable.

When the client's physical inventory takes place before the last day of the year, it is still necessary to perform an accounts payable cutoff at the time of the physical count in the manner described in the preceding paragraph. In addition, the auditor must verify whether all acquisitions taking place between the physical count and the end of the year were added to the physical inventory and accounts payable. For example, if the client takes the physical count on December 27 for a December 31 year-end, the cutoff information is taken as of December 27. During the year-end field work, the auditor must first test to determine whether the cutoff was accurate as of December 27. After determining that the December 27 cutoff is accurate, the auditor must test whether all inventory received subsequent to the physical count, but on or before the balance sheet date, was added to inventory and accounts payable by the client.

Inventory in Transit A distinction in accounts payable must be made between acquisitions of inventory that are on an **FOB destination** basis and those that are made **FOB origin**. With the former, title passes to the buyer when it is received for inventory. Therefore, only inventory received on or before the balance sheet date should be included in inventory and accounts payable at year-end. When an acquisition is on an FOB origin basis, the inventory and related accounts payable must be recorded in the current period if shipment occurred on or before the balance sheet date.

Determining whether inventory has been acquired on an FOB destination or origin basis is done by examining vendors' invoices. The auditor should examine invoices for merchandise received shortly after year-end to determine whether they were on an FOB origin basis. For those that were, and when the shipment dates were on or before the balance sheet date, the inventory and related accounts payable must be recorded in the current period if the amounts are material.

Reliability of Evidence

OBJECTIVE 18-7
Distinguish the reliability of vendors' invoices, vendors' statements, and confirmations of accounts payable as audit evidence.

In deciding on the appropriate evidence to accumulate for verifying accounts payable, it is essential that the auditor understand the relative reliability of the three primary types of evidence ordinarily used: vendors' invoices, vendors' statements, and confirmations.

Distinction between Vendors' Invoices and Vendors' Statements In verifying the amount due to a vendor, the auditor should make a distinction between vendors' invoices and vendors' statements. In examining vendors' invoices and related supporting documents, such as receiving reports and purchase orders, the auditor gets highly reliable *evidence about individual transactions.* A vendor's statement is not as desirable as invoices for verifying individual transactions because a statement includes only the total amount of the transaction. The units acquired, price, freight, and other data are not included. However, a statement has the advantage of including the ending balance according to the vendor's records. Which of these two documents is better for verifying the correct balance in accounts payable? *The vendor's statement is superior for verifying accounts payable* because it includes the ending balance. The auditor could compare existing vendors' invoices with the client's list and still not uncover missing ones, which is the primary concern in accounts payable. Which of these two documents is better for testing acquisitions in tests of controls and substantive tests of transactions? *The vendor's invoice is superior for verifying transactions* because the auditor is verifying individual transactions and the invoice shows the details of the acquisitions.

Difference between Vendors' Statements and Confirmations The most important distinction between a vendor's statement and a confirmation of accounts payable is the source of the information. A vendor's statement has been prepared by an independent third party, but it is in the hands of the client at the time the auditor examines it. This provides the client with an opportunity to alter a vendor's statement or to not make certain statements available to the auditor. A confirmation of accounts payable, which normally is a request for an itemized statement sent directly to the CPA's office, provides the same information but can be regarded as more reliable. In addition, confirmations of accounts payable often include a request for information about notes and acceptances payable as well as consigned inventory that is owned by the vendor but stored on the client's premises. An illustration of a typical accounts payable confirmation request is given in Figure 18-4.

Because of the availability of vendors' statements and vendors' invoices, which are both relatively reliable evidence because they originate from a third party, the confirmation of accounts payable is less common than confirmation of accounts receivable. If the client has adequate internal controls and vendors' statements are available for examination, confirmations are normally not sent. However, when the client's internal controls are weak, when statements are not available, or when the auditor questions the client's integrity, it is desirable to send confirmation requests to vendors. Because of the emphasis on understatements of liability accounts, the accounts confirmed should include large accounts, active accounts, accounts with a zero balance, and a representative sample of all others.

In most instances in which accounts payable are confirmed, it is done shortly after the balance sheet date. However, if assessed control risk is low, it may be possible to confirm accounts payable at an interim date as a test of the effectiveness of internal controls. Then if the confirmations indicate that the internal controls are ineffective, it is possible to design other audit procedures to test accounts payable at year-end.

FIGURE 18-4   Accounts Payable Confirmation Request

ROGER MEAD, INC.   January 15, 2000
Jones Sales, Inc.
2116 Stewart Street
Wayneville, Kentucky 36021

Gentlemen:

Our auditors, Murray and Rogers, CPAs, are conducting an audit of our financial statements. For this purpose, please furnish them with the following information as of December 31, 1999.

(1) Itemized statements of our accounts payable to you showing all unpaid items;
(2) A complete list of any notes and acceptances payable to you (including any which have been discounted) showing the original date, dates due, original amount, unpaid balance, collateral, and endorsers; and
(3) An itemized list of your merchandise consigned to us.

Your prompt attention to this request will be appreciated. An envelope is enclosed for your reply.

                                                      Yours truly,

                                                      Phil Geriovini

                                                      Phil Geriovini, President

---

When vendors' statements are examined or confirmations are received, there must be a *reconciliation* of the statement or confirmation with the accounts payable list. Differences are often caused by inventory in transit, checks mailed by the client but not received by the vendor at the statement date, and delays in processing the accounting records. The reconciliation is of the same general nature as that discussed in Chapter 15 for accounts receivable. The documents typically used to reconcile the balances on the accounts payable list with the confirmations or vendors' statements include receiving reports, vendors' invoices, and cancelled checks.

Our discussion of tests of details of the account payable balance has focused heavily on the typical audit procedures performed, the documents and records examined, and the timing of the tests. We now briefly discuss sample sizes in the audit of accounts payable.

(margin note, handwritten) Can you use monetary unit sampling on A/P? No, will not hit zero balance accts.

Sample Size

Sample sizes for accounts payable tests vary considerably, depending on such factors as the materiality of accounts payable, number of accounts outstanding, assessed control risk, and results of the prior year. When a client's internal controls are weak, which is not uncommon for accounts payable, almost all population items must be verified. In other situations, minimal testing is needed.

Statistical sampling is less commonly used for the audit of accounts payable than for accounts receivable. It is more difficult to define the population and determine the population size in accounts payable. Because the emphasis is on omitted accounts payable, it is essential that the population include all potential payables.

SUMMARY

Figure 18-5 (p. 600) summarizes how the five types of audit tests are used to obtain audit assurance for transactions and accounts in the acquisition and payment cycle. Procedures to gain an understanding of internal control and tests of controls evaluate whether controls

FIGURE 18-5 Types of Audit Tests for the Acquisition and Payment Cycle (see Figure 18-1 on page 583 for accounts)

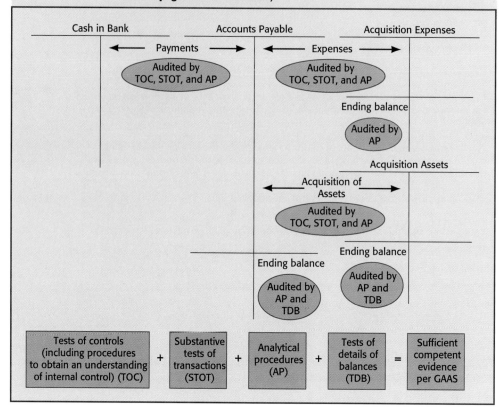

over transactions in the cycle are operating effectively to reduce control risk and thereby reduce substantive testing of ending balances in the related accounts. By combining all types of audit tests shown in Figure 18-5, the auditor obtains a higher overall assurance for transactions and accounts in the acquisition and payment cycle than the assurance obtained from any one test. To increase overall assurance for the cycle, the auditor can increase the assurance obtained from any one of the tests.

ESSENTIAL TERMS

Accounts payable master file—a computer file for maintaining a record for each vendor of individual acquisitions, cash disbursements, acquisition returns and allowances, and vendor balances

Accounts payable trial balance—a listing of the amount owed to each vendor at a point in time; prepared directly from the accounts payable master file

Acquisition and payment cycle—the transaction cycle that includes the acquisition of and payment for goods and services from suppliers outside the organization

Cutoff tests—tests to determine whether transactions recorded a few days before and after the balance sheet date are included in the correct period

Debit memo—a document indicating a reduction in the amount owed to a vendor because of returned goods or an allowance granted

FOB destination—shipping contract in which title to the goods passes to the buyer when the goods are received

FOB origin—shipping contract in which title to the goods passes to the buyer at the time that the goods are shipped

Purchase order—a document prepared by the purchasing department indicating the description, quantity, and related information for goods and services that the company intends to purchase

Purchase requisition—request by an authorized employee to the purchasing department to place an order for inventory and other items used by an entity

Receiving report—a document prepared by the receiving department at the time tangible goods are received, indicating the description of the goods, the quantity received, the date received, and other relevant data; it is part of the documentation necessary for payment to be made

Vendor's invoice—a document that specifies the details of an acquisition transaction and amount of money owed to the vendor for an acquisition

Vendor's statement—a statement prepared monthly by the vendor, which indicates the customer's beginning balance, acquisitions, payments, and ending balance

REVIEW QUESTIONS

18-1 (Objective 18-1) List five asset accounts, three liability accounts, and five expense accounts included in the acquisition and payment cycle for a typical manufacturing company.

18-2 (Objective 18-3) List one possible internal control for each of the six transaction-related audit objectives for cash disbursements. For each control, list a test of control to test its effectiveness.

18-3 (Objective 18-3) List one possible control for each of the six transaction-related audit objectives for acquisitions. For each control, list a test of control to test its effectiveness.

18-4 (Objective 18-3) Evaluate the following statement by an auditor concerning tests of acquisitions and cash disbursements: "In selecting the acquisitions and cash disbursements sample for testing, the best approach is to select a random month and test every transaction for the period. Using this approach enables me to thoroughly understand internal control because I have examined everything that happened during the period. As a part of the monthly test, I also test the beginning and ending bank reconciliations and prepare a proof of cash for the month. At the completion of these tests I feel I can evaluate the effectiveness of internal control."

18-5 (Objective 18-3) What is the importance of cash discounts to the client and how can the auditor verify whether they are being taken in accordance with company policy?

18-6 (Objective 18-3) What are the similarities and differences in the objectives of the following two procedures? (1) Select a random sample of receiving reports and trace them to related vendors' invoices and acquisitions journal entries, comparing the vendor's name, type of material and quantity acquired, and total amount of the acquisition. (2) Select a random sample of acquisitions journal entries and trace them to related vendors' invoices and receiving reports, comparing the vendor's name, type of material and quantity acquired, and total amount of the acquisition.

18-7 (Objectives 18-2, 18-3) If an audit client does not have prenumbered checks, what type of misstatement has a greater chance of occurring? Under the circumstances, what audit procedure can the auditor use to compensate for the weakness?

18-8 (Objective 18-2) What is meant by a voucher? Explain how its use can improve an organization's internal controls.

18-9 (Objective 18-2) Explain why most auditors consider the receipt of goods and services the most important point in the acquisition and payment cycle.

18-10 (Objectives 18-3, 18-6) Explain the relationship between tests of the acquisition and payment cycle and tests of inventory. Give specific examples of how these two types of tests affect each other.

18-11 (Objectives 18-3, 18-4) Explain the relationship between tests of the acquisition and payment cycle and tests of accounts payable. Give specific examples of how these two types of tests affect each other.

18-12 (Objective 18-6) The CPA examines all unrecorded invoices on hand as of February 29, 2000, the last day of field work. Which of the following misstatements is most likely to be uncovered by this procedure? Explain.

    a. Accounts payable are overstated at December 31, 1999.

b. Accounts payable are understated at December 31, 1999.

c. Operating expenses are overstated for the twelve months ended December 31, 1999.

d. Operating expenses are overstated for the two months ended February 29, 2000.*

18-13 (Objective 18-7)   Explain why it is common for auditors to send confirmation requests to vendors with "zero balances" on the client's accounts payable listing, but uncommon to follow the same approach in verifying accounts receivable.

18-14 (Objectives 18-2, 18-7)   Distinguish between a vendor's invoice and a vendor's statement. Which document should ideally be used as evidence in auditing acquisition transactions and which for verifying accounts payable balances? Why?

18-15 (Objective 18-7)   It is less common to confirm accounts payable at an interim date than accounts receivable. Explain why.

18-16 (Objective 18-6)   In testing the cutoff of accounts payable at the balance sheet date, explain why it is important that auditors coordinate their tests with the physical observation of inventory. What can the auditor do during the physical inventory to enhance the likelihood of an accurate cutoff?

18-17 (Objective 18-6)   Distinguish between FOB destination and FOB origin. What procedures should the auditor follow concerning acquisitions of inventory on an FOB origin basis near year-end?

■ MULTIPLE CHOICE QUESTIONS FROM CPA EXAMINATIONS

18-18 (Objective 18-3)   The following questions concern internal controls in the acquisition and payment cycle. Choose the best response.

a. Effective internal control over the purchasing of raw materials should usually include all of the following procedures *except*

(1) systematic reporting of product changes that will affect raw materials.

(2) determining the need for the raw materials prior to preparing the purchase order.

(3) obtaining third-party, written quality and quantity reports prior to payment for the raw materials.

(4) obtaining financial approval prior to making a commitment.

b. Budd, the purchasing agent of Lake Hardware Wholesalers, has a relative who owns a retail hardware store. Budd arranged for hardware to be delivered by manufacturers to the retail store on a COD basis, thereby enabling his relative to buy at Lake's wholesale prices. Budd was probably able to accomplish this because of Lake's poor internal control over

(1) purchase requisitions.

(2) cash receipts.

(3) perpetual inventory records.

(4) purchase orders.

c. Which of the following is an internal control that would prevent paid cash disbursement documents from being presented for payment a second time?

(1) Unsigned checks should be prepared by individuals who are responsible for signing checks.

(2) Cash disbursement documents should be approved by at least two responsible management officials.

(3) The date on cash disbursement documents should be within a few days of the date that the document is presented for payment.

(4) The official signing the check should compare the check with the documents and should deface the documents.

*AICPA adapted.

18-19 (Objectives 18-6, 18-7) The following questions concern accumulating evidence in the acquisition and payment cycle. Choose the best response.

   a. In comparing the confirmation of accounts payable with suppliers and confirmation of accounts receivable with debtors, the true statement is that
   (1) confirmation of accounts payable with suppliers is a more widely accepted auditing procedure than is confirmation of accounts receivable with debtors.
   (2) statistical sampling techniques are more widely accepted in the confirmation of accounts payable than in the confirmation of accounts receivable.
   (3) as compared with the confirmation of accounts payable, the confirmation of accounts receivable will tend to emphasize accounts with zero balances at the balance sheet date.
   (4) it is less likely that the confirmation request sent to the supplier will show the amount owed him than that the request sent to the debtor will show the amount due from him.

   b. Which of the following audit procedures is best for identifying unrecorded trade accounts payable?
   (1) Examining unusual relationships between monthly accounts payable balances and recorded cash payments.
   (2) Reconciling vendors' statements to the file of receiving reports to identify items received just prior to the balance sheet date.
   (3) Reviewing cash disbursements recorded subsequent to the balance sheet date to determine whether the related payables apply to the prior period.
   (4) Investigating payables recorded just prior to and just subsequent to the balance sheet date to determine whether they are supported by receiving reports.

   c. In auditing accounts payable, an auditor's procedures most likely would focus primarily on management's assertion of
   (1) existence or occurrence.
   (2) presentation and disclosure.
   (3) completeness.
   (4) valuation or allocation.

DISCUSSION QUESTIONS AND PROBLEMS

18-20 (Objective 18-3) Questions 1 through 8 are typically found in questionnaires used by auditors to obtain an understanding of internal control in the acquisition and payment cycle. In using the questionnaire for a client, a "yes" response to a question indicates a possible internal control, whereas a "no" indicates a potential weakness.

1. Is the purchasing function performed by personnel who are independent of the receiving and shipping functions and the payables and disbursing functions?
2. Are all vendors' invoices routed directly to accounting from the mailroom?
3. Are all receiving reports prenumbered and the numerical sequence checked by a person independent of check preparation?
4. Are all extensions, footings, discounts, and freight terms on vendors' invoices checked for accuracy?
5. Does a responsible employee review and approve the invoice account distribution before it is recorded in the acquisitions journal?
6. Are checks automatically posted in the cash disbursements journal as they are prepared?
7. Are all supporting documents properly cancelled at the time the checks are signed?
8. Is the custody of checks after signature and before mailing handled by an employee independent of all payable, disbursing, cash, and general ledger functions?

Required
   a. For each of the preceding questions, state the transaction-related audit objective(s) being fulfilled if the control is in effect.
   b. For each internal control, list a test of control to test its effectiveness.

c. For each of the preceding questions, identify the nature of the potential financial misstatement(s) if the control is not in effect.

d. For each of the potential misstatements in part c, list a substantive audit procedure that can be used to determine whether a material misstatement exists.

18-21 (Objective 18-3) Following are some of the tests of controls and substantive tests of transactions procedures commonly performed in the acquisition and payment cycle. Each is to be done on a sample basis.

1. Trace transactions recorded in the acquisitions journal to supporting documentation, comparing the vendor's name, total dollar amounts, and authorization for acquisition.
2. Account for a sequence of receiving reports and trace selected ones to related vendors' invoices and acquisitions journal entries.
3. Review supporting documents for clerical accuracy, propriety of account distribution, and reasonableness of expenditure in relation to the nature of the client's operations.
4. Examine documents in support of acquisition transactions to make sure that each transaction has an approved vendor's invoice, receiving report, and purchase order included.
5. Foot the cash disbursements journal, trace postings of the total to the general ledger, and trace postings of individual cash disbursements to the accounts payable master file.
6. Account for a numerical sequence of checks in the cash disbursements journal and examine all voided or spoiled checks for proper cancellation.
7. Prepare a proof of cash disbursements for an interim month.
8. Compare dates on cancelled checks with dates on the cash disbursements journal and the bank cancellation date.

Required

a. State whether each procedure above is primarily a test of control or substantive test of transactions.

b. State the purpose(s) of each procedure.

18-22 (Objectives 18-3, 18-6) The following misstatements are included in the accounting records of Westgate Manufacturing Company.

1. Telephone expense (account 2112) was unintentionally charged to repairs and maintenance (account 2121).
2. Acquisitions of raw materials are often not recorded until several weeks after the goods are received because receiving personnel fail to forward receiving reports to accounting. When pressure from a vendor's credit department is put on Westgate's accounting department, it searches for the receiving report, records the transactions in the acquisitions journal, and pays the bill.
3. The accounts payable clerk prepares a monthly check to Story Supply Company for the amount of an invoice owed and submits the unsigned check to the treasurer for payment along with related supporting documents that have already been approved. When she receives the signed check from the treasurer, she records it as a debit to accounts payable and deposits the check in a personal bank account for a company named Story Company. A few days later, she records the invoice in the acquisitions journal again, resubmits the documents and a new check to the treasurer, and sends the check to the vendor after it has been signed.
4. The amount of a check in the cash disbursements journal is recorded as $4,612.87 instead of $6,412.87.
5. The accounts payable clerk intentionally excluded from the cash disbursements journal seven larger checks written and mailed on December 26 to prevent cash in the bank from having a negative balance on the general ledger. They were recorded on January 2 of the subsequent year.
6. Each month, a fraudulent receiving report is submitted to accounting by an employee in the receiving department. A few days later, he sends Westgate an invoice for the quantity of goods ordered from a small company he owns and operates in the evening. A check is prepared, and the amount is paid when the receiving report and the vendor's invoice are matched by the accounts payable clerk.

Required

    a. For each misstatement, identify the transaction-related audit objective that was not met.

    b. For each misstatement, state a control that should have prevented it from occurring on a continuing basis.

    c. For each misstatement, state a substantive audit procedure that could uncover it.

18-23 (Objectives 18-5, 18-6, 18-7) The following auditing procedures were performed in the audit of accounts payable:

1. Examine supporting documents for cash disbursements several days before and after year-end.

2. Examine the acquisitions and cash disbursements journals for the last few days of the current period and first few days of the succeeding period, looking for large or unusual transactions.

3. Trace from the general ledger trial balance and supporting working papers to determine whether accounts payable, related parties, and other related assets and liabilities are properly included on the financial statements.

4. For liabilities that are payable in a foreign currency, determine the exchange rate and check calculations.

5. Discuss with the bookkeeper whether any amounts included on the accounts payable list are due to related parties, debit balances, or notes payable.

6. Obtain vendors' statements from the controller and reconcile to a listing of accounts payable.

7. Obtain vendors' statements directly from vendors and reconcile to the listing of accounts payable.

8. Obtain a list of accounts payable. Re-add and compare with the general ledger.

Required

    a. For each procedure, identify the type of audit evidence used.

    b. For each procedure, use the matrix below to identify which balance-related audit objective(s) were satisfied. (Procedure 1 is completed as an illustration.)

    c. Evaluate the need to have certain objectives satisfied by more than one audit procedure.

AUDIT PROCEDURE	BALANCE-RELATED AUDIT OBJECTIVE							
	Detail tie-in	Existence	Completeness	Accuracy	Classification	Cutoff	Obligations	Presentation and disclosure
1			X			X		
2								
3								
4								
5								
6								
7								
8								

18-24 (Objectives 18-3, 18-4)   In testing cash disbursements for the Jay Klein Company, you have obtained an understanding of internal control. The controls are reasonably good, and no unusual audit problems have arisen in previous years.

Although there are not many individuals in the accounting department, there is a reasonable separation of duties in the organization. There is a separate purchasing agent who has responsibility for ordering goods and a separate receiving department for counting the goods when they are received and for preparing receiving reports. There is a separation of duties between recording acquisitions and cash disbursements, and all information is recorded in the two journals independently. The controller reviews all supporting documents before signing the checks, and he immediately mails the check to the vendor. Check copies are used for subsequent recording.

All aspects of internal control seem satisfactory to you, and you perform minimum tests of 75 transactions as a means of assessing control risk. In your tests, you discover the following exceptions:

1. Two items in the acquisitions journal have been misclassified.
2. Three invoices had not been initialed by the controller, but there were no dollar misstatements evident in the transactions.
3. Five receiving reports were recorded in the acquisitions journal at least 2 weeks later than their date on the receiving report.
4. One invoice had been paid twice. The second payment was supported by a duplicate copy of the invoice. Both copies of the invoice had been marked "paid."
5. One check amount in the cash disbursements journal was for $100 less than the amount stated on the vendor's invoice.
6. One voided check was missing.
7. Two receiving reports for vendors' invoices were missing from the transaction packets. One vendor's invoice had an extension error, and the invoice had been initialed that the amount had been checked.

Required

    a. Identify whether each of 1 through 7 was a control test deviation, a monetary misstatement, or both.

    b. For each exception, identify which transaction-related audit objective was not met.

    c. What is the audit importance of each of these exceptions?

    d. What follow-up procedures would you use to determine more about the nature of each exception?

    e. How would each of these exceptions affect the balance of your audit? Be specific.

    f. Identify internal controls that should have prevented each misstatement.

18-25 (Objective 18-3)   You are the staff auditor testing the combined acquisitions and cash disbursements journal for a small audit client. The internal controls are regarded as reasonably effective, considering the number of personnel.

The in-charge auditor has decided that a sample of 80 items should be sufficient for this audit because of the excellent controls. He gives you the following instructions:

1. All transactions selected must exceed $100.
2. At least 50 of the transactions must be for acquisitions of raw material because these transactions are typically material.
3. It is not acceptable to include the same vendor in the sample more than once.
4. All vendors' invoices that cannot be located must be replaced with a new sample item.
5. Both checks and supporting documents are to be examined for the same transactions.
6. The sample must be random, after modifications for instructions 1 through 5.

Required

    a. Evaluate each of these instructions for testing acquisition and cash disbursements transactions.

    b. Explain the difficulties of applying each of these instructions to attributes sampling.

18-26 (Objective 18-3)   Each year near the balance sheet date, when the president of Bargon Construction, Inc., takes a 3-week vacation to Hawaii, she signs several checks to pay major bills during the period she is absent. Jack Morgan, head bookkeeper for the company, uses this practice to his advantage. Morgan makes out a check to himself for the amount of a large vendor's invoice, and because there is no acquisitions journal, he records the amount in the cash disbursements journal as an acquisition from the supplier listed on the invoice. He holds the check until several weeks into the subsequent period to make sure that the auditors do not get an opportunity to examine the cancelled check. Shortly after the first of the year when the president returns, Morgan resubmits the invoice for payment and again records the check in the cash disbursements journal. At that point, he marks the invoice "paid" and files it with all other paid invoices. Morgan has been following this practice successfully for several years and feels confident that he has developed a foolproof method.

Required

   a. What is the auditor's responsibility for discovering this type of embezzlement?
   b. What weaknesses exist in the client's internal control?
   c. What audit procedures are likely to uncover the fraud?

18-27 (Objective 18-6)   You were in the final stages of your audit of the financial statements of Ozine Corporation for the year ended December 31, 1999, when you were consulted by the corporation's president, who believes there is no point to your examining the year 2000 acquisitions journal and testing data in support of year 2000 entries. He stated that (a) bills pertaining to 1999 that were received too late to be included in the December acquisitions journal were recorded as of the year-end by the corporation by journal entry, (b) the internal auditor made tests after the year-end, and (c) he would furnish you with a letter certifying that there were no unrecorded liabilities.

Required

   a. Should a CPA's test for unrecorded liabilities be affected by the fact that the client made a journal entry to record 1999 bills that were received late? Explain.
   b. Should a CPA's test for unrecorded liabilities be affected by the fact that a letter is obtained in which a responsible management official certifies that to the best of his or her knowledge all liabilities have been recorded? Explain.
   c. Should a CPA's test for unrecorded liabilities be eliminated or reduced because of the internal audit tests? Explain.
   d. Assume that the corporation, which handled some government contracts, had no internal auditor but that an auditor for a federal agency spent 3 weeks auditing the records and was just completing his work at this time. How would the CPA's unrecorded liability test be affected by the work of the auditor for a federal agency?
   e. What sources in addition to the year 2000 acquisitions journal should the CPA consider to locate possible unrecorded liabilities?*

18-28 (Objectives 18-2, 18-3, 18-4, 18-6)   Because of the small size of the company and the limited number of accounting personnel, the Dry Goods Wholesale Company initially records all acquisitions of goods and services at the time cash disbursements are made. At the end of each quarter, when financial statements for internal purposes are prepared, accounts payable are recorded by adjusting journal entries. The entries are reversed at the beginning of the subsequent period. Except for the lack of an acquisitions journal, the controls over acquisitions are excellent for a small company. (There are adequate prenumbered documents for all acquisitions, proper approvals, and adequate internal verification wherever possible.)

Before the auditor arrives for the year-end audit, the bookkeeper prepares adjusting entries to record the accounts payable as of the balance sheet date. A list of all outstanding balances is prepared, by vendor, on an accounts payable listing and is given to the auditor. All vendors' invoices supporting the list are retained in a separate file for the auditor's use.

In the current year, the accounts payable balance has increased dramatically because of a severe cash shortage. (The cash shortage apparently arose from expansion of inventory and facilities rather than lack of sales.) Many accounts have remained unpaid for several months and the client is getting pressure from several vendors to pay the bills. Because the

*AICPA adapted.

company had a relatively profitable year, management is anxious to complete the audit as early as possible so that the audited statements can be used to obtain a large bank loan.

Required

    a. Explain how the lack of an acquisitions journal will affect the auditor's tests of controls and substantive tests of transactions for acquisitions and cash disbursements.

    b. What should the auditor use as a sampling unit in performing tests of acquisitions?

    c. Assuming no misstatements are discovered in the auditor's tests of controls and substantive tests of transactions for acquisitions and cash disbursements, how will that result affect the verification of accounts payable?

    d. Discuss the reasonableness of the client's request for an early completion of the audit and the implications of the request from the auditor's point of view.

    e. List the audit procedures that should be performed in the year-end audit of accounts payable to meet the cutoff objective.

    f. State your opinion as to whether it is possible to conduct an adequate audit in these circumstances.

18-29 (Objectives 18-6, 18-7)   Mincin, CPA, is the auditor of the Raleigh Corporation. Mincin is considering the audit work to be performed in the accounts payable area for the current year's engagement.

The prior year's working papers show that confirmation requests were mailed to 100 of Raleigh's 1,000 suppliers. The selected suppliers were based on Mincin's sample, which was designed to select accounts with large dollar balances. A substantial number of hours were spent by Raleigh and Mincin resolving relatively minor differences between the confirmation replies and Raleigh's accounting records. Alternative audit procedures were used for those suppliers who did not respond to the confirmation requests.

Required

    a. Identify the accounts payable balance-related audit objectives that Mincin must consider in determining the audit procedures to be followed.

    b. Identify situations in which Mincin should use accounts payable confirmations and discuss whether Mincin is required to use them.

    c. Discuss why the use of large dollar balances as the basis for selecting accounts payable for confirmation might not be the most effective approach and indicate what more effective procedures could be followed when selecting accounts payable for confirmation.*

18-30 (Objective 18-7)   As part of the June 30, 2000, audit of accounts payable of Milner Products Company, the auditor sent 22 confirmations of accounts payable to vendors in the form of requests for statements. Four of the statements were not returned by the vendors, and five vendors reported balances different from the amounts recorded in Milner's accounts payable master file. The auditor made duplicate copies of the five vendors' statements to maintain control of the independent information and turned the originals over to the client's accounts payable clerk to reconcile the differences. Two days later, the clerk returned the five statements to the auditor with the information on the working paper on page 609.

Required

    a. Evaluate the acceptability of having the client perform the reconciliations, assuming that the auditor intends to perform adequate additional tests.

    b. Describe the additional tests that should be performed for each of the five statements that included differences.

    c. What audit procedures should be performed for the nonresponses to the confirmation requests?

*AICPA adapted.

Statement 1	Balance per vendor's statement	$ 6,618.01
	Payment by Milner June 30, 2000	(4,601.01)
	Balance per master file	$ 2,017.00
Statement 2	Balance per vendor's statement	$ 9,618.93
	Invoices not received by Milner	(2,733.18)
	Payment by Milner June 15, 2000	(1,000.00)
	Balance per master file	$ 5,885.75
Statement 3	Balance per vendor's statement	$26,251.80
	Balance per master file	(20,516.11)
	Difference cannot be located because the vendor failed to provide details of its account balance	$ 5,735.69
Statement 4	Balance per vendor's statement	$ 6,170.15
	Credit memo issued by vendor on July 15, 2000	(2,360.15)
	Balance per master file	$ 3,810.00
Statement 5	Balance per vendor's statement	$ 8,619.21
	Payment by Milner July 3, 2000	(3,000.00)
	Unlocated difference not followed up because of minor amount	215.06
	Balance per master file	$ 5,834.27

18-31 (Objective 18-6) The physical inventory for Ajak Manufacturing was taken on December 30, 1999, rather than December 31, because the client had to operate the plant for a special order the last day of the year. At the time of the client's physical count, you observed that acquisitions represented by receiving report number 2631 and all preceding ones were included in the physical count, whereas inventory represented by succeeding numbers was excluded. On the evening of December 31, you stopped by the plant and noted that inventory represented by receiving report numbers 2632 through 2634 was received subsequent to the physical count, but before the end of the year. You later noted that the final inventory on the financial statements contained only those items included in the physical count. In testing accounts payable at December 31, 1999, you obtain a schedule from the client to aid you in testing the adequacy of the cutoff. The schedule below includes the information that you have not yet resolved.

			INFORMATION ON THE VENDOR'S INVOICE		
Receiving Report Number	Amount of Vendor's Invoice	Amount Presently Included in or Excluded from Accounts Payable*	Invoice Date	Shipping Date	FOB Origin or Destination
2631	$2,619.26	Included	12-30-99	12-30-99	Origin
2632	3,709.16	Excluded	12-26-99	12-15-99	Destination
2633	5,182.31	Included	12-31-99	12-26-99	Origin
2634	6,403.00	Excluded	12-16-99	12-27-99	Destination
2635	8,484.91	Included	12-28-99	12-31-99	Origin
2636	5,916.20	Excluded	01-03-00	12-31-99	Destination
2637	7,515.50	Excluded	01-05-00	12-26-99	Origin
2638	2,407.87	Excluded	12-31-99	01-03-00	Origin

*All entries to record inventory acquisitions are recorded by the client as a debit to purchases and a credit to accounts payable.

Required
a. Explain the relationship between inventory and accounts payable cutoff.
b. For each of the receiving reports, state the misstatement in inventory or accounts payable, if any exists, and prepare an adjusting entry to correct the financial statements, if a misstatement exists.
c. Which of the misstatements in part b are most important? Explain.

PART I

18-32 (Objectives 18-2, 18-3, 18-4, 18-6, 18-7) You are provided with the following information about internal control for materials acquisitions for the Johnson Machinery Company, a medium-sized firm that builds special machinery to order.

Materials purchase requisitions are first approved by the plant foreman, who then sends them to the purchasing department. A prenumbered purchase order is prepared in triplicate by one of several department employees. Employees account for all purchase order numbers. The original copy is sent to the vendor. The receiving department is sent the second copy to use for a receiving report. The third copy is kept on file in the purchasing department along with the requisition.

Delivered materials are immediately sent to the storeroom. The receiving report, which is a copy of the purchase order, is sent to the purchasing department. A copy of the receiving report is sent to the storeroom. Materials are issued to factory employees subsequent to a verbal request by one of the foremen.

When the mailroom clerk receives vendors' invoices, he forwards them to the purchasing department employee who placed the order. The invoice is compared with the purchase order on file for price and terms by the employee. The invoice quantity is compared with the receiving department's report. After checking footings, extensions, and discounts, the employee indicates approval for payment by initialing the invoice. The invoice is then forwarded to the accounting department. Vendor name, date, gross and net invoice amounts, and account distribution are key-entered into the computer system for updating the acquisitions journal and accounts payable master file, and filed by payment date due. The vendor's invoice is filed in the accounting department. The purchase order and receiving report are filed in the purchasing department.

The accounting department requisitions prenumbered checks from the cashier. They are manually prepared and then returned to the cashier, who puts them through the check-signing machine. After accounting for the sequence of numbers, the cashier sends the checks to the accounting department, where they are key-entered for recording cash disbursements and updating accounts payable. The checks are placed in envelopes and sent to the mailroom. At the end of each month, a listing of the accounts payable master file is printed and the total is compared with the general ledger balance. Any differences disclosed are investigated.

Required

 a. Prepare a flowchart for the acquisition and payment cycle for Johnson Machinery Company.

 b. List the controls in existence for each of the six transaction-related audit objectives for acquisitions.

 c. For each control in part b, list one test of control audit procedure to verify its effectiveness.

 d. List the most important internal control weaknesses for acquisitions and cash disbursements.

 e. Design an audit program to test internal control. The program should include, but not be limited to, the tests of controls from part c and procedures to compensate for the weaknesses in part d.

PART II

In confirming accounts payable at December 31, 2000, the following procedures are suggested to you for the Johnson Machinery Company.

 1. Obtain a list of accounts payable at December 31, 2000, from the client and

  (a) foot the list.

  (b) compare the total with balance shown in the general ledger.

  (c) compare the amounts shown on the list with the balances in the accounts payable master file.

 2. Select accounts to confirm.

  (a) Select each account with a balance payable in excess of $2,000.

  (b) Select a random sample of 50 other accounts over $100.

(c) Indicate the accounts to be confirmed on the accounts payable list, make a copy of the list, and give it to the accounts payable clerk along with instructions to type the vendor's name, address, and balance due on confirmations.

3. Compare the confirmations with the accounts payable master file.
4. Have the client's controller sign each confirmation.
5. Have the accounts payable clerk insert the confirmations and return envelopes addressed to the CPA firm in the client's envelopes. The envelopes are also to be stamped and sealed by the clerk. This should all be done under the auditor's control.
6. Mail the confirmations.

Required

Assume that the results of tests of controls in Part I support your preliminary assessment of control risk in the acquisition and payment cycle. Evaluate the procedures for confirming accounts payable.

18-33 (Objectives 18-2, 18-3, 18-4, 18-6)   The following tests of controls and substantive tests of transactions audit procedures for acquisitions and cash disbursements are to be used in the audit of Ward Publishing Company. You have concluded that internal control appears effective and a reduced assessed control risk is likely to be cost beneficial. Ward's active involvement in the business, good separation of duties, and a competent controller and other employees are factors affecting your opinion.

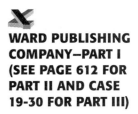

WARD PUBLISHING COMPANY—PART I (SEE PAGE 612 FOR PART II AND CASE 19-30 FOR PART III)

Tests of Controls and Substantive Tests of Transactions Audit Procedures for Acquisitions and Cash Disbursements

1. Foot and crossfoot the acquisitions and cash disbursements journals for 2 months and trace totals to postings in the general ledger.
2. Scan the acquisitions and cash disbursements journals for all months and investigate any unusual entries.
3. Reconcile cash disbursements per books to cash disbursements per bank statement for one month.
4. Examine evidence that the bank reconciliation is prepared by the controller.
5. Determine by observation that a check protector is in use.
6. Inquire and observe whether the accounts payable master file balances are periodically reconciled to vendors' statements by the controller.
7. Examine the log book as evidence that the numerical sequence of checks is accounted for by someone independent of the preparation function.
8. Inquire and observe that checks are mailed by D. Ward or someone under his supervision after he signs checks.
9. Examine initials indicating that the controller balances the accounts payable master file to the general ledger monthly.
10. Select a sample of entries in the cash disbursements journal, and
   a. obtain related cancelled checks and compare with entry for payee, date, and amount, and examine signature endorsement.
   b. obtain vendors' invoices, receiving reports, and purchase orders, and
      (1) examine vendors' invoices to determine that all supporting documents are attached.
      (2) determine that documents agree with the cash disbursements journal.
      (3) compare vendors' names, amounts, and dates with entries.
      (4) determine whether a discount was taken when appropriate.
      (5) examine vendors' invoices for initials indicating an independent review of chart of account codings.
      (6) examine reasonableness of cash disbursements and account codings.
      (7) review invoices for approval of acquisitions by Ward.
      (8) review purchase orders and/or purchase requisitions for proper approval.
      (9) verify prices and recalculate footings and extensions on invoices.
      (10) compare quantities and descriptions on purchase orders, receiving reports, and vendors' invoices to the extent applicable.

(11) examine vendors' invoices and receiving reports to determine that the check numbers are included and the documents are marked "paid" at the time of check signing.

c. Trace postings to the accounts payable master file for name, amount, and date.

11. Select a sample of receiving reports issued during the year and trace to vendors' invoices and entries in the acquisitions journal.

a. Compare type of merchandise, name of vendor, date received, quantities, and amounts.

b. If the transaction is indicated in the acquisitions journal as paid, trace check number to entry in cash disbursements journal. If unpaid, investigate reasons.

c. Trace transactions to accounts payable master file, comparing name, amount, and date.

Required

Prepare all parts of a sampling data sheet (such as the one on p. 461) through the planned sample size for the above audit program, assuming that a line item in the cash disbursements journal is used for the sampling unit. Use either nonstatistical or attributes sampling. For all procedures for which the line item in the cash disbursements journal is not an appropriate sampling unit, assume that audit procedures were performed on a nonsampling basis. For all tests of controls, use a tolerable exception rate of 5 percent, and for all substantive tests of transactions, use a rate of 6 percent. Use an ARACR of 10 percent, which is considered medium. Plan for an estimated population exception rate of 1 percent for tests of controls and 0 percent for substantive tests of transactions.

Prepare the data sheet using the microcomputer (instructor option—also applies to Part II).

PART II

Assume a sample size of 50 for all procedures in Part I, regardless of your answers in Part I. For other procedures, assume that an adequate sample size for the circumstance was selected. The only exceptions in your audit tests for all tests of controls and substantive tests of transactions audit procedures are as follows:

1. Procedure 2—Two large transactions were identified as being unusual. Investigation determined that they were authorized acquisitions of fixed assets. They were both correctly recorded.

2. Procedure 10b(1)—A purchase order had not been attached to a vendor's invoice. The purchase order was found in a separate file and determined to be approved and appropriate.

3. Procedure 10b(5)—Six vendors' invoices were not initialed as being internally verified. Three actual misclassifications existed. The controller explained that he often did not review codings because of the competence of the accounting clerk doing the coding, and was surprised at the mistakes.

Required

a. Complete the sampling data sheet from Part I using either nonstatistical or attributes sampling.

b. Explain the effect of the exceptions on tests of details of accounts payable. Which balance-related audit objectives are affected, and how do those objectives, in turn, affect the audit of accounts payable?

c. Given your tests of controls and substantive tests of transactions results, write an audit program for tests of details of balances for accounts payable. Assume:
(1) the client provided a list of accounts payable, prepared from the master file.
(2) acceptable audit risk for accounts payable is high.
(3) inherent risk for accounts payable is low.
(4) analytical procedure results were excellent.

COMPLETING THE TESTS IN THE ACQUISITION AND PAYMENT CYCLE: VERIFICATION OF SELECTED ACCOUNTS

19

LEARNING OBJECTIVES

After studying this chapter, you should be able to

19-1 Recognize the many accounts in the acquisition and payment cycle.

19-2 Design and perform audit tests of property, plant, and equipment and related accounts.

19-3 Design and perform audit tests of prepaid expenses.

19-4 Design and perform audit tests of accrued liabilities.

19-5 Design and perform audit tests of income and expense accounts.

IMPROPER CLASSIFICATIONS HIDE A GREATER NET LOSS

TV Communications Network (TVCN), a Denver-based wireless cable television company, materially understated losses in its 1992 financial statements by improperly recording $2.5 million of expenses as a direct decrease in stockholders' equity. The misstatement took the company from an actual 1992 net loss of $4.7 million to a reported loss of only $2.2 million.

According to the investigation by the SEC, the expenses charged to equity were from disbursements for the development and distribution of brochures promoting the company's business prospects. The payments should have been expensed and reflected in the income statement as advertising expenses.

The internal controls associated with the advertising expenses were clearly inadequate. TVCN typically did not have invoices or other documentation available when payments were made by the company's president, who controlled the bank account. Because of the lack of adequate documentation, when the financial statements were prepared, TVCN employees responsible for recording the expenses did not have sufficient information to properly classify the disbursements. The SEC found that even when documentation was available, the accounts where the transactions were recorded conflicted with the supporting documentation.

Unfortunately, TVCN's auditor relied on inquiry of the company president as the primary evidence about the nature of the advertising payments. In his substantive testing of transactions exceeding $10,000, the auditor relied on the company controller to identify all transactions meeting the criteria for review. Needless-to-say, the controller didn't present all transactions meeting the $10,000 scope. As you might expect, the SEC brought charges against the auditor for failing to comply with generally accepted auditing standards.

Source: *Accounting and Auditing Enforcement Release No. 534,* Commerce Clearing House, Inc., Chicago.

The last chapter noted that transactions in the acquisition and payment cycle affect several accounts. Acquisitions of assets affect supplies, property, plant and equipment, and prepaid expenses accounts, to name a few. In addition, payments made for services incurred affect many expense accounts. This chapter continues the discussion of the acquisition and payment cycle by highlighting unique audit issues related to other accounts commonly found in the acquisition and payment cycles of most businesses.

The opening vignette about TVCN highlights the importance of understanding the nature of acquisition and payment cycle transactions. Because transactions in this cycle affect numerous accounts in both the balance sheet and the income statement, improperly classified transactions may significantly affect reported results, as they did for TVCN. Therefore, auditors must understand the nature of transactions flowing through the acquisition and payment cycle so that they can effectively evaluate the accounts in the cycle.

Federal Acquisitions Regulations

TYPES OF OTHER ACCOUNTS IN THE ACQUISITION AND PAYMENT CYCLE

OBJECTIVE 19-1
Recognize the many accounts in the acquisition and payment cycle.

Table 19-1 highlights many of the typical accounts associated with transactions in the acquisition and payment cycle. These accounts are common in many types of businesses. As the nature of the industry or the client's business becomes more unique, however, the types of assets, expenses, and liabilities change.

The methodology associated with auditing these accounts is similar to the audits of other accounts discussed in earlier chapters. Figure 19-1 highlights that methodology, which is similar to the methodology shown for the audit of accounts payable in Chapter 18.

The last chapter presented an overview of typical tests of controls and substantive tests of transactions for acquisition and payment cycle transactions, as well as commonly used analytical procedures and tests of details of balances for accounts payable. Later chapters highlight audit issues unique to cash, inventory, and costs of goods sold, which are accounts commonly associated with acquisition and payment cycle transactions. This chapter discusses unique issues for some of the other key accounts in this cycle. In this chapter, we take a closer look at the audit of property, plant, and equipment; prepaid expenses; other liabilities; and income and expense accounts.

TABLE 19-1	Accounts Typically Associated with Acquisition and Payment Cycle Transactions	
Assets	**Expenses**	**Liabilities**
Cash	Cost of goods sold	Accounts payable
Inventory	Rent expense	Rent payable
Supplies	Property taxes	Accrued professional fees
Property, plant, and equipment	Income tax expense	Accrued property taxes
Patents, trademarks, and copyrights	Insurance expense	Other accrued expenses
Prepaid rent	Professional fees	Income taxes payable
Prepaid taxes	Retirement benefits	
Prepaid insurance	Utilities	

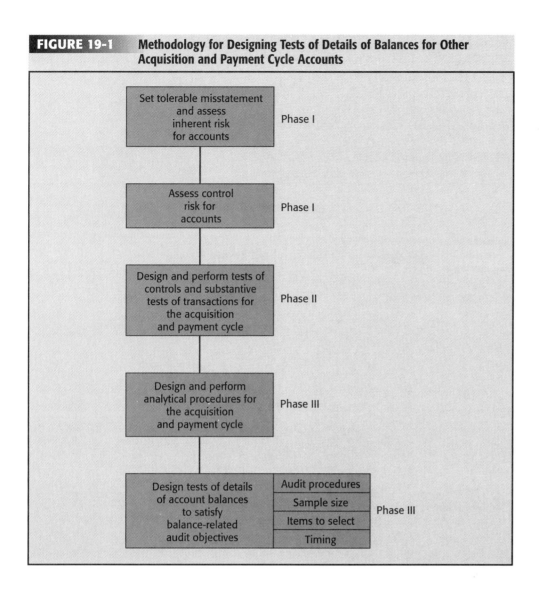

FIGURE 19-1 Methodology for Designing Tests of Details of Balances for Other Acquisition and Payment Cycle Accounts

Set tolerable misstatement and assess inherent risk for accounts — Phase I

Assess control risk for accounts — Phase I

Design and perform tests of controls and substantive tests of transactions for the acquisition and payment cycle — Phase II

Design and perform analytical procedures for the acquisition and payment cycle — Phase III

Design tests of details of account balances to satisfy balance-related audit objectives — Phase III

| Audit procedures |
| Sample size |
| Items to select |
| Timing |

AUDIT OF PROPERTY, PLANT, AND EQUIPMENT

We focus first on issues associated with auditing property, plant, and equipment accounts because many transactions in the acquisition and payment cycle are likely to affect these accounts. Property, plant, and equipment are assets that have expected lives of more than 1 year, are used in the business, and are not acquired for resale. The intent to use the assets as part of the operation of the client's business and their expected lives of more than 1 year are the significant characteristics that distinguish these assets from inventory, prepaid expenses, and investments. Table 19-2 (p. 616) shows examples of some of the typical classifications of property, plant, and equipment accounts.

Because the audits of these property, plant, and equipment accounts are similar, this section focuses on auditing manufacturing equipment to illustrate an approach to auditing all types of property, plant, and equipment accounts. When there are significant differences in the verification of other types of property, plant, and equipment accounts, the differences are briefly discussed.

The accounts commonly used for manufacturing equipment are illustrated in Figure 19-2 (p. 616). The relationship of manufacturing equipment to the acquisition and payment cycle is apparent by examining the debits to the asset account. Because the source of debits in

> **OBJECTIVE 19-2**
> Design and perform audit tests of property, plant, and equipment and related accounts.

Overview of Equipment-Related Accounts

TABLE 19-2	Classifications of Property, Plant, and Equipment Accounts

Land and land improvements
Buildings and building improvements
Manufacturing equipment
Furniture and fixtures
Autos and trucks
Leasehold improvements
Construction-in-process for property, plant, and equipment

Emphasis on current yr. acquisitions

Subsidiary of Equipment.

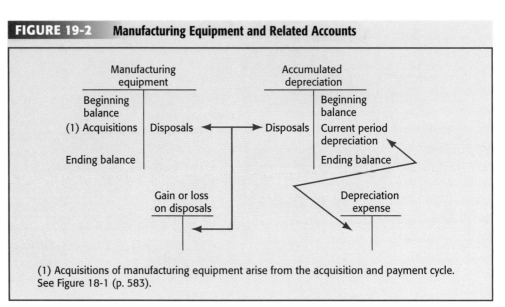

FIGURE 19-2 Manufacturing Equipment and Related Accounts

(1) Acquisitions of manufacturing equipment arise from the acquisition and payment cycle. See Figure 18-1 (p. 583).

the asset account is the acquisitions journal, the accounting system has already been tested for recording current-period additions to manufacturing equipment as part of the tests of the acquisition and payment cycle studied in the last chapter. Because equipment additions are infrequent and may be subject to special controls, such as board of directors approval, the auditor may decide not to rely heavily on these tests.

The primary accounting record for manufacturing equipment and other property, plant, and equipment accounts is generally a **fixed asset master file**. The contents of the fixed asset master file must be understood for a meaningful study of the audit of manufacturing equipment. The master file is composed of a set of records, one for each piece of equipment and other types of property owned. In turn, each record includes descriptive information, date of acquisition, original cost, current-year depreciation, and accumulated depreciation for the property. The totals for all records in the master file equal the general ledger balances for the related accounts. The master file will also contain information about property acquired and disposed of during the year. For disposals, proceeds, gains, and losses will be included.

Manufacturing equipment is normally audited differently from current asset accounts for three reasons: (1) there are usually fewer current period acquisitions of manufacturing equipment, (2) the amount of any given acquisition is often material, and (3) the equipment is likely to be kept and maintained in the accounting records for several years. Because of these differences, the emphasis in auditing manufacturing equipment is on the verification of current-period acquisitions rather than on the balance in the account carried forward from the preceding year. In addition, the expected life of assets over 1 year requires depreciation and accumulated depreciation accounts, as shown in Figure 19-2, which are verified as a part of the audit of the assets. Finally, equipment may be sold or disposed of, triggering a gain or loss entry that the auditor may need to verify.

Although the approach to verifying manufacturing equipment is dissimilar from that used for current assets, several other asset accounts are verified in much the same manner. These include patents, copyrights, catalog costs, and all property, plant, and equipment accounts.

In the audit of manufacturing equipment and related accounts, it is helpful to separate the tests into the following categories:

• Analytical procedures
• Verification of current-year acquisitions
• Verification of current-year disposals
• Verification of the ending balance in the asset account
• Verification of depreciation expense
• Verification of the ending balance in accumulated depreciation

The next several sections highlight the use of these categories of tests in the audit of manufacturing equipment, depreciation expense, accumulated depreciation, and gain or loss on disposal accounts.

As in all audit areas, the nature of the analytical procedures depends on the nature of the client's operations. Table 19-3 illustrates the type of ratio and trend analysis often performed for manufacturing equipment.

Analytical Procedures

As you can see, most of the typical analytical procedures performed relate to assessing the likelihood of material misstatements in the depreciation expense and accumulated depreciation accounts. In a later section, we focus on other substantive tests that are often performed for these accounts.

TABLE 19-3	Analytical Procedures for Manufacturing Equipment
Analytical Procedure	**Possible Misstatement**
Compare depreciation expense divided by gross manufacturing equipment cost with previous years.	Misstatement in depreciation expense and accumulated depreciation.
Compare accumulated depreciation divided by gross manufacturing equipment cost with previous years.	Misstatement in accumulated depreciation.
Compare monthly or annual repairs and maintenance, supplies expense, small tools expense, and similar accounts with previous years.	Expensing amounts that should be capitalized.
Compare gross manufacturing cost divided by some measure of production with previous years.	Idle equipment or equipment that has been disposed of, but not written off.

The proper recording of current-year additions is important because of the long-term effect the assets have on the financial statements. The failure to capitalize a fixed asset, or the recording of an acquisition at the improper amount, affects the balance sheet until the company disposes of the asset. The income statement is affected until the asset is fully depreciated.

Verification of Current-Year Acquisitions

Because of the importance of current-period acquisitions in the audit of manufacturing equipment, seven of the nine balance-related audit objectives for tests of details of balances are used as a frame of reference. (Realizable value and presentation and disclosure are discussed in connection with the verification of ending balances.)

The balance-related audit objectives and common audit tests are shown in Table 19-4. As in all other audit areas, the actual audit tests and sample size depend heavily on tolerable misstatement, inherent risk, and assessed control risk. Tolerable misstatement is of special importance for verifying current-year additions. These transactions vary from immaterial amounts in some years to a large number of significant acquisitions in others. Completeness, accuracy, and classification are usually the major objectives for this part of the audit.

The starting point for the verification of current-year acquisitions is normally a schedule obtained from the client of all acquisitions recorded in the general ledger during the year. A typical schedule lists each addition separately and includes the date of the acquisition, vendor, description, notation of new or used, life of the asset for depreciation purposes, depreciation method, and cost. The client obtains this information from the property master file.

In studying Table 19-4, one should recognize the importance of examining vendors' invoices and related documents in verifying acquisitions of manufacturing equipment. In fact, the most common audit test to verify additions is to examine vendors' invoices and receiving reports. Additional testing besides that which is done as a part of the tests of

TABLE 19-4	Balance-Related Audit Objectives and Tests of Details of Balances for Manufacturing Equipment Additions	
Balance-Related Audit Objective	**Common Tests of Details of Balances Procedures**	**Comments**
Current-year acquisitions in the acquisitions schedule agree with related master file amounts, and the total agrees with the general ledger (detail tie-in).	Foot the acquisitions schedule. Trace the total to the general ledger. Trace the individual acquisitions to the master file for amounts and descriptions.	These tests should be limited unless controls are weak. All increases in the general ledger balance for the year should reconcile to the schedule.
Current-year acquisitions as listed exist (existence).	Examine vendors' invoices and receiving reports. Physically examine assets.	It is uncommon to physically examine acquisitions unless controls are weak or amounts are material.
Existing acquisitions are recorded (completeness).	Examine vendors' invoices of closely related accounts such as repairs and maintenance to uncover items that should be manufacturing equipment. Review lease and rental agreements.	This objective is one of the most important ones for manufacturing equipment.
Current-year acquisitions as listed are accurate (accuracy).	Examine vendors' invoices.	Extent depends on inherent risk and effectiveness of internal controls.
Current-year acquisitions as listed are properly classified (classification).	Examine vendors' invoices in manufacturing equipment account to uncover items that should be classified as office equipment, part of the buildings, or repairs. Examine vendors' invoices of closely related accounts such as repairs to uncover items that should be manufacturing equipment. Examine rent and lease expense for capitalizable leases.	The objective is closely related to tests for completeness. It is done in conjunction with that objective and tests for accuracy.
Current-year acquisitions are recorded in the proper period (cutoff).	Review transactions near the balance sheet date for proper period.	Usually done as a part of accounts payable cutoff tests.
The client has rights to current-year acquisitions (rights).	Examine vendors' invoices.	Ordinarily no problem for equipment. Property deeds, abstracts, and tax bills are frequently examined for land or major buildings.

controls and substantive tests of transactions is often considered necessary because of the complexity of many equipment transactions and the materiality of the amounts. It is ordinarily unnecessary to examine supporting documentation for each addition, but it is normal to verify large and unusual transactions for the entire year as well as a representative sample of typical additions. The extent of the verification depends on the auditor's assessed control risk for acquisitions and the materiality of the additions. The events described in the following box highlight the importance of the auditor understanding the nature of large acquisitions.

AUDIT THAT WHICH IS UNCOMFORTABLE!

"Although this landscaping plan is expensive, the project is long overdue. I heartily approve!" wrote the president of a West Coast company in an internal memo.

One year later, the internal audit department conducted a routine review of expenditures for the relandscaping of the company's corporate headquarters. When the auditors went to the facilities department to get the contract, design blueprint, bidding records, and other supporting documents, the manager informed them that the relandscaping had not been administered by his department, but by the department's vice president and the recently retired former president.

The auditors decided to probe further because the landscaping cost of $1,000,000 seemed excessive, there was no competitive bidding, and the contract was administered by high-level executives rather than those usually administering such contracts.

The contractor initially defended his pricing as reasonable, because of adverse soil and site condition. However, after several intense meetings and discussion of possible legal action, the contractor reluctantly disclosed the true circumstances of the transaction. He was instructed by the vice president and former president to price the project so that it would also cover extensive landscaping and building renovation at each of their homes. The internal auditors' review of the contractor's records confirmed that excess charges of almost $600,000 covered the cost of a pool, hot tub, deck, marble patio, sprinkler system, fountain, dock, landscaping, and extensive building renovation at the homes of both executives. The contractor also said that the former president had contacted him during the audit to discourage cooperation.

The company went public with the audit findings, and the investigative file was turned over to the prosecutor. As a result of their no contest pleas, the two executives were convicted of obtaining money under false pretenses. Virtually all losses were recovered through successful bonding claims. This situation highlights the importance of auditors following up on matters that make them feel uncomfortable.

Source: Courtenay Thompson, "Fraud in the Executive Suite." This article was adapted from pp. 68–69 of the October 1993 issue of *Internal Auditor*, published by The Institute of Internal Auditors, Inc.

Tests for acquisitions are accomplished by comparing the charges on vendors' invoices with recorded amounts. The auditor must know the client's capitalization policies to determine whether acquisitions are recorded in accordance with generally accepted accounting principles (GAAP) and are treated consistently with those of the preceding year. For example, many clients automatically expense items that are less than a certain amount, such as $500. The auditor should be alert for the possibility of material transportation and installation costs, as well as the trade-in of existing equipment.

In conjunction with testing current-period additions for existence and accuracy, the auditor should also review recorded transactions for proper classification. In some cases, amounts recorded as manufacturing equipment should be classified as office equipment or as a part of the building. There is also the possibility that the client has improperly capitalized repairs, rents, or similar expenses. Recall from the opening vignette how poor internal controls over the document preparation at TVCN resulted in significant misclassifications of disbursement transactions.

The inclusion of transactions that should properly be recorded as assets in repairs and maintenance expense, lease expense, supplies, small tools, and similar accounts is a common client error. The error results from lack of understanding of GAAP and some clients' desire to avoid income taxes. The likelihood of these types of misclassifications should be evaluated in conjunction with obtaining an understanding of internal control in the acquisition and payment cycle. If the auditor concludes that material misstatements are likely, it may be necessary to vouch the larger amounts debited to the expense accounts. It is a common practice to do this as a regular part of the audit of the property, plant, and equipment accounts.

Verification of Current-Year Disposals

Transactions involving the disposal of manufacturing equipment are often misstated because company internal controls often lack a formal method to inform management of the sale, trade-in, abandonment, or theft of recorded machinery and equipment. If the client fails to record disposals, the original cost of the manufacturing equipment account will be overstated indefinitely, and the net book value will be overstated until the asset is fully depreciated. Formal methods of tracking disposals and provisions for proper authorization of the sale or other disposal of manufacturing equipment help reduce the risk of misstatement. Finally, there should be adequate internal verification of recorded disposals to make sure that assets are correctly removed from the accounting records.

The auditor's main objectives in the verification of the sale, trade-in, or abandonment of manufacturing equipment are to gather sufficient evidence that (1) existing disposals are recorded and (2) disposals are accurately recorded. The starting point for verifying disposals is the client's schedule of recorded disposals. The schedule typically includes the date when the asset was disposed of, the name of the person or firm acquiring the asset, the selling price, the original cost of the asset, the acquisition date, and the accumulated depreciation of the asset. Detail tie-in tests of the schedule are necessary, including footing the schedule, tracing the totals on the schedule to the recorded disposals in the general ledger, and tracing the cost and accumulated depreciation of the disposals to the property master file.

Because the failure to record disposals of manufacturing equipment no longer used in the business can significantly affect the financial statements, *the search for unrecorded disposals is essential*. The nature and adequacy of the controls over disposals affect the extent of the search. The following procedures are often used for verifying disposals:

- Review whether newly acquired assets replace existing assets.
- Analyze gains and losses on the disposal of assets and miscellaneous income for receipts from the disposal of assets.
- Review plant modifications and changes in product line, property taxes, or insurance coverage for indications of deletions of equipment.
- Make inquiries of management and production personnel about the possibility of the disposal of assets.

When an asset is sold or disposed of without having been traded in for a replacement asset, the *accuracy* of the transaction can be verified by examining the related sales invoice and property master file. The auditor should compare the cost and accumulated depreciation in the master file with the recorded entry in the general journal and recompute the gain or loss on the disposal of the asset for comparison with the accounting records. When *trade-in of an asset for a replacement* occurs, the auditor should be sure that the new asset is properly capitalized and the replaced asset properly eliminated from the records, considering the book value of the asset traded in and the additional cost of the new asset.

Verification of Ending Balance of Asset Account

Two of the auditor's objectives when auditing manufacturing equipment include determining that (1) all equipment owned is recorded and (2) all recorded equipment physically exists on the balance sheet date. In designing audit tests to meet these objectives, the auditor first considers the nature of internal controls over manufacturing equipment. Ideally, the auditor is able to conclude that controls are strong so that the auditor can rely on balances carried forward from the prior year. Important controls include the use of a master file for individual fixed assets, adequate physical controls over assets that are easily movable (such as computers, tools, and vehicles), assignment of identification numbers to each plant asset, and periodic physical count of fixed assets and their reconciliation by accounting personnel. A formal method of informing the accounting department of all disposals of fixed assets is also an important control over the balance of assets carried forward into the current year.

Usually, the auditor does not obtain a list from the client of all assets included in the ending balance of manufacturing equipment. Instead, audit tests are determined on the basis of the master file.

Typically, the first audit step concerns the detail tie-in objective: manufacturing equipment as listed in the master file agrees with the general ledger. Examining a printout of the master file that totals to the general ledger balance is ordinarily sufficient. The auditor may choose to use audit software to foot an electronic version of the master file or manually test-foot a few pages.

After assessing control risk for the existence objective, the auditor must decide whether it is necessary to verify the existence of individual items of manufacturing equipment included in the master file. If the auditor believes there is a high likelihood of significant missing fixed assets that are still recorded on the accounting records, an appropriate procedure is to select a sample from the master file and examine the actual assets. In rare cases, the auditor may believe it is necessary that the client take a complete physical inventory of fixed assets to make sure they actually exist. If a physical inventory is taken, the auditor normally observes the count.

Ordinarily, it is unnecessary to test the accuracy or classification of fixed assets recorded in prior periods because presumably they were verified in previous audits at the time they were acquired. But the auditor should be aware that companies may occasionally have on hand manufacturing equipment that is no longer used in operations. If the amounts are material, the auditor should evaluate whether they should be written down to net realizable value (realizable value objective) or at least disclosed separately as "nonoperating equipment."

A major consideration in verifying the ending balance in fixed assets is the possibility of existing *legal encumbrances* (presentation and disclosure objective). A number of methods are available to determine whether manufacturing equipment is encumbered. These methods include reading the terms of loan and credit agreements and mailing loan confirmation requests to banks and other lending institutions. Information with respect to encumbered assets may also be obtained through discussions with the client or letters to legal counsel. In addition, it is desirable to obtain information on possible liens by sending a form titled *Request for Information Under the Uniform Commercial Code* to the secretary of state or other appropriate officials of the state in which the company operates.

The *proper presentation and disclosure* of manufacturing equipment in the financial statements must be evaluated carefully to make sure that GAAP is followed. Manufacturing equipment should include the gross cost and should ordinarily be separated from other fixed assets. Leased property should also be disclosed separately, and all liens on property must be included in the footnotes.

Verification of Depreciation Expense

Depreciation expense is one of the few expense accounts that is not verified as a part of tests of controls and substantive tests of transactions. The recorded amounts are determined by *internal allocations* rather than by exchange transactions with outside parties. When depreciation expense is material, more tests of details of depreciation expense are required than for an account that has already been verified through tests of controls and substantive tests of transactions.

The most important objective for depreciation expense is accuracy. Two major concerns are involved in the accuracy objective: determining whether the client is following a *consistent depreciation policy* from period to period and whether the client's *calculations are correct.* In determining the former, there are four considerations: the useful life of current period acquisitions, the method of depreciation, the estimated salvage value, and the policy of depreciating assets in the year of acquisition and disposition. The client's policies can be determined by having discussions with appropriate personnel and comparing the responses with the information in the auditor's permanent files.

In deciding on the reasonableness of the useful lives assigned to newly acquired assets, the auditor must consider a number of factors: the actual physical life of the asset, the expected life (taking into account obsolescence or the company's normal policy of upgrading equipment), and established company policies on trading in equipment. Occasionally, changing circumstances may necessitate a reevaluation of the useful life of an asset. When this occurs, a change in accounting estimate rather than a change in accounting principle is involved. The effect of this on depreciation must be evaluated carefully.

A useful method of testing depreciation is to make a calculation of its overall reasonableness. The calculation is made by multiplying the undepreciated fixed assets by the depreciation rate for the year. In making these calculations, the auditor must of course make adjustments for current-year additions and disposals, assets with different lengths of life, and assets with different methods of depreciation. The calculations can be made fairly easily if the CPA firm includes in the permanent file a breakdown of the fixed assets by method of depreciation and length of life. If the overall calculations are reasonably close to the client's totals and if assessed control risk for depreciation expense is low, tests of details for depreciation can be minimized.

In many audits, it is also desirable to check the detail tie-in of a sample of depreciation calculations. This is done by recomputing depreciation expense for selected assets to determine whether the client is following a proper and consistent depreciation policy. To be relevant, the detailed calculations should be tied in to the total depreciation calculations by footing the depreciation expense on the property master file and reconciling the total with the general ledger. If the client maintains computerized depreciation and amortization records, it may be desirable to consider using the computer in testing the calculations.

Verification of Ending Balance in Accumulated Depreciation

The debits to accumulated depreciation are normally tested as a part of the audit of disposals of assets, whereas the credits are verified as a part of depreciation expense. If the auditor traces selected transactions to the accumulated depreciation records in the property master file as a part of these tests, little additional testing should be required for the ending balance in accumulated depreciation.

Two objectives are usually emphasized in the audit of the ending balance in accumulated depreciation:

1. Accumulated depreciation as stated in the property master file agrees with the general ledger. This objective can be satisfied by test-footing the accumulated depreciation or the property master file and tracing the total to the general ledger.
2. Accumulated depreciation in the master file is accurate.

In some cases, the life of manufacturing equipment may be significantly reduced because of such changes as reductions in customer demands for products, unexpected physical deterioration, or a modification in operations. Because of these possibilities, it is necessary to evaluate the adequacy of the allowances for accumulated depreciation each year to make sure that the net book value does not exceed the realizable value of the assets.

AUDIT OF PREPAID EXPENSES

OBJECTIVE 19-3
Design and perform audit tests of prepaid expenses.

We now look at the next major category of accounts in this cycle—prepaid expenses. Prepaid expenses, deferred charges, and intangibles are assets that vary in life from several months to several years. Their inclusion as assets results more from the concept of matching expenses with revenues than from their resale or liquidation value. The following are examples:

- Prepaid rent
- Organization costs
- Prepaid taxes
- Patents

- Prepaid insurance
- Trademarks
- Deferred charges
- Copyrights

One typical difference between these assets and others, such as accounts receivable and inventory, is their immateriality in many audits. Analytical procedures are often sufficient for prepaid expenses, deferred charges, and intangibles. However, in some companies, some of these assets can be significant. Because of this, we next take a look at some of the typical internal controls and related audit tests commonly associated with prepaid expenses.

In this section, the audit of prepaid insurance is discussed as an account representative of this group because (1) it is found in most audits—virtually every company has some type of insurance, (2) it is typical of the problems commonly encountered in the audit of this class of accounts, and (3) the auditor's responsibility for the review of insurance coverage is an additional consideration not encountered in the other accounts in this category.

Overview of Prepaid Insurance

The accounts typically used for prepaid insurance are illustrated in Figure 19-3. The relationship between prepaid insurance and the acquisition and payment cycle is apparent in examining the debits to the asset account. Because the source of the debits in the asset account is the acquisitions journal, the payments of insurance premiums have already been partially tested by means of the tests of controls and substantive tests of acquisition and cash disbursement transactions.

Internal Controls

The internal controls for prepaid insurance and insurance expense can be conveniently divided into three categories: controls over the acquisition and recording of insurance, controls over the insurance register, and controls over the charge-off of insurance expense.

Controls over the acquisition and recording of insurance are a part of the acquisition and payment cycle. These should include proper authorization for new insurance policies and payment of insurance premiums consistent with the procedures discussed in that cycle.

An **insurance register** is a record of insurance policies in force and the expiration date of each policy. Use of an insurance register is an essential control to ensure that the company has adequate insurance at all times. The control should include a provision for periodic review of the adequacy of the insurance coverage by an independent qualified person.

After they have been completed, the detailed records of the information in the prepaid insurance register should be verified by someone independent of the person preparing them. A closely related control is the use of monthly standard journal entries for insurance expense. If a significant entry is required to adjust the balance in prepaid insurance at the end of the

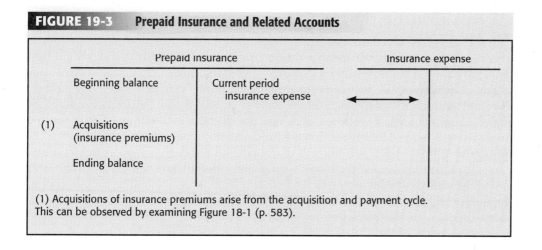

FIGURE 19-3   Prepaid Insurance and Related Accounts

Prepaid insurance		Insurance expense	
Beginning balance	Current period insurance expense		
(1) Acquisitions (insurance premiums)			
Ending balance			

(1) Acquisitions of insurance premiums arise from the acquisition and payment cycle. This can be observed by examining Figure 18-1 (p. 583).

FIGURE 19-4   Schedule of Prepaid Insurance

PBC

Gilman Company, Inc.
Prepaid Insurance
12/31/99

Schedule	9-2	Date
Prepared by	Client/JL	1/20/00
Approved by	GG	1/25/00

Insurer	Policy Number	Coverage	Term
Ever-ready Casualty Co.	IBB-79016 ②	Auto liability, collision, comprehensive, uninsured motorist—covers all autos owned and leased by the company	6/1/98-99 6/1/99-00
Everystate Insurance	74-88-914 ②	Multi-peril—covers headquarters and plant, including contents.	3/15/98-99 ① 3/15/99-00 ①
Standard Surety Co.	1973016 ②	Blanket position bond—$25,000	7/1/98-99
Commercial Bonding Co.	717-639 ②	Commercial blanket bond—$100,000	7/1/99-00

Reconciliation to Insurance Expense (General) Account:

Dependable Insurance	DIC-9161 ②	Personal property—Sales offices	1/1/99-12/31/99

Insurance Expense

① Policy term is 3 years, expiring 3/14/01, premium shown is annual portion. Annual premium is estimated, subject to annual review and adjustment. Premium is payable in monthly installments under terms of contract. (See work paper section CC, Contracts Payable.)

② Reviewed and briefed policies; details of coverage in permanent file. Blanket position bond replaced by commercial blanket bond on expiration.

③ Annual premium adjustment; traced to invoice and voucher.

year, it indicates a potential misstatement in the recording of the acquisition of insurance throughout the year or in the calculation of the year-end balance in prepaid insurance.

Audit Tests

Throughout the audit of prepaid insurance and insurance expense, the auditor should keep in mind that the amount in insurance expense is a residual based on the beginning balance in prepaid insurance, the payment of premiums during the year, and the ending balance. The only verification of the balance in the expense account that is ordinarily necessary are analytical procedures and a brief test to be sure that the charges to insurance expense arose from credits to prepaid insurance. Because the payments of premiums are tested as part of the tests of controls and substantive tests of transactions and analytical procedures, the emphasis in the tests of details of balances is on prepaid insurance.

In the audit of prepaid insurance, a schedule is obtained from the client or prepared by the auditor that includes each insurance policy in force, policy number, insurance coverage for each policy, premium amount, premium period, insurance expense for the year, and prepaid insurance at the end of the year. An example of a schedule obtained from the client

Annual Premium	Prepaid Insurance 1/1/99	Additions	Expense	Prepaid Insurance 12/31/99
6300	2625 *PY*		2625	- √
7000	-	7000	4083 *C*	2917 √
12600	2625 *PY*	1800 ③	4425	- √
15100	-	15100	11954 *C*	3146 √
1200	600 *PY*		600	- √
800	-	800	400 *C*	400 √
	5850	24700	24087	6463
	∧ *PY*	∧	∧	∧ × *GL*
500			500	
			24587	
			∧ *GL*	

PY   Agreed to prior year's schedule of prepaid insurance in working papers

∧   Footed

×   Cross-footed

GL   Agreed to general ledger

C   Unearned premium confirmed by broker; confirmation filed at 9-2/1.

√   Verified calculation

look @ policies, send confirm to ins. company

for the auditor's working papers is given in Figure 19-4. The auditor's tests of prepaid insurance are normally indicated on the schedule.

A major consideration in the audit of prepaid insurance is the frequent *immateriality* of the beginning and ending balances. Furthermore, few transactions are debited and credited to the balance during the year, most of which are small and simple to understand. Therefore, the auditor can generally spend little time verifying the balance. When the auditor plans not to verify the balance in detail, analytical procedures become increasingly important as a means of identifying potentially significant misstatements. The following are commonly performed analytical procedures of prepaid insurance and insurance expense using information on the prepaid insurance schedule similar to the one in Figure 19-4:

• Compare total prepaid insurance and insurance expense with previous years as a test of reasonableness.
• Compute the ratio of prepaid insurance to insurance expense and compare it with previous years.

- Compare the individual insurance policy coverage on the schedule obtained from the client with the preceding year's schedule as a test of the elimination of certain policies or a change in insurance coverage.
- Compare the computed prepaid insurance balance for the current year on a policy-by-policy basis with that of the preceding year as a test of an error in calculation.
- Review the *insurance coverage* listed on the prepaid insurance schedule with an appropriate client official or insurance broker for adequacy of coverage. The auditor cannot be an expert on insurance matters, but his or her understanding of accounting and the valuation of assets is important in making certain that a company is not underinsured.

For many audits, no additional tests need be performed beyond the review for overall reasonableness unless the tests indicate a high likelihood of a significant misstatement or assessed control risk is high. The remaining audit procedures should be performed only when there is a special reason for doing so. The discussion of these tests is organized around the balance-related audit objectives for performing tests of details of asset balances. Realizable value is not applicable.

Insurance Policies in the Prepaid Insurance Schedule Exist and Existing Policies Are Listed (Existence and Completeness) The verification of existence and tests for omissions of the insurance policies in force can be tested in one of two ways: by referring to supporting documentation or by obtaining a confirmation of insurance information from the company's insurance agent. The first approach entails examining insurance invoices and policies in force. If these tests are performed, they should be done on a limited test basis. Sending a confirmation to the client's insurance agent is preferable because it is usually less time-consuming than vouching tests and it provides 100 percent verification.

The Client Has Rights to All Insurance Policies in the Prepaid Insurance Schedule (Rights) The party who will receive the benefit if an insurance claim is filed has the rights. Ordinarily, the recipient named in the policy is the client, but when there are mortgages or other liens, the insurance claim may be payable to a creditor. The review of insurance policies for claimants other than the client is an excellent test of unrecorded liabilities and pledged assets.

Prepaid Amounts on the Schedule Are Accurate and the Total Is Correctly Added and Agrees with the General Ledger (Accuracy and Detail Tie-in) The accuracy of prepaid insurance involves verifying the total amount of the insurance premium, the length of the policy period, and the allocation of the premium to unexpired insurance. The amount of the premium for a given policy and its time period can be verified simultaneously by examining the premium invoice or the confirmation from an insurance agent. Once these two have been verified, the client's calculations of unexpired insurance can be tested by recalculation. The schedule of prepaid insurance can then be footed and the totals traced to the general ledger to complete the detail tie-in tests.

The Insurance Expense Related to Prepaid Insurance Is Properly Classified (Classification) The proper classification of debits to different insurance expense accounts should be reviewed as a test of the income statement. In some cases, the appropriate expense account is obvious because of the type of insurance (such as insurance on a piece of equipment), but in other cases, allocations are necessary. For example, fire insurance on the building may require allocation to several accounts, including manufacturing overhead. Consistency with previous years is the major consideration in evaluating classification.

Insurance Transactions Are Recorded in the Proper Period (Cutoff) Cutoff for insurance expense is normally not a significant problem because of the small number of policies and the immateriality of the amount. If the cutoff is checked at all, it is reviewed as a part of accounts payable cutoff tests.

Prepaid Insurance Is Properly Presented and Disclosed (Presentation and Disclosure) In most audits, prepaid insurance is combined with other prepaid expenses and included as a current asset. The amount is usually small and not a significant consideration to statement users.

OBJECTIVE 19-4
Design and perform audit tests of accrued liabilities.

A third major category of accounts in the acquisition and payment cycle is accrued liabilities. **Accrued liabilities** are estimated unpaid obligations for services or benefits that have been received before the balance sheet date. Many accrued liabilities represent future obligations for unpaid services resulting from the passage of time but are not payable at the balance sheet date. For example, the benefits of property rental accrue throughout the year; therefore, at the balance sheet date, a certain portion of the total rent cost that has not been paid should be accrued. If the balance sheet date and the date of the termination of the rent agreement are the same, any unpaid rent is more appropriately called rent payable than an accrued liability.

A second type of accrual is one in which the amount of the obligation must be estimated due to the uncertainty of the amount due. An illustration is the obligation for federal income taxes when there is a reasonable likelihood that the amount reported on the tax return will be changed after an audit has been conducted by the Internal Revenue Service. Other examples include accrued payroll, accrued payroll taxes, accrued officers' bonuses, and accrued commissions, which were discussed in Chapter 17. The following are other common accrued liabilities:

- Accrued income taxes
- Accrued interest
- Accrued pension costs
- Accrued professional fees
- Accrued rent
- Accrued warranty costs

The verification of accrued expenses varies depending on the nature of the accrual and the circumstances of the client. For most audits, accruals take little audit time, but in some instances, accounts such as accrued income taxes, warranty costs, and pension costs are material and require considerable audit effort. To illustrate, the audit of accrued property taxes is discussed in this section.

Auditing Accrued Property Taxes

The accounts typically used by companies for accrued property taxes are illustrated in Figure 19-5. The relationship between accrued property taxes and the acquisition and payment cycle is the same as for prepaid insurance and is apparent from examining the debits

FIGURE 19-5   Accrued Property Taxes and Related Accounts

Accrued property taxes		Property tax expense	
	Beginning balance		
(1) Payments (property taxes)	Current period property tax expense	⟷	
	Ending balance		

(1) Payments of property taxes arise from the acquisition and payment cycle. This can be observed by examining Figure 18-1 (p. 583).

to the liability account. Because the source of the debits is the cash disbursements journal, the payments of property taxes have already been partially tested by means of the tests of the acquisition and payment cycle transactions.

As for insurance expense, the balance in property tax expense is a residual amount that results from the beginning and ending balances in accrued property taxes and the payments of property taxes. Therefore, the emphasis in the tests should be on the ending property tax liability and payments. In verifying accrued property taxes, all nine balance-related audit objectives except realizable value are relevant. But two are of special significance:

1. Existing properties for which accrual of taxes is appropriate are on the accrual schedule. The failure to include properties for which taxes should be accrued would understate the liability (completeness). A material misstatement could occur, for example, if taxes on property were not paid before the balance sheet date and not included as accrued property taxes.
2. Accrued property taxes are accurately recorded. The greatest concern in accuracy is the consistent treatment of the accrual from year to year (accuracy).

The primary methods of testing for the inclusion of all accruals are (1) to perform the accrual tests in conjunction with the audit of current-year property tax payments and (2) to compare the accruals with those of previous years. In most audits, there are few property tax payments, but each payment is often material, and therefore it is common to verify each one.

First, the auditor should obtain a schedule of property tax payments from the client and compare each payment with the preceding year's schedule to determine whether all payments have been included in the client-prepared schedule. The fixed asset working papers also must be examined for major additions and disposals of assets that may affect the property taxes accrual. If the client is expanding its operations, all property affected by local property tax regulations should be included in the schedule even if the first tax payment has not yet been made.

After the auditor is satisfied that all taxable property has been included in the client-prepared schedule, it is necessary to evaluate the reasonableness of the total amount of property taxes on each property being used as a basis to estimate the accrual. In some instances, the total amount has already been set by the taxing authority, and it is possible to verify the total by comparing the amount on the schedule with the tax bill in the client's possession. In other instances, the preceding year's total payments must be adjusted for the expected increase in property tax rates.

The auditor can verify the accrued property tax by recomputing the portion of the total tax applicable to the current year for each piece of property. The most important consideration in making this calculation is to use the same portion of each tax payment as the accrual that was used in the preceding year unless justifiable conditions exist for a change. After the accrual and property tax expense for each piece of property have been recomputed, the totals should be added and compared with the general ledger. In many cases, property taxes are charged to more than one expense account. When this happens, the auditor should test for proper classification by evaluating whether the proper amount was charged to each account.

A typical working paper showing property tax expense, accrued property taxes, and the audit procedures used to verify the balances is illustrated in Figure 19-6 (pp. 630–631).

AUDIT OF INCOME AND EXPENSE ACCOUNTS

OBJECTIVE 19-5
Design and perform audit tests of income and expense accounts.

The final look at key accounts in the acquisition and payment cycle includes an overview of procedures auditors typically use to determine whether the income and expense accounts in the financial statements are fairly presented in accordance with GAAP. The auditor must be satisfied that each of the income and expense totals included in the income statement as well as net earnings is not materially misstated.

In conducting audit tests of the financial statements, the auditor must always be aware of the importance of the income statement to users of the statements. It is clear that many users rely more heavily on the income statement than on the balance sheet for making decisions. Equity investors, long-term creditors, union representatives, and often even short-term creditors are more interested in the ability of a firm to generate profit than in the historical cost or book value of the individual assets.

Considering the purposes of the income statement, the following two concepts are essential in the audit of income and expense accounts:

1. The matching of periodic income and expense is necessary for a proper determination of operating results. *Revenues + expenses*
2. The consistent application of accounting principles for different periods is necessary for comparability.

These concepts must be applied to the recording of individual transactions and to the combining of accounts in the general ledger for statement presentation.

Approach to Auditing Income and Expense Accounts

The audit of income and expense accounts cannot be regarded as a separate part of the total audit process. A misstatement of an income statement account will almost always equally affect a balance sheet account, and vice versa. The audit of income and expense accounts is so intertwined with the other parts of the audit that it is necessary to interrelate different aspects of testing these accounts with the different types of tests previously discussed. A brief description of these tests serves as a review of material covered in other chapters; more important, it shows the interrelationship of different parts of the audit with income and expense account testing. The parts of the audit directly affecting these accounts are as follows:

• Analytical procedures
• Tests of controls and substantive tests of transactions
• Tests of details of account balances

The emphasis in this section is on income and expense accounts directly related to the acquisition and payment cycle, but the same concepts apply to the income statement accounts in all other cycles.

Analytical Procedures

Analytical procedures were first discussed in Chapter 7 as a general concept and have been referred to in subsequent chapters as a part of specific audit areas. Analytical procedures should be thought of as a part of the test of the fairness of the presentation of both balance sheet and income statement accounts. A few analytical procedures and the possible misstatements they may uncover in the audit of income and expense accounts are shown in Table 19-5 (p. 632). *go back & look @ same*

Tests of Controls and Substantive Tests of Transactions

Tests of controls and substantive tests of transactions both have the effect of simultaneously verifying balance sheet and income statement accounts. For example, when an auditor concludes that internal controls are adequate to provide reasonable assurance that transactions in the acquisitions journal exist, are accurately recorded, correctly classified, and recorded in a timely manner, evidence exists as to the correctness of individual balance sheet accounts such as accounts payable and fixed assets, and income statement accounts such as advertising and repairs. Conversely, inadequate controls and misstatements discovered through tests of controls and substantive tests of transactions are an indication of the likelihood of misstatements in both the income statement and the balance sheet.

Understanding of internal control and the related tests of controls and substantive tests of transactions to determine the appropriate assessed control risk are the most important means of verifying many of the income statement accounts in each of the transaction cycles. For example, if the auditor concludes after adequate tests that assessed control risk can be reduced to low, the only additional verification of income statement accounts such as utilities, advertising, and purchases should be analytical procedures and cutoff tests.

FIGURE 19-6 Schedule of Property Taxes

Gilman Company, Inc.
Property Tax Worksheet
12/31/99

PBC

Schedule	*2-6*	Date
Prepared by	*Client/JL*	*1/15/00*
Approved by	*GS*	*1/20/00*

Tax Bill No.	Area Code	Assessing Authority	Property	Assessed Value ①	Total Tax ②	Date Lien Payable ③	Paid ④	Period Covered
		West Coast Facilities						
526391	51	King County	Westside Warehouse	400000	16000	Jan. 1, 1999	Apr. 30, 2000	1999
526392	51	King County	Headquarters Bldg	250000	10000	Jan. 1, 1998	Apr. 30, 1999 Oct. 31, 1999	1998
						Jan. 1, 1999	Apr. 30, 2000	1999
		Midwest Facilities						
17923	A	Minor County	Manufacturing Plant	2000000	23000	Jul. 1, 1998		Jul. 1, 1998-99
					25000	Jul. 1, 1999	Dec. 31, 1999	Jul. 1, 1999-00

① *Assessed valuation is defined by the laws of both states as 50% of "true and fair value."*

② *Millage rates:*
   King County   .0400 ($40 per $1,000)
   Minor County   .0115 ($11.50 per $1,000) for 1998-99
   *   .0125 ($12.50 per $1,000) for 1999-00*

③ *Laws of both states establish the lien date to be the same as the assessment date; assessment date for the West Coast state is statutorily defined as January 1, and for the Midwest state as July 1.*

④ *Taxes are payable as follows*
   West Coast state — one-half no later than April 30 and the balance no later than October 31, for the preceding calendar year.
   Midwest state — payable in full not later than December 31 following assessment date.

However, certain income and expense accounts are not verified at all by tests of controls and substantive tests of transactions, and others must be tested more extensively by other means. These are discussed next.

Tests of Details of Account Balances

make sure not a capital asset

The amounts included in certain income statement accounts must be analyzed even though the previously mentioned tests have been performed. The meaning and methodology of analysis of accounts are described first, followed by a discussion of when expense account analysis is appropriate.

Expense account analysis is the examination of underlying documentation of the individual transactions and amounts making up the detail of the total of an expense account. The underlying documents are of the same nature as those used for examining transactions

	Prepaid				Accrued		
Beginning Balance	Additions ⑥	Expense	Ending Balance	Beginning Balance	Additions ⑥	Payments	Ending Balance
-0-	16000 √	16000	-0-	⑤ -0-	16000 √	-0-	16000 x
				10000		5000 #	
						5000 #	-0- x
-0-	10000 √	10000 ^	-0- x	-0-	10000 √		10000 x
11500		11500 ^	-0- x	-0-			-0- x
	25000	12500 ^	12500 x	-0-	25000 √	25000 #	-0- x
11500	51000	50000	12500 x	10000	51000	35000	26000 x
⋁ PY	⋁	⋁	GL ⋁	⋁ PY	⋁	⋁	GL ⋁

⑤ *Warehouse certified complete and accepted Dec. 22, 1998, inspected and valued by County in March 1999. Per state law (note 3) assessment date and lien date statutorily set at Jan. 1, 1999.*

⑥ *Liability and deferred charge are recorded by company on the lien date. The deferred charge is amortized monthly and the liability account relieved when installments are paid.*

PY Agreed to prior year's working papers.

√ Agreed to county tax due notice (identified in left column).

^ Agreed to amortization schedule and traced to standard journal entry.

 # Traced to cancelled check and validated receipt.

⋁, x Footed, cross-footed.

GL Agreed to general ledger.

as a part of tests of acquisition transactions and include invoices, receiving reports, purchase orders, and contracts. Figure 19-7 on page 633 illustrates a typical working paper showing expense analysis for legal expenses.

Expense account analysis concentrates on transactions that make up the details of an individual expense account. Although the focus of expense account analysis is on transactions, these tests differ from tests of controls and substantive tests of transactions. Because the tests of controls and substantive tests of transactions are meant to assess the appropriate control risk, they constitute a general review that usually includes the verification of many different accounts. The analysis of expense and other income statement accounts consists of the examination of the transactions in specific accounts to determine the propriety, classification, accuracy, and other specific information about each account analyzed.

TABLE 19-5	Analytical Procedures for Income and Expense Accounts
Analytical Procedure	**Possible Misstatement**
Compare individual expenses with previous years.	Overstatement or understatement of a balance in an expense account.
Compare individual asset and liability balances with previous years.	Overstatement or understatement of a balance sheet account that would also affect an income statement account (for example, a misstatement of inventory affects cost of goods sold).
Compare individual expenses with budgets.	Misstatement of expenses and related balance sheet accounts.
Compare gross margin percentage with previous years.	Misstatement of cost of goods sold and inventory.
Compare inventory turnover ratio with previous years.	Misstatement of cost of goods sold and inventory.
Compare prepaid insurance expense with previous years.	Misstatement of insurance expense and prepaid insurance.
Compare commission expense divided by sales with previous years.	Misstatement of commission expense and accrued commissions.
Compare individual manufacturing expenses divided by total manufacturing expenses with previous years.	Misstatement of individual manufacturing expenses and related balance sheet accounts.

Assuming satisfactory classification results are found in tests of controls and substantive tests of transactions, auditors normally restrict expense analysis to those accounts with a relatively high likelihood of material misstatement. For example, auditors often analyze repairs and maintenance expense accounts to determine whether they erroneously include property, plant, and equipment transactions; rent and lease expense are analyzed to determine the need to capitalize leases; and legal expense is analyzed to determine whether there are potential contingent liabilities, disputes, illegal acts, or other legal issues that may affect the financial statements. Accounts such as utilities, travel expense, and advertising are rarely analyzed unless analytical procedures indicate high potential for material misstatement.

Expense account analysis is often done as a part of the verification of the related asset. For example, it is common to analyze repairs and maintenance as a part of verifying fixed assets, rent expense as a part of verifying prepaid or accrued rent, and insurance expense as a part of testing prepaid insurance.

Expense account analysis is generally not performed for expense accounts that arise from the internal **allocation** of accounting data. These include expenses such as depreciation, depletion, and the amortization of copyrights and catalog costs. The allocation of manufacturing overhead between inventory and cost of goods sold is an example of a different type of allocation that affects the expenses.

Allocations are important because they determine whether an expenditure is an asset or a current-period expense. If the client fails to follow GAAP or fails to calculate the allocation properly, the financial statements can be materially misstated. The allocation of many expenses such as the depreciation of fixed assets and the amortization of copyrights is required because the life of the asset is greater than 1 year. The original cost of the asset is verified at the time of acquisition, but the charge-off takes place over several years. Other types of allocations directly affecting the financial statements arise because the life of a short-lived asset does not expire on the balance sheet date. Examples include prepaid rent and insurance. Finally, the allocation of costs between current-period manufacturing expenses and inventory is required by GAAP as a means of reflecting all the costs of making a product.

FIGURE 19-7 Expense Analysis for Legal Expense

Gilman Company, Inc.
Legal Expenses
12/31/99

Schedule	V-10		Date	
Prepared by	Client/JL		1/21/00	
Approved by	SW		1/28/00	

Acct. 913-Legal Expense

Paid to	For	Date	Amount
② Alexander J. Schweppe	Retainer-12 months @$500	Monthly ①	6000 √
	ABC vs. Carson — patent infringement suit	Apr. 14 Aug. 9	2800 √ 3109 √
② Smith, Tom	Consultation re: inquiry from Consumer Protection Bureau, State Attorney General's office	June 6 July 10	200 √ 200 √
③ L. Marvin Hall	Assistance in collecting overdue receivable from Star Mfg.	Nov. 10	105 √
			12414 GL

① Per minutes of meeting of Board of Directors 1/10/00. Schweppe reappointed general counsel with retainer.

② Attorney's letter requested { Received 1/23/00, all matters listed are covered therein; letters filed in General Section of working papers.

③ Attorney's letter not requested. Per phone conversation with Mr. Hall 1/21/00, he rarely represents the company, and his services have been limited to collection problems. The Star Mfg. matter was closed in October 1999, and he has not been involved in any other matters related to the company since that time.

√ Examined statement and vouchers
∧ Footed
GL Agreed to general ledger

Income statement accounts resulting from allocations are typically not verified as a part of tests of controls, substantive tests of transactions, or tests of details of balance sheet accounts. Analytical procedures are used extensively for verifying allocations, but additional detailed testing often is needed.

In auditing the allocation of expenditures such as prepaid insurance and manufacturing overhead, the two most important considerations are adherence to GAAP and consistency with the preceding period. The two most important audit procedures for allocations are tests for overall reasonableness using analytical procedures and recalculation of the client's results. It is common to perform these tests as a part of the audit of the related asset or liability accounts. For example, depreciation expense is usually verified as part of the audit of property, plant, and equipment; amortization of patents is tested as part of verifying new patents or the disposal of existing ones; and allocations between inventory and cost of goods sold are verified as part of the audit of inventory.

SUMMARY

This chapter concludes the discussion of accounts and transactions in the acquisition and payment cycle. Auditors need to have an understanding of key accounts, classes of transactions, business functions, documents, and records related to acquisition and payment cycle transactions to adequately audit the numerous accounts associated with this cycle. Many of these accounts, such as accounts payable, property, plant, and equipment, depreciation expense, and prepaid expenses, have unique characteristics that affect how the auditor gathers sufficient competent evidence about related account balances. The analysis of the audit tests associated with accounts in this cycle has provided an overview of how auditor's tests in different cycles interrelate to provide a basis for the auditor's verification of many financial statement accounts.

ESSENTIAL TERMS

Accrued liabilities—estimated unpaid obligations for services or benefits that have been received prior to the balance sheet date; common accrued liabilities include accrued commissions, accrued income taxes, accrued payroll, and accrued rent

Allocation—the division of certain expenses, such as depreciation and manufacturing overhead, among several expense accounts

Expense account analysis—the examination of underlying documentation of individual transactions and amounts making up the total of an expense account

Fixed asset master file—a computer file containing records for each piece of equipment and other types of property owned; the primary accounting record for manufacturing equipment and other property, plant, and equipment accounts

Insurance register—a record of insurance policies in force and the expiration date of each policy

REVIEW QUESTIONS

19-1 (Objective 19-2) Explain the relationship between substantive tests of transactions for the acquisition and payment cycle and tests of details of balances for the verification of property, plant, and equipment. Which aspects of property, plant, and equipment are directly affected by the tests of controls and substantive tests of transactions and which are not?

19-2 (Objective 19-2) Explain why the emphasis in auditing property, plant, and equipment is on the current-period acquisitions and disposals rather than on the balances in the account carried forward from the preceding year. Under what circumstances will the emphasis be on the balances carried forward?

19-3 (Objective 19-2) What is the relationship between the audit of property, plant, and equipment accounts and the audit of repair and maintenance accounts? Explain how the auditor organizes the audit to take this relationship into consideration.

19-4 (Objective 19-2) List and briefly state the purpose of all audit procedures that might reasonably be applied by an auditor to determine that all property, plant, and equipment retirements have been recorded on the books.

19-5 (Objective 19-2) In auditing depreciation expense, what major considerations should the auditor keep in mind? Explain how each can be verified.

19-6 (Objective 19-3) Explain the relationship between substantive tests of transactions for the acquisition and payment cycle and tests of details of balances for the verification of prepaid insurance.

19-7 (Objective 19-3) Explain why the audit of prepaid insurance should ordinarily take a relatively small amount of audit time if the client's assessed control risk for acquisitions is low.

19-8 (Objective 19-3) Distinguish between the evaluation of the adequacy of insurance coverage and the verification of prepaid insurance. Explain which is more important in a typical audit.

19-9 (Objective 19-3) What are the major differences between the audit of prepaid expenses and other asset accounts such as accounts receivable or property, plant, and equipment?

19-10 (Objective 19-4) Explain the relationship between accrued rent and substantive tests of transactions for the acquisition and payment cycle. Which aspects of accrued rent are not verified as a part of the substantive tests of transactions?

19-11 (Objective 19-4) In verifying accounts payable, it is common to restrict the audit sample to a small portion of the population items, whereas in auditing accrued property taxes, it is common to verify all transactions for the year. Explain the reason for the difference.

19-12 (Objective 19-4) Which documents will be used to verify accrued property taxes and the related expense accounts?

19-13 (Objective 19-5) List three expense accounts that are tested as part of the acquisition and payment cycle or the payroll and personnel cycle. List three expense accounts that are not directly verified as a part of either of these cycles.

19-14 (Objective 19-5) What is meant by the analysis of expense accounts? Explain how expense account analysis relates to the tests of controls and substantive tests of transactions that the auditor has already completed for the acquisition and payment cycle.

19-15 (Objectives 19-2, 19-5) How would the approach for verifying repair expense differ from that used to audit depreciation expense? Why would the approach be different?

19-16 (Objective 19-5) List the factors that should affect the auditor's decision whether to analyze an account balance. Considering these factors, list four expense accounts that are commonly analyzed in audit engagements.

MULTIPLE CHOICE QUESTIONS FROM CPA EXAMINATIONS

19-17 (Objective 19-2) The following questions concern internal controls in the acquisition and payment cycle. Choose the best response.

a. If preparation of a periodic scrap report is essential in order to maintain adequate control over the manufacturing process, the data for this report should be accumulated in the

    (1) accounting department.   (3) warehousing department.
    (2) production department.   (4) budget department.

b. Which of the following is not an internal control weakness related to factory equipment?

    (1) Checks issued in payment of acquisitions of equipment are *not* signed by the controller.

    (2) All acquisitions of factory equipment are required to be made by the department in need of the equipment.

    (3) Factory equipment replacements are generally made when estimated useful lives, as indicated in depreciation schedules, have expired.

    (4) Proceeds from sales of fully depreciated equipment are credited to other income.

c. With respect to an internal control measure that will ensure accountability for fixed asset retirements, management should implement controls that include

    (1) continuous analysis of miscellaneous revenue to locate any cash proceeds from sale of plant assets.

    (2) periodic inquiry of plant executives by internal auditors as to whether any plant assets have been retired.

    (3) continuous use of serially numbered retirement work orders.

    (4) periodic observation of plant assets by the internal auditors.

19-18 (Objectives 19-2, 19-5)   The following questions concern analytical procedures in the acquisition and payment cycle. Choose the best response.

a. Which of the following comparisons would be most useful to an auditor in auditing an entity's income and expense accounts.
   (1) Prior-year accounts payable to current-year accounts payable.
   (2) Prior-year payroll expense to budgeted current-year payroll expense.
   (3) Current-year revenue to budgeted current-year revenue.
   (4) Current-year warranty expense to current-year contingent liabilities.

b. The controller of Excello Manufacturing, Inc., wants to use analytical procedures to identify the possible existence of idle equipment or the possibility that equipment has been disposed of without having been written off. Which of the following ratios would best accomplish this objective?
   (1) Depreciation expense/book value of manufacturing equipment.
   (2) Accumulated depreciation/book value of manufacturing equipment.
   (3) Repairs and maintenance cost/direct labor costs.
   (4) Gross manufacturing equipment cost/units produced.

c. Which of the following analytical procedures should be applied to the income statement?
   (1) Select sales and expense items and trace amounts to related supporting documents.
   (2) Ascertain that the net income amount in the statement of cash flows agrees with the net income amount in the income statement.
   (3) Obtain from the proper client representatives the beginning and ending inventory amounts that were used to determine costs of sales.
   (4) Compare the actual revenues and expenses with the corresponding figures of the previous year and investigate significant differences.

19-19 (Objective 19-2)   The following questions concern the audit of asset accounts in the acquisition and payment cycle. Choose the best response.

a. In testing for unrecorded retirements of equipment, an auditor most likely would
   (1) select items of equipment from the accounting records and then locate them during the plant tour.
   (2) compare depreciation journal entries with similar prior-year entries in search of fully depreciated equipment.
   (3) inspect items of equipment observed during the plant tour and then trace them to the equipment master file.
   (4) scan the general journal for unusual equipment additions and excessive debits to repairs and maintenance expense.

b. Which of the following is the *best* evidence of real estate ownership at the balance sheet date?
   (1) Title insurance policy.   (3) Paid real estate tax bills.
   (2) Original deed held in the client's safe.   (4) Closing statement.

19-20 (Objectives 19-2, 19-4, 19-5)   The following questions concern the audit of liabilities or income and expense accounts. Choose the best response.

a. Which of the following audit procedures is *least* likely to detect an unrecorded liability?
   (1) Analysis and recomputation of interest expense.
   (2) Analysis and recomputation of depreciation expense.
   (3) Mailing of standard bank confirmation forms.
   (4) Reading of the minutes of meetings of the board of directors.

b. Which of the following *best* describes the independent auditor's approach to obtaining satisfaction concerning depreciation expense in the income statement?
   (1) Verify the mathematical accuracy of the amounts charged to income as a result of depreciation expense.

(2) Determine the method for computing depreciation expense and ascertain that it is in accordance with GAAP.

(3) Reconcile the amount of depreciation expense to those amounts credited to accumulated depreciation accounts.

(4) Establish the basis for depreciable assets and verify the depreciation expense.

c. Before expressing an opinion concerning the audit of income and expenses, the auditor would *best* proceed with the audit of the income statement by

(1) applying a rigid measurement standard designed to test for understatement of net income.

(2) analyzing the beginning and ending balance sheet inventory amounts.

(3) making net income comparisons to published industry trends and ratios.

(4) auditing income statement accounts concurrently with the related balance sheet accounts.

DISCUSSION QUESTIONS AND PROBLEMS

19-21 (Objective 19-2) For each of the following misstatements in property, plant, and equipment accounts, state an internal control that the client could install to prevent the misstatement from occurring and a substantive audit procedure that the auditor could use to discover the misstatement.

1. The asset lives used to depreciate equipment are less than reasonable, expected useful lives.

2. Capitalizable assets are routinely expensed as repairs and maintenance, perishable tools, or supplies expense.

3. Construction equipment that is abandoned or traded for replacement equipment is not removed from the accounting records.

4. Depreciation expense for manufacturing operations is charged to administrative expenses.

5. Tools necessary for the maintenance of equipment are stolen by company employees for their personal use.

6. Acquisitions of property are recorded at an improper amount.

7. A loan against existing equipment is not recorded in the accounting records. The cash receipts from the loan never reached the company because they were used for the down payment on a piece of equipment now being used as an operating asset. The equipment is also not recorded in the records.

19-22 (Objective 19-2) The following types of internal controls are commonly used by organizations for property, plant, and equipment:

1. A fixed asset master file is maintained with a separate record for each fixed asset.

2. Written policies exist and are known by accounting personnel to differentiate between capitalizable additions, freight, installation costs, replacements, and maintenance expenditures.

3. Acquisitions of fixed assets in excess of $20,000 are approved by the board of directors.

4. When practical, equipment is labeled with metal tags and is inventoried on a systematic basis.

5. Depreciation charges for individual assets are calculated for each asset; recorded in a fixed asset master file that includes cost, depreciation, and accumulated depreciation for each asset; and verified periodically by an independent clerk.

Required

a. State the purpose of each of the internal controls just listed. Your answer should be in the form of the type of misstatement that is likely to be reduced because of the control.

b. For each internal control, list one test of control the auditor can use to test for its existence.

c. List one substantive procedure for testing whether the control is actually preventing misstatements in property, plant, and equipment.

19-23 (Objectives 19-1, 19-2, 19-3, 19-5)   The following audit procedures were planned by Linda King, CPA, in the audit of the acquisition and payment cycle for Cooley Products, Inc.

1. Review the acquisitions journal for large and unusual transactions.
2. Send letters to several vendors, including a few for which the recorded accounts payable balance is zero, requesting them to inform us of their balance due from Cooley. Ask the controller to sign the letter.
3. Examine a sample of receiving report numbers and determine whether each one has an initial indicating that it was recorded as an account payable.
4. Select a sample of equipment listed on fixed asset master files and inspect the asset to determine that it exists and to determine its condition.
5. Refoot the acquisitions journal for 1 month and trace all totals to the general ledger.
6. Calculate the ratio of equipment repairs and maintenance to total equipment, and compare with previous years.
7. Obtain from the client a written statement that all mortgages payable have been included in the current period financial statements and have been accurately recorded and that the collateral for each is included in the footnotes.
8. Select a sample of cancelled checks and trace each one to the cash disbursements journal, comparing the name, date, and amount.
9. For 20 nontangible acquisitions, select a sample of line items from the acquisitions journal and trace each to related vendors' invoices. Examine whether each transaction appears to be a legitimate expenditure for the client and that each was approved and recorded at the correct amount and date in the journal and charged to the correct account per the chart of accounts.
10. Examine invoices and related shipping documents included in the client's unpaid invoice file at the audit report date to determine whether they were recorded in the appropriate accounting period and at the correct amounts.
11. Recalculate the portion of insurance premiums on the client's prepaid insurance schedule that is applicable to future periods.
12. When the check signer's assistant writes "paid" on supporting documents, watch whether she does it after the documents are reviewed and the checks are signed.

Required
    a. For each procedure, identify the type of evidence being used.
    b. For each procedure, identify whether it is an analytical procedure, a test of control, a substantive test of transactions, or a test of details of balances.
    c. For each test of control or substantive test of transactions, identify the transaction-related audit objective(s) being met.
    d. For each test of details of balances, identify the balance-related audit objective(s) being met.

19-24 (Objective 19-2)   Hardware Manufacturing Company, a closely held corporation, has operated since 1996 but has not had its financial statements audited. The company now plans to issue additional capital stock to be sold to outsiders and wishes to engage you to audit its year 2000 transactions and render an opinion on the financial statements for the year ended December 31, 2000.

The company has expanded from one plant to three and has frequently acquired, modified, and disposed of all types of equipment. Fixed assets have a net book value of 70 percent of total assets and consist of land and buildings, diversified machinery and equipment, and furniture and fixtures. Some property was acquired by donation from stockholders. Depreciation was recorded by several methods using various estimated lives.

Required
    a. May you confine your audit solely to year 2000 transactions as requested by this prospective client whose financial statements have not previously been audited? Why?
    b. Prepare an audit program for the January 1, 2000, opening balances of the land, building, and equipment and accumulated depreciation accounts of Hardware

Manufacturing Company. You need not include tests of year 2000 transactions in your program.*

19-25 (Objective 19-4)   The following program has been prepared for the audit of accrued real estate taxes of a client that pays taxes on 25 different pieces of property, some of which have been acquired in the current year.

1. Obtain a schedule of accrued taxes from the client and tie the total to the general ledger.
2. Compare the charges for annual tax payments with property tax assessment bills.
3. Recompute accrued/prepaid amounts for all bills on the basis of the portion of the year expired.

Required
    a. State the purpose of each procedure.
    b. Evaluate the adequacy of the audit program.

19-26 (Objective 19-4)   As part of the audit of different audit areas, it is important to be alert for the possibility of unrecorded liabilities. For each of the following audit areas or accounts, describe a liability that could be uncovered and the audit procedures that could uncover it.

    a. Minutes of the board of directors' meetings
    b. Land and buildings
    c. Rent expense
    d. Interest expense
    e. Cash surrender value of life insurance
    f. Cash in the bank
    g. Officers' travel and entertainment expense

19-27 (Objective 19-5)   While you are having lunch with a banker friend, you become involved in explaining to him how your firm conducts an audit in a typical engagement. Much to your surprise, your friend is interested and is able to converse intelligently in discussing your philosophy of emphasizing the study of internal control, analytical procedures, tests of controls, substantive tests of transactions, and tests of details of balance sheet accounts. At the completion of your discussion, he says, "That all sounds great except for a couple of things. The point of view we take these days at our bank is the importance of a continuous earnings stream. You seem to be emphasizing fraud detection and a fairly stated balance sheet. We would rather see you put more emphasis than you apparently do on the income statement."

Required
How would you respond to your friend's comments?

19-28 (Objective 19-5)   Brian Day, a staff assistant, has been asked to analyze interest and legal expenses as a part of the first-year audit of Rosow Manufacturing Company. In searching for a model to follow, Day looked at other completed working papers in the current audit file and concluded that the closest thing to what he was looking for was a working paper for repair and maintenance expense account analysis. Following the approach used in analyzing repairs and maintenance, all interest and legal expenses in excess of $500 were scheduled and verified by examining supporting documentation.

Required
    a. Evaluate Day's approach to verifying interest and legal expenses.
    b. Suggest a better approach to verifying these two account balances.

19-29 (Objectives 19-1, 19-2, 19-5)   In performing tests of the acquisition and payment cycle for the Orlando Manufacturing Company, the staff assistant did a careful and complete job. Because internal controls were evaluated as excellent before tests of controls and substantive tests of transactions were performed and were determined to be operating

*AICPA adapted.

effectively on the basis of the lack of exceptions in the tests of controls and substantive tests of transactions, the decision was made to significantly reduce the tests of expense account analysis. The in-charge auditor decided to reduce but not eliminate the acquisition-related expense account analysis for repair expense, legal and other professional expense, miscellaneous expense, and utilities expense on the grounds that they should always be verified more extensively than normal accounts. The decision was also made to eliminate any account analysis for the acquisition of raw materials, depreciation expense, supplies expense, insurance expense, and the current period additions to fixed assets.

Required

a. List other considerations in the audit besides the quality of internal controls that should affect the auditor's decision as to which accounts to analyze.

b. Assuming that no significant problems were identified on the basis of the other considerations in part a, evaluate the auditor's decision of reducing but not eliminating expense account analysis for each account involved. Justify your conclusions.

c. Assuming that no significant problems were identified on the basis of the other considerations in part a, evaluate the auditor's decision to eliminate expense account analysis for each account involved. Justify your conclusions.

CASES

WARD PUBLISHING COMPANY—PART III (SEE CASE 18-33 FOR PARTS I AND II)

19-30 (Objectives 19-1, 19-2, 19-5)   Examine the tests of controls and substantive tests of transactions results, including the sampling application in Case 18-33 for Ward Publishing Company. Assume that you have already reached several conclusions.

1. Your tests of details of balances for accounts payable are completed, and you found no exceptions.
2. Acceptable audit risk for property, plant, and equipment and all expenses is high.
3. Inherent risk for property, plant, and equipment is high because in the current year, the client has acquired a material amount of new and used printing equipment and has traded in older equipment. Some of the new equipment was ineffective and returned; an allowance was received on others. Inherent risk for expense accounts is low.
4. New computer equipment and some printing equipment are being leased. The client has never leased equipment before.
5. Analytical procedures for property, plant, and equipment are inconclusive because of the large increases in acquisition and disposal activity.
6. Analytical procedures show that repairs, maintenance, and small tools expenses have increased materially, both in absolute terms and as a percentage of sales. Two other expenses have also materially increased, and one has materially decreased.
7. In examining the sample for tests of controls and substantive tests of transactions, you observe that no sample items included any property, plant, and equipment or lease transactions.

Required

a. Explain the relationship between the tests of controls and substantive tests of transactions results in Case 18-33 and the audit of property, plant, and equipment and leases.

b. How would the tests of controls and substantive tests of transactions results and your conclusions (1 through 7) affect your planned tests of details for property, plant, and equipment and leases? State your conclusions for each balance-related audit objective. Do not write an audit program.

c. Explain the relationship between the tests of controls and substantive tests of transactions results in Case 18-33 and the audit of expenses.

d. How would the tests of controls and substantive tests of transactions results and your conclusions (1 through 7) affect your planned tests of details of balances for expenses? Do not write an audit program.

19-31 (Objective 19-2) You are doing the audit of the Ute Corporation, for the year ended December 31, 2000. The following schedule for the property, plant, and equipment and related allowance for depreciation accounts has been prepared by the client. You have compared the opening balances with your prior year's audit working papers.

UTE CORPORATION ANALYSIS OF PROPERTY, PLANT, AND EQUIPMENT AND RELATED ALLOWANCE FOR DEPRECIATION ACCOUNTS YEAR ENDED DECEMBER 31, 2000

Description	Final 12/31/99	Additions	Retirements	Per Books 12/31/00
Assets				
Land	$ 22,500	$ 5,000		$ 27,500
Buildings	120,000	17,500		137,500
Machinery and equipment	385,000	40,400	$26,000	399,400
	$527,500	$62,900	$26,000	$564,400
Allowance for Depreciation				
Building	$ 60,000	$ 5,150		$ 65,150
Machinery and equipment	173,250	39,220		212,470
	$233,250	$44,370		$277,620

The following information is found during your audit:

1. All equipment is depreciated on the straight-line basis (no salvage value taken into consideration) based on the following estimated lives: buildings, 25 years; all other items, 10 years. The corporation's policy is to take one-half year's depreciation on all asset acquisitions and disposals during the year.
2. On April 1, the corporation entered into a 10-year lease contract for a die-casting machine with annual rentals of $5,000, payable in advance every April 1. The lease is cancelable by either party (60 days' written notice is required), and there is no option to renew the lease or buy the equipment at the end of the lease. The estimated useful life of the machine is 10 years with no salvage value. The corporation recorded the die-casting machine in the machinery and equipment account at $40,400, the present value at the date of the lease, and $2,020, applicable to the machine, has been included in depreciation expense for the year.
3. The corporation completed the construction of a wing on the plant building on June 30. The useful life of the building was not extended by this addition. The lowest construction bid received was $17,500, the amount recorded in the buildings account. Company personnel were used to construct the addition at a cost of $16,000 (materials, $7,500; labor, $5,500; and overhead, $3,000).
4. On August 18, $5,000 was paid for paving and fencing a portion of land owned by the corporation and used as a parking lot for employees. The expenditure was charged to the land account.
5. The amount shown in the machinery and equipment asset retirement column represents cash received on September 5, upon disposal of a machine acquired in July 1996 for $48,000. The bookkeeper recorded depreciation expense of $3,500 on this machine in 2000.
6. Crux City donated land and building appraised at $10,000 and $40,000, respectively, to the Ute Corporation for a plant. On September 1, the corporation began operating the plant. Because no costs were involved, the bookkeeper made no entry for the foregoing transaction.

a. In addition to inquiry of the client, explain how you would have found each of these six items during the audit.
b. Prepare the adjusting journal entries with supporting computations that you would suggest at December 31, 2000, to adjust the accounts for the preceding transactions. Disregard income tax implications.*

19-32 (Objective 19-5) You are the manager in the audit of Vernal Manufacturing Company and are turning your attention to the income statement accounts. The in-charge auditor assessed control risk for all cycles as low, supported by tests of controls. There are no major inherent risks affecting income and expense accounts. Accordingly, you decide that the major emphasis in auditing the income statement accounts will be to use analytical procedures. The in-charge auditor prepared a schedule of the key income statement accounts that compares the prior-year totals with the current-year totals and includes explanations of variances obtained from discussions with client personnel. That schedule is included on page 643.

Required

a. Examine the schedule prepared by your staff and write a memorandum to the in-charge that includes criticisms and concerns about the audit work procedures performed and questions for the in-charge auditor to resolve.
b. Evaluate the explanations for variances provided by client personnel. List any alternative explanation to those given.
c. Indicate which variances are of special significance to the audit and how you believe they should be responded to in terms of additional audit procedures.

*AICPA adapted.

Vernal Manufacturing Co.
Income Statement Accounts
12/31/00

Account	Per G/L 12/31/99	Per G/L 12/31/00	Change Amount	Change Percent	Explanations by Client
Sales	$8,467,312	$9,845,231	$1,377,919	16.3	Sales increase due to two new customers who account for 20 percent of volume. Larger returns due to need to cement relations with these customers.
Sales returns and allowances	(64,895)	(243,561)	(178,666)	275.3	
Gain on sale of assets	43,222	(143,200)	(186,422)	−431.3	Trade-in of several sales cars that needed replacement.
Interest income	243	223	(20)	−8.2	
Miscellaneous income	6,365	25,478	19,113	300.3	
	8,452,247	9,484,171	1,031,924	12.2	
Cost of goods sold:					
Beginning inventory	1,487,666	1,389,034	(98,632)	−6.6	Increase in these accounts due to increased volume with new customers as indicated above.
Purchases	2,564,451	3,430,865	866,414	33.8	
Freight in	45,332	65,782	20,450	45.1	
Purchase returns	(76,310)	(57,643)	18,667	−24.5	
Factory wages	986,755	1,145,467	158,712	16.1	
Factory benefits	197,652	201,343	3,691	1.9	
Factory overhead	478,659	490,765	12,106	2.5	
Factory depreciation	344,112	314,553	(29,559)	−8.6	
Ending inventory	(1,389,034)	(2,156,003)	(766,969)	55.2	Inventory being held for new customers.
	4,639,283	4,824,163	184,880	4.0	
Selling, general and administrative:					
Executive salaries	167,459	174,562	7,103	4.2	Normal salary increases.
Executive benefits	32,321	34,488	2,167	6.7	
Office salaries	95,675	98,540	2,865	3.0	
Office benefits	19,888	21,778	1,890	9.5	
Travel and entertainment	56,845	75,583	18,738	33.0	Sales and promotional expenses increased in an attempt to obtain new major customers. Two obtained and program will continue.
Advertising	130,878	156,680	25,802	19.7	
Other sales expense	34,880	42,334	7,454	21.4	
Stationery and supplies	38,221	21,554	(16,667)	−43.6	Probably a misclassification; will investigate.
Postage	14,657	18,756	4,099	28.0	Normal increase.
Telephone	36,551	67,822	31,271	85.6	Normal increase.
Dues and memberships	3,644	4,522	878	24.1	Normal increase.
Rent	15,607	15,607	0	0.0	
Legal fees	14,154	35,460	21,306	150.5	Timing of billing for fees.
Accounting fees	16,700	18,650	1,950	11.7	Normal increase.
Depreciation, SG&A	73,450	69,500	(3,950)	−5.4	Normal change.
Bad debt expense	166,454	143,871	(22,583)	−13.6	Haven't reviewed yet for the current year.
Insurance	44,321	45,702	1,381	3.1	Normal change.
Interest expense	120,432	137,922	17,490	14.5	Normal change.
Other expense	5,455	28,762	23,307	427.3	Amount not material.
	1,087,592	1,212,093	124,501	11.4	
	5,726,875	6,036,256	309,381	5.4	
Income before taxes	2,725,372	3,447,915	722,543	26.5	
Income taxes	926,626	1,020,600	93,974	10.1	
Net income	$1,798,746	$2,427,315	$628,569	34.9	Increase due to increased income before tax.

AUDIT OF THE INVENTORY AND WAREHOUSING CYCLE

20

DON'T IGNORE RED FLAGS

Packard, Packard & Dodge (PP&D) had audited Farago, a commercial finance company owned by a large heavy equipment dealer, for the past 7 years. When equipment was sold on credit by the dealer, the transaction was financed through Farago. If customers defaulted on their loan payments, Farago would repossess the equipment inventory.

In assessing inherent risk for repossessed inventory, the engagement senior, Rich Haney, noted that the commercial finance industry was experiencing problems and that Farago's management was aggressive in its choice of accounting policies and seemed quite concerned about earnings. Rich believed that inherent risk should probably be increased at least to a medium level, leading to increased testing of the repossessed inventory. However, the engagement manager, Jerry Bliss, thought differently. Jerry told Rich, "Nothing has changed on this audit. Just state that risk is low and do the same amount of testing."

In determining the existence of repossessed equipment inventory, PP&D had always relied on internal reports from the branch managers who held the equipment. Based on the prior year's work, Rich concluded that physical inspection was not necessary. In determining the value of equipment inventory, Rich relied on discussions with management, the same as in the prior year. As in the past, management did not get appraisals of the equipment, stating that their familiarity with the industry allowed them to make reasonable estimates. The auditors accepted this without further challenge. Based on finding no significant exceptions, PP&D issued an unqualified report.

When PP&D conducted their audit of Farago the next year, Jerry Bliss had left the firm and a new manager was assigned. Conditions in the commercial finance industry had deteriorated even more during the year, and the amount of repossessed inventory had increased significantly. The listing of repossessed equipment included many large items that had been included in the previous year. The new audit manager insisted on physical inspection of larger repossessed items. The result of this procedure was the discovery that the items did not exist. Investigation revealed that they had been sold and the proceeds recorded against the allowance for uncollectible loans, which was also understated. It was also clear that these practices had existed for at least the past 2 or 3 years.

LEARNING OBJECTIVES

After studying this chapter, you should be able to

20-1 Describe the business functions and the related documents and records in the inventory and warehousing cycle.

20-2 Explain the five parts of the audit of the inventory and warehousing cycle.

20-3 Design and perform audit tests of cost accounting.

20-4 Apply analytical procedures to the accounts in the inventory and warehousing cycle.

20-5 Design and perform physical observation audit tests for inventory.

20-6 Design and perform audit tests of pricing and compilation for inventory.

20-7 Integrate the various parts of the audit of the inventory and warehousing cycle.

T he **inventory and warehousing cycle** is unique because of its close relationships to other transaction cycles. Raw material and direct labor enter the inventory and warehousing cycle from the acquisition and payment cycle and the payroll and personnel cycle, respectively. The inventory and warehousing cycle ends with the sale of goods in the sales and collection cycle.

The audit of inventory, especially tests of the year-end inventory balance, is often the most complex and time-consuming part of the audit. As the example involving the audit of Farago in the opening vignette demonstrates, it is often difficult to establish the existence and appropriate valuation of inventories. Factors affecting the complexity of the audit of inventory include the following:

- Inventory is generally a major item on the balance sheet, and it is often the largest item making up the accounts included in working capital.
- The inventory is in different locations, which makes physical control and counting difficult. Companies must have their inventory accessible for the efficient manufacture and sale of the product, but this dispersal creates significant auditing problems.
- The diversity of the items in inventories creates difficulties for the auditor. Such items as jewels, chemicals, and electronic parts present problems of observation and valuation.
- The valuation of inventory is also difficult because of such factors as obsolescence and the need to allocate manufacturing costs to inventory.
- There are several acceptable inventory valuation methods, but any given client must apply a method consistently from year to year. Moreover, an organization may prefer to use different valuation methods for different parts of the inventory, which is acceptable under GAAP.

This chapter begins the discussion of the audit of the inventory and warehousing cycle by reviewing the business functions in the cycle and the related documents and records.

Inventory Accounting
Scandals

BUSINESS FUNCTIONS IN THE CYCLE AND RELATED DOCUMENTS AND RECORDS

OBJECTIVE 20-1
Describe the business functions and the related documents and records in the inventory and warehousing cycle.

Inventory takes many different forms, depending on the nature of the business. For retail or wholesale businesses, the most important inventory is merchandise on hand, available for sale. For hospitals, it includes food, drugs, and medical supplies. A manufacturing company has raw materials, purchased parts, and supplies for use in production, goods in the process of being manufactured, and finished goods available for sale. We have selected manufacturing company inventories for presentation in this text. However, most of the principles discussed apply to other types of businesses as well.

The physical flow of goods and the flow of costs in the inventory and warehousing cycle for a manufacturing company are shown in Figure 20-1. The direct tie-in of the inventory and warehousing cycle to the acquisition and payment cycle and the payroll and personnel cycle can be seen by examining the debits to the raw materials, direct labor, and manufacturing overhead T-accounts. The direct tie-in to the sales and collection cycle occurs at the point where finished goods are relieved (credited) and a charge is made to cost of goods sold.

The inventory and warehousing cycle can be thought of as comprising two separate but closely related systems, one involving the actual *physical flow of goods,* and the other the *related costs.* As inventories move through the company, there must be adequate controls over both their physical movement and their related costs. The six functions that make up the inventory and warehousing cycle are discussed in the following sections.

Process Purchase Orders

The inventory and warehousing cycle begins with the acquisition of raw materials for production. Whether inventory purchases relate to raw materials for a manufacturer or finished goods for a retailer, it is essential that adequate controls over purchasing are maintained. Purchase requisitions are used to request the purchasing department to place orders for inventory items. Requisitions may be initiated by stockroom personnel or by computer when

FIGURE 20-1   Flow of Inventory and Costs

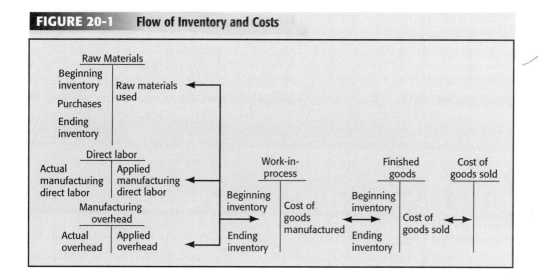

inventory reaches a predetermined level; orders may be placed for the materials required to produce a customer order; or orders may be initiated on the basis of a periodic inventory count by a responsible person. Regardless of the method followed, the controls over purchase requisitions and the related purchase orders are evaluated and tested as part of the acquisition and payment cycle.

Receipt of the ordered materials is also part of the acquisition and payment cycle. Material received should be inspected for quantity and quality. The receiving department produces a receiving report that becomes a part of the necessary documentation before payment is made. After inspection, the material is sent to the storeroom and the receiving documents are typically sent to purchasing, the storeroom, and accounts payable. Control and accountability are necessary for all transfers.

Receive Raw Materials

When materials are received, they are stored in the stockroom until needed for production. Materials are issued out of stock to production upon presentation of a properly approved materials requisition, work order, or similar document that indicates the type and quantity of materials needed. This requisition document is used to update the perpetual inventory master files and to make book transfers from the raw materials to work-in-process accounts.

Store Raw Materials

The processing portion of the inventory and warehousing cycle varies greatly from company to company. The determination of the items and quantities to be produced is generally based on specific orders from customers, sales forecasts, predetermined finished goods inventory levels, and economic production runs. A separate production control department often is responsible for the determination of the type and quantities of production. Within the various production departments, provision must be made to account for the quantities produced, control of scrap, quality controls, and physical protection of the material in process. The production department must generate production and scrap reports so that accounting can reflect the movement of materials in the books and determine accurate costs of production.

Process the Goods

In any company involved in manufacturing, an adequate cost accounting system is an important part of the processing of goods function. The system is necessary to indicate the relative profitability of the various products for management planning and control and to value inventories for financial statement purposes. Two types of cost systems exist, although many variations and combinations of these systems are used: **job cost systems** and **process cost systems**. The main difference is whether costs are accumulated by individual jobs when material is issued and labor costs incurred (job cost) or whether they are accumulated by processes, with unit costs for each process assigned to the products passing through the process (process cost).

Cost accounting records consist of master files, worksheets, and reports that accumulate material, labor, and overhead costs by job or process as the costs are incurred. When jobs or products are completed, the related costs are transferred from work-in-process to finished goods on the basis of production department reports.

Store Finished Goods

As finished goods are completed by the production department, they are placed in the stockroom awaiting shipment. In companies with good internal controls, finished goods are kept under physical control in a separate limited access area. The control of finished goods is often considered part of the sales and collection cycle.

Ship Finished Goods

Shipping of completed goods is an integral part of the sales and collection cycle. Any shipment or transfer of finished goods must be authorized by a properly approved shipping document. The controls for shipment have already been studied in previous chapters.

The physical movement and related documentation in a typical inventory and warehousing cycle is shown in Figure 20-2. The figure reemphasizes the important point that the recording of costs and movement of inventory as shown in the books must correspond to the physical movements and processes.

Perpetual Inventory Master Files

One of the records used for inventory that has not been previously discussed is a **perpetual inventory master file**. Separate perpetual records are normally kept for raw materials and finished goods. Most companies do not use perpetuals for work-in-process.

Perpetual inventory master files can include only information about the units of inventory acquired, sold, and on hand, or they can also include information about unit costs. The latter is more typical of well-designed computerized systems.

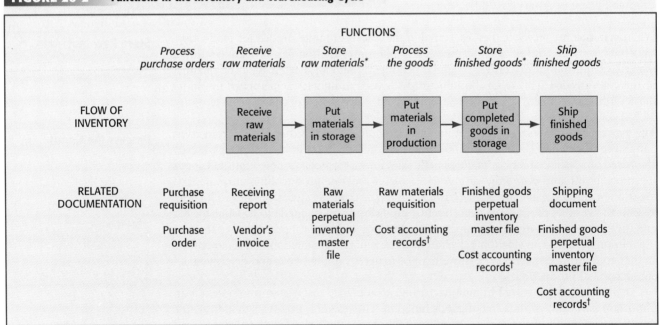

FIGURE 20-2   Functions in the Inventory and Warehousing Cycle

*Inventory counts are taken and compared with perpetual and book amounts at any stage of the cycle. The auditor must determine that cutoff for recording documents corresponds to the physical location of the items. A count must ordinarily be taken once a year. If the perpetual inventory system is operating well, this can be done on a cycle basis throughout the year.

†Includes cost information for materials, direct labor, and overhead.

For acquisitions of raw materials, the perpetual inventory master file is updated automatically when acquisitions of inventory are processed as a part of recording acquisitions. For example, when the computer system enters the number of units and unit cost for each raw material acquisition, this information is used to update perpetual inventory master files along with the acquisitions journal and accounts payable master file.

Transfers of raw material from the storeroom must be separately entered into the computer to update the perpetual records. Typically, only the units transferred need to be entered because the computer can determine the unit costs from the master file. Raw material perpetual inventory master files that have unit costs include, for each raw material, beginning and ending units on hand and unit costs, units and unit cost of each acquisition, and units and unit cost of each transfer into production.

Finished goods perpetual inventory master files include the same type of information as raw materials perpetuals but are considerably more complex if costs are included along with units. Finished goods costs include raw materials, direct labor, and manufacturing overhead, which often requires allocations and detailed record keeping. When finished goods perpetuals include unit costs, the cost accounting records must be integrated into the computer system.

PARTS OF THE AUDIT OF INVENTORY

Now that you are familiar with the business functions and the related documents and records in the inventory and warehousing cycle, we are ready to turn our attention to the audit of the cycle. The overall objective in the audit of the inventory and warehousing cycle is to determine that raw materials, work-in-process, finished goods inventory, and cost of goods sold are fairly stated on the financial statements. The audit of the inventory and warehousing cycle can be divided into five distinct parts.

> **OBJECTIVE 20-2**
> Explain the five parts of the audit of the inventory and warehousing cycle.

This part of the audit of the inventory and warehousing cycle includes the first three functions in Figure 20-2: process purchase orders, receive raw materials, and store raw materials. The internal controls over these three functions are first understood, then tested as a part of performing tests of controls and substantive tests of transactions in the acquisition and payment cycle and the payroll and personnel cycle. At the completion of the acquisition and payment cycle, the auditor is likely to be satisfied that acquisitions of raw materials and manufacturing costs are correctly stated and samples should be designed to ensure that these systems are adequately tested. Similarly, when labor is a significant part of inventory, the payroll and personnel cycle tests should verify the proper accounting for these costs.

Acquire and Record Raw Materials, Labor, and Overhead

Internal transfers include the fourth and fifth functions in Figure 20-2: process the goods and store finished goods. These activities are accounted for in the cost accounting records. These records are independent of other cycles and are tested as part of the audit of the inventory and warehousing cycle.

Transfer Assets and Costs

Recording of shipments and related costs, the last function in Figure 20-2, is part of the sales and collection cycle. Therefore, internal controls over the function are understood and tested as a part of auditing the sales and collection cycle. Tests of controls and substantive tests of transactions should include procedures to verify the accuracy of the perpetual inventory master files.

Ship Goods and Record Revenue and Costs

Observing the client taking a physical inventory count is necessary to determine whether recorded inventory actually exists at the balance sheet date and is properly counted by the client. Inventory is the first audit area for which physical examination is an essential type of evidence used to verify the balance in an account. The example at the beginning of the chapter involving the audit of Farago demonstrates the importance of physically observing inventories that are material to the financial statements.

Physically Observe Inventory

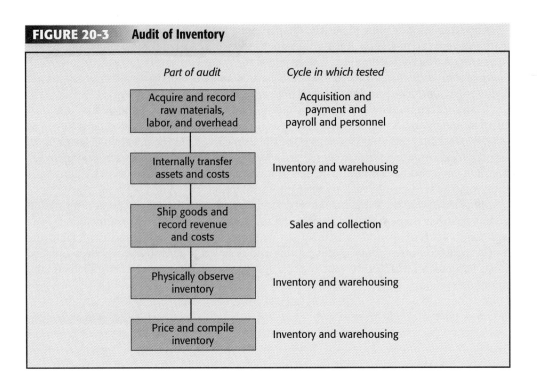

FIGURE 20-3   Audit of Inventory

Part of audit	Cycle in which tested
Acquire and record raw materials, labor, and overhead	Acquisition and payment and payroll and personnel
Internally transfer assets and costs	Inventory and warehousing
Ship goods and record revenue and costs	Sales and collection
Physically observe inventory	Inventory and warehousing
Price and compile inventory	Inventory and warehousing

Price and Compile Inventory

Costs used to value the physical inventory must be tested to determine whether the client has correctly followed an inventory method that is in accordance with GAAP and is consistent with previous years. Audit procedures used to verify these costs are called price tests. In addition, the auditor must verify whether the physical counts were correctly summarized, the inventory quantities and prices were correctly extended, and the extended inventory was correctly footed. These tests are called compilation tests.

Figure 20-3 summarizes the five parts of the audit of the inventory and warehousing cycle. Because of the interrelationships of the inventory and warehousing cycle with other cycles, some parts of the audit of inventory are most efficiently tested with the audit tests of other cycles. As noted in Figure 20-3, the acquisition and recording of raw materials, labor, and overhead is tested as part of the audit of the acquisition and payment and payroll and personnel cycles. The shipment of goods and recording of revenue and related costs is addressed in the audit of the sales and collection cycle. Because these activities involving the audit of other cycles have previously been discussed, they are not addressed in this chapter. However, the results of these tests of other cycles are important to the overall evaluation of the audit of inventory.

The following section discusses the audit of cost accounting. We begin by discussing the internal transfer of assets and costs, which are accounted for in the cost accounting records. The internal transfer of assets and costs is one of the three parts of the audit of the inventory and warehousing cycle that is not tested in other cycles.

AUDIT OF COST ACCOUNTING

OBJECTIVE 20-3
Design and perform audit tests of cost accounting.

Cost accounting systems and controls of different companies vary more than most other areas because of the wide variety of items of inventory and the level of sophistication desired by management. For example, a company that manufactures an entire line of farm machines will have a completely different kind of cost records and internal controls than a steel fabricating shop that makes and installs custom-made metal cabinets. It should also not be surprising that small companies whose owners are actively involved in the manufacturing process will need less sophisticated records than will large multiproduct companies.

Cost accounting controls are those related to the physical inventory and the related costs from the point at which raw materials are requisitioned to the point at which the manufactured product is completed and transferred to storage. It is convenient to divide these controls into two broad categories: (1) physical controls over raw materials, work-in-process, and finished goods inventory, and (2) controls over the related costs.

Almost all companies need physical controls over their assets to prevent loss from misuse and theft. The use of physically segregated, limited access storage areas for raw material, work-in-process, and finished goods is one major control to protect assets. In some instances, the assignment of custody of inventory to specific responsible individuals may be necessary to protect the assets. Approved prenumbered documents for authorizing movement of inventory also protect the assets from improper use. Copies of these documents should be sent directly to accounting by the persons issuing them, bypassing people with custodial responsibilities. An example of an effective document of this type is an approved materials requisition for obtaining raw materials from the storeroom.

Perpetual inventory master files maintained by persons who do not have custody of or access to assets are another useful cost accounting control. Perpetual inventory master files are important for a number of reasons: they provide a record of items on hand, which is used to initiate production or acquisition of additional materials or goods; they provide a record of the use of raw materials and the sale of finished goods, which can be reviewed for obsolete or slow-moving items; and they provide a record that can be used to pinpoint responsibility for custody as a part of the investigation of differences between physical counts and the amount shown on the records.

Another important consideration in cost accounting is the existence of adequate internal controls that integrate production and accounting records for the purpose of obtaining accurate costs for all products. The existence of adequate cost records is important to management as an aid in pricing, controlling costs, and costing inventory.

The concepts in auditing cost accounting are no different from those discussed for any other transaction cycle. Figure 20-4 shows the methodology the auditor should follow in deciding which tests to perform. In auditing cost accounting, the auditor is concerned with

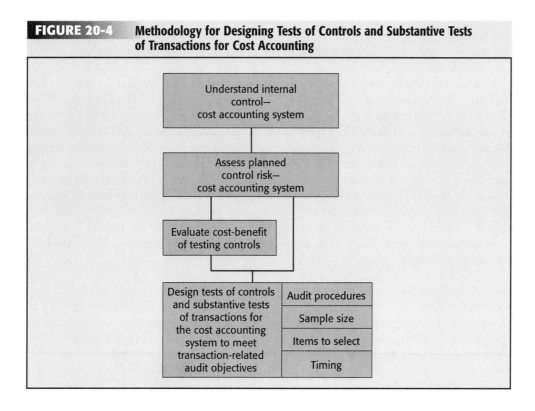

FIGURE 20-4   Methodology for Designing Tests of Controls and Substantive Tests of Transactions for Cost Accounting

four aspects: physical controls over inventory, documents and records for transferring inventory, perpetual inventory master files, and unit cost records.

Physical Controls Auditor's tests of the adequacy of the physical controls over raw materials, work-in-process, and finished goods must be restricted to observation and inquiry. For example, the auditor can examine the raw materials storage area to determine whether the inventory is protected from theft and misuse by the existence of a locked storeroom. An adequate storeroom with a competent custodian in charge also ordinarily results in the orderly storage of inventory. If the auditor concludes that the physical controls are so inadequate that the inventory will be difficult to count, the auditor should expand his or her observation of physical inventory tests to make sure that an adequate count is carried out.

Documents and Records for Transferring Inventory The auditor's primary concerns in verifying the transfer of inventory from one location to another are that the recorded transfers exist, the transfers that have actually taken place are recorded, and the quantity, description, and date of all recorded transfers are accurate. First, it is necessary to understand the client's internal controls for recording transfers before relevant tests can be performed. Once the internal controls are understood, the tests can easily be performed by examining documents and records. For example, a procedure to test the existence and accuracy of the transfer of goods from the raw material storeroom to the manufacturing assembly line is to account for a sequence of raw material requisitions, examine the requisitions for proper approval, and compare the quantity, description, and date with the information on the raw material perpetual inventory master files. Similarly, completed production records can be compared with perpetual inventory master files to be sure that all manufactured goods were physically delivered to the finished goods storeroom.

Perpetual Inventory Master Files Adequate perpetual inventory master files have a major effect on the *timing and extent* of the auditor's physical examination of inventory. When there are accurate perpetual inventory master files, it is often possible to test the physical inventory before the balance sheet date. An interim physical inventory can result in significant cost savings for both the client and the auditor, and it enables the client to get the audited statements earlier. Perpetual inventory master files also enable the auditor to reduce the extent of the tests of physical inventory when the assessed control risk related to physical observation of inventory is low.

Tests of the perpetual inventory master files for the purpose of reducing tests of physical inventory or changing their timing are done through the use of documentation. Documents to verify the acquisition of raw materials can be examined when the auditor is verifying acquisitions as part of the tests of the acquisition and payment cycle. Documents supporting the reduction of raw material inventory for use in production and the increase in the quantity of finished goods inventory when goods have been manufactured are examined as part of the tests of the cost accounting records in the manner discussed in the preceding section. Support for the reduction in the finished goods inventory through the sale of goods to customers is ordinarily tested as part of the sales and collection cycle. Usually, it is relatively easy to test the accuracy of the perpetuals after the auditor determines how the internal controls are designed and decides to what degree assessed control risk should be reduced.

Unit Cost Records Obtaining accurate cost data for raw materials, direct labor, and manufacturing overhead is an essential part of cost accounting. Adequate cost accounting records must be integrated with production and other accounting records to produce accurate costs of all products. Cost accounting records are pertinent to the auditor in that the valuation of ending inventory depends on the proper design and use of these records.

In testing the inventory cost records, the auditor must first develop an understanding of internal control. This is often somewhat time-consuming because the flow of costs is usually integrated with other accounting records, and it may not be obvious how the internal controls provide for the internal transfers of raw materials and for direct labor and manufacturing overhead as production is carried out.

Once the auditor understands internal control, the approach to internal verification involves the same concepts that were discussed in the verification of sales and acquisition transactions. When possible, it is desirable to test cost accounting records as a part of the acquisition, payroll, and sales tests to avoid testing the records more than once. For example, when the auditor is testing acquisition transactions as a part of the acquisition and payment cycle, it is desirable to trace the units and unit costs of raw materials to the perpetual inventory master files and the total cost to cost accounting records. Similarly, when payroll costs data are maintained for different jobs, it is desirable to trace from the payroll summary directly to job cost records as a part of testing the payroll and personnel cycle.

A major difficulty in the verification of inventory cost records is determining the reasonableness of cost allocations. For example, the assignment of manufacturing overhead costs to individual products entails certain assumptions that can significantly affect the unit costs of inventory and therefore the fairness of the inventory valuation. In evaluating these allocations, the auditor must consider the reasonableness of both the numerator and the denominator that result in the unit costs. For example, in testing overhead applied to inventory on the basis of direct labor dollars, the overhead rate should approximate total actual manufacturing overhead divided by total actual direct labor dollars. Because total manufacturing overhead is tested as part of the tests of the acquisition and payment cycle and direct labor is tested as part of the payroll and personnel cycle, determining the reasonableness of the rate is not difficult. However, if manufacturing overhead is applied on the basis of machine hours, the auditor must verify the reasonableness of the machine hours by separate tests of the client's machine records. The major considerations in evaluating the reasonableness of all cost allocations, including manufacturing overhead, are compliance with generally accepted accounting principles and consistency with previous years.

Because the internal controls over cost accounting records vary significantly among organizations, specific tests of controls are not presented here. The auditor should design appropriate tests based on the understanding of the nature of the cost accounting records and the extent to which they will be relied on to reduce substantive tests. The quality of the cost accounting records also affects the use of analytical procedures, which is discussed in the next section.

ANALYTICAL PROCEDURES

Analytical procedures are as important in auditing inventory and warehousing as in any other cycle. Table 20-1 (p. 654) includes several common analytical procedures and possible misstatements that may be indicated when fluctuations exist. Several of those analytical procedures have also been included in other cycles. An example is the gross margin percentage.

OBJECTIVE 20-4
Apply analytical procedures to the accounts in the inventory and warehousing cycle.

After performing the appropriate tests of the cost accounting records and analytical procedures, the auditor is prepared to design and perform tests of details of the ending inventory balance.

METHODOLOGY FOR DESIGNING TESTS OF DETAILS OF BALANCES

The methodology for deciding which tests of details of balances to perform for inventory and warehousing is essentially the same as that discussed for accounts receivable, accounts payable, and all other balance sheet accounts. It is shown in Figure 20-5 on page 654.

TABLE 20-1   Analytical Procedures for the Inventory and Warehousing Cycle

Analytical Procedure	Possible Misstatement
Compare gross margin percentage with that of previous years.	Overstatement or understatement of inventory and cost of goods sold.
Compare inventory turnover (cost of goods sold divided by average inventory) with that of previous years.	Obsolete inventory, which affects inventory and cost of goods sold. Overstatement or understatement of inventory.
Compare unit costs of inventory with those of previous years.	Overstatement or understatement of unit costs, which affect inventory and cost of goods sold.
Compare extended inventory value with that of previous years.	Misstatements in compilation, unit costs, or extensions, which affect inventory and cost of goods sold.
Compare current-year manufacturing costs with those of previous years (variable costs should be adjusted for changes in volume).	Misstatement of unit costs of inventory, especially direct labor and manufacturing overhead, which affect inventory and cost of goods sold.

FIGURE 20-5   Methodology for Designing Tests of Details of Balances for Inventory

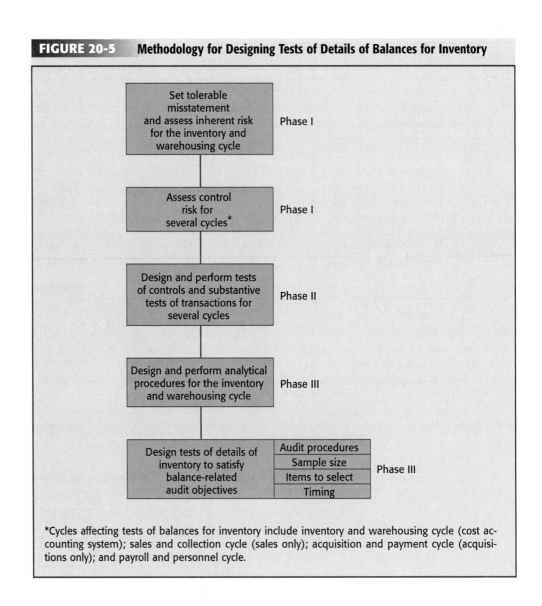

*Cycles affecting tests of balances for inventory include inventory and warehousing cycle (cost accounting system); sales and collection cycle (sales only); acquisition and payment cycle (acquisitions only); and payroll and personnel cycle.

The auditor first sets tolerable misstatement and assesses inherent risk for inventory. Inventory is typically one of the most material items in the financial statements for manufacturing, wholesale, and retail companies. Inherent risk is often assessed at a relatively high level for companies with significant inventory. Inventory may be stored in multiple locations, increasing concerns about the existence of inventory, including the potential for theft. The pricing of inventory is often complex, increasing the risk of misstatement for the accuracy objective. There may also be concerns about inventory obsolescence, which relates to the net realizable value objective.

In assessing control risk, the auditor is primarily concerned about internal controls over perpetual records, physical controls, inventory counts, and inventory pricing. The nature and extent of controls vary widely from company to company. Note that the test results from several cycles other than inventory and warehousing also affect tests of details of balances for inventory.

Because of the complexity of auditing inventory, two aspects of tests of details of balances are discussed separately: (1) physical observation and (2) pricing and compilation. These topics are studied in the next two sections.

PHYSICAL OBSERVATION OF INVENTORY

OBJECTIVE 20-5
Design and perform physical observation audit tests for inventory.

Auditors have been required to perform physical observation tests of inventory since a major fraud was uncovered in 1938 at the McKesson & Robbins Company. The company recorded significant amounts of nonexistent inventory. This was possible because the auditors did not physically observe the inventory. SAS 1 (AU 331) states that the following requirement exists for inventory observation:

> • . . . it is ordinarily necessary for the independent auditor to be present at the time of count and, by suitable observation, tests, and inquiries, satisfy himself respecting the effectiveness of the methods of inventory-taking and the measure of reliance which may be placed upon the client's representations about the quantities and physical condition of the inventories.

An essential point in the SAS 1 requirement is the distinction between the observation of the physical inventory count and the responsibility for taking the count. The client has responsibility for setting up the procedures for taking an accurate physical inventory and actually making and recording the counts. The auditor's responsibility is to evaluate and observe the client's physical procedures and draw conclusions about the adequacy of the physical inventory.

The requirement of physical examination of inventory is not applicable in the case of *inventory in a public warehouse*. The AICPA position on inventory stored in a public warehouse is summarized in the same section of the standard as follows:

> • In the case of inventories which in the ordinary course of business are in the hands of public warehouses or other outside custodians, direct confirmation in writing from the custodians is acceptable provided that, where the amount involved represents a significant proportion of the current assets or the total assets, supplemental inquiries are made to satisfy the independent auditor as to the bona fides of the situation.

The SAS recommends that the supplemental inquiries include the following steps, to the extent that the auditor considers them necessary in the circumstances:

> • Discussion with the owner as to the owner's controls in investigating the warehouse-person and tests of related evidential matter
> • Review of the owner's controls concerning performance of the warehouseperson and tests of related evidential matter
> • Observation of physical counts of the goods whenever practical and reasonable
> • Where warehouse receipts have been pledged as collateral, confirmation (on a test basis, when appropriate) from lenders as to pertinent details of the pledged receipts

Timber Inventory
Estimation Techniques

Regardless of the client's inventory record-keeping method, there must be a periodic physical count of the inventory items on hand. The client can take the physical count at or near the balance sheet date, at a preliminary date, or on a cycle basis throughout the year. The last two approaches are appropriate only if there are adequate perpetual inventory master files.

In connection with the client's physical count of inventory, adequate controls include proper instructions for the physical count, supervision by responsible personnel, independent interval verification of the counts, independent reconciliations of the physical counts with perpetual inventory master files, and adequate control over count sheets or tags.

Inventory Audit Software

An important aspect of the auditor's understanding of the client's physical inventory controls is complete familiarity with them before the inventory begins. This is obviously necessary to evaluate the effectiveness of the client's procedures, but it also enables the auditor to make constructive suggestions beforehand. If the inventory instructions do not provide adequate controls, the auditor must spend more time making sure that the physical count is accurate.

Audit Decisions

The auditor's decisions in the physical observation of inventory are similar to those made for other audit areas and include selecting audit procedures, deciding the timing of the procedures, determining sample size, and selecting items for testing. The last three decisions are discussed next, followed by a discussion of selecting the appropriate audit procedures.

Timing The auditor decides whether the physical count can be taken before year-end primarily on the basis of the accuracy of the perpetual inventory master files. When an interim physical count is permitted, the auditor observes it at that time and also tests the perpetuals for transactions from the date of the count to year-end. When the perpetuals are accurate, it may be unnecessary for the client to count the inventory every year. Instead, the auditor can compare the perpetuals with the actual inventory on a sample basis at a convenient time. When there are no perpetuals and the inventory is material, a complete physical inventory must be taken by the client near the end of the accounting period and tested by the auditor at the same time.

Sample Size Sample size in physical observation is usually impossible to specify in terms of the number of items because the emphasis during the tests is on observing the client's procedures rather than on selecting items for testing. A convenient way to think of sample size in physical observation is in terms of the total number of hours spent rather than the number of inventory items counted. The most important determinants of the amount of time needed to test inventory are the adequacy of the internal controls over the physical counts, accuracy of the perpetual inventory master files, total dollar amount and type of inventory, number of different significant inventory locations, nature and extent of misstatements discovered in previous years, and other inherent risks. In some situations, inventory is such a significant item that dozens of auditors are necessary to observe the physical count, whereas in other situations one person can complete the observation in a short time. Special care is warranted in the observation of inventory because of the difficulty of expanding sample sizes or reperforming tests after the physical inventory has been taken.

Selection of Items The selection of items for testing is an important part of the audit decision in inventory observation. Care should be taken to observe the counting of the most significant items and a representative sample of typical inventory items, to inquire about items that are likely to be obsolete or damaged, and to discuss with management the reasons for excluding any material items.

for Have to do periodic for COGS

By 1970, Crazy Eddie, Inc., a consumer electronics retail company, had forty-three consumer sales outlets, sales of $350 million, reported net income before taxes of $21 million, and a market value of more than $500 million. By the end of 1989, the company had filed for bankruptcy, closed all stores, and liquidated all assets at a huge loss to investors.

Investigation by regulatory authorities found extensive financial fraud, the most important being a $65 million overstatement of inventory. There were extensive lawsuits against many parties, including the CEO, who was found guilty of fraud and sent to prison.

Naturally, the question arose as to why the auditors failed to uncover the fraud in their annual audit. The defense used by the auditor was the difficulty of uncovering the well-conceived fraud. The parties involved in or who knew of the fraud included the acting controller, the director of internal auditing, and the director of accounts payable. One example of fraud was the shipment of inventory from store to store immediately before the auditor arrived to count the inventory. Another was the destruction of documentation to conceal inventory shortages at various locations. The auditor argued that it is almost impossible to uncover fraud when there is extensive collusion. The suit against the CPA firm and other defendants was settled out of court in 1993.

Source: Michael C. Knapp, *Contemporary Auditing: Issues and Cases,* 3rd edition. West Publishing, 1999, pp. 71–80.

Physical Observation Tests

The same balance-related audit objectives that have been used in previous sections for tests of details of balances provide the frame of reference for discussing the physical observation tests. However, before the objectives are discussed, some comments that apply to all the objectives are appropriate.

The most important part of the observation of inventory is determining whether the physical count is being taken in accordance with the client's instructions. To do this effectively, *it is essential that the auditor be present* while the physical count is taking place. When the client's employees are not following the inventory instructions, the auditor must either contact the supervisor to correct the problem or modify the physical observation procedures. For example, if the procedures require one team to count the inventory and a second team to recount it as a test of accuracy, the auditor should inform management if he or she observes both teams counting together.

Obtaining an adequate understanding of the client's business is even more important in physical observation of inventory than for most aspects of the audit because inventory varies so significantly for different companies. A proper understanding of the client's business and its industry enables the auditor to ask about and discuss such problems as inventory valuation, potential obsolescence, and existence of consignment inventory intermingled with owned inventory. A useful starting point for becoming familiar with the client's inventory is for the auditor to tour the client's facilities, including receiving, storage, production, planning, and record-keeping areas. The tour should be led by a supervisor who can answer questions about production, especially about any changes in the past year.

Common tests of details of balances audit procedures for physical inventory observation are shown in Table 20-2 on page 658. Detail tie-in and presentation and disclosure are the only balance-related audit objectives not included in the table. These objectives are discussed under compilation of inventory. The assumption throughout is that the client records inventory on prenumbered tags on the balance sheet date.

In addition to the detailed procedures included in Table 20-2, the auditor should walk through all areas where inventory is warehoused to make sure that all inventory has been counted and properly tagged. When inventory is in boxes or other containers, these should be opened during test counts. It is desirable to compare high dollar value inventory to counts in the previous year and inventory master files as a test of reasonableness. These two procedures should not be done until the client has completed the physical counts.

TABLE 20-2	**Balance-Related Audit Objectives and Tests of Details of Balances for Physical Inventory Observation**	
Balance-Related Audit Objective	**Common Inventory Observation Procedures**	**Comments**
Inventory as recorded on tags exists (existence).	Select a random sample of tag numbers and identify the tag with that number attached to the actual inventory. Observe whether movement of inventory takes place during the count.	The purpose is to uncover the inclusion of nonexistent items as inventory.
Existing inventory is counted and tagged and tags are accounted for to make sure none are missing (completeness).	Examine inventory to make sure it is tagged. Observe whether movement of inventory takes place during the count. Inquire as to inventory in other locations. Account for all used and unused tags to make sure none are lost or intentionally omitted. Record the tag numbers for those used and unused for subsequent follow-up.	Special concern should be directed to omission of large sections of inventory. This test should be done at the completion of the physical count. This test should be done at the completion of the physical count.
Inventory is counted accurately (accuracy).	Recount client's counts to make sure the recorded counts are accurate on the tags (also check descriptions and unit of count, such as dozen or gross). Compare physical counts with perpetual inventory master file. Record client's counts for subsequent testing.	Recording client counts in the working papers on *inventory count sheets* is done for two reasons: to obtain documentation that an adequate physical examination was made, and to test for the possibility that the client might change the recorded counts after the auditor leaves the premises.
Inventory is classified correctly on the tags (classification).	Examine inventory descriptions on the tags and compare with the actual inventory for raw material, work-in-process, and finished goods. Evaluate whether the percent of completion recorded on the tags for work-in-process is reasonable.	These tests would be done as a part of the first procedure in the accuracy objective.
Information is obtained to make sure sales and inventory purchases are recorded in the proper period (cutoff).	Record in the working papers for subsequent follow-up the last shipping document number used at year-end. Make sure the inventory for the above item was excluded from the physical count. Review shipping area for inventory set aside for shipment, but not counted. Record in the working papers for subsequent follow-up the last receiving report number used at year-end. Make sure the inventory for the above item was included in the physical count. Review receiving area for inventory that should be included in the physical count.	Obtaining proper cutoff information for sales and acquisitions is an essential part of inventory observation. The appropriate tests during the field work were discussed for sales in Chapter 13 and acquisitions in Chapter 18.
Obsolete and unusable inventory items are excluded or noted (realizable value).	Test for obsolete inventory by inquiry of factory employees and management, and alertness for items that are damaged, rust- or dust-covered, or located in inappropriate places.	
The client has rights to inventory recorded on tags (rights).	Inquire about consignment or customer inventory included on client's premises. Be alert for inventory that is set aside or specially marked as indications of nonownership.	

An important part of the audit of inventory is to perform all the procedures necessary to make certain that the physical counts or perpetual record quantities were properly priced and compiled. **Inventory price tests** include all the tests of the client's unit prices to determine whether they are correct. **Inventory compilation tests** include all the tests of the summarization of the physical quantities, the extension of price times quantity, footing the inventory summary, and tracing the totals to the general ledger.

OBJECTIVE 20-6
Design and perform audit tests of pricing and compilation for inventory.

The existence of adequate internal controls for unit costs that are integrated with production and other accounting records is important to ensure that reasonable costs are used for valuing ending inventory. One important internal control is the use of **standard cost records** that indicate variances in material, labor, and overhead costs and can be used to evaluate production. When standard costs are used, procedures must be designed to keep the standards updated for changes in production processes and costs. The review of unit costs for reasonableness by someone independent of the department responsible for developing the costs is also a useful control over valuation.

An internal control designed to prevent the overstatement of inventory through the inclusion of obsolete inventory is a formal review and reporting of obsolete, slow-moving, damaged, and overstated inventory items. The review should be done by a competent employee by reviewing perpetual inventory master files for inventory turnover and holding discussions with engineering or production personnel.

Compilation internal controls are needed to provide a means of ensuring that the physical counts are properly summarized, priced at the same amount as the unit records, correctly extended and totaled, and included in the general ledger at the proper amount. Important compilation internal controls are adequate documents and records for taking the physical count and proper internal verification. If the physical inventory is taken on prenumbered tags and carefully reviewed before the personnel are released from the physical examination of inventory, there should be little risk of misstatement in summarizing the tags. The most important internal control over accurate determination of prices, extensions, and footings is internal verification by a competent, independent person.

Pricing and Compilation Controls

| Acquire and record raw materials, labor, and overhead |
| Internally transfer assets and costs |
| Ship goods and record revenue and costs |
| Physically observe inventory |
| Price and compile inventory |

Balance-related audit objectives for tests of details of balances are also useful in discussing pricing and compilation procedures. The objectives and related tests are shown in Table 20-3 (p. 660), except for the cutoff objective. Physical observation, which was previously discussed, is a major source of cutoff information for sales and purchases. Tests of the accounting records for cutoff are done as a part of sales (sales and collection cycle) and acquisitions (acquisition and payment cycle).

The frame of reference for applying the objectives is a listing of inventory obtained from the client that includes each inventory item's description, quantity, unit price, and extended value. The inventory listing is in inventory item description order with raw material, work-in-process, and finished goods separated. The totals equal the general ledger balance.

Pricing and Compilation Procedures

(handwritten annotation: Inventory – w/ cost basis & come up w/)

Valuation of Inventory

(handwritten annotation: Lower of cost or Market basis (replacement cost) Compare to Market)

The proper valuation (pricing) of inventory is often one of the most important and time-consuming parts of the audit. In performing pricing tests, three things about the client's method of pricing are extremely important: the method must be in accordance with GAAP, the application of the method must be consistent from year to year, and cost versus market value (replacement cost or net realizable value) must be considered. Because the method of verifying the pricing of inventory depends on whether items are acquired or manufactured, these two categories are discussed separately.

Pricing Purchased Inventory The primary types of inventory included in this category are raw materials, purchased parts, and supplies. As a first step in verifying the valuation of purchased inventory, it is necessary to establish clearly whether LIFO, FIFO, weighted

Balance-Related Audit Objective	Common Inventory Pricing and Compilation Procedures	Comments
Inventory in the inventory listing schedule agrees with the physical inventory counts, the extensions are correct, and the total is correctly added and agrees with the general ledger (detail tie-in).	Perform compilation tests (see existence, completeness, and accuracy objectives). Foot the inventory listing schedules for raw materials, work-in-process, and finished goods. Trace the totals to the general ledger. Extend the quantity times the price on selected items.	Unless controls are weak, extending and footing tests should be limited.
Inventory items in the inventory listing schedule exist (existence).	Trace inventory listed in the schedule to inventory tags and auditor's recorded counts for existence and description.	The next six objectives are affected by the results of the physical inventory observation. The tag numbers and counts verified as a part of physical inventory observation are traced to the inventory listing schedule as a part of these tests.
Existing inventory items are included in the inventory listing schedule (completeness).	Account for unused tag numbers shown in the auditor's working papers to make sure no tags have been added. Trace from inventory tags to the inventory listing schedules and make sure inventory on tags are included. Account for tag numbers to make sure none have been deleted.	
Inventory items in the inventory listing schedule are accurate (accuracy).	Trace inventory listed in the schedule to inventory tags and auditor's recorded counts for quantity and description. Perform price tests of inventory. For a discussion of price tests, see text material on pages 659–662.	
Inventory items in the inventory listing schedule are properly classified (classification).	Compare the classification into raw materials, work-in-process, and finished goods by comparing the descriptions on inventory tags and auditor's recorded test counts with the inventory listing schedule.	
Inventory items in the inventory listing are stated at realizable value (realizable value).	Perform tests of lower of cost or market, selling price, and obsolescence.	
The client has rights to inventory items in the inventory listing schedule (rights).	Trace inventory tags identified as nonowned during the physical observation to the inventory listing schedule to make sure these have not been included. Review contracts with suppliers and customers and inquire of management for the possibility of the inclusion of consigned or other nonowned inventory, or the exclusion of owned inventory.	
Inventory and related accounts in the inventory and warehousing cycle are properly presented and disclosed (presentation and disclosure).	Examine financial statements for proper presentation and disclosure, including: Separate disclosure of raw materials, work-in-process, and finished goods. Proper description of the inventory costing method. Description of pledged inventory. Inclusion of significant sales and purchase commitments.	Pledging of inventory and sales and purchase commitments are usually uncovered as a part of other audit tests.

average, or some other valuation method is being used. It is also necessary to determine which costs should be included in the valuation of an item of inventory. For example, the auditor must find out whether freight, storage, discounts, and other costs are included and compare the findings with the preceding year's audit working papers to make sure that the methods are consistent.

In selecting specific inventory items for pricing, emphasis should be put on the larger dollar amounts and on products that are known to have wide fluctuations in price, but a representative sample of all types of inventory and departments should be included as well. Stratified variables or monetary unit sampling is commonly used in these tests.

The auditor should list the inventory items that he or she intends to verify for pricing and request the client to locate the appropriate vendors' invoices. It is important that sufficient invoices be examined to account for the entire quantity of inventory for the item being tested, especially for the FIFO valuation method. Examining sufficient invoices is useful to uncover situations in which clients value their inventory on the basis of the most recent invoice only and, in some cases, to discover obsolete inventory. As an illustration, assume that the client's valuation of an inventory item is $12.00 per unit for 1,000 units, using FIFO. The auditor should examine the most recent invoices for acquisitions of that inventory item made in the year under audit until the valuation of all of the 1,000 units is accounted for. If the most recent acquisition of the inventory item was for 700 units at $12.00 per unit and the immediately preceding acquisition was for 600 units at $11.30 per unit, the inventory item in question is overstated by $210.00 (300 $\times$ $.70).

When the client has perpetual inventory master files that include unit costs of acquisitions, it is usually desirable to test the pricing by tracing the unit costs to the perpetuals rather than to vendors' invoices. In most cases, the effect is to reduce the cost of verifying inventory valuation significantly. Naturally, when the perpetuals are used to verify unit costs, it is essential to test the unit costs on the perpetuals to vendors' invoices as a part of the tests of the acquisition and payment cycle.

Pricing Manufactured Inventory The auditor must consider the cost of raw materials, direct labor, and manufacturing overhead in pricing work-in-process and finished goods. The need to verify each of these has the effect of making the audit of work-in-process and finished goods inventory more complex than the audit of purchased inventory. Nevertheless, such considerations as selecting the items to be tested, testing for whether cost or market value is lower, and evaluating the possibility of obsolescence also apply.

In pricing raw materials in manufactured products, it is necessary to consider both the unit cost of the raw materials and the number of units required to manufacture a unit of output. The unit cost can be verified in the same manner as that used for other purchased inventory—by examining vendors' invoices or perpetual inventory master files. Then it is necessary to examine engineering specifications, inspect the finished product, or find a similar method to determine the number of units it takes to manufacture a product.

Similarly, the hourly costs of direct labor and the number of hours it takes to manufacture a unit of output must be verified while testing direct labor. Hourly labor costs can be verified by comparison with labor payroll or union contracts. The number of hours needed to manufacture the product can be determined from engineering specifications or similar sources.

The proper manufacturing overhead in work-in-process and finished goods is dependent on the approach being used by the client. It is necessary to evaluate the method being used for consistency and reasonableness and to recompute the costs to determine whether the overhead is correct. For example, if the rate is based on direct labor dollars, the auditor can divide the total manufacturing overhead by the total direct labor dollars to determine the actual overhead rate. This rate can then be compared with the overhead rate used by the client to determine unit costs.

When the client has standard costs records, an efficient and useful method of determining valuation is by the review and analysis of variances. If the variances in material, labor, and manufacturing overhead are small, it is evidence of reliable cost records.

Cost or Market In pricing inventory, it is necessary to consider whether replacement cost or net realizable value is lower than historical cost. For purchased finished goods and raw materials, the most recent cost of an inventory item as indicated on a vendor's invoice of the subsequent period is a useful way to test for replacement cost. All manufacturing costs must be considered for work-in-process and finished goods for manufactured inventory. It is also necessary to consider the sales value of inventory items and the possible effect of rapid fluctuation of prices to determine net realizable value. Finally, it is necessary to consider the possibility of obsolescence in the valuation process.

INTEGRATION OF THE TESTS

OBJECTIVE 20-7
Integrate the various parts of the audit of the inventory and warehousing cycle.

The most difficult part of understanding the audit of the inventory and warehousing cycle is grasping the interrelationships of the many different tests the auditor makes to evaluate whether inventory and cost of goods sold are fairly stated. Figure 20-6 and the discussions that follow are designed to aid the reader in perceiving the audit of the inventory and warehousing cycle as a series of integrated tests.

FIGURE 20-6   Interrelationship of Various Audit Tests

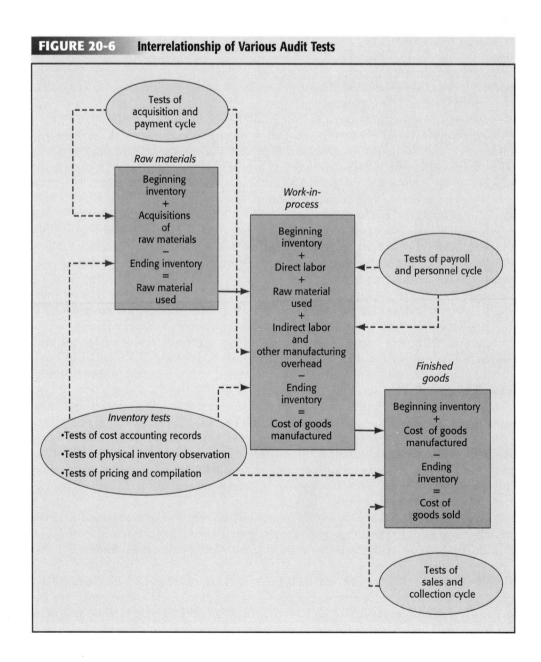

Tests of the Acquisition and Payment Cycle When the auditor verifies acquisitions as part of the tests of the acquisition and payment cycle, evidence is being obtained about the accuracy of raw materials acquired and all manufacturing overhead costs except labor. These acquisition costs either flow directly into cost of goods sold or become the most significant part of the ending inventory of raw material, work-in-process, and finished goods. In audits involving perpetual inventory master files, it is common to test these as a part of tests of controls and substantive tests of transactions procedures in the acquisition and payment cycle. Similarly, if manufacturing costs are assigned to individual jobs or processes, they are usually tested as a part of the same cycle.

Tests of the Payroll and Personnel Cycle When the auditor verifies labor costs, the same comments apply as for acquisitions. In most cases, the cost accounting records for direct and indirect labor costs can be tested as part of the audit of the payroll and personnel cycle if there is adequate advance planning.

Tests of the Sales and Collection Cycle Although the relationship is less close between the sales and collection cycle and the inventory and warehousing cycle than between the two previously discussed, it is still important. Most of the audit testing in the storage of finished goods as well as the shipment and recording of sales takes place when the sales and collection cycle is tested. In addition, if standard cost records are used, it may be possible to test the standard cost of goods sold at the same time that sales tests are performed.

Tests of Cost Accounting Tests of cost accounting are meant to verify the controls affecting inventory that were not verified as part of the three previously discussed cycles. Tests are made of the physical controls, transfers of raw material costs to work-in-process, transfers of costs of completed goods to finished goods, perpetual inventory master files, and unit cost records.

Physical Inventory, Pricing, and Compilation In most audits, the underlying assumption in testing the inventory and warehousing cycle is that cost of goods sold is a residual of beginning inventory plus acquisitions of raw materials, direct labor, and other manufacturing costs minus ending inventory. When the audit of inventory and cost of goods sold is approached with this idea in mind, the importance of ending inventory becomes obvious. Physical inventory, pricing, and compilation are each equally important in the audit because a misstatement in any one results in misstated inventory and cost of goods sold.

In testing the physical inventory, it is possible to rely heavily on the perpetual inventory master files if they have been tested as a part of one or more of the previously discussed tests. In fact, if the perpetual inventory master files are considered reliable, the auditor can observe and test the physical count at some time during the year and rely on the perpetuals to keep adequate records of the quantities.

When testing the unit costs, it is also possible to rely, to some degree, on the tests of the cost records made during the substantive tests of transactions. The existence of standard cost records is also useful for the purpose of comparison with the actual unit costs. If the standard costs are used to represent historical cost, they must be tested for reliability.

[handwritten margin note: If count is wrong, price is wrong, or compilation is wrong — can throw off inventory big time.]

SUMMARY

This chapter discussed the audit of the inventory and warehousing cycle. Because of the difficulties associated with establishing the existence and valuation of inventories, the cycle is often the most time-consuming and complex part of the audit. The cycle is also unique because many of the tests of the inputs to the cycle are tested as part of the audit of other cycles. Tests performed as part of the inventory and warehousing cycle focus on the cost accounting records, physical observation, and tests of the pricing and compilation of the ending inventory balance.

Cost accounting controls—controls over physical inventory and the related costs from the point at which raw materials are requisitioned to the point at which the manufactured product is completed and transferred to storage

Cost accounting records—the accounting records concerned with the manufacture and processing of the goods and storing finished goods

Inventory and warehousing cycle—the transaction cycle that involves the physical flow of goods through the organization, as well as related costs

Inventory compilation tests—audit procedures used to verify whether physical counts of inventory are correctly summarized, inventory quantities and prices are correctly extended, and extended inventory is correctly footed

Inventory price tests—audit procedures used to verify the costs used to value physical inventory

Job cost systems—systems of cost accounting in which costs are accumulated by individual jobs when material is used and labor costs are incurred

Perpetual inventory master file—a continuously updated computerized record of inventory items purchased, used, sold, and on hand for merchandise, raw materials, and finished goods

Process cost systems—systems of cost accounting in which costs are accumulated for a process, with unit costs for each process assigned to the products passing through the process

Standard cost records—records that indicate variances between projected material, labor, and overhead costs, and the actual costs

REVIEW QUESTIONS

20-1 (Objective 20-1)   Give the reasons why inventory is often the most difficult and time-consuming part of many audit engagements.

20-2 (Objectives 20-1, 20-7)   Explain the relationship between the acquisition and payment cycle and the inventory and warehousing cycle in the audit of a manufacturing company. List several audit procedures in the acquisition and payment cycle that support your explanation.

20-3 (Objective 20-1)   State what is meant by cost accounting records and explain their importance in the conduct of an audit.

20-4 (Objectives 20-2, 20-3)   Many auditors assert that certain audit tests can be significantly reduced for clients with adequate perpetual records that include both unit and cost data. What are the most important tests of the perpetual records that the auditor must make before he or she can reduce assessed control risk? Assuming the perpetuals are determined to be accurate, which tests can be reduced?

20-5 (Objective 20-5)   Before the physical examination, the auditor obtains a copy of the client's inventory instructions and reviews them with the controller. In obtaining an understanding of inventory procedures for a small manufacturing company, these deficiencies are identified: shipping operations will not be completely halted during the physical examination, and there will be no independent verification of the original inventory count by a second counting team. Evaluate the importance of each of these deficiencies and state its effect on the auditor's observation of inventory.

20-6 (Objective 20-5)   At the completion of an inventory observation, the controller requested the auditor to give him a copy of all recorded test counts to facilitate the correction of all discrepancies between the client's and the auditor's counts. Should the auditor comply with the request? Why?

20-7 (Objective 20-5)   What major audit procedures are involved in testing for the ownership of inventory during the observation of the physical counts and as a part of subsequent valuation tests?

20-8 (Objectives 20-4, 20-5, 20-6)   In the verification of the amount of the inventory, one of the auditor's concerns is that slow-moving and obsolete items be identified. List the auditing procedures that could be used to determine whether slow-moving or obsolete items have been included in inventory.

20-9 (Objective 20-5) During the taking of physical inventory, the controller intentionally withheld several inventory tags from the employees responsible for the physical count. After the auditor left the client's premises at the completion of the inventory observation, the controller recorded nonexistent inventory on the tags and thereby significantly overstated earnings. How could the auditor have uncovered the misstatement, assuming that there are no perpetual records?

20-10 (Objective 20-5) Explain why a proper cutoff of purchases and sales is heavily dependent on the physical inventory observation. What information should be obtained during the physical count to make sure that cutoff is accurate?

20-11 (Objective 20-6) Define what is meant by compilation tests. List several examples of audit procedures to verify compilation.

20-12 (Objective 20-4) List the major analytical procedures for testing the overall reasonableness of inventory. For each test, explain the type of misstatement that could be identified.

20-13 (Objective 20-6) Included in the December 31, 1999 inventory of the Wholeridge Supply Company are 2,600 deluxe ring binders in the amount of $5,902. An examination of the most recent acquisitions of binders showed the following costs: January 26, 2000, 2,300 at $2.42 each; December 6, 1999, 1,900 at $2.28 each; November 26, 1999, 2,400 at $2.07 each. What is the misstatement in valuation of the December 31, 1999, inventory for deluxe ring binders, assuming FIFO inventory valuation? What would your answer be if the January 26, 2000, acquisition was for 2,300 binders at $2.12 each?

20-14 (Objectives 20-6, 20-7) The Ruswell Manufacturing Company applied manufacturing overhead to inventory at December 31, 1999, on the basis of $3.47 per direct labor hour. Explain how you would evaluate the reasonableness of total direct labor hours and manufacturing overhead in the ending inventory of finished goods.

20-15 (Objective 20-7) Each employee for the Gedding Manufacturing Co., a firm using a job-cost inventory costing method, must reconcile his or her total hours worked with the hours worked on individual jobs using a job time sheet at the time weekly payroll time cards are prepared. The job time sheet is then stapled to the time card. Explain how you could test the direct labor dollars included in inventory as a part of the payroll and personnel tests.

20-16 (Objective 20-5) Assuming that the auditor properly documents receiving report numbers as a part of the physical inventory observation procedures, explain how he or she should verify the proper cutoff of purchases, including tests for the possibility of raw materials in transit, later in the audit.

MULTIPLE CHOICE QUESTIONS FROM CPA EXAMINATIONS

20-17 (Objective 20-1) The following questions concern internal controls in the inventory and warehousing cycle. Choose the best response.

    a. In a company whose materials and supplies include a great number of items, a fundamental deficiency in control requirements would be indicated if
        (1) a perpetual inventory master file is not maintained for items of small value.
        (2) the storekeeping function were to be combined with production and record keeping.
        (3) the cycle basis for physical inventory taking was to be used.
        (4) minor supply items were to be expensed when acquired.

    b. For control purposes, the quantities of materials ordered may be omitted from the copy of the purchase order that is
        (1) forwarded to the accounting department.
        (2) retained in the purchasing department's files.
        (3) returned to the requisitioner.
        (4) forwarded to the receiving department.

c. Which of the following procedures would *best* detect the theft of valuable items from an inventory that consists of hundreds of different items selling for $1 to $10 and a few items selling for hundreds of dollars?

(1) Maintain a perpetual inventory master file of only the more valuable items with frequent periodic verification of the validity of the perpetuals.

(2) Have an independent CPA firm prepare an internal control report on the effectiveness of the administrative and accounting controls over inventory.

(3) Have separate warehouse space for the more valuable items with sequentially numbered tags.

(4) Require an authorized officer's signature on all requisitions for the more valuable items.

20-18 (Objectives 20-1, 20-3) The following questions concern testing the client's internal controls for inventory and warehousing. Choose the best response.

a. When an auditor tests a client's cost accounting records, the auditor's tests are *primarily* designed to determine that

(1) quantities on hand have been computed based on acceptable cost accounting techniques that reasonably approximate actual quantities on hand.

(2) physical inventories are in substantial agreement with book inventories.

(3) the internal controls are in accordance with generally accepted accounting principles and are functioning as planned.

(4) costs have been properly assigned to finished goods, work-in-process, and cost of goods sold.

b. The accuracy of perpetual inventory master files may be established, in part, by comparing perpetual inventory records with

(1) purchase requisitions.

(2) receiving reports.

(3) purchase orders.

(4) vendor payments.

c. When evaluating inventory controls with respect to segregation of duties, a CPA would be *least* likely to

(1) inspect documents.

(2) make inquiries.

(3) observe procedures.

(4) consider policy and procedure manuals.

20-19 (Objectives 20-1, 20-4, 20-5, 20-6) The following questions deal with tests of details of balances and analytical procedures for inventory. Choose the best response.

a. An auditor would be *most* likely to learn of slow-moving inventory through

(1) inquiry of sales personnel.

(2) inquiry of store personnel.

(3) physical observation of inventory.

(4) review of perpetual inventory master files.

b. An inventory turnover analysis is useful to the auditor because it may detect

(1) inadequacies in inventory pricing.

(2) methods of avoiding cyclical holding costs.

(3) the optimum automatic reorder points.

(4) the existence of obsolete merchandise.

c. A CPA auditing inventory may appropriately apply attributes sampling to estimate the

(1) average price of inventory items.

(2) percentage of slow-moving inventory items.

(3) dollar value of inventory.

(4) physical quantity of inventory items.

20-20 (Objectives 20-1, 20-3, 20-5, 20-6, 20-7)   Items 1 through 8 are selected questions typically found in questionnaires used by auditors to obtain an understanding of internal control in the inventory and warehousing cycle. In using the questionnaire for a client, a "yes" response to a question indicates a possible internal control, whereas a "no" indicates a potential weakness.

1. Does the receiving department prepare prenumbered receiving reports and account for the numbers periodically for all inventory received, showing the description and quantity of materials?
2. Is all inventory stored under the control of a custodian in areas where access is limited?
3. Are all shipments to customers authorized by prenumbered shipping documents?
4. Is a detailed perpetual inventory master file maintained for raw materials inventory?
5. Are physical inventory counts made by someone other than storekeepers and those responsible for maintaining the perpetual inventory master file?
6. Are standard cost records used for raw materials, direct labor, and manufacturing overhead?
7. Is there a stated policy with specific criteria for writing off obsolete or slow-moving goods?
8. Is the clerical accuracy of the final inventory compilation checked by a person independent of those responsible for preparing it?

Required
a. For each of the preceding questions, state the purpose of the internal control.
b. For each internal control, list a test of control to test its effectiveness.
c. For each of the preceding questions, identify the nature of the potential financial misstatement(s) if the control is not in effect.
d. For each of the potential misstatements in part c, list a substantive audit procedure to determine whether a material misstatement exists.

20-21 (Objective 20-3)   The cost accounting records are often an essential area to audit in a manufacturing or construction company.

Required
a. Why is it important to review the cost accounting records and test their accuracy?
b. For the audit of standard cost accounting records in which 35 parts are manufactured, explain how you would determine whether each of the following were reasonable for part no. 21.
   (1) Standard direct labor hours
   (2) Standard direct overhead rate
   (3) Standard overhead rate
   (4) Standard units of raw materials
   (5) Standard cost of a unit of raw materials
   (6) Total standard cost

20-22 (Objectives 20-1, 20-3, 20-5, 20-6)   Following are audit procedures commonly performed in the inventory and warehousing cycle for a manufacturing company.

1. Compare the client's count of physical inventory at an interim date with the perpetual inventory master file.
2. Trace the auditor's test counts recorded in the working papers to the final inventory compilation and compare the tag number, description, and quantity.
3. Compare the unit price on the final inventory summary with vendors' invoices.
4. Read the client's physical inventory instructions and observe whether they are being followed by those responsible for counting the inventory.

5. Account for a sequence of raw material requisitions and examine each requisition for an authorized approval.
6. Trace the recorded additions on the finished goods perpetual inventory master file to the records for completed production.
7. Account for a sequence of inventory tags and trace each tag to the physical inventory to make sure it actually exists.

Required

    a. Identify whether each of the procedures is primarily a test of control or a substantive test.

    b. State the purpose(s) of each of the procedures.

20-23 (Objectives 20-1, 20-5, 20-6)   The following misstatements are included in the inventory and related records of Westbox Manufacturing Company.

1. An inventory item was priced at $12 each instead of at the correct cost of $12 per dozen.
2. In taking the physical inventory, the last shipments for the day were excluded from inventory and were not included as a sale until the subsequent year.
3. The clerk in charge of the perpetual inventory master file altered the quantity on an inventory tag to cover up the shortage of inventory caused by its theft during the year.
4. After the auditor left the premises, several inventory tags were lost and were not included in the final inventory summary.
5. When raw material acquisitions were recorded, the improper unit price was included in the perpetual inventory master file. Therefore, the inventory valuation was misstated because the physical inventory was priced by referring to the perpetual records.
6. During the physical count, several obsolete inventory items were included.
7. Because of a significant increase in volume during the current year and excellent control over manufacturing overhead costs, the manufacturing overhead rate applied to inventory was far greater than actual cost.

Required

    a. For each misstatement, state an internal control that should have prevented it from occurring.

    b. For each misstatement, state a substantive audit procedure that could be used to uncover it.

20-24 (Objectives 20-5, 20-6)   Often an important aspect of a CPA's audit of financial statements is his or her observation of the taking of physical inventory.

Required

    a. What are the general objectives or purposes of the CPA's observation of the taking of the physical inventory? (Do not discuss the procedures or techniques involved in making the observation.)

    b. For what purposes does the CPA make and record test counts of inventory quantities during his or her observation of the taking of the physical inventory? Discuss.

    c. A number of companies employ outside service companies that specialize in counting, pricing, extending, and footing inventories. These service companies usually furnish a certificate attesting to the value of the inventory.

        Assuming that the service company took the inventory on the balance sheet date:

    (1) How much reliance, if any, can the CPA place on the inventory certificate of outside specialists? Discuss.

    (2) What effect, if any, would the inventory certificate of outside specialists have upon the type of report the CPA would render? Discuss.

    (3) What reference, if any, would the CPA make to the certificate of outside specialists in his or her short-form report?*

*AICPA adapted.

20-25 (Objective 20-5)   You encountered the following situations during the December 31, 1999, physical inventory of Latner Shoe Distributor Company.

   a. Latner maintains a large portion of the shoe merchandise in 10 warehouses throughout the eastern United States. This ensures swift delivery service for its chain of stores. You are assigned alone to the Boston warehouse to observe the physical inventory process. During the inventory count, several express trucks pulled in for loading. Although infrequent, express shipments must be attended to immediately. As a result, the employees who were counting the inventory stopped to assist in loading the express trucks. What should you do?

   b. (1) In one storeroom of 10,000 items, you have test-counted about 200 items of high value and a few items of low value. You found no misstatements. You also note that the employees are diligently following the inventory instructions. Do you think you have tested enough items? Explain.

   (2) What would you do if you counted 150 items and found a substantial number of counting errors?

   c. In observing an inventory of liquid shoe polish, you note that one lot is 5 years old. From inspection of some bottles in an open box, you find that the liquid has solidified in most of the bottles. What action should you take?

   d. During your observation of the inventory count in the main warehouse, you found that most of the prenumbered tags that had been incorrectly filled out are being destroyed and thrown away. What is the significance of this procedure and what action should you take?

20-26 (Objective 20-5)   In connection with his audit of the financial statements of Knutson Products Co., an assembler of home appliances, for the year ended May 31, 1999, Ray Abel, CPA, is reviewing with Knutson's controller the plans for a physical inventory at the company warehouse on May 31, 1999.

Finished appliances, unassembled parts, and supplies are stored in the warehouse, which is attached to Knutson's assembly plant. The plant will operate during the count. On May 30, the warehouse will deliver to the plant the estimated quantities of unassembled parts and supplies required for May 31 production, but there may be emergency requisitions on May 31. During the count, the warehouse will continue to receive parts and supplies and to ship finished appliances. However, appliances completed on May 31 will be held in the plant until after the physical inventory.

Required

What procedures should the company establish to ensure that the inventory count includes all items that should be included and that nothing is counted twice?*

20-27 (Objective 20-4)   The following are sales, cost of sales, and inventory data for Aladdin Products Supply Company, a wholesale distributor of cleaning supplies. Dollar amounts are in millions.

	1999	1998	1997	1996
Sales	$23.2	$21.7	$19.6	$17.4
Cost of sales	17.1	16.8	15.2	13.5
Beginning inventory	2.3	2.1	1.9	1.5
Ending inventory	2.9	2.3	2.1	1.9

Required

   a. Calculate the following ratios, using an electronic spreadsheet program (instructor's option):
   1. Gross margin as a percentage of sales
   2. Inventory turnover

   b. List several logical causes of the changes in the two ratios.

*AICPA adapted.

c. Assume that $500,000 is considered material for audit planning purposes for 1999. Could any of the fluctuations in the computed ratios indicate a possible material misstatement? Demonstrate this by using the spreadsheet program to perform a sensitivity analysis.

d. What should the auditor do to determine the actual cause of the changes?

20-28 (Objective 20-5)   In an annual audit at December 31, 1999, you find the following transactions near the closing date:

1. Merchandise costing $1,822 was received on January 3, 2000, and the related acquisition invoice recorded January 5. The invoice showed the shipment was made on December 29, 1999, FOB destination.

2. Merchandise costing $625 was received on December 28, 1999, and the invoice was not recorded. You located it in the hands of the purchasing agent; it was marked "on consignment."

3. A packing case containing products costing $816 was standing in the shipping room when the physical inventory was taken. It was not included in the inventory because it was marked "Hold for shipping instructions." Your investigation revealed that the customer's order was dated December 18, 1999, but that the case was shipped and the customer billed on January 10, 2000. The product was a stock item of your client.

4. Merchandise received on January 6, 2000, costing $720 was entered in the acquisitions journal on January 7, 2000. The invoice showed shipment was made FOB supplier's warehouse on December 31, 1999. Because it was not on hand at December 31, it was not included in inventory.

5. A special machine, fabricated to order for a customer, was finished and in the shipping room on December 31, 1999. The customer was billed on that date and the machine excluded from inventory, although it was shipped on January 4, 2000.

Assume that each of the amounts is material.

Required

a. State whether the merchandise should be included in the client's inventory.

b. Give your reason for your decision on each item.*

20-29 (Objective 20-6)   As a part of your clerical tests of inventory for Martin Manufacturing, you have tested about 20 percent of the dollar items and have found the following exceptions:

1. Extension errors:

Description	Quantity	Price	Extension as Recorded
Wood	465 board feet	$ .12/board foot	$ 5.58
Metal-cutting tools	29 units	30.00 each	670.00
Cutting fluid	16 barrels	40.00/barrel	529.00
Sandpaper	300 sheets	.95/hundred	258.00

2. Differences located in comparing last year's costs with the current year's costs on the client's inventory lists:

Description	Quantity	This Year's Cost	Preceding Year's Cost
TA-114 precision- cutting torches	12 units	$500.00 each	Unable to locate
Aluminum scrap	4,500 pounds	5.00/ton	$65.00/ton
Lubricating oil	400 gallons	6.00/gallon	4.50/barrel

*AICPA adapted.

3. Test counts that you were unable to find when tracing from the test counts to the final inventory compilation:

Tag No.	Quantity	Current-Year Cost	Description
2958	15 tons	$75.00/ton	Cold-rolled bars
0026	2,000 feet	2.25/foot	4-inch aluminum stripping

4. Page total, footing errors:

Page No.	Client Total	Correct Total
14	$1,375.12	$1,375.08
82	8,721.18	8,521.18

Required

a. State the amount of the actual misstatement in each of the four tests. For any item for which amount of the misstatement cannot be determined from the information given, state the considerations that would affect your estimate of the misstatement.

b. As a result of your findings, what would you do about clerical accuracy tests of the inventory in the current year?

c. What changes, if any, would you suggest in internal controls and procedures for Martin Manufacturing during the compilation of next year's inventory to prevent each type of misstatement?

20-30 (Objective 20-5) You have been engaged for the audit of the Y Company for the year ended December 31, 1999. The Y Company is in the wholesale chemical business and makes all sales at 25 percent over cost.

Following are portions of the client's sales and purchases accounts for the calendar year 1999.

SALES

Date	Reference	Amount	Date	Reference	Amount
				Balance Forward	
12-31	Closing entry	$699,860			$658,320
			12-27	*SI#965	5,195
			12-28	SI#966	19,270
			12-28	SI#967	1,302
			12-31	SI#969	5,841
			12-31	SI#970	7,922
			12-31	SI#971	2,010
		$699,860			$699,860

PURCHASES

Date	Reference	Amount	Date	Reference	Amount
	Balance Forward				
		$360,300	12-31	Closing entry	$385,346
12-28	†RR#1059	3,100			
12-30	RR#1061	8,965			
12-31	RR#1062	4,861			
12-31	RR#1063	8,120			
		$385,346			$385,346

*SI = Sales invoice.
†RR = Receiving report.

You observed the physical inventory of goods in the warehouse on December 31, 1999, and were satisfied that it was properly taken.

When performing a sales and purchases cutoff test, you found that at December 31, 1999, the last receiving report that had been used was no. 1063 and that no shipments have been made on any sales invoices with numbers larger than no. 968. You also obtained the following additional information.

1. Included in the warehouse physical inventory at December 31, 1999 were chemicals that had been acquired and received on receiving report no. 1060 but for which an invoice was not received until the year 2000. Cost was $2,183.
2. In the warehouse at December 31, 1999 were goods that had been sold and paid for by the customer but which were not shipped out until the year 2000. They were all sold on sales invoice no. 965 and were not inventoried.
3. On the evening of December 31, 1999, there were two cars on the Y company siding:
   (a) Car AR38162 was unloaded on January 2, 2000, and received on receiving report no. 1063. The freight was paid by the vendor.
   (b) Car BAE74123 was loaded and sealed on December 31, 1999, and was switched off the company's siding on January 2, 2000. The sales price was $12,700 and the freight was paid by the customer. This order was sold on sales invoice no. 968.
4. Temporarily stranded at December 31, 1999 on a railroad siding were two cars of chemicals en route to the Z Pulp and Paper Co. They were sold on sales invoice no. 966, and the terms were FOB destination.
5. En route to the Y Company on December 31, 1999, was a truckload of material that was received on receiving report no. 1064. The material was shipped FOB destination, and freight of $75 was paid by the Y Company. However, the freight was deducted from the purchase price of $975.
6. Included in the physical inventory were chemicals exposed to rain in transit and deemed unsalable. Their invoice cost was $1,250, and freight charges of $350 had been paid on the chemicals.

Required

a. Compute the adjustments that should be made to the client's physical inventory at December 31, 1999.
b. Prepare a worksheet of adjusting entries that are required as of December 31, 1999.*

20-31 (Objective 20-6) You are testing the summarization and cost of raw materials and purchased parts inventories as a part of the audit of Rubber Products and Supply Company. There are 2,000 inventory items with a total recorded value of $648,500.

Your audit tests are to compare recorded descriptions and counts with the final inventory listing, compare unit costs with vendors' invoices, and extend unit costs times quantity. A misstatement in any of those is defined as a difference. You plan to use difference estimation sampling.

You make the following decisions about the audit of inventory:

Tolerable misstatement	$16,000
Estimated point estimate	4,000
Acceptable risk of incorrect acceptance	5%
Estimated standard deviation	30
(based on data contained in last year's working papers)	

Required

a. What would be the advantages of using difference estimation compared to nonstatistical sampling?
b. What is the sample size necessary to achieve your objectives using difference estimation.

*AICPA adapted.

c. Without regard to your answer to part b, assume that a sample of 60 items is selected and the following differences between book and audited values are identified (understatements are in parentheses).

Item No.	Difference
1	$19
2	11
3	(19)
4	40
5	90
6	38
7	(90)
8	70
9	(85)
Total	$74

For each of the other 51 items in the sample, there was no difference between the book and the audited values.

Based on this sample, calculate the upper confidence limit of the population misstatement amount at the acceptable risk of incorrect acceptance.

d. Given that actual sample size in part c was smaller than the required sample size in part b, explain why the confidence limits still fall within tolerable misstatement.

20-32 (Objective 20-6)   You are assigned to the December 31, 1999, audit of Sea Gull Airframes, Inc. The company designs and manufactures aircraft superstructures and airframe components. You observed the physical inventory at December 31 and are satisfied that it was properly taken. The inventory at December 31, 1999 has been priced, extended, and totaled by the client and is made up of about 5,000 inventory items with a total valuation of $8,275,000. In performing inventory price tests, you have decided to stratify your tests and conclude that you should have two strata: items with a value over $5,000 and those with a value of less than $5,000. The book values are as follows:

	No. of Items	Total Value
More than $5,000	500	$4,150,000
Less than $5,000	4,500	4,125,000
	5,000	$8,275,000

In performing your pricing and extension tests, you have decided to test about 50 inventory items in detail. You selected 40 of the over $5,000 items and 10 of those under $5,000 at random from the population. You find all items to be correct except for items A through G at the top of page 674, which you believe may be misstated. You have tested the following items, to this point, exclusive of A through G.

	No. of Items	Total Value
More than $5,000	36	$360,000
Less than $5,000	7	2,600

Sea Gull Airframes uses a periodic inventory system and values its inventory at the lower of FIFO cost or market. You were able to locate all invoices needed for your examination.

The seven inventory items in the sample you believe may be misstated, along with the relevant data for determining the proper valuation, are shown below.

INVENTORY ITEMS POSSIBLY MISSTATED

Description	Quantity	Price	Total*
A. L37 spars	3,000 meters	$ 8.00/meter	$24,000
B. B68 metal formers	10,000 inches	1.20/foot	12,000
C. R01 metal ribs	1,500 yards	10.00/yard	15,000
D. St26 struts	1,000 feet	8.00/foot	8,000
E. Industrial hand drills	45 units	20.00 each	900
F. L803 steel leaf springs	40 pairs	69.00 each spring	276
G. V16 fasteners	5.50 dozen	10.00/dozen	55

*Note: Amounts are as stated on client's inventory.

INFORMATION FOR PRICING FROM INVOICES (SEA GULL AIRFRAMES)

Voucher Number	Voucher Date	Date Paid	Terms	Receiving Report Date	Invoice Description
7-68	8-01-94	8-21-94	Net FOB destination	8-01-94	77 V16 fasteners at $10 per dozen
11-81	10-16-99	11-15-99	Net FOB destination	10-18-99	1,100 yards R01 metal ribs at $9.50 per yard; 2,000 feet St26 struts at $8.20 per foot
12-06	12-08-99	12-30-99	2/10, n/30 FOB S.P.	12-10-99	180 L803 steel leaf springs at $69 each
12-09	12-10-99	12-18-99	Net FOB destination	12-11-99	45 industrial hand drills at $20 each; guaranteed for 4 years
12-18	12-27-99	12-27-99	2/10, n/30 FOB S.P.	12-21-99	4,200 meters L37 spars at $8 per meter
12-23	12-24-99	1-03-00	2/10, n/30 FOB dest.	12-26-99	12,800 inches B68 metal formers at $1.20 per foot
12-61	12-29-99	1-08-00	Net FOB destination	12-29-99	1,000 yards R01 metal ribs at $10 per yard; 800 feet St26 struts at $8 per foot
12-81	12-31-99	1-20-00	Net FOB destination	1-06-00	2,000 meters L37 spars at $7.50 per meter; 2,000 yards R01 metal ribs at $10 per yard

In addition, you noted a freight bill for voucher 12-23 in the amount of $200. This bill was entered in the freight-in account. Virtually all freight was for the metal formers.

This is the first time Sea Gull Airframes has been audited by your firm.

Required

    a. Review all information and determine the inventory misstatements of the seven items in question. State any assumptions you consider necessary to determine the amount of the misstatements.

    b. Prepare a working paper schedule to summarize your findings. Use the computer to prepare the schedule (instructor's option).

20-33 (Objectives 20-5, 20-6)   You are observing inventory as a part of the August 31 year-end audit of Engine Warehouse Supply Company, a wholesale and retail engine parts company. Inventory includes a large number of diverse parts varying from small bolts to large engines for earth-moving equipment.

The company has ceased operations during the physical count except for receiving goods from suppliers and making shipments to essential wholesale customers. On the morning of the physical count, which is Saturday, September 2, you record in your working papers the last shipping document and receiving report number issued the previous day. They are 109,314 and 41,682, respectively.

You observe the client's counting procedures and test-count selected inventory yourself. You conclude that the counts and descriptions are accurate. Before you leave the warehouse at the end of the day, after all counting is completed, you do several things:

1. Examine the receiving report book. The last number used was 41,685. The receiving clerk informs you that all goods received on September 2 were kept in the receiving department with other goods received during the past 2 or 3 days.
2. Examine the shipping document book. The last number used was 109,317. The shipping department informs you that three shipments were made before noon, two were made after noon, and one was still in the shipping department.
3. Ask the receiving department to identify all goods received September 1. He identifies receiving reports 41,680 through 41,682 as having been received September 1.
4. Ask the shipping department to identify all goods shipped or sold over the counter September 1. He informs you goods on shipping document 109,311 to 109,313 were shipped September 1. He shows you approximately 300 duplicate sales slips for September 1 over-the-counter sales. September 1 retail sales totaled $12,690, but they were not included in August sales.
5. Examine the client's inventory counts in the receiving department. Inventory had been counted only for receiving reports 41,674 to 41,684.
6. Examine the client's inventory counts in the shipping department. Inventory had been counted only for shipping documents 109,316 and 109,317. Further examination shows that inventory for all shipments made September 2 were included in the counts in the department from which the inventory was taken.

During the year-end audit work you obtain selling prices, costs, terms, and recording data for each receipt and shipment. They are as follows:

ACQUISITIONS OF INVENTORY

Receiving Report No.	Date Shipped	Date Received	Dollar Amount of Acquisition	Included in or Excluded from August Acquisitions Journal	FOB Origin or Destination
41,679	8-29	8-31	$ 860	I	Destination
41,680	8-27	9-01	1,211	I	Origin
41,681	8-20	9-01	193	I	Origin
41,682	8-27	9-01	4,674	I	Destination
41,683	8-30	9-02	450	E	Destination
41,684	8-30	9-02	106	E	Origin
41,685	9-02	9-02	2,800	E	Origin
41,686	8-30	9-02	686	E	Destination

SHIPMENTS OF INVENTORY

Shipping Document No.	Date Shipped	Dollar Amount of Sale	Included in or Excluded from August Sales Journal
109,310	8-31	$ 780	I
109,311	9-01	56	I
109,312	9-01	3,194	I
109,313	9-01	635	I
109,314	9-01	193	I
109,315	9-02	1,621	E
109,316	9-02	945	E
109,317	9-02	78	E
109,318	9-02	3,611	E

Required

Assume that the information you have obtained from the receiving and shipping departments about the September 1 receipts and shipments is accurate.

    a. Prepare all adjustments for cutoff misstatements in accounts payable, assuming that no acquisitions are made for cash.

    b. Prepare all adjustments for misstatements in sales.

    c. What is the amount of the client's misstatement in inventory, assuming a periodic inventory method, and no adjustments in part a or b affected inventory? For retail sales, assume that the gross margin percentage is approximately 30 percent.

    d. How would you determine whether the receiving and shipping departments have given you accurate information about the September 1 receipts and shipments of goods?

AUDIT OF THE CAPITAL ACQUISITION AND REPAYMENT CYCLE

A DISHONEST CLIENT WILL GET THE BEST OF THE AUDITOR ALMOST EVERY TIME

Able Construction Company entered into long-term construction contracts, recognizing income using the percentage of completion method of accounting. This method requires, among other things, an agreement with well-defined, enforceable terms, a reliable method of estimating costs to complete the contracts, and recognition of losses at the time they become known. As part of the audit of Able, its auditors read the contracts for all projects in progress, test costs incurred to date, and assess the ultimate profitability of the contracts, including discussing them with management. A significant part of verifying income under percentage of completion is auditing costs incurred.

In the current year, management's records and schedules of projects indicate that all projects will result in a profit. For each project, there is a separate schedule showing estimated total revenue from the project, costs incurred in the current period, costs incurred to date, estimated total costs, percentage of completion, and profit recognized in the current period. The auditor discussed each project with management, performed audit tests to support the schedule, and concluded that the revenue, expenses, and profit were reasonably stated. Reported income allowed Able to meet several of the restrictive covenants in its loan agreement with the bank.

In fact, Able had incurred a significant loss on one of its major projects. Able engaged a subcontractor to do reconstructive work not anticipated in the original contract bid. In awarding the subcontract, Able entered into an agreement with the subcontractor that the work would not be paid for until after its audit was completed. Management hid the subcontractor's invoices from the auditors as they were received. During the next year, management recognized this loss but doctored the invoices so that it appeared the "unexpected" additional cost was incurred during that year, and that the previous year's statements were correct.

The fraudulent misstatement was discovered several years later when Able went bankrupt and the CPA firm was sued by the bank, which had loaned Able funds to finance construction projects, for performing inadequate audits. The firm was ultimately found not responsible, but only after spending extensive time and large amounts of money defending its audit.

LEARNING OBJECTIVES

After studying this chapter, you should be able to

21-1 Identify the accounts and the unique characteristics of the capital acquisition and repayment cycle.

21-2 Design and perform audit tests of notes payable and related accounts and transactions.

21-3 Identify the primary concerns in the audit of owners' equity transactions.

21-4 Design and perform tests of controls, substantive tests of transactions, and tests of details of balances for capital stock and retained earnings.

The final transaction cycle discussed in this text relates to the acquisition of capital resources in the form of interest-bearing debt and owners' equity and the repayment of the capital. The **capital acquisition and repayment cycle** also includes the payment of interest and dividends. The cycle is important because it is the primary source of financing for most businesses.

Four characteristics of the capital acquisition and repayment cycle significantly influence the audit of these accounts:

1. *Relatively few transactions affect the account balances, but each transaction is often highly material in amount.* For example, bonds are infrequently issued by most companies, but the amount of a bond issue is normally large. Because of their size, it is common to verify each transaction taking place in the cycle for the entire year as a part of verifying the balance sheet accounts. It is not unusual to see audit working papers that include the beginning balance of every account in the capital acquisition and repayment cycle and documentation of every transaction that occurred during the year.

2. *The exclusion of a single transaction could be material in itself.* For example, the omission or incorrect recording of a single debt transaction could have a material effect on the financial statements. Accordingly, a primary emphasis in auditing debt is on the completeness and accuracy of debt.

3. *There is a legal relationship between the client entity and the holder of the stock, bond, or similar ownership document.* As the example involving Able Construction Company in the opening vignette demonstrates, the auditor must be concerned with whether the client has met the requirements of debt or equity agreements. In the audit of the transactions and amounts in the cycle, the auditor must take great care in making sure that the significant legal requirements affecting the financial statements have been properly fulfilled and adequately presented and disclosed in the statements.

4. *There is a direct relationship between the interest and dividends accounts and debt and equity.* In the audit of interest-bearing debt, it is desirable to simultaneously verify the related interest expense and interest payable. This holds true for owners' equity, dividends declared, and dividends payable.

We begin by describing the accounts in the cycle, and how the unique characteristics of the cycle impact the audit of these accounts.

ACCOUNTS IN THE CYCLE

OBJECTIVE 21-1
Identify the accounts and the unique characteristics of the capital acquisition and repayment cycle.

The accounts in a company's capital acquisition and repayment cycle depend on the type of business the company operates and how it is financed. For example, all corporations have capital stock and retained earnings, but some may also have preferred stock, additional paid-in capital, and treasury stock. As with other cycles, cash is an important account in the cycle because both the acquisition and repayment of capital affect the cash account. The following are accounts often found in the cycle:

- Notes payable
- Contracts payable
- Mortgages payable
- Bonds payable
- Interest expense
- Accrued interest
- Cash in the bank
- Capital stock—common
- Capital stock—preferred

- Paid-in capital in excess of par
- Donated capital
- Retained earnings
- Appropriations of retained earnings
- Treasury stock
- Dividends declared
- Dividends payable
- Proprietorship—capital account
- Partnership—capital account

The methodology for designing tests of details of balances for accounts in the capital acquisition and repayment cycle is the same as that followed for other accounts. Figure 21-1 is an example of the methodology applied to notes payable, but it is equally applicable to other accounts in the cycle.

In determining the tests of details of balances for notes payable, the auditor considers tolerable misstatement, inherent risk, control risk, the results of tests of controls and substantive tests of transactions, and the results of analytical procedures. Tolerable misstatement is often set at a low level because it is often possible to completely audit the account balance or the transactions affecting the account balance. Inherent risk is also typically set at a low level because it is usually easy to determine the correct account value. Auditors are normally most concerned about the adequacy of disclosures, such as collateral and covenant restrictions for notes payable.

Because there are usually few transactions in the cycle, control risk and the results of substantive tests of transactions are normally less important for designing tests of details of balances for accounts such as notes payable. For most transactions in the cycle, an important consideration is that they are properly authorized.

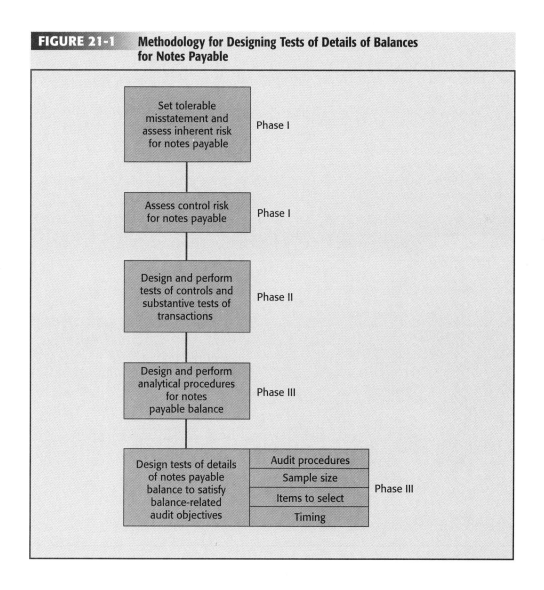

FIGURE 21-1   Methodology for Designing Tests of Details of Balances for Notes Payable

The audit procedures for many of the accounts in the capital acquisition and repayment cycle are best understood by studying representative accounts that are significant parts of the cycle for a typical business. The following sections discuss (1) the audit of notes payable and related interest expense to illustrate interest-bearing capital and (2) the audit of common stock, paid-in capital in excess of par, retained earnings, and dividends.

NOTES PAYABLE

OBJECTIVE 21-2
Design and perform audit tests of notes payable and related accounts and transactions.

A **note payable** is a legal obligation to a creditor, which may be unsecured or secured by assets. Typically, a note is issued for a period somewhere between 1 month and 1 year, but there are also long-term notes of over a year. Notes are issued for many different purposes, and the pledged property includes a wide variety of assets, such as securities, accounts receivable, inventory, and fixed assets. The principal and interest payments on the notes must be made in accordance with the terms of the loan agreement. For short-term loans, a principal and interest payment is usually required only when the loan becomes due; but for loans over 90 days, the note usually calls for monthly or quarterly interest payments.

The accounts used for notes payable and related interest are shown in Figure 21-2 below. It is common to include tests of principal and interest payments as a part of the audit of the acquisition and payment cycle because the payments are recorded in the cash disbursements journal. But because of their relative infrequency, in many cases, no capital transactions are included in the tests of controls and substantive tests of transactions sample. Therefore, it is also normal to test these transactions as a part of the capital acquisition and repayment cycle.

The objectives of the audit of notes payable are to determine whether the following are true:

• The internal controls over notes payable are adequate.

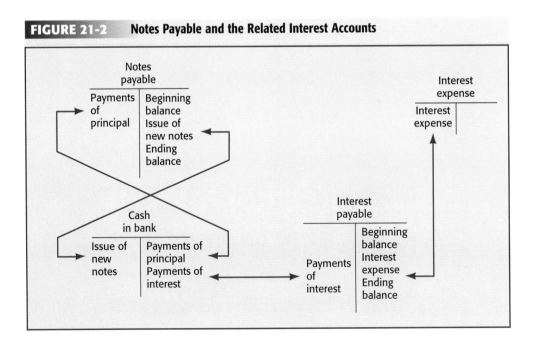

FIGURE 21-2   Notes Payable and the Related Interest Accounts

- Transactions for principal and interest involving notes payable are properly authorized and recorded as defined by the six transaction-related audit objectives.
- The liability for notes payable and the related interest expense and accrued liability are properly stated as defined by eight of the nine balance-related audit objectives. (Realizable value is not applicable to liability accounts.)

There are four important controls over notes payable:

Internal Controls

1. *Proper authorization for the issue of new notes.* Responsibility for the issuance of new notes should be vested in the board of directors or high-level management personnel. Generally, two signatures of properly authorized officials are required for all loan agreements. The amount of the loan, the interest rate, the repayment terms, and the assets pledged are all part of the approved agreement. When notes are renewed, it is important that they be subject to the same authorization procedures as those for the issuance of new notes.
2. *Adequate controls over the repayment of principal and interest.* The periodic payments of interest and principal should be controlled as a part of the acquisition and payment cycle. At the time the note was issued, the accounting department should have received a copy in the same manner in which it receives vendors' invoices and receiving reports. The accounts payable department should automatically issue checks for the notes when they become due, again in the same manner in which it prepares checks for acquisitions of goods and services. The copy of the note is the supporting documentation for payment.
3. *Proper documents and records.* These include the maintenance of subsidiary records and control over blank and paid notes by a responsible person. Paid notes should be cancelled and retained under the custody of an authorized official.
4. *Periodic independent verification.* Periodically, the detailed note records should be reconciled with the general ledger and compared with the note holders' records by an employee who is not responsible for maintaining the detailed records. At the same time, an independent person should recompute the interest expense on notes to test the accuracy and propriety of the record keeping.

Tests of notes payable transactions involve the issue of notes and the repayment of principal and interest. These audit tests are a part of tests of controls and substantive tests of transactions for cash receipts (see Chapter 13) and cash disbursements (see Chapter 18). Additional tests of controls and substantive tests of transactions are often done as a part of tests of details of balances because of the materiality of individual transactions.

Tests of controls for notes payable and related interest should emphasize testing the four important internal controls discussed in the previous section. In addition, the accurate recording of receipts from note proceeds and payments of principal and interest is emphasized.

Tests of Controls and Substantive Tests of Transactions

Analytical procedures are essential for notes payable because tests of details for interest expense and accrued interest can often be eliminated when results are favorable. Table 21-1 (p. 682) illustrates typical analytical procedures for notes payable and related interest accounts.

The auditor's independent estimate of interest expense, using average notes payable outstanding and average interest rates, tests the reasonableness of interest expense, but also tests for omitted notes payable. An illustration of an auditor's working paper where such an analytical procedure has been performed is illustrated in Figure 7-3, page 195. If actual interest expense had been materially larger than the auditor's estimate, one possible cause would be interest payments on unrecorded notes payable.

Analytical Procedures

TABLE 21-1   Analytical Procedures for Notes Payable

Analytical Procedure	Possible Misstatement
Recalculate approximate interest expense on the basis of average interest rates and overall monthly notes payable.	Misstatement of interest expense and accrued interest, or omission of an outstanding note payable
Compare individual notes outstanding with those of the prior year.	Omission or misstatement of a note payable
Compare total balance in notes payable, interest expense, and accrued interest with prior year balances.	Misstatement of interest expense and accrued interest or notes payable

Tests of Details of Balances

The normal starting point for the audit of notes payable is a schedule of notes payable and accrued interest obtained from the client. A typical schedule is shown in Figure 21-3 below and on page 683. The usual schedule includes detailed information of all transactions that took place during the entire year for principal and interest, the beginning and ending balances for notes and interest payable, and descriptive information about the notes, such as the due date, the interest rate, and the assets pledged as collateral.

When there are numerous transactions involving notes during the year, it may not be practical to obtain a schedule of the type shown in Figure 21-3. In that situation, the auditor is likely to request that the client prepare a schedule of only those notes with unpaid balances at the end of the year. This would show a description of each note, its ending balance, and the interest payable at the end of the year, including the collateral and interest rate.

The balance-related audit objectives and common audit procedures are summarized in Table 21-2 (p. 684). Realizable value is not included in the table because it is not applicable

FIGURE 21-3   Schedule of Notes Payable and Accrued Interest

PBC

XYZ Company, Inc.
Notes Payable
12/31/99

Schedule _AA-4_   Date
Prepared by _Client/DB_   _1/12/00_
Approved by _JL_   _1/16/00_

	Date		Face Amount	SECURITY		Balance at Beginning
Payee	Made	Due	of Note	Description	Valuation	of Period
First National Bank	9/30/98	9/30/99	10000	Investments	15000	10000
Second National Bank	9/30/99	9/30/00	10000	Investments	16000	
Third National Bank	10/31/99	10/31/00	10000	Fixed Assets	22000	
			30000		53000	10000 ①
						⋀

① — Traced to prior year audit working papers.   ⑤ — Traced to general ledger.
② — Obtained copy of note included in permanent file.   ⑥ — Recomputed expense and accrued interest; no differences noted.
③ — Examined cancelled note and/or check.   ⋀ — Footed
④ — Agreed to confirmation received from bank.   X — Cross-footed

to notes payable. The schedule of notes payable is the frame of reference for the procedures. Again, the amount of testing depends heavily on materiality of notes payable and the effectiveness of internal controls.

The three most important balance-related audit objectives in notes payable are as follows:

1. Existing notes payable are included (completeness).
2. Notes payable in the schedule are accurately recorded (accuracy).
3. Notes payable are properly presented and disclosed (presentation and disclosure).

The first two objectives are important because a misstatement can be material if even one note is omitted or incorrect. Table 21-2 indicates common procedures to test for the completeness of notes payable. When internal controls over notes payable are weak, it may be necessary to perform extended procedures to test for omitted notes payable. For example, the auditor might send confirmations to creditors that have held notes from the client in the past but are not currently included in the notes payable schedule. The auditor might also analyze interest expense for payments to creditors that are not included in the notes payable schedule, and review the minutes of the board of directors' meetings for authorized but unrecorded notes.

Presentation and disclosure is important because generally accepted accounting principles require that the footnotes adequately describe the terms of notes payable outstanding and the assets pledged as collateral for the loans. If there are significant restrictions on the activities of the company required by the loans, such as compensating balance provisions or restrictions on the payment of dividends, these must also be disclosed in the footnotes.

Figure 21-4 (p. 685) illustrates the major accounts related to notes payable in the capital acquisition and repayment cycle and the types of audit tests used to audit these accounts.

NOTES					INTEREST			
Additions	Payments	Balance at End of Period	Rate	Paid to	Accrued at Beginning of Period	Expense	Paid	Accrued at End of Period
	10000 ③	-0- ④	9¾% ④	Maturity	238	712 ⑥	950 ③	-0-
10000 ②		10000 ④	10% ④	Maturity		250 ⑥		250 ⑥
10000 ②		10000 ④	10% ④	Maturity		167 ⑥		167 ⑥
20000	10000	20000 ⑤			238 ①	1129 ⑤	950	417 ⑤
Ⅶ	Ⅶ	Ⅶ ✗			Ⅶ	Ⅶ		Ⅶ ✗

Balance-Related Audit Objective	Common Tests of Details of Balances Procedures	Comments
Notes payable in the notes payable schedule agree with the client's notes payable register or master file, and the total is correctly added and agrees with the general ledger (detail tie-in).	Foot the notes payable list for notes payable and accrued interest. Trace the totals to the general ledger. Trace the individual notes payable to the master file.	These are often done on a 100 percent basis because of the small population size.
Notes payable in the schedule exist (existence).	Confirm notes payable. Examine duplicate copy of notes for authorization. Examine corporate minutes for loan approval.	The existence objective is not as important as completeness or accuracy.
Existing notes payable are included in the notes payable schedule (completeness).	Examine notes paid after year-end to determine whether they were liabilities at the balance sheet date. Obtain a *standard bank confirmation* that includes specific reference to the existence of notes payable from all banks with which the client does business. (Bank confirmations are discussed more fully in Chapter 22.) Review the *bank reconciliation* for new notes credited directly to the bank account by the bank. (Bank reconciliations are also discussed more fully in Chapter 22.)	This objective is important for uncovering both errors and fraud. These three procedures are done on most audits. Additional procedures to search for omitted liabilities may be necessary if internal controls are weak.
Notes payable and accrued interest on the schedule are accurate (accuracy).	Examine duplicate copies of notes for principal and interest rates. Confirm notes payable, interest rates, and last date for which interest has been paid with holders of notes. Recalculate accrued interest.	In some cases, it may be necessary to calculate, using present-value techniques, the imputed interest rates, or the principal amount of the note. An example is when equipment is acquired for a note.
Notes payable in the schedule are properly classified (classification).	Examine due dates on duplicate copies of notes to determine whether all or part of the notes are a noncurrent liability. Review notes to determine whether any are related party notes or accounts payable.	
Notes payable are included in the proper period (cutoff).	Examine duplicate copies of notes to determine whether notes were dated on or before the balance sheet date.	Notes should be included as current-period liabilities when dated on or before the balance sheet date.
The company has an obligation to pay the notes payable (obligations).	Examine notes to determine whether the company has obligations for payment.	
Notes payable, interest expense, and accrued interest are properly presented and disclosed (presentation and disclosure).	Examine duplicate copies of notes. Confirm notes payable. Examine notes, minutes, and bank confirmations for restrictions. Examine balance sheet for proper presentation and disclosure of noncurrent portions, related parties, assets pledged as security for notes, and restrictions resulting from notes payable.	Proper financial statement presentation, including footnote disclosure, is an important consideration for notes payable.

FIGURE 21-4 **Types of Audit Tests for the Capital Acquisition and Repayment Cycle—Notes Payable (See Figure 21-2 on p. 680 for accounts)**

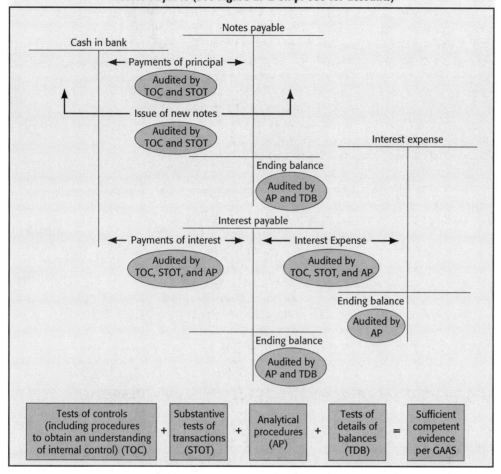

OWNERS' EQUITY

OBJECTIVE 21-3
Identify the primary concerns in the audit of owners' equity transactions.

The previous section discussed the audit of notes payable and related accounts for debt financing. We now turn our attention to the audit of owners' equity. A major distinction must be made in the audit of owners' equity between a **publicly held corporation** and a **closely held corporation**. In most closely held corporations, there are few if any transactions during the year for capital stock accounts and there are typically only a few shareholders. The only transactions entered in the owners' equity section are likely to be the change in owners' equity for the annual earnings or loss and the declaration of dividends, if any. Closely held corporations rarely pay dividends. The amount of time spent verifying owners' equity is often minimal for closely held corporations, even though the auditor must test the existing corporate records.

For publicly held corporations, the verification of owners' equity is more complex because of the larger numbers of shareholders and frequent changes in the individuals holding the stock. In this section, the appropriate tests for verifying the major accounts—capital and common stock, paid-in capital in excess of par, retained earnings, and the related dividends—in a publicly held corporation are discussed. The other accounts in owners' equity are verified in much the same way as these.

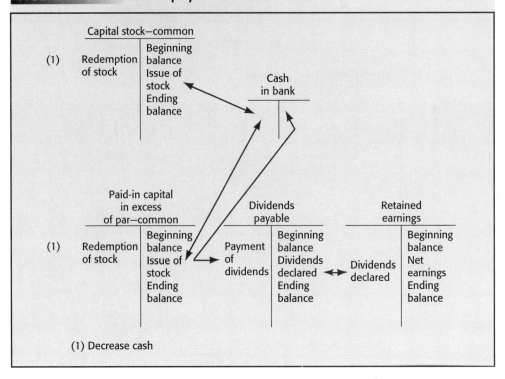

FIGURE 21-5   Owners' Equity and Dividend Accounts

An overview of the specific owners' equity accounts discussed in this section is given in Figure 21-5 above. The objectives of the audit of owners' equity are to determine whether the following are true:

- The internal controls over capital stock and related dividends are adequate.
- Owners' equity transactions are recorded properly, as defined by the six transaction-related audit objectives.
- Owners' equity balances are properly presented and disclosed, as defined by the balance-related audit objectives for owners' equity accounts (rights/obligations and realizable value are not applicable).

Internal Controls

Several important internal controls are of concern to the independent auditor in owners' equity: proper authorization of transactions, proper record keeping, adequate segregation of duties between maintaining owners' equity records and handling cash and stock certificates, and the use of an independent registrar and stock transfer agent.

Proper Authorization of Transactions Because each owners' equity transaction is typically material, many of these transactions must be approved by the board of directors. The following types of owners' equity transactions usually require specific authorization.

Issuance of Capital Stock The authorization includes the type of the equity to issue (such as preferred or common stock), number of shares to issue, par value of the stock, privileged condition for any stock other than common, and date of the issue.

Repurchase of Capital Stock The repurchase of common or preferred shares, the timing of the repurchase, and the amount to pay for the shares should all be approved by the board of directors.

Declaration of Dividends The board of directors should authorize the form of the dividends (such as cash or stock), the amount of the dividend per share, and the record and payment dates of the dividends.

Proper Record Keeping and Segregation of Duties

When a company maintains its own records of stock transactions and outstanding stock, the internal controls must be adequate to ensure that the actual owners of the stock are recognized in the corporate records, the correct amount of dividends is paid to the stockholders owning the stock as of the dividend record date, and the potential for misappropriation of assets is minimized. The proper assignment of personnel and adequate record-keeping procedures are useful controls for these purposes.

The most important procedures for preventing misstatements in owners' equity are (1) well-defined policies for preparing stock certificates and recording capital stock transactions and (2) independent internal verification of information in the records. The client must be certain when issuing and recording capital stock that both the state laws governing corporations and the requirements in the corporate charter are being complied with. For example, the par value of the stock, the number of shares the company is authorized to issue, and the existence of state taxes on the issue of capital stock all affect issuance and recording.

A control over capital stock used by most companies is the maintenance of stock certificate books and a shareholders' capital stock master file. A **capital stock certificate book** is a record of the issuance and repurchase of capital stock for the life of the corporation. The record for a capital stock transaction includes such information as the certificate number, the number of shares issued, the name of the person to whom it was issued, and the issue date. When shares are repurchased, the capital stock certificate book should include the cancelled certificates and the date of their cancellation. A **shareholders' capital stock master file** is the record of the outstanding shares at any given time. The master file acts as a check on the accuracy of the capital stock certificate book and the common stock balance in the general ledger. It is also used as the basis for the payment of dividends.

The disbursement of cash for the payment of dividends should be controlled in much the same manner as has been described in Chapter 17 for the preparation and payment of payroll. Dividend checks should be prepared from the capital stock certificate book by someone who is not responsible for maintaining the capital stock records. After the checks are prepared, it is desirable to have an independent verification of the stockholders' names and the amount of the checks and a reconciliation of the total amount of the dividend checks with the total dividends authorized in the minutes. The use of a separate *imprest dividend account* is desirable to prevent the payment of a larger amount of dividends than was authorized.

Independent Registrar and Stock Transfer Agent

Moscow Central Depository

Any company whose stock is listed on a securities exchange is required to engage an **independent registrar** as a control to prevent the improper issue of stock certificates. The responsibility of an independent registrar is to make sure that stock is issued by a corporation in accordance with the capital stock provisions in the corporate charter and the authorization of the board of directors. The registrar is responsible for signing all newly issued stock certificates and making sure that old certificates are received and cancelled before a replacement certificate is issued when there is a change in the ownership of the stock.

Most large corporations also employ the services of a **stock transfer agent** for the purpose of maintaining the stockholder records, including those documenting transfers of stock ownership. The employment of a transfer agent not only serves as a control over the stock records by putting them in the hands of an independent organization but reduces the cost of record keeping by the use of a specialist. Many companies also have the transfer agent disburse cash dividends to shareholders, thereby further improving internal control.

Audit of Capital Stock and Paid-in Capital

OBJECTIVE 21-4

Design and perform tests of controls, substantive tests of transactions, and tests of details of balances for capital stock and retained earnings.

There are four main concerns in auditing capital stock and paid-in capital in excess of par:

1. Existing capital stock transactions are recorded (completeness).
2. Recorded capital stock transactions exist and are accurately recorded (existence and accuracy).
3. Capital stock is accurately recorded (accuracy).
4. Capital stock is properly presented and disclosed (presentation and disclosure).

The first two concerns involve tests of controls and substantive tests of transactions, and the last two, tests of details of balances.

Existing Capital Stock Transactions Are Recorded This objective is easily satisfied when a registrar or transfer agent is used. The auditor can confirm with them whether any capital stock transactions occurred and the accuracy of existing transactions. Review of the minutes of the board of directors' meetings, especially near the balance sheet date, and examination of client-held stock record books are also useful to uncover issuances and repurchases of capital stock.

Microsoft Stock

Recorded Capital Stock Transactions Exist and Are Accurately Recorded The issuance of new capital stock for cash, the merger with another company through an exchange of stock, donated shares, and the purchase of treasury shares each require extensive auditing. Regardless of the controls in existence, it is normal practice to verify all capital stock transactions because of their materiality and permanence in the records. Existence can ordinarily be tested by examining the minutes of the board of directors' meetings for proper authorization.

Accurate recording of capital stock transactions for cash can be readily verified by confirming the amount with the transfer agent and tracing the amount of the recorded capital stock transactions to cash receipts. (In the case of treasury stock, the amounts are traced to the cash disbursements journal.) In addition, the auditor must verify whether the correct amounts were credited to capital stock and paid-in capital in excess of par by referring to the corporate charter to determine the par or stated value of the capital stock.

When capital stock transactions involve stock dividends, acquisition of property for stock, mergers, or similar noncash transfers, the verification of amounts may be considerably more difficult. For these types of transactions, the auditor must be certain that the client has correctly computed the amount of the capital stock issue in accordance with GAAP. For example, in the audit of a major merger transaction, the auditor has to evaluate whether the transaction is a purchase or a pooling of interests. Considerable research is often necessary to determine which accounting treatment is correct for the existing circumstances. After the auditor reaches a conclusion as to the appropriate method, it is necessary to verify that the amounts were correctly computed.

Capital Stock Is Accurately Recorded The ending balance in the capital stock account is verified by first determining the number of shares outstanding at the balance sheet date. A confirmation from the transfer agent is the simplest way to obtain this information. When no transfer agent exists, the auditor must rely on examining the stock records and accounting for all shares outstanding in the stock certificate books, examining all cancelled certificates, and accounting for blank certificates. After the auditor is satisfied that the number of shares outstanding is correct, the recorded par value in the capital account can be verified by multiplying the number of shares by the par value of the stock. The ending balance in the capital in excess of par account is a residual amount. It is audited by verifying the amount of recorded transactions during the year and adding them to or subtracting them from the beginning balance in the account.

A major consideration in the accuracy of capital stock is verifying whether the number of shares used in the calculation of earnings per share is accurate. It is easy to determine the correct number of shares to use in the calculation when there is only one class of stock and a small number of capital stock transactions. The problem becomes much more complex when there are convertible securities, stock options, or stock warrants outstanding. A thorough understanding of SFAS 128 is important before verifying the number of shares for determining basic and diluted earnings per share.

Capital Stock Is Properly Presented and Disclosed The most important sources of information for determining proper presentation and disclosure are the corporate charter, the minutes of board of directors' meetings, and the auditor's analysis of capital stock transactions. The auditor should determine that there is a proper description of each class of stock, including such information as the number of shares issued and outstanding and any special rights of an individual class. The proper presentation and disclosure of stock options, stock warrants, and convertible securities should also be verified by examining legal documents or other evidence of the provisions of these agreements.

The emphasis in the audit of dividends is on the transactions rather than the ending balance. The exception is when there are dividends payable.

    The six transaction-related audit objectives for transactions are relevant for dividends. But typically, dividends are audited on a 100 percent basis and cause few problems. The following are the most important objectives, including those concerning dividends payable:

1. Recorded dividends exist (existence).
2. Existing dividends are recorded (completeness).
3. Dividends are accurately recorded (accuracy).
4. Dividends as paid to stockholders exist (existence).
5. Dividends payable are recorded (completeness).
6. Dividends payable are accurately recorded (accuracy).

    Existence of recorded dividends can be checked by examining the minutes of board of directors' meetings for authorization of the amount of the dividend per share and the dividend date. When the auditor examines the board of directors' minutes for dividends declared, the auditor should be alert to the possibility of unrecorded dividends declared, particularly shortly before the balance sheet date. A closely related audit procedure is to review the permanent audit working paper file to determine whether there are restrictions on the payment of dividends in bond indenture agreements or preferred stock provisions.

    The accuracy of a dividend declaration can be audited by recomputing the amount on the basis of the dividend per share and the number of shares outstanding. If the client uses a transfer agent to disburse dividends, the total can be traced to a cash disbursement entry to the agent and also confirmed.

    When a client keeps its own dividend records and pays the dividends itself, the auditor can verify the total amount of the dividend by recalculation and reference to cash disbursed. In addition, it is necessary to verify whether the payment was made to the stockholders who owned the stock as of the dividend record date. The auditor can test this by selecting a sample of recorded dividend payments and tracing the payee's name on the cancelled check to the dividend records to make sure that the payee was entitled to the dividend. At the same time, the amount and the authenticity of the dividend check can be verified.

    Tests of dividends payable should be done in conjunction with declared dividends. Any unpaid dividend should be included as a liability.

Audit of Dividends

For most companies, the only transactions involving retained earnings are net earnings for the year and dividends declared. But there may also be corrections of prior-period earnings, prior-period adjustments charged or credited directly to retained earnings, and the setting up or elimination of appropriations of retained earnings.

    The starting point for the audit of retained earnings is an analysis of retained earnings for the entire year. The audit schedule showing the analysis, which is usually a part of the permanent file, includes a description of every transaction affecting the account.

Audit of Retained Earnings

The audit of the credit to retained earnings for net income for the year (or the debit for a loss) is accomplished by simply tracing the entry in retained earnings to the net earnings figure on the income statement. The performance of this procedure must, of course, take place fairly late in the audit after all adjusting entries affecting net earnings have been completed.

An important consideration in auditing debits and credits to retained earnings other than net earnings and dividends is determining whether the transactions should have been included. For example, prior-period adjustments can be included in retained earnings only if they satisfy the requirements of APB opinions and FASB statements.

After the auditor is satisfied that the recorded transactions are appropriately classified as retained earnings transactions, the next step is to decide whether they are accurately recorded. The audit evidence necessary to determine accuracy depends on the nature of the transactions. If there is a requirement for an appropriation of retained earnings for a bond sinking fund, the correct amount of the appropriation can be determined by examining the bond indenture agreement. If there is a major loss charged to retained earnings because of a material nonrecurring abandonment of a plant, the evidence needed to determine the amount of the loss could include significant numbers of documents and records of the plant.

Another important consideration in the audit of retained earnings is evaluating whether any transactions should have been included but were not. If a stock dividend was declared, for instance, the market value of the securities issued should be capitalized by a debit to retained earnings and a credit to capital stock. Similarly, if the financial statements include appropriations of retained earnings, the auditor should evaluate whether it is still necessary to have the appropriation as of the balance sheet date. As an example, an appropriation of retained earnings for a bond sinking fund should be eliminated by crediting retained earnings after the bond has been paid off.

The primary concern in determining whether retained earnings is correctly presented and disclosed in the financial statements is the existence of any restrictions on the payment of dividends. Often, agreements with bankers, stockholders, and other creditors prohibit or limit the amount of dividends the client can pay. These restrictions must be disclosed in the footnotes to the financial statements.

Figure 21-6 illustrates the major accounts related to owners' equity in the capital acquisition and repayment cycle and the types of audit tests used to audit these accounts.

FIGURE 21-6 Types of Audit Tests for the Capital Acquisition and Repayment Cycle—Owners' Equity (See Figure 21-5 on p. 686 for accounts)

This chapter discussed the audit of the capital acquisition and repayment cycle. The cycle is important because it includes the primary sources of financing for most businesses. The cycle often involves few transactions, but the individual transactions are often material, which influences the design and performance of tests in the cycle. The approach to auditing the cycle was illustrated for notes payable, related interest expense and accrued interest, and for owners' equity and related accounts.

ESSENTIAL TERMS

Capital acquisition and repayment cycle—the transaction cycle that involves the acquisition of capital resources in the form of interest-bearing debt and owners' equity, and the repayment of the capital

Capital stock certificate book—a record of the issuance and repurchase of capital stock for the life of the corporation

Closely held corporation—corporation whose stock is not publicly traded; typically, there are only a few shareholders and few, if any, capital stock account transactions during the year

Independent registrar—outside person engaged by a corporation to make sure that its stock is issued in accordance with capital stock provisions in the corporate charter and authorizations by the board of directors; required by the SEC for publicly held corporations

Note payable—a legal obligation to a creditor, which may be unsecured or secured by assets

Publicly held corporation—corporation whose stock is publicly traded; typically, there are many shareholders and frequent changes in the ownership of the stock

Shareholders' capital stock master file—a record of the issuance and repurchase of capital stock for the life of a corporation

Stock transfer agent—outside person engaged by a corporation to maintain the stockholder records, and often to disburse cash dividends

REVIEW QUESTIONS

21-1 (Objective 21-1) List four examples of interest-bearing liability accounts commonly found in balance sheets. What characteristics do these liabilities have in common? How do they differ?

21-2 (Objectives 21-1, 21-2) Why are liability accounts included in the capital acquisition and repayment cycle audited differently from accounts payable?

21-3 (Objective 21-2) It is common practice to audit the balance in notes payable in conjunction with the audit of interest expense and interest payable. Explain the advantages of this approach.

21-4 (Objective 21-2) Which internal controls should the auditor be most concerned about in the audit of notes payable? Explain the importance of each.

21-5 (Objective 21-2) Which analytical procedures are most important in verifying notes payable? Which types of misstatements can the auditor uncover by the use of these tests?

21-6 (Objective 21-2) Why is it more important to search for unrecorded notes payable than for unrecorded notes receivable? Suggest audit procedures that the auditor can use to uncover unrecorded notes payable.

21-7 (Objective 21-2) What is the primary purpose of analyzing interest expense? Given this purpose, what primary considerations should the auditor keep in mind when doing the analysis?

21-8 (Objective 21-2) Distinguish between (a) tests of controls and substantive tests of transactions and (b) tests of details of balances for liability accounts in the capital acquisition and repayment cycle.

21-9 (Objective 21-2) List two types of restrictions long-term creditors often put on companies when granting them a loan. How can the auditor find out about these restrictions?

21-10 (Objective 21-3) What are the primary objectives in the audit of owners' equity accounts?

21-11 (Objectives 21-3, 21-4) Evaluate the following statement: "The corporate charter and the bylaws of a company are legal documents; therefore, they should not be examined by the auditors. If the auditor wants information about these documents, an attorney should be consulted."

21-12 (Objective 21-3) What are the major internal controls over owners' equity?

21-13 (Objective 21-3) How does the audit of owners' equity for a closely held corporation differ from that for a publicly held corporation? In what respects are there no significant differences?

21-14 (Objective 21-3) Describe the duties of a stock registrar and a transfer agent. How does the use of their services affect the client's internal controls?

21-15 (Objective 21-3) What kinds of information can be confirmed with a transfer agent?

21-16 (Objective 21-4) Evaluate the following statement: "The most important audit procedure to verify dividends for the year is a comparison of a random sample of cancelled dividend checks with a dividend list that has been prepared by management as of the dividend record date."

21-17 (Objective 21-4) If a transfer agent disburses dividends for a client, explain how the audit of dividends declared and paid is affected. What audit procedures are necessary to verify dividends paid when a transfer agent is used?

21-18 (Objective 21-4) What should be the major emphasis in auditing the retained earnings account? Explain your answer.

21-19 (Objectives 21-3, 21-4) Explain the relationship between the audit of owners' equity and the calculations of earnings per share. What are the main auditing considerations in verifying the earnings per share figure?

MULTIPLE CHOICE QUESTIONS FROM CPA EXAMINATIONS

21-20 (Objective 21-2) The following multiple-choice questions concern interest-bearing liabilities. Choose the best response.

a. The audit program for long-term debt should include steps that require the
   (1) verification of the existence of the bondholders.
   (2) examination of any bond trust indenture.
   (3) inspection of the accounts payable master file.
   (4) investigation of credits to the bond interest income account.

b. During the year under audit, a company has completed a private placement of a substantial amount of bonds. Which of the following is the *most* important step in the auditor's program for the audit of bonds payable?
   (1) Confirming the amount issued with the bond trustee.
   (2) Tracing the cash received from the issue to the accounting records.
   (3) Examining the bond records maintained by the transfer agent.
   (4) Recomputing the annual interest cost and the effective yield.

c. Several years ago, Conway, Inc., secured a conventional real estate mortgage loan. Which of the following audit procedures would be *least* likely to be performed by an auditor auditing the mortgage balance?
   (1) Examine the current year's cancelled checks.
   (2) Review the mortgage amortization schedule.

(3) Inspect public records of lien balances.

(4) Recompute mortgage interest expense.

21-21 (Objectives 21-2, 21-3, 21-4) The following questions concern the audit of accounts in the capital acquisition and repayment cycle. Choose the best response.

a. During an audit of a publicly held company, the auditor should obtain written confirmation regarding debenture transactions from the

(1) debenture holders.

(2) client's attorney.

(3) internal auditors.

(4) trustee.

b. An audit program for the audit of the retained earnings account should include a step that requires verification of

(1) market value used to charge retained earnings to account for a 2-for-1 stock split.

(2) approval of the adjustment to the beginning balance as a result of a write-down of an account receivable.

(3) authorization for both cash and stock dividends.

(4) gain or loss resulting from disposition of treasury shares.

c. When *no* independent stock transfer agents are employed and the corporation issues its own stocks and maintains stock records, cancelled stock certificates should

(1) be defaced to prevent reissuance and attached to their corresponding stubs.

(2) *not* be defaced, but segregated from other stock certificates and retained in a cancelled certificates file.

(3) be destroyed to prevent fraudulent reissuance.

(4) be defaced and sent to the secretary of state.

DISCUSSION QUESTIONS AND PROBLEMS

21-22 (Objective 21-2) Items 1 through 6 are questions typically found in a standard internal control questionnaire used by auditors to obtain an understanding of internal control for notes payable. In using the questionnaire for a client, a "yes" response indicates a possible internal control, whereas a "no" indicates a potential weakness.

1. Are liabilities for notes payable incurred only after written authorization by a proper company official?

2. Is a notes payable master file maintained?

3. Is the individual who maintains the notes payable master file someone other than the person who approves the issue of new notes or handles cash?

4. Are paid notes cancelled and retained in the company files?

5. Is a periodic reconciliation made of the notes payable master file with the actual notes outstanding by an individual who does not maintain the master file?

6. Are interest expense and accrued interest recomputed periodically by an individual who does not record interest transactions?

Required

a. For each of the preceding questions, state the purpose of the control.

b. For each of the preceding questions, identify the type of financial statement misstatement that could occur if the control were not in effect.

c. For each of the potential misstatements in part b, list an audit procedure that can be used to determine whether a material misstatement exists.

21-23 (Objective 21-2) The following are frequently performed audit procedures for the verification of bonds payable issued in previous years.

1. Obtain a copy of the bond indenture agreement and review its important provisions.

2. Determine that each of the bond indenture provisions has been met.

3. Analyze the general ledger account for bonds payable, interest expense, and unamortized bond discount or premium.
4. Test the client's calculations of interest expense, unamortized bond discount or premium, accrued interest, and bonds payable.
5. Obtain a confirmation from the bondholder.

Required

    a. State the purpose of each of the five audit procedures listed.
    b. List the provisions for which the auditor should be alert in examining the bond indenture agreement.
    c. For each provision listed in part b, explain how the auditor can determine whether its terms have been met.
    d. Explain how the auditor should verify the unamortized bond discount or premium.
    e. List the information that should be requested in the confirmation of bonds payable with the bondholder.

21-24 (Objective 21-2) In conducting an audit of a corporation that has a bond issue outstanding, the trust indenture is reviewed and a confirmation is obtained from the trustee.

Required

List eight matters of importance to the auditor that might be found either in the indenture or in the confirmation obtained from the trustee. Explain briefly the reason for the auditor's interest in each of the items.*

21-25 (Objective 21-2) The Fox Company is a medium-sized industrial client that has been audited by your CPA firm for several years. The only interest-bearing debt owed by Fox Company is $200,000 in long-term notes payable held by the bank. The notes were issued 3 years previously and will mature in 6 more years. Fox Company is highly profitable, has no pressing needs for additional financing, and has excellent internal controls over the recording of loan transactions and related interest costs.

Required

    a. Describe the auditing that you think would be necessary for notes payable and related interest accounts in these circumstances.
    b. How would your answer differ if Fox Company were unprofitable, had a need for additional financing, and had weak internal controls?

21-26 (Objective 21-2) The ending general ledger balance of $186,000 in notes payable for the Sterling Manufacturing Company is made up of 20 notes to eight different payees. The notes vary in duration anywhere from 30 days to 2 years, and in amount from $1,000 to $10,000. In some cases, the notes were issued for cash loans; in other cases, the notes were issued directly to vendors for the acquisition of inventory or equipment. The use of relatively short-term financing is necessary because all existing properties are pledged for mortgages. Nevertheless, there is still a serious cash shortage.

Record-keeping procedures for notes payable are not good, considering the large number of loan transactions. There is no notes payable master file or independent verification of ending balances; however, the notes payable records are maintained by a secretary who does not have access to cash.

The audit has been done by the same CPA firm for several years. In the current year, the following procedures were performed to verify notes payable:

1. Obtain a list of notes payable from the client, foot the notes payable balances on the list, and trace the total to the general ledger.
2. Examine duplicate copies of notes for all outstanding notes included on the listing. Compare the name of the lender, amount, and due date on the duplicate copy with the list.

*AICPA adapted.

3. Obtain a confirmation from lenders for all listed notes payable. The confirmation should include the due date of the loan, the amount, and interest payable at the balance sheet date.
4. Recompute accrued interest on the list for all notes. The information for determining the correct accrued interest is to be obtained from the duplicate copy of the note. Foot the accrued interest amounts and trace the balance to the general ledger.

Required

a. What should be the emphasis in the verification of notes payable in this situation? Explain.

b. State the purpose of each of the four audit procedures listed.

c. Evaluate whether each of the four audit procedures was necessary. Evaluate the sample size for each procedure.

d. List other audit procedures that should be performed in the audit of notes payable in these circumstances.

21-27 (Objective 21-2) The following covenants are extracted from the indenture of a bond issue. The indenture provides that failure to comply with its terms in any respect automatically advances the due date of the loan to the date of noncompliance (the regular date is 20 years hence). List any audit steps or reporting requirements you think should be taken or recognized in connection with each one of the following.

a. The debtor company shall endeavor to maintain a working capital ratio of 2 to 1 at all times, and in any fiscal year following a failure to maintain said ratio, the company shall restrict compensation of officers to a total of $100,000. Officers for this purpose shall include chairman of the board of directors, president, all vice presidents, secretary, and treasurer.

b. The debtor company shall keep all property that is security for this debt insured against loss by fire to the extent of 100 percent of its actual value. Policies of insurance comprising this protection shall be filed with the trustee.

c. The debtor company shall pay all taxes legally assessed against property that is security for this debt within the time provided by law for payment without penalty, and shall deposit receipted tax bills or equally acceptable evidence of payment of same with the trustee.

d. A sinking fund shall be deposited with the trustee by semiannual payments of $300,000, from which the trustee shall, in his discretion, purchase bonds of this issue.*

21-28 (Objective 21-2) The Redford Corporation took out a 20-year mortgage on June 15, 1999, for $2,600,000 and pledged its only manufacturing building and the land on which the building stands as collateral. Each month subsequent to the issue of the mortgage, a payment of $20,000 was paid to the mortgagor. You are in charge of the current-year audit for Redford, which has a balance sheet date of December 31, 1999. The client has been audited previously by your CPA firm, but this is the first time Redford Corporation has had a mortgage.

Required

a. Explain why it is desirable to prepare a working paper for the permanent file for the mortgage. What type of information should be included in the working paper?

b. Explain why the audit of mortgage payable, interest expense, and interest payable should all be done together.

c. List the audit procedures that should ordinarily be performed to verify the issue of the mortgage, the balance in the mortgage and interest payable accounts at December 31, 1999, and the balance in interest expense for the year 1999.

21-29 (Objectives 21-3, 21-4) Items 1 through 6 are common questions found in internal control questionnaires used by auditors to obtain an understanding of internal control for owners' equity. In using the questionnaire for a client, a "yes" response indicates a possible internal control, whereas a "no" indicates a potential weakness.

*AICPA adapted.

1. Does the company use the services of an independent registrar or transfer agent?
2. Are issues and retirements of stock authorized by the board of directors?
3. If an independent registrar and transfer agent are not used:
   (a) Are unissued certificates properly controlled?
   (b) Are cancelled certificates mutilated to prevent their reuse?
4. Are common stock master files and stock certificate books periodically reconciled with the general ledger by an independent person?
5. Is an independent transfer agent used for disbursing dividends? If not, is an imprest dividend account maintained?
6. Are all entries in the owners' equity accounts authorized at the proper level in the organization?

Required

a. For each of the preceding questions, state the purpose of the control.
b. For each of the preceding questions, identify the type of potential financial statement misstatements if the control is not in effect.
c. For each of the potential misstatements in part b, list an audit procedure that the auditor can use to determine whether a material misstatement exists.

21-30 (Objectives 21-3, 21-4)   The following audit procedures are commonly performed by auditors in the verification of owners' equity:

1. Review the articles of incorporation and bylaws for provisions about owners' equity.
2. Review the minutes of the board of directors' meetings for the year for approvals related to owners' equity.
3. Analyze all owners' equity accounts for the year and document the nature of any recorded change in each account.
4. Account for all certificate numbers in the capital stock book for all shares outstanding.
5. Examine the stock certificate book for any stock that was cancelled.
6. Recompute earnings per share.
7. Review debt provisions and senior securities with respect to liquidation preferences, dividends in arrears, and restrictions on the payment of dividends or the issue of stock.

Required

a. State the purpose of each of these seven audit procedures.
b. List the type of misstatements the auditors could uncover by the use of each audit procedure.

21-31 (Objective 21-3, 21-4)   You are engaged in the audit of a corporation whose records have not previously been audited by you. The corporation has both an independent transfer agent and a registrar for its capital stock. The transfer agent maintains the record of stockholders and the registrar checks that there is no overissue of stock. Signatures of both are required to validate certificates.

It has been proposed that confirmations be obtained from both the transfer agent and the registrar as to the stock outstanding at the balance sheet date. If such confirmations agree with the books, no additional work is to be performed as to capital stock.

If you agree that obtaining the confirmations as suggested would be sufficient in this case, give the justification for your position. If you do not agree, state specifically all additional steps you would take and explain your reasons for taking them.*

21-32 (Objective 21-4)   The Rico Corporation is a medium-sized wholesaler of grocery products with 4,000 shares of stock outstanding to approximately 25 stockholders. Because of the age of several retired stockholders and the success of the company, management has decided to pay dividends six times a year. The amount of the bimonthly dividend per share varies depending on the profits, but it is ordinarily between $5 and $7 per share. The controller, who is also a stockholder, prepares the dividend checks, records the checks in the dividend journal, and reconciles the bank account. Important controls include manual check signing by the president and the use of an imprest dividend bank account.

*AICPA adapted.

The auditor verifies the dividends by maintaining a schedule of the total shares of stock issued and outstanding in the permanent working papers. The total amount of stock outstanding is multiplied by the dividends per share authorized in the minutes to arrive at the current total dividend. This total is compared with the deposit that has been made to the imprest dividend account. Because the transfer of stock is infrequent, it is possible to verify dividends paid for the entire year in a comparatively short time.

Required

    a. Evaluate the usefulness of the approach followed by the auditor in verifying dividends in this situation. Your evaluation should include both the strengths and the weaknesses of the approach.

    b. List other audit procedures that should be performed in verifying dividends in this situation. Explain the purpose of each procedure.

21-33 (Objective 21-4) You are a CPA engaged in an audit of the financial statements of Pate Corporation for the year ended December 31, 1999. The financial statements and records of Pate Corporation have not been audited by a CPA in prior years.

The stockholders' equity section of Pate Corporation's balance sheet at December 31, 1999, follows:

Stockholders' equity:

Capital stock—10,000 shares of $10 par value authorized; 5,000 shares issued and outstanding	$ 50,000
Capital contributed in excess of par value of capital stock	32,580
Retained earnings	47,320
Total stockholders' equity	$129,900

Pate Corporation was founded in 1991. The corporation has 10 stockholders and serves as its own registrar and transfer agent. There are no capital stock subscription contracts in effect.

Required

    a. Prepare the detailed audit program for the audit of the three accounts comprising the stockholders' equity section of Pate Corporation's balance sheet. (Do not include in the audit program the verification of the results of the current year's operations.)

    b. After every other figure on the balance sheet has been audited, it might appear that the retained earnings figure is a balancing figure and requires no further verification. Why does the CPA verify retained earnings as he or she does the other figures on the balance sheet? Discuss.*

*AICPA adapted.

AUDIT OF CASH BALANCES

22

SOCIETY EXPECTS A LOT FROM AUDITORS

Bert Sampson was the controller of Pardoe Manufacturing Company. From 1993 through 1998, Bert paid himself an extra $2 million in "bonuses." He did this by transferring funds from the general account, writing checks to himself from the payroll account, destroying the checks when received from the bank, and making entries directly into the Company's computer files to disguise the theft. Bert was able to do this because he had almost complete control of the Company's accounting process.

Jack Baker of Tramenier and Baker, CPAs, was the partner on the Pardoe audit. Although Baker found a strong control environment at Pardoe and a good budgeting and reporting system, he assessed control risk at maximum because there was limited segregation of duties. Accordingly, Baker used a "substantive" approach to the audit. Baker applied tests of details of balances and analytical procedures to the year-end financial statements. He did no tests of controls or substantive tests of transactions.

Because Sampson had lost all of the $2 million and Pardoe had no fidelity bond insurance, the company sued Tramenier and Baker, CPAs, for the loss, claiming breach of contract. Baker's defense was that he had done the audit in accordance with generally accepted auditing standards.

The trial revolved around the testimony of two expert witnesses. The witness for the Company argued that even though the auditors took a substantive approach to the audit, they should have seen that Sampson had the opportunity to commit the theft, extended their audit, and found it.

The expert for the defense argued that a substantive audit approach is allowed by generally accepted auditing standards. Sampson manipulated the records so carefully that the substantive procedures of the various payroll accounts did not indicate that the theft had occurred. Because no "red flags" were evident that would have caused the auditors to extend their tests, the audit was clearly satisfactory.

The jury found against the auditors, and Tramenier and Baker, CPAs, was required to pay approximately $2.3 million in damages. When jury members were interviewed about their decision, they indicated that they didn't really understand the technical nature of the arguments made by the expert witnesses, but it was apparent to them that the people who did the audit were extremely bright and competent. Accordingly, the jury members believed that *the auditors certainly had the ability to find the theft* and the fact that they didn't meant that they failed to perform up to their potential.

LEARNING OBJECTIVES

After studying this chapter, you should be able to

22-1 Show the relationship of cash in the bank to the various transaction cycles.

22-2 Identify the major types of cash accounts maintained by business entities.

22-3 Design and perform audit tests of the general cash account.

22-4 Recognize when to extend audit tests of the general cash account to test further for material fraud.

22-5 Design and perform audit tests of the imprest payroll bank account.

22-6 Design and perform audit tests of imprest petty cash.

Cash is the only account that is included in several cycles. It is a part of every cycle except inventory and warehousing. The audit of cash balances is the last audit area studied because the evidence accumulated for cash balances depends heavily on the results of the tests in other cycles. For example, if the understanding of internal control and tests of controls and substantive tests of transactions in the acquisition and payment cycle lead the auditor to believe that it is appropriate to reduce assessed control risk to low, the auditor can reduce detailed tests of the ending balance in cash. If, however, the auditor concludes that assessed control risk should be higher, extensive year-end testing may be necessary.

Cash is important primarily because of the potential for fraud but also because there may be errors. The opening vignette provides one example of what can happen if an auditor is not careful in assessing risks in auditing the cash account.

CASH IN THE BANK AND TRANSACTION CYCLES

OBJECTIVE 22-1
Show the relationship of cash in the bank to the various transaction cycles.

A brief discussion of the relationship between cash in the bank and the other transaction cycles serves a dual function: it clearly shows the importance of the tests of various transaction cycles to the audit of cash, and it aids in further understanding the integration of the different transaction cycles. Figure 22-1 on page 701 illustrates the relationships of the various transaction cycles, the focal point being the general cash account.

An examination of Figure 22-1 indicates why the general cash account is considered significant in almost all audits even when the ending balance is immaterial. The amount of cash *flowing* into and out of the cash account is often larger than that for any other account in the financial statements. Furthermore, the susceptibility of cash to defalcation is greater than for other types of assets because most other assets must be converted to cash to make them usable.

In the audit of cash, an important distinction should be made between verifying the client's reconciliation of the balance on the bank statement to the balance in the general ledger and verifying whether recorded cash in the general ledger correctly reflects all cash transactions that took place during the year. It is relatively easy to verify the client's reconciliation of the balance in the bank account to the general ledger, but a significant part of the total audit of a company involves verifying whether cash transactions are properly recorded. For example, each of the following misstatements ultimately results in the improper payment of or the failure to receive cash, but none will normally be discovered as a part of the audit of the bank reconciliation:

- Failure to bill a customer
- Billing a customer at a lower price than called for by company policy
- A defalcation of cash by interception of cash receipts from customers before they are recorded, with the account charged off as a bad debt
- Duplicate payment of a vendor's invoice
- Improper payments of officers' personal expenditures
- Payment for raw materials that were not received
- Payment to an employee for more hours than he or she worked
- Payment of interest to a related party for an amount in excess of the going rate

If these misstatements are to be uncovered in the audit, their discovery must come about through the tests of controls and substantive tests of transactions that were discussed in the preceding chapters. The first three misstatements could be discovered as part of the audit of the sales and collection cycle, the next three in the audit of the acquisition and payment cycle, and the last two in the tests of the payroll and personnel cycle and the capital acquisition and repayment cycle, respectively.

Entirely different types of misstatements are normally discovered as a part of the tests of a bank reconciliation. For example,

- Failure to include a check that has not cleared the bank on the outstanding check list, even though it has been recorded in the cash disbursements journal

FIGURE 22-1 Relationships of Cash in the Bank and Transaction Cycles

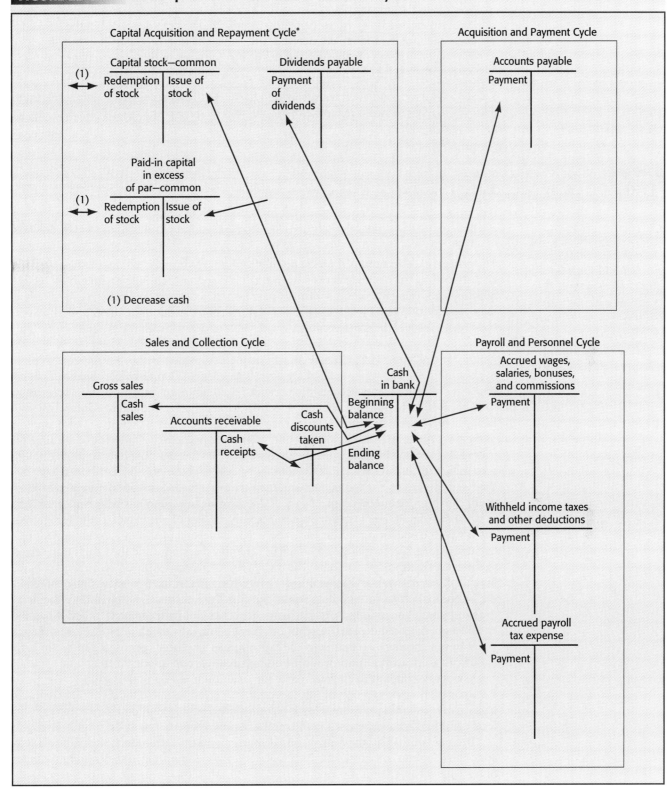

*For simplicity, only owners' equity accounts are shown in this figure. For notes payable accounts, see Figure 21-2 on page 680.

- Cash received by the client subsequent to the balance sheet date but recorded as cash receipts in the current year
- Deposits recorded as cash receipts near the end of the year, deposited in the bank in the same month, and included in the bank reconciliation as a deposit in transit
- Payments on notes payable debited directly to the bank balance by the bank but not entered in the client's records

Before we focus on audit tests related to the client's bank reconciliation, it is helpful to discuss the types of cash accounts commonly used by most companies. This is the subject of the next section.

TYPES OF CASH ACCOUNTS

It is important to understand the different types of cash accounts because the auditing approach to each varies. The following are the major types of cash accounts.

General Cash Account

> **OBJECTIVE 22-2**
> Identify the major types of cash accounts maintained by business entities.

The **general cash account** is the focal point of cash for most organizations because virtually all cash receipts and disbursements flow through this account. The disbursements for the acquisition and payment cycle are normally paid from this account, and the receipts of cash in the sales and collection cycle are deposited in the account. In addition, the deposits and disbursements for all other cash accounts are normally made through the general account.

Imprest Payroll Account

As a means of improving internal control, many companies establish a separate imprest bank account for such things as making payroll payments to employees or separate cash receipts and disbursements accounts for branch banking. In an **imprest payroll account**, a fixed balance, such as $1,000, is maintained in a separate bank account. Immediately before each pay period, one check is drawn on the general cash account to deposit the total amount of the net payroll into the payroll account. After all payroll checks have cleared the imprest payroll account, the bank account should have a $1,000 balance. The only deposits into the account are for the weekly and semimonthly payroll, and the only disbursements are paychecks to employees. For companies with many employees, the use of an imprest payroll account can improve internal control and reduce the time needed to reconcile bank accounts.

A somewhat different type of imprest account consists of one bank account for receipts and a separate one for disbursements. There may be several of these in a company for different divisions. All receipts are deposited in the imprest account, and the total is transferred to the general account periodically. The disbursement account is set up on an *imprest basis*, but in a different manner than an imprest payroll account. A fixed balance is maintained in the imprest account, and the authorized personnel use these funds for disbursements at their own discretion as long as the payments are consistent with company policy. When the cash balance has been depleted, a reimbursement is made to the imprest disbursement account from the general account *after* the expenditures have been approved. The use of such an imprest bank account improves controls over receipts and disbursements.

Branch Bank Account

For a company operating in multiple locations, it is often desirable to have a separate bank balance at each location. **Branch bank accounts** are useful for building public relations in local communities and permitting the centralization of operations at the branch level.

In some companies, the deposits and disbursements for each branch are made to a separate bank account, and the excess cash is periodically electronically transferred to the main office general bank account. The branch account in this instance is much like a general account, but at the branch level.

Imprest Petty Cash Fund

An **imprest petty cash fund** is actually not a bank account, but it is sufficiently similar to cash on deposit to merit inclusion. A petty cash account is often something as simple as a preset amount of cash set aside in a strong box for incidental expenses. It is used for small cash acquisitions that can be paid more conveniently and quickly by cash than by check, or for the convenience of employees in cashing personal or payroll checks. An imprest cash account is set up on the same basis as an imprest branch bank account, but the expenditures are normally for a much smaller amount. Typical expenses include minor office supplies, stamps, and small contributions to local charities. A petty cash account usually does not exceed a few hundred dollars and may not be reimbursed more than once or twice each month.

Excess cash accumulated during certain parts of the operating cycle that will be needed in the reasonably near future is often invested in short-term, highly liquid **cash equivalents**. Examples include time deposits, certificates of deposit, and money market funds. Cash equivalents, which can be highly material, are included in the financial statements as a part of the cash account only if they are short-term investments that are readily convertible to known amounts of cash within a short time and there is insignificant risk of a change of value from interest rate changes. Marketable securities and longer-term interest-bearing investments are not cash equivalents.

Cash Equivalents

    Figure 22-2 shows the relationship of general cash to the other cash accounts. All cash either originates from or is deposited in general cash. The remainder of this chapter focuses on auditing three types of accounts: general cash account, imprest payroll bank account, and imprest petty cash. The others are similar to these and need not be discussed.

FIGURE 22-2 **Relationship of General Cash to Other Cash Accounts**

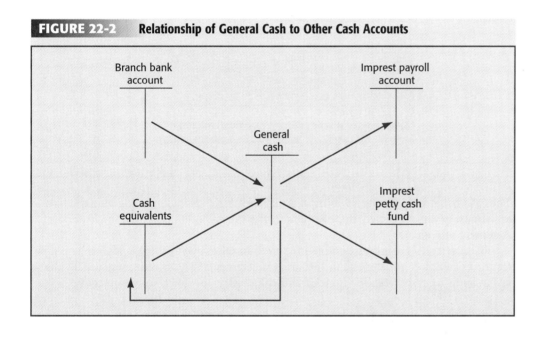

AUDIT OF THE GENERAL CASH ACCOUNT

On the trial balance of Hillsburg Hardware Co., on page 152, there is only one cash account. Notice, however, that all cycles, except inventory and warehousing, affect cash in the bank.

OBJECTIVE 22-3
Design and perform audit tests of the general cash account.

    In testing the year-end balance in the general cash account, the auditor must accumulate sufficient evidence to evaluate whether cash, as stated on the balance sheet, is fairly stated and properly disclosed in accordance with six of the nine balance-related audit objectives used for all tests of details of balances. Rights to general cash, its classification on the balance sheet, and the realizable value of cash are not a problem.

    The methodology for auditing year-end cash is essentially the same as that for all other balance sheet accounts. The methodology is shown in Figure 22-3 (p. 704) and then discussed in detail.

FIGURE 22-3 Methodology for Designing Tests of Details of Balances for Cash in the Bank

Set tolerable misstatement and assess inherent risk for cash in bank — Phase I

Assess control risk for cash in bank — Phase I

Design and perform tests of controls and substantive tests of transactions for several cycles* — Phase II

Design and perform analytical procedures for cash in bank balance — Phase III

Design tests of details of cash in bank balance to satisfy balance-related audit objectives — Audit procedures / Sample size / Items to select / Timing — Phase III

*Cycles affected include sales and collection, acquisition and payment, payroll and personnel, and capital acquisition and repayment.

Set Tolerable Misstatement and Assess Inherent Risk (Phase I)

The cash balance is immaterial in most audits, but cash transactions affecting the balance are almost always extremely material. Therefore, there is often potential for material misstatement of cash.

Because cash is more susceptible to theft than other assets, there is high inherent risk for the existence, completeness, and accuracy objectives. These objectives are usually the focus in auditing cash balances. Typically, inherent risk is low for all other objectives.

Assess Control Risk (Phase I)

Internal controls over year-end cash balances in the general account can be divided into two categories: *controls over the transaction cycles* affecting the recording of cash receipts and disbursements and *independent bank reconciliations.*

Controls affecting the recording of cash transactions have been discussed in preceding chapters, but they are essential in deciding control risk for cash. For example, in the acquisition and payment cycle, major controls include adequate segregation of duties between the check signing and accounts payable functions, signing of checks only by a properly authorized person, use of prenumbered checks printed on special paper, adequate control of blank and voided checks, careful review of supporting documentation by the check signer before checks are signed, and adequate internal verification. If controls affecting cash-related transactions are adequate, it is possible to reduce control risk and therefore the audit tests for the year-end bank reconciliation.

A monthly **bank reconciliation** of the general bank account on a timely basis by someone independent of the handling or recording of cash receipts and disbursements is an essential control over the cash balance. If a business defers preparing bank reconciliations for long periods, the value of the control is reduced and may affect the auditor's assessment of control risk for cash. The reconciliation is important to ensure that the books reflect the same cash balance as the actual amount of cash in the bank after considering reconciling items, but even more important, the *independent* reconciliation provides a unique opportunity for an internal verification of cash receipts and disbursements transactions. If the bank statements are received unopened by the reconciler and physical control is maintained over the statements until the reconciliations are complete, the cancelled checks, duplicate deposit slips, and other documents included in the statement can be examined without concern for the possibility of alteration, deletions, or additions. A careful bank reconciliation by competent client personnel includes the following:

- Compare cancelled checks with the cash disbursements records for date, payee, and amount.
- Examine cancelled checks for signature, endorsement, and cancellation.
- Compare deposits in the bank with recorded cash receipts for date, customer, and amount.
- Account for the numerical sequence of checks, and investigate missing ones.
- Reconcile all items causing a difference between the book and bank balance and verify their propriety.
- Reconcile total debits on the bank statement with the totals in the cash disbursements records.
- Reconcile total credits on the bank statement with the totals in the cash receipts records.
- Review month-end interbank transfers for propriety and proper recording.
- Follow up on outstanding checks and stop-payment notices.

Most accounting software packages incorporate a bank reconciliation as a part of end-of-month procedures. Even though the software reduces the clerical efforts in performing the bank reconciliations, it does not eliminate the need for the preparer to do most of the procedures just identified.

Because of the importance of monthly reconciliation of bank accounts, another common control for many companies is to have a responsible employee review the monthly reconciliation as soon as possible after its completion.

Because the cash balance is affected by all other cycles except inventory and warehousing, an extremely large number of transactions affect cash. The appropriate tests of controls and substantive tests of transactions have been discussed in detail in several earlier chapters as the audit of each cycle was studied.

Design and Perform Tests of Controls and Substantive Tests of Transactions (Phase II)

In many audits, the year-end bank reconciliation is extensively audited. Using analytical procedures to test the reasonableness of the cash balance is therefore less important than it is for most other audit areas.

It is common for auditors to compare the ending balance on the bank reconciliation, deposits in transit, outstanding checks, and other reconciling items with the prior-year reconciliation. Similarly, auditors normally compare the ending balance in cash with previous months' balances. These analytical procedures may uncover misstatements in cash.

Design and Perform Analytical Procedures (Phase III)

The starting point for the verification of the balance in the general bank account is to obtain a bank reconciliation from the client for inclusion in the auditor's working papers. Figure 22-4 on page 706 shows a bank reconciliation after adjustments. Notice that the bottom figure in the working paper is the adjusted balance in the general ledger, which is the balance that should appear on the financial statements. The auditor must determine that the client has made adjustments such as those at the bottom of Figure 22-4 if they are material.

The frame of reference for the audit tests is the bank reconciliation. The balance-related audit objectives and common tests of details of balances are shown in Table 22-1 on page 707. As in all other audit areas, the actual audit procedures depend on the materiality and the risks the auditor has identified in other parts of the audit that are related to cash.

Design Tests of Details of Cash Balance (Phase III)

FIGURE 22-4   **Working Paper for a Bank Reconciliation**

PBC

Clawson Industries
Bank Reconciliation
12/31/99

Schedule	A-2	Date
Prepared by	Client/DED	1/10/00
Approved by	SW	1/18/00

Acct. 101 – General account, First National Bank

Balance per Bank		109713	X A-2/1
Add:			
Deposits in transit			
12/30	10017 √		
12/31	11100 √	21117	
Deduct			
Outstanding checks			
#7993	12/16	3068 ⩔	
8007	12/16	9763 ⩔	
8012	12/23	11916 ⩔	
8013	12/23	14717 ⩔	
8029	12/28	A-7 37998 ⩔	
8038	12/30	A-7 10000 ⩔	<87462>
Other reconciling items: Bank error			
Deposit for another bank customer credited to General account by bank, in error		<15200>	A-3
Balance per bank, adjusted		28168	T/B
		⩔	
Balance per books before adjustments		32584	A-1
Adjustments:			
Unrecorded bank service charge		216	A-3
Nonsufficient funds check returned by bank, not collectible from customer	4200	<4416>	C-3/1
Balance per books, adjusted		28168	A-1
		⩔	

X Traced and agreed to bank confirmation.

√ Traced deposit to the December 1999 cash receipts records and to the January 2000
bank cutoff statement, noting its proper classification as a deposit in transit at
12/31/99.

⩔ Traced check to December 1999 cash disbursements records and to the January 2000
bank cutoff statement, noting its proper classification as an outstanding check at
12/31/99.

T/B Traced to 12/31/99 adjusted trial balance.

⩔ Footed

TABLE 22-1	Balance-Related Audit Objectives and Tests of Details of Balances for General Cash in the Bank	
Balance-Related Audit Objective	**Common Tests of Details of Balances Procedures**	**Comments**
Cash in the bank as stated on the reconciliation foots correctly and agrees with the general ledger (detail tie-in).	Foot the outstanding check list and deposits in transit. Prove the bank reconciliation as to additions and subtractions, including all reconciling items. Trace the book balance on the reconciliation to the general ledger.	These tests are done entirely on the bank reconciliation, with no reference to documents or other records except the general ledger.
Cash in the bank as stated on the reconciliation exists (existence). Existing cash in the bank is recorded (completeness). Cash in the bank as stated on the reconciliation is accurate (accuracy).	*(See extended discussion for each of these.)* Receipt and tests of a bank confirmation. Receipt and tests of a cutoff bank statement. Tests of the bank reconciliation. Extended tests of the bank reconciliation. Proof of cash. Tests for kiting.	These are the three most important objectives for cash in the bank. The procedures are combined because of their close interdependence. The last three procedures should be done only when there are internal control weaknesses.
Cash receipts and cash disbursements transactions are recorded in the proper period (cutoff).	*Cash receipts:* Count the cash on hand on the last day of the year and subsequently trace to deposits in transit and the cash receipts journal. Trace deposits in transit to subsequent period bank statement (cutoff bank statement). *Cash disbursements:* Record the last check number used on the last day of the year and subsequently trace to the outstanding checks and the cash disbursements journal. Trace outstanding checks to subsequent period bank statement.	When cash receipts received after year-end are included in the journal, a better cash position than actually exists is shown. It is called "holding open" the cash receipts journal. Holding open the cash disbursements journal reduces accounts payable and usually overstates the current ratio. The first procedure listed for receipts and disbursements cutoff tests requires the auditor's presence on the client's premises at the end of the last day of the year.
Cash in the bank is properly presented and disclosed (presentation and disclosure).	Examine minutes, loan agreements, and obtain confirmation for restrictions on the use of cash and compensating balances. Review financial statements to make sure (a) material savings accounts and certificates of deposit are disclosed separately from cash in the bank, (b) cash restricted to certain uses and compensating balances are adequately disclosed, and (c) bank overdrafts are included as current liabilities.	An example of a restriction on the use of cash is cash deposited with a trustee for the payment of mortgage interest and taxes on the proceeds of a construction mortgage. A compensating balance is the client's agreement with a bank to maintain a specified minimum in its checking account.

Also, because of their close relationship in the audit of year-end cash, the existence of recorded cash in the bank, accuracy, and inclusion of existing cash (completeness) are combined. These three objectives are the most important ones for cash and therefore receive the greatest attention.

The following three procedures merit additional discussion because of their importance and complexity.

Reconciling Items in the UK

Receipt of a Bank Confirmation The direct receipt of a confirmation from every bank or other financial institution with which the client does business is typically done but not required by auditing standards for every audit except when there is an unusually large number of inactive accounts. If the bank does not respond to a confirmation request, the auditor should send a second request or ask the client to telephone the bank. As a convenience to auditors as well as to bankers who are requested to fill out bank confirmations, the AICPA has approved the use of a **standard bank confirmation form**. Figure 22-5 on page 708

Clawson Industries
Bank Confirmation
12/31/99

Schedule *A-211*	Date
Prepared by *DCD*	*1/10/00*
Approved by *SW*	*1/18/00*

STANDARD FORM TO CONFIRM ACCOUNT
BALANCE INFORMATION WITH FINANCIAL INSTITUTIONS

Clawson Industries
CUSTOMER NAME

Financial
Institution's
Name and
Address

[   ]

First National Bank
200 Oak Street
Midvale, Illinois 40093

[   ]

We have provided to our accountants the following information as of the close of business on **December 31, 1999,** regarding our deposit and loan balances. Please confirm the accuracy of the information, noting any exceptions to the information provided. If the balances have been left blank, please complete this form by furnishing the balance in the appropriate space below.* Although we do not request nor expect you to conduct a comprehensive, detailed search of your records, if during the process of completing this confirmation additional information about other deposit and loan accounts we may have with you comes to your attention, please include such information below. Please use the enclosed envelope to return the form directly to our accountants.

1. At the close of business on the date listed above, our records indicated the following deposit balance(s):

ACCOUNT NAME	ACCOUNT NUMBER	INTEREST RATE	BALANCE*
General account	*19751-974*	*None*	*109,713.11 A-2*

2. We were directly liable to the financial institution for loans at the close of business on the date listed above as follows:

ACCOUNT NO./ DESCRIPTION	BALANCE*	DATE DUE	INTEREST RATE	DATE THROUGH WHICH INTEREST IS PAID	DESCRIPTION OF COLLATERAL
N/A	*50,000.00*	*1/9/00*	*10%*	*N/A*	*General*
N/A	*90,000.00*	*1/9/00*	*10%*	*N/A*	*Security*
N/A	*60,000.00*	*1/23/00*	*11%*	*N/A*	*Agreement*

A L Moore
(Customer's Authorized Signature)

January 3, 2000
(Date)

The information presented above by the customer is in agreement with our records. Although we have not conducted a comprehensive, detailed search of our records, no other deposit or loan accounts have come to our attention except as noted below.

Margaret Davis
(Financial Institution Authorized Signature)

January 10, 2000
(Date)

Vice President
(Title)

EXCEPTIONS AND/OR COMMENTS
None

Please return this form directly to our accountants:

Jones and Smith CPAs
2111 First Street
Detroit, Michigan 48711

*Ordinarily, balances are intentionally left blank if they are not available at the time the form is prepared.
Approved 1990 by American Bankers Association, American Institute of Certified Public Accountants, and Bank Administration Institute. Additional forms available from: AICPA-Order Department, P.O. Box 1003, NY, NY 10108-1003

is an illustration of a completed standard confirmation. As shown in Figure 22-5, it is called a standard form to confirm account balance information with financial institutions. This standard form has been agreed upon by the AICPA and the American Bankers Association.

The importance of bank confirmations in the audit extends beyond the verification of the actual cash balance. It is typical for the bank to confirm loan information and bank balances on the same form. The confirmation in Figure 22-5 includes three outstanding loans. Information on liabilities to the bank for notes, mortgages, or other debt typically includes the amount of the loan, the date of the loan, its due date, interest rate, and the existence of collateral.

Banks are *not responsible* to search their records for bank balances or loans beyond those included on the form by the CPA firm's client. A sentence near the bottom of the form obligates banks to inform the CPA firm of any loans not included on the confirmation *about which the bank has knowledge.* The effect of this limited responsibility is to require auditors to satisfy themselves about the completeness objective for unrecorded bank balances and loans from the bank in another manner. Similarly, banks are not expected to inform auditors of such things as open lines of credit, compensating balance requirements, or contingent liabilities for guaranteeing the loans of others. If the auditor wants confirmation of this type of information, a separate confirmation addressing the matters of concern should be obtained from the financial institution.

After the bank confirmation has been received, the balance in the bank account confirmed by the bank should be traced to the amount stated on the bank reconciliation. Similarly, all other information on the reconciliation should be traced to the relevant audit working papers. In any case, if the information is not in agreement, an investigation must be made of the difference.

Receipt of a Cutoff Bank Statement A **cutoff bank statement** is a partial-period bank statement and the related cancelled checks, duplicate deposit slips, and other documents included in bank statements, mailed by the bank directly to the CPA firm's office. The purpose of the cutoff bank statement is to verify the reconciling items on the client's year-end bank reconciliation with evidence that is inaccessible to the client. To fulfill this purpose, the auditor requests the client to have the bank send directly to the auditor the statement for 7 to 10 days subsequent to the balance sheet date.

Many auditors verify the subsequent period bank statement if a cutoff statement is not received directly from the bank. The purpose of this verification is to test whether the client's employees have omitted, added, or altered any of the documents accompanying the statement. It is obviously a test for intentional misstatements. The auditor performs the verification in the month subsequent to the balance sheet date by (1) footing all the cancelled checks, debit memos, deposits, and credit memos; (2) checking to see that the bank statement balances when the footed totals are used; and (3) reviewing the items included in the footings to make sure that they were cancelled by the bank in the proper period and do not include any erasures or alterations.

Tests of the Bank Reconciliation As stated earlier, a well-prepared independent bank reconciliation is an essential internal control over cash. The reasons for testing the bank reconciliation are to determine whether client personnel have carefully prepared the bank reconciliation and to verify whether the client's recorded bank balance is the same amount as the actual cash in the bank except for deposits in transit, outstanding checks, and other reconciling items. In testing the reconciliation, the auditor can obtain the information for conducting the tests from the cutoff bank statement. Several major procedures are involved:

- Verify that the client's bank reconciliation is mathematically accurate.
- Trace the balance on the bank confirmation and/or the beginning balance on the cutoff statement to the balance per bank on the bank reconciliation; a reconciliation cannot take place until these balances are the same.
- Trace checks written before year-end and included with the cutoff bank statement to the list of outstanding checks on the bank reconciliation and to the cash disbursements journal in the period or periods prior to the balance sheet date. All checks that cleared the bank after the balance sheet date and were included in the cash disbursements journal should also be included on the outstanding check list. If a check was included in the cash disbursements journal, it should be included as an outstanding

check if it did not clear before the balance sheet date. Similarly, if a check cleared the bank before the balance sheet date, it should not be on the bank reconciliation.

- Investigate all significant checks included on the outstanding check list that have not cleared the bank on the cutoff statement. The first step in the investigation should be to trace the amount of any items not clearing to the cash disbursements journal. The reason for the check not being cashed should be discussed with the client, and if the auditor is concerned about the possibility of fraud, the vendor's accounts payable balance should be confirmed to determine whether the vendor has recognized the receipt of the cash in its records. In addition, the cancelled check should be examined before the last day of the audit if it becomes available.
- Trace deposits in transit to the cutoff bank statement. All cash receipts not deposited in the bank at the end of the year should be traced to the cutoff bank statement to make sure that they were deposited shortly after the beginning of the new year.
- Account for other reconciling items on the bank statement and bank reconciliation. These include such items as bank service charges, bank errors and corrections, and unrecorded note transactions debited or credited directly to the bank account by the bank. These reconciling items should be investigated carefully to be sure that they have been treated properly by the client.

Figure 22-6 illustrates how the types of audit tests are used to audit the general cash account. Observe in the figure that tests of controls, substantive tests of transactions, and analytical procedures are done for each transaction cycle involving the cash account.

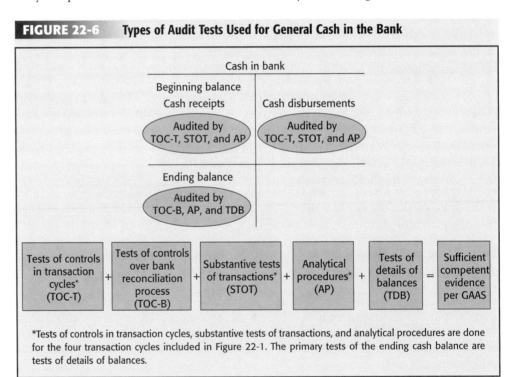

FIGURE 22-6 Types of Audit Tests Used for General Cash in the Bank

Cash in bank

Beginning balance
Cash receipts — Audited by TOC-T, STOT, and AP

Cash disbursements — Audited by TOC-T, STOT, and AP

Ending balance — Audited by TOC-B, AP, and TDB

Tests of controls in transaction cycles* (TOC-T) + Tests of controls over bank reconciliation process (TOC-B) + Substantive tests of transactions* (STOT) + Analytical procedures* (AP) + Tests of details of balances (TDB) = Sufficient competent evidence per GAAS

*Tests of controls in transaction cycles, substantive tests of transactions, and analytical procedures are done for the four transaction cycles included in Figure 22-1. The primary tests of the ending cash balance are tests of details of balances.

FRAUD-ORIENTED PROCEDURES

OBJECTIVE 22-4
Recognize when to extend audit tests of the general cash account to test further for material fraud.

A major consideration in the audit of the general cash balance is the possibility of fraud. The auditor must extend his or her procedures in the audit of year-end cash to determine the possibility of a material fraud when there are inadequate internal controls, especially the improper segregation of duties between the handling of cash and the recording of cash transactions in the accounting records.

In designing audit procedures for uncovering fraud, careful consideration should be given to the nature of the weaknesses in internal control, the type of fraud that is likely to result from the weaknesses, the potential materiality of the fraud, and the audit procedures that are most effective in uncovering the fraud. When auditors are specifically testing for fraud, they should keep in mind that audit procedures other than tests of details of cash balances can also be useful. Examples of procedures that may uncover fraud in the cash receipts area include the confirmation of accounts receivable, tests for lapping, reviewing the general ledger entries in the cash account for unusual items, tracing from customer orders to sales and subsequent cash receipts, and examining approvals and supporting documentation for bad debts and sales returns and allowances. Similar tests can be used for testing for the possibility of fraudulent cash disbursements.

Even with reasonably elaborate fraud-oriented procedures, it is extremely difficult to detect fraud, especially omitted transactions and account balances. If, for example, a company has illegal offshore cash accounts and makes deposits to those accounts from unrecorded sales, it is unlikely that an auditor will uncover the fraud. Nevertheless, auditors are responsible for making a reasonable effort to detect fraud when they have reason to believe it may exist. The following procedures for uncovering fraud that are directly related to year-end cash balances are discussed in this section: extended tests of the bank reconciliation, proofs of cash, and tests of interbank transfers.

Extended Tests of the Bank Reconciliation

When the auditor believes that the year-end bank reconciliation may be intentionally misstated, it is appropriate to perform extended tests of the year-end bank reconciliation. The purpose of the extended procedures is to verify whether all transactions included in the journals for the last month of the year were correctly included in or excluded from the bank reconciliation and to verify whether all items in the bank reconciliation were correctly included. Let us assume that there are material internal control weaknesses and the client's year-end is December 31. A common approach is to start with the bank reconciliation for November and compare all reconciling items with cancelled checks and other documents in the December bank statement. In addition, all remaining cancelled checks and deposit slips in the December bank statement should be compared with the December cash disbursements and receipts journals. All uncleared items in the November bank reconciliation and the December cash disbursements and receipts journals should be included in the client's December 31 bank reconciliation. Similarly, all reconciling items in the December 31 bank reconciliation should be items from the November bank reconciliation and December's journals that have not yet cleared the bank.

In addition to the tests just described, the auditor must also carry out procedures subsequent to the end of the year with the use of the bank cutoff statement. These tests would be performed in the same manner as previously discussed.

Proof of Cash

Auditors sometimes prepare a proof of cash when the client has material internal control weaknesses in cash. The auditor uses a proof of cash to determine whether the following were done:

- All recorded cash receipts were deposited.
- All deposits in the bank were recorded in the accounting records.
- All recorded cash disbursements were paid by the bank.
- All amounts that were paid by the bank were recorded.

A **proof of cash** includes the following:

- A reconciliation of the balance on the bank statement with the general ledger balance at the beginning of the proof-of-cash period
- A reconciliation of cash receipts deposited per the bank with the cash receipts journal for a given period

- A reconciliation of cancelled checks clearing the bank with the cash disbursements journal for a given period
- A reconciliation of the balance on the bank statement with the general ledger balance at the end of the proof-of-cash period

A proof of cash of this nature is commonly called a four-column proof of cash—one column is used for each of the types of information just listed. A proof of cash can be performed for one or more interim months, the entire year, or the last month of the year. Figure 22-7 below shows a four-column proof of cash for an interim month.

FIGURE 22-7   Interim Proof of Cash

Clawson Industries
Interim Proof of Cash
6/30/99

		Schedule	A-5	Date
		Prepared by	JG	7/15/99
		Approved by	RP	7/17/99

Acct. 101 – General account, First National Bank

		5/31/99	Receipts	Disbursements	6/30/99
Balance per Bank	①	121782.12	627895.20	631111.96	118565.36
Deposits in transit					
5/31	②	21720.00	<21720.00>		
6/30	②		16592.36		16592.36
Outstanding checks					
5/31	③	<36396.50>		<36396.50>	
6/30	③			14800.10	<14800.10>
NSF checks	④		<4560.00>	<4560.00>	
To allow for effect of a cash disbursement recorded as a credit item in cash receipts journal			<8500.00>	<8500.00>	
Balance per bank, adjusted		107105.62	609707.56	596455.56	120357.62
Balance per books, unadjusted		107105.62	609707.56	597957.04	118856.14
Bank debit memos	⑤			120.00	<120.00>
Payroll checks erroneously entered in General Disbursements Journal	⑥			<1621.48>	1621.48
Balance per books, adjusted		107105.62	609707.56	596455.56	120357.62

① Per 6/30/99 bank statement.
② Detailed listing filed below; traced to subsequent bank statements.
③ Outstanding-check list filed below; examined cancelled checks.
④ Detailed listing filed below; all NSF items were redeposited in June and had all cleared as of 6/30/99.
⑤ Safety deposit rentals; traced to recording via journal entry.
    Requested list of contents of safety deposit boxes.
⑥ Traced to journal entry correcting error.

The concern in an interim-month proof of cash is not with adjusting account balances, but rather with reconciling the amounts per books and bank.

When the auditor does a proof of cash, he or she is combining substantive tests of transactions and tests of details of balances. For example, a proof of cash receipts is a test of recorded transactions, whereas a bank reconciliation is a test of the balance in cash at a point in time. A proof of cash is an excellent method of comparing recorded cash receipts and disbursements with the bank account and with the bank reconciliation. However, the auditor must recognize that a proof of cash disbursements is not effective for discovering checks written for an improper amount, fraudulent checks, or other misstatements in which the dollar amount appearing on the cash disbursements records is incorrect. Similarly, proof-of-cash receipts is not useful for uncovering the theft of cash receipts or the recording and deposit of an improper amount of cash.

Tests of Interbank Transfers

Embezzlers occasionally cover a defalcation of cash by a practice known as **kiting**: transferring money from one bank to another and improperly recording the transaction. Near the balance sheet date, a check is drawn on one bank account and immediately deposited in a second account for credit before the end of the accounting period. In making this transfer, the embezzler is careful to make sure that the check is deposited at a late enough date so that it does not clear the first bank until after the end of the period. If the interbank transfer is not recorded until after the balance sheet date, the amount of the transfer is recorded as an asset in both banks. Although there are other ways of perpetrating this fraud, each involves the device of increasing the bank balance to cover a shortage by the use of interbank transfers.

A useful approach to test for kiting, as well as for unintentional errors in recording interbank transfers, is to list all interbank transfers made a few days before and after the balance sheet date and to trace each to the accounting records for proper recording. An example of an interbank transfer schedule is included in Figure 22-8. The working paper shows that four interbank transfers were made shortly before and after the balance sheet date.

FIGURE 22-8 Interbank Transfer Working Paper

Clawson Industries
Schedule of Interbank Transfers
December 31, 1999

PBC

Schedule _A-7_
Prepared by _Client/DES_ _1/10/00_
Approved by _SW_ _1/18/00_

Check No. (1)	Disbursements Bank (2)	Amount (3)	Date Recorded in Books (4)	Date Paid by Bank (5)	Receipts Bank (6)	Date Recorded in Books (7)	Date Received by Bank (8)
#8018	First National - general	$20,642 √	12-26-99 ⊗	12-28-99 □	Federal Charter - payroll	12-28-99 Ⓥ	12-29-99 □ Ø
#8029	First National - general	$37,998 √ A-2	12-28-99 √̇	01-02-00 □	Federal Charter - savings	12-29-99 Ⓥ	12-29-99 □ Ø
#8038	First National - general	$10,000 √ A-2	12-30-99 √̇	01-04-00 □	Federal Charter - savings	12-30-99 Ⓥ	01-03-00 □ ⓦ
#8045	First National - general	$21,014 √	01-02-00 ⊗	01-04-00 □	Federal Charter - payroll	01-03-00 Ⓥ	01-04-00 □ Ø

√ *Traced to cash disbursements records.*
Ⓥ *Traced to cash receipts records.*
√̇ *Check included as outstanding on bank reconciliation.*
⊗ *Check not included as outstanding on bank reconciliation.*
ⓦ *Receipt included as a deposit in transit.*
□ *Traced to bank statement.*
Ø *Receipt not included as a deposit in transit.*

Note: Examined cash disbursements and cash receipts records for checks to and deposits from bank accounts. None included except those listed above.

There are several things that should be audited on the interbank transfer schedule.

- *The accuracy of the information on the interbank transfer schedule should be verified.* The auditor should compare the disbursement and receipt information on the schedule to the cash disbursements and cash receipts records to make sure that it is accurate. Similarly, the dates on the schedule for transfers that were received and disbursed should be compared with the bank statement. Finally, cash disbursements and receipts records should be examined to make sure that all transfers a few days before and after the balance sheet date have been included on the schedule. The tick mark explanations on the working paper in Figure 22-8 indicate that these steps have been taken.
- *The interbank transfers must be recorded in both the receiving and disbursing banks.* If, for example, there was a $10,000 transfer from Bank A to Bank B but only the disbursement was recorded, this is evidence of an attempt to conceal a cash theft.
- *The date of the recording of the disbursements and receipts for each transfer must be in the same fiscal year.* In Figure 22-8, the dates in the two "date recorded in books" columns [columns (4) and (7)] are in the same period for each transfer; therefore, they are correct. If a cash receipt was recorded in the current fiscal year and the disbursement in the subsequent fiscal year, it may be an attempt to cover a cash shortage.
- *Disbursements on the interbank transfer schedule should be correctly included in or excluded from year-end bank reconciliations as outstanding checks.* In Figure 22-8, the 12-31-99 bank reconciliation for the general cash account should include outstanding checks for the second and third transfers but not the other two. [Compare the dates in columns (4) and (5).] Understating outstanding checks on the bank reconciliation indicates the possibility of kiting.
- *Receipts on the interbank transfer schedule should be correctly included in or excluded from year-end bank reconciliations as deposits in transit.* In Figure 22-8, the 12-31-99 bank reconciliations for the savings and payroll accounts should indicate a deposit in transit for the third transfer but not for the other three. (Compare the dates for each transfer in the last two columns.) Overstating deposits in transit on the bank reconciliation indicates the possibility of kiting.

Even though audit tests of interbank transfers are usually fraud oriented, they are often performed on audits in which there are numerous bank transfers, regardless of internal controls. When there are numerous interbank transfers, it is difficult to be sure that each is correctly handled unless a schedule of transfers near the end of the year is prepared and each transfer is traced to the accounting records and bank statements. In addition to the possibility of kiting, inaccurate handling of transfers could result in a misclassification between cash and accounts payable. The materiality of transfers and the relative ease of performing the tests make many auditors believe they should always be performed.

ELECTRONIC TRANSFER OF CASH

Many organizations use electronic transfer when they are transferring cash among banks, collecting from customers, and paying vendors. Under these systems, cash is transferred instantly. For example, when Company A collects from Customer X, the cash is instantly transferred from Customer X's bank account to Company A's. There is no check.

Electronic transfers have the potential to improve internal controls in that no cash is handled by employees. However, there is also potential risk of cash thefts through inappropriate cash transfers. It is essential that excellent internal controls are in place for electronic transfers.

AUDIT OF THE IMPREST PAYROLL BANK ACCOUNT

Tests of the payroll bank reconciliation should take only a few minutes if there is an imprest payroll account and an independent reconciliation of the bank account such as that described for the general account. Typically, the only reconciling items are outstanding checks, and for most audits, the great majority clear shortly after the checks are issued. In testing the payroll bank account balances, it is necessary to obtain a bank reconciliation, a bank confirmation, and a cutoff bank statement. The reconciliation procedures are performed in the same manner as those described for general cash except that tests of the outstanding checks are normally limited to a reasonableness test. Naturally, extended procedures are necessary if the controls are inadequate or if the bank account does not reconcile with the general ledger imprest cash balance.

> **OBJECTIVE 22-5**
> Design and perform audit tests of the imprest payroll bank account.

Keep in mind that these procedures pertain only to the imprest bank account, not to the overall payroll cycle. Auditing the payroll cycle was discussed in detail in an earlier chapter.

AUDIT OF IMPREST PETTY CASH

> **OBJECTIVE 22-6**
> Design and perform audit tests of imprest petty cash.

Petty cash is a unique account because it is often immaterial in amount, yet it is verified on many audits. The account is verified primarily because of the potential for defalcation and the client's expectation of an audit review even when the amount is immaterial.

Internal Controls Over Petty Cash

The most important internal control for petty cash is the use of an imprest fund that is the responsibility of *one individual.* In addition, petty cash funds should not be mingled with other receipts, and the fund should be kept separate from all other activities. There should also be limits on the amount of any expenditure from petty cash, as well as on the total amount of the fund. The type of expenditure that can be made from petty cash transactions should be well defined by company policy.

When a disbursement is made from petty cash, adequate internal controls require a responsible official's approval on a prenumbered petty cash form. The total of the actual cash and checks in the fund plus the total unreimbursed petty cash forms that represent actual expenditures should equal the total amount of the petty cash fund stated in the general ledger. Periodically, surprise counts and a reconciliation of the petty cash fund should be made by the internal auditor or other responsible official.

When the petty cash balance runs low, a check payable to the petty cash custodian should be written on the general cash account for the reimbursement of petty cash. The check should be for the exact amount of the prenumbered vouchers that are submitted as evidence of actual expenditures. These vouchers should be verified by the accounts payable clerk and cancelled to prevent their reuse.

Audit Tests for Petty Cash

The emphasis in verifying petty cash should be on testing controls over petty cash transactions rather than the ending balance in the account. Even if the amount of the petty cash fund is small, there is potential for numerous improper transactions if the fund is frequently reimbursed.

An important part of testing petty cash is first to determine the client's procedures for handling the fund by discussing internal controls with the custodian and examining the documentation of a few transactions. As a part of obtaining an understanding of internal control, it is necessary to identify internal controls and weaknesses. Even though most petty cash systems are not complex, it is often desirable to use a flowchart and an internal control questionnaire, primarily for documentation in subsequent audits.

Tests of controls and substantive tests of transactions depend on the number and size of the petty cash reimbursements and the auditor's assessed control risk. When control risk is assessed as low and there are few reimbursement payments during the year, it is common for auditors not to test any further for reasons of immateriality. When the auditor decides to test petty cash, the two most common procedures are to count the petty cash balance and to carry out detailed tests of one or two reimbursement transactions. In such a case, the primary procedures should include footing the petty cash vouchers supporting the amount of the reimbursement, accounting for a sequence of petty cash vouchers, examining the petty cash vouchers for authorization and cancellation, and examining the attached documentation for reasonableness. Typical supporting documentation includes cash register tapes, invoices, and receipts.

Petty cash tests can ordinarily be performed at any time during the year, but as a matter of convenience, they are typically done on an interim date. If the balance in the petty cash fund is considered material, which is rarely the case, it should be counted at the end of the year. Unreimbursed expenditures should be examined as a part of the count to determine whether the amount of unrecorded expenses is material.

SUMMARY

We have seen in this chapter that transactions in most cycles affect the cash account. Because of the relationship between transactions in several cycles and the ending cash account balance, the auditor typically waits to audit the ending cash balance until he or she completes and analyzes the results of tests of controls and substantive tests of transactions for all cycles. As shown in this chapter, tests of the cash balance normally include tests of the bank reconciliations of key cash accounts, such as the general cash account, imprest payroll account, and imprest petty cash fund. If the auditor assesses a high likelihood of fraud in cash, he or she may also perform additional tests, such as extended bank reconciliation procedures, a proof of cash, or tests of interbank transfers.

ESSENTIAL TERMS

Bank reconciliation—the monthly reconciliation, usually prepared by client personnel, of the differences between the cash balance recorded in the general ledger and the amount in the bank account

Branch bank accounts—separate bank accounts maintained at local banks by branches of a company

Cash equivalents—excess cash invested in short-term, highly liquid investments such as time deposits, certificates of deposit, and money market funds

Cutoff bank statement—a partial-period bank statement and the related cancelled checks, duplicate deposit slips, and other documents included in bank statements, mailed by the bank directly to the auditor; the auditor uses it to verify reconciling items on the client's year-end bank reconciliation

General cash account—the primary bank account for most organizations; virtually all cash receipts and disbursements flow through this account at some time

Imprest payroll account—a bank account to which the exact amount of payroll for the pay period is transferred by check from the employer's general cash account

Imprest petty cash fund—a fund of cash maintained within the company for small cash acquisitions or to cash employees' checks; the fund's fixed balance is comparatively small and is periodically reimbursed

Kiting—the transfer of money from one bank account to another and improperly recording the transfer so that the amount is recorded as an asset in both accounts; this practice is used by embezzlers to cover a defalcation of cash

Proof of cash—a four-column working paper prepared by the auditor to reconcile the bank's record of the client's beginning balance, cash deposits, cleared checks, and ending balance for the period, with the client's records

Standard bank confirmation form—a form approved by the AICPA and American Bankers Association through which the bank responds to the auditor about bank balance and loan information provided on the confirmation

REVIEW QUESTIONS

22-1 (Objectives 22-1, 22-2) Explain the relationships among the initial assessed control risk, tests of controls and substantive tests of transactions for cash receipts, and the tests of details of cash balances.

22-2 (Objectives 22-1, 22-2) Explain the relationships among the initial assessed control risk, tests of controls and substantive tests of transactions for cash disbursements, and the tests of details of cash balances. Give one example in which the conclusions reached about internal controls in cash disbursements would affect the tests of cash balances.

22-3 (Objective 22-3) Why is the monthly reconciliation of bank accounts by an independent person an important internal control over cash balances? Which individuals would generally not be considered independent for this responsibility?

22-4 (Objective 22-3) Evaluate the effectiveness and state the shortcomings of the preparation of a bank reconciliation by the controller in the manner described in the following statement: "When I reconcile the bank account, the first thing I do is to sort the checks in numerical order and find which numbers are missing. Next I determine the amount of the uncleared checks by referring to the cash disbursements journal. If the bank account reconciles at that point, I am all finished with the reconciliation. If it does not, I search for deposits in transit, checks from the beginning outstanding check list that still have not cleared, other reconciling items, and bank errors until it reconciles. In most instances, I can do the reconciliation in 20 minutes."

22-5 (Objective 22-3) How do bank confirmations differ from positive confirmations of accounts receivable? Distinguish between them in terms of the nature of the information confirmed, the sample size, and the appropriate action when the confirmation is not returned after the second request. Explain the rationale for the differences between these two types of confirmations.

22-6 (Objective 22-3) Evaluate the necessity of following the practice described by an auditor: "In confirming bank accounts I insist upon a response from every bank the client has done business with in the past 2 years, even though the account may be closed at the balance sheet date."

22-7 (Objective 22-3) Describe what is meant by a cutoff bank statement and state its purpose.

22-8 (Objective 22-3) Why are auditors usually less concerned about the client's cash receipts cutoff than the cutoff for sales? Explain the procedure involved in testing for the cutoff for cash receipts.

22-9 (Objective 22-2) What is meant by an imprest bank account for a branch operation? Explain the purpose of using this type of bank account.

22-10 (Objective 22-4) Explain the purpose of a four-column proof of cash. List two types of misstatements it is meant to uncover.

22-11 (Objective 22-3) When the auditor fails to obtain a cutoff bank statement, it is common to verify the entire statement for the month subsequent to the balance sheet date. How is this done and what is its purpose?

22-12 (Objective 22-4) Distinguish between lapping and kiting. Describe audit procedures that can be used to uncover each.

22-13 (Objective 22-5) Assume that a client with excellent internal controls uses an imprest payroll bank account. Explain why the verification of the payroll bank reconciliation ordinarily takes less time than the tests of the general bank account, even if the number of checks exceeds those written on the general account.

22-14 (Objective 22-6) Distinguish between the verification of petty cash reimbursements and the verification of the balance in the fund. Explain how each is done. Which is more important?

22-15 (Objectives 22-3, 22-4) Why is there a greater emphasis on the detection of fraud in tests of details of cash balances than for other balance sheet accounts? Give two specific examples that demonstrate how this emphasis affects the auditor's evidence accumulation in auditing year-end cash.

22-16 (Objective 22-3) Explain why, in verifying bank reconciliations, most auditors emphasize the possibility of a nonexistent deposit in transit being included in the reconciliation and an outstanding check being omitted rather than the omission of a deposit in transit and the inclusion of a nonexistent outstanding check.

MULTIPLE CHOICE QUESTIONS FROM CPA EXAMINATIONS

22-17 (Objectives 22-3, 22-4) The following questions deal with auditing year-end cash. Choose the best response.

a. A CPA obtains a January 10 cutoff bank statement for his client directly from the bank. Few of the outstanding checks listed on his client's December 31 bank reconciliation cleared during the cutoff period. A probable cause for this is that the client
  (1) is engaged in kiting.
  (2) is engaged in lapping.
  (3) transmitted the checks to the payees after year-end.
  (4) has overstated its year-end bank balance.

b. The auditor should ordinarily mail confirmation requests to all banks with which the client has conducted any business during the year, regardless of the year-end balance, because
  (1) the confirmation form also seeks information about indebtedness to the bank.
  (2) this procedure will detect kiting activities that would otherwise not be detected.
  (3) the mailing of confirmation forms to all such banks is required by generally accepted auditing standards.
  (4) this procedure relieves the auditor of any responsibility with respect to nondetection of forged checks.

c. The usefulness of the standard bank confirmation request may be limited because the bank employee who completes the form may
  (1) not believe the bank is obligated to verify confidential information to a third party.
  (2) sign and return the form without inspecting the accuracy of the client's bank reconciliation.
  (3) not have access to the client's bank statement.
  (4) be unaware of all the financial relationships that the bank has with the client.

22-18 (Objective 22-4) The following questions deal with discovering fraud in auditing year-end cash. Choose the best response.

a. Which of the following is one of the better auditing techniques to detect kiting?
  (1) Review composition of authenticated deposit slips.
  (2) Review subsequent bank statements and cancelled checks received directly from the banks.
  (3) Prepare a schedule of bank transfers from the client's books.
  (4) Prepare year-end bank reconciliations.

b. The cashier of Baker Company covered a shortage in his cash working fund with cash obtained on December 31 from a local bank by cashing an unrecorded check drawn on the company's New York bank. The auditor would discover this manipulation by
  (1) preparing independent bank reconciliations as of December 31.
  (2) counting the cash working fund at the close of business on December 31.
  (3) investigating items returned with the bank cutoff statements.
  (4) confirming the December 31 bank balances.

c. A cash shortage may be concealed by transporting funds from one location to another or by converting negotiable assets to cash. Because of this, which of the following is vital?
  (1) Simultaneous bank confirmations.
  (2) Simultaneous bank reconciliations.
  (3) Simultaneous four-column proofs of cash.
  (4) Simultaneous surprise cash counts.

22-19 (Objectives 22-3, 22-4)   The following are misstatements that might be found in the client's year-end cash balance (assume that the balance sheet date is June 30).

1. A check was omitted from the outstanding check list on the June 30 bank reconciliation. It cleared the bank July 7.
2. A check was omitted from the outstanding check list on the bank reconciliation. It cleared the bank September 6.
3. Cash receipts collected on accounts receivable from July 1 to July 5 were included as June 29 and 30 cash receipts.
4. A loan from the bank on June 26 was credited directly to the client's bank account. The loan was not entered as of June 30.
5. A check that was dated June 26 and disbursed in June was not recorded in the cash disbursements journal, but it was included as an outstanding check on June 30.
6. A bank transfer recorded in the accounting records on July 1 was included as a deposit in transit on June 30.
7. The outstanding checks on the June 30 bank reconciliation were underfooted by $2,000.

Required
   a. Assuming that each of these misstatements was intentional (fraud), state the most likely motivation of the person responsible.
   b. What control could be instituted for each fraud to reduce the likelihood of occurrence?
   c. List an audit procedure that could be used to discover each fraud.

22-20 (Objectives 22-3, 22-4)   The following are misstatements that an auditor might find through substantive tests of transactions or by tests of details of cash balances.

1. The bookkeeper failed to record checks in the cash disbursements journal that were written and mailed during the first month of the year.
2. The bookkeeper failed to record or deposit a material amount of cash receipts during the last month of the year. Cash is prelisted by the president's secretary.
3. The cash disbursements journal was held open for 2 days after the end of the year.
4. A check was paid to a vendor for a carload of raw materials that was never received by the client.
5. A discount on an acquisition was not taken, even though the check was mailed before the discount period had expired.
6. Cash receipts for the last 2 days of the year were recorded in the cash receipts journal for the subsequent period and listed as deposits in transit on the bank reconciliation.
7. A check written to a vendor during the last month of the year was recorded in the cash disbursements journal twice to cover an existing fraud. The check cleared the bank and did not appear on the bank reconciliation.

Required
   a. List a substantive audit procedure to uncover each of the preceding misstatements.
   b. For each procedure in part a, state whether it is a test of details of cash balances or a substantive test of transactions.

22-21 (Objectives 22-3, 22-4)   The following audit procedures are concerned with tests of details of general cash balances.

1. Compare the bank cancellation date with the date on the cancelled check for checks dated on or shortly before the balance sheet date.
2. Trace deposits in transit on the bank reconciliation to the cutoff bank statement and the current year cash receipts journal.
3. Obtain a standard bank confirmation from each bank with which the client does business.
4. Compare the balance on the bank reconciliation obtained from the client with the bank confirmation.

5. Compare the checks returned along with the cutoff bank statement with the list of outstanding checks on the bank reconciliation.
6. List the check number, payee, and amount of all material checks not returned with the cutoff bank statement.
7. Review minutes of the board of directors' meetings, loan agreements, and bank confirmation for interest-bearing deposits, restrictions on the withdrawal of cash, and compensating balance agreements.
8. Prepare a four-column proof of cash.

Required

Explain the objective of each.

22-22 (Objective 22-3)   You are auditing general cash for the Pittsburg Supply Company for the fiscal year ended July 31, 1999. The client has not prepared the July 31 bank reconciliation. After a brief discussion with the owner, you agree to prepare the reconciliation, with assistance from one of Pittsburg Supply's clerks. You obtain the following information:

	General Ledger	Bank Statement
Beginning balance 7/1/99	$ 4,611	$ 5,753
Deposits		25,056
Cash receipts journal	25,456	
Checks cleared		(23,615)
Cash disbursements journal	(21,811)	
July bank service charge		(87)
Note paid directly		(6,100)
NSF check		(311)
Ending balance 7/31/99	$ 8,256	$ 696

June 30 Bank Reconciliation

**Information in General
Ledger and Bank Statement**

Balance per bank	$5,753
Deposits in transit	600
Outstanding checks	1,742
Balance per books	4,611

Additional information obtained is as follows:

1. Checks clearing that were outstanding on June 30 totaled $1,692.
2. Checks clearing that were recorded in the July disbursements journal totaled $20,467.
3. A check for $1,060 cleared the bank but had not been recorded in the cash disbursements journal. It was for an acquisition of inventory. Pittsburg Supply uses the periodic-inventory method.
4. A check for $396 was charged to Pittsburg Supply but had been written on a different company's bank account.
5. Deposits included $600 from June and $24,456 for July.
6. The bank charged Pittsburg Supply's account for a nonsufficient check totaling $311. The credit manager concluded that the customer intentionally closed its account and the owner left the city. The check was turned over to a collection agency.
7. A note for $5,800, plus interest, was paid directly to the bank under an agreement signed 4 months ago. The note payable was recorded at $5,800 on Pittsburg Supply's books.

Required

a. Prepare a bank reconciliation that shows both the unadjusted and adjusted balance per books.

b. Prepare all adjusting entries.

c. What audit procedures would you use to verify each item in the bank reconciliation?

d. What is the cash balance that should appear on the July 31, 1999, financial statements?

22-23 (Objectives 22-3, 22-4)   In the audit of the Regional Transport Company, a large branch that maintains its own bank account, cash is periodically transferred to the central account in Cedar Rapids. On the branch account's records, bank transfers are recorded as a debit to the home office clearing account and a credit to the branch bank account. Similarly, the home office account is recorded as a debit to the central bank account and a credit to the branch office clearing account. Gordon Light is the head bookkeeper for both the home office and the branch bank accounts. Because he also reconciles the bank account, the senior auditor, Cindy Marintette, is concerned about the internal control weakness.

As a part of the year-end audit of bank transfers, Marintette asks you to schedule the transfers for the last few days in 1999 and the first few days of 2000. You prepare the following list:

Amount of Transfer	Date Recorded in the Home Office Cash Receipts Journal	Date Recorded in the Branch Office Cash Disbursements Journal	Date Deposited in the Home Office Bank Account	Date Cleared the Branch Bank Account
$12,000	12-27-99	12-29-99	12-26-99	12-27-99
26,000	12-28-99	01-02-00	12-28-99	12-29-99
14,000	01-02-00	12-30-99	12-28-99	12-29-99
11,000	12-26-99	12-26-99	12-28-99	01-03-00
15,000	01-02-00	01-02-00	12-28-99	12-31-99
28,000	01-07-00	01-05-00	12-28-99	01-03-00
37,000	01-04-00	01-06-00	01-03-00	01-05-00

Required

a. In verifying each bank transfer, state the appropriate audit procedures you should perform.

b. Prepare any adjusting entries required in the home office records.

c. Prepare any adjusting entries required in the branch bank records.

d. State how each bank transfer should be included in the December 31, 1999, bank reconciliation for the home office account after your adjustments in part b.

e. State how each bank transfer should be included in the December 31, 1999, bank reconciliation of the branch bank account after your adjustments in part c.

22-24 (Objective 22-3)   In connection with an audit you are given the following worksheet (see below and on top of page 722):

Bank Reconciliation, December 31, 1999

Balance per ledger December 31, 1999	$17,174.86
Add:	
Cash receipts received on the last day of December and charged to "cash in bank" on books but not deposited	2,662.25
Debit memo for customer's check returned unpaid (check is on hand but no entry has been made on the books)	200.00
Debit memo for bank service charge for December	5.50
	$20,142.61

Deduct:

Checks drawn but not paid by bank (see detailed list below)	$2,267.75	
Credit memo for proceeds of a note receivable that had been left at the bank for collection but which has not been recorded as collected	400.00	
Checks for an account payable entered on books as $240.90 but drawn and paid by bank as $419.00	178.10	(2,945.85)
Computed balance		17,196.76
Unlocated difference		(200.00)
Balance per bank (checked to confirmation)		$16,996.76

Checks Drawn but Not Paid by Bank

No.	Amount
573	$ 67.27
724	9.90
903	456.67
907	305.50
911	482.75
913	550.00
914	366.76
916	10.00
917	218.90
	$2,267.75

Required

    a. Prepare a corrected reconciliation.

    b. Prepare journal entries for items that should be adjusted prior to closing the books.*

22-25 (Objective 22-4)   You are doing the first-year audit of Sherman School District and have been assigned responsibility for doing a four-column proof of cash for the month of October 1999. You obtain the following information:

1.	Balance per books	September 30	$8,106
		October 31	3,850
2.	Balance per bank	September 30	5,411
		October 31	6,730
3.	Outstanding checks	September 30	916
		October 31	1,278
4.	Cash receipts for October	per bank	26,536
		per books	19,711
5.	Deposits in transit	September 30	3,611
		October 31	693

    6. Interest on a bank loan for the month of October, charged by the bank but not recorded, was $596.

    7. Proceeds on a note of the Jones Company were collected by the bank on October 28 but were not entered on the books:

        Principal $3,300
        Interest   307
                $3,607

    8. On October 26, a $407 check of the Billings Company was charged to Sherman School District's account by the bank in error.

*AICPA adapted.

9. Dishonored checks are not recorded on the books unless they permanently fail to clear the bank. The bank treats them as disbursements when they are dishonored and deposits when they are redeposited. Checks totaling $609 were dishonored in October; $300 was redeposited in October and $309 in November.

Required

  a. Prepare a four-column proof of cash for the month ended October 31. It should show both adjusted and unadjusted cash.
  b. Prepare all adjusting entries.

CASE

22-26 (Objective 22-4)   The following information was obtained in an audit of the cash account of Tuck Company as of December 31, 1999. Assume that the CPA has satisfied himself as to the propriety of the cash book, the bank statements, and the returned checks, except as noted.

  1. The bookkeeper's bank reconciliation at November 30, 1999.

Balance per bank statement	$19,400	
Add: Deposit in transit	1,100	
Total	$20,500	
Less: Outstanding checks		
#2540	$140	
#1501	750	
#1503	580	
#1504	800	
#1505	30	(2,300)
Balance per books		$18,200

  2. A summary of the bank statement for December 1999.

Balance brought forward	$ 19,400
Deposits	148,700
	168,100
Charges	(132,500)
Balance, December 31, 1999	$ 35,600

  3. A summary of the cash book for December 1999 before adjustments.

Balance brought forward	$ 18,200
Receipts	149,690
	167,890
Disbursements	(124,885)
Balance, December 31, 1999	$ 43,005

  4. Included with cancelled checks returned with the December bank statement were the checks listed on page 724.
  5. The Tuck Company discounted its own 60-day note for $9,000 with the bank on December 1, 1999. The discount rate was 6 percent. The accountant recorded the proceeds as a cash receipt at the face value of the note.
  6. The accountant records customers' dishonored checks as a reduction of cash receipts. When the dishonored checks are redeposited, they are recorded as a regular cash receipt. Two N.S.F. checks for $180 and $220 were returned by the bank during December. Both checks were redeposited and were recorded by the accountant.
  7. Cancellations of Tuck Company checks are recorded by a reduction of cash disbursements.
  8. December bank charges were $20. In addition, a $10 service charge was made in December for the collection of a foreign draft in November. These charges were not recorded on the books.

9. Check 2540 listed in the November outstanding checks was drawn in 1997. Because the payee cannot be located, the president of Tuck Company agreed to the CPA's suggestion that the check be written back into the accounts by a journal entry.
10. Outstanding checks at December 31, 1999, totaled $4,000, excluding checks 2540 and 1504.
11. The cutoff bank statement disclosed that the bank had recorded a deposit of $2,400 on January 2, 2000. The accountant had recorded this deposit on the books on December 31, 1999, and then mailed the deposit to the bank.

Number	Date of Check	Amount of Check	Comment
1501	November 28, 1999	$ 75	This check was in payment of an invoice for $750 and was recorded in the cash book as $750.
1503	November 28, 1999	$ 580	This check was in payment of an invoice for $580 and was recorded in the cash book as $580.
1523	December 5, 1999	$ 150	Examination of this check revealed that it was unsigned. A discussion with the client disclosed that it had been mailed inadvertently before it was signed. The check was endorsed and deposited by the payee and processed by the bank even though it was a legal nullity. The check was recorded in the cash disbursements journal.
1528	December 12, 1999	$ 800	This check replaced 1504, which was returned by the payee because it was mutilated. Check 1504 was not cancelled on the books.
—	December 19, 1999	$ 200	This was a counter check drawn at the bank by the president of the company as a cash advance for travel expense. The president overlooked informing the bookkeeper about the check.
—	December 20, 1999	$ 300	The drawer of this check was the Tucker Company.
1535	December 20, 1999	$ 350	This check had been labeled N.S.F. and returned to the payee because the bank had erroneously believed that the check was drawn by the Luck Company. Subsequently, the payee was advised to redeposit the check.
1575	January 5, 2000	$10,000	This check was given to the payee on December 30, 1999, as a postdated check with the understanding that it would not be deposited until January 5. The check was not recorded on the books in December.

Required

Prepare a four-column proof of cash of the cash receipts and cash disbursements recorded on the bank statement and on the company's books for the month of December 1999. The reconciliation should agree with the cash figure that will appear in the company's financial statements.*

*AICPA adapted.

PART V
(Chapter 23)

COMPLETING THE AUDIT

The last of the four phases of an audit is completing the audit, which is covered in Chapter 23, the only chapter in Part V. Even when the other phases of the audit are done well, if the completion phase is done poorly, the quality of the audit will be low. If the planning phase (phase I) and the two testing phases (phases II and III) are done well, the completion phase is typically relatively easy.

COMPLETING THE AUDIT

GOOD REVIEW REQUIRES MORE THAN LOOKING AT WORKING PAPERS

Larry Lenape, an audit senior of Santro, Best & Harmon, assigned staff assistant Clawson Little the audit of accounts payable for Westside Industries, a large equipment manufacturer. Accounts payable is a major liability account for a manufacturing company, and testing accounts payable cutoff is an important audit area. Testing primarily involves reviewing the liability recorded by the client by examining subsequent payments to suppliers and other creditors to ensure that they were properly recorded.

Lenape observed that Little was spending a lot of time on the phone, apparently on personal matters. Shortly before the audit was completed, Little announced that he was leaving the firm. Despite Little's distractions due to his personal affairs, he completed the audit work he was assigned within the budgeted time.

Because of Lenape's concern about Little's work habits, he decided to review the working papers with extreme care. Every schedule he reviewed was properly prepared, with tick marks entered and explained by Little, indicating that he had made an extensive examination of underlying data and documents and had found the client's balance to be adequate as stated. Specifically, there were no payments subsequent to year-end for inventory purchases received during the audit period that had not been accrued by the Company.

When Lenape finished the audit, he turned the working papers over to Kelsey Mayburn, an audit manager on the engagement, for her review. She had considerable knowledge about equipment manufacturers and also about Westside Industries. Mayburn reviewed all of the working papers, including analytical procedures performed during the audit. After calculating additional analytical procedures during her review, she contacted Lenape and told him accounts payable didn't seem reasonable to her. She asked him to do some additional checking. Lenape went back and looked at all the documents that Little had indicated in the working papers that he had inspected. It was quickly apparent that Little had either not looked at the documents or did not know what he was doing when he inspected them. There were almost $1 million of documents applicable to the December 31, 1999, audit period that had not been included as liabilities. Mayburn's review probably saved Santro, Best & Harmon significant embarrassment or worse.

LEARNING OBJECTIVES

After studying this chapter, you should be able to

23-1 Conduct a review for contingent liabilities and commitments.

23-2 Obtain and evaluate letters from the client's attorneys.

23-3 Conduct a post–balance-sheet review for subsequent events.

23-4 Design and perform the final steps in the evidence-accumulation segment of the audit.

23-5 Integrate the audit evidence gathered, and evaluate the overall audit results.

23-6 Communicate effectively with the audit committee and management.

23-7 Identify the auditor's responsibilities when facts affecting the audit report are discovered after its issuance.

The entire textbook starting with Chapter 6 has dealt with the first three phases of the audit process shown in the margin below. The last of the four phases of an audit, which is shaded in the figure, is completing the audit. Although completing the audit is covered in only one chapter, the topic is extremely important to auditors. The opening vignette illustrates the importance of careful and thoughtful review of the audit by an experienced and knowledgeable person. There are several other aspects of completing the audit besides reviewing the results that are critical to the success of an audit. The figure in the margin on page 729 shows the six parts of the completing the audit phase that are discussed in this chapter.

REVIEW FOR CONTINGENT LIABILITIES AND COMMITMENTS

OBJECTIVE 23-1
Conduct a review for contingent liabilities and commitments.

Summary of the Audit Process

PHASE I
Plan and design an audit approach

PHASE II
Perform tests of controls and substantive tests of transactions

PHASE III
Perform analytical procedures and tests of details of balances

PHASE IV
Complete the audit and issue an audit report

A **contingent liability** is a potential future obligation to an outside party for an unknown amount resulting from activities that have already taken place. Three conditions are required for a contingent liability to exist: (1) there is a potential future payment to an outside party or the impairment of some other asset that would result from an existing condition, (2) there is uncertainty about the amount of the future payment or impairment, and (3) the outcome will be resolved by some future event or events. For example, a lawsuit that has been filed but not yet resolved meets all three of these conditions.

This uncertainty of the future payment can vary from extremely likely to highly unlikely. SFAS 5 describes three levels of likelihood of occurrence and the appropriate financial statement treatment for each likelihood. These requirements are summarized in Table 23-1. The decision as to the appropriate treatment requires considerable professional judgment.

TABLE 23-1	Likelihood of Occurrence and Financial Statement Treatment
Likelihood of Occurrence of Event	**Financial Statement Treatment**
Remote (slight chance)	No disclosure is necessary.
Reasonably possible (more than remote, but less than probable)	Footnote disclosure is necessary.
Probable (likely to occur) ✓	• If the amount can be reasonably estimated, financial statement accounts are adjusted. • If the amount cannot be reasonably estimated, note disclosure is necessary.

When the proper disclosure in the financial statements of a material contingency is through a footnote, the footnote should describe the nature of the contingency to the extent it is known and the opinion of legal counsel or management as to the expected outcome. Figure 23-1 is an illustration of a footnote for pending litigation and company guarantees of debt.

FIGURE 23-1	Contingent Liability Footnote

There are various suits and claims pending against the company and its consolidated subsidiaries. It is the opinion of the company's management, based on current available information, that the ultimate liability, if any, resulting from such suits and claims will not materially affect the consolidated financial position or results of operations of the company and its consolidated subsidiaries.

The company has agreed to guarantee the repayment of approximately $14,000,000 loaned by a bank to several affiliated corporations in which the company owns a minority interest.

Certain contingent liabilities are of considerable concern to the auditor:

• Pending litigation for patent infringement, product liability, or other actions
• Income tax disputes

Sell product — Adj. entry anytime
warranty Exp *Est. fiab under warr.*
Est. fiab. under warranties *Cash or Inventory or*
Phase IV— *Labor,*
Completing the Audit *or Parts*

- Product warranties *very common*
- Notes receivable discounted
- Guarantees of obligations of others
- Unused balances of outstanding letters of credit

Auditing standards make it clear that management, not the auditor, is responsible for identifying and deciding the appropriate accounting treatment for contingent liabilities. In many audits, it is impractical for auditors to uncover contingencies without management's cooperation.

The auditor's objectives in verifying contingent liabilities are to evaluate the accounting treatment of known contingent liabilities and to identify, to the extent practical, any contingencies not already identified by management.

Closely related to contingent liabilities are **commitments** to purchase raw materials or to lease facilities at a certain price, agreements to sell merchandise at a fixed price, bonus plans, profit-sharing and pension plans, royalty agreements, and similar items. In a commitment, the most important characteristic is the *agreement to commit the firm to a set of fixed conditions* in the future regardless of what happens to profits or the economy as a whole. In a free economy, presumably the entity agrees to commitments as a means of bettering its own interests, but they may turn out to be less or more advantageous than originally anticipated. All commitments are ordinarily either described together in a separate footnote or combined in a footnote related to contingencies.

Many of these potential obligations are ordinarily verified as an integral part of various segments of the engagement rather than as a separate activity near the end of the audit. For example, unused balances in outstanding letters of credit may be tested as a part of confirming bank balances and loans from banks. Similarly, income tax disputes can be checked as a part of analyzing income tax expense, reviewing the general correspondence file, and examining revenue agent reports. Even if contingencies are verified separately, it is common to perform the tests well before the last few days of completing the engagement to ensure their proper verification. Tests of contingent liabilities near the end of the engagement are more a review than an initial search.

The appropriate audit procedures for testing contingencies are less well defined than those already discussed in other audit areas because the primary objective at the initial stage of the tests is to determine the *existence* of contingencies. As you know from the study of other audit areas, it is more difficult to discover unrecorded transactions or events than to verify recorded information. Once the auditor is aware that contingencies exist, evaluation of their materiality and disclosure requirements can ordinarily be satisfactorily resolved.

The following are some audit procedures commonly used to search for contingent liabilities. The list is not all-inclusive, and each procedure is not necessarily performed on every audit.

- Inquire of management (orally and in writing) about the possibility of unrecorded contingencies. In these inquiries, the auditor must be specific in describing the different kinds of contingencies that may require disclosure. Naturally, inquiries of management are not useful in uncovering the intentional failure to disclose existing contingencies, but if management has overlooked a certain type of contingency or does not fully comprehend accounting disclosure requirements, the inquiry can be fruitful. At the completion of the audit, management is typically asked to make a written statement as a part of the letter of representation, which is discussed later in this chapter, that it is aware of no undisclosed contingent liabilities.
- Review current and previous years' internal revenue agent reports for income tax settlements. The reports may indicate areas or years in which there are unsettled disagreements. If a review has been in progress for a long time, there is an increased likelihood of a tax dispute.
- Review the minutes of directors' and stockholders' meetings for indications of lawsuits or other contingencies.

Review for contingent liabilities

Review for subsequent events

Accumulate final evidence

Evaluate results

Issue audit report

Communicate with audit committee and management

Audit Procedures for Finding Contingencies

When do you make an entry for a contingent liab.?
1. probable (likely to occur)
2. the $ amt. can be reasonably estimated

- Analyze legal expense for the period under audit and review invoices and statements from legal counsel for indications of contingent liabilities, especially lawsuits and pending tax assessments.
- Obtain a letter from each major attorney performing legal services for the client as to the status of pending litigation or other contingent liabilities. This procedure is discussed in more depth shortly.
- Review working papers for any information that may indicate a potential contingency. For example, bank confirmations may indicate notes receivable discounted or guarantees of loans.
- Examine letters of credit in force as of the balance sheet date and obtain a confirmation of the used and unused balance.

Evaluation of Known Contingent Liabilities

SANYO

If the auditor concludes that there are contingent liabilities, he or she must evaluate the significance of the potential liability and the nature of the disclosure needed in the financial statements. The potential liability is sufficiently well known in some instances to be included in the statements as an actual liability. In other instances, disclosure may be unnecessary if the contingency is highly remote or immaterial. The CPA firm may obtain a separate evaluation of the potential liability from its own legal counsel rather than relying on management or management's attorneys. The client's attorney is an advocate for the client and often loses perspective in evaluating the likelihood of losing the case and the amount of the potential judgment.

Audit Procedures for Finding Commitments

The search for unknown commitments is usually performed as a part of the audit of each audit area. For example, in verifying sales transactions, the auditor should be alert for sales commitments. Similarly, commitments for the purchase of raw materials or equipment can be identified as a part of the audit of each of these accounts. The auditor should also be aware of the possibility of commitments as he or she is reading contracts and correspondence files.

Inquiry of Client's Attorneys

OBJECTIVE 23-2
Obtain and evaluate letters from the client's attorneys.

give Auditor's report date to return confirm

A major procedure that auditors rely on for evaluating known litigation or other claims against the client and identifying additional ones is the **inquiry of the client's attorneys**. The auditor relies on the attorney's expertise and knowledge of the client's legal affairs to provide a professional opinion about the expected outcome of existing lawsuits and the likely amount of the liability, including court costs. The attorney is also likely to know of pending litigation and claims that management may have overlooked.

As a matter of general practice, many CPA firms analyze legal expense for the entire year and have the client send a standard inquiry letter to every attorney the client has been involved with in the current or preceding year, plus any attorney the firm occasionally engages. In some cases, this involves a large number of attorneys, including some who deal in aspects of law that are far removed from potential lawsuits.

The standard inquiry to the client's attorney, which should be prepared on the client's letterhead and signed by one of the company's officials, should include the following:

- *A list including (1) pending threatened litigation and (2) asserted or unasserted claims or assessments with which the attorney has had significant involvement.* This list is typically prepared by management, but management may request that the attorney prepare the list.
- *A request that the attorney furnish information or comment about the progress of each item listed.* The desired information includes the legal action the client intends to take, the likelihood of an unfavorable outcome, and an estimate of the amount or range of the potential loss.
- *A request for the identification of any unlisted pending or threatened legal actions or a statement that the client's list is complete.*
- *A statement informing the attorney of his or her responsibility to inform management of legal matters requiring disclosure in the financial statements and to respond directly to the auditor.* If the attorney chooses to limit his or her response, reasons for doing so are to be included in the letter.

An example of a typical standard letter sent to the attorney for return directly to the CPA's office is shown in Figure 23-2. Notice in the first paragraph that the attorney is requested to communicate about contingencies up to approximately *the date of the auditor's report.*

FIGURE 23-2   Typical Inquiry of Attorney

BANERGEE BUILDING CO.
409 Lane Drive
Buffalo, New York 10126

January 26, 2000

Bailwick & Bettle, Attorneys
11216–5th Street NE
New York, New York 10023

Gentlemen:

Our auditors, Clarrett & Co., CPAs (1133 Broadway, New York, New York 10019), are conducting an audit of our financial statements for the fiscal year ended December 31, 1999. In connection with their audit, we have prepared and furnished to them a description and evaluation of certain contingencies, including those attached, involving matters with respect to which you have been engaged and to which you have devoted substantive attention on behalf of the company in the form of legal consultation or representation. For the purpose of your response to this letter, we believe that as to each contingency an amount in excess of $10,000 would be material, and in total, $50,000. However, determination of materiality with respect to the overall financial statements cannot be made until our auditors complete their audit. Your response should include matters that existed at December 31, 1999, and during the period from that date to the date of the completion of their audit, which is anticipated to be on or about February 13, 2000.
  Please provide to our auditors the following information:

(1) Such explanation, if any, that you consider necessary to supplement the listed
     judgments rendered or settlements made involving the company from the
     beginning of this fiscal year through the date of your reply.
(2) Such explanation, if any, that you consider necessary to supplement the listing of
     pending or threatened litigation, including an explanation of those matters as to
     which your views may differ from those stated and an identification of the
     omission of any pending or threatened litigation, claim, and assessment or a
     statement that the list of such matters is complete.
(3) Such explanation, if any, that you consider necessary to supplement the
     attached information concerning unasserted claims and assessments, including
     an explanation of those matters as to which your views may differ from those
     stated.

We understand that whenever, in the course of performing legal services for us with respect to a matter recognized to involve an unasserted possible claim or assessment that may call for financial statement disclosure, you have formed a professional conclusion that we should disclose or consider disclosure concerning such possible claim or assessment, as a matter of professional responsibility to us, you will so advise us and will consult with us concerning the question of such disclosure and the applicable requirements of Statement of Financial Accounting Standards No. 5. Please specifically confirm to our auditors that our understanding is correct.
  Please specifically identify the nature of and reasons for any limitations in your response.

Yours very truly,
Banergee Building Co.

Clark Jones

Clark Jones, Pres.

Attorneys in recent years have become reluctant to provide certain information to auditors because of their own exposure to legal liability for providing incorrect or confidential information. The nature of the refusal of attorneys to provide auditors with complete information about contingent liabilities falls into two categories: the refusal to respond due to a lack of knowledge about matters involving contingent liabilities and the refusal to disclose information that the attorney considers confidential. As an example of the latter, the attorney might be aware of a violation of a patent agreement that could result in a significant loss to the client if it were known (**unasserted claim**). The inclusion of the information in a footnote could actually cause the lawsuit and therefore be damaging to the client. Review the attorney concerns described in the box "The Legal View."

If an attorney refuses to provide the auditor with information about material existing lawsuits (asserted claims) or unasserted claims, *the auditor must modify his or her audit report to reflect the lack of available evidence.* This requirement in SAS 12 (AU 337) has the effect of requiring management to give its attorneys permission to provide contingent liability information to auditors and to encourage attorneys to cooperate with auditors in obtaining information about contingencies.

THE LEGAL VIEW

The lawyer is the expert on litigation, yet differences in lawyers' and CPAs' responsibilities with respect to common clients have resulted in contentious difficulties. Although CPAs are responsible for determining there is "adequate disclosure" under Statement no. 5 [SFAS 5] . . . lawyers are responsible for "winning the case." Because information provided by lawyers may affect a case adversely, these responsibilities may conflict.

Many lawyers believe that, despite a client's request they provide the auditor with information, they should be less than candid in letters to CPAs because of concern their replies may

- Impair the client-lawyer confidentiality privilege.
- Disclose a client confidence or secret.
- Prejudice the client's defense of a claim.
- Constitute an admission by the client.

The authoritative guidance for lawyers . . . warns lawyers they must be careful in communications with auditors. Indeed, the first sentence of the ABA statement says, "The public interest in protecting the confidentiality of lawyer–client communications is fundamental."

The ABA statement also says lawyers normally should refrain from expressing judgments on outcome—either likelihood or amount of loss. The net effect is CPAs generally can obtain relatively complete responses on the existence of litigation and the dates when the underlying cause occurred . . . but less complete responses on the likelihood of an unfavorable outcome and the amount of potential loss.

In addition to an implicit hesitancy to provide evidential matter on likelihood and amount of loss, the ABA statement gives lawyers definitions of *probable* and *remote* that are different from those in Statement no. 5:

- **Remote**. The ABA says an unfavorable outcome is remote if the prospects for the client not succeeding in its defense are judged to be extremely doubtful and the prospects of success by the claimant are judged to be slight.
- **Probable**. The ABA says an unfavorable outcome for the client is probable if the claimant's prospects of not succeeding are judged to be extremely doubtful and the client's prospects for success in its defense are judged to be slight.

Source: Excerpted from an article by Bruce K. Behn and Kurt Pany, "Limitations of Lawyers' Letters," *Journal of Accountancy* (February 1995), pp. 62–63.

The second part of completing the audit is the review for subsequent events. The auditor must review transactions and events occurring after the balance sheet date to determine whether anything occurred that might affect the fair presentation or disclosure of the current-period statements. The auditing procedures required by SAS 1 (AU 560) to verify these transactions and events are commonly called the **review for subsequent events** or **post–balance-sheet review**.

The auditor's responsibility for reviewing for subsequent events is normally limited to the period beginning with the balance sheet date and ending with the date of the auditor's report. Because the date of the auditor's report corresponds to the completion of the important auditing procedures in the client's office, the subsequent events review should be completed near the end of the engagement.[1] Figure 23-3 shows the period covered by a subsequent events review and the timing of that review.

OBJECTIVE 23-3
Conduct a post–balance-sheet review for subsequent events.

Real-Time
News Services

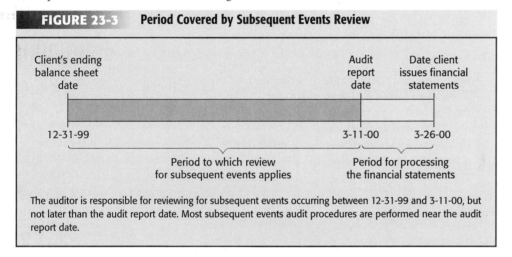

FIGURE 23-3	**Period Covered by Subsequent Events Review**

Client's ending balance sheet date — 12-31-99

Audit report date — 3-11-00

Date client issues financial statements — 3-26-00

Period to which review for subsequent events applies

Period for processing the financial statements

The auditor is responsible for reviewing for subsequent events occurring between 12-31-99 and 3-11-00, but not later than the audit report date. Most subsequent events audit procedures are performed near the audit report date.

Two types of **subsequent events** require consideration by management and evaluation by the auditor: those that have a direct effect on the financial statements and require adjustment and those that have no direct effect on the financial statements but for which disclosure is advisable.

Those That Have a Direct Effect on the Financial Statements and Require Adjustment These events or transactions provide additional information to management in determining the fair presentation of account balances as of the balance sheet date and to auditors in verifying the balances. For example, if the auditor is having difficulty determining the correct valuation of inventory because of obsolescence, the sale of raw material inventory as scrap in the subsequent period would indicate the correct value of the inventory as of the balance sheet date.

Such subsequent period events as the following require an adjustment of account balances in the current year's financial statements if the amounts are material:

- Declaration of bankruptcy by a customer with an outstanding accounts receivable balance because of deteriorating financial condition
- Settlement of a litigation at an amount different from the amount recorded on the books
- Disposal of equipment not being used in operations at a price below the current book value
- Sale of investments at a price below recorded cost

Types of Subsequent Events

Phase IV– Completing the Audit

Review for contingent liabilities

Review for subsequent events

Accumulate final evidence

Evaluate results

Issue audit report

Communicate with audit committee and management

[1]When the auditor's name is associated with a registration statement under the Securities Act of 1933, his or her responsibility for reviewing subsequent events extends beyond the date of the auditor's report to the date the registration becomes effective.

When subsequent events are used to evaluate the amounts included in the statements, care must be taken to distinguish between conditions that existed at the balance sheet date and those that came into being after the end of the year. The subsequent information should not be incorporated directly into the statements if the conditions causing the change in valuation did not take place until after year-end. For example, assume one type of a client's inventory suddenly becomes obsolete because of a technology change after the balance sheet date. The sale of the inventory at a loss in the subsequent period would not be relevant in the valuation of inventory for obsolescence in this case.

Those That Have No Direct Effect on the Financial Statements But for Which Disclosure Is Advisable

Subsequent events of this type provide evidence of conditions that did not exist at the date of the balance sheet being reported on but are so significant that they require disclosure even though they do not require adjustment. Ordinarily, these events can be adequately disclosed by the use of footnotes, but occasionally, one may be so significant as to require *supplementing the historical statements* with statements that include the effect of the event as if it had occurred on the balance sheet date.

Following are examples of events or transactions occurring in the subsequent period that may require disclosure rather than an adjustment in the financial statements:

- Decline in the market value of securities held for temporary investment or resale
- Issuance of bonds or equity securities
- Decline in the market value of inventory as a consequence of government action barring further sale of a product
- Uninsured loss of inventories as a result of fire
- A merger or an acquisition

Audit Tests

Audit procedures for the subsequent events review can be conveniently divided into two categories: procedures normally integrated as a part of the verification of year-end account balances and those performed specifically for the purpose of discovering events or transactions that must be recognized as subsequent events.

The first category includes cutoff and valuation tests done as a part of the tests of details of balances. For example, subsequent period sales and acquisition transactions are examined to determine whether the cutoff is accurate. Similarly, many valuation tests involving subsequent events are also performed as a part of the verification of account balances. As an example, it is common to test the collectibility of accounts receivable by reviewing subsequent period cash receipts. It is also a normal audit procedure to compare the subsequent period purchase price of inventory with the recorded cost as a test of lower of cost or market valuation. The procedures for cutoff and valuation have been discussed sufficiently in preceding chapters and are not repeated here.

The second category of tests is performed specifically to obtain information to incorporate into the current year's account balances or footnotes. These tests include the following.

Inquire of Management

Inquiries vary from client to client but normally are about potential contingent liabilities or commitments, significant changes in the assets or capital structure of the company, the current status of items that were not completely resolved at the balance sheet date, and unusual adjustments made subsequent to the balance sheet date.

Inquiries of management about subsequent events must be held with the proper client personnel to obtain meaningful answers. For example, discussing tax or union matters with the accounts receivable supervisor would not be appropriate. Most inquiries should be held with the controller, the vice presidents, and the president, depending on the information desired.

Correspond with Attorneys

Correspondence with attorneys, which was previously discussed, takes place as a part of the search for contingent liabilities. In obtaining letters from attorneys, the auditor must remember his or her responsibility for testing for subsequent events up to the date of the audit report. A common approach is to request the attorney to date and mail the letter as of the expected completion date for field work.

Review Internal Statements Prepared Subsequent to the Balance Sheet Date The emphasis in the review should be on (1) changes in the business relative to results for the same period in the year under audit and (2) changes after year-end. The auditor should pay careful attention to major changes in the business or environment in which the client is operating. The statements should be discussed with management to determine whether they are prepared on the same basis as the current period statements, and there should be inquiries about significant changes in the operating results.

Review Records Prepared Subsequent to the Balance Sheet Date Journals and ledgers should be reviewed to determine the existence and nature of significant transactions related to the current year. If the journals are not kept up to date, documents relating to the journals should be reviewed.

Examine Minutes Issued Subsequent to the Balance Sheet Date The minutes of stockholders' and directors' meetings subsequent to the balance sheet date must be examined for important subsequent events affecting the current period financial statements.

Obtain a Letter of Representation The letter of representation written by the client's management to the auditor formalizes statements that management has made about different matters throughout the audit, including discussions about subsequent events. This letter is mandatory and includes other relevant matters too. This letter is discussed in detail during the discussion of evidence accumulation, which is the next part discussed in completing the audit.

Occasionally, the auditor determines that an important subsequent event occurred after the field work was completed but *before the audit report was issued.* The source of such information is typically management or the media. An example using the dates in Figure 23-3 on page 733 is the acquisition of another company by an audit client on March 23, when the last day of field work was March 11. In such a situation, SAS 1 (AU 530) requires the auditor to extend audit tests for the newly discovered subsequent event to make sure that it is correctly disclosed. The auditor has two equally acceptable options for expanding subsequent events tests: expand all subsequent events tests to the new date or restrict the subsequent events review to matters related to the new subsequent event. For the first option, the audit report date is changed to the new date. For the second option, the auditor issues a **dual-dated audit report,** which means that the audit report includes two dates. The first date is the date for the completion of field work except for a specific exception. The second date, which is always later, deals with the exception. In the example of the acquisition, assume that the auditor returned to the client's premises and completed audit tests on March 31 pertaining only to the acquisition. The audit report is dual-dated as follows: March 11, 2000, except for note 17, as to which the date is March 31, 2000.

Dual Dating

[handwritten marginalia: Often CPA writes + asks mgmt. to put on letterhead + sign.]

FINAL EVIDENCE ACCUMULATION

In addition to the review for subsequent events, the auditor has several final accumulation responsibilities that apply to all cycles. Four types of final evidence accumulation that are discussed in this section are (1) perform final analytical procedures, (2) evaluate the going concern assumption, (3) obtain a management representation letter, and (4) read other information in the annual report. Each of these is done late in the engagement.

Analytical procedures done during the completion of the audit are useful as a final review for material misstatements or financial problems not noted during other testing and to help the auditor take a final objective look at the financial statements. It is

OBJECTIVE 23-4
Design and perform the final steps in the evidence-accumulation segment of the audit.

Perform Final Analytical Procedures

common for a partner to do the analytical procedures during the final review of working papers and financial statements. Typically, a partner has a good understanding of the client and its business because of ongoing relationships. Knowledge of the client's business combined with effective analytical procedures help identify possible oversights in an audit.

When performing analytical procedures during the final review stage, the partner would generally read the financial statements, including footnotes, and consider (1) the adequacy of evidence gathered about unusual or unexpected account balances or relationships identified during planning or while conducting the audit and (2) unusual or unexpected account balances or relationships that were not previously identified. Results from final analytical procedures may indicate that additional audit evidence is necessary.

Evaluate Going Concern Assumption

SAS 59 (AU 341) requires the auditor to evaluate whether there is a substantial doubt about a client's ability to continue as a going concern for at least 1 year beyond the balance sheet date. That assessment is initially made as a part of planning but is revised when significant new information is obtained. For example, if the auditor discovered during the audit that the company had defaulted on a loan, lost its primary customer, or decided to dispose of substantial assets to pay off loans, the initial assessment of going concern may need revision. A final assessment is desirable after all evidence has been accumulated and proposed audit adjustments have been incorporated into the financial statements.

Analytical procedures are one of the most important types of evidence to assess going concern. Discussions with management and a review of future plans are important considerations in evaluating analytical procedures. Knowledge of the client's business gained throughout the audit is important information used to assess the likelihood of financial failure within the next year.

When the auditor has reservations about the going concern assumption, it is necessary to evaluate management's plans to avoid bankruptcy and the feasibility of achieving these plans. Making the final decision whether to issue a report with a going concern explanatory paragraph is typically time consuming and difficult. Going concern explanatory paragraphs were discussed in Chapter 3.

Obtain Management Representation Letter

SAS 85 (AU 333) requires the auditor to obtain a **letter of representation** documenting management's most important oral representations during the audit. The client representation letter is prepared on the client's letterhead, addressed to the CPA firm, and signed by high-level corporate officials, usually the president and chief financial officer.

There are two purposes of the client letter of representation:

1. *To impress upon management its responsibility for the assertions in the financial statements.* For example, if the letter of representation includes a reference to pledged assets and contingent liabilities, honest management may be reminded of its unintentional failure to disclose the information adequately. To fulfill this objective, the letter of representation should be sufficiently detailed to act as a reminder to management.
2. *To document the responses from management to inquiries about various aspects of the audit.* This provides written documentation of client representations in the event of disagreement or a lawsuit between the auditor and client. Because it is more formal than oral communication, a letter of representation also helps reduce misunderstandings between management and the auditor.

The letter should be dated no earlier than the date of the auditor's report to make sure that there are representations related to the subsequent events review. The letter implies that it has originated with the client, but it is common practice for the auditor to prepare the letter and request the client to type it on the company's letterhead and sign it. Refusal by a client to prepare and sign the letter would require a qualified opinion or disclaimer of opinion.

SAS 85 suggests five categories of specific matters that should be included. The five categories are as follows, with examples in each category.

1. *Financial statements*

   • Management's acknowledgment of its responsibility for the fair presentation in the financial statements of financial position, results of operations, and cash flows in conformity with generally accepted accounting principles
   • Management's belief that the financial statements are fairly presented in conformity with generally accepted accounting principles

2. *Completeness of information*

   • Availability of all financial records and related data
   • Absence of unrecorded transactions

3. *Recognition, measurement, and disclosure*

   • Information concerning fraud involving (1) management, (2) employees who have significant roles in internal control, or (3) others where the fraud could have a material effect on the financial statements
   • Information concerning related party transactions and amounts receivable from or payable to related parties

4. *Significant risks and uncertainties*

   • Unasserted claims or assessments that the entity's lawyer has advised are probable of assertion and must be disclosed in accordance with Financial Accounting Standards Board (FASB) Statement No. 5, *Accounting for Contingencies*
   • Satisfactory title to assets, liens or encumbrances on assets, and assets pledged as collateral
   • Compliance with aspects of contractual agreements that may affect the financial statements

5. *Subsequent events*

   • Subsequent events that have a direct effect on the financial statements and require adjustment
   • Subsequent events that have no direct effect on the financial statements but for which disclosure is advisable

A client representation letter is a written statement from a nonindependent source and therefore *cannot be regarded as reliable evidence.* The letter does provide documentation that management has been asked certain questions to make sure that management understands its responsibilities and to protect the auditor if there are claims against the auditor by management.

In some audits, the auditor may find other evidence that contradicts statements in the letter of representation. In such cases, the auditor should investigate the circumstances and consider whether representations in the letter are reliable.

Read Other Information in the Annual Report

SAS 8 (AU 550) requires the auditor to read **other information included in annual reports** pertaining directly to the financial statements. For example, assume that the president's letter in the annual report refers to an increase in earnings per share from $2.60 to $2.93. The auditor is required to compare that information with the financial statements to make sure it corresponds.

SAS 8 pertains only to information that is not a part of the financial statements but is published with them. Examples are the president's letter and explanations of company activities included in annual reports of nearly all publicly held companies. It usually takes the auditor only a few minutes to make sure that the nonfinancial statement information is consistent with the statements. If the auditor concludes that there is a material inconsistency, the client should be requested to change the information. If the client refuses, which would be unusual, the auditor should include an explanatory paragraph in the audit report or withdraw from the engagement.

EVALUATE RESULTS

OBJECTIVE 23-5
Integrate the audit evidence gathered, and evaluate the overall audit results.

After performing all audit procedures in each audit area, including the review for contingencies and subsequent events and accumulating final evidence, the auditor must integrate the results into *one overall conclusion*. Ultimately, the auditor must decide whether sufficient audit evidence has been accumulated to warrant the conclusion that the financial statements are stated in accordance with generally accepted accounting principles, applied on a basis consistent with those of the preceding year. The five main aspects of evaluating the results are discussed next.

Sufficiency of Evidence

Phase IV–
Completing the Audit

- Review for contingent liabilities
- Review for subsequent events
- Accumulate final evidence
- Evaluate results
- Issue audit report
- Communicate with audit committee and management

The final evaluation of the adequacy of the evidence is a review by the auditor of the entire audit to determine whether all important aspects have been adequately tested, considering all circumstances of the engagement. A major step in this process is to review the entire audit program to make sure that all parts have been accurately completed and documented and that all audit objectives have been met. This review includes deciding whether the audit program is adequate, considering problem areas identified as the audit progressed. For example, if misstatements were discovered during tests of sales, the initial plans for tests of details of accounts receivable may have been insufficient. The final review should evaluate whether the revised audit program is adequate.

As an aid in drawing final conclusions about the adequacy of the audit evidence, auditors often use a **completing the engagement checklist**. Such a checklist is a reminder of aspects of the audit that must not be overlooked. An illustration of part of a completing the engagement checklist is given in Figure 23-4 below.

If the auditor concludes that he or she has *not* obtained sufficient evidence to draw a conclusion about the fairness of the client's representations, there are two choices: additional evidence must be obtained or either a qualified opinion or a disclaimer of opinion must be issued.

FIGURE 23-4   **Completing the Engagement Checklist**

	YES	NO
1. Examination of prior year's working papers		
a. Were last year's working papers and review notes examined for areas of emphasis in the current-year audit?		
b. Was the permanent file reviewed for items that affect the current year?	___	___
2. Internal control		
a. Has internal control been adequately understood?	___	___
b. Is the scope of the audit adequate in light of the assessed control risk?	___	___
c. Have all major weaknesses been included as reportable conditions in a letter to the audit committee or to senior management?	___	___
3. General documents		
a. Were all current-year minutes and resolutions reviewed, abstracted, and followed up?		
b. Has the permanent file been updated?	___	___
c. Have all major contracts and agreements been reviewed and abstracted or copied to ascertain that the client complies with all existing legal requirements?	___	___

An important part of evaluating whether the financial statements are fairly stated is summarizing the misstatements uncovered in the audit. When the auditor uncovers misstatements that are in themselves material, entries should be proposed to the client to correct the statements. It may be difficult to determine the appropriate amount of adjustment because the true value of a misstatement may be unknown; nevertheless, it is the auditor's responsibility to decide on the required adjustment. In addition to the material misstatements, there are often a large number of immaterial misstatements discovered that are not adjusted at the time they are found. It is necessary to combine individually immaterial misstatements to evaluate whether the combined amount is material. The auditor can keep track of these misstatements and combine them in several different ways, but many auditors use a convenient method called an **unadjusted misstatement worksheet** or **summary of possible misstatements**. It is relatively easy to evaluate the overall significance of several immaterial misstatements with this type of working paper. An example of an unadjusted misstatement worksheet is given in Figure 23-5.

The schedule in Figure 23-5 includes both known misstatements that the client has decided not to adjust and projected misstatements, including sampling error. Observe that in the bottom left portion of the working paper there is a comparison of possible adjustments to materiality.

FIGURE 23-5   Unadjusted Misstatement Worksheet

Wixom Manufacturing
Summary of Possible
Misstatements
12/31/99

Schedule   A-3   Date
Prepared by   PR   1/28/00
Approved by   GS   1/31/00

POSSIBLE MISSTATEMENT–OVERSTATEMENT
<UNDERSTATEMENT>

Working Paper Source		Type of Misstatement	Total Amount	Current Assets	Noncurrent Assets	Current Liabilities	Income Before Tax
B-32	Unreimbursed petty cash vouchers	<A>	480	480			480
C-4	Possible underprovision in allowance for uncollectible accounts	<P>	4000	4000			4000
C-8	Accounts receivable/Sales cutoff misstatements	<P>	600	<600>			<600>
D-2	Difference between physical inventory and book figures	<A>	5200	<5200>			<5200>
H-7/2	Unrecorded liabilities	<P>	4850	<2000>	<1850>	<4850>	1000
V-10	Repairs expense items which should be capitalized	<A>	900		<900>		<900>
Totals				<3320>	<2750>	<4850>	<122

<A> Actual population misstatements.
<P> Estimated population misstatements based on the sample, including sampling error.

Conclusions

The net effects of the above items are as follows:

	Possible Overstatements <Understatements>	Materiality
Working capital	$1530	$10000
Total assets	<6070>	20000
Net income before taxes	<1220>	4000

None of these aggregate effects or the individual items has a material effect on the financial statements in total or with respect to the components they pertain to. On this basis, adjustment of any or all of the items is passed.

Paul Roberts
1/28/00

If the auditor believes that he or she *has* sufficient evidence but it does not warrant a conclusion of fairly presented financial statements, the auditor again has two choices: the statements must be revised to the auditor's satisfaction or either a qualified or an adverse opinion must be issued. Notice that the options here are different from those in the case of insufficient evidence obtained.

Financial Statement Disclosures

A major consideration in completing the audit is to determine whether the disclosures in the financial statements are adequate. Throughout the audit, the emphasis is most often on verifying the accuracy of the balances in the general ledger by testing the most important accounts on the auditor's trial balance. Another important task is to make sure that the account balances on the trial balance are correctly aggregated and disclosed on the financial statements. Naturally, adequate disclosure includes consideration of all of the statements, including related footnotes.

The auditor actually prepares the financial statements from the trial balance in many small audits and submits them to the client for approval. Performing this function may seem to imply that the client has been relieved of responsibility for the fair representation in the statements, but that is not the case. The auditor acts in the role of advisor when preparing financial statements, but *management retains the final responsibility for approving the issuance of the statements.*

Review for adequate disclosure in the financial statements at the completion of the audit is not the only time the auditor is interested in proper disclosure. Unless the auditor is constantly alert for disclosure problems, it is impossible to perform the final disclosure review adequately. For example, as part of the audit of accounts receivable, the auditor must be aware of the need to separate notes receivable and amounts due from affiliates and trade accounts due from customers. Similarly, there must be a segregation of current from noncurrent receivables and a disclosure of the factoring or discounting of notes receivable if such is the case. An important part of verifying all account balances is determining whether generally accepted accounting principles were properly applied on a basis consistent with that of the preceding year. The auditor must carefully document this information in the working papers to facilitate the final review.

As part of the final review for financial statement disclosure, many CPA firms require the completion of a **financial statement disclosure checklist** for every engagement. These questionnaires are designed to remind the auditor of common disclosure problems encountered on audits and also to facilitate the final review of the entire audit by an independent partner. An illustration of a partial financial statement disclosure checklist is given in Figure 23-6. Naturally, it is not sufficient to rely on a checklist to replace the auditor's own knowledge of generally accepted accounting principles. In any given audit, some aspects of the engagement require much greater expertise in accounting than can be obtained from such a checklist.

Working Paper Review

There are three main reasons why it is essential that working papers be thoroughly reviewed by another member of the audit firm at the completion of the audit:

1. *To evaluate the performance of inexperienced personnel.* A considerable portion of most audits is performed by audit personnel with less than 4 or 5 years of experience. These people may have sufficient technical training to conduct an adequate audit, but their lack of experience affects their ability to make sound professional judgments in complex situations.
2. *To make sure that the audit meets the CPA firm's standard of performance.* Within any organization the performance quality of individuals varies considerably, but careful review by top-level personnel in the firm assists in maintaining a uniform quality of auditing.
3. *To counteract the bias that often enters into the auditor's judgment.* Auditors must attempt to remain objective throughout the audit, but it is easy to lose proper perspective on a long audit when there are complex problems to solve.

Except for a final independent review, which is discussed shortly, the **review of working papers** should be conducted by someone who is knowledgeable about the client and

FIGURE 23-6   Financial Statement Disclosure Checklist: Property, Plant, and Equipment

1. Are the following disclosures included in the financial statements or notes (APB 12, para. 5):
   a. Balances of major classes of depreciable assets (land, building, equipment, and so forth) at the balance sheet date?
   b. Allowances for depreciation, by class or in total, at the balance sheet date?
   c. General description of depreciation methods for major classes of PP&E (APB 22, para. 13)?
   d. Total amount of depreciation charged to expense for each income statement presented?
   e. Basis of evaluation (SAS 32, AU 431.02)?
2. Are carrying amounts of property mortgaged and encumbered by indebtedness disclosed (FASB 5, para. 18)?
3. Are details of sale and leaseback transactions during the period disclosed (FASB 13, para. 32–34)?
4. Is the carrying amount of property not a part of operating plant—for example, idle or held for investment or sale—segregated?
5. Has consideration been given to disclosure of fully depreciated capital assets still in use and capital assets not presently in use?

Note: Information in parentheses refers to authoritative professional literature.

the unique circumstances in the audit. Therefore, the initial review of the working papers prepared by any given auditor is normally done by the auditor's immediate supervisor. For example, the least experienced auditor's work is ordinarily reviewed by the audit senior. The senior's immediate superior, who is normally a supervisor or manager, reviews the senior's work and also reviews less thoroughly the papers of the inexperienced auditor. Finally, the partner assigned to the audit must ultimately review all working papers, but the partner reviews those prepared by the supervisor or manager more thoroughly than the others. Except for the final independent review, most of the working paper review is done as each segment of the audit is completed.

Independent Review

At the completion of larger audits, it is common to have the financial statements and the entire set of working papers reviewed by a completely independent reviewer who has not participated in the engagement. An **independent review** is required for SEC engagements. This reviewer often takes an adversary position to make sure that the conduct of the audit was adequate. The audit team must be able to justify the evidence they have accumulated and the conclusions they reached on the basis of the unique circumstances of the engagement.

Summary of Evidence Evaluation

Figure 23-7 (p. 742) summarizes the evaluation of the sufficiency of the evidence and deciding whether the evidence supports the opinion. It shows that the auditor evaluates the sufficiency of actual evidence by first evaluating achieved audit risk, by account and by cycle, and then making the same evaluation for the overall financial statements. The auditor also evaluates whether the evidence supports the audit opinion by first estimating misstatements in each account and then for the overall financial statements. In practice, the evaluation of achieved audit risk and estimated misstatement are made at the same time. On the basis of these evaluations, the audit report is issued for the financial statements.

ISSUE THE AUDIT REPORT

The auditor should not decide the appropriate audit report to issue until all evidence has been accumulated and evaluated, including all parts of completing the audit discussed so far. Because the audit report is the only thing that most users see in the audit process and

Review for con-
tingent liabilities

Review for
subsequent events

Accumulate
final evidence

Evaluate results

Issue audit report

Communicate with
audit committee
and management

FIGURE 23-7   **Evaluating Results and Reaching Conclusions on the Basis of Evidence**

the consequences of issuing an inappropriate report can be severe, it is critical that the report be correct.

In most audits, the auditor issues an unqualified report with standard wording. Almost all firms have this report included in a word processing file and need to change only the name of the client, title of the financial statements, and date.

When a CPA firm decides that a standard unqualified report is inappropriate, there will almost certainly be extensive discussions among technical partners in the CPA firm and often with client personnel. Most CPA firms have comprehensive audit reporting manuals to assist them in selecting the appropriate wording of the report they decide to issue.

COMMUNICATE WITH THE AUDIT COMMITTEE AND MANAGEMENT

OBJECTIVE 23-6
Communicate effectively with the audit committee and management.

After the audit is completed, there are several potential communications from the auditor to client personnel. The first three of these communications discussed in this section are required by auditing standards to make certain that the audit committee and senior management are informed of audit findings and auditor recommendations. The fourth item discussed in this section, management letters, is often communicated with operating management.

Communicate Fraud and Illegal Acts

SAS 82 (AU 316) and SAS 54 (AU 317) require the auditor to communicate all fraud and illegal acts to the audit committee or similarly designated group, regardless of materiality. The purpose is to assist the audit committee in performing its supervisory role for reliable financial statements. This requirement indicates the increased concern of the profession over the auditor's responsibility for the detection and prevention of fraud.

Communicate Reportable Conditions

internal control

As discussed in Chapter 10, the auditor must also communicate significant deficiencies in the design or operation of internal control. In larger companies, this communication is made to the audit committee and in smaller companies to the owners or senior management. The nature and form of that communication were discussed in Chapter 10.

Other Communication with Audit Committee

SAS 61 (AU 380) requires the auditor to communicate certain additional information obtained during the audit for all SEC engagements and other audits where there is an audit committee or similarly designated body. This communication is not required for most small nonpublic companies. As with all communications with the audit committee, the purpose is to keep the committee informed of auditing issues and findings that will assist them in performing their supervisory role for financial statements.

The following are major items that must be communicated to the audit committee or similarly designated body under SAS 61:

- Auditor's responsibilities under generally accepted auditing standards, including responsibility for evaluating internal control and the concept of reasonable rather than absolute assurance.
- Significant accounting policies selected and applied to the financial statements, including management's judgments and estimates of accounting-related issues.
- Significant financial statement adjustments found during the audit and the implications of both those that management has chosen to record and those proposed but not recorded.
- Disagreements with management about the scope of the audit, applicability of accounting principles, or wording of the audit report.
- Difficulties encountered in performing the audit, such as lack of availability of client personnel and failure to provide necessary information.

Communication with the audit committee normally takes place more than once during each audit and can be oral, written, or both. For example, issues dealing with the auditor's responsibilities and significant accounting policies are usually discussed early in the audit, preferably during the planning phase. Disagreements with management and difficulties encountered in performing the audit are communicated after the audit is completed, or earlier if the problems hinder the auditor's ability to complete the audit. The most important matters are communicated in writing to minimize misunderstanding and to provide documentation in the event of subsequent disagreement.

Phase IV–
Completing the Audit

Review for contingent liabilities

Review for subsequent events

Accumulate final evidence

Evaluate results

Issue audit report

Communicate with audit committee and management

Management Letters

A **management letter** is intended to inform client personnel of the CPA's recommendations for improving any aspect of the client's business. The recommendations focus on suggestions for more efficient operations. The combination of the auditor's experience in various businesses and a thorough understanding gained in conducting the audit place the auditor in a unique position to provide management with assistance.

Many CPA firms write a management letter for every audit to demonstrate to management that their firm adds value to the business beyond the audit service provided. The intent is to encourage a better relationship between the CPA firm and management and to suggest additional tax and management services that the CPA firm can provide. Some CPA firms generate considerable additional revenue from the additional services.

A management letter is different from a reportable conditions letter discussed in Chapter 10. The latter is required by SAS 60 (AU 325) when there are reportable conditions. It must follow a prescribed format and be sent in accordance with SAS requirements. A management letter is optional and is intended to help the client operate its business more effectively.

There is no standard format or approach for writing management letters. Each letter should be developed to meet the style of the auditor and the needs of the client, consistent with the CPA firm's concept of management letters. It should be noted that many auditors combine the management letter with the reportable conditions letter. On smaller audits, it is common for the auditor to communicate operational suggestions orally rather than by a management letter.

SUBSEQUENT DISCOVERY OF FACTS

OBJECTIVE 23-7
Identify the auditor's responsibilities when facts affecting the audit report are discovered after its issuance.

After the auditor issues the audit report and completes all communications with management and the audit committee, the audit is finished. The next major contact the auditor has with the client is when the planning process for next year's audit begins. Although it rarely happens, if the auditor becomes aware *after the audited financial statements have been issued* that some information included in the statements is materially misleading, the auditor has an obligation to make certain that users who are relying on the financial statements are informed about the misstatements. If the auditor had known about the misstatements before the audit report was issued, the auditor would have insisted that management correct the misstatements or, alternatively, a different audit report would have been issued. When this occurs, it is referred to as subsequent discovery of facts. Although subsequent discovery of facts is not a part of completing the audit, it is included in this chapter because it is easier to understand when compared and contrasted with subsequent events.

The most likely case in which the auditor is faced with this problem occurs when the financial statements are determined to include a material misstatement subsequent to the issuance of an unqualified report. Some possible causes of misstatements are the inclusion of material nonexistent sales, the failure to write off obsolete inventory, or the omission of an essential footnote. Regardless of whether the failure to discover the misstatement was the fault of the auditor or the client, the auditor's responsibility remains the same.

The most desirable approach to follow if the auditor discovers that the statements are misleading after they have been issued is to request that the client issue an immediate revision of the financial statements containing an explanation of the reasons for the revision. If a subsequent period's financial statements are completed before the revised statements would be issued, it is acceptable to disclose the misstatements in the subsequent period's statements. When pertinent, the client should inform the SEC and other regulatory agencies of the misleading financial statements. The auditor has the responsibility for making certain that the client has taken the appropriate steps in informing users of the misleading statements.

If the client refuses to cooperate in disclosing the misstated information, the auditor must inform the board of directors of this fact. The auditor must also notify regulatory agencies having jurisdiction over the client and, when practical, each person who relies on the financial statements, that the statements are no longer trustworthy. If the stock is publicly held, it is acceptable to request the SEC and the stock exchange to notify the stockholders.

It is important to understand that the subsequent discovery of facts requiring the recall or reissuance of financial statements *does not arise from business events occurring after the date of the auditor's report.* For example, if an account receivable is believed to be collectible after an adequate review of the facts at the date of the audit report but the customer subsequently files bankruptcy, a revision of the financial statements is not required. The statements must be recalled or reissued only when information that would indicate that the statements were not fairly presented *already existed at the audit report date.* If, in the previous example, the customer had filed for bankruptcy before the audit report date, there is a subsequent discovery of facts.

In an earlier section, it was shown that the auditor's responsibility for subsequent events review begins as of the balance sheet date and ends on the date of the completion of the field work. Any pertinent information discovered as a part of the review can be incorporated in the financial statements before they are issued. Note that the auditor has no responsibility to search for subsequent facts of the nature discussed in this section, but if the auditor discovers that issued financial statements are improperly stated, he or she must take action to correct them. The auditor's responsibility for reporting on improperly issued financial statements does not start until the date of the audit report. Typically, an existing material misstatement is found as a part of the subsequent year's audit, or it may be reported to the auditor by the client.

Figure 23-8, which includes the same dates as Figure 23-3 on page 733, shows the difference in the period covered by the review for subsequent events and that for the discovery of facts after the audit report date. If the auditor discovers subsequent facts after the audit report date but before the financial statements are issued, the auditor will require that the financial statements be revised before they are issued.

The auditor's responsibility for the period from 3-11-00 to 3-26-00 is the same as that for the period after 3-26-00. If a subsequent event is discovered in this period, one of the two options discussed under the Dual Dating heading on page 735 should be followed.

Commitments—agreements that the entity will hold to a fixed set of conditions, such as the purchase or sale of merchandise at a stated price, at a future date, regardless of what happens to profits or to the economy as a whole

Completing the engagement checklist—a reminder to the auditor of aspects of the audit that may have been overlooked

Contingent liability—a potential future obligation to an outside party for an unknown amount resulting from activities that have already taken place

Dual-dated audit report—the use of one audit report date for normal subsequent events and a later date for one or more subsequent events that come to the auditor's attention after the field work has been completed

Financial statement disclosure checklist—a questionnaire that reminds the auditor of disclosure problems commonly encountered in audits, and that facilitates final review of the entire audit by an independent partner

Independent review—a review of the financial statements and the entire set of working papers by a completely independent reviewer to whom the audit team must justify the evidence accumulated and the conclusions reached

Inquiry of the client's attorneys—a letter from the client's legal counsel informing the auditor of pending litigation or any other information involving legal counsel that is relevant to financial statement disclosure

Letter of representation—a written communication from the client to the auditor formalizing statements that the client has made about matters pertinent to the audit

Management letter—an optional letter written by the auditor to a client's management containing the auditor's recommendations for improving any aspect of the client's business

Other information included in annual reports—information that is not a part of published financial statements but is published with them; auditors must read this information for inconsistencies with the financial statements

Review for subsequent events—the auditing procedures performed by auditors to identify and evaluate subsequent events; also known as a *post–balance-sheet review*

Review of working papers—a review of the completed audit working papers by another member of the audit firm to ensure quality and counteract bias

Subsequent events—transactions and other pertinent events that occurred after the balance sheet date, which affect the fair presentation or disclosure of the statements being audited

Unadjusted misstatement worksheet—a summary of immaterial misstatements not adjusted at the time they were found, used to help the auditor assess whether the combined amount is material; also known as a *summary of possible misstatements*

Unasserted claim—a potential legal claim against a client where the condition for a claim exists but no claim has been filed

23-1 (Objective 23-1)   Distinguish between a contingent liability and an actual liability, and give three examples of each.

23-2 (Objective 23-1)   In the audit of the James Mobley Company, you are concerned about the possibility of contingent liabilities resulting in income tax disputes. Discuss the procedures you could use for an extensive investigation in this area.

23-3 (Objective 23-1) Explain why an auditor would be interested in a client's future commitments to purchase raw materials at a fixed price.

23-4 (Objective 23-2) Explain why the analysis of legal expense is an essential part of every audit engagement.

23-5 (Objectives 23-1, 23-2) During the audit of the Merrill Manufacturing Company, Ralph Pyson, CPA, has become aware of four lawsuits against the client through discussions with the client, reading corporate minutes, and reviewing correspondence files. How should Pyson determine the materiality of the lawsuits and the proper disclosure in the financial statements?

23-6 (Objective 23-2) Distinguish between an asserted and an unasserted claim. Explain why a client's attorney may not reveal an unasserted claim.

23-7 (Objective 23-2) Describe the action that an auditor should take if an attorney refuses to provide information that is within his or her jurisdiction and may directly affect the fair presentation of the financial statements.

23-8 (Objective 23-3) Distinguish between the two general types of subsequent events and explain how they differ. Give two examples of each type.

23-9 (Objectives 23-2, 23-3) In obtaining letters from attorneys, Bill Malano's aim is to receive the letters as early as possible after the balance sheet date. This provides him with a signed letter from every attorney in time to properly investigate any exceptions. It also eliminates the problem of a lot of unresolved loose ends near the end of the audit. Evaluate Malano's approach.

23-10 (Objective 23-3) What major considerations should the auditor take into account in determining how extensive the review of subsequent events should be?

23-11 (Objective 23-3) Identify five audit procedures normally done as a part of the review for subsequent events.

23-12 (Objectives 23-3, 23-7) Distinguish between subsequent events occurring between the balance sheet date and the date of the auditor's report, and subsequent discovery of facts existing at the date of the auditor's report. Give two examples of each and explain the appropriate action by the auditor in each instance.

23-13 (Objective 23-4) Miles Lawson, CPA, believes that the final summarization is the easiest part of the audit if careful planning is followed throughout the engagement. He makes sure that each segment of the audit is completed before he goes on to the next. When the last segment of the engagement is completed, he is finished with the audit. He believes this may cause each part of the audit to take a little longer, but he makes up for it by not having to do the final summarization. Evaluate Lawson's approach.

23-14 (Objectives 23-4, 23-5) Compare and contrast the accumulation of audit evidence and the evaluation of the adequacy of the disclosures in the financial statements. Give two examples in which adequate disclosure could depend heavily on the accumulation of evidence and two others in which audit evidence does not normally significantly affect the adequacy of the disclosure.

23-15 (Objectives 23-4, 23-6) Distinguish between a client letter of representation and a management letter and state the primary purpose of each. List some items that might be included in each letter.

23-16 (Objective 23-4) What is meant by reading other financial information in annual reports? Give an example of the type of information the auditor is examining.

23-17 (Objective 23-5) Distinguish between regular working paper review and independent review and state the purpose of each. Give two examples of important potential findings in each of these two types of review.

23-18 (Objective 23-1) The following questions deal with contingent liabilities. Choose the best response.

a. The audit step most likely to reveal the existence of contingent liabilities is
   (1) a review of vouchers paid during the month following the year-end.
   (2) accounts payable confirmations.
   (3) an inquiry directed to legal counsel.
   (4) mortgage-note confirmation.

b. When obtaining evidence regarding litigation against a client, the CPA would be *least* interested in determining
   (1) an estimate of when the matter will be resolved.
   (2) the period in which the underlying cause of the litigation occurred.
   (3) the probability of an unfavorable outcome.
   (4) an estimate of the potential loss.

c. When a contingency is resolved subsequent to the issuance of audited financial statements, which correctly contained disclosure of the contingency in the footnotes based on information available at the date of issuance, the auditor should
   (1) insist that the client issue revised financial statements.
   (2) inform the audit committee that the report cannot be relied on.
   (3) take no action regarding the event.
   (4) inform the appropriate authorities that the report cannot be relied on.

23-19 (Objective 23-4) The following questions concern letters of representation. Choose the best response.

a. A principal purpose of a letter of representation from management is to
   (1) serve as an introduction to company personnel and an authorization to examine the records.
   (2) discharge the auditor from legal liability for the audit.
   (3) confirm in writing management's approval of limitations on the scope of the audit.
   (4) remind management of its primary responsibility for financial statements.

b. A letter of representation issued by a client
   (1) is essential for the preparation of the audit program.
   (2) is a substitute for testing.
   (3) does not reduce the auditor's responsibility.
   (4) reduces the auditor's responsibility only to the extent that it is relied on.

c. The date of the management representation letter should coincide with the
   (1) date of the auditor's report.
   (2) balance sheet date.
   (3) date of the latest subsequent event referred to in the notes to the financial statements.
   (4) date of the engagement agreement.

d. Management's refusal to furnish a written representation on a matter that the auditor considers essential constitutes
   (1) prima facie evidence that the financial statements are not presented fairly.
   (2) a violation of the Foreign Corrupt Practices Act.
   (3) an uncertainty sufficient to preclude an unqualified opinion.
   (4) a scope limitation sufficient to preclude an unqualified opinion.

23-20 (Objective 23-3) The following questions deal with review of subsequent events. Choose the best response.

a. Subsequent events for reporting purposes are defined as events that occur subsequent to the
   (1) balance sheet date.
   (2) date of the auditor's report.
   (3) balance sheet date but before the date of the auditor's report.
   (4) date of the auditor's report and concern contingencies that are not reflected in the financial statements.

b. An example of an event occurring in the period of the auditor's field work subsequent to the end of the year being audited that normally would not require disclosure in the financial statements or auditor's report would be
   (1) decreased sales volume resulting from a general business recession.
   (2) serious damage to the company's plant from a widespread flood.
   (3) issuance of a widely advertised capital stock issue with restrictive covenants.
   (4) settlement of a large liability for considerably less than the amount recorded.

c. With respect to issuance of an audit report that is dual-dated for a subsequent event occurring after the completion of field work but before issuance of the auditor's report, the auditor's responsibility for events occurring subsequent to the completion of field work is
   (1) extended to include all events occurring until the date of the last subsequent event referred to.
   (2) limited to the specific event referred to.
   (3) limited to all events occurring through the date of issuance of the report.
   (4) extended to include all events occurring through the date of submission of the report to the client.

d. Karr has audited the financial statements of Lurch Corporation for the year ended December 31, 1999. Karr's field work was completed on February 27, 2000, Karr's auditor's report was dated February 28, 2000, and was received by the management of Lurch on March 5, 2000. On April 4, 2000, the management of Lurch asked that Karr approve inclusion of this report in their annual report to stockholders, which will include unaudited financial statements for the first quarter ended March 31, 2000. Karr approved the inclusion of this auditor's report in the annual report to stockholders. Under the circumstances, Karr is responsible for inquiring as to subsequent events occurring through
   (1) February 27, 2000.   (3) March 31, 2000.
   (2) February 28, 2000.   (4) April 4, 2000.

DISCUSSION QUESTIONS AND PROBLEMS

23-21 (Objective 23-1) Elizabeth Johnson, CPA, has completed the audit of notes payable and other liabilities for Valley River Electrical Services and now plans to audit contingent liabilities and commitments.

Required
a. Distinguish between contingent liabilities and commitments and explain why both are important in an audit.
b. Identify three useful audit procedures for uncovering contingent liabilities that Johnson would likely perform in the normal conduct of the audit, even if she had no responsibility for uncovering contingencies.
c. Identify three other procedures Johnson is likely to perform specifically for the purpose of identifying undisclosed contingencies.

23-22 (Objective 23-1)   In an audit of the Marco Corporation as of December 31, 1999, the following situations exist. No entries have been made in the accounting records in relation to these items.

1. The Marco Corporation has guaranteed the payment of interest on the 10-year, first mortgage bonds of the Newart Company, an affiliate. Outstanding bonds of the Newart Company amount to $150,000 with interest payable at 5 percent per annum, due June 1 and December 1 of each year. The bonds were issued by the Newart Company on December 1, 1997, and all interest payments have been met by that company with the exception of the payment due December 1, 1999. The Marco Corporation states that it will pay the defaulted interest to the bondholders on January 15, 2000.

2. During the year 1999, the Marco Corporation was named as a defendant in a suit for damages by the Dalton Company for breach of contract. An adverse decision to the Marco Corporation was rendered and the Dalton Company was awarded $40,000 damages. At the time of the audit, the case was under appeal to a higher court.

3. On December 23, 1999, the Marco Corporation declared a common stock dividend of 1,000 shares with a par value of $100,000 of its common stock, payable February 2, 2000, to the common stockholders of record December 30, 1999.

Required
   a. Define contingent liability.
   b. Describe the audit procedures you would use to learn about each of the situations above.
   c. Describe the nature of the adjusting entries or disclosure, if any, you would make for each of these situations.*

23-23 (Objectives 23-3, 23-7)   The field work for the June 30, 1999, audit of Tracy Brewing Company was finished August 19, 1999, and the completed financial statements, accompanied by the signed audit reports, were mailed September 6, 1999. In each of the highly material independent events (a through i), state the appropriate action (1 through 4) for the situation and justify your response. The alternative actions are as follows:

1. Adjust the June 30, 1999, financial statements.
2. Disclose the information in a footnote in the June 30, 1999, financial statements.
3. Request the client to recall the June 30, 1999, statements for revision.
4. No action is required.

The events are as follows:

   a. On December 14, 1999, the auditor discovered that a debtor of Tracy Brewing went bankrupt on October 2, 1999. The sale had taken place April 15, 1999, but the amount appeared collectible at June 30, 1999, and August 19, 1999.

   b. On August 15, 1999, the auditor discovered that a debtor of Tracy Brewing went bankrupt on August 1, 1999. The most recent sale had taken place April 2, 1998, and no cash receipts had been received since that date.

   c. On December 14, 1999, the auditor discovered that a debtor of Tracy Brewing went bankrupt on July 15, 1999, due to declining financial health. The sale had taken place January 15, 1999.

   d. On August 6, 1999, the auditor discovered that a debtor of Tracy Brewing went bankrupt on July 30, 1999. The cause of the bankruptcy was an unexpected loss of a major lawsuit on July 15, 1999, resulting from a product deficiency suit by a different customer.

   e. On August 6, 1999, the auditor discovered that a debtor of Tracy Brewing went bankrupt on July 30, 1999, for a sale that took place July 3, 1999. The cause of the bankruptcy was a major uninsured fire on July 20, 1999.

   f. On May 31, 1999, the auditor discovered an uninsured lawsuit against Tracy Brewing that had originated on February 28, 1999.

   g. On July 20, 1999, Tracy Brewing settled a lawsuit out of court that had originated in 1996 and is currently listed as a contingent liability.

*AICPA adapted.

h. On September 14, 1999, Tracy Brewing lost a court case that had originated in 1998 for an amount equal to the lawsuit. The June 30, 1999, footnotes state that in the opinion of legal counsel there will be a favorable settlement.

i. On July 20, 1999, a lawsuit was filed against Tracy Brewing for a patent infringement action that allegedly took place in early 1999. In the opinion of legal counsel, there is a danger of a significant loss to the client.

23-24 (Objective 23-5) Mel Adams, CPA, is a partner in a medium-sized CPA firm and takes an active part in the conduct of every audit he supervises. He follows the practice of reviewing all working papers of subordinates as soon as it is convenient, rather than waiting until the end of the audit. When the audit is nearly finished, Adams reviews the working papers again to make sure that he has not missed anything significant. Because he makes most of the major decisions on the audit, there is rarely anything that requires further investigation. When he completes the review, he prepares a pencil draft of the financial statements, gets them approved by management, and has them typed and assembled in his firm's office. No other partner reviews the working papers because Adams is responsible for signing the audit reports.

Required
a. Evaluate the practice of reviewing the working papers of subordinates on a continuing basis rather than when the audit is completed.
b. Is it acceptable for Adams to prepare the financial statements rather than make the client assume the responsibility?
c. Evaluate the practice of not having a review of the working papers by another partner in the firm.

23-25 (Objective 23-4) Leslie Morgan, CPA, has prepared a letter of representation for the president and controller to sign. It contains references to the following items:

1. Inventory is fairly stated at the lower of cost or market and includes no obsolete items.
2. All actual and contingent liabilities are properly included in the financial statements.
3. All subsequent events of relevance to the financial statements have been disclosed.

Required
a. Why is it desirable to have a letter of representation from the client concerning the above matters when the audit evidence accumulated during the course of the engagement is meant to verify the same information?
b. To what extent is the letter of representation useful as audit evidence? Explain.
c. List several other types of information commonly included in a letter of representation.

23-26 (Objective 23-6) In a letter to the audit committee of the Cline Wholesale Company, Jerry Schwartz, CPA, informed them of weaknesses in the control of inventory. In a separate letter to senior management, he elaborated on how the weaknesses could result in a significant misstatement of inventory by the failure to recognize the existence of obsolete items. In addition, Schwartz made specific recommendations in the management letter on how to improve internal control and save clerical time by installing a computer system for the company's perpetual records. Management accepted the recommendations and installed the system under Schwartz's direction. For several months, the system worked beautifully, but unforeseen problems developed when a master file was erased. The cost of reproducing and processing the inventory records to correct the error was significant, and management decided to scrap the entire project. The company sued Schwartz for failure to use adequate professional judgment in making the recommendations.

Required
a. What is Schwartz's legal and professional responsibility in the issuance of management letters?
b. Discuss the major considerations that will determine whether he is liable in this situation.

23-27 (Objective 23-3)   In connection with your audit of the financial statements of Olars Mfg. Corporation for the year ended December 31, 1999, your review of subsequent events disclosed the following items:

1. January 3, 2000: The state government approved a plan for the construction of an express highway. The plan will result in the expropriation of a portion of the land owned by Olars Mfg. Corporation. Construction will begin in late 2000. No estimate of the condemnation award is available. Read item 6 before answering requirement b for this question.

2. January 4, 2000: The funds for a $25,000 loan to the corporation made by Mr. Olars on July 15, 1999, were obtained by him from a loan on his personal life insurance policy. The loan was recorded in the account "loan from officers." Mr. Olars' source of the funds was not disclosed in the company records. The corporation pays the premiums on the life insurance policy, and Mrs. Olars, wife of the president, is the beneficiary.

3. January 7, 2000: The mineral content of a shipment of ore enroute on December 31, 1999, was determined to be 72 percent. The shipment was recorded at year-end at an estimated content of 50 percent by a debit to raw material inventory and a credit to accounts payable in the amount of $20,600. The final liability to the vendor is based on the actual mineral content of the shipment.

4. January 15, 2000: Culminating a series of personal disagreements between Mr. Olars, the president, and his brother-in-law, the treasurer, the latter resigned, effective immediately, under an agreement whereby the corporation would purchase his 10 percent stock ownership at book value as of December 31, 1999. Payment is to be made in two equal amounts in cash on April 1, 2000 and October 1, 2000. In December, the treasurer has obtained a divorce from his wife, who was Mr. Olars' sister.

5. January 31, 2000: As a result of reduced sales, production was curtailed in mid-January and some workers were laid off. On February 5, 2000, all the remaining workers went on strike. To date the strike is unsettled.

6. February 10, 2000: A contract was signed whereby Mammoth Enterprises purchases from Olars Mfg. Corporation all of the latter's fixed assets (including rights to receive the proceeds of any property condemnation), inventories, and the right to conduct business under the name "Olars Mfg. Division." The effective date of the transfer will be March 1, 2000. The sale price was $500,000 subject to adjustment following the taking of a physical inventory. Important factors contributing to the decision to enter into the contract were the policy of the board of directors of Mammoth Industries to diversify the firm's activities and the report of a survey conducted by an independent market appraisal firm that revealed a declining market for Olars products.

Required

Assume that the items described above came to your attention before completion of your audit work on February 15, 2000. For *each* item:

    a. Give the audit procedures, if any, that would have brought the item to your attention. Indicate other sources of information that may have revealed the item.

    b. Discuss the disclosure that you would recommend for the item, listing all details that you would suggest should be disclosed. Indicate those items or details, if any, that should not be disclosed. Give your reasons for recommending or not recommending disclosure of the items or details.*

23-28 (Objective 23-3)   The following unrelated events occurred after the balance sheet date but before the audit report was prepared:

1. The granting of a retroactive pay increase
2. Determination by the federal government of additional income tax due for a prior year
3. Filing of an antitrust suit by the federal government
4. Declaration of a stock dividend
5. Sale of a fixed asset at a substantial profit

*AICPA adapted.

a. Explain how each of the items might have come to the auditor's attention.
b. Discuss the auditor's responsibility to recognize each of these in connection with his or her report.*

23-29 (Objective 23-3)   The philosophy of Irene Hatton, CPA, is to intensively audit transactions taking place during the current audit period but to ignore subsequent transactions. She believes that each year should stand on its own and be audited in the year in which the transactions take place. According to Hatton, "If a transaction recorded in the subsequent period is audited in the current period, it is verified twice—once this year and again in next year's audit. That is a duplication of effort and a waste of time."

Required

a. Explain the fallacy in Hatton's argument.
b. Give six specific examples of information obtained by examining subsequent events that are essential to the current-period audit.

23-30 (Objective 23-2)   In analyzing legal expense for the Boastman Bottle Company, Mary Little, CPA, observes that the company has paid legal fees to three different law firms during the current year. In accordance with her CPA firm's normal operating practice, Little requests standard attorney letters as of the balance sheet date from each of the three law firms.

On the last day of field work, Little notes that one of the attorney letters has not yet been received. The second request contains a statement to the effect that the law firm deals exclusively in registering patents and refuses to comment on any lawsuits or other legal affairs of the client. The third attorney's letter states that there is an outstanding unpaid bill due from the client and recognizes the existence of a potentially material lawsuit against the client but refuses to comment further to protect the legal rights of the client.

Required

a. Evaluate Little's approach to sending the attorney letters and her follow-up on the responses.
b. What should Little do about each of the letters?

CASES

23-31 (Objective 23-5)   In your audit of Aviary Industries for calendar year 1999, you found a number of matters that you believe represent possible adjustments to the company's books. These matters are described below and on page 753. Management's attitude is that "once the books are closed, they're closed," and management does not want to make any adjustments. Planning materiality for the engagement was $100,000, determined by computing 5 percent of expected income before taxes. Actual income before taxes on the financial statements prior to any adjustments is $1,652,867.

Possible adjustments:

1. Several credit memos that were processed and recorded after year-end relate to sales and accounts receivable for 1999. These total $23,529.
2. Inventory cutoff tests indicate that $22,357 of inventory received on December 30, 1999, was recorded as purchases and accounts payable in 2000. These items were included in the inventory count at year-end, and therefore were included in ending inventory.
3. Inventory cutoff tests also indicate several sales invoices recorded in 1999 for goods that were shipped in early 2000. The goods were not included in inventory but were set aside in a separate shipping area. The total amount of these shipments was $36,022. (Ignore cost of sales for this item.)

*AICPA adapted.

4. The company wrote several checks at the end of 1999 for accounts payable that were held and not mailed until January 15, 2000. These totaled $48,336. Recorded cash and accounts payable at December 31, 1999, are $2,356,553 and $2,666,290, respectively.

5. The company has not established a reserve for obsolescence of inventories. Your tests indicate that such a reserve is appropriate in an amount somewhere between $20,000 and $40,000.

6. Your review of the allowance for uncollectible accounts indicates that it may be understated by between $25,000 and $50,000.

Required

a. Determine the adjustments that you believe must be made for Aviary's financial statements to be fairly presented. Include the amounts and accounts affected by each adjustment.

b. Why may Aviary Industries' management resist making these adjustments?

c. Explain what you consider the most positive way of approaching management personnel to convince them to make your proposed changes.

23-32 (Objective 23-6) You are the senior on the audit of Dahlstrom Manufacturing Company. Dahlstrom manufactures various sizes of cardboard boxes. These are customized both in terms of size and printing and are used by producers of various types of retail food products. Your present task is to draft a reportable conditions letter and a management letter to the Company. Your firm prepares these letters using the following process:

1. As work is done, auditors who observe a possible reportable condition or management letter item fill out a form that shows a description of the item and a recommended solution.

2. The senior drafts both the reportable conditions letter and the management letter using word processing software and the firm's standard formats maintained on a computer file for firm use. The standard formats:
   a. Contain standard introduction and ending sections.
   b. Require three segments for each item: description of finding or observation, possible consequences if item is not resolved, and suggestion(s) for resolution.

3. The drafts are reviewed by the manager and discussed with appropriate client personnel. They are then finalized and delivered.

Following is a summary of the reportable conditions and management letter items being suggested by the audit team, in the order in which they were documented. Each item is stated and then followed by a suggested solution.

1. In sampling sales invoices, it was noted that in a sample of 60 items, 4 were recorded on a different date than the day the goods were shipped.

   The Company should batch invoices by the date of shipment, accounting for their numerical sequence, and ensure that the date of shipment is used when the invoices are input into the computer system.

2. While verifying prices on sales invoices, it was noticed that prices charged differed from catalog prices in a number of instances. These price differences were authorized by regional sales managers as per Company policy. However, we also received comments on our accounts receivable confirmation replies that some sales were in dispute, and the credit manager told us that there were some collection problems that arose from pricing differences.

   The Company should consider reviewing its pricing policies and related practices.

3. In conducting our inventory observation, we noted that there was a large buildup of work-in-process inventory between the cutting and printing operations. Workers in the folding/gluing operation were observed idle, waiting for output from printing to continue their work.

   The Company should consider reviewing the design of its production line, and specifically the printing operation, for a possible bottleneck problem.

4. When we conducted our inventory observation we noted a significant amount of cardboard stock (raw material to the production process) that had apparently not been used for some time. It was still bound by strapping and covered with dust.

   The client should determine whether this stock can be used in production, and if not, consider whether it can be sold.

5. In conducting our inventory observation, we observed several wall-hung fire extinguishers that were stamped with an expiration date prior to the date of our observation.

   All fire extinguishers should be kept in working condition.

6. When we counted petty cash at the Oakridge location, we found that the fund contained a personal check for $240 prepared by the fund custodian. The custodian told us it represented a "temporary loan." This is not in accordance with Company policy. We informed the Oakridge manager about this finding.

   The Oakridge manager should review the policy on petty cash funds with the custodian and ensure that the policy is adhered to in the future.

7. In reviewing the cash accounts, we noted that some payroll bank accounts had not been reconciled for more than 60 days.

   All bank accounts should be reconciled monthly.

8. In talking to the manager of the Oakridge location, he told us that he was having difficulty making production decisions because of constant changes in sales forecasts being issued by marketing. He said that if he could receive more stable sales forecast data, he could save significantly on set-up costs and also reduce both raw material and work-in-process inventories.

   The Company should consider reviewing its sales forecasting system with the objective of providing more stable information that is effectively integrated with production planning.

Required

    a. For each of the above eight items, decide whether the item belongs in a reportable conditions letter, a management letter, both, or neither. Document your decisions.

    b. Prepare a draft of the reportable conditions letter for Dahlstrom Manufacturing Company using word processing software and the standard format provided on the CW site (instructor option). The letter should be properly organized and effectively written. Feel free to make any assumptions you believe are reasonable and appropriate.

    c. Prepare a draft of the management letter for Dahlstrom Manufacturing Company using word processing software and the standard format provided on the CW site (instructor option). Note that the management letter can refer to items included in the reportable conditions letter without including details of these items. The letter should be properly organized and effectively written. Feel free to make any assumptions you believe are reasonable and appropriate.

Reference the CW site. This problem requires students to use the Internet to research and classify actual subsequent event disclosures reported in SEC filings.

PART VI
(Chapters 24–25)

OTHER ASSURANCE AND NONASSURANCE SERVICES

Chapter 1 introduced assurance and nonassurance services offered by CPA firms and other types of auditors. The chapters in Part VI expand that discussion. Assurance services other than audits and nonassurance services are increasingly important to both CPA firms and other auditors.

Chapter 24 deals with assurance and nonassurance services, both traditional and emerging, that CPA firms offer. Chapter 25 covers services performed most often by governmental and internal auditors, including internal financial auditing, governmental financial auditing, and operational auditing.

OTHER AUDIT, ATTESTATION SERVICES, AND COMPILATION ENGAGEMENTS

24

LEARNING OBJECTIVES

After studying this chapter, you should be able to

24-1 Understand the level of assurance and evidence requirements for review and compilation services.

24-2 Describe special engagements to review interim financial information for public companies.

24-3 Describe other audit and limited assurance engagements related to historical financial statements.

24-4 Distinguish AICPA attestation standards from auditing standards, and know the type of engagements to which they apply.

24-5 Describe special engagements to attest to prospective financial statements.

24-6 Understand special engagements to attest to internal control, including controls over electronic commerce.

24-7 Describe agreed-upon procedures engagements.

SKEPTICISM APPLIES TO ALL TYPES OF ENGAGEMENTS

Barnhart Construction Company was a contractor specializing in apartment complexes in the Southwest. The owner of the construction company, David Barnhart, reached an agreement with a promoter named Alton Leonard to serve as a contractor on three construction projects Leonard was currently marketing. One problem with the agreement was that Barnhart would not receive final payment for the construction work until all the partnership units were sold.

The first partnership offering was completely sold and Barnhart was paid. Unfortunately, the next two partnerships were not completely sold. To solve this problem, Barnhart loaned money to relatives and key employees who bought the necessary interests for the partnerships to close so that Barnhart would receive the final payment.

Barnhart Construction had a review service performed by Renee Lathrup, CPA, a sole practitioner. She noticed that the accounting records showed loans receivable from a number of employees and individuals named Barnhart. She also observed that the loans were made just before the second and third partnerships closed and that they were in multiples of $15,000, the cost of a partnership unit. Renee asked Barnhart to explain what happened. Barnhart told Renee, "When I received the money from the first partnership escrow, I wanted to do something nice for relatives and employees who had been loyal to me over the years." He told Renee, "This is just my way of sharing my good fortune with the ones I love. The equality of the amounts is just a coincidence."

When Renee considered the reasonableness of this scenario, she found it hard to believe. First, the timing was odd. Second, the amounts seemed to be an unusual coincidence. Third, if he really had wanted to do something special for these folks, why didn't he give them something, rather than loan them money? Renee asked that the promoter, Leonard, send her detailed information on the subscriptions for each partnership. Leonard refused, stating that he was under legal obligation to keep all information confidential. When Renee pressed Barnhart, he also refused further cooperation, although he did say he would "represent" to Renee that the loans had nothing to do with closing the partnerships so that he could get his money. At this point, Renee withdrew from the engagement.

The text material to this point has been primarily about the performing of audits of historical financial statement that are presented in conformance with generally accepted accounting principles (GAAP). We now discuss other types of reports and services offered by CPAs. The example that opened the chapter involved a review of historical financial statements, a limited assurance engagement involving historical financial statements that was first introduced in Chapter 1. CPAs provide many other types of attestation services related to historical financial statements to meet the specific needs of financial statement users. With increases in technology and information, CPAs are increasingly asked to attest to controls and other types of forward-looking information. The level of assurance, extent of evidence, and type of report depend upon the nature of the service offered.

This chapter examines other types of engagements and reports related to historical financial information and several types of attestation engagements, such as reports on forecasted financial statements and reports on internal control over financial reporting. The chapter begins by discussing reviews and compilations of historical financial statements.

REVIEW AND COMPILATION SERVICES

Many nonpublic companies have their financial statements reviewed or compiled by a CPA, instead of having them audited. A company's management may believe that an audit is unnecessary because of the active involvement of owners, and the company may not have significant amounts of debt or other regulatory requirements. The company may engage the CPA to assist in the preparation of financial statements, either for internal use or to provide to creditors or lenders under loan agreements. Depending on the size of the loan, a lender may require compiled or reviewed financial statements, rather than an audit. A review provides limited assurance on the financial statements, whereas a compilation provides no expressed assurance.

The standards for compilations and reviews of financial statements are called **Statements on Standards for Accounting and Review Services (SSARS)**. These statements are issued by the Accounting and Review Services Committee of the AICPA, which has authority equivalent to the Auditing Standards Board for services involving unaudited financial statements of nonpublic (private) companies.

The assurance provided by compilations and reviews is considerably below that of audits. As a result, less evidence is required for these services and they can be provided at a lower fee than an audit. It is interesting to note that the SSARS refer to practitioners performing review and compilation services as accountants, not auditors. Figure 24-1

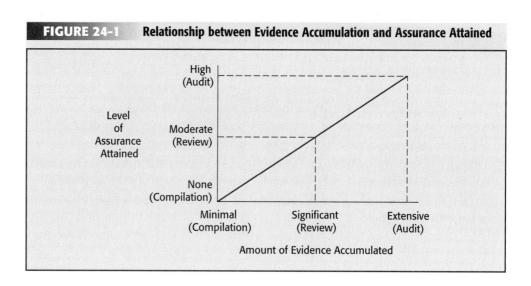

FIGURE 24-1   Relationship between Evidence Accumulation and Assurance Attained

illustrates the difference in evidence accumulation and level of assurance for audits, reviews, and compilations. The actual amount of evidence and assurance for each engagement is not well defined by the profession and depends on the practitioner's judgment.

Because review and compilation services provide less assurance than audits, it is important that the accountant establish an understanding with the client, preferably in a written engagement letter, about the services to be performed. The understanding should include a description of the nature and limitations of the services and a description of the compilation or review report expected to be rendered at the completion of the engagement. The next two sections discuss the requirements for review and compilation services in greater detail.

Review Services

A **review service (SSARS review)** engagement is designed to allow the accountant to express limited assurance that the financial statements are in accordance with GAAP, including appropriate informative disclosures, or an other comprehensive basis of accounting (OCBOA), such as the cash basis of accounting. Accountants performing review services must be independent of the client.

Procedures Suggested for Reviews The evidence for a review engagement consists primarily of inquiries of management and analytical procedures. It should be apparent that the required procedures for a review are substantially less than those required for an audit. A review engagement does not include obtaining an understanding of internal control, tests of controls, substantive tests of transactions, or specific tests of balances such as confirmation of receivables or physical examination of inventory. The following are recommended procedures for a review engagement:

- Obtain knowledge of the accounting principles and practices of the client's industry. The accountant can study AICPA industry guides or other sources to obtain industry knowledge. The level of knowledge for reviews can be somewhat less than for an audit.
- Obtain knowledge of the client. The information should be about the nature of the client's business transactions, its accounting records and employees, and the basis, form, and content of the financial statements. The level of knowledge can be less than for an audit.
- Make inquiries of management. The objective of these inquiries is to determine whether the financial statements are fairly presented, assuming that management does not intend to deceive the accountant. Inquiry is the most important of the review procedures. The following are illustrative inquiries:

  1. Inquire as to the company's procedures for recording, classifying, and summarizing transactions, and disclosing information in the statements.
  2. Inquire into actions taken at meetings of stockholders and board of directors.
  3. Inquire of persons having responsibility for financial and accounting matters whether the financial statements have been prepared in conformity with GAAP consistently applied.

- Perform analytical procedures. These are meant to identify relationships and individual items that appear to be unusual. The appropriate analytical procedures are no different from the ones already studied in Chapter 7 and in those chapters dealing with tests of details of balances.
- Obtain letter of representation. The accountant is required to obtain a letter of representation from members of management who are knowledgeable about financial matters.

SSARS
Representation Letter

Based on these procedures, the accountant may become aware that information is incorrect, incomplete, or otherwise unsatisfactory. Under these circumstances, additional procedures should be performed before the accountant expresses a standard review services report.

Form of Report Figure 24-2 provides an example of the review report issued when the accountant has completed a review engagement and determined that no material modifications are necessary to the financial statements. Three aspects of the report are worth noting:

1. The first paragraph is similar to an audit report except for its reference to a review service rather than an audit.
2. The second paragraph notes that a review consists primarily of inquiries and analytical procedures. This paragraph also notes that a review is substantially less in scope than an audit and that no opinion is expressed.
3. The third paragraph expresses limited assurance *in the form of a negative assurance* that "we are not aware of any material modifications that should be made to the financial statements."

The date of the review report should be the date of completion of the accountant's inquiry and analytical procedures. Each page of the financial statements reviewed should include a reference to "See accountant's review report."

FIGURE 24-2   Example of Review Report

> We have reviewed the accompanying balance sheet of XYZ Company as of December 31, 1999, and the related statements of income, retained earnings, and cash flows for the year then ended, in accordance with Statements on Standards for Accounting and Review Services issued by the American Institute of Certified Public Accountants. All information included in these financial statements is the representation of the management of XYZ Company.
>
> A review consists principally of inquiries of company personnel and analytical procedures applied to financial data. It is substantially less in scope than an audit in accordance with generally accepted auditing standards, the objective of which is the expression of an opinion regarding the financial statements taken as a whole. Accordingly, we do not express such an opinion.
>
> Based on our review, we are not aware of any material modifications that should be made to the accompanying financial statements in order for them to be in conformity with generally accepted accounting principles.

Failure to Follow GAAP If a client has failed to follow GAAP in a review engagement, a modification of the report is needed. The effects of the departure should be disclosed in the report if they have been determined by management or are known as a result of the accountant's review procedures. If the effects have not been determined, that should be stated in the report. The disclosure must be made in a *separate paragraph* in the report. The following is an example of suggested wording:

- As disclosed in note X to the financial statements, generally accepted accounting principles require that land be stated at cost. Management has informed us that the company has stated its land at appraised value and that, if generally accepted accounting principles had been followed, the land account and stockholders' equity would have been decreased by $500,000.

Compilation Services

A **compilation service** engagement is defined in SSARS as one in which the accountant presents information in the form of financial statements that is the representation of management without the CPA firm expressing any assurance on the statements. Many CPA firms prepare monthly, quarterly, or annual financial statements for their clients. These statements are usually for internal use by management, although they may also be provided to external users. When an accountant submits financial statements to a client or other parties, the CPA is required to at least compile the statements. The CPA is not required to be independent to perform a compilation and the financial statements can be issued without additional disclosures.

Requirements for Compilation Compilation does not mean that the accountant has no responsibilities. The accountant is always responsible for exercising due care in performing all duties. In a compilation engagement, the accountant must do the following:

- Possess knowledge about the accounting principles and practices of the client's industry.
- Know the client; the nature of the client's business transactions, accounting records, and employees; and the basis, form, and content of the financial statements. The knowledge can be less than that for a review.
- Make inquiries to determine whether the client's information is satisfactory.
- Read the compiled financial statements and be alert for any obvious omissions or errors in arithmetic and GAAP.

The accountant does not have to make other inquiries or perform other procedures to verify information supplied by the entity. But if the accountant becomes aware that the statements are not fairly presented, he or she should obtain additional information. If the client refuses to provide the information, the accountant should withdraw from the compilation engagement.

Form of Report The form of the compilation report depends on whether management elects to include all the required disclosures with the financial statements. It is also permissible to issue a compilation report when the auditor is not independent, but this must be clearly stated in the report.

- *Compilation with full disclosure.* A compilation of this type requires disclosures in accordance with GAAP, the same as for audited financial statements or reviews. Figure 24-3 shows the appropriate wording in such circumstances.

FIGURE 24-3   Compilation Report with Full Disclosure

We have compiled the accompanying balance sheet of XYZ Company as of December 31, 1999, and the related statements of income, retained earnings, and cash flows for the year then ended, in accordance with Statements on Standards for Accounting and Review Services issued by the American Institute of Certified Public Accountants.

A compilation is limited to presenting in the form of financial statements information that is the representation of management. We have not audited or reviewed the accompanying financial statements and, accordingly, do not express an opinion or any other form of assurance on them.

- *Compilation that omits substantially all disclosures.* This type of compilation is acceptable *if the report indicates the lack of disclosures* and the absence of disclosures *is not*, to the CPA's knowledge, *undertaken with the intent to mislead users.* This type of statement is usually expected to be used primarily for management purposes only.

  Figure 24-4 (p. 762) shows the appropriate wording when the accountant compiles statements without disclosures. In this example, management has also elected not to present the statement of cash flows.
- *Compilation without independence.* A CPA firm can issue a compilation report even if it is not independent with respect to the client, as defined by the *Code of Professional Conduct.* When the accountant lacks independence, the following should be included as a separate last paragraph in either of the two previously discussed reports: "We are not independent with respect to XYZ Company."

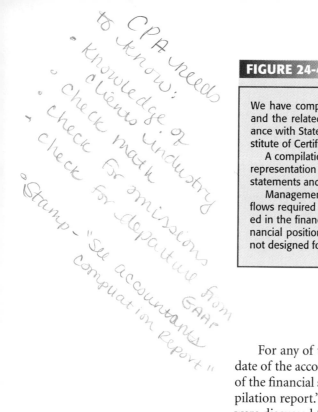

FIGURE 24-4   Compilation That Omits Substantially All Disclosures

We have compiled the accompanying balance sheet of XYZ Company as of December 31, 1999, and the related statements of income and retained earnings for the year then ended, in accordance with Statements on Standards for Accounting and Review Services issued by the American Institute of Certified Public Accountants.

A compilation is limited to presenting in the form of financial statements information that is the representation of management. We have not audited or reviewed the accompanying financial statements and, accordingly, do not express an opinion or any other form of assurance on them.

Management has elected to omit substantially all of the disclosures and the statement of cash flows required by generally accepted accounting principles. If the omitted disclosures were included in the financial statements, they might influence the user's conclusions about the company's financial position, results of operations, and cash flows. Accordingly, these financial statements are not designed for those who are not informed about such matters.

For any of the three types of compilation reports, the following are also required: the date of the accountant's report is the date of completion of the compilation, and each page of the financial statements compiled by the accountant should state "See accountant's compilation report." If the client fails to follow GAAP, the same report modifications exist that were discussed for reviews.

This section discussed the requirements for compilation and review services under SSARS for nonpublic companies. The next section describes reviews of interim financial information for public companies.

REVIEW OF INTERIM FINANCIAL INFORMATION FOR PUBLIC COMPANIES

OBJECTIVE 24-2
Describe special engagements to review interim financial information for public companies.

Reviews of interim financial information are done to help management of public companies meet their reporting responsibilities to regulatory agencies. The SEC requires quarterly financial information as a part of quarterly 10-Q reports. The statements do not have to be audited, and the CPA firm's name need not be associated with the quarterly statements.

However, the SEC requires a footnote in the annual audited financial statements disclosing quarterly sales, gross profit, income, and earnings per share for the past 2 years. Typically, the footnote in the annual statements is labeled *unaudited,* but at a minimum, the CPA firm must perform review procedures of the footnote information. There is no requirement that the review procedures be done quarterly. The review can be done as a part of the annual audit. *Stamped "unaudited"*

The disadvantage of doing the review procedures at the time of the annual audit is that potential discrepancies may arise between the quarterly information in the annual statement's footnote and the quarterly 10-Q reports. Therefore, management often asks auditors to do quarterly reviews of financial statements to maximize the likelihood of consistency between the 10-Q reports and the footnotes to the annual statements.

SAS 71 Reviews

The requirements for reviews of interim information for public companies (**SAS 71 reviews**) are set forth by SAS 71 (AU 722). Even though they are issued by the Auditing Standards Board, the requirements are more closely related to review engagement requirements of SSARS than to audit requirements. The five requirements for review service engagements previously discussed are all applicable to both SSARS and SAS reviews.

Like reviews under SSARS, an SAS 71 review does not provide a basis for expressing a positive-form opinion. There are ordinarily no tests of the accounting records, independent confirmations, or physical examinations.

There are some differences, however, between the two types of reviews. First, because an annual audit is also performed for a client who has an SAS 71 review, the auditor must obtain sufficient information about the client's internal control for both annual and interim financial information. Similarly, because the client in an SAS 71 review is audited annually, the auditor's knowledge of the results of these audit procedures is used in considering the scope and results of SAS 71 inquiries and analytical procedures. Third, under SSARS, the auditor makes inquiries about actions of directors' and stockholders' meetings; under SAS 71, the auditor reads the minutes of those meetings.

The objective of an SAS 71 review is to provide the accountant with a basis for reporting to management, the board of directors, and the stockholders and others on significant matters found through inquiry and analytical procedures. The report on this review is made directly available to management and the directors; it is usually made available to stockholders and others by its inclusion in Form 10-Q, although this is required only when management states in the 10-Q that such a review has been made.

The standard report for interim financial statements that have been reviewed is recommended in SAS 71 and is illustrated in Figure 24-5.

FIGURE 24-5	Example of a Report for Interim Financial Statements for a Public Company

> We have reviewed the consolidated balance sheet of Rainer Company and consolidated subsidiaries as of September 30, 1999, and the related statements of earnings, retained earnings, and cash flows for the three-month and nine-month periods then ended. These financial statements are the responsibility of the company's management.
>
> We conducted our review in accordance with standards established by the American Institute of Certified Public Accountants. A review of interim financial information consists principally of applying analytical procedures to financial data and making inquiries of persons responsible for financial and accounting matters. It is substantially less in scope than an audit conducted in accordance with generally accepted auditing standards, the objective of which is the expression of an opinion regarding the financial statements taken as a whole. Accordingly, we do not express such an opinion.
>
> Based on our review, we are not aware of any material modifications that should be made to the accompanying financial statements for them to be in conformity with generally accepted accounting principles.

The report for a review under SAS 71 is similar to the report for a SSARS review. The standards referred to in the second paragraph are those established in SAS 71. Because the review is conducted according to the requirements of SAS 71, there is no reference to the SSARS in a review report of interim financial information for a public company. Each page of the interim financial information should be clearly marked as "unaudited."

When the auditor determines that there has been a departure from GAAP, the report should be modified. This modification is similar to that used in a review under SSARS, except that the effect of the departure should, if feasible, be stated.

The quarterly data reviewed by the auditor and included as a footnote in the annual audited statements should be labeled "unaudited." A separate review report for this information is not required.

OTHER AUDITS OR LIMITED ASSURANCE ENGAGEMENTS

Earlier in this chapter, we discussed compilation and review services for nonpublic companies, as well as reviews of interim financial information for public companies. We now examine other types of audit and attestation services that fall within the auditing standards but are not audits of historical financial statements in accordance with GAAP. Some of the

OBJECTIVE 24-3
Describe other audit and limited assurance engagements related to historical financial statements.

more important of these services include audits of financial statements prepared on an other comprehensive basis of accounting (OCBOA); audits of specified elements, accounts, or items; information accompanying the basic financial statements; and debt compliance letters. We now discuss each of these services in greater detail.

Other Comprehensive Basis of Accounting

Auditors often audit statements prepared on a basis other than GAAP. SAS 62 (AU 623) provides that generally accepted auditing standards apply to these audit engagements, but the reporting requirements differ somewhat from those described in Chapter 3. The following are bases other than GAAP for which reports may be issued according to the requirements of SAS 62:

- *Cash or modified cash basis.* With cash basis accounting, only cash receipts and disbursements are recorded. Under the modified cash basis of accounting, the cash basis is followed except for certain items, such as fixed assets and depreciation. Physicians and attorneys often follow this accounting method.
- *Basis used to comply with the requirements of a regulatory agency.* Common examples include the uniform system of accounts required of railroads, utilities, and some insurance companies.
- *Income tax basis.* The same measurement rules used for filing tax returns are often used for financial statement preparation, even though this is not in accordance with GAAP. Many small businesses use this method.
- *A definite set of criteria having substantial support.* An example would be the price-level basis of accounting. The method of accounting must be applied to all material items in the financial statements.

For the most part, these audits are done in the same way as those in which GAAP is followed. Naturally, the auditor must fully understand the accounting basis that the client is required to follow. For example, in auditing a railroad, there are complex accounting requirements that require the auditor to have specialized accounting knowledge to conduct the audit.

A concern in reporting on a comprehensive basis is to make sure that the statements clearly indicate that they are prepared on a basis other than GAAP. If the statements imply that GAAP is followed, the reporting requirements of Chapter 3 apply. Consequently, terms such as *balance sheet* and *statement of operations* must be avoided by the client. Instead, a title such as "statement of assets and liabilities arising from cash transactions" would be appropriate for a cash basis statement.

The reporting requirements for audits of these comprehensive bases of accounting include the following.

Introductory Paragraph This paragraph is equivalent to the introductory paragraph of a report on statements that follow GAAP. The statements are identified, and the paragraph states that they were audited. The paragraph also states that the statements are the responsibility of management and that the auditor's responsibility is to express an opinion on them based on the audit.

Scope Paragraph This paragraph is equivalent to the scope paragraph in the ordinary report. It states that the audit was conducted in accordance with generally accepted auditing standards and describes the nature of the audit process.

Middle Paragraph Stating the Accounting Basis This paragraph is unique to this type of report. It states the basis of presentation and refers to a note to the financial statements that describes the basis of accounting followed. It states that such basis is a comprehensive basis of accounting other than GAAP. The note referred to will describe not only the basis followed but also how that basis differs from GAAP. It need not state the effects of the differences in quantitative terms. It is important for the auditor to consider whether the financial statements include all informative disclosures that are appropriate for the basis of accounting used.

Opinion Paragraph The opinion paragraph is comparable to that used in the standard report. It expresses the auditor's opinion with regard to conformity with the basis of accounting described.

If the financial statements are prepared in conformity with requirements of a governmental regulatory agency, a paragraph must be added that restricts the distribution of the report to those within the entity and for filing with the regulatory agency.

Figure 24-6 is a common example of a report prepared on an entity's income tax basis.

FIGURE 24-6   Example of a Report on Income Tax Basis

Independent Auditor's Report

We have audited the accompanying statements of assets, liabilities, and capital—income tax basis of ABC Partnership as of December 31, 1999 and 1998, and the related statements of revenue and expenses—income tax basis and of changes in partners' capital accounts—income tax basis for the years then ended. These financial statements are the responsibility of the Partnership's management. Our responsibility is to express an opinion on these financial statements based on our audits.

We conducted our audits in accordance with generally accepted auditing standards. Those standards require that we plan and perform the audit to obtain reasonable assurance about whether the financial statements are free of material misstatement. An audit includes examining, on a test basis, evidence supporting the amounts and disclosures in the financial statements. An audit also includes assessing the accounting principles used and significant estimates made by management, as well as evaluating the overall financial statement presentation. We believe that our audits provide a reasonable basis for our opinion.

As described in Note X, these financial statements were prepared on the basis of accounting the Partnership uses for income tax purposes, which is a comprehensive basis of accounting other than generally accepted accounting principles.

In our opinion, the financial statements referred to above present fairly, in all material respects, the assets, liabilities, and capital of ABC Partnership as of December 31, 1999 and 1998, and its revenue and expenses and changes in partners' capital accounts for the years then ended, on the basis of accounting described in Note X.

Specified Elements, Accounts, or Items

Auditors are often asked to issue reports on their audit of specific aspects of financial statements. A common example is a special report on the audit of sales of a retail store in a shopping center to be used as a basis for rental payments. Other common examples are reports on royalties, profit participation, and provision for income taxes. The authority for auditing specified elements, accounts, or items is SAS 62 (AU 623) Special Reports.

The type of engagement to be undertaken for specified elements, accounts, or items is usually an audit. Thus, it is typically like an ordinary audit but is applied to less than the full financial statements. There are two primary differences between audits of specified elements, accounts, or items, and audits of complete financial statements:

1. Materiality is defined in terms of the elements, accounts, or items involved rather than in relation to the overall statements. The effect is to ordinarily require more evidence than would be needed if the item being verified were just one of many parts of the statements. For example, if the sales account is being reported on separately, a smaller misstatement would be considered material than when sales is just one account of many being reported on as a part of a regular audit.
2. The first standard of reporting under GAAS does not apply because the presentation of elements, accounts, or items is not a financial statement prepared in accordance with GAAP.

In addition, the auditor must be careful to extend his or her audit efforts to include other elements, accounts, or items that are interrelated with those that are the subject of the engagement. This will cause an increase in audit effort as well. For example, in expressing an opinion on sales, the auditor must also consider the effect of accounts receivable on sales.

Figure 24-7 illustrates a report for royalties, which is a specified account. The format and contents of the report are similar to the standard audit report on the audit of financial statements in accordance with GAAP. However, it must also reflect the following requirements for reporting on specified elements, accounts, or items:

- The specified elements, accounts, or items must be identified.
- The basis on which the specified elements, accounts, or items are presented and the agreements specifying the basis must be described.
- The source of significant interpretations made by the client about the provisions of a relevant agreement must be indicated and described.
- If the specified element, account, or item is presented on a basis that is not in conformity with GAAP or another comprehensive basis of accounting, a paragraph that restricts the distribution of the report to those within the entity and the parties to the contract or agreement must be added.

FIGURE 24-7 **Example of a Report for Royalties**

Independent Auditor's Report

We have audited the accompanying schedule of royalties applicable to engine production of the Q Division of XYZ Company for the year ended December 31, 1999, under the terms of a license agreement dated May 14, 1997, between ABC Company and XYZ Company. This schedule is the responsibility of XYZ Company's management. Our responsibility is to express an opinion on this schedule based on our audit.

We conducted our audit in accordance with generally accepted auditing standards. Those standards require that we plan and perform the audit to obtain reasonable assurance about whether the schedule of royalties is free of material misstatement. An audit includes examining, on a test basis, evidence supporting the amounts and disclosures in the schedule. An audit also includes assessing the accounting principles used and significant estimates made by management, as well as evaluating the overall schedule presentation. We believe that our audit provides a reasonable basis for our opinion.

We have been informed that, under XYZ Company's interpretation of the agreement referred to in the first paragraph, royalties were based on the number of engines produced after giving effect to a reduction for production retirements that were scrapped, but without a reduction for field returns that were scrapped, even though the field returns were replaced with new engines without charge to customers.

In our opinion, the schedule of royalties referred to above presents fairly, in all material respects, the number of engines produced by the Q Division of XYZ Company during the year ended December 31, 1999, and the amount of royalties applicable thereto, under the license agreement referred to above.

This report is intended solely for the information and use of the boards of directors and managements of XYZ Company and ABC Company and should not be used for any other purpose.

It is important to realize that the circumstances and requirements that exist for modifying a report on an audit of GAAP financial statements also apply to special reports on both specific elements, accounts, or items and financial statements prepared on another comprehensive basis of accounting. These modifications would include not only departures from an unqualified opinion but also an explanatory paragraph where appropriate. The form of the modifications would essentially be the same as discussed in Chapter 3.

Clients often request auditors to include additional information beyond the basic financial statements in the set of materials prepared for management or outside users. SAS 29 (AU 551) refers to this additional information as *information accompanying the basic financial statements in auditor-submitted documents.* In the past, the same information was called a *long-form report.* Figure 24-8 illustrates the basic financial statements and additional information.

The profession has intentionally refrained from defining or restricting the appropriate supplementary information included to enable auditors to individualize the information to meet the needs of statement users. However, several types of information are commonly included in the additional information section:

- Detailed comparative statements supporting the control totals on the primary financial statements for accounts such as cost of goods sold, operating expenses, and miscellaneous assets
- Supplementary information required by the Financial Accounting Standards Board or the SEC
- Statistical data for past years in the form of ratios and trends
- A schedule of insurance coverage
- Specific comments on the changes that have taken place in the statements

It is important that the auditor clearly distinguish between responsibility for the primary financial statements and for additional information. Usually, the auditor has not performed a sufficiently detailed audit to justify an opinion on the additional information, but in some instances, the auditor may be confident that the information is fairly presented. The profession's reporting standards require the auditor to make a clear statement about the degree of responsibility he or she is taking for the additional information. Two types of opinions are allowed: a positive opinion indicating a high level of assurance or a disclaimer indicating no assurance. When the auditor issues an opinion on additional information accompanying the financial statements, materiality is the same as that used in forming an opinion on the basic financial statements. As a result, the additional procedures required are less extensive than if the auditor were issuing an opinion on the information taken by itself, such as in a report on specified elements or accounts. The following is an example of

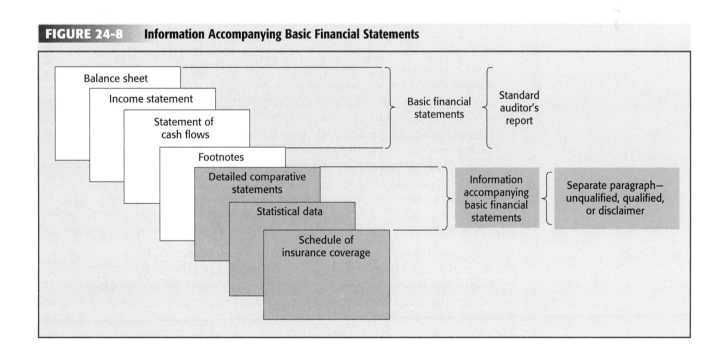

FIGURE 24-8   Information Accompanying Basic Financial Statements

the additional wording to be added to the auditor's standard report when expressing an opinion on the additional information:

- Our audit was conducted for the purpose of forming an opinion on the basic financial statements taken as a whole. The accompanying information on pages x through y is presented for purposes of additional analysis, and is not a required part of the basic financial statements. Such information has been subjected to the auditing procedures applied in the audit of the basic financial statements and, in our opinion, is fairly stated in all material respects in relation to the basic financial statements taken as a whole.

If the auditor decided that sufficient evidence had *not* been accumulated for the additional data to justify an unqualified opinion, SAS 29 requires that a disclaimer paragraph such as the following be added to the standard audit report:

- Our audit was made for the purpose of forming an opinion on the basic financial statements taken as a whole. The accompanying information on pages x through y is presented for purposes of additional analysis and is not a required part of the basic financial statements. Such information has not been subjected to the auditing procedures applied in the audit of the basic financial statements, and, accordingly, we express no opinion on it.

Debt Compliance Letters and Similar Reports

Clients occasionally enter into loan agreements that require them to provide the lender with a report from a CPA as to the existence or nonexistence of some condition. For example, borrowing arrangements may require maintenance of a certain dollar amount of working capital at specified times and an independent accountant's report as to the compliance with the requirement.

Reports on debt compliance and similar engagements are discussed in AU 623, paragraphs .19 through .21. These reports may be issued as separate reports or as part of a report that expresses the auditor's opinion on the financial statements by adding a paragraph after the opinion paragraph. In either case, the following matters are important for the auditor to observe in such engagements:

- The engagement and report should be limited to compliance matters the auditor is qualified to evaluate. Some of the provisions of debt compliance agreements the auditor is normally in a position to verify are whether principal and interest payments were made when due; whether the proper limitations were maintained on dividends, working capital, and debt ratios; and whether the accounting records were adequate for conducting an ordinary audit. However, determining, for example, whether the client has properly restricted its business activities to the requirements of an agreement or if it has title to pledged property are legal questions that the CPA is not qualified to answer. Furthermore, the *Code of Professional Conduct* prohibits the auditor from practicing as an attorney in such circumstances.
- The auditor should provide a debt compliance letter only for a client for whom he or she has done an audit of the overall financial statements. A debt compliance letter on a matter such as the existence of a current ratio of 2.5 or better would be difficult to do without having conducted a complete audit.
- The auditor's opinion is in the form of a *negative assurance,* stating that nothing came to the auditor's attention that would lead the auditor to believe there was noncompliance.

Figure 24-9 on page 769 is an example of a separate report on debt compliance. Note that the final paragraph restricts distribution of the report to the directly affected parties.

Although debt compliance letters are common, they are only part of a broader set of special reports arising from contractual or regulatory requirements. These types of reports also include (1) presentations of financial statements that are in a form required by contract or regulation that are not in conformity with GAAP or another comprehensive basis of accounting and (2) presentations that are in conformity with one of those bases but are

FIGURE 24-9   **Example of Debt Compliance Report**

Independent Auditor's Report

We have audited, in accordance with generally accepted auditing standards, the balance sheet of XYZ Company as of December 31, 1999, and the related statements of income, retained earnings, and cash flows for the year then ended, and have issued our report thereon dated February 16, 2000.

In connection with our audit, nothing came to our attention that caused us to believe that the Company failed to comply with the terms, covenants, provisions, or conditions of sections XX to XX, inclusive, of the Indenture dated July 21, 1997, with First Bank insofar as they relate to accounting matters. However, our audit was not directed primarily toward obtaining knowledge of such non-compliance.

This report is intended solely for the information and use of the boards of directors and managements of XYZ Company and First Bank and should not be used for any other purpose.

---

incomplete. In such cases, the auditor's report should include a separate paragraph clearly stating what the presentation is intended to present. The separate paragraph should also indicate that the statements are not intended to be a complete presentation or are not a presentation in accordance with GAAP. An additional paragraph should also restrict the distribution of the report to the client and appropriate contractual parties or regulatory agencies, except for certain filings with regulatory agencies that are to be included in a document that is distributed to the general public.

ATTESTATION ENGAGEMENTS

OBJECTIVE 24-4
Distinguish AICPA attestation standards from auditing standards, and know the type of engagements to which they apply.

CPAs have increasingly been asked to perform a variety of audit-like, or *attest,* services for different purposes. An example of an **attestation engagement** is a bank that requests a CPA to state in writing whether an audit client has adhered to all requirements of a loan agreement. As specific types of requests became common, specific standards were issued to provide guidance. This guidance was usually in the form of an interpretation of GAAS. But because those standards relate primarily to historical financial statements prepared in accordance with GAAP and the new services often dealt with other types of information, the guidance became difficult to formulate and communicate effectively without disrupting the cohesiveness of Statements on Auditing Standards.

This problem has been addressed by the profession through the issuance of **Statements on Standards for Attestation Engagements (SSAE)**. The original purpose of the statements was to provide a general framework for and set reasonable boundaries around the attest function, including audits of historical financial statements.

In recent years, the Auditing Standards Board has attempted to distinguish between issues that should be addressed by auditing standards and others that should be addressed by attestation standards even though both are attestations. In general, attestations that deal with providing assurance on historical financial statements, including one or more parts of those statements, are addressed in auditing standards. Examples include audits of financial statements prepared in accordance with GAAP or some other comprehensive basis of accounting, audits of only a balance sheet, and audits of individual accounts. All other forms of attestation are addressed in the attestation standards (an exception is reviews of historical financial statements, which are addressed in SSARS). Attestation standards are established by the Auditing Standards Board following the same process used for auditing standards. Attestation standards are labeled as AT rather than AU. As of the date of publication of this text, standards through SSAE 9 have been issued.

Attestation Standards

In 1986, the Auditing Standards Board issued 11 attestation standards that parallel the 10 generally accepted auditing standards. They are included in Table 24-1 along with generally accepted auditing standards for comparison. The attestation standards are stated in sufficiently general terms to enable practitioners to apply them to any attestation engagement, including new types of engagements that may arise.

The most notable differences in the attestation and generally accepted auditing standards are in general attestation standards 2 and 3. Standard 2 requires the practitioner to have adequate knowledge of the subject matter over which there is attestation. For example, if a practitioner is to attest to a company's compliance with environmental protection laws, the practitioner needs a thorough knowledge of the laws and methods that companies use to assure compliance. Standard 3 requires any assertion about which the practitioner is asserting be capable of evaluation against reasonable criteria and be capable of reasonable estimation or measurement. Again, using the example of environmental protection laws, it may be difficult for the practitioner to conclude whether there is compliance because of measurement difficulties and the lack of specific criteria.

Types of Attestation Engagements

The Auditing Standards Board has consciously made the decision to not attempt to define the potential boundaries of attestation engagements except in conceptual terms because new services are likely to arise. For example, PricewaterhouseCoopers has been attesting to the balloting for the Miss America contest for decades, but attesting to compliance with environmental protection laws started only in recent years.

Specific attestation standards have been developed in the following areas: prospective financial statements, pro forma financial information, reports on internal control over financial reporting, compliance with laws and regulations, agreed-upon procedures engagements, and management's discussion and analysis. Standards have been developed for these types of engagements because practitioners are performing these services in sufficiently large numbers to need more specific guidance than is provided by the general attestation standards. The absence of specific standards for a type of service is not intended to imply that it is inappropriate to perform such a service.

Levels of Service

The attestation standards define three levels of engagements and related forms of conclusions: examinations, reviews, and agreed-upon procedures. In addition, compilation engagements are defined for prospective financial statements.

An **examination** results in a conclusion that is in a *positive* form. In this type of report, the practitioner makes a direct statement as to whether the presentation of the assertions, taken as a whole, conforms with the applicable criteria. An example of an examination report written under the general guidance of the attestation standards is shown in Figure 24-10 (p. 772). This is for an engagement to determine that the rate of return on a hypothetical portfolio, based on a brokerage firm's buy–sell recommendations, is correct as represented in the firm's promotional materials.

A report on an examination is unrestricted as to distribution by the client after it is issued. This means that a client can provide the information being examined and the related report to anyone.

In a **review**, the practitioner provides a conclusion in the form of a *negative assurance*. In this form, the practitioner's report states whether any information came to the practitioner's attention to indicate that the assertions are not presented in all material respects in conformity with the applicable criteria. A review report is also unrestricted in its distribution. It is interesting that review engagements are prohibited in most of the engagements where specified attestation standards have been issued. The reason for the prohibition is the difficulty of setting standards for the limited assurance provided by reviews.

In an **agreed-upon procedures engagement**, the procedures to be performed are agreed upon by the practitioner, the responsible party making the assertions, and the specific persons who are the intended users of the practitioner's report. The degree of assurance being conveyed in such a report varies with the specific procedures agreed to and performed.

TABLE 24-1	Comparison of Attestation Standards and Generally Accepted Auditing Standards

Attestation Standards	Generally Accepted Auditing Standards
General Standards	
1. The engagement shall be performed by a practitioner or practitioners having adequate technical training and proficiency in the attest function.	1. The audit is to be performed by a person or persons having adequate technical training and proficiency as an auditor.
2. The engagement shall be performed by a practitioner or practitioners having adequate knowledge in the subject matter of the assertion.	
3. The practitioner shall perform an engagement only if he or she has reason to believe that the following two conditions exist:	
• The assertion is capable of evaluation against reasonable criteria that either have been established by a recognized body or are stated in the presentation of the assertion in a sufficiently clear and comprehensive manner for a knowledgeable reader to be able to understand them.	
• The assertion is capable of reasonably consistent estimation or measurement using such criteria.	
4. In all matters relating to the engagement, an independence in mental attitude shall be maintained by the practitioner or practitioners.	2. In all matters relating to the assignment, an independence in mental attitude is to be maintained by the auditor or auditors.
5. Due professional care shall be exercised in the performance of the engagement.	3. Due professional care is to be exercised in the performance of the audit and the preparation of the report.
Standards of Field Work	
1. The work shall be adequately planned and assistants, if any, shall be properly supervised.	1. The work is to be adequately planned and assistants, if any, are to be properly supervised.
	2. A sufficient understanding of internal control is to be obtained to plan the audit and to determine the nature, timing, and extent of tests to be performed.
2. Sufficient evidence shall be obtained to provide a reasonable basis for the conclusion that is expressed in the report.	3. Sufficient competent evidential matter is to be obtained through inspection, observation, inquiries, and confirmations to afford a reasonable basis for an opinion regarding the financial statements under audit.
Standards of Reporting	
1. The report shall identify the assertion being reported on and state the character of the engagement.	
2. The report shall state the practitioner's conclusion about whether the assertion is presented in conformity with the established or stated criteria against which it was measured.	1. The report shall state whether the financial statements are presented in accordance with generally accepted accounting principles.
	2. The report shall identify those circumstances in which such principles have not been consistently observed in the current period in relation to the preceding period.
	3. Informative disclosures in the financial statements are to be regarded as reasonably adequate unless otherwise stated in the report.
3. The report shall state all of the practitioner's significant reservations about the engagement and the presentation of the assertion.	4. The report shall either contain an expression of opinion regarding the financial statements, taken as a whole, or an assertion to the effect that an opinion cannot be expressed. When an overall opinion cannot be expressed, the reasons therefor should be stated. In all cases where an auditor's name is associated with financial statements, the report should contain a clear-cut indication of the character of the auditor's work, if any, and the degree of responsibility the auditor is taking.
4. The report on an engagement to evaluate an assertion that has been prepared in conformity with agreed-upon criteria or on an engagement to apply agreed-upon procedures should contain a statement limiting its use to the parties who have agreed upon such criteria or procedures.	

FIGURE 24-10 Example of an Examination Report under the Attestation Standards

To Management
Akron Securities, Inc.

We have examined the accompanying statement for investment performance statistics of the Akron Securities Model Portfolio for the year ended December 31, 1999. Our examination was made in accordance with standards established by the American Institute of Certified Public Accountants and, accordingly, included such procedures as we considered necessary in the circumstances.

In our opinion, the statement of investment performance statistics referred to above presents the investment performance of the Akron Securities Model Portfolio for the year ended December 31, 1999, in conformity with the actual results that would have been obtained if the buy–and–sell recommendations for the portfolio were followed as described in the buy–sell recommendations set forth in Note 1.

> Farnsworth & Jackson, P.C.
> Certified Public Accountants
> Akron, Ohio
> February 12, 2000

Accordingly, such reports are limited in their distribution to only the involved parties, who would have the requisite knowledge about those procedures and the level of assurance resulting from them. The report should include a statement of what procedures management and the practitioner agreed to and what the practitioner found in performing the procedures.

Figure 24-11 summarizes the reporting levels for attestation engagements.

FIGURE 24-11 Types of Engagements and Related Reports

Type of Engagement	Amount of Evidence	Level of Assurance	Form of Conclusion	Distribution
Examination	Extensive	High	Positive	General
Review	Significant	Moderate	Negative	General
Agreed-upon procedures	Varying	Varying	Findings	Limited

The remainder of this chapter discusses three common types of engagements for which detailed attestation standards have been issued.

PROSPECTIVE FINANCIAL STATEMENTS

OBJECTIVE 24-5
Describe special engagements to attest to prospective financial statements.

As implied by the term, **prospective financial statements** refer to predicted or expected financial statements in some future period (income statement) or at some future date (balance sheet). An example is management's predictions of the income statement and balance sheet one year in the future.

Most practitioners believe that there are significant opportunities and potential risks for auditors to provide credibility to prospective financial information. It is well accepted that users want reliable prospective information to aid them in their decision making. If auditors can improve the reliability of the information, information risk is reduced in the same way as in audits of historical financial statements. The risks arise because the actual results obtained may significantly differ from the predicted results in the prospective financial statements. Regulators, users, and others may criticize and sue auditors, even if the prospective statements were fairly stated given the available information at the time they were prepared.

There are two general types of prospective financial statements defined in SSAE 1 (AT 200): forecasts and projections. **Forecasts** are prospective financial statements that present an entity's expected financial position, results of operations, and cash flows, to the *best* of the responsible party's knowledge and belief. These are commonly required by banks as a part of loan applications. **Projections** are prospective financial statements that present an entity's financial position, results of operations, and cash flows, to the best of the responsible party's knowledge and belief, given one or more *hypothetical assumptions*. An example is the preparation of projected financial statements assuming that the company is able to increase the price of its primary product by 10 percent with no reduction in units sold.

one best guess

Both types of prospective financial statements are commonly prepared by management, but CPA firms have begun to associate their names with these statements only in recent years. A considerable body of literature has been developed to assist responsible parties in the preparation of both forecasts and projections. This guidance, along with guidance for independent accountants, is presented in the AICPA *Guide for Prospective Financial Statements*. The guidance to preparers constitutes a set of established criteria against which an attestation engagement can be framed.

Prospective financial statements are for either *general* or *limited* use. General use refers to use by any third party. An example of general use is the inclusion of a financial forecast in a prospectus for the sale of hospital bonds. Limited use refers to use by third parties with whom the responsible party is negotiating directly. An example of limited use is the inclusion of a financial projection in a bank loan application document.

Forecasts can be provided for both general and limited use, but projections are restricted to the latter. This is because limited users are in a position to obtain a better understanding of the prospective statements and related circumstances than other parties. For example, a limited user such as a potential venture capital investor can ask the responsible party about the hypothetical assumptions in a projection, whereas a removed user such as a reader of a prospectus cannot. Because users may have difficulty dealing with the meaning of hypothetical assumptions without obtaining additional information, the standards prohibit their general use. An exception to this rule is that a projection may be issued as a supplement to a forecast for general use.

The following types of engagements are permissible for prospective financial statements: an examination, a compilation, or an agreed-upon procedures engagement. Only an examination, which is studied in the next section, is dealt with in this chapter.

An engagement to review a forecast or projection is prohibited. The reason is that a forecast or projection is essentially the result of mechanically applying a set of significant assumptions. It is relatively easy to define an examination as obtaining satisfaction as to the completeness and reasonableness of all the assumptions, and to define a compilation as primarily involving the computational accuracy of the statements, and not the reasonableness of the assumptions. It is difficult to define a meaningful middle ground. For example, none of the assumptions could be excluded because they are all significant. Therefore, being "moderately satisfied" about the assumptions, which is implied by a review service, is likely to confuse users. Rather than confuse users with this dilemma, the AICPA decided in SSAE 1 to allow only the clearer alternatives.

SSAE 1 makes it clear that the practitioner is not attesting to the accuracy of the prospective financial statements. Instead the focus is on examining the underlying assumptions and the preparation and presentation of the forecast or projection. Accordingly, the following are the four elements of an examination of forecasts and projections:

1. Evaluating the preparation of the prospective financial statements
2. Evaluating the support underlying the assumptions
3. Evaluating the presentation of the prospective financial statements for conformity with AICPA presentation guidelines
4. Issuing an examination report

FIGURE 24-12 Example of a Report on a Forecast

We have examined the accompanying forecasted balance sheet, statements of income, retained earnings, and cash flows of Allstar, Inc., as of December 31, 2000, and for the year then ending. Our examination was made in accordance with standards for an examination of a forecast established by the American Institute of Certified Public Accountants and, accordingly, included such procedures as we considered necessary to evaluate both the assumptions used by management and the preparation and presentation of the forecast.

In our opinion, the accompanying forecast is presented in conformity with guidelines for presentation of a forecast established by the American Institute of Certified Public Accountants, and the underlying assumptions provide a reasonable basis for management's forecast. However, there will usually be differences between the forecasted and actual results, because events and circumstances frequently do not occur as expected, and those differences may be material. We have no responsibility to update this report for events and circumstances occurring after the date of this report.

Manford & Brown
Certified Public Accountants
October 15, 1999

These elements are based primarily on accumulating evidence about the completeness and reasonableness of the underlying assumptions as disclosed in the prospective financial statements. This requires the accountant to become familiar with the client's business and industry, to identify the significant matters on which the client's future results are expected to depend ("key factors"), and to determine that appropriate assumptions have been included with respect to these.

The accountant's report on an examination of prospective financial statements should include the following:

- An identification of the prospective financial statements presented
- A statement that the examination of the prospective financial statements was made in accordance with AICPA standards and a brief description of the nature of such an examination
- The accountant's opinion that the prospective financial statements are presented in conformity with AICPA presentation guidelines and that the underlying assumptions provide a reasonable basis for the forecast or a reasonable basis for the projection, given the hypothetical assumptions
- A caveat that the prospective results may not be achieved
- A statement that the accountant assumes no responsibility to update the report for events and circumstances occurring after the date of the report

Figure 24-12 above is an example of a report on an examination of a forecast with an unqualified opinion. Note that the date of the forecasted balance sheet is more than a year later than the report date.

POTENTIAL LEGAL LIABILITY IN PROSPECTIVE FINANCIAL STATEMENTS

A partner in one of the Big Five CPA firms stated recently in an informal meeting that his firm has decided not to do assurance engagements for prospective financial statements because of litigation costs. He reported that his firm calculated their total revenues (not profits) from all prospective financial statement engagements and also calculated all legal costs, including partner and staff time incurred to defend against lawsuits involving these engagements. The firm calculated that legal costs exceeded revenues. The partner said, "You don't have to be a rocket scientist to conclude that if legal costs exceed revenues it's a bad business. Users sue when actual profits are less favorable than those projected regardless of what the CPA firm's report says."

A CPA firm may be engaged to report on an entity's internal control. This may be done for a regular audit client who wants such a report for internal use, for meeting the requirements of a regulatory agency, or for an entity such as an IT service center for the use of its customers and their auditors. The report may cover all or part of internal control, and it may relate to the controls in effect as of a specified date or during a specified period. Reporting on internal control over financial reporting is the subject of SSAE 2.

A major reason for an attestation standard on internal control results from the emphasis on the importance of internal controls by Congress and regulatory agencies. For example, the Federal Deposit Insurance Corporation Improvement Act of 1991 requires management of federally insured depository institutions such as banks and thrifts to report on internal control effectiveness, and the act requires a CPA firm to attest to the report. Other legislative and regulatory proposals have suggested similar requirements for reporting on internal control.

When auditors perform an audit of financial statements, they obtain an understanding of internal control in accordance with the second standard of field work. The scope of the study depends on the extent to which the auditor plans to reduce assessed control risk for the purpose of determining the nature, timing, and extent of related substantive tests. When reduced control risk is planned, the auditor considers the internal controls in effect for the entire audit period. Certain areas are *not* examined if reduced control risk in those areas is not planned.

When the practitioner is engaged to report on internal control under the attestation standards, however, all areas of internal control are included unless specifically excluded by agreement. Also, the time period covered is a matter of agreement. All agreements are made between the auditor and management, but regulatory agency requirements and customers' needs must be considered.

The requirements for an examination of management's assertion about the effectiveness of an entity's internal control are similar to the procedures for assessing control risk on an audit. The following five steps are performed in an examination:

1. *Plan the engagement.* The practitioner, client, and others involved first agree on the areas to be covered and the timing of the study. The practitioner then obtains information about the client's business, industry and regulatory requirements, and the nature of accounting transactions and the record-keeping system. This information provides a basis for planning the most effective approach to the remaining steps.
2. *Obtain an understanding of internal control.* The practitioner obtains detailed information about the transactions, their flow through the system, transaction-related audit objectives, and control activities used to achieve control. The procedures for accomplishing this step are similar to those discussed in Chapter 10.
3. *Evaluate the design effectiveness of controls.* The practitioner should evaluate whether the controls are suitably designed to prevent or detect misstatements in specific financial statement assertions.
4. *Test and evaluate the operating effectiveness of the controls.* These tests are concerned with how the controls are applied and their consistency of application. The methodology for these procedures is similar to the procedures for performing tests of controls in an audit.
5. *Form an opinion about management's assertion regarding the effectiveness of internal control.* The auditor evaluates the results of the tests of controls and any identified control deficiencies to evaluate whether management's assertion about the effectiveness of internal control is fairly stated. A material weakness in internal control generally precludes management from asserting that the entity has effective internal control. Depending on the significance of the weakness, management may qualify its

OBJECTIVE 24-6
Understand special engagements to attest to internal control, including controls over electronic commerce.

Comparison to Requirements for Audits

Requirements for an Examination of the Effectiveness of Internal Control

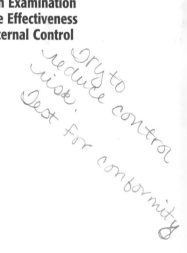

assertion that internal control is effective. The existence of reportable conditions does not preclude management's asserting that internal control is effective, but the practitioner should evaluate whether individual reportable conditions, or the combined effects of reportable conditions, represent a material weakness. Reportable conditions and material weaknesses are defined in SAS 60 (AU 325) and were discussed in Chapter 10. Any reportable conditions or material weaknesses should be communicated to the audit committee or equivalent level.

Figure 24-13 is an example of the report used when the practitioner has examined management's assertion about the effectiveness of an entity's internal control as of a specified date.

FIGURE 24-13 **Example of Report on Effectiveness of Internal Control Over Financial Reporting**

We have examined management's assertion that XYZ Company maintained effective internal control over financial reporting as of September 30, 1999, included in the accompanying management report.

Our examination was made in accordance with standards established by the American Institute of Certified Public Accountants and, accordingly, included obtaining an understanding of internal control over financial reporting, testing, and evaluating the design and operating effectiveness of internal control, and such other procedures as we considered necessary in the circumstances. We believe that our examination provides a reasonable basis for our opinion.

Because of inherent limitations in any internal control, errors or fraud may occur and not be detected. Also, projection of any evaluation of the internal control over financial reporting to future periods is subject to the risk that internal control may become inadequate because of changes in conditions, or that the degree of compliance with the policies or procedures may deteriorate.

In our opinion, management's assertion that XYZ Company maintained effective internal control over financial reporting as of September 30, 1999, is fairly stated, in all material respects, based upon the criteria established in *Internal Control–Integrated Framework* issued by the Committee of Sponsoring Organizations of the Treadway Commission.

This section discussed an examination attestation engagement on the effectiveness of internal control over financial reporting. Two additional attestation services involving internal controls are discussed in the following sections. Reports on internal control for service organizations are attestation engagements, but the guidance for these services is found in the auditing standards. Reports on business practices and controls over electronic commerce are attestation engagements developed from the AICPA Special Committee on Assurance Services.

Internal Control for Service Organizations

Many companies use the services of other organizations for executing and recording transactions and processing related data. For example, many companies rely on outside service organizations to process payroll transactions. Bank trust departments and similar organizations may invest and hold assets for employee benefit plans and also provide accounting information. In assessing control risk for transactions and cycles for these types of service organizations, the auditor should first assess the effect of the service organization on the client's financial statements. The use of such reports will depend on the significance of the assertions involved, the extent of controls at the service organization, and whether auditable data is in the user organization's possession. In some cases, the auditor may rely on the service organization's auditor's report on internal controls at the service organization in obtaining an understanding of internal control and assessing control risk.

SAS 70 (AU 324) provides guidance to (1) auditors who issue reports on the internal control of service organizations *(service auditors)* and (2) auditors of user organizations *(user auditors)* about reliance on the service auditor's report. Service auditors may issue two types of reports:

- Report on controls placed in operation
- Report on controls placed in operation and tests of operating effectiveness

A report on controls placed in operation is helpful in obtaining an understanding of internal control to plan the audit. However, evidence concerning the operating effectiveness of controls is necessary to assess control risk below the maximum. This evidence can be based on the service auditor's report on controls placed in operation and tests of operating effectiveness. This evidence can also come from tests of the user organization's controls over the activities of the service organization, or the user auditor may perform appropriate tests at the service organization. If the user auditor decides to rely on the service auditor's report, he or she should make appropriate inquiries regarding the service auditor's reputation. The user auditor should not make reference to the report of the service auditor in his or her opinion on the user organization's financial statements.

WebTrust Business Practices and Controls Over Electronic Commerce

WebTrust is a service designed to provide reasonable assurance that a company's web site complies with certain principles and criteria for business-to-consumer electronic commerce relating to disclosure of business practices, transaction integrity, and information integrity. A site that meets the *WebTrust* principles is eligible to display the *WebTrust* electronic seal on its transaction or order page.

The *WebTrust* service was developed jointly by the AICPA and the Canadian Institute of Chartered Accountants (CICA). *WebTrust* is an attest service and is performed in the United States under SSAE 1. The *WebTrust* seal is licensed to CPA firms under a licensing agreement in which the firm agrees to follow the professional standards for the program that were developed by a joint AICPA/CICA task force, and take the required continuing education programs on the *WebTrust* principles.

A site is allowed to retain the *WebTrust* seal as long as it remains in compliance with the *WebTrust* principles. These principles require that the CPA verify continued compliance at least every 90 days. The *WebTrust* report for a site is found by clicking on the *WebTrust* seal. Figure 24-14 (p. 778) is an example of a *WebTrust* report.

AGREED-UPON PROCEDURES ENGAGEMENTS

OBJECTIVE 24-7
Describe agreed-upon procedures engagements.

When the auditor and management or a third-party user agree that the audit will be limited to certain specific audit procedures, it is referred to as an agreed-upon procedures engagement. Many practitioners refer to these as procedures and findings engagements because the report emphasizes the audit procedures performed and the findings when the procedures were completed.

The primary appeal to practitioners of agreed-upon procedures engagements is making management or a third-party user specify the procedures they want performed. Imagine the difficulty a CPA firm would face if it agreed to issue an opinion to a federal agency that a company complied with federal affirmative action laws for a 2-year period under compliance attestation SSAE 3. Now assume that the federal agency was willing to specify 10 audit procedures the CPA firm was to perform, which would satisfy the agency. For example, one procedure is to determine that the standard company's employment application form had no reference to age, gender, or race. Assuming the CPA firm and federal agency could agree on the procedures, many CPA firms would be willing to perform the procedures and issue a report of the related findings.

Several professional standards address agreed-upon procedures engagements, but the two primary ones are SAS 75 and SSAE 4. SAS 75 and SSAE 4 are referred to as mirror standards because of their similarity. The two primary differences are as follows:

1. The SASs deal with financial statement items, whereas the SSAEs deal with nonfinancial statement subject matter.

FIGURE 24-14   **Example of a *WebTrust* Report**

We have examined the assertion *[hot link to management's assertion]* by XYZ Company regarding the disclosure of its electronic commerce business practices on its web site and the effectiveness of its controls over transaction integrity and information protection for electronic commerce at *[web site address]* during the period August 1, 1999, through October 31, 1999.

These electronic disclosures and controls are the responsibility of XYZ Company's management. Our responsibility is to express an opinion on management's assertions with regards to the AICPA/CICA *WebTrust* Criteria *[hot link]* based on our examination.

Our examination was conducted in accordance with attestation standards established by the American Institute of Certified Public Accountants and, accordingly, included (1) obtaining an understanding of XYZ Company's electronic commerce business practices and its controls over the processing of electronic commerce transactions and the protection of related private customer information, (2) selectively testing transactions executed in accordance with disclosed business practices, (3) testing and evaluating the operating effectiveness of controls, and (4) performing such other procedures as we considered necessary in the circumstances. We believe that our examination provides a reasonable basis for our opinion.

Because of inherent limitations in controls, errors or fraud may occur and not be detected. Furthermore, the projection of any conclusions, based on our findings, to future periods is subject to the risk that (1) changes made to the system or controls, (2) changes in processing requirements, or (3) changes required because of the passage of time may alter the validity of such conclusions.

In our opinion, during the period August 1, 1999, through October 31, 1999, XYZ Company, in all material respects, based on the AICPA/CICA *WebTrust* Criteria:

- disclosed its business practices for electronic commerce transactions and executed transactions in accordance with its disclosed business practices,
- maintained effective controls to provide reasonable assurance that customers' orders placed using electronic commerce were completed and billed as agreed, and,
- maintained effective controls to provide reasonable assurance that private customer information obtained as a result of electronic commerce was protected from uses not related to XYZ's business.

The CPA *WebTrust* seal of assurance on XYZ's web site for electronic commerce constitutes a symbolic representation of the contents of this report and it is not intended, nor should it be construed, to update this report or provide any additional assurance.

This report does not include any representation as to the quality of XYZ's goods or services nor their suitability for any customer's intended purpose.

2. Management must provide a written assertion for an SSAE engagement but not for an SAS engagement.

Agreed-Upon
Procedures Report

An example of an SAS 75 engagement is performing agreed-upon procedures on the gross sales account for a lease agreement. These engagements are commonly done for retail stores when the store leases from the building owner on the basis of a percent of gross sales. Figure 24-15 illustrates a report for such an engagement, including the three procedures agreed upon and the two findings resulting from the procedures performed.

Agreed-upon procedures engagements under the SSAEs have been permitted and commonly performed since the original issue of the attestation standards. SSAE 4 provides additional guidance to practitioners performing these engagements. An example of such an engagement is performing agreed-upon procedures for a mutual fund in calculating the internal rate of return, beta risk for measuring volatility, and other relevant information pertinent to investors.

FIGURE 24-15 **Example of an Agreed-Upon Procedures Report**

Report of Independent Certified Public Accountants

Board of Directors and Management of Morgil Company

We have performed the procedures enumerated below, which were agreed to by the Board of Directors and management of Morgil Company, solely to assist you in determining the amount of gross sales as defined in the lease agreement dated September 1, 1995, between Rocklin, Inc., lessor, and Morgil Company, lessee, for the year ended December 31, 1999. This engagement to apply agreed-upon procedures was performed in accordance with standards established by the American Institute of Certified Public Accountants. The sufficiency of these procedures is solely the responsibility of the Board of Directors and management of Morgil Company. Consequently, we make no representation regarding the sufficiency of the procedures described below either for the purpose for which this report has been requested or for any other purpose.

The procedures we performed are summarized as follows:

1. We obtained a schedule prepared by management, which reflected gross sales, as defined
2. above, for the year ended December 31, 1999, of $35,675,000.
   We obtained the weekly cash reports submitted by the store manager for the year. These reports show information on gross sales, cash register readings, sales taxes, returns, and allow-
3. ances for discounts and other information.
   We compared monthly summarizations of these reports with the schedule of gross sales and compared approximately 5 percent of the daily cash net receipts shown in the weekly cash reports with the bank statements.

Based solely on the foregoing procedures, we found:

1. The daily cash net receipts shown in the weekly cash reports that we compared with the bank statements to be in agreement.
2. The monthly summarizations to be in agreement with the schedule of gross sales we obtained from management.

These agreed-upon procedures do not constitute an audit or review of financial statements or any part thereof, the objective of which is the expression of an opinion or limited assurance on the financial statements or a part thereof. Accordingly, we do not express such an opinion. Had we performed additional procedures, other matters might have come to our attention that would have been reported to you.

This report is intended solely for the use of the specified users listed and should not be used by those who have not agreed to the procedures and taken responsibility for the sufficiency of the procedures for their purposes.

Renfor Malik and Co CPAs LLP

Chicago, Illinois

SUMMARY

This chapter described many of the special reports and services offered by CPAs. The types of services offered continues to grow and expand as society demands assurance on new and different types of information. Depending on the nature of the service, the guidance for performance of the service may come from auditing standards, attestation standards, or the accounting and review services standards. Table 24-2 provides a summary and examples of the primary categories of services discussed in this chapter.

Type of Engagement	Example	Source of Authoritative Support
Audits of historical financial statements prepared in accordance with GAAP	Audit of General Mills' financial statements	Auditing standards
Reviews or compilations of historical financial statements prepared in accordance with GAAP	Review of Ron's Shoe Store's quarterly financial statements	Accounting and review services standards for nonpublic companies; auditing standards for public companies
Audits or limited assurance engagements other than audits, reviews, or compilations of historical financial statements prepared in accordance with GAAP	Audit of Ron's Shoe Store's ending balance in inventory	Auditing standards
Attestation engagements under the attestation standards	Attestation of General Mills' forecasted financial statements	Attestation standards

ESSENTIAL TERMS

Agreed-upon procedures engagement—an engagement in which the procedures to be performed are agreed upon by the practitioner, the responsible party making the assertions, and the intended users of the practitioner's report; the practitioner's report is presented in the form of a negative assurance

Attestation engagement—one in which a practitioner is engaged to issue a written communication that expresses a conclusion with respect to the reliability of an assertion that is the responsibility of another party

Compilation service—a nonaudit engagement in which the accountant undertakes to present, in the form of financial statements, information that is the representation of management, without undertaking to express any assurance on the statements

Examination—an attest engagement that results in a positive assurance as to whether or not the assertions under examination conform with the applicable criteria

Forecasts—prospective financial statements that present an entity's expected financial position, results of operations, and cash flows for future periods, to the best of the responsible party's knowledge and belief

Projections—prospective financial statements that present an entity's financial position and results of operations and cash flows for future periods, to the best of the responsible party's knowledge and belief, given one or more hypothetical assumptions

Prospective financial statements—financial statements that deal with expected future data rather than with historical data

Review—an attestation engagement that results in a negative assurance as to the practitioner's awareness of any information indicating that the assertions are not presented in conformity with the applicable criteria

Review service (SSARS review)—a review of unaudited financial statements designed to provide limited assurance that no material modifications need be made to the statements in order for them to be in conformity with generally accepted accounting principles or, if applicable, with another comprehensive basis of accounting

SAS 71 reviews—reviews of interim, unaudited financial information performed to help public companies meet their reporting responsibilities to regulatory agencies

Statements on Standards for Accounting and Review Services (SSARS)—standards issued by the AICPA Accounting and Review Services Committee that govern the CPA's association with unaudited financial statements of nonpublic companies

Statements on Standards for Attestation Engagements (SSAE)—statements issued by the AICPA to provide a conceptual framework for various types of attestation services

WebTrust—an attestation service designed to provide reasonable assurance that a company's web site complies with certain principles and criteria for business-to-consumer electronic commerce relating to disclosure of business practices, transaction integrity, and information integrity

24-1 (Objective 24-1)   What is meant by the term level of assurance? How does the level of assurance differ for an audit of historical financial statements, a review, and a compilation?

24-2 (Objective 24-1)   What is a negative assurance? Why is it used in a review engagement report?

24-3 (Objective 24-1)   Distinguish between compilation and review of financial statements. What is the level of assurance for each?

24-4 (Objective 24-1)   Distinguish the three forms of compilation reports that a CPA can provide to clients.

24-5 (Objective 24-1)   List five things that are required of an auditor by SSARS for a compilation.

24-6 (Objective 24-1)   What steps should auditors take if during a compilation engagement they become aware that the financial statements are misleading?

24-7 (Objective 24-1)   What procedures should the auditor use to obtain the information necessary to give the level of assurance required of reviews of financial statements?

24-8 (Objective 24-1)   What should auditors do if during a review of financial statements they discover that generally accepted accounting principles are not being followed?

24-9 (Objectives 24-1, 24-2)   What are the differences between the review reports covered by SSARS and SAS 71?

24-10 (Objective 24-2)   Explain why a review of interim financial statements may provide a greater level of assurance than do SSARS reviews.

24-11 (Objective 24-3)   What is the purpose of an engagement of specified elements, accounts, or items? List the four special requirements for reports on specified elements, accounts, or items.

24-12 (Objective 24-3)   State the reporting requirements for statements prepared on a basis other than GAAP.

24-13 (Objective 24-3)   The Absco Corporation has requested that Herb Germany, CPA, provide a report to the Northern State Bank as to the existence or nonexistence of certain loan conditions. The conditions to be reported on are the working capital ratio, dividends paid on preferred stock, aging of accounts receivable, and competency of management. This is Herb's first experience with Absco. Should Herb accept this engagement? Substantiate your answer.

24-14 (Objective 24-3)   Explain what is meant by information accompanying basic financial statements. Provide two examples of such information. What levels of assurance may the CPA offer for this information?

24-15 (Objective 24-4)   Define what is meant by attestation standards. Distinguish between attestation standards and generally accepted auditing standards.

24-16 (Objective 24-5)   Explain what is meant by prospective financial statements and distinguish between forecasts and projections. What four things are involved in an examination of prospective financial statements?

24-17 (Objective 24-6)   What is an engagement to report on internal control? Explain how the requirements differ from the responsibilities the auditor has for obtaining an understanding of internal control and tests of controls in an audit.

24-18 (Objective 24-6)   Identify the five steps for obtaining an understanding of internal control and tests of controls.

24-19 (Objective 24-6)   Indicate the two types of reports that can be issued on the internal control of service organizations. Indicate how each would affect the assessment of control risk by the user organization's auditor.

24-20 (Objective 24-1) The following are miscellaneous questions about compilation and review services. Choose the best response.

a. A CPA has been engaged to perform review services for a client. Identify which of the following is a correct statement.
   (1) The CPA must perform the basic audit procedures necessary to determine that the statements are in conformity with GAAP.
   (2) The financial statements are primarily representations of the CPA.
   (3) The CPA may prepare the statements from the books but may not assist in adjusting and closing the books.
   (4) The CPA is performing an accounting service rather than an audit of the financial statements.

b. It is acceptable for a CPA to be associated with financial statements when he or she is not independent with respect to the client and still issue a substantially unmodified report for which of the following:
   (1) Audits of companies following GAAP.
   (2) Audits of companies on a comprehensive basis of accounting other than GAAP.
   (3) Compilation of financial statements following GAAP.
   (4) Review of financial statements following GAAP.

c. A CPA is performing review services for a small, closely held manufacturing company. As a part of the follow-up of a significant decrease in the gross margin for the current year, the CPA discovers that there are no supporting documents for $40,000 of disbursements. The chief financial officer assures her that the disbursements are proper. What should the CPA do?
   (1) Include the unsupported disbursements without further work in the statements on the grounds that she is not doing an audit.
   (2) Modify the review opinion or withdraw from the engagement unless the unsupported disbursements are satisfactorily explained.
   (3) Exclude the unsupported disbursements from the statements.
   (4) Obtain a written representation from the chief financial officer that the disbursements are proper and should be included in the current financial statements.

d. Which of the following best describes the responsibility of the CPA in performing compilation services for a company?
   (1) The CPA must understand the client's business and accounting methods and read the financial statements for reasonableness.
   (2) The CPA has to satisfy only himself or herself that the financial statements were prepared in conformity with GAAP.
   (3) The CPA should obtain an understanding of internal control and perform tests of controls.
   (4) The CPA is relieved of any responsibility to third parties.

e. Frank, CPA, performed compilation services omitting substantially all disclosures for a client and issued the appropriate report. Three months after the statements were issued, the client informed Frank that the statements had been given to a bank for a secured loan. Which of the following is appropriate under these circumstances?
   (1) Frank must revise the statements to include appropriate footnotes and attach a revised disclaimer of opinion.
   (2) The client may give the statements to the banker as long as Frank's disclaimer of opinion accompanies the statements.
   (3) The client should retype the statements on plain paper and send them to the banker without Frank's report.
   (4) The client may let the banker review the statements and take notes but should not give the banker a copy of the statements.

f. In performing a compilation of financial statements of a nonpublic entity, the accountant decides that modification of the standard report is not adequate to indicate deficiencies in the financial statements taken as a whole, and the client is not willing to correct the deficiencies. The accountant should therefore
   (1) perform a review of the financial statements.
   (2) issue a special report.
   (3) withdraw from the engagement.
   (4) express an adverse audit opinion.

24-21 (Objective 24-3)   The following questions concern reports issued by auditors, other than those on historical financial statements. Choose the best response.

a. Which of the generally accepted auditing standards of reporting would *not* normally apply to special reports such as cash basis statements?
   (1) First standard.
   (2) Second standard.
   (3) Third standard.
   (4) Fourth standard.

b. An auditor is reporting on cash basis financial statements. These statements are best referred to in his or her opinion by which of the following descriptions?
   (1) Cash receipts and disbursements and the assets and liabilities arising from cash transactions.
   (2) Financial position and results of operations arising from cash transactions.
   (3) Balance sheet and income statements resulting from cash transactions.
   (4) Cash balance sheet and the source and application of funds.

c. Which of the following statements with respect to an auditor's report expressing an opinion on a specific item on a financial statement is correct?
   (1) Materiality must be related to the specific item rather than to the financial statements taken as a whole.
   (2) Such a report can be expressed only if the auditor is also engaged to audit the entire set of financial statements.
   (3) The attention devoted to the specified item is usually less than it would be if the financial statements taken as a whole were being audited.
   (4) The auditor who has issued an adverse opinion on the financial statements taken as a whole can never express an opinion on a specified item in these financial statements.

d. When asked to perform an audit to express an opinion on one or more specified elements, accounts, or items of a financial statement, the auditor
   (1) may *not* describe auditing procedures applied.
   (2) should advise the client that the opinion can be issued only if the financial statements have been audited and found to be fairly presented.
   (3) may assume that the first standard of reporting with respect to GAAP does *not* apply.
   (4) should comply with the request only if they constitute a major portion of the financial statements on which an auditor has disclaimed an opinion based on an audit.

24-22 (Objective 24-3)   The following questions concern information accompanying basic financial statements. Choose the best response.

a. Which of the following best describes the auditor's reporting responsibility concerning information accompanying the basic financial statements in an auditor-submitted document?
   (1) The auditor has no reporting responsibility concerning information accompanying the basic financial statements.
   (2) The auditor should report on the information accompanying the basic financial statements only if he or she participated in its preparation.

(3) The auditor should report on the information accompanying the basic financial statements only if he or she did not participate in its preparation.

(4) The auditor should report on all the information included in the document.

b. Ansman, CPA, has been requested by a client, Rainco Corp., to prepare information in addition to the basic financial statements for this year's audit engagement. Which of the following is the best reason for Rainco's requesting the additional information?

(1) To provide an opinion about the supplemental information when certain items are not in accordance with GAAP.

(2) To provide Rainco's creditors a greater degree of assurance as to the financial soundness of the company.

(3) To provide Rainco's management with information to supplement and analyze the basic financial statements.

(4) To provide the documentation required by the SEC in anticipation of a public offering of Rainco's stock.

c. Ansman, CPA, has been requested by a client, Rainco Corp., to prepare additional information accompanying the basic financial statements for this year's audit engagement. In issuing the additional information, Ansman must be certain to

(1) issue a standard short-form report on the same engagement.

(2) include a description of the scope of the audit in more detail than the description in the usual short-form report.

(3) state the source of any statistical data and that such data have not been subjected to the same auditing procedures as the basic financial statements.

(4) maintain a clear-cut distinction between the management's representations and the auditor's representations.

d. Information accompanying basic financial statements should *not* include

(1) exceptions or reservations to the standard short-form auditor's report.

(2) details of items in basic financial statements.

(3) statistical data.

(4) explanatory comments.

24-23 (Objectives 24-4, 24-5, 24-6) The following questions concern attestation engagements. Choose the best response.

a. Which of the following professional services would be considered an attestation engagement?

(1) A management consulting engagement to provide IT advice to a client.

(2) An engagement to report on compliance with statutory requirements.

(3) An income tax engagement to prepare federal and state tax returns.

(4) A compilation of financial statements from a client's accounting records.

b. Which of the following statements concerning prospective financial statements is correct?

(1) Only a financial forecast would normally be appropriate for limited use.

(2) Only a financial projection would normally be appropriate for general use.

(3) Any type of prospective financial statements would normally be appropriate for limited use.

(4) Any type of prospective financial statement would normally be appropriate for general use.

c. Which of the following best describes a CPA's engagement to report on an entity's internal control?

(1) An attestation engagement to examine and report on management's written assertions about the effectiveness of its internal control.

(2) An audit engagement to render an opinion on the entity's internal control.

(3) A prospective engagement to project, for a period not to exceed 1 year, and report on the expected benefits of the entity's internal control.

(4) A consulting engagement to provide constructive advice to the entity on its internal control.

24-24 (Objective 24-3)   As a part of the audit of Ren Gold Manufacturing Company, management requests basic financial statements, and separately, the same basic financial statements accompanied by additional information. Management informs you that the intent is to use the basic financial statements for bankers, other creditors, and the two owners who are not involved in management. The basic financial statements accompanied by the additional information are to be used only by management. Management requests the inclusion of specific information but asks that no audit work be done beyond what is needed for the basic financial statements. The following is requested:

1. A schedule of insurance in force.
2. The auditor's feelings about the adequacy of the insurance coverage.
3. A 5-year summary of the most important company ratios. The appropriate ratios are to be determined at the auditor's discretion.
4. A schedule of notes payable accompanied by interest rates, collateral, and a payment schedule.
5. An aged trial balance of accounts receivable and evaluation of the adequacy of the allowance for uncollectible accounts.
6. A summary of fixed asset additions.
7. Material weaknesses in internal control and recommendations to improve internal control.

Required
    a. What is the difference between basic financial statements and additional information?
    b. What are the purposes of additional information accompanying basic financial statements?
    c. For the previously listed items (1 through 7), state which ones could appropriately be included as additional information. Give reasons for your answer.
    d. Identify three other items that may appropriately be included as additional information.
    e. Assume that an unqualified opinion is proper for the basic financial statements report, that no testing was done beyond that required for the basic financial statements report, and that only appropriate information is included in the additional information. Write the proper auditor's report.

24-25 (Objective 24-3)   You have been requested by the management of J. L. Lockwood Co. to issue a debt compliance letter as a part of the audit of Taylor Fruit Farms, Inc. J. L. Lockwood Co. is a supplier of irrigation equipment. Much of the equipment, including that supplied to Taylor, is sold on a secured contract basis. Taylor Fruit Farms is an audit client of yours, but Lockwood is not. In addition to the present equipment, Lockwood informs you they are evaluating whether they should sell another $500,000 of equipment to Taylor Fruit Farms.

You have been requested to send Lockwood a debt compliance letter concerning the following matters:

1. The current ratio has exceeded 2.0 in each quarter of the unaudited statements prepared by management and the annual audited statements.
2. Total owners' equity is more than $800,000.
3. The company has not violated any of the legal requirements of California fruit-growing regulations.
4. Management is competent and has made reasonable business decisions in the past 3 years.
5. Management owns an option to buy additional fruit land adjacent to the company's present property.

Required
    a. Define the purpose of a debt compliance letter.
    b. Why is it necessary to conduct an audit of a company before it is acceptable to issue a debt compliance letter?

c. For which of the five requested items is it acceptable for a CPA firm to issue a debt compliance letter? Give reasons for your answer.

24-26 (Objective 24-3)   Independent CPAs customarily issue two types of auditor's reports in connection with an audit of financial statements: an *auditor's report* in connection with financial statements intended for publication and a *report on additional information accompanying basic financial statements* for the purposes of management and other parties.

Required

a. Outline in *general terms* the kinds of materials that are commonly included in the additional information other than those commonly included in basic financial statements.

b. Does the auditor assume the same degree of responsibility for additional information that he or she assumes for individual items in the customary basic financial statements (balance sheet and statements of income, retained earnings, and cash flows)? State the reasons for your answer.*

24-27 (Objective 24-1)   Evaluate the following comments about compiled financial statements: "When a CPA associates his or her name with compiled financial statements, his or her only responsibility is to the client and that is limited to the proper summarization and presentation on the financial statements of information provided by the client. The opinion clearly states that the auditor has not conducted an audit and does not express an opinion on this fair presentation. If users rely on compiled financial statements, they do so at their own risk and should never be able to hold the CPA responsible for inadequate performance. Users should interpret the financial statements as if they had been prepared by management."

24-28 (Objective 24-1)   The items listed below represent a series of unrelated procedures that an accountant may consider performing in an engagement to review or compile the financial statements of a nonpublic entity. Procedures may apply to only one, both, or neither type of engagement.

1. The accountant should establish an understanding with the entity regarding the nature and limitations of the services to be performed.
2. The accountant should make inquiries concerning actions taken at the board of directors' meetings.
3. The accountant should obtain a level of knowledge of the accounting principles and practices of the entity's industry.
4. The accountant should obtain an understanding of the entity's internal control.
5. The accountant should perform analytical procedures designed to identify relationships that appear to be unusual.
6. The auditor should send a letter of inquiry to the entity's attorney to corroborate the information furnished by management concerning litigation.
7. The accountant should obtain a management representation letter from the entity.
8. The accountant should make inquiries about events subsequent to the date of the financial statements that would have a material effect on the financial statements.
9. The accountant should perform a physical examination of inventory.

Required

a. Indicate which procedures are required to be performed on a review engagement.
b. Indicate which procedures are required to be performed on a compilation engagement.*

24-29 (Objective 24-1)   You are doing review services and the related tax work for Regency Tools, Inc., a tool and die company with $2,000,000 in sales. Inventory is recorded at $125,000. Prior-year unaudited statements, presented by the company without assistance

*AICPA adapted.

from a CPA firm, disclose that the inventory is based on "historical cost estimated by management." You determine four facts:

1. The company has been growing steadily for the past 5 years.
2. The unit cost of the typical material used by Regency Tools has increased dramatically for several years.
3. The inventory cost has been approximately $125,000 for 5 years.
4. Management intends to use a value of $125,000 again for the current year.

When you discuss with management the need to get a physical count and an accurate inventory, the response is negative. Management is concerned about the effect on property and income taxes of a more realistic inventory. The company has never been audited and has followed this practice for years. You are convinced, based on inquiry and ratio analysis, that a conservative evaluation would be $500,000 at historical cost.

Required

    a. What are the generally accepted accounting principle requirements for valuation and disclosure of inventory for unaudited financial statements?
    b. Identify the potential legal and professional problems that you face in this situation.
    c. What procedures would you normally follow for review services when the inventory is a material amount? Be as specific as possible.
    d. How should you resolve the problem in this situation? Identify alternatives and evaluate the costs and benefits of each.

24-30 (Objective 24-1) SSARS provide illustrative review procedures for accountants to use as a guideline for conducting reviews. The introduction to the illustrative inquiries states:

> The inquiries to be made in a review of financial statements are a matter of the accountant's judgment. In determining his or her inquiries, an accountant may consider (a) the nature and materiality of the items, (b) the likelihood of misstatement, (c) knowledge obtained during current and previous engagements, (d) the stated qualifications of the entity's accounting personnel, (e) the extent to which a particular item is affected by management's judgment, and (f) inadequacies in the entity's underlying financial data. The following list of inquiries is for illustrative purposes only. The inquiries do not necessarily apply to every engagement, nor are they meant to be all-inclusive.

> The inquiry procedures included in SSARS for the sales and collection cycle are as follows:

Revenue
1. Are revenues from the sale of major products and services recognized in the appropriate period?

Receivables
1. Has an adequate allowance been made for doubtful accounts?
2. Have receivables considered uncollectible been written off?
3. If appropriate, has interest been reflected?
4. Has a proper cutoff of sales transactions been made?
5. Are there any receivables from employees and related parties?
6. Are any receivables pledged, discounted, or factored?
7. Have receivables been properly classified between current and noncurrent?

Required

    a. What other information about accounts receivable and revenue, besides the items listed, would the accountant have to obtain?
    b. Compare the illustrative procedures for review services and those commonly performed for audits. What are the major differences?
    c. Of whom should the accountant make inquiries in a small closely held company?

d. Under what circumstances would procedures beyond those illustrated likely be performed? Be specific.

e. Compare the levels of achieved assurance for review services and audits. Is the achieved level much higher for audits, somewhat higher, or approximately the same? Give reasons for your answer.

24-31 (Objective 24-2) Lucia Johnson, of Johnson and Lecy, CPAs, has completed the first-year audit of Tidwell Publishing Co., a publicly held company, for the year ended December 31, 1999. She has now been asked to do a review of interim financial statements under SAS 71 (AU 722) for the quarter ended March 31, 2000.

Johnson has never done an SAS 71 review, but her firm does extensive compilation and review work. She therefore has one of her most experienced assistants, Fred Blair, do the work. She instructs him to follow the firm's standard review services procedures for SSARS reviews and to do high-quality work because Tidwell is a high-risk client.

Blair completes the review of Tidwell's statements and Johnson carefully reviews Blair's work. No exceptions are found. Each page of the client's financial statements is marked "reviewed." The following report is issued.

SECURITIES AND EXCHANGE COMMISSION

We have reviewed the accompanying balance sheet of Tidwell Publishing Co. as of March 31, 2000, and the related statements of income, retained earnings, and changes in financial position for the year then ended, in accordance with standards established by the American Institute of Certified Public Accountants. All information included in these financial statements is the representation of the management of Tidwell Publishing Co.

A review consists principally of inquiries of company personnel and analytical procedures applied to financial data. It is substantially less in scope than an audit in accordance with generally accepted auditing standards, the objective of which is the expression of an opinion regarding the financial statements taken as a whole. Accordingly, we do not express such an opinion.

Based on our review, we are not aware of any material modifications that should be made to the accompanying financial statements in order for them to be in conformity with generally accepted accounting principles.

Johnson & Levy, CPAs
March 31, 2000

Required
a. Is it appropriate to do a review service for a publicly held company? Explain.
b. Evaluate the approach taken by Johnson and Blair on the engagement.
c. Evaluate the report.

24-32 (Objective 24-3) Bengston, CPA, is conducting the ordinary audit of Pollution Control Devices, Inc. In addition, a supplemental negative assurance report is required to a major mortgage holder. The supplemental report concerns indenture agreements to keep the client from defaulting on the mortgage. Total assets are $14 million and the mortgage is for $4 million. The major provisions of the indentures are as follows:

1. The current ratio must be maintained above 2.3 to 1.
2. The debt/equity ratio must be maintained below 3.0.
3. Net earnings after taxes must exceed dividends paid by at least $1,000,000.

Required
a. Write the appropriate supplemental report if all three indenture agreement provisions have been satisfied.
b. How would the supplemental report change if net earnings after taxes were $1,010,000 and dividends paid were $60,000?
c. Assume the same situation as in part b and also assume that the client refuses to modify the financial statements or disclose the violation of the indenture

agreement provisions on the grounds that the amount is immaterial. What is the nature of the appropriate auditor's report?

d. What is the nature of the appropriate supplemental report if all the indenture agreement provisions have been satisfied but there is a lawsuit against the company that has resulted in disclosure of the lawsuit in a footnote to the financial statements?

24-33 (Objective 24-3)   Quality CPA Review is the franchisor of a national CPA review course for candidates taking the CPA examination. Quality CPA Review is responsible for providing all materials, including cassettes and video material, doing all national and local advertising, and giving assistance in effectively organizing and operating local franchises. The fee to the participant is $1,500 for the full course if all parts of the examination are taken. There are lower rates for candidates taking selected parts of the examination. Quality CPA Review gets 50 percent of the total fee.

The materials for the review course are purchased by Quality CPA Review from Ronnie Johnson, CPA, a highly qualified writer of CPA review materials. Quality CPA Review receives one copy of those materials from Johnson and reproduces them for candidates. Quality CPA Review must pay Johnson a $60 royalty for each full set of materials used and 12 percent of the participant fee for partial candidates. The contract between Johnson and Quality CPA Review requires an audited report to be provided by Quality CPA Review on royalties due to Johnson. Recorded gross fees for the 1999 review course are $1,500,000.

Even before the audit is started, there is a dispute between Quality CPA Review and Johnson. Quality CPA Review does not intend to pay royalties on certain materials. Johnson disagrees with that conclusion but the contract does not specify anything about it. The following are the disputed sales on which Quality CPA Review refused to pay royalties:

1. Materials sent to instructors for promotion	$31,000
2. Uncollected fees due to bad debts	6,000
3. Candidates who paid no fee because they performed administrative duties during the course	16,000
4. Refunds to customers who were dissatisfied with the course	22,000
Total	$75,000

Required

a. Assume that you are engaged to do the ordinary audit of Quality CPA Review and the special audit of royalties for Johnson. What additional audit testing beyond the normal tests of royalties is required because of the special audit?

b. Assume that the financial statements of Quality CPA Review are found to be fairly stated except for the unresolved dispute between Johnson and Quality CPA Review. Write the appropriate audit report.

c. Write the report for total royalties to Johnson, assuming that the information as stated in the case is all correct and the dispute is not resolved.

24-34 (Objective 24-3)   Jones, CPA, has completed the audit of Sarack Lumber Supply Co. and has issued a standard unqualified report. In addition to a report on the overall financial statements, the company needs a special audited report on three specific accounts: sales, net fixed assets, and inventory valued at FIFO. The report is to be issued to Sarack's lessor, who bases annual rentals on these three accounts. Jones was not aware of the need for the report on the three specific accounts until after the overall audit was completed.

Required

a. Explain why Jones is unlikely to be able to issue the audit report on the three specific accounts without additional audit tests.

b. What additional tests are likely to be needed before the report on the three specific accounts can be issued?

c. Assuming that Jones is able to satisfy all the requirements needed to issue the report on the three specific accounts, write the report. Make any necessary assumptions.

24-35 (Objective 24-5)   Carl Monson, the owner of Major Products Manufacturing Company, a small successful longtime audit client of your firm, has requested you to work with his company in preparing 3-year forecasted information for the year ending December 31, 1999, and two subsequent years. Monson informs you that he intends to use the forecasts, together with the audited financial statements, to seek additional financing to expand the business. Monson has had little experience in formal forecast preparation and counts on you to assist him in any way possible. He wants the most supportive opinion possible from your firm to add to the credibility of the forecast. He informs you that he is willing to do anything necessary to help you prepare the forecast.

First, he wants projections of sales and revenues and earnings from the existing business, which he believes could continue to be financed from existing capital.

Second, he intends to buy a company in a closely related business that is currently operating unsuccessfully. Monson states that he wants to sell some of the operating assets of the business and replace them with others. He believes that the company can then be made highly successful. He has made an offer on the new business, subject to obtaining proper financing. He also informs you that he has received an offer on the assets he intends to sell.

Required

    a. Explain circumstances under which it would and would not be acceptable to undertake the engagement.

    b. Why is it important that Monson understand the nature of your reporting requirements before the engagement proceeds?

    c. What information will Monson have to provide to you before you can complete the forecasted statements? Be as specific as possible.

    d. Discuss, in as specific terms as possible, the nature of the report you will issue with the forecasts, assuming that you are able to properly complete them.

24-36 (Objective 24-6)   Warren, CPA, has been approached by Veridyne Co. to accept an attest engagement to examine and report on management's assertion about the effectiveness of Veridyne's internal control over financial reporting as of June 30, 1999, the end of its fiscal year.

Required

    a. Describe the required conditions that must be met for Warren to accept an attest engagement to examine and report on management's assertion about the effectiveness of Veridyne's internal control.

    b. Describe the engagement activities that would be involved in Warren's performing an examination of management's assertion about the effectiveness of Veridyne's internal control.

    c. Warren was asked to perform an examination of Veridyne's internal control over financial reporting. What other types of attest services could Warren provide in connection with Veridyne's internal control, other than an examination.*

---

*AICPA adapted.

INTERNAL AND GOVERNMENTAL FINANCIAL AUDITING AND OPERATIONAL AUDITING

25

LEARNING OBJECTIVES

After studying this chapter, you should be able to

25-1 Explain the role of internal auditors in financial auditing.

25-2 Describe the auditing and reporting requirements under Government Auditing Standards and the Single Audit Act.

25-3 Distinguish operational auditing from financial auditing.

25-4 Provide an overview of operational audits.

25-5 Plan and perform an operational audit.

GOOD AUDITING OFTEN RESULTS IN IMPROVED CASH FLOWS

Sandy Previtz is an experienced internal audit staff person with Erhardt Freight Company (EFC), a long-haul trucking company. EFC has been growing rapidly, adding customers and shipping agents daily, and volume exceeds several thousand shipments per day. To address the growing volume of freight bills and related receivables, EFC implemented a new state-of-the-art computerized information system.

Previtz was assigned to test the accuracy of the aging of the accounts receivable system and the adequacy of the allowance for doubtful accounts. She took an initial sample of 300 freight bills selected at random from a population of 20,000 outstanding freight bills. She used the sample to project an aging and develop an estimate of the required allowance for doubtful accounts. Her tests indicated the allowance could be understated by as much as $1 million.

Previtz informed Martha Harris, the head of internal audit, of the situation. Harris informed the chief financial officer that as long as the tests indicated there could be a material misstatement, EFC must expand the sample until it was clear whether the allowance was materially misstated.

Previtz's second sample increased the total sample to 600 items, with essentially the same results. However, at Harris's request, she analyzed the items from *both* a management and an accounting standpoint. When Harris and Previtz met with the CFO to discuss the updated information, Harris pointed out that the real problem was not the allowance but that receivables were out of control and EFC faced a significant loss in cash flows if management didn't do something about it. The CFO quickly agreed and responded by hiring a team of temporary workers to analyze the aging of all 20,000 freight bills and to institute a large-scale collection effort. Not only did the analysis and collection efforts improve cash flows, it also showed that Previtz's estimate was right on target.

The last chapter discussed several other audit and attestation services provided by external auditors. This chapter examines the activities of other types of auditors. As Sandy Previtz of Erhardt Freight Company demonstrates in the introductory vignette, internal auditors can have a significant impact on a company's operational efficiency and effectiveness, as well as on earnings and cash flow.

Internal and government auditors perform a significant amount of financial auditing similar to that done by CPA firms. CPA firms also do considerable financial auditing of governmental units. The concepts and methodologies discussed throughout this book apply to audits by internal and government auditors. We begin this chapter by examining the role of internal auditors in financial auditing.

INTERNAL FINANCIAL AUDITING

OBJECTIVE 25-1

Explain the role of internal auditors in financial auditing.

As discussed in Chapter 1, internal auditors are employed by companies to do both financial and operational auditing. Their role in auditing has increased dramatically in the past two decades, primarily because of the increased size and complexity of many corporations. Because internal auditors spend all of their time with one company, their knowledge about the company's operations and internal controls is much greater than the external auditors' knowledge.

Internal auditing encompasses the examination and evaluation of the adequacy and effectiveness of the organization's system of internal control and the quality of performance in carrying out assigned responsibilities. The Institute of Internal Auditors *Statement of Responsibilities of Internal Auditing* indicates that internal auditors should do the following:

- Review the reliability and integrity of financial and operating information and the means used to identify, measure, classify, and report such information.
- Review the systems established to ensure compliance with those policies, plans, procedures, laws, regulations, and contracts, which could have a significant impact on operations and reports and should determine whether the organization is in compliance.
- Review the means of safeguarding assets and, as appropriate, verify the existence of such assets.
- Appraise the economy and efficiency with which resources are employed.
- Review operations or programs to ascertain whether results are consistent with established objectives and goals and whether the operations or programs are being carried out as planned.

The objectives of internal auditors are considerably broader than the objectives of external auditors. This provides flexibility for internal auditors to meet company needs. Different companies vary in the extent of internal auditing and the areas on which the internal auditors focus. For example, management of one company may decide that internal auditors should evaluate the internal controls and financial statements of every division annually, whereas others may decide that a 3-year rotation is sufficient. Also, internal audit reports are not standardized because (1) the reporting needs vary for each company and (2) the reports are not relied on by external users.

Institute of Internal Auditors

Professional guidance for internal auditors is provided by the **Institute of Internal Auditors (IIA)**. The IIA is an organization similar to the AICPA that establishes ethical and practice standards, provides education, and encourages professionalism for its approximately 60,000 members. The IIA has played a major role in the increasing influence of internal auditing. For example, the IIA has established a highly regarded certification program resulting in the designation of Certified Internal Auditor (CIA) for those who meet the testing and experience requirements.

The **IIA Practice Standards** include five categories of guidance that encompass both financial and operational auditing: independence, professional proficiency, scope of work, performance of audit work, and management of the internal auditing department. The specific standards supporting these five categories are included in Figure 25-1. A

IIA

SUMMARY OF GENERAL AND SPECIFIC STANDARDS FOR THE PROFESSIONAL PRACTICE OF INTERNAL AUDITING

100 INDEPENDENCE. Internal auditors should be independent of the activities they audit.

110 *Organizational Status.* The organizational status of the internal auditing department should be sufficient to permit the accomplishment of its audit responsibilities.

120 *Objectivity.* Internal auditors should be objective in performing audits.

200 PROFESSIONAL PROFICIENCY. Internal audits should be performed with proficiency and due professional care.

The Internal Auditing Department

210 *Staffing.* The director of internal auditing should ensure that the technical proficiency and educational background of internal auditors are appropriate for the audits to be performed.

220 *Knowledge, Skills, and Disciplines.* The internal auditing department should possess or should obtain the knowledge, skills, and disciplines needed to carry out its audit responsibilities.

230 *Supervision.* The director of internal auditing should ensure that internal audits are properly supervised.

The Internal Auditor

240 *Compliance with Standards of Conduct.* Internal auditors should comply with professional standards of conduct.

250 *Knowledge, Skills, and Disciplines.* Internal auditors should possess the knowledge, skills, and disciplines essential to the performance of internal audits.

260 *Human Relations and Communications.* Internal auditors should be skilled in dealing with people and in communicating effectively.

270 *Continuing Education.* Internal auditors should maintain their technical competence through continuing education.

280 *Due Professional Care.* Internal auditors should exercise due professional care in performing internal audits.

300 SCOPE OF WORK. The scope of internal auditing should encompass the examination and evaluation of the adequacy and effectiveness of the organization's system of internal control and the quality of performance in carrying out assigned responsibilities.

310 *Reliability and Integrity of Information.* Internal auditors should review the reliability and integrity of financial and operating information and the means used to identify, measure, classify, and report such information.

320 *Compliance with Policies, Plans, Procedures, Laws, Regulations, and Contracts.* Internal auditors should review the systems established to ensure compliance with those policies, plans, procedures, laws, regulations, and contracts that could have a significant impact on operations and reports and should determine whether the organization is in compliance.

330 *Safeguarding of Assets.* Internal auditors should review the means of safeguarding assets and, as appropriate, verify the existence of such assets.

340 *Economical and Efficient Use of Resources.* Internal auditors should appraise the economy and efficiency with which resources are employed.

350 *Accomplishment of Established Objectives and Goals for Operations or Programs.* Internal auditors should review operations or programs to ascertain whether results are consistent with established objectives and goals and whether the operations or programs are being carried out as planned.

400 PERFORMANCE OF AUDIT WORK. Audit work should include planning the audit, examining and evaluating information, communicating results, and following up.

410 *Planning the Audit.* Internal auditors should plan each audit.

420 *Examining and Evaluating Information.* Internal auditors should collect, analyze, interpret, and document information to support audit results.

430 *Communicating Results.* Internal auditors should report the results of their audit work.

440 *Following Up.* Internal auditors should follow up to ascertain that appropriate action is taken on reported audit findings.

500 MANAGEMENT OF THE INTERNAL AUDITING DEPARTMENT. The director of internal auditing should properly manage the internal auditing department.

510 *Purpose, Authority, and Responsibility.* The director of internal auditing should have a statement of purpose, authority, and responsibility for the internal auditing department.

520 *Planning.* The director of internal auditing should establish plans to carry out the responsibilities of the internal auditing department.

530 *Policies and Procedures.* The director of internal auditing should provide written policies and procedures to guide the audit staff.

540 *Personnel Management and Development.* The director of internal auditing should establish a program for selecting and developing the human resources of the internal auditing department.

550 *External Auditors.* The director of internal auditing should coordinate internal and external audit efforts.

560 *Quality Assurance.* The director of internal auditing should establish and maintain a quality assurance program to evaluate the operations of the internal auditing department.

Source: *Standards for the Professional Practice of Internal Auditing* (Altamonte Springs, Fla.: Institute of Internal Auditors, 1980), pp. 3–4.

comparison of these standards to the AICPA generally accepted auditing standards on page 30 shows both similarities and differences. **Statements on Internal Auditing Standards (SIASs)** are issued by the Internal Auditing Standards Board to provide authoritative interpretations of the standards.

Relationship of Internal and External Auditors

There are both differences and similarities between the responsibilities and conduct of audits by internal and external auditors. The primary difference is whom each party is responsible to. The external auditor is responsible to financial statement users who rely on the auditor to add credibility to the statements. The internal auditor is responsible to management. Even with this important difference, there are many similarities between the two groups. Both must be competent as auditors and remain objective in performing their work and reporting their results. They both, for example, follow a similar methodology in performing their audits, including planning and performing tests of controls and substantive tests. Similarly, they both use the audit risk model and materiality in deciding the extent of their tests and evaluating results. Their decisions about materiality and risks may differ, however, because external users may have different needs than management has.

External auditors rely on internal auditors through the use of the audit risk model. Auditors significantly reduce control risk and thereby reduce substantive testing if internal auditors are effective. The fee reduction of the external auditor is typically substantial when there is a highly regarded internal audit function. External auditors typically consider internal auditors effective if they are independent of the operating units being evaluated, competent and well trained, and have performed relevant audit tests of the internal controls and financial statements.

Internal Audit WWW

SAS 65 (AU 322) also permits the external auditor to use the internal auditor for direct assistance on the audit. Relying on the internal audit staff for performance of some of the audit testing may allow the audit to be completed in less time and for a lower fee. When direct assistance is provided, the external auditor should assess the internal auditors' competence and objectivity. The work of the internal auditors should be supervised and evaluated as appropriate under the circumstances.

GOVERNMENTAL FINANCIAL AUDITING

The previous section discussed the role of internal auditors. This section examines the activities of government auditors. The federal and state governments employ their own auditing staff to perform audits in much the same way as internal auditors. Chapter 1 briefly discussed the United States General Accounting Office (GAO). All states have their own audit agencies, similar to but smaller than the GAO. In addition, CPA firms do considerable financial auditing of governmental units. For example, some states require the audit of all city and school district financial statements by CPA firms.

GAO Yellow Book

The primary source of authoritative literature for the performance of **government audits** is *Government Auditing Standards*, which is issued by the GAO. Because of the color of the cover, it is usually referred to as the "**Yellow Book**" rather than by its more formal name. The Yellow Book was initially issued in 1972, with subsequent revisions in 1981 and 1994. The initial Yellow Book standards were similar to the GAAS standards but have been expanded in subsequent revisions to provide guidance standards for performance audits. The Yellow Book standards are often called generally accepted government auditing standards (**GAGAS or GAS**).

Financial auditing under the Yellow Book includes audits of financial statements of governmental units, government contracts and grants, internal control, fraud, and other noncompliance with laws and regulations. These categories of information are broader than audits under generally accepted auditing standards and encompass the types of attestation work discussed in Chapter 24 under the attestation standards. It is not surprising, however, that governmental units are as concerned with compliance with laws and regulations as with the reliability of financial statements.

The financial auditing standards of the Yellow Book are consistent with the 10 generally accepted auditing standards of the AICPA. However, there are some important additions and modifications.

- *Materiality and significance.* The Yellow Book recognizes that in government audits the thresholds of acceptable audit risk and materiality may be lower than in an audit of a commercial enterprise. This is because of the sensitivity of government activities and their public accountability.
- *Quality control.* CPA firms and other organizations that audit government entities in compliance with the Yellow Book must have an appropriate system of internal quality control and participate in an external quality control review program. The latter requirement exists for some CPAs, but only as a requirement for membership in the AICPA and/or the audit of public companies.

  Auditors involved in planning, conducting, or reporting on audits under GAGAS must complete 80 hours of continuing professional education in each 2-year period. At least 24 of these 80 hours of training must be in subjects related to the government environment and government auditing.
- *Compliance auditing.* The audit should be designed to provide reasonable assurance of detecting material misstatements resulting from noncompliance with provisions of contracts or grant agreements that have a material and direct effect on the financial statements. The auditor must also apply additional procedures if information comes to the auditor's attention concerning possible noncompliance that would have a material indirect effect on the financial statements.
- *Reporting.* The audit report must state that the audit was made in accordance with generally accepted government auditing standards. In addition, the report on financial statements must describe the scope of the auditors' testing of compliance with laws and regulations and internal controls and present the results of those tests or refer to a separate report containing that information.
- *Working papers.* Audits done in accordance with government auditing standards are subject to review by other auditors and oversight officials. The Yellow Book indicates that working papers should contain sufficient information to enable an experienced reviewer with no previous connection to the audit to ascertain from the working papers evidence that supports the auditors' significant conclusions and judgments.

The additional requirements reflect the emphasis on compliance in governmental audits and the need for quality control due to the complexities of the governmental accounting and auditing environment.

Before 1980, each federal financing agency had its own audit requirements. As a result, recipients of federal funds received multiple audits. This was remedied in 1984 with the passage of the **Single Audit Act**, which provided for a single coordinated audit to meet the audit requirements of all federal agencies. The Single Audit Act of 1984 applied only to audits of state and local governments. The requirements of the act were extended in 1990 to higher-education institutions and other not-for-profit organizations by the Office of Management and Budget (OMB) through the issuance of OMB Circular A-133.

Congress passed the Single Audit Act Amendments of 1996 to relieve the audit burden on small entities receiving federal financial assistance. Some of the significant provisions of the 1996 Amendments include the following:

- The threshold for requiring a single audit was raised from $100,000 to $300,000 to exempt many smaller entities from single audit requirements.
- Statutory coverage of the single audit was extended to not-for-profit organizations, as well as to state and local governments.
- A risk-based approach is to be used in selecting programs for testing.

The Office of Management and Budget issued a revised Circular A-133, *Audits of States, Local Governments, and Non-Profit Organizations,* to provide administrative guidance for implementing the single audit requirements.

Audit Requirements The 1996 Single Audit Act Amendments and OMB Circular A-133 (hereafter referred to collectively as the Act) contain requirements for the scope of the audit, including the following:

- The audit should be in accordance with generally accepted government auditing standards (GAGAS).
- The auditor must obtain an understanding of internal control over federal programs sufficient to support a low assessed level of control risk for major programs.
- The auditor should determine whether the client has complied with laws, regulations, and the provisions of contracts or grant agreements that may have a direct and material effect on each of its major programs.

Association of Government Accountants

The compliance requirements to be met are described in the A-133 *Compliance Supplement,* along with suggested audit procedures. Fourteen types of compliance requirements are identified that should be considered in every audit. In addition, specific requirements for individual federal programs are identified. The following are examples of some specific compliance objectives:

- Whether the amounts reported as expenditures were for allowable services.
- Whether the records show that those who received services or benefits were eligible to receive them.
- Whether matching requirements (where the government unit matches federal funds), levels of effort, and earmarking limitations were met.
- Whether federal financial reports and claims for advances and reimbursements contain information that is supported by the books and records from which the basic financial statements have been prepared.
- Whether amounts claimed or used for matching were determined in accordance with the cost principles and administrative requirements in relevant OMB circulars.

Reporting Requirements The revised OMB Circular A-133 greatly simplified reporting under the Act. The following reports are required:

- An opinion on whether the financial statements are in accordance with GAAP, and an opinion as to whether the schedule of federal awards is presented fairly in all material respects in relation to the financial statements as a whole. Figure 25-2 is an example of a governmental audit report.
- A report on internal control related to the financial statements and major programs.
- A report on compliance with laws, regulations, and the provisions of contracts or grant agreements, where noncompliance could have a material effect on the financial statements. This report can be combined with the report on internal control.
- A schedule of findings and questioned costs.

Note that the auditor's report in Figure 25-2 refers to government auditing standards and also refers to the report on internal control and compliance. The schedule of federal awards is supplemental information, and the opinion on this information is consistent with the auditor's reporting on additional information accompanying the basic financial statements discussed in Chapter 24.

AICPA Guidance for Auditors

From the preceding discussion, one can see that entering the arena of government auditing is a complex undertaking. The auditor must be familiar with both generally accepted auditing standards and a series of government audit documents, laws, and regulations. Thus, the first step in preparing for such an engagement is extensive professional development. In response to the changes arising from the Single Audit Act Amendments of 1996,

FIGURE 25-2 **Example of a Government Audit Report**

We have audited the accompanying general-purpose financial statements of XYZ City as of and for the year ended June 30, 1999, as listed in the table of contents. These general-purpose financial statements are the responsibility of XYZ City's management. Our responsibility is to express an opinion on these general-purpose financial statements based on our audit.

We conducted our audit in accordance with generally accepted auditing standards and the standards applicable to financial audits contained in *Government Auditing Standards,* issued by the Comptroller General of the United States. Those standards require that we plan and perform the audit to obtain reasonable assurance about whether the financial statements are free of material misstatement. An audit includes examining, on a test basis, evidence supporting the amounts and disclosures in the financial statements. An audit also includes assessing the accounting principles used and the significant estimates made by management, as well as evaluating the overall financial statement presentation. We believe that our audit provides a reasonable basis for our opinion.

In our opinion, the general-purpose financial statements referred to above present fairly, in all material respects, the financial position of XYZ City as of June 30, 1999, and the results of its operations and the cash flows of its proprietary fund types and nonexpendable trust funds for the year then ended in conformity with generally accepted accounting principles.

In accordance with *Government Auditing Standards,* we have also issued our report dated *[date of report]* on our consideration of XYZ's internal control over financial reporting and on our tests of its compliance with certain provisions of laws, regulations, contracts, and grants.

The accompanying schedule of expenditures of federal awards is presented for purposes of additional analysis as required by U.S. Office of Management and Budget Circular A-133, *Audits of States, Local Governments, and Non-Profit Organizations,* and is not a required part of the general-purpose financial statements. Such information has been subjected to the auditing procedures applied in the audit of the general-purpose financial statements and, in our opinion, is fairly stated, in all material respects, in relation to the general-purpose financial statements taken as a whole.

revised OMB Circular A-133, and the *Compliance Supplement,* the AICPA issued Statement of Position (SOP) 98-3, *Audits of States, Local Governments, and Not-for-Profit Organizations Receiving Federal Awards.* SOP 98-3 contains guidance for auditors, along with illustrated reporting examples. Additional guidance for auditors can be found in SAS 74 (AU 801), *Compliance Auditing Considerations in Audits of Governmental Entities and Recipients of Governmental Financial Assistance,* and the *Audit and Accounting Guide for Audits of State and Local Governmental Units.*

OPERATIONAL AUDITING

Previous sections of this chapter discussed the financial auditing activities of internal auditors and government auditors. Internal and government auditors, as well as CPA firms, are also involved in operational auditing.

Although **operational auditing** is generally understood to deal with efficiency and effectiveness, there is less agreement on the use of that term than one might expect. Many people prefer to use the terms **management auditing** or **performance auditing** instead of **operational auditing** to describe the review of organizations for efficiency and effectiveness. Those people typically describe operational auditing broadly and include evaluating internal controls and even testing those controls for effectiveness (tests of controls) as a part of operational auditing. Others do not distinguish among the terms *performance auditing, management auditing,* and *operational auditing.*

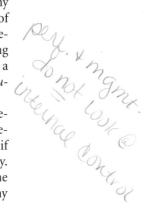

We prefer to use *operational auditing* broadly, as long as the purpose of the test is to determine the effectiveness or efficiency of any part of an organization. Testing the effectiveness of internal controls by an internal auditor is therefore a part of operational auditing if the purpose is to help an organization operate its business more effectively or efficiently. Similarly, the determination of whether a company has adequately trained assembly line personnel is also operational auditing if the purpose is to determine whether the company is effectively and efficiently producing products.

Three major differences exist between operational and financial auditing: purpose of the audit, distribution of the reports, and inclusion of nonfinancial areas in operational auditing.

Purpose of the Audit The major distinction between financial and operational auditing is the purpose of the tests. Financial auditing emphasizes whether historical information was correctly recorded. Operational auditing emphasizes effectiveness and efficiency. The financial audit is oriented to the past, whereas an operational audit concerns operating performance for the future. An operational auditor, for example, may evaluate whether a type of new material is being purchased at the lowest cost to save money on future raw material purchases.

Distribution of the Reports For financial auditing, the report typically goes to many users of financial statements, such as stockholders and bankers; whereas operational audit reports are intended primarily for management. As indicated in Chapter 3, well-defined wording is needed for financial auditing reports as a result of the widespread distribution of the reports. Because of the limited distribution of operational reports and the diverse nature of audits for efficiency and effectiveness, operational auditing reports vary considerably from audit to audit.

Inclusion of Nonfinancial Areas Operational audits cover any aspect of efficiency and effectiveness in an organization and can therefore involve a wide variety of activities. For example, the effectiveness of an advertising program or efficiency of factory employees would be part of an operational audit. Financial audits are limited to matters that directly affect the fairness of financial statement presentations.

Effectiveness versus Efficiency

Effectiveness refers to the accomplishment of objectives, whereas efficiency refers to the resources used to achieve those objectives. An example of effectiveness is the production of parts without defects. Efficiency concerns whether those parts are produced at minimum cost.

can accomp. objective?

what amt. of resources were used to reach goals?

Effectiveness Before an operational audit for effectiveness can be performed, there must be specific criteria for what is meant by **effectiveness**. An example of an operational audit for effectiveness would be to assess whether a governmental agency has met its assigned objective of achieving elevator safety in a city. Before the operational auditor can reach a conclusion about the agency's effectiveness, criteria for elevator safety must be set. For example, is the objective to see that all elevators in the city are inspected at least once a year? Is the objective to ensure that no fatalities occurred as a result of elevator breakdowns or that no breakdowns occurred?

Efficiency Like effectiveness, there must be defined criteria for what is meant by doing things more efficiently before operational auditing can be meaningful. It is often easier to set efficiency than effectiveness criteria if **efficiency** is defined as reducing cost without reducing effectiveness. For example, if two different production processes manufacture a product of identical quality, the process with the lower cost is considered more efficient.

The following are several types of inefficiencies that commonly occur and often are uncovered through operational auditing.

Types of Inefficiency	*Example*
• Acquisition of goods and services is excessively costly.	• Bids for purchases of materials are not required.
• Raw materials are not available for production when needed.	• An entire assembly line must be shut down because necessary materials were not ordered.
• There is duplication of effort by employees.	• Identical production records are kept by both the accounting and production departments because they are unaware of each other's activities.

- Work is done that serves no purpose.

- There are too many employees.

- Copies of vendors' invoices and receiving reports are sent to the production department where they are filed without ever being used.

- The office work could be done effectively with one less administrative assistant.

In Chapter 10, it was stated that management establishes internal controls to help it meet its own goals. The following three concerns in setting up good internal controls were identified and discussed in Chapter 10:

- Reliability of financial reporting
- Efficiency and effectiveness of operations
- Compliance with applicable laws and regulations

The second of these three client concerns is obviously directly related to operational auditing, but the other two also affect efficiency and effectiveness. For example, reliable cost accounting information is important to management in deciding such things as which products to continue and the billing price of products. Similarly, failure to comply with a law such as the Foreign Corrupt Practices Act could result in a large fine to the company.

There are two significant differences in internal control evaluation and testing for financial and operational auditing: the purpose of the evaluation and testing of internal controls, and the normal scope of internal control evaluation.

The primary purpose of internal control evaluation for financial auditing is to determine the extent of substantive audit testing required. The purpose of operational auditing is to evaluate efficiency and effectiveness of internal control and make recommendations to management. The control procedures might be evaluated in the same way for both financial and operational auditing, but the purpose is different. To illustrate, an operational auditor might determine whether internal verification procedures for duplicate sales invoices are effective to ensure that the company does not offend customers but also receives all money owed. A financial auditor often does the same internal control evaluation, but the primary purpose is to reduce confirmation of accounts receivable or other substantive tests. However, a secondary purpose of many financial audits is also to make operational recommendations to management.

The scope of internal control evaluation for financial audits is restricted to matters affecting fairly presented financial statements, whereas operational auditing concerns any control affecting efficiency or effectiveness. Therefore, for example, an operational audit could be concerned with policies and procedures established in the marketing department to determine the effectiveness of catalogs used to market products.

There are three broad categories of operational audits: functional, organizational, and special assignments. In each case, part of the audit is likely to concern evaluating internal controls for efficiency and effectiveness.

Functional Functions are a means of categorizing the activities of a business, such as the billing function or production function. There are many different ways to categorize and subdivide functions. For example, there is an accounting function, but there are also cash disbursement, cash receipt, and payroll disbursement functions. There is a payroll function, but there are also hiring, timekeeping, and payroll disbursement functions.

As the name implies, a **functional audit** deals with one or more functions in an organization. It could concern, for example, the payroll function for a division or for the company as a whole.

A functional audit has the advantage of permitting specialization by auditors. Certain auditors within an internal audit staff can develop considerable expertise in an area, such as production engineering. They can more efficiently spend all their time auditing in that area. A disadvantage of functional auditing is the failure to evaluate interrelated functions. The production engineering function interacts with manufacturing and other functions in an organization.

Organizational An operational audit of an organization deals with an entire organizational unit, such as a department, branch, or subsidiary. An **organizational audit** emphasizes how efficiently and effectively functions interact. The plan of organization and the methods to coordinate activities are especially important in this type of audit.

Special Assignments In operational auditing, **special assignments** arise at the request of management. There are a wide variety of such audits. Examples include determining the cause of an ineffective IT system, investigating the possibility of fraud in a division, and making recommendations for reducing the cost of a manufactured product.

Who Performs Operational Audits

Operational audits are usually performed by one of three groups: internal auditors, government auditors, or CPA firms.

Internal Auditors Internal auditors are in such a unique position to perform operational audits that some people use the terms *internal auditing* and *operational auditing* interchangeably. It is, however, inappropriate to conclude that all operational auditing is done by internal auditors or that internal auditors do only operational auditing. Many internal audit departments do both operational and financial audits. Often, they are done simultaneously. An advantage that internal auditors have in doing operational audits is that they spend all their time working for the company they are auditing. They thereby develop considerable knowledge about the company and its business, which is essential to effective operational auditing.

To maximize their effectiveness for both financial and operational auditing, the internal audit department should report to the board of directors or president. Internal auditors should also have access to and ongoing communications with the audit committee of the board of directors. This organizational structure helps internal auditors remain independent. For example, if internal auditors report to the controller, it is difficult for the internal auditor to evaluate independently and make recommendations to senior management about inefficiencies in the controller's operations.

MAJOR CHANGES SEEN IN ROLE OF INTERNAL AUDITORS

The control environment of major financial institutions has changed dramatically over the last five years in the face of shifting regulations, complex financial instruments, technological breakthroughs, and accelerating customer and stockholder demands. Crippling losses resulting from control failures are prompting far-reaching changes in the internal audit function. Some major changes:

Tension between Roles Traditionally, internal auditors have been the organization's "control conscience," but they are now being asked to provide strategic and operational input. These conflicting roles of both creating and enforcing rules have resulted in tension that must be effectively managed. They also demand new types of skill sets, requiring that auditors have not only technical expertise, but also "live" skills such as communication, decision making, and business analysis.

Risk Management There are two major interrelated trends in the area of risk management: (1) the need for more audit attention to control the risks of derivative financial instruments, and (2) the movement toward integrated financial risk management, a central component of which is "value at risk"—the potential loss from adverse changes in market factors for a specified time period and confidence level.

Electronic Commerce Conducting financial activity in a "paperless" electronic environment poses a major concern. As reliance on computer networks increases, institutions must design and implement control systems that can adequately manage risk, particularly in areas such as data security and integrity, and vulnerability to viruses. Early involvement of internal audit is important in designing and developing new data systems and products, allowing institutions to build internal controls *into* new procedures and systems, as opposed to controlling them after the fact.

Source: "Major Changes Seen in Role of Internal Auditors," *Deloitte & Touche Review* (February 5, 1996), p. 2.

Government Auditors Different federal and state government auditors perform operational auditing, often as a part of doing financial audits. As already discussed, the most widely recognized government auditors group is the GAO, but there are also many state government auditors. Most of these auditors are concerned with both financial and operational audits.

The Yellow Book, which was discussed earlier, defines and sets standards for performance audits, which are essentially the same as operational audits. Performance audits include the following:

- *Economy and efficiency audits.* An **economy and efficiency audit** has as its purpose determining (1) whether an entity is acquiring, protecting, and using its resources economically and efficiently; (2) the causes of inefficiencies or uneconomical practices; and (3) whether the entity has complied with laws and regulations concerning matters of economy and efficiency.
- *Program audits.* A **program audit** has as its purpose determining (1) the extent to which the desired results or benefits established by the legislature or other authorizing body are being achieved; (2) the effectiveness of organizations, programs, activities, or functions; and (3) whether the entity has complied with laws and regulations applicable to the program.

The first two objectives of each of these types of performance audits are clearly operational in nature. The final objective in each is compliance in nature, and was discussed earlier.

To illustrate specific operational activities of a state governmental audit, the following three examples are taken from an article in the publication *Internal Auditor*, discussing auditing for economy and efficiency:

- A separate hospital with its own administrative staff occupied three buildings on the grounds of another state hospital. Our audit showed that the limited workload of the administrative activities of this separate hospital and its proximity to the offices of the main hospital would permit consolidation of the administrative functions of the two hospitals at a savings of $145,000 a year.
- A local school district exercised control over twenty-nine individual facilities. Our audit showed that the unused classroom facilities amounted to about 28 percent or the equivalent of eight schools and that enrollment was continuing to decline. We recommended consolidating and closing of individual facilities to the extent possible. Such action would not only reduce costs but also provide greater flexibility in class sizes and course offerings.
- The outstanding accounts receivable at a teaching hospital increased from $7 million to $11 million during a two-year period. An audit showed that this serious situation was caused, in part, by a lack of aggressive follow-up action, insufficient supervision, and insufficient staff to keep up with an increasing workload.[1]

[1]From *Round Table,* © 1982 by The Institute of Internal Auditors, Inc., 249 Maitland Avenue, Altamonte Springs, Fla. 32701. Reprinted with permission.

CPA Firms When CPA firms do an audit of historical financial statements, part of the audit usually consists of identifying operational problems and making recommendations that may benefit the audit client. The recommendations can be made orally, but they are typically made by use of a management letter. Management letters were discussed in Chapter 23.

The background knowledge about a client's business that an external auditor must obtain in doing an audit often provides useful information for giving operational recommendations. For example, suppose that the auditor determined that inventory turnover for a client slowed considerably during the current year. The auditor is likely to determine the cause of the reduction to evaluate the possibility of obsolete inventory that would misstate the financial statements. In determining the cause of the reduced inventory turnover, the auditor may identify operational causes, such as ineffective inventory acquisition policies, that can be brought to the attention of management. An auditor who has a broad business background and experience with similar businesses is more likely to be effective at providing clients with relevant operational recommendations than a person who lacks those qualities.

It is also common for a client to engage a CPA firm to do operational auditing for one or more specific parts of its business. Usually, such an engagement would occur only if the company does not have an internal audit staff or if the internal audit staff lacks expertise in a certain area. In most cases, a management consulting staff of the CPA firm, rather than the auditing staff, performs these services. For example, a company can ask the CPA firm to evaluate the efficiency and effectiveness of its computer systems.

Independence and Competence of Operational Auditors

Indepence, here, means auditor does not hold another job function in comp. other than the auditor.

The two most important qualities for an operational auditor are *independence* and *competence*.

Whom the auditor reports to is important to ensure that investigation and recommendations are made without bias. Independence is seldom a problem for CPA firm auditors because they are not employed by the company being audited. As stated earlier, independence of internal auditors is enhanced by having the internal audit department report to the board of directors or president. Similarly, government auditors should report to a level above the operating departments. The GAO, for example, reports directly to Congress as a means of enhancing independence.

The responsibilities of operational auditors can also affect their independence. The auditor should not be responsible for performing operating functions in a company or for correcting deficiencies when ineffective or inefficient operations are found. For example, it would negatively affect auditors' independence if they were responsible for designing an IT system for acquisitions or for correcting it if deficiencies were found during an audit of the acquisitions system.

It is acceptable for auditors to recommend changes in operations, but operating personnel must have the authority to accept or reject the recommendations. If auditors had the authority to require implementation of their recommendations, the auditor would actually have the responsibility for auditing his or her own work the next time an audit was conducted. Independence would therefore be reduced.

The Institute of Internal Auditors considers independence of internal auditors critical. It has established in its *Statement of Responsibilities of Internal Auditing* a special requirement for independence, as follows:

• Internal auditors should be independent of the activities they audit. Internal auditors are independent when they can carry out their work freely and objectively. Independence permits internal auditors to render the impartial and unbiased judgments essential to the proper conduct of audits. It is achieved through organizational status and objectivity.

The organizational status of the internal auditing department should be sufficient to permit the accomplishment of its audit responsibilities. The director of the internal auditing department should be responsible to an individual in the organization with sufficient authority to promote independence and to ensure a broad audit coverage, adequate consideration of audit reports, and appropriate action on audit recommendations.

Objectivity is an independent mental attitude that internal auditors should maintain in performing audits. Internal auditors are not to subordinate their judgment on audit matters to that of others. Designing, installing, and operating systems are not audit functions. Also, the drafting of procedures for systems is not an audit function. Performing such activities is presumed to impair audit objectivity.

Competence is, of course, necessary to determine the cause of operational problems and to make appropriate recommendations. Competence is a major problem when operational auditing deals with wide-ranging operating problems. For example, imagine the difficulties of finding qualified internal auditors who can evaluate both the effectiveness of an advertising program and the efficiency of a production assembly process. The internal audit staff doing that type of operational auditing would presumably have to include some personnel with backgrounds in marketing and others in production.

A major difficulty found in operational auditing is in deciding on specific criteria for evaluating whether efficiency and effectiveness have occurred. In auditing historical financial statements, GAAP are the broad criteria for evaluating fair presentation. Audit objectives are used to set more specific criteria in deciding whether GAAP have been followed. In operational auditing, no such well-defined criteria exist.

One approach to setting criteria for operational auditing is to state that the objectives are to determine whether some aspect of the entity could be made more effective or efficient and to recommend improvements. This approach may be adequate for experienced and well-trained auditors, but it would be difficult for most auditors to follow such a poorly defined approach.

Criteria for Evaluating Efficiency and Effectiveness

OBJECTIVE 25-5
Plan and perform an operational audit.

Specific Criteria More specific criteria are usually desirable before operational auditing is started. For example, suppose that you are doing an operational audit of the equipment layout in plants for a company. The following are some specific criteria, stated in the form of questions, that might be used to evaluate plant layouts:

- Were all plant layouts approved by home office engineering at the time of original design?
- Has home office engineering done a reevaluation study of plant layout in the past 5 years?
- Is each piece of equipment operating at 60 percent of capacity or more for at least 3 months each year?
- Does layout facilitate the movement of new materials to the production floor?
- Does layout facilitate the production of finished goods?
- Does layout facilitate the movement of finished goods to distribution centers?
- Does the plant layout effectively use existing equipment?
- Is the safety of employees endangered by the plant layout?

Sources of Criteria The operational auditor can use several sources in developing specific evaluation criteria. These sources include the following:

- *Historical performance.* A simple set of criteria can be based on actual results from prior periods (or audits). The idea behind using these criteria is to determine whether things have become "better" or "worse" in comparison. The advantage of these criteria is that they are easy to derive; however, they may not provide much insight into how well or poorly the audited entity is really doing.
- *Benchmarking.* Most entities subject to an operational audit are not unique; there are many similar entities within the overall organization or outside it. In those cases, the performance data of comparable entities are an excellent source for developing criteria for benchmarking. For internal comparable entities, the data are usually readily available. When the comparable entities are outside the organization, they will often be willing to make such information available. It is also often available through industry groups and governmental regulatory agencies.

- *Engineered standards.* In many types of operational auditing engagements, it may be possible and appropriate to develop criteria based on engineered standards—for example, time and motion studies to determine production output rates. These criteria are often time-consuming and costly to develop because they require considerable expertise; however, they may be effective in solving a major operational problem and well worth the cost. It is also possible that some standards can be developed by industry groups for use by all their members, thereby spreading the cost and reducing it for each participant. These may be groups in the industry of the subject organization, or functional groups such as an IT users' organization.
- *Discussion and agreement.* Sometimes objective criteria are difficult or costly to obtain, and criteria are developed through simple discussion and agreement. The parties involved in this process should include management of the entity to be audited, the operational auditor, and the entity or persons to whom the findings will be reported.

Phases in Operational Auditing

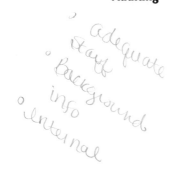

There are three phases in an operational audit: planning, evidence accumulation and evaluation, and reporting and follow-up.

Planning The planning in an operational audit is similar to that discussed in earlier chapters for an audit of historical financial statements. Like auditors of financial statements, the operational auditor must determine the scope of the engagement and communicate it to the organizational unit. It is also necessary to staff the engagement properly, obtain background information about the organizational unit, understand internal control, and decide on the appropriate evidence to accumulate.

The major difference between planning an operational audit and a financial audit is the extreme diversity in operational audits. Because of the diversity, it is often difficult to decide on specific objectives for an operational audit. The objectives will be based on the criteria developed for the engagement. As discussed in the preceding sections, these will depend on the specific circumstances at hand. For example, the objectives for an operational audit of the effectiveness of internal controls over petty cash would be dramatically different from those of an operational audit of the efficiency of a research and development department.

Another difference is that staffing is often more complicated in an operational audit than in a financial audit. This again is because of the breadth of the engagements. Not only are the areas diverse—for example, production control, advertising, and strategy planning—but the objectives within those areas often require special technical skills. For example, the auditor may need an engineering background to evaluate performance on a major construction project.

Finally, it is important to spend more time with the interested parties agreeing on the terms of the engagement and the criteria for evaluation in an operational audit than in a financial audit. This was alluded to in the preceding section for criteria developed through discussion. Regardless of the source of the criteria for evaluation, it is essential that the auditee, the auditor, and the sponsor of the engagement be in clear and complete agreement on the objectives and criteria involved. That agreement will facilitate effective and successful completion of the operational audit.

Evidence Accumulation and Evaluation The seven types of evidence studied in Chapter 7 and used throughout this book are equally applicable for operational auditing. Because internal controls and operating procedures are a critical part of operational auditing, it is common to extensively use documentation, client inquiry, and observation. Confirmation and reperformance are used less extensively for most operational audits than for financial audits because accuracy is not the purpose of most operational audits.

To illustrate evidence accumulation in operational auditing, we return to the example discussed earlier about evaluating the safety of elevators in a city. Assume there is agreement that the objective is to determine whether the inspection is made annually of each elevator in the city by a competent inspector. To satisfy the completeness objective, the auditor would, for example, examine blueprints of city buildings and elevator locations and trace them to the agency's list to ensure that all elevators are included in the population. Additional tests on newly constructed buildings would be appropriate to assess the timeliness with which the central listing is updated.

Assuming that the agency's list is determined to be complete, the auditor can select a sample of elevator locations and evidence can be collected as to the timing and frequency of inspections. The auditor may want to consider inherent risk by doing greater sampling of older elevators or elevators with previous safety defects. The auditor may also want to examine evidence to determine whether the elevator inspectors were competent to evaluate elevator safety. The auditor may, for example, evaluate inspectors' qualifications by reviewing resumes, training programs, competency examinations, and performance reports.

It is also likely that the auditor would want to reperform the inspection procedures for a sample of elevators to obtain evidence of inconsistencies in reported and actual conditions.

In the same manner as for financial audits, operational auditors must accumulate sufficient competent evidence to afford a reasonable basis for a conclusion about the objectives being tested. In the elevator example, the auditor must accumulate sufficient evidence about elevator safety inspections. After the evidence is accumulated, the auditor must decide whether it is reasonable to conclude that an inspection is made annually of each elevator in the city by a competent inspector.

Reporting and Follow-Up Two major differences in operational and financial auditing reports affect operational auditing reports. First, in operational audits, the report is usually sent only to management, with a copy to the unit being audited. The lack of third-party users reduces the need for standardized wording in operational auditing reports. Second, the diversity of operational audits requires a tailoring of each report to address the scope of the audit, findings, and recommendations.

The combination of these two factors results in major differences in operational auditing reports. Report writing often takes a significant amount of time to clearly communicate audit findings and recommendations.

When reports are being rendered on performance audits in accordance with the Yellow Book, specific contents are required. The Yellow Book permits considerable freedom on the form of the report.

Follow-up is common in operational auditing when recommendations are made to management. The purpose is to determine whether the recommended changes were made, and if not, why.

Each issue of the *Internal Auditor,* a bimonthly publication of the Institute of Internal Auditors, includes several internal operational audit findings submitted by practicing internal auditors. In reviewing a multitude of these reported findings, the authors concluded that almost all of them relate to efficiency rather than effectiveness. We believe the reason is that readers of the journal find efficiency findings more interesting reading than those related to effectiveness. If someone can state, for example, that an operational audit resulted in a savings of $68,000, it is likely to be more interesting than reporting on improved accuracy of financial reporting. The following examples from the *Internal Auditor* include two related to effectiveness and the rest to efficiency.

Examples of Operational Audit Findings

Outside Janitorial Firm Saves $160,000

- An internal auditor reviewed the efficiency and effectiveness of the janitorial services furnished by state employees for the buildings in the state capitol complex. The audit disclosed the costs of the janitorial services were excessive when compared with similar services performed by outside janitorial firms. In addition, the auditors found many janitorial tasks were not completed as required, resulting in unacceptable quality. A study of alternative janitorial services indicated equal or better service could be provided by an outside janitorial firm and at a savings of $137,000 a year. The auditor recommended the state seek competitive bids and contract with the janitorial firm submitting the lowest bid that meets the specifications. The resultant contract actually saved more than $160,000, and the quality of the cleaning improved noticeably.

More Timely Credit Memo Processing

- A frequent complaint heard by the internal auditor concerned the inordinate amount of time required to process customers' credit memos. The auditor found the complaint was justified because an average of 14 working days elapsed between the receipt of the request and the actual issuance of the memo. In some cases, as many as 21 working days elapsed before the memo was issued.

  Using a time-phased flowchart, the auditor determined the requests were not moving in an efficient linear flow. As a matter of fact, the time-phased flowchart looked like a zigzag with a bad case of hiccups. The requests moved from the originator for removal of the supporting documents. The request then went back again to one of the approving departments for sorting, coding, and batching. Finally, the request was transmitted to the computer to issue the memo. Each step required from 1 to 5 working days, depending on the workload and complexity of the request.

  The auditor recommended each approving department perform all the required functions the first time it handled the request and substitute well-controlled procedures for after-the-fact approvals in place of the preapprovals. The recommendation was adopted, and credit memos are now being issued within 5 working days after the request is received. The auditor noted a higher degree of customers' satisfaction, and complaints have ceased.

Legislative Auditors Detect $11 Million per Year Insurance Overcharge

- Most states have insurance commissions to monitor and regulate the insurance industry, providing some assurance that insurance premiums are reasonable for the coverage received.

  Two legislative auditors, conducting a comparison with national loss ratios, found the state's property and liability policyholders, on average, had paid too much. In fact, the auditors determined policyholders within the state had overpaid approximately $55.1 million in premiums over 5 years because:

  - Some of the insurance companies charged premium rates developed by regional rating bureaus that use regional—not state—loss statistics. The losses projected by this method were often higher than what actually occurred within the state.
  - In some lines of property and liability insurance, there was inadequate competition to force companies to adopt more competitive rates.
  - The rate increases requested by many insurance companies were not adequately analyzed. As a consequence, these rates were increased when the justification was questionable.

  The auditors recommended the insurance commission regularly monitor the premium-to-loss ratios and implement a plan for each major line of property and liability insurance to get the state's loss ratios in line with the national average.

Use the Right Tool

- The company leased 25 heavy-duty trucks for use by service employees who installed and repaired about 20,000 vending machines in a large metropolitan area. All of the trucks were equipped with hydraulic lift-gates for loading and unloading vending machines.
- The internal auditor found that only a few of the trucks were actually delivering and picking up vending machines. Most of the trucks were used for service calls, which consisted of on-the-scene repair of coin boxes or other simple adjustments not requiring the hydraulic lift-gates.

- The auditor recommended most of the heavy-duty trucks be phased out and replaced by conventional light vans. Management agreed and the savings in lease rates and operating expenses were estimated at $25,000 a year.

Computer Programs Save Manual Labor

- ERISA requires an annual audit of profit-sharing plans. These internal auditors not only tested the finances but also performed an operational review, which provided a number of valuable recommendations to management.

  The IT auditors devised a number of computer-assisted audit programs to test control over enrollment in and termination from the company's profit-sharing plan. The computer assistance saved much manual labor and detected a number of findings such as employees on the plan with less than the required 1 year of service and terminated employees still on the plan. The computer portion of the audit program also detected conflicting data between the payroll and profit-sharing plan master files.

  When shown the results of the audit, management corrected all of the problems and instituted additional controls to prevent the problems in the future. And the additional controls were . . . well, guess. Yep, they wanted the IT auditors to leave their computer programs in the machine. The profit-sharing plan manager uses the programs periodically as a control to detect enrollment errors.

Timely Depositing

- During a cash review, the internal auditor found that bank deposits were not made until several days after the cash and checks were received. The cause was a complicated reconciliation/distribution process requiring 3 to 15 days to complete.

  Management agreed to implement a direct-deposit or electronic-funds-transfer system and to perform the reconciliation/distribution process after the funds were deposited. The system's estimated additional interest is about $120,000 a year.[2]

SUMMARY

This chapter discussed the financial auditing activities of internal auditors and the effect of internal auditors on external audits. We also discussed government auditors and the auditing and reporting requirements under government auditing standards. Increasingly, internal auditors and government auditors, as well as CPA firms, are also asked to perform operational audits of the efficiency or effectiveness of a company or government unit. In these engagements, it is important to determine the appropriate criteria for evaluating efficiency or effectiveness.

ESSENTIAL TERMS

Economy and efficiency audit—a government audit to determine whether an entity is acquiring, protecting, and using its resources economically and efficiently, the causes of any inefficiencies or uneconomical practices, and whether the entity has complied with laws and regulations concerning matters of economy and efficiency

Effectiveness—the degree to which the organization's objectives are accomplished

Efficiency—the degree to which costs are reduced without reducing effectiveness

Functional audit—an operational audit that deals with one or more specific functions within an organization, such as the payroll function or the production engineering function

Government Auditing Standards (GAGAS or GAS)—see Yellow Book

Government audits—financial or operational audits of government agencies or government-funded institutions

IIA Practice Standards—guidelines issued by the Institute of Internal Auditors, covering the activities and conduct of internal auditors

[2]Ibid.

Institute of Internal Auditors (IIA)—organization for internal auditors that establishes ethical and practice standards, provides education and encourages professionalism for its members

Operational auditing—the review of an organization for efficiency and effectiveness. The terms *management auditing, performance auditing,* and *operational auditing* are often synonymous terms

Organizational audit—an operational audit that deals with an entire organizational unit, such as a department, branch, or subsidiary, to determine how efficiently and effectively functions interact

Program audit—a government audit to determine the extent to which the desired results or benefits established by the legislature or other authorizing body are being achieved, the effectiveness of organizations, programs, activities, or functions, and whether the entity has complied with laws and regulations applicable to the program

Single Audit Act—federal legislation that provides for a single coordinated audit to satisfy the audit requirements of all federal funding agencies

Special assignments—management requests for an operational audit for a specific purpose, such as investigating the possibility of fraud in a division or making recommendations for reducing the cost of a manufactured product

Statements on Internal Auditing Standards (SIASs)—statements issued by the Internal Auditing Standards Board to provide authoritative interpretations of the IIA Practice Standards

Yellow Book—a publication of the GAO that is widely used as a reference by government auditors and CPAs who do governmental audit work; the official title is *Government Auditing Standards*

REVIEW QUESTIONS

25-1 (Objective 25-1) Explain the role of internal auditors for financial auditing. How is it similar to and different from the role of external auditors?

25-2 (Objective 25-1) What are the five parts of the scope of the internal auditor's work, according to the IIA Practice Standards?

25-3 (Objective 25-1) Explain the difference in the independence of internal auditors and external auditors in the audit of historical financial statements. How can internal auditors best achieve independence?

25-4 (Objective 25-2) Explain how governmental financial auditing is similar to and different from audits of commercial companies. Who does governmental auditing?

25-5 (Objective 25-2) Explain what is meant by the Single Audit Act. What is its purpose?

25-6 (Objective 25-2) In what ways is the Yellow Book consistent with generally accepted auditing standards, and what are some additions and modifications?

25-7 (Objective 25-2) Identify the primary specific objectives that must be incorporated into the design of audit tests under the Single Audit Act.

25-8 (Objective 25-2) Identify the key required reports of the Single Audit Act and OMB Circular A-133.

25-9 (Objective 25-3) Describe what is meant by an operational audit.

25-10 (Objective 25-3) Identify the three major differences between financial and operational auditing.

25-11 (Objective 25-4) Distinguish between efficiency and effectiveness in operational audits. State one example of an operational audit explaining efficiency and another explaining effectiveness.

25-12 (Objective 25-4) Distinguish among the following types of operational audits: functional, organizational, and special assignment. State an example of each for a not-for-profit hospital.

25-13 (Objective 25-4) Explain why many people think of internal auditors as the primary group responsible for conducting operational audits.

25-14 (Objective 25-4) Explain the role of government auditors in operational auditing. How is this similar to and different from the role of internal auditors?

25-15 (Objective 25-4) Under what circumstances are external auditors likely to be involved in operational auditing? Give one example of operational auditing by a CPA firm.

25-16 (Objective 25-5) Explain what is meant by the criteria for evaluating efficiency and effectiveness. Provide five possible specific criteria for evaluating effectiveness of an IT system for payroll.

25-17 (Objective 25-5) Identify the three phases of an operational audit.

25-18 (Objective 25-5) Explain how planning for operational auditing is similar to and different from financial auditing.

25-19 (Objective 25-5) What are the major differences between reporting for operational and financial auditing?

MULTIPLE CHOICE QUESTIONS FROM CPA, IIA, AND CMA EXAMINATIONS

25-20 (Objectives 25-1, 25-4) The following questions deal with independence of auditors. Choose the best response.

a. The operational auditor's independence is most likely to be compromised when the internal audit department is responsible directly to the
   (1) Vice president of finance.
   (2) President.
   (3) Controller.
   (4) Executive vice president.
   (5) Audit committee of the board of directors.

b. The independence of the internal audit department will most likely be assured if it reports to the
   (1) President.
   (2) Controller.
   (3) Treasurer.
   (4) Audit committee of the board of directors.
   (5) Vice president of finance.

c. Which of the following may compromise the independence of an internal auditor?
   (1) Reviewing IT systems before implementation.
   (2) Performing an audit where the auditor recently had operating responsibilities.
   (3) Failing to review the audit report with the auditee prior to distribution.
   (4) Following up on corrective action in response to audit findings.

d. Internal auditors should be objective in performing audits. Which of the following situations violates standards concerning objectivity?
   (1) The auditor who reviews accounts receivable worked in that department for three months as a trainee two years ago.
   (2) The auditor reviews a department that continues to use procedures recommended by that auditor when the department was established.
   (3) The auditor reviews the same department for 2 years in succession.
   (4) The auditor reviews a department in which the auditor has the responsibility for cosigning checks.

25-21 (Objective 25-2) The following questions deal with governmental auditing. Choose the best response.

a. Which of the following bodies promulgates standards for audits of recipients of federal awards?
   (1) Governmental Accounting Standards Board.
   (2) Financial Accounting Standards Board.

(3) General Accounting Office.

(4) Governmental Auditing Standards Board.

b. When performing the audit of a city that is subject to the requirements of the federal Single Audit Act, an auditor should adhere to
  (1) Governmental Accounting Standards Board General Standards.
  (2) Governmental Finance Officers Governmental Accounting, Auditing and Financial Reporting Principles.
  (3) Government Auditing Standards.
  (4) Securities and Exchange Commission Regulation S-X.

c. When engaged to audit a governmental entity in accordance with Government Auditing Standards, an auditor prepares a written report on internal control
  (1) on all audits, regardless of circumstances.
  (2) only when the auditor has noted reportable conditions.
  (3) only when requested by the governmental entity being audited.
  (4) only when requested by the federal government funding agency.

d. Ward is auditing an entity's compliance with requirements governing a major federal financial assistance program in accordance with the Single Audit Act. Ward detected noncompliance with requirements that have a material effect on the program. Ward's report on compliance should express
  (1) no assurance on the compliance tests.
  (2) reasonable assurance on the compliance tests.
  (3) a qualified or adverse opinion.
  (4) an adverse opinion or a disclaimer of opinion.

25-22 (Objectives 25-3, 25-4, 25-5)   The following questions deal with operational auditing. Choose the best response.

a. Which of the following best describes the operational audit?
  (1) It requires constant review by internal auditors of the administrative controls as they relate to the operations of the company.
  (2) It concentrates on implementing financial and accounting controls in a newly organized company.
  (3) It attempts and is designed to verify the fair presentation of a company's results of operations.
  (4) It concentrates on seeking aspects of operations in which waste would be reduced by the introduction of controls.

b. The evaluation of audit field work of an operating unit should answer the following questions:
  1. What are the reasons for the results?
  2. How can performance be improved?
  3. What results are being achieved?
  What is the chronological order in which these questions should be answered?
  (1) 3—1—2.   (4) 1—2—3.
  (2) 1—3—2.   (5) 2—3—1.
  (3) 3—2—1.

c. Complaints from the public were received about processing automobile license applications in the state department of motor vehicles. You were assigned by the legislative auditor to review this operation. Which of the following should be your first audit step?
  (1) Send out questionnaires to recent licensees.
  (2) Test the system by licensing a vehicle.
  (3) Discuss the nature of the complaints with the chief of the licensing office.
  (4) Discuss the nature of the complaints with several licensing clerks.
  (5) Discuss the nature of the complaints with the director of the state department of motor vehicles.

d. The first step an operational auditor should take in performing a management study to help the director of marketing determine the optimum allocation of the advertising budget to company products is to
   (1) Analyze prior years' advertising costs.
   (2) Hold discussions with media personnel.
   (3) Establish and discuss with the director the key objectives of the study.
   (4) Determine the amount of projected sales for the purpose of establishing the proposed sales budget.
   (5) Do both (1) and (2).

25-23 (Objectives 25-1, 25-4, 25-5) The following questions deal with internal auditing departments and their responsibilities. Choose the best response.

a. Which of the following is generally considered to be a major reason for establishing an internal auditing function?
   (1) To relieve overburdened management of the responsibility for establishing effective systems of internal control.
   (2) To ensure that operating activities comply with the policies, plans, and procedures established by management.
   (3) To safeguard resources entrusted to the organization.
   (4) To ensure the accuracy, reliability, and timeliness of financial and operating data used in management's decision making.
   (5) To assist members of the organization in the measurement and evaluation of the effectiveness of established systems of internal control.

b. Which of the following is generally considered to be the primary purpose of an internal auditor's evaluation of the adequacy of internal control?
   (1) To determine whether the established internal controls are functioning as intended by management.
   (2) To determine the extent of reliance the internal auditor can place on the established internal controls in the process of evaluating the financial statements prepared by the organization.
   (3) To determine whether all risks and exposures of the enterprise have been reduced or eliminated by the established internal controls.
   (4) To determine whether the established internal controls provide reasonable assurance that the objectives and goals of the organization will be met in an efficient and economical manner.

c. With regard to corrective action on audit results, which of the following is not the internal auditor's responsibility?
   (1) Soliciting auditees' suggestions for corrective actions.
   (2) Recommending possible alternative corrective actions.
   (3) Directing the corrective actions.
   (4) Determining that the corrective actions are responsive to the audit results.
   (5) Evaluating new policy statements to determine whether they address the unsatisfactory conditions disclosed in the audit results.

CASES

25-24 (Objectives 25-3, 25-4, 25-5) Saint Gabriel Hospital, which is affiliated with a leading midwestern university, has an extremely reputable research department that employs several renowned scientists. The research department operates on a project basis. The department consists of a pool of scientists and technicians who can be called on to participate in a given project. Assignments are made for the duration of the project, and a project manager is given responsibility for the work.

All major projects undertaken by the research department must be approved by the hospital's administrative board. Approval is obtained by submitting a proposal to the board outlining the project, the expected amount of time required to complete the work, and the anticipated benefits. The board also must be informed of major projects that are terminated because of potential failure or technological changes that have occurred since the time of project approval. An overall review of the status of open projects is submitted to the board annually.

In many respects, profit-making techniques used by business firms are applied to the management of the research department. For example, the department performs preliminary research work on potential major projects it has selected before requesting the board to approve the project and commit large amounts of time and money. The department also assesses the potential for grants and future revenues of the project. Financial reports for the department and each project are prepared periodically and reviewed with the administrative board.

More than 75 percent of the cost of operating the department is for labor. The remaining costs are for materials used during research. Materials used for experimentation are purchased by the hospital's central purchasing department. Once delivered, the research department is held accountable for storage, use, and assignment of cost to the projects.

To protect the hospital's rights to discoveries made by the research department, staff members are required to sign waiver agreements at the time of hire, and at certain intervals thereafter. The agreements relinquish the employees' rights to patent and royalty fees for hospital work.

Saint Gabriel's excellent reputation is due in part to the success of the research department. The research department has produced high-quality research in the health care field and has always been able to generate revenues in excess of its costs. Saint Gabriel's administrative board believes that the hospital's continued reputation depends on a strong research department, and therefore, the board has requested that the university's internal auditors perform an operational audit of the department. As a part of its request for the operational audit, the board presented the following set of objectives which the internal audit is to accomplish.

The operational audit to be conducted by the university's internal audit department should provide assurances that:

- The research department has assessed the revenues and cost aspects of each project to confirm that the revenue potential is equal to or greater than estimated costs.
- Appropriate controls exist to provide a means to measure how projects are progressing and to identify if corrective actions are required.
- Financial reports prepared by the research department for presentation to the administrative board properly reflect all revenues (both endowment and royalty sources and appropriated funding) and all costs.

Required

    a. Evaluate the objectives presented by the administrative board to the university's internal audit department in terms of their appropriateness as objectives for an operational audit. Discuss fully:

        (1) the strengths of the objectives.

        (2) the modifications and/or additions needed to improve the set of objectives.

    b. Outline, in general terms, the procedures that would be suitable for performing the audit of the research department.

    c. Identify three documents that members of the university's internal auditing staff would be expected to review during the audit and describe the purpose that the review of each document serves in carrying out the audit.*

25-25 (Objectives 25-1, 25-4) Lajod Company has an internal audit department consisting of a manager and three staff auditors. The manager of internal audits, in turn, reports to the corporate controller. Copies of audit reports are routinely sent to the audit committee of the board of directors as well as to the corporate controller and the individual responsible for the area or activity being audited.

The manager of internal audits is aware that the external auditors have relied on the internal audit function to a substantial degree in the past. However, in recent months, the

*CMA adapted.

external auditors have suggested there may be a problem related to the objectivity of the internal audit function. This objectivity problem may result in more extensive testing and analysis by the external auditors.

The external auditors are concerned about the amount of nonaudit work performed by the internal audit department. The percentage of nonaudit work performed by the internal auditors in recent years has increased to about 25 percent of their total hours worked. A sample of five recent nonaudit activities are as follows:

1. One of the internal auditors assisted in the preparation of policy statements on internal control. These statements included such things as policies regarding sensitive payments and standards of control for internal controls.

2. The bank statements of the corporation are reconciled each month as a regular assignment for one of the internal auditors. The corporate controller believes this strengthens internal controls because the internal auditor is not involved in the receipt and disbursement of cash.

3. The internal auditors are asked to review the budget data in every area each year for relevance and reasonableness before the budget is approved. In addition, an internal auditor examines the variances each month, along with the associated explanations. These variance analyses are prepared by the corporate controller's staff after consultation with the individuals involved.

4. One of the internal auditors has recently been involved in the design, installation, and initial operation of a new computer system. The auditor was primarily concerned with the design and implementation of internal accounting controls and the computer application controls for the new system. The auditor also conducted the testing of the controls during the test runs.

5. The internal auditors are often asked to make accounting entries for complex transactions before the transactions are recorded. The employees in the accounting department are not adequately trained to handle such transactions. In addition, this serves as a means of maintaining internal control over complex transactions. The manager of internal audits has always made an effort to remain independent of the corporate controller's office and believes that the internal auditors are objective and independent in their audit and nonaudit activities.

Required

  a. Define *objectivity* as it relates to the internal audit function.
  b. For each of the five situations outlined, explain whether the objectivity of Lajod Company's internal audit department has been materially impaired. Consider each situation independently.
  c. The manager of audits reports to the corporate controller.
    (1) Does this reporting relationship result in a problem of objectivity? Explain your answer.
    (2) Would your answer to any of the five situations in requirement b above have changed if the manager of internal audits reported to the audit committee of the board of directors? Explain your answer.*

25-26 (Objectives 25-1, 25-4, 25-5) Lado Corporation has an internal audit department operating out of the corporate headquarters. Various types of audit assignments are performed by the department for the eight divisions of the company.

The following findings resulted from recent audits of Lado Corporation's White Division.

1. One of the departments in the division appeared to have an excessive turnover rate. Upon investigation, the personnel department seemed to be unable to find enough workers with the specified skills for this department. Some workers are trained on the job. The departmental supervisor is held accountable for labor efficiency variances but does not have qualified staff or sufficient time to train the workers properly. The supervisor holds individual workers responsible for meeting predetermined standards

*CMA adapted.

from the day they report to work. This has resulted in a rapid turnover of workers who are trainable but not yet able to meet standards.

2. The internal audit department recently participated in a computer feasibility study for this division. It advised and concurred on the purchase and installation of a specific computer system. Although the system is up and operating, the results are less than desirable. The software and hardware meet the specifications of the feasibility study, but there are several functions unique to this division that the system has been unable to accomplish. Linking of files has been a problem. For example, several vendors have been paid for materials not meeting company specifications. A revision of the existing software is probably not possible, and a permanent solution probably requires replacing the existing computer system with a new one.

3. One of the products manufactured by this division was recently redesigned to eliminate a potential safety defect. This defect was discovered after several users were injured. At present, there are no pending lawsuits because none of the injured parties have identified a defect in the product as a cause of their injury. There is insufficient information to determine whether the defect was a contributing factor.

The director of internal auditing and assistant controller is in charge of the internal audit department and reports to the controller in corporate headquarters. Copies of internal audit reports are sent routinely to Lado's board of directors.

Required

    a. Explain the additional steps in terms of field work, preparation of recommendations, and operating management review that ordinarily should be taken by Lado Corporation's internal auditors as a consequence of the audit findings in the first situation (excessive turnover).

    b. Discuss whether there are any objectivity problems with Lado Corporation's internal audit department as revealed by the audit findings. Include in your discussion any recommendations to eliminate or reduce an objectivity problem, if one exists.

    c. The internal audit department is part of the corporate controllership function, and copies of the internal audit reports are sent to the board of directors.

        (1) Evaluate the appropriateness of the location of the internal audit department within Lado's organizational structure.

        (2) Discuss who within Lado should receive the reports of the internal audit department.*

25-27 (Objectives 25-4, 25-5)   Haskin Company was founded 40 years ago and now has several manufacturing plants in the Northeast and Midwest. The evaluation of proposed capital expenditures became increasingly difficult for management as the company became geographically dispersed and diversified its product line. Thus, the Capital Budgeting Group was organized in 1998 to review all capital expenditure proposals in excess of $50,000.

The Capital Budgeting Group conducts its annual planning and budget meeting each September for the upcoming calendar year. The group establishes a minimum return for investments (hurdle rate) and estimates a target level of capital expenditures for the next year based on the expected available funds. The group then reviews the capital expenditure proposals that have been submitted by the various operating segments. Proposals that meet either the return on investment criterion or a critical need criterion are approved to the extent of available funds.

The Capital Budgeting Group also meets monthly, as necessary, to consider any projects of a critical nature that were not expected or requested in the annual budget review. These monthly meetings allow the Capital Budgeting Group to make adjustments during the year as new developments occur.

Haskin's profits have been decreasing slightly for the past 2 years despite a small but steady sales growth, a sales growth that is expected to continue through 2000. As a result of the profit stagnation, top management is emphasizing cost control and all aspects of Haskin's operations are being reviewed for cost reduction opportunities.

*CMA adapted.

Haskin's internal audit department has become involved in the companywide cost reduction effort. The department has already identified several areas where cost reductions could be realized and has made recommendations to implement the necessary procedures to effect the cost savings. Tom Watson, internal audit director, is now focusing on the activities of the Capital Budgeting Group in an attempt to determine the efficiency and effectiveness of the capital budgeting process.

In an attempt to gain a better understanding of the capital budgeting process, Watson decided to examine the history of one capital project in detail. A capital expenditure proposal of Haskin's Burlington Plant that was approved by the Capital Budgeting Group in 1999 was selected randomly from a population of all proposals approved by the group at its 1998 and 1999 annual planning and budget meetings.

The Burlington proposal consisted of a request for five new machines to replace equipment that was 20 years old and for which preventive maintenance had become expensive. Four of the machines were for replacement purposes, and the fifth was for planned growth in demand. Each of the four replacement machines was expected to result in annual maintenance cost savings of $10,000. The fifth machine was exactly like the other four and was expected to generate an annual contribution of $15,000 through increased output. Each machine had a cost of $50,000 and an estimated useful life of 8 years.

Required

    a. Identify and discuss the issues that Haskin Company's internal audit department must address in its examination and evaluation of Burlington Plant's 1999 capital expenditure project.

    b. Recommend procedures to be used by Haskin's internal audit department in the audit review of Burlington Plant's 1999 capital expenditure project.*

25-28 (Objectives 25-4, 25-5) Lecimore Company has a centralized purchasing department that is managed by Joan Jones. Jones has established policies and procedures to guide the clerical staff and purchasing agents in the day-to-day operation of the department. She is satisfied that these policies and procedures are in conformity with company objectives and believes there are no major problems in the regular operations of the purchasing department.

Lecimore's internal audit department was assigned to perform an operational audit of the purchasing function. Their first task was to review the specific policies and procedures established by Jones. The policies and procedures are as follows:

- All significant purchases are made on a competitive bid basis. The probability of timely delivery, reliability of vendor, and so forth, are taken into consideration on a subjective basis.
- Detailed specifications of the minimum acceptable quality for all goods purchased are provided to vendors.
- Vendors' adherence to the quality specifications is the responsibility of the materials manager of the inventory control department and not the purchasing department. The materials manager inspects the goods as they arrive to be sure that the quality meets the minimum standards and then sees that the goods are transferred from the receiving dock to the storeroom.
- All purchase requests are prepared by the materials manager based on the production schedule for a 4-month period.

The internal audit staff then observed the operations of the purchasing function and gathered the following findings:

- One vendor provides 90 percent of a critical raw material. This vendor has a good delivery record and is reliable. Furthermore, this vendor has been the low bidder over the past few years.
- As production plans change, rush and expedite orders are made by production directly to the purchasing department. Materials ordered for cancelled production runs are stored for future use. The costs of these special requests are borne by the purchasing

department. Jones considers the additional costs associated with these special requests as "costs of being a good member of the corporate team."

- Materials to accomplish engineering changes are ordered by the purchasing department as soon as the changes are made by the engineering department. Jones is proud of the quick response by the purchasing staff to product changes. Materials on hand are not reviewed before any orders are placed.

- Partial shipments and advance shipments (that is, those received before the requested date of delivery) are accepted by the materials manager, who notifies the purchasing department of the receipt. The purchasing department is responsible for follow-up on partial shipments. No action is taken to discourage advance shipments.

Required

Based on the purchasing department's policies and procedures and the findings of Lecimore's internal audit staff,

- a. Identify weaknesses and/or inefficiencies in Lecimore Company's purchasing function.
- b. Make recommendations for those weaknesses/inefficiencies that you identify.*

Use the following format in preparing your response.

Weaknesses/Inefficiencies	Recommendations
1.	1.

25-29 (Objectives 25-4, 25-5) Superior Co. manufactures automobile parts for sale to the major U.S. automakers. Superior's internal audit staff is to review the internal controls over machinery and equipment and make recommendations for improvements when appropriate.

The internal auditors obtained the following information during the assignment:

- Requests for purchase of machinery and equipment are normally initiated by the supervisor in need of the asset. The supervisor discusses the proposed acquisition with the plant manager. A purchase requisition is submitted to the purchasing department when the plant manager is satisfied that the request is reasonable and that there is a remaining balance in the plant's share of the total corporate budget for capital acquisitions.

- Upon receiving a purchase requisition for machinery or equipment, the purchasing department manager looks through the records for an appropriate supplier. A formal purchase order is then completed and mailed. When the machine or equipment is received, it is immediately sent to the user department for installation. This allows the economic benefits from the acquisition to be realized at the earliest possible date.

- The property, plant, and equipment ledger control accounts are supported by lapse schedules organized by year of acquisition. These lapse schedules are used to compute depreciation as a unit for all assets of a given type which are acquired in the same year. Standard rates, depreciation methods, and salvage values are used for each major type of fixed assets. These rates, methods, and salvage values were set ten years ago during the company's initial year of operation.

- When machinery or equipment is retired, the plant manager notifies the accounting department so that the appropriate entries can be made in the accounting records.

- There has been no reconciliation since the company began operations between the accounting records and the machinery and equipment on hand.

Required

Identify the internal control weaknesses and recommend improvements that the internal audit staff of Superior Co. should include in its report regarding the internal controls employed for fixed assets. Use the following format in preparing your answer.*

Weaknesses	Recommendations
1.	1.

*CMA adapted.

INDEX

Note: Essential Terms appear in boldface.

Absence of causal connection, 118–19, 124, 130

Acceptable audit risk, 218, 238, 258, 261, 267, 268
assessing, 263–64
defined, 273
factors affecting, 261–64

Acceptable risk of assessing control risk too low (ARACR), 445, 448–49, 465

Acceptable risk of incorrect acceptance (ARIA), 517, 518, 546

Acceptable risk of incorrect rejection (ARIR), 537–38, 546

Account balances
adjusting, 521–22
internal control, 415

Accounting
defined, 11, 16
distinction between auditing and, 11
separating of custody of assets from, 295–96

Accounting basis, stating in report, 764

Accounting policies, management's responsibilities, 143

Accounting principles
AICPA *Code,* 84, 86, 93
consulting with other accountants, 91

Accounts
accrued property taxes, 627
acquisition and payment cycle, 582, 583, 584, 614
capital acquisition and repayment cycle, 678–80
manufacturing equipment, 615–16
notes payable, 680
payroll and personnel cycle, 558, 559
prepaid insurance, 623
sales and collection cycle, 398–99, 400

Accounts payable, 592
audit objectives, 594
balance-related audit objectives, 585, 596
confirmation, 596, 598
inherent risk, 592
substantive tests of transactions, 581–601
tests of controls, 581–601
tests of details of balances, 592–99
tolerable misstatements, 592

Accounts payable master file, 585, 600

Accounts payable trial balance, 585, 600

Accounts receivable
analytical procedures, 479
confirmation, 483, 488–95
designing tests of details of balances, 482–87
details of balances audit program, 378

Accounts receivable *(contd.)*
inherent risk, 374
lapping, 414, 425
master file, 401
sales and collection cycle, 475–97
tolerable misstatement, 374, 477
trial balance, 401
uncollectible, 403, 413–14

Accounts receivable balance-related objectives, 476, 497

Accounts receivable turnover ratio, 197

Accrual, 627

Accrued bonuses, 569

Accrued commissions, 569

Accrued liabilities, 634
audit of, 627–28

Accrued payroll expenses, 568, 571

Accrued payroll taxes, 569

Accrued salaries and wages, 569

Accrued sick pay, 569

Accrued vacation pay, 569

Accumulated depreciation, 622

Accumulate final evidence, 383

Accuracy
of acquisitions recording, 590
audit objective, 157, 158, 159, 161
capital stock transactions, 688
prepaid insurance, 626–27

Acquisition and payment cycle, 150, 152–54, 582, 600
accounts, 582, 583, 584, 614
accrued liabilities, 627–28
analytical procedures, 594
audit risk, 258
business functions, 583–86
controls, 704
documents and records, 583–86
income and expense accounts, 628–34
internal controls, 587, 589
prepaid expenses, 623–27
property, plant and equipment, audit of, 615–22
substantive tests of transactions, 581–601
tests, 663
tests of controls, 581–601
tests of details of balances, 592–99
transaction-related audit objectives, 589, 591
transactions, 582, 588

Acquisitions journal, 585

Acts discreditable, AICPA *Code,* 84, 96

Actually foreseen and limited classes of persons, 120

Adjusting entry, 233

Adverse opinion, 46, 47, 52, 54, 57, 61, 62

Advertising, AICPA *Code,* 84, 97

Aged trial balance, 482–83, 485, 497

Agreed-upon procedures engagement, 770, 772, 777–79, 780

Agreed-upon procedures report, 779

AICPA, *see* **American Institute of Certified Public Accountants**

Allocation, 634
of expenses, 632, 633
management assertions about, 156, 158, 161
of materiality, 254

Allocation of preliminary judgment about materiality, 251–54, 273

Alternative procedures, 183, 491, 497

American Institute of Certified Public Accountants (AICPA), 28, 37
Accounting and Review Services Committee, 758
Alliance for CPA Firms, 33
Audit Program Generator (APG), 379
Code of Professional Conduct, see Code of Professional Conduct
Committee on Professional Ethics, 29
CPA Vision Project, 28
CPA *WebTrust* services, 4, 777, 778, 780
disciplinary action, 99
Division of CPA firms, 33, 37
Elliott Committee, 4
enforcement of rules of conduct, 99–100
functions, 28–29
government auditing, 796–97
Industry Audit Risk Alerts, 265
preventing lawsuits, 127
Private Companies Practice Section (PCPS), 35
Professional Ethics Division, 95, 99–100
publications of, 29, 32
Quality Control Standards Committee, 33
research, 29, 127
sanctions, 128
SEC Practice Section, 33–34, 35
SOP 98-3, 797
Special Committee on Assurance Services, 4, 5
standards and rules of, 28–29, 127, 128
Statement on Standards for Attestation Engagements, 29
vision for the future, 28
web site, 15

Analysis, 234

Analytical procedures, 164, 185, 186, 203, 372–73
accounts receivable, 479
acquisition and payment cycle, 594
as audit evidence, 188–94

Analytical procedures (contd.)
cash balance, 705
computerized, 196
defined, 189, 382
evidence, 367
evidence mix, 370
financial ratios, 196–203
going concern, 736
for gross percentage, 481
income and expense accounts, 629
inventory and warehousing cycle, 653, 654
manufacturing equipment, 617
misstatements in financial statements, 189
notes payable, 681–82
payroll and personnel cycle, 568
preliminary, 227–28, 229
purposes of, 189, 191, 363
reduction of detailed audit tests, 189–90
review service, 759
sales and collection cycle, 363–65, 374, 479–80
statistical techniques, 194–96
substantive tests of transactions, 368
timing of, 190, 191
types of, 190–94
using effectively, 192
Analytical procedures and tests of details of balances, 163, 164, 380, 381, 382
Antifraud provisions, Securities Exchange Act of 1934, 123
APG, see Audit Program Generator
Application controls, 332–34, 346
categories of, 333
information technology, 336–37
ARACR, see Acceptable risk of assessing control risk too low
ARIA, see Acceptable risk of incorrect acceptance
ARIR, see Acceptable risk of incorrect rejection
ASB, see Auditing Standards Board
Assertions by management, see Management assertions
Assessment of acceptable audit risk, 263–64
Assessment of control risk, 162, 288–89, 305–11, 314, 315
sales and collection cycle, 374, 404, 478
Assessment of inherent risk, 266
sales and collection cycle, 477–78
Assessment of risk, see Risk assessment
Assets, see also Property, plant and equipment
overstatement of, 148
physical control over, 298, 565
separation of duties, 296, 588
Assurance services, 2, 3–6, 16
agreed-upon procedures, 772
examination, 772
on information technology, 4–5
review, 772
review and compilation, 758–62
AT number, 769

Attention directing, 189
Attestation engagement, 769–72, 780
Attestation services, 2–3, 6, 16
Attestation standards, 769–71, 775
Attorneys
contingent liabilities, 734–35
inquiry of client's, see Inquiry of client's attorneys
reluctance to provide information, 732
Attributes, 445, 446, 465
Attributes sampling, 453, 454–58, 465
Audit
accrued liabilities, 627–28
bank reconciliation, 700
capital acquisition and repayment cycle, 677–91
capital stock and paid-in capital, 688–89
cash, 700
cash balances, 699–716
communicating with audit committee and management, 742–43
completing, 727–45
compliance, 12–13, 16
contingent liabilities, 729–730
cost accounting, 650–53
dividends, 689
economy and efficiency audit, 801, 807
evaluate results, 738–41
evidence, see Evidence
final evidence accumulation, 735–38
financial statement cycles, 149–54
functional audit, 799–800
general cash account, 703–10
government audit, 807
imprest payroll account, 715
imprest petty cash fund, 715–16
income and expense accounts, 628–34
internal financial auditing, 792–94
inventory, 649–50
inventory and warehousing cycle, 645–64
notes payable, 680–85
objectives of, 142–43, 154–56
operational, 12, 16, 797–807, 808
organizational audit, 800, 808
owner's equity, 685–90
planning, see Audit planning
prepaid expenses, 622–27
pricing and compilation, 659–62
prior year's audit, 265, 312
process, see Audit process
program audit, 801, 808
property, plant and equipment, 615–22
retained earnings, 689–90
specified elements, accounts or items, 765–66
subsequent discovery of facts, 743–45
Audit assurance, 261, 273
Audit committee, 90–91, 101, 293, 310, 382, 452, 742–43
Audit failure, 113, 130
Audit of historical financial statements, 2–3, 16, 780, 802

Auditing
cycle approach, 150–54, 164
database management systems, 345, 346
defined, 9, 16
distinction between accounting and, 11
economic demand for, 7–9
governmental financial auditing, 794–97
information technology and, 330–47
management auditing, 797
nature of, 9–11
in network environment, 344–45
operational, 12, 16, 797–807, 808
performance auditing, 797, 801
Auditing around the computer, 339, 340, 346
Auditing standards, 28, 29–31, 145, 149
Auditing Standards Board (ASB), 28, 770
Auditing through the computer, 339, 340, 346
Audit objectives, 142–43, 154–63
accounts payable, 594
accounts receivable, 476
analytical procedures, 190
balance related, see Balance-related audit objectives
internal auditors, 792
manufacturing equipment, 620–21
meeting, 160–63
notes payable, 680–81
payroll and personnel cycle, 558
performance audits, 801
transaction-related, see Transaction-related audit objectives
Auditors
approval of by stockholders, 91
control risk assessment, 289
defense against third-party suits, 120–21
defenses against client suits, 117–19
defense under Securities Exchange Act of 1934, 122–24
ethics, see Ethics
external, 13, 794
government auditors, 794–97, 801–2
independent, 10, 13, 16, 58–59, 83, 84, 85, 129, 179
internal, 14, 16, 792–94, 800–801, 802–3
legal liability, 111–31
objectivity of, 83
operational auditors, 797–802
responsibilities of, 143–49
service auditors, 776
user auditors, 776–77
Auditor's opinion, 45
Audit planning, 218–38
analytical procedures, 185
audit risk model, 259
background information, 224–26, 229
client's legal obligations, 226–27
evidence mix, 369–70
internal control, 302
legal obligations, 226, 229
levels of disaggregation, 375

Audit planning (contd.)
operational auditing, 804–5
preliminary analytical procedures, 227–28, 229
preplanning the audit, 219–24, 229, 238
purposes of, 228–29
tests, selecting, 366–69
tests, types of, 360–66
tests of details of balances, 373–75
working papers, 230–37
Audit procedures, 177, 187, 188, 203, 371–72
Audit process, 161, 164
impact of information technology on, 338–43
phase I (plan and design an audit approach), 161–62, 190, 191, 378, 380, 381, 704
phase II (tests of controls and substantive tests of transactions), 162–63, 190, 191, 379–80, 381
phase III (analytical procedures and tests of details of balances), 163, 164, 380, 381, 382
phase IV (complete and issue an audit report), 183, 190, 191, 381, 382–83
summary of, 379–383
Audit program, 178, 203, 232–33
computerized, 376
design format audit program, 411, 425
design of, 371–79
performance format audit program, 411, 425
Audit Program Generator (APG), 378
Audit reports, 10–11, 16, 44–62, 163
adverse opinion, 46, 47, 52, 54, 57, 61, 62
auditor's decision process, 59–61
categories of, 47
disclaimer of opinion, 46, 47, 50, 52, 54, 61, 62
dual-dated audit report, 745
emphasis of a matter, 49, 60
explanatory paragraph, 47–48, 49, 60, 61
GAAP departure, 47–48, 50–52, 55–59, 60, 62
going concern, substantial doubt about, 48–49, 60
introductory paragraph, 44, 51, 56, 57, 61, 764
involving other auditors, 49–50, 60
issuing, 741–42
materiality, 52–55, 59, 60
material uncertainties, 48
modified wording report, 47, 50
more than one condition requiring departure or modification, 60–61
number of paragraphs, 61
opinion paragraph, 45–46, 51, 56, 57, 58, 61, 765
qualified, 47, 51–52, 61, 62
qualified scope and opinion report, 56–57, 61
restricted scope, 50

Audit reports (contd.)
Rule 203 reports, 58
scope paragraph, 44–45, 51, 56, 61, 250, 764
standard unqualified, 44–47, 54, 59, 61, 62
unqualified, 50–52, 54, 59, 60, 62
unqualified with explanatory paragraph or modified wording, 47–50, 61
unqualified report, 742
unqualified shared report with other auditors, 61
when departure required, 50–52
Audit risk, 113, 130, *see also* **Risk**; **Risk assessment**
acceptable, 218, 238, 258, 261, 261–64, 267, 268, 273
control risk, 162, 258, 260, 267, 273, 315
inherent risk, 238, 258, 260, 264–67, 273
for segments, 267–68
Audit risk model, 259, 273
evaluating results, 271
measuring components, 268–69
relationship to sample size for monetary unit sampling, 532
Audit sampling, 438, 465, *see also* Sample selection; Sample size
applicability, 446, 515
attributes sampling, 453, 454–58, 465
case illustration, 458–65
defining sampling unit, 447
difference estimation, 536, 538–44, 546
exception rate, 443–44, 466
judgmental, 439, 466
monetary units sampling, 521–33, 545–46
nonprobabilistic sample selection, 439, 440–41, 466
nonsampling risk, 438, 466
nonstatistical, 439–40, 444–53, 466, 514–21
probabilistic, 439, 440, 441–43, 466
random sample, 441, 466
representative samples, 438, 466
sampling distribution, 453–54, 466
sampling risk, 438, 466
statistical sampling, 439–40, 453–54, 466, 521–38
steps for, 445–58
steps for, summary, 452
stratified sampling, 516, 518, 537, 547
substantive tests of transactions, 437–46, 514
tests of controls, 437–66, 514
tests of details of balances, 513–47
variable sampling, 533–38, 547
Audit tests, *see* Tests
AU number, 32
Authorization
acquisition and payment cycle, 587–88
owners' equity, 686
payroll and personnel cycle, 563
sales and collection cycle, 404
Authorization of transactions and activities, 296–97

Background information, audit planning, 224–26, 229, 262–63
Bad debt expense, 485
Balance-related audit objectives, 155, 158–60, 164, 187
accounts payable, 585, 596
inventory pricing and compilation, 660
manufacturing, 618
notes payable, 682–84
physical inventory observation, 658
tests, 378
tolerable misstatement and risks related to, 268
transaction-related audit objectives and, 379, 380
Bank confirmation, receipt of, 707–9
Bank reconciliation, 704–5
audit of, 700
extended tests of, 711
independent reconciliation, 705
misstatements, 700
payroll bank account reconciliation, 561
tests of, 709–10
working paper for, 706
year-end bank reconciliation, 705, 711
Batch input controls, 337
Big Five international firms, 25
Bill of lading, 400
Bills not paid, documentation for, 595
Bily v. *Arthur Young*, 120
Binomial distribution, 453
Blank confirmation form, 488, 497
Block sample selection, 440–41, 465
Board of Directors, as internal control, 293
Boeing Company, report of management, 143, 144
Bonuses, accrued, 569
Bookkeeping services, 25
Code Rule 101, 89
Book value per common share, 199
Branch bank accounts, 702, 716
Breach of contract, 116
Budgets, 194, 203
Burden of proof, 231
Business failure, 113, 130
Business functions
acquisition and payment cycle, 583–86
inventory and warehousing cycle, 646–49
payroll and personnel cycle, 558–62
sales and collection cycle, 399–403, 424
Business performance measurement services, 6
Business risk, 261, 262, 273
Bylaws, 226, 229, 238

Canadian Institute of Chartered Accountants (CICA), 777
Capital acquisition and repayment cycle, 150, 152–54, 691
accounts, 678–80
audit of, 677–91
audit risk, 258
characteristics of, 678

Capital acquisition and repayment cycle *(contd.)*
 notes payable, 679, 680–85, 691
 tests, 690
Capital stock, 686, 688–89
 transactions recorded, 688
Capital stock certificate book, 687, 691
Capital stock and paid-in capital, audit, 688–89
Caring, as ethical principle, 76
Cash
 audit of, 700, 710
 defalcation, 414, 700
 electronic transfer, 714
 fraud-oriented procedures, 710–14
 interbank transfer, 713–14
 proof of, 711–13
Cash accounts
 general cash account, 700, 702, 703–10, 716
 types of, 702–3
Cash balances, audit of, 699–716
Cash in the bank
 relationship to other transaction cycles, 700, 701
 tests of details of balances, 704
Cash basis accounting, 764
Cash disbursements
 processing and recording, 585–86
 subsequent, 595
Cash disbursements journal, 586
Cash equivalents, 703, 716
Cash ratio, 197
Cash receipts
 cutoff, 485
 processing and recording, 401–2
 proof of, 414, 425
 subsequent to confirmation date, 491–92
 substantive tests of transactions, 412–14
 test of controls, 412–14
Cash receipts journal, 402
Cenco Incorporated v. *Seidman & Seidman,* 117
Certified Internal Auditor (CIA), 792
Certified Public Accountant (CPA), 14, 16
 assurance services, 2, 3–6
 attestation services, 2–3, 6
 criminal liability, 125–27
 disciplinary action, 99–100
 engagement letters, 117, 118, 129, 221, 238
 legal liability, 111–31
 management consulting services, 5
 nonassurance services, 5–6
 requirements, 14, 15
Chart of accounts, 297–98, 315
Check, 586
CIA, *see* Certified Internal Auditor
CICA, *see* Canadian Institute of Chartered Accountants
Citizenship, as ethical principle, 76
Civil liabilities, federal securities laws, 121–25
Classes of transactions in the sales and collection cycle, 399, 424

Classification
 of acquisitions, 590
 audit objective, 157, 158, 159, 161
 prepaid insurance, 626
Client
 defined, 83
 human resource policies, 294, 303
 internal controls, 289
 investee relationship with, 88
 liability to, 115–19
 organizational structure, 294
 personnel, 302–3
 policy and systems manuals, 303
 reason for audit, 221
 rights to accounts receivable, 486
Client records
 Code Rule 501, 96
 confidentiality, *see* Confidentiality
Closely held corporation, 685, 691
Code of Professional Conduct, 81, 82–86, 127
 definitions, 83
 ethical principles, 83
 financial interests and issues, 87–88
 independence, 84, 85, 86–92
 Rule 101, 51, 84, 85, 86–92
 Rule 102, 84, 92
 Rule 201, 84, 93
 Rule 202, 84, 93
 Rule 203, 49, 58, 84, 86, 93
 Rule 301, 84, 94, 230
 Rule 302, 84, 95
 Rule 501, 84, 96
 Rule 502, 84, 97
 Rule 503, 84, 98
 Rule 505, 84, 98
 rules of conduct, 84–100
Collusion, 289, 315
Commissions, 570
 accrued, 569
Commissions, AICPA *Code,* 84, 98
Commitments, 729, 730, 745
Committee of Sponsoring Organizations of the Treadway Commission (COSO), 148, 289
Common law, 116
Comparability, 48
Compare, term defined, 188
Competence
 of client staff, 293
 of operational auditors, 802
Competence of evidence, 178–80, 185–86, 203, 598
Competent independent person, 10
Compilation report, 761
Compilation report with full disclosure, 761
Compilation report that omits substantially all disclosures, 761, 762
Compilation report without independence, 761
Compilation and review standards, 28–29
Compilation services, 760–62, 780
Complete and issue an audit report, 183, 190, 191, 381, 382–83

Completeness
 of acquisitions recording, 590
 audit objective, 157, 158, 159, 161
 management assertions about, 155–56
 prepaid insurance, 626
 sales returns and allowances, 411–12
Completing the engagement checklist, 738, 745
Compliance audit, 12–13, 16, 795
Compliance with standards, AICPA *Code,* 84, 93
Compute, term defined, 188
Computed upper exception rate (CUER), 444, 445, 465
Computer controls, 330
Computer generation of random numbers, 442, 443
Computer service center, outsourcing to, 345
Computer software, *see also* Information technology
 AICPA audit program, 379
 for auditing, 196
 automated working papers, 237
 generalized audit software, 341–42, 346
 parallel simulation, 341, 342
 systems development, 335
Concurring partner review, 33
Confidential client information, 84, 94, 101, 115
Confidentiality
 AICPA *Code,* 84, 94
 exceptions to, 94–95
 lack of privileged communication, 115
 need for, 94
 of working papers, 230–31
Confirmation, 182–84, 186, 203
 accounts payable, 596, 598
 accounts receivable, 483, 488–95
 analysis of differences, 492
 bank confirmation, 707–9
 blank confirmation form, 488, 497
 difference between vendor's statements and, 598
 invoice confirmation, 488, 497
 negative confirmation, 183, 488–90, 497
 positive confirmation, 183, 488, 497
 standard bank confirmation form, 716
 type of, 488–90
Consistency, 48
Constructive fraud, 116
Continental Vending case, 487
Contingent fees, AICPA *Code,* 84, 95
Contingent liabilities
 defined, 728, 745
 review for, 728–32
Continuing education, 33
Contracts, 116, 227
Contributory negligence, 118, 120, 130
Control activities, 295–99, 300, 315
 authorization of transactions, 296–97
 control over assets and records, 298
 documents and records, 297–98
 independent checks, 298–99
 separation of duties, 295–96

Control environment, 292–94, 300, 315
  control activities, 295–99, 300, 315
  information and communication, 299, 300, 315
  monitoring, 299–300, 315
  risk assessment, 294–95, 300, 315
Control risk, 258, 260, 267
  assessed, 313, 451
  assessing, 162, 288, 305–11, 314, 315, 478
  cash balance, 704
  defined, 260, 273
  information technology and, 338–39
  sales and collection cycle, 374–75, 404, 478
Control risk matrix, 308, 309, 315
Controls
  acquisition and payment cycle, 704
  cost accounting, 651
  effectiveness of, 179
  general controls, 338
  inventory, 656
  notes payable, 681
  pricing and compilation, 659
  testing, *see* Tests of controls
  understanding, 31, 162
Corporate by-laws, 226, 229, 238
Corporate charter, 226, 229, 238
Corporate minutes, 226, 229, 238, 689, 729, 735–36
COSO, *see* Committee of Sponsoring Organizations of the Treadway Commission
Cost accounting
  audit of, 650–53
  tests of, 651–52, 663
Cost accounting controls, 651, 664
Cost accounting records, 648, 664
Count, term defined, 188
CPA, *see* **Certified Public Accountant**
CPA examination, 15, 29
  Code Rule 501, 96
CPA firms, 13, 24–25, 37
  activities of, 25–26
  AICPA division, 33–34
  approval of by stockholders, 91
  ethics, 81
  independence, 86, 129
  legal liability, 111–31
  litigation with client, 89
  operational audit, 802
  organizational hierarchy, 26
  organizational structure, 26–27, 84, 98–99, 129, 294
  peer review, 34–35, 95, 128
  quality control procedures for, 33
  staff levels and responsibilities, 27
Credit, granting, 399–400
Credit Alliance v. *Arthur Andersen & Co.,* 120
Credit memo, 402
Criminal liability, 116, 125–27, 130
CUER, *see* **Computed upper exception rate**
Current files, 232–36, 238
Current ratio, 196

Current-year acquisitions, manufacturing equipment, 617–18
Current-year disposals, manufacturing equipment, 620
Customer order, 399
Customer order processing, 399
Cutoff, audit objective, 159, 161
Cutoff bank statement, 709, 716
Cutoff misstatements, 484, 497
Cutoff tests, 597, 600
Cycle approach, 150–54, 164

Database management systems, 345, 346
Debit memo, 585, 600
Debt compliance letters, 768, 769
Debt-paying ability, 196
Debt-to-equity ratio, 198
Declaration of dividends, 687
Deduction authorization form, 559
Defalcation, 145, 266, *see also* Fraud
  cash, 414, 700
  protecting against, 295–96
Depreciation expense, manufacturing equipment, 621–22, 633
Design format audit program, 411, 425
Design of tests, 302
Detail tie-in, audit objective, 159, 161
Detection risk, 302, 313
Difference estimation, 536, 538–44, 546
Directed sample selection, 440, 466
Direct-effect illegal acts, 148, 149
Direct financial interest, 87, 101
Direct projection estimate of misstatement, 256, 273
Disaggregation levels, 375
Disclaimer of opinion, 46, 47, 50, 52, 54, 61, 62
Disclosure, management assertions about, 156, 158, 160, 161
Discreditable acts, AICPA *Code,* 84, 96
Disposals, manufacturing equipment, 620
Dividends
  audit of, 689
  declaration of, 687, 689
  payment of, 687
  stock dividends, 690
  tests of, 689
Documentation, 184, 186, 187, 188, 203
  for bills not paid, 595
  outside documentation, 236
Documents and records
  acquisition and payment cycle, 583–86
  adequacy, 297
  capital stock transactions, 688
  cost accounting records, 664
  examining, 303, 311
  inventory, transferring, 652
  inventory and warehousing cycle, 646–49
  notes payable, 681
  payroll and personnel cycle, 558–62, 563–64
  prenumbered, 405
  sales and collection cycle, 400, 404–5
  standard cost records, 659, 664

Dual-dated audit report, 745
Due care, 83

Earnings per share, 198, 199–200
Economy and efficiency audit, 801, 807
EDI, *see* Electronic Data Interchange
Effectiveness, 12, 807
  of internal control, 179, 369, 775–76
  operational audits, 798
Efficiency, 12, 807
  operational audits, 798
Efficiency ratio, 198, 199
"ElderCare Plus" assurance services, 5
Electronic commerce, 800–801
Electronic Data Interchange (EDI), 184, 369
electronic funds transfer, 402
Electronic information, 184
Electronic transfer of cash, 714
Elliott Committee, 4
Embedded audit module approach, 342–43, 346
Employee fraud, 145
Employment, *see* Payroll and personnel cycle
Engagement letters, 117, 118, 129, 221, 238
EPER, *see* **Estimated population exception rate**
Equipment-related accounts, 615–16, *see also* Property, plant and equipment
Error, 145, 164
Escott et al. v. *Bar Chris Construction Corporation,* 122
ESM Government Securities v. *Alexander Grant & Co.,* 127
Estimated population exception rate (EPER), 445, 449, 466
Estimate misstatements, 256–57
Ethics, 76–101, 101, *see also Code of Professional Conduct*
  AICPA Committee on Professional Ethics, 29
  control environment, 292–93
  defined, 76–77, 101
  difference between CPA and other professionals, 81
  ethical conduct of CPAs, 81
  ethical conduct in professions, 80–82
  ethical dilemma, 77–80, 101
  ethical principles, 76, 83
  ethical rulings, 85–86
  need for, 76
  rationalizing unethical behavior, 78
  why people act unethically, 76–77
Evidence, 10, 16, 175–203
  acquisition and payroll cycle, 598
  agreed-upon procedures, 772
  attestation engagements, 772
  audit tests and, 367
  competence of, 178–80, 185–86, 203
  cost of, 181, 186–87, 367
  decisions, 176–78, 187
  evaluating results and reaching conclusions, 741, 742

Evidence *(contd.)*
    examination, 772
    final evidence accumulation, 735–38
    nature of, 176
    objectivity of, 179
    operational auditing, 804–5
    persuasiveness of, 178–81
    planning, audit risk models for, 272
    relevance of, 178–79
    reliability of, 598
    review, 772
    revising, 272
    risk relationship to, 269
    sample size, 177, 180
    sufficiency of, 31, 180, 203, 738, 741
    timeliness of, 177, 180
    types of, 181–88, 367
Evidence mix, 370–71, 383
Examination, 770, 773, 775–76, 780
Examination report, 772
Examination of supporting
    documents, 235
Examine, term defined, 188
Exception, 445
Exception rate, 443–44, 466
Existence
    audit objective, 156–57, 158, 159, 161
    prepaid insurance, 626
Expectation gap, 114
Expense account analysis, 630–32, 634
Expense accounts, tests of details of
    balances, 569–70
Explanatory paragraph (audit report),
    47–48, 49, 60, 61
Extended audit services, 90
External auditors, 13, 794
External document, 184, 203

Fairness, as ethical principle, 76
Federal Deposit Insurance Corporation
    Improvement Act of 1991, 775
Financial interests and issues, ethics,
    87–89
Financial ratios, 196–203
Financial reporting
    reliability of, 289–90
    risk assessment and, 294–95
Financial statement audit, 2, 11, 12, 16
Financial statement disclosure checklist,
    740, 745, 841
Financial statements
    auditability, 305
    audit of historical financial
        statements, 2–3, 16
    cycles, 149–54
    disclosures, 740
    fraud, 145–48
    information accompanying basic
        financial statements, 767–68
    management's responsibilities, 143
    objectives of audit of, 142–43
    other comprehensive basis of
        accounting (OCBOA), 764
    review and compilation services,
        758–59
Firm, defined, 83

Fixed asset master file, 616, 634
Fixed assets, *see* Property, plant and
    equipment
Flowchart, 303–4, 315
FOB destination, 597–98, 600
FOB origin, 597, 600
Foot, term defined, 188
Footnotes, 487
    contingent liabilities, 728
    review of interim financial
        information, 762
Forecasts, 773, 780
Foreign Corrupt Practices Act of 1977,
    125, 130, 289
Foreseeable users, 120, 130
Foreseen user, 119, 130
Form 8-K (SEC), 36, 122
Form 10-K (SEC), 36, 122, 235
Form 10-Q (SEC), 36
Former practitioners, *Code* Rule 101, 88
Form of organization and name, *Code,*
    26–27, 84, 98
Forms S-1 to S-16 (SEC), 36
Fraud, 145, 164
    auditor's responsibilities for detecting,
        145–47
    cash accounts, 710–14
    communicating to audit committee and
        management, 742
    discovery of, statistics, 291
    fraudulent financial reporting, 145–46,
        147, 164
    management fraud, 145
    misappropriation of assets, 145–46,
        147, 164
    risk assessment for, 145–47
    Securities Exchange Act of 1934, 123
    statistics, 148
Fraud-oriented procedures, 710–14
Fraudulent financial reporting, 145–46,
    147, 164
    misstatements arising from, 265
Functional audit, 799–800, 807

GAAP, *see* Generally accepted accounting
    principles
GAAS, *see* **Generally accepted auditing**
    standards
General Accounting Office (GAO), *see*
    United States General Accounting
    Office
General Accounting Office auditor,
    13, 16
General authorization, 296, 315
General balance-related audit objectives,
    159–60, 161
General cash account, 700, 702, 716
    audit of, 703–10
    fraud-oriented procedures, 710–14
General controls, 332–34, 346
    categories of, 333
    control risk and, 338
    transaction-related audit objectives, 338
General corporation, 26
Generalized audit software (GAS),
    341–42, 346

Generally accepted accounting principles
    (GAAP)
    financial statements not in accordance
        with, 47–48, 50–51
    management assertions, 155
Generally accepted auditing standards
    (GAAS), 29–31, 37, 771
General Partnership, 26
General standards, AICPA *Code,* 84, 93
General transaction-related audit
    objectives, 156–57, 158
General use, 773
Going concern
    analytical procedures to assess, 189
    substantial doubt about, 48–49, 60, 736
Goods, receiving, in acquisition and
    payment cycle, 584
Governmental financial auditing,
    794–97, 807
Government Auditing Standards
    (GAGAS; GAS), 794, 807
Government audit report, 796, 797
Government audits, 794–97, 807
Gross margin percentage, 199
Gross negligence, 116
Gross percentage, analytical procedures
    for, 481

Haphazard sample selection, 441, 466
Hardware controls, 336, 346
Historical financial statements
    audit of, 1–2, 780, 802
    review of, 3
Hochfelder v. *Ernst & Ernst,* 123, 124
Holding the cash receipts book open, 485
Howard Sirota v. *Solitron Devices, Inc.,*
    123–24
Human resource policies, client, 294

IFAC, *see* International Federation of
    Accountants (IFAC)
IIA, *see* **Institute of Internal Auditors**
IIA Practice Standards, 792–94, 807
Illegal acts, 148, 164
    auditing standards, 148
    communicating to audit committee and
        management, 742
Immaterial misstatements, 143, 739
Imprest dividend account, 687
Imprest payroll account, 561, 571, 702,
    716
    audit of, 715
Imprest petty cash fund, 702–3, 716
    audit of, 715–16
Income and expense accounts, audit of,
    628–34
Income tax basis accounting, 764, 765
Independence
    AICPA *Code,* 83, 84, 85, 86–92
    compilation report without
        independence, 761
    of auditors, 10, 13, 16, 58–59, 83, 129,
        179
    of operational auditors, 802
Independence in appearance, 87, 101
Independence in fact, 87, 101

Independence Standards Board, 90, 101
Independent auditors, 10, 13, 16, 58–59
Independent checks, 298–99, 315
Independent reconciliation, 705
Independent registrar, 687, 691
Independent review, 741, 745
Indirect-effect illegal acts, 148–49
Indirect financial interest, 87, 101
Information accompanying basic financial statements, 767–68
Informational schedule, 235
Information and communication, 299, 300, 315
Information and established criteria, 9–10
Information risk, 7–8, 16
Information systems reliability services, 4–5
Information technology (IT), *see also* Computer software
application controls, 332–34, 336–37
assessing risks of, 331–32
assurance services on, 4–5
auditing around the computer, 339, 340, 346
auditing through the computer, 339, 340, 346
back-up and contingency planning, 336
data control, 335
defined, 296, 315
embedded audit module approach, 342–43, 346
general controls, 332–34, 346
hardware controls, 336, 346
input controls, 336, 337, 346
internal control enhanced by, 330
management of, 332, 334
microcomputers and, 343–44
network environment, 344–45
operations, 335
outsourced, 345–47
output controls, 337, 346
parallel simulation, 341, 342, 346
processing controls, 337, 347
security, 335–36
segregation of duties, 331, 334
separation of duties, 296
systems development, 334, 335
test data approach, 339–41, 347
Inherent risk, 238, 258, 260, 267
accounts payable, 592
accounts receivable, 374
assessing, 266, 477–78
cash balance, 704
defined, 260, 273
factors affecting, 264–67
payroll, 568
Initial sample size, 449, 466
Input controls, 336, 337, 346
Inquire, term defined, 188
Inquire of management, 729, 734, 759
Inquiry, 185, 186, 187, 188, 203
client personnel information, 302–3, 311
Inquiry of client's attorneys, 730–32, 745
Institute, defined, 83
Institute of Internal Auditors (IIA), 792–94, 802–3, 808

Institute of Internal Auditors (IIA) Professional Practice Standards, 793
Insurance expense, 623
Insurance register, 623, 634
Integrity
AICPA *Code,* 84, 92
control environment, 292–93
Intentional misstatement, 145
Interbank transfers, tests of, 713–14
Interbank transfer schedule, 713–14
Internal auditing, 90
Internal auditors, 14, 16, 792, 794, 800–801, 802–3
Internal control
account balances, 415
acquisition and payment cycle, 587, 589, 591
auditing around the computer, 339–41, 346
auditing through the computer, 339–41, 346
audit risk and, 258, 259
cash receipts, 412, 413
components of, 292–301
concepts, 288–89
control activities, 295–99, 300, 315
control environment, 292–95, 300, 315
defined, 288, 315
effectiveness of, 179, 369, 775–76
information technology, specific to, 330, 332–37
inventory and warehousing cycle, 649
management's responsibility, 288–89
notes payable, 681
owners' equity, 686–87
payroll and personnel cycle, 563, 564
prepaid expenses, 623–24
procedures to obtain an understanding, 301–5, 315
relationship between operational auditing and, 799
reporting on, 775–77
sales and collection cycle, 404, 405–11
for service organization, 776–77
size of business and, 301
understanding of, 31, 162
Internal control questionnaire, 305, 315
Internal control weakness, 307, 315, 338, 339
Internal document, 184, 203
Internal financial auditing, 792–94
Internal flowchart, 315
Internal revenue agents, 14, 16
Internal verification procedures, 405
International Auditing Practice Committee (IFAC), 32
International CPA firms, 25
International Federation of Accountants (IFAC), 32
International Standards on Auditing (ISAs), 32
Introductory paragraph (audit report), 44, 51, 56, 57, 61, 764
Inventory, 616
audit of, 649–50
cutoff to physical observation, 597

Inventory (*contd.*)
flow of, 647
manufactured inventory, 661
perpetual inventory master file, 648, 652, 664
physical observation, 649, 655–58
price and compile inventory, 650
pricing purchased inventory, 659
in public warehouse, 655
purchased inventory, 659
replacement cost, 661–62
transferring, 652
in transit, 597–98
valuation of, 659–60
Inventory compilation tests, 659, 664
Inventory price tests, 659, 664
Inventory turnover ratio, 197
Inventory valuation, relationship between payroll and, 566
Inventory and warehousing cycle, 150, 152–54, 646, 664
analytical procedures, 653, 654
audit, 645–64
audit risk, 258, 259, 260
business functions, 646–49
documents and records, 646–49
integration of tests, 662–63
internal controls, 649
purchase orders, 646–47, 649
tests of details of balances, 653–55
Investee relationship with client, *Code* Rule 101, 88
Invoice confirmation, 488, 497
ISAs, *see* International Standards on Auditing
Issuance of capital stock, 686
IT, *see* Information technology
Items to select, as audit decision, 177

Job cost systems, 664
Job time ticket, 560
Joint investor, *Code* Rule 101, 88
Joint and several liability, 115, 116
Judgmental sampling, 439, 466

Kiting, 713, 716
Known third party, 119

Lack of duty to perform, 117, 121, 124, 130
LANs, *see* **Local area networks**
Lapping of accounts receivable, 414, 425
Lawsuits, *see* Liability
Lead schedule, 233, 238
Legal documents and records, examining, 226–27
Legal expenses, analysis of, 730
Legal liability, 111–29, 130, 595, 774, *see also* Liability
Legal obligations, audit planning, 226, 229
Lending procedures, *Code* Rule 101, 88
Letter of representation, 736, 745
Letters of credit, 730
Levels of disaggregation, 375
Leverage analysis, 199
Liabilities, accrued, 627–28, 634

Liability
 burden of proof, 231
 chance of client financial failure, 262
 civil, under federal securities laws, 121–25
 criminal, 116, 125–27, 130
 joint and several, 115, 116
 legal concepts affecting, 114–15, 116
 legal environment, 112–33
 preventing, 128–29
 profession's response to, 127–28
 receipt of goods and services, 584
 separate and proportionate, 116
 terms defined, 113–14, 116
 to clients, 115–19
 to third party under common law, 116
 under federal securities laws, 116, 119–21
Liability accounts, payroll and personnel cycle, 568–70
Limited liability company (LLC), 26–27, 129
Limited liability partnership (LLP), 26–27, 114–15, 129
Limited use, 773
Liquidity, 197
Litigation
 client confidentiality, 94–95, 115
 Code Rule 101, 89
Loans, investee relationship with, 88
Local area networks (LANs), 344, 346
Local CPA firms, 25
Lockbox systems, 402

McLean v. *Alexander,* 124
Management
 communicating with, 742–43
 contingent liabilities, 729
 control environment, 293–94
 financial statement disclosures, 740
 illegal acts and, 149
 inquiry of management, 729, 734, 759
 integrity, auditor's evaluation of, 263
 internal controls, 288–89, 293–94
 responsibilities of, 143, 288
 risk assessment by, 294–95
Management assertions, 155–56, 158, 160, 161, 164
Management auditing, 797
Management consulting services, 5, 34
Management fraud, 145
Management letter, 311, 315, 743, 745
Manufactured inventory, pricing, 661
Manufacturing equipment, *see also* Property, plant and equipment
 analytical procedures, 617
 audit objectives, 620–21
 audit of, 615–22
 current-year acquisitions, 617–18
 current-year disposals, 620
 depreciation expense, 621–22
Materiality, 48, 52–55, 250–57
 accounting basis other than cash, 765
 allocate preliminary judgment to segments, 254–56
 bases for, 252

Materiality *(contd.)*
 Code Rule 101, 88
 decisions, 54–55
 defined, 52, 250, 273
 government auditing, 795
 illustrative guidelines, 253
 levels of, 52–53, 59, 60
 non-GAAP condition, 54–55
 preliminary judgment about, 251–54
 qualitative factors, 252–53
 as relative rather than absolute concept, 252
 sales returns and allowances, 411–12
 scope limitations condition, 55
Material misstatements, 52, 62, 143, 250
 audit risk, 258, 260
 potential, 302
Mean-per-unit estimation, 537, 546
Measurability, 54
Member, defined, 83
Microcomputers, auditing and, 343–44
Minutes, **corporate minutes,** 226, 229, 238, 689
Misappropriation of assets, 145–46, 147, 164
Misstatement bounds, 546
Misstatements
 adjusting entries, 233
 bank reconciliation, 700
 cash accounts, 700, 702
 cutoff misstatements, 484, 497
 error v. fraud, 145
 estimate, 256–57
 in financial statements, 744
 fraudulent financial reporting, 265
 immaterial, 143, 739
 intentional, 145
 material, 52, 62, 143, 250, 252
 monetary, 361
 monetary unit sampling, 525–29
 previous year's audit, 265
 projected, 256
 reclassification entries, 233
 sales and collection cycle, 407, 520–21
 summarizing, 739
 tolerable, 254
 unadjusted misstatement worksheet, 739, 745
 unusual fluctuations, 189
Modified cash basis accounting, 764
Modified wording report, 47, 50
Monetary misstatements, 361
Monetary unit sampling (MUS), 521–33, 545–46
Monitoring, 299–300, 315
Monthly statement, 401, 405

Narrative, 303, 304, 315
National CPA firms, 25
Negative confirmation, 183, 488–90, 497
Negligence, 116
Network environment, auditing in, 344–45
Next of kin, *Code* Rule 101, 88
Nonexistent payroll, tests for, 566–67

Nonnegligent performance, 117–18, 120, 124, 130
Nonpartners, *Code* Rule 101, 87
Nonprobabilistic sample selection, 439, 466
Nonprobabilistic sampling, 439, 440–41, 466
Nonpublic companies, review and compilation services, 758–62
Nonresponses, accounts receivable confirmations, 491
Nonroutine transactions, inherent risk, 266
Nonsampling risk, 438, 466
Nonshareholders, *Code* Rule 101, 87
Nonstatistical sampling, 439–40, 466
 application of, 444–53
 differences between monetary unit sampling and, 522–25
 differences variable sampling and, 533
 tests of details of balances, 514–21
Notes payable, 680–85
 accounts, 680
 analytical procedures, 681–82
 audit objective, 680–81
 balance-related audit objectives, 682–84
 controls, 681
 defined, 680, 691
 internal controls, 681
 substantive tests of transactions, 681
 tests of controls, 681
 tests of details of balances, 679, 682–85

Objectivity
 AICPA *Code,* 84, 102
 of auditor, 83
 of evidence, 179
Obligations, management assertions about, 156, 158, 160, 161
Observation, 185, 186, 187, 188, 203
Observe, term defined, 188
OCBOA, *see* Other comprehensive basis of accounting
Occurrence rate, 443–44, 466
Officers' compensation, 570
OMB Circular A-133, 795, 796
Operating and performance ratio, 198
Operational auditing, 12, 16, 797–807, 808
Opinion paragraph (audit reports), 45–46, 51, 56, 57, 58, 61, 765
Ordinary negligence, 116
Organizational audit, 800, 808
Organizational structure
 of client, 294
 of CPA firms, 25–27, 84, 98–99, 129
Other comprehensive basis of accounting (OCBOA), 764
Other information included in annual reports, 745
Out-of-period liabilities tests, 595
Output controls, 337, 346
Outside documentation, 236

Outside specialists, required for audit, 225–26
Outsourcing, of information technology functions, 345–46
Overstatement of assets, 148
Owners' equity
  audit of, 685–90
  internal control, 686–87

Parallel simulation, 341, 342, 346
Parallel testing, 335, 341, 347
Partner rotation, 33
Partners
  Code Rule 101, 87
  legal liability, 115
Payment of dividends, 687
Payments, authorization, 588
Payroll
  imprest payroll account, 561, 571, 702, 715, 716
  nonexistent payroll, 566–67
  payment of, 561
  payment of taxes, 561–62
  records, 560–61
  relationship between inventory valuation and, 566
  tax returns, 561–62
Payroll bank account reconciliation, 561
Payroll check, 561
Payroll expenses, accrued, 568, 571
Payroll journal, 560
Payroll master file, 560–61, 571
Payroll and personnel cycle, 150, 152–54, 571
  accounts, 558, 559
  analytical procedures, 568
  audit objective, 558
  audit risk, 258, 259, 260
  business functions, 558–62
  documents and records, 558–62, 563–64
  internal controls, 563, 564
  liability accounts, 568–70
  payroll taxes, 562, 565, 569
  substantive tests of transactions, 562–67
  tests, 663
  tests of controls, 562–67
  tests of details of balances, 567–70
  transactions, 558
Payroll taxes
  accrued, 569
  withheld, 565, 569
Payroll tax expense, 570
Payroll tax forms, 565
Payroll tax returns, 562
Peer review, 33, 34–35, 37, 95, 128
Performance auditing, 797, 801
Performance format audit program, 411, 425
Permanent files, 231–32, 238
Perpetual inventory master file, 648, 652, 664
Personnel, *see* Payroll and personnel cycle
Personnel records, 559, 581
Persuasiveness of evidence, 178, 203

Petty cash, **imprest petty cash fund,** 702–3, 715–16
Phase I (plan and design an audit approach), 161–62, 190, 191, 379, 381, 382
  accounts payable, 593–94
  cash balance, 704–5
Phase II (tests of controls and substantive tests of transactions), 162–63, 190, 191, 379–80, 381, 382
  cash balance, 705
Phase III (analytical procedures and tests of details of balances), 163, 164, 380, 381, 382
  cash balance, 705
Phase IV (complete and issue an audit report), 183, 190, 191, 381, 382–83
Physical examination, 181–82, 186, 187, 188, 203
Physical inventory, 663
Physical observation, inventory, 649, 655–58
Pilot testing, 335, 347
Plan and design an audit approach, 161–62, 190, 191, 378, 381, 382
Planned detection risk, 258, 260, 273
Planning, *see* Audit planning
Planning and supervision, adequate, 31
Plant equipment, *see also* Property, plant and equipment
  audit of, 615–22
Point estimate, 519, 520, 546
Positive confirmation, 183, 488, 497
Post-balance-sheet review, 733–35, 745
Posting and summarization, audit objective, 157, 158
PPS, *see* **Probability proportion to size sample selection**
Practice of public accounting, defined, 83
Preliminary analytical procedures, 227–28, 229
Preliminary judgment about materiality, 251–54, 273
Prepaid expenses
  audit of, 622–27
  internal control, 623–24
Prepaid insurance, 623–24
Preplanning the audit, 219–24, 229, 238
Presentation and disclosure, management assertions about, 156, 158, 160, 161
Price and compile inventory, 650
Pricing
  manufactured inventory, 661
  purchased inventory, 659
Pricing and compilation
  audit of, 659–62
  controls, 659
  physical inventory, 663
Primary beneficiary, 119
Private Securities Litigation Reform Act, 128, 130
Privileged information, 94, 101, 115
Privity of contract, 116, 117, 119, 121, 131
Probabilistic sample selection, 439, 440, 441–43, 466

Probability proportional to size and stratified sample selection, 442–43
Probability proportion to size sample selection (PPS), 442–43, 523, 547
Procedures for tests of controls, 311–13
Procedures to gain an understanding, 360
Procedures to obtain an understanding, 301–5, 315, 360, 383
  evidence, 367
  evidence mix, 370
Process cost systems, 664
Processing controls, 337, 347
Professional care, due, 31
Professional corporation (PC), 26
Professional ethics, *see Code of Professional Conduct;* Ethics
Professional skepticism, 145
Profitability ratio, 199
Profit margin ratio, 199
Program audit, 801, 808
Projected misstatements, 256
Projections, 773, 780
Proof of cash, 711–13, 716
Proof of cash receipts, 414, 425
Property, plant and equipment, audit of, 615–22
Property taxes, accrued, 627
Proprietorship, 26
Prospective financial statements, 772–74, 780
Prudent person concept, 114, 130
Public companies, review of interim financial information, 762–63
Public interest, 83
Publicly held corporation, 685, 691
Purchase orders, 584, 600
  inventory and warehousing cycle, 646–47, 649
  processing, 646–47
Purchase requisition, 584, 601

Qualified opinion report, 47, 50, 61, 62
Qualified scope and opinion report, 56–57, 61
Quality control, 33–35, 37
  government auditing, 795
  peer review, 34–35, 95, 128
Quality reviews, 35
Quick ratio, 197

Racketeer Influenced and Corrupt Organization Act (RICO), 125, 130
Random numbers, computer generation of, 442, 443
Random number table, 441–42, 466
Random sample, 441–42, 466
Rate authorization form, 559
Ratio estimation, 537, 547
Raw materials, 647, 648, 649, 652
Read, term defined, 188
Realizable value, audit objective, 159–60, 161
Realizable value of accounts receivable, 485, 497
Reasonable assurance, 44, 143–45, 250, 288

Receipt of bank confirmation, 707–9
Receiving report, 584, 596, 601
Reclassification entries, 233
Recompute, term defined, 188
Reconciliation, *see* **Bank reconciliation**
Reconciliation of amounts, 234–35
Records, *see also* Documents and records
    capital stock transactions, 688
    cost accounting records, 648, 664
    physical control over, 565
    shipments and related costs, 649
    standard cost records, 659, 664
Referral fees, AICPA *Code,* 84, 98
Reform Act, *see* Private Securities
    Litigation Reform Act
Regional and large local CPA firms, 25
Regression analysis, 195–96
Related parties, 225, 238
    inherent risk, 265–66
Related party transaction, 225, 238
Relevance, of evidence, 178–79
Reliability
    of evidence, *see* **Competence of
        evidence**
    of financial reporting, 289–90
Remittance advice, 402
Reperformance, 185, 186, 187, 188, 203
Replacement cost, inventory, 661–62
Report, royalties, 766
Reportable conditions, 310, 315
    communicating to audit committee and
        management, 742
Reportable conditions letter, 310
Reporting, 10–11
    government auditing, 795, 796
    on internal controls, 775–77
    operational auditing, 805
    other comprehensive basis of
        accounting (OCBOA), 764–65
    standards, 30, 31
Reports, *see also* **Audit report**
    agreed-upon procedures report, 779
    compilation report, 761
    on effectiveness of internal control, 776
    examination report, 772
    financial auditing, 798
    forecast report, 774
    government audit report, 796, 797
    operational audit, 798
    review report, 760
    special report on audit of sales, 764
    special reports, 768–69
    specified elements, 765–66
    standard interim report, 763
    WebTrust report, 778
Representation letter, 129
Representative sample, 438, 466
Repurchase of capital stock, 686
Research, AICPA, 29, 127
Respect, as ethical principle, 76
Responsibility
    of auditors, 143–49
    as ethical principle, 76, 83
Restatement of torts, 120
Retained earnings, audit of, 689–90
Return on common equity ratio, 199

Returns and allowances, *see* Sales returns
    and allowances
Return on total assets ratio, 199
Revenue transactions, fraud, 148
Review and compilation services, of
    nonpublic companies, 758–62
Review for contingent liabilities, 728–32
Review of historical financial statements,
    3, 16
Review of interim financial information,
    762–63
Review report, 760
Review services, 3, 759, 770, 780
Review for subsequent events, 381,
    733–35, 745
Review of working papers, 740–41,
    745
Revised judgment about materiality,
    272, 273
RICO, *see* Racketeer Influenced and
    Corrupt Organization Act
Rights and obligations, management
    assertions about, 156, 158, 160, 161
Risk, 257–73, *see also* Audit risk
    acceptable audit risk, 218, 238
    assessing, *see* Risk assessment
    fraudulent financial reporting, 147
    information risk, 7–8
    materiality and, 257
    misappropriation of assets, 147
    nonsampling risk, 438, 466
    revising, 272
    sampling risk, 438, 466
    types of, 259–61
Risk assessment, 300, 315
    acceptable audit risk, 263–64
    control risk, 162, 315
    financial reporting and, 294–95
    for fraud, 145–47, 162
    of information technology, 331–32
    inherent risk, 266
Risk management, internal
    auditors, 800
Royalties, report for, 766
Rules of Conduct, *see Code of Professional
    Conduct*
Rusch Factors v. *Levin,* 120

Salaries and wages, accrued, 569
Sales and collection cycle, 150, 152–54
    accounts, 398–99, 400
    accounts receivable, 475–97
    analytical procedures, 363–65, 375,
        479–80
    audit risk, 258
    audit tests in, 365–66
    authorization, 404
    business functions for, 399–403, 424
    case illustration, 416–24, 493–97
    classes of transactions in, 399, 424
    control risk, 374–75, 404, 478
    defined, 399, 425
    documents and records, 400, 404–5
    internal controls, 404, 405–11
    misstatements, 407, 520–21
    separation of duties, 404, 407

Sales and collection cycle *(contd.)*
    substantive tests of transactions, 362,
        364, 375, 406, 407, 411, 479
    tests, 663
    tests of controls, 361, 362, 375, 405–7,
        411, 479
    tests of details of balances, 365, 375,
        475–97
    transaction-related audit objectives,
        406, 410
Sales cutoff, 484
Sales invoice, 401, 402
Sales journal, 401, 483
Sales order, 399
Sales returns and allowances, 402,
    411–12
    cutoff, 484–85
Sales returns and allowances
    journal, 403
Sales transaction-related audit objectives,
    290
Sample exception rate (SER), 445,
    450, 466
Sample selection
    accounts receivable confirmations, 491
    block, 440–41, 465
    directed, 440, 466
    haphazard, 441, 466
    inventory observation, 656
    nonprobabilistic, 439, 440–41, 466
    probabilistic, 439, 440, 441–43, 466
    with probability proportional to size,
        442–43, 523, 547
    random number tables, 441–42, 466
    systematic, 442, 466
    tests of details of balances, 517, 519
Sample size
    accounts receivable confirmations, 491
    attributes sampling, 455–56
    as audit decision, 177
    expanding, 451, 521
    initial sample size, 449, 466
    inventory observation, 656
    tests of details of balances, 517, 519
Sampling distribution, 453–54, 466
Sampling error, 256–57, 273, 438
Sampling risk, 438, 466
SAS 71 reviews, 762–63, 780
SAS number, 32
SASs, *see* **Statements on Auditing
    Standards**
Scan, term defined, 188
Scope and nature of services, 83
Scope paragraph (audit report), 44–45, 51,
    56, 61, 250, 764
Securities Act of 1933, 112, 121–22, 131
Securities Exchange Act of 1934, 112,
    122, 131, 289
    antifraud provisions, 123
    auditor defenses, 124
    Rule 10b-5, 122–24
Securities and Exchange Commission
    (SEC), 36, 37
    Blue Ribbon Committee on Improving
        the Effectiveness of Corporate Audit
        Committees, 293

Securities and Exchange Commission
  (SEC) *(contd.)*
  EDGAR web site, 262
  forms, 36
  reports, 36
  sanctions by, 124
Security, information technology,
  335–36
Segregation of duties
  information technology, 331, 334
  owners' equity, 687
Separate and proportionate liability, 116
Separation of duties, 295–96, 315
  acquisition and payment cycle, 588
  payroll and personnel cycle, 563
  sales and collection cycle, 404, 407
Service auditors, 776
Service center, 345, 347
Service organization, internal controls for,
  776–77
Services, receiving, in acquisition and
  payment cycle, 584
Shareholders, *Code* Rule 101, 87
Shareholders' capital stock master file,
  687, 691
Shipments and related costs, recording of,
  649
Shipping document, 400
Short-term debt-paying ability, 196
Short-term liquidity, 197
SIASs, *see* **Statements on Internal
  Auditing Standards**
Sick pay, accrued, 569
Single Audit Act of 1984, 795, 808
Single Audit Act Amendments of 1996,
  795, 796–97
Software, *see* Computer software
Software Toolworks suit, 124
Solicitation, AICPA *Code,* 84, 97
Special assignments, 800, 808
Specialists, required for audit, 225
Special report on audit of sales, 764
Special reports, 768–69
Specific authorization, 296, 315
Specific balance-related audit objectives,
  160, 161
Specific transaction-related audit
  objectives, 156, 157–58
Specified elements, 765–66
SSAE, *see* **Statements on Standards for
  Attestation Engagements**
SSARS, *see* **Statements on Standards for
  Accounting and Review Services**
SSARS review, 780
Standard bank confirmation form, 707,
  708, 716
Standard cost records, 659, 664
Standard interim report, 763
Standards, *see also* Auditing standards
  AICPA, 28, 29, 33, 127, 128
  attestation standards, 769–71, 775
  of conduct, 85
  of field work (GAAS), 30
  Institute of Internal Auditors
    Professional Practice Standards, 793
  of reporting (GAAS), 30

Standard unqualified audit report,
  44–47, 54, 59, 61, 62
  conditions for, 46–47
  parts of, 44–46
State Board of Accountancy, disciplinary
  action, 100
Statements on Auditing Standards
  (SASs), 28, 31–32, 37
  SAS 1, 32, 655
  SAS 1 (AU 110), 142, 143
  SAS 1 (AU 220), 127
  SAS 1 (AU 230), 145
  SAS 7 (AU 315), 127
  SAS 8 (AU 550), 737
  SAS 21 (AU 435), 224
  SAS 22 (AU 311), 162
  SAS 29 (AU 551), 767
  SAS 39 (AU 350), 254, 256, 444
  SAS 45 (AU 334), 127, 225
  SAS 47 (AU 312), 251, 259, 271
  SAS 50 (AU 625), 91
  SAS 54 (AU 317), 148, 742
  SAS 55, 302
  SAS 56 (AU 329), 189
  SAS 58 (AU 508), 58
  SAS 59 (AU 341), 48, 49, 736
  SAS 60 (AU 325), 310, 743
  SAS 61 (AU 380), 742
  SAS 62 (AU 623), 764, 765, 768
  SAS 65 (AU 322), 794
  SAS 67 (AU 330), 183, 488
  SAS 70 (AU 324), 776
  SAS 71 (AU 722), 762–63
  SAS 73 (AU 336), 225–26
  SAS 74 (AU 801), 797
  SAS 75, 777, 778
  SAS 77 (AU 311), 375
  SAS 78, 289
  SAS 78 (AU 319), 302
  SAS 80, 184
  SAS 80 (AU 326), 369
  SAS 82 (AU 316), 145, 146, 147, 265,
    742
  SAS 83 (AU 310), 221
  SAS 85 (AU 333), 127, 736, 737
  SAS 87, 32
**Statements on Internal Auditing
  Standards** (SIASs), 794, 808
**Statements on Standards for Accounting
  and Review Services** (SSARS), 28,
  758, 780
**Statements on Standards for Attestation
  Engagements** (SSAE), 769, 780
*Statement on Standards for Attestation
  Engagements* (AICPA), 29
Statistical inferences, 535–36, 547
Statistical sampling, 439–40, 453, 466
  monetary unit sampling (MUS),
    522–33
  variables sampling, 533–38, 547
Statistical techniques, 194–96
Statutory law, 116
Stock dividends, 690
Stock transfer agent, 687, 691
Stratified sampling, 516, 518, 537, 547
Subsequent discovery of facts, 743–45

Subsequent events, 745
  cash disbursements, 595
  cash receipts, 491–92
  review for, 382, 733–35, 745
Substantive tests, 362, 383
  ARACR and ARIA, 517, 518
Substantive tests of transactions, 163,
  164, 362, 383
  accounts payable, 581–601
  acquisition and payment cycle,
    581–601
  analytical procedures and, 368
  audit sampling for, 437–46, 514
  cash balance, 705
  cash receipts, 412–14
  cost of evidence, 367
  design of, 371, 403–11, 412–14
  effect of, 415
  evidence, 367
  evidence mix, 370, 371
  income and expense accounts, 629
  notes payable, 681
  payroll and personnel cycle, 562–67
  sales and collection cycle, 362, 364, 374,
    406, 407, 411, 479
Sufficiency, 31
Sufficiency of evidence, 31, 180, 203, 738,
  741
Summarization, audit objective, 157,
  158
Summary acquisitions report, 585
Summary payroll report, 560
Summary of possible misstatements,
  739, 745
Summary of proceedings, 235
Summary sales report, 401
Supporting schedule working papers,
  233–36, 238
Systematic sample selection, 442, 466
Systems development, 334, 335

Tangible net assets-to-equity ratio, 198
Tax services, 25
Technical training and proficiency,
  adequate, 29
Tenants v. *Max Rothenberg and Company,*
  118
TER, *see* **Tolerable exception rate**
Test data approach, 339–41, 347
Test of reasonableness schedule, 235
Tests
  accounts receivable, 475–97, 482–87
  acquisition and payment cycle, 663
  bank reconciliation, 709–10
  capital acquisition and repayment cycle,
    690
  contingent liabilities, 729–730
  cost accounting, 651–52
  design of, 302
  dividends, 689
  general cash, 710
  interbank transfers, 713–14
  nonexistent payroll, 566–67
  notes payable, 681
  owners' equity, 690
  payroll and personnel cycle, 663

Tests *(contd.)*
    physical observation of inventory, 657–58
    prepaid insurance, 624–27
    reduction of, 189–90
    sales and collection cycle, 663
    timing of, 381
    types of, 360–66, 383
    for uncollectible accounts, 414–15
Tests of controls, 162–63, 164, 311, 312, 315, 360
    accounts payable, 581–601
    acquisition and payment cycle, 581–601
    audit sampling, 437–66, 514
    cash balance, 705
    cash receipts, 412–14
    cost of evidence, 367
    design of, 371, 403–11, 412–14, 562–67
    effect of, 415
    evidence, 367
    evidence mix, 370–71
    examples, 363
    income and expense accounts, 629
    notes payable, 681
    payroll and personnel cycle, 562–67
    sales and collection cycle, 361, 362, 375, 405–7, 410, 479
    substantive tests, 369
Tests of details of balances, 163, 164, 269–71, 383
    accounts payable, 592–99
    accounts receivable, 482–87
    audit sampling for, 513–47
    capital acquisition and repayment cycle, 679
    cash balance, 705
    cash in the bank, 704
    cost of evidence, 367
    design of, 373–75, 476–87, 567–70, 653–55, 679
    evidence, 367
    evidence mix, 370
    expense accounts, 569–70
    income accounts, 630
    inventory and warehousing cycle, 653–55
    manufacturing equipment, 618
    nonstatistical sampling, 514–21
    notes payable, 679, 682–85
    payroll and personnel cycle, 567–70
    sales and collection cycle, 365, 375, 475–97
Third-party beneficiary, 116
Third-party liability, 116, 119–21
Third-party suits, auditor defenses against, 120–21

Tick marks, 237, 238
Time card, 560, 571
Time interest earned, 198
Timeliness, of audit evidence, 177, 180
Timing
    accounts receivable confirmations, 490
    of analytical procedures, 190, 191
    as audit decision, 177–78
    as audit objective, 157, 158
    inventory observation, 656
Timing difference in accounts receivable confirmation, 485, 497
Tolerable exception rate (TER), 445, 447, 448, 449, 451, 466
Tolerable misstatement, 254, 273, 516
    accounts payable, 592
    accounts receivable, 374, 477
    cash balance, 704
    payroll, 568
Total payroll, 570
Trace, term defined, 188
Transaction-related audit objectives, 155, 156–58, 164
    acquisition and payment cycle, 589, 591
    balance-related audit objectives and, 378, 379
    cash receipts, 413
    control risk, 290
    dividend audit, 689
    identifying, 307
    payroll, 564
    sales and collection cycle, 406, 410
Transactions
    acquisition and payment cycle, 582, 588
    payroll and personnel cycle, 558
    sales cycle, 296–97
Transaction walk-through, 299, 315
Trial balance (list), 234, 483
Trustworthiness, as ethical principle, 76
Turnover ratios, 197

Ultramares Corporation v. *Touche,* 119, 131
Ultramares doctrine, 119, 131
Unadjusted misstatement worksheet, 739, 745
Unasserted claim, 732, 745
Uncollectible account authorization form, 403
Uncollectible accounts receivable, 403, 414–15, 485, 486
Unethical behavior, defined, 76–77
Uniform system of accounts, 764
Unintentional misstatement, 145
Unit cost records, 652–53
United States General Accounting Office (GAO), 13
    Yellow Book, 794, 795, 801, 808

United States v. *Natelli,* 126
United States v. *Simon,* 125–26
United States v. *Weiner,* 126–27
Unknown commitments, 730
Unpaid fees, *Code* Rule 101, 90
Unqualified audit report with explanatory paragraph or modified wording, 47–50, 61
Unqualified audit reports, 54, 59, 60, 62
    departures from, 50–52, 55–59, 62
    issuing, 742
Unqualified shared report with other auditors, 61
Unusual fluctuations, 189, 203
User auditors, 776–77

Vacation pay, accrued, 569
Valuation, management assertions about, 156, 158, 161
Variables sampling, 533–38, 547
Vendor's invoice, 585, 598, 601
Vendor's statement, 585, 596, 598, 601
Vouch, term defined, 188
Voucher, 585
Vouching, 184, 203

W-2 form, 561
Wages, accrued, 569
WANs, *see* **Wide-area-networks**
Weaknesses, internal control, 307–8, 315, 338, 339
WebTrust assurance services, 4, 777, 778, 780
Wide-area-networks (WANs), 344, 347
Working papers, 230–37, 238
    bank reconciliation, 706
    computerized, 237
    confidentiality, 230–31
    contents and organization, 231, 232
    current files, 232–36
    final review of, 740–41
    government auditing, 795
    interbank transfer, 713
    ownership of, 230
    permanent files, 231–32
    preparation of, 236–37
    purposes of, 230
    supporting schedule working papers, 233–36
Working trial balance, 233, 238
Worksheet, tests of details of balances, 270
Worlds of Wonder suit, 124

Yale Express case, 94
Year-end bank reconciliation, 705, 711
Yellow Book (GAO), 794, 795, 801, 808